CW00642060

WATCHMAKERS AND CLOCKMAKERS OF THE WORLD

WATCHMAKERS AND CLOCKMAKERS OF THE WORLD

Volume I

BY

G. H. BAILLIE

Fellow of the Institute of Physics

N.A.G. PRESS LTD.
LONDON

First Edition . . 1929
Methuen & Co. Ltd., London

Second Edition . . 1947
Third Edition . . 1951
Reprinted as Volume I 1976
Latest reprint .. . 1982

I.S.B.N. 7198 0040 4

Printed in Great Britain by
Morrison & Gibb Ltd, London and Edinburgh

PREFACE TO THE FIRST EDITION

THE first general list of Watch and Clockmakers was published in Britten's *Old Clocks and Watches and their Makers*, and has proved invaluable to collectors and students of horology. It was, though, a list mainly of English makers and, many years ago, I started to supplement it by compiling a list of the foreign makers whose names I found in old books and records and on watches and clocks.

The list of foreign makers grew rapidly, and I was advised to publish it as an appendix to my book on *Watches*. I then found that the Minute-books of The Clockmakers Company of London—a marvellously kept series of records, complete from 1632 to date—had never been thoroughly examined from the point of view of the makers, and I decided to compile a new list of English makers, taking these records as a basis. I am greatly indebted to the Secretary and Court of The Clockmakers Company for their kindness in permitting me to compile the list, to the Librarian of the Guildhall Library for his courtesy in giving me access to the books, and to Miss O'Farrell for her skill in transcribing the manuscripts. The list of English makers so formed has had many additions from a large number of minor sources, and the complete list became too large for publication except in book form.

In the foreign list, Paris figured far too little in view of its importance as a watch and clockmaking centre, and, as far as I have been able to ascertain, no research on Paris makers has ever been made. I determined, therefore, to fill the gap by looking for records in the Bibliothèque Nationale. For a long time the results were meagre. The records of the Paris Corporation, which was founded in 1544 and continued to the Revolution, were burned in the Hotel de Ville and no copies exist. In time, however, the Archives de Paris and the Archives de la Seine yielded many records of makers, and at length the list reached a point when newly discovered records but rarely gave particulars of a maker not on the list. From this I judged that the list had made some headway towards completeness.

The list extends up to 1825, but a few later makers of distinction have been mentioned. After that date there were too many calling themselves watch and clockmakers who were more merchants than craftsmen.

Even with this limitation, the list began to get unwieldy, and I have used various expedients to keep it within the limits of a single volume. The records have yielded many interesting particulars about the makers, but I have in general included only information likely to be useful. I have omitted the names of streets, except where they served to distinguish one maker from another or to indicate probable connection in relationship or business; the inclusion even of those that are known would have increased the size of the list by one-third. Abbreviations have been used freely, and a list precedes the list of makers; they have, though, been chosen so that their meaning is fairly obvious, and they should not prove inconvenient. A number of conventions have been adopted and explained on the pages following this preface, and these should be read before using the list. A considerable amount of space has been saved by giving the geographical position of the smaller towns and villages in a list at the end of the volume, instead of wherever their names occur in the list of makers. Many of them are not found in ordinary atlases, and there remain a few which I have not succeeded in locating, probably on account of a change in the name or its spelling.

At the end of the list of makers is a list of initials and monograms found on watches and clocks; I have included in this the names of makers who may have been the signatories.

An addition, which may be of interest to American collectors, is the list of the names with which the products of the early American watch factories were christened. These names are inserted in the list of makers in alphabetical order and also under the names of the Companies that made the watches.

Though much of the list is the result of research made by me or for me, a great deal is based on the work of other students of horological history, and I acknowledge the great debt I owe to them.

Mr. John Smith, in his *Old Scottish Clockmakers*, has given a most interesting history of the makers of Scotland and of the Corporation of Hammermen in which they were enrolled, and he has, most generously, allowed me to include in my list the names of the makers he has found. I am grateful for similar generosity from Mr. Elis Sidenbladh, who has published an exhaustive list of Swedish makers in his book, *Urmakare i Sverige*; from Mr. Bering Liisberg, whose *Urmagere og Ure i Danmark* is a valuable history of horology with particulars of Danish makers; from M. Alfred Chapuis, the historian of Swiss horology and author of three splendid works, *La Pendulerie Neuchâteloise*, *La Montre Chinoise*, and, in collaboration with M. Edouard Gélis, *Le Monde des Automates*; and from M. Claudius Côte, who with M. Eugène Vial has recently published *Les Horlogers Lyonnais de* 1550 *à* 1650.

M. Théodore Ungerer has not only allowed me to make use of his monograph on *Les Habrecht*, but has sent me the names of Strasbourg makers discovered by him in a search among the archives of the city, and Dr. Rudolph Kaftan, Director of the Uhren Museum in Vienna, has given me the list of makers of the Viennese Corporation compiled by him from the records.

I am indebted to M. Marius Fallet for the makers of Basle, to Herr Giersberg for those of Cologne, to the account of the Pleissner collection, published by the firm of Robert Pleissner, for the list of Dresden makers compiled, I believe, by Herr Max Engelmann, and to Develle's monograph on the Blois makers for many details of this great watchmaking centre; this book presents a vivid picture of the life and work of the craftsmen of the seventeenth century.

The two German periodicals, the *Deutsche Uhrmacher Zeitung* and the *Allgemeine Journal der Uhrmacherkunst*, the Swiss *Journal d'Horlogerie et de Bijouterie*, and the French *Horloger* have always catered for the historian as well as for the technician, and I have gleaned much valuable information from their pages. The German journals in particular have published articles of great interest about horology in Nürnberg and Augsburg by Carl Friedrich and other historians.

I shall be grateful for information about makers and their works, which could be added to the list in the event of a second edition being published.

G. H. BAILLIE

1929

PREFACE TO THE SECOND EDITION

WATCH and Clockmakers of the World was first published in Methuen & Co.'s 'Connoisseur' series in 1929. The present edition contains about 35,000 names of makers of which 10,000 are in addition to the 25,000 names of the first edition.

This addition is due in large measure to the kindness of many friends and readers who have sent me the results of their researches and allowed me to make use of them.

In particular, Mr. Francis Buckley, with his brother, Dr. G. C. Buckley, has compiled from many sources a long list of makers, many hitherto unknown. The manuscript list has been presented to the Guildhall Library. Mr. Francis Buckley has, moreover, published several pamphlets on the work of Tompion, Quare, Graham and Ellicott, in which he has correlated the numbers on these makers' watches with dates obtained from various sources. In the cases of Tompion and Graham, the correlation has reached a point that makes it possible to date a watch by its number within a few years.

A correspondence between number and date, based on Mr. Buckley's researches, has been included under the names of these makers.

Mr. Courtney Ilbert's remarkable collection of clocks and watches has yielded much information, and he has given me invaluable help.

Dr. Iowerth C. Peate, of the National Museum of Wales at Cardiff, has filled a gap in horological history by publishing (1945) a book on the clock and watchmakers of Wales.

Mr. C. Speierdijk, editor of the Amsterdam journal, *Christiaan Huygens*, sent me, just before the war started, a list of Dutch makers, including many Huguenots who fled from France on the revocation of the Edict of Nantes in 1685.

The Rev. N. V. Dinsdale has made an exhaustive search in Yorkshire county records. The results have been published (1946) under the title, *The Old Clockmakers of Yorkshire.*

Mr. W. T. Edgley, himself a collector, has done a like work for the Midlands around Birmingham.

Mr. Stephen Murray published a list of West Country clockmakers in his book on the West Country, and Mr. John T. Marshall published in 1930, in the *Belfast Telegraph*, a list of Ulster makers.

Finally, M. Alfred Chapuis was able during the war to continue his work on horological history and has published several books full of valuable information. I mention two examples of beautiful printing and illustration, *Montres et Emaux de Genève* and *Histoire et Technique de la Montre Suisse*, the latter having M. Eugène Jacquet as joint author.

To all these historians of horology I owe a debt of gratitude for their generosity in allowing me to make use of their work. I am grateful, too, to many others who have helped me on a smaller scale.

Maps of the European countries have been added to the list of place names. They may be of interest in indicating the old watchmaking centres of Europe and in showing places found only in very large scale maps.

A change has been made in recording variants in the spelling of names. In the first edition the list had cross-references from one variant to another, but the finding of fresh sources has increased so greatly the number of variants that this system was found wasteful of space. The cross-references have, therefore, mainly been omitted from the main list and the variants have been collected together in a separate list, which precedes the list of makers.

If a name sought is not found in the main list, it will be found, if there are variants, in this separate list, which will indicate different forms of the name to be sought in the main list.

Many of the variants are obviously due to different scribes taking different views of the spelling of a spoken name, but the earlier makers were not particular in how their names were spelt. I have found different spellings engraved on the plates of two watches by the same maker.

Some of the collections referred to in the first edition have since been dispersed, but the references have been retained.

The list extends, as before, only up to 1825, but includes a few makers of distinction after that date.

The same conventions have been adopted, and readers will find it helpful to read the list of them before consulting the list of makers for the first time.

G. H. Baillie

1947

CONVENTIONS

DATES.—The first and last dates given in respect of a maker are those of the earliest and latest records; they do not indicate birth or death without a preceding 'b.' or 'd.'

The abbreviation 'ca.' before a date applies to that date only. Thus, 'ca.1700-25' indicates that the date 1700 is approximate but that the date 1725 is certain or, at any rate, is believed by the Author to be certain.

'From' or 'To' preceding a date indicates that the maker started or ceased working in the town mentioned at that date.

MASTERSHIP, etc.—'m.1725,' 'CC.1725,' etc., mean that the maker became a master or became free of the Clockmakers Company in 1725.

'1725 m.,' '1725 CC.,' mean that he was master or was free of the CC. generally at some previous unknown date.

In the case of the Paris, Nürnberg and Augsburg corporations, a maker had to present a mastership essay on joining the corporation, even though he may have been already a master. In these towns, therefore, 'm.1725' means that he became a master in the corporation at that date and may have been a master previously. Whenever the record indicated that he was previously a master, the date has been given as '1725 m.,' so the indication 'm.1725' generally has its normal meaning.

The word 'juré' is used to indicate the officer of the corporation charged with the duty of inspecting work and workshops, in all the corporations except that of London. In Paris, the officer was called at different periods 'juré,' 'garde-visiteur' and 'syndic.' In London, the equivalent 'warden' or 'w.CC.' is used.

RELATIONSHIP.—The words 'son' and 'bro.,' when alone after the name, indicate that the maker is the son or brother of the maker *immediately* preceding.

SPELLING.—A list of alternative spellings of makers' names precedes the list of makers. It should be consulted if the name of a maker sought is not in the list of makers.

Some alternative spellings are retained in the list of makers and are in brackets.

The spelling of Christian names found in the records or on clocks and watches has been used and has not been modernized or made uniform; thus, Étienne, Estienne and Étinne are found.

The spelling of place names follows the recommendations of the Royal Geographical Society.

DUPLICATE ENTRIES.—In many cases two entries refer probably to the same maker, more especially among the Paris makers, with unrecorded Christian names. Where identity is merely probable, entries are kept separate, and, where not adjacent, the possible identity is indicated by a reference. There must be many duplicate entries, under different spellings, which have escaped the Author's notice.

WORKS.—All works known to the Author in museums and many in certain private collections have been mentioned, except in the case of some of the later well-known makers, whose works are too numerous to make a list of interest. No attempt, however, has been made to give a complete list of works in private possession or of which the ownership is unknown.

ALPHABETICAL ORDER.—German names with modified vowels, ae, oe and ue, are written with ä, o and ü, except in the case of makers who lived in countries where the diaeresis is not used. Swedish and Danish letters å, ä, ø, o and ü are not given their proper places in the Swedish and Danish alphabets, but, for alphabetical order, are treated as a, o and u. The modern Dutch alphabet has been followed in using ij and not y, except in familiar names such as Huygens.

Names found both with and without 'De,' 'Du,' 'La,' 'Le,' 'Van' and 'Von' are given these prefixes.

'KLEINUHRMACHER' and 'HORLOGER.'—These words are used when found in records because they have no equivalent in English. A Kleinuhrmacher did not make turret clocks, but may have been a house clockmaker or a watchmaker or both. A Horloger may have been a maker of turret or house clocks or watches.

'C.,' 'W.' and 'MATH. INST. MAKER.'—Whenever the record describes a maker as a clockmaker or watchmaker, the entry contains the abbreviation C. or W. It does not, though, follow that a maker described as a watchmaker did not make clocks, or vice versa. When a maker is described as mathematical instrument maker only, he is not known to be a watch or clockmaker. A few such makers are included because the crafts of instrument making and horology were often combined.

ABBREVIATIONS

GENERAL

a. . . . . . apprentice or apprenticed.
al. . . . . . alarum.
an. . . . . . *ante*; before.
Art. . . . . . Article.
astro. . . . . . astronomical, i.e. giving indications of sun, moon, etc. Clocks for astronomical purposes are called Observatory clocks.
aut. . . . . . automaton or automata.
b. . . . . . born.
BC. . . . . . Blacksmiths Company.
br. clock . . . bracket clock.
bro. . . . . . brother.
C. . . . . . clockmaker.
c. . . . . . after 16, 17, etc., century.
ca. . . . . . *circa*; about.
cal. . . . . . calendar.
CC. . . . . . Clockmakers Company, or, with date, free of Clockmakers Company.
cf. . . . . . compare.
chron. . . . . . chronometer.
comp. . . . . . compagnon or journeyman.
crys. . . . . . crystal.
c.secs. . . . . . centre seconds.
cyl. . . . . . cylinder.
d. . . . . . died.
desc. . . . . . described or description.
en. . . . . . enamelled or enamel.
eng. . . . . . engraved or engraving.
esc. . . . . . escape or escapement.
g. . . . . . gold.
hex. . . . . . hexagonal.
hm. . . . . . hall mark.
ill. . . . . . illustrated.
l.CC. . . . . . livery Clockmakers Company.
l.c. clock . . . long-case clock.
m. . . . . . master.
mar. . . . . . married.
math. inst. . . mathematical instrument.
m.CC. . . . master of the Clockmakers Company.
mem. . . . . . memoir.
mid. . . . . . middle.
min. . . . . . minute.
mt. . . . . . movement.
mus. . . . . . musical.
oct. . . . . . octagonal.
p.c. . . . . . pair-case.
prob. . . . . . probable or probably.
pub. . . . . . published.
rep. . . . . . repeating.
½ ¼ rep. . . . half-quarter repeating.
sd. . . . . . signed.
sig. . . . . . signature.
sil. . . . . . silver.
sq. . . . . . square.
str. . . . . . striking.

T.C. . . . . . Turret Clockmaker.
trav. . . . . . travelling.
W. . . . . . watchmaker.
w.CC. . . . . . warden of the Clockmakers Company.

MUSEUMS AND COLLECTIONS

B.M. . . . . . British Museum.
C.A. & M. . . Conservatoire des Arts et Métiers, Paris.
Chamb. coll. . . Collection of the late Major Chamberlain.
coll. . . . . . collection.
Den. coll. . . . Dennison collection.
Furt. M. . . . Furtwangen Museum.
F.W.M. . . . Fitzwilliam Museum, Cambridge.
Gall. . . . . . Gallery.
G.M. . . . . . Guildhall Museum.
K.H.M. . . . Kunsthistorische Museum, Vienna.
M. . . . . . Museum.
M.M.A. . . . Metropolitan Museum of Art, New York.
M.P.S. . . . Mathematische Physikalische Salon, Dresden.
Nat. . . . . . National.
Nord. M. . . . Nordiske Museum, Stockholm.
N.Y. Univ. . . James Arthur coll. in New York University.
Pal. . . . . . Palace, Palais.
S.K.M. . . . Victoria and Albert Museum, S. Kensington.
S.M.S.K. . . . Science Museum, S. Kensington.
Stern. coll. . . Maurice Sternberger coll., formerly on loan to the M.M.A., New York, sold at Christie's in 1937.
Stuttgart M. . . Württembergische Landesgewerbemuseum.
Weth. coll. . . Wetherfield collection, sold and dispersed in 1928.

BOOKS

Baillie . . . . G. H. Baillie. *Watches*. London, 1929.
Britten . . . . F. J. Britten. *Old Clocks and Watches and their Makers*. 6th edition, 1932.
Cec. & Web. . . Cescinsky and Webster. *English Domestic Clocks*. London, 1914.
Côte & Vial . . *Les Horlogers Lyonnais de* 1550 *a* 1650. Lyons, 1927.
Gould . . . . *The Marine Chronometer*. London, 1923.
Les Habrecht . *T. Ungerer*. Strasbourg, 1925.
Liisberg . . . *Urmagere og Ure i Danmark*. Copenhagen, 1908.
Milham . . . *Time and Timekeepers*. New York, 1923.
M. des Aut. . . Gélis et Chapuis. *Le Monde des Automates*. Paris, 1928.
Sidenbladh . . *Urmakare i Sverige*. Stockholm, 1918.
Smith . . . . *Old Scottish Clockmakers*, 1453 *to* 1850. Edinburgh, 1921.

LIST OF NAMES WITH ALTERNATIVE SPELLINGS

Names in italic type are not in the list of makers

Names with alternative spellings which are near each other in the list of makers are not included.

Ackers Akers Acres
Addis Adis
Adfield Atfield
Adis Addis
Affolter Folter
Aicken Aitken
Aieres Aires Ayeres Ayres
Aiken Aicken Aitken
Aikenhead Akenhead
Aires Ayeres Ayres
Airey Ayrey
Aiston Eyston Easton
Aitken Aicken
Akers Ackers Acres
Alar Allard
Aleurs Van Aleurs
Alison Allison
Alkins Allkins
Allan Allen Allin
Allanson Allinson
Allaway Alloway
Allen Allan Allin
Allison Alison
Allkins Alkins
Allman Alman Almond
Alloway Allaway
Allsop Alsope
Allvey Alvey
Alman Allman Almond
Alsope Allsop
Alvey Allvey
Anders Anderes Andries
Annone D'Annone
Apiohn Upjohn
Ataway Atway
Atfield Adfield
Augoille Angoille
Aymes Ames
Ayrey Airey

Backquett Bocquet Bouquet Bucquet
Baddeley Badiley Badley
Bailes Bayles
Bailey Bayley Bayly
Baillet Baillot
Baily Bailey Bayley Bayly
Bain Bayne
Baines Baynes
Baionville De Baionville
Baisley Beasley Beesley
Bamstead Bumstead
Bane Bain Bayne
Banfield Bamfield
Bannister Banister
Barclay Barkley
Barenger Barrenger
Bargeau Barjeau
Barkley Barclay
Bärmann Baermann
Barnard Bernard
Baron Barron
Barraclough Barroclough
Barrie Barril Barry Debary
Barrington Berrington
Barron Baron
Barwin Barbin
Baseley Basely Basley Beasley Beesley
Baterson Batterson
Battie Batty
Baucutt Bawcutt
Bauldwin Baldwin
Baur Bauer
Bawcutt Baucutt
Bayles Bailes
Bayley Bayly Bailey
Bayne Bain
Bazeley Beasley Beesley
Beard Boad
Beasley Beesley
Beddell Bedell Biddle
Beeckman Beckman
Beefield Byfield
Beeling Beeding
Beesley Beasley
Beffield Byfield
Beidelrock Beitelrock
Beifield Byfield
Beigel Biegel
Belle De Belle
Belle Fontaine De Belle Fontaine
Bellinger Billinger
Benguerel-dit-Perrenoud Perrenoud
Bepffen-Hauser Peffenhauser
Berger Bergier Berguer
Bernard Barnard
Berrington Barrington
Berugier Berger Bergier Berguer
Bettwood Bellwood
Beuldet Buldet
Biddle Bedell
Biefield Bifield Byfield
Biegel *Beigel*
Billinger Bellinger
Biör— Björ—
Birch Burch
Birge Burge Burges Burgis
Birley Burley
Birtles Bertles
Bisse Bysse
Bläderl Blöderl Pletterl
Blanc Le Blanc
Blanpignon Blancpignon
Blaundel Blundell
Blederl Blöderl Pletterl
Blick Blecke
Boad Beard
Bocquet Bouquet Bucquet
Boddell Boddle
Boddily Bodily
Boekett Bockelts
Böheimb Böhm
Boillon Bouillon
Boiservoise Boicervoise
Bollinger Bellinger Billinger
Bolton Boulton
Bombourg De Bombourg
Boot Booth
Boquet Bocquet Bouquet Bucquet
Borel Borrel Borrett
Borlet Bourlet
Borrell Borel Borrett
Böttcher Boettcher
Boucquet Bouguet Bouquet Bocquet Bucquet
Boude Bouze
Boufler De Boufler
Boulton Bolton
Bouquet Bocquet Bucquet
Bourbon Boubon

Brackenrig Breakenrig
Bradl Bradel
Bradu Brodu
Braen Bradin
Brafield Brayfield
Bramer Braemer
Brandt Brant
Bratel Bradel
Bremt Van der Bremt
Brian Briand Bryan Bryant
Bridgman Bridgeman
Brockhouse Brookhouse
Brodt Brod
Bron Brun
Brown Browne
Bruer Brewer
Brumstead Bumstead
Brunet Brunnet
Bruse Bruce
Bryan Bryant Brian Briand
Bryce Brice
Bucket Bucquet Bouquet Bocquet
Buhl Boulle
Buldet Burdet
Bulke Bulcke
Burbey Bunby
Burch Birch
Burdet Buldet
Burge Burges Burgis Birge
Burghardt Burkhardt
Buri Burry
Burkhardt Burghardt
Burkelow Burkloe
Burn Burns
Burnstead Bumstead
Bury Burry
Bushman Buschmann
Bussel Van Bussel
Butteu Buteux
Buys Buijs
Bycliff Bilcliff
Byrgi Burgi
Bysse Bisse

Caesar Cesar
Calliber Colliber
Calson Colson
Calston Colston
Campden Camden
Canson Cawson
Cappler Kappler
Carington Carrington
Carruthers Caruthers
Carstens Castens
Carter Carver
Caruthers Carruthers
Carver Carter
Cary Carey
Casinghurst Cassinghurst
Castens Carstens
Caterall Catterall Catherall
Cattin Catin
Cattley Catley
Cauch Canche
Caudwell Cawdwell
Causon Cawson
Cawdry Corderoy Cowdrey [Cowderoy
Cawe Cawne
Cawley Crawley
Cayser Keysen
Chapezeau Chappuzeau
Charlo Charlau
Chastelain Châtelin
Chauanes Chaunes Chavane
Chavane Chauanes
Chavenix Chabenex
Chetenham Cheltenham
Cheyser Keysen
Clair Du Clair
Cleave Cleeve
Clerat Clairat
Cleve Cleeve Cleave

Clewes Clowes
Clock Klok
Cloribos Claribos
Clydesdale Clidsdale
Coatsworth Coatesworth
Cöberle Köberle
Cocquart Cocart
Coelombie Collomby
Coke Cooke
Coleson Coulson Colson Colston
Collambel Colambel
Colley Calley
Collman Coleman
Collomby Coelombie
Collyer Collier
Colman Coleman
Colomb Coulomb
Colomby Collomby Coelombie
Colson Colston Coleson Coulson
Colvil Covill
Comlosy Kamiloschi
Condy Cony
Cordrey Corderoy Cowdrey Cowderoy
Cosine Cusin
Coster Koster
Cottrell Cottrill Cotterel
Couch Crouch
Couldray Coudrey
Coulet Collet
Coulomb Colomb
Coulson Coleson Colson Colston
Cousins Cusins
Cowdrey Cowderoy Corderoy
Crafford Crayford
Crawley Cawley
Creak Creeke
Creitmayer Kreittmaier
Creitzer Kreitzer
Croin Crouin
Crompton Crumpton
Crosland Crosslands
Crosnier Cronier
Crossfield Crosfield
Crosslands Crosland
Crouch Couch
Croudhill Crowdhill
Crumpton Crompton
Culper Külper
Cusin Cosine
Cusins Cousins
Cuyper Cuper
Cuyperus Cuijperus

Daglish Dalgleish
Dalton Dolton
Danson Danton
Darly Darnley
Darrell Dorrell
Daud Dand
Davall Devall
Davidson Davison
Davie Davy
Davison Davidson
Davy Davie
De Barry Debary
De Beaulieu Beaulieu
De Beauvais Beauvais
De Belle Fontaine Belle Fontaine
Debois Desbois
De Bulke Bulcke
Decombaz Descombats
De Graaf Graaf
De Haan Haan
Deierl Deyerl
De la Grange Lagrange
Delalande Lalande
De la Motte Lamotte
De la Place Laplace
De la Planche La Planche
Delarue La Rue
Delaunder Delander
De Laurent Laurent

Délépine Lépine Lespine
De Lisle Lysle
Delphinou Definod
De Mallet Mallet
De Marc Marc
De Molin Molin
De Muyter Muyter
De Nourry Nourry
Derchinger Dörchinger
Derimo Roumieu
De Rivaz Rivaz
Derne Derue
De Romieux Roumieu
Derue Derne
Descamus De Camus
Descharmes De Charmes
Descombats Decombaz
Destape Détape
De Storr Storr
De Val Du Val
Dicks Dix
Dike Dykes
Dirrick Derrick
Disbrowe Desbrow
Dix Dicks
Dodswell Dadswell
Dohrn Dor
Döller Deller
Dolton Dalton
Domvile Dumville
Done Donne Dunn
Dorill Dorrell Darrell
Dort Van Dort
Dorville *Douville* Doville
Dressler Drechsler Trechsler
Dross Droz
Dubois Duboys
Duchene Duchesne
Du Clair Clair
Dudiott Duduict
Du Jardin Jardin
Dumbill Dunbill
Dumville Domvile
Dunckley Dunkley
Dunn Donne Done
Dupny Dupuy

Eagleton Egleton
Easton Eston Eyston
Eccles Ecles
Edlinger Ettlinger
Edy Edey
Eisele Eisler Eysler
Ejdeldinger Aigeldinger
Eliot Elliott
Ells Ellis
Elst Van der Elst
Elwood Ellwood
Emerey Emery
Enew Ennew
Engelschalk Englsalck
Engler Henggler
English Inglish
Ennew Enew
Ennis Enys
Erhardt Ehrhardt
Ervin Irving
Eryles Earles
Estienne Étienne
Eston Easton Eyston
Etchinger Elchinger
Étienne Estienne
Euwa Eyba
Evel Evill
Ewestasce Eustace
Eyre Ayr
Eysler Eisler Eisele
Eyston Eston Easton

Faivre Favre Faver Faure
Falkner Falconer Faulkner
Farmbrough Farnborough
Farris Faris
Fatio Facio
Faulkner Falconer
Faure Faver Favre Faivre
Feilder Fielder
Feirer Feurer
Felter Fetter
Fénil Fétil
Ferster Förster
Ferteau Fetteau
Festeau Ferteau Fetteau
Feurer Feirer
Fietzen Fitzer
Findlay Finley
Finelly Tinelly
Fines Fynes
Finleater Fenleater
Finley Findlay
Firtree Fitree
Fischer Fisher
Flet Le Flet
Floccard Flacard
Fogel Vogel
Forest . Forrest
Forman Foreman
Forrester Forester
Forster Foster
Foulds Fowlds
Foulet Foullet Foulé
Fountain Fontaine
Fowell Fowle
Franck Frank
Francklin Franklin
Franckom Frankcom Frankscom
Frank Franck
Frasar Frisar Frisard Frésard
Fraser Frazer
Frejsar Frisar Frisard Frésard
Frere Féré
Frésard Frisar Frisard
Fridrich Friedrich
Frier Fryer
Frisar Frisard Frésard
Frizard Frisar Frésard
Fryer Frier
Fuillot Foillot
Fulkener Falconer Faulkner
Furnace Furniss
Füter Fueter
Fynes Fines

Gallaway Galloway
Gallet Galle Gallot
Galliard Gaillard
Gallimore Galimore
Gallonde Gallande
Galot Gallot
Gambell Gamble
Gape Grape
Garet Garrett Garratt
Gasnet Gaznet
Gautrier Gaultier
Gebe *Geeb* Gobe
Gérard Girard
Gerardier Girardier
Gertner Gärtner
Geutze Gôtz
Gibs Gib
Giessen Van der Giessen
Gil Gill
Gilbard Gilbert
Gilbraith Galbraith
Girard Gérard
Girle Garle
Glase Glaze
Glaser Glazier
Gold Gould
Gordoune Goodoune
Gould— Gold—
Grainger Granger
Gratrex Greatorex
Greenaway Greenway

Greene Green
Greisbeutel Kreisbeutel
Gretz Grätz
Grey Gray
Grieve Greaves
Grigsby Gregsby
Grinsill Greensill
Groce Grose
Guedon Guiden
Guericke Von Guericke
Guessler Gessler
Gui d'Amour Guydamour
Guignochot Dinocheau
Guilin Guillin Gwillin
Guiot Guyot
Gutheridge Guttridge
Guttbub Gutbub
Guttridge Gutheridge
Guyot Guiot
Gwillin Guillin

Habram Abraham
Häckel Heckel
Haehnel Hähnel
Hafman Hofmann
Hähnel Haehnel
Halaicher Haleicher Halleicher
Halifax Hallifax
Halliwell Hallwell Holliwell
Haltern Von Haltern
Hän Haen
Hanns Hans
Hanscomb Handscomb
Hänzler Hentzler
Harbert Harbottle Herbert
Hardey Hardy
Hardman Heardman
Hardwell Hartwell
Harrald Harold
Harriman Harryman Hariman
Hartwell Hardwell
Hathornthwaite Haythornthwaite Hawthorn
Haughton Houghton
Hauksbee Hawkesbee
Heardman Hardman
Hebstreit Herbstreit
Hechstetter Heckstetter
Heiden Heyden
Hekel Hekhl Hekl Heckel
Helden Holden
Heliger Hediger
Helme Holme
Hemins Hemmings
Henchel Hentschel
Henri Henry
Hensler Henzle Hentzler
Hering Herring
Heward Howard
Hewes Hues Huse Hughes
Hewett Hewitt
Heyer Heijer
Hicnar Hignar
Hietzinger Hitzinger
Higgnett Hignett
Hillyard Hillier
Hilson Hilton
Hinde Hines Hynes
Hinsch Hintsch
Hohenadl Hochenadl
Hoijendijk Hoogendijk
Holden Helden
Holliard Hollier Hollyar Holyer
Holrich Hobrich
Holyer Hollyar Hollier
Hoogendijk Hoijendijk
Hoquet Hoguet
Hornby Hornsby
Hory Ourry *Ory* Houry
Hosser Hoser
Houdin Oudin
Houghton Haughton
Houry Hory Ourry *Ory*

House Howes Howse
Howe How Howie
Howes Howse
Howkins Hawkins
Howse Howes
Hoy Hay
Hoyendijk Hoijendijk Hoogendijk
Huckley Hewkley
Hueit Viet Veit Witte
Hues Hughes Hewes Huse
Huffam Hougham
Hugault Hugot
Hughes Hues Hewes Huse
Hugho Higho
Hulst Van der Hulst
Huntsman Hunstman
Huray Le Huray
Hüs Huse Hughes Hues Hewes
Hutchason Huchason
Hynes Hines Hinde

Ingell Ignell
Ingerham Ingram
Inglish English
Innis Innes
Isles Iles

Jacques Jaques
Jacquet Jaquet
Jakeman Jackeman
Jakob Jacob
Jakobsen Jacobsen
Jameson Jamison
Jaques Jacques
Jaquet Jacquet
Jardin Du Jardin
Jeanes Jeans
Jeeyes Jeyes
Jefferies Jefferys
Jehan Jean
John Jon
Joley Joly
Jollage Jolage
Jon John
Jonod Jornod
Josslin Joselin Joseline
Jovel Jouvel

Kammlosy Kamiloschi Comlosy
Kampe Campe
Kapff Von Kapff
Kellaway Kellway
Kellström Kjellström
Kember Kimber
Kempelen Von Kempelen
Kieding Kjeding
Kimber Kember
Kinnling Kienling
Kirshaw Kershaw
Kiser Kifer
Klainschmidt Kleinschmidt
Klok Clock
Kommenda Comenda
Koster Coster
Kränkel Krenckel
Kreiser Kreizer
Krenckel Kränkel
Kreitzer Kreizer
Kroenkl Kränkel Krenckel
Külper Culper
Künell Hünell
Kürner Kirner

Laar Van Laar
Lacey Lacy
Lagrange De la Grange
Lainé Laisne
Laing Lang
Läisz Laeisz
Lami Lamy
Lamley Lumley Lunley
Lamotte De la Motte

Lamy Lami
Landsdown Lansdowne
Landteck Landeck
Lang Laing
Langcroft Longcraft
Lansdowne Landsdown
Laplace De la Place
La Planche De la Planche
Larçay Larcé Larsé
La Rue Delarue
Lasne Laisne
Lassalle Lasalle
Laud Lode
Laughton Layton Leighton
Laurence Lawrence
Laurent De Laurent
Laurie Lawrie Lowrie
Lauron Loron
Lawell Lowell Lovell
Lawford Lowford
Lawley Lowley
Lawndy Laundy
Lawrence Laurence
Lawrie Laurie Lowrie
Layland Leyland
Layton Leighton Laughton
Lea Leigh
Leabetter Leadbetter
Leake Leek
Leaver Lever
Le Blanc Blanc
Léchot Léchet
Le Compte Leconte Le Count
Ledbetter Leadbetter Leabetter
Lee Lea Leigh
Leech Leach
Leek Leake
Leenert Lindhart
Leenman Van Leenman
Legg Lögg
Le Guay Guay
Leicester Leister Lester Lister
Leigh Lea
Leighton Layton Laughton
Leister Leicester Lester Lister
Lenorman Norman
Le Pelletier Pelletier
Leper Lepper
Lépine Lespine Delépine
Lepper Leper
Le Prévost Le Provost Prévost
Lequin Tequin
Leroux Rou Roux
Le Roy Roy
Leschopié Lechopié
Le Sene Lesney Lesseney
Lespine Lépine Délépine
Lester Leicester Leister Lister
Le Sommelier Sommelier
Lever Leaver
Levi Levy
Levin Lewin
Levissel Leussel
Levy Levi
Lewin Levin
Leyton Layton Leighton Laughton
Lichfield Litchfield
Lichtenstern Liechtenstern
Lietzken Lintzken
Lilley Lilly
Limonière Le Monnière
Linch Lynch
Linck Link
Lindesey Lindsay Linsey Linsley Lyndsay
Line Lyne
Liney Lyney
Link Linck
Linnaker Linaker
Linsey Linsley Lindsay Lyndsay
Lisle Lysle De Lisle
Lister Leister Lester Leicester
Litzken Lintzken
Lod Lode Laud
Loder Loader
Longcraft Langcroft
Loosley Loseley
Louis Louys
Loumes Loomes
Lovell Lowell Lawell
Lowley Lawley
Lowndes Loundes
Lowrie Laurie Lawrie
Lucie Lucy
Ludewig Ludwig
Lundelius Lungdelius
Lynaker Linaker
Lyndsay Lindsay Linsey Linsley
Lyne Line
Lyney Liney
Lysle De Lisle
Lysney Lesseney

McC— Mac—
Mackie Macky
Macy Macey
Madison Maddison
Magnière Manière
Mair Maire Mayr Mayor Mayer Meyer Meier Meye
Mairet Maret
Maistre Maystre
Malet Mallett De Mallet
Man Mann
Manière Magnière
Manoreau Manceau
Manwaring Mainwaring
Marc De Marc
March Marsh Murch
Markie Merchie
Marquet Markwick
Martenet Martinet Martinot
Martineau Martmott
Martin Martins Martyn
Märtz Merz
Masurier Mazurier
Maurice Morris Morice Morrice Morize
Math— Matth—
May— Mey—
Mayer Mayor Mayr Mair Maire Meyer Meier Meye
Maystre Maistre
Mea— Mee— Me—
Medcalf Metcalf
Medhurst Midhurst
Medsger Metzger
Mee—— Me—— Mea——
Meier Meyer Meye Mair Maire Mayr Mayor
Mellen Von Mellen
Mellie Melly
Melzer Möltzer
Menard Mesnard
Menil Mesnil
Mennd Ment
Meraly Moraly
Mercklein Merklein
Merrick Meyricke
Merriman Merryman
Meslin Merlin
Mesnard Menard
Metcalf Medcalf
Metscher Metzger Medsger
Meunier Meusnier
Mey— May—
Meye Meyer Meier Mair Maire Mayr Mayor Mayer
Meynier Moynier
Meyricke Merrick
Meytare Métare
Michell Mitchell
Midhurst Medhurst
Midleton Middleton
Miers Myers
Miles Myles

Millar Miller Müller
Millegg Millögg
Miller Millar Müller
Millikin Mulliken
Mills Milnes Milne Mylne
Millward Milward
Milne Milnes Mills Mylne
Mimess Memess
Mintem Mintern
Miroglio Miroli
Mitchell Michell
Mitchinalle Michinale
Moisan Moysan
Molard Mollard
Mole Moule
Molens Molyns
Molesworth Molsworth
Molin De Molin
Molineaux Molyneux
Mollard Molard
Mollineux Molyneux Molineaux
Mollins Molyns
Molton Moulton
Monck Monk
Monday Munday Munden
Monde Moude
Monier Monnier
Monk Monck
Monkes Monks
Monro Munro
Morel Moret Morrell Murrell
Moreland Morland
Morelley Moraly
Moreton Morton
Morice Morize Morrice Morris Maurice
Morison Morrison
Morrice Morris Morice Morize Maurice
Morton Moreton
Mosley Moseley Mousley Mozley
Mosser Moser
Moth Mott
Moule Mole
Moulton Molton
Mounier Monnier
Mountlow Montlow
Mousley Moseley Mozley
Mowlton Mowtlow Moutlow
Moynier Meynier
Moysan Moisan
Moyse Moise
Mozley Moseley Mousley
Muisard Mussard
Mukle Muckle
Müller Miller Millar
Mulliken Millikin
Mullineux 'Molyneux Molineaux
Müllner Müller Miller Millar
Munday Munden Monday
Munro Monro
Murch March Marsh
Murchi Merchie
Murrell Morell Morel Moret
Mussard Muisard
Myddleton Middleton
Myers Miers
Mylbourne Milborne
Myles Miles
Mylne Milne Milnes Mills

Neal Neill
Neames Nemes
Nedes Needs
Neill Neal
Nepveu Neveu
Nesfel Nestfell
Neue Neve
Neuren Neveren
Neveu Nepveu
Newbald Newbolt
Neweren Neveren
Newson Newton
Newzam Newsam
Nicholls Nichols Nickals Nicoll
Nicklis Nicholas
Nickson Nixon
Nicoll Nicol Nicholls Nickals
Nicot Nicod
Nordling Norling
Norman Lenorman
Norry Nourry
Nourse Nurse
Noway Nawe
Nowan Nawe Nouwen
Nurse Nourse
Nusam Newsam

Oatway Otway
Oijterweer Uijterveer
Okey Oakey
Ol— Oll—
Oltramare Ostramare
Orry *Ory* Ourry Hory
Orton Oughton
Orum Oram
Osede Von Osede
Oth Otte
Oudin Houdin
Oughton Orton
Oultremer Oltramare Ostramare
Ourry Orry Hory
Overklift Van Overklift

Pacey Pasey
Padgett Paget
Paellard Paillard
Pain Payne
Pairas Payras
Paliard Paillard
Pannier Panier
Paplett Puplett
Paratt Parratt
Parkes Parks Parke
Parris Paris
Partin Parton
Paten Patten
Paterson Patterson
Paton Payton Peyton
Patten Paten
Pattenson Pattinson
Patterson Paterson
Pattey Paty
Pattinson Pattenson
Paty Pattey
Paull Paul
Payne Pain
Payton Paton Peyton
Peal Peele
Pearse Pearce Peirce Pierce
Pearson Peirson
Peatling Peytling
Péchot Peschot
Peder Peter Petter
Pedersson Petersen Petersson
Peele Peal
Peerce Peirce Pearce Pierce
Peiras Payras
Peirson Pearson
Peller Pöller
Pen Penn
Perche Porcher
Perey Perrey Pery
Perier Perrier Peryer
Perin Perins Perrin Perrins
Perot Perrot
Perras Payras
Perreton Pereton
Perrey Perey Pery
Perrier Perier Peryer
Perrot Perot
Pery Perey Perrey
Peryer Perier Perrier
Peschka Pesta
Peter Petter
Pett Petty Pettey

Pettygrew Pettigrew
Peyras Payras
Peyton Payton Paton
Pezas Pezar Payras
Pfeffenhauser Peffenhauser
Pfort Fort
Phelippson Philippon
Philip Phillip Philp
Picklmann Pickelmann
Pierce Peirce Pearce
Pierrepoint Pierpoint
Pike Pyke
Pinckart Pinkart
Pine Pyne
Pinfold Penfold
Pinnell Pinell
Pitan Piton Pitton
Pittman Pitman
Pittney Pitney
Pitton Piton
Plaevier Pleuvier
Plairas Payras
Plaire Player
Planner Plumer
Platel Plattel
Pletterl Blöderl
Plevier Plovier Pleuvier
Plewman Plowman
Plötterl Pletterl Blöderl
Plumber Plummer
Plumbly Plumley
Plumer Planner
Plummer Plumber
Pluvier Pleuvier
Plymley Plumley Plumbly
Pohlack Polack
Poireau Poiret Poirot
Polack Pohlack
Polson Poulson
Polton Poulton
Pommel Bommel
Pomroy Pomeroy
Pond Pound
Porcher Perche
Porlack Polack Pohlack
Porteous Porteus
Porthouse Posthouse
Pothier Potier Pottier
Pouchet Ponchet
Poughton Pejon
Poulingue Polingue
Poulson Polson
Poulton Polton
Pound Pond
Preist Priest
Preng Van Preng
Pretty Pritty
Preudhomme Prodhomme
Prévault Prévost
Prichard Pritchard
Priest Preist
Prigtori Praetorius
Prior Pryor
Pritchard Prichard
Pritty Pretty
Prodhomme Preudhomme
Prouvost Prévost
Prudhomme Preudhomme Prodhomme
Prugner Bruckner
Prutscher Brutscher
Pryor Prior
Pülmann Bullmann
Pummeroy Pomeroy
Putley Button
Pyne Pine

Query Quiery

Raillard Rallart
Raiment Rayment
Raine Rainer Rainier
Rainford Rainsford
Ramsey Ramsay
Ranceford Rainsford Rainford
Randloe Randolph Randall
Rasbocks Rusbacks
Rawden Rowden
Rawson Rowson
Rawworth Raworth Roworth
Rayne Rayner Raine Ranier
Raynes Raines
Raynesford Rainsford Rainford
Raynolds Reynolds
Razenhofer Ratzenhofer
Read Reed Reid
Record Ricord Rickard Riccard
Redford Radford
Reed Read Reid
Regeux Regueux
Regnault Renaud Renaut Renault
Reid Reed Read
Reilly Riley Ryley
Reinmann Reimann Reymann
Remsey Ramsay
Renard Von Renard
Renaud Renault Renaut
Rénier Reynier
Reymann Reimann
Reynier Rénier
Riccard Rickard Ricord Record
Rider Ryder
Ridl Riedl
Riebold Rieppolt
Rilley Riley *Rily* Ryley Reilly
Risbie Reisbye
Rivers Riviere
Robartes Roberts
Robbins Robins
Roe Rowe
Roger Rogier
Roi Roy Le Roy
Romeux Romier *Rommieu* Roumieu Derimo
Romsey Rumsey
Rontree Rowntree
Roquet Rocquet
Rou Roux Leroux
Rougier Rogier Roger
Roumieu Romieu Romier Derimo
Roux Leroux
Rowden Rawden
Rowe Roe
Rowntree Rontree
Rowson Rawson
Ryder Rider
Ryley Reilly Riley

Saager Sager
Safley Safely Safly Saifloy
Saigler Sailler Sayller
St. Blimont De Saint-Blimont
St. Jean De Saint-Jean
St. Leu De St. Leu
St. Martin De St. Martin
Saint-Paul De Saint-Paul
Saint-Père De Saint-Père
Salmon Samon
Sanbrooke Sambrook
Sanderacque Sidrac
Sanders Saunders
Sanford Sandford
Sandis Sandys
Sargent Sarjent Sergeant Seargeant
Saunders Sanders
Saunderson Sanderson
Savage Savidge
Savery Savory
Savion Savyon
Sayller Sailler Saigler
Saynoe Stayne
Schäufle Von Schäufle
Schegs Schecks
Scheier Scheirer
Schenberg Schonberg
Schieferdöcker Schifferdöcker

Schiold Schol
Schiøtz Schuetze
Schirmer Schermer
Schleuer Schloer
Schmidt Schmied Schmit
Schneidau Von Schneidau
Schøtte Schuetze
Schumann Schuhmann
Scoles Scones Stones
Scummo Schumo
Seamer Seamour Seymour
Seargeant Sargent Sarjent Sergeant
Sedley Sidley
Segrave Seagrave
Seil Seall
Sellars Sellers
Sergeant Seargeant Sargent Sarjent
Servière Grollier de Servière
Sevestre Senestre
Seymour Seamour Seamer
Sharratt Sherrat
Shearer Sheerer
Shelton Skelton
Sherrat Sharratt
Shurley Shirley
Shurwood Sherwood
Sideracque Sidrac
Sidley Sedley
Sidwell Sedwell
Siedle Sittle
Sime Sym
Simes Sims Simms Symms
Simkin Simkins Simpkin Simpkins
Simkinson Simpkinson Sinkinson
Simmons Simmonds Simons Simonds Symons Symonds
Simms Sims Symms
Simonds Simons Simmonds Simmons Symons Symonds
Simpkin Simpkins Simkin Simkins
Simpkinson Sinkinson
Sims Simms Simes Symms
Sittle Siedle
Skelton Shelton
Skipper Skepper
Skult Schol
Sloper Slipper
Smeeton Smeaton
Smith Smyth
Smithies Smythies
Snack Schnack
Somellier Sommelier
Somers Summers
Soriau Sotiau Souriau
Souley Sonley
Souriau Sotiau
Southgate Suggate
Spear Speer
Spendelow Spendlove
Staptoe Stepstow
Staunton Stanton
Steephens Steevens Stephens Stevens
Stein Von Stein
Stephens Stevens
Stephenson Stevenson
Stewart Stuart
Stiel Steill
Stile Stiles Style Styles
Stirzacker Starzaker
Stoakes Stokes Stocks
Stockdon Stockton
Stockell Stockwell
Stocks Stokes Stoakes
Stokell Stockell Stockwell
Stokheyn Stockheyne
Story Storey
Strachan Strahan Strauchan
Strangfellow Stringfellow
Strebell Streibel
Streetin Streelin
Stringfellow Strangfellow
Stuart Stewart
Suhrbom Zurbun
Sumers Summers Somers
Sumner Sunner
Swayers Swaayen
Sych Sich
Sylver Silver
Sylvester Silvester
Sym Sime
Symms Simms Sims
Symonds Symons Simons Simonds Simmons Simmonds

Tailor Taylor
Tait Tate
Talan Talon
Tarant Tarrant
Tate Tait
Taylor Tailor
Terry Tirry
Terveen Treveen
Thibaud *Thibault* Thibaut Thiébault
Thiriot Thieriot
Thirkelt Threlkeld
Thompson Thomson Tomson
Thoresby Therasby
Thoorn Van der Thoorn
Thorne Thorn
Thouverot Touverez
Threlkeld Thirkeld
Thristram Tristram
Thuillay Du Thuillay
Thümcke Thiemecke
Tifene Tiphesne
Tight Tyte
Tiriot Thieriot
Tirry Terry
Tite Tight Tyte
Toleson Tollison Tolson
Tolley Tolly
Tomegay Thomegay Thomeguex
Tomlyn *Tomlyns* Tomlin Tomlins
Tompkins Tomkins
Tompson Tomson Thompson Thomson
Tornare Tournarre
Tounley Townley
Toutlemonde Toulemonde
Touverez Thouverot
Towneson Townsend
Tranchant Trenchant
Travis Trevis
Trechsler Drechsler
Trenchant Tranchant
Tressler Trechsler
Trevis Travis
Tristram Thristram
Tröffler Treffler
Tunmarck Thunmark
Turbom Zurbun
Turet Thuret
Turveen Treveen
Tyte Tight

Uyterveer Uijterveer

Vaillant Vallant
Valinghauss Vollenhauss
Vallé Vallier
Varneaux Verneaux
Vauchez Vauché Vaucher
Vauguion De Vauguion
Vaulove Vanlove
Vaultrollier Vautrollier
Vauquer Vautier Votier
Veber Weber
Vechelen Van Vechelen
Veit Viet Vié Witte Hueit
Verneaux Varneaux
Verrassat Veyrassat
Vibrandi Wijbrandts
Viet Vié Veit Witte Hueit
Vinco Vinio Vigniaux
Vogelin Vogel

Voice Voyce
Voirin Varin
Volkmer Volckmair Volchamer
Vollant Volunt Volant
Votier Vautier
Voyce Voice
Vuarin Varin
Vuille Wuilly
Vuilleumier Willeumier Willieumier

Waker Walker
Walbank Wallbank
Walden Wallden
Waley Whaley
Walingford Wallingford
Walker Waker
Wallbank Walbank
Wallden Walden
Walley Whalley
Wallström Wahlström
Wareham Warham
Wareing Waring
Warsfold Worsfold
Warswick Worswick
Warton Wharton Worton
Watters Waters
Watton Walton
Weast West
Weber Veber
Wehrle Werrle
Weise Weisse
Wekherlin Weckherlin
Welch Welsh
Wellcome Welcome
Wellowe Willowe
Welsh Welch
Wennock Winnock
Werrle Wehrle
Westlake Weslake
Weston Westen Westin
Wethel Wetherell
Wetherby Weatherby
Wetherall Weatherall
Weybrandt Weijbrandt Wijbrandts
Weych Wych
Weylett Waylett
Whaley Waley
Whalley Walley
Wharton Warton Worton
Whitaker Whittaker
Whitefield Whitfield

Whyatte Wyatt
Wibrants Wijbrandts Weijbrandt
Wideman *Widenmann* Widman Wiedemann
Widenböck Wittenböck
Widtenmann Wiedemann Widemann Widmann
Wiellerme Williarme
Wier Wyer
Wilbrandt Wijbrandts Weijbrandts
Wilcox Wilcocks Willcocks
Wild Wyld
Wilder Wylder
Willcocks Wilcocks
Willes Wills
Willeumier Willieumier Vuilleumier
Willey Wiley
Williard Willard
Willieumier Willeumier Vuilleumier
Willmot Wilmot
Wills Willes
Willson Wilson
Wilmhurst Wilmshurst
Winckler Winkhler Winkler
Winder Window
Winn Wynn
Winton Windon
Wittman Wightmann
Wolf Wolfe Wolff Woolfe
Wolfreston Woolverton Wolverstone
Wood Woods
Woolfe Wolf Wolfe Wolff
Woolverton Wolverstone
Wonostrocht Wanostrocht
Worton Warton Wharton
Wouters Gualtheri
Wuilly Vuille
Würz Wirtz
Wyatt Whyatt
Wybrants Wijbrandts Weijbrandt
Wyer Wier
Wyeth Wyth Wythe
Wyld Wild
Wylder Wilder
Wynman Widman Widemann Wiedemann
Wyrall Wirral
Wyse Wise
Wyth Wythe Wyeth
Wyther Wither

Yateman Yeatman

Ziegelhart Ziegenhirt

ADDENDA

ABADIE, ——. *Toulouse.* 1824. Repaired Hôtel de Ville clock.
ABRAHAM, ——. *Frome.* ca.1820. l.c. clock.
ABRAM, Jean Nicolas. *Montécheroux* (*Doubs*). 1803. Maker of watchmakers' tools.
ACTON, William. prob. *London.* an.1766. Watch.
ADAM, ——. *Udine.* Early 16c. Repaired clock on tower.
ADAMSON, ——. *Paris.* 1791. C. to the Royal family.
ADRIANO, ——. *Rome.* ca.1558.
AFFRES, Jacques. *Castres.* End 16c.
AGAR, Thomas. *London.* ca.1720. g. en. watch.
AGUITON ET ROCHAT, ——. Late 18c. 4 col. g. rep. watch.
AHLEFELDT, Carl Wilhelm von. *Ekenäs* (*Finland*). d.1800. Cartel clock and watch.
ALEXANDRE, ——. *Paris.* Juré 1753.
ALLAMAND ET BERTHOUD, ——. Late 18c. sil. p.c. watch Parisi coll.
ALLAN & CAITHNESS. *London.* 1800-4.
ALLEN, John. *Macclesfield.* ca.1760. l.c. clock.
ALLIER ET BREGUER. *Paris.* ca.1820. Al. watch Parisi coll.
ALLSOP, Joshua. *E. Smithfield.* ca.1710. l.c. clock. cf. ALSOPE.
AMABLE, Marie. ——. Mid. 17c. Oval gilt eng. watch.
ANCOILLE, ——. *Paris.* End 17c. sil. al. watch.
ANSELL, Edward. *Abingdon.* 1730. Lantern clock.
APPS, Robert. *Battle.* ca.1780. l.c. clock. 30-hour locking plate clock ca.1800.
ARLAUD—
Abraham, bro. of Jean. *Geneva.* b.1627, m.1647-86. In *Constantinople* 1647-51, 1666 and 1668.
Lazare, son of Jean. *Geneva.* b.1665, d.1734. Watch Geneva M.
ARMISTEAD, Joseph. *Shoeham.* 1748. Insolvent. W.
ARNOLD, Thomas Wolfgang. *Hamburg.* mar. an.1678.
ASPINWALL, James. *Wigan.* 1712-17.
ATKINSON, William. *Carlisle.* 1777. W.
AUSTIN, John. *Uxbridge.* ca.1705-ca.1725.
AVENALL—
William. *Gravesend.* 1750-60. l.c. clock.
Joseph. *Farnham.* 1st half 18c. l.c. clock, one hand.
AVERY, John. *Boston, U.S.A.* 1726. Maker of clock in old North Church.
AVICE, ——. *Rheims.* Early 18c. watch.

BAILLON, François. *Choudens.* 2nd half 18c. C.
BAILY—
Joel. *Bradford* (*Chester Co., U.S.A.*). b.1732. l.c. clocks.
Emmor, son. *Salem, N.J., Baltimore* and *Ohio.*
BAKER, John. *Hull.* ca.1780. br. clock.
BALISSAT, Peter. *Geneva.* a.1659.
BANCROFT—
——. *Stockport.* ca.1720. l.c. clock.
Titus. *Sowerby Bridge.* 1809. Made clock for Hepptonstall church.
BARKER—
Thomas. *Wigan.* 1738.
Joseph. *Appleby.* Early 19c.
BARLIE, ——. *London.* ca.1770. p.c. watch Parisi coll. prob. same as Thomas BARLEY.
BARNES, Timothy. *Bristol* and *Lichfield, U.S.A.* b. 1760-93.
BAROCCI, Gio. Maria. *Pesaro.* ca.1570, d.1593. Famous maker of complex clocks. Made planetary clock for the Pope.
BARONNEAU, F. *Paris.* Mid. 17c. Watch mt. Gélis coll.
BARWISE, Nathaniel. *London.* ca.1810.
BASTARD, Jean. *Geneva.* a.1638.
BASTIAENS, Mattheus. *Antwerp.* 1596-1608. Repaired clock of St. Jacques.
BASTIEN, ——. *Paris.* 1737. Devised a cal. clock.
BATES, John. *Atherstone.* Late 18c. l.c. clock.
BATTY—
Joseph. *Halifax.* 1767-71.
John. *Halifax.* 1770.
James. *Halifax.* 1770. cf. BATTIE.
BAYER, Johann Georg. *Grosse Glogau.* Early 18c. rep. watch.
BAYLIFFE—
John. *Halifax.* 1765.
J. *Tewkesbury.* 1770.
BÉCHART, François. *Paris.* 2nd half 18c.
BELLAMY, Jean Joseph. *Geneva.* ca.1810. Watch Parisi coll.
BELLE, Josias. *Paris.* b.1628-84.
BELLMAN, ——. *Kendal.* ca.1800. l.c. clock.
BENGUEREL-DIT-PERROUD, Isaac and David, bro. *Fontainemelon.* 1793. Made partnership with J. H. and F. Humbert-Droz, starting the Fontainemelon factory.
BENNY, Jonathan. *Easton, U.S.A.* Late 18c.
BENOIST, Claude. *Toulouse.* 1577. Keeper of clock on Hôtel de Ville.
BERGIER, ——. *London.* ca.1700. p.c. eng. watch.
BERGUILLIER, ——. *Paris.* 1818. Cal. and equation watch.
BERNHARD, Simon. *Prague.* ca.1780. sil. p.c. watch Parisi coll.
BERRY, John, jun. and sen. *London* (*Clements La.*). 1743.
BERTRAM, Gottlieb Friedrich. *Freiberg.* ca.1800. Watch virgule esc.
BERTRAND, ——. *Castres.* 1638.
BEWLAY, Samuel. *London.* ca.1705. sil. p.c. watch.
BEZIÈRES, Janos. *France.* Late 18c. Watch.
BILLINGE, John. *Wigan.* 1671. W.
BILLINGTON, Everard. *Market Harborough.* ca.1750. l.c. clock.
BINET, ——. *Paris.* 1560. C. to the King.
BINGHAM, ——. *London.* ca.1800. Watch.
BINNS—
Robert. *Halifax.* 1710.
James. *Halifax.* 1720-63.
BIRD, Edward. *London* (*Exchange Alley*). Early 18c. l.c. clock.
BISOT, Jacques. *Paris.* ca.1650. C.
BLANCHARD, Charles. *Porrentruy.* 1809-1823. Patented a watch esc.
BLASENS, Lambrech. *Hasselt.* 1560. Replaced chiming mechanism of St. Jacques' clock, Antwerp.
BLONDEL, Marc. *Naples.* Late 18c. Watch.

BOBINET—
Charles. *Geneva.* b.1610, d.1678. See main list for many works.
Abraham, son. *Geneva.* b.1639, d.1688. crys. cross watch M.M.A.
BOLLAND, John. *Halifax.* 1664-82. Repaired church clock.
BORDIER—
Leonard. *Paris.* Late 18c. g. en. watch set pearls and diamonds.
——. *London.* 1785. sig. on dial of Swiss mt.
BORELL, Maximilian. *London.* End 18c. 3-case watch for Turkey.
BORQUIN, ——. *London.* 1782.
BOSCOVICH, R. G. *Milan.* 1770. Invented a compensated pendulum.
BOUCANSON, Louis. *Toulouse.* 1647. Clock on St. Sernin church.
BOUCHIER, ——. *Paris.* ca.1780. Regulator.
BOULANGER, ——. *Paris.* 1793. Took care of Breguet's business while he was in Switzerland.
BOULTON, Matthew. *London* and *Birmingham.* 1760. d.1809. Made elaborate clock cases in French style. Also made clocks.
BOURDILLON, LES FRÈRES. *Geneva.* ca.1780. sil. watch studded diamonds Parisi coll.
BOURET, Samuel. ——. ca.1760. sil. p.c. watch.
BOUSSARD, A. *Toulouse.* 1826. Patented a str. work for clocks.
BOUVEL, ——. *Paris.* Mid. 18c. C.
BOUVRIER, M. *Pittsburgh, U.S.A.* ca.1820.
BOWER, Peter. *Redlinch.* Early 18c. l.c. clock, one hand.
BOYER, François. *Castres.* 1757.
BRAEM, Caspar. *London.* 1743. W.
BRANDHUBER, Johann Leonhard. *Thannhausen.* 1763-75. Made clock for Zipplingen church. Repaired clock of Eschenbach church.
BREGUET, ——. *Besançon.* 1823. Worked at factory.
BRIDGE, Thomas. *Wigan.* 1712-45. l.c. clocks.
BROCHE, Jacques, & Comp. *Berlin.* Late 18c. Watch.
BROCKHURST, Benjamin. *Coventry.* ca. 1705. l.c. clock.
BROEKMAN, C. H. *Delft.* 1658. Fitted pendulum to town clock.
BROMLEY—
Charles. *Halifax.* 1820.
William. *Halifax.* 1816.
William & son. *Halifax.* 1826. Wm. and Richard (son) dissolved partnership.
BROUGH, Henry. *Workington.* ca.1770-91. C.
BROWN, Jonathan C. *Bristol, U.S.A.* b.1807, d.1872.
BRUGEL, G. A. *Venice.* Early 18c. al. watch.
BRUNER, Asmus Birin. *Germany.* 1577. Tower table clock.
BRUYKENS, A. B. *Amsterdam.* ca.1750. sil. p.c. rep. watch Parisi coll.
BUCHANAN, A. D. *Boston.* Early 19c. l.c. clock.
BUCKNEY—
Thomas. *London.* b.1838, d.1900. Succeeded to the firm of E. Dent & Co. in 1860.
Daniel, bro. *London.* b.1845, d.1927. A fine W. Joined the firm of E. Dent & Co. in 1898.
BUHRÉ, Paul. *Chaux-de-Fonds.* From 1815. Firm still in business.
BUPERT, Michel. *Paris.* 1641. C. to duc d'Orléans.
BURCHALL, ——. *London.* 1782.
BURGES, John. *Wigan.* 1710. d.1754. l.c. clock Wigan library.
BURGESS, ——. *London (Old Bailey).* 1780. CC.
BURROUGH—
Edward. *Fordham.* ca.1745. l.c. clock.
John. *Ironbridge.* ca.1770. l.c. clock.
John. *Brampton.* ca.1770.
BURTON & PATTISON. *Halifax.* 1800.
BUSCHENDORF, Karl Friedrich. *Leipzig.* 1805. Pub. 'Gründlicher Unterricht von Thurmuhren.
BUTCHER, Charles. *Bedford.* ca.1735. Watch.
BUTTBUB—
Carel. *Strasbourg.* 1588.
Hanns. *Strasbourg.* 1595.
BUTTERLY, Stephen. *Dartford.* ca.1710-26. l.c. clock.
BUTTERWORTH, ——. *London (Temple La.).* 1782.

CAILLARD, ——. *Paris.* ca.1730. Watch Parisi coll.
CAILLATTE—
Louis. *Geneva.* b.1624-45.
Jean Pierre. *Geneva.* b.1627-66.
Jaques. *Geneva.* b.1634-91.
Daniel. *Geneva.* b.1636, d.an.1662.
Pierre. *Metz* and later *Heidelberg.* b.1640.
Abraham, bro. of Jaques. *Geneva.* b.1642, d.1710. French refugee. Watches Louvre M.M.A. and Gélis coll. Watch in shell-shaped case of garnet, g. en. mountings. Mantel clock.
Matthieu, bro. *Geneva.* 1646-78.
Jean, son of Jean Pierre. *Geneva.* b.1659. Went *Copenhagen.* 1695.
Isaac, son of Jaques. *Geneva.* 1663-1738.
André, son of Abraham. *Geneva.* 1666-1709.
Isaac, bro. *Geneva.* b.1671.
Arni, bro. *Geneva.* 1672-1744.
Pierre, son of Matthieu. *Geneva.* 1670-1723.
Bartholomeus, son of Jean. *Copenhagen.* mar.1726, d.1761. Master of Corporation.
Jacques, son. *Copenhagen.* a.1743.
Jean. *Geneva.* 1693-1763.
David. *Copenhagen.* m.1771.
CALAME, ——. *Hérimoncourt.* 1806. Associated with JAPY in ébauche factory.
CALDANI, ——. *Alessandria.* ca.1780. rep. trav. clock, tortoiseshell case, Parisi coll.
CAMPANI, Giovanni, prob. bro. of P. T. CAMPANUS. *Rome.* 1656-96. Astronomer and optical inst. maker. Rolling ball clock Cassel Landes-M. In 1660 pub. 'Discorso di G. Campani intorno ai suoi muti oriuoli.'
CANNON, Samuel. *Londom.* ca.1740. l.c. clock.
CARR, John. *Coventry.* 1778-98. W. In 1798 said that he made 3,819 watches in the year.
CARTER—
Christopher. *Galby (Leics.).* b.1676. Lantern clock Leicester M.
Morris. *Bishop's Stortford.* ca.1760-84. l.c. clock. W.
CASSIN, Isaac. *Geneva.* a.1688.
CASTILLE, ——. *Paris.* 1824. Device for obtaining any number of divisions from a dividing plate.
CÉZERON, J. *Toulouse.* 1774.
CHAMBERT, Jean. *Toulouse.* 1552. Keeper of clock on Hôtel de Ville.
CHAMP, ——. prob. *London.* an.1766. Watch.
CHARLESON, W. *London.* 18c. p.c. watch.

CHATEL, ——. *Turin.* ca.1750. Watch Parisi coll.
CHEESEBROUGH, Adam. *Penrith.* 1689-1712. l.c. clock. Made clock for Penrith church.
CHENEVIÈRE—
François. *Geneva.* a.1653.
Pierre. *Geneva.* a.1654.
——. *London.* End 17c. en. watch.
CLAVEL, ——. *London.* ca.1750. p.c. watch Parisi coll.
CLERC, ——. *Fleurier.* ca.1800. en. watch.
CLOUGH, John. *Manchester.* Early 18c. l.c. clock.
COATS—
Archibald. *Wigan.* To 1811. C.
James and Robert. *Wigan.* 1794.
James. *Wigan.* 1800-11.
COCHRAN, George. *West Chester, U.S.A.* 1799-1806.
COGNIET, Jacques. *Paris.* ca.1690. Watch Parisi coll. prob. same as COIGNET.
COIJPEL, A. *Paris.* ca.1700. Worker in bronze clock cases.
COLLON, Charles. prob. *London.* an.1766. Watch.
CONNOLD, ——. *Aylsham.* ca.1800. l.c. clock.
COOKE, John. *Runcorn.* d.1818. C. & W.
COPPEN, ——. *Paris.* Late 18c. g. watch.
CORANCEZ, ——. *Paris.* 1799. Devised a bimetallic balance.
CORNISH, Richard. *Westram.* Early 18c. l.c. clock.
CORTÉBERT WATCH CO. *Cortébert* and *Chaux-de-Fonds.* Started 1790, still in business.
CORTHUYS, Herman. *Malines.* 1664. Repaired clock of St. Rombaux.
COUPÉ—
Elizabeth. *Paris.* 1683-8. 'Horlogeusse du Roi.'
Jacques. *Paris.* 1680. C. to the King.
Édouard. *Paris.* 1683. C. to the King.
COURVOISIER, Fritz. *Chaux-de-Fonds.* b.1799, d.1854.
CRISTIN, ——. *Paris.* 1755. Presented a new watch esc. to the Académie.
CROW, George, bro. of Thos. *Wilmington, U.S.A.* d.an.1802.
CURSIN, Louis. *Paris.* End 17c. Watch en. flowers.
CUSIN, Jean. *Geneva.* b.1585, d.1656. crys. cross watch M.M.A.

DALAVAN, Agnes. *London.* 1427. Made clock for new tower in Westminster Pal.
DANCEL, ——. *Paris.* ca.1780. Mantel clock.
DANDILLET, ——. *Beaucourt.* 1800. Associated with JAPY in his ébauche factory.
DARBYSHIRE, Roger. *Wigan.* 1662. d.1690.
DARDENNE, F. *Orléans.* ca.1700. Watch.
DARVILL, Edward. *London.* ca.1780. Large oval p.c. en. watch.
D'AUBESPINE, Colin. *France.* 1421. C. to duke of Burgundy.
DAVEY, ——. *Yarmouth.* Late 18c. l.c. clock.
DAVID, René. *Bordeaux.* ca.1700. eng. sil. watch, en. on cock, Gélis coll.
DAVY, R. *Aylsham.* Late 18c. l.c. clock.
DEACON—
Samuel. *Barton-in-the-Beans.* 1771. Many l.c. clocks.
John. *Leicester.* 1784-98. C. & W.
DECARRO, Jaques. *Geneva.* a.1695.
DEFINOD, Louis. *Grenoble.* 1603.
DEFROCHES, ——. *Courtenay* (*Sens*). 1776. Turret clock.
DEGEN—
Johan Fredrik. *Stockholm.* Late 18c.
Jakob. *Vienna.* b.1761, d.1846.
DEHECQ, F. *Orléans.* End 17c. eng. al. watch.
DEJOUX, Pierre. *Geneva.* a.1679.
DE LA COMBE, Jean Pierre. *Travers.* Mid. 18c. W.
DELAFON, ——. *Avallon.* ca.1700. Clock with semi-circular dial.
DENNISON—
Thomas. *Halifax.* 1814.
Aaron L. *Waltham, U.S.A.,* and *Birmingham.* b.1812, d.1895. In 1849 started the Howard, Davis and Dennison factory at *Roxbury,* later known as the Warren Mfg. Co. and, after moving to *Waltham,* the Boston Watch Co. In 1863 he went to *Zürich* to manufacture watch parts for watches produced by the Tremont Watch Co. in Boston. In 1866, the Co. moved to *Melrose* and failed in 1868. In 1870 he came to *Birmingham* selling his machines to a Co. known later as The English Watch Co. The firm of DENNISON, WIGLY & Co. started a case-making factory in 1874.
DEROCHES FRÈRES ET EYNOUF, ——. ca.1740. rep. watch Parisi coll.
DERVIEUX, V. *Bordeaux.* Late 18c. g. rep. watch.
DESAUX, PÈRE, FILS ET CIE. *Geneva.* ca.1800. en. mandoline watch.
DESBLANCS, ——. *Trévoux.* 1806. Made watch verges by machine.
DEUTZEN, Matthys. *Strasbourg.* 1639.
DE VILLENEUVE, ——. *Paris.* 2nd half 18c. C.
DILGER, Andreas. *Gutenbach.* Late 18c. Musical C.
DIXON, John. *Sowerby Bridge.* 1780.
DOBEL, Robert. *Yeovil.* Late 18c. l.c. clock.
DODSON, ——. *Beeston.* ca.1770-ca.1780. l.c. clock.
DOMINICÉ—
Bernard. *Geneva.* 1685-96.
ET BLONDET. *Geneva.* Early 19c. Watch Parisi coll.
DONCASTER, Thomas. *Wigan.* 1755. d.ca. 1802.
DOUNET, Etienne. *Castres.* 1691.
DOWNES, Robert. *London* (*Soho*). 1748. Insolvent. W.
DROZ, R. *Charleville* (*Ardennes*). 1826 devised a rep. work.
DROZ-MATILE, N. *Chaux-de-Fonds.* ca. 1800. g. watch.
DRURY, C. W. *Banbury.* Early 19c. 30-hour l.c. clock.
DUBOIS—
l'aîné. *Toulouse.* 1680. Watch mt. Gélis coll.
——. *Toulouse.* 1758.
Philippe Henri & Charles, sons of Philippe. *Le Locle.* 1785. Joined their father.
DUCKWORTH—
Richard. *Halifax.* 1651. d.1677. C.
John. *Halifax.* 1651.
DUDAL, Gédéon. *France.* 1757. Devised a fuzee-cutting machine.
DUFALGA, Philippe Cafarello. *Geneva.* 1712. d.1794. g. en. watches Mallet and Gélis colls.
DU MARESQ, Philip. *London.* ca.1660. p.c. watch.
DUMAS—
Antoine. *Toulouse.* 1554. Clock in Cour du Sénéchal.
A. *Toulouse.* Late 16c. Oct. table clock St. Raymond M.
DUMOULIN—
André. *Breslau.* Late 18c. Watch.
Francis. *Montreal.* Late 18c. br. clock.

DUNANT, J. P. *Geneva.* ca.1800. en. watch.
DUNDAS, Charles. *London.* ca.1800. Watch for China.
DUPRÉ, ——. *Paris.* ca.1700. Watch Gélis coll.
DYER, Giles. *Boston, U.S.A.* 1673-80. Made town clock.

EBERLE, Johannes. *Augsburg.* 18c. Watch.
EISENBERG, ——. *Liverpool.* ca.1800. g. watch.
ELLIS, James. *Canterbury.* 1674.
ELRHOW, ——. *London.* Mid. 18c. sig. on rep. watch, with J. B. RILLET. *Geneva* on dial. prob. WOHRLE.
ENGMAN, Carl Fredrik. *Stockholm.* Mid. 18c. l.c. clock.
ENGWAL, Magnus. *Sweden.* 1760. l.c. clock
ÉTIENNE, J. P. *Nancy.* 1810. Pub. 'Notions sur l'horlogerie.'
ETTRY, John. *Horton.* ca.1735. l.c. clock.
EWBANK, George. *Halifax.* 1795.

FABIAN, Christoph. *Forchheim.* 2nd half 16c. Watch in ivory barrel.
FALLER, Matthias. b. in *Neukirch* 1707, d. in *St. Mergen* ca.1790.
FALQUET, Bastian. *Geneva.* a.1663.
FARRER—
Jonathan. *Warlay* (near *Halifax*). b.1671, d.1702.
Jonathan. *Warlay.* 1740.
Joshua. *Brighouse.* 1750.
FAULMIN, John. *London?* Mid. 18c. Watch.
FAVARET, Claude Antoine, aîné. *Morey* (*Hte Saône*). 1804. astro. clock with 8 dials.
FAVRE, Louis. *Naples.* Late 18c.
FAVRE-JACOT, Georges. *LeLocle.* ca.1800. en. watch.
FEHR, Thomas. *Germany.* ca.1760. g. watch.
FENIE, Michel. *Venice.* Mid. 17c. hex. astro. watch.
FERTIG, Jacob. *Vincent* (*Chester Co.*). b.1778, d.1823. l.c. clock.
FIELD, Matthew. *London.* ca.1740. Wall clock.
FINCKH, Hans Martin. *Strasbourg.* 1660.
FIRDIRER, J. *Birmingham.* Early 19c. Watch Birmingham M.
FISCHER, T. *Dresden.* Late 18c. Watch in ring.
FLATHER, William. *Halifax.* 1786-1856.
FLETCHER, John. *Ripponden.* 1740-65.
FLEUTRY, ——. *Paris.* 1789. T.C.
FLOURNOY—
Jean. *Geneva.* a.1691.
P. *Paris.* Mid. 18c. C.
FOIX, Louis de. *Escurial.* 1558. C. to Philippe II.
FOREMAN, ——. *Canterbury.* ca.1800. l.c. clock.
FORFAICT, Abraham. *Sedan.* d.1612.
FOSTER, Jabez. *London.* ca.1660. g. en. watch.
FRANCIS, ——. *Wymondham.* Late 18c. l.c. clock. cf. Richard of *Attleborough.*
FREDONIA WATCH CO., N.Y. 1880. Previously INDEPENDENT WATCH Co. Became PEORIA WATCH Co. in 1886.
FREKE, Daniel. *Bridport* (*Dorset*). ca.1705. l.c. clock.
FRISARD, ——. *Paris.* ca.1800. Watch Parisi coll.
FRITSCHE, Johann Christoph. *Germany.* 18c. p.c. watch.

GALLONDE, Louis Charles. *Paris.* Devised a 4-wheel clock in 1742 and a depth tool in 1751.
GAMBELL, Thomas. *Walton* (*Leics.*). 1704. Lantern clock, iron mt. with dial on front plate.
GAMNETT, Richard. *Alford.* Early 18c. l.c. clock.
GARTLY, John. *Aberdeen.* b.1749, m.1783, d.1827. Made clocks for King's Coll., cathedral and Tolbooth Aberdeen and l.c. clocks. Lever watch with double esc. wheel, Ilbert coll.
GAUKROGER, John. *Halifax.* 1823.
GAY, John. *London.* ca.1800. Watch.
GENTIL, Jean. *Geneva.* a.1672.
GEVRIL, Moyse. *Neuchâtel* or *Le Locle.* 1780. Auto winding watch.
GILBERT, Abraham. *Paris.* ca.1770. rep. watch.
GILFORD, James. *London.* Mid. 18c. sil. repoussé watch.
GILMORE, John. *Battle.* ca.1700. clock.
GIROD-CHANTRONS, ——. *Hérimoncourt.* 1806. Son-in-law of JAPY. Director of ébauche factory.
GLAZE, Edward. *Bridgnorth.* ca.1770. l.c. clock.
GODDELAINE, ——. *Paris.* Mid. 18c. C.
GOEGEL, Joseph. *Friedberg.* ca.1800. rep. watch Parisi coll.
GOTTIER, Grégoire. *France.* Late 18c. g. en. watch.
GOUCHON, Jacques. *Paris.* From 1726. Previously with HANET as HANET ET GOUCHON.
GOUX, François de. *Toulouse.* 1542-51. In charge of clock on Hôtel de Ville.
GRAVER, Thomas. *Manchester.* 1397. Sued by the Prior of Warrington for having made an unsatisfactory clock at a charge of 100s.
GRELET, Theodor. ——. ca.1710. Watch with English type cock Parisi coll.
GRIEDER, ——. *Basle* and *La Neuveville.* 1787.
GRIESSHABER, Gebrüder. *Black Forest.* Late 18c.
GRIFFON, ——. *Toulouse.* 1741. Restored clock on Hôtel de Ville.
GRIME, Thomas. ——. ca.1625. sil. oval watch, calendar ring, no screws.
GRIT, Abel. *Castres.* 1658.
GROCOT, Thomas. *Holywell.* d.1813. W.
GROOTE—
Pieter de. *Antwerp.* 1557. Fitted chiming mechanism to clock of St. Jacques.
Hans. *Antwerp.* 1575-88. Repaired clock of St. Jacques.
Jan de. ——. 1751. Small clock.
GROSVENOR, ——. *London.* 1702.
GUARFFI, ——. *London.* Mid. 18c. p.c. rep. watch.
GUIGUET, ——. *London.* Mid. 18c. sil. p.c. watch.
GUILLENIEZ, ——. *Paris.* ca.1700. Watch Parisi coll.
GUILLIAUMIN, Jehan. Went to *Constantinople* as apprentice in 1602 with RUAUD.
GUY, ——. *Shaston.* ca.1770. l.c. clock.

HADLEY—
Humphrey. *Birmingham.* d.1698.
Humphrey, sen., son. *Birmingham.* 1702-7. Several turret clocks.
Humphrey, jun., bro. *Birmingham.* 1708. d.1770. Made clock for cathedral.
HALL, Thomas. *Runcorn.* d.1818. C. & W.
HALLIFAX, S. *Barnsley.* ca.1730. l.c. clock.
HAMILTON—
George. *London.* ca.1660. g. en. watch.
John. *Glasgow.* 1771-89. l.c. mus. clock.
HAMPSON, Robert. *Wigan.* 1791. Clock Warrington M. sd. at Warrington ca.1800, may be by him.

HANET—
Nicolas. *The Hague.* 1659. *Paris.* d.1726. sil. watch Horstmann coll. sil. watch Gélis coll. Mark of 1672-80 with balance spring. Gilt en. watch ca.1700.
ET GOUCHON. *Paris.* ca.1710. GOUCHON continued alone after 1726. cal. watch Gélis coll.
HANKS, Benjamin. *Litchfield, U.S.A.* 1783. Obtained patent for self-winding clock from Connecticut Assembly.
HANNET, N. *Paris.* ca.1700. al. watch. cf. HANOT.
HARDY—
Edward. *Halifax.* 1780.
Thomas. *Nottingham.* 1799. W. l.c. clock.
HARGREAVES, Thomas. *St. Ives.* Early 18c. Watch.
HARIMAN, Edward. *Workington.* Mid. 18c. l.c. clocks.
HARLEY, Joseph. *Wingrove* (*Wingrave* near *Aylesbury*?). Late 17c. l.c. clock.
HARLOW, Benjamin. *Lane End* (now *Longton, N. Staffs*). ca.1825. l.c. clocks.
HARQUIN, ——. *Paris.* 1733. Devised a watch esc.
HARRISON, Thomas. *Lacks.* 18c. sq. hood l.c. clock.
HART, ——. *N. Walsham.* ca.1800. l.c. clock.
HÄRTEL, Ana Maria. *Augsburg.* Late 18c. Watch, onyx case.
HARWOOD, James. *Halifax.* 1714-21.
HAYLEY, Michael. *Halifax.* 1651. Repaired church clock.
HAZELTON, H. *Armagh.* ca.1780. l.c. clock.
HEATON, ——. *Bierley.* Late 18c. l.c. clock.
HEBDEN, George. *Halifax.* 1816.
HECKEL—
Michael. *Friedberg.* 17c. Table clock in ruby drum glass case.
Johan. *Warsaw.* Early 18c. trav. str. clock.
Michel. ——. ca.1740. al. clock Parisi coll.
HELLIWELL—
Richard. *Halifax.* 1626-32. Repaired church clock.
H. *Leeds.* 1814. l.c. clock.
HENKELS, Jan. *Amsterdam.* End 17c. Watch en. Huaud les jeunes.
HERDL, Christ. *Augsburg.* ca.1700. Watch.
HEYDRICH, Matthias. *Hamburg.* mar. an. 1682.
HEYWOOD, ——. *Carnarvon.* ca.1770. l.c. clock.
HIBBARD, ——. *Willistown, U.S.A.* 1809-1818. l.c. clocks.
HIGOU, Pierre. *Paris.* 1769. Juré.
HILLS, ——. *London* (*Fleet St.*). 1780. CC.
HILTON—
Evan. *Wigan.* 1667. d.1699.
Joh. Nic. *Regensburg.* 18c. Watch.
HINES—
P. *Needham Market.* ca.1750. l.c. clock.
Edward. *Needham Market.* ca.1770. Small l.c. clock.
HOEYSEL, Johann Carl. *Dantzig.* ca.1700. hex. str. al. and cal. watch.
HOHLFELD, ——. *Austria.* b.1711, d.1771.
HOLDSWORTH, Jonas. *Halifax.* 1816.
HOLFOM, Christoph. *Germany.* 1710.
HOLLIWELL, ——. *Birmingham.* Early 19c. l.c. clock.
HOLMES—
Paul. *Lane End* (now *Longton, N. Staffs.*).
James. *Cheadle.* ca.1825. l.c. clocks.
HOLROYD, Richard. *Halifax.* 1820.
HOLT—
William. *Wigan.* b.ca.1735, d.1780. Watch Wigan Library.

HOLT—*continued.*
Matthew, son of Matthew. *Wigan.* b.1745, d.1805.
HONEYBONE, Richard. *Wanborough.* ca. 1735. l.c. clock.
HORN, Johann Antoni. *Dantzig.* 17c. br. clock.
HOUGHTON, Richard. *Wigan.* 1784-1806. C.
HOUTON, Richard. *Oversley Green.* a. to Tompion ca.1705.
HOWES, B. *Downham.* 2nd half 18c. l.c. clock.
HOWLETT & HORNE. *London.* Late 18c. Elaborate mus. table clock.
HOWS, Thomas. *London.* ca.1640. sil. watch 1⅛ in. dia. pinned on cock.
HOWSE, ——. *Swindon.* ca.1770. l.c. clocks.
HOY, D. J. *Mattishall* (near *Norwich*). Late 18c. l.c. clock.
HUBBARD, John. *London* (*Southwark*). ca.1770. l.c. clock.
HUBERT, Paul. *Geneva.* 1683.
HUDDISON, William. *London.* 1816. Watch.
HUGGIN—
Barnard. *Ashwell Thorp.* 18c. l.c. clock.
William & Barnard. *Ashwell Thorp.* 2nd half 18c. l.c. clock.
HUGHES, J. *London* (*Gracechurch St.*). 1780. CC.
HUGUET, Jacques. *Paris.* Late 17c. Fine Boulle br. clock, M. des Arts décoratifs.
HUMPHREYS, ——. *Runcorn.* 18c. l.c. clock.

IBACH, Louis. *Thun.* 1815. g. eng. turned watch.
IGOUT, ——. *Paris.* Juré. 1753.
ILGER, ——. *Paris.* 1774. Supplied watch to the Menus-Plaisirs.
INDEPENDENT WATCH CO. OF FREDONIA. *New York.* 1880. *See* CORNELL WATCH CO. and PEORIA WATCH CO.
INGHELS—
Jean. *Malines.* ca.1540-68. Made chiming mechanism for St. Rombaux church and repaired clock of St. Jacques, Antwerp.
Pierre. *Malines.* 1557-64. Worked with Jean.
Pontius. ——. 1595. Repaired Lübeck clock.
ISABEL, ——. *Rouen.* 1806. Devised a secs. watch.
IVES, Ira. *Bristol, U.S.A.* 1809. Patent for str. part.
IVISON, Henry, bro. of John. *Carlisle.* Early 19c. l.c. clocks.

JACKSON, Thomas. *Boston, U.S.A.* ca.1740. l.c. clock.
JACOB—
M. *Tours.* ca.1650. Watch.
——. *Paris* (*Rue de Colombier*). 1827. Devised a split secs. chronograph.
——. *Paris* (*Bde Montmartre*). 1833. Devised a compensated pendulum.
JAKSON, Joseph. *Paris.* ca.1650. al. wall clock. cf. JACKSON.
JAMES, Eric. *Oldham.* ca.1770. l.c. clock.
JAMOU, William. ——. ca.1625. Watch.
JANS, Joseph. *Passau.* Early 18c. hex. table clock.
JAQUET, Amy Jean. *Paris.* Mid. 18c. C.
JAR, Pierre. *Blois.* Mid. 18c. C.
JARMARD, Jean. *Toulouse.* 1607. Repaired clock on Hôtel de Ville.
JOHANN, Jacob, Baron von Küllmar. *Arnstadt.* ca.1800. Made aut. astro. clocks.
JOHANSSON, H. *Kalmar.* Late 18c. Wall clock.
JOLY—
Pierre. *Paris.* 1530. C. to the King.

JOLY—*continued.*
Jean, son. *Paris.* 1560. C. to Catherine de Médicis.
JONES—
William. *Beccles.* Early 19c. l.c. clock.
D. *Liverpool.* ca.1820. Watch Parisi coll.
JOURDAINSON, William. *London.* 18c. l.c. clock.
JOURDAN, ——. *Vouzon.* ca.1700. Watch Parisi coll. sd. thus on dial and JEORDEAS on plate.
JOYCE, J. & R. *Ruthin.* ca.1795. l.c. clock.
JUDGE, Thomas. *Frome.* ca.1745. l.c. clock.
JULIA, M. *Toulouse.* 1785. Clock.
JURINE, Jean Pierre. *Geneva.* Late 18c. sil. p.c. watch Parisi coll.

KALTENBRUNNER, ——. *Prague.* Early 18c. Watch.
KAUFMANN, Caspar. *Vienna.* Early 19c. g. en. watch.
KELVEY, Robert. *Dover.* Late 18c. l.c. clock.
KENDAL, ——. *Canterbury.* ca.1800. l.c. clock.
KETTERER, Franz. *Schönwald.* b.1675.
KIDD, Joseph. *Swaffham.* ca.1775. l.c. clock.
KINGSLEY, William. *Wigan.* 1811.
KIRK, Nathaniel. *Kibworth* (*Leics.*). ca.1785. l.c. clock Leicester M.
KNIGHT—
Thomas & Mary. *Denmead.* 1761. l.c. clock.
William. *Stafford.* 1813. l.c. clock.
& BUCKNELL. ——. ca.1820. Duplex watch, bimetallic balance.
KNIP, Gerrit. *Amsterdam.* End 17c. g. en. p.c. watch.
KOCH, Hans. *Munich.* 1566-1600. Table clock Hamburg M. dated 1596.
KOPP, Carl Joseph. *Vienna.* Late 17c. Drum table clock.
KRAUSE, Christof. *Loban.* 18c. p.c. watch.
KREUZ, Paulus. *Ibenthal.* b.1730.
KREUZER, Daniel. *Schleswig.* ca.1640. g. en. watch.
KÜHN, Georg Friedrich. *Lübeck.* 1752. Repaired Lübeck clock.
KULLBERG, Victor. *Stockholm* and *London.* b.1824, d.1890. In *Stockholm* till 1849, then with Jürgensen in *Copenhagen.* Went to *London* 1850.
KURTZHALTZ, Johann Gottfrid. *Stockholm.* In 1748 went to *Lübeck.*

LACKER, Joseph Michael. *Rottenlos.* Early 18c. Watch.
LA CROIX, Jacques. *Castres.* 1616.
LADOIREAU, Jean. *Paris.* 1680. C to Louis XIV.
LAMANIÈRE. *v.* MANIÈRE.
LAMBERT, Pierre. *Geneva.* a.1644.
LANDESPERGER, ——. *Prague.* 1787. Repaired town clock.
LANSQUENAY, ——. *Brest.* 1771. Installed LeRoy's and Berthoud's time-pieces for De Borda's voyages.
LASSETER, Charles. *Steyning.* ca.1770. Sun clock.
LAWSON, Ramsay. *Wigan.* mar.1791. C.
LE BRUN, Christoffer. *Copenhagen.* ca.1640. Oct. crys. watch.
LEDERLE, Georg. *Augsburg.* 1667. Made public clock for Florence.
LEE—
Richard. *Halifax.* 1665.
William. *Charleston, U.S.A.* ca.1720-68. l.c. clock. C. & W.
William. *Leicester.* Mid. 18c. l.c. clock.
LEES, Jonathan. *Bury.* ca.1760. l.c. clock.
LE GRAND—
Robert. *Geneva.* Went to *Constantinople* in 1652.

LE GRAND—*continued.*
Simon. *Paris.* 1657. C. to the King.
LE GROS, ——. *Paris.* 1750. Two clocks with terrestial and celestial globes, C.A. & M.
LEICESTER, Laurence. *Wigan.* 1703. d.1711.
LEIGHTON, James. *Warrington.* d.1776. C.
LELIEVRE, ——. *Paris.* d.an.1757. Devised a fuzee-cutting machine.
LENOIR, Jean. *Paris.* 1552. C. to the King.
LESANCHEUR, ——. *Paris.* Mid. 18c. C. to the King.
LEUMAS, *London.* *v.* SAMUEL.
LE VERROUX, Louis. ——. End 17c. str. watch.
LINDSAY, George. *Liverpool.* ca.1820. Watch Parisi coll.
LIPPERD, Joseph. *Brag.* Late 18c. g. rep. watch.
LISLE, Benjamin. *Rotterdam.* 1658. Fitted clock of Schweningen with pendulum.
LISTER, Bromley. *Halifax.* 1800.
LIVERSAY, George. *Prescot.* 1666.
LOMBART, François. *Geneva.* a.1668.
LORRAIN, Charles le. *Castres.* 1690.
LUGG, Jaspar. *Gloucester.* a.1700. l.c. clock.
LUKENS, Isaiah. *Philadelphia.* b.1779, d.1846. l.c. clock.
LULLIN, Jaques. *Geneva.* a.1663.

MACHIEN, ——. *Toulon.* ca.1800. Watch Parisi coll.
MACHON, Abraham. *Geneva.* a.1669.
MACMILLAN, I. *Warley* (near *Halifax*). 1805.
MADIOT, Pre. George. *Milan.* ca.1700. p.c. rep. watch Parisi coll.
MALADIER, ——. *Magdeburg.* ca.1680. Watch tortoiseshell case.
MALCHET, John. *London.* 1675.
MANGIN, J. H. *London.* Early 19c. Watch Parisi coll.
MANIÈRE—
François la. *Toulouse.* 1595. Keeper of clock on Hôtel de Ville.
Jean la. *Toulouse.* 1603. Repaired clock on Hôtel de Ville.
Durand de la. *Toulouse.* 1619. Keeper of clock on Hôtel de Ville.
MANNING, Richard. *Ipswich, Mass.* ca.1760. Wall clock.
MARKWICK, James. *York.* ca.1735. br. clock.
MARQUES, E. *Paris.* Early 18c. Watch.
MARSH, W. *Diss.* Late 18c. l.c. clock.
MARSHALL—
Christopher. *Halifax.* 1624. Repaired church clock.
Thomas. *Halifax.* 1659-63. Repaired church clock.
MARTIN, Thomas, son of Thos. of Wigan. *Wigan.* 1725-44.
MARTINA, Carlo. *Turin.* Early 19c. Watch Parisi coll.
MASCON, Felix P. ——. End 17c. sil. al. watch Parisi coll.
MASON, George. *Horton Curby.* 2nd half 18c. 3-case g. rep. watch.
MASSEY—
& WINDHAM. *London.* 1813. Watch Parisi coll.
Edward John. *Liverpool.* 1838. Patented a spring detent esc.
MATHIEU, ——. *Paris* (*Rue de la Bourse*). 1825. Made ruby cyl. watches and a machine for making them.
MAURER, P. *Berlin.* ca.1660. Table clock.
MAURIS, Jaques. *Geneva.* End 18c. g. en. watch.

MAURY, Julien Girard. *France.* Late 18c. Ruby cyl. watch.
MEGELE, D. *Milan.* Mid. 18c. Made clock for Milan Observatory.
MEIGAN, Edme. *Paris.* 2nd half 17c. sil. watch.
MELLAND, Jean. *Geneva.* 1675.
MELLION, Jacques. *Lisieux.* 1792-1802. Aut. and cal. clock.
MERMILLON FRÈRES & COMP. *Geneva.* Late 18c. Watches Parisi coll.
MERRISON, T. A. *London.* Early 19c. br. clock.
MESNIER, Claude. *Paris.* 1655. C. to duc d'Anjou.
MESTRAL, S. Bastien (Sebastien). *France.* End 17c. Watch, en. on cock, Gélis coll.
METCALF—
James. *Halifax.* 1780.
& NICHOL. *Halifax.* 1800.
George Marmaduke. *London.* 1802.
MÉTRAL, Jean Pierre. ——. 2nd half 18c. Watch Parisi coll.
MICHAUD, Bertrand. *Paris.* 1514. C. to François I.
MICOT, ——. *London.* ca. 1780. p.c. repoussé watch.
MILES, Joseph. *Thaxton.* ca.1745. l.c. clock.
MILHARET, ——. *Paris.* ca.1790. Watch Parisi coll.
MILHAS, Jean Guillaume Gabriel. *Toulouse.* 1720-1802. Made clocks for Dalbade church and the towns of Muret, Auch, Albi and Porlèt-sur-Garonne.
MIROGLIO, Marc. *Geneva.* a.1658.
MITCHELL, George. *Bristol, U.S.A.* b.1774, d.1852.
MOLLET, ——. *Paris.* Mid. 18c. C.
MONDEHARE, J. *London.* ca.1700. rep. br. clock.
MOODY, Leonard. *Ripponden.* d.1791.
MOUCHON, ——. *Paris.* Early 19c. Watch.
MOUJOT, Antoine. *Castres.* 1719.
MOUNTAIN, William. *London.* an.1766. Watch.
MÜLLER—
Hans. *Soleure.* 1566-78. Clock.
Jost. *Strasbourg.* 1577-1633.
Christoph. *Augsburg.* 17c. sq. table clock.
Joh. Jacob. *Strasbourg.* ca.1660. g. en. watch Gélis coll.
Johann Michael. ——. ca.1700. Repoussé trav. clock.
Ferdinand. ——. Early 18c. hex. table clock Parisi coll.
MUNDAY, Joseph. *London.* 1656.

NAPIER, Thomas. *Glasgow.* ca.1770. l.c. clock.
NARDIN, Léonard Frédéric. *Le Locle.* b.1792, d.1859.
NEALE—
James. *Aylesbury.* ca.1715. Wall clock with secs. pendulum.
Francis. *Aylesbury.* ca.1715. l.c. clock.
NELSON, Stephen. *Wigan.* b.1729, d.1807. l.c. clock.
NEUBER, J. C. *Dresden.* Late 18c. Watch.
NEWLAND, ——. *Farnham.* ca.1800. l.c. clock.
NEWTON, Gilbert. *London.* ca.1720. l.c. clock str. every minute.
NICHOLSON, Samuel. *London.* Mid. 18c. sil. p.c. watch repoussé by COCHIN.
NITARDY, Caspar. *Dramburg* (*Pommern*). mar.1694, d.1706. In 1693 made clock for Stettin castle. Court C.
NOIRIET, ——. *Tours.* 1819. Devised a compensated pendulum.
NORMAN—
Matthew. *Sherborne.* ca.1800. l.c. clock
Olof. *Stockholm.* Early 19c. Wall clock

OGDEN—
James. *Soyland* (near *Halifax*). d.1715.
Isaac, bro. *Sowerby.* End 17c.
OLDENBURG, Johann. *Hamburg.* 1648, obtained burghership. d. between 1693 and 1699. g. watch Pleissner coll.
OLDFIELD, Edward. ——. Mid. 18c. l.c. clock.
OLIVET, Pierre. *Geneva.* a.1681.
OLTRAMARE, Stephen. *Geneva.* 1684.
ONNITSCH, ——. *Marburg.* Early 18c. Table clock.
OOSTERWIJK, Adam, son of Severijn. *The Hague.* 1688.
ORR, ——. *Newtownards.* ca.1790. l.c. clock.
OURRY, Louis. *Paris.* Early 18c. str. watch.

PACHMEIER, Anton. *Vienna.* Early 19c. Watch Parisi coll.
PADBURY, Thomas. *Bishop's Waltham.* Late 18c. l.c. clock.
PAGÈS—
Claude. *Toulouse.* 1585-95. Keeper of clock of Hôtel de Ville.
Bernard, son. *Toulouse.* 1645-9. Keeper of clock of Hôtel de Ville.
Jean, son. *Toulouse.* 1649. Added half-quarter chimes to clock of Hôtel de Ville.
PALMER, Anthony. *London.* ca.1770. l.c. clock.
PAPILLON, ——. *Dijon.* Early 18c. Watch.
PARIS, Jean. *Paris.* ca.1660. Watch in filigree case.
PARKER, John. *Greenwich.* d.1766. Widow carries on business.
PARKINSON, Samuel. ——. ca.1765. l.c. clock.
PARLOW, ——. *Montgomery.* Early 19c. l.c. clock.
PARROTT, Samuel. *Grassrigg* (*Westmorland*). 18c. l.c. clock.
PASQUIER, ——. *Paris.* 1773. C. to the King.
PATRON, Jean Abraham. *Geneva.* a.1699.
PEARCE, John. *Chard.* ca.1800. l.c. clock.
PECQUEUR, ——. *Paris.* 1819-24. C. Devised gearing to show primes.
PEGLER, Samuel. *Blandford.* ca.1800. l.c. clock.
PEHE, Bernardo. ——. Mid. 17c. g. en. watch.
PENNANS, J. C. *London.* Early 19c. Fine chiming br. clock.
PEPLOW, William. *Wellington* (*Salop*). a.1805. In *Wellington* ca.1816-25.
PERRET, Phinée. *Switzerland.* b.1777. T.C. Complicated clocks.
PFAFF, Cass. ——. 17c. Table clock.
PIAULT, ——. *France.* 1819. Devised a compensated pendulum with lazy-tongs rod of steel and brass bars.
PICCOT, Jacob. *Geneva.* a.1667.
PINTARD, David. *Paris.* 1652. C.
PIRETTE—
——. *Beaume.* ca.1725. hex. eng. watch Gélis coll.
Bonaventure. *Autun.* ca.1625. Repaired town clock.
PLATT, Oliver. *Wigan.* 1674. W.
PLUMB, David. ——. Early 18c. l.c. chiming clock.
POCOCK, John. *Kilmston* (*Hants*?). 1st half 18c. l.c. clock.
PORTER, S. G. *Oakingham.* ca.1790. l.c. clock.
PORTIER, Pierre. *Paris.* 1565. C. to the City.

POTERAT, ——. *Paris.* 1816. Devised a machine for forging strips for mainsprings.
POYRIER, Henri. *Grenoble.* 1637-47.
PRÉVOST—
D. *Toulouse.* Late 18c. Watch.
Fils. *Toulouse.* ca.1800. Watch Gélis coll.
Frères. *Toulouse.* 1809.
PRIVATE, William. *London.* 1763. g. repoussé watch.
PROUST, Pierre. *Pau.* 1558.

QUARREY, A. prob. *London.* an.1766. Watch.
QUENTIN, Gilles. *Paris.* 1657. C. to Louis XIV.

RACINE, ——. *Besançon.* 1823.
RAFFARD—
David. *Geneva.* a.1675.
François. *Geneva.* ca.1750. Watch.
RAINGO—
Z. J. *Ghent.* 1810. Patented clock with elaborate astro. indications.
Frères. *Paris.* 1824.
RAPER, Sidney. *Thirsk.* Late 18c. Watch.
RATCLIFFE, Nathaniel. *Elland.* 1810.
RAWLING, Peter. *Dover.* 18c. l.c. clock.
RAWLINGS, John. *Stone (Staffs.).* ca.1720. l.c. clocks.
RAYMOND, ——. *London (Leadenhall St.).* 1780. CC.
REDSHAW, John. *Newcastle-under-Lyme.* Early 18c. l.c. clock.
RENSONET, Nicolas. *Herve (Belgium).* 1729. l.c. clock.
RÉVILLON, ——. *Macon.* 1823-7. T.C.
REY, ——. *Paris.* ca.1700. Watch.
REYNOLDS, William. *Launceston.* 18c. l.c. clock.
RHIND, T. *Manchester.* End 18c. l.c. clock.
RICE, ——. *Penrhyn.* Late 18c. l.c. clock.
RICHARDSON, ——. *Goole.* ca.1800. Watch.
RICHTER. Auguste. ——. End 17c. sil. p.c. str. watch.
RIDREAUT, RIDROT. *v.* Ridereau.
RILEY—
Gill. *Todmorden.* 1800.
George. *Halifax.* 1810.
RILLET, J. B. *Geneva.* sig. on dial of rep. watch. *See* Elrhow.
RIPPON—
Richard. *London (King St., Seven Dials).* b.1755, d.1827. Teacher of E. J. Dent. Made rep. mechanisms. Watch mt. G.M.
William Frederick, son. *London.* a.1822, CC. 1831, d.1860. Joined E. J. Dent, his step-father, took his name and succeeded him. Completed the Westminster clock. Experimented with glass springs for chrons.
ROBERT, Jacob. *Switzerland.* b.1792, d.1865.
ROBERTSON, Thomas. *Rothsay.* 2nd half 18c. Wall clock with pendulum above dial.
RODECK BROS. *Vienna.* ca.1820. Trav. clock.
ROGER, ——. *Paris.* 1537. C. to the King and City.
ROGERS, John. *Devizes.* Mid. 18c. l.c. clock.
ROMAN ET CIE. *Constance.* ca.1800. g. en. rep. watch.
ROMILLY ET MONNIER. *Geneva.* ca.1780. g. en. watch set pearls.
ROPER, ——. *Ashwick.* ca.1700. l.c. clock.
ROTHRAM, Thomas. *Lewes.* an.1684. cf. Rotherham.
ROUSSEL, Johannes. *The Hague.* 1658.
ROWE, ——. *London (St. Paul's Churchyard).* 1780. CC.
RUMBALL, Bryan. *Newbury (Berks.).* d.1685. Lantern clock.
RUNDLE, John. *Bratton.* Mid. 18c. l.c. clock.
RUSSELL—
Henry. *Hardock.* Late 18c. l.c. clock.
——. *Buxton* (near *Norwich*). Early 19c. l.c. clock.

SABLON, ——. *Castres.* 1772.
SAINTON, ——. *Toulouse.* 1773-83.
SALZENBERG, J. C. ——. 18c. p.c. watch.
SAMM, Edward. *Linton.* ca.1760. l.c. clock.
SAMUEL, S. *Louth.* Early 19c. l.c. clock.
SARTORI, Gallüs. *Bamberg.* 17c. sq. table clock.
SAUDE, Pierre. *Paris.* 1658. C. to Louis XIV.
SCHEFER, Gaspar. *Thorn.* 2nd half 17c. Table clock Parisi coll.
SCHMIDT, Georg. *Neustadt.* ca.1780. aut. rep. watch.
SCHÜTZ, George. *Königsberg.* 17c. oct. table clock.
SCHWANDER, Jacob. *La Neuveville.* 1787.
SCHWILGUÉ, ——. *Schlestadt.* 1816. Clock with ecclesiastical cal.
SEAMARK, Thomas. *Harborough.* ca.1775. l.c. clock.
SEINE-RUE, Pierre de. *Paris.* 1560. C. to the City.
SENIN, Pierre. *Paris.* ca.1700. sil. dial.
SEON, Pierre. *Geneva.* a.1663.
SHAW—
E. *Edinburgh.* ca.1800. p.c. watch.
Abraham. *Billingborough.* 1806. Verge watch.
James. *Halifax.* 1800-20. l.c. clock.
SHEPHERD—
William. *Kempston.* ca.1700. Watch.
——. *Sheffield.* ca.1740. l.c. clock. Shephard.
James. *Edinburgh.* ca.1800. Pocket chron.
SIDWELL, Robert. *Nuneaton.* ca.1750. l.c. clock.
SIMPSON—
John. *Wigton.* b.1736, d.1796. Fine maker. l.c. clocks.
John, son. *Wigton.* b.1757, d.1837. l.c. clocks.
SKEDGE, Charles. *Norwich.* Mid. 18c. l.c. clock.
SLACK, Joseph. *Ipstones (Staffs.).* 18c. l.c. clock with moving figures in arch.
SMALLWOOD, Jonathan. *Lichfield.* ca.1700. br. clock.
SMITH—
Thomas. *Wigan.* 1755. C.
Thomas. *Leighton.* ca.1770. lc. clock.
John. *Widnes.* d.1803.
W. *Crowland.* Early 19c. l.c. clock.
SOAMES, Thomas. *London.* 1656.
SOURDETAL, ——. *Paris.* Early 18c. sil. str. eng. watch.
SPRAKEL, Jurrien. *Zutphen.* 1652-85. Made clocks for Groningen, Arnhem cathedral and carillons for Amsterdam.
SPRINGALL, ——. *Norwich.* Early 19c. l.c. clock.
STAFFORD, T. *London (Chelsea).* Late 18c. trav. clock.
STAHL, Michael. *Lübeck.* 1629. Repaired Lübeck clock.
STAMROD, T. *Barnsley.* 1780-90.
STEELE, George. *Bath.* ca.1760. Watch.
STEINER, Louis. *London.* ca.1750. mus. br clock.
STEPHENS, William. ——. 1705. l.c. clock.
STERLING, John. *London.* Late 18c. br. clock.
STEYR, Is. Eb. *Germany.* Early 17c. str. watch. cf. Steir.
STOKES, John. *St. Ives.* ca.1720.
STORER, James. *London.* 1798.

STRIBLING, ——. *Stowmarket.* Late 17c. l.c. clock.
STRINGFELLOW, Thomas. *Halifax.* 1748. Insolvent.
SUMMERFIELD, ——. *London* (*Westminster*). 1751. W.

TALBOT, C. *Tuxford.* 1670. Made church clock.
TARTS, Jno. *London.* 2nd half 18c. Sig. on many watches for Dutch market. May be J. STRATTON.
TAYLOR—
John. *Ormskirk.* ca.1725. year l.c. clock.
James. *Ormskirk.* 1st half 18c. clock.
TEMPEL, Gabriel. *Innsbruck.* ca.1800. Watch Parisi coll.
TERRY—
Samuel, bro. of Eli. b.1774, d.1852. *E. Windsor, U.S.A.*, till 1818, then *Plymouth.* Worked alone till 1829; then went to *Bristol*, with his sons Ralph and John B., still as Samuel Terry, Plymouth. Retired 1834. Wooden clocks and mirror clocks.
Eli & Samuel. *Plymouth, U.S.A.* 1824-7. Shelf clock M.M.A.
THIERRY, Niel. *Rouen.* 19c. en. watch in form of apple.
THIOLET, L'aîné. *Paris.* Late 18c. br. clock.
THOMPSON—
Joseph. *Cirencester.* Early 18c. l.c. clock.
James. *Pittsburgh.* ca.1815.
THORN, Abram William. ——. ca.1680. hex. table clock.
THORNTON, Thomas. ——. 1810. Verge watch.
THRELKELD, ——. *Newcastle-on-Tyne.* ca. 1710. sil. p.c. watch.
TICHELMANS, Heynderick. *Lierre.* 1571. Repaired clock of St. Jacques, Antwerp.
TIMMERMAN, Jan. *Antwerp.* Made clock for St. Jacques in 1507.
TOLPUTT, James. *Dover Castle.* 18c. l.c. clock.
TONSPET, Joseph. *Augsburg.* Mid. 18c. 4-col. g. rep. watch.
TRIBE, Daniel. *Portsmouth.* Mid. 18c. mus. clock.
TROUT, Thomas. *London.* Early 18c.
TROUTBECK, W. *Leeds.* Early 18c. l.c. clock. sil. al. watch.
TUNN, James. *London.* ca.1700. br. clock.
TYACKE, George. *Breage.* ca.1800. l.c. clock.

ULPH, ——. *Stalham.* ca.1800. l.c. clock.

VAISSIÈRES, Pierre. *Castres.* End 16c.-1625. Sil. eng. watch Toulouse M.
VALLET, Antoine Leon. *Paris* (*Rue du fg du Temple*). 1824.
VAN CALL, Jan. *Arnhem.* 1652-8. Fitted pendulum to cathedral clock.
VAN DER CLOESEN, Jacob. *Leyden.* Early 18c. l.c. clock.
VAN DER DUSSEN, Willem. *Dordrecht.* d. 1689.
VAN DER ELST—
Loys. *Antwerp.* 1614-55. Fitted carillon to clock of St. Jacques.
Hans, son. *Antwerp.* 1655. Assisted his father.
VAN DOERNE, Anthonis. *Antwerp.* 1543-53. Repaired clock of St. Jacques.
VAUGHAN, Richard. *Watlington.* Late 18c. l.c. clock.
VERNEDE—
Pierre. *Agen.* ca.1640. Watch Gélis coll.
Pierre. *Bordeaux.* ca.1650. g. en. watch.
VERNON, Richard. *Liverpool.* ca.1705. Sun & moon watch.
VIALA, DUPIN ET ARGAND. *Geneva.* Early 19c. g. watch set pearls.
VILBAR, ——. *Paris.* 1787. C. to the Queen.
VIVIEN, Jean. *Paris.* ca.1800. g. en. watch.
VOGLER, Johann Michael. *Herrieden.* ca. 1700. hex. str. & rep. clock.
VOICE. *v.* VOYCE.
VOYCE, George. *Dean.* 1717. l.c. clock.
VUILLEUMIER, D. L., **ET FILS.** ——. Early 19c. str. rep. watch Parisi coll.

WALLER & STRAUB. *Norwich.* ca.1800. l.c. clock.
WALLETZKI, Joh. *St. Petersburg.* ca.1760. Watch Parisi coll.
WALLS, Brownker. *London.* Early 18c. l.c. clock.
WARR, E. *Bristol.* End 18c. l.c. clock.
WEBB & SON. *Newbury.* 1770-early 19c. Watch and l.c. clock.
WEHRLE—
Eusebius, bro. *Simonswald.* Mid. 18c. mus. C.
Martin, bro. *Simonswald.* Mid. 18c. mus. C.
WELCH, John. *Chesham.* ca.1700. 30-hour br. clock.
WEST, G. *Docking* (near *King's Lynn*). 1780-1790. l.c. clock.
WEYMAN, James. *Appleby.* Early 19c.
WHARTON, ——. *Harling* (18m. SW. of *Norwich*). Early 19c. l.c. clock.
WHITE—
Thomas. *Fairford.* ca.1700. l.c. clock.
James. *Paris.* 1812. Patented a construction of clock.
WHITFIELD—
John. *Clifton* (*Westmorland*). 18c. l.c. clock.
R. T. *Tanfield* (*Westmorland*). 18c. l.c. clock.
WHITTON, Francis. *Norwell.* ca.1740. l.c. clock.
WICK, Emil. *Basle.* b.1816, d.1894. Maker of elaborate ant. clocks.
WILKES, William. *Stratford-on-Avon.* 1756. l.c. clock.
WILKINSON—
Abe. *Midgley.* 1769.
Joseph. *Penrith.* 1790-1820.
WILLIAMS, H. *Llancarfan.* Early 18c. l.c. clock.
WILSON—
John. *Peterborough.* 1757-95. l.c. clock. W.
George. *Appleby.* Early 19c. l.c. clocks.
WINCH, Joseph. *Uxbridge.* ca.1700. Marqueterie l.c. clock.
WINSTANLEY—
William. *Wigan.* ca.1770-ca.1785. l.c. clocks.
Abraham. *Wigan.* 1811. C.
WISHBORNE, John, sen. *Gloucester?* ca. 1740. l.c. clock.
WITHERSTON, J. *Hereford.* ca.1690. br. clock.
WOHRLE. *v.* ELRHOW.
WRIGHT, B. *London.* ca.1800. l.c. clock.

YORKE, G. *London* (*Strand*). Early 19c. br. clock.
YOUNG—
Thomas. *London.* ca.1710. l.c. clock.
William. *London* (*Butcher Hall La.*). 1776. Watch.

ZEIDLMEIR, M. *Munich.* Mid. 18c. p.c. repoussé watch.
ZOLLING, Hans Andreas. *Hamburg.* mar. an.1664.

CONTENTS

A

AAGAARD, Christian. *Copenhagen.* m.1776.
AAMANN, Emanuel. *Copenhagen.* m.1812.
AARON, Abraham. *Plymouth.* 1818.
ABBAS, Gottfridus. *Germany.* 17c. Sundial Fränkel coll.
ABBATI (ABBATY, ABASTY).
Bernardin. *Paris,* 1559. C. to Henri II.
Jean, son. *Paris,* 1597. *Blois* for 13 years. *La Rochelle,* 1614. *Blois,* 1623. d.1624. Watch Liverpool M.
ABBETS, James. *Albany, N.Y., U.S.A.* To 1760. W.
ABBIS, J. *London.* 1807.
ABBOTT—
Richard. *London.* a.1668.
Peter. *London (Gutter Lane).* 1699, d.1728. Watch.
Philip. *London.* a.1695, CC.1703-33. l.c. red lacquer clock Weth. coll.
Peter. *London.* a.1709, CC.1719.
John. *London.* 1703.
William. *Sarson.* Early 18c. l.c. clock.
Thomas. *London.* a.1718, CC.1740.
John, son of Philip. *London.* a.1724.
John, son of Peter. *London.* 1740.
John. *London.* 1787. C. Arrested for making agreement to work in Petersburg.
John Q. *London.* CC.1788-1800. l.c. clocks.
William. *Prescot.* 1790-5. W.
Thomas. *London.* 1808-20. Watch mt.maker.
John. *Manchester.* 1813. W.
Francis. *Manchester.* 1825-40. Pub. book on management of public clocks.
ABBY, George. *Liverpool.* 1805-07. W.
ABDY, William. *London.* 1768-90.
ABEL—
Peter Michael. *Copenhagen.* m.1747.
Peter, son. *Copenhagen.* a.1766.
ABELING (ABELLING), William. *London.* 1817-40. br. clock.
ABERCROMBIE, James. *Aberdeen.* 1730.
ÅBERG—
Daniel. *Norrköping.* 1760. d.ca.1780. 2 watches, one Nord. M.
Jonas. *Norrköping.* b.1760, d.1826. 2 watches.
Petter. *Linköping.* 1799. d.ca.1817. Watch.
ABERLEY, Joseph. *London.* a.1664.
ABILLAN, Étienne. *Blois.* 1617-29.
ABLITT, John. *Ipswich.* m.1819. Watch.
ABRAHAM—
——. *Lyons.* 1620-30, perhaps Abraham LAMUSSE.
——. *London (Lamb Court).* 1751. W.
Thomas. *Liverpool.* 1754, d.1767. W. Also ABRAM.
Jacob. *London.* 1769. Bankrupt.
John. *Warrington.* d.1776. W.
Miles. *Newport Pagnell.* 1772-8. W.
E. *Olney.* 1773. g. p.c. watch.

ABRAHAM—*continued.*
Simon. *Portsea.* 1795. Watch.
B. *Yeovil.* d.1797. C. & W.
Elizabeth, widow. *Yeovil.* 1797. Carried on his business. l.c. clock.
H. *Taunton.* ca.1800.
M. *London.* 1805-08. W.
Joseph. *London (Greenwich).* 1812-24. Watch.
John. *London (Bishopsgate).* 1820. W.
——. *Southampton.* Early 19c. Watch.
Joseph. *Liskeard.* Early 19c. Watch.
ABRAHAMS—
Aaron. *London.* a.1730.
Zarah. *London.* a.1730.
Abraham. *London (Dukes Pl.).* 1751. W.
Zachariah. *London (Leadenhall St.).* 1763. W.
Samuel. *Sandwich.* 1783-99. W.
J. *Dover.* 1785.
Henry. *London.* 1802-25. W.
——. *Hythe.* 1806.
Isaac. *London.* 1817-24. W. & C.
John. *London (Steward St.).* 1821-5. W.
Phineas. *Hull.* 1823-36.
ABRAMS, John. *Warrington.* 1776.
ABRATHAT, William James. *London.* a.1749.
ABSOLON ——. *London.* 1770. l.c. clock.
ACAM, Robert. *London.* a.1767, CC. 1774-1824.
ACASTLE—
Robert. *Taunton.* ca.1660. Watch Ilbert coll.
Thomas. *Taunton.* ca.1670. Watch.
ACEY, Peter. *York.* 1656. Clock.
ACHARD—
George. *Geneva.* ca.1780. g. aut. watch.
George, et fils. *Geneva.* ca.1780. rep.watches in rich cases.
ET CIE. *Geneva.* Late 18 and early 19c. cal. and secs. watch. g. en. watch S.K.M.
ACHER—
——. *Paris.* 1740 m.
Pierre François. *Paris,* m.1746.
ACHURCH—
William. *London.* a.1691, CC.1699-1743.
Thomas. *London.* a.1699.
William, son of William. *London.* a.1716.
ACKERMANN—
Wolff Ernst. *Fürth.* d.1751.
Johann Christoph. *Basle.* 1767. Of *Leipzig.*
ACKERS, William. *London.* 1706. p.c. watch S.K.M.
ACKLAM, John Philip. *London.* 1820-25. W.
ACKRILL, Thomas. *Birmingham.* 1808. C.
ACKROYD, Thomas. *Leeds.* 1797. W.
ACOTT—
William. *London.* a.1784, CC.1791-1824.
John. *London.* a.1791.
ACRES, Edward. *Sittingbourne.* d.1767.
ACRIN, ——. *Paris.* 1812.

ACTON—
John. *London.* CC.1677.
Thomas. *London.* CC.1677
Edward. *London.* a.1686.
Abraham. *London.* a.1694, CC.1710-32.
Abraham, son. *London.* CC.1738.
S.E. ——. ca.1770. Watch mt.
ADAIR—
James. *Stranraer.* 1820.
Stair. *Stranraer.* 1820.
ADAM—
Melchior. *Paris.* ca.1610. Watch M.M.A.
Elias. *England.* 1627. Dial M.M.A.
Johan. *Karlskrona.* comp. 1695. d.1753.
Père et fils. *Geneva.* ca.1770. Painters on enamel.
Johann Ludwig. *Berlin.* 1785-90.
ADAMI, Jacob Ludwig. *Berlin.* 1791-5. *v.* ADAMY.
Carl Jacob. *Berlin.* 1794.
ADAMS—
Thomas. *London.* a.1704.
Henry. *London.* a.1716.
Edmond. *London.* a.1716.
George. *London.* a.1721.
George. *London* (*Fleet St.*). a.1739, CC.1752-1795. Seconds timing mt. G.M.
——. *Leigh.* 1757. Watch.
John. *Halesowen.* ca.1760.
John. *London* (*Moorfields*). l.CC.1766, d.1777.
Hector. *London.* an.1771. Watch.
John. *London* (*Maiden Lane*). a.1764, CC. 1772-94.
Samuel. *Bromley* (*Kent*). an.1775. Watch.
Clement. *Stamford.* an.1777. Watch.
Thomas. *London.* a.1773.
Thomas. *London.* a.1776.
Nathaniel. *Stowmarket.* 1784. W.
Stephen & Son. *London.* 1785.
C. & J. *London.* 1788.
& HOTHAM. *London.* 1795. Watch N.Y.Univ.
William. *London.* 1795.
John. *Pembroke.* 1795.
Thomas. *Middlewich.* 1795. C. & W.
William. *Exeter.* 1795. W.
Nathan. *Boston, U.S.A.* 1796-1825.
Henry. *London* (*Hackney*). 1799-1811.
Francis Bryant. *London* (*Clerkenwell*). a.1792-1825. Watch.
Benjamin. *London.* a.1792.
Cornelius. *London.* a.1796.
Thomas. *London.* a.1800.
John. *London.* a.1804.
Thomas F. *Baltimore, U.S.A.* 1804-07. W.
F. *London* (*St. John's Sq.*). 1809-11.
William. *Boston, U.S.A.* 1809-25. W.
William & Samuel A. Eaton. *Boston, U.S.A.* 1816-21.
Elizabeth. *London.* 1817-24.
Charles. *Drogheda.* 1820-4.
Francis Bryant, son of Francis Bryant. *London.* a.1821, m.CC.1848.
George William, son of Francis Bryant. *London.* a.1822, CC.1829.
Joshua. *Magherafelt.* 1824.
Samuel. *Boston, U.S.A.* 1825. C.
'J. C. ADAMS.' Sig. on 1871-4 watches of CORNELL WATCH CO.
'ADAMS ST.' Sig. on watches of the WALTHAM WATCH CO. from 1878.
ADAMSEN, Johan Gottfred. *Copenhagen.* m.1779. Master of Corporation 1793-5.
ADAMSON—
Humfry. *London.* 1668-82. Clock for Whitehall Chapel. Tortoise-shell br. clock Weth. coll.
John. *London.* CC.1686.
Thomas. *Burnley.* d.1699. W.
Anna. *London.* 1696. Watch.
Gottfried. *Karlskrona.* 1750. d.1765. l.c. clock. Also ADAMSEN.

ADAMSON—*continued.*
Johan Friedrich. *Karlskrona.* m.1759-80. l.c. clock. Prob. same as ADAMSSON.
& MILLENET. *Paris.* 1770. g. en. watch, S.K.M.
Gustav Adolph. *Karlskrona.* a.1760. *Paris.* m.1788.
John. *Thirsk.* 1772. Watch.
John. *Liverpool.* 1781-96. Watchcase maker.
Samuel. *London.* an.1786. Watch.
Thomas. *Liverpool.* 1811-16. W.
John. *London.* CC.1813.
——. *Anstruther.* 1818.
ADAMSONE, ——. *Paris.* 1775-1819. Clock Nat. M. Stockholm.
ADAMSSON—
Johan Frederic. *Kalmar.* 1750. *v.* ADAMSON.
Petter Anders. *Kristianstad.* Comp. 1763.
Gottfried. *Lund.* b.1775, d.1840.
ADAMY—
I. P. *Stettin.* 18c. Table clock Feill coll.
——. *Berlin.* 1786. *v.* ADAMI.
ADCOCK, William. *London.* a.1747.
ADDIS—
Robert. *Bristol.* 1720.
William, son. *London* (*Birchin La.*). a.1738, CC.1745, m.CC.1764, d.1785. rep. watch G.M.
George Curzon, son. *London* (*Cornhill*). CC. 1780, l.CC.1787-99. cyl. mt. G.M. br. clock ill. Cec. & Web.
ADDISON—
Edmond. *London.* a.1678.
Thomas. *Ulverstone.* d.1767. C.
T. *Liverpool.* Mid. 18c. Watch.
John. *London.* a.1758.
Joshua. *London.* 1775-1800. Watch Den. coll.
John. *York.* 1789. Watch.
Joseph. *London* and *Quernmore.* 1817. W.
John. *Guildford.* Early 19c. watch.
George. *Belfast.* 1824.
ADEANE—
Henry. *London.* a.1667, CC.1675-1712.
Henry, son. *London.* CC.1706-16.
ADEIRES, Joseph. *London.* an.1765. Watch.
ADELAAR, G. *Rotterdam.* 1821-30.
ADELDINGER, Sebastian. *Vienna.* Early 18c. Small gilt br. clock Arts M. Prague.
ADELINE FRÈRES. *Paris.* 1812.
——, L. *Paris.* 1814-20.
ADERLEY, ——. *Wolverhampton.* an.1746.
ADFIELD, ——. *Brentford.* an.1751. cf. ATFIELD.
ADIS, Thomas. *London.* a.1736.
ADKINS, Thomas. *London.* a.1716, CC.1745. Watch.
ADLINGER, Michael. *Vienna.* m.1781.
ADLINGTON, John. *London.* l.CC.1806-17.
ADMIRAUD (ADMYRAULD)—
Germain. *Paris.* 1767. Sil. al. watch Bourges M. by him or bro.
Nicolas, brother. *Paris.* 1767.
ADNEY—
Richard. *London.* 1744-67. Watch.
Thomas. *London.* CC.1767.
ADOR, ——. *Berne.* 1758. From *Vuiteboeuf.* Founded a watch factory with CHRISTIN or BONARD, which failed in 1762.
ADRIE, John. *Romsey.* 1747.
AEBY, Nicolaus. *Berne.* 18c. Watch Fränkel coll.
AETZLI, Josef. *Soleure.* ca.1770. From *Subingen.*
AGAMBAR, William. *London.* a.1823.
AGAR—
John. *York.* 1741. d.1808. l.c. clocks, br. clock. *v.* Thos. below.
Seth. *York.* 1743.
John. *York.* 1760. d.1815.
Edward. *New York.* 1761.

AGAR—*continued.*
Charles. *Pontefract.* 1779.
John. *Malton.* 1782.
Thomas. *York.* 1791. Partner with his father John. d. 1807. Watch.
John. *York.* 1807.
Francis. *York.* 1808.
Thomas. *Bury.* ca.1820.
AGASSE, Thomas. *Rouen.* m.1655.
AGERON, François. *Paris.* m.1741-79. Two g. en. watches. str. cal. clock Bernal sale.
AGGAS, Robert. *Norwich.* 2nd half 18c. l.c. clock.
AGRELL, Johan Mathias. *Sölvesberg,* 1822. *Kristianstad,* 1830-46. Verge watch.
AGTERVELD, J. *Amsterdam.* 1822. W.
ÅHLSTRAND, Nils. *Göteborg.* 1818.
ÅHLSTROM, Anders. *Marstrand.* 1793.
ÅHMAN—
Mathias. *Mariestad.* Mid. 17c. hex. table clock.
Joh. *Stockholm.* b.1710, d.1762.
Måns. *Stockholm.* 1782-90.
AHNS, J. *Derby.* 1750. Watch.
AHRENS, F. H. 1818. Court C. Large stand clock with special chron. escapement.
ÅHSTRÖM, Nils. *Göteborg.* 1814.
AIBAUD, ——. *Paris.* 1787.
AICH, Constantin. *Stockholm.* comp. 1751.
AICKEN—
James. *Cork.* 1763. W.
George. *Cork.* 1763 CC., d. 1813. mus. clock Dublin M. Watch. Also AICKIN.
George, son. *London.* a.1763, CC.1777.
Greaves. *Newry.* 1820.
AIGELDINGER, M. *Trälleborg* and *Malmö.* b.1772, d.1849.
AIKINSON, Peabody. *Concord, U.S.A.* 1790.
AIMÉ, ——. *Paris.* 1795. Watch.
AIMERY, ——. *Paris.* 1681 m.
AINGE, Alexander. *London.* a.1749, CC.1766-1783.
AINGER, Nathaniel. *London.* a.1795.
AINGS, Edward. *London.* a.1813.
AINSWORTH—
Robert. *Liverpool.* d.1747. W.
John. *Chelmsford.* 1759. Bankrupt. W.
Daniel. *London.* 1761. Insolvent. W.
George. *Warrington.* 1807. Pinion maker.
AIRES, ——. *London (Leicester Fields).* an. 1784. Watch.
AIREY—
John. *Hexham.* 1784-95. W. Also AIRCEY. cf. AYREY.
Smith. *Sunderland.* 1820.
AIRY, George Biddell. *London.* b.1802, d.1892. Astronomer Royal; many publications on horology.
AISH, Simon. *Sherborne.* ca.1700-ca.1750. l.c. clock. Watch.
AISTROP, John. *London.* a.1764. Bankrupt 1774.
AITCHISON—
Robert. *Edinburgh.* a.1756, d.1790.
Alexander. *Edinburgh.* a.1765.
William. *Edinburgh.* 1807.
AITKEN—
John. *Edinburgh.* a.1750, d.1779.
John. *London.* an. 1777-1826. Award from Soc. Arts for a detached escapement.
George. *Edinburgh.* 1781-5.
David. *Carnwath.* 1790-1850. Also AIKEN.
AKCED, *v.* DECKA.
AKENHEAD, John. *London.* an.1777. Watch.
AKERES, Jonathan. *London.* a.1697.
ÅKERMAN, Hans P. *Göteborg.* 1817-20.
AKERS, James. *Derby.* ca.1800. Watches Den. coll. and Derby M.
AKROYD, Thomas. *Leeds.* 1798. W.
ALAIN, Nicolas. *Rouen.* a.1701.
ALAIS—
Moïse. *Blois.* m.1630, d.1632.
Veuve. *Blois.* 1639.
ALAMBY, ——. *London.* an.1796. Watch.
ALATHEY, Daniel. *London.* 1752. Watch.
ALBAN, Augustin. *Paris.* 1771 m.
ALBE (ALBO), Jean. *Fontainebleau,* 1539; *Lyons,* 1561. Made two clocks for François I, and was C. to Henri II.
ALBERT—
Isaac. *London.* a.1721, CC.1732-7.
——. *Paris.* 1807-25.
'ALBERT CLARK.' Sig. on 1870 watches of the NEW YORK WATCH Co.
ALBIN—
Johan Gustav. *Stockholm.* 1792-1809. Wall clock and watch.
J. G. *Norrtälje.* 1830-5.
ALBINO, Agostin. *Cadiz.* 1806. d.1813. C. to the King. Sent by Spanish Navy to study chron. making in Paris.
ALBOUET, ——. *Paris.* 1783.
ALBOUT, Jean Augustin. *Paris.* 1754-74.
ALBRECHT—
Hans. *Strasbourg.* 1630.
——. *Berlin.* ca.1690. Sq. table clock.
Michael Georg. ——. ca.1714. g. rep. watch.
Johann Georg. *Zelechow, Poland.* ca.1715. Gilt repoussé watch S.K.M.
Johann Christian. *Fürth.* d.ca.1820.
J. G. *Berlin.* 1812.
Johan Magnus. *Växjö.* b.1796, d.1845.
ALBURG, James. *London.* an.1771. Watch.
ALCE, Henry. *Lewes.* a.1716.
ALCOCK—
Thomas. *London.* 1630. w.CC.1645. d.an. 1655. Petitioner for incorporation of CC. cal. watch ill. Britten.
Elias. *London.* 1650-75.
John. *London.* 1650-70.
John. *London.* 1720. Night dial.
George. *London.* 1770-83.
John. *London.* 1772-5.
James. *London.* 1790.
ALCORNE—
Richard. *Edinburgh.* a.1694-1738.
James, son. *Edinburgh.* 1733-60.
ALDEN—
J. *London.* Late 18c. br. clock.
& ELDRIDGE. *Bristol, U.S.A.* 1820.
ALDER—
C. G. *Blyth.* 18c. l.c. clocks.
Joseph. *London.* 1762. Watch.
Brian. *London.* a.1770.
ALDERHEAD, John. *London.* 1783-8.
ALDERMAN, Edwin. *London.* 1818. l.CC. 1822-34.
ALDERSON, Josiah. *London.* a.1749, CC. 1758-61. Watch.
ALDRED—
Leonard. *London.* CC.1671-86. Maker of repute.
John. *London.* a.1686.
ALDRIDGE—
Daniel. *London.* a.1680.
Edward. *London.* a.1704. br.clock.
John. *London.* a.1717, CC.1726, d.1745.
Thomas. *London.* a.1753, CC.1769.
Thomas. *Deal.* 1784-91. W.
James. *London.* 1815-25.
ALDWINE, ——. ——. 1761. Watch.
ALDWORTH, Samuel. *Oxford* and *London.* CC.1697. Watch S.K.M.
ALEHOUSE, John. *London.* a.1788.
ALEMAN, John Frederick. *London.* a.1715.
ALENSON, ——. *Bristol.* an.1801. Watch.
ALEVA—
Willem. *Joure.* 1727.
Folkert. *Joure.* 1775.
Wiebe, son. *Joure.* ca.1800.
ALEXANDER—
John. *Edinburgh.* a.1667-1707.

ALEXANDER—*continued.*
Thomas. *London.* a.1698.
Robert. *Edinburgh.* 1708-18.
Isaac. *Nottingham.* 1745-60. Watch.
Robert. *Leith.* 1751-73. l.c. clock.
Robert. *Edinburgh.* 1761.
Robert. *Wigton.* 1770.
James Alexander. *London.* Mid. 18c. Watch Wakefield M.
Isaac. *Birmingham.* 1780. Watch.
John. *Edinburgh.* 1790.
Solomon. *Portsea.* 1795. W.
R. *Chippenham.* 1795. C. & W.
Alexander. *Pentonville.* 1795. C. & W.
Robert. *Leith.* an.1764. d.1830.
E. *London.* 1802-04.
A. *London.* 1805-07. W.
G. *Hull.* Early 19c. Watch.
& Co. *London.* 1820. Watch G.M.
William. *Westminster.* Early 19c. br. clock ill. Cec. & Web.
William. *London* (*Newington Causeway*). 1825.
'ALEXANDER.' Sig. on 1869-70 watches of the UNITED STATES WATCH CO.
ALEXANDRE—
Nicolas. *Paris.* m.1781-9.
——. *Paris* (*Rue St. Martin*). 1812.
ALFORD, Peter Joseph. *London.* a.1762.
ALGAR, Samuel. *London.* a.1749.
ALIBERT—
F. *Paris.* 1807-25. g. watch. mus. boxes and singing birds.
Frères. *Paris.* Early 19c. cyl. watch S. & A.M.
ALIMENIS, *v.* CAMPANUS.
ALISON—
James. *Edinburgh.* 1641-7. Made 'knok' for tower of Magdalen Chapel.
John. *Leith.* 1796.
John. *Montrose.* 1798-1822.
ALKAR, John. *Wigan.* 1790-1820 CC. Watch.
ALKINS, ——. *London.* 1666. W.
ALLAM—
Andrew. *London.* a.1656, CC.1664, d.1674. Lantern clock. l.c. clock Webster coll.
Michael. prob. *London.* 1723. Bankrupt.
Robert. *London.* a.1730, CC.1742-65. rep. watch mt.
William. *London.* CC.1743-85. 2 watch mts. G.M. g. en. watches M.M.A. and Stern. coll. rep. watch Marryat coll. Watch mt. Oldham M.
& CLEMENTS. *London.* 1764-95. g. en. watch London M. br. clock.
John. *London.* an.1777-98. Watch.
& STACY. *London.* 1781-5.
& CAITHNESS. *London.* 1805. Successors to ALLAM & CLEMENTS. br. clock ill. Cec. & Web.
ALLAMAND—
Jean Marc. *Geneva.* ca.1770-98. Juré.
Frères. *Geneva.* Early 19c. g. cyl. rep. watch. *v.* GENEQUAND-ALLAMAND.
ALLAN—
William. *Aberdeen.* 1703.
W. *London.* 1750-85. rep. watch mt.
George. *Montego Bay* (*Jamaica*). 1782-7. W.
Richard. *York.* 1796. Watch.
John. *Edinburgh.* 1800.
William. *Aberdeen.* 1807.
James. *Kilmarnock.* 1807.
ALLANSON, William. *Liverpool.* 1796-1805. W. cf. ALLINSON.
ALLARD (ALAR)—
Charles. *Paris.* m.1756.
Jean Claude. *Paris.* m.1757-89.
——. *Paris.* 1807-25.
ALLATSON, Richard. *London.* 1808. W.
ALLAWAY—
John. *London.* a.1681, CC.1695-1704.
Stephen. *London.* a.1736.
ALLBRIDGE, Samuel. *London.* a.1786.
ALLEBACH, Jacob. *Philadelphia.* 1825-40.
ALLEMAND, Benjamin. *Basle.* 1751. From *Lausanne.*
ALLEMANT, Jacques. *Paris.* m.1746.
ALLEN—
Elias. *London.* 1620. m.CC.1636, d.1654. Dials B.M. and Old Ashmolean M.
James. *London.* 1644. W.
John. *London.* CC.1653.
Nathaniel. *London.* a.1658, CC.1662.
Thomas. *London.* a.1663.
John. *London.* a.1671.
Richard. *London.* a.1696.
John. *London.* a.1703, CC.1720.
John. *London.* a.1710.
Daniel. *London.* 1732.
William. *London.* a.1736, CC.1745-60.
John. *London.* a.1737, CC.1753.
Charles. *London.* a.1747, CC.1763-9.
T. W. *London* (*Drury Lane*). an.1762. Watch.
James. *London.* 1761-1800. Awarded prize of 100 guineas for engine dividing by Board of Longitude. Watch.
Charles. *London* (*Shoe Lane*). CC.1770-5.
John. *Northwich.* ca.1770. Watch mt. Grosvenor M. Chester.
George. *London* (*Temple Bar*). CC.1771.
George. *London* (*Fleet St.*). CC.1776-81. Was abroad in 1784.
Richard Wyatt. *Macclesfield.* 1779.
Joseph. *London* (*Christ's Hosp.*). a.1773, CC.1781-1810.
George. *London* (*New Bond St.*). 1781-5.
Thomas. *Deptford.* an.1789. Watch.
Richard. *Pangbourne.* 1785. Watch mt. Buckley coll.
Fisher. *London* (*Thames St.*). an. 1791. Watch.
Thomas. *Buckingham.* ca.1790 CC.
Samuel. *London.* a.1785.
Philip. *Macclesfield.* 1795. Watch.
Peter. *S. Molton.* 1795.
John. *London* (*Aldersgate St.*). 1795. Watch-case maker.
John. *London* (*Bell St.*). 1795. Shagreen case maker.
William. *London.* a.1795.
George. *London* (*Red Lion Pass.*). 1805-24.
Thomas. *Salford.* 1808-13. C.
Charles. *London.* a.1813.
Richard. *Dublin.* 1820-4. Also ALLIN.
Thomas. *Corsley.* Early 19c. Watch.
——. *Wantage.* ca.1825.
ALLÉOUD, Pierre. *Geneva.* b.1741-85.
ALLETT (ALLET, ALLATT), George. *London.* a.1683, CC.1691. br. clock Weth. coll. l.c. clock, lacquer and gesso on oak, ill. Cec. & Web.
ALLGOOD, A. *Ledbury.* Early 19c. Watch.
ALLIÉ, Moïse. *Geneva.* Early 19c. c.secs. equation watch mt. Geneva M.
ALLIER—
——. *Paris* (*Rue St. Antoine*). 1807-24.
——. *Paris* (*Rue de la Barillerie*). 1812.
le jeune. *Paris.* 1824.
ALLIEZ—
TÉROND, & Co. *Geneva.* ca.1825. g. watch.
BACHELARD & TÉROND FRÈRES. *Geneva.* 1829. Four colour g. rep. watch Feill coll. Three g. en. watches M.M.A.
v. TÉROND, ALLIEZ & BACHELARD.
ALLIN—
Thomas. *Manchester.* ca.1820.
John. *London.* a.1823.
James. *London.* a.1825.
ALLING, Richard. *London.* a.1710, CC.1722.
ALLINGHAM, ——. *Croydon.* an.1752. Watch.
ALLINSON, William. *Liverpool.* ca.1770. cf. ALLANSON.

ALLISON, Gilbert. *Sunderland.* ca.1770. d.1810. W. l.c. clock.
Robert. *Berwick.* 1809.
ALLIX, Peter. *London.* an.1744. Watch.
ALLKINS, Thomas. *West Bromwich.* Early 19c. Watch.
ALLMAN—
Andrew. *London.* 1656. CC.1664.
William. *London.* a.1764-98. Till 1772 partner with John KENTISH and J. A. MANGAAR.
ALLON, William. *London.* a.1795.
ALLOWAY, Joshua. *London.* a.1726.
ALLPORT, Samuel. *Birmingham.* 1790-1836. br. clock. Watch.
ALLREY, Thomas. *London.* a.1750.
ALLSOP, Joshua. *Northamptonshire.* CC.1689. Maker of repute. l.c. clock. Watch. cf. ALSOPE.
ALLSOPP, John. *London.* a.1786, CC.1794. From *Quebec.* cf. ALSOPE.
ALLVEY—
Henry. *London.* a.1773, CC.1784.
v. ALVEY.
ALMAN—
Ralph. *v.* ALMOND.
Isaac. *Bristol.* 1794-7.
Robert. *Bristol.* 1801. W.
Aaron. *Bristol.* 1812-18. W.
W. *London* (*Woolwich*). 1817-24. W.
ALMCRANTZ, Peter. *Stockholm.* 1815-20.
ALMEIDA,——. *Cadiz.* 2nd half 18c. Watch.
ALMGREN, Johem. *Örebro.* 18c. l.c. clock.
ALMOND—
William. *London.* CC.1633-70.
Ralph. *London.* a.1637, CC.1646, m.CC. 1678. Also ALMAN.
John, son. *London.* CC.1671.
ALMROTH, Chr. Ad. *Göteborg.* b.1792, d.1822.
ALRICHS—
Jonas. *Wilmington, Del., U.S.A.* b.1759, d.1802.
Jacob. *Wilmington, Del., U.S.A.* b.1775, d.1857.
Jonas & Jacob. *Wilmington, Del., U.S.A.* 1795. Firm dissolved 1797.
& M'CLARY. *Wilmington.* 1810-13. Partnership of Jacob with Samuel M'CLARY.
ALSOPE (ALSOP)—
Joshua. *London.* 1689,CC.—ca.1710. l.c. clock. cf. ALLSOP.
John. *London.* a.1788.
John. *London* (*Lambeth*). 1820. cf. ALLSOPP.
ALSTED, Jens Chr. *Copenhagen.* m.1738.
ALSTON—
John. *Leith.* 1794.
John. *Edinburgh.* 1806.
John. *Edinburgh.* 1811.
ALT, Johann Jakob. *Basle.* b.1725, d.1812. Gross and Kleinuhrmacher.
ALTENBURG, J. C. *Hamburg.* 1815-21.
ALTSTEDT, F. *Cologne.* 1813.
ALVEY (ALLVEY)—
Samuel. *London.* a.1750, CC.1757-62.
Henry Quiat. *London.* a.1773, CC.1794-1808.
Thomas, son. *London.* a.1794, CC.1804.
ALWIN, ——. *London.* an.1773. Watch.
ALYETE, Anthelmo. *Autun.* 1485. Made new clock for Cathedral.
AMABRIC—
Abraham. *Geneva.* 1760-88. g. en. watch M.M.A.
Ami, son. *Geneva.* ca.1800-42. Watch N.Y. Univ.
Jean Louis David, brother. *Geneva.* ca.1800.
David, brother. *Geneva.* ca.1800.
Frères. *Geneva.* ca.1800. g. en. watches in form of shield and urn. Urn watch Feill coll.
ÅMAN—
Mathias Mauritz. *Köping* and *Stockholm.* m.1770-86.

ÅMAN—*continued.*
C. *Söderhamn.* b.ca.1770-1810.
Emanuel. *Örebro.* 1800.
J. *Lund.* b.1786, d.1849.
AMANDRIEZ, Jean François. *Paris.* m.1777-1789.
AMANT—
——. *Paris.* ca.1730-49. An eminent maker. Devised pin-wheel escapement for clocks.
Jean Louis (l'aîné), son. *Paris* (*Faubourg St. Martin*). m.1751-89.
Jean (le jeune). *Paris* (*Quai Pelletier*). m. 1755-89.
Anne Henry. *Paris.* m.1759, d.1773.
——. *Paris.* d.1785. Prob. one of the preceding.
Veuve. *Paris* (*Rue St. Denis*). 1785-89.
Fester. *Philadelphia.* 1793.
ÅMARCK, Niclas. *Stockholm.* 1751-99. br. clock.
ÅMARK, Mick. *Stockholm.* Early 18c. br. clock.
AMAURY, ——. *Le Havre.* 2nd half 18c.-1822. en. watch. Watch detent esc. jump c.secs. Ilbert coll.
AMBROGIO DA MILANO. *Genoa.* 1357. First keeper of Genoa clock.
AMBROSE—
Edward. *London.* CC.1637.
Edward. *London.* a.1634.
David. *London.* CC.1669.
Daniel. *London.* 1805-08. Or AMBROSS.
'AMERICAN WATCH CO.' Predecessors of the WALTHAM WATCH Co. Sig. on watches, 1860-72.
AMERY, Amos. *London* (?). an.1778. Watch.
AMES—
Richard. *London.* a.1648, CC.1656, m.CC. and d.1681. Lantern clock. Also AYMES.
William, son. *London.* a.1675, CC.1682-93.
Katharine. *London.* 1684.
Thomas. *Cleobury.* an.1780. Watch.
AMEY, John. *London.* a.1712-44.
AMEZ-DROZ, ——. *Geneva* and, later, *London.* 1800. Singing birds.
AMI, Théodore. *Geneva.* ca.1825.
AMIET, Isaac. *Boudry.* 1755. Modified clock on the Tour Marfaux.
AMIRAULT—
Louis Henry. *Paris.* Juré 1762.
Nicolas. *Paris.* m.1764. Expert on Bastille clock made by QUILLET.
Germain. *Paris.* m.1764.
AMMON, Johann. *Vienna.* 1765. Mechanician. Made mus. aut.
AMONTONS, Guillaume. *Paris.* b.1663, d. 1705. Able mechanician. Pub. book on a water clock in 1695.
AMOROSI, Pellegrino. *Rome.* 2nd half 18c. br. clock.
AMOS, William David Samuel. *London.* a.1819.
AMOURETTE, ——. *Abbeville.* End 17c. Lantern clock.
AMPE, Henry. *London.* a.1807. Also AMPS.
AMYOT (AMYOTT)—
Peter. *Norwich.* Late 17c. Lantern clocks, skeleton watch and mt. G.M.
Thomas. *London.* 1750-70. Watch G.M.
Peter. *Norwich.* b.1733, d.1799. CC. Large watch Ilbert coll.
& BENNETT. *Norwich.* 1790. Partnership with the preceding. Pub. book by J. Bennett.
ANCELET or **ANCELOT DU CHEMIN.** *Besançon.* 1459. Serrurier-horlogeur from Germany. Made clock for St. Jean Church. *v.* DUCHEMIN.
ANCRUM, Thomas. *Edinburgh.* a.1703.
ANDELES, Teddo. prob. *Friesland.* 2nd half 18c. p.c. g. watch Leeuwarden M.
ANDERES, Joseph. *Vienna.* m.1771.

ANDERSON—
William. *London*. CC.1649.
William. *London*. a.1646.
Robert. *London*. a.1691 to Thos. TOMPION. 6 months' l.c. clock.
Charles. *Aberdeen*. 1699.
John. *London*. a.1696.
Hugh. *London*. a.1737, CC.1745-55. mt. maker.
John. *London*. a.1740.
Alexander. *Liverpool*. an.1760-ca.1780. Watch Liverpool M.
Richard. *London* and *Preston*. 1767-78. W.
Robert. *Liverpool*. an.1774. Watch.
William. *Lancaster*. an.1762, d.1801.
John. *London*. CC.1776-86. Watch.
John. *Dundee*. 1776-1802.
George. *London*. 1777. Sued for putting Cabrier's name on watches.
George. *Liverpool*. ca.1780. Watch.
Alexander. *London*. an.1780. Watch.
Richard. *Preston*. ca.1780-95. Watch mt. Preston M.
William. *Hull*. 1784. W.
John. *London*. a.1783.
Samuel Thornton. *London*. a.1783, CC.1801-1811.
& ROBINSON. *Lancaster*. 1789. Dissolved partnership.
Sarah. *London*. 1789 CC.
Joseph. *London*. a.1791.
George. *London*. 1805-11. W.
William. *London*. 1805-08. Watch N.Y. Univ.
Henry. *Tullialan*. 1820.
William. *St. Andrews*. b.1790, d.1867.
David D. *Marietta, U.S.A.* 1821-4.
& SON. *London*. 1822-4. W.
Edmund. *London*. a.1822.
——. *Huddersfield*. Before 1828.
James. *Carrickfergus*. 1824.
Edward Charles. *London*. 1825-50. W.
F. *London* (*King St.*). Early 19c. Watch.

ANDERSONE, David. *Aberdeen*. 1597. Made 'sun horologe' on Aberdeen tolbooth.

ANDERSSON—
Anders. *Göteborg*. 1691-4.
Lars. *Karstorp*. 1775. l.c. clock.
Gustav Er. *Sweden*. Late 18c. Large mus. clock.
Nils. *Malmö*. b.1790, d.1871.

ANDERTON—
John. *London*. a.1716-53. rep. watch Den. coll.
——. *London*. a.1718.
——. *Liverpool*. ca.1750. Watch N.Y. Univ.
——. *London* (*Soho*). d.1765, W.
William. *London*. a.1805, CC.1818. Watch.

ANDERVALT, Pasquale. *Trieste*. 1850. Maker of repute. Made clocks wound by variations in barometer. Clock wound by generating hydrogen gas G.M.

ANDRÉ—
Jean. *Lyons*. a.1600, m.1605-19.
Camille. Prob. of Swiss family. ca.1700. Enameller of watch by Tompion B.M.
Jean. *Geneva*. b.1646, d.1714. Painter on enamel. Pupil of Pierre HUAUD. Watches Côte and Feill colls. and two others.
Père et Fils. ——. ca.1695. Sig. on en. on watch by P. MARTIN Ilbert coll.
Louis. *La Rochelle*. 1758-90.
Augustin. *Paris*. 1764 m.-1780.
Noel Augustin. *Paris*. m.1771-89. Employed at the Manufacture d'Horlogerie.
v. LANDRE.

ANDREAS—
Jacobi. *Vadstena*. 1406. d.1438. str. clock for Vadstena cloister.
Joh. Georg Adam. *Fürth*. d.1741. Maker of repute.

ANDREW—
J. *Dublin*. an.1757-80. Watch.

ANDREW—*continued*.
William. *Perth*. a.1791-5.
Alexander. *London*. 1820. W.
Joseph. *London*. 1820. W.

ANDREWS—
Robert. *London*. a.1661, CC.1709-17.
Ezekiall. *London*. a.1674. Went to the Indies.
Isaac. *London*. a.1674.
John. *London* (*Leadenhall Street*). a.1680, CC.1688-1715. Watch.
James. *London*. a.1686.
Thomas. *London* (*Leadenhall St.*). a.1686, CC.1705-22. l.c. marqueterie clock.
Thomas. *London*. a.1688.
Richard. *London*. a.1695, CC.1703-30. Watch.
Robert. *London*. a.1695, CC.1710-44. Watch.
William, son of John. *London*. a.1708, CC. 1719-27.
Richard. *London*. a.1710.
James. *London*. CC.1719.
Benjamin. *London*. a.1710, CC.1741-52.
Thomas. *London*. a.1716.
Thomas. *London*. a.1728-60. Watch.
Richard. *London*. a.1730.
Richard. *London* (*W. Smithfield*). 1743-52.
William. *London*. a.1742.
Thomas. *Steyning*. ca.1760. l.c. clock.
William. *London*. a.1756, CC.1767-83.
Nathaniel James. *London* (*Grub St.*). CC. 1772.
Thomas. *Sheffield*. 1774. W.
Samuel. *Bristol*. 1774.
Nathan. *Sheffield*. 1782. Murdered.
Joseph. *London*. an.1784. Watch.
Thomas. *Dover*. 1784. Watch.
W. H. *Royston*. ca.1790. CC.
Eliza. *London*. 1790-1812. en. watch set pearls F.W.M. Watch mt. G.M.
Benjamin. *St. Austell*. 1791. l.c. clock.
Haydock. *Dublin*. 1795. W
Richard. *London*. a.1798.
Kendrick. *London* (*Hoxton*). ca.1800. Watch.
William. *London*. a.1802.
John Richard. *London*. a.1813.

ANDRIES (**ANDRIESEN, ANDERS**)—
Johannes. *Grouw*. 1759-64. l.c. and table clock.
Klaas Johannes, son. *Grouw*. b.1761. l.c. and table clock.
Johannes Klaas, son. *Grouw*. 1800-31.

ANDS, ——. *Vienna*. 18c. g. en. watch M.M.A.

ANGELIQUE, ——. *Neuchâtel*. 1686. 'Maistre horlogeur.' Repaired the town clocks.

ANGELY (**ANGELLI**)—
Étienne. *Montpellier*. 1679 m.
Pierre, son. *Lyons*. 1678 comp., mar. 1679.
Jehan. *Paris*. 1686.

ANGEVIN, ——. *Paris*. 1812-25. Clock.

ANGOILLE—
Jean. *Paris*. m.1690, juré 1712. Watch.
Jean. *Moulins*. End 17c. Watch Den. coll.
——. *Paris*. 1768.

ANGOT, Isac. *Amsterdam*. 1681. A Huguenot refugee from France.

ANGUS, George. *Aberdeen*. 1790. d.1830.

ANICH, Peter. *Innsbruck*. b.1723, d.1766. Astronomer and mathematician. Made fine astro. clocks.

ANISSE, J. *Paris*. ca.1660. circ. g. chased watch.

ANITO, Nicola. *Rome*. 1796. Repaired the Farnese planisphere clock and made a set of drawings in 24 sheets of all its parts, with description, in the Vatican library, Cod. Vat. Lat. 12946. *v.* FELICETTI and FACCINI.

ANJOU, Jean Gustave. *Stockholm*. 1771-90. *Uppsala* in 1779. Watch.

ANNAT, Nicholas. *London*. a.1673.

ANNESS—
William. *London*. CC.1796, l.CC.1802-21. Watch, br. clock.
v. ANNS.

ANNIN, M. *New York.* 1786.
ANNOTT, Charles. *London.* a.1674.
ANNS, Benjamin. *Highworth.* 1770. C.
James. *Highworth.* mar.1777. 'Eminent' W.
——. *Eye.* 1785. C. & W. Also ANNESS.
ANSART, Pierre. *Paris.* m.1767-89.
ANSELL (ANSELME)—
Richard. *London.* a.1672, CC.1680.
George. *London* (*Moorfields*). a.1766, l.CC. 1791-1821. Spring maker.
George, son. (*London.*) a.1792, CC. 1796-1825. Spring maker.
John, son. *London.* a.1803.
Thomas. *Abingdon.* From 1780-ca.1810.
ANSERMIER, Jean Rodolphe. *Chaux-de-Fonds.* 1799. Maître pendulier. Made mus. mts.
ANSTEY, John. *London.* a.1683.
ANTES, John. *London.* 1787. p.c. pocket chron. G.M.
ANTHEAUME, Jean Baptiste. *Paris.* m. 1784-9.
ANTHONY—
Anthony. *London.* 1529-31. C. to Henry VIII. Paid 10 guineas for a clock in a case of gold in 1531.
William. *London.* b.ca.1764, d.1844. Famous maker. Verge watch Chamb. coll.; large g. en. watch set pearls and diamonds. Made many watches for China.
John. *Maidenhead.* an.1784. Watch.
ANTIS, John. *Fulneck,* near *Leeds.* 1805. Prize from Soc. of Arts for a clock escapement.
ANTOINE, ——. *Paris.* 1772.
ANTONI—
Georg. *Neustadt* (*Vienna*). Late 18c. Large astro. l.c. clock Uhren M. Vienna.
P. J. *Copenhagen.* m.1819.
ANTRAM—
Joseph. *London.* a.1697, CC.1706. d.1723. W. & C. to George I. l.c. clock. p.c. str. watch Fränkel. coll. g. repoussé watch Arts M. Prague.
Joshua. *London.* 1712. l.c. clocks.
APFELDERN, Hans. *Basle.* 1630. From *Breslau.*
APIOHN, Henry. *London.* a.1649.
APPEL, Bernhard. *Oberhausen.* 1756.
APPELHOKE, Hinrik. *Brunswick.* 1443-9.
APPERLEY, Thomas. *London.* 1807CC.
Mary, daughter. *London.* CC.1807.
APPLEBY—
Edward. *London.* 1681 CC.
Edmund. *London.* CC.1712. Watch.
Joshua. *London.* a.1705 to QUARE, CC.1719, m.CC.1745-59.
Thomas. *Manchester.* 1791-3. W.
Thomas. *London.* ca.1800. br. clock.
John James. *London.* CC.1823.
APPLEGARTH, Thomas. *London.* a.1664, CC.1674.
APPLETON—
William. *Prescot.* an.1765. Watch.
John. *Liverpool.* 1777. W.
William. *Widnes.* an.1791. Watch.
John. *Liverpool.* 1810-24. W.
'APPLETON TRACY & CO.' Predecessors of the WALTHAM WATCH Co. Sig. on watches 1859-69.
APPLEY, Edmund. *London.* a.1670, CC. 1677-93. br. clock.
ARBITT, S. *London.* an.1772. Watch.
ARBOE, Jørgen Peter. *Bornholm.* 1787.
ARCH, Samuel. *London.* 1795. W.
ARCHAMBO, John. *London.* 1720-50. br. clock and l.c. clocks. Musical watches with bells, Webster and Olivier colls. l.c. clock in Chippendale 'Director' style case. Watch mt. Oldham M.
ARCHDEKIN, Michael. *Dublin.* 1769-1800. W.
ARCHER—
Henry. *London.* Admitted BC. 1628 as 'english forrin.' CC. 1632. d.1649. First warden of CC. The BC. in 1633 petitioned to disfranchise him. Oval watch, sil. covers, Webster coll. Watch Miller coll.
John. *London.* a.1650, CC.1660.
Walter. ——. ca.1700. Lantern clock.
Edward. *London.* a.1702, CC.1712, d.1734.
John. *London.* a.1734.
John. *London.* a.1737.
Richard Sewell. *London.* CC.1758.
John. *Liverpool.* 1777. W.
William. *London.* a.1769.
Robert. *London.* an.1781. Watch.
Richard. *Stow-in-Wold.* 1795. l.c. clock.
Samuel. *London* (*Leather Lane*). 1790-7.
Succeeded by Samuel junior. *London* (*Leather Lane* then *Kirby St.* and *Hatton Gdn.*). 1797-1824.
Thomas. *London.* CC.1815-24. Watch.
Samuel William. *London* (*Hackney*). 1817-24.
George. *Rochdale.* ca.1820.
ARCHIMBAUD, Jean. *Lyons.* 1653. From *Geneva.*
ARCHINARD—
——. *Paris.* 1817.
Farjon et Olivet. *Paris.* 1818.
J. L. *Paris.* 1819-21. Successor to preceding.
ET CIE. ——. Early 19c. g. en. watch M.M.A.
v. GUIRODON.
ARCUTT, George. *London.* a.1697.
ARDEN, Samuel. *London.* a.1809.
ARDERN, John. *Liverpool.* 1777-84. C.
ARDESOIF, Thomas. *Paris.* m.1752.
ARDIN, John Jacob. *Cologne.* m.1703.
ARDING—
John. *London.* a.1699.
John. *London.* a.1703.
ARDIOT, ——. *Paris.* 1772-1812.
ARENBERG, Gustav. *Copenhagen.* m.1798.
ARGAND—
L'aîné. *Geneva.* Mid. 18c. 3-case sil. watch.
Jacques. *Geneva.* b.1733, d.1782.
J. L. *Paris.* 1760-77. rep. watch M.M.A.
& SALOMON. *Paris.* End 18c. Watch.
ARGANT, ——. *Paris.* 1749m.
ARGO, ——. *Peterhead.* 1784.
ARIELL—
James. *London.* a.1792, CC.1812-25. mt. maker.
John, son. *London.* a.1807-39.
Samuel, brother. *London.* a.1804, CC.1822, l.CC.1823.
ARIS—
Samuel. *London.* 1743-7. Shagreen watch.
John. *London.* a.1731, CC. 1764-92. Shagreen case-maker.
John, & Co. *London.* 1781-92.
——. *Uppingham.* 1798. W. cf. AVIS.
ARKINSTALL, Francis. *Market Drayton.* Early 19c. Watch.
ARLANDEAU—
——. *Paris.* 1735 m.
Jean Philippe. *Paris.* 1743 m.
ARLANDY—
John. *London.* CC.1682. Chainmaker.
Robert. *London.* a.1697. Bankrupt 1743. Chainmaker.
ARLAUD—
Anthoine. *Geneva.* 1617. Protestant refugee from the Auvergne. Sil. gilt eng. cross watch Wallace coll. crys. cross watch M.M.A.
Étienne. *Grenoble.* 1637. Son of Anthoine.
Henri. *Geneva.* b.1630, d.1689.
Henry. *London.* 1650-85. Watch ill. Britten. Watch en. Huaud le puisné.
Jean. *Geneva* and *Basle.* 1657.

ARLAUD—*continued.*
Benjamin. *London* (?). ca.1680. Watches B.M. and Munich M.
Lazare. *Geneva.* ca.1700. Watch.
François. *Geneva.* b.1720-76. Mém. to Soc. des Arts on a depth tool for crown wheel.
——. *Geneva.* ca.1800. Painter on enamel.
ARLOTT (**ARLOT**)—
Thomas. *Sunderland.* 1780-91. l.c. clock.
William. *Sunderland.* 1801-20. W.
ARLUDE, Claude. *Paris.* Juré 1692.
ARMAGNAC—
——. *Paris.* 1807. d.1810.
Veuve. *Paris.* 1811-13.
ARMAND—
Michel. *Grenoble.* 1703.
Jean Abraham. *Copenhagen.* b.1732 .d.1819. Marine chron. Fränkel coll.
Jean Victor. *Paris.* m.1773-89.
Johan Vilhelm, son of J. A. *Bornholm.* b.1762-1806. Chron. maker.
ARMIGER, Joseph. *London.* CC.1688.
ARMINGAU, ——. *Paris.* 1812.
ARMITAGE—
Richard. *London.* a.1791.
& Moore. *London.* 1799. W.
Thomas. *Manchester.* ca.1815.
ARMOUR—
John. *Kilmaurs.* 1780-1808.
Joseph Rowland. *London.* a.1810.
ARMSTRONG—
John. *London.* a.1716, CC.1724.
John. *London.* a.1720.
John. *London.* a.1725.
Edward. *London.* a.1736.
George. *London.* an.1780.
J. *Liverpool.* 2nd half 18c. Watch mt.
——. *Newcastle.* ca.1790. l.c. clocks.
J. *London.* 1805-08.
Thomas. *Manchester.* 1804-20. C.
John. *Newcastle.* mar.1803-16. C. & W.
Thomas. *Kirkham.* mar. 1804.
Thomas. *Poulton* (*Lancs.*). 1808. C.
D. *London.* Early 19c. Watch.
George. *Gateshead.* an.1818.
Thomas. *Liverpool.* 1825. W.
ARNAUD—
——. *Grenoble.* Mid. 17c. From *Geneva.*
Antoine. *Paris.* m.1780-1812. 4-colour gold watch.
ARNOLD—
Thomas. *London.* a.1687, CC.1703. Fine watch Chamb. coll.
Thomas. *Hamburg.* Early 18c. watch Nat. M. Stockholm.
Edward. *London.* a.1737-75.
Thomas. *London* (*Fetter Lane*). a.1742, CC. 1750-72. Watch.
John. *Coventry.* 1760. C. & W.
Edward. *St. Neots.* 1772. Succeeded Joseph Eayre. C. & W.
John. *London.* b.1736, CC.1783, d.1799. One of the most famous English makers. Had a chron. factory at *Chigwell.* Made rep. watch set in ring for George III in 1764. Invented helical balance spring for chrons. and a detent escapement similar to the modern chron. escapement. Also end curves for helical balance spring and several compensation balances (Patents No. 1113 of 1775 and No. 1328 of 1782). Was the principal chron. maker of his day. Two marine chron. and 2 pocket chron. and 2 watches G.M. cyl. watch S. & A.M. Pocket chron. rep. helical spring No. 37, h.m. 1778 Ilbert coll. Pump winding verge watch Den. coll.
& Son. *London.* 1787-99. Firm of John and his son J. Roger. Three pocket and a marine chron. G.M. Watch mt. with helical gold balance spring Ilbert coll. Regulator Weth. coll.
William. *London.* Late 18c. g. watch S.K.M.

ARNOLD—*continued.*
Edward. *Leicester.* 1794. C. & W.
John. *London.* a.1782.
John Roger. *London.* Son of John I., a. to his father in 1783 and later to A. L. Breguet. CC.1796, m.CC.1817, d.1843. Patented a compensation balance in 1821. Many watches and chron. Stem wind watch dated 1824 Ilbert coll.
John Fitzwilliam. *London.* a.1789. W.
John. *London* (*Pentonville*). 1799-1824.
John. *London* (*Hoxton*). 1805-08. W.
Nicholas, ——. 1813. Watch.
Charles. *Eltham.* CC.1824.
John Roger, & Dent. *London.* 1830, dissolved 1840. On John R.'s death in 1843, the business was taken over by Charles Frodsham.
ARNOLTS, Thomas Wolffgang. *Hamburg.* ca.1635. Watch ill. Britten.
ARNOTT—
Thomas. *London.* a.1764. Watch.
Richard. *London.* CC.1808-20.
ARNOULT, ——. *Paris.* 1825.
ARNOUX—
Jean François. *Paris* (*Rue des Tournelles*). m.1741.
Jean Baptiste. *Paris.* m.1788
——. *Paris.* 1810-13.
ARONDELL, Laurence. *London.* 1568. Frenchman.
ARSANDEAUX, ——. *Paris.* 1780. Planetarium C.A. & M.
ARSAUD, Henry. ——. Mid. 17c. en. watch Gotha M.
ARSENIUS, Gualterus. *Louvain.* ca.1535-71. Nephew of Gemma Frisius. Famous math. inst. maker. Fine Astrolabes Archaeological M. Madrid and Old Ashmolean M.
ARSYE, I. *Namur.* Early 18c. sheep's head clock.
ARTHAUD—
Louis. *Lyons.* b.1612, 1637 m., d.1662. Astro. watch B.M. ill. Vial & Côte. Watch S.K.M.
Olivier. *Lyons.* 1679-83. 'Armurier et horloger.'
François. *Paris.* m.1764.
ARTHAULT—
——. *Paris.* ca.1745 m.
Jacques André. *Paris.* m.1756-89.
Pierre Marie. *Paris.* m.1756.
ARTHUR—
William. *London.* a.1669, CC.1676-81.
Jean. *Paris.* m.1757-89. 'Un des plus renommés, est des plus à la mode pour les montres à répétition.' Watch M.M.A.
Charles. *London* (?). an.1780. Watch.
'The Arthur Wadsworth.' Sig. on 1867-9 watches of the Newark Watch Co.
ARTOULÉ, Pierre André. *Paris.* m.1744.
ARTUS, Claude. *Paris.* 1678 juré. Fine boulle br. clock Pal. de Pau, Paris.
ARWEN, William. *Huddersfield.* 1785-95.
ARWIG, Anton. *Vienna.* m.1788.
ÄRZT—
Marcus. *Munich.* ca.1600. Astro. clock Munich M.
Johann Martin. *Munich.* Court C.1752. Town C. 'Mechanicus' to the Bayerische Akad. der Wiss. 1773. Went to *Vienna* 1793. d.1800. Very famous maker of aut. clocks.
Franz Egydius. *Vienna.* m.1794.
'ASA FULLER.' Sig. on 1869-70 watches of the United States Watch Co.
ÅSBERG, G. J. *Söderköping.* 1820-35.
ASH—
——. *London.* 1630. Subscribed for incorporation of CC.
Ralph. *London.* CC.1646.
Edward. *London.* a.1700.

ASH—*continued.*
Lawrence. *Philadelphia.* 1762. C. & W.
John. *London.* an.1774. Watch.
Robert. *London (Cheapside).* CC.1820-5.
ASHBOURNE, James. *London.* a.1663.
ASHBROOKE—
Thomas. *London.* a.1685.
John. *London.* a.1686-ca.1710. .c. clock M.M.A.
Thomas. *Manchester.* 1788-92. C. & W.
ASHBURNE, Leonard. ——. 1730. Invented a clock lamp showing time by oil consumption.
ASHBY—
Joseph. *London.* a.1664, CC.1674-95.
James. *Boston, U.S.A.* 1769.
ASHCROFT, John. *Liverpool.* 1816-29. W.
ASHENHEIM, Jacob. *Edinburgh.* 1818-38.
ASHER, Joseph. *London.* 1802-11.
ASHFORD, Richard Henry. *London.* a.1820, CC.1827.
ASHLEY—
James. *London.* a.1647, CC.1655.
James. *London.* a.1755, CC.1763.
Charles. *London.* a.1761. Watch.
James. *London.* a.1766.
John Powell. *London.* a.1786-1805.
Edward. *London.* a.1812-21.
& MAUSER. *London.* 1823-35. Devised variant of cylinder escapement.
ASHMAN, Thomas. *London.* a.1719.
ASHMORE—
Thomas. *London.* a.1719.
Robert. *London (Bridgewater Sq.).* 1782-97. Watch.
Edward, son. *London.* a.1782.
ASHNESS, George. *Macclesfield.* 1772. C.
ASHTON—
Thomas. *London.* 1654 CC.
Miles. *London.* a.1663.
John. *London.* a.1671.
John. *London.* a.1672.
Charles. *Chester.* 1683. Watch.
Thomas. *London.* a.1687.
John. *Whiston.* d.1738. W.
Samuel. *Ashbourne.* 1753. C. & W.
Thomas. *Macclesfield.* ca.1760-95. Watch mt.
——. *Gee Cross, Lancs.* 2nd half 18c. l.c. mus. clock.
H. *Ashbourne.* ca.1780.
& Son. *Ashbourne.* 1791-5. C. & W.
Thomas. *Tideswell.* an.1795. W.
John. *Leek.* 1795. C. & W.
Samuel. *Stockport.* 1803. C.
ASHURST—
William. *London.* CC.1699.
James. *Chorley.* d.1793.
ASHWELL—
Nicholas. *London.* a.1642, CC.1649.
John. *London.* 1805-08.
ASKE, Henry. *London.* a.1669, CC.1676-97.
ASKELL, Elizabeth. *London.* a.1734.
ASKEQUITH, Edward. *London.* a.1735.
ASKEYEN, John. *London.* a.1716.
ASKWITH, John. *York.* 1740. W.
ASLATT, Thomas. *London.* an.1722. l.c. clock. Watch.
ASLING, E. *Birmingham.* 1790.
ASPDIN, James. *Leeds.* d.1788.
ASPINWALL (ASPINALL)—
Thomas. ——. ca.1605. Watch ill. Britten.
Samuel. ——. ca.1655. Watches Miller and Gélis colls.
Josiah. *London.* CC.1675. Watch with balance spring of two turns and straight screw regulator, prob. by him or the preceding, Webster coll.
John. *Liverpool (Dock Gates).* 1781-1800. W.
Thomas. *Manchester.* 1787-92. C. & W.
Henry. *Liverpool.* 1790-6. l.c. clock.

ASPINWALL (ASPINALL)—*continued.*
John. *Liverpool (Wapping).* 1800. W.
Robert. *Liverpool.* 1807-24 CC. W.
ASPREY, William. *London.* 1820-5.
ASSELIN—
Francis. *London.* CC.1687. French. br. clock.
Stephen. *London.* ca.1700. br. clock Ilbert coll. Watch.
Jean Baptiste. *Rouen.* 1694. In charge of town clock.
Michael Jean Nicolas, son. *Rouen.* 1732. In charge of town clock.
ASSELYNNE, ——. *London.* 1717. Engraver. French.
ASSOM, John. *London.* a.1700.
ASSUR, Isaac. *Hamburg.* 1801-15.
ASTHALTER, Ludwig. *Vienna.* m.1804.
ASTLEY, Edward. *London.* a.1713.
ASTON—
John. *London.* a.1739.
George. *Bilston.* 1781. C.
ÅSTRÖM—
Nils. *Hälsingborg.* b.1784, d.1852.
Nils. *Söderhamn.* 1815-20.
A. *Norrköping.* 1825-35. g. cyl. str. watch.
ASTWOOD, Joseph. *London.* a.1659.
ATCHE, Valentin Kruse. *Copenhagen.* m.1798.
ATCHISON—
Robert. *London.* a.1753, CC.1760-1819.
William. *London.* a.1760.
ATFIELD, James. *Brentford.* 1712.
ATHERN (ATHEN), John. *Norwich.* an.1760. Watch.
ATHERTON, Nathan, jun. *Philadelphia.* 1825. W.
ATKINS (ATKIN)—
Joseph. *London.* a.1654.
Samuel. *London (Temple Bar).* b.1697, d.1768. 'Eminent' C. & W.
Jonathan. *London.* a.1689.
Henry. *London.* a.1713.
Samuel. *London.* a.1733-65. W.
Francis. *London (Clement's Lane).* b.1730, a.1746, CC.1759, m.CC.1780, d.1809. *v.* ATKINS & SON. Watch mt. G.M.
Samuel, & Son. *London (Temple Bar).* 1763.W.
William. *Chipping Norton.* 1764. C. & W.
Robert. *London (Salisbury St.).* 1770-85. g. watch Den. coll.
John. *London,* an.1781. Watch.
George, son of Francis. *London (Clement's Lane and Fenchurch St.).* b.1767, CC. 1788, m.CC.1845, d.1855.
& Co. *Bourne.* Late 18c.
Joshua. *Chipping Norton.* Late 18c. CC.
——. *Eastbourne.* End 18c. CC.
M. T. *London.* End 18c.
John. *London.* a.1784.
& SON. *London (Clement's Lane).* 1795-1811. Continuation of firm of Francis ATKINS.
Robert. *London.* a.1782-1800. g. rep. cyl. p.c. en. watch F.W.M.
William. *London.* a.1786.
R. & J. *London.* 1799-1824. mt. makers.
Francis. *Liverpool.* 1800.
Robert. *Liverpool.* 1810-29. W.
W. *Poplar.* Early 19c. Chron. W. & C.
W. *London (Hoxton).* Early 19c.
John. *London (Clerkenwell).* 1817-24. W.
Henry Michael. *London.* a.1811.
Thomas Carpenter. *London.* a.1814.
John. *Sunderland.* 1820.
William. *Wexford.* 1824.
Francis. *Liverpool (St. John St.).* 1825.
Francis. *Liverpool (Lord St.).* 1825.
Rollin. *Bristol, U.S.A.* 1826. C.
Ireneus. *Bristol, U.S.A.* 1830. C.
Samuel Elliott, son of George. *London.* a. 1821, CC.1831, m.CC.1881 and 1889, d.1898. cyl. watch G.M.

ATKINSON—
James. *London.* CC.1667-99. Math. inst. maker.
Joseph. *London.* 1687 CC.
John. *London* (*Aldersgate St.*). 1749. Watch.
Thomas. *Dublin.* 1766-74. W.
Thomas. *Lancaster* and *Ormskirk.* 1767. C.
Samuel & Robert. *London.* an.1768. Watch.
James. *Gateshead.* 1770-7.
Joseph. *Gateshead.* 1775, d.ca.1804. l.c. clocks. Watch. Widow, Mary, continues.
Thomas. *Ormskirk.* 1784.
Robert. *London.* a.1772.
——. *Carlisle.* 1777. W.
Richard. *Liverpool.* 1785-96. W
v. DAWSON & ATKINSON.
Thomas. *Dublin.* 1795. W.
Mary. *Baltimore, U.S.A.* 1802-07. W. & C.
M. & A. *Baltimore, U.S.A.* 1804.
Thomas. *Gateshead.* 1809-11. W.
William, son of Richard. *Liverpool.* 1817. W.
John. *Wirksworth.* an.1816. Watch.
Samuel. *Drogheda.* 1820-4.
Robert. *Liverpool.* 1825.
Thomas Benjamin. *London.* a.1817, CC.1829.

ATLEE—
Henry. *London.* a.1662, CC.1672.
Roger. *London.* a.1664.

ATMORE, ——. *London.* 1735. Watch.

ATTEMSTÄTTER, David. *Augsburg.* d. 1617. Very fine clock, sil. with en. K.H.M.

ATTMORE, Marshall. *Philadelphia.* 1824.

ATTWELL—
——. *Romford.* Late 18c.
William. *London.* 1805. CC.1811. Watch.
W. H., junior. *London.* 1817-24. W.
Robert. *London.* 1817-24. W.

ATWAY (ATAWAY), John. *Three Mile Cross* (*Berks.*). d.1756. C.

ATWOOD (ATTWOOD)—
Thomas. *London.* an.1774. Watch.
W. *Lewes.* Late 18c. W. to the King and Queen. Watch.
George. *London.* 1805-21.
M. *London.* 1821.

AUBAN, Leonard. *Copenhagen.* 1756-66. Court C. Swiss.
——. *Switzerland.* ca.1770.

AUBER, Daniel. *London.* Late 18c. rep. duplex watch.

AUBEREY, William. *London.* an.1794. Watch.

AUBERT—
Estienne. *Lyons.* 1661. Settled in *Paris* 1667 m.-1685.
Étienne. *Rouen.* 2nd half 17c. en. watch Arts M. Prague.
Denis. *Blois.* m.1662-1703.
Pierre, son. *Blois.* m.1703.
John Jenkell. *London.* a.1731.
Jean Jacques. *Paris.* 1737. 'Horloger du Roi.'
l'aîné. *Paris.* 1789-1824. Mantel clock, Mobilier National, Paris. Fine cal. and c.secs. clock, Pal. de Fontainebleau.
D. F. *Geneva.* Early 19c. Watch in finger ring Feill coll.

AUBOURG—
Jacques. *Blois.* comp.1663-70.
Louis, son. *Blois.* m.1696.

AUBREIN, Laurent. *Lyons.* 1492.

'AUBURNDALE ROTARY.' Sig. on 1877 watches of the AUBURNDALE WATCH Co.

'AUBURNDALE TIMER.' Sig. on 1877-81 watches.

AUBURNDALE WATCH CO. *Auburndale. Mass.* Watches sd. as two preceding, and 'Bentley' and 'Lincoln' in 1879.

AUCH, Jakob. *Seeberg.* b.1765. *Weimar,* 1798, d.1842. Court C. Pub. 2 books on horology. Large g. astro. watch Schloss M. Berlin. Lever watch Furt. M.

AUCKLAND, William. *London.* an.1782. Watch.

AUDEBERT—
D. *Amsterdam.* ca.1725. l.c. clock. Watch mt.
——. *Paris* (*Rue Montagne Ste Geneviève*). 1807-25. cf. AUDIBERT.

AUDEMARS, J. Louis. *Brassus.* b.1782-ca. 1840. An eminent maker. Started factory with P. S. MEYLAN for parts of complex watches. Made demi-Breguet calibres.

AUDÉOUD-CHENEVIÈRE. *Geneva.* Early 19c.

AUDIAUX, Thomas. *Paris.* Juré 1752.

AUDIBERT, Jean Pierre. *Paris* (*Rue du Petit-Pont*). m.1756-89. cf. AUDEBERT.

AUDIERNE, Jean Louis. *Paris.* m.1787-1813.

AUDINET, ——. *Paris.* Early 18c. Boulle clock.

AUDLEY, Joseph. *London.* a.1683 to TOMPION.

AUDRAS, Pierre. *Rouen.* 1607.

AUGÉ, Jean Antoine René. *Paris.* m.1788.

AUGHTON, R. *London.* Mid. 18c. l.c. clock Virginia M.

AUGIER, Jehan. *Paris.* 1600-20. Sig. to Statuts of Paris Corporation of 1600. Registered a private punch mark in 1620. Fine en. watch Louvre.

AUGUIER, ——. *Nogent.* ca.1620. Watch G.M.

AUGUSTIN—
——. *Vienna.* 1700.
——. *Paris.* 1810-25.

AULD, William. *Edinburgh.* 1795-1823. *v.* REID & AULD.

AULT—
Thomas. *London* (*Hoxton*). a.1770-1808.
William, son. *London.* a.1803. Watch.
Thomas. *London* (*Soho*). 1822-4.
Thomas. *London* (*Leicester Sq.*). 1822-5.

AUMAN, Mathias. *Mariestad.* 1750-4.

AUMONT—
Jacques. *Paris* (*Rue de la Huchette*). m.1777-1789.
Jean Baptiste. *Paris* (*Rue de la Juiverie*). m.1788.

AUNALE, ——. *Gravesend.* an.1743. Watch.

AUNGIER, Thomas. *London.* a.1696.

AURELIUS (Pater) à San Daniele. *Vienna.* 1770. Astro. clock.

AUSENDER, Grenado. *London.* 1.CC.1812-1817.

AUSIN, Prob. *France.* Early 17c. Sig. on gilt cross watch, crys. covers, Wallace coll.

AUSTEN—
John. *London.* CC.1712-25. br. clock.
——. *Cork.* 1740-60. Made 3-wheel clock.
Robert. *Challock.* ca.1780. l.c. clock Virginia M.
John. *London* (*St. John's Wood*). Early 19c. Watch.

AUSTIN—
John. *London.* CC.1712.
Henry. *London.* a.1700-20 CC.
John, son. *London.* a.1725.
Paul. *London.* a.1726.
James. *London.* a.1731.
John. *London* (*Shoreditch*). an.1745. Watch.
——. *Romsey.* an.1761. Watch.
William. *London.* a.1762.
Richard. *London.* CC.1769-1817.
Aaron. *Bristol.* 1775-97.
Isaac. *Philadelphia.* 1785-1805.
Thomas. *London* (*Soho*). 1802-04.
Thomas. *London* (*Fulham*). 1805-24.
Richard, son of Richard. *London.* CC.1817.
& Co. *London.* 1820-5.
A. *London.* 1820.
Thomas. *Bristol.* 1825.

AUTRAM, ——. *London.* 1720. sil. watch M.M.A.

AUTRAN—
——. *Pforzheim.* 1765. From *Geneva.*
——. *Paris.* ca.1790 g. en. watch S.K.M.
Charles. *Geneva.* 1792.
AUTRAND, Les Frères. *Paris.* Late 18c. 4-colour g. watch.
AUTRAY—
François. *Paris.* m.1737-50. Watch.
Claude. *Paris.* m.1784-9.
Fils. *Paris* (*Rue d'Aboukir*). 1809-25. Pedometer winding cyl. watch mt. Ilbert coll.
——. *Paris* (*Quai des Ormes*). 1811-24.
AUZIÈRE—
Georges. *Geneva,* 1770. *Ferney,* ca.1790. *Besançon,* 1795. d.1799. In 1795 was given a concession to start a factory at Besançon, which failed.
Jacques. *Geneva.* ca.1770-89.
AVARD, Joseph. *Bristol.* 1794. Bankrupt. Partner in AVARD & HALL.
AVELINE—
Daniel. *London.* a.1723, l.CC.1731, m.CC. and d.1771. Watch-case maker.
Richard. *London.* l.CC.1766.
AVELLOT, Émile. *Lyons.* ca.1625. Oval watch B.M.
AVELOT, Mathieu. *Rouen.* 1607. 'Orlogiographe.'
AVENALL (AVENELL)—
Thomas. *London.* 1700-10. CC.1705.
Edward. *London.* a.1698, CC.1706-49. Watch mt. G.M.
Richard. *London.* an.1726. Watch.
John, son of Edw. *London.* a.1724, CC. 1735-56.
William. *Alresford.* 1760. l.c. clock.
Philip. *Farnham,* 1765. *London,* 1775. Watch.
Richard. *Bagshot.* 1791. W.
William. *Farnham.* 1795. C.
AVERILL, John. *London.* 1622. Alien.
AVERY—
——. *Boston, U.S.A.* 1726. Maker of clock in old North Church.
John. *Preston, U.S.A.* 1732-94.

AVERY—*continued.*
Amos. *London.* 1767-9. Bankrupt.
Andrew. *London* (*Paul's Alley*). a.1760, CC. 1777-88.
Philip, son. *London* (*St. Dunstan's Hill*). a. 1781, CC.1802-04.
Joseph, son. *London.* a.1804, CC. 1811.
'T. M. AVERY.' Sig. on watches of ELGIN NATIONAL WATCH Co. from 1876.
AVIS, William. *Uppingham.* 1795. W. cf. ARIS.
AVRIL—
Théodore. *Paris.* ca.1750. In charge of clocks of Fontainebleau. g. watch Pal. du Cinquantenaire, Brussels.
——. *London.* ca.1750. Watch Ilbert coll.
——. *Paris.* 1812-23.
AVYCE, Damien. *Rouen.* 1575.
'A. W. Co. WALTHAM.' Sig. on watches of AMERICAN WATCH Co. from 1800. Predecessor of the WALTHAM WATCH Co.
AXFORD, George. *London.* an.1775. Watch.
AYERES, Richard. *London.* CC.1680.
AYLOFFE—
Elizabeth. *London.* a.1678.
John. *London* (?). an.1782. Clock.
AYQUET, Jehin, dit Jehin de Lyon. *Lyons.* 1395. 'Rappareille l'horloge de la chambre de Mons.' (Monseigneur.)
AYR (EYR), Benjamin. *Edinburgh.* a.1765-70.
AYRE—
Henry. *Gateshead.* ca.1820. l.c. clock.
Thomas. *Dublin.* 1824.
AYRES—
Samuel. *London.* a.1664.
Richard. *London.* a.1670, CC.1680-98.
& BENNETT. *London.* 1815-25.
AYREY, John. *Hexham.* 1779, d.1806. W. cf. AIREY.
AYSHFORD,——. *Crawley.* Early 19c. Watch.
AZEMARD—
Jacques. *Geneva.* ca.1770-91. Watch.
Pierre Barthélemy. *Paris.* m.1779-89.
AZIRE, Peter. *London.* an.1753. Watch.

B

BAATEN, F. *Rotterdam.* 1821-30.
BABB, Thomas. *London.* a.1712.
BACCUET, F. *London.* 1st half 18c. Watch Chamb. coll. g. repoussé watch.
BACHAN, H. *London.* d.1768. W.
BACHELARD, ——. *Paris.* 1807-18.
BACHELDER, Ezra. *Danvers, U.S.A.* b. 1764, d.1859.
BACHELET, Nicolas. *Paris.* 1544-7. Founder member of Paris corporation. Took a key as his mark.
Matieu. ——. 16c. Circ. table clock Feill coll.
BACHELIER—
Jean. *Rouen.* m.1658.
Daniel. ——. Astro. clock M.P.S. Dresden.
BACHHOFEN, Felix. *Switzerland.* 1675-89. Changed clock of St. Peter's Church, Zürich, to pendulum.
Hans Konrad. *Zürich.* 2nd half 17c. Noted maker of pendulum clocks.
Heinrich. *Zürich.* 1730. Made clock for Fraumünsterkirche.
BACHIN, L. *Filipstad.* 1697. l.c. clock.
BACHLATT, Matthew. *England.* 1544. French.
BÄCHLER, Joh. Caspar. *Germany.* ca.1800. Pedometer winding cal. watch M.P.S. Dresden.
BACHMAN, John. *Bachmanville, Lancaster, U.S.A.* b.1798. l.c. casemaker; put his own name on clocks.
BACHMANN, Samuel. *Basle.* a.1666.
BACHMAUER, ——. *Westheim.* 1756.
BACHNER, Michael. *Vienna.* m.1818. l.c. clock Uhren M. Vienna.
BACKENHILL, ——. ——. an.1770. Watch.
BACKHOUSE—
James. *Lancaster.* 1726. d.1747. W.
William. *London.* a.1749.
BACKMAN—
Christian. *Stockholm.* 1738. d.1750. Director of a clock factory.
Olof. *Stockholm.* 1768-71. Wall clock.
BÄCKMAN, Fredrik. *Göteborg.* b.1754, d.1818. br. clock and watch.
BÄCKVALL, Paul Eric. *Stockholm.* 1810-35. l.c. clock and watch.
BACLE—
Jacques. *Geneva.* b.1733-71.
Fils. *Geneva.* an.1762. Watch.
BACON—
John. *London.* CC.1639.
Thomas. *Tewkesbury.* 1708-50. Watch S.K.M.
Charles. *London.* a.1711, CC.1719.
Samuel, *Annapolis.* 1752. a. in London, 1747. W.
Thomas. *London.* a.1780, CC.1791-1824.

BACOT, Peter. *London.* ca.1700. Watch G.M.
BADDELEY—
Phineas. *London.* a.1652, CC.1661.
John. *Tong.* ca.1720-66, then *Albrighton* to 1780. C. & W. Prob. two makers.
William. *Birmingham.* 1781. C.
George. *Newport (Shropshire).* 1784.
Thomas. *Albrighton.* 1795. C.
BADDY, Ben. *London.* 1743. Bankrupt.
BADGER—
Henry. *London.* a.1672.
John. *London.* 1720-2 CC.
John. *London.* a.1720.
John. *London.* a.1731.
Thomas. *London.* a.1772.
BADIER, ——. *Paris.* 1812.
BADILEY, Richard. *London.* a.1702. l.c. clock.
BADIN, Balthazard. *Paris.* m.1786.
BADLEY, Thomas. *Boston, U.S.A.* 1712.
BADOLLET—
Pierre. *Geneva.* b.1578.
Pierre. *Geneva.* b.1614.
Antoine. *Geneva.* b.1640.
Benedict. *Geneva.* b.1673.
Jean. *Geneva.* b.1678.
Daniel. *Geneva.* b.1678.
Jean Marc. *Geneva.* b.1681.
Pierre. *Geneva.* b.1684.
Abraham. *Geneva.* b.1707.
Gabriel. *Geneva.* b.1720.
Daniel. *Geneva.* b.1736.
Zacharie Nicolas. *Geneva.* b.1737.
Jean Jacques. *Geneva.* b.1756-1829. en. cyl. watch.
Jacob Daniel. *Geneva.* b.1765.
——. *Paris.* 1807-25.
Jean Moïse. *London.* b.1811-54. Later in *Geneva.* Eminent maker of chron. and complex watches.
Gustave. *Geneva.* b.1855, d.1924. The last member of this family of watchmakers, with unbroken succession from 16c.
BAEKAERT, Le. *Paris.* ca.1775. crys. watch Ilbert coll.
BAERMANN, Andreas. *Schwarzwald.* ca. 1750.
BAFFERT, ——. *Paris.* ca.1780. Clock S.K.M. on alabaster pillar.
BAGGS, Samuel. *London.* 1817-30.
BAGHIJN, Adrian van. *Amsterdam.* 1750. Maker of repute.
BAGLEY—
Thomas. *London.* CC.1658, d.1679.
Thomas. *London.* a.1656, CC.1664.
Samuel. *London.* a.1757.
Richard, father and son. *Cork.* 1820.
William. *Cork.* 1820. Watch.

BAGLINE, Thomas. *London.* a.1779.
BAGNALL—
William. *Boston, U.S.A.* Early 18c. 8-day clocks.
Benjamin. *Charleston, U.S.A.* 1712-40.
Benjamin. *Boston, U.S.A.* 1733. W.
Samuel, son of Benj. (1). *Charleston* and *Boston, U.S.A.* 1740-60. l.c. clock M.M.A.
Benjamin. *Philadelphia.* 1749-53. W.
William. *Dudley.* ca. 1760.
John. *Dudley.* 1762-91. C. & W. Also BAGNELL
Benjamin. *Boston, U.S.A.* 1770-ca.1800.
William, jun. *Cannock.* 1779. C. & W.
John. *West Bromwich.* Went to *Walsall* in 1781.
Charles. *London.* an.1777-84.
BAGNELL—
William. *London.* a.1712, CC.1719.
William. *London.* a.1734.
Samuel. *London.* a.1749.
Henry. *London* (*Bell Lane*). d.1783. CC. Watch.
Henry, son. *London* (*Windsor St.* and *Bishopsgate St.*). a.1783, CC.1795, l.CC. 1802-17.
Henry, son. *London.* a.1810.
BAGOT, ——. *London.* 1749. W.
BAGSHAW—
Edward. *London.* a.1681, CC.1691-1722.
William, son. *London.* CC.1722.
Henry. *London.* 1808. Watch Ilbert coll.
BAGWELL—
Richard. *London* (*Queen St.*). 1779-94. W.
John, son. *London.* a.1779.
BAHN, ——. *Strasbourg.* an.1781. Watch.
BAHRMAN—
H. E. *Stockholm.* 1790-5.
Bengt. *Stockholm.* 1825-35. Wall clock.
BAILES, John. *London* (*Westminster*). 1799.
BAILEY—
Jeffrey. *London.* a.1637, CC.1646, m.CC. 1674-97. Also BAYLIE. Lantern clock G.M.
Edward. *London.* CC.1658. Also BAYLEY.
John. *London.* 1719-29. br. clock. Watch mt. Buckley coll.
Jeremiah. *London.* CC.1724-6.
James. *London.* a.1720. Watch.
John. *London.* a.1732.
——. *Paris.* 1750.
Francis. *London.* an.1758. Watch.
Henry. *London.* a.1759.
Charles. *London.* a.1766-1800. Watch mt. G.M.
John. *Hanover, U.S.A.* 1770-1815.
John. *London.* CC.1771-1812. Watch S.K.M.
James. *London.* a.1780.
William. *Maidstone.* an.1785. Watch.
Catherine. *London.* 1795. Watchcase maker.
——. *Chippenham.* ca.1800. br. clock Virginia M.
J. *Horncastle.* an.1807. Watch.
John. *Boston, U.S.A.* 1803-16. W.
Charles. *London.* a.1817.
William. *Philadelphia.* 1819. C.
William. *Philadelphia.* 1820. W. & C.
BAILHON, Joseph. *London.* 1714.
BAILIE, William. *Downpatrick.* 1824.
BAILLER, François. *Paris.* m.1742.
BAILLET, ——. *Paris.* 1772. cf. BAILLOT.
BAILLEU, Peter. *London.* a.1712.
BAILLON—
Jean. *Rouen.* m.1659, juré 1663-72.
Étienne, son. *Rouen.* m.1691. Dumb rep. watch.
Albert. *Paris.* End 17c. Watch Den. coll.
François. *Paris.* 1749.
Jean Baptiste. *Paris.* 1751. d.ca.1770. C. to Queen Marie Leszinska, and later to Marie Antoinette. Very famous maker. en. watch S.K.M. Watch M.M.A. str. trav. clock C.A. & M. Watch Schloss M. Berlin.

BAILLON—*continued.*
G. *Paris.* ca.1750. Clock.
Estienne. *Paris.* an.1774. Watch.
Jean Baptiste Albert. *Paris.* m.1772-84. g. en. watch Stern. coll. en. watches Feill coll.
R. *Paris.* an.1783. Watch.
B. *Paris.* an.1783. Watch.
BAILLOT—
——. *Paris.* ca.1730 m.
Pierre, son. *Paris.* m.1737. cf. BAILLET.
BAILLY—
l'aîné. *Paris.* 1750-75. Famous maker. Clock on elephant's back ill. Britten. Boulle clock Schloss M. Berlin.
Claude François. *Morbier.* 1766-74.
William. *York.* an.1778. Watch.
——. *Besançon.* 1775.
Fils. *Paris.* ca.1780, d.1821. C. to Napoleon. g. rep. watch. Clocks in Palais de Compiègne, Fontainebleau, Trianon, Légion d'honneur, Bourbon, and in the Mobilier National, Paris.
——. *Paris* (*Rue de Richelieu*). 1812.
Veuve. *Paris* (*Place St. Germain des Prés*). 1812-25.
BAILLY-SALINS, Pierre Joseph. *Morbier.* 1774.
BAIN—
John. *Stirling.* 1786.
Alexander. *Edinburgh.* b.ca.1811, d.1877. Devised clocks driven electrically by current from plates buried in the earth. Invented the electro-chemical printing telegraph.
BAINBRIDGE, George. *Dublin.* 1766-95. W.
BAINES, George. *London.* a.1784.
BAINS, John. *Snaith.* ca.1770-95.
BAIOLE, Jean. *Autun.* 1377. A payment 'pro rologio moderando.'
BAIRD—
John. *London* (*Strand*), 1775; (*Hatton Garden*), 1820. Watch.
George. *Carlisle.* 1811-29. l.c. and wall clocks. Watch.
W. & J. *London.* 1815-25. Watch mt. detent esc. Ilbert coll.
BAIRNSFATHER, Alexander. *Edinburgh.* a.1780-7.
BAK, Abraham. *Amsterdam.* Mid. 18c. br. clock.
BAKER—
Richard. *London* (*Lombard St.*). CC.1685, d.1710. Maker of repute. rep. br. clock Weth. coll. str. watch Marryat coll.
Jane, widow. *London.* 1710.
William. *London.* a.1710.
Richard, son of Richard. *London.* CC.1727.
Thomas. *Portsmouth.* an.1753. Watch.
Pointer, son of Richard. *London* (*Ludgate Hill*). CC.1758-78. rep. watch.
Thomas. *London.* ca.1760-74. Watch.
Henry. *Town Malling.* an.1768-84. Watch.
John. *London* (*Covent Garden*). 1768. CC. 1781-99. p.c. tortoise-shell watch G.M. prob. by him. Succeeded by Richard Heap.
William. *London.* CC.1779. Watch.
Richard, son of Pointer. *London.* a.1775.
Henry. *London* (*Westminster*). CC.1781-90. W.
Joseph. *Appleby.* an.1784. Watch.
Richard. *Tamworth.* 1784-95. W.
Edward. *London.* 1785-1821. Duplex watch G.M.
William. *West Bromwich.* ca.1790. l.c. clock.
P. *Newark.* d.1800. C. & W.
John. *Plymouth Dock.* 1795. C. & W.
Henry. *London.* a.1793.
John Culmer. *London.* a.1795.
John. *London* (*Rotherhithe Wall*). a.1806, CC.1813.
Simon. *Limpsfield.* Early 19c. Watch.
& Son. *Boughton.* Early 19c. Watch.

BAKER—*continued.*
William. *Shrewsbury.* Early 19c. Watch.
George. *Providence, U.S.A.* 1824.
Benjamin H. *Philadelphia.* 1824. W.
Benjamin F. *Philadelphia.* 1825.
BAKEWELL, Thomas. *London.* CC. 1654-1665. Lantern clock.
BAL—
Imbert. *Avignon.* 1613. Restored belfry clock with LOIAL & NICOLAS.
J. *Tholen.* ca.1800.
BALCH—
Daniel. *Newburyport, U.S.A.* 1760-90.
Daniel, son. *Newburyport.* 1782-1818.
Thomas H., bro. *Newburyport.* 1790-1818.
Charles H. *Newburyport.* b.1787-1808.
Benjamin. *Salem, U.S.A.* 1837.
BALCHIN, ——. *London.* an.1749. Watch.
BALDETUS DE COULOMBY. *Paris.* 1420.
BALDWEIN, ——. *Marburg.* 1561-8. Made with BUCHER a monumental astro. clock for August I of Saxony, M.P.S. Dresden. Also a very complex astro. clock for Wilhelm IV of Cassel in Cassel Landes-M.
BALDWIN—
Christopher. *London.* a.1656.
Thomas. *London.* a.1678, CC.1685, d.1737. Watch mt. Buckley coll.
Robert. *London.* a.1682.
John. *London.* a.1691.
John. *Faversham.* an.1739. Watch.
J. *Andover.* 1763. d.1776. C. & W.
William. *Croydon.* 1774. Insolvent. C. & W.
Mrs. *Andover.* 1779. W.
Jedediah. *Hanover, U.S.A.* 1780.
Henry Smith. *London.* a.1778, CC.1785.
Jeremiah. *Basingstoke.* 1791.
Thomas. *Dublin.* 1795.
George. *Sadsburyville, U.S.A.* 1808-32.
Antony. *Lancaster, U.S.A.* b.1783, d.1867. l.c. clocks.
William. *London.* a.1804.
Jabez. *Boston, U.S.A.* 1812.
& JONES. *Boston, U.S.A.* 1812.
BALDWYN, Thomas. *London.* a.1699, CC. 1706-35.
BALE—
Thomas. *London.* CC.1704.
Thomas. *London* (*Essex St.*). CC.1724-7.
BALES, John. *Bungay.* 1791. C. & W.
BALESTRI, Domenico. *Florence.* 1649. Employed by Vincenzo GALILEI to make a pendulum clock after his father's design.
BALFOUR—
Joseph. *London.* a.1753, CC. 1761.
B. *London.* 1800. Watch Ilbert coll.
BALL—
John. *London.* CC.1637.
Victor. *London.* 1647. Not admitted to CC.
John. *Liverpool.* 1699-1703.
Thomas. *London.* a.1711, CC.1724.
Jonathan. *London.* 1743. Watch.
William. *Bicester.* ca.1760. l.c. clock ill. Britten. Watch.
Edward. *London.* 1790.
Thomas. *Liverpool.* 1816. W.
BALLACH, C. *London.* Early 19c. Watch.
BALLALOUD, ——. *Cluses.* 1715. Introduced watchmaking into the villages near Geneva.
BALLANTINE, William. *Edinburgh.* a.1798.
BALLANTYNE—
James. *Edinburgh.* a.1756.
William. *Edinburgh.* 1778-1806.
William. *London.* 1815-42.
BALLARD—
William. *London.* a.1707, CC.1736.
John. *London.* CC.1768.
William, son of William. *London.* CC.1792. (*Fetter Lane*) 1799; (*Holborn*) 1808.
William. *London.* CC.1813.
——. *Cranbrook.* Early 19c. Watch.
BALLART, I. *Bourges.* ca.1600. Oval en. watch Louvre ill. Baillie.
BALLAUF, Anton. *Günzberg.* 1791-5. Kleinuhrmacher.
BALLE, John. *Exeter.* 18c. l.c. clock.
BALLEURE, Anthony. *London.* 1744. C.
BALLIF, F. *Neuenstadt* and *Basle.* 1801.
BALLON, Étienne. *Paris.* m.1740.
BALLUE, Jean. *Yvercrique.* 1704. Repaired church clock of Auffay.
BALMER, Thomas. *Liverpool.* 1820-5. W.
BALSAM, James. *London.* an.1791. Watch.
BALSTERS, G. *Amsterdam.* ca.1800.
BALTAZAR (BALTAZARD, BALTHAZARD)—
Jean Baptiste. *Paris.* 1675 m.
Maximillian. *Paris.* an.1731. Watch.
Charles. *Paris.* Early 18c.
Marc Antoine. *Paris.* m.1739.
Jean Guillaume. *Paris.* m.1740.
Michel Antoine. *Paris.* m.1744-69.
Noel. *Paris.* ca.1760, d.1786. g. en. watch S.K.M. 4-colour g. watch. Cartel clock, Pal. de Justice, Paris.
Louis Charles. *Paris* (*Rue du Boule*). m.1763-1789.
Cadet. *Paris.* 1769. C. to Mesdames filles de Louis XV. Clock Art M. Boston.
Michel Antoine. *Paris* (*Rue de Harlay*). m.1778-89. Monteur de boîtes.
Jean Baptiste. *Paris.* 1778 comp. Mantel clock, Pal. de Fontainebleau.
——. *Paris* (*Place Dauphine*). 1786.
——. *Paris* (*Rue de la Calandre*). d.1823.
Fils. *Paris* (*Rue de la Calandre*). 1812-24.
BALTZER, I. H. *Frankfurt-a.-O.* Early 19c. Made lever esc. with pallets embracing two teeth.
BAMBER, Thomas. *London.* an.1753. Watch.
BAMBRIDGE—
John. *London.* an.1762. Watch.
John. *Dublin.* 1786-1800.
BAMFIELD (BANFIELD)—
William. *London.* a.1753.
Thomas. *London* (*St. John's St.*). a.1762, CC.1773.
John. *London.* a.1781-1817. Watch.
BAMFORD—
Cornelius. *London.* a.1716.
Luke Exall. *London.* mar.1764. W.
BANBURY—
John. *London.* a.1675, CC.1686-1704.
Thomas. *London.* a.1796.
BANCE, Matthew. *Hungerford.* 1793-7. W.
BANCROFT—
John. *Scarborough.* End 18c. From *London.*
William. *Scarborough.* Early 19c.
BANGER, Edward. *London.* a.1687, CC. 1695-1713. Nephew and assistant to Thomas TOMPION. Many fine clocks and watches sd. THO. TOMPION EDWD. BANGER.
BANGILONER, ——. *London.* ca.1660. W.
BANGUERELLE, ——. *Paris.* 1812.
BANISTER—
Henry. *Weobly.* 1737. Insolvent. C.
Henry. *London.* ca.1750. br. clock Apothecaries Co.
James. *Wrexham.* an.1768. *Ellesmere* in 1773. Watch.
Richard. *Coleshill.* 1783-95. Watch. T.C.
Joseph. *Colchester.* 1790-1836. Partner with HEDGE. Patented a crutch for clocks.
William. *London.* a.1807.
W. H. *London* (*Princes St.*). 1815-24. W.
BANK, B. & A. *London.* Early 19c. Watch.
BANKES—
William. *London.* a.1690, CC.1698-1733.
John. *Liverpool.* 1790-1800. W.
George. *London.* ca.1790. Watch Ilbert coll.
BANKS—
——. *Nottingham.* End 17c. Watch.
John. *London.* a.1714-25. Bankrupt.

BANKS—*continued.*
Robert. *London.* a.1732, CC.1750-3.
William. *London.* a.1734.
James. ——. an.1776. Watch.
J. *Nottingham.* 2nd half 18c. Watch mt.
James. *Oldham.* 1791. Watch.
R. *Plymouth Dock.* an.1795. Watch.
Thomas. *London.* a.1786.
John. *London.* a.1791.
——. *Dublin.* an.1819. Watch.
Joseph. *Philadelphia.* 1819. W.
James. *London.* Early 19c. Watch.
John. *Parsonstown.* 1824.
BANNER, Richard. *Liverpool.* 1734.
BANNICKER, Paul. *Paris.* Late 18c. g. en. watch Carnegie M.
BANNISTER—
Anthony. *London.* a.1708, CC.1715-36.
William. *Liverpool.* 1734-54. C. Also BANISTER.
Thomas. *Liverpool.* 1734. Also BANISTER.
Henry. *Lichfield.* 1791-5. C. & W.
John. *Newport* (*I. of W.*). 1795. Watch. Also BANISTER.
Thomas. *London.* 1801. mus. br. clock ill. Cec. & Web.
James. *London.* CC.1818-35. Watch.
T. & J. *London.* 1822-5. Also BANISTER.
BANNY, T. *London* (*Horsleydown*). 1817-24. W.
BANRUCKE, Bene. ——. Late 18c. p.c. g. en. watch Feill coll.
BANSTEIN, John. *Philadelphia.* 1791.
BANTING, William. *London.* CC.1646.
BANTON, ——. *London.* an.1752. Watch.
BAPTISTE, ——. *London.* an.1787. Watch.
BARACHIN, Stephen. *London.* CC.1687. W. French.
BARADELLE, ——. *Paris.* ca.1730. Compass.
BARANCOURT, Pierre Michel. *Paris.* m. 1779, juré 1783-9. Vase clock.
BARANDA, François. *Paris.* m.1741.
BARAT, Philippe. *Paris.* Juré 1764.
BARBE, Joseph. *Paris.* 1777 m.-1810.
BARBER—
Jonas. *London.* CC.1682-9. W.
Richard. *London.* a.1710.
Joseph. *London.* a.1721.
Thomas, jun. *Portsmouth.* an.1757. Watch.
Michael. *London.* a.1769.
John. *Stratford.* an.1777. Watch.
John. *Lincoln.* 1777. Bankrupt.
John. *Stafford.* an.1779. Watch.
Benjamin. *Deptford* and *Red Lion St., London.* 1785-94. Livery Goldsmiths Co. br. clock Virginia M.
John. *Newark.* 1786-95. Succeeded Wm. BARNARD.
William. *London.* 1786-94.
James. *London.* 1790.
James. *York.* 1790-1814. Partner with CATTLE.
John. *Droitwich.* 1791. W.
James. *Newcastle-under-Lyme.* 1795. C.
Charles. *London.* a.1786, CC.1796-1804.
Aquila. *Bristol.* 1797-1830. W. & C. Clock in Council House.
Joseph. *London.* 1799.
John. *London* (*Stratford*). 1799-1811. W.
& WATKINS. *London* (*Stratford*). 1805-08.
Thomas. *London.* 1810-17. c.secs. ruby cyl. watch Ilbert coll.
Richard Price. *Bristol.* 1812. W. & C.
& WHITWELL. *York.* Early 19c.
William. *Mullingar.* 1824.
BARBERET—
Jacques. *Paris.* ca.1640. Fine en. watch Mallett coll. Fine sil. watch with sig. 'J. BARBARET' over sig. 'LOYS GUION À DIJON, Louvre.' Oval sil. watch, Pal. du Cinquantenaire, Brussels.

BARBERET—*continued.*
Jean. *Paris.* ca.1650. str. watch F.W.M. oct. sil. watch Blot-Garnier coll.
R. *St. Fleurs.* 2nd half 17c. Watch Gélis coll.
BARBERIOS, Felice. *Milan.* 1680. Astro. clock in Sacristy of S. Maria delle Grazie.
BARBET—
——. *Paris.* 1732 m.
Michel François, son. *Paris.* m.1740.
BARBIER—
Bernardin. *Lons-le-Saunier.* 1578. Modified turret clock at Boudry.
Jean. *Pernes* (*Avignon*). 1627. Re-made clock of Monmoiron.
Jacques, dit Brunet. *Lyons.* 1669. From *Geneva.*
Louis Étienne. *Lyons.* b.1677 in Rome. Lyons 1698-1704 m.
Pierre. *Boudry.* 1755.
Charles François. *Paris.* m.1770.
le jeune. *Paris* (*Quai des Ormes*). 1772-89. Maker of repute. Made carillon clocks.
Jean Jacques (l'aîné). *Paris* (*Rue du Fg. St. Antoine*). 1776 m.-1789.
Michel. *Paris* (*Place des Grands Cordeliers*). 1778. m.1783-9.
Jean Denis Marguerite. *Paris.* m.1785.
le jeune. *Paris* (*Rue du Fg. St. Antoine*). 1807-12.
——. *Paris* (*Rue Grenetat*). 1812-25.
BARBIES, ——. *Paris.* 1772.
BARBIN (BARWIN), ——. *Göggingen.* 1756.
BARBOT, ——. *London.* ca.1780. Aut. mus. clocks. Two in Peiping M. and one in Palace M. Pekin.
BARCLAY—
Peter. *Lochwinnoch.* 1706.
Samuel. *v.* BARKLEY.
Hugh. *Edinburgh.* a.1717, d.1749.
John. *London* (*Bull Yd., Fan St.*). a.1779. CC.1787-96.
C. *London.* ca.1810. Watch.
Thomas. *Montrose.* 1811-22.
James. *London.* 1821-4. Watch.
BARCOLE, John. *London.* a.1638, CC. 1647.
BARDOLPH, Thomas. *London.* a.1695.
BARDOT ET FILS. *Paris.* 1825.
BARFOOT, James. *Wimborne.* 1785.
BARFORD, Thomas. *London.* a.1656.
BARGEUX, A. *Pars.* 1767-75.
BARGNOULZ, Gédéon. *Amsterdam.* 1689. Huguenot refugee from *Mer.*
BARIDON, J. A. *Geneva.* ca.1800. d.1844. Several fine turret clocks.
ET FILS. *Geneva.* 1823. Remontoir regulator.
BARILLET le jeune. *Paris.* Late 18c.-1810. Cartel clock.
BARINTON, John. *London.* an.1701. Watch. Perhaps BERRINGTON.
BARJEAU, Peter. *London.* an.1746. Watch and l.c. clock.
BARJON, John. *London.* CC.1685. W.
BARKED, John. *London.* a.1732.
BARKER—
William. *London.* CC.1632.
Daye. *London.* Early 18c. Bankrupt 1749. Small hex. table clock.
William. *London.* a.1699.
John. *London.* a.1732.
William. *Wigan.* ca.1760. l.c. clock S.K.M.
Thomas. *London.* a.1755-1813. Watches.
Richard. *London.* an.1773. Watch.
B. B. *New York.* 1786-90.
Charles. *Dublin.* 1795.
——. *Brighton.* ca.1800. CC.
William. *Boston* (*Howe St.*), *U.S.A.* 1800-13.
William. *London.* 1805-11.
William. *Boston* (*Town Dock*), *U.S.A.* 1806-25.
Edward. *London.* 1806-21. W.

BARKER—*continued.*
Bryan Blake, son. *London.* CC.1806.
John. *London.* a.1806, CC.1813.
W. K. *Beccles.* Early 19c. Watch.
Robert. *Chichester.* Early 19c. Watch.
BARKLEY—
Samuel. *London.* a.1715 to Geo. GRAHAM. CC.1722-51. Was Graham's foreman and executor and succeeded him, entering into partnership with Thos. COLLEY.
& COLLEY. *London.* From 1751 to 1754. l.c. clock Weth. coll. ill. Britten, sd. 'Graham's Successors.' *v.* COLLEY & PRIEST.
BARKMAN—
Olof. *Jönköping.* 1774. d.ca.1802. g. watch.
Johan. *Jönköping.* 1811-14.
BARLEY, Thomas. *London.* an.1774. Watch.
BARLOW—
Edward. *London.* b.1636, d.1716. Very able horologist. Invented rack striking work for clocks ca.1676. Also repeating work for watches in 1686 and a cylinder-type escapement in 1695. Also BOOTH. *v.* Wm. HOUGHTON.
Thomas. *London.* CC.1692. Sheep's-head clock Bourges M. prob. by him.
John. *Rochdale.* d.1769.
William. *Ashton.* 1760. Watch.
Benjamin. *Ashton* and *Oldham.* 1773-80. l.c. c.secs. clock. ill. Cec. & Web. Watch Buckley coll.
James. *Oldham.* 1775.
John. *Oldham.* 1780. l.c. clock.
James. *Northwich.* 1795.
J. H., & Co. *London.* 1812-20. Watch.
Thomas. *Rochdale.* ca.1820.
BARLY & UPJOHN. *London.* an.1791. Watch.
BARMONT, ——. *Paris.* 1823.
BARNARD—
Nicholas. *London.* a.1662.
John. *London* (*St. John's St.*). a.1675 CC. 1682-96.
Francis. *London.* a.1675.
Ralph. *London.* a.1678.
Mary. *London.* 1698.
Richard. *London.* a.1725.
Robert. *London.* a.1726, CC.1740.
Philip. *London.* 1st half 18c. l.c. clock.
William. *Newark.* b.1707-84. Many l.c. clocks.
Thomas. *London.* 1783-1823.
——. *Sittingbourne.* End 18c.
John, son of John. *London.* a.1793.
BAYLEY & SON. *London.* 1795.
& KIDDER. *London.* 1809-12.
BARNARDISTON, John. *London.* a.1697, CC.1714. l.c. clock.
BARNED—
Israel, & Co. *Liverpool.* 1814-24.
John, & Co. *Liverpool.* 1816-21.
BARNES—
Ri. *Worcester.* ca.1610. Watch S.K.M.
Richard. *Worcester.* ca.1710.
George. *London.* a.1693.
James. *London.* a.1696.
Joseph. *London* (*Strand*). a.1716-48. Took over David HUBERT's business in or before 1747.
Thomas. *London.* a.1727.
Robert. *Liverpool.* 1754. Went *Birmingham* 1775-8. C. & W.
John. *London.* 1770-93. Livery Barbers' Co.
Thomas. *Lichfield, U.S.A.* b.1760-90.
Samuel. *London.* an.1776-1808.
George. *Northampton.* 1804-12. C. & W.
T. *Leicester.* 1815. C. & W.
George. *London.* a.1802.
BARNET, Dimanche. *Autun.* a.ca.1565.
BARNETT—
John. *London.* a.1675, CC.1682-1700. l.c. clock Weth. coll. br. clock.

BARNETT—*continued.*
John. *London.* a.1697.
Richard. *London.* a.1704.
Dilks. *London.* a.1704.
Mary. *London.* a.1705.
Micajah. *London.* a.1743.
Felix. *London.* a.1747.
Joseph. *Birmingham.* 1770-5.
William. *Sevenoaks.* 1771. Bankrupt. W.
John. *Tavistock.* 1795. l.c. clock.
David. *London.* 1805-24.
J. *London.* 1809-24.
Michael. *London.* 1820.
Charles. *Liverpool.* 1825. W.
BARNHILL, Robert. *Philadelphia.* 1777. W.
BARNISH, John. *Rochdale.* 1776-1814. l.c. clock.
BARNOU, ——. *Paris.* 1812.
BARNS—
Henry. *London.* a.1711.
Robert. *Birmingham.* 1781. W. cf. BARNES.
Richard. *Manchester.* 1804. W.
Ann. *London.* 1805-08.
BARNSLEY, William. *Birmingham.* 1774-81. C.
BARNWELL—
Richard. *London.* a.1698, CC.1712, d.1719.
Anne, widow. *London.* 1719-28.
Richard, son. *London.* a.1721.
BAROCCI, Gio. Maria. *Urbino.* ca.1570. Made planetary clock for the Pope.
BARON—
Guiot. *France.* 1412. C. to the duc de Bourgogne.
Edmund. *London.* a.1693.
Jean. *Utrecht.* 1725. Watches B.M. and Staats M. Amsterdam. Watch mt. G.M.
David. *Haarlem.* 1736.
——. *London.* ca.1750.
J. *London.* an.1775. Watch.
John. *Cove* (*Munster*). 1824.
James. *Mallow* (*Munster*). 1824.
ET LEFEBVRE. *Paris.* 1810-13.
ET CIE. *Paris.* 1814. Successors.
BARONNEAU—
Louys. *Paris.* 1640-64. C. to the Queen. Watch g. filigree and another sil. al. Blot-Garnier coll. Watch mt. G.M. Fine en. watch Ilbert coll. Fine Boulle br. clock Pal. de Pau, Paris.
Joseph. *Paris.* 1681 m., juré 1690.
Louys. *Paris.* 1728-60. 'Horloger à la Reine.'
BARPUTT, John. *London.* an.1773. Watch.
BARR—
Jean de. *Strasbourg.* 1494. Repaired clock in Cathedral tower. Barr is a small town in the Vosges.
Lazarus de. *Strasbourg.* 1505. Clock with jacquemarts.
Thomas. *Lewes.* Late 17c. Lantern clock.
Martin. *London.* a.1778.
——. *Bolton.* 1790. l.c. clock ill. Cec. & Web.
William. *Dublin.* 1802. Watch N.Y. Univ.
BARRACLOUGH, George. *London.* 1776. Shagreen case maker.
BARRAL, Abraham. *Geneva.* ca.1760-77.
BARRARD, William Thomas. *London.* a. 1717
BARRATT, P. *London.* 1785-1830. g. watch G.M.
BARRAUD—
Henry. *London.* 1633 CC.
Paul John. *London* (*Fleet St.*). 1790.
Francis. *London* (*Fleet St.*). 1790.
Paul Philip. *London* (*Cornhill*). l.CC.1796, m.CC.1810-11, d.1820. Partner with W. HOWELLS and G. JAMISON for making MUDGE's Timekeepers. Fine pocket watch and chron. maker. Marine and 2 pocket chrons. G.M. Rep. watch with sapphire cyl. Chamb. coll.

BARRAUD—*continued.*
Frederick Joseph, son. *London.* a.1799, CC.1806-25. W.
& Sons. *London.* 1811-35. g. watch G.M.
John, son of Paul P. *London.* a 1806, CC. 1813, l.CC.1814.
James, brother. *London.* a.1807, CC.1815, l.CC.1824.
——. *Paris.* 1809-55. Mantel clock, bronze by Ravrio, made for Napoléon, Pal. de l'Elysée. Clock Pal. de la légion d'honneur.
BARRELET, Louis. *Boveresse.* 1755-9.
BARRENGER—
Philip. *London.* 1745-1808. W.
——. *Brighton.* an.1790. Watch.
BARRETT—
Simon. *London.* a.1668, CC.1678.
Robert. *London.* CC. 1687. W.
Henry. *London.* a.1684, CC.1692.
Samuel. *London.* a.1693, CC.1701.
Thomas. *London.* CC.1702.
Thomas. *Canterbury.* Late 17c. Watch.
Skelton. *London.* a.1710. Watch mt. S.K.M.
William. *Bath.* 1722-34. W.
——. *Stowmarket.* 18c. l.c. clock.
S. H. *London.* an.1781. Watch.
E. *Blandford.* Late 18c. g. en. Watch.
William. *Corscombe.* Late 18c. C.
John. *London.* a.1775.
Daniel. *Chatham.* ca.1800 CC.
Henry William. *London.* CC.1802-40. Watch.
John. *London.* 1805-24.
BARRIDGE, John. *London.* a.1654.
BARRINGTON—
Samuel. *Limerick.* d.1693. Clock and chime maker.
Urian. *London.* a.1677, CC.1684-1734. Also Berrington.
Urian, son. *London.* a.1705.
Isaac. *Dublin.* 1820-4. Watch.
BARRIOS, Adam. *Kingston (Jamaica).* Early 19c.
BARRITIUS (BARRITY), Jacobus. *Leeuwarden.* ca.1610. Oval crys. cal. watch, g. and en. mounts Mallet coll.
BARROCLOUGH—
John. *London.* a.1747.
George. *London.* a.1751.
BARROLL, John. *London.* a.1701.
BARRON—
Antoine. *Paris.* b.1748, guillotined 1794.
John. *Aberdeen.* b.1765, d.1852. Watch.
John, & Son. *Aberdeen.* Early 19c.
BARROW—
Nathaniel. *London.* a.1653, CC.1660, m. CC.1689-99. cal. watch and str. watch G.M. str. watch S.M.S.K. str. watch Den. coll. l.c. clock ill. Cec. & Web.
John. *London.* a.1671, CC.1681, m.CC. 1714-7. Watch Ilbert coll.
Samuel. *London.* a.1688, CC.1696-1704. l.c. clocks.
William John. *London.* 1700 CC.
John. *London.* CC.1704.
James. *London.* Early 18c. Watch.
William, son of W. J. *London.* a.1700, CC. 1710. d.1736. 'Noted' C. l.c. lacquer clock Nord. M. 3 l.c. clocks Nat. M. Stockholm.
George. *London.* a.1706.
Daniel. *Frodsham.* d.1731. C.
Anne. *London.* 1733.
Samuel. *Philadelphia.* From 1771. Previously in *London.* Said he worked for John Harrison.
William. *Woolton.* an.1775. Watch.
Thomas. *Stockport.* 1784. Watch.
Thomas. *London.* a.1778.
William. *Liverpool.* 1816-21. W.

BARRY—
Marc. Prob. *Blois.* 1616.
Blaise. *Blois.* m.1620.
Josué. *Blois.* 1627. d.1631. Also Joseph Barril.
Dominique de. *Neuchâtel.* 1702.
Robert or Richard. *London.* 1770.
Standisk. *Baltimore, U.S.A.* 1784-1804. W. *v.* Joseph Rice.
Walter. *London.* 1790.
——. *Bristol.* 1792-5. Partner in Barry & Green.
John. *Bolton-le-Moors.* ca.1820.
Thomas. *Bolton-le-Moors.* ca.1820.
Joseph. *Cork.* 1824.
William George. *London.* a.1819.
BARSTON, John. *London.* 1737. Bankrupt.
BART, R. *London.* an.1791. Watch.
BARTELS—
Hinrich. *Neumünster.* Early 18c. Watch Feill coll.
Hinrich Wilhelm. *Ritzebüttel.* 1821.
Wed. *Amsterdam.* 1822-5.
BARTH, Johan Nicolai. *Copenhagen.* m.1773.
BARTHEL, Joh. Jac. *Fürth.* d.1809.
BARTHELET, ——. *Besançon.* 2nd half 18c. Fine cartel clock.
BARTHET, E. *Marseilles.* ca.1840. Marine chron. G.M.
BARTHLEWSKY, Mathias. ——. 1788. Iron br. clock Elbing M.
BARTHOLDI, Johan Jacob. *Copenhagen.* m.1787.
BARTHOLOMEW—
John. *London.* a.1668, CC.1675-85.
Edward. *Sherborne.* 1720. C.
James. *Sherborne.* 1750. C.
Josiah. *London.* 1799-1842. Watch for Turkey B.M.
E. & G. *Bristol, U.S.A.* ca.1820.
BARTHOLOMY—
Abraham. *Paris.* 1749m. g. en. watch set diamonds and rubies, for Turkey, Lincoln M. g. en. watch with obscene paintings Gélis coll.
Anne. *Paris.* m.1749. Son of a master.
Daniel. *Paris.* m.1758-67. Four colour g. watch Feill coll. prob. by him.
BARTHROP, Walter. *Ixworth.* 1769. Insolvent.
BARTLE, George. *Brigg.* 18c. l.c. clock.
BARTLES, Edward. *Liverpool.* ca.1770.
BARTLETT—
John. *Chester.* 1642. Dial M.M.A.
Samuel. *Norwich.* an.1742. l.c. clock. Watch.
'P. S. Bartlett.' Sig. on watches of the American Watch Co., 1861-78. Predecessor of the Waltham Watch Co.
BARTLEY—
& Eggert. *Bristol.* 1810-15.
Mark. *Bristol.* 1816-50.
Andrew. *Bristol.* 1825-50.
BARTLIFF—
George. *York.* 1801. W.
Robert. *York.* 1807. Settled at *Malton.* Watch.
BARTMANN, Matthäus. *Neukirch.* ca.1790. Wall clock Furt. M.
BARTON—
Samuel. *London* and *Manchester.* CC.1640. Watch.
John. *London.* a.1657.
James. *Ormskirk.* d.1718. C.
John. *Ormskirk.* 1723. Insolvent. C.
John. *Peterborough.* an.1762. Watch.
John. *Manchester.* 1746, d.1770. C. Made cyl. watches.
Thomas. *Manchester.* 1755, d.1791. In 1782 sold his business to Runcorn. Watch.
T. & J. *Manchester.* 1764-75. Partnership of preceding and following. Watch mt.

BARTON—*continued.*
John. *Manchester.* 1764-73.
William. *London.* 1767-1811. Watch.
James. *Whitehaven.* ca.1770.
James. *London.* 1771. Son-in-law of John Harrison. Watch with en. portrait of Harrison, Webster coll. ill. Baillie.
John. *London.* 1780.
John. *Saffron Walden.* 1790. Watch.
——. *Wainfleet.* ca.1790 CC.
Thomas. *London* (*Leather Lane*). 1794-1823.
Thomas. *Manchester.* 1795. Bankrupt.
James. *Birmingham.* 1804. Watch mt.
Thomas, son of Thos. *London.* a.1794.
Mathias. *London.* a.1797, CC.1804.
James. *London.* 1820.
George. *Wicklow.* 1824.
James. *Sheffield.* 1825.
BARTONHEAD—
Thomas. *Bristol.* 1710.
Thomas. *Elburton.* 1739.
BARTRAM—
Simon. *London.* 1630-60. Petitioner for incorporation of CC. m.CC.1650. d.1660. Watch M.M.A. oct. crys. watch.
William. *London.* a.1677, CC.1684-1716.
BARTS, George Frederick. *London.* Late 18c. Watch mt. G.M.
BARTSKAER, Wulff. *Aarhus.* 1631.
BARUCH, Jean. *Basle.* 1753.
BARUGH—
William. *London.* a.1709, CC.1716.
Anne. *London.* 1737. d.1742.
BARWELL—
Richard. *London.* CC.1705. Watch.
Bartholomew. *New York.* 1749-60. From *Bath.* C.
BARWICK—
George. *Norwich.* 1788.
William. *London.* a.1775.
A. & B. *London.* 1794-6.
James. *London.* a.1790, CC.1798-1809.
BARWISE—
Lott. *Cockermouth.* ca.1770-91. l.c. clock.
John. *London.* 1790. d.1842. Chairman of British Watch Co. Watch and pocket chron. G.M. cyl. watch S.M.S.K. Regulator St. James's Palace. Watch Den. coll.
William. *London.* 1799-1808. W.
Charles. *London.* 1809-11.
& Sons. *London.* 1819-23.
Weston and John. *London.* 1825.
BASAMOYNG, ——. *London.* an.1748. Watch.
BASCHET, Étienne (l'aîné). *Paris.* m.1778-..1789.
BASCHLE, Martin. *Basle.* b.1645, d.1675. Kleinuhrmacher.
BASFORD, Daniel. *Wem.* 1795. C.
BASH, James. *London.* CC.1729.
BASHLIN, ——. *London.* 1744. Watch.
BASIRE, John. *London.* a.1748, CC.1756, l.CC.1766-86. cyl. jewelled c. secs. mt. Buckley coll.
BASKERVILLE—
Thomas. *London.* a.1731, CC.1738-52.
Richard. *London.* a.1741, CC.1749-72. Clock in Sacristy of Bruges Cathedral.
John. *London.* d.1761. Watchcase maker.
BASNET, James. *Liverpool.* 1825. C.
BASOMOINE, ——. *London.* ca.1740. Watch Ilbert coll.
BASS—
George. *London.* a.1715, CC. 1722.
John. *London.* an.1758. Watch.
BASSARD, Pierre. *The Hague* (?). Early 17c. Watch. Ryksmuseum Amsterdam. cf. Batard.
BASSELET—
Pierre François. *Paris.* m.1760.
Veuve. *Metz.* 1789.
BASSELIER, Fabrique de. *St. Petersburg.* ca.1810. Watch mt. Ilbert coll.
BASSELIN, Mathieu. *Paris.* d. between 1544 and 1547. Founder member of Paris corporation.
BASSEREAU—
Hilaire. *Paris.* d.ca.1810. Horloger de l'Empereur et Roy. Pedometer winding watch for Turkey. Pocket chron. Ilbert coll.
Veuve. *Paris.* 1811-25.
Fils. *Paris* (*Rue Neuve des Petits Champs*). 1812.
BASSERT, Martin. *Paris.* 1773.
BASSET—
Guillaume. *Lyons.* 1653. d.1657. Keeper of clock of St. Jean.
Thomas. *London.* a.1668.
Jean Jacques Louis. *York.* 1771. W.
——. *Ipswich.* 1795. Succeeded by R. Cole.
George Francis. *Philadelphia.* 1797. W.
John Francis. *Philadelphia.* 1798. W.
BASSETT—
Stephen. *London.* a.1717.
John. *London.* a.1732.
Charles. *London.* 1790.
N. B. *Albany, U.S.A.* 1813.
BASSOT, ——. *Paris.* 1750-1825. Clock ministère de la Guerre, Paris. g. en. cyl. watch.
BAST, T. *London.* Early 18c.-1756. Watches Huddersfield M. and Den. coll.
BASTABLE, William. *London.* Early 19c. Watch.
BASTARD—
Louis. *Lyons.* 1608. d.1611.
Louis. *Lyons.* 1658. d.ca.1661. From *Geneva.*
Thomas. *Blandford.* ca.1750. l.c. clock.
BASTON, ——. *London.* an.1753. Watch.
BASTIEN, ——. *London.* 1547. 'Haurologier' to Cromwell. Keeper of Westminster clock.
BATARD—
Pierre. *The Hague.* Mid. 17c. circ. crys. watch M.P.S. Dresden. cf. Bassard.
Jean André. *Geneva.* ca.1770-91.
Fils. Prob. *Geneva.* 1788-1815. Springmaker who sd. his springs.
BATCHELOR—
William. *Battle.* a.1731.
John. *London.* a.1760.
William. *Dundee.* 1816.
BATE—
Anthony. *Dublin.* 1766-80. l.c. clock. W.
Richard. *Atherstone.* ca.1795.
James. *London.* a.1780.
Robert Brettel. *London.* 1815 CC. math. inst. maker. Pocket compass G.M.
BATEMAN—
Nathaniel. *London.* a.1714 CC.
Nathaniel, son. *London.* a.1740, CC.1747-50.
Mary. *London.* a.1722.
William. *London.* a.1756.
Samuel. *London* (*Old Bailey*). 1769. Insolvent. W.
Andrew. *London.* a.1776, l.CC.1812, d.1816. Firm continued to 1824.
P. & A. *London.* 1798-1818.
Samuel. *London.* 1799. W.
Teresa. *London.* 1820-5.
BATES—
Thomas. *London.* a.1677, CC.1684-97.
Joseph. *London.* a.1678, CC.1687-1706.
Henry. ——. ca.1695. l.c. clock.
William. *London.* 1727. Watch.
Aaron. *London.* 1730. Watchcase maker. Sd. AB.
James. *London.* 1738. Bankrupt.
John. *London.* a.1740.
John. *Kettering.* 1768-1800 CC. W.

BATES—*continued.*
Edward. *London* (*St. Bartholomew the Less*). 1778. W.
Edward. *London.* a.1778.
Robert. *Exeter.* 1785. Succeeded Thos. UPJOHN. Succeeded by T. TUCKER. 1789. C. & W.
Edward. *Cuckfield.* 1791. C. & W.
Simeon. *London.* 1795. Bankrupt.
Robert. *Atherstone.* 1795. C. & W.
Thomas. *Market Harboro'.* From 1783-ca. 1800 CC. W.
John. *London.* a.1796.
Joshua. *Huddersfield.* 1814. Watches.
& LOWE. *London.* 1817-24. Clock.
BATESON, John. *Boston, U.S.A.* 1720. d.1727.
BATGER, John. *London.* a.1703.
BATH (BATHE)—
William. *Bristol.* 1751. From *Paris. Bath.* 1755. *Bristol.* 1758. W.
Thomas. *London.* a.1749, CC.1757-84. W.
James. *Cirencester.* 1812 CC. Clock. Watch.
BATHALL, W. *London.* an.1757. Watch.
BATHY, Jacques. *Paris.* 1609. Proposed as juré, but not elected.
BATLEY, Thomas. *London.* an.1777. Watch.
BATSON, Richard. *London.* a.1700.
BATT—
Benjamin. *London.* a.1764.
William. *Petersfield.* 1771.
BATTAILE, James. *London.* Early 19c. Watch.
BATTAS, Jean. *Paris.* d. before 1773.
BATTEN—
John. *London.* CC.1668-84.
Edward. *London.* a.1670.
& Co. *London.* 1820.
BATTERSBY, George. *Manchester.* 1694. C.
BATTERSON—
Robert. *London.* a.1686, CC.1693-1701. Also BATERSON. l.c. lacquer clock.
Henry. *London.* a.1694, CC.1701-11.
James. *London.* a.1696. l.c. clock.
James. *New York* and *Boston.* 1707-30.
BATTEY, John. *London.* a.1748.
BATTIE(BATTY), James. *Sheffield.* 1790-7. W.
BATTIN, Thomas. *London.* a.1654, CC. 1661-3.
BATTINSON, John. *Burnley.* ca.1820.
BATTLE, William. *London.* a.1705.
BATTY, Edward. *Lancaster.* 1825. W.
BAUCUTT, William. *London.* a.1723.
BAUD, Jean. *Lyons.* mar. 1611, comp.
BAUDET, ——. *Paris.* 1822-5. Cal. watch.
BAUDIN—
Jacques François. *Paris.* m.1787.
——. *Paris* (*Rue des Petits Carreaux*). 1807-25.
——. *Paris* (*Rue Croix des Petits-Champs*). 1812.
——. *Paris* (*Cour St. Guillaume*). 1822.
BAUDIT—
Lagier. ——. End 18c. Trav. clock Feill coll.
G. *Hamburg.* 1801.
BAUDOIN, Nicolas. *Paris.* 1675. Juré.
BAUDOUIN, Pierre. *Paris.* d.1785.
BAUER—
Carl. *Amsterdam.* ca.1650. sil. cross watch, double folding cover.
Joh. Jacob. *Lissa.* Late 17c. hex. table clock Fränkel coll.
Caspar. *Vienna.* m.1717. Also BAUR.
J. L. *Berlin.* 1718. Made a fine clock given by Wilhelm I to Peter the Great, in the Hermitage.
Aloisius. *Fürth.* d.1784.
Caspar. *Vienna.* Mid. 18c. Watch mt. Arts M. Prague.
Johann Christoph. *Leipzig.* 1763. Town C.
Dominikus. *Vienna.* m.1794.
Ch. —. 1798. Pub. a book on watches.

BAUGH—
Anne. *London.* 1737.
Valentine. *Abingdon, U.S.A.* 1820-30. C.
BAUGHAM, John. *London.* a.1739.
BAULER, James. *Leeds.* 1800.
BAULLIER—
——. *Paris.* 1807-13.
ET GUYERDET. *Paris.* 1818-21. Successors.
BAUMANN—
Johann Michael. *Burgau.* ca.1750-76.
Johann Jacob, son. *Augsburg.* comp. 1767, m.ca.1770-99.
BAUMGARTEN, ——. *Cassel.* 1825. Court C.
BAUMGARTINGER—
Johann Valentin. *Mergentheim.* 1757. Made clock for Eschenbach church.
Johann Leonhard. *Thannhausen.* 1763-75. Made clock for Zipplingen church.
Johann Erasmus. *Mergentheim.* 1776-82. Made clock for Ellingen.
Franz. *Thannhausen.* 1789. Made clock for Lichtenau.
Joseph. ——. 1807. Made clock for Segringen church.
BAUMGARTNER, Gottfr. *Fürth.* d.1813.
BAUNACH, Michael. *Würzburg.* m.1798. C.
BAUNE, George. *Bristol.* 1758. d.1787. W.
BAUSSARD, ——. *France.* 1790. Water clock C.A. & M.
BAUSSE, ——. *Paris.* 1807-24.
BAUTTE—
Jean François. *Geneva.* b.1772, d.1837. Eminent maker. Specialized in very thin watches. g. en. mandolin and circ. watches M.M.A. Partner with MOULINIÉ as MOULINIÉ ET BAUTTE, and later as MOULINIÉ, BAUTTE ET MOYNIER, then BAUTTE ET MOYNIER, and last as J. F. Bautte.
& MOYNIER. *Geneva.* Early 19c. g. cyl. watch set pearls and rubies on seed pearls F.W.M. ill. Baillie. Pearl studded watch Carnegie M. Watch with en. map of Italy Fränkel coll. Two g. en. watches M.M.A., one en. Signs of Zodiac. *v.* MOYNIER.
& Co. *Geneva.* ca.1825. g. en. watch Fränkel coll.
BAUVES, Gilles. *Paris.* m.1770-1815.
BAVERSTOCK, John. *London.* a.1767.
BAVID, W. & J. *London.* 1820.
BAVIUS, Franciscus. *Leeuwarden.* 1761. l.c. mus. clock.
BAWCUTT, Thomas. *London.* a.1748. Watch.
BAWDYSON, Allaine. *London.* 1550. C. to Edward VI.
BAWN, W. *London.* Late 18c. Watch.
BAX, Philip. *London.* a.1720.
BAXTER—
Charles. *London* and *St. Neots.* a.1673, CC. 1681-83. Watch.
Matthew. *St. Neots.* Early 18c. Watch Den. coll.
John. *London.* 1743. Watch.
Joseph. *London.* a.1736.
James. ——. a.1744.
John. *London.* a.1762.
John. *London.* a.1786.
William. *London.* 1800. Watch.
John. *Monaghan.* 1824.
James. *Liverpool.* 1825. W.
BAYARD, Thomas. *Geneva.* d.1553. 'Horrologier.' Native of Lorraine. Refugee after Edict of Châteaubriand, 1551.
BAYER—
Martin. *Annaberg.* Juré 1605.
William. *London.* 1623. Lantern clock.
BAYES—
John. *London.* CC.1646, w.CC.1658-64, d. before 1675. Fine eng. watch S.K.M.
Benjamin, bro. *London.* a.1661, CC.1675.
BAYFORD, George. *London.* a.1682.

BAYLE, Thomas. *London.* CC.1703.
BAYLES, George. *London.* a.1788.
BAYLEY—
William. *London.* a.1654, CC.1663.
Edward. *London.* CC.1658. Also BAILY.
John. *London.* a.1681, CC.1708-29.
John. *London.* a.1692. cf. BAYLY.
Jeremiah. *Bardfield.* 1731. Insolvent. W.
Edward Branston. *London.* a. 1728, CC.1738-1765.
George. *London.* Mid. 18c. rep. watch mt.
Thomas. *Buxton.* 1757. W.
Samuel. *London.* an.1758. Watch.
James. *London.* a.1749.
Joseph. *London.* a.1760.
James. *London.* a.1760, CC.1768.
John. *Hanover, U.S.A.* 1770-1815.
Josiah. *London.* a.1770, CC.1778.
Barnard. *London (Bridgewater Sq.).* 1777. W.
Barnard, son. *London.* a.1777, CC.1784-95. Watches Ilbert coll.
Thomas. *London.* CC.1786, l.CC. 1787-1820. Watch mt. G.M.
Thomas. *Burton.* ca.1790 CC. cf. BEALEY.
Richard. *Cork.* ca.1790 CC.-1824.
Simeon C. *Philadelphia.* 1794.
& UPJOHN. *London (Clerkenwell).* To 1792. Partnership of Richard B. and Peter U. l.c. clock ill. Cec. & Web.
B., & Son. *London.* 1794.
Richard. *London.* 1799-1808.
Calvin. *Hingham, U.S.A.* 1800.
Joseph. *Hingham, U.S.A.* 1808.
John. *Hingham, U.S.A.* 1815-20.
BAYLIS—
Samuel. *London.* a.1720.
John. *Norwich(?)* an.1752. Watch.
——. *Margate.* 1793-5.
BAYLY—
John. *London.* CC.1700. cf. BAYLEY.
——. *Exeter.* 1778. W.
Richard, jun. *Folkestone.* In 1780 came from Ashford. W.
BAYNAM, Samuel. *London.* a.1725.
BAYNE (BANE), John. *Stirling.* 1777-90.
BAYNES, Robert Burdon. *London.* a.1822. *v.* BAINES.
BAYNHAM, Benjamin. *Limerick.* 1820-4.
BAYR, Georg. *Holland.* ca.1640. circ. watch and tulip watch B.M.
BAYSE, Thomas. *London.* CC.1695.
BAYSSALLANCE, Michael. *London.* 1737. Bankrupt.
BAZIN, Pierre. *Paris.* 1675 m.-ca.1700.
BEACE, T. —— an. 1766. Watch.
BEADLE—
William. *London.* a.1667.
Thomas. *London.* a.1760.
BEAKE—
Jonathan. *London.* a.1717, CC.1724-45.
John Covell, son. *London.* a.1745, CC.1752.
BEAL, Samuel. *Sheffield.* 1825.
BEALE—
John. *London.* a.1658.
Robert. *London.* a.1677.
Hamilton. *London,* a.1737.
——. *Canton (China).* 1790-ca.1810 in firm of Cox & BEALE, then Cox, BEALE & LAURENT, and then alone.
William. *London.* 1805. Lever watch S.K.M.
Josiah. *Twickenham.* 1805-24. W.
William. *Twickenham.* 1809-11. W.
James. *London.* 1817-25.
John. *Oundle.* Early 19c. Watch.
BEALEY, Thomas. *Burton.* an.1764. Watch. cf. BAYLEY.
BEAN—
Edward Lloyd. *London.* a.1772.
Edward. *Kingston (Kent).* an.1792. Watch.
John. *London (Hackney).* 1807-24.
J. *London (Clapham).* 1809-11.
James. *London.* a.1808.
BEAR, Robert. *Hertford.* ca.1800, CC. Watch.
BEARCOCK, John. *Chatteris.* 1771-91. T.C.
BEARCROFT, Samuel. *London.* a.1801, CC. 1808.
BEARD—
William. *London.* a.1667.
Cornelius. *London.* a.1670.
Thomas. *London.* a.1684, CC.1692.
John. *London.* 1742. Watch.
Duncan. *Appoquinemonk, U.S.A.* 1755. d.1797. Clock.
'S. M. BEARD.' Sig. on watches 1869-70 of the UNITED STATES WATCH CO.
BEARE—
John. *Barnstaple (Pilton).* 1780.
Peter. *Nottingham.* 1795. Wooden C.
BEASLEY, Thomas. *London.* a.1676, CC. 1683-1711. Also BASELY.
Nathaniel. *London.* a.1686, CC.1694-1707. Also BAISLEY and BAZELEY.
Thomas. *London.* a.1708. Also BEZELEY.
John. *London.* a.1709, CC.1719-32. Also BASELY, BAZELEY, BEESLEY, and BEZELEY.
William. *London.* a.1712. Also BASELEY.
John. *London.* CC.1725. Also BASELY.
E. *London.* 1805-08. W.
BEATSON, Thomas. *London.* End 18c. cyl. p.c. watch Ilbert coll.
'BEATSON.' On M'CABE's lowest grade watches.
BEAU, J. B. *Clermont.* Late 18c. Metal watch.
BEAUCHAMP—
George. *London.* b.1706, d.1769. C. & W.
& FINCKLY. *London.* an.1736. Watch.
John. *Croydon.* a.1737.
R. *London.* 1820. W.
BEAUFORD, J. *London.* an.1782. Watch.
BEAUFORT—
Jacques Étienne. *Paris.* m.1776-89.
——. *Paris.* 1822-5.
BEAUFOY, Mark. *England.* 1820. Used wooden pendulum rod.
BEAULIEU—
Étienne. *Basle.* 1673.
Gédéon de. *Basle.* m.1675. *Strasbourg,* 1681. *Düsseldorf,* 1685, from *Mer (Blois).* Watch after 1685 Münich M.
BEAUMARCHAIS, *v.* CARON.
BEAUMONT—
Simon. *Paris.* 1675 m.
Philip. *London.* a.1689.
William. *Shoreditch.* 1766. W.
Robert. *London.* 1772. Watch mt. maker.
William, son of Wm. *London.* a.1766.
Alfred. *Paris.* ca.1780. Watch N.Y. Univ.
Joseph. *Howden (Yorks).* 1784-95. W.
BEAUNETT, F. *London.* an.1755. Watch.
BEAUPOIL—
Salomon. *Lyons.* 1677. From *Châtellerault.*
Isac. *Amsterdam.* 1689. *Copenhagen.* 1713. d. 1737. From *Châtellerault.* Also BOPOEL and BOVEL.
BEAURIEUX, Jean Jacques. *Paris,* m.1787-9.
BEAUVAIN, ——. *Paris.* 1600. Sig. to Statuts of Paris corporation.
BEAUVAIS—
Anthoine de. *Paris.* 1544. Petitioner for incorporation of Paris clockmakers.
Gilles. *Lyons.* 1615 comp.
Guillaume. *Paris.* 1630-46. Sig. to Statuts of Paris corporation of 1646. Registered a private punch mark in 1630.
——. *Paris.* 1671.
Simon. *London.* CC.1690-1730. Eminent maker. str. rep. watch Den. coll. Watch sd. Simon and Paul an.1713.
Paul. *London.* an.1704-ca.1730. Lapis lazuli watch, set diamonds and emeralds, Bernal sale. g. p.c. watch with flick back minute hand Ilbert coll.

BEAUVAIS—*continued.*
Nicolas. *Rouen.* 1740. Made a new clock for St. Maclou.
BEAUVARLET, Josse Adrien. *Paris.* m. 1763-89.
BEAUVILLAIN, Charles. *Paris.* 1740. Cartel clock Schloss M. Berlin.
BEAVAN, William. *Ross.* an.1776. Watch.
BEAVER, Robert. *London.* a.1714.
BEAVINGTON, William. *Stourbridge.* 1795. Watch N.Y. Univ.
BEAVIS—
George. *London.* CC.1687. Chainmaker.
Elijah. *London.* 1725-9. Bankrupt.
William. *London.* an.1761. Watch.
BECH, Jørgen. *Copenhagen.* m.1798.
BECHER, J. J. *Mainz.* 1680-2. Made clock wound by fall of rainwater falling from roof. Proposed winding clocks by thermometer. Pub. 'De nova temporis demetiens ratio,' London, 1680, and 'Närrische Weissheit,' Frankfort, 1682.
BECHOT, ——. *Paris.* 1819-25.
BECHTEL, Henry. *Philadelphia.* 1817. W.
BECK—
Richard. *London.* a.1646, CC.1653-8. eng. watch.
Nicholas. *London.* a.1660, CC.1669-93.
John. *London.* a.1673, CC.1681. Assistant to Daniel QUARE. Also BECKE.
Joseph. *London (Long Lane).* CC.1701.
John. *London.* a.1696.
Philip. *London.* a.1724.
Christopher. *London (St. John St.* and *Aldersgate St.).* CC.1761, l.CC. 1787, d.1811.
Michael Peter. *Copenhagen.* 1767. m.1774.
Alexander. *London* (?). an.1781. Watch.
John, son of Christopher. *London.* a.1782.
Kirstine Marie. *Copenhagen.* 1806.
James, son of Christopher. *London.* CC. 1811-20. Chron. maker.
Hamilton. *London.* a.1809. From *Bombay.*
BECKAERT, ——. *Paris.* an.1772. Watch.
BECKER—
Antonio. *Frankfurt-a.-M.* ca.1740. g. en. watch.
Joseph Frederick. *Berlin.* 1794. Wooden C.
Gustav. *Freiburg (Silesia).* b.1819, d.1885. Established factory with large output of clocks and regulators.
BECKERS, Antoine. *Paris.* m.1775-89.
BECKETT (BECKET, BECKITT)—
Gilbert. *London.* 1678. Watch.
John. *London.* a.1698.
Thomas. *Bishop Auckland.* b.1723, d.1803, C. & W.
Mann. *Stockton.* 1753. l.c. clocks.
Thomas. *Durham.* 1767-95. Watches. C.
Mann. *Durham.* ca.1780-95 CC. C. & W.
Francis. *Chester-le-Street.* ca.1770-91.
W. *Sedgefield.* b.1737, d.1812. W.
Sir E. *v.* DENISON.
BECKFORD—
——. *Bristol.* an.1778. Watch.
William. *Lancaster.* an.1789. Watch.
BECKMAN—
Daniel. *London.* a.1671, CC.1680-1726. Also BEECKMAN.
John. *London.* 1689. CC.1695-8.
Anders. *Stockholm.* comp. 1716, m.1721, d.1736.
Daniel, son of Daniel. *London.* CC.1726.
Fredric. *Göteborg.* b.1754, d.1818. br. clock and watch.
BECKNER, Abraham. *London.* CC.1652, w.CC.1665, d.1667. str. watch ill. Britten.
BECKOVER, R. *London.* Late 18c. rep. watch mt.
BECKWITH—
William. *London (Rotherhithe).* 1790.
William. *Harwich.* Early 19c. Watch.
BECQUEREL, ——. *Paris.* 1822-5.
BECQUET, ——. *Paris.* 1814. W. to Napoleon.
BECQUEUR, Abraham. *Rouen.* m.1645.
BECTON, Ham. *London.* a.1809.
BEDELL—
Joseph. *London.* a.1676, CC.1684.
Michael. *London.* an.1774. Watch.
BEDFORD—
Helkiah. *London.* CC.1667-71. math. inst. maker.
Samuel. *London.* a.1691. mar.1698.
Francis. *London.* a.1697.
John. *London.* a.1732.
John. *Reading.* Left in 1768. Formerly at *Pembridge.*
William. *London.* ca.1790. Watch G.M.
Isaac. *Dublin.* 1795-1824. W.
BEDKE, Christian. *Hanover.* 1606. Made clock for the Marktkirche.
BEDWARD, Thomas William. *London.* a. 1809.
BEDWELL, Jeremiah. *London.* a.1720.
BEE, Thomas. *London.* a.1776.
BEECH, Joseph. *London.* a.1740.
BEECHING—
——. *Ashburnham.* ca.1750. l.c. clock.
Stephen. *Maidstone.* an.1791. Watch.
Elizabeth. *Maidstone.* 1791-5. W.
& EDMELL. *Maidstone.* Early 19c. Watch.
BEECK, Huybert. *Amsterdam.* 1671.
BEEDING, Edward. *London.* a.1732.
BEEFORTH, John. *York.* 1680. W.
BEEG, Christiana. *London.* CC.1698. W.
BEELS, Robert. *Lynn.* 2nd half 18c. l.c. clocks.
BEER, Johann. *Ulm.* ca.1730. Table clock Ulm M.
BEESLEY—
John. *London.* a.1709, CC.1719-32. Also BEASLEY.
John. *Liverpool.* Mid 18c. Watch N.Y. Univ.
James. *Manchester.* 1766-87. l.c. clock and watch.
Ann, dau. of John. *London.* CC.1769.
Thomas. *Liverpool.* ca.1818-29. Watch and chron. maker.
Richard and George. *Liverpool.* 1825. Watch N.Y. Univ.
BEET, ——. *London.* 1744. Watch.
BEETON—
John. *London.* an.1781. Watch.
Ham. *London.* a.1809.
BEGER, Charles. *London.* a.1726.
BEGG—
John. *Glasgow.* 1800.
John. *Edinburgh.* 1804-07. W. to the King.
BEGGS, Thomas. *Glasgow.* 1822-41.
BÉGUET, ——. *Paris.* 1787-9.
BEHAM—
Moritz. *Vienna.* 1559. rect. stand. clock sd. 'Me fecit Magister Mavricivs Behaeme in Vienna Anno 1559.'
Hans Sebald. *Nürnberg.* b.1500. *Frankfurt-a.M-.* d.1550. Engraver. Copied on clock by Jeremias Metzker in K.H.M.
Jacob. *Vienna.* ca.1650. Falling ball clock B.M.
BEHOE, John. *London.* 1727-54. W.
BEIER, James. *Vienna.* Early 18c. Fine l.c. Boulle-work clock Hofburg, Vienna.
BEIJDROCK, Lor. *Lüblin.* Mid. 18c. trav. clock Ashmolean M.
BEILBY—
William. *Durham.* an.1752. Watch.
Ralph. *Newcastle-on-Tyne.* 1767. Engraver of clock dials.
& HAWTHORN. *Newcastle-on-Tyne.* 1790-1802. Watch.

BEITELROCK—
Jos. *Constance.* Late 17c. Also BEIDELROCK. Square table clock.
Johann. *Augsburg.* m.ca.1736. Juré 1740-57. Watch mt.
BEITH, Robert. *Dublin.* 1795-1824.
BEITLER, Mathias. *Onolzbach.* 1582-1616. Designed watch-cases.
BEK, James. *London.* Early 19c. Watch.
BEKERS, ——. *Paris.* 1807-25.
BEL, Michel (or Marie) Hyacinthe. *Paris.* m.1785-9.
BELCHER—
Thomas. *London* (*Brownlow St.*). a.1741, CC.1750-77.
Joseph. *London.* a.1750.
BELHOMME, Pierre Jean Baptiste. *Paris.* m.1755-1814.
BÉLIARD—
Dominique. *Paris.* ca.1700-36 m. Watch Gélis coll. Also BELLIARD.
Pierre. *Paris.* m.1740.
François. *Paris.* m.1749. Juré 1771-89.
Pierre François (l'aîné), son. *Paris.* m. 1774-89.
François. *Paris.* 1774. m.1777, juré 1781-9. C. to Louis xv from 1781.
Julien Antoine (le jeune), bro. of P. F. *Paris.* 1779-1812. m.1796, juré 1788.
Veuve (of Pierre). *Paris.* 1789.
——. *Paris.* 1814-18.
BELICHON, Claude. *Lyons.* 1636-59.
BELK, William. *London.* 1790. *Philadelphia.* 1796. Dissolved partnership BRAMBLE & BELK in 1790.
BELKNAP—
Ebenezer. *Boston, U.S.A.* 1806-13. W.
Ebenezer. *Boston, U.S.A.* 1818-25. C. Perhaps same as preceding.
William A. *Boston, U.S.A.* 1818. W.
BELL—
Charles. *London.* a. ca.1646.
Benjamin. *London.* a.1649, CC.1657, m.CC. 1682-98. Watch with hour, minute and seconds hands G.M.
Henry. *Edinburgh.* 1660.
Henry. *London.* (*Lothbury*). Late 17c. br. clock.
John. *London.* a.1671-85 CC.
Matthew. *Edinburgh.* a.1680.
Daniel. *London.* a.1683.
Joseph. *London.* a.1684, CC.1691.
Thomas. *London.* a.1691.
——. *Cambusnethan.* 1700.
John. *London.* a.1698.
John. *London.* a.1699, CC.1719-51. l.c. clock and watch.
Edward or Edmond. *London.* a.1704.
John. *London.* a.1709.
John. *New York.* 1734.
John. *London.* a.1732.
Robert. *London.* 1744. Watch.
James. *London.* a.1737.
William. *London.* a.1747.
Thomas. *London* (*Whitechapel*). 1758. Bankrupt.
William. *London* (*Spitalfields*). 1766-74.
Boucher. *London.* a.1761, CC.1772.
Andrew. *Haddington.* 1769-90.
Peter. *Garstang.* ca.1770-95.
Joseph. *London* (*Bunhill Row*). ca.1770-99. br. clock M.M.A.
James. *Cambusnethan.* 1770-90.
William. *London.* a.1767.
Thomas. *London.* a.1768.
Ephraim. *London.* an.1775. Watch.
Joseph. *Twickenham.* an.1781. Watch.
William. *Newcastle-on-Tyne.* an.1791. Watch.
Thomas. *Newcastle-on-Tyne.* 1785.
Alexander. *St. Andrews.* 1785.
Alexander. *Glasgow.* 1790.
William. *Cambusnethan.* 1790-1820.

BELL—*continued.*
John. *Hexham.* ca.1790-1827.
Joseph. *Doncaster.* 1794. C. & W.
Edward. *Uttoxeter.* 1795. C. & W.
John. *Doncaster.* 1795. W.
H. *Lancaster.* d.1801.
Succeeded Thos. WARSWICK.
Succeeded by Thos. DICKINSON.
Joseph. *London.* a.1792.
David. *Stirling.* 1801-50.
William. *Philadelphia.* 1805. C. & W.
John. *London* (*Tottenham Ct. Rd.*). 1805-1808. W.
William. *London.* CC.1815-18.
J. *London* (*Golden Sq.*). 1817-24. mus. C.
James. *Belfast.* 1820.
Dawson. *Strabane.* 1820-4.
J. *Norwich.* Early 19c. Watch.
Joseph. *Coleraine.* 1824.
W. *Lurgan.* 1824.
Thomas. *Liverpool.* 1825. W.
BELLAMY—
A. *London.* 1775. *Geneva.* 1800.
Joseph. *Grimsby.* Early 19c. Watch.
BELLARD, John. *London.* CC.1674. Went abroad in 1689. Watch.
Veuve, et MESTRAL. Prob. *Paris.* ca.1800. Watch S.K.M.
BELLE-FONTAINE, ——. *Burgundy.* Early 18c. Devised anchor recoil esc. for clocks with two independently pivoted pallets.
BELLEMAY, Peter. *London.* 1743. Watch.
BELLER, Rodolphe. *Chaux-de-Fonds.* 1806-1809.
BELLIARD—
Louis. *Blois.* m.1675.
v. BÉLIARD.
BELLICHON, Claude. *Lyons.* 1636-59.
BELLING, John. *Bodmin.* 1740. l.c. clock.
BELLINGE, James. *Liverpool.* ca.1770.
BELLINGER—
Richard. *London.* a.1676 to Edward EAST. CC.1686.
John. *London.* a.1677, CC.1686-1721.
Charles. *London.* a.1686.
John, son of John. *London.* a.1706, CC.1725.
James. *London.* 1731 CC.
John, son. *London.* a.1730.
William, brother. *London.* a.1732.
BELLMAN—
William. *Broughton* (*Lancs.*). 1784.
Daniel. *Broughton* (*Lancs.*). ca.1820. l.c. clock. Watch mt. Platt Hall M. Manchester.
BELLON, Capt. Peter. *London.* 1662.
BELLOT—
——. *Paris.* 1795. Petitioned with LEMAIRE for permission to start a watch factory at Versailles.
J. *Geneva.* Early 19c.
BELLUNE, Peter. *London.* 1630-64 CC.
BELLWOOD, John. *Keswick.* an.1751. Watch Den. coll.
BELON, Pierre. *Paris.* 1646-9. C. to the Reine Mère. Sig. to Statuts of 1646 of Paris guild. crys. cross watch.
BELTON, Edward. *London.* 1723. Bankrupt.
BELTZ—
Jean Adam. *Paris.* m.1785-9.
——. *Paris* (*Rue St. Denis*). 1807-25.
——. *Paris* (*Rue Dauphine*). 1818-20.
BEMOGAUD, ——. *Lyons.* 1638 m.
BÉNARD—
F. *Paris.* ca.1600. Oval watch with sundial M.M.A.
Jehan. *Paris.* 1611. Watch with sundial B.M. Oval watch M.M.A.
Claude. *Blois.* m.1634-42.
BENBOW—
John. *Northwood* (*Salop*). b.1696, d.1806. C. & W.

BENBOW—*continued.*
T. *Northwood.* 1785. Watch with twin wheel verge esc. Ilbert coll.
Thomas. *Newport* (*Salop*). 1778-ca.1800.
Thomas. *Tullamore.* 1824.
BENBRICK, James. *London.* a.1671.
BENBRIDGE, Thomas. *London.* a.1669, CC. 1683.
BENCE, Stephen. *London.* an.1723. Watch.
BENCHING, Edward. *London.* a.1659.
BENCROFT, Titus. *London.* 1775.
BENDALL—
Walter. *London.* a.1704.
William. *London.* an.1796. Watch.
BENDELE, Johann Michael. *Augsburg.* b. 1734, m.1763-86. In *Ansbach* 1772.
BENECH, Anthony. *London.* a.1722.
BENEDICT—
S. W. *New York.* Early 19c.-1835. Watch N.Y. Univ.
BROTHERS. *New York.* Founded 1819.
BENESTON, Joseph. *London.* a.1802. From *Dominica, W. Indies.*
BENGG, Paulus. *Zug.* 1612, d.1642. Able maker. crys. heart watch Blot-Garnier coll. Crucifix clock Zürich Landes-M.
BENGGRAF—
Caspar. *Neustadt-a.-d.-Saale.* m.1794.
Caspar der Jüngere. *Neustadt-a.-d.-Saale.* m.1826.
BENGO, Alexander. *London.* an.1771. Watch.
BENGUEREL-DIT-JACOT—
Abram. *Fontainemelon.* 1745-80. Maker of clocks with wooden wheels.
David. *Fontainemelon.* 1745-80. 'Maître horloger en bois.'
Abram David. *Fontainemelon.* 1775.
Daniel. *Fontainemelon.* 1780. Maker of clocks with wooden wheels.
BENHAM, John. *Cullompton.* 18c. l.c. clock.
BENJAMIN—
Joel. *London* (*Minories*). 1820-4. W.
M. *London.* 1820. W.
Joel. *London* (*St. Mary Axe*). 1822-4.
Barzillai. *New Haven, U.S.A.* 1823.
BENKER, J. *London.* 18c. Watch Fränkel coll. probably Dutch.
BENLEY & BECK. *London.* Early 19c. Watch. cf. BENTLEY & BECK, but sig. on watch is clear.
BENN—
Thomas. *London.* a.1660.
Robert. *London.* CC.1716-40. br. clock.
Anthony, son. *London.* CC.1742, m.CC. 1763, d.1764.
Thomas, bro. *London* and *Clifton.* CC. 1764-86.
Thomas, son. *London.* a.1764, CC.1771, l.CC.1773.
John. *Bristol.* an.1773. Watch.
William. *London.* CC.1786.
BENNER, Johannes. —— ca.1650. Table clock.
BENNETOT, ——. *Paris.* 1812.
BENNETT—
Mathew. *Dorchester.* 1650. C.
Thomas. *London.* a.1667.
John. *London.* a.1670, CC.1677-1709.
Richard. *London.* a.1671.
Samuel. *London.* a.1673.
William. *London.* a.1675, CC.1692-1722.
William. *London.* a.1677, CC.1687-1702.
Mansell. *London.* CC.1688-1711. l.c. clock S.K.M. Watch mt.
Thomas. *London.* a.1696.
George. *London.* a.1697, CC.1702-22.
John. *London.* a.1702, CC.1712-52.
Samuel. *London.* a.1705, CC.1716-62.
John. *Bristol.* CC.1712. cf. John below.
Richard. *London.* a.1707, CC.1715-29.
Samuel. *London.* a.1709.
Thomas. *London.* a.1710, CC.1720-2. l.c. clock Weth. coll.

BENNETT—*continued.*
John. *London.* a.1715.
Anne. *London.* 1725.
Samuel. *London.* a.1720,CC.1742-56. Watch.
William. *London.* a.1721, CC.1729-48.
John. *London.* CC.1733.
William, son of George. *London.* a.1729.
George. *London.* CC.1739.
John. *Bristol.* 1743. cf. John above.
Giles. *Malmesbury,* 1752-66. W.
——. *Gosport.* an.1755. Watch. BENNET.
——. *Camerton.* d.1779. W.
John Webb. *London.* an.1770. Watch.
B. *London.* 1778. Watch Ilbert coll.
John. *Helstone.* 1779. Watch.
Henry. *London.* a.1771.
James. *London.* a.1780.
James. *Norwich.* a. to and partner with Peter AMYOT from 1790-9.
Samuel. *London.* a.1786.
William. *Salisbury.* ca.1790 CC.
James. *Uttoxeter.* 1795. C. & W. BENNET.
Edward. *East Dereham.* 1797. W.
Charles. *London.* a.1797. CC.1824.
George. *Greenwich.* 1802-11. W.
Richard. *London.* CC.1813-17.
John. *Greenwich.* 1817-24. W.
William. *Liverpool.* ca.1820.
Thomas. *Liverpool.* 1825. W.
BENNINGS, ——. *Windsor.* an.1758. Watch.
BENNIWORTH—
Thomas. *St. Albans.* an.1773 CC. Watch.
William. *St. Albans.* ca.1780 CC. In partnership with Thomas.
BENOIST, Martin or Mathurin. *Paris.* Early 16c.-1554. Keeper of Henri de Vic's clock on Palais de Justice. Founder member of Paris corporation. Made clock of Chât. d'Anet.
BENOIT—
J. F. *Nancy.* 1730-80. Watch and l.c. clock.
Louis. *Paris.* d.an.1772.
Louis. *Ponts de Martel* and *La Sagne.* b. 1732, d.1825. Painter on enamel, noted for his blacks and purples. Decorated the automata of JACQUET-DROZ and MAILLARDET.
Abraham. *Geneva.* b.1738-70.
Jacques. *Geneva.* b.1747-70.
Alexandre. *Cottendart* (*Bôle*). 1828-31. C. of repute.
Achille Hubert. *Versailles.* b.1804, d.1895. Famous maker. Designed several watch remontoirs and an escapement. Director of royal factory at Versailles, and, later, of the École d'Horlogerie at Cluses. Many fine watches.
Gérard, *v.* GÉRARD.
BENSON—
John. *London.* a.1652, CC.1669-1709. l.c. clock.
Samuel. *London.* a.1692, CC.1700-30.
Abraham. *London.* Early 18c. Fine g. en. and repoussé p.c. watch.
William. *London.* an.1771. Watch.
George. *London.* an.1786. Watch.
& HELL. *London.* Late 18c. Spring makers who sd. their springs.
Richard. *Liverpool.* 1816-21. W.
BENT, John. *London.* a.1734.
BENTE, ——. *Fredericia.* m.1788.
BENTLEY—
——. *London.* an.1754. Watch.
John. *Stockton-on-Tees.* 1760. Watch.
John. *Thirsk.* 1760-91. l.c. clock.
James. *London.* a.1765.
——. *Darlington.* 1776. C. & W.
Richard. *Stockton-on-Tees.* 1774-84. Watch.
Samuel. *Kingsbridge.* Late 18c. l.c. clock. Watch with painting under horn S.K.M.
John. *London.* a.1796, CC.1813-23. br. clock ill. Cec. & Web. Watch.

BENTLEY—*continued.*
& BECK. *London.* 1815-24. Made a Congreve clock. mus. br. clock.
Matthew. *London.* a.1810.
'BENTLEY.' Sig. on 1879 watches of AUBURNDALE WATCH CO.
BENTON—
Edward. *London.* a.1778.
Benjamin. *London.* a.1779.
BENTWE, Martin. *Vienna.* ca.1740. 2 br. clocks Uhren M. Vienna.
BENYON, ——. *London.* 1744. Watch.
BENZ, Ludwig. *Basle.* 1776-1850.
BERAIN, Jean Louis. *Paris.* b.1637, d.1711. Designed many clock cases.
BERAND, William. *Croydon.* 1757-72. Watch.
BÉRANGER, Antoine. *Paris.* m.1777-89.
BERARD, Jean Louis Gédéon Hippolite. *Geneva.* ca.1770-91.
BERAUD—
Rene. *La Rochelle.* 1572, d.an.1615. C. to town in 1580.
Isaac. *La Rochelle.* 1599.
Henri. *Sedan.* ca.1600. Watch Soltykoff coll.
A. *Blois. v.* BÉRAULT.
Henry. *London.* 1633 CC.
James. *London.* a.1632.
Stephen. *London.* 1670 CC.
BÉRAULT—
Abel. *Blois.* mar.1593. *Paris.* 1607. d.ca. 1620. Always sd. 'BÉRAUD.'
Abel, son. *Blois.* b.1587, d.1677. Mainly an engraver.
Jean, bro. *Blois.* comp. 1626-49.
John. *London.* a.1691.
BERBETTE, Louis. *Chaux-de-Fonds.* 1781-1804. cal. and mus. clocks.
BERBRUN, ——. *Paris.* 1807.
BERCHENET, Jean. *Neuchâtel.* 1413.
BERCKMANN, Samuel. *Augsburg.* ca.1680. 10-sided table clock. sq. table clock Feill coll.
BERENTZ, Hindrich. *Stockholm.* comp.1695.
BERG—
F. L. *Augsburg.* 1719. Table clock G.M.
Nils. *Stockholm.* m.1751-90. 2 br. clocks in Nord M. and Nat. M. Stockholm. Wall and 2 l.c. clocks. trav. clock and watch.
Claes. *Stockholm.* 1762-82. Wall and 4 br. clocks and watch.
Johan. *Stockholm.* 1784.
Nils. *Linköping.* 1802-05. 2 trav. clocks; watch Nord M.
Hans Christian. *Copenhagen.* m.1806.
Nils. *Karlstad.* 1816-46.
N. D. *Sala.* 1816-26.
Gustav. *Stockholm.* 1819-20.
Johan Fredrik. *Stockholm.* 1823-46.
BERGAUER—
Johann Michael. *Innsbruck* and *Vienna.* m.1757. Clock with sundial.
C. *Vienna.* 1770. Court C.
BERGEAU (BERGEO), Peter. *London.* a. 1715-ca.1770. Watch Den. coll.
BERGENAT, ——. *Chaux-de-Fonds.* 1789.
BERGER—
François. *Paris.* 1675 m. str. and al. trav. clock Den. coll. sq. watch mt. Ilbert coll.
——. *Paris.* 17c. en. watch Blot-Garnier coll. Perhaps same as BERGIER.
Isach. *Copenhagen.* m.1753. g. en. watch. Watches Nat. M. Copenhagen and Palace M. Pekin.
Stephanus. *Vienna.* m.1757.
Jean Marc. *Geneva.* ca.1770-91.
——. *Brün.* Late 18c. p.c. watch with tortoise-shell covered painting.
Friedrich. *Fürth.* d.ca.1820.
——. *Brün.* End 18c. Watch.
Andreas. *Giebelstadt.* m.1807.
BERGERET—
Claude. *Besançon.* 1481. Keeper of clock on St. Étienne.
Jean. *Dijon.* 1592. Repaired clock on Notre Dame.
BERGH, P. V. D. *Rotterdam.* Mid. 18c. Br. clock.
BERGHUIS, P. B. *Spijk.* ca.1800.
BERGIER—
Clément. *Geneva.* 1559. Maker of repute; from *Lyons.*
Abraham. *Lyons.* mar. 1589. *Grenoble* and *Lyons,* 1597-1616. *Lyons,* 1624-42. Watch mt.
L. *Grenoble.* ca.1600. Several watches.
Pierre, son of Abraham. *Lyons,* 1601-12. Also *Grenoble,* 1633-41. 'Armorier et horloger du Roi.'
Pierre. *Grenoble.* 1603. d. before 1612.
——. *Paris.* ca.1650. Watch B.M. en. watch Blot-Garnier coll.
Jean. *Grenoble.* 1648-69.
BERGKUMMER, F. *Essen.* ca.1750. Watch Manx M.
BERGLIN—
Georg. *Västerås.* 1737. Made clock for St. Jacob's church, Stockholm. 2 l.c. clocks.
Hans. *Kristinehamn.* 1750.
Johan. *Västerås.* 1750. l.c. clock.
Johan. *Örebro.* m.1750.
Leonard, son. *Örebro.* comp. 1750.
BERGLUND, Johan Olof. *Västerås.* 1824-35.
BERGMAN, Johan. *Stockholm.* 1794-1815. Wall clock ill. Sidenbladh.
BERGMILLER, ——. *Paris.* 1809-25. Clock. Succeeded ROUVIÈRE.
BERGNER, Carl Fredrik. *Stockholm.* 1763. m.1766-78.
BERGSTEN—
H. *Lindesberg.* Mid. 18c. br. clock.
Petter. *Lidköping.* 1761-70.
Eric. *Nyköping.* 1801. d.1814. Made turret, wall and br. clocks and a str. and rep. watch.
BERGSTENSSON, Johan Eric. *Nyköping.* 1817. d.ca.1832.
BERGSTRÖM, Peter. *Karlskrona.* 1820-5.
BERGUER—
Samuel. *Chaux-de-Fonds.* 1749. d.1777. C. Also BERGER.
Jonas. *Chaux-de-Fonds.* 1781. C. Also BERGER.
Frederick. *London.* 1805-24. Also BERUGIER.
John. *London.* 1809-24. Watch.
Francis. *London (Holborn).* 1820. Watch.
Joseph. *London.* 1820. Also BERUGIER.
BERINGER, D. *Germany.* 2nd half 18c. Dial M.M.A.
BERKELEY, Thomas. *London.* a.1676, CC., d.ca.1685.
BERLIÉ, ——. *Paris.* End 18c. en. watch.
BERLIER, Pierre. *Paris.* m.1603.
BERLING—
——. *Uppsala.* b.1787-1826. Prob. same as following.
Carl Fredrik. *Göteborg,* 1815-18. *Stockholm,* 1836-40. *Visby,* 1845. Watch Nord. M. by him or preceding.
G. *Kalmar.* 1819.
Fredrik. *Västervik.* 1822.
C. F. *Kalmar.* 1830. Prob. Carl Fredrik.
BERLINGER, Ignatius. *Vienna.* ca.1800. Large astro. regulator Hofburg, Vienna.
BERLINGUART, Carl. *Berlin* and *Basle.* 1721-5.
BERMAN, Jacob, & Co. *London.* 1820-30. Wooden C.
BERNARD—
M. *Paris.* 1600. Signatory to Statuts of Paris corporation. M. perhaps error for N. below. oct. sil. eng. watch.

BERNARD—*continued.*
Nicolas. *Paris.* ca.1600. oct. crys. watch and Limoges en. watch M.M.A.
Nicolas, prob. son. *Paris.* 1636-46. Signatory to Statuts of Paris corporation of 1646. Registered a private punch mark in 1636. 2 watches S.K.M., one with very fine painted enamels ill. Baillie. Watch M.M.A. g. en. watch Gélis coll.
A. *Paris.* Mid. 17c. sil. str. watch B.M.
Abraham. *Bristol.* 1763-70. W.
Daniel Gaspard. *Geneva.* ca.1770-91.
Joseph. *Geneva.* ca.1770-91.
Nicolas. *Paris.* 1791.
BERNARDINE, James. *London.* a.1797.
BERNARDINO DAGLI OROLOGI. *Padua.* 1510-51. Repaired clock on the Rigobello tower of Ferrara.
BERNARDOT ET GENDRE. *Clermont.* Mid. 18c. g. rep. watch.
BERNAUDA, ——. *Paris.* 1812.
BERNCASTLE, ——. *Lewes.* an.1814. Watch.
BERNE, Jean Zacharie. *Paris.* m.1763-89.
BERNHARD (BERNHARDT)—
Martin. *Landsberg.* 1728-50.
Martin. *Göggingen.* ca.1750 comp.
Wilhelm. *Weimar.* 1822.
BERNIER—
Sauvaire. *Manosque* (*Avignon*). ca.1620. Made clock for Beaumont d'Apt.
Benoît. *Lyons.* 1625 comp.
François. *Paris.* m.1746.
Pierre. *Paris.* ca.1750. Mantel clock.
Michel. *Geneva.* ca.1770-88.
——. *Paris.* 1812.
BERNINCK, Jan. *Amsterdam.* ca.1720-ca. 1750. Watch en. G. BOUVIER and repoussé H. MANLY, B.M.
BERNOULLI—
Jean. *Neuchâtel.* b.1667, d.1748. Eminent mathematician. Mem. on spiral springs to the Acad. Roy. des Sciences, 1736.
Daniel. *Basle.* b.1700, d.1782. Eminent mathematician. In 1747 gained prize of the Acad. Roy. des Sciences for mem. on finding the longitude.
BERON, Marc. *La Rochelle.* 1627.
BERQUIZ, Francis. *London.* 1815-30. Watch Horstmann coll.
BERRANGER, ——. *Paris.* 1812.
BERRIDGE—
John. *London.* 1738. Clock.
John. *Boston.* Mid. 18c. l.c. equation clock. Watch.
Robert. *London,* a.1746-95. l.c. clocks.
John. *London* (*Oxford St.*). 1784.
William. *London* (*Oxford Rd.*). 1785-95. C. & W. l.c. and br. clock.
John Blissbury. *London.* CC.1793-99.
William. *London* (*Holles Rd.*). 1799-1824.
BERRIE, James. *London.* d. an.1774. Watch.
BERRINGER, Henry. *London.* a.1784.
BERRINGTON—
John. *London.* a.1681.
Urian. *v.* BARRINGTON.
John. *Bolton-le-Moors.* ca.1820.
John Johnson. *Bolton-le-Moors.* ca.1820.
James. *St. Helens.* ca.1820.
BERRISFORD, Edward. *London.* a.1663.
BERROLLAS, Joseph Anthony. *London* and *Paris.* 1800-30. A very able W. Patented a repeater in 1808, an alarm watch in 1810, and pump winding in 1827.
BERROW—
John. *London.* a.1675.
John. *London.* a.1711.
BERRY—
Samuel. *London.* a.1631.
John. *London* (*Clement's Lane*). a.1674,CC. 1688, m.CC.1723-44. l.c. clocks Salters Co. and Merchant Taylors Co. Watch Den. coll. str. watch mt. G.M. prob. by him.
John. *London.* a.1684, CC.1692.
John. *London.* a.1687, CC.1697.
Francis. *Hitchin.* ca.1700. l.c. clock. ill. Cec. & Web.
Samuel. *London.* a.1698, CC.1705-43.
Henry. *London.* a.1714.
John. *London.* CC.1728-54.
John. *Manchester.* 1738-62. Watch.
Robert. *Hitchin.* 1743. C.
John, or Robert, son. *London.* a.1743.
A. *London.* an.1752. Watch.
John. *Canterbury.* an.1753. Watch.
William. *London.* a.1752-ca.1780. l.c. clock.
James. *Pontefract.* an.1769. Watch.
Edward. *London.* an.1789. Watch.
William. *Minehead.* 1791-5. C.
Arthur. *Liverpool.* 1815-24. W.
Edward. *Liverpool.* 1825. W.
BERSEAU, ——. *London.* an.1775. Watch.
BERT, Thomas. *Lewes.* 1716. C.
BERTAUD (BERTHAULT), ——. *Paris.* 1809-12.
BERTEL—
Sigmund. *Cologne.* 1797.
H. *Cologne.* 1813.
BERTHERAN, I. *France.* Mid. 16c. Triangular case of table clock S.K.M.
BERTHOUD—
Ferdinand. *Paris.* b.1727, d.1807. Went to Paris to Julien LE ROY in 1745. A most eminent horologist and maker of clocks, watches and chrons.; did much experimental work on timekeepers; devised the spring detent prob. independently of EARNSHAW. Pub. 'L'Art de régler les pendules,' 1759. 'Essai sur l'Horlogerie,' 1763. 'Traité des Horloges Marines,'1773. 'Éclaircissements sur l'Invention des Horloges Marines,' 1773. 'Les Longitudes par la mesure du Temps,' 1775. 'De la mesure du Temps,' 1787. 'Traité des Montres à Longitudes,' 1792. 'Suite du Traité des Montres à Longitudes,' 1797. 'Histoire de la mesure du Temps,' 1802. 'Supplément au Traité des Montres à Longitudes,' 1807. C. to the King and the Marine. Membre de l'Institut. F.R.S. London. Made first chron. 1754, sent for trial 1761. Mantel clock S.K.M. 3 clocks Wallace coll. 2 watches G.M. Year regulator and 2 others and 18 marine chrons. C.A. & M. Equation, c.secs. dumb rep. watch going a month, ca.1760, Ilbert coll. Watch Fränkel coll. rep. watch M.P.S. Dresden. Fine cartel clock Mobilier National, Paris. g. watch Nat. M. Stockholm.
Pierre, bro. *Couvet.* 1740-67. W. & C.
Jean Henri, bro. *Paris.* 1742-92.
Armand. *Paris.* m.1753.
Abram Henry. *Couvet.* 1778-1807. One of the foremost C. at Couvet.
Pierre Louis, son of Pierre. *Paris.* b.1754, d.1813. Successor to Ferdinand. C. to the Observatoire and the Bureau des Longitudes. Wrote 'Entretiens sur l'horlogerie.' Made many watches and clocks and about 150 chrons. Used cylindrical balance springs in watches and conical balance springs in 1793. Pedometer winding c.secs. watch Ilbert coll.
Jean Henri, bro. *Couvet.* 1758. Later at Paris with FERDINAND.
Isaac, bro. *Couvet, Fleurier* and *Paris.* 1749-1798. W. & C.
Abram. *Fleurier.* 1754.
Jonas Henri. *Couvet.* 1756. d.1820. Made complex clocks.
Pierre Frédéric. *Couvet.* 18c.

BERTHOUD—*continued.*
Henri, nephew of Ferdinand. *Couvet.* 1779. C.
Daniel Henry. *Paris* (*Pont St. Michel*). m.1784-9.
Abram David. *Plancemont-sur-Couvet.* 1787-1789.
Claude. *Paris.* End 18c. en. watch.
Charles Henri, son of Abram Henry. *Couvet.* 1803. C.
Frères. *Paris.* From 1813. Firm composed of Louis and Charles Auguste, sons of Pierre Louis. 'Horlogers de la Marine.'
Veuve. *Paris.* 1817-19. 'Horloger de la Marine.'
BERTHOUD-DU-FOUR, Pierre. *Couvet.* 1688. Repaired clock of Couvet.
BERTIN—
——. *Paris* (*Rue Bar de Bac*). 1822-5.
——. *Paris* (*Rue Française*). 1824.
BERTLES (BIRTLES)—
Edward. *Liverpool.* 1777-96. C.
John. *Market Harborough.* an.1788-95. Watch.
BERTON, ——. *Paris.* Late 18c.-1825. Cartel clock, Ministère de la Marine, Paris.
BERTRAM, William. *London.* 1729. m.CC. 1732, d.1733.
BERTRAND—
Michaud or Michel, dit Pothier. *Paris.* 1540-1547. C. to François I. Founder member of Paris corporation.
Pierre. *Lyons.* 1603-20. From *Geneva.*
Joseph. *Paris.* m.1746. Juré 1763-9.
Antoine. *Paris.* m.1750.
François. *Paris.* m.1759.
Claude Joseph. *Paris.* Juré 1771.
Joseph Charles (or Claude) Paul. *Paris.* (*Rue Montmartre*). m.1772-89. Watch mt. G.M. Remontoir cal. clock C.A. & M.
Robert. *London.* 1790.
Charles. *Paris.* ca.1800. g. en. watch.
——. *Paris* (*Rue de la Paix*). 1818.
Veuve. *Paris* (*Rue de la Paix*). 1822-5.
BERWICK, Abner. *Berwick, U.S.A.* 1820.
BESCHEDT, ——. *Bruges.* 16c. Mentioned by Dubois.
BESCHET, ——. a. *Besançon. Lyons,* 1757. Application for mastership refused.
BESCK—
Zackarias. *Stockholm.* 1697. d.1727. br. and l.c. clocks.
Johan, son. *Linköping.* 1705-17.
Anders, bro. *Nyköping.* 1716. d.1729. Wall clock.
Zackarias, bro. *Stockholm.* d.1727.
BESHOLT, Peter. *London.* 1622. Alien.
BESNARD—
André *Paris.* m.1606. Juré 1616.
Nicolas. *Blois.* 1663.
BESSEL, Friedrich Wilhelm. *Germany.* b. 1784, d.1846. Eminent mathematician and astronomer; wrote on pendulums and their suspensions.
BESSIN, Pierre. *Rouen.* 1717 m.
BESSIRE, Jacob. *Péry.* 1800.
BEST—
J. *London.* an.1752. Watch.
Robert. *London.* CC.1783-1820. Bankrupt 1796. en. watch.
Thomas. *London.* an.1761-90. Watches for Dutch market and mus. clocks. 3-case quarter str. trav. clock, Ilbert coll.
——. *Lewes.* an.1765. Watch.
Thomas. *Newcastle-on-Tyne.* 1785. en. watch.
& Son. *Ilminster.* 1793-7. C.
William. *Ballymena.* 1824.
BESTWICK—
Richard. *London.* 1660-73. C.
Katharine, widow. *London.* 1672 CC.
Henry, son. *London.* a.1678, CC.1686.

BETHELL—
George. *London.* an.1757. Watch.
Thomas. *London.* an.1763. Watch.
R. *London.* 2nd half 18c. Watch mt.
William. *London.* CC.1770.
John. *Stowmarket.* From 1791-5. From *London.* C. & W.
John. *Warrington.* ca.1820.
BETHMANN, Louis. *Leipzig.* ca.1800. Stop watch M.P.S. Dresden.
BETHNAN, Robert. *Paris.* m.1767-89.
BETON, John. *London.* 1800. Watch Den. coll.
BETSON, Thomas. *London.* ca.1740-80. Watch Chamb. coll.
BETTERTON, H. *London.* an.1773-ca.1780. Watch G.M.
BETTINSON, Solomon. *Newark.* 1750-96. l.c. clock. Also BETTISON.
BETTS—
Samuel. *London.* 1645. d. before 1675. CC. Maker of repute. br. clock Weth. coll. Fine en. watch G.M. circ. sil. cal. watch Mallett coll. Sil. watch filigree case Ilbert coll. Watch ill. Britten.
Job. *London.* CC.1656-82.
Samuel. *London.* a.1675, CC.1682-1700. br. clock Weth. coll.
Joseph. *London.* 1706 CC.
John. *London.* 1720. Watchcase maker. Sd. IB.
——. *King's Lynn.* an.1782. Watch.
BETZMAYR, Johan Simon. *Danzig.* ca.1750. sil. trav. clock.
BEURLING, Peter Henric. *Stockholm.* b. 1763, d.1806. Had a large workshop, continued by widow till 1830. Watch Nord. M. Many wall clocks. br. clock.
BEURNIER, Frères. *Seloncourt.* 1820. Started factory for ébauches.
BEURRIER, ——. *Paris.* 1825.
BEVAN—
——. *London.* CC. d.an.1680.
John. *Marlborough.* an.1753. Watch.
——. *Wigan.* ca.1820.
BEVANS, William. *Norristown, U.S.A.* 1816.
BEVASS, Joseph. *London.* an.1762. Watch.
BEVENS, William. *Philadelphia.* 1811-13.
BEVERIDGE, George. *Kettle.* 1799-1842.
BEVERLEY—
James. *London.* a.1684, CC.1691. rep. br. clock ill. Cec. & Web., and watch.
Thomas. *Caister.* 1791. C.
BEVERN, Charles. *London.* an.1757. Watch.
BEVIL, C. P. *Ipswich.* Early 19c. Watch.
BEVIS, ——. *London.* an.1765. Watch.
BEW, William. *London.* a.1731.
BEWICK, Thomas. *Newcastle-on-Tyne.* a. 1767, d.1828. Engraver of clock dials.
BEWLEY, Joseph. *London.* an.1783. Watch.
BEXINGER, Jo. Anthony. *Salzburg.* Late 17c. rep. watch M.M.A.
BEXLEY, James. *Liverpool.* 1825. W.
BEYEL, P. A. *Amsterdam.* 1822. W.
BEYENDOFF—
George. *London.* a.1751.
David. *Dublin, London* and *Liverpool.* a. 1753-70. Watchcase maker.
BEYER—
Hans. *Strasbourg.* 1587.
John. *London.* CC.1769.
Carl August. *Dresden.* m.1807.
G. C. *Newton Abbot.* Early 19c.
BEYNON, Jeffrey, *Cardiff.* 1775. C. & W.
BEYSSAC, Antoine. *Rouen.* m.1653-67. Introduced the pendulum at Rouen. 'Ayant l'art et le secret de faire les mouvemens des horloges à pendule et y ayant très bien réussy à ceux de St. Ouen et Bonnes-Nouvelles à Rouen.' Repaired clock of Notre Dame, Dijon.
BEZAR, Stephen. *London.* CC.1648.

BEZART, Guillaume. *Rouen.* 1735. Repaired Rouen Cathedral clock.
BEZENCENET—
Abram. *Boveresse.* 1734-49. W. & C.
Abram Henri. *Môtiers.* 1749. C.
Jean François. *Couvet.* 1757-72. C.
Jean Louis. *Boveresse (Switzerland).* 1758-1776. C.
Abram Henri. *Boveresse.* b.1774, d.1861. Made mus. clocks and chron.
BIANCO, Guglielmo. *Genoa.* 1413. Keeper of clock on campanile of St. Siro.
BIAUDET, ——. *Rolle.* an.1717. Watch.
BIBBY—
William. *London.* 1805-08. W.
Thomas. *Liverpool.* 1825. W.
BIBLEY, John. *London.* 1790.
BICK—
Johan Friedrick. *Elverfeld.* 1749. Wall clock Staats M. Amsterdam.
John. *London.* an.1764. Watch.
BICKEL—
Franz Anton. *Augsburg.* comp. ca.1783-1800.
Johann. *Fürth.* d.ca.1822.
BICKERSTAFF—
William. *Liverpool.* 1790-1829. W.
Peter. *Liverpool.* 1807-29. W.
Robert. *Liverpool.* 1818-29.
BICKERTON—
William. *Cambridge.* 1758. W.
William. *Downham Market.* 1773. W.
BICKLE, R. H. *Bishop's Nympton.* 2nd half 18c. l.c. clock.
BICKLEY, Thomas. *London.* 1790.
BICKLMANN, Ph. Ja. *Linz.* Mid. 18c. Watch in snuff-box with portrait of Maria Theresa.
BICKNELL, Francis. *London.* a.1653, CC. 1665.
v. CAITHNESS & BICKNELL.
BIDARD, ——. *Alençon.* ca.1730. str. rep. al. c.secs. watch desc. by Thiout.
BIDAULT—
Claude. *Paris.* 1628. d.1652. C. to Louis XIII and XIV.
Henri Auguste. *Paris.* 1641-86. C. to Louis XIV, appointed 1652.
Augustin François. *Paris.* 1687-1718. d. before 1727. C. to Louis XIV.
BIDDELL, ——. *London.* ca.1800. br. clock.
BIDDLE—
Joseph. *London.* CC.1684-1705.
Henry. *London.* an.1761. Watch. l.c. clock.
Owen. *Philadelphia.* 1764. d.1799.
John. *London.* a.1762.
BIDDLECOMBE—
Thomas. *Stourton Caundle.* 1720. C.
William. *Stourton Caundle.* 1750. C.
BIDERMAN, Jean Marc André. *Geneva.* ca.1770-91.
BIDLAKE—
James. *London (Minories).* an.1762-95. C. & W.
James, son. *London (Sun St.* and *Chiswell St.).* a.1772, CC.1779-1825.
Thomas. *London (Minories).* 1792. Watch.
Thomas, son. *London.* a.1792, CC.1809-18.
James. *London.* a.1800-35. In partnership with following as J. & J. H. BIDLAKE.
James Hodgson. *London (Chiswell St.).* a.1801, CC.1809, l.CC.1818.
James, & Son. *London (Chiswell St.).* 1820-1840.
BIEGEL, Henry W. *Philadelphia.* 1813.
BIELAUSCHEK, Franciscus. ——. ca.1700. Table clock.
BIELER, ——. *Bienne.* ca.1790. cal. watch mt. S.M.S.K.
BIENTOURNÉ, ——. *Paris.* 1812.
BIERFELDER—
Erasmus. *Steppach.* 1756-70.
Joseph, son. *Augsburg.* 1791. comp. in *Steppach* ca.1783.
BIESTA, Jean. *Paris.* m.1759-89.
BIGARD—
——. *Paris.* 1735 m.
Jean Noel. *Paris.* m.1743.
BIGG, Benjamin. *London.* a.1678.
BIGGEN (BIGGIN)—
——. *London (Westminster Bridg Rd.).* 1805-08.
William. *London (Lambeth).* 1809-11.
BIGGER—
Gilbert. *Dublin.* 1783. *Baltimore, U.S.A.*, in partnership with CLARKE for one year, then alone until 1807.
& CLARKE. *Baltimore, U.S.A.* 1784. From *Dublin.* C. & W.
William. *Baltimore.* 1802.
BIGGS—
Edward or Edmond. *London.* a.1695.
John. *London.* a.1714.
William. *London.* a.1771.
Richard. *Salisbury, Romsey* and *London.* 1776 insolvent in London. Back in *London* ca.1800. CC.
BIGNEL—
Richard. *London.* CC.1719.
Richard. *London.* a.1717.
BIGNELL—
Thomas. *London.* a.1769.
Charles. *London.* a.1818.
BIGOT, ——. *Rouen.* Juré 1777.
BIGRAVE, John. *London.* Early 19c. Watch.
BILAN, Jean. *Paris.* 1780 comp.
BILBIE—
Thomas. *Bristol.* 1768.
Thomas. *Chewstoke.* 1774. l.c. clock.
John. *Oxbridge.* b.1734, d.1767.
Edward. *Chewstoke.* an.1785. Watch.
BILCLIFF (BYCLIFF)—
John. *York.* 1617. 'Clocksmith.'
Robert. *York.* 1627. W.
John, son of John. *York.* 1639. W.
Robert, son of Robert. *York.* 1653. C.
BILDSTEIN, ——. *Önnestad, Kristianstad.* 18c. l.c. clock.
BILL—
Thomas. *London.* 1758. Bankrupt. W.
John. *Doncaster.* ca.1770.
BILLARD, ——. *Marseilles.* an.1762. Watch.
BILLE, John. *London.* CC.1687-99. W.
BILLÉ, Isaïe. *Lyons.* 1657 comp.
BILLETER, Albert. *Chaux-de-Fonds.* 1815. d.1895. Also *Italy, Spain* and *Paris.* Made complex clocks; in 1840 a l.c. clock going 250 days, showing mean and sidereal time, equation, days, months, years, moon and signs of zodiac.
BILLIÉ, Jean. *Grenoble.* 1680.
BILLINGE—
Charles. *Liverpool.* 1774-84. W.
Topham. *Liverpool.* 1790-6. W.
James. *Liverpool.* 1795. W.
William. *Liverpool.* 1796-1824.
BILLINGER (BELLINGER), John. *London.* CC.1637.
BILLINGHAM, Robert. *London.* a.1735.
BILLINGHURST—
William. *London.* a.1668 CC.
Anthony. *London.* a.1672, CC.1681.
William. *London.* a.1694.
Henry. *London (Aldersgate St.).* a.1749, CC.1757, l.CC.1766, d.1777.
BILLINGS, ——. *London.* an.1766. Watch.
Joseph. *Reading, Penna.* 1770. C.
BILLINGTON—
Joseph. *Chester.* 1670. C.
Robert. *London.* a.1735 CC.1742-59.

BILLON—
Charles, & Co. *Philadelphia.* 1796.
Charles. *Philadelphia.* 1802-19.
BILLOP, William. *London.* a.1681. CC.1688.
BILLOT (BILLOD, BILODET), Abraham. *Val de Morteau.* 1648. Made clock for Dole.
BILLOW, Charles, & Co. *Boston, U.S.A.* 1796.
BILSON, William. *London.* a.1783.
BIMSON, Laurence. *Prescot.* 1795. Watch toolmaker.
BINCH—
Thomas. *Mansfield.* 1737. l.c. clock.
James. *Liverpool.* 1777-81. C.
BINDER, Joh. Vinz. *Vienna.* Early 19c. en. watch in form of violin.
BINDITH, S. P. *Mainz.* 1st half 18c. Watch N.Y. Univ.
BINDLEY, John. *London.* a.1674.
BINET—
Pierre. *Niort.* ca.1575.
Antoine, son. *Blois.* mar. 1609, d. an.1616.
Abraham Gédéon. *Geneva.* b.1725, d.1800. Invented a wheelcutting machine.
BINÉTRUY, Charles. *Paris.* 1807-25.
BING—
Thomas. *London.* an.1761-ca.1785. Dutch type watch Glasgow Art Gall.
John. *Ramsgate.* d.1790 CC.
BINGHAM & BRICERLY. *Philadelphia.* 1778-99.
BINGLEY—
Giles. *London.* a.1692. Bankrupt 1720.
John. *London.* an.1769. Watch.
——. *London* (*Clerkenwell*). 1778.
Thomas. *London* (*Golden Lane*). 1799. W.
Thomas. *London* (*Bunhill Row*). 1805-08. W.
BINKS—
Thomas. *Birmingham.* ca.1740.
——. *London.* ca.1820. Watch mt. G.M.
BINLEY, J. W. *London.* 1790.
BINNY (BINNIE)—
Daniel. *Edinburgh.* a.1747-79. Succeeds his uncle And. Dickie in 1765.
& Gordon. *Edinburgh.* 1774.
BION, Nicolas. *Paris.* b.1652, d.1733. Famous math. inst. maker, and pub. book on inst. in 1725.
BIRCH—
Thomas. *London.* a.1649, CC.1658-1724. Lantern clock.
Thomas. *London.* a.1675, CC.1682.
Samuel. *London.* a.1715.
Richard. *Birmingham.* 1776-87. l.c. clock.
John. *London.* a.1782.
Humphrey. *Hoddesdon.* 1793-7. W.
John. *London* (*Islington*). 1805-08.
Joseph. *Liverpool.* 1805. W.
James. *Liverpool.* 1811-29. W.
BIRCHALL—
& Harper. *London.* an.1732. Watch.
& Son. *Warrington.* ca.1770-95. C. & W.
M. *Derby.* 1770-90. Watch Den. coll.
Joshua. *Liverpool.* 1781-7. W.
Thomas. *Nantwich.* 1784. br. clock.
George. *Warrington.* an.1793-ca.1820. Watch.
William. *Liverpool.* 1796. W.
William. *London* (*Hatton Garden*). 1799-1808. W.
William. *London* (*Clerkenwell*). 1809-24. W.
George. *Warrington.* ca.1820. Watch mt.
BIRCHOLL, ——. *Shrewsbury.* an.1774. Watch.
BIRD—
Michael. *Oxford* and *London.* a.1648, CC. 1682-1713. br. clock. Issued token coins in Oxford in 1668.
William. *London.* a.1667.
John. *Belfast.* 1667. C.

BIRD—*continued.*
Luke. *London* (*Old Bailey*). a.1675, CC. 1683-1705.
Edward. *London.* 1684. C.
William. *London.* a.1696.
Nathaniel. *London.* CC.1693. l.c. clock.
Thomas. *London.* a.1721. Watch.
William. *London.* a.ca.1726, CC.ca.1749.
Samuel. *London.* a.1740.
Luke. *London.* 1750 CC.
William. *Faversham.* 1752. From London. W.
John. *London.* 1765. Expert at examination of Harrison's chron.
William. *London.* 1769. Insolvent. W.
William. *Seagrave.* an.1778. Watch.
William. *London.* 1785 CC. Watch.
Richard. *London.* 1790.
Edward. *Bristol.* 1791-1818. Succeeded Joseph Wood. W. br. clock ill. Cec. & Web.
John. *Amersham.* ca.1800 CC. From *London.*
Samuel Joseph. *London.* CC.1813.
Samuel Joseph, son. *London.* a.1822.
Charles. *Liverpool.* 1818-29.
BIRDSELL, ——. *London.* an.1742. Watch.
BIRDWHISTELL—
Francis. *London.* a.1675, CC.1687-93.
James. *London.* a.1682.
Isaac. *London.* a.1682, CC.1692-1725. Fine watch.
Thomas, bro. of Francis. *London.* 1689. CC. 1694-1702.
John. *London.* a.1711, CC.1718.
BIRGE, John. *Bristol, U.S.A.* 1812, d.1862.
BIRKHEAD—
John. *London.* a.1722.
Charles. *London.* a.1754.
Worthley. *Shoreditch.* 1796. Watch.
Peter, son. *London.* a.1796. Watch.
BIRLEY—
John. *Sheffield.* ca.1700. Watch mt. Huddersfield M.
Samuel. *Birmingham.* Early 19c. Watch.
BIRNEY, A. G. *Barbadoes.* Early 19c.
BIRNIE—
William. *Templepatrick* and *Dublin.* ca.1750-1767. Also Birney.
Laurence, son. a. to his father, then *Philadelphia.* 1774.
John. *Templepatrick.* 2nd half 18c. l.c. clocks.
BISBEE, J. *Brunswick, U.S.A.* 1798-1825.
BISHOP—
John. *Maidstone.* ca.1650. Lantern clock.
John. *London.* a.1700.
John. *London.* a.1720.
Samuel. *London.* an.1730. Watch.
John. *Deptford.* 1748. Bankrupt. W.
John. *London.* a.1747.
Samuel. *London.* 1769. CC.1781-1808.
Thomas. *London.* 2nd half 18c. Watch mt.
George. *Redmile.* an.1789. Watch.
James. *Musselburgh.* 1787.
James. *Edinburgh.* 1794.
James. *London* (*Fetter Lane*). 1809-11.
Thomas. *London.* a.1808, CC.1816.
Robert. *London.* a.1809.
Thomas. *London.* CC.1815, 1.CC.1818.
James Griffin. *London.* 1815-24.
John. *Sherborne.* Early 19c. Watch.
& Bradley. *Plymouth, U.S.A.* 1825-30.
BISLETT, ——. *Wincanton.* Early 19c. Watch.
BISSAC, Nicolas. *Geneva.* 1562. 'Tourneur et horlogeur'; refugee from *Burgundy.*
BISSE, Edward. *London.* CC.1632. Table clock with al. above S.K.M. Prob. same as Bysse.
BISSET—
——. *London.* 1742. Watch.

BISSET—*continued.*
David. *Perth.* an.1764-5. Watch.
William. *Dundee.* 1781.
William. *Perth.* 1808.
BISSETT, James. *London.* CC.1815-24. Watch.
BISSON—
François Bourgeois. *Paris.* m.1775-89.
Louis Pierre. *Paris.* Juré 1786-1809. Mantel clock, marble and ormolu.
BISTRUP, Christian. *Bornholm.* Late 18c.
BITEROST, Heinrich. *Basle.* 1670.
BITTLESTON, John. *London.* 1765. CC. 1781-94. Astro. watch Den. coll.
BIXLER, Christian. *Easton, U.S.A.* 1785-1830. Reputed maker of 8-day clocks.
BIZET, Jean Auguste. *Paris.* m.1787. Watch mt. G.M.
BIZONVAL, ——. *Paris.* 1819.
BIZOT, Étienne François. *Geneva.* ca.1770-1791.
BJÖRKDAHL, Jon. Dan. *Västerås.* b.1764, d.1810.
BJÖRKHOLM, Lars. *Köping,* 1750-3; *Nyköping,* 1754.
BJÖRKLING, Anders. *By, Dalarne.* End 18c. l.c. clock.
BJÖRKMAN—
Peter. *Västerås.* 1750. inst. maker.
Lars. *Västerås.* 1750. inst. maker.
P. *Kristianstad.* Early 19c. Wall clock.
BJÖLIN, Pehr. *Falun.* 1794.
BJÖRNBERG, Benjamin. *Stockholm.* 1815. Watch.
BJURMAN, Adolph Frederic. *Norrköping.* b.1743, d.1812. Wall and br. and trav. clock. 2 watches.
BJURQVIST, Hans. *Göteborg.* b.1750, d.1810.
BLAAMAN, Frans Ludvig. *Bornholm* and *Copenhagen.* m.1799.
BLACK—
James. *Dublin.* an.1772. Watch.
John. *Edinburgh.* a.1771-7.
William. *London* (*Wapping*). an.1773-1808. W.
James Henry. *London.* a.1802.
Andrew. *Glasgow.* 1818.
James. *Kirkcaldy.* 1820-37.
George. *Lurgan.* Early 19c. Watch.
M. *Calcutta.* Early 19c.
BLACKBOROW, James. *London.* a.1701, CC.1711, w.CC. and d.1746. g. p.c. repoussé watch Carnegie M.
BLACKBOURNE, William. *London.* a.1731, CC.1739-50.
BLACKBURN—
Robert. *London.* CC.1720.
James. *Prescot.* d.1774. Watch wheel finisher.
Richard. *London.* an.1757. Watch.
Ralph. *London.* an.1778. Watch.
William. *London* (*Shoe Lane*). CC.1768-75.
William. *London.* CC.1786, l.CC. 1787, d.1817.
Thomas. *London* (*Little Britain*). an.1770. CC.1799, l.CC.1812. Watch.
Robert. *London.* a.1796.
William, son of Thos. *London.* a.1807.
Robert. *Liverpool.* 1817-29. W.
Thomas. *Liverpool.* 1818. W.
John. *Liverpool.* 1821-9. W.
BLACKETER, Peter. *London.* CC.1786.
BLACKETT, John. *London.* l.CC.1809-23.
BLACKFORD, John. *London.* a.1770.
BLACKHAM, George. *Newry.* 1820-4.
BLACKHURST, J. *Weaverham.* Early 19c. Watch.
BLACKIE—
George. *Musselburgh.* 1795-1844. l.c. clock.
George. *London.* b.1813, d.1885. Watch and marine chron. G.M.

BLACKMORE—
John. *London.* a.1688.
John. *Rochester.* 1716. W.
William. *London.* an.1745. Watch.
Thomas. *London.* a.1755.
James. *Sidmouth.* 1795. l.c. clock. Watch.
Thomas. *Liverpool.* ca.1820.
BLACKSHAW, John. *London.* a.1740.
BLACKWELL—
John. *London.* a.1720.
J. *London.* 1820. W. en. telescope watch.
BLACKWOOD—
Thomas. *Kinnoul.* 1798.
William. *N. Shields.* 1820-7. l.c. clocks.
BLAESLI, Christian. *Chur, Basle.* 1673.
BLAGBURN, John. *Durham.* 1812.
BLAGROVE, Henry. *London.* an.1728. Watch.
BLAIKIE, William. *Edinburgh.* 1726.
BLAIN, Jaques François. *Geneva.* ca.1770-91.
BLAINVILLE, ——. *Rouen.* End 18c. Watch M.M.A.
BLAIR—
Thomas. *Perth.* 1746.
Andrew. *Edinburgh.* a.1775.
BLAKAY, Guillaume. *Paris.* m.1750.
BLAKE—
Jonas. *London.* a.1702.
Charles. *Salisbury.* an.1737. Watch.
Caleb. *London.* an.1762. Watch.
James. *London.* an.1768. Watch.
John. *Croydon.* 1767-84. W.
William. *London.* an.1769-1808. W.
Jonathan. *Fulham.* 1758-1808. Watch.
James. *London.* a.1794.
Joseph. *Bristol.* 1825.
BLAKEBOROUGH—
Henry. *Burnley.* ca.1820.
——. *Keighley.* Early 19c. Watch Horstmann coll.
William. *Pately Bridge.* Early 19c. Watch S.K.M.
BLAKECRUM, ——. *London.* 1743. Watch.
BLAKELEY, George. *Liverpool.* 1816. W.
BLAKEWAY—
Thomas. *Rushbury.* 1766. C.
Charles. *Albrighton.* 1774-95. C. & W. 'Wheels cut for clockmakers at 6*d.* per set and Dyal Plates engraved at 2*s.*6*d.* each.'
Thomas. *Wenlock.* 1795. C. & W.
BLAKEY, William. *London.* a.1701. *Paris.* 1774-55. Granted an exclusive privilege to make and sell pinion steel in France, promising to sell at one-third less than English steel. Wrote an account of springmaking pub. Amsterdam 1780.
BLANC (LE BLANC)—
Jean. *Lyons.* 1610. comp.
Denis. *Montpellier* (*Blois*). 1619-22.
Jean. *Geneva.* mar. ca.1745-70.
Père et fils. *Geneva.* Late 18c. g. en. watch S.K.M.
Isaac. *Geneva.* ca.1800. Painter on enamel.
Lewis. *Philadelphia.* 1810. W.
Célestin fils. *Couvet.* Early 19c. Exported clocks to Italy.
Fils. *Paris.* Late 18c. Watch. br. clock with watch mt. Furt M.
Fils aîné. *Paris* (*Rue St. Honoré*). 1807-09.
Fils. *Paris* (*Palais Royal*). 1807-25.
——. *Paris* (*Rue des Vieux Augustins*). 1810-1813.
J. B. *Paris* (*Rue Quinquempoix*). 1823.
ET DE RIAZ. *Paris.* 1825.
BLANCHARD—
Charles. *London.* b.1688, d.1768. C.
Abraham. *London.* an.1744. Watch.
——. *Geneva.* 1800. Singing birds.
William. *Hull.* 1822-36.
BLANCHER, James. *Attleborough.* an.1774-1791. Watch. l.c. clock.

BLANCHET—
André. *Orléans.* 1600.
Guy, son. *Blois.* comp. 1619. d.ca.1625.
BLANCHETON, Jean. *Lyons.* 1607. d. between 1629 and 1636. oct. sil. watch Reichenberg M.
BLANCHIN—
Zacarie Nicolas. *Paris.* m.1735.
Louis. *Paris.* m.1738.
BLANCHON—
Pierre. *Rouen.* m.1696.
Hélie, son. *Rouen.* m.1696.
BLANCKEN, Thomas Hermann. *Brunswick.* 1534. 'Seigermacher.'
BLANCMAVY, ——. *Paris.* 1814.
BLANCPAIN, Frédéric le jeune. *Villeret.* End 18c. Founded a business still existing.
BLANCPIGNON, Antoine. *Lyons.* 1630-31. Also BLANPIGNON.
BLAND—
John. *London.* a.1714. Watch.
Thomas. *London.* an.1755. Watch.
——. *Howden (Yorks.).* ca.1770-95. W.
B. *Reading.* an.1785. Watch.
BLANDFORD—
G. *Buckingham.* an.1773. Watch.
Thomas. *London.* a.1776.
BLANDY—
James. *London.* 1758. Watch Horstmann coll.
William. *London.* a.1803.
BLANFORD, George. *London.* a.1783.
BLANK—
Franz Benno. *Steppach,* 1770. *Augsburg,* 1786.
Alf. *Cannstätt.* Early 19c. g. en. lute watch Fränkel coll.
BLANVALET, ——. *Geneva.* ca.1800.
BLASER—
Mathys. *Berne.* 1712. Repaired clock on Zeitglockenturm.
Christ. *Boveresse.* 1749. C.
Jean Louis. *Boveresse.* a.1749.
Louis. *St. Imier.* ca.1792.
BLASSER, Johann Ignati. *Augsburg.* m.1786-1795.
BLATTER—
Pierre. *Chaux-de-Fonds.* 1779-1803. C.
Joseph. *Berlin.* 1794.
BLATTET, Daniel Samuel. *Paris.* m.1766.
BLAVET, ——. *Paris.* ca.1810. Bronze worker. Made clock cases.
BLAYLOCK—
John. *Longtown.* 1791. C.
John. *Carlisle.* Early 19c.
J. & W. *Carlisle.* 1820. l.c. clock.
BLAZE, John. *London.* a.1714.
BLEAK, John. *London.* an.1776. Watch.
BLECKE (BLECHE or BLICK)—
Johan Heinrich. *Copenhagen.* comp. 1709, m.1712-28. From *Westphalia.* Turret C.
Franz Henrik. *Copenhagen.* m.1740.
BLED, ——. *Paris.* 1812-25. Mantel clock.
BLEEKE, Joseph. *London.* a.1695.
BLENHAM, William. *London.* End 18c. en. watch.
BLENKINSOP, ——. *N. Shields.* an.1780. Watch.
BLESSING, Martin. *Moscow,* 1809. *Furtwangen,* 1814. b.1774, d.1847. Famous mus. C.
BLETHIN, William. *Pembroke.* 1795. C.
BLEW, William. *London.* an.1769. Watch.
BLIGH, John. *London.* 1783. p.c. watch G.M.
BLIN, Julien. *Paris.* m.1775-89.
BLINCO, Richard. *London.* a.1716.
BLINKER, Thomas. *London.* ca.1770. l.c. clock ill. Cec. & Web.
BLINKHORNE, Thomas. *London.* a.1729.
BLINKO—
John. *London.* a.1811, CC.1819.
William. *London.* a.1814.
BLINMAN—
Thomas. *Bristol.* 1807.
Thomas, & Co. *Bristol.* 1818-30. C.
BLINTSCH, Gottfried. *Basle.* 1769.
BLISS, Ambrose. *London.* CC.1653-61.
BLISSET—
James. *London.* a.1770.
Isaac. *London.* 1820.
BLITHE, James. *London.* ca.1760. Watch mt. Buckley coll.
BLOCHET, ——. *Paris.* ca.1710. sil. rep. watch.
BLOCK, Francis. *London.* a.1689.
BLÖDERL (BLÄDERL, PLÖTTERL), Frantz. *Vienna.* m.1764.
BLODWELL, Thomas. *London.* a.1719.
BLOIS, Alexandre. *Paris.* m.1683.
BLOMBERG—
Martin. *Stockholm.* d.1690. Court C. br. clock.
Mathias. *Gäfle.* 1750-4.
Anders M. *Stockholm.* 1811-20. Rack clock and wall clock.
BLOMQUIST, Fredric. *Åbo.* b.1740, m.1766, d.1796. Wall clocks and watches.
BLOND, Charles. *Dieppe.* 18c. Ivory dials B.M. and Ilbert coll. Compass.
BLONDEAU, ——. *Paris.* 1815. C.
BLONDEL—
Paul. *Amsterdam.* 1686. Huguenot refugee from *Châlons.*
Nicolas. *Paris.* m.1743-89.
ET MELLY. *Geneva.* Early 19c. g. en. watch M.M.A.
BLONNAY, ——. *Paris.* ca.1800. g. en. watch.
BLOODWORTH, John. *London.* a.1758.
BLOOMER, Lewen. *London.* a.1714.
BLOOMHALL, Charles. *London.* 1799.
BLOS, L. *Frankfort.* 2nd half 18c. 4-colour gold watch set pearls.
BLOWERS—
Edward. *Beccles.* 2nd half 18c. l.c. clocks.
Isaac. *Beccles.* 2nd half 18c. l.c. clocks.
BLOWSKI, Elias. *Lumensteira.* 1568. Circ. table clock with al. above, Nat. M. Prague.
BLUCK, W. *London.* 1779-ca.1800. Dissolved partnership with James YOUNG in 1779.
BLUDWICK—
John. *London.* a.1722.
Henry. *London.* a.1726.
BLUEMCKE, Johan Georg. *Copenhagen.* m.1756. From *Königsberg.*
BLUKAERT, Jean François. *Paris.* m.1746.
BLUMB, Joseph. *'Germaine.'* Late 18c. Watch M.M.A.
BLUMFIELD, John. *Norwich.* 1782. d.1815. CC.
BLÜMMER, Heinrich. *Leipzig.* 1800.
BLUMMINGER, Wilhelm. *Nürnberg.* Burgher in 1564.
BLUNDELL—
John. *London (Greenwich).* a.1678-ca.1730. CC. br. and l.c. clock. Also BLAUNDEL.
Richard. *London.* CC.1682-1717.
Joseph. *Dublin.* 1703. d.1732.
William. *London.* a.1706, CC.1716.
Thomas. *Dublin.* 1733. d.1775. Watch Belfast M.
Thomas. *Dublin.* 1766-1824.
Thomas. *Liverpool.* 1818-36. W.
BLUNDY—
Charles. *Charleston, U.S.A.* 1760. From *London.* W.
Joseph. *London.* a.1772-95.
BLUNSCHI, Wolfgang. *Zug.* b.1703, d.1734.
BLUNT—
——. *London.* 1744. Watch.

BLUNT—*continued.*
Edward. *London (Islington).* a.1752, CC. 1763-1815.
Samuel Corbit, son. *London.* a.1781-1811.
John. *London (Hoxton).* 1824.

BLÜNTZEL, ——. *Oberhausen.* 1756 comp.

BLUXOME, Isaac. *Liverpool.* ca.1820.

BLY, Christopher. *London.* 1744. W.

BLYTH, Robert. *London.* a.1790.

BOAD—
Thomas. *London.* a.1684, CC.1692-4.
Thomas, son. *London.* CC.1744-72.

BOARDMAN—
& DUNBAR. *Bristol, U.S.A.* 1811.
Chauncey. *Bristol, U.S.A.* 1813-45. Wooden wall clocks and, later, brass shelf clocks.
& WELLS. *Bristol, U.S.A.* 1815.

BOBERG—
Henric. *Skeninge.* ca.1800. trav. clock.
Henric. *Örebro.* 1810. d.1821.

BOBILIER, ——. *Besançon.* 1703. Several br. clocks of poor quality.

BOBINET—
Père Pierre. *France.* b.1593-1654. Author of works on dialling.
Abraham. *Paris.* Prob. son. 1630-60. crys. cross watch M.M.A.
Charles, son of Pierre. *Paris.* ca.1650. en. watch crys. cover M.M.A. crys. and sil. cross watch S.K.M. circ. crys. watch S.K.M. crys. watch F.W.M. crys. watch B.M. ill. Baillie. sil. skull watch Bernal sale. Fine en. watch. Basle M. crys. cross watch Gélis coll.

BOCHARD, ——. *Compiègne.* 1426. Keeper of clock on St. Jacques.

BOCHERON, J. *Autun.* ca.1600.

BOCK—
Albrecht. *Frankfort.* m.1599. Very fine book watch Städtische Historische M.
Johann. *Frankfort.* 1640. Oval watch M.M.A. circ. watches B.M., S.K.M. and M.P.S. Dresden. Clock K.H.M.

BÖCK—
Johann. *Vienna.* m.1797.
Martin. *Vienna.* m.1812.

BOCKAU, B. F. *Stockholm.* 1787. 2 watches.

BOCKELTS (BOCKEL, BOEKETT), Mathys. *Haarlem.* 1610-ca.1630. Oval watch S.K.M. crys. watch Ilbert coll.
Jan, Janns or Jansen. *The Hague, Aachen* and *Amsterdam.* 1607-ca.1640. Watches B.M. and Stern coll. Fine eng. oval watch with sundial, Mallett coll.

BOCKETT, Richard. *London.* 1712. l.c. clock. Watch.

BOCKH, Josephus. *Lintz.* ca.1720. Rep. watch Ilbert coll.

BOCKSTÖRER, Conrad Eberhard. *Berlin.* 1794.

BOCKSTÖVER, J. H. *Hamburg.* 1801.

BOCQUET—
Claude. *Rouen.* m.1658. Prob. of same family as BOQUET and BOUQUET.
Jean. *Paris.* m.1780-9.

BODDIMAN, William. *London.* a.1750.

BODDINGTON—
John. *London.* a.1726, CC.1734.
John. *London.* a.1725.
William. *London.* a.1758.

BODDLE, Jonah. *London.* a.1730, CC.1741.

BODE, William. *Philadelphia.* 1796-1806. W.

BODEKER, Jost. *Warburg.* 1587. d. prob. after 1626. Made clock for Osnabrück Dom with foliot and, as alternative, a device which probably was a conical pendulum.

BODENHAM, Edward. *London.* a.1709, CC. 1719. Bankrupt 1725. Transported for theft 1735. Watch mt.

BODHAM, Stephen. *London.* a.1680 CC.

BODILY—
Elizabeth. *London.* a.1683, CC.1692.
N. *London.* 1825. W. & C.

BODIN, ——. *Angers.* 1729. Restored clock on cathedral.

BODKIN, John. *Donaghadee.* 1824.

BODLE—
Nicholas. *East Grinstead.* 1714.
Charles. *East Grinstead.* a.1714.
——. *Westerham.* an.1771. Watch.

BODMER—
Johann George. *Dresden.* m.1710. From *Freiberg.*
Johannes. *Basle.* 1752. From *Zürich.*

BODOT, Pul. *Paris.* 1650.

BODY—
John or Robert. *London.* a.1715.
Obadiaha. *Battle.* a.1716-31.
Abraham. *Battle.* 1763. C. & W.
Abraham. *Cranbrook.* an.1774. Watch.
Henry. *Battle.* 1791. C.

BOETTCHER, A. *Dantzig.* 1741. Carillon for St. Katharinenkirche.

BOFENSCHEIN, ——. *Paris.* 1807-13. aut. and mus. clocks.

BOGARDUS, Everardus. *New York.* 1698.

BÖGLE, Joseph. *Augsburg.* 1759. comp.

BOGNER, Joseph Benedikt. *Augsburg.* m.1769-99.

BOHEMUS, Chasparus. *Vienna.* 1568. Table clock M.M.A.

BÖHM—
Jacob. *Vienna.* m.1668. Also BÖHEIMB.
Marcus. *Augsburg.* Juré 1702. d.ca.1726. Fine table clock ill. Britten. Wall clock Ilbert coll.

BOHNE, Hans. *Hagen (Brunswick).* 1595. From *Nürnberg.*

BÖHRINGER, Jakob Traugott. *Dresden.* b.1820, d.1901. Eminent maker.

BOICERVOISE (BOISERVOISE)—
——. *Paris.* 1811-16.
Fils. *Paris.* 1821-5. Successor.

BOIFFLER, ——. *London.* ca.1800. mus. l.c. clock.

BOILE, Patrick. *Tuam.* 1824.

BOILEAU—
J. *Edinburgh.* an.1780. Watch.
——. *Paris.* 1811-25.

BOILLAT—
——. *Soleure.* ca.1800. Watch Chamberlain coll.
——. *Aux Breuleux.* ca.1800. Watch Ilbert coll.

BOILLON—
Jean. *Montbéliard.* 1598. d.an.1603. From *Lyons.* Also BOUILLON.
Claude Ignace. *Morteau.* 1779-91. Turret clocks.

BOILTEUX, ——. *Paris.* 1821.

BOIMOND, Fs. Pre. *Carouge.* ca.1780.

BOIS, Balthazar. *Cologne.* 1604.

BOIS-DE-CHESNE, John Francis. *Charleston, U.S.A.* 1750. From *London.* C. & W.

BOISGOUTIER—
Jean Denis. *Paris.* m.1750.
——. *Paris.* 1822.

BOISLANDON, ——. *Metz.* Early 17c. Watch École d'horlogerie, Geneva.

BOISSEAUX, René Hubert. *Paris.* m.1756.

BOISSON—
Etinne. *London.* ca.1700. Watch Webster coll. Watch, wandering hour figure, Den. coll.
M. *London.* ca.1750. Watches M.M.A. and Den. coll. g. en. watch set stones Stern coll.
Marc François. *Geneva.* 1770-98 juré.

BOISTOUT, ——. *Hüningen.* ca.1820. Ilbert coll.

BOITEAU, S. *Paris.* 1695. Watch Den. coll.

BOITISSANDEAU, ——. *France.* Early 18c. Devised a repeating mechanism for clocks separable from the mt.
BOIZARD, Gerard Urbain. *Paris.* m.1781.
BOIZOT, ——. *Paris.* ca.1775. Bronze worker. Made clock cases.
BOLD—
T. *Warrington.* an.1762. d.1795.
John. *Warrington.* an.1769-95. Watch.
William. *Prescot.* an.1785. d.1797. Watch.
Matthew. *Prescot.* 1795. Watch tool-maker.
John. *Liverpool.* 1818-24. W.
George. *Liverpool.* 1825. W.
Joshua. *Liverpool.* 1825. W.
BOLEY, Richard. *London.* 1729. Insolvent.
BOLLIER, ——. *Paris.* an.1774. Watch.
BOLLAND, John Henry. *London.* a.1821.
BÖLLER, Joseph. *Würzburg.* m.1727. W.
BOLLERMANN—
Georg. *Würzburg.* m.1782. W.
Caspar. *Würzburg.* a.1785, m.1796. W.
Adam, son of Georg. *Würzburg.* m.1814. W.
Friedrich, bro. *Würzburg.* m.1823. W.
BOLLES, ——. *Berlin.* 1812.
BOLLOGNIEL (BOLOGNIEL), ——. *Paris.* 1811-24.
BOLTON—
John. *Chester-le-Street* and *Durham.* b.1761, d.1821. l.c., br., inn and turret clocks. Watch.
Thomas. *Manchester.* an.1791. Watch.
BOLUMEY, ——. *Paris.* an.1762. Watch.
BOMAN—
Hans. *Gäfle.* m.1780, d.an.1805. Watch.
Anders, son. *Gäfle.* 1808-25.
BOMMEL (POMMEL)—
Melchior. *Nürnberg.* Burgher in 1642.
Johann Melchior, son. *Nürnberg.* b.1644, d.1719. Watch Feill coll.
Leonhard. *Nürnberg.* ca.1720. Watch Stuttgart M. Watch with secs. dial Munich M.
BOMPARD, ——. *Paris.* ca.1800. Table clock mt. G.M.
BON—
Jean François. *Dijon.* 1430. In charge of clock of Notre Dame; added half hour striking.
Philippe. *Geneva.* 1557. Refugee from *Lorraine.*
Jonas. *Coffrane.* 1751. C.
Jean. *Coffrane.* 1787-90. C.
BONANDREA, Nicolò di. *Fabiano.* 1443. Keeper of Spezzia clock.
BONARD, ——. *Romainmôtier.* 1758. Started a watch factory with Ador at *Berne* with loan from the town. Failed in 1762, and factory taken over by Michod. cf. Christian.
BONATERRE, Jean. *Paris.* 1786.
BONBRUICT, Jean. *Blois.* 1632. d.1678. Trav. clock Ilbert coll.
BOND—
Thomas. *London.* a.1685-9 CC.
J. *London.* an.1775. Watch.
J. *York.* an.1775. Watch.
Thomas. *London.* an.1780. Watch.
Richard. *Bilston.* 1791. C. & W.
William. *Boston, U.S.A.* 1793-1809. Wall clocks. Made first American chron. 1812.
William, & Son. *Boston, U.S.A.* 1813. The firm still exists as chron. makers.
H. *Cirencester.* Early 19c. Watch.
Charles. *Boston, U.S.A.* 1825.
'Bond St.' Sig. on watches of the American Watch Co. from 1886; predecessor of the Waltham Watch Co.
BONDU, ——. *Paris.* 1789.
BONE, William. *Essex.* ca.1790.
BONELLI, Pamfilio. *Rome.* 1590. C. to Sixtus v.
BONES, Thomas. *Maldon.* an.1758. Watch.
BONET, Joseph. *London.* CC.1719.
BONEY, *v.* Bonny.
BONFANTI, Joseph. *New York.* 1823.
BONFILS, David. *Geneva.* ca.1770-91.
BONFLEUR, Andrew. *London.* CC.1804.
BONHÖFER, Joseph. *Hagen (Brunswick).* 1593.
BONIN, Jean. *La Rochelle.* 1690. d.1692. C. to town.
BONIUS, Johannes. *Holland.* ca.1600. Dial and astrolabe Miller coll.
BONNA Frères. *Geneva.* Late 18c. and early 19c. Fine g. en. lyre watch.
BONNAR—
Robert. *Dunfermline.* 1733.
Mrs. *Edinburgh.* 1802.
BONNAUD, ——. *Philadelphia.* 1799.
BONNEFOY, ——. *London.* 1723. Watch.
BØNNELØCKE, Jeppe Larsen. *Copenhagen.* m.1766.
BONNER—
Charles. *London.* a.1650, CC.1659, d.1682. Watch.
Jasper, son. *London.* a.1681, CC.1688.
Charles. *London.* a.1691-1715 CC.
Jasper. *London.* CC.1704.
Charles. *London.* a.1693, CC.1705-17. l.c. clock Weth. coll. sd. 'Bonnor.'
Thomas. *London.* 1729. Insolvent.
John. *London (Aldersgate St.).* 1744. W.
Joseph. *London.* an.1765. Watch.
Thomas. *London.* 1784-90.
BONNET—
André. *Paris.* m.1788.
Élie. *Geneva.* Early 19c.
J. P. *Geneva.* 1825. Watch.
BONNEUX or **BONNEUIE,** C. *Paris.* 1640. Watch en. by Vauquer, Bernal sale. Watch F.W.M.
BONNEY, Thomas. *London (Horsleydown).* 1802-24.
BONNICK, William. *London.* a.1771.
BONNIER, Amy. ——. Mid. 18c. Watch mt. Arts M. Prague.
BONNY—
——. *London.* 1790-1820. rep. c.secs. watch.
Caleb. *Padstow.* 1791-ca.1810 C. Also Boney.
BONS, Simon Peter. *London.* 1797. W.
BONTÉ—
Charles Frédéric. *Copenhagen.* m.1761-72. Court C. From *Paris.*
Laurens. *Haarlem.* 1785.
BONTEMPS—
——. *Paris.* 1812-24.
Blaise. *Paris.* 1868. Manufactured singing birds.
BONUS, Simon Peter. *London.* a.1781, CC. 1790-1808.
BONVALLET, Louis Antoine. *Paris.* m.1756-1808.
BONYER, Peter. *London.* ca.1775. mus. br. clock Virginia M.
BOOKER—
Richard. *London.* CC.1694-9.
Thomas. *London (Grub St.).* a.1752, CC. 1759-75.
Nugent. *Dublin.* 1774-80. l.c. clock.
Thomas. *Liverpool.* 1805. W.
BOOKLESS, Peter. *Edinburgh.* 1798.
BOOLE, Jonathan. *London.* a.1676.
BOONE, Edward. *London.* a.1681, CC.1691-1693. Watch.
BOOSEY—
John. *London (King St.).* CC.1773-89.
Thomas, son. *London (Broad St.).* a.1782, CC.1792, l.CC.1812.
BOOT—
John. *Sutton-in-Ashfield.* ca.1750. l.c. clocks.

BOOT—*continued.*
John, junior. *Sutton-in-Ashfield.* ca.1775. l.c. clock.
John and William. *Sutton-in-Ashfield.* 1780. l.c. clock.
Elizabeth. *Sutton-in-Ashfield.* End 18c.
John. *Huddersfield.* ca.1770.
George. *Manchester.* 1772-1814. W.
John. *Manchester.* 1775-94. W.
Charles. *Manchester.* 1797-1809. W.

BOOTH—
Edward, *v.* BARLOW.
Joshua. *Manchester.* ca.1700. C.
Benjamin. *Pontefract.* Early 18c.-1791. Watch Den. coll.
George. *Manchester.* 1758-88. W.
John. *Wakefield.* an.1765-97. Watch.
James. *Frodsham.* d.1781. C.
John. *London.* an.1773. Watch.
James Bowker. *Manchester.* 1772-1814. Watch Platt Hall M. Manchester.
Benjamin. *London.* ca.1780. Watch M.M.A.
James. *Rochester* and *London.* CC.1778, l.CC.1781, d.1822. Watch mt.
James. *Pontefract.* ca.1780.
John. *Manchester.* 1782-95. W.
Richard. *London* (*Alfred Ct.*). a.1773, CC. 1785-1800.
William. *Hull.* 1784. W.
William. *London.* CC.1790.
John. *Congleton.* 1790. C. & W.
John. *Bridport.* 1790. C.
John. *Huddersfield.* 1795.
Charles. *Manchester.* 1800. C. & W.
Richard, son of Richard. *London.* a.1795-1814 CC.
Joseph, son of James. *London.* a.1796.
Samuel, bro. *London.* a.1799-1825.
G. W. *Selby.* ca.1800 CC. Clock.
Mrs. *Huddersfield.* 1802. W.
George. *Aberdeen.* an.1818. Watch.
William. *Leeds.* 1817.
John. *Stalybridge.* ca.1820.
John. *Aberdeen.* 1820-46.
G., & Son. *Aberdeen.* 1820-46.
James. *Dublin.* 1824.
William. *Wexford.* 1824.

BOOTY—
Henry. *London.* a.1760-1808. W.
Alexander. *London.* a.1764, CC.1776.

BOR, J. *Paris.* ca.1600. Clock with minute hand driven by fuzee on separate dial. Cross watch Den. coll.

BORCHARDT, Lorenz. *Rostock.* 1641. Made the clock in the Marienkirche.

BORDEAUX,——. *London.* an.1745. Watch.

BORDENN, A. *Amsterdam.* ca.1800-22.

BORDIER—
Pierre. *Geneva.* ca.1630-50. Famous en. painter. Painted watch presented by Parliament to Gen. Fairfax.
Étienne. ——. Mid. 17c. crys. and en. cross watch.
Denis. *Geneva.* b.1629, d.1708. 12-lobed crys. watch Louvre. Oval sil. scalloped watch M.M.A.
François. *Geneva.* 1660-1722.
Frères. *Geneva.* ca.1725. g. en. watch.
Jacques. *Paris.* m.1766.
Pierre François. *Paris.* 1766 comp.
A. *Geneva.* ca.1785. Watch.
Léonard. *Geneva.* ca.1800. Mandoline watch M.M.A. Watch S.K.M. ¼ rep. Chamb. col. g. en. watch Fränkel coll. Metal en. watch set jargoons Carnegie M.
Frères. *Geneva.* 1815-30. g. en. watch set pearls. en. apple watch. g. en. watch S.K.M. g. en. shell watch Stern. coll. Two four-colour g. watches M.M.A.
——. *Paris.* 1822-5.

BORDOT, ——. *Paris.* 1825.

BOREHAM—
John. *London.* ca.1720. l.c. clock.
John. *London.* a.1750.
——. *London* (*Old St.*). 1799.
William. *London* (*Hoxton*). 1802-08.
William. *London* (*St. Giles*). 1805-08.

BOREMAN, William. *London.* ca.1790. T.C.

BOREL—
Claude. *Val-de-Travers.* d.1713.
François Louis. *Couvet.* 1740. C.
Jacob, son. *Couvet, Môtiers* and *Neuchâtel.* a.1735, d.1779. Many clocks.
Jean Jacques. *Couvet.* a.1751.
François Antoine. *Couvet.* b.1767, d.1827. Maker of repute of turret and mus. clocks and trav. clocks.
——. *Paris.* 1772-5.
François Louis, son of Jacob. *Chaux-de-Fonds.* a.1773-7.
Jean Henri. *Couvet, Fontaines* and *London.* a.1780-1821.
Abram, Henri. *Couvet.* a.1786.
——. *Geneva.* 1794. *v.* HUMBERT.
ET FAVRE. *Neuchâtel.* 1794-1804. 2 clocks.
Abram Louis. *Couvet.* 1796 C.
Jacob Henri. *Chaux-de-Fonds.* a.1804-15. C.
Louis. *Couvet.* 1816. C.
Constant. *Florence.* b.1790.
Henri Constant. *Chaux-de-Fonds.* b.1790, d.1849. C. of repute.
Henri Selim. *Couvet.* b.1792, d.1870.
Ferdinand. *Couvet.* 1820.
Abram Louis. *Couvet.* b.1794, d.1873. C. of repute.
Pierre Auguste. *Switzerland.* b.1798, d.1895. C.
Célestine. *Boveresse.* ca.1800-50.
Jonas Henry. *Neuchâtel.* 1829.
Alphonse Henri. *Couvet.* b.1814, d.1894.
Amédée Philippe. *v.* BORREL.

BOREL-JAQUET, Abram. *Côte Bertin.* b. 1731, d.1815. Many clocks.

BORELL, M. M. *London.* End 18c. 3-case en. watch M.P.S. Dresden. cf. BORRETT.

BORFORD, F. *London.* an.1756. Watch.

BORG—
Eric. *Uddevalla.* b.1747. *Göteborg.* 1778. d.1812.
Sven Jakob. *Göteborg.* b.1786, d.1824.
Peter, son of Eric. *Göteborg.* 1815-18.

BORGELIN, Fr. *St. Petersburg.* ca.1790. 8-day watch mt. Ilbert coll.

BORLE, Abram Louis. *Chaux-de-Fonds.* 1790. Watch Chamb. coll.

BORNAND—
Jean François. *Ste. Croix.* 1754. Turret clocks.
Frères. *Ste. Croix.* Founded 1825. Makers of mus. mechanism.

BORNET, André. *Paris.* m.1788.

BORNNEJUS, C. C. *Stockholm.* Early 19c. l.c. clock.

BOROCK, Frédéric. *Geneva.* Mid. 18c. Watch.

BORRADAILE, W. *London.* 1820.

BORRE, Bendt Henrik. *Copenhagen.* m.1798.

BORREL, Amédée Philippe. *Paris.* b.1818, d.1887. Pupil and successor to J. WAGNER, neveu. Famous T.C.

BORRELL, Henry. *London.* 1794-1840. mus. C. & W. Watch ill. Britten. rep. br. clock ill. Cec. & Web. *v.* MARKHAM, MARKWICK.

BORRETT—
George. *Stowmarket.* 1755. Watch mt. G.M.
M. M. *London.* ca.1790. Watch G.M. cf. BORELL.

BORROUGH, John. *Brampton.* ca.1770.

BÖRSDORFER, Johannes. *Augsburg.* 1698. oct. watch Bernal sale.

BORWELL, ——. *London.* an.1741. Watch.

BOSCH—
Baltasar. *Cologne.* 1st half 17c. Fine cal. watch Feill coll.
Ulrich. *London.* CC.1652. From *Cologne.*
BÖSCH, Andreas. *Lüneberg.* 1620. Made turning globe 3½ metres diam. with seats inside showing stars and planets, for Friedrich III.
BÖSCHEL, Joseph. *Würzburg.* m.1819.
BOSEN, ——. *Paris.* 1806. Watch.
BOSLEY—
Joseph. *London.* a.1718, CC.1725-55. Also BOSELEY. Patented the use of high-numbered pinions. Watch S.M.S.K.
Charles. *London.* a.1725, CC.1749, 1.CC. 1766. Successor to William KIPLING. l.c. clock.
BOSQUET, Jean. *Paris.* m.1780.
BOSSET—
J. Jaque André. *La Neuveville.* 18c. watch G.M.
——. *Paris.* 1807-23.
BOSSHARDT—
Johannes. *Basle.* b.1718, d.1794. Town C.
J. J., son. *Basle.* b.1749, d.1799. Town C. br. clock Basle M. sd. 'BOSSARDT FILS.'
Johann Heinrich, bro. *Basle.* Town C. from 1794.
BOSTOCK, William. *London.* a.1731. Watch.
BOSTON, Beverley Butler. *London.* a.1750.
'BOSTON WATCH CO.' Predecessor of the WALTHAM WATCH Co. Sig. on 1853 watches.
BOSWELL—
Thomas. *London.* a.1707.
——. *Birmingham.* d.1786. W.
George. *Chester.* 1781. d.1787. W.
BOTAT—
Henri. *Autun.* 1384-93.
Jean. *Autun.* 1393.
BOTHAMLEY—
William. *Kirton.* In 1757 went to *Spalding.* C. & W.
Jarkinson. *Boston.* 1791. C. & W.
BOTHEZEAU, Jacques. *Paris.* m.1759.
BOTJES, Wildrik. *Nieuwe Pekela.* b.1814, d.1874. Made two orreries.
BOTTE, Gt. *Haarlem.* 1792.
BÖTTNER, Hans. *Cassel.* 1545-53.
BOTTOM, John. *London.* a.1760. From *Russia.*
BOTTOMLEY, T. *Boston.* 1784. W.
BOUBON (BOURBON), ——. *Paris.* 1808-1825. g. en. watch.
BOUCAUMONT, Pierre Marie François. *Paris.* m.1752.
BOUCHÉ, ——. *Paris (Rue du Vert Bois).* 1812.
BOUCHER—
Marc. *Paris.* m.1770.
John. *London.* 1775.
Ponce. *Paris.* m.1785-9. Fine g. and jasper watch, set cameo and diamonds.
——. *Loches.* ca.1790. Watch Chamb. coll.
John. *Birmingham.* 1808. C.
W. *London.* 1820.
Achille. *Paris.* 1812-25. C.
BOUCHERET—
Jacob. *London.* CC.1728.
John. *London.* 1750.
BOUCHET—
Jacob. *London.* a.1714, CC.1729.
John. *London.* a.1741.
Jean Louis. *Paris.* 1762-89. Horloger du Roi. Vernis Martin and bronze br. clock Archives Nationales, Paris.
——. *Paris.* Early 19c. C.
BOUDON, J. *St. Flour.* ca.1600. oct. watch ill. Britten, Blot-Garnier coll.
BOUDRY, ——. *Tourcoing.* Late 18c. Wall clock gridiron pendulum, Elbing M.
BOUFFARD, Abraham. *La Rochelle.* 1664.
BOUFFÉ, Louis. *Saumur.* ca.1700. Watch Webster coll.
BOUGHS, Charles. *London.* 1805-08. W.
BOUGON, ——. *Paris.* 1808.
BOUGREAU, Nicolas. *Poligny.* Early 19c. l.c. clock M.M.A.
BOUHIER—
——. *Lyons.* 1538.
Pierre. *Besançon.* 1604.
BOUHIN, Jean. *Niort.* 1570. Clock for town with elaborate automata. Described in MS. No. 1744 in Bibl. Nat. Paris.
BOUIC, dit LECOMTE. *Paris.* 1825. C.
BOUILLARD, Paul. *London.* ca.1775. Watch.
BOUILLIER, Albert. *Rouen.* a.1667.
BOUILLON—
Nicolas. *Blois.* comp. 1635, m.1636, d.1659. *v.* BOILLON.
BOULANGER, David. *London.* a.1691.
BOULÉ, Fils. *Verneuil.* ca.1770. Watch mt. Buckley coll.
BOULLE (BOULE, BUHL), André Charles. *Paris.* b.1642, d.1732. Installed at Louvre as ébéniste to the King in 1673. Famous chaser and inlayer. Inlay of tortoise-shell and brass known by his name.
BOULLOT, Georges. *Besançon.* 1592. Serrurier. In charge of clock of St. Pierre.
BOULLYER, Gilles. *Blois.* 1628. d. an.1635.
BOULT, Joseph. *London.* a.1702, CC.1710-1725. Bankrupt.
BOULTON—
William. *London.* a.1700.
Robert. *Wigan.* ca.1770-91. C.
James. *London.* a.1766.
William. *London.* a.1769.
BOULU, ——. *Paris.* 1807-17. C. to the duchesse de Suède. Mantel clock Pal. de Rambouillet.
BOUMA—
Engele Klazes. *Joure.* 1775.
Jan Engeles, son. *Joure.* ca.1800.
Engele Jans, son. *Joure.* ca.1825.
BOUQUET (BOUGUET, BOUCQUET, BUCQUET, BUCKET or BACKQUETT)—
Martin. *Lyons.* 1611 m., d.1630.
David. *London.* Admitted B.C. 1628, CC. 1632. d.1665. French. A fine maker. en. watch set stones B.M. ill. Baillie. crys. cross watch. oval sil. watch. Fine en. watch Pal. du Cinquantenaire, Brussels. str. cal. watch Mallett coll. en. watch set stones Ilbert coll. Watch Gélis coll.
Nicolas. *Lyons.* 1647 m.-87. Watch. Perhaps the same as Nicolas of Paris. Fine cal. monstrance clock.
Solomon, son of David. *London.* a.1641, CC.1650-74, d. an.1677. Maker of repute.
David, bro. *London.* a.1652-62 CC.
Hector. *London.* a.1656.
David. *London.* a.1662.
Dorcas. *London.* 1677-94.
Solomon, son of Solomon. *London.* 1680. CC.1683-1700. Also BOQUET. Watch B.M.
Nicolas. *Paris.* ca.1690. Watch with en. portraits of the Apostles. en. cross watch Schloss M. Berlin. Perhaps the same as Nicolas of Lyons.
——. *Dole (Jura).* 1712. Made a watch for the town council.
David Alexander. *London (Cannon St.).* a.1786, CC.1793-1824.
John. *London.* a.1798.
BOURBELIN, ——. *Paris.* m.1608.
BOURCHIER, William. *London.* 1817-35. chron. and rep. W.
BOURDET (BOURDAIS)—
Jean. *Blois.* 1605. comp., d.1623.
Nicolas. *Paris.* m.1754.

BOURDIER—
Jean Simon. *Paris.* m.1787-1825. Remontoir clock C.A. & M. Mantel clock Ministère de la Guerre, Paris. Singing bird.
Fils. *Paris.* 1822.

BOURDILLON—
Augustin. *Stockholm.* b.1729, d.1799. A famous maker. g. en. watch Stern. coll. 4 watch mts. Nord. M. 2 g. watches Nat. M. Stockholm ill. Sidenbladh. 3 trav., 2 br. and wall clock.
——. *Paris.* an.1770. Watch.
& BERNIER. *Geneva.* ca.1770. 4-colour g. watch.
& FAUCONNET. *Geneva.* End 18c. Watch mt. with inverted fuzee Ilbert coll.

BOURDON, Pierre. *Geneva.* 1703. Pub. 'Essais de Gravure . . . dans le goût de l'Art propre aux Horlogeurs . . .'

BOURGAUD, Hugues. *Annonay* and *Lyons.* mar. 1637-58.

BOURGEOIS—
Nicolas. *Grenoble.* 1656-1704.
Jacques. *Paris.* 1685 m.
——. *Copenhagen.* End 17c. French refugee.
Jean Bernard. *Paris.* 1740. Offered a post in Madrid by King of Spain.
Benoist Gabriel. *Paris.* m.1739.
Claude. *Grenoble.* Mid. 18c.
Jean François. *Paris.* m.1761.
Jean Baptiste. *Paris.* 1773.
Pierre Antoine. *Paris.* m.1779-89.

BOURGET, Jean Pierre. *Lyons.* mar. 1647 m.-82.

BOURLET (BORLET), Théodore. *Lyons.* mar. 1649-81. Went to *Grenoble.*

BOURN—
Loder. *Canterbury.* an.1750. Watch.
George. *London.* an.1759. Watch.

BOURNE—
Henry. *London.* a.1761.
Samuel. *London.* an.1785. Watch.

BOURQUIN—
Nicolas. *Paris.* 1544-7. Founder member of Paris corporation.
Guillaume. *Convers.* 1733.
Le Jeune. *Switzerland.* Mid. and late 18c. rep. watch S.M.S.K. Watch with fly-back hour hand Ilbert coll.
Adam. *Villeret.* b.1735-67.
David. *Villeret.* m. ca.1777. Partner with Bénédict FRÉSARD.
Antoine. *Paris.* m.1781.
Philippe. *Sonvilier.* 1782.
Jean Pierre. *Sonvilier.* 1782.
David Louis, le jeune. *Villeret.* End 18c. Founded an important business with his two bros. following.
Victor. *Villeret.* End 18c.
Henri. *Villeret.* End 18c.
Bénédict. *Renan.* ca. 1810.
——. *Paris.* 1822-5.

BOURRELIER, Léonard. *Geneva.* b.1688, d.1755.

BOURRET, —— *Paris.* Late 18c. Mantel clock.

BOURRIT, J. D. *Geneva.* Late 18c.-ca.1835. g. en. watch M.M.A.

BOURSAULT—
Hélie. *Châtellerault.* ca.1680. Watch G.M.
I. *Paris.* End 17c. Watch Den. coll.
——. *Ferney.* 1770. *v.* SERVANT.

BOURSEAUX, James. *London.* a.1715.

BOUSQUET, Félix. *Paris.* 1825.

BOUSSARD, ——. *Paris.* 1812. Watch Ilbert coll.

BOUSSART, Jean. *Rouen.* 1711 m. Repaired clock of St. Laurent.

BOUSSOT DE VILLENEUVE, Jacques. *Paris.* m.1742-89.

BOUTET, ——. *Geneva.* ca.1825. Watch mt. Ilbert coll.

BOUTROUS, ——. *Blois.* 1617 comp.

BOUTTEFEOY, Jean. *Paris.* 1774.

BOUVAIST, ——. *Paris.* 1812.

BOUVERAT, ——. *Paris.* 1812-25.

BOUVET, George. *London.* a.1730-52. CC.

BOUVIER—
Pierre. *Geneva.* mar. an.1640.
Louis, son. *Lyons.* mar. 1661-6 m.
Étienne. *Lyons.* b.1642-89 m.
Amy. ——. ca.1700. Large p.c. watch F.W.M.
Charles François. *Geneva.* mar. an.1727-56.
Guillaume. *Paris.* ca.1740. en. painter. 2 cases B.M., 1 Lincoln M.
Jean. *Geneva.* b.1727-56.
Gaspard. *Geneva.* b.1737.
Pierre. *Paris.* 1749 comp.
Frères. *Geneva.* End 18c. Large g. c.secs. watch Carnegie M.
——. *Paris.* 1812.

BOUVILLON—
Jehan. *Paris.* 1544-7. Founder member of Paris corporation.
Jacques. *Paris.* 1544-7. Founder member of Paris corporation.

BOUWER, W. *Rotterdam.* ca.1800.

BOUZE (BOUDE), David. *Haarlem.* 1716.

BOVARD, ——. *Paris.* 1812.

BOVE, ——. *Paris.* 1772.

BOVERICK, Sobieski. *London,* 1745. *Edinburgh,* 1770. *Newcastle-on-Tyne,* 1785. W.

BOVET—
Jean Frédéric. *Fleurier.* d.1818.
Henri. *Berlin.* 1800.
Frédéric, son of J. F. *Fleurier.* b.1786. In *London,* 1815. *Fleurier,* 1840. d.1850.
Alphonse, bro. *Fleurier.* b.1788. *London,* 1815. d.1850. *v.* Edouard.
Gustave, bro. *Fleurier.* b.1790, d.1835.
Edouard, bro. *Fleurier.* b.1797. Went *Canton,* 1818. *Fleurier,* 1826. *Besançon,* 1832. d.1849. In 1822 started with Alphonse a society for commerce in watches for China, which lasted till 1864.
Charles Henri, bro. *Fleurier* and *Canton.* b. 1802. Went *Canton.* 1824; returned *Fleurier,* 1839.
——. Watches by Bovet of London or Fleurier sent to China in large quantity, sd. 'Bovet London,' or 'Bovet Fleurier,' or 'Tevob,' or in Chinese. Watches for China by Bovet were made till 1864.

BOWDEN—
George. *Liverpool.* 1784. W.
Ambrose. *Plymouth.* 18c. l.c. clock.
——. *East Grinstead.* an.1780. Watch.

BOWDINGIS (BOWDOWINGIS), Adrian. *Edinburgh.* 1595.

BOWEN—
Francis. *London.* a.1647, CC.1655. Lantern clock.
Richard. *London.* a.1650, CC.1657. d. before 1677. p.c. chased watch.
Mary widow. *London.* 1677-1710.
Richard, son. *London.* a.1670, CC. 1678-86. Watch Bernal sale. Advertised a watch wound without key.
John, bro. *London.* a.1677, CC.1710. Watch.
Thomas, bro. *London.* a.1684.
John. *Bristol.* 1722-34.
Walter. *London.* a.1717.
James. *London.* an.1763. Watch.
Thomas. *London.* a.1765.
William. *London.* a. 1768.
David. *Canterbury.* Late 18c.-1815. Regulator Buckley coll. C. & W.
Thomas. *Bridgend.* 1795. W.
Thomas. *London* (*Charing Cross* and *Half Moon St.*). a.1784, CC.1796, l.CC.1810-1818.
O. *Merthyr Tydvil.* ca.1800 CC.

BOWEN—*continued.*
John. *London* (*Long Acre* and *Coventry St.*). ca.1800. T.C.
& Downes. *London.* 1802-08. W.
Frederick Charles Peoly. *London.* a.1801.
& Holt. *London.* 1820. T.C.
'C. T. Bowen.' Sig. on 1871-4 watches of the Cornell Watch Co.
BOWER—
Thomas. *London.* a.1711.
William. *Charleston, U.S.A.* 1772. C. & W.
Michael. *Philadelphia.* 1790-1800.
John. *Kirriemuir.* 1802.
Arthur. *Killarney.* 1824.
BOWERS—
Robert. *Chester.* 1783-97.
William. *Chesterfield.* ca.1800. Watch.
George. *Kilnesh.* 1824.
BOWIE—
William. *Edinburgh.* 1719.
——. *Kirkcaldy.* 1779.
John. *Stirling.* 1811.
James. *Kirkcaldy.* 1825.
BOWKER—
David. *London.* 1622. Alien.
Mrs. *Manchester.* 1762. W.
BOWLE, John. *Wimborne.* 1790.
BOWLER, James. *Stourbridge.* 1772. C.
BOWLES—
Joseph. *Aylsham.* 1752. C. & W.
Joseph. *Norwich.* In 1752 went to *London.*
Robert. *King's Lynn.* From 1766. C. & W.
Joseph. *Wimborne.* 1784-95. W.
John. *Poole.* 1795.
John. *Wimborne.* 1795.
Thomas. *London.* a.1806.
BOWLEY (BOWLY)—
Devereux. *London.* a.1710, CC.1718, m.CC. 1759, d.1773. rep. clocks. Maker of repute.
John. *London.* an.1762. Watch.
John. *London.* a.1758. Watch.
BOWLING, William. *Leeds.* 1798. C.
BOWMAN—
James. *London.* a.1723, CC.1743.
Daniel. *Morpeth.* 1820. l.c. clocks.
Joseph. *New Holland, U.S.A.* ca.1800.
Joseph, son. *Strasbourg, Lancaster, U.S.A.* b.1799, d.1891. Noted maker, many l.c. clocks.
BOWN, John. *Matlock.* an.1788. Watch.
BOWNE, Samuel. *New York.* 1751.
BOWRA—
T. *Sevenoaks.* an.1773. Watch.
William. *Sevenoaks.* mar.1789.
John. *Sevenoaks.* ca.1800. Watch.
John. *London.* 1820.
——. *Epsom.* Early 19c. Watch.
BOWRING—
——. *Exeter.* Early 19c.
——. *London.* Early 19c. Watch.
BOWTELL—
Samuel. *London.* a.1673, CC.1681-1707.
William. *London.* a.1694, CC.1703-27. Watch mt. sil. cock, Buckley coll. Also Bowter.
John. *London.* a.1744.
BOWTON, Daniel. *London.* a.1792.
BOWYER—
William. *London.* 1626-47. Subscribed at incorporation of CC. Lantern clock dated 1626 Webster coll.
John. *London.* ca.1685. mus. lantern clock ill. Cec. & Web.
Michael. *London.* an.1774. Clock.
BOX—
Edward. *Chichester.* 1800. W.
J. *London.* ca.1800. g.watch.
BOXELL, ——. *Brighton.* 18c. Watch.
BOXER—
Michael. *Folkestone.* an.1791-5. Watch.
Thomas. *Sandwich.* Early 19c. Watch.
BOYCE—
James. *London.* a.1685. CC.1692-1712. l.c. clock. sil. mounted br. clock.
Thomas. *London.* a.1687, CC.1702.
John. *London.* 1708 CC.
Lawrence. *Puddletown.* 1719. Made church clock at Bere Regis.
——. *Gloucester.* d.1732.
Charles. *London.* a.1730.
John. *London* (*Blue Anchor Alley*). 1770. C.
N. *London.* an.1774. Watch.
Robert. *London.* an.1778. Watch.
Thomas. *London.* a.1770.
BOYD—
James. *London.* d.1771. Watch.
William. *Belfast.* 1807. Partner with Job Rider.
Thomas. *Philadelphia.* 1807. W.
& Richards. *Philadelphia.* 1808. W.
James. *Cupar-Fife.* 1818.
BOYENTON, Thomas. *London.* a.1756.
BOYER, William. *London.* a.1753.
BOYES, William. *London.* a.1814.
BOYET, William. *London.* a.1751.
BOYFIELD—
Richard. *Melton Mowbray.* 1784-95. W.
Thomas. *Melton Mowbray.* 1791-5. C. & W.
BOYLAN & SON. *Dublin.* 1824. C.
BOYLE—
Richard. *London.* a.1652, CC.1660.
William. *London.* 1800-21.
BOYLES—
Philip. *London.* a.1768.
John. *London.* a.1770.
BOYNTON, James. *Howden* (*Yorks.*). ca. 1770-95. W.
BOYS, Laurence. *Deal.* 1737. C. & W.
BOYSON, ——. *London.* Early 18c. Watch.
BOYVEAUX, Jean. *Blois.* m.1641.
BOZEK, Josef. *Prague.* b.1782, d.1835. Able chron. maker.
BRABANT, Peter. *London.* 1723. Insolvent.
BRABNER, William A. *Boston.* 1825. C.
BRACE—
Joshua. *Chepstow.* 1763. Repaired Westbury Church clock.
Thomas. *Worcester.* 1786. Bankrupt. W.
Rodney. *N. Bridgewater, U.S.A.* ca.1830. Wooden looking-glass clock ill. Milham.
BRACEBRIDGE—
Edward. *London.* 1799-1815. Partner with Wm. Pleace 1796-99.
& Sons. *London.* 1811-24.
J. & E. C. *London.* 1820-40.
BRACHER—
——. *Paris.* 1792. *v.* Bruce, Bracher et Cie.
Jonathan. *London.* a.1803.
BRACHET—
——. *Seguret* (*Avignon*). 1728-60. Repaired clocks of Carpentras and Monteux.
——. *Versailles.* 1756. Invented a machine to cut files, approved by the Acad. des Sciences.
BRACKENRIDGE—
James. *Kilmaurs.* 1726.
Alexander. *Kilmarnock.* 1820.
BRACKLEY, George. *London.* a.1669, CC.1677-90.
BRADBORNE, John. *Westerham.* 1744. W.
BRADBURY, Matthew. *Bolton-le-Moors.* ca. 1820.
BRADDOCK, Joseph. *London.* a.1810.
BRADDON, Thomas. *Plymouth Dock.* 1795. C. & W.
BRADEL—
Antoni. *Augsburg.* 1736. m.1739-70. Also Bradl. sd. 'A.B.' Very fine g. watch chiselled in high relief. Watch in steel case with four-colour g. Feill coll.
Nikodemus. *Augsburg.* m.1753-70. p.c. sil. watch M.M.A. sd. 'Bratel Nicodemus.'

BRADEL—*continued.*
Joseph, bro. of Antoni. *Oberhausen.* 1756-70. Kleinuhrmacher.
BRADFORD—
Thomas. *London.* a.1673, CC.1680-7. l.c. clock ill. Cec. & Web.
Thomas. *London.* a.1680, CC.1692-1715. Watch.
Robert. *London.* ca.1700. Watch.
Thomas. *London.* a.1700, CC.1710-70. Watch G.M.
John. *London* (*Holborn*). a.1725-ca.1775. Bankrupt 1743. p.c. watch S.M.S.K.
James Woolman. *London* (*Holborn*). 1743. Bankrupt.
James. *Buckingham.* 1751. C.
James. *Salisbury.* 1771. Previously worked for Geo. GRAHAM.
George. *London* (?). an. 1773. Watch.
Richard. *London.* an.1774. Watch.
S. *Totnes.* 2nd half 18c. l.c. clock.
J. *Liverpool.* 1816. Watch S.K.M. ill. Baillie.
Henry. *London.* 1820.
Nathaniel. *Enniskillen.* 1824.
Robert. *Rathfryland.* 1824.
BRADIER, John. *Philadelphia.* 1802. W.
BRADIN (BRAEN), Caspar. *London.* a. 1696, CC.1715.
BRADLEY—
Henry. *London.* a.1667, CC.1681-91.
John. *London.* a.1671.
Langley. *London.* a.1687, CC.1695, m.CC. 1726-38. A famous maker. Made clocks for St. Paul's, London, ca.1706, and St. Giles', Edinburgh. In 1738 appointed keeper of St. Paul's clock at £100 p.a. Watches Soane M. and B.M. mt. G.M. l.c. clocks Weth. coll. Watch ill. Britten. l.c. clock ill. Cec & Web.
Nathaniel. *London.* 1720-3. Insolvent.
Luke. *London.* CC.1726.
Benjamin, son of Langley. *London.* a.1721, CC.1728-36.
William. *Worcester.* 1728. Watch Horstmann coll.
L. & B. *London.* 1734.
Thomas. *London.* a.1737.
Joseph. *Worcester.* an.1744-9. W.
Samuel. *Worcester.* 1744. d.1783. W.
Thomas. *Ilkston.* 1760.
Thomas. *Brigg.* an.1765. Watch.
William. *Worcester.* 1774, d.1783.
John. *Halifax.* 1784. Bankrupt 1793. W.
William. *London* (*Shoreditch*). 1790-1808. Watch Den. coll.
Thomas. *Mansfield.* 1791-5. C & W.
Thomas. *Gloucester.* 1795. W.
John. *Leeds.* 1795. W.
John. *Blackburn.* ca.1820.
James Gibbon. *Liverpool.* 1825. W.
BRADON—
——. *Paris.* ca.1750 m.
Arnoult Joseph. *Paris.* m.1757.
BRADSHAW—
John. *London.* a.1651, CC.1658.
Henry. *London.* a.1687, CC.1696-1724.
Richard. *London.* a.1713, CC.1725-39. Watch G.M.
Edward. *London* (*Johnson's Ct.*). a.1721, CC.1736-73. d. an.1777.
Thomas. *London.* a.1728.
John, son of Henry. *London.* CC.1731.
Edward. *London.* an.1745. Watchcase maker.
Thomas. *Manchester,* to 1765. Succeeded by John.
& RUBERY. *Coventry.* ca.1760.
John. *York,* 1762. *Manchester,* 1765-1814. C. & W. Watch Platt Hall M. Manchester. Succeeded Thos. *v.* COOPER and BRADSHAW.
Thomas. *London* (*Middle Moorfields*). 1778. Bankrupt. W.

BRADSHAW—*continued.*
Thomas. *Manchester.* 1764. Made cyl. watches.
John. *London.* a.1784.
William. *Coventry.* 1795.
John. *Coventry.* 1795.
& RYLEY. *Coventry.* Early 19c.
T. *Canterbury.* 1804. C. & W.
William. *Liverpool.* 1810-29. Watch.
William. *London.* a.1802.
Robert. *Dublin.* 1820-4.
John. *Liverpool.* 1825. W.
Matthew. *Liverpool.* 1825. W.
BRADSTOCK, John. *London.* a.1812.
BRADSTREET, Robert. *Rochester.* b.1737, d.1795. W.
BRADT, Anton. *Augsburg.* ca.1750. Watch.
BRADY—
James. *London.* a.1808.
Edward. *Tuam.* 1824.
Sampson. *Antrim.* 1824.
BRAEMER (BRAMER)—
Gerrett Paulus. *Amsterdam.* ca.1730. Watch G.M. rep. watch S.K.M. ill. Baillie. Sun and moon hour indicator watch Carnegie M. Watch Den. coll. l.c. clock.
Pieter. *Amsterdam.* ca.1750. l.c. clock.
Paulus et Zoon. *Amsterdam.* ca.1750. p.c. g. watch Blot-Garnier coll.
Willem Jan. *Amsterdam* and *Zwolle.* 18c. Watch Staats M. Amsterdam.
BRAENDL, ——. *Steinamanger* (*Hungary*) and *Paris.* 1814. Skeleton clocks with column dials.
BRAETZ, ——. *Berlin.* 1792.
BRAHAM—
James. *Torquay.* Early 19c. From *Liverpool.* C. to Duchess of Clarence.
John. *London.* Early 19c. Watch.
BRAHE, Tycho. *Prague.* b.1546, d.1601. Famous astronomer. Made 3 clocks for his observations, one with wheel of 1,200 teeth.
BRAHIER, Angélique. *Paris.* Late 18c. Watch mt. Glasgow Art Gall.
BRAILEY, ——. *London.* an.1719-ca.1750. Watch.
BRAILLARD, ——. *Besançon.* 2nd half 18c. Fine crucifix clock.
BRAITHWAITE—
John. *London.* a.1760, CC.1768. d.1797.
George, son. *London.* CC.1797-9.
——. *Kendal.* an.1816. Watch.
William. *Hawkshead.* ca.1820.
BRALLE FRÈRES. *Paris.* 1786. François Jean BRALLE was granted in 1787 the privilege to establish a watch and clock factory in Paris and to call it 'Manufacture royale d'Horlogerie.' Associated with Vincent. The factory failed before 1792.
BRAMBLE—
William. *London.* 1784-1804.
& BELK. *London.* 1790. Dissolved partnership.
William. *Liverpool.* 1790. W.
Joseph. *London.* 1805-20. Clock.
BRAMLEY—
John. *Andover.* 1791-5. C. & W.
I. & H. *London.* 1820. g. cyl. rep. cal. watch M.P.S. Dresden.
BRAMPSTON, Stephen. *Hull.* an.1792. Watch.
BRANCHE, Antoine. *Grenoble.* 1597-1604.
BRANCHU—
Jean François. *Geneva.* mar. an.1750-70.
Guillaume, son. *Geneva.* 1770.
Bénédict. *Geneva.* 1770.
Pierre Antoine. *Geneva.* 1772.
BRAND—
Basil. *London.* a.1660.

BRAND—*continued.*
Alexander. *Edinburgh.* 1711-57. Clock in Magdalen Chapel.
James. *Edinburgh.* 1732-93.
George. *London.* a.1764.
Robert. *London.* a.1773.
John. *Dumfries.* 1790-1802.
William. *London.* a.1795.
James. *London.* Early 19c. Watch.
BRANDECK, Kaspar. *Vienna.* m.1799.
BRANDENBURG, Rudolf. *Bergzabern.* 1579. Made aut. clock for castle of Johann I, Herzog von Zweibrücken.
BRANDER—
G. F. *Augsburg.* Mid. 18c. Dial B.M.
& MATTHEY. *Philadelphia.* 1797.
James. *Keith.* b.1788, d.1835.
BRANDHUBER—
Franz Anton. *Thannhausen.* 1776. Turret C.
Reymund, bro. *Thannhausen.* 1776.
Joseph, bro. *Thannhausen.* 1776.
BRANDLING, William. *London.* a.1720.
BRANDON, Benjamin. *London.* a.1681, CC. 1689.
BRANDOUL, Gilequin. *Paris.* 1401.
BRANDRETH—
Joseph. *London.* a.1711, CC.1718.
Benjamin. *Middlewich.* d.1742.
James. ——. an.1766. Watch.
Obadiah. *Middleswich.* an.1766-95. Watch.
BRANDS & MATTHEY. *Philadelphia.* 1799.
BRANDT—
Clement. *Neuchâtel.* 1623. 'Pfiffer et Horlogier.'
Abram. *Neuchâtel.* 1623-46. Town C.
Pierre. *Chaux-de-Fonds.* 1689-1727.
Jacob. *Montbéliard.* 1693-1743 m.
David. *L'Abbaye.* 1705-33. 'Horloger de clochers et armurier.'
Isaac. *Chaux-de-Fonds.* 1715-27.
Joachim. *Göteborg.* 1732-51. l.c. clock Göteborg M.
Daniel. near *Chaux-de-Fonds.* b.1718, d. 1768.
Daniel. *Chaux-de-Fonds.* a.1740-1828. Several clocks.
Joachim. *Copenhagen.* m.1777. Master of Corporation, 1795-1800. Watch Chamb. coll.
David. ——. ca.1790. Watch.
BROWN & LEWIS. *Philadelphia.* 1795. W.
& MATHEY. *Philadelphia,* 1795-9. W.
Amie. *Paris.* 1800. Prob. Aimé.
Aimé & Charles. *Philadelphia.* 1800-13. cf. preceding and two below.
Frédéric. *Péry.* 1810. Later *Renan.*
Charles. *London* (*Compton St.*). 1813-35. mus. W. Lever mt. G.M.
Aimé. *Philadelphia.* 1817-31.
Charles. *London* (*Jermyn St.*). 1822-4.
Robert, & Co. *Chaux-de-Fonds.* ca.1825. g. en. watch.
BRANDT-DIT-GRIEURIN—
Pierre. *Chaux-de-Fonds.* 1648. d.1727. 'Horloger et Armurier.' Turret clocks.
Jacob, son. *Chaux-de-Fonds.* 1673. d.1743. Worked with Isaac. Turret clocks.
Daniel, bro. *Chaux-de-Fonds.* 1695. W. & C.
Abram, bro. *Chaux-de-Fonds.* 1711. d.1715. Watches, clocks and turret clocks.
David, bro. *Chaux-de-Fonds.* 1705. d.1733. Turret clocks.
Isaac, bro. *Chaux-de-Fonds.* 1715. d.1727. C.
Daniel, son. *Switzerland.* b.1718, d.1768.
Jacob, bro. *Dunkerque.* 1745.
Jacob. *Chaux-de-Fonds.* 1730.
Suzanne. *Switzerland.* d.1743. 'Orlogeuse.'
Jean François. *Montbéliard.* 1752.
Abram. *Chaux-de-Fonds.* 1784.

BRANDTMAIR, Melchoir. *Vienna.* m. 1741.
BRANQUE, Michel. *Paris.* m.1744.
BRANSTON—
Robert. *London.* a.1740.
John. *London.* ca.1800. Watch Ilbert coll.
BRANT—
Richard. *London.* a.1649 CC.
Richard. *London.* a.1692, CC 1700.
BRASIER—
William. *London.* 1785. W.
John, son. *London.* a.1785.
BRASS, Thomas. *Guildford.* an.1767-84. Watch. l.c. clock. br. clock.
BRASSETT—
John. *London.* a.1744-55. Watch.
Charles. *London* (*E. Smithfield*). an.1773. Watch.
BRASSEUR, ——. *Paris.* 1772-1823.
BRATTEL—
John. *London* (*Old St.*). a.1751, CC.1761-70.
Lewis. *London.* CC.1787.
BRAUN—
Stöffel. *Bischofszell* (*Basle*). 1667.
Johann Georg. *Augsburg.* 1712. Left *Augsburg* 1735.
Johann Jonas. *Fürth.* d.1809.
Anton. *Vienna.* m.ca.1781. str. and rep. trav. clock Ilbert coll.
Georg. *Neukirch.* 1800. Wall clock Furt. M.
BRAUND—
John. *Hatherleigh.* 2nd half 18c. l.c. clock.
William. *Dartford.* Early 19c. Watch.
BRAUNER, Joseph. *Vienna.* m.1804.
BRAUNMILLER, Joseph Anton. *Augsburg.* a.ca.1777, comp. ca.1785, m.1792.
BRAY—
John. *London.* a.1717, CC.1733.
Robert. *London.* a.1718, CC.1728-43. Agate case watch Ilbert coll.
Thomas. *London.* a.1753.
Francis. *London.* a.1768.
Thomas. *London.* an.1778-1825. g. en. watch Fränkel coll.
Edward. *London.* a.1798.
BRAYFIELD (BRAFIELD)—
William. *London.* a.1671, CC.1678-92.
Thomas. *London.* a.1675, CC.1682-1725. l.c. clock.
William. *London.* CC.1712.
John. *London.* CC.1716. Bankrupt 1729.
Thomas. *London.* a.1742, CC.1762.
BRAYLEY—
Joseph. *London.* a.1794, CC.1802.
& STREET. *Bridgwater.* 2nd half 18c. l.c. clock.
John, bro. of Joseph. *London.* a.1802.
Joseph. *Nottingham.* 1814. W.
BRAYLY, John. *London.* a.1802.
BRAZART, Charles Laurent. *Paris.* m.1777.
BRAZIER—
——. *London.* End 17c. Watch Ilbert coll.
John. *London.* a.1811, CC.1819.
Amable. *Philadelphia.* 1796-1825.
BREACH, William. *London.* a.1763, CC.1773.
BREADSTEAD, ——. *London.* an.1788. Watch.
BREADY, C. L. *Philadelphia.* 1808. C.
BREAKENRIG—
Robert. *Edinburgh.* 1757-70. Able maker. Made clock with very early duplex escapement.
Robin. *Edinburgh.* 1761.
John. *Edinburgh.* 1767-1800.
Alexander, son. *Edinburgh.* 1800-26.
James, son of Robert. *Edinburgh.* 1802-06.
BREAMES, Leonard. *London.* CC.1633.
BRÉAN, ——. *Paris* (*Rue du Bac*). 1787-9.

BRÉANT—
Jean Nicolas Michel. *Paris* (*Rue St. Martin*). m.1778-89. Mantel clock, Pal. de l'Élysée. Lyre clock Ministère des Finances, Paris.
Jacques Thomas. *London.* 1788 m.
BRÉANT DE BAILLET. *Paris* (*Rue N. D. des Champs*). 1789.
BREARLEY—
James. *London.* an.1774. Watch.
James. *Philadelphia.* 1793-1824.
BREBANT, Peter. *London.* ca.1710. Watch.
BRECKELL—
Richard. *New York.* 1755. C.
Richard. *Holmes.* d.1756.
BRECKENRIDGE, Alexander. *Edinburgh.* 1799-1848.
BRECKLEY, John. *Canterbury.* 1784. W.
BREDERODE, Johan. *The Hague.* 1750. Watch mt. S.K.M.
BREDON—
Isaac. *Grenoble.* 1648. From *Geneva.*
Jean. *Grenoble.* 1649. From *Geneva.*
BREDRUP, Reïnholt P. A. *Copenhagen.* m.1824.
BREDU, John. *London.* an.1751. Watch.
BREESE, James. *Wisbech.* Early 19c. Watch.
BREETZ—
C. *Berlin.* 1786-94.
A. *Berlin.* 1794.
Friedrich. *Berlin,* 1812.
BREGUET—
Rodolphe. *Neuchâtel.* 1594. 'Horloger de la Ville.'
Abraham-Louis. *Paris.* b.1747, d.1823. At *Neuchâtel* till ca.1769. Started in Paris 1776, but watch No. 1 is of 1787. Elected to Acad. des. Sci. One of the most famous makers and the last of the great artist-craftsmen. All his watches show perfect workmanship, originality in design and beauty in form. Many watches bearing his name were made outside and finished in his workshop. There are innumerable watches bearing his name in forgery. He made many improvements, including the parachute ca.1790, and the tourbillon in 1801, also many self-winding watches. Was the first to make lever esc. with lift partly on the pallets and partly on the teeth. The overcoil balance spring is known by his name. Draw was absent from early levers, but used after 1814. Most important collections contain genuine and forged watches. The late Sir David Salomons had a collection of 102 watches and 6 clocks by Breguet. Subscription watches B.M. ill. Baillie, G.M. & S.M.S.K. str. cyl. watch and mus. rep. cyl. watch S.M.S.K. Tourbillon watches G.M. and Ilbert coll. The latter, of 1808, was the first made. Verge watch Den. coll. Pedometer winding rep. watch No. 27 (1791), several watches and pedometer, Ilbert coll. Regulators Buckingham Palace and C.A. & M.
Louis Antoine, son. *Paris.* b.1776, retired 1833, d.1858.
Louis Clément François, son. b.1804, d.1883. Famous maker and mechanician. Invented many recording instruments. Applied electricity to clocks and established electrically synchronized clocks in Paris.
Louis Antoine, son. b.1851, d.1882.
BREGUET ET FILS. *Paris.* 1816 to date. This firm was composed of Breguet, A. L. and his son, and later by his grandson and great-grandson, who brought in Edward BROWN as successor, and he was succeeded by his sons Edward and Henry.
BREGUET, PÈRE ET FILS. This style is on the case of a detent watch dated 1824, Ilbert coll.
BREGUET ET NEVEU. *Paris.* ca.1830. Also BREGUET, NEVEU ET CIE. Style of firm of BREGUET ET FILS for a short time.
BREIDENBAUCH, L. *Philadelphia.* 1807. W.
BREIL, Adrianus. *Zittau.* End 17c. str. and al. hanging plate clock Feill coll.
BREITHAUPT, ——. *Cassel.* 1772. Court mechanic.
BRENKELAAR, Jan. *Amsterdam.* Early 18c. p.c. sil. and tortoiseshell watch Feill coll.
BRENNER—
Steffen. *Copenhagen.* 1556-1602. Court C. in 1563. With Johan SIBE made a magnificent astro. clock; made sil. table clock dated 1556, both in Rosenborg Castle.
Jørgen, son. *Kronborg.* 1585. Court C.
BRENT—
Nicholas. *London.* a.1649.
——. *London.* Early 19c. Watch.
BRENTNALL, Thomas. *Sutton Coldfield.* 1795.
BRENTWOOD, William. *London.* 1776. Watch Nos. 6180-9412.
BRERETON, Henry William. *London.* a.1780, CC.1791.
BRESEMER, Andres Ludewig. *Berlin.* 1785-1793. C.
BRESHARD, ——. *Copenhagen.* ca.1740. g. en. rep. watch.
BRESSEL, Sebastian. *Augsburg.* comp. 1743, d. 1751. From *Friedberg.*
BREST—
John. *London.* an.1769. Watch.
Edward. *Prescot.* ca.1770-95.
BRET, ——. *Paris.* 1811-25.
BRETON, ——. *Paris.* 1772.
BRETONNEAU, Auguste. *Paris.* 1638-1643. Registered a private punch mark in 1638. en. watch M.M.A. circ. g. watch with champlevé en. Watch mt. Glasgow Art Gall.
BRETT—
& Co. *Portsmouth.* an.1763. Watch.
——. *London.* an.1769. Watch.
George. *London.* a.1804.
BRETTSCHNEIDER, Carl Gotthelf. *Berlin.* 1780-86. C.
BREVET, ——. *Paris.* 1681 m.
BREW, Christopher. *Liverpool.* 1825. W.
BREWER—
William. *London.* a.1654.
Edward. *London.* a.1665.
John. *London.* a.1670, CC.1677-84.
John. *Rochdale.* 1720. C.
James. *Darlaston.* an.1756. Watch.
Edward. *London.* 1761.
William. *Philadelphia.* 1774-1824.
Richard. *Preston.* 1781. Insolvent. W.
Richard. *London.* 1783. C. Lancaster freeman.
Isaac. *Philadelphia.* 1813.
William. *Blackburn.* 1814-24.
J. *London.* 1815.
Thomas. *Preston.* ca.1820. W.
E. *London.* Early 19c.
BREWTON, Robert. *London.* a.1660.
BREYNTON, Vaughan. *London.* a.1681, CC. 1693.
BRIAN—
Robert. *London.* a.1662.
Antoine Julien. *Paris.* m.1782-9.
BRIAN, T. *v.* BRYANT.
BRIAND, George. *London.* 1748. Insolvent.
BRIANSON, Edward. *London.* CC.1768.
BRICE—
Clement. *London.* a.1689.
John. *Sandwich.* an.1761. Watch.
William. *Sandwich.* 1795. Watch.
John. *London* (*Islington*). ca.1800.
BRICERLY, ——. *Philadelphia.* 1778-99. Partner with BINGHAM.
BRICK, Richard. *London.* an.1786. Watch.

BRICKENDEN, Nat. *London.* a.1651.
BRICKER, William. *London.* a.1728, CC. 1736-65.
BRICKHILL, James. *London.* a.1648.
BRIDGE—
Thomas. *London.* ca.1700. l.c. clock Weth. coll.
Thomas. *Bolton.* 1717. C.
Samuel. *London.* a.1762.
BRIDGEMAN—
Edward. *London.* a.1655, CC.1662-1703.
John. *London* (*Chequer Alley*). 1782. W.
James, son. *London* (*Church Row*). a.1782, CC.1801-24.
James, son. *London.* a.1816.
BRIDGEN, Henry. *London.* a.1675, CC.1682-1684.
BRIDGER—
Samuel. *London.* a.1697, CC.1703. Bankrupt 1729.
Jane. *London.* a.1704.
BRIDGES—
Thomas. *Edinburgh.* a.1691.
Henry. *Waltham Abbey.* 1730-41. Monumental astro. clock ill. Britten.
John. *London.* an.1767. Watch.
P. *London.* Mid. 18c. g. repoussé watch.
William. *London.* a.1785.
James Colman. *Okehampton.* 1795. C. & W.
John. *Ipswich.* 1798-1820. C. & W.
John. *London.* a.1789.
BRIEGEL, Martin. *Vienna.* mar. ca. 1780-1811. Restored Olmütz clock.
BRIGGS, John. *London.* CC.1669-75. Watch glass cutter.
John. *London.* a.1713. Watch.
Francis. *London.* a.1718.
Stephen. *London.* a.1718.
Richard. *London* (*Whitecross St.*). a.1748, CC.1756-68.
Alexander. *Edinburgh.* a.1762.
Thomas. *London.* an.1775. Watch.
'J. A. Briggs.' Sig. on 1870 watches of the New York Watch Co.
BRIGHT—
John. *London.* an.1769-90. Watch.
Jerome. *Saxmundham.* mar.1790. C. & W.
Isaac. *Sheffield.* 1797-1817. W.
& Sons. *Sheffield* and *Buxton.* 1817-36.
P. *Doncaster.* an.1822. Watch.
BRIGHTEL, H. C. *The Hague.* Late 17c. Large clock gilt and covered with sil. filigree S.K.M.
BRIGHTRIDGE—
Thomas. *London.* a.1700.
Matthew. *London.* a.1756.
Henry William. *London.* a.1779, CC.1790.
BRIGSTOCK, William. *London.* an.1784. Watch.
BRILLE, ——. *Paris.* ca.1750. Clock.
BRILLON, Jacob. *London.* an.1777. Watch.
BRIMBLE, John. *Bristol.* 1785-1801. W.
BRIN, — —. *Paris.* 1812-21.
BRINCK, Olof C. *Västerås.* m.1816-46. Wall clock.
BRINDEAU, ——. *Paris.* ca.1780-1823. Sig. on dial of mantel clock, Ministère de la Guerre, Paris.
BRINDLE—
James. *Liverpool.* 1818-21. Watch N.Y. Univ.
Ralph. *Liverpool.* 1825. W.
BRINDLEY, James. *Mansfield.* 1791-5. C.
BRINGHURST, Joseph. *Philadelphia.* 1813.
BRINK, J. Ten. *Amsterdam.* ca.1800.
BRINKLEY—
William. *London.* a.1756, CC.1766.
William. *Harwich.* b.1744, d.1780. W.
BRINKLOW—
J. L. *Bath.* 1778. From *London.* W.
James. *Jamaica.* 1789. W.
BRINKMAN, George. *London.* 1802-40.
BRINTZINGHOFFER, F. *Philadelphia.* 1804. W.
BRISBOROUGH, John. *England.* 1544.
BRISCARD, Gilles Jean Baptiste. *Paris.* m. 1772-89.
BRISCOE, Thomas Charles. *London.* a.1764.
BRISSET, Claude François. *Paris.* m.1765.
BRISSON—
Jean. *Paris.* 1675 m.-1693.
Pierre. *Paris.* m.1744.
Louis Pierre. *Paris.* m.1775.
BRISTOW—
John. *London.* a.1653.
Timothy. *London.* a.1691.
Thomas. *Bristol.* 1781.
William George. *London.* 1790-1820. Trunk clock G.M.
BRITISH WATCH CO. *London.* 1843. Formed to manufacture watches by tools designed by Ingold. Opposed by watch trade and forced to close.
BRITLEY, John. *London.* an.1767. Watch.
BRITTAIN—
James. *London.* a.1703.
John. *London.* an.1784. Watch.
Henry. *Norwich.* 1795.
BRITTAINE—
Boaz. *London.* a.1670, CC.1679.
Stephen. *London.* a.1684, CC.1692, d. an. 1720.
Stephen, son. *London.* a.1720, CC.1728.
BRITTEN—
Francis. *London.* a.1702.
Thomas George. *London.* a.1802.
BRITTON—
James. *London.* 1748. Insolvent.
John. *London.* an.1771. Watch.
M. *Devizes.* d.1777. W.
John. *London.* a.1774.
BRITZLI, Jakob. *Mainz.* End 17c. Swiss.
BROAD—
Thomas. *London.* a.1674, CC.1682.
William. *London* (*Clerkenwell* and later *Leadenhall St.*). CC.1792, l.CC. 1811-20. Watch.
Richard. *Bodmin.* 1795. W.
R. *London.* 1820.
H. B. *London.* Early 19c. Watch.
BROADBELT—
——. *Knaresborough.* 1797. C. & W.
George. *Gateshead.* 1811-33.
BROADBENT, Joshua. *London.* an.1753. Watch.
BROADHEAD, Benjamin. *London.* a.1702. CC.1709-19.
BROADHURST—
George. *Liverpool.* 1816. W.
James. *Liverpool.* 1818-29. W.
William. *Liverpool.* 1825. W.
BROADLEY, James. *London.* 1772.
BROADWATER, Hugh. *London.* 1689. CC. 1692. W.
BROADWAY, Thomas. *London.* a.1648.
'BROADWAY.' Sig. on 1872 watches of American Watch Co., predecessor of the Waltham Watch Co.
BROADWOOD, ——. *London.* 1795. Watch.
BROCHARD, Bernard. *Paris.* m.1787. 'Monteur de boîtes.'
BROCHE, Jacques. *Berlin.* 1771.
BROCK—
Benjamin. *Bristol.* 1775-ca.1794. CC. W.
Thomas. *Bristol.* 1792. Watch.
Aunger. *Mullingar.* 1824.
BROCKBANK—
John. *London* (*Old Jewry* and later *Cooper's Ct., Cornhill*). a.1761. CC.1769, l.CC. 1777-1806. C. & W. 3 watch mts. and cyclometer G.M.
Myles, bro. *London.* a.1769, CC.1776, l.CC. 1796, d.1821.
John & Myles. *London.* Firm of the two brothers to 1806, styled 'Brockbanks.'

BROCKBANK—*continued.*
John Edward, son of John. *London.* a.1787, CC.1807.
William. bro. *London* (*Cooper's Ct., Cornhill*). a.1794, CC.1807-18. Succeeded to the firm of BROCKBANKS with his brother until 1814. Myles rejoined the firm between 1807 and 1814.
Henry. *Bootle.* ca.1800. Watch.
& GROVE. *London.* Partnership with Myles to 1814.
& Co. *London.* 1815.
& ATKINS. *London.* 1815-35. Firm of BROCKBANKS with George ATKINS, and after 1821 with Samuel Elliot Atkins. 2 marine chron. G.M.
ATKINS & SON. *London.* 1840.
ATKINS & MOORE. *London.* ca.1850. Karrusel watch G.M.

BROCKBANKS. *London.* 1791-1835. 3 marine and 4 pocket chron. and watch G.M. One of the pocket chrons. is a rep. and an exceptionally fine watch. Pocket chron. M.P.S. Dresden. *v.* BROCKBANK.
BROCKE, Jaques. *Berlin.* an.1818. Watch.
BROCKEDON, F. *Totnes.* 18c. l.c. clock.
BROCKHURST, John. *London.* a.1699.
BROCKLAND, John. *London.* an.1784. Watch.
BROCKLES, Thomas. *London.* a.1701.
BROCKLESSE, Thomas. *London.* a.1699.
BROCKUS, Charles. *London.* a.1737.
BROCOT—
——. *Paris.* 1824. C.
Achille. *Paris.* b.1817, d.1878. An eminent maker. Devised the form of anchor escapement and the adjustable pendulum suspension known by his name, and the free escapement called *à mise d'aplomb seul.*

BROD (BRODT)—
Johann Georg. *Augsburg.* m.1755-92.
Johann Georg. *Augsburg.* m.1786-93. sil. trav. clock Feill coll. by him or preceding.
Joseph Ignati. *Augsburg.* b.1756, comp. 1774, m.1791-8.

BRODERICK—
Creasey. *Boston.* 1791. C. & W.
——. *Spalding* and *Holbeach.* Early 19c. CC.
William. *Dublin.* 1824. Watch N.Y. Univ.

BRODERSEN, Ludvig. *Denmark.* m.1759.
BRODIE—
Hugh. *London.* a.1772, CC.1779-1811.
Hugh, son. *London* (*City Road*). CC.1811.
John. *Wooler.* Early 19c. Watch.

BRODON—
Nicolas. *Paris.* 1674 juré-1684.
——. *Paris.* 1681 m. Not Nicolas or Gilles Nicolas.
Gilles Nicolas, son. *Paris.* m.1684. Watch Feill coll. prob. by him.
Nicolas. *Paris.* m.1744-75.
Pierre Joseph. *Paris.* m.1772-89.

BRODRICK, William. *Clonmel.* 1820.
BRODU, James. *London.* an.1726. Watch. Also BRADU.
BROE, Henrie. *London.* 1622-62 CC. Alien.
BROEKHUYSEN, A. V. *Gorinchem.* Early 18c. Watch Staats M. Amsterdam. Fine p.c. sil. watch G.M.
BROEKMAN, Caspar. *Gorinchem.* 1756.
BROGAN, Philip. *Waterford.* 1824.
BROGDEN—
Robert. *York.* 1713-63. C.
John. *London.* Mid. 18c. br. clock.
Joseph. *York.* 1774. W.
James. *London.* 1770-99. Livery Goldsmiths Co. Clock.
William. *London.* an.1786. Watch.
Joseph. *London.* 1790.
& MARRIOTT. *London.* 1799-1805. Successors to James. br. clock.

BROILLAT (BROLLIAT), Henri. *Colombier.* 1791-1822.
BROMFIELD, ——. *Chatham.* 1707. 'Clocksmith.'
BROMHALL, Woorsley. *London.* a.1726, CC.1735.
BROMLEY, ——. *Horsham.* 1804. Watch.
BRONDER—
Caspar. *Cologne.* m.1723. Kleinuhrmacher.
Adolphus. *Cologne.* a.1726.

BRONIKOFF, ——. *Wjatka* (*Russia*). Early 19c. Watch entirely of boxwood, Fränkel coll.
BRONNE, Peter. *England.* ca.1700. l.c. clock.
BRONSON, ——. *Stowmarket.* an.1766. Watch.
BRONZIER, Ravico. *Paris.* ca.1800. Mantel clock.
BROOK—
Edmund. *London.* a.1702, CC.1709.
John. *Battle.* a.1726. From *Hoe.*
John. *Wakefield.* b.1732, a.1751.
William. *London* (*Clerkenwell*). 1791-4.
John Walter. *London.* CC.1803, l.CC.1812-1821.
Richard. *London.* Early 19c. Watch.

BROOKE—
John. *London.* CC.1632.
George. *London.* a.1671, CC.1681-1701.
Edward. *London.* a.1681.
B. *London.* 1743. Watch.
Samuel. *London.* a.1760, CC.1770.
William. *London.* 1787-95.
George. *London.* Late 18c. Watch mt. S.K.M.

BROOKES—
Edward. *London.* a.1683, CC.1690.
John. *London.* a.1685.
Edward. *London.* a.1722.
George. *London.* a.1723.
Henry. *London.* a.1748.
Thomas. *London.* CC.1766-93.
William. *Stow-in-the-Wold.* ca.1800.

BROOKHOUSE—
R. *Easingwold.* ca.1800. Watch.
& TUNNICLIFF. *Derby.* 1820. Ceased 1829. W. Advertised a rolling detached lever esc.

BROOKMAN, John. *London.* a.1755.
BROOKS—
Samuel. *London.* a.1680.
John. *London.* a.1693.
Edward. *London.* a.1693.
Robert. *London.* CC.1733.
Thomas. *London.* a.1729, CC.1738.
William. *London* (*Aldgate*). a.1731, CC.1754, l.CC.1776. Watch.
Thomas. *London.* a.1746.
William. *London* (*Old St.*). CC.1760-87.
Robert. *Ipswich.* Retired 1768. W.
John. *London* (*Bridgewater Sq.*). a.1766, CC. 1773-1813.
John. *London* (*Bunhill Row*). a.1767, CC. 1777, l.CC.1787.
Susannah Christina. *London.* a.1771.
John. *London* (*Fleet Market*). 1780-7.
Thomas. *London.* a.1773.
William. *London* (*Upper Thames St.*). 1781-1790.
William. *London.* a.1777. CC.1787-1800.
Thomas. *London* (*Golden La.*). a.1779. CC. 1787-95.
William. *London* (*Pentonville*). Late 18c. Watch mt.
Samuel. *London* (*St. John St.*). a.1789, CC. 1798. l.CC.1812-15
C. *Stamford.* ca.1800.
John. *London.* 1805.
Thomas. *London.* CC.1805.
Thomas. *London.* CC.1823.
Charles. *London.* CC.1824.

BROOKSTED, John. *London.* a.1671.
BROOM, ——. *London suburbs.* 1662.

BROOME—
Thomas. *London*. CC.1652. Casemaker.
Thomas. *London*. 1734. g. mounted agate watch Blot-Garnier coll. en. watch Palace M. Pekin.
BROOMHALL, Charles. *London*. Late 18c. Succeeded by his son-in-law, SHEARSMITH.
BROSSE, ——. *Bordeaux*. 1816-40. 3 clocks C.A. & M.
BROST, John. *Liverpool*. 1825. W.
BROSTEN, Johan. *Stockholm*. comp. 1734-1743.
BROSTER, John. *Liverpool*. 1796. W.
BROSY—
Abbott. *London*. 1680.
Michael. *Germany*. Late 17c. Watch.
Johann Paul. *Friedberg (Augsburg)*. 1732-41. br. clock Feill coll.
BROTHERTON—
John. *London*. 1755. Watchcase maker.
Edward. *London*. a.1787.
BROUC (BROUÉ), ——. *Paris*. 1816-21.
BROUGH—
John. *London*. a.1780.
Samuel. *London (New St. Cloth Fair)*. a. 1784, l.CC.1792-1825. Watchcase maker.
William Thomas, son. *London*. a.1810.
BROUGHAM, George. *Baltimore, U.S.A.* 1774. From *London*. C. & W.
BROUGHT, Henry. *Workington*. ca.1770-1791 C.
BROUMWELL, John. *London*. 1727. W.
BROUNNER, ——. *Lucerne*. 18c.
BROUWER, Gerrit. *Holland*. 18c. Table clock.
BROWN—
Andrew. *Edinburgh*. a.1665, m.1675, d.1712. A famous maker. Clock on Magdalen Chapel. l.c. clock.
James. *Croydon*. CC.1687.
John. *Edinburgh*. a.1680-1710.
Philip. *London*. a.1680, CC.1688. Also BROWNE.
Richard. *Romford*. an.1692. Watch.
Samuel. *London*. ca.1700. Watch.
Thomas. *London*. CC.1703.
Jonathan. *London*. a.1699.
Robert. *Edinburgh*. a.1702.
John. *London*. a.1703.
George. *Linlithgow*. 1710.
James. *Aberdeen*. 1720.
John, son of John. *Edinburgh*. 1720-50. Treasurer to Incorporation of Hammermen.
Henton. *London*. a.1714, CC.1726, m.CC. 1753, l.CC.1766, d.1775. Also BROWNE. An able watchmaker.
William. *London*. a.1714.
Samuel. *London*. a.1715.
Abel. *London*. a.1717.
James. *Elgin*. 1726-68.
William. *London*. a.1718.
George. *Brighton*. 1728. C.
William. *Edinburgh*. 1733.
John. *Brighton*. a.1728.
Joshua. *Liverpool*. 1734-73. C.
Philip. *London*. a.1732.
James, son of Henton. *London*. a.1735, l.CC.1766, m.CC.1770, d.1781.
Benjamin. *Newcastle-on-Tyne*. an.1746. Watch.
John. *Elgin*. 1743.
Thomas. *Birmingham (Digbeth* and *Bull Ring)*. 1745, d.1802. In *Bull Ring* from 1751. l.c. clock. Watches Birmingham M. and Den. coll.
William. *London*. a.1738.
Thomas. *London*. a.1738, CC.1747, l.CC. and d.1767.
Garven. *Boston, U.S.A.* 1750-76 C.
Samuel. *Edinburgh*. 1750-87 CC. Son of John (1720-50). In partnership with George SKELTON, 1784. Watch.

BROWN—*continued*.
Edward. *Norwich*. an.1756. Watch. l.c. clock. Also BROWNE.
Henry. *Liverpool*. 1761-96. W.
Joseph. *Worcester*. 1766-96. C. & W.
Thomas. *Chester*. 1766-84. *Stockport*. 1795-1801.
James. *London*. CC.1767.
Robert. *London*. CC.1768.
Aaron. *Erith*. an.1769. Watch.
Thomas. *London (Moorfields)*. 1768.
Joseph. *Kirkcaldy*. 1769.
Jonathan. *Harwich*. d.1808. W.
George. *Beverley*. 1770-91.
Nathaniel. *Manchester*. 1770-1800. Watch. l.c. clock ill. Cec. & Web.
James. *Birmingham*. an.1771. Watch.
William. *Yoxford*. Also at *Harleston* from 1771-84. C. & W.
Robert. *London*. CC.1771.
John. *Edinburgh*. a.1763-76.
Murdoch. *Edinburgh*. 1772.
John. *Manchester*. 1772-81. C. & W. Watch advertised for with purchaser's cypher on cock.
Thomas. *Norwich*. an.1775. Watch.
Ranock. *London*. an.1775. Watch.
George. *London*. CC.1773-81.
John. *London (Fleet St.)*. a.1766, CC.1773-1795.
Nathaniel. *London*. ca.1780. Watch.
Joseph. *London*. a.1770.
Ralph. *London*. a.1772.
Malcolm. *Edinburgh*. 1778.
Thomas. *Birmingham (Moat Row)*. 1781. W.
& SKELTON. *v.* Samuel above.
D. *Birmingham*. 1782.
John. *St. Andrews*. 1783.
Anthony. *London*. a.1777.
Samuel. *London*. a.1777.
John. *London (Charing Cross)*. 1785-1811. Watch.
John. *London*. CC.1786.
——. *Portsmouth*. 1789. W.
Gawen. *Boston, U.S.A.* 1789-1800. W.
John. *London (Soho)*. 1790.
John. *Bristol*. 1790. Left 1792. W. Succeeded Thos. PIERCE.
Joseph. *Ledbury*. 1791-5.
James. *Pateley Bridge*. 1792. C. & W.
J. *Thornbury*. From 1792. Previously *Bristol*.
James. *London*. a.1781.
William. *London*. a.1787.
William. *London (Piccadilly)*. ca.1800. Watch with name of WALLERIUS, Norrköping on dial in case with obscene paintings Feill coll.
William. *London*. a.1790.
Isaac. *Liverpool*. 1796-1818. C.
John. *London*. a.1793, CC.1807.
John. *London (Soho)*. 1799.
James. *London (Portman Sq.)*. 1799-1840.
John. *London*. a.1794.
John. *Lancaster City, U.S.A.* ca.1800. l.c. clocks.
——. *Epsom*. ca.1800.
B. *London*. 1802-04.
Daniel. *London*. an.1806.
Thomas. *London (Clerkenwell)*. 1805-08. W.
Mrs. *Birmingham*. In 1806 succeeded by William HOUGH.
Charles. *London*. a.1797.
John. *London (Old St.)*. 1805-08.
Thomas. *Liverpool*. 1807-24.
John. *London (Manchester Sq.)*. 1809-11.
John. *London (Featherstone St.)*. 1809.
James. *Liverpool (Whitechapel)*. 1811-29. W.
Jonathan. *London*. a.1808.
Joseph. *Sheffield*. 1817-28.

BROWN—*continued.*
Richard. *London.* a.1810.
Isaac. *Newark.* an.1819. Watch.
John. *Harleston.* an.1820. Watch.
John. *Philadelphia.* 1819-22. W.
Thomas. *Manchester.* 1820-36.
William. *N. Shields.* 1820-47.
George. *London* (*Clerkenwell*). 1820. Watch.
James. *Liverpool* (*Richmond Row*). 1821. W.
Henry. *London.* a.1818.
James. *London* (*George St.*). 1820-40. W.
John. *London* (*George St.*). 1820. W.
T. *London* (*Goswell St.*). 1820. W.
& MARSTON. *Brighton.* 1822. C. & W.
William. *Philadelphia.* 1823-37. W.
William. *Roscrae.* 1824.
Samuel. *Cookstoun.* 1824.
——. *Southampton.* Early 19c.
James. *Winchester.* Early 19c.
Benjamin. *London.* Early 19c. Watch.
Thomas. *Auchtermuchty.* 1825.
Henry. *London.* CC.1825.
Alexander. *Liverpool.* 1825. W.
Francis. *London.* a.1820.
Edward. *Paris.* b.1829, d.1895. Head of BREGUET ET FILS, *q.v.*
v. BROWNE.

BROWNBILL—
James. *Liverpool* (*Prussia St.*). 1767-1814.
John. *Liverpool.* 1769-84. W.
Thomas. *Liverpool.* 1777-84. W.
Henry. *Leeds.* From 1777-95. l.c. clock ill. Britten.
John. *Liverpool* (*St. Paul's Sq.*). 1800-03. W.
Thomas. *Liverpool.* 1803-18. W.
John. *Liverpool* (*Pownall Sq.*). 1807-16. W.
John. *Liverpool* (*Prussia St.*). 1816-29. W.
Thomas. *Leeds.* 1817-26. Watch.
John. *Liverpool* (*Williamson St.*). 1825. W.
James. *Liverpool.* 1825. W.

BROWNE—
Matthew. *London.* CC.1633.
John. *London.* CC.1652, m.CC.1681-1701.
Thomas, son. *London.* a.1653, CC. 1676-87. Small lantern clock.
John. *London.* CC.1667. math. inst. maker.
Richard. *London.* a.1668, CC.1675-90. Lantern and l.c. clock.
Thomas. *London.* a.1669.
Richard. *London.* a.1671.
Philip. *London.* a.1680, CC.1688. Also BROWN.
Robert. *London.* a.1684.
Moses. *London.* a.1687.
John. *London.* a.1687.
Charles. *London.* a.1692.
James. *London.* a.1696.
Nicholas. *London.* a.1698.
Jonathan. *Lavington.* ca.1710. l.c. chimney clock ill. Cec. & Web.
William. *London.* a.1705, CC.1719-32.
George. *Lewes.* a.1720.
William. *London.* a.1729.
Roger. *London.* a.1730.
Michael. *London.* a.1741.
Ranock. *London.* CC.1799. Partner with John PERIGAL.
William. *Liverpool.* 1774. Bankrupt. C.
Edward. *Norwich.* ca.1775. l.c. clock.
Robert. *Bottisdale.* 2nd half 18c. l.c. clock.
John. *London* (*Seven Dials*). 1799.
John. *Kinsale.* 1820-4.
Adam. *Comber.* 1824.

BROWNING—
James. *London.* a.1650.
Isaac. *Penrith.* ca.1770-95.
Henry. *Bury St. Edmunds.* 1783. W. l.c. clock.

BROWNLESS, George. *Staindrop.* 1746. d.1799. Watch Den. coll.

BROWNLETT, ——. *Leeds.* ca.1790 CC.

BROWNLIE—
Alexander. *Edinburgh.* a.1710-39.
Alexander. *Edinburgh.* a.1740.
William. *Hamilton.* 1800.

BROWNSWORD, P. *Derby.* 1814. Watch.

BROYART, Charles Laurent. *Paris.* m.1777-1789.

BRUCE—
David. *Aberdeen.* 1538. Keeper of clock in Tolbooth.
Thomas. *London.* a.1645.
James. *Edinburgh.* 1718.
James. *London.* CC.1721.
William. *Edinburgh.* 1743.
Henry. *London.* a.1738.
George. *London.* an.1745. Watch.
William. *Edinburgh.* 1757.
BRACHER ET CIE. *Paris.* 1792. English. Petitioned the Government for 100,000 livres to start a factory for watch and clock tools at Paris.
Thomas. *Leicester.* 1791. C. & W.
Robert. *Edinburgh.* 1797.

BRUCKNER (PRUGNER), Nicolas. *Strasbourg.* 1497-1557. Astrologer, worked on design for a new clock at Strasbourg to replace Habrecht's, but without result.

BRUDER, Ignatz. *Simonswald* and *Waldkirch.* b.1780, d.1845. Went to *Waldkirch* in 1834. A famous maker of aut. organs and mus. clocks. Wrote a book on them in 1829. Known as 'Uhren-Nazi.'

BRUECHNER, Baltser. *Copenhagen.* 1689.

BRUEL, ——. *Paris.* Late 18c. Mantel clock Ministère des Finances, Paris.

BRUFF, James. *New York.* 1766. C. & W.

BRUGERCIA, C. *London.* 1820-4. Mus. clocks and snuff-boxes.

BRUGUIER, Charles Abram. *Geneva.* b.1788, d.1862. Improved the mechanism of singing birds and produced them in large number.

BRUIJGOM, M. *Rotterdam.* ca.1800.

BRUIJN, J. *Amsterdam.* 1822. Wall clock Nord. M. trav. clock Nat. M. Stockholm.

BRULEFUR, Jean. *London.* ca.1690. l.c. clock S.K.M.

BRULFER—
Pierre. *Paris.* 1678 m.
Louis. *London.* End 17c. l.c. and br. clock.
Louis. *Paris.* m.1741.
Louis. *Paris.* m.1751.
Jean Baptiste (le jeune). *Paris.* m.1754-89.
——. *Paris.* 1807-22.

BRUMMER (BRÜMMER), ——. *Vienna.* m.1803.

BRUN—
Niclaus. *Basle.* 1550-71. Also BRON.
Jacob. *Copenhagen.* 1645-61.
Daniel. *Geneva.* ca.1750-71.
FRÈRES. *Chaux-de-Fonds.* 1784.
Antoine. *Paris.* m.1787.
——. *Paris* (*Rue St. Honoré*). 1809-12.
——. *Paris* (*Rue Thévenot*). 1809.

BRUNEL, ——. *Avignon.* 1779-89. Made clock of his invention for town, but had to replace it by an ordinary clock.

BRUNELL, Johan. *Arboga.* m.1822-6.

BRUNN, Jan. *Amsterdam.* 18c. Watch Staats M. Amsterdam.

BRUNNER, Kaspar. *Berne.* 1526, d.1565. Went to *Nürnberg* in 1541 where he was appointed caster of cannon. Renewed 1527-1530 famous clock in Zeitglockenturm.

BRUNNET (BRUNET), ——. *Paris.* 1824.

BRUNSLEY, William. *London.* ca.1670. Token coin in B.M.

BRUNTON—
Walter. *Edinburgh.* 1771-1808.
Patrick. *Dalkeith.* 1788.

BRUNWIN, Henry. *London.* a.1768, CC. 1775, d.1790. *Watch.*

BRUSE, Henry. *London.* a.1738.

BRUSH, James. *Dublin.* 1774-80.
BRUSHFIELD—
George. *Ashford.* 1814. W.
Joseph Blackden, son. *London.* a.1814.
BRUTON—
Thomas. *London.* CC.1778-1811.
Thomas. *Bristol.* 1781.
BRUTSCHER—
Melcher. *Stockholm.* 1643, d.1676.
Johan, son. *Stockholm.* 1671.
BRUYKESSEL—
Gaspard. *Lucerne* and *Berne,* 1522-67. Went Berne in 1547. Town C. from 1554. T.C.
Gaspard, son. *Berne.* d.1583. First house C. in Berne.
BRY, Ami. *Geneva.* b.1750. In partnership with Jacques COULIN and Jean FLOURNEY, 1784-1800.
BRYAN—
Robert. *London.* a.1662.
Richard. *London.* a.1683, CC.1696.
Samuel. *London.* a.1685.
Robert. *London.* a.1698.
Lancelot. *London.* a.1711.
James. *London.* a.1718.
Samuel. *London.* a.1718, CC.1765.
John. *London (Aldersgate St.).* a.1727-73. CC. Wall clock.
William, son of Samuel (2). *London.* a.1765, CC.1772.
John. *London (Shadwell).* CC.1773-1804.
James, son of John (1). *London.* a.1773.
Samuel, son of Samuel (2). *London (Chequer Alley).* a.1773-1811.
John, son of John (2). *London.* a.1781
Thomas, son of Samuel (2). *London.* a.1783.
John. *Belfast.* 1824. Watch.
BRYANS, Richard. *London.* a.1785.
BRYANT—
George. *London.* a.1657.
Thomas. *London.* CC.1773, d.1815.
& SON. *London.* 1781. C. & W.
John. *Hertford.* b.1748, d.1829. Many fine clocks.
Robert. *London.* a.1788.
Thomas. *London.* a.1801.
Francis. *London.* 1808 CC.
BRYCE, Clement. *London.* a.1689.
BRYERS, Arthur. *Liverpool.* 1800-03. Later at *Chester.*
BRYGER, Peter. *Hälsingborg.* b.1764, d.1837.
BRYGGER, Peter. *Helsingør.* m.1811.
BRYSON—
Robert. *Edinburgh.* b.1778, d.1852. F. Roy. Soc. Ed. Very fine maker; made sidereal clock for Edinburgh Observatory.
Alexander, son. *Edinburgh.* b.1816, d.1866. F.R.S.E. C. for Scotland to the Queen. Eminent maker. Invented many devices for electrical and other clocks.
Robert, bro. *Edinburgh.* d.1886. Carried on business as Robert Bryson & Son.
BRYZELIUS, ——. *London.* an.1760. Watch.
BUARDSELL, William. *London.* CC.1771-5.
BUCHAN, Archibald. *Kinnoul.* 1800-33.
BUCHANAN—
James. *London.* a.1702.
Charles. *London.* an.1769. Watch.
Archibald. *Dublin.* 1795-1800. l.c. clock. W.
John. *Ashton-under-Lyne.* ca.1820.
Thomas. *Dublin.* 1820-4. Fine duplex watch Chamb. coll.
BUCHEGGER, Joseph. *Scharnstein.* End 18c. en. watch Den. coll.
BUCHER (BUCHART)—
Hans. *Marburg.* 1568. From *Augsburg.* Became burgher in Marburg 1570. Made with BALDWEIN a monumental astro. clock in M.P.S. Dresden.
Jean. *Stettin.* Early 19c.

BUCK—
Edward. *London.* CC.1632.
John. *Chester.* 1680. W.
Richard. *London.* a.1718, CC.1725-37. Bankrupt.
William. *Bristol.* 1801-30. W. & C.
BUCKE, George. *Bungay.* From 1765. l.c. clock.
BUCKEL, John. *London.* a.1697.
BUCKENHAM, Joseph. *London.* an.1710. Watch. Prob. BUCKINGHAM.
BUCKENHILL—
John. *London.* a.1664, CC.1672-85. sil. eng. watch.
Edward. *London.* a.1672, CC.1687.
BUCKFORD, William. *Liverpool.* ca.1795. W.
BUCKINGHAM, Joseph. *London.* an.1766. Watch.
BUCKLAND—
Thomas. *Greenwich.* an.1775-ca.1790 CC. Watch.
Henry. *Greenwich.* 1795. W.
John. *London.* 1799-1804. br. clock.
William. *Thame.* 1800. C. & W.
BUCKLE, Peter. *London.* a.1741.
BUCKLEE—
Henry. *London.* 1779-86. CC.
David. *London.* CC.1785, l.CC.1787-1822.
BUCKLEY—
T. *London.* an.1775. Watch.
James. *London.* a.1767.
John. *Canterbury.* From 1781. Retired 1805. C. & W.
Samuel. *Philadelphia.* 1811. W.
John. *Ashton-under-Lyne.* ca.1820.
BUCKMAN, George. *Baltimore, U.S.A.* 1802. W.
BUCKNALL, Thomas. *Berkhampstead.* Mid. 18c. Watch, shagreen case.
BUCKNELL—
James. *Crediton.* End 17c. l.c. clock. Watch Exeter M.
William. *Crediton.* 1795. C. & W.
William. *London (Westminster).* 1816-25. Watch mt. Glasgow Art Gall.
BUCKNER—
Philip. *London.* a.1660, CC.1667-81.
Richard. *London.* CC.1701.
Edward. *London.* 1706 CC.
BUCKSHER, John. *London.* a.1775-1820.
BUCKTROUT, Richard. *Howden (Yorks.)* and *Wakefield.* 1784. Watch.
BUCKWELL, E. *Brighton.* 1819. C. to the King and to the Prince Regent. Watch.
BUCQUET (BUCKQUIT)—
David Alexander. *London.* a.1786, CC.1793-1824. Also BOUQUET.
John. *London.* a.1798.
Daniel. *London.* 1815-25.
BUDD, Nathaniel. *London.* an.1775. Watch.
BUDGEN (BUDGEON)—
William. *Reigate.* 1710-13. C.
Thomas. *Croydon.* 1737. l.c. clock ill. Cec. & Web. Watch.
William. *Croydon* and *London.* 1750-1824. CC. Watch.
BUFFET, John. *Colchester.* 1721-35. Watch and l.c. clock.
BUGBIRD, Joseph. *London.* a.1724.
BUGBY, John. *London.* a.1722.
BUGDEN, David. *London.* a.1804.
BUGLAS, C. *Berwick-on-Tweed.* an.1787. C. & W.
BUGNON, Jean. *Paris.* m.1765. g. rep. watch Den. coll.
BUHR, Lars. *Norrköping.* 1727.
BUIJS—
M. *Amsterdam.* 18c. p.c. sil. watch.
H. *Amsterdam.* 1822. W.
P. *Amsterdam.* 1822. W.
BUIJSEN, M. Zoon. *Amsterdam.* ca.1800. Watch Staats M. Amsterdam.

BUILLO, Noel. *Lyons.* 1536.
BUJARD & CO. *Pforzheim.* End 18c. Watch in Dresden china cane handle, M.M.A.
BÜK, F. *Bregenz.* Early 19c. Pedometer winding watch G.M.
BULCKE (BULKE), Jacques de. *London.* 1599. str. drum watch. 2 oval watches. Employed to repair clocks 'remayning in riche peeces of Plate within our Tower of London.' Appears to have worked also in *Paris.*
BULDET (BEULDET, BURDET, BURDEL)—
Hugues. *Lyons.* 1619-27.
Jean Baptiste, son. b.1627-69.
BULET, D., Fils. *Geneva.* 18c. cal. watch.
BULGIN, M. *Leatherhead.* ca.1800.
BULKDAY (BULKELEY), Thomas. *London.* a.1707, CC.1715-27.
BULL—
Rainulph (Randolph). *London.* 1582-1617. Keeper of Westminster Pal. clock. C. to the King. circ. str. watch Mallett coll. ill. Baillie. Watch Gélis coll.
Edmund. *London.* 1610-30. 2 watches S.K.M. p.c. watch G.M. Watches F.W.M. and Gélis coll.
Emmanuel. *London.* an.1618. C. to the King. Perhaps same as Edmund.
George. *London.* 1622.
William. *London.* 1622. Alien.
John. *London.* 1630-2. Subscriber for incorporation of CC.
Nicholas. *London.* a.1679.
John. *London.* a.1691.
John. *London.* a.1702.
Thomas. *London.* a.1717.
Charles. *London.* a.1742.
——. *Rochester.* an.1753. Watch.
Isaac. *Dublin.* 1766-95. W.
William. *London (Stratford).* 1770-1804. 2 br. clocks ill. Cec. & Web.
T. *London.* an.1774. Watch.
John. *Bedford.* Early 19c.
——. *Bristol.* Early 19c. Watch.
BULLBY, John. *London.* CC.1632.
BULLER, ——. *Abingdon.* an.1759. Watch.
BULLIMORE, Henry. *London.* a.1687.
BULLINE, Ben. *London.* 1763-9. Insolvent. Watch and l.c. clock.
BULLINGFORD—
——. *Liverpool.* Early 19c. Watch.
C. *London.* Early 19c. Watch.
BULLMANN, BÜLMANN or **PÜLMANN,** Jacob. *Nürnberg.* m.1498, d.1535. Famous locksmith, clock and aut. maker. Mentioned by Dopplmayr as Hanns, in error.
BÜLLMANN, Johann Daniel. *Fürth.* 1757.
BULLOCH, William. *Dublin.* 1820.
BULLOCK—
Richard. *London.* a.1715.
Edward. *Oswestry.* Early 18c. l.c. clock.
Zephaniah. *Widcombe (Bath).* ca.1740.
Edmund. *Ellesmere (Salop).* ca.1740. l.c. lacquer clock ill. Cec. & Web.
Thomas. *Bath.* 1767. Watch.
James. *London (Leather Lane).* 1776-94. Marine chron. Ilbert coll.
John. *Bishops Waltham.* 1785.
William. *Widcombe (Bath).* d.1790.
Edward, son. *London.* a.1776.
William. *Bath.* 1795-1826. Watch.
William. *Dublin.* 1824.
BULLOT ——. *Paris.* 1824.
BULMAN—
Caspar. *Nürnberg.* Went to *Berlin,* 1544.
Jacob. *Nürnberg.* *v.* BULLMANN.
BULMER, Henry. *Liverpool.* 1825. W.
BULSTROD, William. *London.* a.1671.
BULT, James. *London.* ca.1780. Watch.
BULTY, Daniel. *London.* a.1655, CC.1663. Also BULTE.
BUMEL, Michel. *Nürnberg.* 1601.
BUMSTEAD, Robert. *London.* a.1700, CC. 1707-36. p.c. rep. watch Den. coll. Also BRUMSTEAD, BURNSTEAD AND BAMSTEAD.
BUNBERRY, Dutton. *Chester.* 1637. C.
BUNBY, John. *London.* a.1729.
BUNCE—
Matthew. *London.* a.1684.
Matthew. *London.* a.1689, CC.1698.
John. *London.* a.1713.
James, son of Matthew. *London.* CC.1721.
Thomas. *Wantage.* 1795. C.
BUNDGAARD, Jens Villadsen. *Salling.* ca. 1750.
BUNEL, ——. *Avignon.* 1779. Remade town clock.
BUNN—
James. *London.* a.1697.
——. *Dorchester.* an.1736. Watch.
Peter. *London.* a.1789.
'BUNN.' Sig. on 1870-82 watches of ILLINOIS SPRINGFIELD WATCH Co.
BUNNET—
William. *London.* ca.1760. Watch.
Jacob. *Ipswich.* From 1779. W.
BUNON—
Étienne. *Rouen.* 1654 m.
——. *Paris.* 1772-89. Cartel clock Carnavalet M.
BUNTING—
William. *London.* a.1637, CC.1645.
Joshua. *London.* a.1648.
Joshua. *London.* a.1651.
BUNTON, ——. *North Walsham.* Up to 1789. W.
BUNYAN, Robert. *Lincoln.* 1784-95. W. Inn clock ill. Cec. & Web.
Henry. *Lincoln.* 1791-5. W.
BURBANK, W. *London.* an.1769. Watch.
BURBRIDGE, ——. *Edinburgh.* 1673.
BURCH—
John. *London.* a.1713.
Thomas E. *London.* Mid 18c. p.c. sun and moon hour indicator watch.
W. *Chelmsford.* 1811. W.
William. *Maidstone.* From 1795-1813. Watch.
William, son. *London.* a.1813.
BURCHETT—
Philip. *London.* CC.1705-15.
John. *London.* a.1721, CC.1731-49.
John, son. *London.* a.1743, CC.1751.
BURCKHART, Joseph. ——. Mid. 18c. Watches Nat. M. Prague and Schloss M. Berlin.
BURDEN, ——. *London.* 1743. *Watch.*
BURDET, Richard. *London.* 1743. Insolvent.
BURDETT—
Henry. *London.* a.1723, CC.1734-7.
Thomas. *London.* 1759.
BURDGE, Nicholas. *Galway.* 1820-4.
BURDITT, Joseph. *London.* CC.1805-10. Also BURDETT.
BURELET, Jean Jacques. *Chaux-de-Fonds.* a.1749.
BURFIELD, Robert. *Arundel.* 1784-95. W.
BURFORD—
Benjamin. *London.* a.1734.
John. *London* (?) an.1773. Watch.
BURGE, Caleb. *London.* a.1682.
BÜRGEL, Martin. *Vienna.* 1810.
BURGER—
Wolfgang. *Bayreuth.* Early 18c. Watch N.Y. Univ.
Georg Matthias. *Nürnberg.* b.1750, d.1825.
Paul Georg. *Fürth.* d.ca.1800.
George. *Kingston.* Early 19c.
BURGES—
John. *Toxteth Park.* d.1716. W.
Samuel. *London.* a.1706.

BURGES—*continued.*
——. *Portsmouth.* Early 18c. Watch Horstmann coll.
John. *London.* a.1712.
Thomas. *Gosport.* an.1740-ca.1750. Watch mt.
John. *London (Jermyn St.).* Before 1762. Watch.
Charles. *London.* 1765. Watch G.M.
——. *Liverpool.* ca.1790. l.c. clock.
John. *Stirling.* 1806.
BURGESS—
Elias. *London.* a.1673, CC.1681-1702. l.c. clock Weth. coll.
John. *Liverpool.* d.1716. W.
Charles, son. *London.* a.1702. Watch.
William. *London.* a.1703.
Samuel. *Manchester.* d.1753. C.
Bazaliel. *Liverpool.* 1761-7. W.
George. *London (Cheapside).* a.1770, CC. 1780-95. Watch.
James. *London.* a.1782.
Anthony. *London.* 1793. Livery Farriers Co.
Richard. *Manchester.* 1793. From *Stockport.* C. & W.
——. *Fordingbridge.* Early 19c. Watch.
BURGHARDT, Heinrich. *Leipzig.* 1814. cf. BURKHARDT.
BURGI (BURGIUS, BYRGI), Justus (Jobst, Jost). *Cassel* and *Prague.* b.1552, d.1632. Mechanician to Wilhelm IV of Hessen-Cassel from 1579 and to his son Moritz from 1595. C. to Rudolph II at Prague 1603-22. Very famous maker. Extremely fine crys. case clock with armillary sphere K.H.M. Another clock K.H.M. with pendulum attributed to him. Clockwork celestial globe in Adelmann sale. Very fine clockwork globe C.A. & M. Celestial globe clock Gotha M. Very fine sq. astro. table clock Cassel Landes-M. Said to have used logarithms and compiled tables, but never published.
BURGIS—
John. *London.* 1630-2. Subscriber to incorporation of C.C. Oval watch ill. Britten.
Thomas. *London.* a.1647.
John. *London.* a.1673.
Elias. *London.* a.1673, CC.1681-94. l.c. clock Weth. coll. Also BURGES.
Charles Edward. *London.* a.1678. l.c. and br. clocks.
John. *London.* a.1709.
William. *London.* CC.1770.
BURKE—
James. *Dublin.* 1820.
John. *Galway.* 1824.
W. *Kingston.* Early 19c.
BURKET, Edward. *London.* a.1700.
BURKHARDT—
Jakob. *Basle.* 1779.
& BRANDT. *Chaux-de-Fonds.* ca.1800. Very small watch M.M.A.
Heinrich Gabriel. *Leipzig.* comp. 1801. cf. BURGHARDT.
BÜRKI, Georg Urban. *Soleure.* ca.1780. *Pforzheim.* 1785.
BURKITT, ——. ——. an.1764. Watch.
BURKLOE, Samuel. *Philadelphia.* 1794-1818. W.
BURLEIGH—
Ninyan. *Durham.* CC.1692. br. clock. Watch.
Nicholas. *Durham.* an.1773. Watch.
BURLERET, Antoine. *Besançon.* 1554-64. Serrurier. In charge of clock of St. Pierre.
BURLEY, T. *Sheffield.* Early 18c. Watch Den. coll.
BURN—
Joseph. *West Bromwich.* 1781. C. & W. Succeeded John BAGNALL.

BURN—*continued.*
Peter. *London.* a.1778-1820.
Richard. *Liverpool.* 1784. W.
James. *London.* a.1780.
David. *Edinburgh.* 1798.
BURNABY, Thomas. *London.* a.1697.
BURNAP, Daniel. *East Windsor, U.S.A.* End 18c. C.
BURNE, James. *Chester.* an.1774. Watch.
BURNET—
Thomas. *London.* Early 18c. sil. p.c. watch.
John. *Tarves.* 1810-46.
BURNETT—
Richard. *London.* a.1695, CC.1706. sil. watch Feill coll.
Philip. *London.* CC.1715.
Nathaniel. *London.* an.1762. Watch.
William. *London.* an.1770. Watch.
Charles. *London.* an.1770. Watch.
John. *London (Rosemary Lane),* an.1770-1825. Watch.
BURNHAM, John. *London.* a.1747.
BURNOT, Edme. *Brussels.* Mid. 17c. Very fine en. watch.
BURNS—
Richard. *Liverpool.* 1770. *Manchester,* 1778-1806. C. & W.
Joseph. *Walsall.* 1765-95. l.c. clock.
David. *Mid-Calder.* 1797.
Robert. *Melrose.* d.1832.
Hugh. *Philadelphia.* 1811.
BURQUI, Wolff. *Middelburg.* Mid. 18c. sil. p.c. watch Feill coll.
BURR—
James. *Bristol.* 1754-83.
& WOOD. *Bristol.* 1775-83.
BURRAGE, John. *Annapolis, U.S.A.* Left in 1769. C. & W.
BURRELL—
Mary. *Wiston.* a.1718.
William. *London.* a.1726.
——. *Collingham.* 1800. Turret clock Sutton-on-Trent Church.
BURRILL, Boys Err. *London.* a.1776, CC. 1796-1817.
BURROUGH, T. *Devizes.* an.1787. Watch.
BURROWES, Thomas. *Strasbourg, Lancaster, U.S.A.* Came *U.S.A.* from *Ireland* 1784-1810, then returned to *Ireland.* Back in U.S.A. 1822. l.c. clocks.
BURROWS—
John. *London.* a.1697.
John. *London.* a.1707.
Thomas. *London.* a.1748.
Joseph. *London.* a.1763, CC.1773, l.CC. 1803, d.1816.
William James, *London (Barbican).* CC.1772-1781.
James. *London.* 1805-35.
BURRY (BURY or **BURI)**—
Jakob. *Basle.* m.1586-91.
Hans Jakob. *Basle.* 1609.
Jakob. *Basle.* 1625.
Jakob. *Basle.* 1642-71.
Herzog. *Basle.* 1667.
Leonhard. *Basle.* b.1633, m.1669, d.1706. Eminent maker, started watchmaking in Basle. Oval crys. watch Spitzer coll. sd. 'Bury.' Watch Gélis coll.
Jakob, son. *Paris.* b.1663, went Paris 1686, d.1722. Watch Basle M. Very fine crucifix of wood and sil. with hour and moon dial on upper part and astro. cyl. dials on ends of arms, Feill coll.
Leonhard, bro. *Basle.* b.1672, m.1697, d.1730.
Leonhard, son. *Basle.* b.1700, m.1730, d.1766.
BURSCOUGH, Thomas. *London.* a.1693.
BURSON, George. *London.* a.1742, CC.1749.
BURT, ——. *Deptford.* d.1774. C. & W.
BURTENWOOD, James. *London (Wapping).* 1799-1804.

BURTON—
Abraham. *London.* a.1650, CC.1657. Watch.
John. *London.* a.1672.
Roger. *London.* a.1678.
William. *London.* a.1681.
Samuel. *Hawkshead.* 1690. l.c. clock.
Thomas. *Hawkshead.* 1690.
John. *London (Mincing Lane).* 1726. W.
William. *London.* 1744-70. Watch Oldham M. and clock.
William. *Kendal.* ca.1750. Clock.
John. *London.* a.1744.
Francis. *London.* 1763, d.1772. W.
Emanuel. *Kendal.* 1760-ca.1800. l.c. clock.
William, son of Wm. *London.* CC.1770.
John. *London.* a.1718, l.CC.1776.
Caesar Lewis. *London.* a.1766.
Samuel. *Morley.* d.1785. C.
Emanuel, jun. *Kendal.* 1790-1828.
John. *Cranbrook.* 1795. W.
James. *Whitehaven.* 1795. Watch.
James. *London (Carey St.).* 1805-19. W.
James. *London (Bethnal Green).* 1805-08. W.
Thomas. *London.* 1809-24.
T. *N. Shields.* 1811.
William. *S. Shields.* 1820-47.
Jonathan. *Ulverstone.* ca.1820.
Isaac. *Ulverstone.* 1820-9.
John. *London.* a.1816.
William. *Dunse (Scotland).* 1824.

BURWASH, William. *London.* 1799-1824. Watchcase maker.

BUSBY—
——. ——. an.1744. Watch.
Samuel. *Dublin.* an.1772. Watch.
William. *London.* 1805-08. W.

BUSCH—
Abraham Alb. *Hamburg.* 1680-ca.1720. Watches Feill coll. and Cassel Landes-M.
Erich. *Hamburg.* Late 17c. Watch Cassel Landes-M.
Franz Anton. *Mainz* and *Cologne.* 1772.

BUSCHBERG, Carl Ludwig. *Berlin.* 1780-1805. C.

BÜSCHENBERG, Friedrich. *Cothen (Basle).* 1760.

BUSCHMANN—
Caspar. *Augsburg.* b.1512, d.1613. Clock M.P.S. Dresden.
Caspar, son. *Augsburg.* d.1589.
Caspar, son. *Augsburg.* 1590-1611. Clock sd. 'Casparus Buschman, Automarius in Augusta, 1611.'
Matthäus, son. *Augsburg.* d.1636. W. Oval al. watch Fränkel coll.
Johannes, bro. *Augsburg.* m.1620-57. Guild of Watchmakers in 1657. Watches and clocks in Palace of Grossen-Behringen in Saxe-Coburg-Gotha, in Maximilian M. in Augsburg and in K.H.M.
David, son. *Augsburg.* 1640. d.1712. Watch M.M.A. Large sil. al. watch Ilbert coll. ill. Britten. Clock and watch K.H.M. Clock with sundial. Magnificent pair of column clocks, Neue Hofburg, Vienna. Skull watch Webster coll. Fine rect. clock supported by Atlas, with semi-circ. dial also forming sundial, Feill coll.
Hans. *Augsburg.* ca.1670. Clock ill. Britten. Ebony stand clock B.M. Clock in K.H.M. with sundial, compass and armillary sphere.
John. *London.* CC.1692-1725. W. German, came from *Hagen.* Wandering hour figure watch M.P.S. Dresden. p.c. sil. watch Feill coll.
Johann. *Germany.* Early 18c. Large g. watch Feill coll.
Georg Adam, son of David. *Augsburg.* b.1697, d.1756.
John Baptist. *London.* CC.1725, l.CC.1786. Fine p.c. g. repoussé rep. watch.

BUSCHMANN—*continued.*
John Baptist William, son. *London.* CC.1774. Also BUSHMAN.

BUSH—
James. *London.* a.1720, CC.1729-70.
Richard Rumley. *London.* a.1761.
Walter, son of James. *London.* CC.1770, d.1803.
Henry. *London.* a.1777.
William. *London.* a.1782.
William. *Bristol.* 1794-1801. W.
George, son of Walter. *London.* CC.1813.
George, *Easton, U.S.A.* 1812-37. C.
James. *London.* 1820.

BUSHEL—
Robert. *Liverpool.* 1734.
Thomas. *Liverpool.* 1761. W.

BUSHELL—
Edward. *London.* a.1687.
Samuel. *London.* a.1690.

BUSHMAN—
John. *London.* CC.1687-ca.1710. Watch showing hours and mins. in openings, S.K.M. Watches G.M., M.M.A. and Ilbert coll. Lantern clock. rep. br. clock Virginia M.
John Baptist. *v.* BUSCHMANN.
John Baptist William, son. *v.* BUSCHMANN.
Joseph. *London.* a.1752, CC.1759.
William. *Woolwich.* ca.1790 CC.
William. *London (Stratford).* 1805-08 CC.

BUSK, James. *London.* 1820. mt. maker.

BUSLEY, Charles. *London.* an.1753. Watch.

BUSMAN, S. *London.* Early 18c. sil. p.c. watch with en. portrait in case Feill coll.

BUSS, Jakob. *Basle.* 1790.

BÜSSARD, Ct. *Montmollin* and *Corcelles.* 1819-43. C.

BUSSEY—
James. *Bristol.* 1816-18. C.
James, jun. *Bristol.* 1825-30. C.

BUSSY, William. *London.* a.1714.

BUST, William. *Hull.* 18c. Clock.

BUTCHER—
Gersham. *London.* a.1711.
Gersham, son. *London.* a.1739, CC.1749.
Nathaniel. *Stradbroke.* 1738. Insolvent, C.
Henry. *London.* a.1742, CC.1760-91.
William. *London.* a.1747.
Benjamin, son of Henry. *London (Billingsgate).* CC.1781, l.CC.1812-20.
Thomas. *London.* a.1783.
Benjamin Henry. *London.* CC.1813.
William, son. *London.* CC.1815, l.CC.1820.
Henry Charles, bro. *London.* CC.1818.

BUTEUX—
Abraham. *London.* a.1736.
Isaac. *London.* a.1772. Also BUTTEU.

BUTLER—
John. *London.* a.1709.
Edward. *London.* a.1716.
John. *London.* a.1717, CC.1724-38. Watch.
P. *London.* ca.1750. Watch Horstmann coll.
Thomas. *London.* a.1742.
James. *Bolton-le-Moors.* 1760-95. l.c. clocks. Watch.
James. *Nantwich.* 1771. Watch.
William. *London.* an.1776. Watch.
Abraham. *Northwich.* 1784. C.
Edward. *Burton-on-Trent.* 1791. C. & W.
Caleb. *Christchurch.* 1791. W.
Edward. *Tutbury.* 1795. C. & W.
Joseph. *London.* a.1799.
John. *Reading.* Early 19c.
Jacob. *Bolton-le-Moors.* 1814-24.

BUTT—
T. *London.* Mid. 18c. Watch Ilbert coll.
H. *London.* 1758. Watch Den. coll.
John. *London.* an.1761. Watch.
Robert. *London.* an.1767. Watch

BUTTERFIELD—
——. *Paris.* d.1724. Well-known math. inst. maker. sil. sundials B.M., G.M. and Fränkel coll.
Thomas. *London.* a.1719-44. Watch. Inn clock.
Edward. *London.* a.1720.
F. *London.* an.1769. Watch.
John. *Todmorden.* ca.1780-1814.
BUTTERLY, William. *Dartford.* 1791. C.
BUTTERWORTH—
Samuel. *Packer.* d.1796. C.
Thomas. *London* (*Bethnal Gr.*). 1805-08.
BUTTON, J. & F. PUTLEY. *London.* 1788. Bankrupt.
BUTZ, Hans. ——. ca.1630. Gilt shell watch Arts M. Prague.
BUTZENGEIGER, H. *Germany.* Late 18c. Worked to improve Harrison's chron.
BUXTON—
Wilson. *London.* a.1726, CC.1733-7.
Henry. *Wolverhampton.* 1748-75. l.c. clock.
Edward. *London.* an.1770. Watch.
Samuel. *Diss.* an.1773. Watch. l.c. clock.
BUYET, C. Massart. *Amsterdam.* 1822. W.
BUZ—
Johannes. *Augsburg.* ca.1625. Watch S.K.M. ill. Baillie.
Hanns. *Germany.* ca.1625. Watch mt. B.M.
BUZOT, Joseph. *Paris.* m.1771-89.
BYAN, Pierre de. *Montbéliard.* 1501.
BYARD, John. *London.* an.1786-1811. Watch
BYÉ, Henri. *Paris.* ca.1400-28. Keeper of clock on the Palais de Justice.
BYFIELD (BIFIELD, BIEFIELD, BEIFIELD, BEEFIELD, BEFFIELD)—
William. *London.* a.1711. Watch.
George. *London.* an.1770-86. Watches Ilbert coll. and N.Y. Univ.
Charles. *London.* an.1770. p.c. g. watch.
Christopher. *London.* an.1777. Watch.
BYFORD, William. *London.* CC.1815-35. W.
BYLES, Henry Aishley. *London.* a.1777.
BYNGERTS, Carl Fredric. *Göteborg.* b.1795, d.1831.
BYRNE—
James. *Athlone.* 1820.
C. *Dublin.* Early 19c. Watch.
BYRON (BYROM)—
William. *Cork.* 1824. Watch.
Martin. *Fermoy.* 1824.
William. *Tralee.* 1824.
BYSSE, Edward. *London.* ca.1630 CC. Fritillary niello watch B.M. ill. Baillie. Prob. same as BISSE.
BYWORTH—
George. *London.* a.1796, CC.1815.
Thomas. *London.* a.1799, CC.1815-40. W. & C.

C

CABAN (**CABANT**), Jean Charles. *Paris.* m.1763-89. 'Monteur de boîtes.'
CABANEL—
Louis. *Geneva.* ca.1770-91.
——. *Paris.* 1812.
CABANIS, Jean Pierre. *Geneva.* ca.1760-82. From *Languedoc.*
CABASSÉ, ——. *Paris.* 1788.
CABLE—
Peter. *Diss.* 1784. W.
John Robert. *London.* a.1813.
CABOT—
Guillaume. *London.* 1654. Journeyman. Prob. same as following.
Guillaume. *Rouen.* m.1657.
Jacques, son. *Rouen.* m.1701.
Nicolas Antoine. *Paris.* m.1748.
Jean Vincent. *Paris.* m.1755.
Jacques Innocent. *Rouen.* 1768 m.
——. *Paris* (*Quai de la Mégisserie*). 1812.
CABRI, Paul Salomon. *Geneva.* ca.1770-91.
CABRIER—
Charles. *London* (*Lombard St.*). CC.1697-1724. Watches B.M., G.M. and Fränkel coll. Fine astro. br. clock Feill coll.
Charles, son. *London.* a.1719, CC.1726, m.CC.1757-72. Famous maker. 2 watch mts. G.M. Watches London M. and M.M.A. Aut. watch M.P.S. Dresden. Fine watch and chatelaine, set agate and diamonds, Winter Pal. Petrograd. g. watch Nat. M. Stockholm. p.c. g. rep. watch Feill coll.
John, son of Charles (1). *London.* CC.1730-1736.
Charles, son of Charles (2). *London.* 1752. CC.1755. d.1777. Famous maker. Watches in G.M., F.W.M., Chamb. coll., Fränkel coll., Peiping M. and Carnegie M.
Rebecca, sister. *London.* 1778. Continued business for a short time alone and then with Gabriel Leekey.
& Leekey. *London.* 1778-1804.
Robert. *London.* an.1783. Watch.
Leekey & Son. *London.* 1795-1805.
Favey & Exchequer. *London.* 1795.
Favey & Son. *London.* 1799-1804.
CABRY, Jean. *Grenoble.* 1624-45. C. to the Princess of Piedmont.
CACHARD—
——. *Paris.* ca.1780-1802. Successor to Ch. Le Roy. Mantel clocks Garde Meuble, Paris, and Château de la Malmaison, and Hamburg M. für Kunst und Gewerbe.
Gasper. *London.* 1820-5. W. & C.
CACKETT—
Thomas. *Canterbury.* 1748. W.
Thomas. *Cranbrook.* an.1762. Retired 1774. Watch.
CADE—
Simon. *London.* a.1680, CC.1688-1730.
& Robinson. *London.* 1820-5. br. clock Weth coll. ill. Britten.
CADGELL, Thomas. *London.* a.1682.
CADIER, ——. *Paris.* an.1713. rep. watch Gélis coll.
CADMAN, George. *London.* a.1729.
'C. M. CADY.' Sig. on 1871-4 watches of Cornell Watch Co.
CAFFAUT—
Charles François. *Paris.* 1751 m.
Veuve (of preceding). *Argenteuil.* 1789.
CAFFIÉRI, Philippe. *Paris.* b.1714, d.1774. Bronze caster and chiseller of great renown. Many clock cases.
CAGÉ, ——. *Paris.* 1812-23.
CAHILL, John. *London.* a.1796.
CAHUC, Zachariah. *London.* a.1765.
CAILLARD, J. M. C. *Paris.* 1810-25. g. rep. watch.
CAILLATTE—
Abraham. *Geneva.* b.1642, d.1710. French refugee. Watches Louvre, M.M.A. and Gélis coll. Watch in shell-shaped case of garnet. en. g. mountings. Mantel clock.
Jean. *Copenhagen.* End 17c.
Bartholomeus. *Copenhagen.* mar. 1726, d.1761. Master of Corporation.
Jacques, son. *Copenhagen.* a.1743.
David. *Copenhagen.* m.1771.
CAILLAUD—
——. *Paris* (*Rue du Four St. Germain*). 1807-25.
——. *Paris* (*Rue Richelieu*). 1824.
CAILLE—
Louis. *Paris.* Early 17c. sil. p.c. watch Fränkel coll.
Moïse. *La Rochelle.* 1681.
——. *Paris.* Early 18c. Fine Boulle cartel clock.
Claude. *Paris.* m.1739.
Louis. *London.* ca.1770. Watches G.M. and Fränkel coll.
——. *Paris.* 1786.
CAILLOT, ——. *Paris.* ca.1790-1823. Watch.
CAILLOUET, ——. *Paris.* 1808-15.
CAIN, William. *Liverpool.* 1825. W.
CAITHNESS & BICKNELL. *London.* Early 19c. Watch.
CAJETANO, *v.* San Cajetano.
CALAME—
Daniel. *Le Locle* and *Les Brenets.* a.1754.
Jacques. *Le Locle.* 1794. C.
David. *London.* 1799. W.
——. *Paris.* ca.1790-1825. Fine mantel clock.

CALAME-BESSON—
Josué. *La Brevine.* 1790. C.
Jonas Frédéric. *Les Gras* and *La Brevine.* 1821-31. C.
CALAME-ROSSET, Jean Pierre. *Chaux-de-Fonds.* b.1769, d.1833. C. Many clocks.
CALBECK, John. *London.* a.1672.
CALCOT, Tobias. *London.* CC.1664.
CALCUTT, Peter. *Roscommon.* 1824. W.
CALDECOTT, John. *Huntingdon.* 1795. W.
CALDER—
John. *Glasgow.* 1775-1816.
John. *Glasgow.* 1814-28.
John. *Edinburgh.* 1819.
CALDERWOOD—
Thomas. *London.* a.1717, CC.1724.
Andrew. *Philadelphia.* 1802-20. W.
CALDWELL—
John. *Glasgow.* 1812.
William. *Glasgow.* 1820-37.
James. *Coleraine.* 1820-4.
'CALIFORNIA WATCH CO.' Sig. on 1876 watches. Successor to CORNELL WATCH Co.
CALIM, Pietro. *Genoa.* 1677-85. German. Keeper of clock on Palazzo delle Compere.
CALINO, Jacob. *Fürth.* 1722. Maker of repute. cf. CATINO.
CALL, *v.* VAN CALL.
CALLAM—
Robert. *London.* an.1760. Watch.
Alexander. *London.* 1790-1808 CC.
Charles. *Edinburgh.* 1804.
Archbald. *Douglas.* d.1834.
CALLAUD, ——. *Paris.* 1825.
CALLÉ ——. *Paris.* Early 19c. Mantel clock.
CALLENDER, James. *Edinburgh.* a.1731.
CALLERSTRÖM—
Anders. *Stockholm.* 1769, d.ca.1775. Watch Nord. M. br. clock.
Lars. *Stockholm.* 1780. d. an.1790. Watch Nord. M.
Johan Er. *Stockholm.* 1817-30. 2 trav. and br. clocks and watch.
CALLET, François. *Paris.* b.1774, d.1798. Prof. of Mathematics. Pub. 'Essai sur les échappements.'
CALLEY, Joseph. *London.* a.1744, CC.1752.
CALLIDON, G. *London.* an.1777. Watch.
CALLIER, ——. *Paris.* 1825.
CALLIS, Robert. *London.* CC.1764.
CALLMAN, Eric. *Stockholm.* 1747. d.1759. 2 watches.
CALLON, Thurston. *London.* an.1765. Watch.
CALLWOOD—
John. *Liverpool.* 1790-6. C.
Susannah. *Liverpool.* 1803-05. C.
CALNEN, Patrick. *Dublin.* 1795.
CALTON, William. *London.* a.1792.
CALUNG, Johann Jacob. *Cologne.* m.1727. Kleinuhrmacher.
CALVAT, Antoine. *Berlin.* 1770.
CALVER—
John. *Woodbridge.* 1739-47. l.c. clock. Watch mt.
——. *London.* an.1755. Watch.
James. *Woodbridge.* From 1774. C. & W.
——. *Diss.* 1791. W.
William. *Eye.* 1812. Watch Ilbert coll.
CALVERT, Nicholas. *London.* a.1655.
CALVISI, Giovanni Battista. *Florence.* End 18c. Made a Franklin clock.
CAM, William. *London.* CC.1686-90. Lantern and l.c. clock.
CAMAL, Peter. *Brussels.* an.1778. Watch.
CAMBRIDGE—
Samuel. *London.* a.1683, CC.1698.
John. *London.* 1703 CC.
CAMDEN—
William. *London.* a.1701, CC.1708-51. Also CAMPDEN. Watch B.M. l.c. clock.

CAMDEN—*continued.*
Richard. *London.* a.1709.
William, son of William. *London.* CC.1751.
John. *London.* an.1811. Watch.
CAMEEL—
Caspar. *Strasbourg.* 1622.. Also KAMEHL. oct. watch S.K.M. crys. watch made for Christian IV in Rosenborg Castle. Oval str. and al. watch Gélis coll.
Georg. *Strasbourg.* 1650.
CAMELIN—
Pierre. *Avignon.* 1638-70. Town C.
Baptiste. *Avignon.* 1670-6. Town C.
CAMERER—
ROPP & Co. *London.* 1788-94.
A., & Co. *London.* 1799-1840. Wooden C.
Laurence. *London.* 1802.
CAMERINI, ——. *Turin.* 1656. 2 table clocks Webster coll. with pendulums, one dated 1656.
CAMERON—
A. *Liverpool.* d.1800. W.
James. *Edinburgh.* a.1776.
Hugh. *Johnshaven.* 1780-90.
John. *Perth.* 1795.
Alexander. *Selkirk.* 1816. W.
Angus. *London.* a.1809.
James. *Dundee.* Early 19c. Watch.
D. *London.* 1823. Pump wind watch Ilbert coll.
Alexander. *Dundee.* 1828-37. Watch.
CAMM, James or Thomas. *London.* a.1793.
CAMMANS, John. *London.* a.1716.
CAMOZZI, C. *Bicester.* Early 19c. Watch.
CAMPANI, Giovanni. *Rome.* ca.1700. Rolling ball clock Cassel Landes-M.
CAMPANUS—
Matthaeus, de Alimenis. *Rome.* 1661-78. A priest with mechanical tastes. Author of two books, 'Nuova invenzione d'orivoli giustissimi ad uso della navigazione,' 1672, and 'Horologium solo naturae motu, atque ingenio dimetiens . . . ,' Amsterdam, 1678. Shows an impracticable clock with two pendulums. Became famous for his work in making telescope lenses.
Petrus Thomas. *Rome.* 1683. Night-light clock with moving hour figure in temple case, and crank connection to pendulum, Ilbert coll.
CAMPBELL—
Hugh. *Edinburgh.* a.1692.
Archibald. *Gourock.* b.1698, d.1807. W.
William. *Stirling.* 1745.
Charles. *Bo'ness.* b.1732, d.1812.
John. *Harwich.* d.1760. W. Succeeded by John PAGE.
Neal. *Aylesbury.* an.1762. Watch.
Francis. *London.* a.1755.
Alexander. *London.* an.1772-ca.1800. Watch.
John. *Campbell's Town, Annapolis.* an.1773. Watch.
Robert. *Edinburgh.* 1778-94.
James. *London.* an.1782. Watch.
Charles. *Philadelphia.* 1796-1802.
Alexander. *Philadelphia.* 1798. W.
John. *Edinburgh.* 1799-1819.
& BEATON. *London.* ca.1800.
F. *Oswestry.* ca.1800.
James. *Edinburgh.* a.1803-10.
Isaac. *Philadelphia.* 1813-24.
John. *Glasgow.* 1823.
William. *Downpatrick.* 1824.
CAMPE, Thomas. *London.* a.1672.
CAMPER, Peter. *London.* a.1712.
CAMPEY, Joseph. *York.* 1758. C.
CAMPIN, ——. *Norwich.* Late 18c. Inn clock.
CAMPION, Thomas. *London.* End 17c. Gilt metal en. watch.
CAMPLESHON, Hannah. *London.* a.1722.
CAMPLIN, Joseph. *Bristol.* 1794-1812.

CAMUS—
Jean. *Blois.* 1611.
Jacques. *Paris.* 1674. Juré. Also LE CAMUS.
——. *Paris.* 1722. Made clock going for one year. Perhaps DE CAMUS.
Charles Étienne Louis. *Paris.* b.1699, d.1768. Prof. of math. Pub. Mem. on the form of teeth for clocks in 1733 which appears in Thiout's 'Traité d'horlogerie,' 1741, and in Camus' 'Cours de Mathématiques,' Vol. 4. 'Theorie des Engrenages.' 1749.
Guillaume. *Paris.* m.1780-9. 'Monteur de boîtes.'
CANARIES, James. *London.* a.1700.
CANBY, Charles. *Wilmington, U.S.A.* b. 1792, retired 1852.
CANCHE, Jacques (James). *London.* 1689. CC.1692. p.c. al. watch B.M. Also CANCH and CAUCH.
CANDONE, Jehan. *France.* 1403. C. to the duc de Bourgogne.
CANN—
John. *London.* a.1647, d.1654. CC.
Judah. *London.* a.1650.
William. *London.* 1687. CC.
James. *London.* a.1775.
CANNON—
John. *London.* a.1715, CC.1723-32.
William. *Philadelphia.* a.1738.
John. *Marlborough.* an.1756. Watch. l.c. clock.
John. *Highworth.* 1739. C.
John, son. *London.* a.1739.
CANT—
——. *London.* an.1743. Watch.
James. *Perth.* 1824.
CANTER & SON. *London.* an.1783. Watch.
CANTERBURY,——. *London.* 1744. Watch.
CANTIS, John. *London.* a.1799.
CANVIN, John. *London.* an.1757. Watch.
CAPELL—
William. *London.* a.1728.
Thomas. *London.* an.1786. Watch.
CAPOBIANCO, Giorgio. *Schio.* 1550.
CAPON—
Katherine. *London.* a.1737.
Francis. *Bridgewater.* 1795. W.
CAPPELEN, ——. *Aarhus.* m.1777.
CAPPER—
Samuel. *London.* a.1674.
Michael. *Philadelphia.* 1799.
CAPPS—
Robert. *London.* a.1761-87. W.
Frederick Daniel, son. *London.* a.1787.
CAPT—
Jean Antoine. *Geneva.* ca.1760-73.
& FREUNDLER. *Geneva.* ca.1790-1829.
Henri Daniel. *Geneva.* 1802-11. In firm with Isaac Daniel PIGUET.
CAPT. DE LA FALCONNIÈRE, C. *Geneva.* Early 19c.
CAPUSEAU, Pierre. *Lyons.* 1677. Went to PERSIA.
CARACCIA, ——. *London.* Early 19c. Watch.
CARAVIAGGIO, Bernardo. *Pavia.* 16c.
CARBONELL, ——. *London.* 1738. W.
CARBOUET, ——. *Paris.* 1812.
CARCAIN, ——. ——. Mid. 17c. sil. watch in form of shell.
CARCEL—
Bernard Guillaume (l'aîné). *Paris.* m.1778-1812.
Alexandre (le jeune). *Paris.* m.1788-1825.
CARD—
Edmund. *London.* a.1672, CC.1680.
James. *London.* a.1760.
CARDAN, Hieronymus. *Bologna* and *Rome.* b.1501, d.1576. Treats of clocks in 'De varietate rerum.'
CARDINAUX, ——. *Paris.* 1807-13.
CARDOUIN, J. *Paris.* 2nd half 18c. Four-colour g. and en. watch Feill coll.
CAREFUL, P. *Coventry.* an.1785. Watch.
CAREL, Louis. *Moulins.* 1443-55. 'Maistre faiseur de mouvemens d'orloiges.' Made a jacquemart for the town clock.
CARELS, Joseph. *Philadelphia.* 1718. W.
CARESWELL, Francis. *Shrewsbury.* 1783-95. *v.* CARSWELL.
CAREY—
George. *London.* a.1671, CC.1679-84. Also CARY.
Thomas. *London.* a.1691, CC.1705-10.
Henry. *London.* a.1769.
CARL, Dionisius. *Krems.* ca.1740. Watch Ilbert coll.
CARLENIUS—
Johan. *Åmål.* 1787-94.
Petter. *Kristinehamn.* 1794.
CARLESS, Charles. *Gainsborough.* 1795.
CARLET, ——. *Paris.* 1812.
CARLETON, Robert. *London.* a.1687.
CARLEY—
Jonathan. *London* and *Thetford.* Early 19c. Watch.
George. *Diss.* Early 19c. Watch.
CARLILL, James Bellamy. *York.* In 1799 dissolved partnership with Jas. PRIDGIN. W.
CARLIN, Martin. *Paris.* ca.1770. Clock in Louvre by Carlin et Gouthière.
CARLOW, P. *London.* 1780-1800. p.c. g. watch.
CARLSON, C. *Sweden.* ca.1790. br. clock.
CARLSSON, Anders. *Stockholm.* 1814-25. 2 wall clocks.
CARLTON, C. *London.* an.1772. Watch.
CARLYON, James. *London.* a.1722.
CARMAN, Samuel. *Harleston.* Early 19c. Watch.
CARMICHAEL—
John. *Greenock.* 1750-1800. Clock in Greenock church. l.c. clock.
James. *Edinburgh.* 1796.
——. *London.* Early 19c. Watch.
CARNABY, John. *Newcastle.* 1778.
CARNE, John. *Penzance.* Late 18c. Watch.
CARNES, John. *Liverpool.* Early 19c. Watch.
CAROLAN—
Edward. *Dublin.* 1780.
James. *London.* 1820.
Edward M'Donnell. *Carrickmacross.* 1824.
CAROLUS, S. *London.* an.1783. Watch.
CARON—
Daniel. *Lizy-sur-Ourcq.* ca.1720.
André Charles, son. *Paris.* b.1697, d.1775. C. to Louis xv. Very fine Boulle l.c. clock, Hofburg, Vienna, prob. by him.
ET LÉPINE. *Paris.* 1756-ca.1760. *v.* LÉPINE.
Peter Auguste, son. *Paris.* b.1732, d.1799. Famous maker. C. to the King in 1755. Wrote 'Le Barbier de Seville,' etc., under name of Beaumarchais. Made a very small watch for Mme de Pompadour. Devised the double virgule escapement, and accused J. A. LEPAUTE of copying it. The Acad. des. Sci. decided in his favour. Made a ring watch with bezel winding for Mme Pompadour. No example of his work known.
François Modeste. *Paris.* m.1770, juré 1788.
——. *London.* Late 18c. l.c. clock Uhren M. Vienna.
CAROVAGIUS, Bernhard. *Pavia.* 1500-50. Made clock for Alciati which sounded alarum, struck light and lit lamp.
CARPENTER—
John. *London.* a.1715.
Henry. *London.* a.1735.
Charles. *London.* a.1743.
Thomas. *London (St. John's St.).* CC.1767. l.CC.1787-1800. Ruby cyl. watch G.M.

CARPENTER—*continued.*
William. *London* (*Soho*). 1770-1805 CC. Gilt mus. aut. clock made for India, S.K.M., and two elaborate aut. mus. clocks Peiping M. by a Wm. Carpenter.
Richard. *Leeds*. an.1775. Watch.
Richard. *London*. an.1776. Watch.
David. *London*. a.1778.
William. *London*. a.1783.
Thomas. *London*. 1795. Watchcase maker.
Thomas, son of Thos. (1). *London*. a.1791.
William. *London*. a.1792.
William. *London* (*St. Martin's Lane*). 1799-1811.
Richard, son of Thos. (2). *London*. a.1793.
William. *London* (*Hoxton*). 1805-24. Watch.
Anthony. *New Holland, U.S.A.* b.1790, d.1868. l.c. clocks.

CARPENTRAS, Guillaume de. *Aix. Lyons*, 1476. 'Astrologien et faiseur d'orloges.'

CARQUILLOT, Jean. *Abbeville*. ca.1680. str. and al. watch G.M.

CARR—
T. *London*. an.1771. Watch.
Mary. *England*. 1789. Watch Ilbert coll.
William. *England*. Early 19c. br. clock.

CARRACK, Robert. *London*. a.1721.

CARRÉ—
Jean. Prob. *Paris*. ca.1650. Watch mt. B.M.
Paul. *La Rochelle*. Protestant banished in 1661.
Daniel. Prob. *Paris*. ca.1690. cal. watch G.M.
Jean Baptiste. *Paris*. 1747 comp.
Louis David. *Paris*. m.1748, juré 1767, d.1779.
Pierre Jean, son of J. B. *Paris*. a.1747.
Joseph Claude. *Paris*. m.1778-89. Also CARRÉE.

CARRELL—
John & Daniel. *Philadelphia*. 1785. C. & W.
John. *Philadelphia*. 1791.

CARRIER, Jean. *Paris*. m.1776.

CARRINGTON—
James. *London*. a.1709, CC.1717, m.CC. 1768.
Robert. *London* (*Lillipot La.*). a.1736, CC. 1743. l.CC.1766, d.1792.
Thomas. *London* (*Bishopsgate*). a.1740, CC. 1748, l.CC.1766-93. Partner with Thomas GIBBONS to 1755.
William. *London*. a.1741. Watch.
Richard. *London* (*Old Bethlem*). a.1751, CC.1759-84. Watch and clock.
Robert, son of Robert. *London*. a.1758.
George, bro. *London*. a.1773, CC.1782.
Robert, son of Robert (2). *London* (*Castle St.*). CC.1790.
Harry Charles, son of Richard. *London*. a. 1785, CC.1791. Went to *Basingstoke*.
Thomas, bro. *London*. CC.1796.

CARRISOL (**CARRISOT**), Jean. Prob. *Geneva*. Early 19c. Spring-maker who sd. his springs.

CARROLI—
Christianus. *Königsberg*. ca.1700. hex. table clock.
William. *Cork*. 1824.

CARRON, Samuel. *London*. 1689. CC.

CARRS, John. *London*. a.1793.

CARRUTHERS—
George. *Walsall*. an.1775. Watch.
George. *London*. 1783-1804. l.CC. W. *v.* CARUTHERS.
——. *Pershore*. ca.1800. l.c. clock.
James. *Belfast*. 1819-24. Watch Belfast M.

CARSTENS—
Heinrich. *Lübeck*. 1650. Famous maker. Watch B.M.
John. *London*. CC.1707.

CARSWELL—
Joseph. *Hastings*. 2nd half 18c. l.c. clock.
& HARPER. *Shrewsbury*. Late 18c. *v.* CARESWELL.
John. *London*. a.1804, CC.1819.

CART—
Pierre. *Paris*. 1817-23.
Philippe. *Paris*. 1824.

CARTE—
John. *Coventry*. 1689. CC.1695. *London* in 1698. Watch Marryat coll.
J. *Hamburg*. Early 18c. Prob. the preceding. MS. Treatise on Watchmaking in Bodleian. Made 8-day watch for Landgrave of Cassel.

CARTELLIER, Thomas. *Geneva*. a.1623.

CARTER—
Thomas. *London*. a.1651, CC.1659.
John. *London* (*St. James' St.*). a.1669-95.
Francis. *London*. a.1670.
Thomas. *London*. a.1674.
William. *Philadelphia*. 1683. d.1738. W.
Samuel. *London*. a.1683.
Thomas. *London*. a.1690, CC.1699.
Thomas. *London*. a.1694.
William. *Ampthill*. ca.1700-40. l.c. clock ill. Cec. & Web.
William. *London* and *Cambridge*. an.1714-ca.1720. Watch. Den. coll.
Thomas. *London*. a.1711.
Thomas. *London*. a.1712.
Hewes. *London*. a.1716.
Leon Augustus. *London*. a.1717, CC.1725.
John. *London*. a.1720, CC.1728-72. 2 l.c. clocks ill. Cec. & Web.
William. *London*. a.1725-94. Watch mt. G.M.
Christopher. *London*. a.1728.
James. *London*. 1733 CC.-1760. l.c. clock.
Robert. *London*. a.1731.
Edmond. *London*. a.1732, CC.1740.
Thomas. *Bishop Auckland*. 1745. C. & W.
Edmond. *London*. a.1739, CC.1749.
Edmond. *London*. a.1739, CC.1776.
Samuel. *London*. a.1747.
——. *Bishop's Stortford*. ca.1760-84. l.c. clock. W.
William. *Uxbridge*. an.1774. Watch.
William. *Preston*. ca.1770.
William. *London* (*Bermondsey*). 1770-99.
Joyce. *London*. CC.1776.
William. *Ripon*. an.1790-5. W.
& SON. *Ripon*. ca.1790.
William. *London* (*Tooley St.*). 1795.
William, jun. *London* (*Tooley St.*). 1805-25. Watch.
Jacob. *Philadelphia*. 1806. W. cf. CARVER.
J. *London* (*Mile End*). 1806-20. W.
William. *London*. a.1808-26.
James. *Warrington*. ca.1820.
John. *Warrington*. ca.1820.
Robert. *Warrington*. ca.1820.
Richard. *Liverpool*. ca.1820.
M. *London*. 1820-4.
William. *Walthamstow*. 1821. Clock.
J. *Nottingham*. Early 19c. Watch.
John. *London*. a.1817, CC.1829, m.CC.1856, 1859 and 1864, d.1878. Lord Mayor.
Herbert Watkins. *London*. a.1818.
Thomas. *Philadelphia*. 1823. W.

CARTHEW, Thomas. *London*. a.1751.

CARTIER—
Jacques. *London*. 1635-80. Watch en. by Huaud le puisné, Fränkel coll.
Jacques & André. *London*. ca.1680. g. en. watch.
Germain. *Geneva*. ca.1770-91.
——. *Paris*. 1825.

CARTWRIGHT—
Thomas. *London*. a.1693. d.1741. W. to Queen Anne and King George I. Watch mt. with sil. and crys. cock G.M. Watch Den. coll. Watch Ilbert coll. with 'Watch-

CARTWRIGHT—*continued.* maker to the Prince,' and 'Horologius Principis.'
George. *London.* a.1698, CC.1706-14. Watch B.M.
William. *London.* a.1705, CC.1714-29. l.c. clock.
N. *London.* Early 18c. Watch mt. with sil. pillars G.M.
Robert. *London.* a.1729.
William. *Oxford.* 1759. Previously in *London.* T.C.
John. *Cheadle.* d.1789.
CARTY, William. *Dublin.* 1820.
CARUS, Henry. *London.* a.1709. *Paris.* 1733. p.c. str. trav. clock S.K.M.
CARUTHERS, George. *London.* a.1760, CC. 1773, l.CC.1788. cf. CARRUTHERS.
CARVELL, William. *London.* a.1726.
CARVER—
Isaac. *London.* CC.1667-89. math. inst. maker. Watch.
Jacob. *Philadelphia.* 1785-1825.
G. *Philadelphia.* 1797. W.
CARWELL, Thomas. *Redbourn.* an.1778, Watch.
CARY—
George. *London.* a.1671, CC.1679-84. Also CAREY.
Margaret. *London.* a.1703.
Robert. *London.* a.1707. Watch.
James. Mid. 18c. Watch.
John. *London.* a.1790. From *Shepton Mallett.*
James. *Brunswick, U.S.A.* 1808-50. C.
CASCOYN, Anne. *London.* a.1732. Prob. error for GASCOYNE.
CASE, Rastus. *London.* 1760. Watch mt.
CASHMORE, M. J. *London.* 1820. W.
CASIMIR—
——. *Paris.* ca.1750 m.
François. *Paris.* a.1758.
CASIMIRE, Josiah. *London.* a.1715.
CASPER, Nathaniel. *London.* 1825-40.
CASS—
George. *London.* a.1760, CC.1771-1817. l.c. clock.
John. *London.* an.1771. Watch.
CASSIN, Jean François. *Paris.* m.1786, juré 1787.
CASSINGHURST, Christopher. *London.* a.1690.
CASSINI, Jacques. *Paris.* b.1677, d.1756. Devised a compensated pendulum, desc. in mem. pub. 1741.
CASSWAY, Charles. *London.* a.1656.
CASTAGNET, Jacques Joseph. *Paris.* m. 1776, juré 1780-9.
CASTAN, STEPHEN & CO. *Philadelphia.* 1819. W.
CASTANG, Philip. *London.* 1777. Watch G.M.
CASTANIER, Jacques. *Geneva.* ca.1760. gilt en. watch. sil. repoussé watch.
CASTEL FRÈRES. *Bourg.* 1767-ca.1770. Took over a watch factory at Bourg which the Province had started in 1764. Watch sd. CASTEL, ca.1700, Gélis coll. *v.* SAVARIN.
CASTELL—
Edward. *London.* 1744. Watch.
John. *London.* 1778. Shagreen case maker.
CASTENS, John. *London.* a.1700, CC.1707.
CASTER, William. *London.* a.1690, CC.1697.
CASTERTON—
James. *London.* a.1794, CC.1803, l.CC. 1812-15.
James, son. *London.* a.1815.
CASTING, John. *London* (?). an.1778. Watch.
CASTLE, Edmund. *London.* a.1750.
CASTON (COSTEN)—
John. *Kirkham.* ca.1770. d.1803.
William. *Kirkham.* ca.1780.
CATCHPOOL—
Thomas. *London* (*Richmond*). Early 19c. Rack lever watch mt. G.M.
W. *London* (*Richmond*). 1817-24.
William. *London.* 1825. W.
CATEL, Pierre Fréderic. *Berlin.* 1770. astro. clock.
CATER—
——. *London.* 1672. Widow.
William. *London.* a.1698.
Stephen. *Charleston, U.S.A.* 1744-8. C. & W.
J. *London.* Mid. 18c. g. watch Gemeente M. The Hague.
CATERMOUL, John. *London.* a.1796.
CATES, John. *London.* a.1715.
CATHERALL, J. *Chorley.* 1814. cf. CATTERALL.
CATHERWOOD—
William. *London.* a.1761.
Joseph. *London.* 1790-1815. Regulator clock Virginia M. Watch Ilbert coll.
John. *London.* 1795.
J., & Son. *London.* 1817-24. Successors.
CATHRO—
G. & R. *London.* 1802-25.
——. *Dundee.* 1823. chron. maker.
Thomas G. *Quebec.* Early 19c. Lever watch Chamb. coll.
CATIN (CATTIN)—
Jean Baptiste. *Fort-du-Plane* (*Franche-Comté*). 1734-46. Designed an equation mechanism and an alarum detent. *v.* OUTHIER.
Maximin, bro. *Fort-du-Plane.* 1734.
Les Frères. *Fort-de-Plane.* 1734. The two preceding. Made clock for St. Maurice, Besançon. The present clock of Autun Cathedral was made in 1751 by a Catin of Franche-Comté.
Jean Norbert (dit DES BOIS). *Paris.* m. 1786-9.
J. L. *Chaux-de-Fonds.* End 18c.
CATINO, Jacob. *Fürth.* 1720. cf. CALINO.
CATLEY (CATTLEY), Daniel. *London.* CC. 1731, d.1779.
CATLIN (CATLING)—
Daniel. *King's Lynn.* Late 17c. and early 18c. Lantern and l.c. clock.
William. *London.* an.1773. Watch.
Daniel. *King's Lynn.* 1784. W.
CATLINGTON, ——. *London.* d.1778.
CATMUR, Thomas. *London.* a.1724.
CATON—
Gilbert. *London.* a.1737, CC.1747-52. Watchcase maker.
Francis. *London.* a.1783.
CATT, John. *London.* 1762.
CATTAERT, ——. *Paris.* 1812.
CATTANEO, P. *Croydon* and *Reigate.* Early 19c. Watch.
CATTELL—
William. *London.* a.1664, CC.1672-94. Lantern clock.
Thomas. *London.* a.1681, CC.1688-1714. Also CATTLE.
Thomas. *London.* a.1691.
William. *York.* 1822. W.
CATTERALL—
Benjamin. *Chester.* mar.1698. W.
Peter. *Liverpool.* 1763-74. W.
John. *Liverpool.* 1790-1829. W.
Joseph. *Chorley.* ca.1820. cf. CATHERALL.
CATTLE & BARBER. *York.* ca.1790-1810.
CATTLES *v.* HAMPTON, PRINCE & CATTLES
CATTON—
William. *London.* a.1792.
Richard. *London.* CC.1819. Duplex watch.

CAUCHARD, Dennis. *Bruges.* ca.1620. oct. crys. watch Lincoln M.
CAUDWELL, Edward. *Ashbrook* (*Blewbury*). 18c. l.c. lacquer clock.
CAUSARD, Georges. *Paris.* m.1770-89. Mantel clock Ministère de la Marine, Paris. Clock on elephant N.Y. Univ. l.c. clock.
CAUSTON—
Robert. *London.* a.1794.
R. H. *St. Albans.* Early 19c.
CAUTEREAU, ——. *Paris.* 1600. Signatory to Statuts of Paris Guild.
CAUVIÈRE, Étienne. *Lyons.* a.1603, m.1606.
CAVE—
W. *York.* 1794.
James. *Liverpool.* 1800-29. W.
CAVELL—
——. *Ipswich.* 1st half 18c. Painted l.c. clock Norsk Folke M. Oslo.
Nathaniel. *Ipswich.* 1784. W.
CAVENDISH, Richard. *London.* CC.1808, l.CC.1810. br. clock.
CAVIT, Ebenezer. *Bungay.* 1784. *Bedford.* 1785-1808. C. & W. Partnership with Thos. CLARE dissolved.
CAWDRON—
George. *London.* a.1675, CC.1684-94.
William. *London.* a.1710.
CAWDWELL, Thomas. *London.* a.1733, CC. 1742.
CAWKITT, Joseph. *London.* a.1695.
CAWKUTT, Thomas. *London.* a.1693.
CAWLEY—
Robert. *Chester.* 1728, d.1743. W.
Robert. *Chester.* 1762-97. W. l.c. clock Virginia M.
William. *London.* CC.1775.
Robert, jun. *Chester.* d.1781.
Samuel. *London.* 1802-08.
CAWNE, Robert. *London.* a.1668, CC.1676.
CAWOOD, John. *London.* a.1742.
CAWSON (CAUSON)—
James. *Liverpool* and *Greta Bridge.* 1779-1818. C. Lancaster freeman.
Edward, bro. *Lancaster.* 1779. C.
——. *Liverpool.* ca.1790. CC.
William, son of James. *Liverpool.* 1817. W. Lancaster freeman.
Eleanor. *Liverpool.* 1825.
CAWTHORN, Samuel. *London.* 1765. Livery Goldsmiths Co.
CAYGILL, Christopher. *Askrigg.* 2nd half 18c. l.c. clock.
CAZEAU, Pierre. *Paris.* m.1749.
CEASER, J. *London.* 1743. Watch.
CEASLEY, William. *London.* a.1787.
CECIL, Charles. *Philadelphia.* 1808. C.
CEDERGRÉN, Johan Fredrik. *Stockholm.* b. 1774, d.1839. 2 lever watches, br. and wall clock Nord. M.
CEDERLUND, Jonas. *Stockholm.* b.1768, d.1857. Court C. 5 br. and wall clocks and 3 watches. Clock in Nat. M. Stockholm ill. Sidenbladh.
CELLIER—
——. *Neuenstadt.* 1801.
FRÈRES ET SCHEFFER. *Paris.* 1813.
MESTRAL ET SCHEFFER. *Paris.* 1814. Successors.
CERET, *v.* DUFOUR.
CERET-CALAS, Louis. *Geneva.* 1811.
CERISEY, Nicolas. *Rouen.* a.1667.
CERLOTTI, Labruccio. *Lucca.* 1391. Made town clock.
CESAR—
Daniel. *London.* a.1696, CC.1703.
Edward. *London.* a.1799.
CETTI—
I. & Co. *London.* Early 19c. Watch.
J. *Buckingham.* Early 19c. Watch.
CEULEN, *v.* VAN CEULEN.
CEXT, Catharine. *London.* a.1722.
CEYBELS, ——. *Paris.* 1812-24.
CHABENEX, John. *London.* an.1710. Watch. Also CHAVENIX.
CHABIVAN ET CIE. *Geneva.* ca.1800. g. en. watch.
CHABRIER, ——. *Avignon.* 1667.
CHABROT, Pierre. *Lyons.* 1659 m.
CHADWELL, Nathaniel. *London.* 1725. Bankrupt.
CHADWICK—
John. *Liverpool.* 1790-6.
John. *Manchester.* 1804-13. C.
Joseph. *Boscowen, U.S.A.* 1810-31. C.
Joseph. *London.* CC.1815-40. W.
CHAGRIN, Desiré. *Marville* (*Lorraine*). b. 1741, d.1812. Made many turret clocks for the monasteries of the Doctrine Chrétienne.
CHAGUET, Antoine Martin. *Paris.* 1773. Engraver.
CHAIGNEAN, John. *London.* a.1733.
CHAILLY, ——. *Lille.* Late 18c. Mantel clock. cf. CHALY.
CHAIS, J. *Geneva.* ca.1710. Cast sil. skull watch.
CHALANDE, ——. *Boudry.* 1713.
CHALAS (SCHALASS)—
Rodolphe. *Reconvilliers* and *Chaux-de-Fonds.* 1773-6.
Jean Pierre, son. *Chaux-de-Fonds.* a.1765-1792.
CHALK—
James. *London* (*Bishopsgate St.*). a.1789, CC.1796, l.CC.1812-22. W.
James. *London* (*New Road, Whitechapel*). CC.1810.
William. *London.* a.1810.
CHALKE, James. *London.* CC.1796-1807.
CHALKHILL, ——. *London.* an.1748. Watch.
CHALKLIN (CHALKLEY)—
John. *Canterbury.* 1761, d.1766. Watch, 'An ingenious artificer.'
John, son. *London.* a.1774.
CHALLARD, William. *London.* a.1737 CC 1749.
CHALMERS—
George. *Dublin.* 1766-80. W.
William. *London.* ca.1768. Watch.
David. *Edinburgh.* 1803-19.
CHALON, Jean Jaques. *Geneva.* ca. 1750-70.
CHALONS, Louis. *Paris.* m.1757, juré 1786-9.
CHALY, ——. *Lille.* 1772. cf. CHAILLY.
CHAMAU, Paul. *London.* 1702. Watch.
CHAMBERLAIN (CHAMBERLAINE, CHAMBERLAYNE, CHAMBERLIN)—
Thomas. *Chelmsford.* ca.1630-40. Watch B.M. str. and cal. watch S.K.M.
Nathaniel. *Chelmsford.* a.1650, CC.1685, m.CC.1717-22. Also shop in *London* for repairs to his own watches. Watch Den. coll.
Nathaniel. *London.* a.1651, CC.1659-94. Watch mt. Ilbert coll.
Daniel. *Chelmsford* and *London.* a.1660.
Thomas. *London.* a.1676, CC.1687.
Joseph. *Norwich.* 1687. Watch.
John. *London.* a.1691.
Charles. *London.* a.1723.
Thomas. *London.* a.1724.
Henry. *Tiverton.* ca.1800. l.c. clock.
CHAMBERS—
Thomas. *Westminster.* 1662.
Edward. *London.* a.1670.
Jonathan. *London.* ca.1690. l.c. clock Weth. coll.
Charles. *Deen.* ca.1700. Lantern clock Virginia M.
Stephen. *London.* a.1697.
Thomas. *London.* a.1699.
Robert. *London.* a.1711, CC.1734-58.

CHAMBERS—*continued.*
——. *Dublin.* an.1774. Watch.
John. *London.* Late 18c. Watch G.M.
George. *Gateshead.* 1775-95. C. & W.
John George. *Gateshead.* 1800. l.c. clocks.
James. *Liverpool.* 1825. W.

CHAMBLEY—
E. or F. *Newcastle-on-Tyne.* ca.1790 CC.
John. *Wolverhampton.* 1780-95. lc. clock. W. cf. CHUMBLEY.

CHAMBON—
Mathieu. *Paris.* 1750 m.-1774.
Jean. *Paris.* m.1766-89. cal. watch Den. coll. Watch with auxiliary decimal dial and two minute hands Ilbert coll.

CHAMBRÉ, ——. *France* or *Lorraine.* 1760. Devised the method of making watch-glasses since known by his name.

CHAMBROT, ——. *Paris.* 1816-25.

CHAMEL, Jean. *Avignon.* 1493-1500. Keeper of clock on Hôtel de Ville.

CHAMOY, ——. *Paris.* 1813-25.

CHAMPAGNE—
Jean Louis. *Paris.* m.1785-9.
——. *Paris.* 1812.

CHAMPAGNIEU—
Antoine. *Lyons.* mar. 1627, d.1629.
Claude. *Lyons.* mar. 1627, d.1658. al. watch B.M. oct. crys. watch Côte coll.

CHAMPEAU, Jean. *Paris.* Juré 1675.

CHAMPELON, Jacques. *Paris.* m.1610.

CHAMPENOIS, Rémond. *Paris.* 1675 m. sil. skull watch F.W.M. Small g. en. watch M.P.S. Dresden.

CHAMPION—
John. *London.* 1540.
Robert. *Wells.* 1630.
Isidore. *Paris.* 1631. Registered a private punch mark. Juré 1657. Cross watch.
John. *London.* CC.1640.
John. *London.* CC.1651-76.
Denis. *Paris.* 1662-1706. C. to duc and duchesse d'Orléans. Watch Besançon M.
Jean. *Amsterdam.* 1681. Huguenot refugee from France.
Charles. *Paris.* Juré 1691.
John. *London.* 1730-79. g. p.c. watch S.K.M. p.c. watch, outer case agate, belonged to Emperor of China, M.M.A. g. en. watch, set stones, Fränkel coll. rep. watch mt. G.M.
Isidore Guillaume. *Paris.* Juré 1752.
G. S. *Paris.* Mid. 18c. Boulle-work br. clock Pal. de Pau, Paris.
François Barnabé. *Paris.* 1753. Prob. son of Isidore.
Charles. *Paris.* 2nd half 18c. Boulle-work clock. Equation clock C.A. & M. Bronze elephant clock Feill coll. prob. by him.
George. *London.* an.1780. Watch.
P. *London.* an.1793. Watch.
——. *Paris.* 1807-25.

CHAMPOT, Nicolas. *Paris.* Juré 1675.

CHAMPURY, Jacques. *France.* ca.1770. g. en. watch Blot-Garnier sale.

CHANCE—
B. *London.* ca.1720. Filigree watch B.M.
John. *Chepstow.* 1783-91. Repoussé watch.
W. & G. *London.* Early 19c. Watch.

CHANCELLOR—
John. *London.* a.1775, CC.1788-90.
John. *Dublin.* 1820-31. Award from Soc. Arts for a clock escapement.
& SONS. *Dublin.* Early 19c.

CHANCEY, James. *London.* 1741. Watch G.M.

CHANDFLOWER, Samuel. *London.* a.1733.

CHANDLEE—
Benjamin. *Philadelphia.* 1710, d.1747.
Benjamin. *Nottingham, Maryland, U.S.A.*, to 1710. *Wilmington,* d.1745. Clock.

CHANDLEE—*continued.*
John, son. *Wilmington, U.S.A.* mar. 1749. W.
Benjamin. *Chester Co. Penna.* 1763. W.

CHANDLER—
John. *London.* a.1699.
Edward. *London.* a.1717, CC.1724-37, d. an. 1742.
Timothy. *Concord, U.S.A.* b.1760, d.1846.
& SON. *London.* 1803. Watch Ilbert coll.
Robert. *London.* Early 19c. Watch.

CHANDLESS, H. *London.* Early 19c. Watch.

CHANSON, ——. *Geneva.* Early 19c.

CHANTER, Thomas. *London.* an.1762. Watch.

CHANTEREAU(**CHANTROT**), Louis. *Paris.* m.1787-93. Petitioned the Govt. for 20,000 livres to enable him to perfect the watch-making at Planchet-les-Mines in Lorraine. Secretarial note on petition 'Rien à faire.' A second petition made to the revolutionary Govt. g. en. watch.

CHANVELL, James. *London.* CC.1699.

CHAPEAU, Peter. *London.* an.1726-46. Watch mt. Arts M. Prague.

CHAPELAIN (CHAPIN), ——. *Paris.* 1819-1823.

CHAPLIN—
William & Thomas. *Bury St. Edmunds* from 1776-90. C. & W. Wm. d.1799. Thos. continued to 1810.
John. *London.* a.1796.

CHAPMAN—
Thomas. *London.* a.1648.
Thomas. *London.* a.1659.
Simon. *London.* a.1667, CC.1675. Went abroad 1689.
Samuel. *London.* 1676.
John. *London.* a.1679.
Titus. *London.* a.1683. Watch.
John. *London.* a.1714.
Peter. *London.* a.1730, CC.1737-47.
William. *London* (*Southwark*). an.1747. Watch.
William. *London.* a.1756-94.
Richard. *London.* a.1762, CC.1770.
John. *Loughborough.* an.1778-95. Watch.
Thomas. *London.* a.1782, CC.1790-1808. Watch.
D. *Chatham.* Late 18c. Watch.
John. *London.* a.1788.
John. *Watford.* 1795. C. & W.
William. *Belfast.* ca.1800. Watch Belfast M.
John. *London.* ca.1800. Watch Glasgow Art Gall.
D. *Hythe.* mar.1805. W.
Richard William Hare. *London.* a.1814.
George. *London.* a.1815.

CHAPO—
Philippe Auguste (le jeune). *Paris.* 1756-89.
Pierre Philippe (l'aîné). *Paris.* m. 1786-9.
Veuve (of Ph. Aug.). *Paris.* 1789.

CHAPONNIÈRE—
Jean Pierre François. *Geneva.* ca.1770-88.
——. *Geneva.* ca.1800. Painter on enamel.

CHAPPELL (**CHAPPLE**)—
Robert. *London.* CC.1720. Sheep's-head clocks.
Thomas. *London* (*Gt. Tower St.*). 1754-63. Watch.

CHAPPERON, Denis. *Paris.* 1675 m.

CHAPPUIS—
Pierre. *Lyons.* 1545-7. From *Geneva.*
Sébastien. *Lyons.* mar. 1659. *Geneva,* 1664. *Constantinople,* 1668. Also CHAPUIS.
Jubilé. *Geneva.* 1800. c.secs. watch Geneva M.
M. *Geneva.* 1813.
aîné. *Geneva.* 1814.
DONDEY ET DUPRÉ. *Geneva.* 1815-17.

CHAPPUZEAU, John Christian. *London.* an. 1717-23. Insolvent.
CHAPTON, William. *London.* Late 18c. Watch.
CHAPUIS—
——. *Geneva.* 1787. Made fine watches for Jaquet-Droz and Leschot.
A. *Paris.* 1824.
CHAPUY-LÉPINE, Jean Paul. *Paris.* 1810-1827. Purchased RAGUET-LÉPINE's business and traded as 'Lépine horloger.' Sold business in 1827 to DESCHAMP. C. to the Empress.
CHARAS, Charles Samson. *London.* CC. 1692. French.
CHARBON, Pierre. *Geneva.* ca.1770-91.
CHARD—
Sébastien. *Lyons.* Early 17c. Watch Garnier coll. Prob. CLÉARD.
——. *Chester.* ca.1810. Clock.
CHARDENON, ——. *Valenciennes.* 1754. aut. clock.
CHARLAU (CHARLO, CHARLAY), Pierre. *Copenhagen.* b.1710 in the Hague. Came Copenhagen 1727, m.1740, d.1773. Court C. g. en. watch Rosenborg Castle.
CHARLE, George. *London.* 1794-1840. Watch Ashmolean M. for Turkish market.
CHARLES—
John. *London.* a.1698.
D. *Kent.* 1760. Watch.
Antoine. *Magdeburg.* 1746. A famous maker. Translated Sully's 'Règle Artificielle du Temps.' Watch Schloss M. Berlin.
William. *Chepstow.* an.1763. Watch.
Nicolas. *Paris.* m.1773-80. Metronome C.A. & M.
Charles. *Chepstow.* ca.1800. l.c. clock.
John. *Portsea.* ca.1800.
——. *Paris.* 1817-25. g. en. watch showing hours in opening, Fränkel coll.
CHARLESON—
C. *London.* ca.1720. rep. watch mt. Buckley coll.
J. G. *London.* 1st half 18c. Watch.
S. F. *London.* ca.1750. Watch Strasbourg M. g. repoussé watch.
J. *London.* 1763. Watch Ilbert coll.
D. *London.* Late 18c. and early 19c. Watches.
CHARLESWORTH, John. *London.* a.1676-1685. Watch.
CHARLIER—
——. *Paris.* ca.1745 m.
Jean Louis, son. *Paris.* m.1756.
CHARLSON, P. *London.* 1758-64. sil. p.c. en. watch Carnegie M.
CHARLSTROM, William. *London.* a.1790, CC.1802, l.CC.1810-38.
CHARLTON—
John. *London.* 1630, CC.1632, m.CC.1640-1646. Petitioner for incorporation of CC. Watch scalloped sil. case Ilbert coll.
Daniel. *London.* a.1637.
Mationah. *London.* a.1721, CC.1729-44.
Robert. *London.* a.1725.
John. *Durham.* 1785-1820. l.c. clocks. W.
John. *Edinburgh.* 1792.
CHARLWOOD, Thomas. *London.* a.1703.
CHARMAN, ——. *London.* ca.1805. Duplex watch Ilbert coll.
CHARMES, *v.* DE CHARMES.
CHARMOT, ——. *Paris.* 1823.
CHARMY, Pierre. *Lyons.* 1776-88. Fitted dead-beat escapement to astro. clock of St. Jean.
CHARNOCK, James. *London.* a.1693.
CHAROST—
Jean. *Paris.* m.1737.
Philippe Jacques. *Paris.* m.1748.
Jean François. *Paris.* m.1765-89.
CHARPENTIER—
Pierre. *Geneva.* 1558. Refugee from *Orléans.*
——. *Paris.* ca.1755 m.
Germain. *Paris* (*Rue de la Monnaie*). m. 1763-89.
Antoine. *Paris.* m.1776.
Edme. *Paris.* m.1776.
——. *Paris* (*Rue du Roule*). 1807-12.
——. *Paris* (*Rue de la Monnaie*). 1825.
CHARRAS, Charles. *Glasgow.* 1717.
CHARRINGTON, S. *London.* m.CC. and d.1768.
CHARRIOT, William. *London.* a.1773.
CHARROLOIS, François. *Grenoble.* ca.1640. From *Conflans* in Poitou.
CHARRON, Louis. *La Rochelle.* 1665.
CHARTERS, Deckford. *Edinburgh.* a.1783.
CHARTIER—
Pierre. *Blois.* b.1618, m. goldsmith 1638-83. Painter on enamel; specialized in flowers.
Philippe dit Champmarqué. *Blois.* 1664. d.1694. circ. table clock.
Isaac. *London.* 1768-97. l.c. clock.
CHARWELL, James. *London.* ca.1740. p.c. rep. watch S.K.M. Watch Den. coll.
'CHAS. E. HOWARD.' Sig. on 1871-5 watches of the NEW YORK WATCH Co.
'CHAS. FARGO.' Sig. on watches of the ELGIN NATIONAL WATCH Co. from 1872.
'CHAS. G. KNAPP.' Sig. on 1869-70 watches of the UNITED STATES WATCH Co.
CHASE—
Richard. *London.* a.1672.
George. *London.* a.1732.
Edmund. *London.* a.1755.
CHASSEREAU—
Edward. *London.* CC.1803-14.
Robert. *London.* 1805-24. Watch London M.
CHASSEUR, ——. *London.* ca.1700. Clock ill. Britten.
CHASTAIGNIER—
Pierre. *La Rochelle.* 1695-1710.
Jean. *La Rochelle.* 1698.
Étienne. *La Rochelle.* 1698. Watch sd. CHATAIGNER Ilbert coll.
CHASTELAIN (CHATELAIN)—
Claude. *Lyons.* 1651 m. d.1671.
François Charles. *Paris* (*Rue St. Louis du Palais*). m.1784-9. Watch with decimal minute hand Ilbert coll.
——. *Paris* (*Rue des Pretres St. Germain*). 1807.
——. *Paris* (*Vielle rue du Temple*). 1812-25.
Ami. *Cortébert.* 1820-ca.1830. From *Tramelan.* The only maker in Cortébert. Made verge clocks in black cases.
CHASTY—
William. *Teignmouth.* ca.1800. l.c. clock.
Robert. *Hatherley.* d.ca.1850.
CHATBOURNE, John. *London.* a.1677.
CHATELIN, ——. *Paris.* 1812.
CHATER—
James. *London.* a.1718, CC.1726, d.1762. Eminent W. mus. br. clock.
Thomas. *London.* a.1740.
Eliezer, son of James. *London* (*Exchange Alley*). CC.1751, l.CC.1766, m.CC.1772, d.1777.
James, son of James. *London.* a.1746, CC. 1753-85.
Eliezer & James. *London.* 1764. Watch Ilbert coll.
James, & Son. *London.* 1753-84.
Richard, son in preceding. *London.* 1785. Carried on business alone.
William. *London.* a.1749.
John. *London.* CC.1766.
Richard, bro. of Eliezer. *London* (*Cornhill*). a.1774, CC.1781, l.CC.1803, d.1811.
Nathaniel. *London.* CC.1782.

CHATER—*continued.*
& LIVERMORE. *London.* 1787-1808.
James. *Nottingham.* 1795-9. W.
William. *London.* 1805-24.
CHATFIELD, John. *London.* 1675-83. Free of BC.
CHATHAM, William. *London.* ca.1760. Watch.
CHATILLON, Joseph Guillaume. *Paris.* m. 1778.
CHATOUREL, ——. *Paris.* 1812-25.
CHAUDEY, ——. *Paris.* 1824.
CHAUDFLOWER, Samuel. *London.* a.1733.
CHAUDOIR, Louis François Guillaume. *Geneva.* ca.1770-92.
CHAUDRON—
P. *Philadelphia.* 1797. W.
J. *Philadelphia.* 1798. W.
Simon. *Philadelphia.* 1799-1813.
S., & Co. *Philadelphia.* 1800-11.
Edward. *Philadelphia.* 1817.
CHAUFFERT, ——. *Paris.* 1818.
CHAULAT, Pierre Béate. *Chaux-de-Fonds.* 1784.
CHAULEY, ——. *La Brévine.* 1815-20.
CHAUMONT, ——. *Paris.* Early 19c. Mantel clock.
CHAUNES (CHAUANES)—
——. *Paris.* 1580-1620. Watch.
le jeune. prob. *Paris.* ca.1650. Watches M.M.A. and Stern. coll. Prob. same as CHAVANE.
CHAUNTER, John. *Gosport* and *Calne.* 1806. Previously in *Exeter.* W.
CHAUVELL—
James D. *London.* ca.1700. rep. watch S.K.M.
George. *London.* 1743-ca.1790. Watch Ilbert coll.
CHAUVET—
Pierres. *France.* 1st half 18c. p.c. rep. watch G.M.
Jean Sébastien. *Paris.* m.1770.
——. *Geneva.* an.1781. Watch.
CHAUVIN—
David. *Lyons.* 1692-7.
Jean Baptiste. *Paris.* m.1765.
CHAUVOT, Alexis Joachim. *Paris.* m.1760.
CHAVANE—
Moïse. *Grenoble.* 1651.
le jeune. Prob. *Paris.* sil. watch Gélis coll. Prob. same as CHAUNES.
CHAVIN, James. *London.* a.1676.
CHAWNER, Edward. *London.* a.1764.
CHAZOT, François. *Lyons.* 1658.
CHEDEL—
——. *Les Brenets.* 1735. Several makers of this name.
——. *Paris.* 1812.
CHEENY, J. *East Hartford, U.S.A.* 1790. C.
CHEESE—
Samuel. *London.* an.1774. Watch, engine-turned case.
Thomas. *Milton (Canterbury).* d.1779. Sarah, widow, continues the business.
CHEESEBROUGH, Aaron. ——. 1689. l.c. clock.
CHEESEMAN—
Daniel. *London.* a.1691, CC.1699-1722.
John. *London.* a.1695.
CHEESWRIGHT, Benjamin. *London.* a. 1711.
CHEETHAM—
Samuel. *Middleton.* d.1769. C.
Peter Wood. *Bredbury (Stockport).* 1785. C.
Joseph. *Leeds.* 1794-1826. l.c. clock and turret clocks.
——. *Sutton.* ca.1800.
Richard. *Leeds.* 1825. W.
CHELTENHAM (CHETENHAM), Michael. *London.* a.1698, CC.1712-20.
CHEMELLE, Elizabeth Claude. *Paris.* 1776-1789.
CHENAUD, ——. *Paris.* 1812.
CHENET, Michael Maximilien. *Paris.* m. 1789.
CHENEVIÈRE—
Urbain. *Geneva.* 1st half 18c. p.c. rep. watch Arch. M. Geneva.
Louis. *Geneva.* 1802. Son-in-law of J. F. LESCHOT.
ET DEONNA. *Geneva.* Early 19c. cyl. watch.
Richard. *Geneva.* 1819. Awarded prize for watch by Soc. des Arts.
CHENEY—
Withers. *London.* a.1646, CC.1657. Elected m.CC.1695, but did not serve.
John. *London.* a.1700.
Timothy. *Manchester, U.S.A.* b.1730, d. 1795. C.
Benjamin. *Manchester, U.S.A.* 2nd half 18c. C.
CHEREY, ——. *Besançon.* ca.1750. Fine br. clocks in Vernis Martin.
CHERITON, George. *London.* a.1685.
CHÉRON, Jean. *Blois.* 1661-7.
CHERONNET, ——. *Paris.* 1812.
CHERRINGTON, John Stanley. *London.* CC.1814-22. W.
CHERRY, John. *London (Islington).* 1793-7. W.
CHERVILLIÉ, Élie Claude. *Paris.* m.1776.
CHESNEAU, J. *Orléans.* ca.1610. oct. sil. watch Mallett coll. ill. Baillie.
CHESNON—
Salomon. *Blois.* b.1572, d. an.1634. Made clock for Marie de Médicis. 2 watches Louvre by him or his son. Watch with sundial Blot-Garnier coll. Watches Mallett and Miller colls.
Salomon, son. *Blois.* a.1626, d.1683. Watch B.M. piqué outer case. Fine g. en. watch Fränkel coll. Oval watch Gélis coll.
Pierre, son. *Blois.* m.1672. Huguenot. Went to *Amsterdam* 1686.
CHESTER—
George. *New York.* ca.1735-57. From *London.*
William Thompson. *London.* 1743. Shagreen watch G.M.
George. *London (Moorfields).* an.1770. Watch.
William. *London (Shoreditch).* 1802-24. Watch N.Y. Univ.
'CHESTER WOOLWORTH.' Sig. on 1870-5 watches of NEW YORK WATCH CO.
CHETWOOD, John. *London.* a.1692.
CHEUILLARD—
Jean. *Blois.* 1610. d.1631.
Barthélemy, son. *Blois.* a.1636-77.
CHEVAL, Jean. *Angers.* 14c. Cannonier. Repaired the 'grant aurlauge.'
CHEVALLIER (CHEVALIER)—
Nicolas. *Blois.* 1578. d.1586.
Robert. *Blois.* b.1584, d.1636. en. watch Olivier coll.
Nicolas, son. *Blois.* 1639-69.
François. *Lyons.* 1665-82.
Fut. *Paris.* 2nd half 18c. Boulle br. clock S.K.M.
——. *Paris.* ca.1750. C. to Louis xv.
& CIE. *Geneva.* ca.1750. en. watch Art M. Boston.
& CIE. *Paris.* 1760-90. Many en. watches.
Samuel. *Geneva.* b.1735-68.
Joseph, bro. *Geneva.* b.1742-68.
Jean Pierre, bro. *Geneva.* 1770.
——. *Honfleur.* 1772. Watch Chamb. coll.
& COCHET. *Paris.* 1790-1805. g. watch Fränkel coll. Watch Stads M. Amsterdam.
——. *Geneva.* ca.1800. Painter on enamel.
P. & CIE. *Paris.* an.1801. Watch.
l'aîné. *Paris.* Late 18c. and early 19c. en.

CHEVALLIER (**CHEVALIER**)—*continued.* watches G.M. and Fränkel coll. Clock Louvre.
A. *Paris.* Early 19c. Pocket sundial G.M.
CHEVENIÈRE, Pierre. ——. Late 17c. sil. watch set garnets.
CHEVENIX, P. D. *London.* ca.1770. p.c. g. rep. watch, agate panels, F.W.M. g. en. rep. watch Mallett coll.
CHEW, William. *London.* a.1719.
CHEYNE, Wither. *London.* 1689-96. CC.
CHEZINSKI, Anton Joseph von. *Breslau.* ca. 1810. Maker of repute.
CHIGNELL, Robert. *London.* 1761.
CHILCOTT—
Richard. *London.* a.1683, CC.1690-1721. l.c. clock.
John, son. *London.* CC.1721.
CHILD—
Richard. *London.* CC.1632, w.CC.1641, d. an.1650. cf. CHILDS.
Henry. *London.* CC.1641, m.CC. and d. 1665. Lantern clock.
Ralph. *London.* a.1654, CC.1661.
Henry. *London.* a.1670, CC.1677-96.
John. *London* (*Cripplegate*). CC.1769.
Samuel. *London.* ca.1770. br. clock.
John Anthony. *London.* a.1790.
John. *Philadelphia.* 1813-25.
& PALMER. *London.* 1820.
True W. *Boston, U.S.A.* 1825. C.
CHILDS—
Richard. *London.* B.C.1630. cf. CHILD.
Thomas. *London.* a.1695.
Francis. *London.* a.1783.
CHILETT, Thomas. *Bristol.* 1772. Partner with W. WADY.
CHILTON—
Thomas. *London.* ca.1700. Lantern clock.
Thomas. *London.* a.1731, CC.1738-60. l.c. clock Virginia M.
CHIOUT, ——. *Paris.* an.1777. Watch.
CHIPP, Robert. *London.* a.1679.
CHIPPENDALE, Gilbert. *London.* 1776. Bankrupt. *Halifax.* ca.1780. l.c. clock.
CHIPPERFIELD, George. *London.* a. 1774.
CHISHOLM, Adam. *Dumfries.* 1780-1821.
CHISMAN—
George. *London.* CC.1772.
Timothy, son. *London.* a.1772, CC.1779, m.CC.1803, d.1821.
CHISWELL, Nathaniel. *London.* a.1695.
CHITTENDEN, William. *Cranbrook.* From 1773. C. & W.
CHIVERS—
John. *London.* an.1747. Watch.
Nathaniel. *London.* a.1755.
CHOAT, Joseph. *London.* a.1788.
CHODOWIECKI, Daniel Nicola. *Berlin.* b. 1726, d.1801. Painter on enamel. Watch Olivier coll.
CHOICE, William Edward. *London.* a.1812.
CHOLLET—
Jean Baptiste. *Paris.* m.1779.
Jean Baptiste. *Philadelphia.* 1819.
CHOLLWELL, Edward. *London.* a.1715.
CHOPARD—
Jean Louis. *Sonvilier.* 1781.
François Louis. *Sonvilier.* 1783.
Frédéric. *Sonvilier.* ca.1795. Good maker.
CHOPE, William. *Hartland.* 18c. l.c. clock.
CHOPEAU, Philippe Auguste. *Paris.* m.1743.
CHOPIN—
——. *Paris* (*Palais Royal*). 1808-11.
ET PONCE. *Paris* (*Palais Royal*). 1812-16.
——. *Paris* (*Rue St. Denis*). 1822-5.
CHOTARD, Paul. *London.* a.1720, CC.1742-1747.
CHOUDENS, Jean. *Geneva.* ca.1690. Square en. watch Bernal sale.
CHOUEF, F. Prob. *France.* Early 17c. Watch Webster coll.
CHOUEN, Perrin. *Parthenay.* 1408. 'Aflogeur.'
CHOUTEAU, Nicholas René. *Paris.* m.1738.
CHRÉTIEN—
Noël. *Paris.* m.1684.
——. *Paris.* 1812.
CHRISTENSEN—
Jens. *Randers.* 1769.
P. *Newport.* Early 19c. Watch.
CHRISTIAN, John. *Aylsham* and *Norwich.* ca.1745, d.1788. In partnership with Thos. PAGE. l.c. lacquer clock ill. Cec. & Web.
CHRISTIE—
Gabriel. *Edinburgh.* a.1736.
Alexander. *Dublin.* 1774-95. W.
James. *Perth.* 1820-43. Two of the same name.
William. *London.* 1825-40.
CHRISTIN—
——. *Berne.* Late 17c. g. watch en. by Les frères Huaud.
——. *Berne,* 1758. *Pforzheim,* 1765. From *Geneva.* Founded a watch factory with Ador, which failed in 1762. cf. BONARD.
——. *Paris.* 1772.
CHRISTMAS—
James. *London.* a.1682.
J. *North Walsham.* From 1789. C. & W.
CHRISTOFLE, ——. *Paris.* 1812.
CHUBB, William. *London.* a.1700.
CHUMBLEY, John. *Wolverhampton.* ca. 1780. cf. CHAMBLEY.
CHUMLEY, Thomas Pittom. *London.* a.1788.
CHUNE, Thomas. *Shifnal.* 1795.
CHUPER, Paul. *Geneva.* a.1664. Prob. CUPER.
CHUR, Georg Melchior. *Munich.* 1717-51. an.1717 in *Holland,* where he learnt to make long pendulum clocks.
CHURCH—
Francis. *London.* a.1718.
Richard. *London.* a.1724.
John. *London.* a.1760.
Thomas. *Norwich.* 1784-95. W.
James. *London.* a.1793.
John Michael Charles. *London.* a.1802.
CHURCHILL—
Charles. *London.* 1787. c.secs. watch Glasgow Art Gall. Watch N.Y. Univ.
Samuel. *Dorchester.* Late 18c. Watch.
CHURCHMAN, Michael. *London.* a.1685. CC.1694.
CHUTTER, Nathaniel. *London.* 1683. C.
CHZERNIAW, J. ——. 1624. Hex. table clock Damiano coll.
CIARUGI, Giovanni Carlo. *Rome.* ca.1550. Table clock with detachable alarum.
CIBELIUS, Benno. *Hassfurt.* m.1823.
CIRNEY, André. *Besançon.* 1653.
CLAES, ——. *France.* ca.1375. C. to Charles V of France.
CLAGGET—
William. *Newport, U.S.A.* b.1696, d.1749. l.c. clock M. of Art, Boston.
Thomas. *Newport, U.S.A.* 1730-49. Very small l.c. clock M.M.A.
CLAIR, Augustin. *Strasbourg.* 1702.
CLAIRAT (**CLERAT**)—
Jean. *Neuchâtel.* 1647-68.
Rodolphe, son. *Neuchâtel.* 1677-90.
CLANFIELD, Henry. *London.* a.1699, CC. 1707.
CLAPHAM, George. *Brigg.* 1767. C.
CLAPOT, D. *London.* 18c. Watch.
CLAPPERTON, Giedon. *Edinburgh.* a.1777.
CLARE—
Peter. *Manchester.* 1764-1811. C. & W.
Thomas. *Warrington.* ca.1790. l.c. clock, Battersea en. dial, Weth. coll.
Joshua. *Kimbolton.* Late 18c. Watch.
Peter, son of Peter. *Manchester.* b.1781, d.1851.

CLARE—*continued.*
Thomas. *Bedford.* ca.1800. Watch. Partnership with J. CAVIT dissolved 1808.
H. J. *London.* Early 19c. Watch.
CLAREBURG, John. *York.* 1371. Made York Minster clock.
CLARIBOS (CLORIBOS), Jan. *Haarlem.* 1785.
CLARIDGE—
Benjamin. *London.* a.1705.
Robert. *London (Finchley).* a.1794, CC. 1802, l.CC. and d.1812.
CLARK (CLARKE)—
Humphrey. *London.* 1632 CC.
George. *London.* CC.1632.
John. *London.* a.1626 under BC.
John. *Bristol.* ca.1635. Watch B.M.
William. *London.* a.1647, CC.1654.
Humphrey. *London* and *Hertford.* a.1657, CC.1668-81. Lantern clock.
Edmund. *London.* a.1665.
William. *London.* a.1668.
Joseph. *Chester.* 1680. W.
Thomas. *London.* a.1674.
Mary. *London.* a.1674.
John. *London.* a.1675.
Elizabeth. *London.* a.1676.
John. *London.* a.1681.
Andrew. *London.* a.1682.
John. *London.* a.1682, CC.1691-5.
John Stanford. *London.* a.1686, CC.1696-1725. Watch.
Samuel. *London.* a.1687-1736.
William. *London.* a.1688.
John. *London.* a.1696, CC.1701.
Thomas. *London.* a.1698, CC.1709.
& DUNSTER. *London.* Early 18c. p.c. rep. watch S.K.M. Watch Stads M. Amsterdam.
Henry. *London.* a.1699.
Henry. *London.* a.1703.
James. *Frome.* ca.1715. Watch.
Thomas. *London.* a.1711, CC.1720.
John. *London.* a.1712.
Richard. *London.* a.1713, CC.1720-45. cal. watch.
Francis. *London.* 1723-9. Insolvent.
Valentine. *London.* 1723. Insolvent.
John. *London.* a.1716.
George. *London (Leadenhall St.).* 1725. l.CC.1787. Fine table clock Weth. coll. Watch mt. G.M. Watch Den. coll. Sheep's-head clock, Turkish figures. l.c. clock Virginia M.
Edward. *London.* a.1718.
Mark. *London.* a.1719.
Thomas. *Ashton (Devon).* 1731. C.
Cornelius. *Cartmel Fell.* 1733, d.1762. W. Lancaster freeman.
John. *Frome.* 1734. T.C. Invented a wheel-cutting engine for large clocks.
John. *London.* a.1725.
Benjamin. *London.* a.1727.
Benjamin S. *Wilmington, U.S.A.* 1737-50.
James. *London.* a.1734-74. Bankrupt.
William. *London (Bishopsgate St.).* 1743-53. Watch.
Robert. *London (Old Fish St.).* 1747. Watch.
Cureton. *London.* a.1735, CC.1747-52.
John. *London.* a.1738.
Benjamin. *London.* a.1742.
Andrew. *Edinburgh.* 1753-64.
Smith Fleetwood. *London.* a.1747.
Samuel. *London.* a.1748.
Robert. *Middlesex.* 1756. C.
Edward. *London (Piccadilly).* d.1766. W.
Rand. *London.* a.1749.
William. *Ousebridge (Yorks.).* ca.1760-76C.
Charles. *Dublin.* an.1762. Watch.
George. *London (Whitechapel).* ca.1760. T.C.
Charles. *London (Fetherstone St.).* 1761-83.

CLARK (CLARKE)—*continued.*
Solomon. *Shoreditch.* 1762. C.
William. *London.* a.1753-72.
Christopher. *Dublin.* 1766-80. Watch mt.
Thomas, son of Cornelius. *Cartmel Fell.* 1767. W. Lancaster freeman.
Richard. *Charleston, U.S.A.* 1767. From *London.* C. & W.
J. *Dublin.* an.1771. Watch.
Richard. *London.* d.1790.
Edward. *London.* a.1755.
John. *London.* a.1756.
James. *London (Newgate St.).* a.1760, CC. 1768-78.
William. *London.* a.1762.
Edward. *London (Bearbinder Lane).* 1770.
E. *Coningsby.* ca.1770. l.c. clock.
Thomas. *Ulverstone.* ca.1770-95.
Robert Cowell. *London.* a.1756, CC.1774-1801. Watch.
Richard. *London.* a.1766.
Robert. *London.* a.1768.
William. *York.* 1776-84. W.
Christopher. *Dublin.* an.1778. Watch.
Randell. *London.* CC.1778.
Edward Weeks. *London (Threadneedle St.).* 1779. W.
& SMITH. *London (Threadneedle St.).* 1779. Bankrupt. Partnership of preceding with Chas. SMITH.
Ephraim. *Philadelphia.* 1780. Retired 1813. Watch N.Y. Univ.
David, son of Chas. *London.* a.1776.
Joseph. *London.* a.1779.
Nathaniel. *London (Shaftesbury Pl.).* CC. 1782-99.
John. *Sudbury (Suffolk).* 1784-95. W.
Ambrose. *Philadelphia* and *Baltimore.* 1784. *v.* BIGGER & CLARKE.
George. *London (Aldersgate St.).* 1784-1804. Bankrupt 1795. Watch No. 18198 an.1794.
William. *Morpeth.* 1784-1805 CC. C. & W.
Robert. *Charleston, U.S.A.* 1785. C. & W. and Math. Inst. maker.
William. *London.* a.1779.
John, son of R. Cowell. *London.* a.1780.
John. *London (Primrose St.).* CC.1788. Watchcase maker.
Richard, son. *London (Spitalfields).* a.1781, CC.1790, l.CC.1792.
Francis. *London.* 1790.
James. *Edinburgh.* 1791-1835. Many turret clocks.
Samuel, sen. *Hinckley.* 1793-7. C.
Samuel, jun. *Hinckley.* 1793-7. C.
Fleetwood. *King's Lynn.* To ca.1794.
John. *Bristol.* 1794.
Richard. *London.* 1795. Watchcase maker.
David. *London.* 1795. Watchcase maker.
& SON. *London.* 1795. Not CC.
William. *Long Buckby.* 1795. W. l.c. clock.
Edward. *Philadelphia.* 1797. W.
William Richard. *London.* a.1784, CC.1803-1820.
Benjamin, son of Ephraim. *Philadelphia.* 1791-1848.
James. *Bristol.* 1797.
William, son of R. Cowell. *London.* a.1789-1824. W.
John. *London (Mark Lane).* 1799-1824. br. clock.
John. *Philadelphia.* 1799.
Joseph. *London (Islington).* 1799.
& CALLOW. *London.* 1800. Watchcase makers.
William. *London (King St.).* 1800-15.
John. *Greenock.* ca.1800.
William. *London (Soho).* 1802-04.
Elias. *Philadelphia.* 1802.
Joseph. *London.* 1802-08.
Richard, son of R. Cowell. *London.* a.1794.

CLARK (CLARKE)—*continued.*
Theodore Cuthbert. *London* (*Clerkenwell*). 1804 CC.
George. *London.* a.1796.
William. *Greenock.* 1805.
M. *Blyth.* 1805. W.
James. *London* (*Bethnal Gr.*). 1805-08.
William. *Cerne Abbas.* 1806. C.
Robert. *York* and *Hull.* 1807. C.
Heman. *Plymouth Hollow, U.S.A.* 1807. a. to Eli TERRY.
Ephraim & Charles. *Philadelphia.* 1808-11.
Robert. *London.* a.1803.
John. *London* (*Bethnal Gr.*). 1809-24.
Charles. *Philadelphia.* 1809-14. W.
Jesse. *Philadelphia.* 1809-14. W.
Daniel. *Waterbury. U.S.A.* 1810-15. Started clockmaking with Zenas COOK and William PORTER; failed ca.1815.
& SON. *Morpeth.* 1812. Watch.
Henry. *London.* CC. and l.CC.1812, w.CC. 1825.
Ellis. *Philadelphia.* 1813-48.
Benjamin & Ellis. *Philadelphia.* 1813-40.
& HUTCHINSON. *Philadelphia.* 1813.
Charles. *Edinburgh.* 1814.
Richard. *London.* Early 19c. Lever cal. watch, 2 dials, S.M.S.K.
Richard, & Son. *London.* Early 19c. g. en. watch and chatelaine B.M.
Thomas. *Leeds.* 1817. C.
William. *London.* CC.1819.
William. *Liverpool.* ca.1820. C.
T. C. *Ulverstone.* ca.1820.
Michael. *Morpeth.* 1820.
William. *Dublin.* 1820.
Samuel. *Coventry.* 1821. Lever watch mt. Ilbert coll.
Richard. *Newport.* Early 19c. Watch.
Michael Faircloth. *London.* a.1815.
George James. *London.* a.1817.
John. *Greenock.* 1822-37.
William. *Parsonstown.* 1824. W.
James. *Ballinasloe.* 1824.
Philip. *Nenagh.* 1824.
Jane. *Wellington.* ca.1825. Watch Shrewsbury M.

CLARKSON—
John. *London.* a.1649, CC.1657-80.
George. *London.* a.1726.
Samuel. *London.* an.1762. Watch.
Hewitt. *Wolverhampton.* 1762-80. C. & W. From *London.*
John. *London.* an.1783. Watch.
John. *Liverpool.* 1825. W.

CLARY, ——. ——. ca.1790. en. watch set pearls M.M.A.

CLAUDE—
——. *Lyons.* 1544-52 and 1581. Prob. two men, who may have been Claude de SAINT-PAUL and Claude GODON.
Abraham. *Annapolis, U.S.A.*, 1773. W. In partnership with Charles JACOB for one year.
Alphonse. *Paris.* 1824.
v. TOURNARRE.

CLAUDE-MARIE, Abram Louis. *Fontaines.* 1787-1802. Able C.

CLAUDON—
James. *London.* an.1761. Watch.
John George. *Charleston, U.S.A.* 1773. From *London.* W.

CLAUS, John. *London.* a.1716.

CLAUSEAU, Louis. *Avignon.* 1676, d.1732. C. & W. Repaired clock of Sorgue. Made clock for Caderousse.

CLAUZIER, Claude. *Paris.* m.1692.

CLAVEL, ——. *Switzerland.* ca.1770.

CLAVERIE, Daniel. *Paris.* 1674 juré. cf. CLAVIER.

CLAVETÉ, ——. *La Rochelle.* ca.1650.

CLAVIER, Daniel. *Paris.* 1679 juré-1685. cf. CLAVERIE.

CLAXTON—
Richard. *London.* a.1638, CC.1646.
Thomas. *London.* CC.1646, m.CC.1670, d. an.1680.

CLAY—
William. *London.* 1652-80. p.c. watch with balance spring of one turn G.M. Watch Taunton M. One-hand clock with minute-showing device, ill. Britten. Lantern clock Weth. coll.
Samuel. *London.* a.1680, CC.1687. d. before 1706.
Jeremiah, son. *London.* a.1706.
Charles. *Stockton.* 1716. d.1740. In *London* (*Strand* and *St. James'*) 1736. CC. opposed petition for patent for rep. and mus. watches. Organ clock and cal. clock Duke of Sussex sale. mus. clock ill. Britten. l.c. cal. clock Weth. coll.
Charles. *London.* ca.1730-50. C. to George II. Watch S.K.M. in outer case of crys. crys. skeleton watch. Watches London M. and Gotha M. Turret clock for St. James's Palace. mus. clock ill. Britten.
William. *London.* ca.1750. l.c. red lacquer clock ill. Cec. & Web.
Joseph. *London.* an.1768. Watch.
John. *London.* an.1771. Watch.
B. *London.* 2nd half 18c. Watch.
C. *Gainsborough.* 1762. W.

CLAYPOT, Dennis. *York.* 1697. W.

CLAYTON—
David. *London.* a.1719, 1732 CC., d.1772.
Humphrey. *London.* a.1721.
Caleb. *London.* a.1725, CC.1734.
John. *Prescot.* d.1754. C.
John. *Charleston, U.S.A.* 1743. Previously *London* and *Jamaica.*
Peter. *Liverpool.* 1754. W.
B. *London.* an.1760. Watch.
John. *London.* ca.1770. Watch Chamb. coll.
John. *Blackburn.* 1770-95.
William. *London.* an.1780. Watch.
Charles. *London.* an.1781. Watch.
Martin. *Manchester.* 1790-1820. CC. W.

CLEAK—
Adam. *Bridport.* 1785. C.
John. *Bridport.* 1800. C.

CLEAR, ——. *Minchinhampton.* 1768. W.

CLÉARD, Sébastien. *Lyons.* a.1612-27 comp. Oval watch Ilbert coll.

CLEARE, William. *London.* a.1688.

CLEAVE, George. *London.* 1784. wooden C.

CLEE, William. *London.* a.1761.

CLEER, Tobias. *London.* a.1713.

CLEETER, William. *London.* a.1700, CC. 1709.

CLEEVE—
William. *London.* CC.1654-68.
Edward. *London.* a.1710. Also CLEVE.

CLEFS, ——. *Paris.* 1807.

CLEGG, Joseph. *London.* an.1761. Watch.

CLEGHORN—
Samuel. *London.* 1790-1808. T.C. Partner with Wm. PLEACE till 1796.
S., & Sons. *London.* ca.1800.

CLELAND—
John. *Edinburgh.* a.1761-84. Partner in GIBSON & CLELAND till 1773. Fine watch Soc. Antiquaries of Scotland M.
v & MOLLISON. *Edinburgh.* 1785-90.

CLEMEN, Michal. *Cöllen a.d. Spree.* 1662. sq. table clock Feill coll.

CLEMENT—
Edward. *London.* a.1662, CC.1671-87.
Edward. *Exeter.* 1671.
William. *London.* CC.1677, m.CC. 1694-9. Also CLEMENTS. First to use anchor escapement in clocks, probably invented ca.1676 by Hooke; first used spring steel

CLEMENT—*continued.*
for hanging the pendulum. l.c. clocks Weth. coll. and Virginia M. l.c. clock with anchor Deutsches M. Munich. l.c. clock, 1¼ secs. pendulum ill. Cec. & Web. Small lantern clock.
William. son. *London.* a.1684-1706.
William. *Totnes.* an.1701. Watch.

CLÉMENT—
Pierre. *Blois.* m.1647-73.
Pierre. *Paris.* 1700. Registered a private punch mark.
Antoine. *Paris.* 1739 m.
François. *Paris.* m.1743.
Claude. *Paris.* m.1743, juré 1767-74.
Louis. *Paris.* m.1778-89.
Anselme. *Paris.* m.1785-9.
——. *Paris.* 1807-13.

CLEMENTS—
Robert. *London.* a.1679, CC.1686-1707.
Thomas. *London.* a.1767. br. clock.
William. *Faversham.* 1775. W.
Harry. *London.* a.1768.
Thomas. *Liverpool.* ca.1790. br. clock ill. Cec. & Web.
Robert. *London.* 1775. Watchcase maker. Insolvent.
John. *London.* 1799-1840. Watch.
John. *Oxford.* 1808-18.

CLEMENTSON, Edward. *Melton Mowbray.* 1784.

CLEMISON, George. *Ulverstone.* 1763. C.

CLEMSON, Richard. *London.* a.1661, CC. 1673.

CLENT, George. *London.* a.1684.

CLENTON, ——. ——. an.1781. Watch.

CLER or **CLERC,** *v.* LE CLER.

CLERC—
Claude. *Lyons.* 1570 m.
Clément. *Lyons.* 1571 m.
Claude. *Lyons.* 1636 m.
J. H. *Môtiers,* 1754-66. l.c. clock.
Jean Pierre. *Paris.* m.1776.
Pierre François. *Chaux-de-Fonds.* 1784.

CLERÉE (CLÉRET),——. *Paris.* 1812-15.

CLERGET, ——. *Paris.* 1807-18.

CLERK, Daniel. *Amsterdam.* ca.1715. Watch G.M.

CLERKE—
John. *Brentwood.* ca.1780.
George. *London* (*Aldersgate*). CC.1782, l.CC.1786, d.1802. Watch Den. coll. Also CLERK.
George, son. *London.* a.1792, CC.1802, l.CC.1810-25. Watch N.Y. Univ. Also CLERK.
G. & N. *London.* 1805-18. Firm of George, son, & Nathaniel.
Nathaniel. *London.* 1805-19. Watches Den. coll. and N.Y. Univ.
Thomas. *London* (*Clothfair*). 1809. W.
Nathaniel, son. *London.* a.1809.

CLERMONT, ——. *Paris.* 1681 m.

CLETIEZ—
——. *Paris.* ca.1750 m.
Jean Joseph. *Paris.* m.1762-89.

CLEVELAND—
Henry. *London.* a.1792, CC.1799.
William. *Connecticut.* Late 18c.

CLEVELEY, Thomas. *Shrewsbury.* an.1778. Watch.

CLEVER, Nathaniel. *London.* a.1727.

CLEVERLEY—
Charles. *London.* a.1714.
Edward. *London.* 1817-24.

CLIDSDALE (CLYDESDALE)—
Robert. *Edinburgh.* a.1738-86.
Hugh. *Edinburgh.* a.1762-1821.

CLIFFORD, ——. *Ashby-de-la-Zouch.* an. 1755. Watch.

CLIFT—
William. *London.* a.1670.
Thomas. *Hull.* 1st half 18c. l.c. lacquer clock Weth. coll. Watch.
Nathaniel. *Hull.* 1784. W. Also CLIFF.
Thomas. *Beaminster.* d.1793. C.
Jonas. *London.* CC.1808.

CLIFTON—
Thomas. *London.* CC.1651.
Thomas. *London.* a.1678, CC.1687-1720. Insolvent.
John. *London.* an.1732. Watch.
John. *Liverpool.* 1777-90. l.c. clock.

CLINCH—
George. *London.* Mid. 18c. Inn clock Virginia M.
James. *Galway.* 1820-4.

CLINTON, James. *London.* 1744. Watch.

CLITHEROW, Thomas. *Liverpool.* 1825. chron. maker.

CLIVERDON—
Thomas. *London.* CC.1722-52.
Richard, son. *London.* a.1752, CC.1762.

CLOCK, R. *Amsterdam.* ca.1680. Watch Ryks M.

CLODER, Johann Paulus. *Venice.* 1756. Prussian. Keeper of clock of S. Marco and repaired it.

CLODION, Michel Claude. *Nancy* and *Paris.* b.1728, d.1814. Eminent bronze worker; made many clock cases.

CLOESE, *v.* VAN DER CLOESEN.

CLONMEL, ——. *London.* 1721. Watch.

CLOPTON, William. *London.* a.1655.

CLOSON (CLOSSON), Peter. *London.* 1630. w.CC.1636-53. Subscribed to incorporation of CC. Lantern clocks Weth. coll. and N.Y. Univ.

CLOTEAU, Pierre. *Paris.* 1746 juré.

CLOTHEN, Conrad de. *Zürich.* 1366. Made clock on St. Pierre's church.

CLOUD, Ralph. *Beaminster.* 1740, d.1764. C.

CLOUET, Gabriel. *Paris.* a.1748.

CLOUGH, Edward. *London.* 1630-83. Watches B.M. and Ilbert coll.

CLOUGHS, Ralph. *London.* an.1773. Watch.

CLOUTMAN, John. *London.* a.1805.

CLOUZIER, ——. *Paris.* ca.1750. g. en. rep. watch. cf. CLAUZIER.

CLOVI, J. *Rome.* 1741. Metal spherical watch Carnegie M.

CLOWES (CLOWS, CLEWES, CLEWS)—
James. *London.* CC.1671-89. A famous maker. l.c. clock Weth. coll. br. clock ill. Cec. & Web.
John. *London* (*Russell Ct.*). CC.1672, w.CC. 1713. br. and l.c. clock. Made a 'rich pendulum weekly clock' for the King.
Ralph. *London* (*Aldersgate St.* and later *Green Arbour Ct.*). a.1695, CC.1703-66. l.c. clock ill. Cec. & Web.
John, son of John. *London.* a.1709.
Ralph, son of Ralph. *London.* a.1766.
B. *Liverpool.* 1775. W.
Thomas. *Nantwich.* 1795. CLEWS.
John. *Liverpool.* 1825. C.

CLUER—
Obadiah. *Lewisham.* a.1682, CC.1709. l.c. clock.
Jesse, son. *London.* a.1737.

CLUGH, Peter. *London.* a.1755.

CLUNY, ——. *Paris.* 1812.

CLUSERET, Nicolas. *Paris.* 1675 m.

CLUTTERBUCK, John. *London.* an.1761. Watch.

CLYATT—
Samuel. *London.* a.1663, CC.1672-1714.
Abraham. *London.* CC.1680-1713.
Samuel, son of Samuel. *London.* CC.1702.
John, bro. *London.* a.1698, CC.1708.
Abraham, bro. *London.* CC.1708.

CLYATT—*continued.*
William. *London.* CC.1709.
Lemuel. *London.* a.1703, CC.1712-23.
Erastus. *London.* a.1704.
CLYMER, Marmaduke. *Bristol.* 1785-1830. W.
CNAPP, Oege. *Sneek.* 1768.
COALES, W. P. & D. *Newport.* Early 19c. Watch.
COATES—
Ralph. *Darlington.* 1686. Made St. Cuthbert's clock.
William. *London.* a.1706. Watch.
John. *London.* ca.1740. l.c. clock.
John. *Tetbury.* an.1759. Watch.
Robert, *v.* COATS.
Archibald, *v.* COATS.
John. *Cirencester.* 1778-1812.
W. & F. *Cirencester.* 1786-1812. Watch and br. clock.
William. *Cirencester.* 1792-1812.
B. *Wakefield.* 1808. W.
& SON. *Wakefield.* Early 19c.
COATESWORTH, Thomas. *London.* a.1790.
COATS—
Robert. *Hamilton.* 1745-61.
Archibald. *Wigan.* 1767. d.1797. l.c. clock ill. Cec. & Web. Watch mt.
Robert. *Wigan.* d.1800. C. Also COATES.
James. *London* (*Clerkenwell*). a.1781, CC. 1788-1822.
James. *Horncastle.* Retired 1797. C. & W. Succeeded by John LAMB.
James. *Stourbridge.* d.1812. C. & W.
John Hardwick, son. *London.* a.1813, CC. 1822.
COATSFEILD, John. *London.* a.1682.
COATSWORTH, John. *London.* an.1706. Watch.
COBB—
William. *York.* 1659. W.
John. *London.* a.1692, CC.1703-34. Watch.
John. *London.* a.1734.
COBBETT, George. *London.* a.1802, CC. 1810. W.
COBHAM—
Joshua. *Liverpool.* 1674. Watchcase maker.
——. *Dundee.* an.1740. Watch.
——. *Dublin.* an.1748. Watch.
Stockley. *London* (*Bunhill Row*). a.1723, CC.1737, d.1787.
John. *London.* a.1729. CC.1737. d.1780. Watch.
James. *London.* a.1732, CC.1739-64.
John, son of John. *London.* CC.1790.
COBURN, ——. *London.* an.1775. Watch.
COCART (**COCQUART**), Juan. *Madrid.* 1590. C. to Philip II of Spain. Native of Brussels. Sundial.
COCHET—
Alexandre. *Grenoble.* 1672-1715.
Alexandre. *Morez.* 1773.
COCHIN—
Jeremy. *Cassel.* Appointed Court C. in 1687.
Daniel. *Geneva* in 1732, later *Paris* (?)-1770. Fine repoussé worker. Two examples G.M. and one on watch by C. UIJTERWEER, Feill coll.
COCHRAN—
Samuel. *London.* 1768. Watch.
& SHAW. *Belfast.* 1820.
Edward. *Belfast.* 1824.
COCHRANE—
Thomas. *Edinburgh.* 1754-62.
Thomas. *Glasgow.* 1810.
COCK—
Charles. *London.* a.1714, CC.1736-57.
John. *London.* ca.1760. l.c. clock. Pinchbeck watch Carnegie M.
Charles. *Macclesfield.* d.1782. C.
Joseph. *London.* Early 19c. Watch.
COCKBURN—
Adam. *Haddington.* 1804-43. Then went to Canada.
William. *Haddington.* 1814.
William. *Sunderland.* 1820.
COCKEY—
William. *Wincanton.* Early 18c. l.c. clock.
Edward. *Warminster.* an.1753-ca.1780. l.c. clock.
COCKINGS, Benjamin. *Bridgewater.* 1795. W.
COCKRAN, Samuel. *London* (*Wapping*). 1790-3.
COCKSHUTT (**COCKSHOOT**)—
Edmund. *Liverpool.* 1785-1811. W.
William. *Liverpool.* 1790-1824. W.
Ann. *Liverpool.* 1813-24. W.
Thomas. *Liverpool.* 1821. W.
CODEVELLE—
——. *Paris.* 1750-72. Made cyl. watches.
——. *Paris.* 1812.
COE—
——. *London.* an.1750. Watch.
William. *Cambridge.* 1795.
COELOMBIE, Jan. *Haarlem.* 1755.
COENRAATS, Hans Eschlinger. *Amsterdam.* 1667.
COEUR—
Edme. *Paris.* m.1759, juré 1787-9.
Edme, son. *Paris.* m.1781-9.
Jean Pierre, bro. *Paris.* m.1786-9.
Père. *Paris* (*Rue de la Verrerie*). 1809-18. One of the two preceding.
Fils, son. *Paris* (*Rue St. Honoré*). 1811-25.
COFFEY, William. *Tullamore.* 1824.
COFFIN-CHEVALIER, ——. *Paris.* 1811-1813.
COFFINS, Richard. *Crewkerne.* 1795. W.
COGGER—
John. *London.* a.1699.
Thomas. *Hastings.* Early 19c. Watch.
COGHILL, James. *Glasgow.* 1811.
COHEN—
Samuel. *London.* Late 18c. Watch Belfast M.
Samuel. *Plymouth.* 1795.
A. J. *Hamburg.* 1804-21.
Levy. *London.* 1805-08. W.
A. E. *Hamburg.* 1815.
S. J. *London.* 1817-24. W.
A. S. *London.* 1820.
Daniel. *Liverpool.* 1825. W.
COIGLEY, James. *Liverpool.* 1818-29. W.
COIGNET—
Antoine. *Paris.* 1665-76 juré. Made the Samaritaine clock.
Jacques. *Paris.* 1676 m., juré 1691. Watch G.M. by him or following.
Jean. *Paris.* 1676 m.
COLAMBELL, Anthony. *London.* 1776-1824. Tortoise-shell watchcase maker.
COLARD, Paul. *London.* an.1751. Watch.
COLBORNE, Thomas. *London.* a.1818.
COLE—
Humphrey. *London.* 1568-97. Sundials Old Ashmolean M. and B.M.
Henry. *London.* a.1695.
John. *London.* a.1706.
Edward. *London.* a.1715, CC.1721, d.1771.
——. *London* (*Aldersgate St.*). d.1731. W.
Richard. *London.* a.1718.
Daniel. *London.* a.1719, CC.1726.
John. *London.* a.1721, CC.1729-60. l.c. clock.
John. *London.* a.1722, CC.1729, d.1744.
Richard. *London.* a.1736.
Benjamin. *London.* CC.1733. Pedometer B.M.
Charles. *London.* ca.1750. Watch mt.
James. *Norwich.* an.1758. Watch.
Thomas. *London.* 1754-63.
Joseph. *London.* a.1753.
John. *Epsom.* an.1774. Watch.
Aquila. *London.* a.1768, CC.1780.

COLE—*continued.*
William. *London.* a.1777-1800.
John. *London.* a.1782.
Richard. *Ipswich.* a.1785-1822 CC. Succeeded BASSET. Watch.
Richard. *Coventry.* 1793. Patented an escapement.
William. *London.* a.1790-1804.
James Ferguson. *London.* b.1799, d.1880. One of the finest makers of watches, clocks and chrons. Patented a detached esc. in 1821. Invented in 1830 a 'resilient' lever esc. in which the pallets bank on the esc. wheel teeth, in 1840 a 'double rotary' esc. and in 1859 a lever esc. with negative draw. A resilient lever watch G.M.
Richard Stinton, son of Richard. *Ipswich.* a.1823.

COLEBORNE—
John. *London.* a.1719.
John. *London.* a.1734.

COLEMAN (COLMAN)—
Francis. *Ipswich.* ca.1700-40. Watch Den. coll. l.c. clock. Watch mt. G.M.
Stephen. *London.* a.1704.
John. *London.* a.1732.
John. *London.* a.1735.
Charles. *London.* a.1760.
William. *London.* a.1767.
George. *London.* a.1784. br. clock.
John. *London (Tottenham Ct. Rd.).* CC. 1781-4. mus. br. clock.
Obadiah. *Bristol.* 1781-1801. C. & W.
William. *London (Arthur St.).* 1790.
Joseph. *London (Stratford).* 1802-08. W.
William. *Greenwich.* 1805-08.
Thomas. *London (Westmoreland St.).* a. 1794, CC.1806, l.CC.1813-40. W.
——. *London (Kennington).* 1809-11. W.
James. *Belfast.* 1819-24.
Henry Samuel. *London.* a.1823.
& CHAPMAN. *Liverpool.* 1825. W.

COLES—
John. *London.* a.1707.
Francis. *London.* a.1721.
Francis. *Bishops Lydeard.* an.1760. Watch.
James. *London (Grub St.* in 1767, *Old St.* in 1778). a.1753, CC.1760-78.
Stephen. *London.* a.1763.
Abraham. *London.* a.1768, CC.1775-81. Bankrupt.
Richard. *Buckingham.* mar.1786. C. & W.
Edward, son of James. *London.* a.1778. W.
M. A. *London.* 1790.

COLESON, John. *London.* a.1699.

COLGATE, George. *London.* Early 19c. Watch.

COLHOUN—
James, & Son. *Londonderry.* 1820.
James, junior. *Londonderry.* 1820-4. Watch N.Y. Univ.
William. *Londonderry.* 1824.

COLIAU, Antoine. *Paris.* 1786-9. Fine turning drum clock.

COLIAUD, ——. *Lyons.* 1708. Prob. same as COLLIOT.

COLIN, Marmaduke. *London.* 1672. Watch.

COLINGSBY, Robert. *London.* a.1792.

COLIS, Jean François. *Charenton.* 1786. Replaced LÉVEQUE (*q.v.*) as manager of watch factory.

COLLAD, John. *London.* ca.1710. Watch mt. Ilbert coll.

COLLADON—
——. *Geneva.* a.1674.
Henry Gabriel. *Geneva.* ca.1760-71. en. watch set stones M.P.S. Dresden.
François, et Edme. *Geneva.* ca.1770. Four colour g. watch M.P.S. Dresden.
FRÈRES. ——. 2nd half 18c. Prob. the preceding. g. en. watch.

COLLADON—*continued.*
Louis Henry Gédéon. *Geneva.* mar. ca.1760-1771.
ET FILS. *Geneva.* End 18c. Copper en. watch Fränkel coll.

COLLARD—
Leonard. *London.* a.1675.
Nicolas. *Paris.* m.1778-89.
——. *Paris.* 1812.

COLLAS, ——. *Paris.* 1812.

COLLAVIN, ——. *Geneva.* 1698.

COLLES—
Charles. *London.* a.1696.
Nicholas. *Kilkenny.* 1820-4.

COLLET—
Amy. *Blois.* comp. 1619. Also COULET.
Thimothée. *Rouen.* m.1652, juré 1659. circ. al. cal. watch B.M. Fine oval cal. watch Fränkel coll.

COLLETT—
John. *London.* an.1774. Watch.
Thomas. *London (Acton).* an.1786-1824. Watch.
John. *London (Stratford).* a.1789-99. l.c. clock and watch.
John. *London (Chelsea).* 1805-21.
Elizabeth. *London (Chelsea).* 1822-4.
W. H. *Uxbridge.* Early 19c.

COLLEY—
Richard. *London (Fleet St.).* d.1736. 'Eminent W.'
John. *London.* a.1736, CC.1749-63.
Thomas. *London (Fleet St.).* 1751. d.1771. a. to and succeeded Geo. GRAHAM. *v.* BARKLEY & COLLEY. p.c. g. rep. watch sd. 'Graham's Succr. Tho. Colley' Ilbert coll. Colley worked alone from 1754.
Joseph. *London.* CC.1752. Also CALLEY.
George. *London (St. Sepulchre).* d. an.1765.
& PRIEST. *London.* 1762. Successors to Thomas.
John, son of John. *London.* a.1763.
James, son of George. *London.* a.1765.
Matthew. *Windsor.* an.1779. Watch.
Thomas, son of Thomas. *London.* a.1772.

COLLIBER (CALLIBER)—
John. *London.* a.1690, CC.1703-54.
Thomas, son. *London.* CC.1726-40.

COLLIER—
Benjamin. *London.* a.1684, CC.1693-1730. Maker of repute. l.c. clock ill. Cec. & Web. br. clock ill. Britten; rep. watch; p.c. watch G.M. l.c. green lacquer clock Weth. coll. Also COLLYER.
Benjamin. *London.* a.1697.
William. *London.* a.1699.
William. *London.* 1712-45. Ring dial M.M.A.
John. *London.* 1716 CC.
Robert. *London.* a.1730, CC.1738-51.
Bernard Jacques. *Paris.* 1728. m.1743, juré 1780-9. Devised a rep. work with all-or-nothing. desc. in Gallon, 'Machines et Inventions,' Vol. v.
Samuel. *Eccles.* ca.1770. l.c. clock.
John. *London.* a.1768, CC.1777.
Peter. *Manchester.* From *Warrington.* 1784-1788. CC. Watch.
David. *Etchells.* d.1792. C.
——. *Newport (Salop).* 1787. C. & W.
Archibald. *London.* ca.1790-1825.
Henry. *London.* a.1785.
Thomas, son of Archibald. *London.* a.1801.
Marshall. *London.* CC.1818.

COLLIN—
——. *Paris.* 1786 m.-1825. Watch N.Y. Univ.
Daniel. *Cambridge.* 1818. Watch.

COLLING—
Andreas. *Augsburg.* ca.1730. Watch Carnegie M.
Martin. *Copenhagen.* m.1784.

COLLINGRIDGE, Edmund (Edward). *London.* a.1792, CC.1800, l.CC.1810-24.
COLLINGS—
James. *London.* a.1773.
& TYRER. *London.* 1820.
COLLINGWOOD—
Thomas. *London.* a.1724, CC.1734-66.
Samuel John, son. *London.* a.1747, CC.1759, l.CC.1787, d.1816.
John. *London.* an.1782. Watch.
Robert. *Rochdale.* ca.1820.
Matthew. *Alnwick.* 1820-55.
COLLINS—
Robert. *London.* a.1646.
Peter. *London.* a.1679, CC.1687-99.
John. *London* (*Gt. Old Bailey*). a.1693, CC.1701-16. Also COLLINGS.
Clement. *London.* a.1697, CC.1705.
John, son of John. *London.* a.1716, CC. 1726.
John. *London.* a.1718, CC.1727. rep. watch.
Alcock. *London.* a.1732.
Charlemain. *London.* a.1736.
Richard Barrett. *London.* a.1738, CC.1751. 'Clocksmith.'
Thomas. *Doncaster.* an.1766. Watch.
William. *London.* an.1778. Watch.
John. *Wattisfield.* b.1750, d.1829.
Joseph. *Emsworth.* 1784. W.
J. B. *Northampton.* Late 18c.-1808.
Elizabeth. *London.* 1795. Shagreen case maker.
Richard. *Margate.* 1795. W.
Charles Augustus. *London.* a.1793.
Robert. *London.* a.1793.
Francis. *London.* a.1800.
John. *Liverpool.* 1825.
COLLINSON, James. *London.* 2nd half 18c. Shagreen watch.
COLLIOT—
François. *Lyons.* 1699-1725.
Antoine. *Lyons.* 1700-37.
COLLIS—
Charles. *London.* 1st half 18c. Watch mt.
Richard. *Romford.* a.1768-1824.
COLLISON, Peter. *London.* a.1800.
COLLMAN, Isaac. *London.* a.1711.
COLLO, Dedie. *England.* 1544. French.
COLLOMBY (COLOMBIER)—
Jacob. *London.* ca.1660. Watch.
Jaques. ——. 1663. Prob. same as Jacob. Watch M.M.A. crys. cross watch.
Estienne. ——. ca.1660. crys. cross watch in sil. filigree case, Mallett coll.
Henri. *Basle*, 1670. *Hüningen*, 1679-99. Native of *Geneva.* Maker of repute. Watches S.K.M. ill. Baillie, Nat. M. Munich and Mallett coll.
Jean Pierre, bro. *Basle* and *Hüningen.* 1684. Native of *Geneva.*
Abraham. *Geneva.* 1745-ca.1760. g. p.c. watch and g. en. watch S.K.M. 3-case 4-colour g. watch Den. coll. Watches Fränkel coll., Stads M. Amsterdam and M.P.S. Dresden.
Abraham. *London.* ca.1750. Perhaps same as above. cal. watch S.K.M. cf. COLLUMBELL.
& ESQUIVILLON. ——. ca.1750. sil. watch case repoussé by COCHIN, Nat. M. Stockholm.
v. COELOMBIE.
COLLOT—
Jean. *Paris.* m.1744.
Jean Rémy. *Paris.* m.1766.
COLLUMBELL, ——. *London.* an.1756. mar.1770. Watch. cf. Abr. COLLOMBY.
COLMER, William. *London.* a.1748.
COLOMB—
Charles Frédéric. *Fontaines* and *Chaux-de-Fonds.* 1782-1805. Able turret C.
——. *Le Locle.* 1800. C.
COLOMBEL—
François. *Rouen.* m.1660.
François. *Rouen.* a.1660.
COLON, Renaud. *Neuchâtel.* 1492. Repaired clock of the Collégiale.
COLSON—
Richard or John. *London.* a.1637. CC.1646-1697.
——. *Penzance.* 1795.
COLSTON—
John. *London.* CC.1646.
John. *London.* CC.1653.
Richard, son. *London.* CC.1682-1709. Clock Battle Abbey. l.c. clock Weth. coll. sil. watch with fine piqué tortoise-shell outer case, S.K.M. Watch Den. coll. Watch ca.1720 with hand for minutes and opening for hours, M.M.A.
Thomas, son. *London.* a.1702.
COLVILLE, Cornelius. *London.* a.1737.
COLVIN, Walter. *Trenton, U.S.A.* 1785.
COLYER, A. *Witham.* Early 19c. Watch.
COMANS, Louis. *London.* 1744. W.
COMBAS, ——. *Paris.* 1812.
COMBAULT (COMBAUX)—
Jacques. *Paris.* m.1776-89.
Claude Joseph. *Paris.* m.1781. Watch.
COMBE, ——. *Paris.* Early 19c.
COMBER—
William. *Lewes.* Retired 1775. Succeeded by Thos. HARBEN.
Richard. *Lewes.* b.1742, d.1824. l.c. clock Weth. coll. Good maker.
COMBES—
Fisher. *London.* 1730. CC.
John. *London.* a.1772, CC.1779. Watch mt. G.M.
George. *London.* a.1772.
COMBRET—
Pierre. *Lyons.* 1570. d.1622. An eminent maker. Shell watch S.K.M. Oval watch Louvre. Cross watch and astro. watch M.M.A. Watch Schloss M. Berlin. crys. watch Petit Palais, Paris. oct. watch Dijon M. oct. crys. watch Spitzer coll. Oval watch and oct. crys. watch Côte coll. 3 ill. Vial & Côte.
Hugues, son. *Lyons.* b.1596, d.1669. sil. tulip watch Pal. du Cinquantenaire, Brussels.
Jacques. *Blois.* 1630-47. Had relations with *Lyons.*
Claude, son of Hugues. *Lyons.* b.1636-59 m.
COMENDA (KOMMENDA), Karl. *Vienna.* m.1817.
COMFORT, William. *London.* CC.1646-56.
COMLEY, Thomas. *London.* 1780-90. Watch G.M.
COMLOSY (KAMELOSY)—
Karl. *Vienna.* m.1781. Watch.
Joseph. *Chaux-de-Fonds.* 1784.
COMMANDER, Samuel. *London.* a.1796.
COMMINGES, ——. *Paris.* 1817-25.
COMMON, Weeks. *Peckham.* ca.1750 Watch.
COMPANY, David. *London.* an.1707. Watch.
COMPIGNÉ, David. *Winchester.* 1718. br. and l.c. clock. Cal. watch Ilbert coll.
COMPLIN, Henry. *London.* a.1699.
COMPORT—
Ebenezer. *London.* a.1720, CC.1728-50.
Joseph, son. *London.* a.1750, CC.1767-75.
COMPTON—
Adam. *London.* CC.1716.
John, E., jun. *Winchester.* 1795 CC.
John. *Calne.* 1795. C.
COMTESSE—
Frédéric. *Chaux-de-Fonds.* ca.1750. C.
Isaac. *Couvet.* 1760. C. Several clocks.
Jonas Pierre. *Ponts-de-Martel.* 1800. C Several clocks.
Jules. *Stockholm.* 1817-25.

COMTOSI—
Lorentz. *S. Germany*. ca. 1800. 'Klein und Gros Hoff Uhrenmacher Im Hoch Fürstl. Stifft Kempten.' cal. br. clock Furt. M.
Paul. *Vienna*. Mid. 18c. Watch mt. Arts M. Prague.
CONANT, Elias. *Bridgwater, U.S.A.* 1776-1812. Then *Lynn* to 1815.
CONDEN, Robert. *London*. 1780-5.
CONDLIFF—
Joseph. *Chapel-en-le-Frith*. 1791. C.
Martin. *Sheffield*. 1797. C.
James. *Liverpool*. 1818-36.
CONDUITT, Sam. *London*. a.1671.
CONDY (CONEY). Thomas. *London*. a.1684. CC.1692-1725.
CONGREVE, William. *London*. 1808-23. Comptroller of Woolwich Laboratory. A very ingenious mechanic; patented in 1808 clock with ball rolling down zigzag grooves on an inclined plane ill. Britten. Designed skeleton clock made by MOXON, Buckingham Palace.
CONIBERE, Samuel. *Ashburton*. 1791. C. & W.
CONING, Richard. *Boston, U.S.A.* 1796. C.
CONNATLY, William. *London*. a.1816.
CONNELL—
William Beto. *London*. a.1770.
William. *London*. a.1817.
CONNESANT, John. *London*. a.1707.
CONNIGERVITS, William. *London*. a.1804, CC.1811.
CONNOCKE—
Gilliam. *London*. 1583. C. From *Holland*.
CONNOR—
James. *London*. a.1813.
John. *Dublin*. 1820-4.
CONNY—
John. *London*. a.1630 under BC. CC.1640.
John. *London*. a.1710. cf. CONY.
CONOR, H. *London*. 1743. Watch.
CONQUER, Patrick. *Perth*. a.1790.
CONQUEROR, Peter. *Berwick-on-Tweed*. 1806-27. l.c. clocks.
CONRAD—
——. ——. 1362. A German who failed to replace the Ferrara clock and 'se absentavit per fugam.'
Hans. *Augsburg*. 1586. Made clock for Fredrik II of Denmark.
H. *Amsterdam*. ca.1715. g. p.c. en. watch.
Ludwig. *Magdeburg*. 1802. Made clocks with light-striking device.
CONRARD, Paul. *Liége*. Mid. 18c. br. clock.
CONSTABLE—
Daniel. *London* (*Little Grays Inn Lane*). an. 1707. Watch.
Daniel. *London* (*Fleet Lane*). a.1714-30. Insolvent.
W. & G. *London*. 1805-08.
William. *Dundee*. 1806-28. Watch N.Y. Univ.
George. *Cupar-Fife*. 1814.
CONSTANSSOIS, *v.* LE COUSTANÇOIS.
CONSTANT, Pierre. *Basle*. 1686. From *Coulommiers*.
CONSTANTIN—
Moïse. *Geneva*. 1750-1800. g. shield-shaped watch S.K.M. Watch Chamb. coll. Watch in form of melon.
Vincent. *Dieppe*. Mid. 18c. sil. watch S.K.M.
François. *Geneva*. b.1787, d.1854. Partner from 1819 in VACHERON & CONSTANTIN.
CONSTANTINE—
John. *London* (*Westminster*). an.1707-27. Watch.
John. *London*. a.1709, CC.1716.
CONWAY—
John. *Poole*. 1750. C.
Timothy. *Cork*. 1783. d.1804.

CONWAY—*continued.*
G. *London*. 1800-30. p.c. g. watch, filigree case, F.W.M.
John. *Sturminster*. Early 19c. Watch.
CONY, John. *London*. 1764.
CONYERS—
Richard. *London*. a.1672, CC.1689, d. an. 1708.
Richard, son. *London*. a.1708, CC.1716-26.
Thomas. *London*. an.1772. Watch.
Thomas. *London*. a.1809.
COOK—
Jonathan. *London*. 1684.
John. *London*. a.1715.
John. *Aylesbury*. an.1765. Watch.
Stephen. *London*. an.1767. Watch.
Robert. *London*. a.1766-1808.
Richard. *London*. a.1766.
Joseph. *Aylesbury*. an.1777. Watch.
J. *Trafford*. ca.1775. Watch mt. Buckley coll.
John. *London*. a.1773, CC.1785.
John. *London*. a.1778.
William. *Kingston* (*Surrey*). an.1773-95 CC. Watch.
Joshua. *London*. 1790.
John. *Whitchurch* (*Hants*). 1791. W.
John. *London* (*Islington*). 1793-7. W.
Benjamin. *London* (*Hackney*). 1802-04. W.
Zenas. *Waterbury, U.S.A.* 1810-15. Started clockmaking with Daniel CLARK and William PORTER; failed ca.1815.
John. *Strabane*. 1820-4.
COOKE—
Lewis. *York*. 1614-32. C. Petitioner for incorporation of CC.
John. *London*. 1622. a. to Cornelius MELLIN. crys. watch with 4-wheel train Wallace coll.
John. *London*. a.1641, CC.1649-56.
Thomas. *London*. a.1649.
John. *London*. a.1655, CC.1662. l.c. clock.
Robert. *London*. CC.1667. math. inst. maker.
Thomas. *London*. CC.1669-1702. l.c. clock.
William. *London*. a.1673, CC.1681. Escaped from prison 1697. Also COKE.
Thomas. *London*. a.1682, CC.1699.
John. *London*. a.1684.
Edward. *London*. a.1687.
George. *London*. a.1694-1723. Bankrupt.
Richard. *London*. a.1696.
William, son of William. *London*. CC.1708.
John. *London*. a.1700, CC.1713-18.
Joseph. *London*. a.1706, CC.1715.
Stephen. *London*. a.1717.
Job. *London*. a.1743, CC.1750.
Julius. *London*. a.1748.
Thomas. *London*. a.1751.
Henry. *London*. a.1753.
John. *London*. a.1754.
John. *London* (*Aylesbury St.*). a.1759, CC. 1775-86.
Thomas. *London*. a.1762.
Joseph. *London*. a.1781.
Robert. *Pentonville*. 1791. C. & W.
Robert. *London*. a.1787.
S. *London*. 1788. Watch.
George. *London*. a.1792.
Charles. *London*. a.1796.
James. *London* (*Romford*). 1809-11. W.
Charles James. *London*. a.1799.
Thomas. *London*. a.1803.
John. *London*. a.1809.
Thomas. *Loughborough*. an.1822. Watch.
J. *Cambridge*. Early 19c.
COOKSON, Thomas. *Ulverston*. 1820.
COOLEY, Henry. *London*. 1768. Watch.
COOMBE—
William. *England*. 1777-87. Submitted a marine timekeeper for test in 1779. Pub.

COOMBE—*continued.*
'Researches on a measure of time for determination of the longitude at sea.'
Joseph. *Bristol.* 1784.
COOMBES (COOMBS)—
William. *London.* a.1689-97.
James. *London.* CC.1719.
Joseph. *London.* a.1712, CC.1720.
Fisher. *London.* a.1721, CC.1728-37.
John. *London.* a.1772.
Benjamin. *Bath.* an.1772. Watch.
Joseph. *Melksham.* 1791-5. W.
COOPER—
Hugh. *London.* a.1646, CC.1653, d. an. 1674.
Stephen. *London.* a.1675.
James. *London.* a.1693.
Samuel. *London.* a.1701.
William. *London.* a.1708.
Richard. *London.* a.1711.
William. *London.* a.1720.
John. *Cardiff.* ca.1705. p.c. watch, portrait of Queen Anne, Ilbert coll.
Edward. *London.* Early 18c. Watch Den. coll.
Joseph. *Shrewsbury.* 1714 C.
John. *London* (*W. Smithfield*). 1747. W.
William. *Derby.* 1760-1802. C. & W.
George. *London.* an.1772. Watch.
Joseph. *Whitchurch* (*Salop*). 1773.
John. *Colchester.* 2nd half 18c.
& HEDGE. *Colchester.* an.1780. l.c. clock. Watch.
& SON. *Derby.* 2nd half 18c. Watch.
James. *London.* a.1779-ca.1790. p.c. watch Ilbert coll.
& BRADSHAW. *Manchester.* 1790. Partnership of James C. and John B. dissolved.
Richard. *Gibraltar.* ca.1790 CC.
Thomas. *London.* a.1787-1800.
Thomas. *Newport* (*Salop*). 1795 C.
Thomas. *London.* a.1789, CC.1798.
Thomas. *London* (*E. Smithfield*). 1799.
William. *London* (*Old Bailey*). 1805-08.
Isaac. *London.* a.1799.
William. *Hamilton.* 1808-24.
John. *London.* a.1802, CC.1813.
William. *London* (*Gee St.*). 1820-40. W.
William. *London* (*Goswell St.*). 1820.
Thomas Frederick. *London.* 1820-40. W. of repute. Supplied the American market.
——. *Bristol.* Early 19c. Watch.
——. *Colchester.* 1825. Lever watch Ilbert coll. *v.* John above.
COOS & ROSS. *London.* an.1778. Watch.
COOTE, Thomas. *Dublin.* 1733-47. br. clock.
COOTH, John. *London.* ca.1700. Watch Ilbert coll.
COPE—
Peter. *London.* CC.1638.
W. *London.* an.1769. Watch.
William. *London.* a.1770.
Benjamin. *Franche.* 1786. W.
Charles John. *London.* 1815-30. Expert on Earnshaw's chron.
COPELAND, Alexander. *London.* CC.1809-1824.
COPES, James. *London.* 1663. Watch.
COPPELL, John. *Liverpool.* 1816-18. W.
COPPET—
R. A. *London.* Mid. 18c. en. watch.
Clément Courta. *Switzerland.* Mid. 18c. Watch Fränkel coll.
COPPIN, John. *London.* a.1698.
COPPING, George. *London.* a.1654.
COPPINGER, Francis. *Bandon.* 1820.
COPPLESTONE, William. *London.* a.1683.
'COQUAI.' ca.1670. Sig. on trav. clock with min.hand, M.P.S. Dresden.
COQUERELLE, Pierre, l'aîné. *Paris.* 1774 m.
COQUET, ——. *Paris.* 1821-4.
COQUIN, Vincent Marie. *Paris.* m.1764-1789.
CORBELLY, Elias William. *London.* a.1758.
CORBET—
Nathan. *London.* 1721.
Robert. *Glasgow.* 1822-41.
CORBETT—
Samuel. *London.* a.1765.
Samuel. *Hadleigh* and *Dedham.* 1768-ca. 1790 CC. Watch G.M.
CORBITT, Benjamin. *London.* a.1682.
CORBORT, Nathaniel. *London.* 1719. W.
CORBYN, & Co. *London.* ca.1800. Watch Ilbert coll.
CORDELL, Thomas. *London.* a.1708.
CORDELLIERS, D. L. *Lyons.* Clock Cassel Landes-M.
CORDER, William. *Derby.* an.1689. Watch.
CORDEROY (CAWDRY)—
Thomas. *London.* a.1663, CC.1670.
Philip. *London.* a.1672, CC.1679-97.
Walter. *London.* a.1692.
CORDIER, ——. *Paris.* 1819. Clock in polished steel case.
CORDING—
Joseph. *London* (*Holborn*). 1801. Watch.
William. *London.* an.1802. Watch.
John. *London* (*Strand*). 1820.
CORDINGLY, Thomas. *Leeds.* 1817-26. Watch N.Y. Univ.
CORDON, Richard. *London.* a.1720, CC. 1729.
CORDWELL, Robert. *London.* mar. 1625. C.
CORGEE, Arthur. *Philadelphia.* 1823. C.
CORK, ——. *London.* 1742. Watch.
CORKER, Daniel. *London.* 1817-40.
CORLESS, John. *London.* 1815. Math. Inst. maker.
CORLYES, Richard. *Stockport.* an.1766. Watch.
CORMASSON, François Casimir. *Paris.* d. 1773.
CORMICK, Nicholas. *London.* a.1812.
CORMIER, Pierre. *France.* 1481. Repaired clock for Louis XI at Plessis du-Parc.
CORMIS, ——. *Geneva.* ca.1790. Painter on enamel of great repute for portraits.
'CORN, JAN. MANN.' 2nd half 17c. Sig. on sil. bud watch Nat. M. Munich.
CORNAH, James. *Lancaster.* 1785. Bankrupt. *Manchester.* d.1795. W.
CORNBER, ——. *Lewes.* ca.1800. c.secs. cyl. watch.
CORNELIUS—
Klensmed (Cornelius the locksmith). *Nyköping.* 1590. Made clock for the castle.
Jacob. *London.* ca.1620 CC. Table clock. Fine blue en. watch with flowers in relief, Webster coll. ill. Baillie.
CORNELL—
Michael. *Cologne.* 1634. Kleinuhrmacher.
C. *Royston.* Early 19c. Watch.
CORNELL WATCH CO. *Chicago.* Issued watches in 1871-4 with sigs.: 'Paul Cornell,' 'J. C. Adams,' 'Geo. F. Root,' 'John Evans,' 'H. N. Hibbard,' 'E. S. Williams,' 'C. T. Bowen,' 'C. M. Cady,' 'Geo. W. Waite, 'Ladies Stem Wind.'
CORNELL WATCH CO. *San Francisco.* Successor, issued watches in 1875 with the sig. 'C. & L. Kidder, San Francisco,' and was succeeded in 1876 by the CALIFORNIA WATCH CO.
CORNER, Jonathan. *Dorchester.* an.1762. Watch.
CORNEU, Peter Daniel. *London.* ca.1730.
CORNFORTH—
——. *Stokesley.* 1746. Lantern clocks.
W. B. *Macclesfield.* Early 19c.
CORNIQUET, Philippe Jacques. *Paris.* m. 1785-1813. astro. and cal. clock. Mantel clock Pal. de l'Élysée.

CORNISH—
Michael. *London.* CC.1661-93.
John. *London.* a.1654.
William. *London.* a.1659.
Robert. *Dartford.* an.1777. Watch.

CORNU—
Peter Daniel. *London.* a.1719.
——. *Montpellier.* Mid 18c. Watch mt. G.M.
——. *Châlons.* ca.1800. Mantel clock Virginia M.
——. *Paris.* 1812.

CORNWALL—
Thomas. *Dublin.* 1766-74. W.
James. *Liverpool.* ca.1820.

CORNWELL—
Daniel. *London.* Mid. 18c. Watch.
Daniel. *Billericay.* 1791. W.

CORP—
Timothy. *London.* 1784.
William. *London.* Early 19c.

CORRALL—
Francis. *London.* 1720-32. CC.
Thomas Tissier. *Lutterworth.* an.1756-95. Watch.
William. *Lutterworth.* Mid. 18c. Watch.
Powell. *Lutterworth.* 1777-95. C.

CORRIE, Philip. *Langholm.* 1770-1817. l.c. clock.

CORRIER, Jean. *Paris.* m.1772-1812.

CORRY, —— *Colchester.* an. 1718. Sun and moon watch.

CORSAN, ——. *London* (*Wapping*). Early 19c. Watch.

CORSTON, John. *London.* ca.1745. Watch mt. Buckley coll.

CORT, Benjamin. *London.* a.1713.

COSBEY, Robert. *London.* a.1646, CC.1653-1689.

COSENS—
Nicholas. *York.* 1638. Sand-glass maker.
Nathaniel. *Bristol.* 1781-97. C.
William. *London.* 1805-08.

COSHER, Thomas. *London.* 1799. W.

COSI, Anthony. *Basle.* 1685. From *Geneva.*

COSINE—
Alexander. *London.* 1622. Alien. Prob. CUSIN.
John. *London.* 1622. Alien. Prob. CUSIN.

COSMAN, Philip. *Amsterdam.* ca.1790.

COSSWORTH, John. *London.* CC.1678. Engraver.

COSTA, Jh. *Marseilles.* ca.1790. 4-colour g. str. watch with 5-bell carillon, Wallace coll., sd. 'Jh. Costa Amateur d'Horlogerie à Marseille.'

COSTALA, Thomas. *Liverpool.* 1781-4. W.

COSTEN, *v.* CASTON.

COSTER—
Salomon. *Haarlem.* ca.1575.
Robert. *London.* a.1647, CC.1655.
Salomon or Samuel. *Haarlem, Amsterdam* and *The Hague.* 1646 m. d.1659. Made the first pendulum clocks for HUYGENS, and obtained Netherlands patent in 1657. The first pendulum clock in the Rijks M. The Hague is sd. 'SAMUEL COSTER—HAGHE. met Privilege 1657.' Watch fishskin p.c. Ilbert coll. en. watch Gélis coll., both sd. Salomon. Trav. clock. Large oval watch Stads M. Amsterdam, sd. Samuel Koster, Haarlem.
William. *London.* CC.1660.
Robert. *London.* a.1695.
Thomas. *London.* a.1699.
Thomas. *London.* a.1756, CC.1764.
James. *Henley* and *Gt. Marlow.* ca.1800. Watch.

COTEAU, Jean. *Sèvres.* b.ca.1739, d. after 1810. Painter on enamel. Dials in Mobilier Nat., Carnavalet M. and Dijon M.

COTHER—
William. *London.* CC.1668.
John, son. *London.* a.1667.

COTHORNE, John. *London.* an.1763. Watch.

COTMORE, Thomas. *London.* a.1790.

COTSWORTH, John. *London.* b.ca.1637, CC.1669, d.1732. W. l.c. clock.

COTTEREL (COTTRELL, COTTRILL)—
William. *London.* a.1687, CC.1694, d.an. 1752. Watch.
John. son. *London.* CC.1721-34, d.an. 1752. l.c. clock Virginia M. Also COTTRELL.
John George, son. *London.* a.1752.
John. *Brecon.* 1780. W. COTTRELL.

COTTEY, Able. *Philadelphia.* mar. ca.1690-1710. W.

COTTIER, ——. *Ramsay, I. of Man.* 1794. Watch.

COTTIN (COTTIN-DESBOIS), Jean Norbert. *Paris.* m.1786.

COTTLE, Thomas. *Crewkerne.* 1795. C.

COTTON—
John. *London.* a.1683, CC.1695. Watch, sun and moon hour indicators, Den. coll.
Charles. *London.* a.1707.
John. *London.* a.1711, CC.1719-52. Worked for Pepys. Fine g. en. watch.
& REEVES. *London.* 1762.
Benjamin. *Hurley.* 18c.
James. *Tamworth.* 1772. C. & W.

COTTONBELT, John. *London.* a.1718. CC. 1729-47. Watch.

COUCH, Francis. *London.* an.1774. Watch.

COUCHE, Charles. *London.* a.1719, CC. 1727-37.

COUDREY (COULDRAY or COULDROY)—
Julien. *Blois.* 1504. d.1530. C. to Louis XI and François I. Famous maker. Prob. the first French W. Made two daggers with watches in hilts for King in 1518; made cal. and astro. clock for Tours and clock for Fontainebleau.
Guillaume. *Blois.* 1532-47. C. to Francis I; C. to town of Blois. Made clock for St. Martin Vendôme, 1533.
B. (Couldroit). *France.* Mid. 16c. Small hex. stand clock B.M.
Julien. *Blois.* mar. 1572, d.1586.

COUET, ——. *Paris.* 1812.

COUETTE, Pierre. *La Rochelle.* 1668.

COUGNARD, Abraham. *London.* a.1695. An apprentice of the same name was bound to Jonas THORELET in Rouen in the same year.

COUGNEFORT, Jean. *Rouen.* 1634. Repaired clock of St. Maclou.

COUILLARD, Jean François Marie. *Paris.* m.1779.

COULIN—
FRÈRES. *Geneva.* ca.1780. en. watch.
Jean François. *Geneva.* 1794-8. Director, with PLAN, of State factory; a juré.
Jacques, and Ami BRY. *Paris* and *Geneva.* 1784-1800. g. en. watch S.K.M. rep. aut. watch Marryat coll. Fine 3-case g. en. watch.
——. *Geneva.* Early 19c. Several en. watches.

COULOMB, Charles Augustin. *Paris.* 1790. Wrote a memoir on pivot friction.

COULON, Charles. *London.* 1743-68. Watch.

COULSON—
Henry. *Penzance.* ca.1790 CC.
Robert. *London.* CC.1791, l.CC.1810-38.
William. *N. Shields.* 1811-27. l.c. clocks.
William. *London.* a.1805, CC.1814.

COULTON—
Richard. *London.* a.1641.
Francis. *London.* CC.1690.
John. *York.* 1701. C.

COULTON—*continued.*
William, son. *York.* 1739. l.c. clock. Watch.
Francis, bro. *York.* 1757. C.
John. *Ulverstone.* ca.1820.
COUNIE, Joseph Simon. *Paris.* m.1778.
COUNSELL, E. *Faringdon.* Early 19c. Watch.
COUPE, James. *London.* Mid. 17c. en. watch.
COUPÉ—
——. *Paris.* Late 17c. Sig. 'Coupe, Anglois, Horlogeur du Roi' on steel watch, crystals front and back, formerly in Shandon coll. Perhaps James above.
Elizabeth. Watch plate Olivier coll. eng. 'Elizabeth Coupé, Angloise, Horlogeuse du Roi.' Prob. early 18c.
COUPLIER, Pierre. *Rouen.* 1701 m.
COUPPEY, Jean André. *Paris.* m.1764. Went to *Vienna* 1773. C. to the King and the city of Paris. Several astro. clocks.
COUPSON—
Achille Louis. *Paris.* m.1737, d. an.1789. He, or the following, was mentioned by L. Berthoud as eminent. A watch with straight spring was approved by the Acad. des Sciences, in 1764.
Jean Achille. *Paris.* m.1760.
Veuve (of A. L.). *Paris.* 1789.
——. *Paris.* 1807-11.
COUR, ——. *Paris.* 1812.
COURCAULT, ——. *Paris.* ca.1690. Boulle clock.
COURGOU, Charles. *Amsterdam.* 1687. Huguenot refugee from *Mer.*
COURIEULT, Gabriel. *Paris.* 1779-93. Made clock for Marie Antoinette.
COURT—
Jean. *Grenoble.* 1643-69.
——. *Paris.* 1787.
Isaac. *Henley-in-Arden* and *Solihull.* 1743-1801. al. attachment for watch.
Thomas. *Leamington.* ca.1790.
Henry. *London.* l.CC.1822.
——. *Paris.* 1824.
COURTANVAUX, Marquis de. *Paris.* 1768. Pub. Journal of voyage for trying Le Roy's chrons.
COURTAULD—
Augustin. *London.* a.1732, CC.1748-51. Watchcase maker.
Samuel. *London.* an.1775. Watch.
COURTENER, ——. *Strasbourg.* End 18c. Watch mt. Ilbert coll.
COURTER, Edward. *Ruthin.* 1772. C.
COURTIN, ——. *Paris.* 1812-25.
COURTNEY, John. *London.* CC.1768.
COURTOIS—
——. *Paris.* 1750-72. Cartel clock ill. Britten. Invented sliding carillon barrel moved by cam, approved by Acad. des Sciences.
——. *St. Malo.* 2nd half 18c. g. en. watch.
——. *Paris.* 1823.
COURTONNE, ——. *Paris.* 1786.
COURVOISIER—
Jean. *Sonvillier.* 1630. C.
-Folter *v.* Folter.
David Louis. *Paris.* m.1765, d.1773.
Louis. *Chaux-de-Fonds.* b.1758, d.1832. Maker of great repute.
——. *Paris.* 1764. Cartel clock ill. Britten.
& Houriet. *Le Locle.* ca.1775-1804. Partnership of David Courvoisier and Jacques Frédéric Houriet. Very fine l.c. and astro. clocks. Watch N.Y. Univ.
Henri Louis, son of Louis. *Chaux-de-Fonds.* b.1796, d.1868.
Frédéric Alexandre. *Chaux-de-Fonds.* b. 1799, d.1854.
& Compe. Also Frères. Firm composed of Henri and Frédéric at *Chaux-de-Fonds.*

COURVOISIER—*continued.*
g. rep. aut. watch M.M.A. Keyless watch Fränkel coll.
et Cie. *Paris, Chaux-le-Fonds* and *Geneva,* 1811-ca.1835. g. 8-day watch M.P.S. Dresden. g. watch M.M.A. *v.* Robert.
Frères. *Le Locle.* 1801-04.
David. *Hamburg.* 1801-04.
Henri Edouard. *Chaux-de-Fonds.* 1823.
COURVOISIER-DIT-CLÉMENT—
Daniel. *Chaux-de-Fonds.* 1681. d.1689. Made clock for La Sagne.
Daniel. *Chaux-de-Fonds.* 1754-65.
COURVOISIER - DIT - VOISIN, Abram. *Chaux-de-Fonds.* 1799. C.
COURVOISIER - SANDOZ, P. F. *Hamburg.* 1801-04.
COUSIN—
Abraham. *Blois.* 1587.
Joseph. Simon. *Paris.* m.1778, juré 1782-9.
——. *Paris* (*Rue du Harlay*). 1787-9.
——. *Paris* (*Rue des Fosses St. Germain*). 1789.
COUSINS, Thomas. *London.* a.1777.
COUSTEILL, John. *Edinburgh.* a.1694-1715.
COUSTOS, James. *London.* an.1769. cyl. watch.
COUTHER, Thomas. *London.* an.1811. Watch.
COUTIER, ——. Prob. *France.* ca.1670. Chased sil. bud watch.
COUTTS, James. *Perth.* 1800-48.
COUTURE, Jean Joseph. *Paris.* m.1778-89.
COUTURIER—
Jean. *Lyons.* 1461. d.1464. Keeper of Cathedral clock.
Étienne Claude. *Paris* (*Rue de Berry*). m. 1768-1823. g. watch.
Jeune. *Paris* (*Rue du Caire*). 1808-12.
——. *Paris* (*Rue d'Anjou*). 1812.
COVELL—
Richard. *London.* a.1671.
John. *London.* 1764 CC.
COVELLE & ROMILLY. *Geneva.* ca.1800. 4-colour g. watch.
COVENTRY—
Carr. *London.* a.1649, CC.1657-60.
William. *Newcastle-o.-T.* 1778-87. C. & W.
Thomas. *London.* a.1774.
COVER, John. *London.* an.1768. Watch.
COVERDALL, Daniel. *London.* a.1683.
COVERLEY, J. *London.* an.1771. Watch.
COVILL (or **COLVIL**), John. *Alford.* 1795, d.1810. C. & W.
COVINGTON, William. *Stony Stratford.* 1785.
COWAN, James. *Edinburgh.* a.1744, d.1781. One of the most famous Scottish makers. br. clock ill. Britten, Weth. coll. Clock in Signet Library, Edinburgh. Fine verge watch. Chamb. coll.
COWARD—
William. *London.* a.1673, CC.1681-84.
& Co. *London.* Late 18c. Watch.
William. *Lancaster.* 1797-1824.
COWDELL, William. *London.* a.1700.
COWDEN, ——. *London.* an.1788. Watch.
COWDEROY—
R. F. *London.* mid. 18c. Fine lever watch Chamb. coll. Watch N.Y. Univ.
William. *London.* a.1811, CC.1820.
John. *London.* CC.1826.
COWDREY, John. *London.* a.1746.
COWELL—
John Flower. *London.* a.1724, CC.1734-75.
John or Joseph. *London.* a.1737.
John. *London* (*Pope's Head Alley, Cornhill*). a.1752, CC.1759, l.CC.1781-99. cyl. watch G.M. g. watch Den. coll.
W. *London.* an.1769. Watch.
Joseph. *London.* 1799-1804.
COWEN, Henry. *London.* 1809-11.

COWLEY—
Richard. *London.* a.1748.
J. *London.* an.1778. Watch.
Thomas. *London.* an.1778. Watch.

COWLING—
John. *London.* a.1712.
Joseph. *Greenwich.* d.1822.
Richard. *London.* ca.1800. Watch N.Y. Univ.
Edward. *Richmond (Yorks.).* 1784-1820. W.
George. *London.* 1810. Watch Oldham M.

COWNDEN, William. *London.* a.1755.

COWPE—
James. *London.* CC.1654.
Edward. *London.* CC.1687. W.
——. *Paris.* ca.1685. 'Horlogier Anglois du Roi à Paris.' br. clock.

COWSELL, Samuel. *Lincoln.* From 1772. C. & W.

COWTAN—
John MacMilvan. *London.* CC.1825.

COX—
William. *London.* CC.1636.
Thomas. *London.* a.1696, CC.1708-27. g. and agate watch.
John. *London.* a.1702.
Edmund. *London.* a.1719.
Benjamin. *London.* a.1726, CC.1734.
Samuel. *London (Long Acre).* an.1747. Watch.
Jason. *London (Long Acre).* 1747-51. Watch. l.c. clock.
Whyman. *London.* a.1751.
James. *London.* 1760. d.1788. A very able maker; made many automata, a clock wound by barometric changes (ill. Britten), and another wound by the opening and shutting of a door. Catalogues of his aut. pub. in 1772 and 1774. Elaborate watch B.M. with dials on both sides. Watch London M. Most of his automata went to China; and there are 11 clocks in the Palace M. Pekin and 7 in the Peiping M., mostly very elaborate mus. and aut.
Thomas. *Thornbury.* d.1784. W. Called 'very eminent.'
Mary, widow. *Thornbury.* 1784.
James, & Son. *Canton, China.* 1783-90, then bankrupt. Successors to James Cox. Pedometer winding cyl. watch Ilbert coll.
& Beale. *Canton.* 1790. Successors to James Cox & Son.
Robert. *Christchurch.* 1791. W.
Beale & Félix Laurent. *Canton.* 1792. Successors to Cox & Beale.
——. *Devizes.* an.1795. Watch.
Thomas. Prob. *London.* 1795. W.
Joseph. *London.* a.1800.
Benjamin. *Philadelphia.* 1811-13.
Henry. *Nottingham.* 1818. W.
Henry. *London.* a.1819.
Richard. *Bristol.* 1825-30. W. & C.

COXALL—
John Cay. *Granada.* an.1776. Watch.
Samuel. *Royston.* 1795. C. & W.

COXETER—
Nicholas. *London.* a.1638, CC.1646, m.CC. 1671-7, d.1679. A famous maker. Lantern clock and l.c. clock Weth. coll.
John. *London.* a.1638, CC.1646, m.CC.1661-1663.
William. *London.* a.1647, CC.1654.
Thomas. *London.* CC.1673.

COXHEAD, William. *Reading.* Early 19c. Watch.

COXWORTHY, Thomas. *Plymouth Dock.* 1795. C. & W.

COZENS—
William. *London (Finsbury Place).* 1808. d.1842. chron. W. & C.
William & Son. *London.* 1815-40. W.

COZENS—*continued.*
Joseph B. *Philadelphia.* 1817-25.
William. *London (Goswell St.).* 1817-19.
Josiah B. *Philadelphia.* 1819-24. W.

CRABB—
——. *Salisbury.* an.1782. Watch.
James. *Whitehaven.* 1820.

CRABTREE, William. *London.* a.1772.

CRADDOCK, Thomas. *London.* a.1736.

CRADOCK, William. *London (Shadwell).* 1802-08.

CRAFT—
David. *London.* a.1702-23. Bankrupt.
W. *London.* 1773-96. aut. clock. en. painting on watch by Windmills, Stern. coll. sd. 'W. Craft fect. 1782.'

CRAFTS, Frederick. *London.* a.1753.

CRAGG—
Richard. *London.* a.1652, CC.1660.
Samuel. *London.* a.1690.
James. *Milnthorpe.* 1779. C. Lancaster freeman.
Thomas. *Horsham.* ca.1785. CC.
John. *London.* a.1780, CC.1788-1811.
John. *Southampton.* ca.1790. br. clock Ilbert coll. T.C.
James. *Manchester.* 1804. C.
Elizabeth. *Manchester.* 1813. C.
Isaac. *London.* CC.1815-24. W.

CRAIG—
Robert. *Kilmaurs.* 1740.
& Nevill or Newell. *London.* an.1744. Watch.
Robert. *Kilmarnock.* 1748.
John. *London.* an.1752. Watch.
James. *Glasgow.* 1760. Fine l.c. astro. clock.
Charles. *Dublin.* 1766-74. rep. watch mt.
John. *Newcastle-o.-T.* 1790-1820.
David. *Dalkeith.* 1798-1804.
John. *London.* 1799. W.
Richard. *Dublin.* 1820-4.

CRAIGNEAN, John. *London.* a.1733.

CRAMBER, R. P. *London.* 1810. Watch. Den. coll.

CRAMBROOK, W. *Deal.* 1818.

CRAMMILLION, Peter. *London.* 1744. Watchcase maker.

CRAMP—
Richard. *Canterbury.* 1775. W.
Thomas. *Liverpool.* 1790-6. W.

CRAMPERN—
John. *Newark.* 1770. Went to *Tuxford* in 1786. l.c. clock dial ill. Britten. l.c. clocks.

CRAMPTON—
Edward. *Newark.* ca.1760-90. l.c. clocks.
Thomas. *Dublin.* an.1775. Watch.

CRANAGE—
Thomas Stokes. *Liverpool.* 1790-1836. W.
Francis. *Liverpool.* 1796. W.
John. *Liverpool.* 1818-29. W.
Joseph. *Liverpool.* ca.1818.

CRANBROOK—
G. *London.* an.1773. Watch.
Stephen. *Dover.* 1791-5. W.

CRANE—
Thomas. *London.* a.1682.
Thomas. *London.* a.1683.
Philip. *London.* an.1745. Watch.
John. *Bromsgrove.* 1800.
S. *Massachusetts.* ca.1800. br. clock.
George. *Worcester.* 1819. C. & W.

CRANFIELD—
Henry. *London.* CC.1707.
John. *London (Clerkenwell).* 1780.
John, son. *London.* a.1780.

CRANMER, Charles. *London.* ca.1800. Verge watch G.M.

CRANSHAW, Andrew. *Rotherham.* Early 19c. l.c. year clock. cf. Crawshaw.

CRASET, J. *Amsterdam.* 1822-5. Watch Staats M. Amsterdam.

CRATHERN, Francis. *London.* a.1748.

CRATZER (KRATZER). Nicholas. *Oxford.* b.1487-1547. Came to England 1517 as prof. in astronomy. C. to Henry VIII. Bavarian. 'Deviser of the King's horologes.' Dial made for Cardinal Wolsey Old Ashmolean M.

CRAVEN, Thomas. *London.* CC.1688. W.

CRAWFORD—
James. *Newcastle-o.-T.* 1766-78. Watches.
Alexander. *Scarborough.* ca.1770-91.
John. *London.* a.1761.
——. *Arundel.* an.1774. Watch.
David. *Newcastle-o.-T.* 1778. Sold stock 1783. W.
William. *Glasgow.* 1799.
Robert. *Dunse.* 1803.
William. *Ballymena.* 1824.
Robert. *Demerara.* Early 19c.

CRAWFORTH, William. *London* (?) an. 1778. Watch.

CRAWLEY—
Thomas. *London.* CC.1660.
William. *London.* a.1748, CC.1756.
J. *London.* 2nd half 18c. Watch.
Thomas. *London.* a.1773.
Richard. *London.* a.1779.
Robert. *London.* a.1796.
Abraham. *Boston, U.S.A.* 1816 C.

CRAWSHAW—
Thomas. *Rotherham.* ca.1770-95.
Andrew. *Rotherham.* 1810-28. Verge watch, pump-winding, Chamb. coll. cf. CRANSHAW.

CRAYFORD, Francis. *London.* a.1710, CC. 1718.

CRAYLE (CRAILL)—
William. *London.* d.an.1626. a. to Robert Grinkin.
Richard. *London.* b.1600. Admitted BC. 1626. Retired 1660, d.1671. Petitioner for incorporation of CC. Very small oval sil. watch S.K.M. ill. Baillie. Watch ill. Britten. German type watch with dumb-bell foliot Stern. coll.
William. *London.* b.1630, d.1710. Watch with wandering hour figure Webster coll. br. clock with two hands.

CRAYTHORN, John. *Maidstone.* an.1747. Watch.

CRAYTON, William. *London.* 1773. Sig. on many Dutch watches. Prob. an imaginary name.

CREAK—
William. *London.* 1754-63. A fine maker. g. repoussé watch S.K.M. Watch G.M. br. clocks. Watch Stads M. Amsterdam. rep. movement S.M.S.K. Also CREACK.
George. *London.* an.1768. Watch.

CREASER, Thomas. *York.* 1815-22. W.

CREASY, Edmund. *London.* a.1803.

CREED—
Thomas. *London.* CC.1668-99. Lantern clock by him or following.
Thomas. *London.* CC.1674.
Robert. *London (Fleet St.).* a.1689 to Thomas Tompion. CC.1699-1733.
Robert, son. *London.* CC.1733.

CREEDE, John. *London.* CC.1728-72, d.an. 1774.

CREEKE, Henry. *London.* CC.1655-7.

CREIG, Joseph. *Maryport.* 1820.

CREIGHTON, David. *Greenock.* 1821.

CREMER—
Richard or Gilbert. *London.* a.1717.
J. T. *Chelmsford.* Early 19c. Watch.

'CRESCENT STREET' and 'CRESCENT GARDEN.' Sigs. on watches of the AMERICAN WATCH Co. of 1869 and 1877 respectively; predecessor of the WALTHAM WATCH Co.

CRESPE, Francois. *Geneva.* 1792-1804. Director of state factory; wrote 'Essai sur les montres à répétition.'

CRESSENT, Charles. *Paris.* b.1685, d.1768. Eminent bronze worker. Made clock cases.

CRESSINER, Amos. *London.* an.1729. Watch.

CREWDSON, Richard. *London.* a.1742.

CREWKERNE, Thomas. *London.* an.1747. Watch.

CREYTON, John. *Manchester.* 1804. C.

CRIBB, William. *Coventry* and *London.* 1816. d.1876. chron. W. & C. Regulator clock Virgina M.

CRIBLEZ—
Théophile. *Péry.* ca.1785.
Abram. *Péry.* ca.1785.
Jean Henri. *Péry.* ca.1785.

CRICHTON—
John. *Leith.* 1793-1800.
John. *Dundee.* 1795.
David. *Glasgow.* 1822.

CRIGHTON, William. *London.* a.1716.

CRIPPEL—
Valentine. *London.* an.1764. Watch.
Walter. *London.* an.1764. Watch.

CRIPPLE—
William. *London.* a.1694, CC.1702, d.an. 1737.
Edward, son. *London.* a.1719.
William, bro. *London.* CC.1750-4.

CRIPPS—
Thomas. *London.* an.1757. Watch.
R. *Bath.* 1819. Watch.

CRISP—
Nicholas. *London.* 1754-9.
John. *London.* a.1760, CC.1770-83.
William. *Wrentham.* 1775. W. l.c. clock.

CRISWELL, Daniel. *London.* 1743. Insolvent.

CRITCHLEY—
William. *London.* an.1775. Watch.
Robert. *Liverpool.* 1805-29. W.
William. *Liverpool.* 1810-29. W.
Joseph. *Liverpool.* 1818-21. W.
Richard. *Liverpool.* ca.1820.

CRITTENDEN, John Chapman. *Sittingbourne.* an.1796. Watch.

CROCKER—
——. *London.* an.1704. Watch.
James. *London.* a.1709, CC.1716.
William Westcott. *London.* a.1818.

CROCKFORD—
Matthew. *London.* a.1650, CC.1658-73. Lantern clock.
Matthew, son. *London.* CC.1693-1718.

CROFT—
John. *London.* a.1658, CC.1665.
Robert. *Plymouth Dock.* ca.1790 CC.
William. *London.* 1805-08. W.
William. *London.* a.1821.

CROFTS—
Thomas, sen. *Newbury.* ca.1790 CC.
Thomas. *Newbury.* 1795. C. & W.

CROIST, Guillemin. *Dijon.* 1391-5. Keeper of 'reloige.'

CROLL, Colin. *Edinburgh.* 1804-08. *Perth,* 1818. chrons., rep. and mus. watches and clocks.

CROLLE, Matthew. *London.* 1761. Watch.

CROME—
Robert or Edmond. *London.* a.1644.
Robert. *London.* a.1655.

CROMPTON—
Andrew. *London.* a.1695.
Adam. *London.* CC.1716.

CRONAGE, Thomas. *Liverpool.* ca.1820. Prob. same as CRANAGE.

CRONHIORT, Carl Gustaf. *Åby* b.1694, d.1774. C. from 1742.

CRONIER (CROSNIER)—
Antoine. *Paris.* m.1763-89.
Jean Baptiste François. *Paris.* m. 1781-93. Clock Wallace coll. Watch with double virgule escapement G.M. Cartel clock, Ministère de la Guerre, Paris. Mantel clock Nat. M. Stockholm. Watch Besançon M.
Philippe. *Paris.* b.1773. Worked for ROBIN.
Antoine. *Paris.* b.1776. Worked for ROBIN.
FILS. *Paris.* 1807-25.
——. *Paris (Rue d'Orléans St. Honoré).* 1812.
jeune. *Paris (Place des Trois Maries).* 1812.
——. *Paris (Rue St. Honoré).* 1812.

CROOKE (CROOK)—
Sampson. *London.* a.1661, CC.1668-87.
Isaac. *London.* a.1675.
Richard. *London.* a.1715.
Peter. *London.* a.1717, CC.1724.
Joseph. *London (Dorrington St.).* CC.1770-97.
William. *Devizes.* an.1775. Watch.
Benjamin. *Hackney (London).* CC.1784-1824. l.c. clock ill. Cec. & Web.
Robert, John, son of Jos. *London.* a.1792.
William, bro. *London.* a.1802.

CROOKS—
George. *Chester.* 1732. W.
& BURN. *Edinburgh.* 1796.

CROOKSEND, Thomas. *London.* an.1771. Watch.

CROONE, Henry. *London.* a.1743.

CROOT, William. *London.* a.1779.

CROQ, Guillaume. *Rouen.* m.1658.

CROSBEY—
Robert. *London.* 1680. Not CC. l.c. clock, one hand.
William. *Dover.* an.1778. Watch.

CROSFIELD, John Johnson. *London.* CC. 1794.

CROSLAND, ——. *Wakefield.* 1802. W.

CROSS—
James. *London.* a.1687.
William. *London.* a.1722. Watch.
James. *London (Fleet St.).* 1762. Insolvent in *Fetter Lane* in 1774. W.
Francis. *Feversham.* 1784. W.
John. *Liverpool.* 1790-1800.
Edward. *London (Fore St.).* 1790-1824. Watch mt.
William. *Trowbridge.* 1795. W.
James. *Perth.* 1800-31.
Edward, son of Edward. *London.* a.1822.
John. *London.* 1802-40. Watch mt. Ilbert coll.
——. *Wallingford.* an.1821. Watch.

CROSSE, Richard. *London.* a.1701.

CROSSGROVE, James. *London.* d.1765. W.

CROSSLANDS—
John Haywood. *London (Hoxton).* a.1773, CC.1785-1818.
James, son. *London.* CC.1818.

CROSSLEY—
James. *London.* 1776-1818.
Jonas. *Manchester.* 1796. g. en. watch with pearls Ilbert coll.
Humphrey. *Manchester.* 1804-20 .
John B. *London.* 1820-50 CC.
Henry. *Manchester.* ca.1820. Watch N.Y. Univ.

CROSTHWAITE—
John. *Dublin.* 1760-1800. Experimented with pendulum supported by steel knife edges on diamond plates, and pub. desc. in 1788 and 1800.
T. & SON. *Dublin.* 1800. W.
& HODGES. *Dublin.* Early 19c.

CROTTET, Franz. *Augsburg.* End 18c. From *Fribourg.* Kleinuhrmacher.

CROUCH—
George. *London.* CC.1668.
Edward. *London.* a.1682, CC.1691, m.CC. 1719-23.
Samuel. *London.* a.1694.
Joseph. *London.* a.1702.
Robert. *London.* a.1715, CC.1722.
John. *London (Charing Cross).* 1774. Insolvent.
Thomas. *St. Ives.* an.1780. Watch.
Robert. *Hertford.* 1795. C. & W.
Robert. *London.* 1809-11. W.

CROUCHER, Joseph. *London.* CC.1827. Associated with John Gottlieb ULRICH. Remontoir marine chron. G.M. Pub. 'Analytical Hints' on his chrons.

CROUCHLEY, Thomas. *Prescot.* 1773-82. W.

CROUIN—
Jacques. *Blois.* mar. 1659-69.
Jean. *Blois.* 1669-87. Also CROÏN and CROYN.
Jacques. *Blois.* m.1676.

CROUTTE, Mathieu. *St. Nicolas d'Aliermont* (near *Dieppe*). End 17c. Said to have started the clock industry there with PAPIN.

CROW—
Nathaniel. *London.* a.1654, CC.1661.
George. *Wilmington, U.S.A.* mar. 1746, d.1772. Several clocks.
Thomas, son. *Wilmington.* 1770. d.1824. Many clocks.
Francis. *Faversham.* 1780-95. C. & W.
John. *Wilmington.* 1797. W. & C.
Francis. *Margate.* ca.1800.
Edward. *Faversham.* ca.1800.
Joseph. *London.* a.1803.

CROWDER, ——. *London (Southwark).* 1731. W.

CROWDHILL (CROUDHILL). Thomas. *London.* 1790.

CROWFORTH, N. *Arundel.* an.1773. Watch.

CROWLEY—
John. *Philadelphia.* 1805-25.
& FARR. *Philadelphia.* 1823-5.

CROWN, ——. *London.* an.1748. Watch.

CROWTHER—
Samuel. *London.* 1784.
William. *London.* Early 19c. Watch.

CROYMARIE—
Jehan. *Le Puy.* mar. an.1595.
Guillaume. *Lyons.* a.1610.
P. *France.* ca.1620. crys. watch B.M. ill. Baillie.

CRUCIFEX—
Robert. *London.* CC.1689-1747. br. and l.c. clocks. Also W.
John. *London.* CC.1712-26. Sheep's head clocks. Lantern clock ill. Cec. & Web. Two lantern clocks Feill coll.
John. *London.* a.1714-70. Red lacquer br. clock, Turkish figures, ill. Cec. & Web. l.c. clock.
Peter. *London.* a.1716.
Robert. *London.* CC.1745.

CRUDELI, Domenico. *Rome.* Early 18c. br. clock.

CRUFF, Thomas. *London.* a.1759.

CRUICKSHANKS, George. *Elgin.* 1820-1837.

CRUKSHANKS, Johne. *Aberdeen.* 1453. Keeper of Aberdeen 'orloge.'

CRULEY, John. *London.* 1710.

CRUMP (CRUMPE)—
Henry. *London.* CC.1667-88.
Richard. *London.* a.1749, CC.1757.
Thomas. *London.* a.1762.
Thomas. *Liverpool.* 1790-1811.
Thomas. *London.* CC.1793.

CRUMPTON, Wilkinson. *London.* a.1749, CC.1756, d.1821. g. watch Den. coll.

CRUN, William. *Haverford West.* 1795. W.

CRUNDEN—
John. *London.* a.1718.
John. *London.* a.1722.
CRUNDWELL, ——. *Tunbridge.* Early 19c. Watch.
CRUNWELL, ——. *Frant.* 1817. W.
CRUTCHFIELD—
Thomas. *Arborfield.* Early 18c.
Richard. *Arborfield.* an.1775. Watch.
H. *Reading.* mar. 1795. C. & W.
CRUTTENDEN—
Thomas. *London,* a.1668.
Thomas. *London* and *York.* a.1670, CC.1677, d.1698. C.
CRUVELIER, Jullien. *Paris.* 1674 juré.
CSACHER, C. *Prague.* 1725. Maker of repute.
CUBÄUS, Johann E. *Fürth.* d.1793.
CUBLEY, Thomas. *London.* 1820. T.C.
CUCKOW, Thomas. *London.* a.1750.
CUDWORTH—
William. *London.* CC.1769.
Benjamin. *London.* a.1766.
Benjamin. *London.* a.1769, CC.1779-1802.
CUE, William. *London.* a.1679, CC.1691.
CUEL, Charles Louis. *Paris.* b.1808, d.1873. Eminent maker. Worked with MOTEL and ROZÉ on chrons. Devised many tools.
CUENDET—
——. *Switzerland.* ca.1810. Maker of mus. mechanism.
Samuel. *London.* 1815-24. C.
CUENIN—
Ferdinand. *Basle.* 1756.
——. *Besançon.* ca.1790. Watch with decimal dial Ilbert coll.
CUFF—
James. *London (R. Exchange).* CC.1699-1716. l.c. clock.
John. *London.* CC.1718.
William. *Shepton Mallet.* 1750-95. l.c. clock.
Robert. *Glastonbury.* 1795. C.
John. *London (Regent St.).* ca.1820. Watch.
James Symes, son of Wm. *London.* a.1809.
CUIJPERUS, M. O. *Grouw.* 1797. d.1830. br. clock.
CUISIN, Nicolas Louis. *Paris.* m.1766-89.
CUISINIER, Nicolas. *Paris.* Mid. 17c. Watch F.W.M. ill. Baillie.
CULLEN—
William. *London.* an.1778. Watch.
James. *London.* a.1787.
John. *Armagh.* 1824.
CULLIDON, Andrew, *Dublin.* 1780.
CULLIFORD, John. *Bristol.* 1692.
CULPEPER, Edmund. *London.* 1666. Dial Old Ashmolean M.
CULPER, Johann. *Brieg.* 1677-1746. Trav. clock Damiano coll. Also KULPER.
CULVER—
Hassell. *London.* a.1773.
William. *London.* a.1793.
'H. Z. CULVER.' Sig. on watches of NATIONAL WATCH CO. OF CHICAGO, 1867-75.
CULVERWELL, William. *London.* a.1724.
CUMMING—
John. *Edinburgh.* a.1737.
Alexander. *Edinburgh* and *London.* b.ca. 1732, CC.1781, d.1814. A very famous chron. and C. Appointed expert by Act of 1761 on Harrison's timepiece. cyl. watch mt. G.M. Watch mt. with ruby cyl. Ilbert coll. Barograph clock Buckingham Pal. br. clock ill. Cec. & Web. and Weth. coll. Large Chippendale br. clock. Pub. 'The Elements of Clock and Watch Work,' 1766. Three MSS. in G.M.
George. *Newcastle-o.-T.* and *Sunderland.* Bankrupt 1778. W.
James. *Edinburgh.* a.1761.
Charles. *Edinburgh.* a.1772.

CUMMING—*continued.*
James. *Falmouth.* 1784. W.
——. *Thorverton.* 18c. l.c. clock.
John. *London.* 1816-40. W.
CUMMINGS—
William. *London.* a.1750.
John. *London.* an.1773. Watch.
CUMMINS—
Thomas. *Stockton (Durham).* ca.1790 CC.
Thomas. *London.* CC.1806-20.
CUMMON, Thomas. *London.* a.1799.
CUMPSTEY, Richard. *Liverpool.* 1796-1800. W.
CUNDEE—
Stephen. *London.* a.1744, CC.1751-91.
Stephen, son. *London.* a.1785, CC.1797-1822.
CUNNINGHAM—
Hugh. *Dublin.* 1755. d.1777. rep. watch. Also CUNINGHAM.
James. *London.* an. 1776. Watch.
James. *Haddington.* 1776.
Thomas. *London.* a.1768.
W. & A. *Edinburgh.* 1790-1845.
Robert. *London.* 18c. circ. wall clock Fränkel coll.
CUNON, M. Jacobi. *Germany.* 1581. Pub. 'Brevis descriptio automati Horlogii.'
CUPER—
Barthélemy. *Blois.* 1555-1611.
Paul, son. *Blois.* 1582-1618. Commissaire of the king's artillery. Watch Louvre. circ. al. clock M.M.A. crys. watch without frames, dated 1634, by him or Pierre; circ. table clock by him or preceding, both Stern. coll.
Pierre (1), son of Paul. *Blois.* mar. 1590-1617. Table clock Garnier coll. ill. Develle, also watch.
Lewes. *London.* 1622. Alien. Also CYPER.
Jonas. *London.* 1622. Alien.
Josias, son. *Blois.* comp. 1618. *London.* 1622. BC.1628, CC.1632-4. Bloodstone watch Webster coll. Watch Liverpool M.
Paul (2), son of Paul (1). *Blois.* 1603. d.1622. C. to the King and commissaire of his artillery.
Michel, son of Paul (1). *Blois.* mar. 1613, d.1634. C. to S.A.R. Gaston d'Orléans. oct. sil. watch Spitzer coll.
Barthélemy, son of Paul (1). *Blois.* mar. 1613, d.1638. C. to the Queen. circ. sil. watch Petit Palais.
Louis, son of Paul (1). *Blois,* 1613. *London.* 1629. CC.1632. Later *Blois.*
Pierre (2), son of Pierre (1). *Blois.* b.1604, a.1617-28. *Constantinople,* 1630-9.
Abraham, son of Pierre (1). *London.* b.1611, a.1629 to Louis. *Blois,* 1636-42.
Barthélemy (2), son of Barthélemy (1). *Blois.* a.1638. sil. eng. watch.
Simon (1), son of Michel. *Blois.* mar.1655-1686.
Abel, son. *London.* End 17c.
Pierre, bro. *London.* End 17c.
Simon (2), bro. *Blois.* b.1656-95. Watch mt. Glasgow Art Gall. prob. by him.
Simon (3), son. *Blois.* b.1696, m.1720.
Paul Vincent, son. *Blois.* b.1737, d.1821.
Louis Augustin, son. *Blois.* b.1772, d.1852.
Charles Raoul, son. *Blois.* b.1801, d.1875.
CURAIN, Jean. *Paris.* m.1782-9. 'Monteur de boîtes.'
CURE, Louis. *Philadelphia.* 1819.
CURETON, ——. *London.* an.1765. Watch.
CURGENSEN, Henry. *London.* an.1764. Watch.
CURLE, John. *Kelso.* an.1780. Watch.
CURRENT, John. *London.* 2nd half 18c. en. watch.
CURREY, Matteus. *Stockholm.* 1716. English.
CURRIE, Thomas. *Edinburgh.* 1793-1804.

CURRIER, Robert. *London.* a.1701.
'CURRIER.' Sig. on 1870-5 watches of ILLINOIS SPRINGFIELD WATCH Co.
CURTEEN, William. *London.* CC.1766. Watch mt.
CURTELL, Jacob. *Torned.* 1806.
CURTIS (CURTICE)—
John. *London.* a.1664, CC.1671.
Greenway. *Oxford* and *London.* a.1694. Clock London M. Lantern clock Virginia M.
Henry. *London.* a.1700.
John. *London.* a.1715. g. en. watch ca. 1760 perhaps by him.
Elisha. *London* (*Southwark*). a.1752, CC. 1766-74.
Solomon. *Philadelphia.* d.1793.
William. *Axbridge.* 1795. W.
William. *Exeter.* 1795-1805. Watch Exeter M.
Lemuel. *Concord* and *Burlington, U.S.A.* b.1790, d.1857. Banjo clock ill. Milham.
CUSIN—
Jehan. *Autun.* 1562-8. Keeper of cathedral clock from 1568.
Noel (1). *Autun.* mar. 1542, d. an.1585. Keeper of cathedral clock to 1559.
Noel, son. *Autun.* b. an.1585, d.1656. Square table clock Louvre, 1622.
Charles, son of Noel (1). *Geneva.* 1574-90. Gained great repute, but left owing money to the town.
Jean. *Blois.* comp.1613. crys. cross watch Spitzer coll.
Noel. *Blois.* comp. 1613.
Abraham. *Nevers.* 1593-1666. Of great repute in Nevers. Oval watch mt. Ilbert coll.
CUSIN—*continued.*
Abraham. *St. Léonard de Corbigny.* m.1651-1682. str. watch M.M.A.
On. *Autun.* Early 17c. str. watch B.M.
Jacques. *Geneva.* ca.1750-80.
CUSINS—
Thomas. *London.* a.1725, CC.1735-9.
Thomas. *London.* a.1739.
CUSONS, Thomas. *Crewkerne.* 1772. W.
CUSSET, ——. *Paris.* Early 19c.
CUSTANS, Stephen, & Co. *Philadelphia.* 1819. W.
CUSTER, Jacob. D. *Norristown, U.S.A.* b.1805, d.1872. l.c. and turret C. Watch mt. An early American W. starting in 1840.
CUTBUSH, John. *Maidstone.* 1744. C.
CUTHBERT—
Amariah. *London.* a.1687, CC.1694-7.
James. *London.* a.1715.
James. *Perth.* 1735-55.
John. *Perth.* 1764.
Thomas. *Wantage.* 1764.
J. *London.* 1784-90.
Samuel. *London.* a.1789.
CUTLER—
George. *London.* a.1692.
John. *Albany City, U.S.A.* 1822. W.
CUTLOVE, John. *Harleston.* 2nd half 18c. C.
CUTRIFFIN, Jacques. *Romans.* 1411-14. Repaired Grenoble clock.
CUTTING, Christopher. *London.* a.1687, CC. 1695-1715.
CYRAIL, François. *Paris.* m.1788.
CYVRAIS, François. *Paris.* m.1788.
CZAPEK ET CIE. *Geneva.* Early 19c. en. watch set pearls.

D

DAADELBEEK, W. Van. *Utrecht.* 18c. Stand clock.
DABERT, ——. *Paris.* 1811-23.
DA CAPRIGLIA, Giuseppe. *Padua.* 1665. Pub. the first book on clockmaking, 'Misura del Tempo, cioè Trattato d'Horologij da Ruota.'
DACHSELHOFER, Johannes. *Hüningen.* 1723.
DADSWELL (DODSWELL)—
John. *Burwash.* d.1790. C. & W.
Thomas. *Burwash.* 1790.
Edward. *Eastbourne.* 1795. W.
DAENLER, Pierre. *Convers.* 1778. C.
DAFO, Abel. *Rome.* ca.1620. From *Geneva.* C. and goldsmith.
DAFT, Thomas. *Philadelphia.* 1775. From *London.*
DAGAN, ——. *Paris.* 1823.
DAGLISH, Joseph. *Alnwick.* 1790-5. Many l.c. clocks. W.
DAGONEAU—
Antoine. *Grenoble.* 1628-34.
Philibert. *Grenoble.* 1629-1700. Fine repoussé watch with hour figures I to VI and 7 to 12 over them, Webster coll. ill. Baillie.
Antoine. *Grenoble.* Baptized 1641.
François. *Grenoble.* 1664-1742.
DAGUE, ——. *Paris.* 1821.
DAGUET, ——. *Fribourg.* 1768.
DAHLBLOM, C. L. *Strömstad.* 1815. d.1835.
DAHLGREN, ——. *Trollhätten.* 18c. Watch Nord. M.
DÄHLING, August. *Hamburg.* 1821.
DAHLSTRÖM, Israel. *Stockholm.* b.1762, d.1829. Clock in cabinet Nat. M. Stockholm.
DAILLÉ, ——. *Paris.* 1765. C. to Mme la Dauphine. Clock Wallace coll.
DAIMES, Jonathan & William Orpwood. *Ipswich.* Early 19c. Watch.
DAIMLEVILLE, Pierre. *Lille.* 1379.
DAIN, François. *Paris.* Late 17c. sil. watch.
DAINTRY, ——. *London.* an.1773. Watch.
DAKIN, James. *Boston, U.S.A.* 1796. W.
DAKING, Richard. *Halstead,* 1772. C. & W.
DAL, Søren. *Skanderborg.* 1588. Court locksmith; repaired clock on castle.
DALAHOYDE, Bernard. *Dublin.* 1795. W.
D'ALBRET—
Robin. *Rouen.* 1469-79. Repaired al. clock of St. Ouen church.
Étienne, son. *Rouen.* 1484.
DALE—
Thomas. *London.* a.1700. Watch.
Robert. *Wellingborough.* 1747. W. From *London.*
William. *London.* ca.1760. br. clock.
Roger. *London.* an.1767, d.1781. Watch.

DALE—*continued.*
Joseph. *London.* an.1767. Watch.
Richard. *Whitchurch.* From 1774.
Anna. *Atherstone.* 1795. C. & W.
DALEIZETTE, ——. *Ferney.* 1770. Director of factory.
D'ALEMAIGNE, Jehan. *Paris.* 1401. C. to the duchesse d'Orléans.
DALGARNO, Alexander. *Aberdeen.* d.1851.
DALGLEISH—
John. *Edinburgh.* 1742. d.1771. l.c. clock. Watch mt. R. Scottish M.
Laurence. *Edinburgh.* 1771-1821 CC.
& Dickie. *Edinburgh.* 1791.
Robert. *Falkirk.* 1820.
DALIN, Hindrich. *Strängnäs.* 1750.
DALL, Thomas. *Dundee.* 1819.
DALLAS—
Joseph. *Perth.* 1760-3.
James. *London.* 1800-20. Watch. Made pocket chron. for Duke of Sussex.
DALLAWAY & SON. *Edinburgh.* 1785-1812. Dial makers.
DALLE ANCORE, Ambrogio. *Venice.* 1497. Made the two life-size Moor aut. for the San Marco clock.
DALLINGTON, William. *London.* Mid. 18c. g. watch Schloss M. Berlin. Watch N.Y. Univ.
DALMASH, John James. *London.* a.1718.
DAL NEGRO, ——. *Padua.* 1816. Pub. 'Nuovo metodo di misurare le piu minute frazioni del tempo.'
DALRYMPLE—
John. *Dublin.* 1766-74. W.
Hannah. *Dublin.* 1780.
A. ——. 1788. Pub. 'Instructions concerning Chronometers or Timekeepers.'
William. *Edinburgh.* a.1781.
James. *Dublin.* 1795. W.
John. *Dublin.* 1795-1824. W.
DALTON—
Thomas. *London.* an.1742. Watch.
Jacob. *London.* Mid. 18c. g. rep. watch Den coll.
Daniel. *Church Lawford.* an.1759. Watch.
Isaac. *London.* an.1770. Watch.
John. *London (Clerkenwell).* CC.1777, l.CC. 1788-1828. W.
Robert. *London (Clerkenwell).* a.1777-1808. Watchcase maker.
Charles, son. *London.* a.1808.
DALZIEL, James. *Fraserburgh.* 1798-1815.
DAMBERGER, Carl. *Leitershofen.* 1756.
D'AMBOURNAY, Jean. *Grenoble.* 1413. Repaired town clock.
D'AMI-GOUGE, ——. *Paris.* 1789. C. to Louis xvi.

DAMMANT, B. *Colchester*. Early 18c. Lantern clock and watch.
D'AMOUR, Guy. *Paris*. an.1794. Watch.
DAN—
Jean Daniel. *Geneva*. In 1770 went to *Berlin* with Louis TRUITTE as managers of the Fabrique royale d'horlogerie. DAN left in 1775.
DAN, TRUITTE ET MOURIER. *Geneva*. Up to 1770. *v*. TRUITTE.
DANAHY, Daniel. *Cork*. 1824.
DANBECK—
Abraham. *Augsburg*. b.1649, d.1734. Famous aut. maker.
Christoph Theodor. *Augsburg*. b.1689, d. 1749. Famous aut. maker.
DANBY, D. *London*. an.1761. Watch.
DANCART, E. *Namur*. 18c. l.c. clock.
DANCE, Sarah. *London*. a.1736.
DAND (DAUD), Tobias. *London*. 1662.
DANE—
John. *London*. an.1783. Watch.
Thomas. *London*. 1790-1825.
S. *London*. 1802-04.
F. *London*. 1820.
DANEL—
——. *London*. ca.1730. Watch G.M.
Pierre. *Geneva*. b.1734, d.1778. Painter on en. for dials.
DANELL, Joseph. *London*. 1825. W.
DANFRIE (DANFERY)—
Philippe. *Rouen* and *Paris*. b.ca.1532, d. 1606. C., inst. maker and engraver.
Philippe, son. *Rouen*. d.1604.
DANGERS, ——. *London*. 2nd half 18c. Fine g. and jasper watch.
DANGLEFIELD, Samuel. *Eltham*. 1805-08. mt. maker.
DANIEL—
Nicolas, *Rouen*. 1554-78. In charge of town clock.
Romain. *Rouen*. 1578.
——. *Paris*. ca.1650. Watch.
Stephen. *London*. CC.1698. W.
Robert. *London*. CC.1708.
Jacques Barthélemy. *Paris*. m.1754-89.
Benjamin. *London*. a.1746.
John Christmas. *London*. a.1755. Watch.
Thomas. *London*. CC.1773-83.
Thomas. *Kirkham*. ca.1775. Watch.
Phineas. *Bristol*. 1785-1800.
& JACKSON. *Bristol*. To 1798. Partnership with Phineas. rep. watch.
Thomas. *Bristol*. 1787. W.
H. *Faringdon*. Early 19c. Watch.
Henry. *Liverpool*. 1824-36.
Henry. *Bristol*. 1825-30.
J. & H. *Liverpool*. 1825. W. cf. H. & J. DANIELS.
DANIELIS, Canziano. *Udine*. 1780. Pub. 'Informazione delle cagioni per cui sogliono variare le mostre . . .'
DANIELL—
William. *London*. CC.1632.
Edward. *London*. CC.1647-89.
Isaac. *London*. CC.1648, w.CC.1674, d.1682.
Henry. *London*. a.1646.
Thomas. *London*. a.1646, CC.1656.
Anne, widow of Isaac. *London*. 1682.
Edward. *London*. a.1686.
James. *New Romney*. 1779. d.1788. C. & W.
Robert. *Plymouth Dock*. 1791. W.
DANIELS—
F. *Leighton*. ca.1760. Watch.
H. & J. *Liverpool*. ca.1820. cf. J. & H. DANIEL. Lever watch mt. S.M.S.K.
DANIELSEN, Lars Jacob. *Bergen*. 1815 m.
DANIELSON, ——. *London*. an.1785. Watch.
DANN, John. *East Derham* and *London*. 1761. Bankrupt.
DANNBORN—
Georg Steph. *Fürth*. d.1820.
Magnus. *Fürth*. d. 1823.
DANNENBERGER, Johann Peter. *Berlin*. 1769-88. C.
DANNER, Alexander. *Lancaster City, U.S.A.* ca.1800. Clockcase maker.
D'ANNONE, Niklaus. *Basle*. m.1678, d.1703. Very able maker; made clock for Louis XIV for Versailles. astro. clock Basle Hist. M.
DANSAYS, Peter. *London*. 1751-76. W.
DANTAN, Ami. *Paris*. m.1754-80.
DANTEL—
Jacques. *Chaux-de-Fonds*. 175 8 C.
Johannes. *Augsburg*. 1772-88. aut. wooden clocks.
DANTHOINE, Daniel. *Grenoble*. 1669-79.
DANTI, Piervincenzo. *Perugia*. 1488. d.1512. Goldsmith and math. inst. maker.
DANTINE, ——. *Paris*. 1810-25.
D'ANTOING, Nicolle. *Cambrai*. 1529. Made an al. clock.
DANTON—
Robert. *London*. a.1670, CC.1678.
Cuthbert. *Chester-le-Street* and *Durham*. 1765. Bankrupt 1776. C. & W.
DA PONTE, Christoforo. *Parma*. 1537. With Lionello RAINERI made a clock for the Rigobello tower of Ferrara.
DARBY—
Mary. *London*. a.1714.
John. *London*. an.1767. Watch.
James. *London*. an.1786. Watch.
John. *London*. 1802-40. W.
Bartholomew. *London*. 1805-07. W.
DARBYSHIRE, Matthew. *Leeds*. 1785.
DARGENT—
James. *London*. CC.1700-27.
Mary Ann, dau. *London*. a.1714.
Peter, bro. *London* (*Westminster*). a.1749-61. Watch.
DARIER—
David. *Geneva*. b.1770, d.1829. Started machine production of hands in 1801, and in 1823 promoted the Geneva school of horology.
——. *Geneva*. ca.1800. Painter on enamel.
——. *Paris*. 1817-20. Represented David.
Hugues, son of David. *Geneva*. b. 1804, d.1879. Started first production of cases by machine with Pierre LACROIX ca.1855.
DARKE, John. *Barnstaple*. 1791. C. & W.
DARKIN, Charles. *London*. a.1714.
DARLING—
Sir Robert. *London*. a.1731, CC.1740, l.CC. 1766-9.
John or James. *London*. a.1749.
Robert. *Edinburgh*. 1788-1825.
Robert. *Haddington*. 1796.
Robert. *Lauder*. 1797.
William. *York*. 1825.
DARLOW, Thomas. *London*. a.1685, CC. 1692-1708.
DARMEZIN, Charles Thomas. *Paris*. m. 1770-89. Mantel clock.
DARMIER, ——. *London*. an.1772. Watch.
DARMSTED, Jacob Michael. *Copenhagen*. m.1718-21.
DARNFORD, ——. *London*. an.1787. Watch.
DARNLEY, Matthias. *London*. a.1735, CC. 1759-71.
DARRAS—
——. *Paris*. 1740 m.
Jacques. *Paris*. m.1740.
Louis Anne. *Paris*. m.1787-1810.
DARRELL—
Francis. *London*. a.1693. Watch.
Joseph. *London*. 1815.
DARROW, Elijah. *Bristol, U.S.A.* 1824. Partner with Chauncey JEROME.

DARTNALL (DARWELL), Thomas, *London.* a.1701, CC.1713.
DARVILL—
George. *London.* 1766. p.c. watch G.M.
John. *London.* 1802-08. W.
DARWELL, Robert. *London.* a.1698, CC. 1708.
DARY, Bartholomew. *London.* a.1677.
DASER, John George. *London.* 1817-24. Cyl. watch Ilbert coll.
DASHPER, Frederick. *London.* a.1796-1840.
DASHWOOD, Joseph. *London* (*Walworth*). 1805-08.
DASYPODIUS, Conrad. *Strasbourg.* b.1531 d.1601. Mathematician who supervised building of the second Strasbourg clock by the Habrechts in 1570. Pub. 'Warhafftige Ausslegung des astronomischen Vhrwercks zu Strassburg. . . ,' Strasbourg, 1576, with re-issue in 1580.
DAU—
Christian. *Fredericia.* m.1775.
Vilhelm. *Copenhagen.* m.1824.
DAUBANCOURT, ——. *Paris.* 1820-5.
DAUNT, Joseph. *Northampton.* 1795. W.
DAUNTENEY, Laurence. *London.* 1576.
DAUPHIN—
J. A. *Amsterdam.* ca.1800.
H. *Amsterdam.* 1822. W.
DAUSTRY, L. Hubert. *Toulouse.* Mid. 17c. Trav. clock Gélis coll.
DAUTEL, ——. *Paris.* 1784-1825. Mantel clock Ministère de la Guerre, Paris.
DAUTHIAU, ——. *Paris.* 1735-67. C. to the King. Made astro. clock designed by PASSEMENT.
DAUZET, Louis. *Paris.* a.1748.
DAVENHILL, William. *London.* an.1774. Watch.
DAVENPORT—
William. *London.* a.1669. Accused of counterfeiting 1679.
William. *London.* a.1684.
William. *London.* a.1695, CC.1706.
Basil. *London.* a.1717.
James. *London* (*Bells Bdg.*). 1776. W.
——. *London.* ca.1780. Large rep. watch shagreen case Peiping M.
DAVENS, ——. *London.* an.1764. Watch.
DAVERILL, John. *London.* CC.1636.
DAVETT, Abraham. *London.* 1662.
DAVEY—
Thomas. *Chesterfield.* an.1758. Watch.
Robert. *Aldeburgh.* 1760. d.1786 at *Hoveton.*
Peter. *Rochford.* an.1763.
Samuel. *Norwich.* 1784. l.c. clock.
James. *Wells* (*Norfolk*). 1795. W.
William. *Penzance.* 1795.
E. *Lewes.* ca.1800. Watch mt. N.Y. Univ.
v. DAVY.
DAVID—
Louis. Prob. *Germany.* 16c. Table clock ill. Britten.
Jacques. *Paris.* 1657 juré.
Jacques, son. *Paris.* m.1657.
Antoine. *Lyons.* 1703-30.
Frater, à S. Cajetano. *Vienna.* b. 1726, d. 1796. Part maker of very complex astro. clock at Zwettl, Austria.
——. *Paris.* Early 19c. mus. works, singing birds and aut.
DAVIDGE—
William. *London.* a.1737.
John. *London.* 1802-04.
DAVIDS, Gerhard. *Hamburg.* 1801-21.
DAVIDSON—
John. *Whitehaven.* Later *Cow Cross* (*Middlesex*). 1772. Insolvent. W.
C. *London.* ca.1775. Watch.
John. *London.* an.1775. Watch.
Robert. *London.* an.1777. Watch.
T. & R. *London.* an.1797. Watch.

DAVIDSON—*continued.*
Charles. *Forfar.* 1798-1815.
Nean. *Dunse.* 1798-1820. Watch.
James. *Dundee.* 1813-37.
John. *London.* 1816-24. C.
James. *Girvan.* 1820-37.
DAVIE—
John. *Linlithgow.* 1753-84.
Christopher. *Linlithgow.* 1783-1832.
Elizabeth. *Peterborough.* In 1795 succeeded her nephew Amos PEARSON. C. & W.
Joseph. *London.* 1820-40. W. & C.
DAVIES—
Samuel. *London.* a.1714.
Simon. *London.* a.1748, CC.1757.
Edward. *Ellesmere.* Mid. 18c. l.c. clock.
H. *London.* an.1774. Watch.
Richard. Left *Gloucester* 1769. W.
William. *Chester.* 1770.
William, & Thomas BRADSHAW. *London.* 1775. Dissolved partnership.
John. *London.* a.1766.
John. *Chester.* 1777. W.
Thomas. *Monmouth.* 1777. W.
James. *London.* a.1773.
John. *London.* a.1789.
James. *Haverford West.* Late 18c.
——. *Swansea.* Late 18c.
James. *Gloucester.* 1795. W. cf. J. DAVIS.
David. *Cardigan.* 1795.
——. *Shrewsbury.* 1795.
William. *Liverpool.* 1805-14.
Charles. *Birmingham.* 1808. W. & C.
Samuel. *Liverpool.* 1810. W.
Thomas. *Liverpool.* 1825. W.
Owen. *Llanidloes.* ca.1825. Watch.
v. also DAVIS.
DAVIS—
Samuel. *London.* a.1640, CC.1647-82.
Tobias. *London.* a.1646, CC.1653-70.
Samuel, son of Samuel. *London.* CC.1673-1706.
Thomas. *London.* a.1667, CC.1674-99.
Benjamin. *London* (*Thames St.*). CC.1678-1680. l.c. clock.
John. *Windsor.* 1678-89. l.c. clock. Carillon clock in Curfew Tower, Windsor Castle.
William. *Boston, U.S.A.* 1683. From *England.*
Aubrey. *London.* a.1679. l.c. clock Weth. coll.
William. *London.* 1686. Tortoiseshell br. clock.
William. *London.* a.1680.
Jeffry. *London.* a.1683, CC.1690.
John. *London* a. to Quare 1685, CC.1697-1736. Watch Ilbert coll.
William, son of Thomas. *London* (*Chancery La.*). a.1692, CC.1699-1743.
Foulke. *London.* a.1694.
Thomas. *London.* a.1694.
Joseph. *London* (*Wapping Dock*). ca.1705-11. l.c. clock ill. Cec. & Web.
Andrew. *London.* Early 18c. l.c. clock Weth. coll.
John. *London.* a.1699.
Jenkin. *London.* 1714-21.
George. *London.* a.1708, CC.1720-6.
Thomas. *London.* CC.1726. Watch. l.c. clock ill. Cec. & Web.
Richard. *London.* a.1717.
Brian. *London.* a.1717.
Jeremiah. *London.* a.1719-35 CC.
James. *London.* a.1722, CC.1732-42.
Richard. *London.* a.1725.
John. *Windsor.* 1739. W.
James. *London.* a.1733.
Joseph Henry. *London.* a.1734.
Theophilus. *London.* a.1736, CC.1764-60.
John. *London.* a.1739.
James. *London.* a.1744.
Charles. *London.* a.1746, CC.1753-6.

DAVIS—*continued.*
Thomas. *London* (*Hoxton*). a.1749, CC.1757-1775.
George. *London.* a.1751.
James. *Dublin.* an.1762. Watch.
James. *London.* an.1762. Watch.
Bartholomew. *Preston.* an.1763. Watch.
G. *London.* 18c. Dial M.M.A.
David. *London* (*Davies St.*). an.1768. Retired 1772. Watch.
William. *London.* a.1753.
John. *London.* a.1760, CC.1768.
Thomas. *London.* a.1764.
William. *London.* CC.1774.
Samuel. *London.* an.1774. Watch.
Richard. *London.* an.1775. Watch.
Robert. *London.* an.1775. Watch.
William. *Birmingham.* 1775.
J. *Gloucester.* 1776. W. cf. James DAVIES.
James. *London.* a.1770.
Robert. *London.* a.1771-90.
Joseph. *London.* a.1772.
William. *London.* a.1773.
John. *London.* a.1775.
Ebenezer. *London.* a.1777.
John. *Windsor.* 1784.
Richard. *London.* a.1782-1800.
John. *London.* a.1782.
John. *London.* a.1786.
Isaac. *Dublin.* 1795. W.
Jesse. *Trowbridge.* 1795. W.
Charles. *Alcester.* 1795. C. & W. l.c. clock.
William. *London.* a.1789, CC.1806, l.CC. 1812-23. Watch.
Moses. *London* (*Shoreditch*). 1799.
G. *Sunderland.* ca.1800. Watch.
James. *London.* a.1796, CC.1803.
John. *New Holland, U.S.A.* 1802. C.
E. *N. Shields.* d.1805. W.
David. *London* (*Strand*). 1802-04.
Moses and David. *London* (*St. Mary Axe*). 1805-08.
Thomas. *London.* 1805-08.
R. C. *London* (*Goswell St.*). 1805-08.
Moses. *London* (*Leicester Sq.*). 1809-11.
Daniel. *London* (*St. Mary Axe*). 1809-11.
J. *Chepstow.* 1810. Bankrupt. W.
John. *London.* a.1804, CC.1818.
Henry. *London.* a.1805.
John. *Dublin.* Early 19c. Watch mt. S.K.M.
James. *Leominster.* Early 19c. Watch mt. Horstmann coll.
T. *Worcester.* In 1816 succeeded John SCANDRETT.
D. & M. *London* (*St. Mary Axe*). 1817-24.
J. *London* (*Woolwich*). 1817-24.
John. *Philadelphia.* 1818. W.
Samuel. *London.* a.1820.
Joseph. *London* (*Holborn Hill*). 1820.
D. James. *London.* 1820.
Jacob. *Bath.* 1825.
PALMER & Co. *Boston, U.S.A.* Early 19c.

DAVISON—
William. *London.* CC.1686-1703. Maker of repute.
William. *London.* a.1700.
John. *London.* an.1776-ca.1790. Watch.
Richard. *London* (*Crown St.*). a.1795, CC. 1815-23.

DAVY—
——. *Fakenham.* Late 18c.
Samuel. *Norwich.* 1772-95. W.
Samuel. *Aylsham.* 1795.
v. DAVEY.

DAWES—
Thomas. *Northampton.* 1745, d.1773. C. & W.
Thomas. *Chester.* d.1779.
William Matthias. *London.* a.1801.
James. *London* (*Islington*). an.1773-ca.1810.
James. *Attleborough.* 1799. C. & W.

DAWES—*continued.*
W. *Antigua.* Early 19c.
John. *Whitehaven.* 1820.

DAWKES, John. *London.* a.1698, CC.1707-1711.

DAWLE, John. *London.* a.1716.

DAWSON—
Thomas. *London.* 1630. CC.1632-6. Petitioner for incorporation of CC.
William. *London.* a.1659.
John. *London.* a.1681, CC.1688-1718. l.c. clock.
Richard. *London.* 1721. Insolvent.
Thomas. *London.* a.1719.
Joseph. *Bewdley.* 1746. W.
& PAYNE. *London.* an.1752. Watch.
Thomas. *London.* an.1788. Watch.
& ATKINSON. *Bath.* 1795.
William. *London.* CC.1778, l.CC.1801, d.1820.
John. *London.* CC.1796.
Matthew. *Haddington.* 1798-1843.
George. *Sudbury.* 18c. l.c. clock. Watch.
Jonas. *Philadelphia.* 1813-24.
James. *London.* Early 19c. Watch.

DAWTREY, James. *London.* a.1736.

DAX, Joseph. *Hannstetten.* 1756.

DAXON, Edward. *London.* a.1726.

DAY—
Edmund. *London.* ca.1600. circ. gilt drum-type watch S.K.M.
Matthew. *Saffron Walden.* 1626.
Jacob. *Saffron Walden.* 1635-7.
Isaac. *London.* a.1673, CC.1679-1714.
Thomas. *London.* a.1683, CC.1691.
Edmund. *London.* a.1684, CC.1692-1720. l.c. clock Weth. coll.
Jacob, son of Isaac. *London.* a.1694.
Samuel. *Saffron Walden.* 1740.
Jeremiah. *London.* a.1753.
James. *London.* an.1766. Watch.
Richard. *London.* an.1768. Watch.
William. *London.* an.1768. Watch.
John. *Wakefield.* b.1729, d.1801. C. & W. l.c. clock.
John. *London.* a.1766, CC.1775-1812. Watch N.Y. Univ.
Henry. *London.* an.1775. Watch.
Titus. *London.* an.1784, Watch.
Richard. *London.* 1781-1808.
Christopher. *S. Molton.* 2nd half 18c. l.c. clock.
Samuel. *London.* 1790-1803. Patented a watchman's clock.
Robert. *Norwich.* 1795.
Israel. *Baltimore, U.S.A.* 1802-07. W. & C.
Henry. *London.* a.1803.
William Archer. *London* (*Cornhill*). CC. 1820.
John. *Grantham.* an.1822. Watch.

DAYNES, William. *London.* a.1700.

DEACLE, Joana. *London.* a.1672.

DEACON—
F. *Barton-in-the-Beans.* 1776. C.
John. *London.* a.1773, CC.1781.
John. *London.* a.1774.
J. *Leicester.* ca.1790.
Daniel. *London.* 1802-04. Watch.
William Archer. *London.* a.1803, CC.1820.
& SON. *Leicester.* 1815. C. & W.
Josiah. *London.* a.1820.
'J. W. DEACON.' Sig. on 1869-70 watches of the UNITED STATES WATCH CO.

DEADMAN, Thomas. *London.* a.1771

DEAKIN—
Henry. *Worcester.* 1751. C. & W. Also DEYKIN.
Alexander. *London.* an.1759. Watch.
——. *London.* 2nd half 18c. Watch.

DEAKINS, Thomas. *London.* a.1805.

DE ALBERTIS, Io. Bapta (Giovanni Baptista). *Brescia.* 1685. Table clock Ilbert coll.

DEAN—
George. *London.* a.1662, CC.1671-80, d. an.1692. Engraver.
Richard. *London.* a.1716.
George. *London.* a.1775.
Thomas. *London (Cripplegate).* 1817-19.
Thomas. *London (St. Swithin's La.).* CC. 1819-40. Watch.
Joseph. *Clitheroe.* ca.1820.
William Henry. *London.* a.1817.
John Travers. *London.* a.1825.

DEANE—
John. *Chester.* 1696. W.
John. *London.* an.1710. Watch.
William. *London.* 1720. Dial Old Ashmolean M.
Richard. *London.* a.1716.
Phineas. *London.* a.1723, CC.1734-42.
Thomas. *London.* CC.1734-7. Also DEAN.
Phineas, son of Phineas. *London.* CC.1766.
George. *London.* a.1775.

DEANS, John. *Haddington.* 1803.

DEAP, T. *London.* ca.1800.

DEAR, William. *London.* a.1790.

DEARDS, John. *London.* an.1748. Watch.

DEARE—
John. *London.* 1709. Made 'a gold watch so little as to be set in a ring with 22 diamonds round, and so small that a mil'd sixpence covers the watch and diamonds.
John. *Youghal.* 1820-4.

DEARMER—
John. *London.* a.1672, CC.1680-1708.
Abraham. *London.* a.1692, CC.1709-30.
Caleb. *London.* a.1708.
John. *London.* a.1721, CC.1735.

DEARSLEY, Edward. *London.* a.1736.

DEATH—
Isaac. *London.* 1750.
Isaac. *Maldon.* 1772. Watch Exeter M.

DEAUPONT, ——. *London.* an.1759. Watch.

DE BAGHIJN, Adriaan. *Amsterdam.* 1710-50. Watch.

DE BAJONVILLE (BAIONVILLE), Charles. *Blois.* 1611-19. From *Orléans.*

DEBANFRE, Peter. De Baufre's name as spelt in his patent.

DEBARY—
Henry. ——. ca.1700. en. watch B.M. sil. watch with en. portrait of Count Tolstoy, Minister of Peter the Great, formerly in Shandon coll.
Dominique. *Geneva.* b.1671, d.1736. In *Hüningen* and *Basle* ca.1702.
Samuel. *Basle.* 1744. From *Geneva.*

DE BAUDE, Ernoulet. *Burgundy.* 1399-1402. C. to the duc de Bourgogne.

DE BAUFRE—
Pierre (DEBEAUFRE, Peter). *Paris,* 1675 m. *London (Church St., St. Annes).* CC.1689-1722. Patented jewelling in 1704 with FACIO and Jacob (below). Invented club-footed verge escapement. Read paper on a pirouette watch before Acad. R. des Sciences. Pirouette watch with secs. hand and 2 mts. G.M. Watch Louvre ill. Baillie. en. and filigree watch M.M.A. Watches Cluny M. ill. Baillie and Gotha M. br. lacquer clock. Fine watch, set stones, dated 1722, Mallett coll. ill. Baillie. Watch and rep. watch Den. coll. p.c. g. watch M.P.S. Dresden.
Jacob. *London (Church St., St. Annes).* 1704. *v.* Pierre.
James. *London (Church St., St. Annes).* CC.1713-50. g. watch, set agates, S.K.M. rep. watch S.M.S.K. sil. watch G.M. repoussé by Cochin. p.c. en. watch Ilbert coll.
John. *London.* a.1722.
Peter. *London.* 1769. W.

DE BAY—
Jean Baptiste. *Paris.* m.1777-89. Mantel clock Pal. de Fontainebleau.
——. *Paris (Rue St. Honoré).* 1812.

DE BEATE, Pierre. ——. 1377. C. to Charles, Duke of Burgundy.

DE BEAUMONT, Robin. *Paris.* 1782-9. Deputy C. to Louis XVI.

DE BEEFE—
Gilles. *Liége.* ca.1700. Maker of repute. l.c. clock.
François. *Maestricht.* 18c. Gilt wood table clock Feill coll.

DE BELLE, Jean François. *Paris.* m.1781-early 19c. g. aut. watch Gélis coll. Pair aut. vase clocks Madrid Pal. Clock Pal. de Fontainebleau.

DE BELLE FONTAINE, Peter. *London.* 1805-08. W.

DE BELLY, John Peter. *London.* 1792. Bankrupt. C. & W.

DEBENHAM—
John. *Tiverton.* Left in 1726. C.
——. *Sudbury.* 18c. l.c. clock.
Robert. *Melford.* 1784-95. W.

DE BENNEVILLE, N. *Philadelphia.* 1820. W.

DE BETHUNE, ——. *France.* 1727. Devised an escapement with two geared balances for watches and a double lever recoil escapement for clocks.

DEBEU, Jacques. *Paris.* m.1741-56.

DEBEUVE, Symon. *Cambrai.* 1600. Repaired palace clock.

DEBOMBOURG—
Pierre. *Lyons.* mar. ca.1633-61 m.
Jean, son. *Lyons* b.ca.1634, d.1694 m.
Pierre, bro. *Lyons.* 1656-83 m.
Pierre, son of Jean. *Lyons.* b.1661-1708.
Pierre. *Lyons.* b.1689-1754.

DE BON, Jacques. *Paris.* 1776. d.1789. C. to the duc d'Orléans. rep. cyl. sweep secs. watch Chamb. coll.

DE BOUFLER—
Andrew. *London.* a.1762, CC.1770-1808.
William. *London.* a.1765-1811.
John, son of Andrew. *London.* a.1805.

DE BOURGES, Jehan. *Paris.* 1544-7. Founder member of Paris corporation.

DEBRAM, ——. *Newport.* ca.1800.

DE BREST, Robin. *Rouen.* 1451. 'Orlogier.'

DE BRÜHL, Comte J. M. 1771. Pub. in London 'A Register of one of Mr. Mudge's Timekeepers.'

DE BRY, Theodore. b. *Liége* 1561, d. *Frankfort* 1623. Celebrated engraver. Many engravings on watch cases copied from his work.

DEBURGES—
Jacob. *Blois.* 1591-1643. Of English origin.
Jacob. *Paris.* 1668-93. al. watch.

DE BURK, Daniel. ——. ca.1800. Watch with pedometer sd. 'Ralph Gout' on dial, Marryat coll.

DECACHENT, Stephen. *Manchester.* 1794. W.

DE CAMUS (DESCAMUS), François Joseph. *Paris, Holland* and *London.* b.1662, d.1732. Scientist, mathematician and mechanician. Pub. in 1722 'Traité des forces mouvantes,' describing some water-clocks.

DE CAUS—
Solomon. *Paris, London* and *Heidelberg.* b.1576, d.ca.1635. Pub. 'Les Raisons des forces mouvantes,' which treats of water-clocks.
Lucas. *Norwich.* an.1718. Watches Den. coll. and l.c. clock.
——. *Paris.* 1812-24. C. Successor of GUYDAMOUR. Also DECAUX.

DECELE, Samuel. *Norwich.* ca.1710. Lantern clock.

DE CHAMBON, Guillaume. *Riom.* 1380. Keeper of town clock.
DE CHARMES (DES CHARMES), Simon. *London.* 1688. CC.1691-1730. Frenchman. p.c. ½ ¼ rep. watch and 2 mts. G.M. p.c. g. watch London M. p.c. g. shagreen rep. watch Ilbert coll. Red lacquer rep. br. clock ill. Cec. & Web.
David, son. *London.* CC.1692-1740, d. an. 1755. W. of great repute.
DE CHARMIÈRES, ——. *Paris.* 1767. Pub. 'Mém. sur l'observation des Longitudes en Mer,' and other works.
DE CHATEAUBLANC, Bourgeois. *Paris.* 1746. Exhibited aut. made by him.
DECHIEN, Jean. *Angers.* 1432. 'Aurelogier.'
DE CHOUDENS—
Jean. *Rouen.* ca.1680. Watch S.K.M. en. by les deux frères Huaut and ill. Britten. sq. watch en. flowers and figures, Bernal sale. p.c. sil. rep. watch Feill coll. ca. 1720 sd. DECHOUDENS LONDON.
v. ESQUIVILLON and VIVIEN.
DECKA, John. *London.* a.1749, CC. 1757-1806. l.c. clock. Also sd. 'AKCED.'
& MARSH. *London.* an.1780-90. T.C.
DECKER, ——. *Nürnberg.* b.1677, d.1713. Designed watch-cases.
DECLÉ—
Jacques Charles. *Paris.* 1748. Juré 1754-60.
Pierre. *Paris.* m.1756.
Pierre Charles. *Paris.* m.1762.
——. *Paris.* 1810-14.
DE COLLEVILLE, Pierre. *Rouen.* 1381.
DE COLOGNY, ——. *Geneva.* 18c. sil. watch.
DE COLOMBY, Baudet. *Paris.* 1411-20. *Rouen,* 1437-57. In charge of Rouen town clock 1448. Repaired clocks of the Archevęché and of St. Laurent.
DECOMBAZ, Gédéon. *Geneva.* Mid. 18c. Watch Olivier coll.
DE COMBES—
Gédéon. ——. ca.1660. circ. agate watch.
V. *Schleswig.* ca.1740. Watch.
DECOR, Aimé. *Paris.* Late 18c.-1812. Four-colour g. watch Gélis coll.
DECOURTEAU, I. *Niort.* Late 16c. Watch.
DECOVIGNY, ——. *Paris.* Early 18c. Watch.
DECRAN, ——. *Paris.* 1812.
DECROSE, ——. *Gex.* 1735. Master of J. A. LÉPINE. Watch N.Y. Univ.
DE CRÜE, ——. *Geneva.* 18c. g. watch.
DE DIANO, Jorge. *San Yste.* 1556. Assistant to Giovanni Torriano, C. to Charles v.
DEE—
William. *London.* a.1720, CC.1729-1758, d. an.1762.
John or William, son. *London.* a.1744.
DEEME, Henry. *Honiton.* ca.1740. br. clock.
DEERING, John Jeffkins. *London.* a.1780.
DEÉVALO, Hans. *Madrid.* 1535. str. monstrance clock Fränkel coll.
DE FÉLAINS, Jehan. *Rouen.* 1389. d. 1414. Keeper and prob. maker of town clock of Rouen which had been begun by DE LECTRE.
DE FETTER, J. *Rotterdam.* 2nd half 18c. l.c. mus. clock.
DEFIENS, Louis. *Huy.* 1372. Erected a clock and bell on the Chateau de Golzinnes for Catherine de Savoie, comtesse de Namur.
DEFINE, Jullian. *Geneva.* 1598 'me orollieur.'
DEFINOD (DELPHINOU, DE FINAULX)—
Louis. *Lyons.* mar.1633-60.
——. *Grenoble.* 1651.
Vincent, son of Louis. *Lyons.* b.1636-59 m.
Jacob, bro. *Lyons.* b.1637-59 m.
David. *Cassel.* 1717. Watches in Cassel Landes-M. and Stuttgart M.
DE FOBIER, Pierre. *Geneva.* 1559. Refugee from Languedoc.
DE FOBIS (DE FOBYS), Pierre. *Lyons.* b.ca.1507-75. Watch.
DEFOE, Daniel. *London.* a.1767.
DE FOIGNY, Joseph. *Lyons.* 1691. Juré in 1708. From *Geneva.* Watch Geneva M.
DE FONTAYNE, James. *London.* 1716-29. Bankrupt. br. clock ill. Cec. & Web.
DEFORGES, ——. *Dijon.* ca.1700. Watches Den. coll. and M.P.S. Dresden.
DEFRANCE, ——. *Paris.* 1746-1812. aut. maker.
DEFRANCS, ——. *Paris.* 1825.
DEFREAS, Nicholas. *London.* 1685 not CC.
DEFRESNE, ——. *Beaune.* 1698.
DE FRIBOURG, Jacquet. *Romans.* 1414. 'Maitre constructeur d'horloges.' Repaired Grenoble clock.
DE GAND, Pérart. *Tournai.* 1383. Erected clock taken from Courtrai to Dijon.
DEGEN—
Matthäus. *Germany.* ca.1640. Two watches K.H.M.
Jakob. *Vienna.* m.1793.
DE GENNES, ——. *Oxford.* 1683. Pub. in Phil. Trans. Vol. xii a desc. of an inclined plane clock.
DÉGLANE, ——. *Paris.* 1812.
DEGMOIS, ——. *Paris.* 1812.
DEGOUZÉE-BLANC, ——. *Paris.* 1824. Complex clocks and watches.
DE GRANGE, *v.* MORICAND.
DE GRÈGES—
Antoine. *Rouen.* 1606-25. Founder member of Rouen corporation.
Antoine le jeune. *Rouen.* 1617. Founder member of Rouen corporation.
DE GRESILLIER, ——. *Paris.* 1823.
DE GROOT, H. *Holland.* Early 19c. Watch Stads M. Amsterdam.
DEGUAY, ——. *Paris.* 1812. T.C.
DEHECQ, Pierre. *La Rochelle.* 1693.
DE HEMANT, Charles Nicolas. *Paris.* m. 1750-89.
DE HINDE, Peter. *London.* d. an.1609. C.
DEIPHOLTH, Johan. *The Hague.* 17c. Dial B.M.
DEIS, Johann Michael. *Friedberg.* 18c. Rep. and al. trav. clock Fränkel coll.
DEISLER, I. D. *Zittau.* End 18c. Wooden table clock Feill coll.
DEJEAN—
——. *Paris.* 1788.
——. Detmold. Early 19c. Court clock-maker.
DE JORÈS, Px. *Lorient.* Late 18c. g. en. watch Feill coll.
DE KUIPER, Marinus. *Harlingen.* 1740. Clock Stads M. Amsterdam.
DE LA BALLE—
Francis. *London.* 1743. W.
Erasmus. *London.* an.1755. Watch.
& Co. *London (Soho).* 1755. W.
DE LA BUSSIÈRE—
Jacques. *Rouen.* m.1646.
Jacques. *Rouen.* m.1659.
DE LA CHANA, Daniel. *London.* CC.1687. French. Engraver.
DE LA CHAUSSÉE, fils. *Paris.* 1772. Made turret clock for Notre Dame.
DELACHAUX—
Josué. *Chaux-de-Fonds.* 1759. C.
Josué, son. *Valangin.* a.1759-79. C.
David. *Paris.* m.1776.
Daniel. *Paris.* 1788.
Philip H. *Philadelphia.* 1820. W.
DE LA CORBIÈRE—
——. *Geneva.* 1760.
——. *Nimes.* Early 19c. g. cyl. pedometer winding watch.
DELACROIX—
Jacob. ——. Early 17c. Watch Besançon M.
Lewis. *London.* a.1715.

DELACROIX—*continued.*
Jean. *Paris.* m.1741.
Jean. *Paris.* m.1751.
Jacques François. *Paris.* m.1778-89.

DELACROSE, ——. *Paris.* 2nd half 18c. g. en. rep. watch.

DE LA FAUDRIÈRE, ——. *Paris.* Early 18c. Improved the wheel cutting machines brought to Paris by SULLY.

DELAFEUILLE—
E. *Paris.* 1610. Watch Spitzer coll., sil. eagle with child on back.
——. *Geneva.* 1674.
Jacques. *Paris.* m.1746.
Benedict. *Paris.* m.1754-89.

DE LA FONS—
David. *London.* a.1724.
John. *London (Pinner's Court).* CC. 1789-1794. W.
John. *London (Threadneedle St.* and *St. Swithin's Lane).* 1790. d.1822. Patented a clockwork log. Awarded prize by Soc. Arts for a watch escapement; desc. pub. in Nicholson's Jl. Vol. i, 1802.
John. *London (Bank).* 1809-11.
Henry Peter Burning. *London.* a.1807, CC. 1814.
John. *London (Warnford Ct.)* . 1817-24.

DE LA FONTAINE, David. ——. Late 17c. en. watch.

DE LA FOSSE—
Samuel. *London.* 1689. CC.1692-4. French.
Jean Charles. *Paris.* Late 18c.-1825. Mantel clock Ministère de la Marine, Paris.

DE LA GARDE—
Jean. *Blois.* 1524-52.
Jacques. *Blois.* 1551-65. 'Aurelogeur.' One of the most famous makers of Blois. Spherical watch Louvre. Earliest French watch known, dated 1551, ill. Baillie. Watch dated 1565. Small clock.
Jean, son. *Blois.* 1580-1621. 'Horloger du Monsieur frère du roi' (duc d'Anjou).
Antoine, son of Jacques. *Blois.* mar. 1580. d. between 1588 and 1618.
Abraham, son of Jacques. *Paris,* 1591. *Blois,* 1600. *Paris,* 1621. C. to the Dowager Queen, Catherine de Médicis, in 1588, and to the King in 1591. Elected juré of the corporation of Paris, 1611. Oval sil. watch Webster coll.
Jacques, son of Antoine. *Paris.* m.1613. *Blois,* 1617. d.1669.
Antoine, son of Abraham. b.1606, m.1631, d.1670. Spring-maker after 1654.
Thomas François. *Paris.* m.1738.
——. *Riom.* ca.1800. Mantel clock Feill coll.

DE LA GARDETTE, Louis Mathieu. *Paris.* m.1767-89.

DE LA GRANGE—
Guy. *Lyons.* 1567. d.1606.
——. *Paris.* Mid.18c.

DELAHAY, Peter. *London.* an.1772. Watch.

DELAHAYE, Pierre. *Paris.* m.1782-9.

DE LA HIRE, Philippe. *Paris.* b.1640, d.1718. Prof. of mathematics. Used a zigzag spring attached to one arm of the balance. Wrote on epicycloids for wheel teeth and pub. many articles on clocks and watches in the Mém. de l'Acad. R. des Sciences.

DE LA HOUILLIERE, Thomas. *London.* an. 1725. Watch.

DE LA HOUSSAYE, ——. *Paris.* 1823. C.

DE LA HOYDE, ——. *Dublin.* 1786-96. CC. Made cyl. watches.

DELAITRE—
——. *Paris.* ca.1750 m.
Jean François, son. *Paris.* m.1758.

DELALANDE—
Lefrançois. *Paris.* b.1732, d.1807. Eminent mathematician and astronomer. Wrote articles in Lepaute's book on the form teeth and on the pendulum.
Honoré Pierre. *Paris.* m.1773-89.
Veuve. *Paris.* 1809.

DE LA LONDE, Martin. *Fauville.* 1633. Made clock for St. Laurent, Rouen, which was rejected as bad.

DELAMARCHE—
——. *Paris.* ca.1740 m.
Jacques François Henry. *Paris.* m.1745.

DELAMARE, Louis François. *Paris.* m.1747.

DE LA MOTTE, N. L. *Rouen.* 1761 m.

DELANDE, Pierre. *Paris.* d. an.1630. Enameller in Limoges en. of a watch in M.M.A.

DELANDER (DE LANDRE, DELAUNDER)—
Peter. *London.* CC.1641-62. Maker of repute. Oval watch ill. Britten.
Nathaniel. *London.* CC.1668-1705. Maker of repute. g. rep. watch Den. coll.
James. *London.* CC.1668-1704. Maker of repute.
John. *London.* CC.1675-87.
Daniel. *London (Devereux Ct.* an.1714 *Fleet St.).* a.1692, CC.1699. d.1733. A famous maker. Succeeded by Nathaniel. Invented a spring to secure watch cases. l.c. equation clock going a year Weth. coll. ill. Britten. l.c., br. and wall clock. Weth. coll. p.c. cyl. watch S.M.S.K. Watch and rep. mt. G.M. str. watch London M. Independent c.secs. stop watch, earliest known, ca.1705, Ilbert coll. rep. watch Marryat coll. Watch M.M.A. l.c. clock with duplex escapement. l.c. clock ill. Cec. & Web. Two l.c. clocks and br. clock Virginia M.
John. *London.* CC.1705-36.
Nathaniel, son of Daniel. *London (Royal Exchange* in 1730. *Fleet St.* in 1755). CC. 1721, m.CC. 1747, d.1762. Succeeded Daniel.
John. *London (Fleet St.).* a.1734, CC.1744-1752.

DELANESY, Nicolas Pierre. *Paris.* m.1764.

DELANOYE—
André. *Paris.* an.1750. m. Watch.
Veuve. *Paris.* 1789.

DELAPE, aîné. *Paris.* 1810.

DE LA PLACE—
Jean Baptiste. *Paris.* m.1758.
——. *Rouen.* 1763 m., juré 1779. Put ¼ str. to clock of St. Martin du Pont.

DE LA PLAINE—
Guillaume. *Blois.* 1551-62.
Roger. *Blois.* mar. 1580.

DE LA PLANCHE—
Étienne. *Geneva.* a.1705. d. an.1770.
Jean Lazare, son. *Geneva.* ca.1740-70.

DELAPONTE, Charles. *London.* an.1771. Watch.

DE LA PORTE—
C. H. *Delft.* 1720. sil. and tortoise-shell p.c. watch S.M.S.K.
Henry. *London.* a.1783.

DE LA REUSSILLE, David. *La Reusille (near Tramelan).* a.1765. Made watches for export.

DE LA ROCHE, Jean Pierre. *Blois.* 1667. Watch Gilles coll.

DELAROUNAT, Jean Baptiste. *Paris.* m. 1784-9. Watch N.Y. Univ.

DELARUE—
Jean Anthony. *London.* 1683.
Nicolas. *Paris.* m.1770.

DE LA RUELLE—
André. *Paris (Rue St. Martin).* m.1762-89.
Nicolas. *Paris (Rue de Richelieu).* m.1770-89.
——. *Paris (Rue du Bouloi).* 1786.

DE LARY, Jules. *Paris.* Juré 1684.

DELASONS, John. *London.* an.1777-97. Watch.

DELASSALLE (DE LA SALLE)—
James. *London.* an.1780. Watch.
Thomas. *London* (*St. Catherine's Stairs*). 1799-1824.
John. *London.* 1809-11.
& MILLER. *London.* 1811 dissolve partnership.
James Thomas. *London* (*Cannon St.*). CC. 1816-40. Watch Den. coll.

DELASTRE, Pierre. *Blois.* m.1664-76.

DELATOUCHE, ——. *Paris.* 1821.

DELAUNAY-BOURDILE, ——. *Paris.* 1824. mus. clocks and watches.

DELAUNCE, James. *London.* CC.1678.

DELAUNE, Étienne. *Paris.* b.1529, d.1583. Famous engraver. Many engravings on watch-cases copied from his work.

DELAUNEY—
Nicolas. *Paris.* Juré 1734.
Peter. *London.* 1815-25.

DE LAURENT, Jean. *Lyons.* a.1640.

DELAVALL, Lewis. *London.* an.1773. Watch.

DE LAVANS, ——. *Besançon.* 1599.

DELAVERSPERRE, William. *London.* CC. 1650.

DE LA VIEVILLE, ——. *Dieppe.* Early 18c. sil. p.c. watch S.K.M.

DELAVILLE—
James. *London.* a.1662.
John. *London.* a.1662.

DE LA VOIPIÈRE—
Pierre. *Rouen.* m.1679-90. In charge of Rouen Cathedral clock.
——. *Rouen.* Juré 1774-9.

DE LAWNCE, Peter. *London.* CC.1650.

DELAWNE, Nathaniell. *London.* 1622. a. to Cornelius Mellin.

DELDEVEZ, ——. *Paris.* 1812-25.

DELEAMONT—
Jean Pierre François. *Geneva.* b.ca.1718, d.1820. Painter of en. dials.
Étienne. *Geneva.* ca.1770-91.
Jean Antoine. *Paris* and *Geneva.* ca.1785. g. en. watch.

DELECLUSE, Pierre Nicolas. *Paris.* m.1738.

DE LECTRE, Jourdain. *Rouen.* ca.1385. Began clock for town.

DELEGALLE, Robert. *London.* a.1768.

DE LE HAEIRE, Andrien. *Cambrai.* 1558. 'Horloger-serrurier.'

DELEIDERIÈRE, Jean Louis. *Geneva.* ca. 1770-91.

DÉLÉMONT, ——. *Paris.* Early 19c. Watch.

DE LENGAINE, John. *London.* a.1713.

DE LEPÉE, Louis. *Paris.* m.1755.

DÉLÉPINE, Borromée. *St. Nicholas d'Aliermont.* Early 19c. Founded clock factory and later acquired that of PONS DE PAUL. In 1855 the firm was DÉLÉPINE & CANDEY.

DELESAIVES, Claude. *Paris.* m.1784-9.

DELESPÉE, L. *Paris.* 1st half 18c. g. en. watch Gélis coll.

DE LESPINASSE, ——. *Paris.* Late 18c. Pair of obelisks with clock, barometer and meridian dial, Wallace coll.

DELETRÉE, Jean. *Paris.* 1768.

DELIER, Thomas. *London.* an.1774. Watch.

DELILE, Jerôme. *Paris.* m.1770.

DELILLE, Jacob. *Vienna.* m.1792.

DELINGENDER, C. C. *Paris.* an.1674. Watch.

DELINOLLE, F. *Orléans.* ca.1720. al. watch F.W.M.

DELISAIRE, Claude. *Paris.* m.1784.

DE LISLE, ——. *Paris.* ca.1720. sil. rep. watch Ilbert coll.

DELISLE & FRÈRES MORICAND (DELISLE & MORICAND). *Geneva.* Late 18c. g. en. watch. 4-colour g. and en. watch.

DELL—
James. *London.* a.1761, CC.1768.
Joseph. *London.* an.1776. Watch.

DELLAMARE, Peter. *London.* 1523-71. 'Frenche clokemaker.' Born in Normandy.

DELLAMY, ——. *London.* d.1772.

DELLAWAS, Johann. *Prague.* 2nd half 18c. Watch mt. Arts M. Prague.

DELLCOURT, Bartholomew. *Beverley.* an. 1753. Watch.

DELLE—
Johann Nikolaus. *Augsburg.* m.1732, juré 1736-57, d. an.1769. g. repoussé watch Schloss M. Berlin.
Anton. *Vienna.* m.1751.

DELLER (DÖLLER), Christian. *Vienna.* m.1801.

DELLESSER, Ellis. *Liverpool.* ca.1820.

DELLUNG, Paul. *London.* a.1659.

DELMAR, Edward. *London.* CC.1821.

DE L'OBEL, ——. *Paris.* an.1776. Watch.

DELOLM, ——. *Brunswick.* Early 19c.

DELOLME, Henry. *London.* Early 19c.

DELOM, Martin. *Geneva.* Early 19c.

DE LONGASTRE, Ricquier. *Valenciennes.* 1546. Made a new clock for Cambrai Cathedral.

DELOR, ——. *Paris.* 1812.

DELORCHE, ——. *Paris.* 1798. Petitioned for a grant to make marine chrons.

DE LORME—
Timothée. *Rouen.* m.1663.
Jean Philippe. *Paris.* Juré 1736.
Henri Philippe. *Paris.* 1742 juré. al. watch given by Nelson to Capt. Rose. Boulle br. clock, Pal. de Pau, Paris, prob. by him.
Jean François. *Geneva.* ca.1770-91.
Michel. *Paris.* 1780.

DE LOUDEREAU, ——. *Amsterdam.* 1688. From *Geneva.*

DEL RIO, P. F. Manuel. *Santiago.* 1759. Pub. in Spanish a large treatise on Clocks and Watches, with a second edition, Madrid, 1798.

DE LUC, J. A., F.R.S. *London.* 1815. Pub. art. in Phil. Mag. on rates of clocks.

DE LUCCA, Johann. *Vienna.* m.1739. br. clock Uhren M. Vienna.

DELUNESY, ——. *Paris.* 1779-86. Two fine clocks Wallace coll.

DELUPONTA, Charles. *London.* 1739. Watch.

DEL VALLE, Vincent. *Gibraltar.* ca.1820. Watch.

DELVAUX, ——. *Paris.* 1812.

DELYNNE, ——. *Paris.* 1st half 18c. g. en. rep. watch Gélis coll.

DE MAFFÉ, Alexandre. *Geneva.* 1715. From *Dauphiné.*

DEMAINGE, ——. *N. France.* 1400.

DE MALLET, P. *London.* Late 18c. rep. watch.

DEMAND, ——. *Paris.* 1824.

DE MARC—
Evangéliste. *Geneva.* 1559. Refugee from *Foligno.*
Louis. *Grenoble.* 1603.

DEMARIN, James. *London.* a.1763.

DEMARQUE—
Loys. *Poitou* and *Avignon.* 1597-1611. Remade Caen clock. Made clock for Orange.
Jean, son. *Avignon.* 1611. Made clock for Malemort with his father.

DEMAS, Hippolyte. *Blois.* m.1682-6.

DE MASSO, Michel. *Lyons.* 1654 m., d.1691.

DEMAYNE, Anthony. *Woodbridge.* 1784. l.c. clock. W.

DEMELAIS, ——. *London.* ca.1740. Watches Ilbert and Den. colls.

DEMER (THEMER)—
Ignatius. *Vienna.* m.1720. trav. clock Den. coll.
——. *Paris.* 1812.

DE MERGUE, ——. *Paris.* 1692. Maker of repute.
DEMESMAY, ——. *La Brévine.* 1815-30. C.
DE MESSY, Jehan. *Hesdin.* 1398. 'faiseur d'orloges.'
DEMET, Antoine. *Lyons.* mar. an.1577.
DE METZ, Pierre. *Romans.* 1411. Worked on Grenoble clock.
DE MEURE, A. *Brussels.* 2nd half 18c. aut. mus. clock.
DEMEZA, G. E. *London.* 1825. Watch N.Y. Univ.
DE MIERE, F. *Amsterdam.* ca.1690. Watch en. Huaud le puisné ill. Britten.
DEMILT, Thomas & B. *New York.* 1805.
DE MIRE, Théodore. *Paris.* 1674 juré.
DEMMEL, Johann. *Würzburg.* m.1780-98. C.
DEMMILEVILLE, Pierre. *Lille.* 1393. Keeper of town clock and fixed the 'rouage de la demie.'
DEMOISEL, Aymé. *Basle.* 1670. From *Geneva.*
DEMOLE (DEMOLE-CHÂLON), ——. *Geneva.* 1798. d.1810. Associated with MAGNIN. Able chron. maker.
DE MOLIN, Nicolas. *Basle.* 1718. From *Bourg-en-Bresse.*
DEMOLLES, Antoine. *Geneva.* ca.1770-91.
DEMOLYN, John. *England.* 1544. French.
DE MONCHAINE, Heliodore Jacques Pierre. *Paris.* m.1771.
DEMONCHANIN, Pierre. *Paris.* m.1746-69.
DE MONTFERRAT, Raymond. 1466. Made clock for town of Orange.
DE MONTIGNY, Henri. *Vincennes.* 1390.
DE MORLIER, Maillet. *France.* Early 18c. Devised a modified verge escapement, and an anchor recoil escapement for clocks with two independently pivoted pallets.
DE MOUCHIE, John. *London.* 1622. Alien.
DEMPSTER, Marc Anthony. *York.* 1825. W.
DE MYLIUS, Albert. ——. 1791. Finished one of Hahn's planetaria.
DENBIGH, William. *London.* a.1793.
DENCH, William. *London.* a.1811, CC.1835.
DENDELOT, L'Abbé. *France.* Early 18c. Devised a watch wheel and pinion-cutting engine.
DENHAM, Charles. *Durham.* 1820-40.
DENIAU, Claude. *Blois.* m.1639-64.
DENIÈRE—
——. *Paris.* Late 18c. and early 19c. Bud watch.
ET MATELIN. *Paris.* ca.1815. Bronze workers. Made clock-cases.
DENIS—
——. *Paris.* 1748 m.
J. Louis. *Fragnée.* 1776. l.c. clock.
DENISARD, ——. *Paris.* 1807-14.
DENISART—
Jean Pierre. *Paris.* m.1770-89.
——. *Paris (Rue de Thiouville).* 1807-14.
DENISON, Edmund Beckett (Baron Grimthorpe in 1886). *London.* b.1816, d.1905. Designed Westminster clock (Big Ben), with its gravity escapement. Pub. 'Clocks Watches and Bells.'
DENMAN—
Thomas. *Chester.* 1775. C. & W.
Thomas. *London.* a.1794.
Jeremiah. *London.* a.1795.
George Frederick. *London.* a.1813, CC. 1821. Watch.
DENN, —— *London.* an.1732. Watch.
DENNE, John. *London.* 1817-24. chron. W. & C.
DENNETT—
John. ——. 1789.
Richard. *Newport (I.O.W.).* 1793-7. W.
James. *St. Helens.* ca.1820.
DENNICKEN, Octavy Johann. —. Late 17c. Table clock.
DENNIS—
Francis. *London.* a.1667, CC.1672-81.
Thomas. *London.* a.1672.
Peter. *London.* a.1704, CC.1712-32.
George. *London.* a.1713.
Thomas. *London.* a.1717.
——. *Torrington.* 18c. l.c. clock.
John. *London.* an.1762. Watch.
DENNISON—
James. *London.* a.1720.
Aaron L. *Waltham, U.S.A.*, and *Birmingham.* b.1812, d.1895. Started watch factory at *Roxbury* in 1853 and at *Waltham* with Howard in 1854. Came to *Birmingham* and started factory for watch-cases.
'DENNISON, HOWARD & DAVIS.' Sig. on Dennison's watches 1854-6.
DENODON—
Michel. *Blois.* mar. 1585-1623.
Abraham. *Blois.* mar. 1617-42.
DENOYELLE, Ferdinand Philippe. *Paris.* m.1788.
DENRICK & PHILLIPS. *London.* an.1786. Watch.
DENSTON, Robert. *London.* a.1711.
DENT—
William. *London.* CC.1674-1703. A famous maker.
Robert. *London.* a.1671, CC.1681-91. Watch.
Robert. *Lincoln.* Early 18c.-1795. Watch.
William. *London.* a.1702.
Edmund. *London.* a.1739, CC.1747.
William. *Scarborough.* an.1756. Watch.
Edward John. *London.* b.1790, d.1853. A celebrated maker. Worked with Richard RIPPON ca.1810, on his own account in 1814, in firm of ARNOLD & DENT 1830-40, and then alone. Made some lever watches with one tooth esc. wheel to design of Chas. MacDowell. Made clock for Royal Exchange, and received order for Westminster (Big Ben) clock, which was completed by his stepson Frederick. Obtained prize for chron. in 1829. Wrote several pamphlets on chrons.
DENTAND—
Isaac. ——. Early 18c. sil. chased watch Nat. M. Stockholm.
F. *Geneva.* Early 18c. 8-day watch Feill coll.
DENTON—
——. *London.* an.1723 Watch.
Robert. *Oxford (High St.).* 1740-90. l.c. clock.
William. *Oxford (Corn Market).* 1750-64. W.
William & Samuel. *Oxford (Corn Market).* 1756. W.
Thomas. *Abingdon.* 1758. W.
Samuel. *Oxford (High St.).* ca.1760, d.1796. W.
Samuel. *London.* a.1765.
John. *London.* a.1767. Watch.
Joseph. *Hull.* l.c. clock.
Samuel, son of Samuel of Oxford. *London.* a.1790.
Frederick. *Rotherham.* Early 19c.
& FOX. *Hull.* Early 19c. Watch.
DEONNA, Jean. *Geneva.* 1722.
DE PAILLOT, ——. *London.* an.1781. Watch.
DE PAP, Balthasar. *Liége.* 1612. Oct. crys. watch.
DÉPARCIEUX, ——. *Paris.* 1739. Mathematician. Mem. on a copper and steel compensating pendulum.
DE PASS, Simon. *London.* Early 17c. Engraver. Fine work on a watch by Onesiphorus Helden.

DE PENNA, Don Nicolas. *Madrid.* 1760. Pub. on regulating timekeepers, in Spanish.
DEPIGNY, ——. *Geneva.* End 18c. Early Lepine watch Geneva M.
DE PLAT, A. *Ghent.* 2nd half 18c. l.c. mus. clock.
DEPONT, ——. *London (Islington).* an.1751. Watch.
DEPOSAY—
Jacques. *Lyons.* mar. 1609. From *Blois.*
Isaac. *Blois.* 1634.
DEPREE, Elie. *London.* CC.1634.
DE PRESLES, Jehan. *Paris.* 1544. Petitioner for incorporation of Paris Guild.
DE PULTER, ——. *Amsterdam.* 1723. rep. watch Chamb. coll.
DERBY—
Aron. *London.* a. 1687. Watch.
Thomas. *London.* an.1769. Watch.
DERCHE, ——. *Paris.* 1810.
DERDIER, ——. *Paris.* Late 18c. Ormolu clock.
DERE, ——. *London.* an.1758. Watch.
DEREY, John. *London.* a.1694.
DERHAM, William, F.R.S. *Upminster.* b. 1657, d.1735. Author of 'The Artificial Clockmaker,' which had five English, two French and two German editions.
DERIAT, Étienne. *Basle.* 1752.
DERIAZ, Étienne. *Geneva.* 1770. Prob. the preceding.
DE RIBAUCOURT, André (Alexandre). *Paris.* m.1770-89. Dead-beat escapement C.A. & M.
DERIMO, Lewis. *London.* 1711 CC.
DERISSOOD, ——. *London.* 18c. Watch Bourges M.
DERNE, Ch. *Nancy.* ca.1630. Watch Feill coll. in fluted sil. case. cf. Derue.
DE RO, ——. *London.* ca.1625. From *Flanders.* Advertised a perpetual motion clock.
DEROCHES FRÈRES. *Geneva.* ca.1720-19c. Watches S.K.M., Wallace coll., M.M.A., Den. and Fränkel colls. and M.P.S. Dresden.
DEROUSSENT, ——. *Paris.* 1822.
DE ROUVROY, Jean. *Amiens.* 1446. Locksmith and C. to the town.
DERRICK—
William. *London.* a.1769, CC.1777-93. Bankrupt. Also Dirrick.
& Phillips. *London.* 1784. Partnership with preceding, dissolved 1785.
DERRINGS, John. *London.* an.1757. Watch.
DERSSIGNY, Pierre. *Paris.* b.1646. Watch M.M.A.
DERUE, Louis. *Nancy.* ca.1640. Watch B.M. in fluted sil. case. cf. Derne.
DERUZE, P. *Jamaica.* Early 19c.
DERWOOD, W. M. *London.* an.1787-ca. 1800. Watch.
DE SAINT-BÉATTE, Pierre. *Paris.* 1364-91. Made clock for Charles v for Chât. de Beauté, and 'un petit aurloge.' Went to Avignon in 1375 to work on a turret clock on the palace of the Popes.
DE SAINT-BLIMONT, Jean Antoine. *Paris.* m.1738.
DE SAINT-JEAN, Jean Baptiste. *Paris.* m. 1760-89. Picture aut. clock C.A. & M.
DE ST. LEU, Daniel. *London.* 1753-97. Succeeded by Rivers & Son, W. to the Queen in 1765. Fine en. watch, rep. watch, and p.c. g. str. watch G.M. Watch, set diamonds, London M. rep. cyl. watch Den. coll. Very fine br. clock in sil. case for Spanish Court.
DE SAINT-MARTIN—
Antoine. *Paris.* Juré 1737.
François Pierre. *Paris.* m.1770-89.
Jean Joseph. *Paris.* m.1781.
DE SAINT-PAUL—
Claude. *Lyons.* 1545. d. between 1560 and 1571.
Jean. *Lyons.* 1567.
Denis. *Geneva.* 1573-1623. Refugee from *Lyons.*
DE SAINT-PÈRE—
Claude. *Paris.* ca.1760 m.
Veuve. *Paris.* 1789.
DE SALLE, ——. *Caen.* Early 18c. Watch Den. coll. Perhaps same as following.
DE SALLES, François. *Rouen.* a.1695.
DE SALVI, ——. *Italy.* 1565. Ring dial Old Ashmolean M.
DESARGUES, Gaspard. *Lyons.* b.1593, d. 1662. Mathematician. Said by De la Hire to have been the first to show the properties of the epicycloid for wheel teeth.
DES ARTS (DESARTS)—
——. *Geneva.* a.1655.
& Cie. *Geneva.* 1775-ca.1800. En. watch rep. by turning the pendant knob.
DESAUX, François. *Geneva.* ca.1750-73.
DES BINS, Pierre. *Paris.* 1700. Registered a private punch mark.
DESBOIS—
Jacob. *London.* CC.1730. Also Debois.
& Wheeler. *London.* 1790-1835. Watch G.M.
Daniel. *London.* 1800-40.
v. Cottin.
DESBOROUGH, Christopher. *London.* a. 1658, CC. 1665.
DESBROW—
Elizabeth. *London.* a.1676.
Robert. *London.* a.1696, CC.1705.
DESBUIS, Pierre. *Paris.* 1675 m.
DESCHAMPS—
Étienne. *Paris.* m.1764-89.
Jean. *Paris.* m.1776-89.
François. *Paris.* m.1782-9.
André. *Paris (Place Baudoyer).* m.1788-1825. 2 clocks C.A. & M. by him or preceding.
——. *Paris.* 1823-53. Succeeded Chapuy in Lépine's business. Succeeded by Fabre.
DESCHEUR, P. *Paris.* 1600. Sig. to Statuts of Paris corporation.
DESCHURINES, ——. *London.* an.1755.
DESCOMBATS—
Jean Louis. *Geneva.* b.1747, m.1787. Made fine watches for Jaquet-Droz and Leschot.
Jean Jacques. *Geneva.* ca.1775-91.
DESCOMBES—
Jaques. ——. ca.1700. Watch with en. sd. 'Les deux frères Huaud les jeunes.' Ilbert coll.
Salomon. *Lausanne.* 1744-56. Clock.
Jacot. *Vienna.* ca.1780. g. en. watch in form of apple.
Jacob. *Paris.* 1782.
DESCURE, Marin. *Lyons.* 1536.
DESEINE—
——. *Paris.* 1680 m.
Mathieu, son. *Paris.* m.1690.
DESENCLOS, ——. *Paris.* 1812.
DESERVE, ——. *Paris.* 1772.
DESESCURES, Blaise. *Riom.* 1616. Oval watch Miller coll.
DESESSART (DESESSARS, DESESAR)—
Abraham. *London.* CC.1682, d.1739. W.
James. *London.* a.1698, CC.1707.
George. *London.* a.1702.
——. *Paris.* 1807-12.
DESFLÈCHES—
Jacques. *Lyons.* a.1668, m.1681-1707. Also a caster of bells.
Jérôme. *Lyons.* 1693 m.-1715.
DESFONTAINE, Louis Martin. *Paris.* m. 1788.
DES FOUNTAINES, Jacobus. *London.* an. 1692. Watch.

DES GRANGES—
Peter. *London* (*Wardour St.*). an.1775-84. W.
Peter. *London* (*Cockspur St.*). 1816-42. Succeeded RECORDON. Watch Chamb. coll.
DESHAIS, Matthew. *London.* an.1710. Watch.
DESHAYES—
Pierre. *Rouen.* 1642-63. Made clock for St. Laurent, Rouen.
Étienne. *Rouen.* 1701 m.
——. *Paris.* Early 19c. Made clocks with pendulum connected to train by crank and connecting rod. Specialized in dividing machines. Watch Gélis coll. Devised a lever esc. with a one tooth esc. wheel.
DESINARD, J. *London.* ca.1730. Watch.
DESMARAIS, Peter. *London.* 1794 and early 19c. g. dead secs. and g. cyl. c.secs. watches.
DESMARES, ——. *Versailles,* 1738. *Paris,* 1750. Elaborate picture aut. clock M. des Arts-Décoratifs, Paris, ill. M. des Aut.
DESNOYERS, ——. *Paris.* 1824.
DE SOIGNIES—
Mathieu. *Valenciennes.* 1396-1409. Remade Cambrai Cathedral clock.
Jacques. *Valenciennes.* 1426. Repaired Cambrai Cathedral clock.
DE SOMMAVAL, ——. *Rouen.* Juré 1774.
DESONNAZ, Jean. *Geneva.* ca.1750-72.
DESPRÉAUX, Pierre. *Lyons.* a.1625.
DESRIFFARD, Philippe Jacques. *Paris.* m. 1776.
DESSAULES—
Samuel Henry. *Valangin.* 1790-6.
Henri Louis. *Fontaines.* a.1805.
DESSOULAVY, Jonas Pierre. *Neuchâtel* and *Chaux-de-Fonds.* b.1803, d.1876. Many clocks.
DESTACHES, John. *London.* CC.1661.
DESTAVE, Jean Joseph. *Paris.* m.1784.
DESTIGNY, ——. *Rouen.* 1825. Pub. in 'C. R. de l'Acad. de Rouen,' 'notice sur un instrument destiné à régler les pendules.'
DESTOUCHES—
——. *Middelburg.* ca.1800.
——. *Paris.* 1809-24. *v.* FONTANIÉ.
DE SUFRY, ——. *Geneva.* ca.1825. g. en. cyl. watch.
DESVIGNES & ATKINS. *London.* 1797. Watch-case makers. Dissolved partnership.
DE TAL, Sour. *Paris.* Early 18c.
DÉTAPE—
Noel Marie. *Paris.* m.1788.
——. *Paris.* 1807-25. Temple clock, Palais de Pau, Paris.
aîné. *Paris* (*Place d'Austerlitz*). 1812.
Alexandre. *Paris* (*Rue de l'Arbre sec*). 1812.
DETAU, ——. *France.* Late 18c. Clock.
D'ETCHINGER, *v.* ELCHINGER.
D'ETOUR, ——. *Paris.* Late 18c. Marble and ormolu mantel clock. cf. DETAU.
DE TUDERT, Jean. *Geneva.* a.1665.
DEUTKE, Jørgen. *Copenhagen.* 1645-61.
DE VAILLY, Dom Charles. *France.* 1690. A Benedictine who devised the form of water-clock with falling drum. Example C.A. & M.
DE VAL, Gabriel. *Paris.* 1674 juré. *v.* DU VAL.
DE VALENTINE (DE VALENCIENNES), Henri. *Lyons.* 1394. Keeper of clock of St. Jean.
DEVALL, John. *London.* a.1670, CC.1677.
DE VALS, Hans. *Madrid.* 1533-ca.1580. C. to Philip II of Spain. Clock with lamp, Spitzer sale.
DE VASSALIEU, Humbert. *Lyons.* 1523-57.
DE VAUGUION, Daniel. *London.* an. 1762. Watch. br. clock.
DEVAULX, S. *Paris.* Early 19c. C. to Mademoiselle d'Orléans. g. en. watch M.M.A.
DE VAUX—
Nicolas. *Geneva.* 1594.
Pierre. *Compiègne.* 1657. Repaired clock on belfry.
DE VEILLE, Jacques. *Angers.* ca.1640. Sil. skull watch Ilbert coll.
DEVEMMEL, Benjamin. *London.* 1743. Watch.
DEVERBERIE—
& CIE. *Paris.* ca.1800. Fine ormolu mantel clock.
J. F. *Paris.* ca.1800. l.c. clock.
DEVERELL—
John. *Boston, U.S.A.* 1796-8. W.
Charles Holman. *London.* a.1789.
DEVERILL—
John. *London.* an.1779. Watch.
Samuel. *London.* a.1822.
DEVEY, William. *Dudley.* 1791. W.
DEVEYRAZ, ——. *Geneva.* 1668.
DE VIC, Henry. *Vic in Lorraine.* 1370. Made clock for Palais de Justice, Paris.
DE VIENNE, Gaspard. *Paris.* 1772.
DEVILLAINE, ——. *Paris.* 1805. Lyre clock.
DE VILLE—
Estienne Simon. *Paris.* m.1767, juré 1784-9.
Siméon. *Paris.* Juré 1786.
——. *Paris.* 1807.
DEVIS—
William. *London* (*Fleet St.*). 1751, d.1763. Watch Belfast M. T.C. Succeeded by John NEWTON.
John. *London* (*Lambs Conduit St.*). 1770. CC.1781-5. g. en. watch.
DEVITT, Robert. *London.* a.1764.
DEVLIN, James. *Ardee.* 1824.
DEVON, James. *London.* a.1799.
DEVOY, Henry. *London.* 1706. W.
DEVRAINVILLE, ——. *Paris.* 1815-21. aut. maker.
DE VREESE, John. *London.* 1683. W.
DE VRIES—
Sijbren Gellius. *Joure.* Late 18c.
J. C. *Amsterdam.* ca.1800.
DEVRINE, ——. *Paris.* 1824.
DEWE—
John. *London* (*Southwark*). a.1726, CC. 1733-64. l.c. lacquer clock.
John, son. *London.* a.1764.
DE WELLKE, Christian. *London.* 1620-30. Petitioner for incorporation of CC. A Mr. Dewell, prob. the same, subscribed. Admitted BC. 1628, desc. as 'Polander.' Table clock Webster coll.
DEWEY, William. *London.* ca.1835. Maker of Dutch clocks.
DEWHURST, William Bolton. *Clitheroe.* 1820. Watch.
DE WIT, Jan. *Hoorn.* ca.1800.
DEWMELANE, John. *London.* 1568. French.
DE WOLDE, Ernoulet. *Burgundy.* 1399-1400 C. to the duc de Bourgogne. Apparently the same as DE BAUDE.
DEXTER—
William. *London.* an.1763. Watch.
M. *London.* an.1763-ca.1790. Watch mt. G.M.
'DEXTER ST.' Sig. on watches 1871-75 of the NATIONAL WATCH CO. OF CHICAGO.
DEY—
Laurent. *Paris.* m.1744. Watch mt. with sil. pillars and cock.
Nicolas Laurent, son. *Paris.* m.1765-89.
DEYERL (DEIERL), Johann. *Vienna.* m. 1748.
DEYKIN—
Thomas. *Worcester.* ca.1710-50.
Henry, son. *Worcester.* 1751-88. Watch. Also DEAKIN.

D'HAUTEL aîné. *Paris.* 1807.
D'HÉRISSART, Philippe Charles. *Paris.* 1783.
DHILGERS, ——. *Paris.* 1807.
DHINSSEAU, Adam. *London.* a.1701.
DIARD, ——. *Angers.* 1770. Re-made clock on Cathedral.
DIAS, Elias. *London.* an.1776. Watch.
DIBBINS, James. *London.* a.1808.
DIBIFORD, ——. *London.* an.1771. Watch.
DIBON, James. *London.* a.1706, CC.1713-25.
DICK—
William. *London.* a.1723.
Charles. *London.* an.1772. Watch.
James. *Ayr.* d.1800.
DICKENS—
John. *London.* a.1680, CC.1688-95.
John. *Bath.* 1755-ca.1800. C. & W. Watch.
DICKER—
Thomas. *Silchester.* 1736-56. *Reading* from 1756, d.1774. l.c. clock.
Thomas, jun. *Mortimer.* Went to *Reading* in 1756. W.
Thomas. *Reading* and *Wokingham.* 1774-97. Son and successor of Thos. of Silchester. Lacquer inn clock.
DICKERSON—
Daniel. *Yarmouth.* ca.1750. l.c. clock.
Daniel. *Framlingham.* an.1767-90. Watch. l.c. clock.
Daniel. *Harleston.* From 1791. l.c. clock.
Benjamin. *London.* an.1761. Watch.
——. *Ipswich.* an.1791. Watch.
DICKIE—
Andrew. *Stirling.* 1723-39. Watch mt. G.M.
Andrew. *Edinburgh.* 1735. d.1765. rep. Watch S.K.M. g. c.secs. watch, balance under dial and g. c.secs. cyl. watch Ilbert coll.
Andrew. *Dunfermline.* 1752.
Andrew. *London.* 1756, d.1772. Appointed expert by Act of 1761 on Harrison's timepiece. l.c. clock.
William. *London.* an.1757. Watch.
Alexander. *Edinburgh.* a.1762-1808. g. watch Glasgow Art Gall. cyl. mt. with steel escape wheel G.M.
William. *Dunfermline.* 1780.
v. DALGLEISH & DICKIE.
David. *London.* a.1808.
DICKINSON—
John. *Warrington.* 1722. C. DICKONSON.
Richard. *Liverpool.* 1734, d.1743. Watch Den. coll.
——. *Boston.* ca.1790 CC.
John. *London.* a.1768, CC.1790.
Thomas. *Lancaster.* In 1801 succeeded H. BELL.
Robert. *York.* 1810-23. W.
Thomas. *Manchester.* 1817-24. C. Lancaster freeman.
Thomas. *Lancaster.* ca.1820. Prob. same as preceding.
——. *Boston.* Early 19c.
John. *Philadelphia.* 1823-5.
DICKMAN—
John. *Leith.* 1800-50.
C. F. *Luleå.* 1810-30.
DICKS—
William. *London.* 1772. Bankrupt. cf. DIX.
W. *Warminster.* an.1777. Watch.
DICKSON—
Charles. *Dundee.* 1722.
Peter. *London.* an.1777. Watch.
John. *Edinburgh.* a.1790.
James. ——. ca.1800. Watch S.K.M.
DIDEROT, ——. *Paris.* 1748. Pub. 'Resistance de l'air au mouvement des pendules.'
DIEBOLD, Johann. *Augsburg.* m.1741-70.
DIEBOLDER—
Michel. *Basle.* m.1572-82.
Baltazar, bro. *Basle.* m.1578-1605.

DIEBOLDER—*continued.*
Hans, son of Michel. *Basle.* 1598. d.1634.
Michel, bro. *Basle.* 1598.
Mathis. *Basle.* 1620.
Johannes, son of Hans. *Basle.* 1646-58. Made clock for Allschwil.
DIEFLER, Georg. *Mainz.* 1782. Court C.
DIEM, Jacob. *Tübingen.* 1589. aut. clock for Esslingen.
DIENSTER, ——. *Amsterdam.* ca.1700. g. en. watch.
DIETERS, C. *Assen.* ca.1800.
DIETRICH, Joh. Mich. *Fürth.* d.1802.
DIETSCHI, Pancratz. *Fribourg.* 1584-94. Showed an astro. clock on model of the Strasbourg clock. Made clock for the Tour de l'Horloge, Berne. Passerace TROCHE appears to be an alternative name.
DIETZ, Lucas Georg. *Hamburg.* 1801-21.
DIEU—
R. *Paris.* Late 16c.-1612. crys. en. watch Spitzer sale. Watch Gélis coll.
v. LEDIEU.
DIGBY—
Charles. *London.* a.1721-60. rep. watch.
Edward. *London.* ca.1750. en. watch.
William. *Dublin.* 1766-80. W.
William. *London.* 1820.
DIGHTON—
William. *London.* a.1687.
Joseph. *London.* a.1743.
DIGNE, Pierre. *Paris.* 1773.
DIJKHOF, Barend. *Haarlem.* 1717.
DIKE—
Nathaniel. *London.* CC.1663.
Joseph. *London.* 1701 CC.
DILGER—
Simon. *Schollenbach.* b.1672. In 1720 was one of the first to start clockmaking in the Schwarzwald.
J. *Neustadt.* d.1780. First maker of the larger 24-hour Schwarzwald wall clocks, called Schottenuhren.
Friedrich, son. *Schollenbach.* 1750. Studied in Paris.
Michael. *Neukirch* and *St. Märgen.* 1750-70. One of the first to make cuckoo clocks. Wall clock Furt. M.
Joseph. *Neukirch.* ca.1770. Wall clock Furt. M.
Johannes. *Glottertal.* ca.1785. Wall clock Furt. M.
DILKER, Leonhard. *Thumenberg.* b.1536, d.1603.
DILLINGTON, ——. *London.* ca.1750. Watch.
DILLON, Jonathan. *Waterford.* 1820-4.
DIMIER—
Jean Antoine. *Geneva.* b.1795, d.1863.
Charles Louis, son. *Chaux-de-Fonds.* b. 1822, d.1896.
Auguste Antoine, bro. *Chaux-de-Fonds.* b. 1824, d.1891.
FRÈRES ET CIE. *Fleurier.* Early 19c. Watch mt. S.M.S.K.
DIMSDALE—
John. *London.* a.1758, CC.1766.
William. *London.* a.1789.
DIMUND, John. *London.* CC.1786.
DINGLEY—
Robert. *London.* a.1661, CC.1668-1706. l.c. clock. 2 watches Bernal sale.
William. *London.* a.1661.
DINGWALL—
John. *London.* 1771. Cyl. watch.
& Co. *London.* ca.1800. en. watch London M.
DINMORE—
John. *London.* an.1749. Watch.
Henry. Prob. *Derby.* an.1760. Watch.
DINNIS, Francis. *London.* CC.1666-91. Engraver.

DINOCHEAU—
Jacques. *Blois.* m.1664-7. Also Guignochot.
Michel. *Blois.* m.1670-91.
DIODONON, Georges. *Paris.* m.1744.
DIPPLE, Francis. *Warwick.* 1795. Watch.
DIRING, ——. *Berlin.* 1794. C. cf. DURING.
DIRKS, Jacob. *Franeker.* 1701. Small turret clock.
DISLEY—
William. *London.* a.1809.
Thomas. *Madras.* Early 19c.
DISOLEY, ——. *Avignon.* 1747.
DISON—
John. *St. Ives.* an.1770-72. Watch.
Jeremiah. *Cambridge.* ca.1800. *Chatteris* from 1802. C. & W.
DISTAVE, Jean Joseph. *Paris.* 1780 comp., m.1784-9.
DISTURNELL—
William. *London.* a.1750, CC.1759-63.
Philip. *London.* a.1759, CC.1769.
John. *London.* a.1763.
DITCHFIELD, Richard. *London.* CC.1677-1687.
DITMAN, M. *Brussels.* Mid. 17c. oct. crys. watch Pal. du Cinquantenaire, Brussels.
DITZ, Martin. *Nordheim-v.-d.-Rhön.* m. 1825.
D'IVERNOIS—
——. *Geneva* and *Paris.* 1768-72. Made rep. watches in rings.
Veuve. *Paris.* Early 19c.
DIVIZIOLI, Giovanni Battista and Giovanni Francesco. *Cremona.* 1588. Re-made clock on the tower of the Piazza del Duomo.
DIX—
——. *London.* 1743. Watch. cf. DICKS.
William. *London.* a.1752.
Joseph. *Philadelphia.* 1769. W.
DIXON—
William. *London.* a.1686.
Thomas. *London.* a.1699.
Edward. *London.* a.1748, CC.1757.
John. *London.* a.1748, CC.1756.
Jonathan. *Macclesfield.* 1773, d.1779.
George. *London.* an.1781. Watch.
James, son of John. *London.* CC.1789, l.CC. 1791.
John. *Leicester.* 1794. C. & W.
Walter. *London.* a.1801.
E. *Hexham.* Early 19c. Watch.
Joseph. *London.* a.1807.
George James. *London.* a.1809, CC.1816.
Charles. *Lisburn.* 1820-4.
DOBB, William. *London.* a.1639, CC.1646.
DOBBIE—
William. *Falkirk.* 1768.
John. *Edinburgh.* 1783.
John. *Glasgow.* 1802-26.
John. *Prestonpans.* 1820.
Andrew. *Glasgow.* 1820-48.
George. *Falkirk.* 1821-50.
William. *Falkirk.* 1821-45. C. to the Queen. Watch.
DOBBIN, William. *Leeds.* 1817. C.
DOBEL, E. *Yeovil.* 18c. l.c. clock. Watch.
DOBIE, John. *Tanfield.* 1796. Watch. Later J. & T.
DOBREE, Elisha. ——. an.1762. Watch.
DOBSON—
William. *London.* CC.1670-84. Maker of repute. Lantern clock.
John. *London.* a.1698, CC.1714-44.
Arlander. *London* (*Covent Garden*). 1744. d. 1772. 'Eminent' W. en. watch S.K.M. rep. watch Den. coll.
Thomas. *London* (*Rosamon St.*). a.1738, CC. 1746-87.
Abraham. *London.* an.1774. Watch.
Charles. *London.* l.CC.1776. str. and al. trav. clock Fränkel coll.
Joshua. *London.* 1795.
Jonathan. *London.* a.1810.

DOBSON—*continued.*
Thomas. *Leeds.* 1817.
——. *Beeston.* 1822.
DOCAGNE. ——. *Le Havre.* 18c. Watch Bourges M.
DOCKSEY, John. *Bristol.* 1774. W.
DODD—
Joseph. *London.* a.1758.
Matthew. *London.* a.1764.
William. *London.* 1805-21.
Philip George. *London.* a.1816.
DODDERIDGE, Thomas. *London.* a.1703.
DODDINGTON, John. *London.* a.1685.
DODDS—
Joseph. *London* (*Aldersgate St.*). CC.1794, l.CC.1795, d.1817. an. 1793 partner with John TROUTBECK.
Joseph, son. *London.* a.1807, CC.1814.
Moses. *Sunderland.* 1820.
DÖDERLEIN, Johann W. *Fürth.* d.1802.
DODGE, Seril. *Connecticut.* Late 18c.
DODGSON, Thomas. *London.* a.1727.
DODS, Andrew. *Selkirk.* 1785.
DODSELL, Thomas. *East Grinstead.* 1795. C.
DODSON, John. *London.* a.1654.
DODSWORTH, John. *London.* CC.1648-51.
DOGGETT, Robert. *London.* an.1779. Watch.
DOGUINET, Adrien. *Paris.* 1685 m.
DOHERTY, James. *Clonmel.* 1820.
DOHOO, Martin. *London.* 1772. Insolvent. From *Hamburg.*
DOIG—
Alexander. *Edinburgh.* 1811.
Alexander. *Musselburgh.* 1814-36.
William. *Polmont.* 1825.
DOKE, Richard. *Liverpool.* 1825. W.
DOLAY, Michel. *Paris.* m.1784-9. 'Monteur de boîtes.'
DOLCAS, Robert. *Northwich.* 1795. C. & W.
DOLD, Johann. *Schönwald.* 1810. Maker of boxwood watches.
DOLL, ——. *Paris.* 1812.
DOLLERY, J. *London.* an.1783. Watch.
DOLLEY—
Thomas. *London* (*Quakers Bdg.*). CC.1772 1792.
Thomas. *London.* l.CC.1796, m.CC.1808, d.1821.
John, son. *London.* l.CC.1804.
DOLLOND, ——. *London.* End 18c. Pedometer Ilbert coll.
DOLPHIN—
Robert. *London.* ca.1770. Watch.
Peter. *London.* an.1773. Watch.
DOLTON, John. *London.* a.1773, CC.1784.
DOMINICÉ—
——. *Geneva.* 1685.
——. *Paris.* an.1747. Watch.
DOMINICK—
Frederick. *Philadelphia.* 1768-74. C. & W.
Bernhardus. *Philadelphia.* 1775. W.
DOMINIQUE, Claude. *Paris.* 1657. Juré.
DOMINY—
Allen. *London.* an.1775. Watch.
——. *Devonport.* ca.1800.
DOMVILE—
Nathaniel. *Wilmslow.* d.1839.
Nathaniel, son. *Stockport.* 1820-42.
v. DUMVILLE.
DON—
Robert. *London.* a.1719.
James. *London.* an.1776. Watch.
George. *Glasgow.* 1804.
DONALD—
John. *London.* CC.1771.
James. *Edinburgh.* a.1815.
DONALDSON—
J. *London.* Late 18c. br. clock.
Thomas. *London.* 1799-1811.
Alexander. *Wigton.* 1810. l.c. clock.
G. *London.* Early 19c.

DONDAINE, Pierre Léonard. *Paris.* m. 1785-1789.
DONDENE, Jean. *Basle.* 1674. From *Geneva.*
DONDI DALL'OROLOGIO, Giovanni. *Padua.* b.1318, d.ca.1380. The most remarkable of early horologists. Professor of astronomy, medicine and logic in different universities. In 1364 completed, after 16 years' work, a clock and planetarium showing movements of sun, moon and planets, of which he left in MSS. a detailed description. ill Baillie. He was given the title of dall'Orologio, which his descendants bear to this day.
DONE—
William. *Manchester.* an.1778-95. W. & C.
William. *Worcester.* 1795. C.
DONELAN, James. *Philipstoun.* 1824.
DONISTHORPE—
George. *Birmingham.* 1755-1801. T.C. Made clock for Aston Hall. Watch and l.c. clock.
Joseph. *Normanton.* an.1770. Watch.
J. or G. *London.* an.1775, Watch.
William. *Loughborough.* an.1780. Watch.
Richard. *Loughborough.* 1791-5. C.
Groves. *Hinckley.* 1793-7. W.
Joseph. *Leicester.* 1794. C. & W.
J. *Loughborough.* an.1822. Watch.
DONKING, James. *Liverpool.* 1825. C.
DONNARD, ——. *Paris.* ca.1790. Crys. watch with train mounted in crys. and virgule esc. Ilbert coll.
DONNE—
Anthony. *London.* a.1707-49 CC.
Robert. *London.* a.1719, CC.1736-94.
Anthony, son of Ant. *London.* a.1742.
Robert, bro. *London.* a.1747.
& Bowen. *London.* an.1768. Watch.
Thomas. *London.* 1784. W.
Griffith. *London.* a.1794.
DONNINGTON, Richard. *London.* a.1783.
D'ONS-EN-BRAY, ——. *Bercy.* 1732. Metronome C.A. & M. Made clock wound by opening of a door.
DONZE, Johs. ——. Early 19c. sil. cal. watch.
DOOGAL & RUSSEL. *New York.* 1805.
DOOLITTLE, Isaac. *New Haven, U.S.A.* 1769-1810. C.
DOORE, Robert. *London.* a.1663, CC.1671-1684.
DOOREY—
Thomas. *London.* a.1758, CC.1766, d.1790.
John, son. *London* (*Tooley St.*). CC.1790-1812.
John George. *London.* CC.1816.
DOPPELMAYR, Johann Gabriel. *Nürnberg.* 1730. Pub. 'History of Nürnberg craftsmen.
DOR (DOHRN), Christoffel. *Marburg.* 1581. Made aut. clock for Rathaus. Fine table clock Cassel Landes-M.
DORCHESTER, James. *London.* an.1772. Watch.
DÖRCHINGER (DERCHINGER), Joseph. *Vienna.* m.1717.
DORE, Thomas. *London.* a.1753, CC.1765.
D'OREGNY, Robert. *Senlis.* 1381-97. C. to the duc d'Orléans.
DORER, Franz Joseph. *Kronstadt* (*Siebenbürgen*). 1826. Took out Austrian patent for winding a watch by a disk in the pendant. Regulator Hofburg, Vienna.
DORGUEIL, ——. *Toulouse.* 18c. Clock Gélis coll.
DORIA—
Antonio. *Venice.* 1795-1827. Keeper of clock of S. Marco and repaired it 1820.
Giovanni, son. *Venice.* b.1795-1860. Keeper of clock from 1827.
DORIN, Jacob. *Paris.* 1675 m.
DÖRING, N. *Konitz* and *Elbing.* 1780. d. 1785. Town C. in *Elbing* and, an.1780, in *Konitz.*
DORLEY, F. S. *London.* an.1781. Watch.
DORLING, Bilby. *Bury St. Edmunds.* 1775. W. l.c. clock.
DORMAN, John. *London.* an.1771. Watch.
DORMER—
James. *London* (*Whitecross St.*). a.1735, CC.1742-55.
P. *London.* ca.1800. Watch Glasgow Art Gall.
Edward. *London.* 1820. Watch Chamb. coll.
DORRELL (DORILL)—
Francis. *London.* CC.1702. d. an.1755. l.c. clocks.
John, son. *London* (*St. Giles, Cripplegate*). a.1725, CC.1732.
Francis, bro. *London* (*Whitecross St.*). a. 1731, CC.1755-80. br. clock.
William, son. *London* (*St. Martin-in-the-Fields* and *Bridgewater Sq.*). a.1768, CC. 1784-1810.
DORSCH, Christoph. *Fürth.* d.1702.
DORSET, William. *London.* ca.1790. Watch mt. S.K.M.
DORWES, ——. *London.* ca.1760. Sig. on watch Chamb. coll.
DOSSETT, Gregory. *London.* a.1651, CC. 1662-77.
DOTTERL (DÖTTERL), Sigmund. *Vienna.* m.1793.
DOTY, John F. *Albany, U.S.A.* 1813-22. W.
DOUBLET, David. *London.* a.1701.
DOUBROG, J. *London.* 1776. Skeleton watch.
DOUÉ, Edme. *Paris.* m.1770.
DOUFFNER—
Frans Savery. *Stockholm.* 1785-1819. Wooden C.
Fr. H., prob. son. *Stockholm.* 1815-20. Wooden C.
DOUGAL, George. *Edinburgh.* 1819.
DOUGHTY—
Tobias. *London.* a.1688, CC.1696.
John. *York.* 1772. W. & C.
John. *London.* an.1778. Watch.
William P. *London.* 1820.
DOUGLAS—
John. ——. an.1744. Watch.
James. *Edinburgh.* a.1759.
Robert. *Bolton-le-Moors.* ca.1770-95. Watch.
Robert. *Liverpool.* 1781-1824. W. cf. Duglass.
James. *Dundee.* 1794. Watch.
Robert. *Prescot.* 1795. C. & W.
Walter. *Dollar.* 1795.
Alexander. *Edinburgh.* 1817.
Samuel. *Liverpool.* ca.1820.
Walter. *Douglas.* 1820.
John W. *Hamilton, Bermuda.* Early 19c.
John. *Dumbarton.* 1824.
DOUGLASS—
John. *London.* an.1744. Watch.
James. *Chertsey.* 1768-91. Bankrupt.
John. *New Haven. U.S.A.* 1800-20.
DOULL, James. *Philadelphia.* 1825-49.
DOURDON, C. J. *Paris.* 1814-25.
DOUTA, Simon. *Gruyères.* 2nd half 17c. Lantern clock Virginia M.
DOUTREUVE, ——. *Paris.* 1818-25.
DOUTY, Henrick. *Philadelphia.* 1774.
DOUW, Simon. *Rotterdam.* 1658. Huygens proceeded against him for making pendulum clocks.
DOUXSAINT, James. *London.* a.1717.
DOVAL, ——. *La Brévine.* 1815-20. C.
DOVE—
Arthur. *London.* CC.1659-68. Watch.
Henry. *London.* CC.1667.
Robert. *London.* CC.1671.

DOVE—*continued.*
William. *London.* a.1701. Watch.
John. *London.* an.1765. Watch.
Joseph. *London.* an.1777. Watch.
DOVERDALE, Goddard. *London.* a.1699.
DOVERS, Robert. *Gloucester.* 1766. Went *Bath.* 1769. From *London.* C. & W. Watch Ilbert coll.
DOVEY, Thomas. *Worcester.* an.1820. Watch.
DOVILLE (DOUVILLE or **DORVILLE),** Noel. *Lyons.* 1529 m.-1546.
DOW, James. *London.* a.1792.
DOWARD, Thomas. *Manchester.* 1804. W.
DOWDNEY, Burrows. *Philadelphia.* 1768.
DOWELL—
John. *London.* a.1731.
Daniel. *Liverpool.* 1790-6. W.
DOWIG, George. *Baltimore.* 1784. W.
DOWLAND, ——. *London.* an.1772. Watch.
DOWN, ——. *London.* an.1784. Watch.
DOWNER, Theodore. *London.* a.1795.
DOWNES—
Christopher. *London.* CC.1632.
Jeremiah. *London.* a.1689.
John. *London (Hoxton).* a.1707-21.
Thomas. *London.* a.1714.
John. *London.* CC.1725.
John, son. *London (Norman St.).* a.1732, CC.1746, d.1774.
Arthur. *London (Dolphin Ct.).* 1743-70. W.
Arthur. *Charleston, U.S.A.* 1765-8.
Michael. *London.* 1781.
Roger. *London.* 1783.
Robert. *London (Clerkenwell).* an.1779-90. l.c. clock.
Robert. *London (Long Acre).* 1800-25. W.
John. *London (Clerkenwell).* 1799-1824.
John. *London (Bunhill Row).* 1802-08.
Joseph. *London (Clerkenwell).* a.1799-1808.
Robert. *London (Pentonville).* 1805-08.
DOWNEY, James. *Philadelphia.* Early 19c. Watch N.Y. Univ.
DOWNHAM, William. *London.* an.1783. Watch.
DOWNIE—
John. *Edinburgh.* 1745.
William. *Edinburgh.* a.1745, d.1776. mus. clock.
David. *Edinburgh.* 1812.
DOWNING—
Samuel. *Liverpool.* 1767, d.1788. W.
John. *Liverpool.* 1770-1807.
DOWNINGE, Humfrey. *London.* 1637-62.
DOWNS—
Valentine. *Louth.* 1791-5. C.
Benjamin. *Mansfield.* 1795-1801.
Ephraim. *Bristol, U.S.A.* 1825.
DOWNUM, Samuel. *Colchester.* 1751 went to *Sudbury.* C. & W.
DOWSE—
Gabriel. *London.* a.1649.
William. *London.* a.1713.
David. *London.* an.1776. Watch.
DOWSET—
John. *London.* a.1693.
Daniel. *London.* a.1702.
DOWSETT—
Thomas. *London.* a.1695.
Jeremiah. *London.* a.1701, CC.1708.
Charles. *Margate.* mar.1799 CC.
DOWSON—
Anthony. *London.* a.1699.
John. *London* and *Bath.* 1770-3. p.c. rep. watch G.M.
& ATKINSON. *Bath.* 1791.
William. *Halesworth.* 1795. W.
Ann. *Bath.* ca.1800.
DOYEN—
——. *Paris.* 1735 m.
Francois Jacques. *Paris.* m.1743.
DOYLE—
Edmund. *Kilkenny.* ca.1810-24. Watch mt. Dublin M.
John. *London.* 1820.
DRABBLE—
Joseph. *London.* 1720-80. br.clock.
Joseph, son. *London.* a.1795.
DRACQUES, J. *Nérac.* 1st half 17c. Fine watch in form fleur-de-lys, Louvre.
DRAKE—
John. *London.* 1629 BC.-1659. Watch Den. coll. Subscriber to incorporation of CC. The BC. in 1633 petitioned to disfranchise him.
Mark. ——. a.1753.
Richard. *Beaminster.* 1750. l.c. clock.
William. *London.* 1761-8.
William. *London.* a.1790.
Thomas. *London.* a.1794.
DRAPER—
Simeon. *London.* a.1688.
John. *London.* a.1695, CC.1703-26. l.c. clock M.M.A.
James. *London.* a.1704, CC.1712.
John. *London.* a.1732.
Paul. *London.* a.1749.
William. *London.* an.1767. Watch.
Charles. *London.* 1774. Watch Ilbert coll.
John. *Chelmsford.* 1775. W.
Thomas. *London.* an.1777. Watch.
John. *London.* a.1775.
John. *London (Gt. Sutton St.).* CC.1787, l.CC.1794.
William. *Maldon.* 1791-5. W.
George. *Manchester.* 1813. C.
DRAREG, In. *London.* ca.1720. Sig. on gilt metal watch. GERARD reversed, but no London maker of this name known.
DRAUDIUS, Georgius Clem. *Giessen.* 1732. Pub. book on old water clocks in Latin.
DRÄXINGER, Leopold. *Vienna.* m.1780.
DRAYCOTT—
Francis. *London.* a.1671, CC.1678.
John. *London.* a.1703.
John. *Hertford.* 1742. W.
DRAYSEY, John. *London.* a.1778, CC.1795-1813.
DRAYTON—
Thomas. *Chardstock.* b.1715, d.1788. C.
James, son. *Chard.* b.1742. C.
Thomas, son. *Chard.* C. b.1768. Succeeded his father.
DRECHSLER (DRESSLER), Paul. *Dresden.* 1653-68. Started the clockmakers' guild in *Dresden* in 1668. Perhaps of the same family as TRECHSLER.
DREIJER—
Herman. *Stockholm.* m.1709-49. Court C. Fine watch.
Erich, son. *Danzig.* 1733-7.
DREIZ, Lukas. *Königshofen-im-Grabfeld.* m. 1810.
DRESCHER—
Aron. *Rotterdam.* ca.1800.
Simon. *Manchester.* 1824-36. Watch mt. Platt Hall M.
DREW—
Robert. *Chester.* 1676. C.
Thomas. *London.* a.1671.
John. *London.* a.1676, CC.1684, d.1713. l.c. clock.
Edward. *London.* a.1683, CC.1692.
Thomas. *London.* a.1740.
Thomas. *London.* a.1754-1808.
Benjamin. *Shipton.* 1784.
Stephen. *London.* an.1792. Watch.
William. *London.* 1809-11.
Mary. *London.* 1817-24.
DREWER, James. *London.* 1727. W.
DREYER, Nicolaus. *Hamburg.* Early 18c. sil. watch.
DREYSS, ——. *Paris.* 1812.

DRIAEN, A. *Rotterdam.* ca.1625. Trav. clock Stern coll.
DRIE, Jean. *Paris.* 1675 m.
DRILLS, John. *London.* 2nd half 18c. Watch.
DRING, ——. *London.* an.1770. Watch.
DRINKWATER, John. *Liverpool.* 1777. W.
DRITCHLER—
John. *Leeds.* 1798. Wooden C.
John, & Co. *Manchester.* 1804.
DRIVER—
Richard. *London.* a.1696.
John. *London.* an.1762. Watch.
DROESHOUT, John. *London.* CC.1632.
DRON—
Pierre Frédéric. *Paris.* m.1776.
Alexandre Humbert. *Paris.* m.1776.
DRONDELLE, Laurent. *Geneva.* 1555. Refugee from *Paris.*
DRONGELEN, Willem Van. *Haarlem.* 1716.
DROSADE—
Samuel. *London.* CC.1675-95. Watch.
Robert, son. *London.* a.1695.
DROTZ, A. *Berlin.* 1806.
DROUOT—
——. *Paris.* (*Quai de la Grève*). 1807.
jeune. *Paris* (*Place Maubert*). 1807-24.
——. *Paris* (*Rue du Roule*). 1812.
DROUX, Jean. *Paris.* m.1683.
DROYER, Nicholas. *Hamburg.* 1st half 18c. Watch.
DROYNOT (DROUYNOT)—
Pierre. *Poitiers.* 1623.
——. *Poitiers.* Early 18c. Monstrance clock, set diamonds and stones, Grüne Gewölbe.
DROZ—
Jean Pierre. *Basle, Paris, La Ferrière* and *Chaux-de-Fonds.* b.1686, d.1764. A very fine C.; numerous complex l.c. and br. clocks in museums at Chaux-de-Fonds, Le Locle and Neuchâtel.
Pierre. *Chaux-de-Fonds.* 1719.
Abraham. *Chaux-de-Fonds.* a.1711-50.
Jean Jacques. *Hüningen.* 1720-44. From *Chaux-de-Fonds.*
Daniel. *Chaux-de-Fonds.* 1733-8. 'Maître horlogeur très expert.' Sd. 'Droz sur le Pont.' Fine br. clock Morges town hall.
Frederico. *Chaux-de-Fonds.* b.1729, d.1753.
Pierre Frédéric. *Le Locle.* b.1748. m. in *Paris.* 1776.
Jean Pierre. *Chaux-de-Fonds.* Late 18c. C. to the Bishop of Basle.
ET PERRET. *St. Imier.* End 18c. Watch N.Y. Univ.
(Henry Lewis Jaquet) & MAILLARDET (Henry). *London.* 1790 dissolve partnership. Mus. C.
Humbert. *Philadelphia.* 1796. d.1813. Also DROSS.
le jeune. *Rouen.* 1799. Watch.
Charles A. *Philadelphia.* 1808-41. Also DROSS.
Olivier. *Renan.* ca.1810.
Charles, & Sons. *Philadelphia.* 1813. Also DROSS.
——. *Paris.* 1819-24.
Jaquet, *v.* JAQUET-DROZ.
DROZ-DIT-BUSSET—
Daniel. *Chaux-de-Fonds.* 2nd half 17c. Complicated clock.
Adam, son. *Chaux-de-Fonds.* 1700-39. Many clocks.
Pierre Frédéric, son. *Chaux-de-Fonds.* b. 1723-70. Also at *Val-de-Travers. Berlin* in 1770.
Isaac. *Les Planchettes.* 1727.
Abram. *Chaux-de-Fonds.* 1752.
Daniel, son. *Chaux-de-Fonds.* a.1759-ca. 1780. br. clock.
DRUCKENBRODT, Urban. *Strasbourg.* ca. 1650. Fine sil. cal. watch.
DRUENNE, Charles. *Paris.* m.1788.
DRUET, Pierre. *Serrières.* 1674.
DRUMMOND—
Francis. *London.* a.1676 CC.
John. *Brechin.* 1789.
John. *Edinburgh.* 1794.
Thomas. *Liverpool.* 1818-29.
J. M. *London.* Early 19c. Watch.
DRURY—
James. *London.* a.1687, CC.1694, m.CC. 1728, d.1740. g. p.c. en. watch F.W.M. l.c. clock.
D. *London.* End 17c. Clock.
John, son of Jas. *London.* CC.1720-74.
James, son of John. *London* (*Clerkenwell*). a.1741, CC.1751, d.1811.
James Francis, son. *London.* a.1765.
William. *Banbury.* 1784.
——. *Oxford.* ca.1790 CC.
John Peter. *London.* CC.1811.
DRUSSUT, ——. *London.* 1635. Prob. same as DROESHOUT.
DRUYER, Charles Pierre. *Paris.* m.1785-1810.
DRYDEN, ——. *London.* Early 19c.
DRYER, Samuel. *London.* ca.1700. Watch Ilbert coll.
DRYSDALE—
James. *Edinburgh.* 1742.
Edward. *London.* a.1769.
William. *Edinburgh.* 1786. d.1823.
William. *Dunbar.* 1791. d.1839.
William. *Edinburgh.* 1812-23.
Walter Scott. *Edinburgh.* 1812-29.
William. *Philadelphia.* 1817-50.
DRYSELIUS, E. F. *Karlskrona.* 1825-37.
DUANCHAP, *v.* PANCHAUD.
DUAIME, Pierre. *Geneva.* ca.1770-91.
DUBAGERA, Claude. *Paris.* m.1780.
DUBANT, ——. *Grenoble.* ca.1690. Watch.
DUBARE, ——. *Neuchâtel.* ca.1660-1708. From *Geneva.*
DUBBAR, Hugh. *London.* a.1648.
DUBELLIS, G. *Marseilles.* ca.1700. Watch Gélis coll.
DUBEDAT, John. *London.* 1774.
DU BEZZY, Jean Baptiste. *Lyons.* a.1604.
DUBIÉ—
J. *Paris.* ca.1635. oct. crys. and topaz watch ill. Britten.
——. *Blois.* ca.1635. One of the earliest painters on enamel.
DUBIED—
D. *Les Geneveys.* ca.1800. Clock.
Abram Henri. *Chaux-de-Fonds.* 1811-13. C.
DUBOIS—
Jacob. *London.* a.1714, CC.1730.
Jacob. *Paris.* 1730. Watch N.Y. Univ.
Winand. *Liége.* ca.1740. l.c. clock.
Philippe. *Le Locle.* b.1738, d.1808. About 1770 exported wooden clocks into Germany.
——. *Brulon.* Mid. 18c. br. clock.
Daniel. *Le Locle.* 1752. C. rep. clock.
Germain. *Paris.* m.1757-89. Pillar clock Wallace coll. cal. watch Blot-Garnier coll.
François. *Paris.* m.1764-89.
David Frédéric. *Chaux-de-Fonds.* 1769-75. Associated with the JAQUET-DROZ.
FRÈRES. *Chaux-de-Fonds.* 1769-75. Firm with the preceding.
ET FILS. *Paris.* 1770-1800. c. secs. pirouette watch mt. G.M. Watch Wallace coll. rep. watch Chamb. coll.
A., aîné. *Chaux-de-Fonds.* ca.1770. sil. gilt en. watch.
Abram. *Le Locle.* 1777. Several small clocks.
Pierre. *Paris.* m.1778-89.
Philippe, et Fils. *Le Locle.* Founded 1785, and still in business. Watch S.M.S.K.
D. F. *Paris.* Late 18c. Prob. David Frédéric. g. en. watch.

DUBOIS—*continued.*
Samuel. *Le Locle.* 1792. Made mus. mechanism.
Charles François. *Chaux-de-Fonds.* b.1776, d.1848. Case painter and gilder of repute.
William. *New York.* 1805. W.
——. *Paris.* 1807-22. Successor to GERMAIN.
Fils. *Paris (Rue St. Honoré).* 1812.
——. *Paris (Rue de Nazareth).* 1812.
Charles Daniel. *Chaux-de-Fonds.* 1813. Maker of mus. watches.
Abram Louis. *Basle.* 1816. From *Chaux-de-Fonds.*
Justin. *Chaux-de-Fonds.* b.1802-38. C.
Frédéric William. *Le Locle.* b.1811, d.1869. Fine C. Several astro. clocks. Endeavoured to start industry of marine chrons.
Pierre. *Paris.* Wrote 'Histoire de l'Horlogerie,' 1849.
DUBOSC, Louis. *Rouen.* 1701 m.
DUBOULE—
——. *Paris.* 1552. C. to the city.
Martin. *Lyons.* 1603. comp. from *Geneva.* Watches Mallet coll. and Reichenberg M. sd. 'M. Duboule' prob. by him.
Jean Baptiste, son. *Geneva.* 1616-ca.1640. Large astro. watch B.M. Lion watch ill. Britten. Tulip watch Wallace coll. Death's-head watches Louvre and Olivier coll. Tulip watch Cluny M. Watches Webster and Mallett colls. ill Baillie.
Samuel Abraham. *Geneva.* ca.1750-75.
——. *London.* an.1777. Watch.
DUBOYS—
——. *Auxerre* ca.1650. Sil. crucifix watch. Ilbert coll.
Jean. *Lyons.* 1685.
DU BREUCQ, Andrieu. *Grantmont.* 1602. Repaired Cambrai Cathedral clock.
DUBREUIL, ——. *Beaugency.* ca.1750. g. en. watch Blot-Garnier coll.
DUBROCHET, Grégoire. *Lyons.* 1601. comp.
DUBROG, J. *London.* an.1765. Watch.
DUBUC—
aîné. *Paris.* ca.1780-1819. C. Supplied American market. Mantel clock, Palais de l'Élysée.
le jeune. *Paris.* ca.1807-12. C. Mantel clock, Ministère de la Guerre, Paris.
DUBUCQ, ——. *Paris.* 1818.
DUBUISSON—
Pierre. *Rouen.* a.1649.
Guillaume. *Paris.* 1771.
François. *Paris.* 1771.
——. *Paris.* End 18c. en. painter of watches and clock dials.
DUBUSC, James. *London.* a.1711.
DUCANE, ——. *London.* an.1758. Watch.
DUCASTEL, Isaac. *London.* CC.1703-14.
DUCELTE, Jean. *Paris.* 1773 m.
DUCHAFFAT, Anton. *Ulm.* mar. 1722, d.1745. French. inst. maker.
DUCHEMIN—
Ancelot. *Besançon.* 1439-61. Made clock for St. Jean.
Jean. *Besançon.* 1478-1514. Repaired clocks of St. Étienne and St. Jean.
Lyon. *Besançon.* 1523.
Pierre. *Besançon.* 1533-8.
Jean. *Brussels.* 1535-49. C. to Charles v.
Dr. *Rouen.* 1570. oct. crys. watch Bernal sale.
Timothée. *Lyons.* 1585 m.
Antoine Nicolas. ——. m.1739.
——. *Paris.* 1822-5.
DUCHENE—
——. *Geneva.* Late 18c.
ET CIE. *Geneva.* Late 18c. g. en. rep. watch set pearls.

DUCHENE—*continued.*
Luigi (Lous or Ls.), et Fils. *Geneva.* 1790-1820. g. spherical watch S.K.M. Watches with aut. F.W.M. and Fränkel coll. Lyre watch. 4-colour g. watches Carnegie M. and M.M.A. Egg-shaped watch.
Etienne. Prob. *Geneva.* Early 19c. Four-colour g. watch M.M.A.
——. *Paris (Rue de la Barillerie).* 1812.
Alexandre, et Cie. *Paris.* 1813-20.
FRÈRES ET CIE. *Geneva.* 1829.
DUCHER, Hans. *Nürnberg.* ca.1580. Dial B.M.
DUCHESNE—
——. *The Hague.* ca.1650. Made 'Haagsche Klokjes.'
Pierre. *Paris.* 1675 m.
Claude. *London.* 1689. CC.1693-1730. *Paris* an.1689. His equation clock desc. in Gallon, 'Machines et Inventions,' Vol. IV. Two fine cal. and mus. clocks Dresden M. l.c. and br. clocks. Regulator mt. C.A. & M. l.c. clock Virginia M.
Jérémie, son of Pierre. *Geneva.* 1702. Also DU CHÈNE.
François Houet. *Paris.* 1726. Juré 1735-41. One of the principal Paris makers. Watch B.M. 2 watches Fränkel coll.
F. *London.* ca.1730. Watch Ilbert coll.
Antoine. *Paris.* m.1739.
Johannes. *Amsterdam.* ca.1750. 2 fine l.c. clocks ill. Britten.
Jean Ursin. *Paris.* 1771 m.-1789.
DUCHY, ——. *London.* 1778.
DUCIMIN, Jacob. *Amsterdam.* ca.1630. Large oval watch M.M.A. Prob. one of the Rouen family DUCHEMIN.
DUCK—
Henry. *London.* a.1700.
Joseph. *London.* a.1709.
Richard. *London.* a.1727.
Richard. *Ipswich.* an.1742. Watch. l.c. clock. Prob. same as above.
G. *London.* ca.1750. en. vase with rep. watch Palace M., Peking.
Henry. *London.* an.1769. Watch.
DUCKLESS, John. *London.* a.1805.
DUCKWORTH, R. *Halifax.* d.1677. C.
DU CLAIR—
Claude. *Lyons.* mar. 1625, d.1649. crys. cross watch Côte coll. ill. Vial & Côte.
Jean Baptiste, son of DU CLAIR-VALLIER. *Lyons.* b.1657-94.
DU CLAIR-VALLIER—
Jean Baptiste. *Lyons.* b.ca.1636, m.1652, d.1699. Grandson of Jean VALLIER.
Jean Baptiste, son. *Lyons.* b.1657-94.
DUCLARDG, ——. *London.* 1535. 'To a Frenchman called Duclardg for 3 dials and a clock 15 li.' Privy Purse Expenses.
DU CLÉRON—
Claude. *Lyons.* 1593 m. d.1637. Maker of repute. Watch M.M.A. ill. Vial & Côte.
Floris, son. *Lyons.* b.1604-59 m.
DUCLOS, ——. *Paris.* 1820. Made clocks of papier-mâché called 'Carthorloges.'
DUCLOSIER, Pierre. *Paris.* m.1675.
DUCLOUX, Moyse. *Paris.* m.1758-64.
DUCOMMUN—
Jean Jacques. *Chaux-de-Fonds.* 1723-50. C.
Jonas Frédéric. *Chaux-de-Fonds.* b.1727, d.1798. C.
J. P. *London.* 1756. Watch, jasper case, Stern coll.
Jean Pierre. *Chaux-de-Fonds.* 1740-1804. rep. and mus. clocks.
Jonas Pierre. *Chaux-de-Fonds.* b.1743, d. 1816. Very able maker. Numerous sd. clocks. Also at *Le Locle.*
Aimé, son. *Chaux-de-Fonds.* b.1760, d.1811. Regulators.

DUCOMMUN—*continued.*
Jean Frédéric. *Chaux-de-Fonds.* 1757-85. C.
Charles. *Chaux-de-Fonds.* 1779. C.
FRÈRES *Chaux-de-Fonds.* 2nd half 18c. br. clock.
Jonas Frédéric. *Chaux-de-Fonds.* 1785.
Balthazard. *Chaux-de-Fonds* and *Fontaines.* 1790.
David Louis. *La Brévine.* 1790. C.
A. L. *Philadelphia.* 1796.
——. *Paris.* 1812.
Abraham, et Cie. *Philadelphia.* Early 19c. Lever watch Gélis coll.
Henry. *Philadelphia.* 1819-50.
Henri. *Chaux-de-Fonds.* b.1798, d.1826. Several Louis XVI clocks.

DUCOMMUN-DIT-BOUDRY—
Abram. *Chaux-de-Fonds.* 1680. d.1729. Made very complex aut. clock.
Pierre. *Chaux-de-Fonds, Yverdon, Neuchâtel* and *Lausanne.* b.1680, d.1760. Reputed maker of turret and complicated clocks. Made clocks for Yverdon and Payerne. l.c. clock Vieux-Vevey M.
David, bro. *Chaux-de-Fonds* and *Yverdon.* b.1682, d.1762.
Jean Pierre. *Chaux-de-Fonds.* b.1690, d. 1762. l.c. clock.
Abram, son of Abram. *Chaux-de-Fonds* and *Les Brenets.* b.1700, d.1755.
Philippe, son of David. *Yverdon.* b.1720-49.
Frédéric. *Madrid.* 1756-8.
Frédéric. *Chaux-de-Fonds.* 1761-74. C.
Daniel. *Chaux-de-Fonds.* 1774. d.ca.1779. C.
François. *Chaux-de-Fonds.* b.1763, d.1839. A famous maker. Several planetary mts. in Neuchâtel and Chaux-de-Fonds M.

DUCOMMUN-DIT-PETITJEAN—
Jean Pierre. *Chaux-de-Fonds.* b.1713, d. 1751.
Jonas Pierre. *Chaux-de-Fonds.* b.1725, d. 1794.

DUCOMMUN-DIT-TINNON—
Daniel. *Chaux-de-Fonds.* 1716-66. Turret and house C. of repute.
Jean Pierre, bro. *Chaux-de-Fonds.* 1739-49. C.
Frédéric, bro. *Chaux-de-Fonds.* 1739-ca. 1790. T.C.
Abram Louis, son of Daniel. *Chaux-de Fonds.* b.1721, d.1819. Turret C.
Daniel, bro. *Chaux-de-Fonds.* 1772. Turret C.
Ferdinand. *Chaux-de-Fonds.* 1753. C.

DUCOMMUN-DIT-VERRON, Jonas Pierre. *Chaux-de-Fonds.* b.1727, d.1787.
Abram Louis. *Chaux-de-Fonds.* *v.* DUCOMMUN-DIT-VERRON FRÈRES, but worked alone in 1745.
Charles. *Chaux-de-Fonds.* *v.* DUCOMMUN-DIT-VERRON FRÈRES.
FRÈRES. *Chaux-de-Fonds.* 1750-89. A very important firm of the three men above. Many clocks.
Jean Jacques. *Chaux-de-Fonds.* b.1756, d. 1811. C.
David. *Chaux-de-Fonds.* 1781. Maker of carillons for clocks.
Ami. *Chaux-de-Fonds.* 1806-29. Fine C.

DUCOMUN, Ferdinand Louis. Prob. *Switzerland.* Early 19c. g. en. watch.

DUCOMUN - DIT - BOUDRILE, Charles. Prob. *Switzerland.* End 18c. cal. watch mt. G.M.

DU CONSEIL—
Jean. *Rouen.* 1426-8. Repaired the clock of the Archeveché.
Jacques. *Rouen.* 1431. Repaired the clock of the Archeveché.

DU COTY (DU COSTY)—
——. *Paris.* ca.1750 m.
Nicolas Garcil. *Paris.* m.1758-89.

DUCRET—
Matthieu. *Les Montagnes Neuchâteloises.* 1700. Wooden C.
——. *Paris.* 1812.

DUCROQ, Guillaume. *Rouen.* a.1654.

DUDDERIDGE, ——. *London.* an.1789. Watch.

DUDDS—
Joseph. *London.* CC.1732, l.CC. 1766-70. l.c. lacquer clock. crys. watch and chatelaine, Winter Pal. Petrograd.
James. *London.* an.1762. Watch.

DUDIOTT, James. *London.* 1622. Alien. Prob. DUDUICT.

DUDLEY, ——. *Philadelphia.* 1784.

DUDRIER, Joseph Florimond. *Paris.* m. 1750.

DUDSON, Simon. *London.* a.1647, CC.1654.

DUDUICT—
Jacques. *Blois.* mar.1599, retired 1645. str. watch G.M. Pub. in 1631 'Nouveau sciatère pour fabriquer toutes sortes d'horloges solaires.'
Daniel, bro. *Blois* and *Paris.* mar. 1604, d.1636. In *Paris,* 1628-34. en. watch B.M.
Jacques, son of Jacques. *Blois.* 1621. d.1631.

DUE, William. *London.* a.1701.

DUEBER-HAMPDEN WATCH CO. *Canton, Ohio.* Succeeded the HAMPDEN WATCH Co. of Springfield, Mass., U.S.A., which had watches sd. 'Perry' ca.1880, 'Hayward' ca.1881, 'State Street' ca.1881.

DUER, Pierre. ——. ca.1640. Watch B.M.

DUET, Pierre. *Paris.* ca.1730. Watch M.M.A.

DUFALGA, Ppe. *Geneva.* 1775. g. en. watches Mallet and Gélis colls.

DU FAY, ——. *Paris.* 1727. Pub. desc. of an equation clock in Mém. de l'Acad. R. des Sciences.

DU FEY, Nicolas. *Rouen.* 1701 m.

DUFF—
James. *Edinburgh.* 1758-74.
David. *Edinburgh.* 1806.
James. *Burntisland.* 1812.
James. *London.* CC.1819. W.

DUFFEE, ——. *London.* an.1790. Watch.

DUFFET—
John. *Bristol.* 1767.
Charles, son. *Bristol.* 1774.
Elizabeth. *Bristol.* ca.1780. Watch.

DUFFIELD, Edward. *Philadelphia.* 1741, d. 1803. C.

DUFFILL, William. *London.* a.1771.

DUFFNER—
Johann. *Schönwald.* b.1673. One of the first C. in the Schwarzwald.
Anton. *Furtwangen.* b.1752, d.1832. mus. C. of repute. mus. clock Furt. M.

DUFGATE, Francis. *Holt* (*Norfolk*). 1784-95. W.

DUFLOS, Louis Jacques. *Paris.* m.1784-1825.

DUFOSSÉ, Pierre Antoine. *Paris.* m.1752.

DUFOUR—
Abraham, ——. ca.1630. Watch F.W.M.
Pierre. *Paris.* ca.1630. Watch Bernal sale.
Jacques, ——. ca.1650. Fine en. cal. watch.
Henri. *Blois.* 1662. d.1689. Watch.
Denis. *Blois.* ca.1670.
Isaac. *Geneva.* 1684. Watch.
Paul. *Geneva.* End 17c.
——. *Paris.* ca.1700. Watch B.M. ill. Baillie.
Jean Jacques. *Geneva.* b.1732-68.
——. *London.* Mid. 17c. Fine watch, outer case lapis-lazuli, set diamonds, Winter Pal. Petrograd.
L. *Geneva.* ca.1770-1800. en. watch, set pearls and diamonds, F.W.M. Large al. watch Den. coll.

DUFOUR—*continued.*
ET CERET. *Ferney.* 1770. Managed the MANUFACTURE ROYALE DE FERNEY.
CERET & CIE. *Ferney.* 1770. en. watch with portrait of le maréchal de Saxe.
Jacques Léon. *Paris.* m.1782-9.
Philippe. *Geneva.* 1784-1810. Then went to *Milan*; returned *Geneva* ca.1825, and founded firm of GABAREL & DUFOUR. d. 1850.
——. *Cartigny.* 1785.
——. *Constance.* 1787.
——. *Geneva.* ca.1800. Painter on enamel.
——. *Paris.* 1812.
DUGARD, ——. *Paris.* 1813-24.
DUGAY, ——. *Paris.* 1812.
DUGGAN—
Thomas. *Liverpool (Dawson St.).* 1781. W.
Thomas. *Liverpool (Dock).* 1781. W.
DUGLASS, Robert, & Co. *Liverpool.* ca.1820. cf. DOUGLAS.
DUGMORE, ——. *London.* an.1772. Watch.
DUGRANDMESNIL—
——. *Paris.* 1735 m.
Claude. *Paris.* m.1743.
Claude Antoine, son. *Paris.* m.1765.
DUGUÉ—
——. *Paris.* Early 17c. Oval watch with sundial Ilbert coll. Prob. DUGUET.
Pierre Charles. *Paris.* m.1717-89.
DUGUET, Jehan. *Paris.* 1606 juré.
DUHAMEL—
Clément. *Rouen.* 1601-17. Watch. Repaired clock of St. Maclou.
Pierre. *Blois.* Early 17c. *Geneva,* 1663. crys. cross watch École d'Horlogerie, Geneva, and sq. watch.
Pierre. *Paris* and *Geneva.* ca.1650-86. en. watch. ill. Baillie. Prob. the preceding.
Barthélemi. ——. ca.1700. Watch.
Isaac. *London.* 1731-55. 3-case watch G.M. Clock Buckingham Palace.
Pierre. *Paris.* 1791.
DU HOCQ, Michel. *Paris.* 1675 m.
DUILLIER *v.* FACIO.
DU JARDIN, Jehan. *Blois.* 1530-47. C. to François I. Re-made Angers Cathedral clock in 1544.
DUJARDIN, ——. *Versailles.* ca.1700. Boulle br. clock.
DUKE—
Nathaniel. *London.* a.1656, CC.1663.
Joseph. *London.* a.1666, CC.1682-1706.
Joseph. *London.* CC.1671.
Joseph, son. *London.* CC.1728.
George. *London.* an.1806. Watch.
William. *Kingston.* Early 19c.
DUKES, John. *London.* a.1796.
DUKEY, William. *London.* an.1757. Watch.
DUKKE, Frederik. *Copenhagen.* 1797.
DULIN—
William Thomas. *London.* CC.1816-30. Watch N.Y. Univ.
William Ephraim, son. *London.* a.1821.
DULIS, Pieter. *Amsterdam.* 18c.
DU LUC—
Jean Baptiste. *Paris.* m.1771-1811.
Veuve. *Paris.* 1812.
DU MAS, Anthoine. *Paris.* 1544-7. Founder member of Paris corporation.
DUMAS, Jean Daniel. *La Brévine.* 1793. C.
DUMBELL—
Joseph. *Liverpool.* 1800-29. W.
Joseph. *Kirkdale.* 1813. W.
Thomas. *Kirkdale.* 1816. W.
Thomas. *Rochdale.* ca.1820. Watch Oldham M.
John. *Liverpool.* 1825. Watch N.Y. Univ.
DUMESNIL, Anthony. *Boston, U.S.A.* 1796-1807. W.
DUMILOW, William. *Coventry.* 1702. W.
DÜMMLER, Conrad. *Fürth.* d.ca.1813.
DUMOCK, N. *Stockport.* ca.1800. Watch.
DUMONT—
David. *Rouen.* m.1663.
FRÈRES (Claude Guillaume and Pierre François). *Besançon.* 1693-1726. The most famous makers of Besançon. Made clock on Hôpital St. Jacques in 1704. Watches Besançon M. and Fränkel coll. Three fine Boulle br. clocks.
Jean Pierre. *Hauts-Geneveys.* 1778.
J. F. *Rouen.* 1789. In charge of town clock.
Charles François. *La Brévine.* 1815-20. C.
DUMONT-SANDOZ, David Louis. *La Brévine* and *Ronde-Chaux.* b.1783, d .1857. Several clocks.
DUMONT-DIT-VIELJEAN, Daniel. *Chaux-de-Fonds.* 1734-52.
DUMONT - DIT - VUATEL, David Louis. *Chaux-de-Fonds.* 1727. C.
DUMVILLE, John. *Nether Alderley.* d.1797.
DUN—
Henry. *London.* CC.1677.
William. *Glasgow.* 1779-1803. In firm of NAPIER & DUN.
DUNANT—
Louis. *Lyons.* 1640 m.-1649.
David. *Grenoble.* 1654. From *Geneva.*
William. *London.* an.1760-5. en. watch.
DUNBALL, Richard. *London.* a.1786, CC. 1793, l.CC.1812-15.
DUNBAR—
James. *Edinburgh.* a.1710.
George. *London.* 2nd half 18c. Watch mt.
Butler. *Bristol, U.S.A.* 1810-15. Made wooden wall clocks with Titus Herriman.
James. *Perth.* 1820.
George. *Cootehill.* 1824.
DUNBARTON, ——. *London.* an.1772. Watch.
DUNBILL (DUMBILL), Joshua. *Prescot.* Early 19c. Watch.
DUNCAN—
Robert. *London.* a.1716.
Andrew. *Edinburgh.* a.1727.
Thomas. *Edinburgh.* a.1729.
& ROBERTS. *London.* an.1758. Watch.
James. *London (Chancery Lane).* 1780-1819. Watch Chamb. coll.
Alexander. *Elgin.* 1785.
James. *Old Meldrum.* 1785-95.
Thomas. *London.* an.1792. Watch.
George. *London.* ca.1800. Watch.
James. *London (St. James's St.).* 1805-25.
Robert. *London.* Late 18c.-1815. Watches N.Y. Univ. and Ilbert coll.
Andrew. *Aberdeen.* 1824.
James. *London (Old Bond St.).* 1824. Watch.
Archibald. *Antrim.* 1824.
John. *Antrim.* 1824.
John. *Kilileigh.* 1824.
——. *Omagh.* 1824.
DUNCKS, Thomas. *London.* a.1722.
DUNCOMBE—
George. *London.* a.1719.
Richard. *London.* a.1760, CC.1770, l.CC. 1775.
Richard. *London.* w.CC.1795, m.CC. 1798.
DUNDAS, James. *Edinburgh.* a.1710.
DUNDASS, Robert. *Dartmouth.* an.1788. Watch.
DUNESME, Maurice (or Marie) Jean Claude Legoix. *Paris.* m.1762-89.
DUNG, ——. *London.* an.1770. Watch.
DUNHEIM, Andrew. *New York.* 1775.
DUNKERLEY, ——. *London.* 1785. W.
DUNKERTON, Robert. *London.* a.1738. Watch.
DUNKLEY—
Benjamin. *London (Tooting).* 1770-1804. l.c. clock.
William. *London.* a.1763.

DUNKLEY—*continued.*
Thomas. *London (Hounslow).* 1795-1811. W.
William. *London (Goswell St.).* 1805-20.
J. *London (Bethnal Gr. Rd.).* Early 19c. T.C.

DUNLOP—
Andrew. *London.* CC.1701-32. g. rep. watch S.M.S.K. Watches Den. coll. Turret clock.
Conyers. *London.* a.1725, CC.1733, m.CC. 1758, d.1779. g. en. rep. watch G.M. g. rep. watch Den. coll.
Alexander. *London.* an.1745. Watch.
Anne. *London.* Mid. 18c. Watch.
Charles. *London.* a.1733-ca.1750. cyl. watch mt. Buckley coll.
J. Sonly. ——. ca.1770. Watch mt. Buckley coll.
Christopher. *London.* an.1772. Watch.
Stephen. *London.* an.1778. Watch.
Conyers. *London.* 1790-3.

DUNN—
Henry. *London.* CC.1677.
Benjamin. *London.* a.1691.
Benony. *London.* a.1691.
Hugh. *London.* a.1716.
Anthony. *London.* CC.1719-36.
William. *London.* an.1761. Watch.
Malcolm. *Edinburgh.* 1764.
Charles. *London (Fleet Mkt.).* CC.1773-96.
Samuel. *London.* 1787. Pub. Tables for finding the longitude by Timekeepers.
Francis. *Dublin.* 1795. W.
Robert. *London.* 1799.
——. *Bolton.* Early 19c. Watch.
Thomas. *Berwick-on-Tweed.* 1820.
John. *Hull.* 1823-36.

DÜNNEBIER—
Ehrenfried. *Dresden.* m.1703, d.1736. p.c. watch Ilbert coll.
Johann Christoph. *Dresden.* m.1721.

DUNNING, C. *London.* Late 18c. Watch.

DUNOD—
Prosper. *Besançon.* 1599.
Claudio. *Munich.* 1679-96. Court C.
Claude. *Düsseldorf.* 1711-14. Sundial maker. Compass dial with geared minute dial M.M.A.

DUNOIS, ——. *Paris.* 1768.

DUNSFORD, Martin. *Ashburton.* 1787. l.c. clocks.

DUNST, Carl. *Munich.* 18c. Small brass br. clock Feill coll.

DUNSTAN, James. *Falmouth.* 1784. W.

DUNSTER—
Charles or Daniel. *London.* a.1695.
Roger. *London.* ca.1700. Watch and br. clock Stads M. Amsterdam.
R. *Amsterdam.* Early 18c. l.c. clock. Watch en. Huaut Frères.

DUNSTON, Paul. *London.* a.1687.

DUNYS, Pierre. *Rouen.* ca.1500. Remade clock of Fécamp church.

DUPAN, ——. *Paris.* Mid. 18c. Fine ormolu clock.

DUPARC, —— *Paris.* 1812-23.

DUPAS, ——. *Paris.* 1810-55. Mantel clock.

DUPASQUIER—
Jonas. *Fleurier.* 1739-66.
Jean Jacques. *Paris.* a.1767.
François. *Paris.* m.1776-89.

DUPENGOLD, Paul. *London.* 1764.

DUPERCHE, ——. *Paris.* 1818-24.

DUPERRET, Daniel Henri. *La Brévine.* b. 1767-86. C.

DUPIAT (DUPIAZ), Jacques. *Geneva.* ca. 1770-94. *v.* FLESSIÈRES.

DUPIN, Paul. *London* and *Geneva.* ca.1710-1767. 3-case rep. watch repoussé by Moser, G.M. rep. watch B.M. rep. watch, set stones, F.W.M. l.c. clock.

DUPLESSIS, Guillaume Louis. *Paris.* 1772.

DUPLEX, ——. Prob. *Geneva.* Early 19c. comp.

DUPLOCK—
Charles. *London (Southwark).* 1790-1819. Watch G.M. br. clock.
& WIGGINS. *London (Southwark).* 1817-25. W. & C.

DUPNEY, Adrian. *Plymouth.* 1734.

DUPNY, Stephen. *London.* a.1734.

DUPONCHEL, Guillaume. *Paris.* Juré 1739-1745.

DUPONT—
——. *Castres.* ca.1650. cal. watch B.M. Watch, with sundial and compass, Bernal sale.
Peter. *London (Ivy Lane).* 1754-70. l.c. clock.
Samuel. *Paris.* 1755. C. to the King. Made clock dials of painted glass to imitate enamel; method approved by Acad. R. des Sciences. Cartel clock.
Paul. *London (Ivy Lane).* 1760-90. Watch G.M.
Antoine. *Geneva.* ca.1770-90.
Jean Jaques. *Geneva.* ca.1775-91.
F. P. *Rotterdam.* Late 18c.
——. *London (Bedford Sq.).* 1794.
Charles. *London (Cockspur St.).* From 1797. RECORDON & C. DUPONT bought Josiah EMERY's business in 1795. Recordon retired end of 1796 and Dupont carried on alone. Made watches for China.
FRÈRES. *Geneva.* Early 19c. g. en. watch M.P.S. Dresden.
——. *Paris.* 1813.
J. P. *Rotterdam.* 1821-30.

DUPPA, Charles. *London.* a.1646.

DUPPE, ——. *Gorinchem.* ca.1800.

DUPRÉ—
Léonard. *Paris.* 1544-7. Founder member of Paris corporation.
——. *Abbeville.* 1772.
——. *Paris.* 1812.

DUPREE, Elias.] *Holland.* 1635.

DUPUIS—
Jean. *Paris.* 1675 m.
Jean. *Amsterdam.* 1682. Huguenot refugee from Dieppe.
Jean Laurent. *Paris.* m.1772.
J. L. *Amsterdam.* Late 18c. Prob. Jean Laurent. Watch Stads M. Amsterdam.
Louis Jacques. *Yverdon.* a.1791. C.
——. *Paris.* 1809-17.

DU PUY—
Jean. ——. 1525. Made clock for Mormoiron (Avignon).
Gilles. *Geneva.* 1573. Refugee from *Rheims.*

DUPUY—
Benoist. *Paris.* 1675 m.
Jacques. *Paris.* Went to *Neuchâtel* 1688. d.1696. Watch Ilbert coll. marked Neuchâtel.
Audran. *London.* a.1713.
Adrian. *Plymouth.* mar. 1734. W. Prob. the preceding.
Odran. *Philadelphia.* 1735. Perhaps the preceding.
Stephen. *London.* a.1734.
Louis. *Verrières.* 1755.
John. *Philadelphia.* 1770-1803. C. & W.
John. *Reading, Pa., U.S.A.* 1777. W.

DUQUESNE, ——. *Paris.* ca. 1700. sil. al. watch Carnegie M.

DUQUET—
Étienne. *Rouen.* m.1658.
——. *France.* 1733. Devised a water clock, desc. in Gallon, 'Machines et Inventions.' Vol. VI.

DURADE, Abel. *Geneva.* Early 18c. In *Holland.* ca.1770. en. watch. Watch Besançon M.

DURAND—
Jacques. *Blois.* m.1605. *Romorantin* in 1625. d.an.1632.
Pierre. *Rouen.* m.1617.
Jacques. *Blois.* comp. 1639.
Jean. *Rouen.* Juré 1649. Also DURANT. Fine g. watch en. flowers.
Jean Louis. *Geneva.* End 17c. Painter on enamel. Watch Gélis coll.
Pierre. ——. ca.1680. al. watch, 3 cases Ilbert coll.
——. *London.* ca.1700. sil. watch, set carnelians.
Pierre, *Paris.* m.1772-89. sil. watch Fränkel coll.
Pierre. *Paris.* m.1777.
——. *Paris* (*Rue du Mont Blanc*). 1807-12.
DURANDEAU, Philip. *London.* a.1775.
DURANT—
P. *Rouen.* ca.1590-ca.1610. oct. watch Louvre. Oval eng. watch. Cast sil. shell watch Ilbert coll.
Oswald. *London.* 1630. w.CC.1645. d.an. 1655. Petitioner for incorporation of CC. Book watch Blot-Garnier coll.
John. *London.* a.1633.
Richard. *London.* a.1784.
William. *Yarmouth.* 1795.
——. *Paris* (*Rue du Mont Blanc*). 1807-09.
Veuve. *Paris* (*Rue du Mont Blanc*). 1815-21.
——. *Paris* (*Rue de la Chaussée d'Antin*). 1822-4.
Veuve. *Paris* (*Rue de la Chaussée d'Antin*). 1825.
DURDENT, Andrew. *London.* a.1655, CC. 1662.
DUREPORT—
——. *Paris.* 1685 m.
Jean Baptiste, son. *Paris.* m.1692.
DURER, A. *Germany.* 17c. Dial M.M.A.
DURHAM—
Stephen. *London.* a.1716.
William. *Edinburgh.* a.1809-50.
William. *Dunbar.* 1820.
DÜRING, Christoph. *Berlin.* 1785-92. cf. DIRING.
DÜRINGER, Hans. *Dantzig.* 1464, d.1477. astro. clock in St. Marienkirche.
DURKS, Rinse. *Grouw.* 1750. d.1787. br. clock Friesch M.
DURNASSIO, Gregorio. *Genoa.* 1364. Second keeper of Genoa clock.
DÜRNER, ——. *Oberhausen.* 1756 comp.
DURONAT, François. *Paris.* 1609 juré.
DU ROUSSEL, ——. *Geneva* and *Neuchâtel.* 1758.
DURRAN, J. H. *Banbury.* Early 19c.
DURRAND, P. *London.* Early 19c. cyl. watch S.M.S.K.
DURRANT—
Charles. *England.* 1544. French.
Richard. *London.* Early 19c. Watch.
——. *Beccles.* Early 19c. Watch.
DÜRRSTEIN, Johannes and Friedrich, brothers who founded the Union Uhrenfabrik in *Glashütte* in 1885.
DURSEN, William. *London.* 1784 l.CC.
DURU—
Guillaume. *Blois.* comp. 1642.
——. *Paris.* 1650-ca.1700. al. watch Den. coll.
——. *Paris.* 1812.
DURVAL, Gédéon. *Paris.* m.1746.
DURWARD, Joseph. *Edinburgh.* 1775-1819.
DUSEIGNEUR, Pierre. *Geneva.* Late 18c. g. cyl. rep. watch.
DUSSAU, ——. *Paris.* 1807-10.
DUTACH, John. *London.* 1662.
DUTCH, Stephen. *Boston, U.S.A.* 1800-18. W.
DUTCHBOURNE, Allen. *London.* a.1750.
DUTEMPS, Claude. *Blois.* End 17c.
DUTENS—
——. *Paris.* ca.1700. Watch M.P.S. Dresden.
Peter. *London.* 1743-ca.1760. rep. watch mt. G.M. Fine g. p.c. repoussé watch.
George. *London.* Mid.18c. Watch M.M.A.
DUTERRAU—
Daniel. *London.* 1752.
James. *London.* an.1770. Watch.
v. PERIGAL & DUTERRAU.
DUTERTRE—
Jean Baptiste. *Paris.* 1715-42. An eminent maker. Invented duplex escapement with two balances geared together. Said by his contemporaries to have devised the first free escapement for watches. A marine timekeeper with two geared pendulums desc. in Gallon, 'Machines et Inventions,' Vol. v. Many watches. g. watch, set diamonds, emeralds and rubies, M.M.A. Very small watch Chamb. coll. Marine clock with two pendulums C.A. & M. Made two fine en. watches for the Russian Court. Bronze case clock.
Charles. ——. 1720. Trav. clock, Turkish figures.
Jean Abraham, son of Jean B. *Paris.* m.1739.
Nicolas Charles, bro. *Paris.* b.1715, m.1739, juré 1775, d.1793. His equation clock desc. in Gallon, 'Machines et Inventions,' Vol. VII.
Jean Pierre. *Paris.* m.1757.
Charles, son of N. C. *Paris.* m.1758. Ormolu clock S.K.M.
Jean Baptiste. *Paris.* m.1758.
DU THUILLAY, ——. *Hall.* 1738. Watch S.K.M. set in mother-of-pearl plaque with stones and cameos. Watch Gotha M.
DUTOUR—
Jean Baptiste Gervais. *Paris.* m.1767-89.
Étienne Anne, son. *Paris.* m.1775.
DUTRAMBLE, ——. *Geneva.* 1818. Springmaker who sd. his springs.
DUTTON—
Edmund. *London.* a.1737, CC.1744.
William. *London.* a.1738, CC.1746, l.CC. 1766-94. Partner with MUDGE, and succeeded him in 1771. l.c. clock ill. Britten.
Benjamin. *London.* an.1776. Watch.
W. & SONS. *London.* ca.1775. rep.cyl. watch mt. Ilbert coll.
Matthew, son of William. *London* (*Fleet St.*). a.1771, CC.1779, m.CC.1800-25. *v.* Thomas.
William. *London.* a.1773.
Thomas. *London.* a.1776, CC.1791, l.CC. 1796-9. Partner with Matthew.
John. *Liverpool.* 1780-1829. W.
Samuel. *Huxley.* Late 18c. Watch mt. Grosvenor M. Chester.
Thomas. *Bath.* ca.1790 CC.
Junior. *London.* ca.1795. Watch mt. Ilbert coll.
& SONS. *London.* 1795-1824. l.c. clock ill. Cec. & Web.
Matthew and Thomas. *London.* 1799-1804. l.c. clock Weth. coll.
Matthew, son of Matthew. *London.* a.1799, CC.1815.
Matthew, & Sons. *London.* 1815-25. W. & C.
DUUS, Simon. *Hamburg.* Late 16c. Made clock for the mother of Christian IV of Denmark.
DU VAL (DUVAL)—
Jean Gaspard. ——. ca.1600. oct. crys. watch M.M.A. crys. shell watch Spitzer sale.
J. B. *Paris.* Juré 1613. en. watch F.W.M. by him or Gabriel.
Gabriel. *Paris.* 1675 m., juré 1684. Prob. same as Gabriel DE VAL.

DU VAL (DUVAL)—*continued.*
Robert. *Rouen.* m.1673.
Ozias. *Paris.* 1680 m.
François. *Paris.* m.1680. Watch S.K.M. by him or one of preceding.
Nicolas, son of Robert. *Rouen.* m.1696.
Frédéric. ——. *Paris.* Early 18c. Boulle br. clock.
Gédéon. *Paris.* ca.1745. br. clock Nat. M. Stockholm.
Abraham. *Paris.* 1749 m.
Jean Michel. *Paris.* m.1752.
Henry. *Paris.* d.1773.
Benoît. *Paris.* m.1771-89.
——. *Rouen.* Juré 1774-8.
Jean, et Fils et Cie. *London.* Late 18c. Ring watch Den coll.
Auguste. *Neuchâtel.* 1793.
Frédéric. *Paris.* Early 19c. 4-colour g. watch Fränkel. coll.
——. *Paris (Rue du Temple).* 1812.
Aîné. *Paris (Quai Pelletier).* 1813-25.
——. *Paris (Quai de la Mégisserie).* 1814-23.

DUVAN, ——. *Paris.* 1824.

DUVAUX, ——. *Dole.* 18c. Made a clock for Pesmes.

DU VERGER, Jean. *Lyons.* 1436. d.1453.

DUVERNOIS, ——. *Paris.* Late 18c. Specialized in ring watches.

DUVERNOY, David Frédéric. *Paris.* m. 1776.

DU VIVIER—
François. *Rouen.* 1759-64. Double virgule watch mt. Ilbert coll.
L'aîné et fils. *Rouen.* Late 18c. g. rep. watch Gélis coll.

DUVOYE, ——. *Paris.* 1824. C.

DUWALL, Axel Johan Diedric. *Sala* b.1787, d.1847.

DUXBURY—
Edmond. *London.* a.1675.
Daniel. *London.* a.1696.

DWERRIHOUSE (D WERRYHOUSE)—
Thomas. *Garston.* 1774. Watch S.M.S.K.
John. *London (Charles St.).* an.1773. CC. 1781-1805. br. clocks. Watch No. 1948 dated 1789 Ilbert coll.
& CARTER. *London.* 1802-23. br. clock Weth. coll. and ill. Cec. & Web. Watch mt.
CARTER & SON. *London.* 1808-15. cyl. p.c. watch S.M.S.K.
CARTER & CO. *London (Davies St.).* 1825. sil. lever watch G.M.
& OGSTON. *London (Davies St.).* 1836. Also OGSTON & BELL.
& BELL. *London.* 1840.

DYDE—
Thomas. *London.* 1662-88 CC. Lantern clock ill. Britten. Gilt en. watch set. jargoons Ilbert coll.
John. *London.* 1675. BC.

DYER—
Samuel. *London.* a.1696.
John. *London.* a.1718. Watch.
Thomas. *Abbots Leigh.* an.1776. Watch.
William. *Barnstaple.* 1784-91. C.
——. *Boston, U.S.A.* 1820. *v.* SAWIN & DYER.
Henry. *Carlow.* 1820-4.

DYKES, Samuel. *London.* an.1779. Watch.

DYRING, Adolf Fredrik. *Göteborg.* 1822-5.

DYSON—
John. *London.* a.1687, CC.1695.
Joseph. *Kawmarsh.* 18c. l.c. clock.
John. *Birmingham.* 1801-08. W. & C.
Mrs. *Birmingham.* 1808. C. & W.
Zaccheus. *Sheffield.* 1817. Watch.
Henry. *Manchester.* ca.1820.
J. & SONS. *Sheffield.* 1821. C. & W.

DYTE, John. *London.* Early 19c. Watch.

DYVEN, Jean. *Lund.* 14c.

E

EADIE, Andrew. *Perth.* a.1794.
EAGLE—
John. *London.* a.1683, CC.1690-1712. l.c. clock Weth. coll. ill. Britten.
Nathaniel. *London.* an.1789. Watch.
EAGLESFIELD, William. *London.* a.1723.
EAGLESHAM, William. *London.* a.1809.
EALAND, B. C. *Dartford.* Early 19c. Watch.
EAMONSON, Benjamin. *London.* a.1770.
EAMPS, ——. *Petersfield.* Early 19c.
EARLE—
Thomas. *London.* CC.1720.
Edward. *London.* a.1750, CC.1757.
Daniel. *London.* an.1778. Watch.
Thomas. *Rye.* an.1778. Watch.
v. REYNOLDS & EARLE.
EARLES (ERYLES)—
——. *London.* 1630. Subscribed for incorporation of CC.
John. *London.* 1700-15.
EARNS—
James. *Edinburgh.* a.1712.
——. *London.* an.1776. Watch.
EARNSHAW—
Thomas. *London (High Holborn).* b.1749, d.1829. Devised spring detent chron. escapement, and did much to develop the chron.; awarded £3,000 by Board of Longitude. His chron. were desc. in a pub. by the Commissioners of Longitude in 1806. He appealed about the award in 1808 and a Parliamentary report was pub. in 1809. ½ ¼ rep. cyl. duplex, lever and chron. watches S.M.S.K. cyl. watch mt. G.M. Verge watch with ruby roller pallets Ilbert coll. p.c. pocket chron. G.M. and M.P.S. Dresden.
Laurence. *Mottram.* d.1767. Astro. clock.
Thomas. *Aston-under-Lyne.* 1774 in prison for debt. W.
James. *London.* a.1770.
Thomas, son of Thomas. *London (High Holborn* and, in 1835, *Fenchurch St.).* 1825-50. Succeeded to his father's business, and was succeeded by his son Thomas.
EARP, Robert. *Castle Donnington.* Late 18c. l.c. clock.
EARPE, ——. *Dublin.* an.1778. Watch.
EASEY, John. *London* a.1740.
EAST—
Jeremy. *London.* ca.1600, CC.1640-61. oct. crys. watch Webster coll. Watch with sil. cock and without screw Marryat coll.
Edward. *London.* ca.1610. CC.1632, m.CC. 1645 and 1652, d.ca.1693. The most celebrated of early English makers. W. to the King. Perhaps two makers of the same name. Very fine oct. crys. watch and watch in tortoise-shell case B.M. ill. Baillie. Three

EAST—*continued.*
watches and two mts. G.M. Watch in form of melon studded turquoises in Ashmolean M. Very beautiful blue en. watch, ill. Baillie. and eng. sil. watch S.K.M. sil. watch Webster coll. Five watches M.M.A. Trav. cal. and al. clock Ilbert coll. l.c. and br.clocks Weth. coll. Five watches and several clocks ill. Britten. sil. skull watch sold Munich in 1917. Miniature 8-day lantern clock, with pendulum; l.c. clock, short pendulum; year cal. and l.c. night clock, all ill. Cec. & Web. l.c. clock Virginia M.
Daniel. *London.* d.1672.
James. *London.* C. to the Queen in 1662.
Nathaniel. *London.* 1670. Worked for the Court.
Jeremiah. *London.* a.1653.
John. *London.* a.1654.
Thomas. *London.* a.1670, CC.1677-1707.
Peter. *London.* 1689. CC.1692.
Edmund or Edward. *London.* a.1688. CC. 1696. Watch mt. ca.1700, Ilbert coll.
Edward, son of Thomas. *London.* a.1699, CC.1710-35.
James. *London.* a.1710. Watch.
Jordan, son of Edmund. *London.* CC.1724.
Edward. *London.* a.1736, CC.1743.
Thomas. *London.* a.1749.
John, son of Edmund. *London.* CC.1757.
John, bro. *London (Cannon St.).* CC.1765.
John, son of John (2). *London.* a.1757.
EASTCOTT, Richard. *Exeter.* 18c. l.c. clock.
EASTLAND, Thomas. *London.* 1744-51. Watch.
EASTMAN—
Henry. *Exeter.* 1795.
Henry. *London (Tooting).* 1805-08.
EASTON—
Edward. *London.* a.1700, CC.1788.
John. *Petworth.* 1784.
EASTWOOD, William. *Burnley.* ca.1750-95.
EATON—
John. *London.* a.1715.
William. *London.* a.1747.
James. *London.* 1790. Watch mt. G.M.
Richard. *London.* Late 18c. Copper en. watch Fränkel coll.
Thomas. *London.* 1802-08. mt. maker.
James. *Boston, U.S.A.* 1806. W.
Samuel A. *Boston, U.S.A.* 1825. W.
EAVE, John. *London.* 1788-93. C.
EAYRE—
Thomas. *Kettering.* 1720-50. A good maker of turret and l.c. clocks.
Joseph. *St. Neots.* 1761. d.1772. Made carillon for Hemel Hempstead church.

EBBELTOFF, Severin. *Jönköping*. d.1773. l.c. clock.
EBBEN, William. *London (Islington)*. 1817-1840.
EBBS, John. *Dublin*. 1766-74. W.
EBEL, Michael. *Basle*. 1672. From *Leipzig*.
EBERHARDT, Gotthilf Anton. *Gotha*. 1812. Pub. a book on Turret clocks.
EBERL, Benedict. *Vienna*. m.1751.
EBERMAN—
John. *Lancaster City, U.S.A.* b.1749, d. 1835. Made Court House clock.
Jacob, bro. *Lancaster City*, 1773-1837. l.c. clocks.
John, son. *Lancaster City*. 1776-1846. Many l.c. clocks.
Joseph, bro. *Lancaster City*. 1780-1844. Many good l.c. clocks.
Gottlieb. *Lancaster City*. 1782. C.
EBHER—
Isaac. *Steyer*. 1617-mid. 17c. Wood and sil. crucifix clock Feill coll. Stackfreed str. watch Ilbert coll.
Sigmund. *Steyer*. 18c. aut. maker.
EBORALL, Thomas. *London*. 1762. W.
EBRART, ——. *Paris*. m.1602.
EBSWORTH—
John. *London*. a.1657, CC.1665, m.CC.1697-1703. Good maker of lantern clocks. str. watch Mallett coll. ill. Baillie. mus. br. clock, l.c. clock Weth. coll. Sheep's-head clock Glasgow Art Gall. Chiming br. clock Feill coll. br. clock with single barrel for going and striking.
Christopher. *London*. a.1662, CC.1669.
EBY, Christian. *Manheim, Lancaster, U.S.A.* 1830-60. Fine maker of l.c. clocks.
ECCLES—
John. *Chester*. 1734. W.
——. *Macclesfield*. an.1754. Watch.
ECHSTEDT, Jacob. *Elbing*. ca.1640. sil. watch with filigree outer case.
ECK—
Francis. *Northampton*. 1777. W.
& Collins. *Northampton*. 1795. W.
ECKEGREN, Daniel. *Copenhagen*. m.1821. Master of Corporation 1842-6.
ECKEN—
William. *London*. a.1752.
Barnaby. *London*. a.1757.
ECKERT—
Heinrich. ——. 1st half 18c. Watch mt. Arts M. Prague.
Carl. *Breslau*. 18c. Bronze br. clock Feill coll.
ECKHARD, P. J. *Brunswick*, 1802. Clock with optical projector throwing an image of dial on wall.
ECKHERT, ——. *London*. Mid. 18c. sil. p.c. rep. watch.
ECKLER, Jørgen. *Copenhagen*. 1585. Court C.
'ECKLICOT.' *London*. Sig. on watch G.M. Prob. an imitation of Ellicott.
ECLES, Henry. *London*. a.1654.
EDARD DE LA PLANTE. ——. *Paris*. 1812.
EDBOROUGH, James. *London*. a.1779.
EDDLING, William. *London*. an.1772. Watch.
EDDOWES, Timothy. *London*. a.1763.
EDELINE, ——. *Paris*. 1764 m.
EDEN—
William. *London*. a.1719, CC.1726.
Thomas. *London*. a.1724.
John. *London*. a.1749, CC.1759.
Ralph. *Liverpool*. 1773-96. W.
Francis. *Liverpool*. 1813-29. W.
John William. *Bristol*. 1825-30. W.
v. Van Eden.
EDENBURY, John. *London*. a.1783. CC. 1791-1802.
EDEY, Richard. *London*. a.1700, CC.1716. Insolvent 1720. Also Edy.
EDGAR—
Benjamin. *London*. a.1770.
Marmaduke. *London*. an.1784. Watch.
EDGECUMBE—
——. *London*. an.1751. Watch.
John. *Bristol*. 1794-1812. W. & C.
John and Nicholas. *Bristol*. 1818. W. & C.
John and Nathaniel. *Bristol*. 1830. W. & C.
EDING, Edward. *London*. 1744. Watch.
EDINGTON, ——. *London*. ca.1800. W.
EDKINS, J. *London (Kensington)*. Early 19c.
EDLIN—
John. *London*. a.1676, CC.1687-1703.
George. *London (Aldgate)*. a.1789, CC.1810-1815.
Shovel Thomas. *London*. a.1792.
John. *London*. 1805-08.
EDLYNE, Edgar. *London*. a.1740, CC.1747-51. br. clock.
EDMARK, O. P. *Mariestad*. d.1801.
EDMONDS (EDMUNDS)—
Eliza. *London*. a.1679 CC.
James. *Charleston, U.S.A.* 1745. From *London*. C. & W.
Jacob. *London*. a.1737.
John. *London*. an.1767. Watch.
D. *Kendal*. an.1772. Watch.
Charles. *London (St. Martin's le Grand)*. CC.1772-1814. Watch N.Y. Univ.
B. *Liverpool*. 1778-1829. W.
D. *Dublin*. ca.1780. Watch mt. Dublin M.
D. *Liverpool*. 1780. Watch Ilbert coll.
John. *Bristol*. 1781. C.
John. *Shrewsbury*. an.1783. Watch.
D. *Liverpool*. 1787-1810. W.
P. *Dublin*. an.1797. Watch.
John. *London*. 1820-30. Watch.
EDMONDSON—
John. *London*. a.1660.
John. *Liverpool*. 1775-96.
EDRIDGE, William. *London*. a.1793, CC. 1802.
EDROP, James Robert. *London*. a.1808.
EDROPE, George. *London*. an.1779. Watch.
EDSOLT, Heinrich Arnold. *Friedberg*. 1732.
EDWARD—
Clement. *Devonshire*. 1671.
'Edward Bevin.' Sig. on 1867-9 watches of Newark Watch Co.
EDWARDS—
William. *London*. 1630 BC.
Joseph. *London*. a.1655.
Thomas. *London*. a.1680.
Nicholas. *London*. a.1687.
Isaac. *London*. a.1710, CC.1719. Shagreen case watch.
George. *London*. a.1716.
John. *Edinburgh*. 1725.
John. *Annapolis, U.S.A.* 1735. W.
William. *London (Holborn* and *Cheapside)*. 1744-93. Livery BC. Succeeded by Christ. Moon. Clock Peiping M. Watch.
——. *Cambridge*. an.1753. Watch.
Adam. *London*. an.1753, Watch.
Thomas. *London*. a.1749-66 CC. Watch.
James. *London (Holborn)*. ca.1760-78. Bankrupt. Watch.
John. *London*. an.1761. Watch.
George. *London*. a.1756, CC.1763.
Richard. *Portsmouth*. an.1766. Watch.
John (3). *London*. a.1760, CC.1775-7.
John. *Norwich*. 1770-84. l.c. clock.
Benjamin. *Bungay*. 18c. l.c. clock.
James. *Norwich*. an.1773. Watch.
James. *Cork*. an.1776. Watch.
William, jun. *London (High Holborn)*. an. 1776-85. Watch.
Philip. *London*. an.1776. Watch.
David. *London*. a.1768.
Charles. *London*. 1775 CC.-1811.

EDWARDS—*continued.*
James, jun. *Norwich.* 1782. C. & W.
Thomas. *Salisbury.* an.1783. Gilt wood cartel clock. Watch.
John. *Bristol.* 1780.
William. *Bristol.* 1781.
D. *Liverpool.* 1785. W.
James, son of John (3). *London* (*Fleet St.*). a. 1780, CC.1788-90. Very small br. clock.
Edward. *Bishopscastle.* 1791. C. & W.
Thomas. *Bromsgrove.* 1791. C.
George. *London.* CC.1792-1813.
James. *Stourbridge.* ca.1795.
Richard. *Southampton.* 1795.
Edward. *London.* an.1796. Watch.
Joseph. *London.* a.1789.
William. *London.* a.1791.
Philip. *London.* 1799. W.
Phineas. *London.* 1799.
William. *Derby.* 1801-25.
& LORIMER. *London.* 1805-08.
James. *London* (*Goswell St.*). CC.1808-19.
James, son of James. *London* (*Commercial Rd.*). a.1808-20.
James. *London* (*Limehouse*). 1817-19.
James. *London* (*Cheapside*). CC.1818-24.
James. *London* (*Whitechapel*). 1820.
I. *London* (*Whitechapel*). 1820.
John. *Alloa.* 1820.
Robert. *London* (*Goswell St.*). 1820.
Henry William. *London.* a.1814.
T. *Godalming.* Early 19c. Watch.
Thomas. *Llangollen.* Early 19c. Lever watch mt. Glasgow Art Gall.

EDWARDSON, John. *Liverpool.* 1754-61. W.

EDWIN—
John. *London.* a.1736, CC.1743-68. Watch engraver.
'EDWIN ROLLO.' Sig. on 1868 watches of the UNITED STATES WATCH CO.

EFFINGTON, John. *London.* CC.1702.

EGAN, Hugh. *London.* a.1717.

EGAR, Samuel. *Spalding.* 1795. C. & W.

EGBY, John. *Congleton.* 1784. W.

EGERSLEY, James. *London.* a.1660.

EGERT, ——. *Berlin.* 1786.

EGERTON—
Isaac. *London.* a.1723.
Thomas. *London.* a.1792.

EGGER, John Sebastian. *Berlin.* 1786.

EGGERZ, Carl Benedictus. *Stockholm.* 1742. m.1745, d.1756. Two watches.

EGGLESTON, R. *Hull.* d.1779.

EGLAN—
Philip Franz. *Würzburg.* m.1802. C.
Caspar. *Würzburg.* m.1807. C.

EGLETON—
Christopher. *London.* a.1683, CC.1695-1730. p.c. sil. watch G.M.
George. *London.* a.1763.

EGRAAD, J. *Amsterdam.* 1822. W.

EGUET, Philibert & Victor. *Malvilliers.* 1820. Founded an ébauche factory, moved in 1834 to *Corgémont.*

EGUET-MAILLARDET, Charles Louis. *Fontaines,* 1791. *Paris,* 1806. *Rouen,* 1807. *London. Fontainemelon,* 1823. *Cernier,* 1830.

EHRBAHR—
Conrad. *Berlin.* 1780-85.
Johann Friedrich. *Berlin.* 1785.

EHRENBERG—
Andreas. *Angelholm.* 1787.
Gilius. *Angelholm.* comp. 1787.
Johan Rth. *Elberfeldt.* ca.1790. g. en. watch.
Ernst Petter. *Söderköping,* 1820-5. *Nyköping,* 1830-5. *Örebro,* 1840-6. W. & C.

EHRHARDT (ERHARDT)—
Johann Christoph. *Augsburg.* 1726-ca.1740. Watch with fly-back minute hand in Vernis Martin outer case B.M. ill. Baillie. g. rep. watch.

EHRHARDT (ERHARDT)—*continued.*
William. *Birmingham.* b.1831, d.1898. Founded a watch factory in Birmingham in 1874.

EHRLING, Daniel. *Nyköping.* m.1819-25.

EICHELAR, Lourens. *Holland.* ca.1760. l.c. clock Boymans M. Rotterdam.

EICHLER—
Johann Georg. *Frankfurt a. M.* d.1758. Town C.
Heinrich. *Augsburg.* ca.1750.

EICHMANN, Johann Friedrich. *Hamburg.* 1815-21.

EICKSTEL, Johan. *Germany.* ca.1600. Table clock. Tower clock Feill coll.

EIDSFORTH, Charles. *London.* a.1764.

EIFFE, James Sweetman. *London.* b.1800, d.1880. Able chron. maker. Regulator Weth. coll.

EIJKMEYER, J. *Rotterdam.* 1821-30.

EIJSBOUTS, B. *Asten.* ca.1800.

EIMMART, Georg Christoph. *Nürnberg.* b.1638.

EINBERGER, Johann. *Lauffen.* Early 19c. sil. p.c. watch. Clock Uhren M. Vienna.

EISELE—
J. *Nürnberg.* 1725. Watch M.M.A. Perhaps same as EISLER.
W. A. *Brussels.* ca.1760. Watch M.M.A.

EISEN, Heinrich. *Nürnberg.* m.1503-15. 'Hormacher.'

EISENHARD, Louis. *Geneva.* Early 19c. Pocket chron. with double spiral, Chamb. coll.

EISENREICH, Joseph. *Vienna.* m.1802.

EISGRUBER, Sebastian. *Vienna.* m.1797.

EISINGA, Eise. *Franeker.* 18c. Planetarium desc. by Van Swinden.

EISLER, ——. *Nürnberg.* 1730. Standing clock Munich Nat. M. *v.* EISELE and EYSLER.

EITERBICHLER—
Joseph. *Nürnberg.* 1800.
Joseph. *Augsburg.* m.ca.1805.

EKEBECK, Sven. *Linköping.* 1754-73. l.c. clock Nord. M.

EKEGREN—
Nils. *Karlshamn.* b.1754, d.1826.
Jeremias. *Karlskrona.* b.1782, d. 1847. Watch.
Simon. *Karlshamn.* 1816-46.
P. *Växjö.* 1819-20.
P. M. *Kalmar.* 1820. d.1830. Prob. same as above.
N. *Kalmar.* 1820-40.
Heinrich. *Geneva.* b.1824, d.1896. Chron. maker of repute.

EKELUND, Eric. *Köping.* 1752.

EKEROTH, Jakob. *Stockholm.* comp. 1751, m.1755, d.1766. Fine watchmaker. Four watches, one in Nat. M. Stockholm, ill. Sidenbladh.

EKINS, Charles. *London.* a.1677.

EKMAN, Fredric. *Västerås.* b.1758, m.1792, d.1828. Partner with J. D. BJÖRKDAHL, 1798-1810.

EKRALL, William. *London.* an.1765. Watch.

EKSTRÖM, Jonas. *Stockholm.* b.1735. d.1769. Two br. clocks.

ELCHINGER, Hans Conrad. *Amsterdam.* 1625-50. Very fine watch B.M., en. sd. 'J. Toutin.' ill. Baillie. hex. table clock Garnier coll. oct. crys. watch Spitzer coll.

ELCOCK, John. *Hursley.* Early 19c. Watch.

ELDER, James. *London.* 1775. Watch.

ELDON, W. *London.* 2nd half 18c. Watch M.P.S. Dresden.

ELDRED, Dodson. *London.* a.1753, CC. 1782.

ELDRICK, Hay. *Kirkwall.* 1823. d. 1832.
ELDRIDGE—
John. *London.* a.1669, CC.1677. l.c. clock.
Francis. *Gloucester.* 1760-95. W.
William. *London.* a.1802.
ELEER, Michael. *Dublin.* 1824.
ELEMENT, William. *London.* an.1803. Watch.
ELEY—
William. *London.* a.1748.
James. *London (Fenchurch St.).* a.1753, CC. 1761, l.CC.1776-87. Watch.
ELFES—
Benjamin. *London.* a.1666, CC.1674.
Thomas. *London.* a.1671.
ELFFROTH—
Carl Ludwig. *Berlin.* 1780-9. mus. clock Märkische M. Berlin.
Johann Daniel. *Berlin.* 1780-7. C.
ELFORT—
Colin. *Avignon.* 1470. Belfry clock begun by him.
Johann. *Vienna.* m.1816.
ELFSTRAND, Anders. *Stockholm.* comp. 1769.
ELFSTRÖM—
Petter. *Lovisa.* 1763-88. Watches and wall clocks.
Johan Gustaf, son. *Lovisa.* 1789-1805.
ELGIN NATIONAL WATCH CO., successor to the NATIONAL WATCH CO. OF CHICAGO, which made watches with the following sigs.:—'B. W. Raymond,' 'H. Z. Culver,' 'J. T. Ryerson,' 'H. H. Taylor,' 'G. M. Wheeler' between 1867-75; 'Matthew Laflin,' 1868-75; 'Lady Elgin,' 1869-75; 'Francis Rubie,' 1870-8; 'Gail Borden,' 1871-5; and 'Dexter Street,' 1871-5. The Elgin National Watch Co. made:—'Chas. Fargo,' 1872; 'T. M. Avery' and 'M. D. Ogden,' 1876; 'Inter-Ocean' and 'Leader,' 1877.
ELGSTRAND, ——. *Eskilstuna.* 1824.
ELIAS, Johannes. *Amsterdam.* 18c. l.c. clock in Ryks M. Amsterdam.
ELISHA, Caleb. *London.* 1820-40. br. clock.
ELKES, James. *London.* a.1787, CC.1819.
ELKINS, William. *London.* a.1696, CC.1710-1730. Partner with WINDMILLS.
ELLAM, William. *Sutton (Lancs.).* d.1777. *v.* ERLAM.
ELLARD, John William. *London.* a.1753.
ELLEIS, David. *Aberdeen.* 1560.
ELLET, William. *London.* CC.1771.
ELLICOTT—
John. *London (Austin Friars* and later *Swithin's Alley, R.Exchange).* a.1687, CC. 1696, w.CC. and d.1733. Watch mt. ca. 1710 Buckley coll. with rivetted bar for 3rd and 4th wheels and only 1/5 inch between plates. Early mts. had sig. under cock. 'An ingenious watchmaker of great note.'
John, F.R.S. *London (Swithin's Alley, R. Exchange).* b.1706, d.1772. Fellow and on Council of Royal Society. One of the most eminent English makers; invented a compensation pendulum; developed use of cylinder escapement. C. to the King. Pub. in Phil. Trans. two articles on clocks, in 1739 and 1753 and an equation of time table. sil. rep. watch B.M. br. clock and four watches G.M., of which two are early cyl's. g. watch and l.c. clock Stern. coll. cyl. c. secs. equation watch Webster coll. cyl. equation and year cal. watch, with c.secs. on back, Marryat coll. two br. and one l.c. clock ill. Britten. Three br. clocks ill. Cec. & Web. A rough guide to the dates corresponding to watch Nos. is: 1730, No. 400. 1740, No. 1800. 1750, No. 3250. 1760, No. 4770. 1770, No. 6435. 1780, No. 7620. 1790, No. 8450. 1800, No. 8760. 1810, No. 9074. The series continuing with John's successors. The earliest cyl. watch known (Ilbert coll.) has No. 2042. Up to No. 4354, about 1758, watches were sd. Jno. Ellicott. Afterwards, prob. when Edward came into partnership, they were sd. Ellicott, and this sig. continued after the death of John, the firm retaining the title, John Ellicott & Son.

ELLICOTT—*continued.*
Jeremiah. *London.* 1708 CC.
John, & Son. *London.* 1758-85. Partnership of John and his son Edward. p.c. cyl. watch S.M.S.K.
Joseph. *Bucks County, Pa. & Baltimore.* b. 1732. Went *Baltimore* 1775, d.1780. Planetarium and mus. l.c. clock playing 24 tunes in Philadelphia.
Edward, son of John (2). *London (R. Exchange).* 1758, d.1791. W. to the King. l.c. clock Virginia M.
James. *London.* 1772. Watch Ilbert coll.
Andrew. *Baltimore, U.S.A.* 1778-80. C.
John. *London.* CC.1782-95. W.
Edward, son of Edw. *London.* CC.1795, m.CC. and d.1835.
Edward, & Sons. *London.* 1785-1811 next style of firm of John Ellicott & Son.
William. *London.* an.1792. Watch.
& TAYLOR. *London.* 1811-30 next style of firm of Edw. Ellicott & Sons. cyl. rep. watch S.M.S.K. Pocket chron. G.M. br. clock ill. Cec. & Web.
& SMITH. *London.* 1830-40 next style of firm.
ELLIONEDY, Louis. *Vienna.* Early 19c. en. mussel shell watch.
ELLIOTT—
John. *London.* a.1681-1722. Watch.
Joseph. *London.* a.1696.
Henry. *London.* CC.1688. l.c. clock Weth. coll.
Henry, son. *London.* a.1704, CC.1720.
Henry. *London.* a.1705.
Thomas. *Greenwich.* an.1720. Watch.
Thomas. *London.* a.1721.
Matthew. *London.* 1744-52. W.
——. *Plymouth.* an.1747. Watch.
Thomas. *London.* a.1744, CC.1751.
Joseph Moseley. *Berkhampstead.* 1759-84. Retired.
James. *London (Oxford St.).* an.1770. Watch.
R. *London.* an.1773. Watch.
Thomas. *Nottingham.* an.1776, retired 1788. W.
William. *London.* 2nd half 18c. Watch.
William. *London.* a.1787.
John or Joseph Moseley. *London.* 1790-1812. The correct name appears to be John, but, on the Patent Specification, is Joseph. Patented in 1804 and 1806 a rep. mechanism without train, actuated by turning the pendant. Pub. desc. in Trans. Soc. Arts. 1804. Lever watch. br. clock Weth coll. Inn clock.
Thomas, jun. *London.* an.1805. Watch.
John. *Ashford.* 1805. Watch.
——. *Philadelphia.* 1819.
ELLIS—
Jacob. *York.* 1636. W.
Henry. *London.* a.1654.
James. *London.* a.1658, CC.1667-81.
Richard. *London (Westminster).* a.1673, CC. 1683, d.1749. br. clock.
Thomas. *London.* a.1672, CC.1682-87.
Paul. *London.* CC.1682-1701.
Isaac. *London.* a.1716.
Edward. *London.* a.1716.
John. *London.* a.1718, CC.1726.
Bownest. *London.* a.1735.
Brown. *London.* a.1736.

ELLIS—*continued.*
John. *Sherborne.* 1750. Watch Ilbert coll.
James. *Canterbury.* 1764. W.
Joseph. *London.* an.1774. Watch.
William. *London.* an.1777-1808. l.c. clock. Watch.
v. Mowray & Ellis.
Richard. *London.* CC.1777.
Henry. *London.* a.1781.
Thomas. *London.* a.1783.
Joseph. *London.* a.1784.
Thomas. *London.* a.1788.
Henry. *Exeter.* mar. 1815. Watch.
Griffith. *London.* a.1805.
John. *London* (*Old Broad St.*). CC.1817, l.CC.1822.
Theophilus. *London.* 1817-24. W.
William. *Wrexham.* Early 19c. Watch.
Richard. *London.* a.1818, CC.1825.

ELLISON—
Caleb. *London.* a.1691.
Henry. *Childwall.* d.1750. C.
William. *London.* an.1778. Watch.
James. *London.* an.1784. Watch.
Robert. *Eccleston.* d.1798.
John and Timothy. *Liverpool.* 1805-07.
John. *Liverpool.* 1810.
Robert. *Liverpool.* ca.1820.
Thomas. *York.* 1826. W.

ELLISTON, Robert. *London.* 1790.
ELLSWORTH, John. *London.* 1809-11.
ELLWOOD—
Martin. *London.* CC.1687-1700. Watch G.M. l.c. clock Virginia M. An able maker.
John. *London.* a.1683.
John. *London* (*Whitefriars*). CC.1702, d. 1734. l.c. clock. Watch.
Thomas. *London* (*Fleet St.*). 1725. Insolvent.
James. *London.* CC.1734.

ELLWORTHY, William James. *London.* 1761. Insolvent.
ELMES—
William. *London.* CC.1667-82. math. inst. maker.
Joseph. *London.* a.1673.
Richard. *London.* a.1696, CC.1708-30.
Roger. *London.* a.1701.
Richard, son of Richard. *London.* CC.1747.

ELMQWIST, N. M. *Asa, Hjälmaryd.* 18c. Watch mt. Nord. M. trav. clock. Prob. same as Hjelmqvist.
ELPHICK, Thomas. *London.* a.1797.
ELSDON, Edward. *Newcastle.* Early 19c. Watch.
ELSEGOOD, William. *Norwich.* 1752.
ELSON—
David. *London.* CC.1646.
Joseph. *London.* an.1775. Watch.

ELSTICK, Edward. *London.* d.1772. W.
ELTON—
John. *London.* a.1668, CC.1675.
Thomas. *London.* CC.1677-1707.
Abner. *London.* a.1714.

ELVINS, William. *Baltimore, U.S.A.* 1799-1802. W. & C.
ELVIUS, P. *Sweden.* 1738. Pub. an art. on pendulums in Latin.
ELY, ——. *London.* an.1789. Watch.
ELZHÖNY, ——. *London.* Mid. 18c. repoussé watch.
EMAN, John. *London.* a.1669,
EMANUEL—
Levy. *London.* an.1777. Watch.
Levi. *Canterbury.* an.1781. Watch.
Michael. *Portsea.* Bankrupt 1795. W.
E. *Deal.* 1797. W.
Joel. *London.* 1815-24.
Lewis. *London.* 1820-5. Watch.
E. *London.* 1820.
M. and E. *London.* 1822-4.

EMANUEL—*continued.*
Brothers. *London.* Early 19c. g. and tortoiseshell watch for Turkey Feill coll.
& Co. *London.* Early 19c. g. en. watch.

EMBDEN, George. *London.* 1805-08. W.
EMBLEY, Robert Ellis. *London.* a.1798, CC. 1812.
EMDIN, Michael Gomport. *Plymouth* and *London.* Insolvent 1781.
EMERAL, Richard. *London.* 1762.
EMEREY, Richard. *London.* a.1753, CC.1763.
EMERSON—
James. *London.* a.1703.
Robert. *London* a.1789.
——. *London.* an.1806. Watch.
James. *Bristol.* 1822.

EMERTON, Benjamin. *London.* a.1742.
John. *London.* an.1762. Watch.
v. Emmerton.

EMERY—
Josiah. *London.* b. prob. 1725, d.1797. CC. 1781. Succeeded by Recordon & Dupont and in 1796 by Dupont. Native of *Geneva.* An eminent maker. L. Berthoud said his work was particularly fine in all essentials, without unnecessary show. Made many watches with lever escapements, the first in 1774. Was the first to apply draw to the lockings. Submitted four timekeepers to the Board of Longitude for trial between 1792 and 1796, but without success. Two watches G.M., one ruby cyl., with helical spring and compensation curb, and the other g. lever with pivoted impulse pin. Cyl. en. watch S.M.S.K. Lever watches, helical spring, Ilbert and Den. colls. mus. br. clock. br. clock Weth. coll. Part of marine chron. C.A. & M.
James. *London.* a.1752.
John. *London.* an.1762. Watch.
E. *London.* an.1775. Watch.
Thomas. *London.* an.1783. Watch.
Ezekiel. *Southampton.* 1795.

EMMERSON, Henry. *Newcastle-o.-T.* mar. 1699. W.
EMMERTON—
William. *Wootton-under-Edge.* 1779. d.1793. His son opened a shop in *Woburn,* but d. 1794.
v. Emerton.

EMMERY, Jules. *La Sagne.* Early 19c. Watch with sweep seconds and ¼ seconds hands, Chamb. coll.
EMMETT, Thomas. *London.* CC.1813, l.CC. 1819-24. Watch-hand maker.
EMMOSER, Gerhard. *Augsburg.* Mid. 16c. Made astro. clocks for Ferdinand i and Maximilian ii.
ENDELL, Adam. *Stockholm.* 1800-05. Watch mt. Nord. M.
ENDERBY—
——. *London.* an.1745. Watch.
Thomas. *Potton.* an.1775. Watch.

ENDERLIN—
Jakob. *Basle.* b.1628. *Breslau,* 1648. *Basle,* 1658. d.1699. Turret and house C.
Johann Heinrich, son. *Basle.* b.1672, d.1716.
Hans Johann Jakob, bro. *Basle.* b.1675, d.1736. C. to the town. Turret clock made for Hässingen (Alsace) in Basle M. Turret and house C.
Hans Georg, bro. *Basle.* b.1678, d.1754. C. to the town from 1736. Turret and house C. Watch Basle M. with en. on cock.
William Andreas, son of Jakob. *Basle.* b. 1681, d.1733. Watches Basle M. with en. on cocks.
Hans Jakob. *Basle.* b.1707, d.1732.
Abraham, son of Wilhelm. *Basle.* b.1719. Went to *Strasbourg* 1763.
Reinhard, bro. *Basle.* b.1721, d.1755. Turret and house C.

ENDERLIN—*continued.*
——. *Paris.* Early 18c. Eminent W. & C. Devised a clock escapement with 2 wheels and 1 pallet, and equation and cal. mechanisms. Wrote article on the irregularities of pendulums in Thiout's book.
Reinhard, nephew. *Basle.* 1750-60. Kleinuhrmacher. Watch Stuttgart M.
ENDERSCH, Johann Friedrich. *Elbing.* b. 1705. Sundial maker.
ENDRES, ——. *Gratz.* ca.1750. g. repoussé watch.
ENDT, Theobald. *Philadelphia.* 1742. C.
ENEROTH, Hans. *Norrköping.* 1761-70. Two l.c. clocks. *v.* ENROTH.
ENEW, William. *London.* a.1687.
ENGAZ, ——. *Paris.* ca.1790-1825. Clock ill. Britten.
ENGBERG—
Niels. *Copenhagen.* m.1769.
Johan. *Stockholm.* b.1793, d.1834.
ENGE, Alexander. *London.* an.1772. Watch.
ENGEL—
D. *Westzaan.* 17c. C.
David Guillaume. *Douanne Glèresse, Chaux-de-Fonds.* b.1737, d.1800. Many mus. and other clocks.
Henri Louis. *Chaux-de-Fonds.* b.1781-1813.
Lars. *Nakskov.* 1820 m.
ENGELBRECHT—
Joan. *Beraun.* 1681-4. Two sundials, one sil. with finely chased signs of zodiac, Arts M. Prague.
Lorentz. *Vienna.* ca.1700. crys. cross watch M.M.A.
Joan. *Beraun.* 1776-1804. Five dials Arts M. Prague. Dial Old Ashmolean M.
ENGELBRECHTEN, Eduard. *Stockholm.* 1815-46. Two wall clocks and br. clock.
ENGELBREIT—
Valentin. *Waldaschach.* m.1797.
Andreas. *Waldaschach.* m.1809.
Franz. *Waldaschach.* m.1824.
ENGELHARD, Jan. *Holland.* Early 18c. Watch Stads M. Amsterdam.
ENGELSCHALK (ENGELSHALKH)—
Benedict. *Thorn.* ca.1600. oct. crys. watch.
Johann. *Prague.* ca.1650-1700. Maker of repute. sil. watch. hex. table clock Fränkel coll.
Johann Georg. *Augsburg.* 1681. aut. mus. clock Nat. M. Munich sd. 'Engelshalkh Johann Georg in Fridberg' prob. by him.
Ferdinand. *Prague.* ca.1700. Hex. table clock Uhren M. Vienna. Perhaps same as following.
Ferdinand. *Würzburg.* m.1721. *Friedberg* to 1720 and from 1727. d.1730.
Georg Konrad Ignatz, son. *Würzburg.* a. 1739, m.1754-94. W.
Johann. *Pesth.* Mid. 18c. Stand clock Feill coll.
Franz. *Prague.* 2nd half 18c. Watch Nat. M. Prague.
ENGER, Amund Andersen. *Christiania.* 1789 m.
ENGERINGH, Cs. *Dordrecht.* ca.1780. aut. clock C.A. & M.
ENGHART, Carl Friedrich. *Augsburg.* 1760 comp., m.1767.
ENGIN, Francis. *London.* 1746-50. Watch in porcelain case.
T. *London.* an.1759. Watch.
James. *London.* an.1770. Watch.
ENGLAND, John. *London.* a.1692.
ENGLEFIELD, James. *London.* a.1714.
ENGLISH—
Isaac. *London.* a.1734.
John. *London.* a.1787.
David. *Manchester.* 1813. W.
Mary. *Manchester.* ca.1820.
ENGLOIS, George. *London.* a.1638.
ENGLSALCK, Johann Christian. *Germany.* 18c. sil. watch Fränkel coll. Prob. same name as ENGELSCHALK.
ENGLUND—
Petter. *Fräkentorp.* 18c. Wall clock.
Olof. *Södertälje.* 1805-10.
ENGSTEDT, P. *Härnösand.* b.1798-1846.
ENGSTRÖM—
——. *Köping.* 1816.
Eric. *Stockholm.* 1820.
ENGUERRANT—
Jacques. *Blois.* mar. 1594-1639.
Jacques. *Blois.* comp. 1633.
ENGUI—
Fer. *London.* an.1762. Watch.
James. *London.* an.1775. Watch.
ENGVALL, Jonas Isak. *Sweden.* 18c. l.c. clock.
ENNEW, Barnard. *London.* a.1733.
ENNS, D. K. ——. 17c. Crucifix clock with sundial on back, Old Ashmolean M.
ENON, Charles. *London.* a.1667.
ENQVIST, Jonas. *Norrköping.* b.1758, d.1802. Watch mt. Nord. M.
ENROTH, Hans. *Västervik.* 1750. *v.* ENEROTH.
ENSCHEDE, Johannes. *Haarlem.* 1673.
ENSWORTH—
Robert. *Liverpool.* 1734.
Peter. *Liverpool.* 1795. W.
ENT, John. *New York.* 1758. *Philadelphia.* 1763. d.1794.
ENTWISLE, Laurence. *London.* a.1638.
ENWOOD, Samuel. *London.* a.1662.
ENYS—
Edward. *London.* a.1650, CC.1658-1702. Also ENNIS.
Edward, son. *London.* CC.1684-9.
EOFF & HOWELL. *New York.* 1805. W.
EPENOY, ——. *Paris.* 1812.
EPP—
Johann Conrad. *Fürth.* d.1748.
Johann. *Fürth.* d.1790.
Andreas. *Fürth.* d.ca.1820.
EPPINGER, Joachim. *Augsburg.* 1764. d. 1771. Wooden clocks and mus. aut.
EPPNER, Wilhelm. *Chaux-de-Fonds.* ca. 1810-75. Very able maker.
ERB—
Zacharias. ——. Early 17c. Table clock with standing figure of Christ, Webster coll.
Albrecht. *Vienna.* m.ca.1661. Fine maker. Watches in K.H.M. and M.M.A. Square table clock. br. clock Furt. M. Trav. clock Virginia M.
Franz Antoni. *Vienna.* m.1714.
ERBURY, Henry. *London.* a.1642, CC.1650-1656.
ERDENEST, ——. *Paris.* 1812.
ERDTSIECK, M. J. *Haarlem.* ca.1800.
ERIC (ERICK)—
William. *London.* CC.1730-69. Watch.
Samuel. *Gravesend.* 1756. W.
ERICKE—
Robert. *London.* a.1706, CC.1719-44.
Samuel. *London.* 1744. Insolvent.
John. *London (Size Lane).* 1761. Insolvent.
William. *London (Size Lane).* CC.1730. d.1772. Watch.
Sen. *London (Size Lane).* d.1771. W.
ERICSSON, Petter. *Stockholm.* 1820. d.1867.
ERIPEAUX, Claude Antoine. *Paris.* 1766 m.
ERLAM, Percival. *Sutton (Lancs.).* 1788. Insolvent. *v.* ELLAM.
ERLIN, Edward. *London.* ca.1740. Watch. Prob. same as following.
ERLING, Edward. *Chiswick.* an.1743. Watch.
ERNST—
Jerg. *Germany.* ca.1620. Oval watch B.M. oct. crys. watch M.P.S. Dresden.

ERNST—*continued.*
Peter. *Växjö.* b.1714. *Stockholm,* 1753. d. 1784. Well-known maker. Many clocks and watches. Examples in Nord. M. and Berzelius M. Astro. clock Vetenskap Observatory. Nine examples ill. Sidenbladh.
Joseph Ignatius. *Augsburg.* m.1756-86.
Ignatz. *Augsburg.* ca.1780-6.
——. *Stockholm.* ca.1780. Pedometer Gotha M.
Jerg. *Augsburg.* End 18c. sil. clock with cameos, K.H.M.
——. *Aarau* and *Basle.* 1790.
Leopold, son of Ignatz. *Augsburg.* comp. 1786-98.
ERRARD, Étienne Théodore. *Chaux-de-Fonds.* 1784.
ERRINGTON, Thomas. *London.* a.1754.
ERTL, Joseph. *Aichach.* 1738.
ESCABASSE—
Jean. *Paris* (*Quai Bourbon*). m.1785-89.
——. *Paris* (*Pont Marie*). 1789.
ESCHINARDI, Francesco. *Italy.* 1762. Pub. 'Regola di trasmettere il tempo ordinario degli Oriuoli in pendolo.'
ESCOURT, Robert. *Bristol.* 1775. W.
ESCUREL, Jeremias. *Basle.* 1670. From *Montbéliard.*
ESPER, ——. *Munich.* 1806. Made a set of escapements for the Soc. des Arts de Genève.
ESPERSEN, N. *Bornholm.* Late 18c.
ESPINO, Francisco Antonio. *Valencia.* 1802. Pub. book on regulating clocks and watches.
ESQUIVILLON—
Antoine. *Geneva.* ca.1720-32.
& DE CHOUDENS. *Paris.* 1765-1830. g. en. watch S.K.M. Two watches M.M.A. p.c. sil. and tortoiseshell watch Feill coll. *v.* COLLOMBY.
FRÈRES ET DE CHOUDENS. *Paris.* ca.1775-ca. 1830. en. watch G.M. Watch S.M.S.K. g. rep. watch M.M.A. en. watch set pearls Marfels coll. 4-colour g. watch Fränkel coll. rep. watch set pearls M.P.S. Dresden. en. watch Carnegie M. p.c. g. en. watch Feill coll.
FRÈRES. *Geneva.* ca.1800. Many watches.
ESSERT, Jean Pierre. *Côte-aux-Fées.* ca.1700.
ESSEX—
Joseph. *Edinburgh.* 1711.
Joseph. *Boston, U.S.A.* 1712.
Richard. *London.* a.1725.
ESTER—
Henry. Prob. *France.* ca.1630. A fine maker who has signed many watches, but never with the name of a town. Tulip watch and oval watch B.M. en. watch with signs of zodiac on dial K.H.M. Cross watch Louvre. crys. watch Ilbert coll. Pelican watch and en. watch S.K.M. ill. Baillie.
Estienne. Prob. *France.* ca.1630. crys. sphere watch with signs of zodiac on dial, Spitzer coll. sil. al. watch B.M. en. watch Ilbert coll.
ESTERBY, James *Clonmel.* 1824.
ESTERLIE, John. *New Holland, U.S.A.* 1812-30. German. l.c. clocks.
ESTEVÉ, ——. *Paris.* 1825.
ESTHER—
Daniel. *Basle.* 1665. From *Geneva.*
Thomas. *Morpeth.* Early 19c. Watch.
ESTIENNE, ——. *Paris.* Early 18c. g. watch.
ESTIER, ——. *Paris.* ca.1750. g. en. watch Blot-Garnier coll.
ESTON, Edward. *London.* a.1651.
ESTWICK, ——. *London.* an.1747. Watch.
ESUOLILA, ——. *London.* an.1776. Watch.
ETHERINGTON—
George. *London.* CC.1684, m.CC.1709, d.1729. Succeeded by his assistant Thos. HAYDON. br. clock. l.c. clocks. Two watches G.M., one rep. p.c.watch S.M.S.K. p.c. str. watch Ilbert coll.

ETHERINGTON—*continued.*
Thomas. *York.* 1684. W.
John. *London.* 1727. Watch.
Thomas, son of Thos. *York.* 1727. W.
Thomas, son. *York.* 1740. W.
John. *Duffield.* 1784. W.
William, son. *York.* 1788. W.
ÉTIENNE—
——. *Lyons.* 1466-82. 'Maistre relogié et serrurier.'
Frédéric. *Paris.* 1824.
ETTLINGER (EDLINGER), Michael. *Vienna.* m.1781.
ETTRY, Abram. *Flushing.* ca.1740. br.clock.
ETTY, Marmaduke. *London.* CC.1716-33.
ETZELL, Jerome Godfrey. *London.* a.1738.
EUDE, Joseph François. *Paris.* m.1786-89.
EULER, Leonard. *St. Petersburg.* b.1707, d. 1783. Famous mathematician. In 1760 pub. art. on the form of teeth for wheels.
EUSTACE, Richard. *London.* a.1687.
EVA, Richard. *Falmouth.* 1784. W.
EVANDER, Gun. *Stockholm.* 1748.
EVANS—
Thomas. *London.* a.1648, CC.1673-87.
Henry. *London.* a.1668, CC.1682-1709.
George. *London.* a.1692.
John. *London.* a.1697.
Thomas. *London.* a.1710, CC.1718.
Thomas. *London.* CC.1720-49. Watch.
John. *London.* a.1720.
Michael. *London.* a.1729.
S., and William FURNISS. *New Castle County, U.S.A.* ca.1740. l.c. clock.
James. *London.* a.1735, CC.1749-81. Partner with R. and Peter HIGGS.
Thomas. *London.* CC.1751.
James. *Shrewsbury.* 1763. Watch. C.
Thomas. *New York.* 1760-1804. C. & W. From London.
William. *Stratford-on-Avon.* 1762.
Joseph. *London.* an.1763. Watch.
Evan. *Builth.* 1765-91. W.
Thomas. *London.* CC.1769.
Caleb. *Pontypool.* 1772-6. W.
William. *London.* an.1774.
James. *London* (*Sweetings Alley* and later *Royal Exchange*). 1773-1805. Livery Skinners Co. Many clocks and watches for Spain sd. Diego Evans, Bolsa Real, or London. Associated with HIGGS, and many clocks and watches sd. Higgs and Evans. Also sig. of James Evans, R. Exchange on an aut. mus. br. clock for China, Virginia M. Sig. of J. & Son, R. Exchange on watches an.1796 to 1799, and of James & Son, Sweetings Alley, 1805.
David. *Baltimore.* 1773-8. C.
David. *London* (*Sweetings Alley*). 1775-1825. Also associated with HIGGS.
Caleb. *Bristol.* 1775. W.
John. *London.* an.1778. Watch.
& BARNETT. *Shrewsbury.* 1778.
John. *Hertford.* 1784.
Thomas, son of Jas. *London* (*Sweetings Alley*). CC.1788-93.
Richard. *Oswestry.* 1788-95. W.
& SON. *London* (*Sweetings Alley*). 1790.
——. *Bridge Town, Barbados.* ca.1790 CC.
Thomas. *Dudley.* ca.1790. l.c. clock.
Price. *Shrewsbury.* an.1793. Watch.
Peter. *Gloverstone* (*Chester*). 1795. C.
Evans. *Liverpool.* 1796. W.
William. *London* (*Clerkenwell*). 1799-1816. Math. Inst. maker.
Dymoke. *London.* a.1790, CC.1800-24.
——. *Kidderminster.* ca.1800.
Samuel. *London.* a.1796, CC.1822.
James. *London.* a.1799, CC.1816.

EVANS—*continued.*
John. *London.* a.1801.
& Son. *London* (*St. John's Sq.*). 1808-11.
Joseph. *London* (*St. John's Sq.*). 1809-11.
James, son of Thos. *London* (*Sweetings Alley*). CC.1811-24.
Thomas Simpson. *London.* CC.1813-17.
William M. *Philadelphia.* 1813-48.
James William. *London.* CC.1816.
——. *Welshpool.* an.1820. Watch.
Thomas. *Aberdare.* Early 19c. Watch.
William. *Shrewsbury.* Early 19c.
Robert. *Ware.* mar.1823. C. & W.
John Windus, son of Dymoke. *London.* CC.1824.

EVELEIGH, George. *Beaminster.* d.1784. C.

EVENS—
Robert. *London.* a.1706. cf. following.
Robert. *Halstead.* ca.1720. Lantern clock ill. Britten.
Robert. *Halstead.* 1795. W.
Evan. *Totnes.* 2nd half 18c. l.c. clock.

EVERELL, John. *London.* a.1698-1747. Watch.

EVEREST, Edward. *London.* a.1674.

EVERETT, John. *London.* an.1724. l.c. clock Schloss M. Berlin. Watch mt.

EVERS, Peter. *Chester.* 1791. C. & W.

EVERT, John Thomas. *London.* a.1787.

EVES, John. *London.* 1809-11.

EVESON, Richard. *London.* a.1760.

EVETT—
Robert. *London.* CC.1636.
George. *London.* a.1701.

EVILL (EVEL)—
William. *Bath.* an.1762. Watch.
William & John. *Bath.* 1776, dissolve partnership. Wm. continues in following firm.

EVILL (EVEL)—*continued.*
Naish & Stroud. *Bath.* 1780.
William & James. *Bath.* 1787. Partnership dissolved in 1790. James continues.

EVISON, Francis. *London.* a.1783.

EVRARD, Leonard. *Namur.* 1677. 'Maître harquebusier et horlogier.' Repaired town clock with Gilles Thiry.

EWER—
John. *London.* a.1687. l.c. and br. clocks. Watch.
Thomas. *Clare.* 1795. W.

EWERL, Wene. *Vienna.* ca.1720. Wall clock Uhren M. Vienna.

EXCHAGNET, Louis. *London.* 1790.

EXELBY (EXCELBY)—
James. *London.* a.1710, CC.1718-54. Watches and l.c. clocks.
James. *London.* a.1737.

EXETER, Francis. *London.* an.1776. Watch.

EYBA (EUWA), Joseph. *Leitershofen.* 1756-1770.

EYRE—
Richard. *London.* a.1638-89 CC.
John. *London.* a.1696, CC.1703-33.
Robert. *London.* 1703 CC.
Mary. *London.* a.1739.
William. *London.* CC.1821.

EYRICH, Johann Baptist. *Würzburg.* m.1796. Mantel clock Luitprandt M. Watch Besançon M.

EYRIER, Esprit. *Avignon.* 1725-53. Made elaborate aut. clock.

EYSLER, Meinhard. *Nürnberg.* Burgher in 1570. Kleinuhrmacher.

EYSTON—
Thomas. *London.* CC.1651-3.
Edward. *London.* CC.1659-97.

EZEKIEL, ——. *Exeter.* 1794. Watch.

F

FABER, Joseph. *London.* a.1678.
FABIAN, Michael. *Thorn.* 2nd half 17c. Table clock with two hands Feill coll.
FABRE—
Gilbert. *Paris.* 1602-08 juré. oct. eng. watch.
——. *Paris.* 1832-53. Purchased Lepine's business.
FABRICIO, Paulo. *Vienna.* 1573-9. Mathematician. Designed planetarium and calendar of the Olmütz clock.
FABRY—
Pierre. *Lyons.* 1548-51.
——. *Paris.* 1600. Signatory to Statuts of Paris Guild. Prob. same as Fabre.
Jean. *Grenoble.* 1626. Came from *Paris.*
FABY, ——. *London.* d.1767. Native of *Geneva.*
FACCINI, Bernardo. *Venice* and *Piacenza.* 1725. Made a complex planisphere clock for the Duchessa di Parma, now in the Vatican, desc. Hor. Jl. 1941. The clock was designed by Montanari. *v.* Anito.
FACCIOLI, Gian Francisco. *Venice.* 1774. Made a clock going by weight for 48 days, which could also be wound by the wind.
FACIO DE DUILLIER (FATIO), Nicholas. *London.* b.1664, d.1753. Fellow of Roy. Soc. and Acad. des Sci. In *Paris* 1683, then in *The Hague* and went to *London* 1687. Swiss geometrician. Optical worker in London, had the idea of piercing stones for watch jewels and, with Debaufre, took out a patent in 1704. Pub. 'Description d'une pièce d'horlogerie.' Geneva. 1704.
FADENIL, V. *Paris.* 1822-5.
FAGARD, Nicolas. *Paris.* 1765. Bankrupt 1780.
FAGE, Edward. *London.* CC.1667. math. inst. maker.
FÄGERSKYLT, Petter. *Kristinehamn.* 1787.
FAGERSTRÖM, Peter. *Växjö.* b.1789, d. 1848.
FAGG, John. *Margate.* ca.1800.
FAGUILLON, ——. *Hesdin* (*Pas de Calais*). 18c. Watch mt. G.M.
FAHLBORG—
Johan Fredrik. *Vasa* (*Finland*) and *Uppsala.* b.1770, d.ca.1800.
Adolf Fredrik, son. *Vasa* and *Uppsala.* b. 1794, d.1861.
A. F. *Härnösand.* 1816-20. Prob. same as above.
FAHLÉN, Math. *Stjärnsund.* 18c. l.c. clock.
FAHY, Peter. *London.* a.1710.
FAIERS, H. H. & Co. *London.* Early 19c Watch.
FAIN, Pierre. *Blois.* m.1677.
FAIRBAIRN, Andrew. *Edinburgh* 1807-34 l.c. clocks. Succeeded by J. Robertson.
FAIRBRIDGE, John William. *London.* a. 1803.
FAIRBROTHER, Philip. *London.* 1817-24.
FAIRCHILD, David. *London.* 1749. W.
FAIRCLOUGH—
Thomas. *London.* CC.1660.
Henry. *Liverpool.* 1773-96. W.
Edward. *Liverpool.* 1774-1803 CC. Watch Den. coll.
Richard. *Liverpool.* 1781-96. W.
Richard. *Dublin.* Early 19c. Watch.
Thomas. *Dublin.* 1824.
FAIRER, William. *London.* Early 19c. Watch Ilbert coll.
FAIREY—
——. *London.* an.1751. Watch.
John. *London* (*Shoreditch*). 1805-11.
John. *London* (*Ratcliff Highway*). 1815-40. Watch sd. 'Yeriaf' G.M.
Richard. *London.* 1816-40. Watch Den. coll. br. clock.
FAIRFAX, William. *London.* a.1685.
FAIRFIELD, ——. *Dublin.* an.1744. Watch.
FAIRGREIVE, James. *Edinburgh.* a.1783-1794.
FAIRHOLM, Robert. *Edinburgh.* a.1739-43.
FAIRHURST, John. *Liverpool.* 1824-36.
FAIRMAN—
John. *London.* a.1738, CC.1769.
Josiah. *London.* a.1771.
Thomas Henry. *London.* a.1776, CC.1794. d.1799.
FAIRWEATHER, John. *Edinburgh.* 1749.
FAIVRE, ——. *Trévillers.* Early 19c. Started factory for clock mts.
FAIZAN—
Pierre. *Geneva.* ca.1770-91.
Louis. *Geneva.* 1776.
——. *Paris.* 1812.
FAKKELER, L. *Amsterdam.* 1822. C.
FAKLER, C. *Amsterdam.* 1822. C.
FALCHNER, Martin. *Oberhausen.* 1756. Kleinuhrmacher.
FALCK, Carl. *Norrköping.* 1777-85. Watch mt.
FALCKE, *v.* Falke.
FALCON, Jean Michel Antoine. *Chaux-de-Fonds.* a.1769.
FALCONER, William. *Laurencekirk.* 1784.
FALDO—
Robert. *London.* an.1710. Watch.
Thomas. *Shefford.* Mid. 18c. l.c. clock.
FALÉONI, ——. *Paris.* Early 19c. g. en watch.
FALIS, Johann. *Vienna.* m.1786.
FALISSE, ——. *Paris.* 1824. C.

FALK, ——. *Göteborg.* 18c. Watch mt. Nord. M.
FALKE, Johann Heinrich. *Leipzig.* ca.1760. Watch mt. S.K.M.
FALKENGREN—
Carl. *Ystad.* 1783. d.1795.
Jakob. *Växjö.* 1812.
FALLER—
Johann. *Neukirch.* ca.1785. Two wall clocks Furt. M.
——. *Paris.* 1821-3.
Mathias. *Bristol.* 1825.
——. *Norwich.* ca.1825. Watch.
FALLERY—
——. *London.* ca.1740. sil. en. watch.
Daniel Pierre. *Geneva.* ca.1750-71.
Jean Jacques, bro. *Geneva.* ca.1750-70.
FALLOW—
Matthew. *Liverpool.* 1805-14. C.
Joseph. *Newcastle-on-Tyne.* 1815. Wooden C.
William & Co. *Liverpool.* 1816. Wooden and brass C.
Matthew, & Co. *Manchester.* ca.1820.
J., & Co. *Manchester.* ca.1820.
& Kromer. *Newcastle-on-Tyne.* 1820.
FALOISE, ——. *Paris.* Late 18c. C.
FALQUÉ, Louis. *Paris.* m.1776.
FAMEL, Charles. *Paris.* m.1741.
FAR, *v.* Farr.
FARBOCK, John. *London.* 1708. Watch.
FARCY, Jean. *Paris.* m.1767-89. 'Monteur de boîtes.'
FARDEL—
——. *Paris.* ca.1760 m.
Louis Henry. *Paris.* m.1766.
FARDEN, John. *Woodstock.* 1780. From *Deddington.*
FARDOIL—
Jacques. *Blois.* 1627. d. between 1651 and 1664.
Jacques, son. *Blois.* m.1664-94.
Pierre. *Blois.* 1664-9.
Pierre, son. *Blois.* 1684. *Paris.* d.1722.
Peter. *London.* 1700. p.c. g. watch Ilbert coll.
Nicolas. *Paris.* m.1717-89.
——. *Paris.* 1725. Prob. Nicolas. Devised a wheel-cutting engine desc. Thiout. Clock with 2 balances and clock with a vertical line dial, and several wheel- and fuzee-cutting machines in C.A. & M.
Jean. *Paris.* Early 18c. sil. rep. watch Carnegie M.
FARDON—
John. *Deddington.* 1772-91. C. & W.
John. *London.* an.1776. Watch.
Thomas. *Deddington.* 1791. W.
FAREMAN, Michael. *London.* a.1799.
FARET, Jean. *Paris.* 1780.
FAREWELL, John. *London.* a.1686, CC. 1697-1731.
FARFLER—
Stephan. *Nürnberg* and *Altdorf.* b.1633, d. 1689. Made clocks of wood, bone and metal, and added chimes to Altdorf clock. Made a device for turning a sand-glass at regular intervals.
Theodor. *Fürth.* 1650-75.
FARGE, Jean Baptiste. *Paris.* Juré 1738.
FARINE—
Jean Baptiste. *Paris.* d.1777.
et Racle. *Paris.* Mid. 18c. Fine watch with champlevé en.
FARIS (FARRIS)—
William. *London.* d.1728.
William, son. *Annapolis.* 1757, d.1804. From *Philadelphia.* l.c. mus. clock. Month clocks.
William, son. *Annapolis.* b.1762-88. *Norfolk, Va.* 1792-5. *Edinton* (*N. Carolina*). 1797.
Hyram, bro. *Annapolis.* b.1769, d.1800.
FARJAIRE, ——. *Paris.* 1812.
FARJON, Archinard. *Geneva.* ca.1800. g. en. skull watch Ilbert coll.
FARLAM, Ebenezer. *London.* a.1707.
FARLEY—
James. *London.* an.1762. Watch.
Thomas. *Faversham.* 1778-95. W.
Thomas. *Dublin.* 1820.
R. ——. 1825. Pub. art. on a 'Self-regulating pendulum.'
FARMBROUGH, Edward. *London.* CC. 1687.
FARMER—
Thomas. *London.* 1646 CC.
Thomas. *London.* CC.1653-60.
John. *London.* CC.1657-62.
James. *London.* a.1661.
Richard. *London.* a.1675, CC.1683. d. an. 1732.
Richard. *Abingdon.* 1688 CC.
Thomas. *London.* a.1682, CC.1690.
Thomas or William. *London.* a.1747.
Thomas. *Stockton.* ca.1770-95. W.
John. *Philadelphia.* 2nd half 18c. W.
John. *London.* 1817-24. Watch.
FARMILOE, William. *London.* 1799-1808.
FARNBOROUGH, Richard. *London.* a.1685.
FARNELL, William. *Rotherham.* 1825.
FARNHAM—
John. *Winchester.* 1428.
Thomas. *Bridport.* 1780. C.
FARNSWORTH, James. *London.* a.1802.
FARNUM—
Henry. *Connecticut.* Late 18c.
Rufus. *Connecticut.* Late 18c.
FARNWORTH—
Joseph. *Nottingham.* 1784-1815. C. & W.
John. *Mansfield.* 1791-5. C. & W.
George. *London.* a.1789, CC.1797.
FARQUHAR—
Andrew. *Edinburgh.* 1768.
William. *Dublin.* 1824.
FARQUHARSON—
Charles. *Edinburgh.* a.1722.
Charles. *Dundee.* 1733-42.
Lauchlin. *Perth.* a.1743.
Alexander. *Edinburgh.* a.1749.
——. *London.* an.1764. Watch.
——. *Paris.* an.1783. Watch.
George. *London.* CC.1789-93.
FARR—
David. *London.* 1662.
George. *London.* a.1703.
John. *Bristol.* ca.1790, CC.-1801. W.
John and Stephen. ——. 1815-18. W.
Thomas. *Bristol.* 1820-30. Fine verge watch G.M. Ruby cyl. watch Ilbert coll.
John C. *Philadelphia.* 1824-40. W.
FARRER—
Samuel. *York.* 1648. W.
Thomas. *Saxmundham.* 1784. W.
Benjamin. *Pontefract.* ca.1820. l.c. clocks.
FARRINGTON, Thomas. *Bristol.* 1819-52. C.
FARROW—
——. *London.* an.1747. Watch.
John. *London.* 1817. CC.1820-4.
FASOLDT, C. *Albany, New York.* b.1818. Started watch factory in 1861. d.1898. Invented a peculiar double-wheel lever escapement, called 'Fasoldt's chronometer.' Example in Ilbert coll.
FASSY (FASY), C. *Stockholm.* 18c. Watch mt. Nord. M.
FASTEAU LE JEUNE. *Paris.* 1730. br. clock.
FAT, Caspar. *Augsburg.* 1570.
FATET, ——. *Paris.* 1764.
FATHERSON, S. *London.* an.1789. Watch.
FATON, ——. *Paris.* 1812.
FATTON, Frederick Louis. *London.* 1822-4. Patented a marking chronograph.

FAUCON, ——. *Rennes.* 1st half 17c. 6-lobed watch M.M.A.
FAUJOUX, ——. *London.* an.1757. Watch.
FAULCON, Benjamin. *London.* an.1752. Watch.
FAULDS, James. *Kilmarnock.* d.1796.
FAULKNER (FALKNER)—
Edward. *London.* a.1692, CC.1702, m.CC. 1734-44. l.c. clock ill. Cec. & Web. Shagreen case watch. Also FULKENER.
William. *London* (*Shoe Lane*). a.1754, CC. 1761, d.1812. Watch-case maker.
William, son. *London* (*Shoe Lane*). a.1788, CC.1796, d.1814.
John. *London.* a.1791.
FAULKS, Robert. *London.* a.1712, CC.1723.
FAURE—
Claude. *Avignon.* 1676-1709. Fitted pendulum to clock on Hôtel de Ville. cf. FAVRE.
——. *London.* ca.1750. Prob. Henrique FAVRE. Wheel-dividing plate C.A. & M.
Fr. *Pontarlier.* 1805. Pub. a book on watches.
FAURET, J. *Paris.* Late 17c. Clock Pal. de Pau, Paris.
FAUVEL—
Jacques. *Rouen.* a.1695.
Charles. *Paris.* 1764 date of his wife's death.
FAVER, John. *London.* an.1753. Prob. Henrique FAVRE. Agate watch. g. repoussé watch F.W.M. ill. Baillie.
FAVEROLLE, Nicolas. *Paris.* m.1752.
FAVEY—
& SON. *London.* 1799-1804.
Albert Francis. *London.* CC.1804.
FAVIER, ——. *Geneva.* an.1800. Watch.
FAVRAT, BLANCHARD ET FERRETTE. *Porrentruy.* 1811. Started a watch factory which failed.
FAVRE (FAURE)—
François. *Lyons.* 1648-59. From *Bourg-en-Bresse.* 'Très expert et adroit.'
Claude. *Lyons.* 1656 m.-1665. Also FAIVRE.
Claude, son. *Lyons.* 1658 m. Prob. Claude FAURE.
Charles. *Lyons.* 1671 m.
Eléazar. *Lyons.* 1678 m.-1717 juré.
Balthasar. *Basle.* 1689. From *Geneva.* Prob. same as Baltazard.
Jean. *Avully* (*Geneva*). 1697.
Baltazard. *Geneva.* 1702. cf. Balthasar above.
Abram. *Basle.* 1708-10. From *Geneva.*
Antoine, son of Eléazar. *Lyons.* 1718.
——. *London.* ca.1720. Sig. on g. repoussé work.
Henrique. *London.* ca.1730. br. clock. *v.* FAVER and FAURE.
Henry. *London.* Prob. same as Henrique.
Théodore. *Geneva.* ca.1750-70.
Antoine. *Couvet.* 1760-80. C.
Isaac. *Valangin* and *Neuchâtel.* b.1750, d. 1816. Maker of repute.
J. B. *Geneva.* b.1751, d.1807. Painter on enamel.
Fils. *Le Locle.* an.1780. Watch.
Abram David. *Neuchâtel.* 1790-1809.
Louis. *Berlin.* 1792-1809. Granted concession in 1793 for a watch and clock factory.
John James. *Philadelphia.* 1797. W.
Henry. *London.* 1800-24. br. clock. W. to the Prince Regent and the Duke of York.
François. *Switzerland* and *Besançon.* 1800-1814.
——. *Paris.* 1810-24.
ET TRINCAT. *Paris.* 1824.
FAVRE-BULLE, Frédéric Louis. *Le Locle.* b.1770, d.1849. One of the most eminent makers of the Neuchâtel district. Duplex watch S.M.S.K.
FAVRE-DIT-COLLAIN, Bernardin. *Rouen.* m.1653.
FAVRE-MULLER, ——. *Neuchâtel.* 1805.
FAWCETT (FAWCET)—
William. *London.* a.1638.
John. *Dublin.* 1780. Watch Horstmann coll.
'FAYETTE STRATTON.' Sig. on 1868 watches of the UNITED STATES WATCH CO.
FAYRER—
William. *London.* Left in 1773. W.
Thomas. *Lancaster.* 1744-78. Bankrupt. C.
James. *London.* 1810-19. Award by Soc. Arts for 3-wheel sidereal regulator.
FAZAKERLEY—
Thomas. *London.* 1765, sold his stock. W. & T.C.
John. *Liverpool.* 1766. W.
Thomas. *Prescot.* 1771. W.
William. *Prescot.* 1786. W.
FAZY—
Jean. *Moscow.* b.1734-65. g. en. watch S.K.M. cf. Jean of Stockholm and Geneva.
Jean. *Stockholm.* 1760. g. en. watch Nord. M.
Marc Conrad. *Moscow.* b.1740. C. to the Russian court. Started with Jean a factory at *Moscow* in 1765.
Jean. *Geneva.* 2nd half 18c. g. en. watch S.K.M. cf. Jean of Moscow and Stockholm.
Théodore Michel. *Moscow.* b.1773. Jeweller to the Czar.
J., ET FILS. *Geneva.* ca.1800. en. watch set diamonds Carnegie M.
FEAR, James. *Berwick.* Late 18c. l.c. clock.
FEARN, John George. *London.* 1810-40. Duplex watch mt. Ilbert coll.
FEARNLEY, Peter. *Wigan.* 1778-1820.
FEARON, Daniel. *London.* an.1774. Watch.
FEATHERSTONE—
Samuel. *London.* a.1760.
William. *Newcastle-on-Tyne.* 1766-95. W.
FEATLEY—
Charles. *London.* a.1775.
George. *London.* a.1803, CC.1811.
FEATON, John. *London.* a.1732.
FÉAU, Nicolas. *Marseilles.* 1st half 17c. C. to Henrietta Maria, wife of Charles I of England. Astrolabe table clock, Petit Palais, Paris. Table clock Blot-Garnier coll.
FEDERSPIEL, Peter. *Augsburg.* Juré 1742. Town C.
FEDERWISCH, J. C. *Hamburg.* 1815.
FEENSTRA—
H. *Leeuwarden.* 1763.
J. *Leeuwarden.* ca.1800. Trunk clock.
FEEVINGS, John. *Torrington.* Early 19c. Watch.
FEHMEL, Andreas. ——. Late 17c. Table clock ill. Britten.
FEHR—
Jean Antoine. *Geneva.* ca.1770-90.
H. C. *Rotterdam.* ca.1800.
FEHRENBACH, Cölestin. *Griessbach.* ca. 1780. Wall clock Furt. M.
FEHRINGER, Joseph. *Loich.* ca.1800. A parson. Astro. wall clock Uhren M. Vienna.
FEIL, ——. *Paris.* 1824. Turret C.
FEILHAUER, Johann Niklaus. *Basle.* 1725. From *Strasbourg.*
FEIRER, Johanes Baptista. *Augsburg.* 18c. Trav. clock Feill coll.
FELD—
Johann Andreas. *Hamburg.* 1815.
Johann Nicolaus. *Hamburg.* 1815.
FELDT—
Marx. *Nürnberg.* d.1602. inst. maker.
Martin. *Nürnberg.* d.1602. inst. maker.
FELFORTH, Isaac. *London.* a.1715.
FELICETTI, Thoma. *Naples.* 1796. en. watch. Wrote a description of the Farnese planisphere clock, MS. in Vatican, Cod. Vat. Lat. 12946. *v.* ANITO and FACCINI.
FELISE, Jacques. *Paris.* m.1785.

FELIZOT, ——. *Paris.* 1733. Showed to the Acad. R. des Sciences a watch proof against shocks.

FELL—
William. *London.* a.1695, CC.1705-40. Watch.
John, son. *London.* a.1720, CC.1727-78.
James. *Lancaster.* 1767. W.
Joseph. *Ulverstone.* From 1778. C. & W.
Peter. *Garstang.* ca.1820.

FELLETREY, ——. *Châlon-sur-Saône.* 1467.

FELLINGHAM, Robert. *Prescot.* 1795.

FELLOWES, Thomas. *London.* a.1679.

FELLOWS—
William. *London.* an.1751. Watch.
John. *London.* a.1803.

FELMINGHAM—
Robert. *Stradbroke.* 1788-91. l.c. clock.
——. *Bungay.* Early 19c. Watch.

FELMORE, E. *London.* 2nd half 18c. Shagreen watch.

FELS, George. *London.* ca.1685. p.c. watch Ilbert coll.

FELSCH, ——. *Berlin.* 1812.

FELSZ—
Johann Gottlob. *Altenburg.* 1819 m.
Johann Wilhelm. *Altenburg.* m.1819.

FELT—
Hans. *Nürnberg.* m.1564. inst. maker.
Eberhard. *Nürnberg.* 1682. inst. maker.

FELTHAM—
John. *Blandford.* 1791. W.
Thomas Hall. *Salisbury.* 1791. C.
W. *Harleston.* 1813. C. & W.

FELTON—
George. *Birmingham.* 1795-1801. W. & C l.c. clocks.
George. *Bridgnorth.* 1780. C.

FEMERITTÉ, Antoine. *Paris.* 1629. C. to Louis XIII.

FENESTRE, Peter. *London.* a.1722, CC.1732.

FENESTRIER, Jean. *Grenoble.* 1616.

FENLEATER (FINLEATER). Alexander. *Baltimore, U.S.A.* 1807. W.

FENN—
Thomas. *London.* a.1647, CC.1657-87. circ. sil. watch Ilbert coll.
John. *Westminster.* 1662.
Robert, son. *London.* a.1680, CC.1687-1705. l.c. clock Weth. coll. Watch.
Daniel. *London* (*Warwick Lane* and later *Newgate St.*). a.1725, CC.1737, m.CC.1766-1804.
Daniel, son. *London.* CC.1767, m.CC.1791.
Samuel. *London.* CC.1767, m.CC.1793, d.1821.
Isaac. *London.* 1769. 'Makes stop watches with four hands, to denote the sixtieth part of a second.' Sale of his stock in 1777.
Joseph. *London.* CC.1777. d. an.1822.
Daniel and Samuel. *London.* 1785-1804.
Joseph. *London.* l.CC.1822, m.CC.1842-64. W. & C.

FENNELL—
Richard. *London* (*Kensington*). a.1669, CC. 1679-1705. br. and l.c. clocks. Gilt metal case br. clock Prestige coll.
John. *London.* a.1669, CC.1679.
Henry Hebden. *London.* a.1764.

FENNER—
Benjamin. *London.* a.1717. Watch.
William. *Birmingham.* ca.1790. l.c. clock.

FENNYMORE, Christopher. *London.* an. 1796. Watch. cf. FINNYMORE.

FENTHAM, T. *London.* Late 18c. Watch.

FENTON—
John. *London.* a.1655, CC.1662. l.c. clock Virginia M.
James. *York.* 1740. C.
Edward. *London.* a.1731, CC.1739.
William. *Newcastle-o.-T.* 1778-90. l.c. clocks. Watch.

FENTON—*continued.*
William. *London.* 1784. Watch.
——. *Chesterfield.* ca.1800.
Thomas. *Bristol.* 1794-1801. W. & C.

FENU,——. *Paris.* an.1776. Watch.

FENWICK—
W. *Spanish Town, Jamaica.* 1795. C. & W.
Father and son. *Crieff.* 1800-76.
John. *S. Shields.* 1820.

FENZEL, Conrad. *Fürth.* d.1832.

FERAND, ——. *Paris.* 1812.

FERCHLIN, Gustavus (or Just). *Copenhagen.* m.1697. Turret C.

FÉRÉ (FERE, FRERE), Adrien Jean Baptiste. *Paris.* m .1786-9.

FERGUSON—
James. *London.* b.1710, d.1776. An eminent astronomer and mechanician. Pub. 'Tables and Tracts . . . ' London, 1771. 'Select Mechanical Exercizes . . .,' dealing with clocks, and 'An introduction to Electricity,' London, 1775, containing the first English reference to electric clocks. Made orreries and a 3-wheel and other special clocks. Compass dial M.M.A.
Alexander. *Edinburgh.* a.1754-72.
William. *Alnwick.* 1767. Watch.
——. *London.* an.1777. Watch.
Alexander. *Dundee.* 1777.
Alexander. *Cupar-Fife.* 1780.
George. *Perth.* a.1791.
Robert. *Newcastle-o.-T.* 1804. C. & W.
Thomas. *Newcastle-o.-T.* 1811. C.
George. *Philadelphia.* 1820. W.
John. *Ballina.* 1824.

FERLITTE—
Gautier. *Geneva.* 1599-1633.
François. *Geneva.* 18c. 4-colour g. watch Fränkel coll.

FERMENT—
John. *London.* CC.1679. French. W. Table clock.
Philip. *London.* 1689-1701 CC.
Paul. *London.* Mid. 18c. Watch mt. S.K.M.

FERNAL—
John. *Wrexham.* ca.1780. Watch.
John. *Chester.* 1784.

FERNER, Eric. *Gäfle.* 1821-5.

FERNEY, *v.* MANUFACTURE ROYALE.

FERNOT, Jean. *Montbéliard.* 1785. 'Serrurier horloger.'

FÉRON, André. *Paris.* m.1767-89. Watch mt. C.A. & M. Machine for cutting escape wheels and filecutting machine C.A. & M. Perpetual cal. watch and a watch showing the Republican calendar, approved by Acad. des Sciences 1772.

FERRACINA, Bartolommeo. *Bassano.* 1750-1760. Re-made Venice clock.

FERRAL & ROUSSEAU. *London.* an.1777. Watch.

FERRAND—
Benjamin. *London.* a.1774.
——. *Paris.* 1812-24.

FERRAR, John. *London.* CC.1693-1705. cf. FERRERS.

FERRARI, Lorenzo. *Parma.* 1824. Astro. clock predicting eclipses.

FERRARO, Niccolò. *Genoa.* 1395. Keeper of Genoa clock. 'Nuper electo magistro orologii.'

FERRER, Guglielmus. *Pontefract.* 1707. Fine tortoiseshell br. clock.

FERRERS, John. *London.* 1715-19. l.c. clock. cf. FERRAR.

FERRIER—
Laurent. *Avignon.* 1590-1630. Town C.
Pierre. *Feurs.* 1606.
Antoine. *Paris.* 1607, d.1622. C. to the King. Watch B.M. with sundial sd. 'Ferrier.'

FERRIER—*continued.*
Guillaume, son. *Paris.* 1622-4. C. to the King. en. watch formerly in Shandon coll.
C. *Lyons.* 1695. d.1707.
James. *London.* a.1783.
J. A. *Valence-sur-Rhône,* 1811.
William Thornton. *Hull.* 1822-36.

FERRIÈRE—
Abraham. *Geneva.* ca.1770-88.
——. *Paris.* 1822.

FERRIS—
James. *London.* a.1783.
Benjamin. *Philadelphia.* 1802-11. Later *Wilmington.*
Ziba, bro. *Wilmington, U.S.A.* b.1786, d. 1875.
James. *Poole.* 1810. C.
Benjamin, & J. McElwee. *Philadelphia.* 1813.

FERROL, Joseph. *London.* an.1772. Watch.

FERRON—
John. *London.* CC.1692. rep. watch, dial set diamonds, Lincoln M.
Lewis. *London.* a.1720. l.c. clocks.
Abraham. *London.* a.1725, CC.1737-56.
John or Jacob. *London.* a.1737.
Michael, son of Abraham. *London.* a.1753, CC.1769, l.CC.1786.
Michael. *London.* 1793 l.CC. *Gt. Missenden,* 1821.

FERROT—
Philippe. *Paris.* 1775-1800. g. rep. watch.
& Fazy. Prob. *Geneva.* Late 18c. 4-colour g. watch Den. coll.
——. *Geneva.* Early 19c. Copper en. watch Fränkel coll.

FERRY—
Maurice Bernard. *Paris.* 1579. C. to Henri III.
M. *London.* an.1773. Watch.
John. *London.* an.1774. Watch.

FERSCHNER, Andreas. *Vienna.* m.1749.

FERTBAUR (FERTHBAUER), Phillipp. *Vienna.* m.1795. Pub. a desc. of some clocks in 1798.

FERTEAU (FESTEAU, and cf. Fetteau)—
Siméon François. *Paris* (*Rue de Montmorency*). m.1750-89.
François Bonaventure, l'aîné, son. *Paris* (*Rue St. Martin*). m.1779, juré 1788. Keeper of Bastille clock. Clock Bernal sale.
Jean Louis, bro. *Paris* (*Rue aux Ours*). m. 1783-1812. Lyre clock.
Le Jeune. *Paris.* Early 19c. Mantel clock M.M.A. Prob. the preceding.

FERTIG—
Benjamin. *Philadelphia.* 1811.
Jacob. *Philadelphia.* 1811.

FERVEZ, ——. *Paris.* 1811.

FESSARD, Pierre. *Paris.* m.1771.

FESSLER, Andreas. *Hasenried.* Early 19c. Skeleton watch.

FESTIN, Christian. *Angers.* 1659. Replaced town clock.

FÉTIL—
Pierre. *Orléans.* b.1753-1814. Maker of repute. Pub. in 1802 'La Théorie de l'horlogerie réduite en tableaux.'
Cadet. *Paris.* 1807-12. Also Fénil.

FÉTINE, ——. *Paris.* 18c. g. en. watch set diamonds.

FETINER, ——. *Paris.* 1812.

FETTEAU—
——. *Paris.* 1745 m. cf. Ferteau.
Jacques François, son. *Paris.* m.1751. cf. Ferteau.

FETTER—
Nicholas. *London.* CC.1632-56.
Thomas. *London.* CC.1710.

FETTERS, Henry. *London.* 1630. CC.1653-1664.

FEUILLET, Pierre. *Beauvais.* 1744. Fitted pendulum to clock of St. Étienne.

FEURER (FEIRER)—
Johann Baptist. *Augsburg.* comp. 1761, m. 1768-95.
Franz Xavier. *Augsburg.* m.ca.1805.

FEVER, ——. *London* (*Soho*). 1711. W.

FEVRIER—
——. *Paris.* 1600. Signatory to Statuts of Paris corporation.
——. *Geneva.* 1765. Tried to go to Russia at request of Catherine II, but was arrested in France for taking a French workman.
George. *Paris.* 2nd half 18c. Watch mt. Arts M. Prague.

FEWELLER (FEWLER). *Liverpool.* 1761-81. C.

FEYHEL, Martin. *Augsburg.* Went to the Dresden Court in 1578. C. Made pedometer for August of Saxony.

FIACRE, Clément. *Paris.* ca.1700. Watch.

FIAULT, Pierre Paul. *Paris.* m.1751.

FICH, Hans. *Copenhagen.* m.1757.

FICHTNER—
Andreas. *Dresden.* m.1681-1700. sil. watch Fränkel coll.
Andreas Gottlieb. *Dresden.* m.1722.
Andreas. *Marburg.* 1750.

FIDELIUS, ——. *Bremen.* Mid. 18c. l.c. clock Schloss M. Berlin.

FIDGETT, William. *Bermondsey* and *London* (*Bell Court*). CC.1789, l.CC.1812-25. Watch G.M.

FIEFFÉ—
Jacques. *Paris.* 1544-7. Founder member of Paris corporation.
Jean Jacques. *Paris.* Juré 1747-89.
Jean Nicolas. *Paris.* m.1752.
Nicolas. *Paris.* m.1754.
Alexandre. *Paris.* m.1757.
Jean Claude. *Paris.* m.1757-89.
——. *Paris* (*Quai Pelletier*). 1812.

FIELD—
William. *London.* a.1725, CC.1733-63. Watch and mt. G.M.
William. *Bungay.* 1750. C. & W.
James. *Dunstable.* an.1758. Watch.
Thomas. *London.* a.1744.
Nath. *London.* an.1768. Watch.
J. *London.* an.1775. Watch.
Charles. *London.* a.1785.
Thomas. *Bath.* Started 1773 CC.-1812. l.c. clock and watch.
John. *Evesham.* d.1785. C.
Daniel. *Luton.* 1785.
Robert, jun. *Frant.* 1790. C. & W.
Daniel. *Hitchin.* 1795. W.
Daniel. *London.* 1799.
T. W. *Aylesbury.* ca.1800. Watch.
George. *London.* 1800. Watch.
James. *Hertford.* ca.1800. l.c. clock. Watch. N.Y. Univ.
Joseph. *London.* a.1792.
Matthew. *London.* a.1792.
Peter. *New York.* 1805.
Peter, jun. *New York.* 1805.
W. *Bath.* 1819.
Simon. *Liverpool.* 1825. C.

FIELDER—
Thomas. *London.* a.1678, CC.1687, m.CC. 1715-19.
William. *London.* a.1799.

FIELDERS, Henry. *Atherstone.* 1796.

FIELDHOUSE, Benjamin. *Leominster.* 1756. Watch.

FIELDSHAW, James. *Leeds.* 1770-87. Watch Ilbert coll.

FIELDSON, Henry. *Atherstone.* ca.1790.

FIELDING—
Nathaniel. *London.* 1805-09.
George. *London.* a.1817.

FIELDUS, Henry. *Tamworth.* 1784. W.

FIERET, ——. *Montpellier*. ca.1620. Oval sil. al. watch, compass and sundial in cover. Oval crys. watch formerly in Shandon coll.
FIFE, William. *Edinburgh*. a.1780.
FIFIELD—
Benjamin. *London*. a.1695.
Joseph. *Winchester*. ca.1800.
FILE, John. *London*. a.1746.
FILLIAT (FILIAT, FILLAT), Étienne. *Lyons*. 1617 m.-1623.
FILLING, Franziskus Salesius. *Freiburg-i.-Br*. ca.1750. br.clock Furt. M.
FILON (FILLON)—
Charles. *Paris*. m.1751.
Claude Charles François. *Paris*. m.1782-9.
Barthélemy. *Geneva*. 1791.
——. *Paris*. 1807-23.
FINCH—
Daniel. *London*. a.1667.
John. *London*. a.1668, CC.1675, m.CC.1706, d.an.1713. Watch, l.c. clock Weth. coll.
Thomas. *London* (*St. Martins*). CC.1670-1706. Watch Den. coll.
Simon. *London*. a.1678, CC.1706.
N. *London*. a.1682, CC.1691.
William. *London*. a.1683, CC.1691-1715. l.c. clock.
Robert. *London*. a.1683, CC.1691-1711. Watch Glasgow Art Gall.
Jacob. *London*. a.1686.
James. *London*. a.1700.
Katherine. *London*. 1719. W.
Richard. *London*. a.1725, CC.1733-62.
& SIMS. *London* (*Lombard St.*). 1743. Watch mt. Ilbert coll.
Richard. *London* (*Lombard St.*). 1744.
Thomas. *London*. a.1743.
William. *Halifax*. an.1757. Watch S.M.S.K.
& BRADLEY. *London and Halifax*. ca.1760.
John. *Dublin*. an.1770. Watch.
G. *London*. an.1772. Watch.
FINCHETT, Arnold. *London*. Mid. 18c. Night clock Ilbert coll.
FINDLAY, William and George. *London* (*Whitechapel*), 1805-08; (*Chelsea*), 1822-4.
FINDLER—
Joseph. *Liverpool*. 1796. Wooden C.
John. *Liverpool*. 1800. Wooden C.
FINDLEY, J. *London*. 1820.
FINDLOW—
Zachariah. *London*. a.1699.
Charles. *London*. a.1756.
FINE, Oronce. *Paris*. b.1494, d.1555. Mathematician. Devised water clocks and a complex astro. clock in library of St. Geneviève, Paris.
FINER—
Thomas. *London*. 1794. Partner in the following.
& NOWLAND. *London*. 1805-25. al. watches S.M.S.K. and Chamb. coll.
FINES (FYNES), John. *London*. a.1688.
FINÉS, ——. *Paris*. 1824.
FINISTER, James. *London*. a.1786.
FINK, Cyriakus. *Würzburg*. m.1745. br. clock Luitprandt M.
FINLEY—
John. *Baltimore, U.S.A*. 1754. C.
James. *Newcastle-o.-T*. 1782-4. C. & W.
FINLOW, Zachariah. *London*. a.1699.
FINMORE, John Thomas. *London*. a.1790.
FINNEY—
Joseph. *Liverpool*. 1734-61. C. & W.
John. *Liverpool*. 1754. C.
John. *Charleston, U.S.A*. 1754. C. & W.
Joseph. *Liverpool*. 1770-96. l.c. mus. clock and watch.
William. *Liverpool*. 1821-9. W.
Richard. *Liverpool*. 1825. W.
FINNIE, Henry. *London*. a.1721, CC.1729.
FINNYMORE, ——. *London* (*Hatton Garden*). d.1767. cf. FENNYMORE.

FIORELLI, Raffaele. *Rome*. ca.1780. Made clocks for the Torre Capitolina, the Basilica Vaticana and the town of Foligno, so arranged that any arbor could be removed without dismantling the clock.
FIREBUCK, William. *London*. an.1766. Watch.
FIRSTENEF, ——. *Friedberg*. Early 18c. Stand clock Feill coll.
FISCHER, Johan Henrik. *Copenhagen*. m. 1709. From *Altona*. Kleinuhrmacher.
Konrad Michael. *Onolzbach*. 1742-72. Court C.
Ignatius. *Augsburg*. Mid. 18c. Watch N.Y. Univ.
Michael. *Aachen*. ca.1750. Table clock.
Conrad. *Stockholm*. 1755-9.
Rudolf. *Basle*. 1763. Turret clocks.
Bent. *Copenhagen*. m.1771.
Johann Benjamin. *Dresden*. 1780. Court C. Granted permit to start a factory in Grossenhain. Ring watch Grüne Gewölbe.
John. *London*. 1783. Patented a pedometer and watch.
Johann. *Augsburg*. 1787. Turret C.
Johann. *Munich*. ca.1790. 8-day watch mt. Ilbert coll.
FISH—
Henry. *London* (*R. Exchange*). 1736. d.1774. Watch.
William. *London*. 1737. Watch Den. coll.
John. *London*. CC.1766-77.
Robert. *London*. an.1769. Watch.
Henry, & Co. *London*. 1770-5.
Samuel. *London*. an.1774. Watch.
George. *Northampton*. 1795.
Robert. *London* (*St. Martins le Grand*). 1775-1825.
John, son. *London*. a.1805.
Robert Howard. *London* (*Dean St.* and *Greek St.*). CC.1813-24.
FISHBURN, Robert. *Carlow*. an.1777. Watch.
FISHER—
Charles. *London*. a.1679.
Ebenezer. *London*. a.1687.
Theophilus. *London*. ca.1700. sil. and shagreen watch S.M.S.K.
Rebeckah. *London*. a.1715.
Ebenezer. *London*. a.1716, CC.1725-38.
John. *Rotherhithe*. d.1750. 'Eminent' W.
John. *Preston*. 18c. Clock.
John. *London*. a.1746, CC.1763.
William Park. *London*. ca.1760.
Joseph. *London*. a.1753.
Daniel. *London*. 1770.
Henry. *Preston*. ca.1770-95. Watch mt. l.c. clock.
William. *London*. an.1773. Watch.
William. *Sutton Coldfield*. 1773.
David. *London*. an.1773. Watch.
Daniel. *London*. an.1790. Watch.
Daniel, & Son. *London* (*Finsbury*). 1790-1805.
John. *York, Pa., U.S.A*. 1790. C.
Richard. *Liverpool*. 1790-1836. W.
& SONS. *London* (*Moorfields*). 1791-1808. Cyl. watch Ilbert coll. Also D. FISHER & SONS.
James. *Preston*. ca.1800.
Edwin. *Bath*. 1819-26.
Joseph William. *London*. a.1815.
FISHWATER, John. *London*. a.1709, CC. 1726.
FISHWICK, George. *London*. 2nd half 18c. Watch.
FISKE, Thomas. *Stowmarket*. 1777-84. W.
FISTER, Amon. *Philadelphia*. 1794. W.
FITCH, William. *London*. a.1803.
FITCHEW, William. *London*. a.1811.
FITE, John. *Baltimore, U.S.A*. 1807-17.

FITGEN (FITTGEN), Jacob Hans. *Cologne.* 1718-30.

FITREE (FIRTREE), Samuel. *London.* 1790-3.

FITTER—

F. R. ——. Mid. 17c. Oval sil. watch Mallett coll.

John. *Battersea.* CC.1685. Watch showing hours and minutes, with a seconds dial on top plate ill. Britten.

Thomas. *London (Clerkenwell Gr.).* CC. 1710-37.

Thomason, son. *London.* a.1731-83. Watch.

Thomas. *Eton.* an.1764. Watch.

FITTON—

Thomas. *London.* a.1638.

Charles. *London.* a.1667, CC.1674.

Daniel. *London.* a.1675.

FITZ, Thomas. *Salisbury.* 1795. W.

FITZER (FITZEN, FIETZEN)—

Benjamin. *Worcester.* 1771. From *London.* C. & W.

William. *Liverpool.* 1811-29.

FITZGERALD, William Bolster. *Newcastle (Munster).* 1824.

FITZHERBERT, John & Andrew. *London.* an.1799. Watch.

FITZJAMES, Thomas. *London.* a.1648.

FITZWALTER, John. *Beaulieu (Hants).* 1538-42. Keeper of clock.

FITZWATER, Henry. *London.* a.1719-34 CC.

FIVEY, George. *Dublin.* 1795. br.clock. Watch N.Y. Univ.

FIZET, Robert Abraham. *Paris.* m.1756.

FLACARD (FLOCCARD), ——. *Paris.* 1812-25. Succeeded PERETTON.

FLACK, George. *London.* 1817-24.

FLADGATE—

John. *London (Conduit St.).* a.1743. CC. and d.1781. For a period up to 1775 he was in partnership with Richard Wilder, as FLADGATE & WILDER. The business was carried on by his widow to 1793. Clock B.M. g. repoussé watch S.K.M. l.c. lacquer clock.

Thomas. *London.* an.1772. Watch.

FLAMENVILLE, ——. *Paris.* 1727. Devised a modified verge escapement.

FLAMEYER, B. *London.* 1760. Watch mt. G.M.

FLANT (FLANC), Jehan. *Geneva* and *La Rochelle.* a.1584. d.1616. C. to the town of La Rochelle from 1599. Fine astro. watch B.M. ill. Baillie, with cal. starting 1610. Watches Louvre and Gélis coll.

FLASCHKE—

Andre. *Vienna.* m.1780.

Tobias. *Vienna.* m.1788. Also FLASGE.

FLASHMAN—

George. *Exeter.* 1765. C. & W.

George. *London.* 1790-1815. Succeeded by TUNNELL.

FLECHY, ——. *Paris.* 1824.

FLEET, James. *London.* a.1776, CC.1813.

FLEETWOOD—

Thomas. *Liverpool.* 1754. W.

Joshua. *Liverpool.* ca.1760. Watch mt. Buckley coll.

Robert. *London.* 1763. d.an.1794. Livery Goldsmiths Co. br. clock. g. rep. watch Den. coll. Watch mt. with ruby cyl. and steel esc. wheel Ilbert coll. Mus. aut. clock Peiping M.

Thomas. *London.* an.1773. Watch.

John. *London.* 1780. d.1812.

Mrs. George. *Liverpool.* 1796.

James. *Liverpool.* ca.1820.

FLEGG, William. *London.* a.1821.

FLEIGEL, Joseph. *Stadt-am-Hof.* Late 18c. p.c. rep. watch M.M.A.

FLEISCHER, Jakob. *Friedberg.* Mid. 18c. Watch mt. Arts M. Prague.

FLEMING—

Andrew. *London.* a.1717, CC.1726.

Curtis. *London (Shadwell).* CC.1768, l.CC. 1771-1806.

James. *Liverpool.* 1790-1829. W.

Hugh. *Dublin.* 1795. W.

Richard. *Liverpool.* 1810. W.

David. *London.* 1817-24. W.

Ignatius. *Waterford.* 1824.

——. *Omagh.* 1824.

Thomas. *Liverpool.* 1825. W.

C. *Manchester.* Early 19c. Watch.

FLESCHELLE, L. *London.* 1817-25. C.

FLESSIÈRES, ——. *Geneva.* 1794. Started with DUPIAT the second machine factory under public subvention, but failed to maintain his promises. Went to *Versailles* in 1795.

FLETCHER—

Daniel. *London.* CC.1646, d.an.1664.

John. *London.* a.1654.

John. *London.* a.1655.

Daniel, son of Daniel. *London.* a.1664.

Thomas. *London.* CC.1676-93.

Edward. *London.* a.1679, CC.1697-1707.

Bazil. *London.* a.1692.

Thomas. *London.* a.1698.

Robert. *Roby-within-Huyton.* d.1743. C.

John. *London.* a.1727, CC.1744.

Richard. *London.* ca.1760. Watch mt. Oldham M.

William. *Leeds.* 1770-1801. l.c. clocks. Also W.

William Kimber. *London.* a.1768.

Cecilia. *Rotherham.* ca.1770-95. C.

John. *Holbeck.* d.1787. C.

Thomas. *Chester.* 1781-93.

John. *Leeds.* d.1797.

Robert. *Chester.* 1784-1820. l.c. clock ill. Cec. & Web. Watch.

Tobias. *Barnsley.* 1790. d.1811. l.c. clocks.

James. *Rotherham.* 1790-1818. W.

William. *Bristol.* 1797. W.

Thomas. *Newcastle-o.-T.* 1801-50. C. & W.

Thomas. *Barnsley.* 1802.

Thomas. *Liverpool.* 1805. C.

Charles. *Barnsley.* 1807-22.

Thomas. *Gateshead.* 1811.

Thomas. *Leeds.* 1817-26.

Robert Graham. *Edinburgh.* 1825-51.

Charles. *Philadelphia.* 1825.

James. *Liverpool.* 1825.

William Frederick, son of Thomas. *Barnsley.* d.1908.

FLEURDAU, Pierre. *Amsterdam.* 1688. Huguenot refugee from *Châtellerault.*

FLEUREAU—

Esaye. *London.* ca.1710. Watch N.Y. Univ. l.c. clock Weth. coll.

Peter. *London.* an.1776. Watch.

FLEURET, Donat Jean. *Geneva.* ca.1760-87.

FLEURIEU, Charles Pierre. *Paris.* Pub. in 1768 an attack on Le Roy's memoir on his chron. and in 1773 an account of the voyage made to try Berthoud's chron.

FLEURY—

——. *Paris.* ca.1750.

Jean (Jacques) François. *Paris.* m.1759-89.

Mathurin Jacques Edme. *Paris.* m.1783.

Louis Pierre Jean Chrisostome. *Paris.* m. 1788.

——. *St. Eloy.* str. watch Den. coll.

FLEUTRY, Jacques François. *Paris.* d.1765.

FLEXNEY, Henry. *London.* a.1656.

FLIEGER, Heinrich. *Günzburg.* Went *Augsburg* 1783-99.

FLIGHT—

Blair. *Kinross.* 1775-99.

Alexander. *Cupar-Fife.* 1820-35.

FLINDELL, Benjamin. *London.* a.1714.

FLING, Daniel. *Philadelphia.* 1811-20.
FLINT—
Henry. *London.* a.1700.
William. *Charing.* b.1733. d.1795. C. & W.
William. *Ashford.* ca.1800. Watch.
FLOCKHART—
John. *Edinburgh.* 1797.
Andrew. *London.* 1815-25.
FLODTER—
Paul. *Prague.* 2nd half 18c. Watch mt. Arts M. Prague.
Michael. *Prague.* 2nd half 18c. Watch mt. Arts M. Prague.
FLOOD—
Humphrey. *London.* 1607-17. Supplied a clock, set diamonds and rubies, to James I. Possibly a goldsmith only.
Joseph. *London.* a.1717.
John. *London.* a.1718.
Edward. *London.* a.1723.
FLOOK—
John. *Bristol.* 1747.
John. *London.* 1754. Watch.
FLOOKS, William. *London.* a.1783.
FLORET, Jean. *Grenoble.* 1389-92. 'Relogier.' Made first public clock of Grenoble.
FLOTE, George. *London.* 1805-08. mus. C. & W.
FLOURNEY, Jean. *Geneva.* 1784-1800. *v.* BRY.
FLOURNOY, Henry. *France.* Late 17c. Watches Den. coll. and S.K.M.
FLOWER—
George. *London.* a.1670, CC.1682-9. Watch with eng. steel outer case ill. Britten.
John. *London.* CC.1728-30.
Thomas. *London.* CC.1730. g. watch.
John. *London.* a.1724, CC.1734.
Henry. *Philadelphia.* 1753. W. & C. of repute. Made l.c. mus. clocks.
Edward (FLOWERS). *London.* 1783. g. watch.
John. *London.* a.1790.
John. *London.* a.1808.
FLOYD—
William. *London.* a.1660.
Thomas. *Charleston, U.S.A.* 1767. C.
FLOYER, Sir John. *London.* 1690-1710. Physician who used a seconds watch for pulse counting and pub. 'The Physician's Pulse Watch,' London, 1707 and 1710.
FLUDGATE, Thomas. *London.* Mid. 18c. cyl. watch mt. G.M.
FLÜGGER, Gottfried Bernhardt. *Berlin.* 1808.
FLUX, Thomas. *London.* a.1774.
FLY—
C. *London.* an.1778. Watch.
Joseph. *London.* 2nd half 18c. Watch mt.
FOCQ, Nicholas. *Maubeuge.* 1751.
FODEN, Thomas. *Congleton.* 1753-85.
FÖDERL, Christian. *Vienna.* m.1803.
FOGARTY, James. *London.* a.1818.
FOGG—
John. *London.* a.1727, CC.1735.
John. *London.* a.1750, CC.1759.
James. *London.* a.1759.
Hugh. *London.* 1770.
John. *Liverpool.* 1807-29. W.
FOGGO, James. *London.* 1799-ca.1820. Fine watch style of Breguet.
FOGO, Hugh. *London.* an.1772. Watch.
FOHMANN, P. A. F. *Fürth.* d.1830.
FOILLOT (FUILLOT), Étienne. *Lyons.* 1567. d.ca.1589.
FOKIBRIKS, Johan. *Copenhagen.* 1703. Kleinuhrmacher.
FOL (LE FOL)—
Jean François. Prob. *Paris.* ca.1700. circ. eng. watch.
Jean. *Paris.* 1770-88. C. to Louis XVI from 1777 and W. to King of Poland. Watch

FOL (LE FOL)—*continued.*
Horstmann coll. g. en. watch, set diamonds. Watch mt. Arts M. Prague. Cartel clock.
FOLGHAM, John. *London.* 1752. Shagreen case maker.
FOLIN—
Jeune. *Paris.* ca.1770. Mantel clock Nat. M. Stockholm.
Nicolas Alexandre. *Paris.* m.1789.
——. *Paris.* 1807-13. cf. FOLLIN.
——. *Paris (Passage des Panoramas).* 1812.
——. *Paris (Rue St. Martin).* 1812.
FOLKINGHAM, Denny. *London.* a.1718.
FOLLAND, William. *Exeter.* 1795. Watch mt. Horstmann coll.
FOLLET, ——. *Sidmouth.* 2nd half 18c. l.c. clock.
FOLLETT—
Richard. *London.* a.1653.
——. *Lichfield.* an.1767. Watch.
Mary. *London.* Mid. 18c. Watch.
FOLLIN, ——. *Paris.* 1819. cf. FOLIN.
FOLLON, Dennis. *London.* a.1749.
FOLMAR, Andrew. *New York.* 1805. W.
FOLTER (AFFOLTER), Jean Rodolphe. *Le Locle.* 1751-85. Fine C. In partnership with Jonas Pierre COURVOISIER. Very fine Louis XV clock sd. 'COURVOISIER-FOLTER.'
FOLZ, Jacob André. *Geneva.* b.1798, d.1847.
FONNEREAU—
Zacharie. *La Rochelle.* a.1618-26 at *Lyons.* At *La Rochelle* from 1641. d.an.1683. oct. crys. watch S.K.M. sil. oct. watch Côte coll. Two crys. cross watches Petit Pal. Paris. circ. sil. watches Mallett, Ilbert, Gélis and Dutuit colls.
Pierre. *La Rochelle.* mar. 1672. d.ca.1710. g. en. watch.
James. *London.* 1653. Frenchman.
FONTAC, ——. *London.* 1794. Watch Den. coll.
FONTAINE—
Abraham. *Geneva.* b.1721-68.
& TORIN. *London.* an.1747. Watch. Moses F. & Daniel T. Also FOUNTAIN.
John. *London.* a.1748, CC.1759.
John & Moses. *London.* an.1766. Watch.
Jaques François, son of Abraham. *Geneva.* ca.1760-91.
Jean. *Paris.* 1807-24.
FONTANA—
C. *High Wycombe.* Early 19c. Watch.
——. *Exeter.* Early 19c. Watch.
FONTANIÉ, ——. *Paris.* 1825. Successor to DESTOUCHES.
FOOT, Robert. *Edinburgh.* a.1755-98.
FOOTE, William. *London.* CC.1726-42. Watches Den. and Horstmann colls.
FORBES—
Charles Henry. *London.* a.1711.
Thomas. *London.* a.1725.
Edward. *Liverpool.* 1803-29. W.
John. *London.* 1820.
Joshua. *Liverpool.* 1825. W.
FORBUS, Thomas. *London.* a.1723.
FORCHER, Jean. *Paris.* m.1764-89.
FORCHIER, John. *London.* 1694.
FORD—
Henry. *London.* a.1647.
Robert. *London.* a.1652.
William. *London.* a.1692-1701 CC.
Thomas. *London (Princes St. Barbican).* a. 1716, CC.1724-64.
John. *London.* 1723. Watch.
John. *Aylesbury.* 1725. Insolvent. W.
Robert. *London.* a.1730.
Southerland. *Charleston, U.S.A.* 1741. C. & W.
James. *London (Long Lane).* an.1761. Watch.
John. *London.* a.1761.
John, son of Thomas. *London.* CC.1752.

FORD—*continued.*
William. *London.* CC.1770.
John. *London.* a.1785, CC.1800.
George. *Lancaster City, U.S.A.* 1811. d. 1842. English. l.c. clocks.
William. *Leith.* a.1813-30.
FORDERER, John. *Birmingham.* 1775-95. Watch Birmingham M.
FORDHAM—
Thomas. *London.* CC.1687. W.
Joseph. *Braintree.* 18c. l.c. clock.
Thomas, jun. *Bishop Stortford* 1776, *Braintree* 1779. C. & W.
John. *Coggeshall.* 1784. C.
James. *Dunmow.* 1793. C.
FORDYCE, George. *England.* 1794. Devised a form of compensation pendulum, and pub. a desc. in Phil.Trans.
FOREMAN—
Francis. *London.* 1620. w.CC.1634. d.1649. Petitioner for incorporation of CC. Also Forman.
Michael. *London.* CC.1805, l.CC.1812.
William. *Petersburg.* d.1830.
John. *London.* a.1800.
George. *London.* a.1806.
FORESTER (FORRESTER), Joseph. *London (Hammersmith).* 1805-08. Watch.
FORFAICT (FORFAIT or **FORFECT)**—
Augustin. *Sedan.* d.1587. Watch in B.M.; one of the earliest known French watches ill. Baillie.
Jacob, son of Augustin Forfaict. *Sedan.* 1582-1637. Fine maker. oct. watch Louvre. Oval eng. watch Ilbert coll.
Isaac, bro. *Sedan.* 1585. Watches Cluny M. and Blot-Garnier coll.
Nicolas. *Paris.* 1606-13. Juré. Watches M.M.A. and Gélis coll.
FORMANT, Philip. *London.* CC.1687-95. Engraver.
FORNELIUS, Laurent. *Uppsala.* 1630. Pub. 'Horologium astronomicum.'
FORNET, Jean. *Geneva.* d.1560.
FORRER, ——. *Vienna.* 1780. Made watch with pedometer winding.
FORREST—
Nathaniel. *London.* a.1672.
Matthew. *London.* a.1672.
Joseph. *London.* a.1681, CC.1692.
Robert. *London.* a.1754.
James. *Edinburgh.* a.1763.
Peter, & Co. *Edinburgh.* 1783-96.
Simon. *Lanark.* 1800-37.
Thomas. *London.* a.1799.
Daniel. *Edinburgh.* 1820-38.
David. *Edinburgh.* 1823.
FORRETTE, John. *London.* 1694.
FORREY, Christian. *Lampeter & Lancaster Co., Pa., U.S.A.* 1773. W.
FORSAITH, John. *London.* 1759. Watch Ilbert coll.
FORSBERG—
Jacob. *Stockholm.* b.1760, d.1806. Wall clock.
Carl Johan. *Stockholm.* 1813.
FORSHAW, John. *Prescot.* 1788. Watch toolmaker.
FORSMAN—
Anders. *Jönköping.* 1752-4. br. and l.c. clocks.
Erik. *Linköping.* b.1755, d.1815. Also Forssman.
FORSSELL—
Johan. *Åbo.* 1741-50.
Michael. *Stockholm.* 1770. d.1780. Year clock. Also Forsell.
——. *Kristinehamn.* 1787.
FORSTER—
William. *London.* CC.1660. Also Foster.
Clement. *London.* a.1670, CC.1682-89.
William. *London.* a.1672, CC.1681-83.

FORSTER—*continued.*
John. *London.* a.1680, CC.1689. Also Foster.
Joseph, *v.* Foster.
Jacob. *London.* a.1690. Also Foster.
Humphrey. *London.* a.1706.
John. *London.* CC.1726.
Henry. *London.* a.1729.
Richard. *London.* a.1736.
Edward. *Carlisle.* 1750-1813. l.c. clocks.
Charles. *London.* an.1757. Watch.
James. *Norwich.* b.1743, d.1789. C. & W.
Thomas. *London.* an.1778. Watch.
Thomas. *Lichfield.* 1780. l.c. clock. Watch.
John. *Liverpool.* 1784. W.
——. *Sheerness.* ca.1790 CC.
Isaac. *London (Holborn).* 1793. Watch.
——. *Harwich.* ca.1800.
——. *Paris.* 1812.
Thomas. *London.* a.1799.
Joseph. *London.* CC.1815.
Thomas and David. *Dublin.* 1824.
v. Foster.
FÖRSTER (FERSTER), Johann Andreas. *Vienna.* m.1753. sil. p.c. rep. watch.
FORSTMANN, C. W. *Halle* (?). 1779. Pub. book on watches.
FORSYTH, James. *London.* 1790.
FORT (PFORT)—
Christophe. *Montbéliard.* 1571-86. 'Faiseur d'horloges.'
Henry. *Paris.* 1807-25. C.
FORTE, John. *London.* a.1660, CC.1672-99. Watch.
FORTH, Thomas. *London.* an.1775. Watch.
FORTIN—
——. *Paris.* 1735 m.
Michel. *Paris.* m.1743, juré 1762.
N. *Paris.* Mid. 18c. Fine Boullework br. clock Pal. de Pau, Paris.
Augustin. *Paris.* m.1752, juré 1769-72. Watch B.M.
Jean. *Paris.* Juré 1768.
FORTUNA, Lawrence. *London.* ca.1560-71. b. in Normandy. Servant to Peter Dellamare.
FOSBROOK—
T. *Coventry.* ca.1765. l.c. clock.
William. *Coventry.* an.1778. Watch.
FOSS, Thomas. *London.* 1782-94.
FOSSARD—
Pierre Jacques. *Paris.* m.1739.
Pierre. *Paris (Rue St. Antoine).* m.1771 1825.
Jean Baptiste Pierre. *Paris (Rue Grenéta).* m.1785-9.
——. *Paris (Rue de l'arbre sec).* 1807-25.
——. *Paris (Rue des Prouvaires).* 1807-10.
——. *Paris (Rue St. Martin).* 1807-22.
——. *Paris (Rue du fg. St. Antoine).* 1812.
FOSSETT—
Bryan. *London.* a.1730.
& Harrison. *London.* an.1753. John F. and Ralph H.
FOSSEY—
Joseph. *London.* a.1712.
John. *London.* 1723. Insolvent.
FOSTER—
Joseph. *London (Exchange Alley.).* a.1684, CC.1691-1707. Watch, sun and moon hour indicators, Den. coll. Also Forster.
John. *London.* a.1684.
John. *London.* a.1693, CC.1726-38.
John. *London.* a.1699.
Edward. *London.* a.1721.
John. *London.* a.1726.
Joseph. *London.* a.1728-39 CC.
S. *London (Birchin Lane).* an.1755. Watch.
John. *London (Aldersgate St.).* a.1744, CC. 1756-69.
Charles. *London.* an.1765. Watch.
James. *Peaseley Cross.* an.1767. Watch.

FOSTER—*continued.*
John. *Liverpool.* 1774-81. W.
Sim. *London.* an.1775. Watch.
William. *Manchester.* ca.1780-1809. l.c. clock F.W.M.
James. *Ashburton.* 2nd half 18c. l.c. clock.
J. *Peterborough.* 1798. C. & W.
John. *Sutton (Lancs.).* d.1806. W.
Robert. *London.* a.1795.
Henry. *Manchester.* 1813.
Thomas. *Tiverton.* Early 19c. Watch.
Joseph. *Carlow.* 1820-4.
John. *Liverpool.* 1824-36. W.
FOTHERGAILE, James. *London.* a.1659.
FOTHERGILL, William. *Manchester.* 1813. C.
FOUBERT—
Théodore. *Blois.* a.1621-41.
——. *Paris (Rue du Bac).* 1813-25. C. to the Duchesse de Berry.
——. *Paris (Rue de Grenelle St. Honoré).* 1821.
FOUCHER—
Blaise. *Blois.* comp. 1623, m.1631, d.1662. Very fine en. watch B.M. ill. Baillie.
Blaise. *Blois.* 1660-98.
Paul. *Paris.* b.1811, d.1882. Fine maker of chronographs. Pub. books on cyl. esc. and on wheel teeth.
FOUCHY, Grandjean de. *Paris.* 1742. Pub. art. on turret clocks in Mém. de l'Acad. R. des Sciences.
FOUGELBERG, Erik. *Linköping.* b.1776, d.1850.
FOUGERET, ——. *Paris.* 1788.
FOULÉ—
——. *Paris.* 1735 m.
Pierre Louis. *Paris.* m.1743.
FOULGER—
Samuel. *London.* a.1764, CC.1778.
Samuel, son. *London (Ratcliffe Highway).* l.CC.1812-19.
James, son. *London.* a.1822. CC.1843.
FOULK, Humphrey. *London.* a.1646.
FOULKES—
David. *London.* a.1671-80.
Robert. *London.* 1737 CC.
FOULLET (FOULET, FOULLÉ)—
Louis. *Paris.* 1756-72.
Antoine André. *Paris.* m.1782-9.
FOULQUIER, Marc Antoine. *Geneva.* ca. 1770-91.
FOULSTON, Laurence. *London.* 1568. Frenchman.
FOUQUÉ, le père. *Paris.* Mid. 18c. Fine Boulle-work br. clock Pal. de Pau, Paris.
FOUQUET—
Claude. *Blois.* 1615-37.
Claude, son. *Blois.* comp. 1617.
Pierre. *Lyons.* 1645 m.-1667.
——. *Paris.* 1822.
FOURNEAU, J. J. *Liége.* Mid. 18c. g. en. watch.
FOURNERAT, Guillaume Charles. *Paris.* m.1775-89.
FOURNIER—
——. *Paris.* 1740 m.
Louis, son. *Paris.* m.1748.
——. *Paris.* 1810-17.
FOUSTON—
——. *Hull.* ca.1790 CC.
John. *New York.* 1805. W.
FOWKES—
Gabriel. *Lewisham.* Early 18c.—1759. l.c. clock.
Gabriel, son. *London.* a.1759.
Gabriel. *Dartford.* 1791. C.
FOWLDS (FOULDS)—
Allan. *Kilmarnock.* b.1719, d.1799. *v.* Fowles.
Andrew. *London.* ca.1770. Watch.
James. *Kilmarnock.* 1820.
FOWLE (FOWELL)—
Edward. *London.* CC.1670.
Thomas. *East Grinstead.* ca.1710. Clock ill. Cec. & Web.
Humphrey. *Westerham.* 1769. W.
Richard. *East Grinstead.* 1783-95. Watch.
Nathaniel. *Boston, U.S.A.* 1803. W.
John. *Boston, U.S.A.* 1805-13. W.
John and Nathaniel. *Boston.* 1805-09.
William. *Uckfield.* 1816. W.
FOWLER—
Robert. *London.* CC.ca.1650.
John. *London.* 1737. Dial Old Ashmolean M.
George. *London.* a.1730.
Richard. *London.* a.1733.
Edward. *London.* an.1757. Watch.
Thomas. *London (Michel St.).* CC.1775-1786.
P. *London.* an.1785. Watch.
William. *London.* 1782. Watch.
Robert. *York.* 1810-26. *Leeds.* 1841. W.
George. *York* and *Doncaster.* 1819.
FOWLES, Allen. *Kilmarnock.* 1771. 3-case watch. Prob. Allan Fowlds.
FOX—
Charles. *London.* a.1655, CC.1662. Lantern and br. clock.
Mordecai. *London.* CC.1687. Maker of repute.
John. *London.* a.1726.
Thomas. *London.* a.1736-90.
Benjamin. *London.* a.1755.
Joseph. *London.* a.1763, CC.1770.
Thomas. *Sleaford.* 1771. W.
Joseph. *Higham Ferrars.* an.1772. Watch.
Isaac. *London.* 1772-94. br. clock.
Isaac, jun. *London.* an.1778. Watch.
John. *Alverton.* Late 18c. l.c. clock.
& Sons. *London.* ca.1780. Mus. aut. clock Peiping M.
E. *Ely.* Early 19c. Watch.
FOXALL, Thomas. *Rotherhithe.* ca.1760. T.C.
FOXTON, James. *Sutton (Ashfield).* Late 18c.
FOY—
James. *Taunton.* 1784. W.
Robert. *Taunton.* 1784. W.
John. *Taunton.* 1784. W.
Samuel. *Dublin.* 1824. C.
FOYNETT, D. *London.* an.1757. Watch.
FRAENDORFFER, John. *London.* a.1752.
FRAGNEAU, Pierre Paul. *Paris.* 1780 m.-1789.
FRAIL, William. *London.* 1820-4.
FRAMES, George. *Gateshead.* 1811-33. l.c. clocks.
FRAMPTON, Abraham Newhouse. *London.* a.1795.
FRANCE, Richard. *Warrington.* d.1740. C.
FRANCES, George. *London.* a.1700.
FRANCESCHI—
Barthélemy. *Avignon.* 1701. Town C.
Louis. *Turin.* 1st half 18c. str. watch.
FRANCIS—
Balmer. *London (Windmill Ct., Smithfield).* a.1709, CC.1731, d.1774.
John. *London.* 1736. Watch.
B. *London (Crown Ct.).* an.1742. Watch.
Bellingham. *London.* 1742. Perhaps Balmer.
Matthew. *London (Tooley St.).* 1765. W.
& Vuille. *Baltimore, U.S.A.* 1766. C. & W.
Basil. *Baltimore, U.S.A.* 1768. *Albany, N.Y.*, from 1773. From *London.* W. A Basil was a. in London in 1761.
Richard. *London.* 1778. W.
W. *Birmingham.* ca.1740.
Richard. *Attleborough.* 1795. l.c. clock. W.
William. *London.* a.1800, CC.1808, l.CC. 1810.
'Francis Rubie.' Sig. on 1870-8 watches of the National Watch Co. of Chicago.

FRANCISCONI, Octavio. *Lyons.* mar. 1647. From *Lucca.*
FRANCK, Andreas. *Eskilstuna.* 1750-4.
FRANCOIS—
——. *Cologne.* 1585. From *Berlin.*
Hélie. *Paris.* 1600. Sig. to Statuts of Paris corporation.
——. *Metz.* 18c. Watch Fränkel coll.
Antoine. *Paris.* m.1766-89. Very fine vase clock.
Marc Auguste Jules. *Geneva.* ca.1770-91.
FRANK—
Andro and James. *Peebles.* 1564-70.
Thomas. *Nürnberg.* 1600.
FRANKCOM—
George. *Portsea.* Late 18c. Watch.
Charles. *Bath.* Late 18c.-1819.
& MOWAT. *Bath.* Early 19c.
FRANKFELD, L. & Co. *Geneva.* Early 19c. Watch in pencil case.
FRANKLAND, ——. *Leyton.* an.1773. Watch.
FRANKLIN—
Joseph. *London.* a.1679. l.c. clock.
William. *London.* an.1701. Watch.
Thomas. *London.* a.1692.
William. *London.* a.1697, CC.1712-25. Also FRANKLYN and FRANCKLIN.
Francis. *London.* a.1713.
William. *London.* a.1720, CC.1731.
Benjamin. *Philadelphia* and *London.* b.1706, d.1790. Celebrated physicist. Made clocks with 3 wheels and 2 pinions. Desc. of a clock in Nicholson's Operative Mechanic, 1825.
William. *London.* a.1725.
John. *Cranborne.* 1750. C.
George. *London.* an.1777. Watch.
William. *Yarmouth.* an.1789. Watch. Also FRANKLYN.
William. *London.* 1790-1810. Shagreen case-maker.
John George. *London.* a.1794.
BROTHERS. *Edinburgh.* 1820-35.
L. *Portsea.* Early 19c. Watch.
——. *London.* Early 19c. Watch.
A. *Manchester.* Early 19c. Watch.
John. *Westbury.* 1825. Watch.
FRANKLING, William. *London.* a.1796.
FRANKS, ——. *Tiverton.* 1771.
FRANKSCOM, George. *London.* a.1787. CC.1801.
FRANKSON, ——. *London.* an.1783. Watch.
FRANKTON, Thomas. *London.* a.1805.
FRANLAY,——. *London.* an.1775. Watch.
FRANTZ, Johann. *Würzburg.* m.1740. C.
FRANZE, F. X. *Landsberg.* 18c. Watch B.M.
FRARIN, Philibert. *Geneva.* 1748.
FRARY FRÈRES. ——. Late 18c. Ring watch.
FRASER—
Nicholas. *Haddington.* 1636.
John. *London.* a.1681.
——. *London.* Late 18c. Pedometer Den. coll. cf. FRAZER.
James. *Perth.* a.1795.
William. *Lincoln, Lancaster, U.S.A.* b.1801, d.1877. l.c. clocks.
William. *Philadelphia.* 1825.
FRAUDÉ—
Jacques. *Blois.* 1552-98. 'Orlogeulx.'
Pierre. *Blois.* 1636. d.1672.
FRAUENPREISS, Johann. *Dresden.* m.1696.
FRAUMONT-CORDENI, ——. *Paris.* 1823.
FRAUNCIS, the Clockmaker. *London (Blackfriars).* 1576.
FRAY, James. *London.* a.1726, CC.1733-7.
FRAZER—
——. *London.* 1785-8. Pedometer G.M. p.c. en. watch Carnegie M.
John. *London.* a.1797.
David. *Longford.* 1824.
FREALE, W. *Bath.* 1819.
FREARSON—
John. *London.* a.1680, CC.1689.
John. *London.* a.1775.
FRECH, Andreas. *Brunswick.* 1624. sq. table clock.
FREDELET, Estevenin. *Besançon.* 1454-97. German locksmith. Keeper of clock on St. Étienne in 1497.
'FREDERICK ATHERTON.' Sig. on 1867 watches of the UNITED STATES WATCH CO.
'FREDERICK BILLINGS.' Sig. on 1871-5 watches of the NEW YORK WATCH CO.
FREDMAN—
Andreas Andersson. *Stockholm.* 1705. m. 1712, d.1737. trav. clock Nord. M.
Johan, son. *Stockholm.* b.1712, m.1736, d.1767. Court C. 1745. l.c. clock ill. Sidenbladh. 2 br. clocks.
Carl, bro. *Stockholm.* b.1717. *Naples,* 1740. d.ca.1800.
FREE, John. *Oxford.* 1705-25. d. an.1728. Widow continued business. Watch Ashmolean M.
FREEBODY, John. *London.* a.1671.
FREEMAN—
John. *London.* CC.1646, d.1679.
Anthony. *London.* a.1653.
Stafford. *London.* a.1656, CC.1663-79.
Edward. *London.* 1697.
Thomas. *London.* a.1686, CC.1698.
Thomas. *London.* a.1688.
James. *London.* a.1708, CC.1718, d.1736.
George. *London.* a.1711-18. Partner with Henry SMITH. W.
Isaac. *London.* CC.1733.
James. *London (Little Moorgate* to 1773. Then *Strand).* a.1726, CC.1736, d.1778. Patented a stop-watch.
James. *London.* CC.1767.
John. *London.* CC.1772.
William. *London.* an.1774. Watch.
Walter. *Hawick.* 1780.
Joseph. *London.* a.1778.
Thomas. *London.* Late 18c. Watch mt. S.K.M.
Drury. *London.* a.1782, CC.1789-1824. Watch-key maker.
Henry. *London.* a.1807, CC.1814.
Francis. *Sheffield.* 1817. C. & W.
Edward Drury, son of Drury. *London.* CC. 1822.
John. *Waterford.* 1824.
Nathaniel. *Enniscorthy.* 1824-42. Watch N.Y. Univ.
FREÉN, Carl Fred. *Mariefred.* 1816-23. Clock.
FREEPORT WATCH CO. *Freeport, Illinois, U.S.A.* 1874. Successor to MOZART WATCH CO. *v.* UNITED STATES WATCH CO.
FREESTONE, Thomas. *Ipswich* and *Bury.* 1765-78. Bankrupt. At *Ipswich* an.1765. l.c. clock.
FREETHY, John. *London.* a.1672.
FREGE, Christian Gottlob. *Leipzig.* 1814.
FREISTADT, A. ——. Late 17c. hex. table clock.
FREMI, ——. *Paris.* 1764 m. cf. FRÉMY.
FREMIN—
Jaques. *Geneva.* 1594. From *Paris.* Granted burghership for repairing clock on Pont de Rosne.
A. *France.* ca.1600. g. en. watch, crys. cover, Spitzer coll. 8-lobed crys. watch, Webster coll. ill. Baillie.
FRÉMON, Pierre. *Blois.* comp. 1627.
FRÉMY—
Jean Baptiste. *Paris.* m.1742.
Jean (Julien) Nicolas. *Paris.* m.1742-89.
——. *Paris (Rue Guénégaud).* 1812.
FREMYN, Jacques. *Geneva.* a.1600.

FRENCH—
James. *London.* an.1747. Watch.
Francis. ——. Mid. 18c. Watch Den. coll.
Thomas. *Norwich.* From 1751. C.
Cuthbert. *London.* ca.1760-1808. Watch.
James Ormsby. *Baltimore, U.S.A.* 1771. From *Dublin.* C. & W.
Edward. *London.* CC.1782, l.CC.1811, d.1822. Watch G.M.
Matthew. *London* (*Sutton St.*). 1782. W.
John. *London.* 1783-ca.1795. br. clock ill. Cec. & Web. al. watch.
John, son of Matthew. *London.* a.1782.
Henry, bro. *London.* a.1784-99. W.
Mrs. *Yalding.* 1801. C. & W.
R. V. *Maidstone.* ca.1800.
Santiago James Moore. *London* (*R. Exchange* and *Sweetings Alley*). CC.1810-40. chron. and W. Rack lever watch G.M. prob. by him.
James. *Bristol.* 1825-30. Watch.

FRENCHAM—
James. *London.* a.1691, CC.1698-1710.
Mary. *London.* 1721.

FRENZEL, Jonas. *Oberhausen.* 1756. Klein-uhrmacher.

FRÉSARD—
Bénédict. *Villeret.* ca.1777. Partner with David BOURQUIN and the two following.
Josué. *Villeret* and *Paris.* ca.1790.
Adam. *Villeret* and *Vienna.* ca.1790.
——. *Bienne.* 1790. C. and aut. maker. cf. FRISARD.

FRESH, H. *London.* an.1732. Watch.

FRESHFIELD—
James. *London* (*Smithfield*). CC.1774-1803. p.c. g. watch.
James William, son. *London.* a.1790, CC. 1801-20.
Frederick, bro. *London.* a.1803, CC.1815, l.CC.1816. Also Francis.

FRETHY, John. *London.* a.1672.

FREULER, Hans Jakob. *Basle.* 1719-58. W.

FREUNDLER, C. B., ET CIE. *Geneva.* Early 19c. en. watch M.P.S. Dresden.

FREWIN, Samuel. *Bristol.* 1812-18. W.

FREY—
Lorenz. *St. Märgen.* 1680. Said to have been the first clockmaker in the Schwarzwald. *v.* HENNINGER and KREUZ.
Remigius. *Basle.* 1705.
Lorenz. *Basle.* 1744.
Anthony. *Oberhausen* (*Augsburg*). 1770.

FREYMANN, Konrad. *Basle.* 1760.

FRIAND, Josué. *Paris.* 1771.

FRICK, Kaspar. *Vienna.* 18c.

FRICKER, Onophrius. *Soleure.* 1563.

FRIDEBECK, Hans. *Copenhagen.* 1792.

FRIDEL, ——. *Paris.* 1812-24.

FRIDGE, James. *Leeds.* 1798. W.

FRIE, Georg. *Zittau.* ca.1745. Court C. br. clock.

FRIEDRICH (**FRIDRICH**), Johann. *Vienna.* m.1805.

FRIEND, ——. *Totnes.* 2nd half 18c. l.c. clock.
W. *Newton Abbot.* Early 19c. Watch.

FRIER—
John. *London.* a.1785.
Stephen. *London.* a.1790.

FRIESE, J. *Strasbourg.* 1791. Pub. a desc. of the Strasbourg clock.

FRIGG, Alexander. *Edinburgh.* a.1759.

FRIM, ——. *France* or *Switzerland.* ca.1780. g. en. watch Stern coll.

FRIQUET, Michel. *Paris.* m.1736.

FRISAR (**FREJSAR, FRASAR**), Abraham. *Vienna.* m.1781.

FRISARD (**FRIZARD**), Jacob. *Geneva, Bienne* and *London.* b.1753, d.1812. Famous maker of singing birds. cf. FRÉSARD.

FRISBY—
John. *London.* 1817-25.
M. *London.* 1817-19.

FRISCHE, Nicasius. *Nürnberg.* 1565.

FRISKE, Hans. *Stockholm.* 1799.

FRISQUET, Peter. *London.* 1768-75.

FRITH, Edward. *London.* a.1714, CC.1738.

FRITSCHEMANN, Guntripheier. *Ulm.* 1407. Made the Rathhaus clock at Basle.

FRITZ—
——. *Miesbach.* d.an.1815. Turret C.
C. F. *Hamburg.* 1815-21.

FRIZELL, Lewis. *Duncannon.* 1824.

FRIZON, V. *Paris.* Early 18c. Watch Bourges M.

FROCKSHAM, John. *London* (*Enfield*). 1817-1824. Perhaps FRODSHAM.

FRODSHAM—
William. *London* (*Red Lion Sq.*). b.1728, CC.1781, d.1807. Expert on Harrison's and Earnshaw's chrons.
William. *London.* a.1760.
David. *Liverpool.* 1774. C.
Edward. *London* (*Kensington*). an.1787. Watch.
William, & Son. *London.* 1790. Firm of William (1) and his son. g. lever watch Den. coll. Watch sd. Wm. Frodsham, jun.
William, son of Wm. (1). *London* (*Holborn*). 1798.
William James, F.R.S., grandson of William (1). *London* (*Change Alley*). b.1778, CC. 1802, m.CC.1836, d.1850. Partner with William PARKINSON.
John, grandson of Wm. (1). *London* (*Gracechurch St.*). b.1785, CC.1822, l.CC.1830, d.1849. Partner with BAKER.
& BAKER. *London.* 1809-11.
Henry, son of William James. *Liverpool.* a.1823.
George, bro. *London* (*Change Alley*). ca. 1825. Succeeded his father, William James.
John, bro. *London.* a.1826, CC.1840.
Charles, bro. *London* (*Finsbury Pavement* and *Strand*). b.1810, CC.1854, m.CC. 1855. After 1843 the firm was ARNOLD & FRODSHAM. A very able maker and writer.
William Edward, bro. *London.* a.1823.
Henry John, son of John (1). *London.* a.1830, CC.1838.

FROIDEVAUX, François Joseph. *Chaux-de-Fonds* and *Berne.* a.1774-1812. rep. al. watch Chamb. coll. Br. clock.

FROISSARD, ——. *Geneva.* ca.1800. Pearl decorated mus. aut. watch ill. Britten.

FROMANTEEL—
Ahasuerus. *London.* BC.1630, CC.1632-56. Turret C.
Ahasuerus. *London.* CC.1655.
John. *London.* a.1651, CC.1663-81. Entered service of Salomon COSTER from Sep. 1657 to May 1658. l.c. clock Weth. coll. l.c. and br. clocks ill. Cec. & Web.
Ahasuerus. *London.* a.1654, CC.1663-85. A very famous maker; was the first to make pendulum clocks in England in collaboration with HUYGENS. The earliest dated 1658 is in the Prestige coll. l.c. clock G.M. br. clock ill. Cec. & Web.
Abraham. *London.* a.1662, CC.1680-1711. Watch with wandering hour-figure and fuzee winding both ways, Webster coll., prob. by him ill Baillie. Watch with sun and moon hour indicator, Mallett coll. ill. Baillie.
Daniel, son of Ahasuerus. *London.* a.1663.
Ahasuerus, son. *London.* a.1679.
——. *Amsterdam.* an.1699. Watch. l.c. clock ill. Cec. & Web.
& CLARKE. *London.* ca.1700. Watches

FROMANTEEL—*continued.*
London M., S.M.S.K. and Carnegie M. l.c. clock Weth coll. rep. watch Den. coll. Pair of clocks Pal. M. Pekin.
FRONE, John. *London.* a.1720.
FRONMILLER, Hans. *Augsburg.* 16c. aut. work of Neptune and a turtle, K.H.M.
FROOME, Michel. *London.* a.1717.
FRÖSELL, Anders. *Stockholm.* 1817-35. br. clock.
FROST—
John. *London (Cornhill).* 1757. Watch G.M.
——. *London (Chiswell St.).* an.1762. Watch.
——. *Colchester.* an.1773. Watch.
Thomas. *London.* a.1772.
Robert. *Nottingham.* an.1777. Watch.
Jonathan. *Exeter.* an.1783. Watch.
William. *Liverpool.* 1796. W.
Henry. *London.* 1805-08. W.
John. *London (Clerkenwell).* a.1799, CC. 1809, l.CC.1816.
FROWDE (FROUDE), John. *London.* a.1646, CC.1654-74.
FRUGARD, John. *Edinburgh.* 1701.
FRÜHWALD, Stephan. *Fürth.* d.1804.
FRY—
——. *London.* 1747. W.
John. *Melksham.* an.1758. Watch.
William. *London (Phillip Lane).* a.1779, CC.1786-1807.
John Robert. *London.* a.1788.
Samuel. *Dublin.* ca.1810. Watch mt. Ilbert coll.
Cornelius. *London.* a.1823.
FRYDAY, William. *London.* a.1730.
FRYER—
——. *London.* an.1720. Watch.
William. *York* and *Pocklington.* 1809. W.
John. *York* and *Pocklington.* 1812-23. W. rep. br. clock.
William, jun. *Leeds.* 1817-26. W.
FUERSTENFELDTER (FUERSTEN-FELDER)—
Benedikt. *Friedberg.* Late 16c. and early 17c. Watch and hex. table clock S.K.M. hex. min. rep. table clock Webster coll. str. rep. trav. clock Fränkel coll.
Gotthardt. *Friedberg.* 1770.
FUETER, ——. *Berne.* 1st half 18c. Watch.
FULLER—
William. *London.* CC.1675-99. l.c. clock ill. Cec. & Web.
Jonathan. *London.* Early 18c. Watch Stern. coll.
Samuel. *London.* 1810-25. W.
Matthias. *Bristol.* 1817. Wooden C.
Daniel. *London.* 1820.

FULLFORD, Richard. *Fareham.* Early 19c. Watch.
FULLUM, George. *London.* a.1649.
FULTHORP, John. *London.* a.1741.
FULWELL, Henry. *London.* a.1649.
FUNCK, ——. *Berne.* 1782. aut. picture ill. M. des Aut.
FUNK, Lars. *Bornholm* and *Copenhagen.* Late 18c.
FURBISS, William. *Windsor.* 1784.
FURET—
l'aîné (André). *Paris.* 1691 m.-ca.1740. One of the principal Paris makers. cf. FAURET. Clock Wallace coll. Small br. clock B.M.
Jean André. *Paris.* d.1778.
Jean Baptiste André. *Paris.* m.1743-89. C. to Louis XVI. Mantel clock Louvre.
Jacques Louis. *Paris.* m.1763-89.
FURLEY, Ralph. *Prescot.* 1795. W.
FURNACE, George. *Dublin.* 1751-74. Watch Den. coll.
FURNER—
Francis. *Rochford, Essex.* 1794. W.
Francis, son. *London.* a.1794.
FURNESS—
Joseph. *Monk Wearmouth.* 1790-1800. W.
John. *London.* 1820.
FURNEY, James. *London.* a.1727.
FURNIFULL, Richard. *London.* a.1715, CC. 1722-78.
FURNISH, ——. *London.* an.1755. Watch.
FURNISS—
John. *Yarmouth.* an.1781. Watch.
Joseph. *Uppingham.* 1795. W.
Henry. *London.* Early 19c. Watch.
v. EVANS & FURNISS.
FURNIVAL—
Thomas. *Taunton.* 2nd half 18c. l.c. clock.
Benjamin. *Stockport and Oldham.* 1790-1800. Watch mt. Oldham M.
FURORIS, Jean. *Bourges.* 17c. Astro. clock.
FURSE, Gregory. *Truro.* 1795. C. & W.
FÜRSTENFELDTER, *v.* **FUERSTENFELDTER.**
FURTENBACH, Martin. *Augsburg.* 1535. math. inst. maker.
FÜSSLIN, David. *Basle.* 1805. From *Stuttgart.*
FUTERS, William. *London.* a.1820.
FYNES, James. *London.* a.1688.
FYRBACH, Claus Henriksen. *Copenhagen.* m.1731, d.1743. Turret C.
FYVIE, George. *Dublin.* ca.1750. Small br. clock.

G

GABEREL & DUFOUR. *Geneva.* ca.1825. *v.* Philippe DUFOUR.
GABLENTZ, Georg Andreas. *Glatz.* ca. 1700. circ. table clock Arts M. Prague.
GABORY, M. *Angers.* 1770. Pub. a book on Timekeepers.
GABRIEL, ——. *London.* 1st half 18c. Hex. table clock Arts M. Prague.
GABRIELLI, James Vincent. *London.* a.1820.
GABRY, ——. *Liancourt.* 1819. Devised a form of night-light clock.
GABYD, James. *London.* an.1779.
GAD, Johan Jakob. *Copenhagen.* m.1785. Turret C.
GADESDON, William. *London.* a.1770.
GADFORD, William. *London.* an.1770. Watch.
GADSBY, Thomas. *Leicester.* 1815-26. Watch.
GAGÉ, —. *Paris.* 1818.
GAGNEBIN—
Daniel. *Chaux-de-Fonds* and *Renan.* b.1709, d.1781. Clocks and watches. Trav. str. clock.
Major. *Chaux-de-Fonds.* 1785. Invented machine for drilling mus. barrels.
GAIGNON (GAGNON), Michel. *Lyons.* 1664.
GAIL, ——. *Paris.* 1812.
'GAIL BORDEN.' Sig. on 1871-5 watches of the NATIONAL WATCH CO. OF CHICAGO.
GAILL, Mattheis. Prob. *Switzerland.* ca.1670. trav. clock S.K.M. Clock Ilbert coll.
GAILLARD—
Nicolas. *Lyons.* 1555. d.1602. Oval watch sd. 'N. Galliard' M.M.A.
Pierre. *Basle.* 1665. From *Geneva.*
Pierre. *Geneva.* ca.1770-91.
GAILLION, ——. *Paris.* ca.1780. Watch, porcelain case, M.P.S. Dresden.
GAINSBOROUGH, John, jun. *Sudbury.* In 1743 went to *Beccles.* W.
GAIREN—
David. *Berne.* 1815.
Isaac. *Berne.* 1815.
GAKEMAN, ——. *London.* an.1745. Watch.
GALABIN, John. *Greenwich.* 1761. W.
GALAIS, L'Abbé. *Paris.* 1784. Made a meridian sundial striking a bell, by burning of a thread holding the hammer. Devised a clock wound by windmill; desc. pub. in Mém. de l'Acad. R. des Sciences, 1766.
GALBRAITH—
Richard. *London.* an.1773. Watch.
Patrick. *Philadelphia.* 1784-1817. W.
GALE—
James. *London.* CC.1780-7. Watch.
John. *London.* 1790-1840. Watch.
William. *London.* a.1786.
GALES—
Daniel. *London.* a.1727. Watch.
——. *London.* an.1758. Watch.
GALIAY—
Philippe. *Paris.* ca.1720. Fine l.c. equation clock.
——. *Paris.* 1816-23.
John P. *Boston, U.S.A.* 1825. W.
GALILEI—
Galileo. *Pisa, Florence* and *Padua.* b.1564, d.1642. Celebrated physicist and astronomer. Discovered the approximate law of the pendulum. Described its application to a clock in a private letter in 1641. Models in S.K.M. and G.M.
Vincenzo, son. Began to have a clock made after his father's design in 1649, by Domenico BALESTRI, but died before its completion.
GALIMORE (GALLIMORE), Joseph. *Salford.* 1790-1813. C.
GALINDO, Joseph. *London.* 1751. Bankrupt. W.
GALLAND, Antoine Gabriel. *Paris.* m.1778-1807.
GALLANDE (GALLONDE), Louis Charles. *Paris.* m.1737-75. Devised an anchor esc. and a c.secs. clock desc. in Mem. de l'Acad. des Sciences, 1740. Regulator C.A. & M.
GALLE—
Arndt. *Württemberg.* Went to Cassel 1626 as Master of the Mint.
——. *Paris.* 1806. Worker in bronze and C. Clocks Pal. de Fontainebleau and Mobilier National, Paris. cf. GALLET.
GALLER, Jakob. *Danzig.* b.1688-1720.
GALLEST, A. *Abbeville.* ca.1680. Watch mt. B.M.
GALLET, ——. *Paris (Rue de la Vieille Monnaie).* 1812. cf. GALLE.
GALLINGTON, John. *Stratford (Essex).* a. 1777.
GALLMAYR, Joseph. *Munich.* 1727. d.1790. A remarkable mechanic who made 52 aut. and clocks for the Bavarian Court. A celestial globe with clockwork in Fugger M. Augsburg. Made a pedometer winding watch before 1776. Repaired aut. clock of Munich in 1749.
GALLOCK, John. *Rochford (Essex).* 1795.
GALLOIS—
James. *London.* 1743. Watch.
François. *Paris.* m.1746.
GALLON, William. *Sunderland.* 1820.
GALLOT (GALOT), Augustin. *Paris.* m. 1758-89.
GALLOTT, Isaac. *London.* a.1655.

GALLOWAY—
John. *London.* a.1683.
William. *Dalry (Ayr).* 1776. l.c. clock.
Walter. *Kilbirnie.* 1776-80. l.c. clock.
John. *Leeds.* 1817. C.
Mathew. *Leeds.* 1817. C.
James. *Leeds.* 1817. C.

GALOPIN—
Frères et Cie. *Geneva.* Early 19c.
Louis. *Paris.* 1815-25.

GALPIN, Thomas. *Wimborne.* 1612.

GALT—
Jean. *Paris.* Juré 1742.
Peter. *Baltimore, U.S.A.* 1802. W.

GALWARD, Joseph. *Sevenoaks.* Late 18c. Perhaps Gatward.

GAMAGE, Philip. *London.* a.1694.

GAMARD, Antoine Simon. *Paris.* m.1740-1749. C. to Louis xv.

GAMBELL—
Matthew. *London.* a.1784.
William. *London.* a.1795.

GAMBET, ——. *Rouen.* 2nd half 18c. Watch.

GAMBEY, Louis Henry. *Paris.* m.1788-1825. Finished clock begun by Noblet for Auxerre.

GAMBIER—
Mary Magdalen. *London.* a.1728.
——. *London.* an.1783. Watch.

GAMBLE—
Thomas. *London.* a.1651, CC.1657.
Henry. *Pudsey.* d.1780. 'Eminent' C.

GAMBLI, Johann Rudolph. *St. Gall.* Late 16c. Drum al. watch B.M.

GAMMAGE, Thomas. *London.* CC.1814-40. mus. C.

GAMMON—
George. *London.* 1769. Insolvent.
William. *Hereford.* d.1795. W.
Richard. *London.* a.1775. Watch.
Thomas. *Hereford.* 1774, d.1786. CC. Watch Ilbert coll.
Maria, widow. *Hereford.* 1786-93. Carried on Thos' business.
George, bro. of Thos. *Hereford.* 1786-98. Was assistant to Thos. and worked with Maria.
William, son of William. *London* and *Birmingham.* a.1795, CC.1814. W. l.c. clock.

GAMMOND, Richard. *London.* an.1783. Watch.

GAMOD, G. *Paris.* 1646. Sig. to Statuts of Paris corporation. Two en. watches M.M.A.

GAMOT, Josse. *Beuille.* ca.1660. circ. sil. eng. watch.

GAMPERT, Johann. *Vienna.* m.1801.

GANDER, Jacob. *Schwarzwald.* 1793. mus. clock with metal and glass bells.

GANDO, Nicolas. *France* or *Switzerland.* ca. 1670. cf. Gandouz *v.* Grando. cal. watch Nat. M. Munich. sq. sil. eng. watch S.K.M.

GANDON, W. *London.* an.1754. Watch.

GANDOUZ, Nicolas. *Geneva.* 1665 m. cf. Gando.

GANDY—
Samuel. *Cockermouth.* 1768. l.c. clocks.
Richard. *London.* 1820. W.

GANEL, Guillaume. *Lyons.* 1508-15.

GANOT, Nicolas. *Paris.* 1675 juré.

GANS, ——. *Nürnberg.* 17c. Crucifix clock Bernal sale.

GANSBEEK, Marinus. *Haarlem.* 1743.

GANSBERG, ——. *Paris.* 1825.

GANT, ——. *Woodbridge.* Early 19c. Watch.

GANTER—
Anton. *Neukirch.* ca.1770.
Jakob, son. *Neukirch.* ca.1790.

GANTHONY—
Richard. *London (Lombard St.).* a.1785, CC. 1794, m.CC.1828, d.1845. g. lever watch G.M. l.c. clock ill. Cec. & Web.
Richard Pinfold, son. *London (Cheapside).* 1821. m.CC. and d.1845.
Richard, bro. *London.* a.1813. CC.1820, d.1825.

GANZENBERGER, Johann Heinrich. *Fürth.* d.1824.

GANZINOTTO, Cristofero. *Genoa.* 1667. d.1670. 'Horologiorum fabro.' Renewed clock on Palazzo delle Compere.

GAPE, Thomas. *London.* a.1714.

GARAN, Jean Antoine. *Paris.* m.1782.

GARANDEAU (GARAUDRAN),——. *Paris.* 1579-1600. cf. Gavandeau. C. to the Queen. Sig. to Statuts of Paris corporation, 1600. en. watch Blot-Garnier coll Oval watch with émail en resille sur verre, Petit Palais, Paris.

GARAUDEL, E. *Verdun.* Early 17c. oct. crys. watch Wallace coll. cf. Géraudel.

GARBET, Gabriel Benoît. *Paris.* m.1770-89.

GARBETT—
Jere. *London.* a.1736, CC.1768.
Jeremiah. *Newcastle-o.-T.* 1754-6. Watch. C. Prob. same as above.

GARBRANTSZOON, Andries. *Haarlem.* 1562

GARBROUND, John. *London.* a.1654.

GARCIN—
A. *London.* an.1755. Watch.
——. *Paris.* 1812.

GARD—
James. *London.* a.1710.
Henry. *Exeter.* 1787-1803. l.c. clock.
William. *Exeter.* ca.1790 CC. l.c. clock,

GARDE, James. *London.* a.1710. br. clock.

GARDEN—
William. *London.* CC.1712.
Phillips. *London.* 1742-62.
Edward. *London.* an.1775. Watch

GARDENER (GARDINER)—
John. *London.* a.1675, CC.1682.
John. *Croydon.* CC.1687.
Ambrose. *London.* 1698 CC.
Obadiah. *London (Fleet St.).* a.1700, CC. 1712-27.
Giles. *London.* a.1712.
Richard. *London.* a.1749.
Joseph. *Lancaster.* 1767. d.1771.
William. *London.* a.1764, CC.1771.
Patrick. *Perth.* a.1779-1800.
Henry. *London (Norton Folgate).* 1790-1804.
Patrick. *Edinburgh.* 1812.
Henry. *London.* CC.1814.
James. *Perth.* 1825-42.

GARDIER, Daniel. *London.* an.1776. Watch.

GARDNER—
Thomas. *London.* CC.1689-1724. l.c. clock Weth. coll.
Margaret. *London.* 1692 CC.
William Obadiah. *London.* CC.1711.
William. *London.* a.1716, CC.1735.
John. *London.* a.1722.
Timothy. *London.* a.1727-62. Watch mt. G.M.
Thomas. *London (Minories).* 1740. d.1770. l.c. clock Virginia M. Watch.
John. *London.* a.1735, CC.1747-52. Watch mt.
Joseph. *London.* CC.1769.
John. *London.* a.1769.
William. *Sandwich.* 1742. 'Clocksmith.' l.c. clock.
William. *Woodbridge.* ca.1800.
Edward. *London.* a.1794.
R. L. *Belfast.* 1805-18. Partner with Job Rider 1805-07 and with R. Neill 1809-18. Watch sd. 'Gardner & Neill,' S.K.M.
Henry. *Belfast.* 1819-24.

GARDNER—*continued.*
Peter. *Perth.* 1820.
John. *Carlisle.* 1820. l.c. clock.
William. *Hull.* 1820.
William. *Penrith.* Early 19c.
GAREST (GARET)—
Jean Pierre. *Paris.* m.1776-89.
——. *Paris.* 1807-20.
GARFIELD, James. *London.* 1698. W.
GARFOOT, William. *London.* a.1673, CC. 1680-1701. Watch.
GARFORTH & SIDGWICK. *Skipton-cum-Craven.* 1792. C.
GARIOT, Charles. *Paris.* m.1783-9.
GARIQUES, ——. *Paris.* 1789.
GARLAND—
John. *London.* a.1753. CC.1760, l.CC.1767. Watch.
E. *Rugby.* an.1820. Watch.
GARLE—
Richard. *London.* a.1682.
Thomas. *London.* a.1706, CC.1720-44.
Thomas, son. *London.* CC.1747. m.CC. 1769-76.
GARLICK, Theophilus. *Wolverhampton.* d. or retired 1746. W.
GARLIN, Pierre Louis. *Paris.* 1772.
GARMENT—
Michael. *London.* a.1756, CC.1768.
William. *London.* 1762.
GARNACHE, ——. *Les Gras.* Early 19c.
GARNAULT—
Jacobus. *The Hague.* ca.1695. Watch mt. Ilbert coll. Prob. the same as the following.
J. *Moscow.* ca.1725. Watches Ilbert and Fränkel colls.
——. *Toulouse.* Late 18c. Watch.
GARNEI, ——. *Karlstad.* 1787.
GARNER—
William. *London.* a.1713.
Joseph. *London.* a.1754.
Thomas. *London* (*Aldersgate*). CC.1767-1808. Watch mt.
GARNES, John. *Liverpool.* 1825. W.
GARNETT—
John Anthony. *London.* a.1672. Went to *France.*
Jeremie. *London.* 1684-91. CC. From *Geneva.*
William. *London.* ca.1700. Watch.
John. *London.* an.1753. Watch.
William. *Upper Holland.* d.1755. Watch toolmaker.
Thomas. *Sutton* (*Lancs.*). d.1760. Watch toolmaker.
C. *London.* an.1775. Watch.
Thomas. *London.* an.1783. Watch.
Thomas. *Rainhill.* 1786. W.
William. *Cronton.* d.1796.
GARNIER—
F. *Paris.* 1740 m. Watch.
François Armand, son. *Paris.* m.1751.
Carl Hubert. *Stockholm.* 1785-95. Also GARNEY. Clock.
——. *Paris* (*Rue Grenetat*). 1812.
Jean Paul. *Paris.* b.1801. d.1869. Eminent maker and mechanician. Devised several escs. and instruments. First applied electric transmission to clocks in France in 1847.
Paul. *Paris.* d.1917. An eminent C. who made an exceptionally fine collection of early watches, of which 56 were given to the Louvre in 1916, and are described in a good illustrated catalogue.
GARNON, Barnett. *London.* 1662.
GARNOT—
Pierre. *Compiègne.* 1530. 'Serrurier et aorlogeur.' Made aut. clock for belfry.
——. *Paris.* 1646. Sig. to Statuts of Paris corporation.
GARNOU, David. *Amsterdam.* 1681. Huguenot refugee from France.
GARON—
Peter. *London* (*St. Bartholomew's Lane* and later *St. Giles, Cripplegate*). a.1687, CC. 1694-1723 insolvent. Bankrupt in 1709. Watch B.M. rep. watch S.M.S.K. mt. G.M. Watch with turning hour circle and l.c. clock ill. Britten. Watch Feill coll. en. by J. André. Watch with en. on cock Arts M. Prague. en. watch Gélis coll. p.c. sun and moon watch Ilbert coll. l.c. clock ill. Cec. & Web.
Peter, son. *London* (*Shoreditch*). a.1713-23.
——. *Paris.* 1822-5.
GARRAUX, Isaac. *Chaux-de-Fonds.* 1815-1820.
GARRAWAY, C. *London* (*Westminster*). Early 19c.
GARRÉ, ——. *Paris.* 1791. Carillon clock.
GARRETT (GARRATT)—
Ferdinando (GARET, Fernando). *London.* 1613-22. Watch B.M. Watch with crys. covers Stern. coll.
Charles. *London.* a.1683, CC.1690-1714.
John. *London.* a.1696.
Charles, son of Charles. *London.* CC.1720.
Hugh. *Ormskirk.* ca.1770, d. 1800. Watch mt. G.M.
William. *London.* an.1777-1815. g. rep. watch Den. coll.
Philip. *Philadelphia.* 1802-25. W.
Henry. *Ormskirk.* ca.1820.
GARRIGUES, Antoine. *Paris.* m.1782-1812.
GARRISON, Tobe. *Ipswich.* an.1752.
GARRON, Vincent. *Paris.* 1764 m.-1771. g. en. watch Stern. coll.
GARROT, John. *Warrington.* ca.1770-95.
GARSHALL, Daniel. *London.* a.1700.
GARSINE, John. *London.* a.1657.
GARTH—
John. *London* (*Clerkenwell*). 1755-64. Watch.
John. *London.* a.1764.
John. *Knaresborough.* ca.1800.
Thornton. *Knaresborough.* 1822.
GARTHWAITE, John. *Colne.* ca.1820.
GARTLY, John. *Aberdeen.* 1799-1810. Lever watch with double escape wheel Ilbert coll.
GÄRTNER (GERTNER)—
Andreas. *Dresden.* 1727. Geographical clock with 360 dials, M.P.S. Dresden.
Math. *Vienna.* m.1742.
GARTON, Thomas. *London.* a.1668.
GARTY—
George. *Dublin.* 1795. W.
William. *Dublin.* 1824.
GASCOIGNE (GASCOYNE)—
Samuel. *London.* a.1668, CC.1676-88. Watch.
Richard, bro. of Sam. *London.* a.1676.
William. *Newark.* ca.1700. d.1740. l.c. clock.
Owin. *Newark.* Early 18c. l.c. clock.
Richard. *London.* a.1710.
Knight. *London.* a.1773.
v. CASCOYN.
GASDON, William. *London.* a.1700, CC. 1712-24. Watch Ilbert coll.
GASKELL, William. *Liverpool.* 1816-29. W.
GASKILL, Thomas. *Knutsford* (*Cheshire*). 1784-95. Also GASKELL.
GASKIN, John. *Dublin.* 1766-1824. Watch Den. coll.
GASPARO, Dominican brother. *Forli.* 1395. 'Eccellente maestro ed ingegnere.' Made clock for the tower of the Palazzo Pubblico.
GASS—
William. *London.* a.1740, CC.1749, d.1806. Watch.
David, & Co. *London.* 1815-25. W.
GASSARE, François. *Paris.* m.1750.

GASTEIGER, Hans. *Munich.* 1562. Large tower clock with astrolabe dial, Old Ashmolean M. cf. GASTINER.
GASTELIER, Jean Paul. *Paris.* m.1741.
GASTELL, James. *London.* a.1806.
GASTIN, Joachim. *Paris.* ca.1775. Watch mt. Debaufre esc. Ilbert coll.
GASTINER, M. Hans. ——. Early 17c. Clock on figure of Atlas, Stern. coll. cf. GASTEIGER.
GASTON-JOLY—
——. *Paris* (*Rue Pavée, St. Sauveur*). 1807-1823 C.
Père. *Paris* (*Bd. Poissonnière*). 1815.
GATE—
Archer. *London.* a.1674.
Thomas. *Carlisle.* ca.1770-95.
Robert. *Hexham.* b.1781. d.1809. W.
GATEHOUSE, William. *London.* a.1741.
GATES—
J. *London.* an.1773. Watch.
Francis. *London.* an.1783. Watch.
GATFORD, William. *Uxbridge.* an.1774. Watch.
GATTINO, Jakob. *Ansbach.* 1705-11. d. an. 1736. Court C.
GATTON—
George. *London.* ca.1760. Watch mt. Buckley coll.
Edward. *London.* an.1768. Watch.
Edward. *Liverpool.* 1769-73. W.
GATWARD—
Thomas. *London.* a.1693.
Samuel. *London.* a.1751.
Joshua. *Sevenoaks.* 1784. CC. W.
Joseph. *Bristol.* 1785. W.
Joseph. *London.* 1790.
Benjamin. *Hitchin.* 1795. W.
J. *Hitchin.* ca.1800. From *London.*
Joseph. *Tonbridge.* Early 19c. Watch.
Thomas. *Saffron Walden.* b.1802, d.1863.
GAUCHER, Jean. *Paris.* 1584. C. to Henri III at the Château of St. Germain-en-Laye.
GAUCHERON, Matthew. *London.* ca.1730, retired 1774. Succeeded VITU. From *Hesse Cassel.*
GAUD, Jean Auguste. *Geneva.* Early 19c. cf. GAUDY.
GAUDEBY—
aîné. *Paris.* 1812.
jeune. *Paris.* 1812.
GAUDIN—
Lewis. *London.* 1742. Watch.
F. *Nyon.* Mid. 18c. Crys. watch.
Antoine. *Paris.* m.1788.
GAUDRON (GAUDERON)—
Antoine. *Paris.* 1675 m., juré 1689.
Pierre. *Paris.* 1690-1730. An eminent maker. C. to the Regent. Boulle br. clock S.K.M. Fine Boulle-work mantel clock, Pal. de l'Élysée, Paris. Boulle-work clock Schloss M. Berlin. Another ill. Britten. Wall clock Cassel M. Watches C.A. & M., Ilbert, Den., Feill and Fränkel colls. and Carnegie M. Art. on repairing watches in Thiout's book.
GAUDY—
——. *London.* 1st half 18c. g. watch.
J. A. *Geneva.* ca.1740-ca.1780. Watch G.M. g. en. watch. cf. GAUD.
GAUER, Wolf Heinrich. *Königsberg.* ca.1675. Hex. table clock Ilbert coll.
GAULARD, ——. *Rennes.* Mid. 18c. Watch N.Y. Univ.
GAULIN, Antoine. *Paris.* m.1788-1825.
GAULT—
Guillaume. *Paris.* 1685 m.
Denis. *Paris.* m.1741.
Pierre Mathurin, son. *Paris.* m.1757.
Désiré Edme. *Paris.* m.1763.
GAULTIER (GAUTRIER), Pierre Laurent. *Paris.* 1767 m.-1789.
GAUNT—
John. *London.* a.1753.
Joseph. *London* (*Aldersgate Bars*). a.1754, CC. 1761, d.1815.
John, son. *London.* CC.1815, l.CC.1824.
Thomas, bro. *London.* CC.1815. W.
GAUP, Johannes. *Basle.* 1764. From *Lindau.*
GAUTHORNY, Richard. *London.* ca.1820. Clock Virginia M. perhaps GANTHONY.
GAUTIER (GAUTHIER)—
——. *Avignon.* 1617. Repaired clock of St. Augustin.
Antoine. *Blois.* m.1646, d.1670.
Louis. *Paris.* 1681m. g. en. watch Gélis coll. g. watch en. les frères Huaud.
Pierre. *Paris.* ca.1710. Perhaps same as preceding. Watch M.M.A.
——. *Rouen.* Early 18c. Watch N.Y. Univ.
William. *London.* 1723. Insolvent.
Michel Victoire. *Paris.* m.1752.
——. *Le Gras.* 1824.
GAUTRIN—
P. L. *Paris.* b.1737-99. In 1799 petitioned for an award for a watch with only one wheel, stating that he had sold one 15 years before to 'Louis Capet.' A secs. watch by him approved by the Acad. des Sci.
——. *Paris* (*Place de l'Hotel de Ville*). 1812-1825.
GAUTRON, Jacques. *La Rochelle.* 1691-1716. C. to the town. Made clock for St. Barthélemy.
GAUVER, Jean. *Paris.* Juré 1740.
GAVANDEAU, Claude. *Paris.* m.1608. cf. GARANDEAU.
GAVELL—
Benjamin. *London.* a.1753, CC.1761.
William. *London.* a.1761.
GAVELLE (GAVEL)—
James. *London.* CC.1682-1700. An alien. br. clock.
Jean Jacques. *Paris* (*Rue de la Huchette*). m. 1753, juré 1778-89.
Charles Antoine. *Paris.* m.1754, juré 1758.
Bernard. *Paris.* 1764 m.-1775.
Pierre (l'aîné), son of Jean Jacques. *Paris* (*Rue St. Denis*). m.1771, juré 1785-9. Mantel clock.
Maurice Jacques (le jeune), bro. *Paris* (*Rue aux Ours*). m.1780-9.
——. *Paris* (*Rue St. Martin*). 1812-21.
GAVEY, Edward. *London.* 1755. Sold his stock.
GAW, William P. *Philadelphia.* 1819.
GAWTHORNE, Thomas. *London.* a.1702. Went to *Paris.*
GAY—
André. *Grenoble.* 1554-70.
Joseph. *London.* an.1757-ca.1760. Watch.
Ante. *Turin.* 1st half 18c. str. rep. watch. g. en. watch Gélis coll.
David. *Geneva.* ca.1780-92.
Fils. *Paris.* ca.1795. g. en. watch, set pearls. g. en. watch S.K.M.
——. *Paris.* 1822-4.
GAYDON, J. *Barnstaple.* 2nd half 18c. l.c. clock. Watch.
GAYESON, ——. *Paris.* an.1786. Watch.
GAYNET, Jeremiah. *London.* an.1767. Watch.
GAZE, S. B. *London.* 1817-24.
GAZEY, Peter. *London.* a.1735.
GAZUET (GASNET), Jerome. *London.* CC. 1682-1700. W. from *Geneva.* Lantern and l.c. clock.
GEAL, John. *London.* an.1777. Watch.
GEAR, George. *London.* a.1782.
GEARY, William. *London.* a.1707. Watch.
GEATER, Henry. *Bristol.* 1825-30. W. & C.
GEBEL—
ET FADEUILLE. *Paris.* 1820-3.
——. *Paris.* 1824.

GEBHARDT—
Heinrich. *Strasbourg*. 1631. d.ca.1662. sil. al. watch B.M. crys. fleur de lys watch Marryat coll.
J. B. *Strasbourg*. 1st half 17c. Watch Louvre.
Joh. Jacob. *Strasbourg*. 1st half 17c. sil. circ. watch B.M.
Hans Jacob. *Strasbourg*. 1663.
Heinrich. *Strasbourg*. ca.1760.
GEDDES—
James. *Edinburgh*. a.1728, d.1755.
Charles. *London, Boston, U.S.A., New York* from 1760. *Halifax, Nova Scotia*. b.1749, d.1810.
GEDDY, James. *Williamsburg* (*Baltimore, U.S.A.*). 1774.
GEE—
William. *Warrington*. 1750. W.
John. *London*. an.1757. Watch.
Richard. *Cronton*. 1770. W.
GEESON, George. *London*. an.1780. Watch.
GEEVERS, S. *Rotterdam*. 1821-30.
GEGENREINER—
Franz Xavier. *Augsburg*. Early 18c. trav. clock G.M.
Franz Xavier. *Augsburg*. 1760-88. Turret and br. C. Possibly the same as preceding or his son.
GEGYE, Rene. *Charleston, U.S.A.* 1740. C. & W.
GEIGER—
Johann Friedrich. *Langensalza*. End 17c. hex. table clock B.M.
E. T. *Fürth*. d.1749.
Johann David. *Leipzig*. Early 18c. Watch Schloss M. Berlin. cf. GEYGER.
GEIJER, Sebastian. *Åbo*. comp. 1770. Clock.
GEILING, Peter. *Fürth*. d.1795.
GEILL, Matthias. *Germany*. 18c. Mantel clock.
GEISER—
Jean. *Les Eplatures*. 1805-17. C.
Jonas, son. *Chaux-de-Fonds*. 1811. Skeleton clock Chaux-de-Fonds M.
David, son. *Chaux-de-Fonds*. 1816. d.1857. C.
Frères. *Chaux-de-Fonds*. 1815-30. Firm of David, Jonas and Lucien (a case maker).
GEISS, J. J. C. *Fürth*. d.1791.
GEISSHEIM, Smod. *Augsburg*. ca.1625. p.c. sil. and tortoise-shell watch.
GEISSLER—
Franziskus. *Augsburg*. m.1748-53. From *Längkirchen*.
——. *Berlin*. d.1797.
J. G. *Halle*. Pub. in 1793 a large work in 10 vols., 'Der Uhrmacher oder Lehrbegrif der Uhrmacherkunst.'
GEIST—
Kilian. *Vienna*. 18c.
Thomas Narcissus. *Augsburg*. a.ca.1778, comp. 1783, m.1793.
GELAT, Samuel. *Paris*. 1675 m.
GELDARTE, John. *York*. 1674. W.
GELL—
John. *York*. 1634. W.
John, son. *York*. 1663. W.
GELLS, Thomas. *London*. CC.1720.
GEMBS, Melchoir. *Basle*. m.1600-25. From *Württemberg*.
GEMIN, Guillaume. *Geneva*. 1586. Refugee from *Antwerp*.
GEMINUS, Antonio. *Rome*. 1589. Ring dial Old Ashmolean M.
GEMMA—
Reynier, called Frisius. *Louvain*. b.1508, d.1555. Mathematician. Proposed the use of timekeepers for ascertaining the longitude.
Gualterus, nephew. ——. 1564. Inst. maker. Astrolabe.
GEMMEL, Mathew. *New York*. 1805. W.
GEMMING, Johann. *Fürth*. d.ca.1800.
GEMPLE, Johann Gervasius. *Olmütz*. 1746. Restored Olmütz clock.
GENDLE, Thomas. *Plymouth*. 1795.
GENEQUAND-ALLAMAND. *Geneva*. Early 19c.
GENERY, John. *London*. a.1823.
GENSPACHER, Fr. Bernardus. *Kaisheim*. b.1723, d.1794. From *Verona*. br. clock Feill coll.
GENT, Joseph. *Walsall*. 1805. C. & W.
GENTIL—
Bartholomin. *Dijon*. 1412-15. 'Serrurier.' Keeper of town clock.
Frères. *Chaux-de-Fonds*. 1804.
Perret. *Paris*. 1810. br. clock.
GENTILHOMME—
——. *Paris*. 1810. C.
Veuve. *Paris*. 1824.
GENTSCHEL, ——. *Strasbourg*. ca.1780. 4-colour g. watch.
'GEO. F. ROOT.' Sig. on 1871-4 watches of the CORNELL WATCH CO.
'GEO. SANCE RICE'. Sig. on 1871-5 watches of the NEW YORK WATCH CO.
'GEO. W. WAITE.' Sig. on 1871-4 watches of the CORNELL WATCH CO.
GEOFFROY, ——. *Paris*. 1819-25.
GEORG, Balthasar. *Strasbourg*. mar. 1680.
GEORGE—
Andrew. *London*. a.1649.
Louys. ——. 17c. Fleur-de-lys crys. watch Mallet coll.
Richard. *London*. a.1674, CC.1681, d.1712.
Richard. *London*. a.1710-25. Bankrupt.
Peter. *London*. a.1730. Watch.
Thomas. *London*. an.1748. Watch.
Walter. *London*. an.1751. Watch.
Jérémie. *Geneva*. 1748.
ET NEVIR. *Berlin*. Mid. 18c. Clock in cabinet, Breslau Schloss M.
Alexander. *London*. an.1776. Watch.
Louis. *Berlin*. 1769-96. C. to the King. Watch. Also GEORGES.
Walter. *Carmarthen*. 1769-76. Watch.
Louis et Compagnie. *Berlin*. ca.1815. Lever watch Ilbert coll.
John. *Dublin*. 1824.
'GEORGE CHANNING.' Sig.on 1868 watches of the UNITED STATES WATCH CO.
'GEORGE WALKER,' Sig. on 1871-5 watches of the NEW YORK WATCH CO.
GEORGÉ, ——. *Paris*. 1807-15.
GEORGES—
l'orlogier. *Lyons*. 1545.
——. *Paris*. 1812.
GÉRARD—
——. *Avignon*. 1404. Worked for Benoît XIII.
Jean. *Castelnau*. 1634. 'Horrologeur.'
Jean Benoît. *Paris*. m.1743, juré 1758-69. Clock mt. C.A. & M. cf. GIRARD.
——. *Metz*. ca.1765. 4-colour g. en. watch.
Benoist. *Paris*. Late 18c. Perhaps same as J.B. Clock with Dresden porcelain figures.
——. *Paris* (*Rue du Coq St. Honoré*). 1807-1825.
In. *London*. *v*. DRAREG.
GÉRAUDEL, ——. *Verdun*. 2nd half 17c. Watch. cf. GARAUDEL.
GERBE, François. Prob. *France*. ca.1700. Watch F.W.M.
GERBEL, F. ——. ca.1720. Watch Ilbert coll.
GERBER, Caspar. *Fürth*. d.ca.1820.
GERCKE, Daniel Friedrich. *Hamburg*. 1801-1821.
GERDTS, Martin. *Hamburg*. 1680. Watch and aut. mus. clock Cassel Landes, M.
GERDUM, ——. *Colberg*. 18c. Mantel clock Feill coll.

GERICKE, ——. *Paris.* 1824. C.
GERING—
Daniel. *Stockholm.* m.1749, d.1797.
Daniel. *Greiffswald.* 2nd half 18c. Watch with twin wheel verge esc. Ilbert coll.
GERMAIN—
Henri. *Grenoble.* 1679 from *Blois.*
——. *Paris.* 1825.
GERMONT, ——. *Paris.* 1812.
GERMÜLLER, Johann Karl. *Augsburg,* comp. 1784: then *Vienna*; *Augsburg,* m.1795.
GERNGROSS, Gottlieb. *Marburg.* 1773.
GERNON, Bernard. *London.* CC.1659-63.
GERON, A. *Paris.* Late 18c. Four col. g. watch Feill coll.
GÉRONDET (GIRONDET)—
Manuel. *Geneva.* d.1553. Refugee from *France.*
Hugues. *Geneva.* d.1555. Refugee from *France.*
GERRARD—
Richard. *London.* an.1689. Watch.
John. *London.* 1714-ca.1735. br. clock and rep. watch G.M. l.c. clock Virginia M.
William. *Liverpool.* 1825. W.
William. *Turriff.* a.1812, d.1872.
GERRISH, William. *Bristol.* 1818. W.
GERRITS, L. S. *Amsterdam.* 1822. W.
GERRO, ——. *Paris.* 1769. g. en. watch Stern. coll.
GERSELAT, Antoine. *Grenoble.* 1670.
GERSTNER, F. prob. *Vienna.* Early 19c. Sig. under cock of watch mt. sd. Carl KRATZSCH, Feill coll.
GERUNG, Ludwig. *Nürnberg.* m.1470. 'Orelmacher.'
GERVAIS, ——. *Paris.* ca.1600.
GESCHEID—
Johann Friedrich. *Dresden.* m.1773, d.1803.
Gottlieb Samuel. *Dresden.* m.1819, d.1822.
GESSLER (GUESSLER)—
Emanuel. *Basle.* 1751. d.1755. Watch Basle M.
Melchior, son. *Basle.* 1763. m.1771. Kleinuhrmacher.
GESTERMANN, Joseph. *Vienna.* m.ca.1737.
GETLAT, Joseph. *Merville.* Mid. 18c. Watch mt. Arts M. Prague.
GETTER, William. *London.* a.1750.
GETWOOD, James. *Portarlington.* 1824.
GEUDER, Johann Paulus. *Fürth.* d.1792.
GEVRIL—
Les Frères. *Chaux-de-Fonds.* 1740-50. rep. Louis XIV. clock.
Jacques. *Chaux-de-Fonds,* 1750. *Madrid,* 1758. d.1767. Clock.
GEX, Jean Samuel François. *Paris.* m.1780-9. g. en. watch Feill coll.
GEYBELS, ——. *Paris.* 1807-12.
GEYGER, Johann David. *Dresden.* m.1704. sil. clock set cameos and stones. cf. GEIGER.
GEYMÜLLER, Joseph. *Grosse Glogau.* Early 18c. Watch M.P.S. Dresden.
GHERRALD, Richard. *London.* 1689 CC.
GIB (GIBB, GIBS)—
William. *Rotterdam.* ca.1710-ca.1770. Watch S.M.S.K. Three watch mts. G.M. Watch mt. École d'Horlogerie, Geneva. p.c. watch, repoussé sd. D. COCHIN, Ilbert coll. l.c. clock ill. Britten.
Pieter. *Rotterdam.* Early 18c. Watch Staats M. Amsterdam. Watch mt. G.M.
William, jun. *Rotterdam.* Mid. 18c. Watch Ilbert coll.
James. *Stockton-on-Tees.* 1779. W.
GIBB, James. *Stirling.* 1770.
GIBBINGS, ——. *St John's, Newfoundland.* ca.1800.
GIBBON—
John. *London* (*Clerkenwell Gr.*). 1772. W.
Alexander & John. *London.* (*Wapping*). 1805-08.
GIBBONS (GIBBINS)—
Benjamin. *London.* CC.1721 Watch.
Richard. *London.* a.1723, C.C.1730-7.
Edward. *London.* CC.1735-41.
Thomas. *London.* a.1737.
Benjamin. *London.* CC.1750, d.1769.
Thomas. *Philadelphia.* 1751. From *London.*
Thomas. *Bristol.* 1759. W.
Edward. *Birmingham.* 1780.
John. *London.* a.1773.
Joshua. *London.* 1809-24.
John. *London* (*Goswell St.* and *King St.*). a.1803, CC.1811-40. W.
Harry. *London* (*Bermondsey St.*). a.1809, CC.1826.
GIBBS—
Walter. *London.* a.1639, CC.1648-1700.
Thomas. *London.* a.1672, CC.1681, m.CC. 1711-17. Watch.
Joshua. London. a.1689, CC.1700-23.
William. *London.* a.1700, CC.1707, d.1750. Watch. l.c. clock Virginia M.
Joseph. *London.* 1710 CC.
John. *London.* 1714 CC.
Solomon. *London.* a.1708, CC.1716-35.
John. *London.* a.1713, CC.1721-34.
Edmund. *London.* a.1721.
John. *London.* a.1723, CC.1736.
Michael. *London.* a.1724.
Edward. *London.* a.1726.
Frederick. *London.* a.1731.
Robert. *London.* a.1731.
Stephen. *London.* a.1733, CC.1748-64. Watch N.Y. Univ.
William. *London.* a.1736.
James. *London* (*Fleet St.*) a.1736, CC.1744-1772.
Edmund. *London.* 1744-92. Watch.
Richard. *London.* an.1745. Watch.
Daniel. *London.* an.1757. Watch.
John, son of Wm. *London.* a.1749.
Isaac. *London.* an.1762. Watch.
George. *London.* an.1775. Watch.
Daniel. *London.* a.1776.
Thomas. *London.* Late 18c. Watch mt. S.K.M.
Richard. *London* (*Fish St. Hill*). CC.1815, l.CC.1818.
GIBERT, ——. *Paris.* 1st half 18c. g. en. watch Gélis coll.
GIBOLET, ——. ——. 18c. rep. watch.
GIBSON—
Benjamin. *London.* a.1650.
James. *London.* a.1669. Maker of repute.
Robert. *Ecclefechan.* 1710. d.1778. l.c. clock.
James. *London.* 1727-60.
Joseph. *Ecclefechan.* ca.1750. l.c. clock.
James. *London.* a.1746.
Mary. *London* (*Newgate St.*). 1753-5.
Daniel. *Liverpool.* 1754-61. W.
Peter. *London.* an.1756. Watch.
James. *Newcastle-o.-T.* 1759-66 From *London.*
James Luke. *London* (*Fleet St.*). an.1762, d.1767. Watch.
John. *London.* an.1762. Watch.
M. *London.* ca.1760. T.C.
John. *Beith.* 1761-1837.
John. *Edinburgh.* a.1758-80. l.c. mus. clock.
& CLELAND. *Edinburgh.* 1767-73.
William. *Barnard Castle.* ca.1770-95. C. & W.
Edward. *London* (*Bishopsgate St.*). a.1766, CC.1777, m.CC.1802-15.
Adam. *Dunse.* 1777.
John. *Alnwick.* an.1781-1827. Watch.
John. *Kelso.* ca.1790.
John. *Edinburgh.* a.1780.
Andrew. *London.* 1802-08.
John. *London* (*Sweetings Alley*). CC.1806,

GIBSON—*continued.*
l.CC.1812-24. Chron. and W. Fine duplex watch G.M.
James. *Glasgow.* 1809-25.
John. *Glasgow.* 1809.
John. *London (Bartholomew Lane).* 1809-11. W.
Robert. *Dumfries.* 1820.
George. *North Shields.* 1820-50.
John. *Saltcoats.* 1820-7.
GIBSTED, John. *London.* an.1785. Watch.
GIDE—
Xavier. *Paris.* m.1762-89. Watch, Meissen porcelain case, B.M.
David, ET BLONDET FILS. *Paris.* ca.1780. g. en. flagon watch F.W.M. g. en. spherical watch Fränkel coll. g. en. basket watch.
Quidon Remond, et Cie. *France.* Late 18c. g. en. watch Fränkel coll.
David. *Paris.* ca.1800. en. lyre watch M.P.S. Dresden.
——. *Paris.* 1822-4.
GIDEON, Robert. *London.* a.1684, CC.1691-1725.
GIDMAN, Thomas. *Liverpool.* 1825. W.
GIEBICKE, Friedrich Wilhelm. *Augsburg.* m.1747-70. From *Berlin.*
GIERCKE, Jacob. *Willensis.* 1660. br. clock.
GIERS, A. *Borås.* 1825-46. Wall and br. clocks.
GIFFART, Samuel. *London.* a.1752.
GIFFIN—
George. *London.* a.1733. CC.1740.
Edward Burr. *London (Holborn).* a.1758, CC.1766-78.
GIFFORD—
Thomas. *London.* a.1685, CC.1692.
Philip. *London.* a.1695.
Thomas. *London.* a.1755.
——. *Dorking.* 1769. W.
GILBERT—
Faustin Augustine. *London.* a.1653, CC.1661.
Thomas. *London.* a.1656.
Richard. *London.* a.1664.
Joseph. *London.* a.1682.
William. *London.* a.1685, CC.1695-1703.
Charles. *London.* a.1690, CC.1700-09. g. en. watch M.M.A.
Richard. *Bristol.* 1711. cf. Richard above.
Thomas. *London.* a.1715.
Thomas, son of William. *London.* CC.1733-1736.
——. *Paris.* 1st half 18c. Boulle clocks Reichenberg M. and Schloss M. Berlin.
William. *London.* a.1747, CC.1767.
Thomas. *Lichfield.* 1775. Nephew and partner of Hannah STRIPLING.
John. *London.* a.1780.
——. *Paris.* ca.1790. g. en. watch Stern. coll.
William. *Southampton.* 1790. Dissolved partnership with Thomas MATCHAM.
Edward. *Chichester.* ca.1790 CC.
William. *Gosport.* 1795 CC. W. l.c. clock.
Thomas. *Pengelly.* 1795.
Thomas. *Rugelly.* 1795.
& HELMSLEY. *Chichester.* ca.1800. W.
——. *Northiam.* ca.1800.
J. *Moscow.* ca.1800.
Thomas. *Hythe.* Early 19c. Watch.
Davies, M.P. *Tredrea (Cornwall).* CC.1823.
GILBERTSON—
John. *Newcastle-o.-T.* 1747, d.1750. C. & W. *v.* SMOULT & GILBERTSON.
Sarah, widow of John. *Newcastle-o.-T.* From 1750.
John. *Ripon.* an.1764-95. l.c. clocks. Watch.
GILBOURNE, Edward. *London.* a.1720.
GILCHRIST (GILDCHRIST)—
Archibald. *London.* CC.1729-41.
John. *Kilsyth.* 1820.
GILDER—
John. *London.* a.1711.
John. *London.* a 1757-99. W.
GILDERED, John. *London.* a.1765.
GILES—
Robert. *London.* a.1711.
Daniel. *London (Clerkenwell).* 1791. W.
——. *Maidstone.* Early 19c.
GILEVART, ——. *Paris.* 1611. Ceased to be juré, prob. dead.
GILGOUR, Thomas. *Elgin.* 1697.
GILGUD, Johann Georg. *Brünn.* 2nd half 18c. Watch mt. Arts M. Prague.
GILIUS, ——. *Stockholm.* 1600-10. Prob. same as Gilius VON DER PLATZ.
GILKES—
Richard. *London.* a.1678, CC.1686-1703. Also GILKS.
George. *London.* a.1693.
——. *Burford.* an.1768. Watch.
Richard. *Adderbury.* 1771. l.c. clock.
Tobias. ——. an.1774. Watch.
Daniel. *London.* 1802-04.
M. *London.* 1822-4.
GILKS—
Robert. *London.* 1693.
John. *Shipton.* an.1758-84. Watch.
GILL—
John. *London.* a.1700, CC.1707.
William. *Maidstone.* Early 18c. l.c. clock.
Henry. *Kings Lynn.* 1729. Insolvent. C.
Thomas. *Birmingham.* 1748-66. From *Liverpool.*
William. *Rotterdam.* 1773-94. Watch sd. GIL L'AINÉ.
Thomas. *London.* an.1779. Watch.
George. *London.* a.1775.
Caleb. *Hingham, U.S.A.* 1785.
Leavitt. *Hingham, U.S.A.* 1785.
William. *Hastings.* 1795. W.
Wilfred. *Winster.* 1795. W.
James Henry. *Liverpool.* 1796-1800. W.
Daniel. *Rye.* 1795.
Thomas. *London.* a.1802.
P. & SON. *Aberdeen.* Early 19c. Watch.
GILLANDER, J. *London.* Mid. 18c. Watch.
GILLAS, Peter Fransen. *Bergen.* 1754 m.
GILLE (GILLES)—
l'égaré. *Paris.* 1663. Orfèvre du roi. Made en. watch-cases.
Pierre. *Paris.* m.1746.
Jean. *Paris.* m.1753.
Guillaume. *Paris.* m.1753.
l'aîné. *Paris.* ca.1760-90. Many clocks, one Louvre, bronze by St. Germain. Watch in eng. steel and gold.
Guillaume Jean, fils. *Paris (Rue St. Denis).* m.1765-86.
Fils. *Paris (Rue Montorgueil).* 18c.
Fils de Pierre. *Paris.* 1779.
——. *Paris. (Rue des Blancs-Manteaux).* 1812.
GILLESPEY—
Charles. *London.* a.1734.
Charles. *Dublin.* 1747. d.1771. Watch mt.
GILLET—
Michel. *Blois.* 1622-31.
Pierre Noël. *Paris.* m.1779.
Jean Louis Gabriel. *Paris.* m.1786-9.
GILLETT—
Charles. *Manchester.* 1772-94. Prob. the following.
Charles Edward. *Manchester.* b.1745, d. 1819. l.c. mus. clock. W.
Edward. *Manchester.* an.1773. W.
& HEALEY. *Manchester.* 1777-93. Partnership of C. E. Gillett with John Healey.
Charles Edward, & Son. *Manchester.* 1790-1800. W.
Hugh. *London.* 1799. W.
GILLIER, C. *Berne.* ca.1630. Oval watch B.M.

GILLIES—
William. *St. Ninians.* 1775.
Robert. *Beith.* 1780.
GILLIUSSON, William. *Stockholm.* 1603. Made clock for the Tre Kronor Tower.
GILMORE—
James. *Stewartstown.* 1824.
Patrick. *Bray* (*Leinster*). 1824.
Robert. *Cookstoun.* 1824.
GILMOT, Harie (Henry). *Edinburgh.* 1711.
GILOT (GILLOT)—
——. *Paris* (*Rue du Cimetière St. Nicolas*). Late 18c.-1812. Mantel clock.
——. *Paris* (*Rue St. Denis*). 1812.
GILPIN, Edmund (Edward). *London.* 1630-1677. Petitioner for incorporation of CC. Fine circ. sil. eng. watch and two others Mallett coll. ill. Baillie. Oval cal. watch Fränkel coll. Oval watch Ilbert coll.
GIMBLETT—
John. *Birmingham.* 1768-81. Watches.
& VALE. *Birmingham.* 1770. Watches.
GIMLINGHAM, John. *London.* a.1764, CC. 1772-94.
GIMSON, S. *March.* Early 19c.
GIN, William. *Perth.* 1778.
GINDRE, ——. *Paris.* 1824.
GINDREAUX, David Louis. ——. ca.1770. Louis xv chiming clock.
GINN, William. *London.* CC.1699-1723.
GIOQUE, ——. *Chaux-de-Fonds.* 1784.
GIOVANNI—
degli Organi. 1354. *v.* ORGANI.
di Venezia. *Avignon.* 1363. Made a clock for the inner Papal chamber.
da San Vincenzo. *Genoa.* 1364. 'Magister relorii.' Third keeper of Genoa clock.
di Syon. *Genoa.* 1377-82. Fourth keeper of Genoa clock.
de Barlono. *Genoa.* 1385-1408. Fifth keeper of Genoa clock.
dalle Ancore. *Venice.* 1551.
GIPFEL, Gabriel. ——. ca.1610. Magnificent g. en. and crys. monstrance clock, set diamonds and rubies, and g. en. crys. watch Grüne Gewölbe, Dresden.
GIRARD—
——. *Avignon.* 1503. Keeper of town clock.
Marc. *Blois.* mar.1593, d.ca.1616. Of German origin. Name Gerrart and Gyrardt. crys. watch M.M.A. Watch Stads M. Amsterdam.
Théodore, son. *Blois.* b.1596, comp. 1619, d.1680. en. watch set stones Ilbert coll. Watch Bernal sale.
Marc, son. *Blois.* 1652-99. g. en. watch M.M.A.
Louis. ——. Early 18c. Watch N.Y. Univ.
FRÈRES. *Carouge.* 1740. g. en. watch S.K.M.
Phillipe. *Paris.* m.1747.
——. *Caen.* 18c. Watch Bernal sale.
Jacob, l'aîné. *Paris.* 1772.
Benoît. *Paris.* 1781. Cartel clock with dial and mt. acting as pendulum. cf. GÉRARD.
Charles (or Claude) Silvain. *Paris.* m.1786.
Claude Antoine. *La Brévine.* 1798. C.
——. *Paris* (*Rue du Harlay*). 1812.
——. *Paris* (*Rue Montmartre*). 1813-25.
frère et soeur. *Paris.* 1819-24.
——. *Nantes.* 1823. Re-made Angers cathedral clock.
Constant Othenin. *Chaux-de-Fonds.* 1845-50. Partner with C. ROBERT. Then alone as GIRARD-PERREGAUX. Eminent maker. Pocket chron. with spherical balance spring, and a tourbillon watch with chron. esc., both Chamb. coll.
GIRARD-DIT-GUERRE, ——. *Hüningen.* a.1680. From *Geneva.*
GIRARDIER, Charles. l'aîné. *Geneva.* 1780-1805. Awarded prize for watch in 1792 by Soc. des Arts. aut. watch. rep. watch. Watch Arch. M. Geneva.
GIRARDOT, Claude. *Paris.* m.1674.
GIRAUD—
Jean Jacques. *Lyons.* 1678 m. From *Gex.*
Jacques André. *Copenhagen.* m.1753.
Benoît. *Paris.* m.1774-89.
Jean Jacques. *Paris.* m.1785-9.
Christophe. *Geneva.* ca.1770-1814. g. lever. rep. watch.
GIRGL, Andreas. *Munich.* Court C.1713, d.1739.
GIRLINGTON, John. *London.* a.1681.
GIROD—
Jean Gaspard. *Geneva.* ca.1620. Astro. watches B.M. and Den. coll.
Jaques. *Coppet.* 2nd half 17c. Watches Ilbert and Den. colls.
James. *London.* 1689. CC.1692-ca.1700. Frenchman. br. clock. Watch Ilbert coll.
——. *Paris.* ca.1770. 4-colour g. watch Nat. M. Stockholm.
& JACOB. *London.* ca.1790. g. en. watch.
Barthélemy. *Paris.* 1810-6. Associated with Jacques Barthélemy VACHERON, in representing the firm of VACHERON.
——. *Paris.* 1823.
GIROUD—
Jean Pierre. *Les Brenets.* 1766-85. Able maker.
——. *Paris.* 1810-9.
Abram Louis. *La Brévine.* 1815-20.
GIROUST—
Alexander. *London.* 1728-39. Lacquer br. clock M.M.A.
Philippe. *Paris.* m.1784-9.
GIROUX, André François. *Paris.* m.1767-89.
GISCARD—
William. *Ely.* b.1749, d.1812. C. & W.
John. *Swaffham.* ca.1800.
William. *Downham.* ca.1800. Watch.
GISSEY, ——. *Paris.* 1812-19.
GITEAU (GITAU, GITEAUX), ——. *Paris.* 1811-24. Pupil of BREGUET. g. en. cyl. watch.
GITTER, John. *London.* a.1683.
GIULIONI E MODER. *Florence.* Early 19c.
GIVELL, Richard. *London.* an.1787. Watch.
GLADDISH, William. *Yalding.* 1788-94. C. & W.
GLADMAN—
Thomas. *London.* a.1711. Watch.
Johan. *Stockholm.* b.1731, d.1800. Several g. watches, one Nord. M. ill. Sidenbladh.
& WILLIAMS. *London.* 1764. From Geo. GRAHAM.
John. *London.* an.1770-ca.1790. Watch.
GLADSTONE—
Thomas. *London.* a.1694, CC.1703-29 Insolvent.
John. *Biggar.* b.1772, d.1851.
GLAESNER & PREUD'HOMME. *Lyons.* 1782. Tried to start a French factory with workmen from *Geneva.* In 1795 Glaesner started a factory with N. C. LEMAIRE at *Versailles,* which lasted till 1801. g. rep. watch. Two en. watches by Glaesner.
GLAISHER, George. *London.* 1775. Sold wooden clocks at 7*s.* 6*d.* to 18*s.*
GLANEY, ——. *London.* an.1755. Watch.
GLANVILLE—
Serjeant. *London.* a.1748.
David. *Waterford.* 1775-1824. Watch N.Y. Univ.
GLASCO—
Thomas. *Dublin.* an.1756-80. Watch.
Philip. *Dublin.* ca.1800. l.c. clock. Watch.
GLASS—
John. *Edinburgh.* 1692.

GLASS—*continued.*
Christoph. *Augsburg.* Early 18c. comp.
John. *London.* a.1752.
James. *Bristol.* 1825-30.
GLASSBROOK, James. *London.* an.1778. Watch.
GLATZ & WUNDERLEY. *Manchester.* ca.1820.
GLAUDE, Quintinus. *Rotterdam.* 1684.
GLAVE, John. *London.* a.1768, CC.1782-1814.
GLAZE, Thomas. *Bridgnorth.* ca.1790-early 19c. Watch S.K.M. l.c. clock.
GLAZEBROOK, John. *Mansfield.* ca.1780. l.c. clocks.
GLAZER, J. *Rotterdam.* 1821-30.
GLAZIER (GLASER), William. *London.* a.1658, CC.1666-89.
GLEAVE—
Matthew. *W. Derby.* d.1705. Watch mt. G.M.
John. *Liverpool.* 1805-29. W.
GLEICHAUF, Benedict. *Vienna.* m.1771.
GLENCK—
A. *Prague.* Early 18c. Watch.
Johannes. *Prague.* Late 18c. g. en. watch Fränkel coll.
GLENNY—
Joseph. *London (Clerkenwell).* a.1784, CC. 1791, l.CC.1810. Watch-case maker.
Joseph, *London (Hoxton Sq.).* 1799. W.
George, son of Joseph (1). *London (Waterloo Pl.).* a.1807, CC.1819.
Joseph. bro. *London.* a.1811.
GLIMMANN, J. G. *Lüneberg.* 1821.
GLORIA—
Jacques. *Rouen.* 1696. Juré 1701-04. Watch Den coll. cal. watch with balance spring Gélis coll. rep. watch mt. Ilbert coll.
——. *Rouen.* 1753 m. Watch mt. Arts M. Prague.
GLORIOD, ——. *Les Gras.* 1825.
GLOSSOP, Robert. *London.* ca.1800. Watch.
GLOTZ, Simon. *Nürnberg.* Burgher in 1565. 'Urlemacher.'
GLOVER—
Samuel. *London.* a.1686, CC.1694-1717.
Richard. *London.* b.1676, mar. 1698. Comp. W.
Daniel. *London.* a.1687, CC.1699. Watch ca. 1705 Ilbert coll.
John. *London.* CC.1700-20. Watch Ilbert coll.
Richard. *London.* a.1695, CC.1703, d.an. 1751.
John Smith. *London.* a.1717.
Thomas. *London.* a.1717.
Thomas. *London.* a.1721.
John, son of John. *London.* CC.1731.
Thomas. *London.* a.1732, CC.1746-63.
James. *Prescot.* d.1765. W.
Boyer. *London.* CC.1746, w.CC. and d. 1768.
William. *London.* an.1753. Bankrupt 1757.
William. *Worcester.* 1751. Retired 1758. C. & W.
William, nephew. *Worcester.* 1758-67. Opened shop in *Tewkesbury* in 1764. From *London.*
William. *Worcester.* 1764-71. Opened shop in *Tetbury* in 1764. Prob. same as above.
William. *Chester.* d.1772. W.
James. *London.* a.1751, CC.1764.
Thomas. *London.* a.1755, CC.1767.
Samuel. *London.* 1772-1811 CC.
Ralph. *London (Hanover Sq.).* 1773, *(Pimlico)* 1799. Watch.
Thomas. *London.* d.1785.
Thomas. *Rainhill.* d.1786. W.
George. *London.* a.1781.
John. *London.* a.1786.
Benjamin. *London.* 1775.

GLOVER—*continued.*
Joseph. *London (Half Moon St.).* an.1776. Watch.
William. *Ledbury.* 1784-95. C. & W.
John. *Bungay.* 1791. l.c. clock.
Joseph. *Leicester.* 1791-5. W.
John. *Prescot.* d.1801. W.
Stephen. *London (Petticoat Lane).* CC.1792, l.CC.1795-1811.
William. *Bristol.* 1792-1801. W.
Samuel. *London.* 1811 CC.
William. *Boston, U.S.A.* 1818-25. W.
James. *Manchester.* ca.1820. cyl. fuzee watch by him or following.
John. *Manchester.* ca.1820.
Thomas. *Kells.* 1824.
W. *Limerick.* 1824.
GLOYDE, ——. *London.* 1771.
GLÜCK—
Adam. *Augsburg.* Mid. 17c. Heliotrope watch B.M. Tulip watch Bernal sale. Stand clock.
Georg. *Berlin.* Mid. 17c. sil. eng. book watch B.M. ill. Baillie.
GLÜCKSTEIN, Anton. *Vienna.* m.1798.
GLUMMER, Peter. *London.* 1582. C. 'of the Frenche church.'
GLYD, James. *London.* 1752. Watch. Ring dial Old Ashmolean M.
GLYNN (GLYNNE)—
Richard. *London.* a.1696, CC.1705-23.
Henry. *London.* an.1761. Watch.
GNASH, Charles. *Liverpool.* ca.1820.
GOAD, John. *London.* an.1760. Retired 1774. Watch.
GOALLON, James. *London.* 1622. Alien.
GOATER, John. *Winchester.* Early 19c.
GOATLEY—
——. *Ramsgate.* ca.1790 CC.
——. *Canterbury.* Early 19c.
GOBART—
James. *London.* 1695.
Matthew. *London.* an.1731. Watch.
GOBBI, A. *Swaffham.* Early 19c. Watch.
GOBDCHILD, John. *London.* a.1710.
GOBE (GEBE, GEEB), Hans. *Dresden.* 1558. d.1574. Court C. Two instruments M.P.S. Dresden.
GOBELS, Jan. *Amsterdam.* 1767. l.c. clock.
GOBERT—
Philippe. *Paris.* 1675 juré.
Peter. *London.* CC.1687. Frenchman. W.
Matthew. *London.* Mid. 18c. Piqué tortoise-shell watch.
GODARD, Simon. *Paris.* 1600. Sig. to Statuts of Paris corporation. crys. watch.
GODBED—
William. *London.* a.1638, CC.1646, d.1664. Watch B.M.
William. *London.* 1665. W.
Matthew. *London.* a.1657.
GODDARD—
Rymon, ——. ca.1600. Oval crys. watch. Perhaps Simon GODARD.
John. *London.* 1615-18. Native of *Paris.*
Thomas. *London.* a.1638.
Isaac. *London.* a.1675, CC.1684-99. l.c. clock.
Thomas. *London (Shoe Lane).* a.1685-1723. Bankrupt.
Nicholas. *Newark.* 1710. d.ca.1741. l.c. clocks.
Benjamin. *London.* a.1692, CC.1701-26. l.c. clock.
Christopher. *London (Little Britain).* 1729. CC.1756-61. Bankrupt. br. clock. Watch.
John, bro. *London, China & London.* CC. 1758-72. Bankrupt.
Henry. *Tenterden* to 1767, then *Dover.* Watch.
Edward. *London (Helmet Row).* 1780, CC. 1787-99.

GODDARD—*continued.*
Francis. *London.* 1790-1825.
Benjamin. *London (Bethnal Gr.).* 1792.
Florimond. *London.* 1794-7. Watch.
William. *London (Shoreditch).* a.1792, CC. 1800.
Luther. *Shrewsbury, U.S.A.* 1809-17. The first American to make watches in quantity; he made 500 from 1809 to 1817.
T. *London (Rathbone Pl.).* 1815-20.
George S. *Boston, U.S.A.* 1816-25. W.
George S., and William GRUBB, jun. *Boston, U.S.A.* 1816. W.
Thomas. *London (Hoxton).* 1817-24.
'L. GODDARD & Co.' Sig. on Goddard's watches, 1809-17.
GODDE—
Jean. *Paris.* m.1691-1729. Watch Den. coll. Clock in Boulle case sd. J. Godde Laisné. Made clock for Louis XIV.
Jean Jacques. *Paris.* m.1769.
J. J., fils. *Paris.* 1779.
——. *London.* 2nd half 18c. Table clock.
GODDEN—
Thomas. *London.* a.1767.
Thomas. *London.* a.1771, CC.1779-96.
John. *Town Malling.* 1784.
GÖDE, Hans. *Stettin.* 1672-1701. Sig. on case of table clock with mt. by Chr. Klein.
GODEFROY—
——. *Besançon.* d.1720. Wall clock.
——. *Paris.* Mid. 18c. Watch mt. Arts M. Prague.
GODEMAR—
Antoine. *Geneva.* ca.1770-1800. Associated with Moïse Pouzait. Taught in the first school of horology in 1788.
Guillaume. *Geneva.* Early 19c.
Frères. *Geneva.* 1814-24.
Antoine. *Paris.* 1814-24. Agent of Godemar Frères.
GODET—
Jean Antoine. *Basle.* 1719. From *Geneva.*
——. *Paris.* 1807-09.
GODFREY—
Henry. *London.* CC.1685-1707. Watch.
John. *London.* a.1682.
John. *London.* a.1708.
Benjamin. *London.* ca.1730.
Elizabeth. *London.* 1741-60.
——. *Sudbury.* 2nd half 18c. l.c. clock.
Abraham. *Kidderminster.* Till 1795 partner with Barnett LEVY.
——. *Plymouth.* 1795. C. & W.
George. *London.* 1799-1824. W.
GODIN—
Pierre. *Paris.* m.1693.
——. *Paris.* ca.1770. Clock Peiping M.
GODLONTON, Charles. *London.* a.1767.
GODLYMAN, Peter. *Hurley.* b.1694, d.1720. Clock.
GODNEY, J. *London.* 1825.
GODON—
Claude. *Lyons.* 1563-95. Made and repaired several turret clocks.
François Louis. *Paris.* m.1787-90. C. to the Court of Spain. Several fine clocks, ormolu and porcelain; one sold for £2100.
GODQUIN, Jean. *Rouen.* 1670. Made a pendulum for Rouen Cathedral clock.
GODRIN, Antoine. *Paris.* 1675 m.
GODSCHALK, Jacob. *Philadelphia.* 1771.
GODSELL, Richard. *London.* a.1757.
GODWIN, ——. *London.* an.1773. Watch.
GOEDEIJ, Nicolas. ——. ca.1630. oct. crys. watch B.M.
GOERING, B. *Chaux-de-Fonds* and *Ottensen.* b.1785.
GOEWELL, ——. *London.* an.1780. Watch.
GOFF—
William. *London.* Mid. 18c. p.c. g. watch.
Thomas. *London.* 1790. W.
GOFFE, William. *London.* Early 19c. Watch.
GOGAY, Am. *London.* Early 19c. Watch Den. coll.
GOHIER, Daniel. *The Hague.* 2nd half 18c. p.c. g. watch Stads M. Amsterdam.
GOLAI, Élizée. *Môtiers.* a.1737. C.
GOLAY—
Moïse and Isaac, bros. *Bellefontaine.* 1737. Made clock for Sentier.
Pierre Henri. *Vallée de Joux.* b.ca.1725.
Abel. *Le Chenit.* ca.1775.
Louis. *Le Chenit.* 1800. Maker of mus. mechanism and singing birds.
Elisée. *Piguet-Dessus.* 1853. Invented a perpetual calendar for watches.
GOLAY-JORDAN, ——. *Vallée de Joux.* b. ca.1730.
GOLD—
Abel. *London.* an.1691. Watch.
Christopher. *London.* ca.1760-74. Watch B.M.
John. *London.* an.1776-ca.1800. Watch.
GOLDBY, T. *London.* an.1773. Watch.
GOLDER, Thomas. *London.* a.1718.
GOLDIN, William. *London.* a.1716.
GOLDING—
Edward. *London.* a.1703. Watch. Also GOULDING.
John. *London (Execution Dock).* an.1773-1775. Watch. T.C.
GOLDNEY, Thomas. *London.* 1815-25.
GOLDSBOROUGH—
Newbury. *London.* a.1732.
George. *Scarborough.* ca.1770.
William. *Scarborough.* 1795. W.
James. *London.* 1800.
GOLDSMITH—
John. *London.* a.1674, CC.1681-9.
Thomas. *London.* a.1683, CC.1692-1703.
William. *London.* a.1708, CC.1719-47.
John. *London.* a.1708.
John. *London.* a.1711, CC.1720.
George. *London.* an.1769 Watch.
T. *Douglas (I. of Man).* Early 19c. C. & W.
John. *London.* 1805-11. C.
James. *London.* 1805-11. W.
GOLDSWORTHY, Edward. *London (Chelsea).* ca.1790-1820. T.C. Succeeded by KNOWLES.
GOLDWIN—
Henry. *London (Borough).* 1751. W.
John. *London.* an.1776. Watch.
GOLE—
James. *London.* 1791. W.
James, son. *London.* a.1791.
GOLL, Gabriel. *Basle.* a.1652-79.
GOLLAND, R. *London.* 1820. W.
GOLLING—
Andreas. *Augsburg.* 1712 m.-1746. d. an. 1755. *Vienna, Gratz, Prague* and *Breslau.* sil. watch Feill coll. Table clock.
Malthias. *Munich.* Court C. 1739, d.1772.
Johann Martin. *Augsburg.* m.1744-57. 4-colour g. watch Fränkel coll.
Leopold. *Augsburg.* m.1748-53.
Johann Georg. *Augsburg.* m.1748-70.
Joh. Simpert. *Fürth.* ca.1750. Went *Augsburg* 1789. d.ca.1800.
——. *London.* an.1762. Watch.
Anselm Benedikt. *Augsburg.* m.ca.1770, juré 1776-93. str. rep. trav. clock Feill coll.
Johann Nikolaus. *Günzburg.* 1770.
Ant. ——. 2nd half 18c. Metal watch.
Christoph Jakob. *Augsburg.* m.ca.1787-99.
Johann Friedrich. *Augsburg.* m.1802.
Johann Friedrich. *Vienna.* m.1818. g. en. watch.
GOLLOP, James. *Dorchester.* 1724.
GOLTON, Kerkby. *London.* a.1700.
GOM, Daniel. *Lyons.* mar.1629-70. From *Pomerania.* C. to the town. Made clock

GOM—*continued.* for Hôtel de Ville 1651. circ. cast silver watch Fränkel coll. crys. cross watch Lemberg M.
GOMARD, ——. *Paris.* 1790.
GOMBAULT, Jacques. *Paris.* 1776 m.
GOMBAUX, ——. *Nancy.* 18c. g. watch.
GOMET, Étienne. *Paris.* m.1776-89.
GOMM, William. *London.* a.1720.
GOMPERTZ, Benjamin. ——. 1817. Wrote art. on pendulums vibrating between cheeks in Jl. of Sci. and the Arts, Vol. 3.
GONDEVILLE, Jacob. *Geneva.* a.1594.
GONESSOT, Denis. *Paris.* 1675 m.
GONNOUILHON & FRANCOIS. *Geneva.* Early 19c. rep. cyl. watch.
GONON (GONNON)—
Bertrand. *Thiers,* 1637 m. *Lyons,* 1638-65. crys. cross watch Côte coll. ill. Vial & Côte.
Jean Baptiste. *Lyons.* 1659-63.
Jean Baptiste. *Milan.* 17c. Perhaps same as preceding. Very fine astro. br. clock.
GONTARD, ——. *Paris.* Early 19c. en. watch.
GONTHIER, ——. *Geneva.* ca.1800. Painter on enamel.
GOOCH—
John. *London (Gt. Arthur St.).* CC.1779-90.
Thomas. *London.* a.1778-1824.
William. *London.* a.1784.
Thomas. *London (Clerkenwell).* 1799-1803. Watch-case maker.
Albert Woodroffe, son. *London.* a.1803-24.
John. *London (Bunhill Row).* 1820.
H. *London.* 1825. W.
GOOD (GOODE)—
John. *London.* a.1671. CC.1678-1711. Writer on dialling.
Charles. *London (Strand).* CC.1686, d.1730. br. and l.c. clocks Weth. coll. Watch Den. coll. and mt. G.M.
John, nephew and a. *London (Strand).* 1726. Insolvent 1743. W.
Thomas. *London.* a.1700.
Charles. *London.* 1714. Not CC.
Savil. *London (Little Carter La.).* CC.1767.
W. J. *London.* an.1776. Watch.
Henry. *London.* an.1780. Watch.
Samuel. *Seaton.* 18c. l.c. clock.
John. *London.* 1780-94. p.c. g. cyl. c.secs. watch G.M.
John. *Athlone.* 1824.
GOODALE, Thomas. *London.* a.1713.
GOODALL—
Adam. *Edinburgh.* a.1744.
James. *London.* 1776. Watch Ilbert coll.
George. *Tadcaster.* Late 18c. Watch.
Charles. *London.* 1795-1824. Watch.
v. GOODHALL.
GOODBED, William. *London.* ca.1620. Watch. cf. GODBED.
GOODCHEAP, William. *London.* a.1794.
GOODCHILD—
John. *London.* CC.1725.
Richard. *Canterbury.* 1756. W.
Richard. *Harbledown.* 1767. W.
GOODEA, T. *Paris.* 1st half 18c. Boulle-work br. clock.
GOODERE, Ephraim. *Worcester.* mar.1782-1796 CC. W.
GOODFELLOW—
John. *Stirling.* 1765.
William. *London.* 1790.
W. *Dublin.* Late 18c. rep. watch mt.
William. *Philadelphia.* 1795-1813. Father and son.
William Richard. *London.* a.1810, CC.1817.
GOODFRIEND, John. *London.* d.1751. 'Eminent C. & W.'
GOODGE, James. *London.* a.1777.
GOODHALL—
William. *London.* a.1751, CC.1765-72.
George. *Aberford.* an.1775-95. Watch.
v. GOODALL.
GOODHUE, D. T. *Providence, U.S.A.* 1824.
GOODHUGH, Richard. *London.* 1825-40. br. clock.
GOODIE, Jeremiah. *London.* a.1753.
GOODING—
Josiah. *Bristol, R.I., U.S.A.* 1788-mid. 19c. Also *Dighton, Mass.*
William. *Manchester.* 1804.
Henry. *Boston, U.S.A.* 1810-25. W.
GOODLAD, Richard. *London.* CC.1689.
GOODLIN, Peter. *London.* CC.1637.
GOODMAN—
Timothy. *Towcester.* Late 17c. Lantern clock.
Thomas. *Charleston, U.S.A.* 1733. From *London.* W.
Charles. *London.* an.1774. Watch.
George. *London.* 1771-80. p.c. g. en. watch G.M. p.c. g. rep. watch M.M.A.
Henry. *London.* ca.1800. Watch London M.
John. *London.* 1805-08.
GOODOUNE, John. *Edinburgh.* 1680.
GOODRICH—
William. *London.* a.1689.
Simon. *London.* 1799. Award from Soc. Arts for clock with pendulum driven by a crank.
GOODWIN—
William. *London* and *Stowmarket.* a.1675-1720. Watch and l.c. clock. Lantern clock Virginia M.
William or Richard. *London.* a.1723.
Robert. *Worsted.* 18c. l.c. clock.
& Co. *London (Whitecross St.).* 1770. W.
John. *London (Strand).* 1770-1811. en. watch.
William. *Nottingham.* From 1789-1818. C. & W.
Samuel. *Philadelphia.* 1820. W.
Henry. *Newark.* 1825-40. l.c. clock.
GOODYEAR—
John. *London.* a.1714, CC.1722.
Joseph. *London.* a.1723, CC.1732.
GOODYER, Joseph. *London.* CC.1789.
GOOLAN, James. *Glasgow.* d.1763. W.
GOORE—
Thomas. *London.* a.1705, CC.1716.
Moses. *London.* an.1756. Watch.
GOOS, Anthony. *Amsterdam.* 1670.
GORDING, William. *Dublin.* 1787. g. watch.
GORDON—
Thomas. *Edinburgh.* a.1688, d.1743. An eminent maker. l.c. clock ill. J. Smith. Watch mt. Roy. M. Edinburgh.
John. *London (Ludgate St.).* a.1689, CC. 1698-1723. br. clock. Watch Ilbert coll.
Patrick. *Edinburgh.* a.1699, d.1749. l.c. clock.
David. *Dublin.* ca.1723. Partner with W. SINCLAIR.
Alexander. *Dundee.* 1729.
James. *Edinburgh.* 1734.
Hugh. *Aberdeen.* 1748-90. p.c. g. watch.
Robert. *Edinburgh.* 1750.
William. *London.* an.1756. Watch.
John. *Edinburgh.* a.1747-99.
Thomas. *Edinburgh.* a.1748. *New York,* 1759. Watch.
John. *London.* a.1749.
Alexander. *Dublin.* 1756. d.1787. Watch Den. coll.
Thomas. *New York.* 1758-71. From *London.*
James. *London.* an.1767. Watch.
David. *Dublin.* an.1768. Watch. cf. David above.
James. *Perth.* 1771-96.
John. *Bristol.* an.1787. Watch.
William. *Lauder.* a.1780-1805.

GORDON—*continued.*
James. *Beith.* 1790.
William. *London (Islington).* 1795-1811. W. & FLETCHER. *Dublin.* 1795-1824. Watch.
James. *Dublin.* 1795. W.
Adam. *Edinburgh.* 1797.
George. *Perth.* a.1795-1810.
William. *Edinburgh.* 1811.
James. *London.* a.1806.
James. *Ballymoney.* 1824.
Hugh. *Madras.* Early 19c.
William. *Dufftown.* Early 19c.
GORDONE, Thomas. *Aberdeen.* 1595.
GORET—
Claude. *Abbeville.* ca.1685. p.c. watch Ilbert coll.
Jean. *Paris.* Juré 1748-69.
Louis. *Paris.* m.1754, juré 1770-89.
André. *Paris.* m.1770.
C. *Abbeville.* 2nd half 18c. Bronze mantel clock Feill coll.
GORFIN, ——. *London.* Early 19c.
GORGAS—
Jacob. *Ephrata, Lancaster, U.S.A.* Came from *Germany.* ca.1760, d.1829. Well-known maker of l.c. clocks.
Solomon, son. *Ephrata.* ca.1780. l.c. clock.
Joseph, bro. *Ephrata.* ca.1780.
GORHAM, James. *London.* 1820-40.
GORLE, ——. *Winchester.* 1705.
GORROM, William. *Canterbury.* an.1788. Watch.
GORSLOW, Richard. *London.* a.1650.
GORST, Thomas. *London.* a.1777.
GORSTIDGE, Samuel. *Liverpool.* 1825.
GORSUCH—
Thomas. *Shrewsbury.* 1728. A fine maker. Watch mts. Oldham and Liverpool Ms. Watch with glass on cock Ilbert coll.
——. *Liverpool.* 1811-14.
GOSBEL, Daniel. *London.* a.1717.
GOSLEE, Richard. *London.* a.1787.
GOSLING, Thomas. *London.* a.1769, CC. 1777-99. Watch-case maker.
GOSS, John. *Salisbury.* 1795. W.
GOSSAGE, W. *Leamington Spa.* ca.1830. Patented an alarm attachment for watches; example Ilbert coll.
GOSSE—
Jeremiah. *London.* a.1660, CC.1667.
John. *London.* a.1662.
GOSSELIN—
——. *Paris.* 1735 m. Watch Ilbert coll.
Jean Baptiste. *Paris.* m.1743.
Jean Philippe. *Paris.* m.1752, juré. Clock.
——. *Paris (Rue Grenetat).* 1812-25.
GOSSET, ——. *Paris.* 1812-15.
GOSSIER, Jacques. *Rouen.* m.1703. Watch Gélis coll.
GOSSOIN, ——. *Val de Grace.* 1667. Made clock for town.
GOSTLING, William. *Diss.* From 1774-91 CC. l.c. clock. W.
GÖTHE, Johann Andreas. *Dünster & Frankfurt a. M.* b. 1733, d. 1788. l.c. clock Goethe House, Frankfurt.
GOTOBED—
T. *Eton.* 1784.
R. *Eton.* ca.1790 CC. W.
William. *Eton.* Retired 1813. C. & W.
GOTSALL—
Thomas. *London.* a.1787.
William. *London.* a.1789.
GOTTHELF, Carl. *Berlin.* 1791.
GÔTZ (GEUTZE), Martin. *Montbéliard.* 1555. From *Berne.*
GÖTZ—
Jörg. *Basle.* 1670. From *Urach.*
Georg. *Basle.* 1671. From *Württemberg.*
GOUBERT, James. *London.* CC.1690-1701. French.
GOUGH—
William. *Devizes.* 1st half 18c. Watch mt.
William. *London.* an.1726-ca.1760. Watch G.M. with sliding piece in pendant for telling time by touch.
GOUGIN, ——. *Paris.* 1825.
GOUIN—
Daniel. *Lyons.* 1650. Said to have completed clock on Hôtel de Ville.
Jacques. *Paris.* 1675 juré.
GOUJON—
Stephen. *London.* CC.1725, m.CC.1760-78.
Peter, son. *London.* a.1742. Watch mt.
Samuel, bro. *London (Newgate St.).* CC. 1763-93.
Samuel, son. *London.* CC.1793, l.CC.1802-1813.
GOULARD—
Jean dit Martinot. *Paris.* 1663. d.1692. C. to Louis XIV in 1663.
Jérôme, son. *Paris.* 1692-1702. C. to Louis XIV.
GOULD—
Christopher. *London.* CC.1682, d.1718. A maker of great repute, especially of l.c. clocks. str. and rep. watch B.M. Watch M.M.A. Four l.c. clocks Weth. coll., including one very small and one very fine lacquer clock ill. Cec. & Web.
Abel. *London.* a.1673, CC.1683-90. l.c. clock Weth. coll. Watch.
James. *London.* 1699 CC.
Charles. *London.* a.1701. Watch.
William. *London.* a.1720.
Thomas. *London.* ca.1750-88. Watches. London M. and Schloss M. Berlin.
John. *London.* an.1771. Watch.
George. *S. Molton.* 1784-95. W. l.c. clock.
——. *Bishop's Nympton.* Late 18c. l.c. clock.
GOULDEN, William. *London.* an.1772. Watch.
GOULLE, Marin. *Rouen.* 1552.
GOULLONS (GOULLENS)—
——. *Paris.* ca.1640-60. A very fine W. Exceptionally fine en. watch S.K.M. ill. Baillie. g. en. watch G.M. Three en. watches M.M.A. and two Gotha M. Very fine painted en. watch Nat. M. Stockholm. Watch Webster coll.
——. *Marseilles.* ca.1670. en. watch ill. Britten.
GOUMARD, Jean Béate. *Chaux-de-Fonds.* 1784.
GOUNOUILHON—
Pierre Simon. *Geneva.* b.1779. Came to *Geneva* 1799, d.1847. Maker of repute. g. cyl. rep. watch. mus. rep. watch mt. Ilbert coll.
ET FRANÇOIS. *Geneva.* Early 19c. g. watch ruby cyl. Ilbert coll. g. rep. lever watch.
GOURDIN (GOURDAIN), Nicolas. *Paris.* 1740. Juré 1747. Devised a dead beat esc. desc. in Gallon, 'Machines et Inventions,' Vol. 7. Experimented on curve of balance spring. Fine cartel clock, bronze by Ch. Cressent, Pal. de Justice, Paris.
GOURIEULT—
Gabriel. *Paris.* ca.1760.
Veuve. *Paris.* 1789.
GOURION, ——. *Geneva.* End 18c. watch.
GOURIOU, ——. *Geneva.* End 18c. watch.
GOURLEY (GOURLIE), Robert. *New York.* 1805.
GOUSSET—
Sylvain. *Blois.* 1629.
Denis. *Paris.* m.1690-5.
GOUSTET, ——. *Paris.* 1802-06.
GOUT—
Ralph. *London.* 1770-1836. Bankrupt in 1796, when his stock included many watches for the Spanish and Indian markets, and

GOUT—*continued.*
pedometer watches. br. clock. Pedometer with watch, Marryat coll., F.W.M., G.M., S.M.S.K., Ilbert and Den. colls. Watch London M. Pedometer Fränkel coll.
William. *London.* 1794.
GOUTHIÈRE, Pierre. *Paris.* b.1732, d.1813. Maker of ormolu clock cases. Fine porcelain vase clock S.K.M.
GOUTIER, ——. ——. ca.1600. oct. crys. watch.
GOVETT, George. *Philadelphia.* 1811-19.
GOW—
William. *London.* a.1745-87. Watch.
William. *Edinburgh.* 1779.
GOWETH, John. *Oxford.* an.1701. Watch.
GOWLAND—
Robert. *London.* an.1773. Watch.
Clement. *Sunderland.* 1780-1800. W.
——. *Blyth.* mar.1809. W.
James. *London.* Early 19c. W. & T.C. & chron. maker.
GOYON (GOJON), Louis. *Lyons.* 1620 m.-1627. Perhaps same as GUYON, comp. 1600.
GRAAF, Abraham de. *Haarlem.* 1775.
GRACE—
Thomas. *London.* a.1704. br. clock.
Thomas. *London.* a.1709.
William. *Cronton.* an.1771. Watch.
Edward. *London (Swan Alley).* CC. 1773-86.
William. *Liverpool.* 1810-29. W.
GRADDELLE, Isaac. *France.* Early 17c. sq. en. watch.
GRADLEY, ——. *London.* an.1755. Watch.
GRADWELL, Augustine. *London.* a.1738.
GRAF—
Simon. *Leipzig.* 1663. Complex watch Schramberg M. cf. GRASTE.
Johann Paulus. *Munich.* 1756. Court C. 1772, d.1788. Fine maker. Several clocks Munich Residenz.
GRÄFE, Johann Wilhelm. *Dresden.* m.1785, d.1789.
GRAFTON—
J. *London.* an.1770. Watch.
R. *London.* an.1778. Watch.
A. *London.* an.1787. Watch.
T. *London.* an.1793. Watch.
GRAHAM—
George. *London.* b.1673, a.1688, CC.1695, m.CC.1722, d.1751. One of the most eminent English makers. Fellow of Roy. Soc. and contributed many papers. Improved or perhaps invented cylinder escapement. He used the verge up to 1726 and then mainly the cyl. Devised but did not use the gridiron pendulum in 1715. Devised the mercury compensation pendulum, desc. in Phil. Trans. Vol. 34, 1726. Was assistant to TOMPION from 1696, in partnership with him ca.1711-13, succeeded him, and is buried with him in Westminster Abbey. He nearly always repeated the watch No. on the pillar plate and beneath the cock. Approx. corresponding dates and Nos. are, for plain watches, 1715, No. 4660. 1725, No. 5260. 1735, No. 5610. 1745, No. 6180. 1750, No. 6480, and, for rep. watches. 1720, No. 480. 1730, No. 620. 1740, No. 790. 1750, No. 960. There are many contemporary forgeries. Many fine watches and br. clocks. l.c. clocks very rare. Six watches and l.c. clock G.M., one, dated 1751, a cyl. c.secs. watch. Several watches S.M.S.K. Watch B.M. cyl. watch dated 1733. rep. watches Den. coll. Watch M.P.S. Dresden. br. clock with dead-beat escapement. br. clock ill. Cec. & Web. Watch Gotha M. Four l.c. and two br. clocks and regulator showing mean and solar time, Weth. coll.

GRAHAM—*continued.*
William. *London (Lombard St.).* 1728. Pub. an equation table. rep. watch S.K.M. l.c. clock.
William. *Philadelphia.* 1733. W.
J. *Kirkintilloch.* 1735.
Reynold. *London.* a.1736.
Robert. *Sunderland* and *Monk Wearmouth.* 1754 and earlier. Advertised that he finished new watches from the beginning.
William. *Hexham.* 1758. C.
John. *London.* 1762. g. p.c. rep. repoussé watch. l.c. clock Weth. coll.
——. *Edinburgh.* an.1758. C.
William. *Bellingham.* 1785. l.c. clocks.
Thomas. *Bellingham.* 1785-1827.
Charles. *Edinburgh.* a.1782-90.
James. *Glasgow.* 1793.
Frank. *Newcastle-on-Tyne.* b.1775, d.1855.
Charles. *London.* 1802-08.
James. *London.* 1802-08.
Daniel. *New York.* 1805.
George. *London.* a.1805.
George. *Cockermouth.* 1820-47. W.
GRAHM, P. (or L.). *Ystad.* End 17c. Fine hex. table clock.
GRAÎNÉ, ——. *Paris.* 1786-9.
GRAINGE, John. *London.* an.1772. Watch.
GRAINGER—
Richard. *London.* a.1685-98 CC.
——. *London.* ca.1825. Watch.
GRAIPAIR, ——. *Paris.* 1773.
GRAN, Magnus. *Uddevalla.* 1794.
GRANBERG, Jonas Mathias. *Stockholm.* 1763.
GRAND—
Aymé. *Lyons.* mar. an. 1650. From *Gex.*
——. *London.* an.1768. Watch.
GRANDCHAMPS, ——. *Paris.* 1825.
GRANDEROY, M. L. *Paris.* Early 18c. Watch N.Y. Univ. cf. GRANDROY.
GRANDIDIER, Jérémie. *Amsterdam.* 1681. Huguenot refugee from *Sedan.*
GRANDJEAN—
David Henri. *Le Locle.* b.1774, d.1845. A fine maker. aut. watches and singing birds and watches showing time in apertures.
FRÈRES. *Hamburg.* 1801-04.
Felix. *Chaux-de-Fonds.* 1807. Partner in ROBERT, COURVOISIER & CIE.
F. *Paris.* 1811-24.
A. F. *Hamburg.* 1815.
Henri. *Le Locle.* b.1803, d.1879. A famous maker of precision watches and chrons. Exported to Brazil.
GRANDO, Nikolas. *France* or *Switzerland.* ca.1680. sil. watch in form of dove. Prob. GANDO.
GRANDPERRIN (GRANDPERIN)—
Hugues. *Besançon.* 1638. Keeper of the town clocks.
Gabriel Joseph. *Paris.* m.1782-9.
——. *Paris (Rue St. Honoré).* 1807-25. Watch N.Y. Univ.
GRANDPRE, William. *London.* 1773. W.
GRANDROY, Nicholas. ——. ca.1705. Watch mt. Ilbert coll. cf. GRANDEROY.
GRANDVOISMET, ——. *Paris.* 1813-25.
GRANGE, C. *London.* an.1772. Watch.
GRANGER—
Galien. *Angers.* 1571-4. Town C.
René, son. *Angers.* 1617. Town C.
Jean. *Paris.* 1678 m.-1685.
Richard. *London.* a.1685, CC.1695.
GRANGIER (GRANGÉ)—
Marc. *France.* ca.1650. Watch ill. Britten. Watch Gélis coll.
Louis. *Châtellerault.* a.1656 *Geneva.*
GRANJA, Jean. *Avignon.* 1496. Made new clock for belfry with RAFIN.
GRANLÖF, ——. *Nora.* d.an.1790.

GRANLUND—
Wilhelm. *Tottesund.* End 17c.
Isaac. *Örebro.* 1815-35.
GRANON, Jacques. *Lyons.* 1599 m. Made clock for Abbaye de St. Antoine.
GRANSAY, John. *London.* an.1771. Watch.
GRANT—
William. *London.* CC.1660.
Thomas. *London.* an.1717. Watch.
William. *Edinburgh.* a.1750-5.
William. *London.* an.1765. Bankrupt in 1779. Watch.
Richard. *London.* ca.1765. br. clock ill. Cec. & Web.
——. *Taunton.* an.1770. Watch.
Edward. *London* (*Long Acre*). CC.1769-96.
George. *London.* an.1773. Watch.
James. *London.* an.1778. Watch.
William. *London.* a.1767.
John. *London* (*Fleet St.*). CC.1781, w.CC. and d.1810. An eminent maker. Four fine watches and regulator and a rack lever mt. G.M., including a watch with lever esc. having esc. wheel at right angles to train. Inn clock. br. clock.
George. *Edinburgh.* a.1776.
William. *London.* a.1777.
John. *London* (*Cockspur St.*). an.1801. Watch.
John. *London.* a.1791.
John. *London* (*Kennington Green*). 1799-1811.
John, son of John. *London* (*Fleet St.*). b. 1796, l.CC.1817, m.CC.1838-67. Duplex watch S.M.S.K. Watch London M.
John. *Glasgow.* 1818-41.
William. *Perth.* 1820.
William. *London* (*Aldgate High St.*). 1820.
H. *London.* 1st half 19c. Duplex rep. mt. G.M.
GRANTHAM—
James. *London.* 1730-70. 3-case g. repoussé watch F.W.M. ill. Baillie. Porcelain case watch G.M. Watch Liverpool M.
William. *London.* ca.1750. g. repoussé watch.
John. *London.* Mid. 18c. g. rep. agate watch Stern. coll.
George. *London.* an.1772. Watch.
GRANVILLE, Richard. *London.* an.1765. Watch.
GRAPE—
Richard. *London.* a.1685.
Thomas. *London.* CC.1721.
John. *London.* 1737. Watch and mt. G.M.
GRASHAM, James. *London.* an.1744. Watch.
GRASS, Thomas. *London.* an.1783. Watch.
GRASSELI, P. A. *Geneva.* Early 19c. g. eng. watch M.M.A.
GRASSENHULLER,Johannes. *Leipzig.* Mid. 18c. Watch.
GRASSL, Lorenz. *Augsburg.* ca.1700. Sundial B.M. Two pocket sundials and compass G.M. Two compass dials M.M.A.
GRASSTON, John. *London.* an.1759. Watch.
GRASTE, Simon. *Leipzig.* ca.1685. Watch Ilbert coll. cf. GRAF.
GRÄT, Philip. *Lintz.* ca.1695. trav. clock ill. Britten.
GRATERY, Joseph de. *Chaux-de-Fonds.* 1787-98. C.
GRATHORN, Jonathan. *Beverley.* ca.1690. Watch Ilbert coll.
GRATREX—
Edward, *Birmingham.* 1720-55. Watch mt. Birmingham M. l.c. clocks.
Robert. *London.* a.1784, CC.1791-1815.
GRATTE—
Henricus. *London.* Late 17c. Astrolabe cal. clock.
Henry. *London.* Early 19c. Sphere clock.
GRATTON, C. *London.* an.1775. Watch.
GRATZ, Joseph. *Oberhausen.* 1755.
GRÄTZ (GRETZ), Johann Georg. *Vienna.* m.1792.
GRAUPNER—
Paul. *Dresden.* m.1696.
Johann Gottlieb. *Dresden.* m.1716-39. Table clock Schloss M. Berlin. p.c. sil. trav. clock Feill coll.
J. G. *Augsburg.* ca.1720. Magnificent en. clock Grüne Gewölbe, Dresden.
Paul Gottfried. *Augsburg.* m.1726, juré 1735-53. d.an.1757. Wall clock.
Christian Friedrich. *Dresden.* m.1741.
——. *Berlin.* ca.1780. g. rep. watch M.P.S. Dresden.
GRAVANT, ——. *Paris.* b.1774-1825. Worked for ROBIN.
GRAVE—
Joseph. *London.* a.1687.
George. *London.* 1820-40. Watch.
GRAVELL—
& SON. *London.* 1783-1825. cyl. watch Ilbert coll.
& TOLKEIN. *London.* 1795-1820. C. Successors to Eardley NORTON.
William. *London* (*W. Smithfield*). 1810 CC.
William, son. *London* (*Charterhouse Sq.*). a. 1810, CC.1818, m.CC.1840-50.
Henry. *London.* a.1820.
GRAVEREAU, Étienne. *Paris.* m.1770-89.
GRAVES—
James. *London.* CC.1676-91.
Benjamin. *London.* a.1668, CC.1676, m.CC. 1705, d.1731.
Benjamin, son of Jas. *London.* a.1684.
William. *York.* 1730. W.
William. *Leicester.* an.1781. Watch.
GRAVIER, ——. *Geneva.* Early 19c.
GRAVIST, James. *London.* an.1776. Watch.
GRAWLAND, Clement. *Sunderland.* 1820.
GRAY (GREY)—
Timothy. *London.* CC.1633. A well-known maker.
John. *London.* a.1680-ca.1720. rep. watch. l.c. clock.
William. *London.* a.1691. Watch.
George. *London.* a.1702.
Benjamin. *London.* b.1676, d.1764. C. to George II from 1744. In *Pall Mall* in 1727, then *St. James' St.* and returned to *Pall Mall* in 1752. g. rep. watch, two movements and pedometer, G.M. oct. crys. watch Spitzer coll. Watch Ilbert coll. and mt. Buckley coll. l.c. clock Weth. coll.
Robert. *London.* 1709. Sundial Ilbert coll.
Joseph. ——. Early 18c. Watch mt. G.M.
Henry. *London.* 1718. CC.
Nathaniel. *London.* an.1723. Watch.
George. *London.* 1725. Insolvent. Watch.
George. *London.* a.1728.
& VULLIAMY. *London* (*Pall Mall*). 1743-62. Partnership of Benjamin GRAY and Justin VULLIAMY, his son-in-law. Very fine makers. Two l.c. clocks Weth. coll. Two watches G.M. g. rep. watch Carnegie M. Watch mt. Oldham M.
Thomas. *London* (*Noble St.*). an.1753. Watch.
Joseph. *London.* an.1755. Watch.
Alexander. *Elgin.* 1754-74.
Joseph. *Durham.* an.1756, d.1768. l.c. clocks. Watch. Succeeded by John NICHOLSON.
James. *London.* ca.1760.
Joseph. *London.* a.1756.
Henry. *London.* an.1768. Watch. GREY.
William. *Windsor.* d.1784. C. & W.
John. *London* (*Gray's Inn La.*). a.1762. CC. 1769-1817. Watch G.M.
Edward. *London.* an.1772. Watch.
John. *Durham.* 2nd half 18c. Watch. GREY.
James. *Edinburgh.* a.1765-1806. Clock C.A.

GRAY (**GREY**)—*continued.*
& M. A fine maker.
James. *Elgin.* 1772.
Francis, bro. of John. *London.* a.1769.
Nathaniel. *London.* an.1775. Watch.
Joseph. *Tamworth.* an.1776. Watch.
James. *Perth.* 1777-1807. GREY.
Adam. *London.* an.1780-1812. Watch.
& CONSTABLE. *London.* ca.1780. Watches G.M. and F.W.M.
Thomas. *London* (*Strand* and *Sackville St.*). 1780-1808. g. lever watch. g. en. watch, set pearls, Den. coll.
John. *London.* a.1773.
William. *Huntly.* d.1799.
William. *Liverpool.* an.1802. Watch.
James, son of James. *Edinburgh.* 1805-36. l.c. clock Weth. coll. ill. Britten, by him or his father.
J. & R. *Belfast.* 1819.
John. *Belfast.* 1824. GREY.
John. *Dublin.* 1824. C.
Joseph. *Duncannon.* 1824.
E. *Calcutta.* Early 19c.

GRAYAM & CO. *London.* ca.1800. Watch mt. Ilbert coll.

GRAYDON, George. *Dublin.* 1764. d.1805. Inn clock Dublin M. W.

GRAYE, ——. *London.* 1630. Subscribed for incorporation of CC.

GRAYHAM—
Charles. *London.* ca.1750. g. repoussé rep. watch.
Timothy. *Workington.* ca.1770-95. C.

GRAYHURST—
Michael, & Co. *London* (*Strand*). 1802-04.
Peter. *London* (*Strand*). 1805. Watch Vernis-Martin outer case, G.M.
& HARVEY. *London* (*Strand*). 1805-30. Watch.

GRAYSON—
William. *Henley-on-Thames.* a.1780. ca. 1825.
James. *Liverpool.* 1805-14. W.

GRAZNET, Abraham David. *London.* a.1699 CC.

GREATBACK, Richard. *Birmingham.* 1808. W. & C.

GREATHEAD, William. *London.* 1785. Tortoise-shell case maker.

GREATOREX—
Ralph. *London.* a.1639, CC.1653-68.
Henry. *London.* a.1703, CC.1712-14.

GREAVES (GRIEVE)—
John. *Birmingham.* b.1684, d.1771. W.
William. *York.* 1730, d.1796. W.
John. *Newcastle-o.-T.* an.1746. W. Also GRIEVE.
Richard. *Newcastle-o.-T.* an.1749. Watch.
William. *Newcastle-o.-T.* ca.1758-78. Watch.
——. *Bedale.* ca.1770-95. C. & W.
Thomas. *Birmingham.* 1770-1808. Watches, l.c. clocks.
William. *Market Harborough* and *Kettering.* an.1771. Watch.
Robert. *Macclesfield.* 1786.
Thomas. *Newcastle-o.-T.* 1778-1820.
Thomas. *Manchester.* 1800. W.
Thomas. *Liverpool.* 1825. W.

GRÉBAN—
Alphonse. *France.* End 16c. C. to Henri IV. Circ. str. table clock Garnier coll.
Jehan. ——. Early 17c. Oval watch Stern. coll. prob. *Germany.*

GRÉBAUVAL—
Jean. *Rouen.* 1597.
Gamaliel. *Rouen.* mar. 1608, m.-1617. Founder member of Rouen corporation.
Hiérosme (Jérôme). *Rouen.* 1614. Juré 1652-5. Oval watches B.M. and Louvre. Founder member of Rouen corporation.

GRÉBAUVAL—*continued.*
S. B. Prob. *Rouen.* Oval watch B.M.
Robert. *Rouen.* 1617 m.-1620. Founder member of Rouen corporation. oct. watch G.M., and watch Rouen M. sd. 'R. Grebeauval.'
Pierre. *Rouen.* 1617 m.-1652. Watch Louvre. Founder member of Rouen corporation.
Pierre. *Nantes.* ca.1650. str. watch Ilbert coll.
Guillaume. *London,* a.1655. *Rouen,* m.1659. Journeyman to David BOUQUET.
Claude. *Rouen.* m.1652.

GREBAY, Philippe. *Paris.* 2nd half 18c. sil. al. watch S.K.M.

GREBE, Heinrich. *Cassel.* Burgher in 1640. Wall clock dated 1653 in Cassel Landes-M.

GREBERT, Pierre Marie. *Paris.* m.1787-1813. Mantel clock, Château de la Malmaison.

GREDIN—
——. *Paris.* ca.1755 m.
Jacques Jérôme. *Paris.* m.1762.

GREEN (GREENE)—
James. *London.* a.1651, CC.1664. Lantern clock.
George. *London.* a.1661.
James. *London.* a.1678. CC.1685. GREENE.
James. *Gloucester.* ca.1685. Watch. GREENE.
Edward. *London.* a.1682.
Nathan. *London.* a.1688.
Nathaniel. *London.* CC.1695. GREENE. Prob. the preceding.
Ernest. *Wallingford.* ca.1700.
John. *London.* a.1704, CC.1712. Sheep's-head clock.
James. *Althorp.* 1712-36. C.
John. *London.* CC.1716. GREENE.
Richard. *London.* a.1696. GREENE.
Edward. *London.* a.1704. GREENE.
Francis. *London.* a.1707.
Joseph. *London.* a.1713, CC.1723-7.
James. *London* (*Fenchurch St.*). a.1722. m.CC.1784-1804. In *Philpot Lane* 1787. Appointed by Act of 1761 expert on Harrison's timepiece. Watch Den. coll.
Edmond. *London.* a.1722-46. GREENE.
Peter. *Liverpool.* 1734.
James. *London.* a.1736, CC.1747, l.CC.1770-1777. Also GREENE.
John. *London.* a.1737, CC.1747-60. Watch, Turkish figures, G.M. l.c. clock. Also GREENE.
George Smith. *Leicester, Cirencester* in 1750. Then *Ross.* d. *Oxford* 1762. W.
James. *Nantwich.* ca.1760, d.1782. Succeeded by his dau. g. en. watch Fränkel coll.
Samuel. *London* (*Hart St.*). 1766-76.
Samuel. *London* (*St. James's St.; Bunhill Row* in 1795). a.1754, CC.1772, l.CC. 1787-1817.
Robert. *Liverpool.* 1767. W.
George. *London.* ca.1770. rep. mt. Ilbert coll.
Margaret. *London.* 1770.
Francis. *London.* a.1763.
James. *Easingwold.* ca.1770-90.
William. *London* (*Fenchurch St.*). an.1777. Watch.
Charles. *Bristol.* 1779-84. Of HORWOOD & GREEN.
Samuel. *London* (*Bunhill Row*). a.1769, CC. 1787-99.
Thomas. *Liverpool.* 1781-1800.
Robert. *Edinburgh.* 1781-1834.
Thomas. *Bristol.* 1781-1801. W. Of GREEN & BARRY.
Mrs. *London* (*St. Martin's Lane*). 1783. Sale of stock.
Thomas. *Liverpool.* 1784. W.
Thomas. *Baldock.* 1784-91. C. & W.

GREEN (**GREENE**)—*continued.*
Ambrose. *London.* a.1784.
William. *London.* a.1785, CC.1798.
Edward. *London* (*Rotherhithe*). CC.1790-1808. Watch.
Edward. *South Mimms.* ca.1790.
Edward. *London* (*Albemarle St.*). 1792-1800. CC.
& Barry. *Bristol.* 1792-1813. W.
Samuel. *Tenbury.* 1795. C.
William. *Newbury.* 1795. W.
& Ward. *London.* 1795. g.en.watch F.W.M.
John. *Boston, U.S.A.* 1796. W.
John. *Philadelphia.* 1796.
John. *London* (*Goswell St.*). 1799. W.
James. *Liverpool.* 1800-29. W.
& Bentley. *England.* ca.1800. br. clock.
S. *Bradford.* ca.1800. l.c. clock.
John. *London* (*Old St.*). 1808. W.
H. *London* (*Old St.*). 1809-11. W.
John. *London* (*St. Luke's*). 1809-11.
John. *London* (*Clerkenwell*). 1809-11.
Francis. *London.* 1812 CC.
William. *Bristol.* 1812-18. W. & C.
Thomas. *Bristol.* 1815-18. W.
William. *London.* CC.1815, l.CC.1824.
Daniel. *London.* a.1810.
D. *London.* 1817-24. Wooden C.
William. *Nottingham.* 1818. C. & W.
Thomas. *London.* a.1812.
Samuel. *Boston, U.S.A.* 1820. W.
William. *Prescot.* ca.1820.
William Thomas. *London.* a.1815.
William. *Grantham.* Early 19c. Watch.
jun. *Clifton.* Early 19c.
William. *London.* a.1822.
Peter. *Bristol.* 1825-30. W. & C.
W. *Bristol.* 1825-30. W.
Samuel, jun. *Boston, U.S.A.* 1825. W.
William. *Liverpool.* 1825.

GREENALL, William. *Liverpool.* 1811-29. W.

GREENER—
C. & F. *Liverpool.* 1821. Wooden C. Watch mt. Platt Hall M. Manchester. Also Greener & Co.
& Chièsa. *Liverpool.* 1825.

GREENFIELD, William Richard. *London.* a.1807, CC.1814.

GREENHILL—
Nathaniel. *London.* a.1674.
John. *Maidstone.* Early 18c. l.c. clock Virginia M.
Samuel. *Canterbury.* 1723. Bankrupt.
Edward. *St. Albans.* 1795. W.
William. *London.* d.1830.

GREENHOW, Joseph. *Chelmsford.* Early 19c. Watch.

GREENING—
Peter. *London.* a.1716.
William. *London.* a.1816.
Charles. *Bristol.* 1825-30. W. & C.
Charles, son. *Bristol.* 1830.

GREENLY—
Philip. *London.* a.1710.
Edward William. *London.* a.1791.

GREENSILL—
Joseph. *London.* an.1775. Watch.
Edward Quin. *London.* a.1769. Also Grinsill.

GREENWAY—
Edmond. *London.* a.1701.
Richard. *London.* a.1705, CC.1718-27. d. an.1737.
William. *London.* a.1732, CC.1748.
Ricard. *London.* a.1736, CC.1745.
Joseph. *London.* a.1737, CC.1747-62.
John. *London.* a.1740.
John. *London.* a.1753-62 CC.

GREENWELL, Whitfield. *London.* 1762-9. Insolvent. W.

GREENWOOD—
Thomas. *London.* a.1764.
John. *London.* 1769. d.1808. W.
Charles. *London.* a.1794.
John. *Rochester.* 1795.
John, son of John. *London.* a.1808.

GREER, John. *Carlisle, U.S.A.* d.1774. C. & W.

GREEVE, James. *London.* an.1762. Watch.

GREGG—
Francis. *London.* a.1691-1747. *Gt. Russell St.* in 1711. *St. James'* 1714-29 bankrupt, *York St.* 1743 insolvent. l.c. clock Weth. coll. Two rep. watch mts. G.M. en. rep. watch Ilbert coll.
Richard. *London.* 1738, d. 1758. *Brentford* in 1738, *St. James' St.* 1742. W. to the King and keeper of the Palace clocks. en. watch M.M.A.

GRÉGOIRE—
Laurent. *Grenoble.* 1573-1611.
Jean. *Blois.* 1626. d.ca.1664. Watches B.M. and Gélis coll. trav. str. clocks, Petit Palais and Blot-Garnier coll. Watch, en. dial, Carnegie M.
Jean, son. *Blois.* 1651. d.1668.
Antoine, bro. *Blois.* m.1662.
P. *Blois.* 2nd half 17c. trav. str. clock Arch. M. Geneva.
——. *Paris.* 1807-25.

GREGORY—
Jeremie. *London* (*R. Exchange, Cornhill*). CC.1652, m.CC.1665, d.1685. Maker of repute. trav. clock S.K.M. sil. al. watch G.M. Watch M.M.A. Watches Den. coll.
James. *London.* a.1650, CC.1657.
Thomas. *London.* a.1650, CC.1671.
Thomas. *London.* CC.1673.
Robert. *London.* a.1670, CC.1678-90.
Jeremiah. *London.* a.1686, CC.1694-1734.
John. *London* (*Houndsditch, Basinghall St.,* in 1779). a.1764, CC.1771-6.
——. *Antigua.* ca.1790 CC.
——. *Basingstoke.* 1793. Watch. br. clock.
Thomas. *Odiham.* 1795. C.
Thomas. *Liverpool.* 1796. W.
William. *Dublin.* 1799. Watch N.Y. Univ.
William. *London.* 1805-24. W.
Charles. *London.* a.1805.
Henry. *London.* a.1812.
Olinthus. L.L.D. *London.* Pub. art. in Phil. Mag. on the rates of Pennington's astro. clock in 1819, and a Treatise of Mechanics dealing with horology in 1826.
James. *Ormskirk.* ca.1820. Watch mt. G.M.

GREGSBY, Edmund. *Sittingbourne.* 1673. Lantern clock Ilbert coll. Also Edward Grigsby.

GREGSON—
John. *London.* a.1689.
Pierre. *Paris.* 1778-90. Englishman. C. to the King. Three en. watches S.K.M. ill. Baillie. en. watch, set pearls, F.W.M. rep. watch S.M.S.K. g. en. watches Carnegie M., Nat. M. Stockholm, Fränkel, Feill and Gélis colls., cyl. watch mt. Buckley coll., g. en. watch, virgule esc., set pearls Ilbert coll.
——. *Geneva.* ca.1790. g. en. watch M.M.A.
John. *London.* 1795-1804. W. to the Prince of Wales. Watch Boston M.
& Jefferson. *London.* 1800-07. Successors. Also Jefferson & Gregson.
John. *Lancaster.* 1815.
John. *Ulverstone.* ca.1820.

GREIG—
James. *Perth.* a.1765-1800.
John. *Perth.* 1801-09.
David. *Perth.* 1810-37.
James Gibson. *Edinburgh.* 1819.
Charles. *London.* a.1822.

GREINER, Michael. *Marktheidenfeld.* m. 1794.
GREIR, Henry. *London.* a.1710.
GRELLMANN, Tobias. *Zeitz.* ca.1660. Night clock Gotha M.
GREMONT (GREMOUD), Michel (or Nicolas) Antoine. *Paris (Creteil).* m.1765-1789.
GRÉMY—
Louis. *Blois.* mar.1613-21.
Michel, son. *Blois.* m.1664-90.
GRENAT, Junior. *Utrecht.* ca.1700. Watch Gélis coll.
GRENDON, Henry. *London.* CC.1640. Watches S.K.M., F.W.M. and M.M.A.
GRENIER—
Bois. *Flanders.* Early 18c. br. clock mt. Glasgow Art Gall.
——. *Rouen.* 1780-90. Invented a 'balancier de pendule à secondes,' desc. in Rozier, 'Observations sur la Physique,' vol. 16.
GRENOBLE, Martin. *London.* an.1794. Watch.
GRENUS, Théodore. *Geneva.* Mid. 18c. Watch Geneva M.
GRENVILLE, Jonathan. *Brighton.* 1799. W.
GREPIN, François Henri. *Paris.* m.1776-89. Four col. g. watch.
GREPPEL—
Walter. *London.* an.1764. Watch.
Valentine. *London.* an.1764. Watch.
GRESHAM, ——. *Mansfield.* Early 19c. Watch.
GRESSE, Pierre. *Geneva.* ca.1770-91.
GRESY, David. *Neuchâtel.* 1600. Keeper of the clock on the Hôpital.
GRETTON, Charles. *London.* a.1662, CC. 1672, m.CC.1700-33. A very fine W. & C. Lantern, br. and l.c. clocks Weth. coll. Four p.c. watches G.M., one of 1702 with ruby top jewel to verge, and one str. Watch with secs. dial Ilbert coll. l.c. and br. clocks ill. Cec. & Web.
GREVILLE—
John. *London.* a.1675.
Obadiah. *London.* an.1773. Watch.
GREYSON, Thomas. *London.* an.1777. Watch.
GRIBBIN—
& Wallace. *Belfast.* 1819.
Edward. *Belfast.* 1824.
GRIBELIN—
Simon. *Blois.* 1588. mar. 1593-1633. Table clock Gélis coll.
Abraham, prob. son. *Blois.* b.1589, d.1671. C. to Louis XIII. A very famous maker. mt. of shell watch B.M. Watch S.K.M. (1614). Watch Spitzer coll., with sundial and compass in case. circ. sil. str. watch. Watch with sundial Old Ashmolean M.
Isaac, bro. *Blois.* Juré goldsmith 1634. d.an.1661. Painter on enamel.
Nicolas. *Paris.* b.1635, d.1715, juré in 1684. Watches B.M. ill. Baillie, S.K.M., Louvre and Olivier coll. Square watch M.M.A. Watches Ilbert and Den. colls. Fine Boulle br. clocks Mobilier National and Pal. de l'Elysée, Paris, and Schloss M. Berlin.
Simon. *London.* 1661. CC.1686-1733. From *Blois.* Engraver. Pub. a book of designs in 1700.
GRICE—
Thomas. *London.* a.1667, CC.1675.
William. *Ormskirk.* 1687.
William. *London.* a.1687.
James. *Kingston (Surrey).* 1744. W.
Henry Lee. *London (Hammersmith).* an. 1769. Watch.
Job. *Lancaster.* 1797-1830.
GRIDIN, ——. *Paris.* Mid. 18c. watch S.K.M.
GRIEBEL—
——. *Strasbourg.* ca.1770. g. en. watch Stern. coll.
Frères. *Paris.* 1807-20. C.
——. *Paris (Rue Vivienne).* 1812. Night clocks.
GRIEL, Jean. *Rouen.* a.1652.
GRIELL, Samuel. *London.* a.1648.
GRIESENBECK, Christian. *Augsburg.* 1650. Watch Cassel Landes-M.
GRIEURIN, *v.* Brandt-dit-Grieurin.
GRIFFEN, Henry. *New York.* 1805. W.
GRIFFIN—
John. *London (Cripplegate).* a.1713, CC. 1720-34.
Henry. *London.* a.1716-24. Bankrupt.
George. *London.* a.1733, CC.1740-62.
Joseph. *Willenhall.* 1769. C.
George. *London.* CC.1769.
Edward Burr. *London.* 1770. Watch-case maker.
Paul. *London.* an.1773. Watch.
Robert. *London.* an.1785. Watch.
Charles Michael. *London.* a.1781.
Robert. *London.* a.1786.
& Adams. *London (Strand).* ca.1800. Watch.
George. *London.* a.1818.
GRIFFING, Thomas. *London.* a.1751, CC. 1758.
GRIFFIS—
Richard. *Sutton Coldfield.* 1749.
Paul. *London* and *Birmingham.* 1773-1808. Watch Birmingham M. l.c. clocks.
Thomas. *Birmingham.* 1782. Goes weekly to *Sutton Coldfield.* l.c. clocks.
GRIFFITH (GRIFFITHS)—
James. *London.* CC.1667. math. inst. maker.
Robert. *London.* a.1695, CC.1706-25. Watch.
Thomas or George. *London.* a.1712, CC. 1720.
William. *London.* a.1732, CC.1744.
Frances. *London.* a.1738.
Charles. *London.* a.1738.
Richard. *London.* a.1753-90. l.c. clock. g. watch, outer case of mother-of-pearl, Den. coll.
Paul. *London.* an.1772. Watch.
Jonathan. *London.* an.1774. Watch.
Thomas. *Hereford.* an.1789. Watch.
Benjamin. *Dudley.* 1790. l.c. clock.
John Charles. *Monmouth.* 1791-5. W.
Edward. *Charleston, U.S.A.* 1796. W.
Edward. *London (Hatton Gdn.* and later *Holborn).* a.1789, CC.1802, l.CC.1810-25.
D. *Carnarvon.* b. 1800, d. 1894. Watch.
GRIFFON, Joseph. *Paris.* m.1770.
GRIFI, Pietro. *Pesaro.* Late 16c.
GRIGBY, John. *London.* a.1722.
GRIGG, John. *London.* a.1684.
GRIGNION—
Daniel. *London.* b.1684, d.1763. Native of France. In England from 1688. His watch No. 396 was lost in 1726.
Thomas, son. *London.* b.1713, d.1784. Watch S.K.M. p.c. sil. watch and cyl. rep. watch G.M. Improved the cylinder escapement.
Daniel & Thomas. *London.* 1730-50. rep. watch Den. coll. rep. and ¼ str. br. clock ill. Cec. & Web.
& Son. *London.* 1775-83. Clock and watch mt. G.M.
Pierre. *Paris.* m.1770-89.
Thomas. *London.* 1790-1825. cyl. watch Chamb. coll. cyl. mt. G.M.
GRIGOR, George. *Elgin.* 1805.
GRIGSON—
Philip. *London.* a.1663.
Benjamin. *London.* a.1709.
v. Gregson.

GRILLAUD, Jean Claude. *Paris.* 1763 m.
GRILLET—
René. *Paris.* 1678. *Amsterdam.* 1681. Invented a calculating machine.
G. *Geneva.* ca.1700. Al. watch Ilbert coll.
GRILLIAT, ——. Prob. *London.* 1729. His scheme for stamping watch dials opposed by CC. on petition of John Hoddle and John Stafford, watch engravers.
GRILLIÉ, Jean. *Blois.* 1652. Painter on enamel.
GRIMALDE—
Peter. *London.* 1800-10. Chron. maker and W. of repute.
Samuel. *London.* 1804-08. W.
& JOHNSON. *London.* 1809-25. W. & C.
Samuel. *Edinburgh.* 1819-22.
GRIMAR, ——. *Ath.* Early 18c. rep. and al. table clock Den. coll.
GRIMES—
Edward. *London.* a.1640.
Thomas. *London.* CC.1671-84. A famous maker.
William. *London.* CC.1682-92. l.c. clock.
William. *London.* a.1695.
GRIMKIN, Richard. *London.* an.1658. Watch.
GRIMLEY, William. *London.* a.1687, CC. 1694.
GRIMM—
Hans. *Nürnberg.* m.1563.
Paulus. *Nürnberg.* 1619. Clock on Klarakirche.
GRIMSHAW, John. *Liverpool.* 1810-29. W.
GRINDALL, Matthew. *Leeds.* ca.1790. Watch.
GRINDLE, James. *London.* an.1781. Watch.
GRINDLEY, William. *London* (*Moorfields*). 1820.
GRINDON—
Henry. *London.* 1633 CC.
John. *St. Albans.* 1749. W.
W. *London.* Early 19c.
GRINFELDTER, Gabriel. *Germany.* Mid. 17c. br. clock Gélis coll.
GRINKIN—
Robert. *London.* Master in BC.1609, CC. 1632, m.CC.1648, d.1660. Watch B.M. Oval watch Nat. M. Munich, with silk thread on fuzee. Watches M.M.A., F.W.M. ill. Baillie, Nat. M. Copenhagen and Den. coll. crys. watch Webster coll.
Edmund. *The Hague.* 1650-80. sil. watch with g.en. decoration Mallett coll.
GRINLING, Robert. *Yarmouth.* d.1790 when old. l.c. clock.
GRINNARD, Thomas. *London.* an.1776. Watch.
GRINTMAN, Hendrik. *Haarlem.* 1774.
GRIOT, ——. *Paris.* 1764 m.
GRISAZ, Jean Baptiste. *Chaux-de-Fonds.* 1784. Worked on the Jaquet-Droz aut.
GRISLEY, Joseph. *London.* a.1695.
GRISWOLD, Thomas. *London.* a.1770.
GRITTO, Bartolomeo. *Italy.* 17c. inst. maker.
GRITTON, Samuel. *London.* a.1749.
GRIVET, Jean Pierre. *Geneva.* ca.1770-91.
GRIZEL, John. *London.* a.1679, CC.1687.
GROB, Arbogast. *Winterthur* and *Basle.* 1541-7.
GROCE, Philippe. *Paris.* End 18c. Four col. g. en. watch Feill coll.
GROCOT, Thomas. *Liverpool.* Late 18c. Watch mt.
GROGNON, ——. *Paris.* 1807.
GROGNOT, ——. *Paris.* 1810-12. C.
GROHEL, ——. *France.* ca.1800. Mantel clock, porcelain case, Virginia M.
GROHMANN, Fr. *Billin.* 1824. Watch with ivory works Schloss M. Berlin.
GROLLIER DE SERVIÈRE—
Nicolas. *Lyons.* b.1593, d.1686. Designed and made a number of freak clocks described in a book pub. by his grandson, 'Recueil d'ouvrages curieux du cabinet de M. Grollier de Servière.' *Lyons,* 1719 and 1733.
Gaspard, son. *Lyons.* b.1646, d.1716. Also a mechanician. Grand Prieur de l'Abbaye de Savigny.
GROLLMESS, Joh. Carl. *Fürth.* d.1740.
GRÖNBERG, M. *Lidköping.* 1819-25.
GRONDEL, Joseph. *Cologne.* 1797.
GRÖNSTRAND, Anders. *Stockholm.* comp. 1751-73.
GROOM—
John. *Edinburgh.* 1703.
T. *London.* an.1778. Watch.
GROOME, Frederick. *London.* a.1740.
GROS—
Philippe. *Paris.* 1780. C. to the Ministère de la Marine. g. rep. watch Den. coll. Fine mantel clock, Ministère de la Marine, Paris.
Amy. *Paris.* m.1783-9. 'Monteur de boîtes.'
Raphael. *St. Pierre-en-Grandvaux.* 1786.
——. *Paris.* 1818-25. Successor to PAILLARD.
GROSCLAUDE—
Abraham. *Basle.* 1760. From *Le Locle.*
Auguste. *Les Brenets.* Early 19c. Worked with Olivier QUARTIER on wheel-cutting machines.
GROSE—
Richard. *London.* CC.1632. Also GROCE.
Anthony. *London.* CC.1658-64.
GROSJEAN, François. *Avignon.* 1688. Keeper of town clock.
GROSS—
Anton. *Vienna.* m.1814.
Franz. *Arnstein.* m.1823.
GROSSER—
Fr. Adam. *Fürth.* d.1803.
Joh. Jacob. *Augsburg.* ca.1750 comp.-1764. Went *Fürth* 1768. d.1829.
Johann. *Fürth.* d.1841.
G. Christoph. *Fürth.* d.1842.
Joh. Heinrich. *Fürth.* d.1846.
GROSSMANN—
Moritz. *Glashütte.* b.1826, d.1885. Established a factory and the horological school at Glashütte. Won prize of British Horological Inst. for Essay on the Lever Escapement in 1863.
Jules. *Berlin, Paris, London, Chaux-de-Fonds* and *Le Locle.* b.1829, d.1907. Head of École d'horlogerie at Le Locle. Author of 'Horlogerie théorique.' Specialized in precision work.
GROSSOEUVRE—
Gaspard. *Rouen.* 1558-77.
Laurent. *Rouen.* 1594.
GROSVENOR & JONES. *London.* 1817-24.
GRÖTTNER, Gottl. Ferdinand. *Stockholm.* 1800. Watch.
GROTTY, Jérôme. *Geneva.* Early 18c. al. watch.
GROUNDES, Jonathan. *London.* Early 18c. Watch G.M. Prob. a forgery of Jonathan LOUNDES.
GROUNDS, Gabriel. *Dutton.* d.1724. W.
GROUSE, ——. *London.* an.1747. Watch.
GROUT—
William. *London.* a.1648, CC.1660.
John. *London.* a.1723.
William. *Philadelphia.* 1816. W.
GROVANT, ——. *London.* an.1749. Watch.
GROVE—
George. *London.* a.1638.
Thomas. *London* (*Wood St.*). CC.1715.
George. *London.* a.1707, CC.1715.
William. *London.* a.1720.
Richard. *London* (*Wood St.*). a.1749, CC. 1760, l.CC.1787-1817.

GROVE—*continued.*
John. *London (Shoreditch).* CC.1766, d.1802.
George. *London (Bishopsgate St.).* CC.1787-1791.
Richard. *Upton.* 1791. W.
Robert. *London.* a.1790.
Benjamin, son of John. *London.* a.1792.
R. *London (Blackman St.).* 1799.
William. *London.* CC.1802.
Samuel. *London.* a.1798.
George. *London (Wood St.).* 1809. l.CC. 1812, d.1814.
William Robert. *London.* CC.1811-15. Partner with Myles BROCKBANK.
Elizabeth. *London (Wood St.).* 1817-24.

GROVES—
Richard. *London.* a.1754.
Thomas. *Birmingham.* 1770-97.
William. *London.* a.1776.
George. *London.* 1790.

GROWEL, Germain. *Abbeville.* 1st half 18c. Watch Pal. du Cinquantenaire, Brussels.

GRUAU, Thomas. *Blois.* 1543. Repaired clock of Amboise.

GRUBB—
Charles Steward. *London.* an.1755. Watch.
——. *Stoke Newington.* an.1779. Watch.
William, jun. *Boston, U.S.A.* 1816-18. W. Previously partner with G. S. GODDARD.

GRUBE, Peter. *Dresden.* m.1669.

GRUBER—
Hans. *Nürnberg.* m.1552, d.1597. Master of locksmiths guild. Watches S.K.M. Watch 0.9 inch diam. Nürnberg M. Stackfreed watch mt. with minute hand Ilbert coll. Clocks Nürnberg M., Stuttgart M. and K.H.M. Made clock for Fredrik II of Denmark. Sd. HG, with crossed spades between the initials.
Michael. *Nürnberg.* Burgher in 1607. str. watches B.M. and Stern. coll.
Andreas. *Vienna.* m.1801.

GRUDAN, Pierre. *Perigueux.* 1492. 'Relogier.'

GRUET, A. *Geneva* and *Septmoncel.* 1664. Introduced chains for fuzees.

GRULLA, Medauro. *Madrid.* 1792. Pub. 'Arte de Gobernar los Reloxes por la Eguacion del Tiempo.'

GRUNDEL, Peter. *Stockholm.* 1586-94. a. in *Hamburg,* then *Nürnberg.* Came *Sweden* 1586. Court C.

GRUNDH, Jonas. *Malmö.* 1709.

GRUNDLER—
Andreas. *Friedberg.* Mid. 18c. trav. clock Ashmolean M.
Johann Nepomuk. *Augsburg.* m.1757, d. 1790.

GRUNDSTRÖM, Johan Gustaf. *Stockholm.* 1820-46.

GRUNKET, ——. *Berlin.* ca.1750. g. watch.

GRUSELL—
Mats Matsson. *Stjärnsund.* b.1679, d. 1766.
Joh., son. *Stjärnsund.* ca.1730. l.c. clock.
Mathias. *Lögdö* and *Lagfors.* b.1730, d.1792.

GRZESKEWITZ, J. H. *Hamburg.* 1821.

GSELL—
Lorentz. *Basle.* 1667 from *St. Gallen.*
Georg. *Schwarzwald.* ca.1780.

GUALTHERI, Pibo (Pybe WOUTERS). *Leeuwarden.* b.ca.1580-1635. inst. maker.

GUARANA, Padre Pietro. *Venice.* 1750.

GUARNERIO, P. *Huntingdon.* Early 19c. Watch.

GUAY, ——. *Paris.* 1809-25.

GUAYNON—
Jacob. *Blois.* mar. 1628-32. comp. at *Lyons* 1625.
Paul. *Blois,* m.1635. *Menars,* 1645-9.

GUDGEON—
Stephen. *London.* 1720-31 CC.
Samuel. *London.* an.1770. Watch.

GUDGEON—*continued.*
John. *Bury St. Edmunds.* 1785-1801. Partner with LUMLEY. Watch.
junior. *Bury St. Edmunds.* Early 19c. Watch.

GUDIN, Jacques Jérôme. *Paris.* 1750. m. 1762, d.1789. Worked with FURET. Mantel clock Windsor Castle ill. Britten. Watch Chamb. coll. g. en. watch set pearls M.P.S. Dresden. Equation regulator C.A. & M. g. watch with case and mt. set stones. 4-colour g. watch Carnegie M. l.c. clock, mounts by Caffieri. g. watch and cartel clock Nat. M. Stockholm.

GUENOT, Jean. *Dijon.* 1458. Re-made clock of Notre Dame and added a moon.

GUENOUX, Charles Théodore. *Paris.* m. 1764-89.

GUEPIN—
John. *London.* a.1687.
Isaac. *Lewes.* an.1705-18. Watch.

GUERARD—
——. *Bayeux.* 1772.
Jean Adrien. *Paris.* m.1776.

GUERBE, Nicolas François. *Paris.* m.1770.

GUÉRIN—
Jacques. *Lyons.* a.1623.
Jean Nicolas. *Paris.* m.1746.
Louis. *Geneva.* 1811.
——. *Paris.* 1812-22.

GUERINT, Sébastien François. *Geneva* and *London.* b.1791, d.1870. Invention of engine-turning wrongly attributed to him. Engine-turning was practised in 1670, though not on watches.

GUÉRLIN, Jean Paul. *Berlin.* Early 19c. A clever maker specializing in very thin cyl. watches.

GUÉROULT, ——. *Avranches.* Mid. 18c. cal. crucifix clock.

GUEST—
Ralph. *Prestwich.* d.1728. C.
George. *London.* a.1762. Watch.
John. *London (Fleet Market).* a.1781, CC. 1797, l.CC.1802-21.
William. *Windsor.* 1795. W.

GUETIER, ——. *Rouen.* Juré 1774-6.

GUEX, ——. *Paris.* ca.1790. g. en. watches set pearls Ilbert, Den. and Feill colls. g. en. watch M.P.S. Dresden. g. en. watch in form of vase. g. en. lyre watch.

GUGELMANN, Hans Michel. *Basle.* m. 1698-1720. Turret clocks.

GUGEMUOS, ——. *Warsaw.* Early 18c. str. al. trav. clock Fränkel coll.

GUGERI, Dominic. *Boston.* Early 19c. Watch.

GUIBERT—
Amiel. *Avignon.* 1474-1504. Finished clock on belfry begun by ELFORT in 1472. Keeper of Avignon clock.
Pierre. *Rouen.* m.1659.

GUIBET (l'aîné). *Paris.* ca.1790 - 1825. Marble and ormolu clock S.K.M. Also GUIBERT.

GUICHARD, Laurence. *London.* a.1766.

GUICHON, Nicolas Pierre. *Paris.* 1779.

GUIDEN—
& CIE. *Paris.* 1795-1821. g. watch. Also GUEDON.
GAND ET CIE. *Paris.* 1822-5.

GUIGNARD—
Jacques. *Blois.* a.1635, m.1643-56.
Ambroise. *Chaux-de-Fonds.* 1784.
& MONARDA. *Geneva.* Early 19c. g. en. watch M.P.S. Dresden.
George. *Geneva.* Early 19c. g. en. watch M.M.A.

GUIGNON, Stephen. *London.* a.1785.

GUIGUER—
Anthony. *London.* CC.1687. 8-day watch.
——. *Amsterdam.* Mid. 18c. Watch Den. coll.
GUILE, John. *Philadelphia.* 1819-24.
GUILLARMOD, F. Vt dit. ——. ca.1800. Four col. g. watch Gélis coll.
GUILLAUME—
——. *Montbéliard.* 1547.
——. *Paris.* 1812-25.
C. & A. *London.* 1820. W.
GUILLAUMIN, Jehan. *Geneva.* a.1602.
GUILLE, Henri. *Rouen.* a.1656.
GUILLEBERT—
Pierre. *Rouen.* a.1649.
Noël. *Rouen.* Juré 1691-4.
GUILLEMAIN, Nicolas Louis. *Paris.* m.1743.
GUILLEMET, ——. *Neuchâtel.* 1380. Made clock of the Collegiale.
GUILLEMIN, ——. *Lyons.* 1461-4.
GUILLERMIN, Antoine. *Crépignat (Bourg).* 1515. Called to Geneva to repair clock of St. Pierre.
GUILLET—
Paul Philippe. *Paris.* m.1757.
Antoine Léandre. *Paris.* m.1788.
——. *Paris (Rue Culture Ste Catherine).* 1812.
GUILLIN (GUILIN, GWILLIN), Ely. *London.* CC.1647.
GUILLON, Antoine. *Nantes.* 1621. d.1649.
GUILLOT, ——. *Paris.* 1807.
GUILLOTEAU, ——. *Paris.* 1823.
GUILMETIN, ——. *Paris.* 1867. Invented clocks which swung and acted as their own pendulums.
GUINAND—
Guillaume. *Lyons.* 1670-86.
Jacques Abram. *Les Brenets.* 1783-91. C.
Pierre. *Fontaines.* 1787-1802. Very able C.
Ernest. *Switzerland.* d.1879. An eminent maker.
GUINTRAND, ——. ——. Re-made clock of *Cadenet (Avignon).*
GUINZER—
Pierre. *Le Locle.* 1812. C.
David. *Chaux-de-Fonds.* 1813-25. C.
GUION, Louis. *Dijon.* End 16c. Watches Louvre and Olivier coll.
GUIOT (GUYOT)—
Guillaume. *Rome.* 1611.
——. *Paris.* ca.1715. Wall clock.
——. *Paris.* 1789.
——. *Paris.* 1810-15. C. to the Queen of Holland.
Veuve. *Paris.* 1819-25.
GUIOTT, John. *London.* a.1732.
GUIRODON—
Et Cie. *Geneva.* Early 19c g. en. watch set stones M.M.A.
Et Archinard. *Geneva.* Early 19c. g. en. watch M.M.A.
Père. *Geneva.* 1821.
GUISE—
Samuel. *London (Wapping).* a.1791, CC. 1799-1807.
Thomas. *London.* a.1807, l.CC.1815.
GUITAU (GUITEAU), ——. *Paris.* 1812-25.
GULDAU, Franz. *Pressburg.* Late 18c. Mantel clock Arts M. Prague.
GULDBRANDSEN, Hans Peter. *Flensborg.* m.1811.
GULDEN & COUNIS. *Geneva.* Early 19c.
GULLFIN, ——. *London.* an.1771. Watch.
GULLIAM, William. *Falmouth.* 1795. C. & W.
GULLIFORD—
John. *Bristol.* 1st half 18c. l.c. clock.
Robert. *Chipping Ongar.* 1788. C. & W.
GULLOCK
Philip. *London.* 1794.
John. *Rochford (Essex).* 1795.
GULLON, John. *London.* a.1714.
GUNARD-DIT-VENDÔME, Michel. *Rouen.* 1720-62 from *Alisay.* Repaired town clock and clock of St. Laurent.
GUNCKEL, ——. *Berlin.* ca.1760. g. en. watch.
GUNDY, William. *London.* a.1750.
GUNKLE, John. *Ephrata, Lancaster, U.S.A.* In business 1830-40. German. A good maker of l.c. clocks.
GUNN—
William. *Wallingford.* ca.1740. l.c. clock.
William. *London.* an.1751. Watch.
GUNTER—
Hildesley. *London.* a.1693.
Richard. *London.* 1790-1808.
GÜNTER—
Leonhard. *Basle.* m.1645, d.1680.
Hans Georg Johann, son. *Basle.* m.1671, d.1726. Kleinuhrmacher.
GUNTHER, Hans. *Strasbourg.* 1587.
GÜNTHER—
Wolffgand, *Gedau.* Late 17c. hex. table clock Fränkel coll.
Simon. *Dantzig.* Late 17c. hex. table clock.
GUNTON, Henry. *Norwich.* Early 19c. Watch.
GURDON—
Joseph. *Oxford.* an.1762. Watch.
Benjamin. *Daventry.* 1795. C. & W.
GURNETT, William. *London.* a.1698.
GURNEY—
Ezekiel. *London.* a.1692.
Joseph. *Bristol.* From 1783-94.
GURR, George. *Ewhurst.* Early 19c. Watch.
GUSSINKLA, W. *Aalten.* 1815. Clock as pendulum bob, Stads M. Amsterdam.
GUSTERMAN, Johann Georg. *Steppach.* 1756-70.
GUT—
Wilhelm. *Augsburg.* Early 18c. comp.
Christian. *Augsburg.* m.1727, juré 1742.
GUTBUB (GUTTBUB)—
Carl. *Strasbourg.* 1571.
Hans. *Strasbourg.* 1587.
GUTCH, John. *London.* CC.1673. Casemaker.
GUTHERIDGE, William. *London.* a.1720, CC.1728.
GUTHRIE—
William. *London.* a.1734.
Nicol. *Glasgow.* 1764. Clock.
Charles. *Calcutta.* ca.1800.
GUTKAES, John. Christ. Fried. *Dresden.* m. 1815, d.1845. Court C. 1842. Pocket chron. Fränkel coll.
GÜTLE, Friedrich Christoph. *Nürnberg.* 1800. Watch Stuttgart M. g. watch Feill coll.
GUTSCH (GÜTSCH), Claus. *Rothweil.* 1401. Made complex clock for Villingen Münster.
GUTTENTAG, J. *Stockholm.* 1812-15.
GUTTRIDGE, Joseph. *London.* a.1761, CC. 1768.
GUVANE, Patrick. *Edinburgh.* 1552.
GUY—
Henry. *London.* a.1660.
Samuel. *London.* a.1692. l.c. clock.
Henry. *London.* a.1695, CC.1702-41.
Henry. *London.* a.1702.
Charles. *London.* a.1707, CC.1714-17.
Henry, son of Henry. *London.* a.1722, CC. 1736.
Joseph. *London (Cold Bath Fields).* an.1778. Watch.
James. *London (Bloomsbury).* CC.1778-1830.
John. *Liverpool.* 1780-96. W.
E. *London.* 1809-24. W.
GUYARD, ——. *Paris.* m.1657.

GUYDAMOUR—
Edme Philippes. *Paris.* m.1784-9. Mantel clock, Pal. de l'Élysée, Paris.
Veuve. *Paris.* 1807-11.

GUYE—
Pierre. *Fleurier.* 1691-1765.
Abram. *Côte aux Fées.* 1710.
Pierre, son of Pierre. *Verrières.* 1711. d.1743.
David, son. *Môtiers.* 1731-62. C.
David Henri, son. *Verrières.* 1755-66. W. & C. of repute.
Jean Pierre, bro. *Verrières.* 1755-75. C. of repute.
Abram Louis, bro. *Perpignan* and *Spain.* b.1741, d.1821. W. & C.
Clos Henry. *Reus.* ca.1790. en. watch, set pearls.
——. *Geneva.* ca.1800. rep. watch mt. S.M.S.K.
——. *Paris.* 1812.

GUYENET—
David Henri. *Couvet.* 1745-77. C.
Henri Ferdinand. *Couvet.* a.1786-94. C.

GUYERDET (jeune). *Paris.* 1825. Clock. g. en. cyl. watch. Wall clock.

GUYMER, *v.* GYMER.

GUYON—
Pierre. *Geneva.* 1599. 'Orollageur.'
Louis. *Lyons.* comp. 1600. *v.* GOYON.
Jean Louis. *Grenoble.* 1692 from *Remorey* (*Doubs*).

GUYOT, H. Fr. *Boudevilliers.* Early 19c. Clock.

GUYTARD, ——. *La Rochelle.* 1679.

GWILLIN—
Eli. *London.* CC.1647.
Thomas. *London.* a.1782.

GWILT, Richard. *London.* an.1776. Watch.

GWINN, Thomas. *Ripley.* Early 19c. Watch.

GWINNELL, J. *London.* 1809-24. W.

GWÜNISER, Franz. *Leitershofen.* 1756.

GWYNN—
Thomas. ——. End 18c. l.c. clock. Perhaps GWINN.
William. *Liverpool.* 1816.

GYBERG—
Pehr. *Lund.* b.1756, d.1818.
Jon. *Kristianstad.* b.1760, d.1809.
Lars. *Åmål.* b.1768, d.1846.

GYDE, John. *London.* an.1764. Watch.

GYLES, Fletcher. *London.* a.1753.

GYLKS, Richard. *Devizes.* 1791-5. C. & W.

GYMER, Robert. *Norwich.* d.1751. Watch. l.c. clock.

GYOTT—
Abraham. *London.* CC.1648-64.
Abraham. *London.* a.1648.

GYROD, Gabriel. *Dover.* an.1772. Watch.

GYSWYT, *Amsterdam.* 1822. W.

H

HAACK, Ernst David Friedrich. *Berlin.* 1785-1840. C.

HAAKMA—

A. & J. *Leeuwarden.* End 17c. p.c. rep. watch.

Sikke Arents. *Leeuwarden.* 1732-60. Town C.

Theunis. *Leeuwarden.* 1743-57. Table clock.

A. & T. *Leeuwarden.* 1743-55. Partnership of the brothers Arents and Theunis, dissolved in 1755. Watch and table clock.

Sicco. *Leeuwarden.* 1765-80. l.c. clock.

H. *Leeuwarden.* 1784. l.c. mus. clock.

HAAN, Michel de. *Rotterdam.* 1750. g. watch Ryks-M. Amsterdam.

HAAS, David Sigmund. *Augsburg.* b.1685, d.1742. Famous maker. Clock presented by Maria Theresa to Prince Josias zu Coburg-Saalfeld, Gotha M.

HAASE, Johann Jakob. *Augsburg.* 1732. Kleinuhrmacher.

HAAVELSEN, Halvor. *Christiania.* 1754 m.

HABEL, Joh. Georg. *Geneva.* ca.1770. Mandoline watch M.M.A.

HÄBERL, Johann Paulus. *Augsburg.* m.ca. 1770, juré 1776-95. ½ ¼ rep. watch.

HÄBERLÉ, ——. *Paris.* Mid. 18c. Fine steel and g. watch.

HÄBERLE—

Johann George. *Ludwigsburg.* ca.1650.

Christoph. ——. Mid.17c. hex. str. rep. al. table clock Feill coll.

Friedrich Wilhelm. *Cannstätt.* 1779.

HABERMEHL—

Josua. *Regensburg,* 1576. *Prague,* 1581. inst. maker. Dial, Old Ashmolean M. Proportional compasses Nat. M. Prague. Quadrant, Old Observatory M. Prague.

Erasmus. *Prague.* 1585. d.1606. inst. maker to Rudolf II. Many fine examples of his work. Astrolabe Old Ashmolean M.

HABERSTROH, Johann George. *Berlin.* 1790, d.1794. Wooden C.

HABL, Norbert. ——. Late 18c. p.c. sil. and tortoiseshell watch Feill coll.

HABRAM—

François Isaac. *Montbrison.* mar. 1785-94. Also ABRAHAM.

Pierre. *Paris.* m.1788.

HABRECHT—

Joachim. *Schaffhausen.* 1537-58. astro. and aut. clock on Tour du Marché, Soleure, 1545; and astro. clock on Frohnwagturm Schaffhausen in 1564, still working, both ill. 'Les Habrecht'; also clock on St. Jean Schaffhausen.

Hans, son. *Zürich.* b.1540, d.ca.1594. C. to the town.

HABRECHT—*continued.*

Isaac (1), bro. *Strasbourg.* b.1544, d.1620. The most famous C. of his time. With his brother Josias, made the second Strasbourg clock; made astro. clocks for Heilbronn and Ulm, and the magnificent aut. and mus. clocks in B.M. and Château de Rosenborg, Denmark, both ill. 'Les Habrecht.' Two MSS. on the Strasbourg clock, dated 1571 and 1574, in Bibl. régionale, Strasbourg.

Josias, bro. *Strasbourg.* b.1552, d.ca.1575; *Kaiserswerth,* ca.1566. Made, but left incomplete, clock on Chateau de Kaiserswerth.

Hans Heinrich, son of Josias. *Bremen* and *Vienne.* b.ca.1574.

Hans Heinrich, son of Hans. *Zürich.* b.1575.

Abraham (1), son of Isaac. *Strasbourg.* b. 1578, d.ca.1636.

Issaac (2), bro. *Strasbourg.* b.1589, d.1633. Physician, mathematician and astronomer.

Daniel. *Strasbourg.* Early 17c. Watch, steel mt.

Caspar, son of Hans. *Zürich.* b.ca.1592.

Abraham (2), son of Isaac (1). *Strasbourg* and *Ratisbonne.* b.1608, d.1686. Maker of the first known l.c. clock, but with foliot, a mus. and aut. clock in the Hotel de Ville, Ratisbonne, ill. 'Les Habrecht,' and a clock on the Brücktor.

Isaac (3), bro. *Strasbourg.* b.1611, d.1686. 'Münster - Uhrmacher.' Crucifix clock Strasbourg M., two Madonna clocks, one in National M., Munich, and a hanging clock, all ill. 'Les Habrecht.'

Daniel (2), bro. *Strasbourg.* b.1616, d.1684. Tulip and skull watches, ill. 'Les Habrecht.' sil. skull watch Feill coll. Stand clock.

Isaac (4), son of Abraham (2). *Ratisbonne.* b.1641, d.1667. Turret C.

Daniel (3), son of Daniel (2). *Strasbourg.* b.1651, d.ca.1695. Table clock Stuttgart M., ill. 'Les Habrecht.'

Abraham (3), son of Isaac (3). *Strasbourg.* b.1654, d.1728. Very fine table clock, Strasbourg M., ill. 'Les Habrecht.'

Johannes, son of Abraham (2). *Ratisbonne.* b.1655, d.1701.

Abraham (4), son of Abraham (3). *Strasbourg.* b.1693, d.1732.

HACK, Grace. *London.* a.1692.

HACKER—

A. *Prague.* Early 18c. Sundial Fränkel coll.

William. *Swaffham.* an.1755. Watch.

HACKETT—

Simon. *London.* CC.1632, m.CC.1646, d. 1664. Two watches S.K.M. ill. Baillie.

HACKETT—*continued.*
g. watch F.W.M. sd. 'Simon Hacke.' Watch M.M.A.
John. *London.* a.1718.
Richard. *Harringworth.* an.1771. Watch.
P. *Harrington.* Late 18c. Watch mt.
HÄCKLER, F. *Prague.* Late 18c. Watch Nat. M. Prague.
HACKNEY—
A. & T. *London.* an.1755. Watch mt.
Thomas. *London.* an.1764. Watch.
William. *London.* an.1773. Watch.
HADDACK, William. *Bath.* 1798-1819. br. clock.
HADDERSICH, Job. *London.* a.1718.
HADDOCK—
John. *London.* a.1722.
Charles. *London.* a.1737.
Richard. *London.* 1748. Insolvent.
HADDON, Charles. *London.* an.1780. Watch.
HADEN, William. *Stourbridge.* 1754. W.
HADKIN, Robert. *Liverpool.* 1805. W.
HADLAND, Thomas. *London.* Early 19c. Watch.
HADLEY—
Humfrey. *Birmingham.* 1708, d.1770. C.
Thomas, son. *Birmingham.* 1780-90.
HADWEN—
Isaac. *Liverpool.* 1754-81. l.c. clock.
Joseph. *Liverpool.* 1761-6. C.
Hannah. *Liverpool.* 1767 C.
Isaac. *Liverpool.* 1800 CC. W.
HADWIN, Isaac. *Sedberg.* 1700. l.c. clock.
HAEHNEL—
Christian. *Zwickau.* 1695.
Chr. Heinrich, son. *Fürth.* b.1695, d.1754. br. clock with cycloidal cheeks.
C. H. *London.* ca.1750-67. sil. p.c. watch G.M. g. repoussé watch S.K.M. Watch with four portraits of Emperor Joseph II and his wife in Vernis Martin on outer case M.M.A.
HAEN, A. J. *Osch.* ca.1800.
HAERTEL, ——. *Hanau.* 1768. cyl. watch Ilbert coll.
HAGBERG, Jonas. *Kristianstad.* 1787-94.
HAGDON, William. *London.* an.1761. Watch.
HAGELTHORN, J. P. *Ängelholm.* b.1798, d.1852.
HAGEMANN, Gottlieb. *Schwerin.* b.1792, d.1894.
HAGEN, Hans. *Worms.* End 16c.
HAGER—
Melchior. *Erfurt.* 1st half 17c. oct. crys. watch Arts M. Prague.
Wolfgang. *Wolfenbüttel.* b.1643, d.1705. Court mechanician and C. Large watch.
D. P. *Wolfenbüttel.* Early 18c. Thiout describes a very complex astro. watch by him.
HAGERT, Jöran Gabriel. *Åbo.* 1762. d.an. 1775.
HAGGER, James. *London.* a.1694, d.an.1735. br. clock. Watch.
HAGGET, Joseph. *London.* a.1786.
HAGUE, Thomas. *London.* a.1718.
HAHN—
Philipp Matthäus. *Kornwestheim* and *Echterdingen.* b.1739, d.1790. A celebrated W. & C. and an exceptionally able mechanician. Developed the cyl. escapement. Pub. art. on Improvements in Watches, in Actis Acad. of Erfurt, 1784. Many fine complicated watches in Bassermann-Jordan, Feill and Kock colls., Stuttgart M., M.P.S. Dresden. Astro. clocks in Stuttgart, Furt., Gotha, Breslau, Nürnberg M., in Bassermann-Jordan and other colls. Planetarium Furt. M. Life written by Max Engelmann, Berlin 1923.
Georg David Polykarp. *Kornwestheim.* b. 1747, d.1814. Assistant to P. M. Hahn. Night-light clock dated 1776.

HAHN—*continued.*
E. S. Gottfried. . *Echterdingn* b.1749-1801. Assistant to P. M. Hahn.
Christoph Matthäus, son of P. M. b.1767, d.1833. *Echterdingen* and *Stuttgart.* Court mechanician at Stuttgart 1790. Watches and astro. clocks. Fine sil. cal. watch.
Christian Gottfried, bro. b.1769. *Stuttgart* to 1795, later *Berlin,* and in 1798 *Philadelphia.* Court mechanician in *Berlin.* Watch Stuttgart M.
Johann Georg, bro. *Stuttgart.* b.ca.1770, d.1813. Court mechanician ca.1806.
Gottlieb, bro. *Echterdingen.* ca.1780. Assistant to his father, P. M.
Andreas Leonhard. *Nürnberg.* 1790-1810. Watch Stuttgart M.
Gebrüder (Christoph and Christian; also J. Georg and Christian). *Stuttgart.* 1791. Watches.
——. *Paris.* 1811-25. mus. and aut. clocks.
HÄHNEL—
C. *Fürth.* d.1754.
C. H. *London.* v. HAEHNEL.
HAID, John. *London.* a.1659.
HAIDEN, Christian. *Nürnberg.* 1574. Made watches for Emperor and Empress.
HAILES—
Samuel. *London.* a.1730.
Thomas. *London* (*Huggin La.*). a.1769, CC. 1778.
HAIMMERT, Martin. *Nürnberg.* Burgher in 1582.
HAINARD, Louis. *Couvet.* 1807-12. C.
HAINAUT, Robert Louis. *Rouen.* b.1813. d.1901. Well-known maker and writer on horology and on Rouen clock.
HAINES—
Francis. *London.* a.1696, CC.1706. Watch.
Robert. *Marlborough.* 1773, retired. W.
Robert. *Oxford.* From 1778-95. C. & W.
James. *London* (*Hackney Rd.*). a.1780, CC. 1793-1808.
Charles. *Swindon.* ca.1800.
HAINKS, John. *London.* a.1728, CC.1750-64.
HAIR, William. *Birmingham.* ca.1780-1808. Clock mt. S.K.M. Watch Birmingham M. W. & C.
HALAND, ——. *London.* an.1770. Watch.
HALBERT, William. *Glasgow.* 1800-18. Watch N.Y. Univ.
HALDANE—
James. *Edinburgh.* 1811.
Charles. *Edinburgh.* 1825.
HALDER—
Heinrich. *Basle.* ca.1370, d.ca.1410. Made clocks for Basle Münster in 1370, Strasbourg 1373, Lucerne, in the Graggenthurm, in 1385.
Hänsly (or Hensli). *Basle.* 1413.
HALDING, John. *London.* an.1743. Watch.
HALE—
Richard. *London.* a.1733.
Thomas. *London.* a.1753.
William. *London.* CC.1769.
Stephen. *London* (*Highgate*). an.1772-1808. Watch.
Joseph. *Bristol.* an.1772. Watch.
W. H. *Devizes.* an.1778. Watch.
William. *London.* a.1780.
Thomas. *London.* a.1783.
Robert. *London.* 1805.
George Long. *London.* 1805-08.
Thomas. *London* (*Old St.*). a.1798, CC.1815.
James, son. *London.* a.1816. CC.1834.
HALER, William. *London.* 1747. Watch.
HALESWORTH, Inggate. ——. Late 18c. Watch.

HALEY—
Samuel. *London.* a.1657.
Thomas. *N. Walsham.* an.1743. *Norwich* from 1753, then *London* (*Oxford St.*)-1781. Watch mt. G.M.
John. *Wrexham.* an.1767. Watch sd. JOHN YELAH Nat. M. Cardiff.
Thomas. *Wrexham.* an.1767. Watch.
& SON. *London.* an.1774. Watch.
Charles. *London* (*Wigmore St.*). a.1762, CC. 1781-1825. A famous maker. Patent for a marine chron. in 1797. l.c. clock Weth. coll. br. clock, pocket chron. and remontoir mt. G.M. 3-case duplex watch S.M.S.K. Watch Den. coll. Pocket chron. Ilbert coll.
& MILNER. *London* (*Wigmore St.*). 1799-1815. br. clock Virginia M.
junior. *London* (*Cleveland St.*). an.1801. Watch.
John. *London.* 1802-07.

HALFHIDE, Edward. *London.* a.1817.

HALFORD—
George. *London.* a.1703.
John. *London.* 1st half 18c. p.c. g. watch. l.c. clock.
George. *Doncaster.* 1784. W.

HALINS, Nicolas. *Troyes.* 1535. Flemish. Re-made jacquemarts for the Cathedral clock.

HALKED (HALHED)—
Thomas. *London.* a.1693, CC.1702-16.
Robert. *London.* a.1694.

HALL—
John. *Kirkcudbright.* 1576.
Ralph. *London.* CC.1638.
Peter. *London.* CC.1648.
Christopher. *London.* a.1646, CC.1655.
John Baptist. *London.* a.1669-80. l.c. clock.
Thomas. *London.* a.1675, CC.1695-9. l.c. clock.
Samuel. *London.* ca.1680. Watch Ilbert coll.
William. *London.* a.1680. l.c. clock.
Joseph. *London.* a.1684. Lantern clock.
William. *London.* a.1687.
William. *London.* a.1695.
Michael. *London.* a.1695.
William. *London.* a.1699.
George. *London.* a.1702, CC.1710.
Edward. *London.* a.1703, CC.1710.
William. *Woodborrow.* Early 18c. l.c. clock.
Samuel. *Bickerstaffe.* 1737. W.
James. *London.* 1720-5. Insolvent.
Henry. *London.* 1738 CC.
Robert. *London* (*Drury Lane*). 1743. W. & C.
Stephen. *London.* a.1748.
William. *London.* a.1750.
Martin. *Yarmouth.* 1752. l.c. clock.
John. *London.* an.1763. Watch.
Robert. *Wells* (*Norfolk*). d.1788. Business continued by his widow Dorothy and her son from London.
John. *Beverley.* ca.1770-95 C.
Christopher. *Dublin.* an.1775. Watch.
Richard. *London.* an.1776. Watch.
T. *Edinburgh.* 1774. C. & W.
John. *London.* a.1767.
Thomas. *London.* a.1770.
Joseph. *Birmingham.* 1781-1806. C. & W.
John, & Sons. *Beverley.* 1784.
John. *Bristol.* d.an.1793. Partner in AVARD & HALL.
William. *N. Shields.* d.1807. W.
Thomas. *Romsey.* an.1788. Watch. l.c. clock.
Harry. *London.* Late 18c. Watch Glasgow Art Gall.
James. *Whitehave* an.1792. Watch.
Nathaniel. *London.* (*Bishopsgate St.*). a.1784, CC.1792-1811.
Eaton. *Liverpool.* 1795. W.

HALL—*continued.*
John. *Grimsby.* 1795. C. & W.
Hilkiah. *London.* a.1795.
John. *Birmingham.* 1801-08.
Christian. *Lititz, Lancaster, U.S.A.* b.1775, d.1848. German. l.c. clocks.
Andrew. *London.* 1802-04. Later *Hatfield.* Watch.
John. *Philadelphia.* 1802-25.
William. *London* (*Blackfriars*). 1805-08.
Asa. *Boston, U.S.A.* 1806. W.
Joseph. *Alston.* 1810. C. & W.
William. *Nottingham.* 1814. C & W.
John. *London.* 1817.
Charles. *London.* a.1810, CC.1815-20. W.
Robert. *Newmarket.* Early 19c. Watch.
Peter. *Philadelphia.* 1819-22.
Jacob. *London.* CC.1825.
Thomas. *Liverpool.* 1825. Chron. maker.

HALLAM—
George. *London.* an.1772. Watch.
Edward. *Lutterworth.* 1791-5. C. & W.
John. *Nottingham.* 1799. W.
John. *London* (*Finsbury*). 1809-11. W.
John. *London* (*Tottenham*). 1809-11. W.
J. & T. *Nottingham.* 1814. Watch.
& STEVENSON. *Nottingham.* 1818.

HALLAND, Richard. *York.* an.1778. Watch.

HALLBÄCK, J. H. *Halmstad.* 1820-46.

HALLBERG, Nils. *Linköping.* d.1751.

HALLEICHER (HALEICHER, HALAICHER)—
Hans Otto (Johann Oth). *Augsburg.* ca.1670. crys. cross watch Spitzer coll. aut. table clock B.M. aut. clock Gotha M. Clock worked by rolling sphere, M.P.S. Dresden. hex. table clock Ilbert coll.
Matthäus. *Augsburg.* Juré 1702. en. watch Ilbert coll.

HALLET, William. *London.* mar.1771.

HALLEWAY, ——. *London.* End 17c. Watch Den. coll.

HALLEY—
William. *London.* a.1663.
Richard. *London.* a.1716.
William. *Wells* (*Somerset*). 1795. C.
Thomas Douglas. *London.* a.1802.

HALLGREN, Carl. *Copenhagen.* m.1797.

HALLIE, Thomas. *Glasgow.* 1721.

HALLIFAX—
John. *London* (*Old Bailey*). 1730-55. l.c. and br. clocks. mus. str. and chiming br. clock ill. Cec. & Web. Watch.
John. *Barnsley.* d.1750. l.c. clock.
Joseph, son. *Barnsley.* From 1750.
George. *Doncaster.* 1750-91. Watch.
John. *London* (*Fleet St.*). d.1758.
George. *London.* an.1758. Watch.
C. *London.* 1783. g. 3-case watch M.M.A.

HALLING—
Francis. *London.* a.1714.
Ole Gothard. *Copenhagen.* m.1764.

HALLIWELL—
Richard. *London.* a.1735.
William. *Chorley.* ca.1770-95.
John. *Warrington.* 1790-1820. C.
William. *Blackburn.* 1795. Watch Blackburn M. Perhaps Wm. above.
George. *New York.* 1805. W.
James. *Chorley.* ca.1820.
——. *Leeds.* 1825. C.

HALLOWAY, William. *Blackburn.* ca.1770-1795. W.

HALLOWS—
Jonathan. *Liverpool.* 1810-29. W.
John. *Liverpool.* 1813-18. W.

HALLS—
Thomas. *Romsey.* Mid. 18c. lc. clock.
Francis. *London.* ca.1775. l.c. clock. Watch.

HALLSTEDT, Johan Petter. *Skara.* 1819-46.

HALLSTRÖM, Johan Gustaf. *Helsingör.* m. 1821.
HALLUM—
Robert. *London.* an.1751. Watch.
Richard. *London.* an.1767. Watch.
John. *London* (*Shoreditch*). 1820.
HALLUS, Franciscus. *Liége.* 1659. Professor of Mathematics. Designer of elaborate sun-dial Whitehall Palace, of which he wrote 'Explicatio Horologii in Horto Regis,' London, 1659.
HALLWELL, John. *Warrington.* 1749. Bankrupt. cf. HALLIWELL.
HALLY—
Thomas. *London.* Late 17c. br. clock and watch.
——. *Glasgow.* an.1742. Watch.
HALONER, Grégore. *Blois.* 1621.
HALSALL—
Gilbert. *Hale.* d.1767. W.
Henry. *Halewood.* d.1767. W.
Edward. *Liverpool.* d.1783. W.
Richard. *Hale.* an.1797. Watch. cf. HORSEHILL.
Francis. *Hale.* an.1799. Watch.
William. *Bristol.* 1812-18. W.
Edward. *Bristol.* 1825-30. Chron. W. & C.
HALSEY—
George. *London.* a.1680, CC.1687-92.
Richard. *London.* Late 17c. Watch.
John. *London.* a.1733, CC.1766.
Edmund. *London.* an.1762. Watch.
Thomas. *London.* an.1765. Watch.
HALSON—
James. *London.* a.1784.
Charles. *London.* 1799-1804. W.
HALSTEAD (HALSTED)—
Richard. *London.* a.1661, CC.1669. d.an. 1678.
Robert. *London* (*Fleet St.*). 1662. CC.1668, m.CC.1699-1734. Watch in agate case Mallett coll. by him or the preceding. Sun and moon watch Ilbert coll.
Charles. *London.* a.1670, CC.1677-1710. sil. rep. watch, ca.1710, Ilbert coll.
John, son of Robert. *London.* CC.1698-1710. l.c. clock. Watch mt. G.M. Watch given by Queen Anne to Duchess of Marlborough, Bernal sale. Vase clock, ca.1750, Palace M. Pekin, may be by him.
George, bro. *London.* CC.1710.
Dorothy. *London.* 1705.
William. *London.* a.1705, CC.1715-18.
John. *London.* a.1710.
Maud. *London.* CC.1786.
HALVORSEN, Jens. *Copenhagen.* m.1824.
HAM—
John. *London.* a.1673.
Daniel. *Stockholm.* 1727-9.
Richard. *London.* an.1768. Watch.
William. *London.* a.1767.
John. *London* (*Snow Hill*). CC.1817, l.CC. 1821-40. W. mt. with Enderlin escapement G.M. Watch N.Y. Univ.
HAMAN, Peter. *London.* an.1816. Watch.
HAMBERGER, Georg Ehrhard. *Göttingen.* 1758. Read a paper on Clocks and Watches before the Soc. of Göttingen, pub. in Beckmann's 'History of Inventions.'
HAMBLETON—
George. *London.* CC.1669-82. W. & C.
J. *London.* an.1773. Watch.
William. *London.* a.1785.
HAMBLEY, William. *Falmouth.* 1784-95. C. & W.
HAMDEN, John. *London.* a.1638.
HAMEL, Clément. *Rouen.* 1596-1617. Founder member of Rouen corporation.
HAMER, ——. *London.* an.1723. Watch.
junior. *London.* an.1749. Watch.
HAMERSLEY, William. *London.* a.1805, CC.1813.
HAMERTON, Charles. *London.* a.1761, CC. 1768.
HAMILTON—
George. *London.* a.1690.
Richard. *London.* CC.1712-58. en. watch Gélis coll. by him or George.
Robert. *London.* a.1768, CC.1775.
The Rev. Dr. Robert. *London.* CC.1786, m. CC.1792-1825.
James. *London.* ca.1800. Watch.
J. & Co. *London.* 1800. Watch N.Y. Univ.
James. *Paisley.* 1820.
William. *Londonderry.* 1824.
HAMLET, Thomas. *London.* 1795-1832. Early lever watch Chamb. coll. Very small g. cyl. watch. Duplex watch mt.
HAMLEY—
J. Osbertus. *London* (*Holborn*). 1775-1840. Watch.
J. O., & Son. *London.* 1810-40.
O. James. *London* (*Duke St.*). 1815-20.
HAMLIN, Richard. *London.* 1677.
HAMLYN—
Thomas. *London.* a.1638.
Thomas, jun. *Ashburton.* 1791. C. & W.
HAMMARIN, Johan Petter. *Uppsala.* 1755-1765.
HAMMOND—
Henry. *London.* a.1672, CC.1680-99.
John. *London.* a.1676.
Anthony. *London.* a.1681.
James. *London.* a.1715.
Edward. *London.* a.1728.
Thomas Cundall. *Richmond* (*Yorks.*). 1825. W.
HAMMOON, William. *London.* an.1777. Watch.
HAMNET, S. *London.* an.1770. Watch.
HAMNSTEDT, P. *Stockholm.* b.1767, d.1805.
HAMOND, Samuel. *Battle* (*Sussex*). 1726. C.
HAMPDEN WATCH CO., *v.* DUEBER-HAMPDEN WATCH CO.
HAMPSON—
Thomas. *Wrexham.* 1728, d.1755. Clocks.
Joseph. *Wrexham.* 1772.
Robert. *Bury.* 1787. C.
& THELWELL. *Manchester.* ca.1820. Watch.
Robert. *Manchester.* ca.1820.
HAMPTON—
Edward. *London.* ca.1680. Watch Mallett coll. ill.Baillie.
W. *London.* an.1771. Watch.
Richard. *London.* ca.1780. en. metal watch S.K.M.
& PRINCE. *York.* an.1785. Watch.
Robert. *Manchester.* 1797-1804. W.
PRINCE & CATTLES. *York.* an.1827. Watch.
HAMSON, Thomas. *Liverpool.* 1800-03. C.
HAMY, William. *Dublin.* Early 19c. Watch.
HANBURY, John. *London.* 1664.
HANCE, David. *London.* a.1797.
HANCOCK—
——. *London.* an.1740. Watch. Dial maker.
Jeremiah. *Gloucester.* 1769-95. W.
John. *Leeds.* Went to *Bradford* (*Yorks.*) in 1780-4. W.
John. *Yeovil.* 1791. l.c. clock.
& Cox. *York.* Early 19c. Watch.
Anthony. *Otley.* 1822.
HANCORNE—
Thomas. *London.* CC.1659, w.CC. 1683-1707. Also HANCORN.
William. *London.* a.1668, CC.1676-86.
James. *London.* a.1675.
HAND—
Joseph. *London.* an.1775. Watch.
Thomas. *Naas.* 1824. Watch Belfast M.
HANDE, Thomas. ——. 1662 CC. Watch in tulip form B.M.
HANDISIDE, George. *London.* 1728, d.1742. br. clock. Watch Ashmolean M.

HANDLEY & MOORE. *London.* 1802-24. br. clock ill. Cec. & Web.
HANDS, Timothy. *London.* ca.1750-65. Watch mt. G.M.
HANDSCHUER, Jos. *Fürth.* d.ca.1800.
HANDSCOMB—
Ebenezer. *Woburn.* an.1764. Ampthill. an. 1787-91. Watch.
Benjamin. *London.* a.1804.
HANDY—
William. *London.* a.1701.
George. *Uxbridge.* Early 19c. Watch.
HANE, Daniel. *Vienna.* m.1800.
HÄNEL, Johann. *Schwarzenberck.* 1573. 'Schlosser, Uhr und Büchsenmacher.'
HANET—
N. *Paris.* 1680. sil. watch Horstmann coll. sil. watch Gélis coll., mark of 1672-80, with balance spring.
Stephen. *London.* 1725-c1750. rep. watch.
John George. *London.* an.1755-ca.1775. Watch in onyx box.
HANFORTH, Robert. *London.* a.1776.
HANG, ——. *Augsberg.* 1636. W. Prob. HAUG.
HANKIN, John. *London.* an.1743. Watch.
HANKINS, John. *Clapton.* an.1774-ca.1800. Watch.
HANLEY, ——. *Dublin.* Early 19c. Watch.
HANLON, W. *Dublin.* 1824. Watch.
HANMAN, John. *London.* an.1778. Watch.
HANNA, ——. *Dublin.* an.1775. Watch.
HANNAM, Edward. *London.* a.1770.
HANNAY—
William. *Paisley.* 1805.
George. *Workington.* Early 19c. Watch.
HANNI, Franz. *Belp* (near *Berne*). 1785.
HANNING—
Anders. *Gäfle,* 1759. *Uppsala,* 1763-65. Turret clock and watch Nord. M.
Anders. *Karlskrona.* 1773.
HANNINGTON—
William. *Glasgow.* 1796. d.1812.
William. *London.* ca.1800. Watch.
HANOT, Nicolas. *Paris.* 1675 m.
HANRIOT, ——. *Paris* and *Mâcon.* 1816-36. Award from Soc. Arts for an escapement.
HANS (HANNS, HANNSS)—
——. *Cologne.* 1544. 'Oermacher.'
——. *Copenhagen.* 1573. Made clock for Frederick II.
Johann Mathias. *Göggingen.* 1756-60.
Christophe. *Paris.* 1788 m.
HANSARD, William Drake. *London.* CC. 1788-94.
HANSCHE, Gustav. *Berlin.* d.1900. Court C.
HANSEL, James. *Philadelphia.* 1819-25.
HANSEN—
Oluf. *Copenhagen.* m.1759.
Morten. *Copenhagen.* m.1770.
Johannes. *Copenhagen.* m.1770.
Rasmus. *Laaland.* m.1794.
HANSET, Jn. Jh. *Brussels.* ca.1800. Court C. Equation regulator.
HANSLAPP—
Robert. *London.* a.1646, CC.1653.
William. *London.* a.1654, CC.1663.
HANSON—
George. *London.* a.1688, CC.1695-97.
Mary. *London.* 1718.
George, son. *London.* a.1718.
Thomas. *London.* a.1745.
George. *Windsor.* 1784-1823. Watch S.K.M. br. clock, tortoise-shell case. Lyre clock Windsor Castle ill. Britten.
& ASHING. *London.* 1799.
William. *Windsor.* ca.1800. Watch.
& SON. *Windsor.* Early 19c.
HANSSEN, Frederik. *Kolding.* 1586. Court C.
HANSSON—
Sven. *Jämtland.* Early 18c. Maker of carved wood wall clocks with one hand, known as 'Jämtland' or 'Sven Hans' clocks.
Jeppe. *Stockholm,* comp. 1770. *Laholm,* 1778. d.an.1785.
HANUSH, ——. *Prague.* ca.1497. Astronomer and astrologer. Prob. made clock for town hall, which has been attributed to Anton Pohl.
HANWELL, Zachariah. *London.* a.1686. CC. 1694-1708. l.c. clock.
HAPPACHER—
Philip. *Vienna.* m.1818. sil. rep. watch, painted dial. aut. watch.
Jacob. *Vienna.* m.1819.
HARBEN—
Perkins Robert. *London.* a.1772.
Thomas. *Lewes.* 1772. Watch.
SON & JESSE. *Lewes.* 1793. Firm with Thos.
HARBERG, Petter. *Härnösand.* 1770-80.
HARBUD—
James. *London* (*Cow Cross*). a.1756, CC. 1767-1805.
Jeremiah, son. *London.* a.1784, CC.1793, l.CC.1812-38.
HARCOURT, ——. *London* (*Westminster*). 1469.
HARD, ——. *Paris.* 1789.
HARDACRE, John. *Leeds.* 1817. C.
HARDE, Nicolas. *Paris.* 1674 juré.
HARDEL—
Louis Michel. *Paris.* m.1753, juré 1769-86.
Louis Maurice. *Paris.* m.1777.
HARDEMAN—
Samuel.•*Bridge and Canterbury.* In partnership with Wm. NASH 1762-94 and then alone. Watch.
William. *Bridge.* Early 19c.
HARDERWIJK, C. *Amsterdam.* 1822. W.
HARDGRAVE, John. *Sleaford.* 1795.
HARDIE, John. *Morpeth.* 1820. l.c. clock. cf. HARDY.
HARDING (HARDIN)—
John. *London.* CC.1685. Maker of repute.
Francis. *London.* a.1673, CC.1687.
John. *London.* a.1709.
John. *London.* a.1709, CC.1721-45. p.c. g. watch.
John. *London.* a.1711.
Joseph. *London.* a.1734, CC.1744, l.CC. 1766, d.1778. *St. John St.,* 1745. *St. John's Lane,* 1752. *Old Jewry,* 1768-75. Watch mt. G.M. g. watch S.K.M. Also HARDIN.
Robert. *London* (*Long La.*). a.1745, CC. 1753-73.
John. *Abingdon.* 1764, d.1783. Watch.
John. *London.* a.1756.
William. *London.* a.1761. W.
Robert, son of Jos. *London.* a.1764.
Richard. *London.* an.1776. Watch.
Charles. *Sidmouth.* 2nd half 18c. l.c. clock.
H. *Reading.* From 1783. C. & W.
Charles. *Ashburton.* 1791. C. & W.
Charles. *London.* Early 19c. Watch. Also HARDIN.
Samuel. *London.* 1810-23. Watch mt. S.K.M.
John. *London.* 1817-24. W.
HARDINGE, Thomas. *Speke.* an.1786. Watch.
HARDLEEVEN, Barnard. *Haarlem.* 1689.
HARDMAN—
Simon. *Munich.* Early 18c. Boulle br. clock Feill coll.
Jacob. *London.* a.1714, CC.1720-45. Also HEARDMAN.
John. *Wavertree.* d.1773. W.
John Gerard. *Liverpool.* 1748-73. W.
Henry. *Liverpool.* 1767-73. W.
Gerrard. *Whiston.* 1771. W.

HARDMAN—*continued.*
Thomas. *London* (*Clerkenwell*). 1792. W.
Thomas, son. *London.* a.1792.
Lawrence. *Liverpool.* 1825. W.
HARDSTAFF, Zachariah. *London.* a.1655.
HARDWELL—
Robert. *Andover.* 1791. Also HARTWELL.
——. *Whitchurch* (*Hants*). Early 19c.
HARDWICK, Joseph. *London.* a.1793.
HARDWIDGE, William. *London.* 1820.
HARDY—
Edme. *Paris.* m.1740.
François Edme. *Paris.* m.1743-89.
John. *London* (*Ball Court*). a.1739, CC. 1746, l.CC.1766-93. Watch case maker, Mark J.H.W.
Thomas. *London.* a.1751.
Thomas. *London* (*Rosamonds Row*). a.1760, CC.1767-89. Watch N.Y. Univ.
Edward. *Hull.* ca.1770-90.
John. *Morpeth.* ca.1770-1811. W. cf. HARDIE.
James. *London.* an.1772. Watch.
George. *Macclesfield.* 1772. C. Also HARDEY.
William. *Charleston, U.S.A.* 1773. From *London.* C. & W.
Charles. *London.* an.1775. Watch.
Jonathan, son of John. *London.* a.1766, CC. 1774.
Horace, bro. *London.* CC.1774-1805.
Robert, bro. *London* (*Newgate St.*). a.1769, CC.1776-1808.
George. *Altrincham.* an.1778. Watch.
Samuel, son of John. *London* (*Somerset St., Aldgate*). CC.1778-1805.
John. *London* (*Bridgewater Sq.*). 1783.
John. *London.* d.1814.
J. *Ashtead.* 1795. W.
William. *London.* l.CC.1796.
——. *Nottingham.* 1799. W.
John. *Preston.* 1802-21. C. & W.
Robert. *London.* CC.1802.
William. *London.* 1800-30. A fine maker of clocks and chron. Regulator with his escapement and mercury pendulum. Prize from Soc. Arts for a compensation balance. Arts. by him in Jl. Soc. Arts in 1804, 1807, 1818, 1821, and 1825.
Richard. *Newark.* 1820-30.
& CHRISTIE. *Manchester.* ca.1820.
Thomas. *London.* 1822-4. Chron. maker.
HARE—
James. *London.* a.1774.
Alexander. *London.* an.1776. CC.1781-1824. Watch G.M.
David. *Calcutta.* ca.1800.
Abraham. *London.* 1815.
HAREL, ——. *Paris.* 1811-25.
HARFORD, William. *Bath.* 1795.
HARGREAVE, Thomas. *London.* 1723. Insolvent.
HARGREAVES (HARGRAVES), Thomas. *Settle.* ca.1770-95. C.
HARGROVES, William. *London.* a.1688.
HARIMAN (HARRIMAN, HARRYMAN), John. *Workington.* ca.1770 1811. l.c. clock. Watch.
HARISON, ——. *London.* Early 19c. Sig. on watch.
HARKER, George. *London.* a.1815.
HARLAND—
Henry. *London.* a.1647, CC.1654-64.
Thomas. *Norwich, U.S.A.* 1773-1807. From *London.* l.c. clock M.M.A. ill. Milham.
Thomas. *New York.* 1805.
John. *Sheffield.* 1825. W.
HARLE, George. *London.* a.1701.
HARLEY—
William. *Shrewsbury.* an.1755. Watch.
George. *Shrewsbury.* 1784. W.

HARLEY—*continued.*
& SON. *Shrewsbury.* 1795-1802. Watch Ilbert coll.
R. *Bury St. Edmunds.* mar.1794. W.
Joseph. *London.* 1799. W.
Samuel. *Shrewsbury.* an.1801. Watch.
HARLING, William. *London.* an.1761. Watch.
HARLOW, Samuel Boulton. *Ashbourne* and *Birmingham.* 1789-1813. Invented a ratchet watch-key and pub. 'The Clockmaker's Guide to Practical Clockwork,' 1813.
HARMAN—
John. *London* (*Hart St.*). a.1681. Watch. Also HARMER.
William. *London.* a.1726.
Philip. *London.* a.1751.
James. *London.* an.1769. Watch.
HARMANT—
Philippe. *Paris.* ca.1760.
Veuve. *Rouen.* 1789.
HARMER—
Jasper. *London.* 1685-1716. Watch G.M.
Richard. *London.* an.1773. Watch.
John, *v.* HARMAN.
HARMON, ——. *Cork.* an.1788. Watch.
HARMSEN, Peter. *Hamburg.* Mid. 18c. rep. watch.
HARMSWORTH, John. *London.* 1820. W.
HARMWOOD, John. *London.* a.1731, CC. 1739.
HARNER—
J. *Colyford.* 2nd half 18c. l.c. clock.
——. *Membury.* 2nd half 18c. l.c. clock.
HAROLD, Richard. *London.* a.1682, CC. 1690-1705.
HARPER (HARPUR)—
Henry. *London* (*Cornhill*). a.1657, CC.1664, d.1708. l.c. clock, Ironmongers Company. Watch and mt. G.M. en. watch ill. Britten. sil. eng. watch Ilbert coll. Watch Mallett coll., with hour figures on square plaques irregularly placed. ill. Baillie.
Edward. *London.* a.1695.
v. BIRCHALL & HARPER.
John. *London.* a.1725-69. Bankrupt.
Thomas. *Shrewsbury.* an.1748-57. Watch.
Richard. *Shrewsbury.* 1766, d.1791. 'Eminent W.'
Thomas. *London* (*Monmouth St.*). a.1760, CC.1771-77. l.c. clock.
William. *London.* a.1766.
——. *Shrewsbury.* ca.1790 CC. In firm of CARSWELL & HARPER.
Samuel. *Ayr.* 1799.
Thomas. *London* (*Curtain Rd.*). 1799.
John. *London* (*Goswell St.*). 1802-24. C.
Joseph. *London.* 1805-08. W.
Richard. *Liverpool.* 1805-16. Watch Ilbert coll.
Benjamin. *Stoke.* Early 19c. Watch.
James. *Nottingham.* 1815. C. & W.
John. *London* (*St. John St.*). 1817-24. W.
HARPLETT, Cornelius. *London.* a.1659.
HARRACHE, Thomas. *London* (*Pall Mall*). an. 1751-73. Watch.
HARRINGTON—
John. *London.* a.1733, CC.1740.
——. *Liverpool.* 1790. Watch.
——. *Warrington.* ca.1810. Watch.
HARRIS—
John. *London* (*Old Bailey*). 1622. CC.1632, m.CC.1641, d.1655.
John. *Burford.* 1631.
Richard. *London.* 1641. Made clock for St. Paul's, Covent Garden, said, on insufficient evidence, to have been with pendulum.
Jacob. *London.* a.1646.
John. *London* (prob. *Holborn Bridge*). CC. 1659, m.CC.1688-99. br. clock ill. Britten.

HARRIS—*continued.*
George. *London.* a.1668, C.C.1674, d.1680. Spring maker.
John. *London.* CC.1677.
Mary, widow of George. *London.* 1680-8.
Anthony. *London.* CC.1683. Lantern and l.c. clock.
John. *Oxford.* 1684.
Benjamin. *London.* a.1677 to Tompion.
Thomas. *London.* ca.1685. br. clock ill. Cec. & Web.
Ebenezer. *London.* a.1682.
John. *London.* CC.1690. l.c. clock Weth. coll.
Charles. *London.* a.1686, CC.1695-1720.
Charles, son of John. *London.* a.1687, CC. 1695.
George. *London* (*Cripplegate*). mar.1699. W.
Francis William. *London.* a.1691, CC.1702-1725.
John. *London.* a.1692.
Richard. *London.* a.1693.
Samuel. *London.* a.1695, CC.1708-1730. l.c. clock.
John. *London.* a.1698.
Henry. *London.* a.1705, CC.1712. Watch.
William. *London* (*St. Michael's Lane*). 1720-1731.
John. *London.* a.1717, CC.1737.
Thomas. *London.* a.1720, CC.1733-60.
Christopher. *London* (*Grays Inn* and later *Leadenhall St.*). a.1721, CC.1729-45. Watch.
William, son of Francis William. *London.* a.1721, l.CC.1776.
George. *London.* a.1724.
Benjamin. *London.* a.1727.
Joseph. *Maidstone.* an.1743-ca.1760. Watch. T.C.
William Aaron, son of Wm. *London.* a.1735, CC.1743-73.
Robert. *London.* ca.1745-50. l.c. clock ill. Cec. & Web.
Robert. *London.* a.1741, CC.1750.
Edward, son of Henry. *London.* a.1742. Watch.
Henry, bro. *London.* CC.1752.
James. *Maidstone.* an.1754. Watch.
John. *London.* a.1752.
James. *London.* a.1753, CC.1762.
James. *London.* a.1755.
William. *London.* a.1756.
Richard. *London* (*Old Jewry*). a.1760, CC. 1770-94.
John, son of William Aaron. *London.* a.1761, CC.1772.
John, son of John. *London.* CC.1766.
——. *Westerham.* an.1769. Watch.
Thomas. *London.* 1770. Patented a dial with rotating centre or rotating figures.
Richard. *Wellington, Salop.* ca.1770. C. W.
——. *Ipswich.* an.1775. Watch.
Solomon. *London.* an.1779. Watch.
William, son of William Aaron. *London.* a. 1765.
William. *London* (*Goswell St.*). CC.1781-1790.
William. *Bridgnorth.* ca.1780. C.
William. *London* (*Bridgewater Gdns.*). 1781.
Thomas. *Bideford.* 1781. l.c. clock.
William. *Chippenham.* 1782. Watch Ilbert coll.
Christopher. *London* (*Old Jewry*). CC.1782-1823. Watch G.M.
E. *Warrington.* Late 18c. Watch Den. coll.
Charles. *London.* 1784. W.
Samuel, son of James. *London.* CC.1787.
John. *Deptford.* 1791. W.
Nathaniel. *London.* 1794. Watch G.M.
John. *London* (*Old Jewry*). a.1782, CC. 1795-1811.

HARRIS—*continued.*
William. *Hatherleigh.* 1795. C. & W.
William. *London* (*Goswell St.*). a.1788, CC. 1796, m.CC.1830-2.
Henry. *London* (*Curtain Rd.*). 1799-1825. W.
Matthew. *Bath.* 1800-19. W.
John. *London.* a.1793.
Samuel, son of Richard. *London.* CC.1802.
John. *London* (*E. Smithfield*). 1802-08. W.
Lazarus. *London.* 1802-24. W.
Nathaniel. *London.* 1802-08.
William. *London.* CC.1804, l.CC.1806-25.
Thomas, son of Matthew. *Bath.* a.1800.
Thomas. *Bath* (*Upper Borough Wall*). 1812-1825.
Solomon. *London.* a.1805, CC.1823.
Clement. *London* (*Cornhill*). CC.1816, l.CC. 1825-40. Chron. maker to East India Co. Marine chron. G.M. Min. rep. watch mt. Ilbert coll.
John. *London* (*Minories*). 1820.
Robert. *Paisley.* 1820.
John James. *London* (*E. Smithfield*), 1820; (*Nightingale Lane*), 1825-40. W.
Richard Joshua. *London.* a.1815.
Clement, son of Clement. *London.* a.1820.
Thomas. *Bath* (*Southgate St.*). 1825.
Charles. *Liverpool.* 1825. W.
William. *Liverpool.* 1825. W.
W. *Newmarket.* Early 19c. br. clock N.Y. Univ.

HARRISON—
George. *London* and *Liverpool.* a.1689, CC. 1698-1719. Maker of repute. Watch.
William. *London.* a.1692, CC.1699.
Anthony. *London* (*Birchin Lane*). a.1693, CC.1701-26. Bankrupt. rep. watch Den. coll.
James. *Barrow.* 1715-50. l.c. clock G.M. with grasshopper escapement and gridiron pendulum.
John, bro. *London.* b.1693, d.1776. In *Barrow* until 1735 except for a visit to London in 1728. The most remarkable man in the history of horology. Son of a carpenter; self-educated; made l.c. clock in 1715 now in G.M. First used in 1725 gridiron compensation pendulum and invented grasshopper escapement before 1728. Produced his No. 1 marine timepiece in 1735, No. 2 in 1739, No. 3 in 1757 and No. 4 in 1759. The last was tried in 1761 on a voyage to Jamaica and lost only five seconds. On the return, after five months, the error was under two minutes. This performance gained for him, eventually, the Government award of £20,000. Nos. 1, 3 and 4 are at the R. Observatory, Greenwich, No. 2 in the S.M.S.K., No. 5 in the G.M. l.c. clocks in S.K.M. and R. Astro. Soc. l.c. clock with frames, wheels and pinions of oak, made while in Barrow, G.M.
Thomas, son of Anthony. *London.* a.1717.
James. *London.* a.1720, CC.1737-51.
Joseph. *London.* a.1738.
C. *England.* b.1725-1810. Math. Inst. maker. sil. compass dial Old Ashmolean M.
Ralph. *London.* a.1742, CC.1751-60. In the firm of Fossett & Harrison.
John. *Liverpool.* Prob. d.1753. W.
Jasper. *Newcastle-o.-T.* an.1756. Watch.
Robert. *London.* a.1749, CC.1757.
George. *London.* 1762. Watch case maker.
William, son of John. *London* (*Holborn*). a. 1752, CC.1763, d.1816. Fellow of the Roy. Soc. Assisted his father in construction of Nos. 4 and 5, and took charge of the trial of No. 4. No. 5 is sd. 'John Harrison & Son.'

HARRISON—*continued.*
William. *London* (*Salisbury St.* and later *Chandos St.*). CC.1766-81. cyl. trav. clock and cyl. watch, ca.1800, Ilbert coll., by him or Wm. below.
Thomas. *Liverpool.* 1770-1803. Watch, Debaufre escapement, S.M.S.K.
John. *Norwich.* 2nd half 18c. l.c. clock M.M.A.
William. *London.* a.1762.
Edward. *Warrington.* ca.1770-95. Watch.
George. *Southminster.* 1775. C. & W.
Richard. *London.* an.1776. Watch.
George. *London.* a.1767.
James. *London.* a.1767, CC.1776.
David. *London.* a.1768.
John. *London.* a.1768. c.secs. watch, dated 1784, S.M.S.K., perhaps by him.
Charles. *London.* a.1771.
John. *Newcastle-o.-T.* 1779-95. str. chiming and rep. br. clock ill. Cec. & Web. W.
Robert. *Edinburgh.* a.1776.
Thomas. *London.* a.1776, CC.1786.
James. *London.* a.1778.
James and Lemuel. *Waterbury, U.S.A.* 1790-1830. Wooden clocks.
Thomas. *London* (*Fetter Lane*). 1799-1804.
Thomas. *London* (*St. George in the East*). 1805-08.
& Son. *Liverpool.* 1805-07.
Samuel, son of James. *London* (*Queen Ann St.*). CC.1807.
James, grandson of John. *Barton-on-Humber* and *Hull.* 1810-35. Turret C. of repute. Prize from Soc. Arts for a detached escapement applied to Filey Church clock, desc. in Trans. Soc. Arts, 1831.
& Finney. *Liverpool.* 1810.
Thomas. *London.* l.CC.1812, d.1820. cyl. mt. G.M.
John. *London.* a.1806.
William. *London.* 1815 CC.
James. *Boston, U.S.A.* 1816-18. C.
E. *Warrington.* Early 19c. Watch.
William Hart. *Chepstow.* 1822-48.
Richard Joshua. *London.* a.1815.
Thomas. *London* (*Ratcliffe Highway*). 1820.
John. *Liverpool.* 1824-9. Watch N.Y. Univ.

HARRISS, William. *Chippenham.* 18c. l.c. clock.

HARROCKS—
Joshua. *Lancaster* and *Eamont Bridge.* 1748-1759. Turret clocks.
John. *Aughton.* an.1769. Watch.
John, son of Joshua. *Nantwich.* 1783. Lancaster freeman.

HARROD, John. *London.* a.1762.

HARRY, John. *Penryn.* 1784. W.

HARRYS, Thomas. *London.* 1671. Made St. Dunstan's clock with Jacks.
William. *Cardiff.* 1734.

HARSCH, Johann Michael. *Berlin.* 1785-1836.

HARSTAFFE, Zachariah. *London.* a.1655.

HART—
Benjamin. *London.* a.1699.
John. *London* (*St. Martin's Lane*). a.1713, CC.1720. Retired 1772.
Henry. *London.* CC.1720.
William. *London.* an.1740. Watch.
John. *Yarmouth.* 1759. C.
——. *Bristol.* 1769. Watch Ilbert coll.
Edward. *London.* a.1766, CC.1773.
——. *Nottingham.* ca.1790 CC.
Samuel. *Plymouth.* 1795. W.
Emanuel. *Plymouth.* 1795. W.
Stephen & Maurice. *London.* 1799-1818.
Stephen, & Co. *London.* 1802-04.
H. & M. *London.* 1809-11.
N. *London.* 1815-24. Later N. Hart & Son. Watch.
William. *Nottingham.* 1815. W.

HART—*continued.*
& Harvey. *London.* 1817-24.
Alpha. *Goshen, N.Y.* 1820. Wooden clock.
John & Robert. *Glasgow.* 1821. Made clock dials illuminated by gas which was turned on and off by the clock.
Thomas. *Ballycastle.* 1824.

HARTEK, Kaspar. *Vienna.* m.1799. Turret C.

HARTEL—
Johann. *Aichach.* 1738. Kleinuhrmacher.
Philipp. *Burghausen.* a.1742-85. Kleinuhrmacher.
Johann Christian, son. *Augsburg.* m.1785, d.1791. From *Dillingen.* g. watch Fränkel coll. prob. by him.

HARTFORD, John. *London.* CC.1632.

HARTICH, Johann Wolfgang. *Augsburg.* m. 1712-70 juré.

HARTINGUE, Claude François. *Paris.* 1773.

HARTLEY—
John. *Halifax.* ca.1770. l.c. clock.
Jeremiah. *Norwich.* an.1777. Clock.
John. *London.* 1784-99.
Levi Henry. *London.* a.1807.

HARTMANN—
Georg. *Nürnberg.* b.1489, d.1564. math. inst. maker. Two astrolabes Old Ashmolean M. Star dial M.P.S. Dresden.
Thomas. *Augsburg* and *Wald.* 1729 comp.-1746.
Johann Georg. *Jena,* 1752. *Halle,* 1756. Pub. 'Nöthige Unterricht von Verbesserung der Sack-Uhren.'
Valentin. *Oberhausen.* 1756. Turret C.
Paulus. *Vienna.* m.1763-early 19c. g. cal. watch.
——. *Vienna.* 1769. Chiming turret clock Uhren M. Vienna. Prob. the preceding.
——. *Berlin.* ca.1770. Court C. Table clock.
Johann Kaspar. *Vienna.* m.1794-early 19c. en. bud watch.
——. *Paris.* 1808-25.

HARTOG, L. *Rotterdam.* ca.1800.

HARTSHORNE—
William. *Broseley.* 1793. Watch.
Alexander. *London.* 1820.

HARTSTONGE, Henry. *Dublin.* 1795. W.

HARTUNG, Georg. *Karlstadt-am-Main.* m. 1821. C.

HARTWELL—
Francis. *London.* a.1678.
——. *London* (*Hatton Garden*). 1780. W.
Elizabeth. *Uttoxeter.* 1795.
Robert. *Nottingham.* 1799. W.
v. Hardwell.

HARVEY—
Benjamin (*alias* Munday). *London.* a.1661.
Samuel. *London.* a.1686, CC.1696. Watch.
John. *London.* a.1691.
Alexander. *London.* a.1717, CC.1726-31.
Thomas. *London* (*Fenchurch St.*). 1753. Watch.
Edward. *Rochdale.* 1758. W.
John. *Weymouth.* 1760-91. C. & W.
——. *Brentwood.* an.1763. Watch.
Eleanor, widow. *Brentwood.* 1772.
James. *Abergavenny.* 1777-95. From London. C. & W.
E. *Launceston.* 1791. C. & W.
John. *London* (*Fenchurch St.*). a.1776, CC. 1789-1804; (*Falcon St.*), 1809-25. W.
Bennett. *Weymouth.* Late 18c. Watch mt.
George. *St. Ninians,* 1805. *Stirling,* 1834. Watch.
Thomas. *York.* 1808. W.
Alexander. *Sanquhar.* 1811.
& Denton. *England.* Early 19c. br. clock.
Robert. *Liverpool.* Early 19c. Watch.
George. F.R.S.E. *Edinburgh.* 1824. Pub.

HARVEY—*continued.*
several arts. on the effects of magnetism on chron.
& Co. *London.* ca.1825. Watch.
HARWARD, Robert. *London.* a.1713, CC. 1730.
HARWOOD—
Benjamin. *London.* BC.1626.
Laurence. *London.* d.1716.
Charles. *London.* a.1742. Watch.
William. *London.* an.1769. Watch.
Robert. *Bridlington.* 1784.
Taylor. *Cambridge.* 1791 CC.
HASE—
Nicolaus. *Dresden.* 1650. Court C.1654. Sq. table clock.
Jacob. *Germany.* 18c. sil. str. watch Fränkel coll.
HASIUS—
Isaac. *Haarlem.* Late 17c. g. watch en. by Huaud le puisné, Blot-Garnier coll. Watch, sun and moon hour indicators, Stads M. Amsterdam.
Jacob. *Amsterdam.* 1682-ca.1725. Watches Stads M. Amsterdam and Den. coll. l.c. clock Ilbert coll.
HASKEN, Isaac. *London.* a.1804.
HASLAM, Joseph. *London.* a.1742.
HASLEDEN, Thomas. *Prescot.* 1795. W.
HASLER—
Hans Leo. *Nürnberg.* 1564-1612. Said to have been the first to apply str. work to watches.
René. *Tramelan.* Early 19c. Watch.
HASLEWOOD—
Thomas. *London.* an.1724. Watch.
Samuel. *Stamford.* an.1770. Watch.
Roger. *London.* a.1793.
HASLIP, William. *Wenlock.* an.1793. Watch.
HASLUCK, Jacob. *London.* ca.1695. Watch with sun and moon hour indicators M.M.A.
HASSELL—
Joshua. *London.* a.1725, CC.1733-71.
Thomas. *London.* a.1736.
James. *Bewdley.* an.1771. Watch.
HASSENIUS, James. *London.* CC.1682. In 1698 went to Russia, his native country. Watch Den. coll. mt. G.M. l.c. month clock. l.c. clock ill. Cec. & Web.
HASSWELL, Leonard. *London.* a.1721.
HASTINGS, David. *Alnwick.* 1758-95.
HASTLER, John. *London.* 1769. Insolvent.
HASTY—
James. *London.* an.1778. Watch.
& Son. *Shrewsbury.* an.1784. Watch.
HASUM, William. *London.* an.1773. Watch.
HASWALL, Alexander. *London.* 1780-94. Duplex watch mt. S.M.S.K.
HASWELL, David. *London.* an.1760. Watch.
HASWHITTLE, Robert. *London.* an.1756. Watch.
HATCH—
John. *London.* a.1685, CC.1693.
George. *Hatfield.* ca.1690 CC.
George. *St. Albans.* ca.1800.
HATCHMAN, James. *London.* a.1673, CC. 1680-98.
HATFIELD—
David. *Bosworth.* a.1732 in *London.* Watch.
Hallows. *London.* a.1791, CC.1805-22.
HATHAWAY—
William. *London.* a.1726, CC.1735.
John. *London.* a.1756.
HATHORN, John. *Lancaster.* an.1755. Watch.
HATT—
John. *London.* a.1726.
William. *London.* a.1753.
HATTLEY, John. *London.* 1783.
HATTON—
Peter. *Stafford.* ca.1725. l.c. clock.
Thomas. *London* (*Old Bailey*). an.1757-74. Pub. 'Introduction to the Mechanical part

HATTON—*continued.*
of Clock and Watch Work,' London, 1773. Watch.
John. *Stafford.* an.1770. Watch.
Samuel. *London.* an.1772. Watch.
Thomas. *Preston.* 1774. Bankrupt. From London.
J. *London.* ca.1780. p.c. watch Ilbert coll.
Nathaniel. *London.* a.1782.
Joseph Yorke. *London* (*Tooley St.*). a.1785, CC.1796, l.CC.1810-30. Watches. br. clock.
Charles. *London.* a.1790.
James. *London.* CC.1799, l.CC.1810-15. Chron. maker. l.c. clock.
Christopher, son of Thomas. *London.* a. 1799, CC.1815.
& Harris. *London.* 1816-24. Chron. makers.
George Cooper. *Lancaster.* 1825. W.
William. *Liverpool.* 1825. W.
William. *London.* ca.1825. Watch.
HAUBERG, J. V. *Dantzig.* Early 19c.
HAUCHART, ——. *Paris.* 1812-5.
HAUER, Nicolas. *Paris.* 1674 juré.
HAUG—
Carol. *Feuchtwangen.* 1555. Made clock for Kirchberg.
Christoph. *Augsburg.* 1622. Table clock with aut. lion Feill coll. *v.* Hang.
HAUGHTON—
Richard. *London.* a.1682, CC.1690-1707.
George. *London.* 1724. l.c. clock.
William. *London.* a.1737, CC.1746-1777.
R. *London* (*Fetter Lane*). ca.1770. l.c. clock Virginia M.
James. *London.* CC.1770-84.
Ann. *London.* 1784 CC.
James, son of James. *London.* a.1796.
James. *London* (*Horsleydown*). 1805-20.
William. *London.* a.1804.
HAUKSBEE, John. *London.* a.1695, CC.1709. *v.* Hawkesbee.
HAUPOISE, ——. *Caen.* Early 19c. Lever rep. watch S.M.S.K.
HAUPT, Georg. *Stockholm.* End 18c. l.c. clock, Nat. M. Stockholm.
HAURY, Jse. *Arbourg.* ca.1800. Watch.
HAUSCHILDT, ——. *Berlin.* 1794.
HAUSCHULTZ, Carl Gottfred. *Copenhagen.* m.1798.
HAUSDORFER, Jos. *Vienna.* m.1787.
HAUSER—
Albertus. *Eichstätt.* 1st half 18c. Watch Feill coll.
Eduard. *Lenzkirch.* b.1825, d.1900. Developed clockmaking in the Schwarzwald and founded Lenzkirch factory.
HAUSIGK, Johann Gottlieb. *Dresden.* m.1751, d.1795.
HAUSSEN, B. ——. ca.1810. Trav. clock Ilbert coll.
HAUT, V. *London.* 1731. Sig. on repoussé work of watch.
HAUTEFEUILLE, Jean de (L'Abbé). *Orléans.* b.1647, d.1724. Made several inventions in horology, desc. in 'Pendule perpetuelle avec un nouveau balancier,' Paris, 1678. 'Avis aux horlogers . . .,' Paris, 1692. 'Inventions nouvelles,' Paris, 1717. Deux problèmes d'horlogerie . . .,' Paris, 1718. 'Horloge circulaire élastique centrifuge' and 'Pendule dont les vibrations sont horizontales,' Orléans, 1720. 'Construction nouvelle de trois montres portatives,' Paris, 1722. Claimed priority over Huygens for the balance spring in 1675, apparently without justification, in a pamphlet, 'Factum . . . touchant les Pendules de Poche, contre M. Huygens,' Paris, 1675. Invented rack-lever escapement in 1722.

HAUTEMANIÈRE—
Jean Baptiste. *Paris.* m.1765.
Charles Guillaume. *Paris.* m.1778-89.
HAUTON, John. *London.* 1716 CC.
HAUTSCH—
Hans. *Nürnberg.* ca.1640. Made an elaborate aut. work.
Gottfried, son. *Nürnberg.* 1662-92. Made aut.
HAVELLAND—
William Thomas. *London.* a.1783, CC.1792.
& STEPHENS. *London.* 1795-ca.1810. br. clock.
HAVELOCK, G. *Guisborough.* 1700.
HAVEN, Thomas. *London.* CC.1652.
HAVES, Peter. *London.* 1662.
HAVILAND, Richard. *Cirencester.* 1820.
HAWES—
William. *London.* 1741. g. repoussé watch Carnegie M.
James. *London.* a.1785.
Alfred. *London.* ca.1825. Watch.
HAWKE, Charles. *Wickham Market.* 1810.
HAWKES—
Susan. *London.* a.1683.
John. *London.* a.1752.
J. *Walsall.* 1802. C. & W.
J. *Albrighton.* 1810. C. & W.
HAWKESBEE, Benjamin. *London.* CC.1709. *v.* HAUKSBEE.
HAWKESWORTH—
John. *London.* a.1697, CC.1710-9.
Edward. *Cork.* 1824.
HAWKINS—
William. *London.* a.1676, CC.1684. l.c. clock Weth. coll. ill. Britten.
Richard. *London.* a.1677.
George. *London.* a.1688.
John. *London.* a.1695.
Marke. *Bury St. Edmunds.* Early 18c. l.c. clock. Watch.
Thomas. *London.* a.1703, CC.1711.
Daniel. *London.* a.1718.
James. *London.* a.1722, CC.1730-40.
William. *Bury St. Edmunds.* 1st half 18c. l.c. clock Weth. coll. Watch mt.
——. *Salisbury.* an.1771. Watch.
Thomas or George. *London.* a.1765, CC. 1772.
Thomas. *London.* CC.1777-1810. cyl. mt. G.M.
Thomas. *London.* a.1771.
Richard. *London.* an.1787. Watch.
Joseph. *Axminster.* 1795. C. & W.
Henry. *Plymouth.* 1795. W.
William. *Southampton.* Early 19c.
HAWKSEY, Enoch. *Nantwich.* d.1799.
HAWLEY—
Henry. *London.* 1680 CC.
J. T., & Co. *London.* 1795-1825. W. to the King. br. clock.
Thomas & Co. *London (Strand).* 1795-1828. Prob. the preceding. Used Savage's 2-pin lever esc. Watch Ilbert coll.
John. *London (Coventry St.).* 1805-08.
John & Charles. *London (Coventry St.).* 1820.
HAWTHORN—
D. *Darlaston.* ca.1705. l.c. mus. clock ill. Cec. & Web.
John. *Newcastle-o.-T.* 1755. d.1779. Many watches. Also HAWTHORNTHWAITE and HAYTHORNTHWAITE.
Margaret, widow. *Newcastle-o.-T.* d.1782.
Edward. *London.* Late 18c. Watch mt. G.M.
v. BEILBY & HAWTHORN.
HAWTING, John. *Oxford.* 1765. d.1791. W.
HAWTYEN, Samuel. *London.* a.1690.
HAY—
George. *London.* a.1705.
Alexander. *Edinburgh.* 1718.

HAY—*continued.*
Thomas. *Bishops Castle.* ca.1770. Watch Shrewsbury M.
William. *London.* CC.1774.
John. *London.* 1770. Watch.
Thomas. *Kelso.* 1778-1814. Also HOY.
Andrew. *Edinburgh.* a.1777.
James. *London.* a.1785.
James. *Inverness.* 1793.
George. *York.* 1808. W.
John. *Leith.* 1822.
——. *Wolverhampton.* Early 19c.
Thomas William. *Shrewsbury.* Early 19c. Watch Shrewsbury M.
HAYCOCK, Nathaniel. *London.* 1802-08. W.
HAYD, Christian. *Olmütz.* 1687-90. Repaired town clock.
HAYDEN—
William. *London.* *v.* HAYDON.
Richard. *London.* a.1714, CC.1733-45.
William. *London.* a.1731, CC.1746-54.
Thomas. *Dudley.* ca.1760-70. l.c. clock.
Samuel. *Boston, U.S.A.* 1796-1809. W.
Henry. *Carrick-on-Suir.* 1824.
HAYDON—
William. *Croydon.* CC.1687-91.
William. *London (Theobalds Row).* a.1707, CC.1717-49. Watch.
Thomas. *London (Strand).* a.1715-31.
Joseph. *London.* a.1719.
William. *London (Red Cross Sq.).* 1767.
Joseph. *London.* a.1760.
William. *Dorchester,* then *Poole* from 1774. Insolvent.
John. *London.* a.1771, CC.1790.
John. *London (Cheapside).* CC.1784, l.CC. 1790-1804.
Charles. *London.* a.1804.
Edward. *London.* CC.1818.
HAYES—
Walter. *London.* CC.1654, m.CC.1680, d. 1685. Dial M.M.A. sd. W. HAYES prob. by him. Universal ring dial. Old Ashmolean M.
Edmund. *London.* a.1675, CC.1682.
John. *London.* a.1676.
William. *London.* a.1686.
James. *London.* a.1693.
Thomas. *London.* a.1704.
John. *London.* a.1716-31.
John. *Wrexham.* 1747-1822. Watch.
Francis. prob. *London.* an.1757. Watch.
Frederick. *London.* an.1767. Watch.
William. *Warrington.* 1782. Watch Den. coll.
Christopher. *Oldham.* ca.1820.
HAYFORD, William. *London.* 1820-4. Watch.
HAYLER, William. *Chatham.* an.1769-Early 19c. l.c. clock. Watch.
HAYLES, Edward. *London.* a.1802.
HAYLEY, William. *London.* 1790.
HAYLOR, Charles. *London.* Late 18c. Watch N.Y. Univ.
HAYN, Carl Sigismund. *Sprottau.* ca.1700. hex. table clock.
HAYNES—
John. *London.* CC.1676.
William. *London.* a.1680, CC.1703.
John. *London.* a.1698.
Francis. *London.* CC.1707-14. Watch.
Sarah. *London.* a.1727.
William. *London.* a.1731, CC.1741.
George. *London.* a.1797.
v. KENTISH & HAYNES.
Samuel. *Cork.* 1824.
HAYTER—
William. *London.* a.1685, CC.1694.
John, jun. *Wells (Somerset).* 1795. W.
——. *Bath.* 1812.
——. *Bristol.* 1819. W.

HAYTHORNTHWAITE (HATHORNTH-WAITE)—
Peter. *Kirkby Lonsdale.* 1709. C. Lancaster freeman.
John, son. *Kirkby Lonsdale.* 1744. C. Lancaster freeman.
Peter, son. *London.* 1783. W. Lancaster freeman.
John, *Newcastle-o.-T.* *v.* HAWTHORN.
HAYTON, F. *London.* Mid. 18c. Watch mt.
HAYWARD—
William. *London.* a.1713, CC.1720-46.
George. *London.* a.1775.
D. *London.* an.1795. Watch.
Robert. *London (Horsleydown).* 1805-11.
Robert. *London (Dockhead).* 1820-4. Watch N.Y. Univ.
John. *London.* 1820.
T. H. *Winchester.* Early 19c. Watch.
'HAYWARD.' Sig. on watches, ca. 1881, of the HAMPDEN WATCH CO.
HAYWOOD—
William. *London.* an.1722. Watch.
Peter. *Crediton.* 1766. Patented a calendar ring.
Joshua. *Manchester.* ca.1770. Watch mt. Platt Hall M. Manchester.
John. *London.* an.1775. Watch.
Samuel. *Norwich.* an.1777. Watch.
William. *London.* 1809-11.
HAZARD, Jérémie Pierre. *Paris.* m.1776.
HEAD—
James. *Evesham.* d.1774. W.
Joseph. *Evesham.* an.1756. Watch.
James. *Burford.* an.1757. Watch.
Joseph. *Cirencester.* an.1768. Watch.
HEADACHE, Thomas. *London.* a.1776, CC. 1784.
HEADDING, Richard William. *London.* a. 1804, l.CC.1812, d.1821.
HEADWORTH—
Phineas. *London (Islington).* a.1789-1840.
J. *London.* 1817-24.
HEADY, George. *London.* a.1675, CC.1682-1694.
HEALER, George. *Wantage.* Early 19c. Watch.
HEALEY—
Thomas. *London.* a.1705.
Benjamin. *London.* an.1776. Watch.
John. *Manchester.* 1777-1814. Watch Platt Hall M.Manchester. Partner with GILLETT.
Thomas. *Manchester.* ca.1820.
HEAP—
Richard. *London (Maiden Lane).* 1802-25.
Richard. *London (Covent Gdn.).* 1820. Succeeded John BAKER.
HEAPES, James. *Didsbury.* an.1793. Watch.
HEAPY, John. *Stockport.* an.1773. Watch.
HEARD, William. *Hartland.* 2nd half 18c. l.c. clock.
HEARDMAN—
Jacob. *London.* a.1714, CC.1720-45. Also HARDMAN.
Jacob. *London.* CC.1746.
John, son. *London.* a.1735, CC.1749.
v. also HARDMAN.
HEARN, Joseph. *London.* a.1690.
HEARNE—
——. *London.* 1630. Subscribed for incorporation of CC.
Henry. *London (Westminster).* 1776. Bankrupt. Watch.
Henry. *Westbury.* 1795. C. & W.
HEART, Henry. *Plymouth.* an.1778. Watch.
HEASLEY, John. *London.* a.1737.
HEASMAN, Walter. *Lindfield.* 1788. Watch.
HEATH—
Benjamin. *London.* a.1661.
Peter. *London.* a.1727.
Gabriel. *London.* a.1736.
Thomas. *London.* 1745. Math. Inst. maker.

HEATH—*continued.*
John. *London.* 1751. Shagreen case maker.
John. *London.* a.1744.
Thomas. *London.* a.1748, CC.1762. Universal ring dial Old Ashmolean M.
Hiram. *London.* a.1751.
& WING. *London.* an.1778-ca.1800. Clockwork orrery Old Ashmolean M.
William. *Moreton-in-Marsh.* Early 19c.
HEATHCOTE—
Timothy. *London.* CC.1698-1729.
Edward. *London.* a.1725, CC.1733.
HEATHER—
Nicholas. *London.* a.1694.
William. *London.* 1701 CC.
Peter. *London.* a.1700.
HEATHERLEY, Richard. *London.* a.1766.
HEATON—
Thomas. *Manchester.* 1804.
Thomas. *Sheffield.* 1817-28. W.
HEAVISID, Michael. *London.* a.1707.
HEBB, John. *London.* a.1728, CC.1736.
HEBBART, John. *Brentford.* an.1769. Watch.
HEBDITCH, Richard. *Bristol.* 1630. Made clock for castle.
HEBER, ——. *Paris.* 1812.
HEBERT—
Abraham. *London.* a.1648.
James. *London.* CC.1682. W.
J. *Brighton.* ca.1715. Watch G.M.
Anthony. *London.* CC.1725.
Henry. *London.* CC.1734.
Mary. *London.* CC.1795.
L. *London (Chelsea).* 1813-28. Award from Soc. Arts for his experiments on using graphite as lubricant.
E. C. *Amsterdam.* 1822. W.
HEBLER, Francis. *London.* 1784.
HEBLETHWAITE, Nathaniel. *London.* a. 1783.
HEBLING, Frederick. *London.* 1808-24. Wooden C.
HEBRAT—
——. *Paris.* 1612 m.
Jean. *Brussels.* 1640. en. watch B.M.
HECHTEL, Johann Conrad. *Ansbach.* Early 18c. en. watch Stern. coll. br. clock.
HECKEL—
Johann. *Friedberg.* m.1722. p.c. shagreen watch Ilbert coll. Also HECKL.
Antonius. *Vienna.* m.1724. sil. trav. clock Carnegie M. Also HECKL and HEKHL.
Francesko. *Friedberg.* ca.1730. str. rep. al. and cal. trav. clock M.P.S. Dresden.
Augustin. *Vienna.* m.1754. Also HÄCKEL.
Joseph Antoni. *Friedberg.* 1700.
Conrad. *Vienna.* m.1783.
Jacob. *Vienna.* m.1787. Also HEKHEL and HEKL.
——. *London.* *v.* LEKCEH.
Franz Xaver. *Vienna.* m.1810. Also HÄCKEL.
Anton Felix. *Vienna.* m.1815. Also HEKEL.
Anton Jacob. *Vienna.* m.1818. Also HEKEL.
Franz Xaver. *Vienna.* m.1819. Also HEKEL.
HECKER, Joh. Ferd. *Cologne.* 1797.
HECKLE—
James. *Liverpool.* 1816.
Anthony. *Liverpool.* ca.1820.
Alanson. *Liverpool.* 1824-9.
HECKMANN, H. *Cologne.* 1813.
HECKSTETTER, Joseph. *London.* a.1687, CC. 1694-1704.
HEDENQUIST, Peter. *Uppsala.* b.1740, d. 1796.
HEDGE—
Nathaniel. *Colchester.* ca.1740-80. Lantern and l.c. clocks. Watch.
John. *Colchester.* d.1778. W.
Nathaniel, jun. *Colchester.* From 1765-90. W.
Thomas & John. *Colchester.* 1774-8. W.
Thomas. *Colchester.* 1784-95. W.

HEDGE—*continued.*
v. COOPER & HEDGE.
& BANISTER. *Colchester.* ca.1800. l.c. clock. Watch N.Y. Univ.
& HEDGE, jun. *Colchester.* ca.1800.
N., & Son. *Colchester.* 1799.
HEDGER, George. *London.* 1820-5. Watch.
HEDIGER, J. *Zug.* 1st half 17c. Watch Louvre. Oval crys. watch Feill coll. Also HELIGER.
HEDIN, Lars Petri. *Jönköping.* 18c. l.c. clock and wall clock Nord. M.
HEDLEY, Amos. *Stamford.* 1751. W.
HEDMAN, L. *Stockholm.* ca.1750. p.c. watch.
HÉDOUIN-DUTERTRE, ——. *Paris.* 1812. Succeeded FALOISE. C.
HÉDOUX, Pierre François. *Paris.* m.1758.
HEDSTRÖM, Ephraim. *Stockholm.* b.1775, d.1816. Two wall and three br. clocks, one Nord. M. g. cyl. watch.
HEELE, Solomon. *London.* a.1730.
HEELEY—
Benjamin. *Deptford.* an.1747. Watch.
Joseph. *Deptford.* 1747. Watch.
HEER, Jost. *Cassel.* ca.1590. From NASSAU.
HEERDEGEN, R. A. *Fürth.* ca.1760. sil. watch.
HEERMAN, John. *London.* CC.1691. Dutchman. W. of repute.
HEGER, Georg. *Vienna.* m.1798.
HEGGLIN (HEGLINA), Antoni. *Zug.* Early 18c. Watch.
HEHSEN, ——. *Paris.* 2nd half 18c. g. en. watch M.P.S. Dresden.
HEIDE, Peter. *Copenhagen.* 1724.
HEIDEMARK, P. *London.* 1777. Watch Belfast M.
HEIDENREICH, Niels. *Copenhagen.* m. 1797-1802.
HEIDER, August et Comp. *Hamburg.* 1821.
HEIDT, Gustave. *Paris.* 1775.
HEIDTMANN, Laurits. *Haderslev.* 1618. Made clock for Christian IV of Denmark.
HEIGEL, Martin. *Stadtamhof.* 1730. g. p.c. watch K.H.M. Clock Cassel Landes-M.
HEIGHEMORE, Nathaniel. ——. 1633. Quadrant dial Ilbert coll.
HEIJER, J. M. *Amsterdam.* ca.1770. cal. watches Den. and Ilbert colls.
HEIJMAN, Johan Fredrick. *Stockholm.* m. 1742, d.1778. Court C.
HEIL, Franz. *Kissingen.* m.1812.
HEILMANN, J. C. *Altenburg.* Early 19c. Watch Fränkel coll.
HEIM, Matthias. *Gütenbach.* ca.1770. Wall clock Furt. M.
HEIN, Hans. *Helsingör.* m.1791.
HEINIMANN, Samuel. *Basle.* 1744.
HEINLEIN, *v.* HENLEIN.
HEINRICH, Peter. *Prague.* 1816. Made an aut. trumpet player.
HEINTZELMAN, John Conrad. *Manheim, Lancaster, U.S.A.* b.1766, d.1796. l.c. clocks.
HEINZ (HEINTZ), Georg. *Vienna.* m.ca. 1671.
HEISE, Johann Konrad. *Cassel.* ca.1770. Several clocks and watches Cassel Landes-M.
HEISS, Georg. *Cologne.* 1730.
HEITZMANN—
George. *London.* 1799-1808. Wooden C.
John, & Co. *London.* 1805-08. Wooden C.
Jules. *Paris.* Early 19c. mus. clocks.
Joachim. *Paris.* Early 19c.
HELBIG (HELBING), Heinrich. *Vienna.* m. 1783. g. en. watch.
HELDEN—
Onesiphorus. *London.* 1630. CC.1632, w. CC.1646-8. Petitioner for incorporation of CC. Very fine pierced and eng. str. watch with portrait of Charles I. Also HOLDER.
Cornelius. *London.* a.1686.
HELE, *v.* HENLEIN.
HELDSTOCK, William. Prob. *London.* an. 1773. Watch.
HÉLEY, ——. *Paris.* 1812.
HELFENZRIEDER, Johann. *Ingolstadt.* Late 18c. Prof. of math. and physics. Pub. two books on Turret clocks in 1789 and 1792.
HELFER-OLIVA, Daniel. *Dantzig.* 1722. Repaired Dammthor clock.
HÉLIE—
Charles. *Paris.* m.1774.
v. HÉLYE.
HELLAM—
James. *London.* a.1682, CC.1690-1700.
George. *Bishop Stortford.* an.1762. Watch.
HELLBERG—
A. *Sweden.* Late 18c. Wall clock. Watch mt. Nord. M.
C. E. *Sundsvall.* 1823.
N. *Sundsvall.* 1825.
HELLIWELL, William. *Leeds.* 1815-26. C.
HELLMAN, ——. *Kungsbacka.* 1819-23.
HELLMERS, Peter Herman. *Hamburg.* 1804-1821.
HELLSTEN, Carl. *Falun.* 1750-4.
HELM, ——. *Ormskirk.* 1761.
HELME—
Nestor. *London.* a.1674.
John. *London.* a.1774.
HELMS, Johann Friedrich. *Hamburg.* 1801-1804.
HELMSLEY, *v.* GILBERT & HELMSLEY
HELMSTINE, ——. *Stockholm.* 2nd half 18c. Watch Stads M. Amsterdam.
HELOR, John. *London.* 1731. W.
HELOT—
Samuel. *Paris.* d.1689 m.
Charles. *Amsterdam.* 1686. Huguenot refugee from *Paris.*
Jean. *Amsterdam.* 1687. Huguenot refugee from *Rouen.* g. watch en. Huaud Mallett coll.
John. *London.* an.1730. Watch.
HELSBY—
Samuel. *Liverpool.* 1821-9. W.
Thomas, & Sons. *Liverpool.* 1825. W.
HÉLYE—
Charles. *Paris* (*Rue Dauphine*). m.1776-89.
Antoine. *Paris* (*Rue Aubry le Boucher*). m. 1779-89.
v. HÉLIE.
HÉMEL, Jean. *Paris.* 1771 m.
HEMING, Thomas. *London.* 1744-75.
HEMINGWAY, John. *Manchester.* ca.1820. Also HEMMINGWAY. Watch.
HEMMEN, Edward. *London.* 1710-60. Watch mt. G.M. Watch London M.
HEMMERLING—
Jean George. *Vevey.* 1724. Made clock for St. Jean. 1733.
F. H. *Vevey.* Mid. 18c. Made clock for Hôtel de Ville.
HEMMING, Charles. *London.* a.1679.
HEMMINGS—
Thomas. *London* (*Air St.*). 1744. d.1777. W. & T.C.
William. *London.* an.1751. Watch.
HEMMINS (HEMINS)—
Joseph. *Banbury.* 1741. Made clock for Banbury Church, now in S. Newington Church.
Edward. *Bicester.* d.1744. 'Ingenious C.' rep. br. clock.
HEMON, ——. *Paris.* 1812. C.
HEMONY, Hans. *Zütphen.* Mid. 17c. Famous maker of carillons.
HEMSLEY, Richard. *London.* a.1722.

HÉNARD—
Jean François. *Paris.* m.1736.
Veuve. *Paris.* 1789.
HENCHE, Uldrich. *London.* 1605. Clock at Whitehall, 'in manner of a branch.'
HENCHER, Thomas. *Musselburgh.* 1776.
HENCHOZ—
Louis. *London.* 1744. Insolvent.
——. *Paris.* 1775 m.
HENCKE, Johann Gottlieb. *Ansbach.* 1751-1755. Town C.
HENDERSON—
John. *London.* 1662 CC.
Robert. *Scarborough.* ca.1705-50. l.c. clock. Watch.
Eunice. *London.* a.1712.
Robert. *Edinburgh.* 1750. Watch S.K.M.
William. *Edinburgh.* a.1760.
George. *Edinburgh.* a.1762.
Robert. *London.* 1768-1805. br. clock. mus. clock Peiping M. Watch.
Thomas. *London.* an.1777. Watch.
Thomas. *Hull.* 1770. Watch.
Francis. *Musselburgh.* 1790.
Francis. *Edinburgh.* 1794.
James. *Dublin.* 1795-1824.
John. *Edinburgh.* a.1795-1808. W. to the King.
R. T. *London.* 1800.
John. *Dunfermline.* 1820.
George. *Ballibay.* 1824.
John. *Monaghan.* 1824.
Ebenezer. *Dunfermline.* 1826.
HENDON, James. *London.* an.1772. Watch.
HENDRICK—
John. *Liverpool.* 1790-1814.
John & Peter. *Liverpool.* ca.1820. br. clock, inlaid brass.
HENDRICKSON, John. *London.* 1652.
HENDRIE, James. *Wigton.* b.1680-1721. l.c. clocks.
HENDRIKS, Obbe. *Harlingen.* 18c. l.c. clock.
HENDSCHELL, *v.* HENTZSCHELL.
HENDY, Walcott. *London.* a.1710.
HENEY, Richard. *London.* a.1646.
HENFREY, William. *Leicester.* 1815. C. & W.
HENGEL, Georg. *Vienna.* m.1786.
HENGELER, Johann Michael. *Münich.* 1799-1802.
HENGGELER—
Antoine. *Chaux-de-Fonds.* 1784-1803. C.
Christian. *Chaux-de-Fonds.* 1813-40. C.
François, son of Antoine. *Chaux-de-Fonds, Basle, France,* and *Germany.* 1816-21. C.
HENKELS, Jan. *Amsterdam.* 1780. Watch Gemeente M., The Hague. cal. and mus. l.c. clock.
HENLEIN, Peter. *Nürnberg.* b.ca.1479, d. 1542. Master locksmith in 1509. At his death called 'vrmacher.' The first man known to have made a watch, about 1510. The Raths of Nürnberg ordered several watches from him between 1521 and 1525. Cocclaeus calls him Hele and Dopplmayr Heinlein, but in the Nürnberg Archives he is always referred to as Henlein.
HENLEY—
——. *York.* an.1765. Watch.
J. *London.* an.1801. Watch.
HENNEQUIN, ——. *Paris.* 1812-25.
HENNER—
Georg. *Heidelberg.* ca.1700. sil. trav. clock.
Johann. *Würzburg.* m.1709, d.1756. Court C. A good maker. sil. watch S.K.M. p.c. sil. chased watch Luitprandt M. g. watch Feill coll. hex. table clock and stand clock.
ET TRAUNER. *Würzburg.* 1753-6. Partnership with his son-in-law, Johann TRAUNER. Watch Luitprandt M.
HENNING, Henry. *Lymington.* an.1782-95. Watch.
HENNINGER, Simon. *St. Georgen.* End 17c. Said to have been the first C. in the Schwarzwald. *v.* FREY.
HENNINGK, ——. *Brunswick.* 1499-1505. 'Seigermacher.'
HENRICH, ——. *Cologne.* 1586. From *Kaiserswerth.*
HENRIOT, ——. *Geneva.* a.1790. 4-colour g. watch S.K.M. ill. Baillie.
HENRISON, Mos. *London.* ca.1730. g. rep. watch.
HENRY—
Claude. *Lyons.* a.1595, m.1610-23. d. an. 1628. Oval sil. watch Spitzer coll. Watch Fränkel coll.
Adrien. *Blois.* 1653-60.
Peter. *London.* an.1745. Watch.
Stephen. *London.* a.1760.
Pierre. *Paris (Quai de l'Horloge).* b.1744, d. 1806. C. to the King. Nephew of J. A. LEPAUTE and in his business. When J. B. LEPAUTE retired in 1789, worked with Pierre Basile LEPAUTE, retiring in 1798. His son Augustin Michel established himself as HENRY NEVEU LEPAUTE. *v.* LEPAUTE.
Léopold (SCHARFFENSTEIN dit L. Henri). *Paris.* m.1782-9.
——. *Falmouth.* ca.1790 CC.
——. *Geneva.* ca.1800. Painter on enamel.
——. *Belfast.* ca.1800. Watch Belfast M.
Augustin Michel *v.* A. M. H. LEPAUTE.
W. & S. *London.* 1802-04.
Stephen. *London (Pentonville).* 1802-04.
W. & P. *London.* 1805-11.
William. *London (Coldbath Fields).* 1805-11.
Stephen. *London (Brook St.).* 1810-40.
William. *London (Islington).* 1820.
Patrick. *Dublin.* 1824.
William. *Cork.* an.1827. Watch.
'HENRY RANDEL.' Sig. on 1869-70 watches of the UNITED STATES WATCH Co.
HENSELER, D. *Cologne.* 1813.
HENSHAW—
Walter. *London.* CC.1667, m.CC.1695-1707. math. inst. maker.
John, son. *London.* a.1689, CC.1696-1716.
——. *London (High Holborn).* 1748. W.
Isaac. *London.* Early 19c. Watch.
HENSON, William. *London.* a.1799, CC.1807.
HENTSCHEL, J. J. *Strasbourg.* ca.1770. rep. watch.
HENTZLER—
Joseph. *Vienna.* m.1778. Also HÄNZLER and HENZLE.
Frantz. *Vienna.* m.1815. Also HENSLER.
HENTZSCHELL—
Johann Erhardt. *Giessen.* 1698. Planisphere and l.c. clock Cassel Landes-M.
Johann Jakob. *Basle.* 1745. From *Darmstadt.* Hanging night-light clock.
HEPBURN, John. *Perth.* 1769.
HEPP, Ulrich. *Augsburg.* 1766.
HEPPET, James. *Didsbury.* d.1781. W.
HEPTON—
Thomas. *Northallerton.* ca.1770-1823.
William. *Northallerton.* 1777-1858. Watch.
HERALD, ——. *London.* an.1744. Watch.
HERAPATH, William. *London.* 1825. Pub. art. in Phil. Mag. on a 'New Compensation Pendulum.'
HERBAULT, Louis François. *Paris.* m.1743, juré 1761-89. br. clock Bernal sale.
HERBEAU, ——. Late 18c. g. en. watch S.K.M. g. watch Fränkel coll.
HERBERT—
Edward. *London.* a.1657, CC.1664-77.
Cornelius. *London (London Br.).* a.1660, CC.1667-89. Watch mt. G.M. Watch Ilbert coll. Also HARBERT and HARBOTTLE.
William. *London.* a.1663, CC.1671-1715. Watch Den. coll.

HERBERT—*continued.*
Thomas. *London* (*Whitehall*). CC.1676-1708. C. to the King. Tortoise-shell br. clock Weth. coll.
John. *London.* a.1672, CC.1682-1713.
Evan. *London.* a.1680, CC.1691. Watch.
Cornelius, son of Cornelius. *London* (*London Br.*). a.1690, CC.1700, m.CC.1727, d.1751. A fine maker. l.c. clock Weth. coll. Also HARBERT and HARBOTTLE.
Morgan. *London.* ca.1700. str. watch Den. coll.
Edward, son of John. *London.* CC.1711-40.
Henry, son of William. *London.* CC.1714.
Cornelius, son of Cornelius (2). *London.* a.1727, CC.1735-74. sil. str. watch.
——. *Oxford.* an.1755. Watch.
William. *London* (*Fenchurch St.*). 1779.
Robert. *S. Shields.* an.1782. Watch.
William. *Edinburgh.* a.1785-91.
L. *London.* 1828. Pub. art. in Trans. Soc. Arts on the 'Application of prepared Plumbago instead of oil for Chronometers.'
HERBIER, P. *Grenoble.* Early 17c. crys. en. cross watch.
HERBIN, Jean Pierre. *Paris.* m.1788.
HERBSTREIT (HERBSTRIETH, HEBSTREIT)—
Jakob. *Hinterzarten* (*Schwarzwald*). 1730-1760.
Jakob, son. *Hinterzarten* and *Neukirch.* 1770. d.1801. The Black Forest type of small hanging clock was first made by him; called 'Jockele-Uhren' after him.
HERCLEN, Peter. *Vienna.* d.1662.
HERDMAN, Robert. 1728. *Belfast.* C.
HEREFORD, Joseph. *London.* an.1789. Watch.
HERGAULT, Auguste. *Paris.* 1824.
HERGETT, J. A. *Cassel.* ca.1725.
HERING, Joseph. *London.* an.1742. Watch. cf. HERRING.
HERITAGE, ——. *Stratford-on-Avon.* an. 1800. Watch.
HERLIN, Sigfred. *Copenhagen.* m.1811.
HERMAN—
Dom Joseph. *Gruyère.* b.1752, d.1820. Monk who made clock with ingenious automata, ill. M. des Aut.
Peter. *Leeds.* 1817. C.
HERMANN—
Christoph. *Friedberg.* mar.1731.
Carl. *Pfersen.* 1770.
Johann Gottlob. *Leipzig.* 1814.
HERMANT, A. J. *Paris.* 1809-25.
HERMELINK—
W. *Amsterdam.* ca.1750. mus. br. clock.
Jan. *Amsterdam.* 2nd half 18c. l.c. clock.
HERN, John. *London.* a.1802.
HERNE, Edward. *London.* a.1680.
HERON—
Henry. *London.* a.1632. Under BC.
J. *Newtown* (*Wales*). ca.1750. Watch Nat. M. Cardiff.
Erskine. *Edinburgh.* a.1752. *Charleston, U.S.A.* 1765. C. & W.
Isaac. *New Jersey.* 1764. *New York.* 1766-1780. Watch of English make G.M.
William. *Donegal.* ca.1780. Clock.
William. *Newtownards.* 1784.
John. *Greenock.* 1797-1822.
William. *Liverpool.* 1800-03. W.
George. *Newcastle-o.-T.* Early 19c. Watch.
Alexander. *Newtownards.* 1824.
HÉRON, Pierre. *Paris.* m.1788.
HEROY, Noel. *Paris.* 1783.
HERR, B. Jacob. *Fürth.* d.1779.
HERRDEGEN, R. A. *Fürth.* d.ca.1800.
HERRFLING, ——. *Fürth.* d.ca.1820.
HERRICK, Henry. *London.* a.1800.
HERRING—
Joshua. *London* (*Cornhill*). 1742, d.1763. br.clock.
Mark. *London* (*Cornhill*). an.1760. Watch.
Joseph. *London.* l.CC.1767-1804. *Farringdon* in 1793. W. cf. HERING.
Richard. *Newark.* 1791-1810. l.c. clocks. Watch.
Thomas. *London.* ca.1800. l.c. clock.
Charles. *East Grinstead.* Early 19c. Watch.
William Hawley. *London.* a.1815.
HERRIS, William. *London.* a.1682.
HERRMANN & CO. *Kings Lynn.* Early 19c. Watch.
HERRON, John. *Blyth.* Early 19c. Watch.
HERRSTRÖM—
Daniel. *Stockholm.* 1788-90. Wall and br. clocks and watch.
Magnus. *Stockholm.* 1795-1800.
HERSANT, Pierre. *Blois.* mar.1638. *Paris,* 1639. d. *Blois,* 1662.
HERSENT—
——. *Paris* (*Rue Pierre Lescot*). 1810.
——. *Paris* (*Rue St. Honoré*). 1810-12.
HERTNER, James. *Belfast.* 1824.
HERTZ, Girarde. ——. Early 19c. g. mus. rep. watch.
HERVAIS, ——. *Paris.* 1818-25. Watches and pedometers.
HERVÉ, ——. *Paris.* Mid. 18c. g. engine turned watch Gélis coll.
HERVEY—
William. *Brentford.* an.1773. Watch.
C. P. *New York.* Early 19c.
HERZOG, Johann Jakob. *Basle.* b.1650, a.1662, d.1708.
HESBERT, Jean. *Rouen.* m.1663.
HESCOTT, Richard. *Prescot.* ca.1760. Watch.
HESELWOOD, David. *Hull.* ca.1770.
HESKETH, William. *Liverpool.* 1825. W.
HESKEY, Henry. *Manchester.* 1781. W.
HESPE, Andr. Ad. *Hannover.* 18c. Watch Cassel Landes-M.
HESS—
Leonhard. *Stavanger.* m.1758.
L. *Zürich.* 1780.
Leonhard. *Bergen.* m.1785-1800. Watch Furt. M.
Rosetta. *Liverpool.* 1825. W.
HESSE—
Henry. *London.* 1775.
John. *London.* a.1768.
HESSEN, André. *Paris.* m.1775-90; then *Stockholm.* C. to French King's brother. Pub. 'Mém. sur l'Horlogerie.' London. 1785. g. en. watch Fränkel coll. l.c. clock. Fine mantel clock. g. rep. watch. Watch with special lever escapement. Many works sd. in Paris. One sd. in Stockholm.
HESSENBOS, P. *Amsterdam.* 1822. W.
HESSICHTI, Dionistus. *Pomerania.* 1627. Book-watch ill. Britten, from Bernal sale. Made for Bogislaw XIV.
HESSIG, Samuel. *Arad.* Early 19c. sil. watch Fränkel coll.
HESTER—
Henry. *London.* CC.1671, d.1717.
Henry, son. *London.* a.1679, CC.1689-1707.
William. *London.* a.1695.
Thomas. *London.* a.1702.
HETON, James. *London.* a.1697.
HEUREUT, Lewis L. *London.* an.1778. Watch.
HEURTAULT, Daniel. *Lyons.* 1626 comp.
HEURTIER, Pierre. *Paris.* m.1757.
HEUSS, Jörg (Georg). *Nürnberg.* m.1499. d. after 1520. A locksmith. Renewed the clock and aut. on the Frauenkirche, 1506-1509.
HEWER, George. *Essington.* 1st half 18c. Watch.
HEWERDINE, ——. *Stilton.* Early 19c. Watch.

HEWES—
——. *London*. 1630. Subscribed for incorporation of CC. *v.* HUE.
Robert. *Colchester*. 18c. l.c. clock.
HEWFELT, Andreas. *Nürnberg*. Burgher in 1487. 'Ormacher.'
HEWINS, Edward. *Bicester*. ca.1700. Lantern clock.
HEWISON, Charles. *London*. 1798. Watch N.Y. Univ.
HEWITSON, Thomas. *London*. a.1748.
HEWITT (HEWETT)—
Alexander. *London*. a.1685. CC.
Thomas. *London*. a.1685.
George. *Marlborough*. ca.1720-69. Maker of astro. and mus. clocks. l.c. clock.
John. *London*. 1724 CC.
Alexander. *London*. a.1714, CC.1725, d. 1746. Watch mt.
Benjamin. *London*. a.1715, CC.1724.
James. *Sunderland*. 1749-52. W.
Alexander, son of Alex. *London*. a.1743.
Thomas. *London*. a.1749.
William. *London* (*Tooley St.*). 1765. CC. 1771-85.
John. *London*. a.1761.
Richard. *London*. an.1772. Watch.
Samuel. *London*. a.1764.
Joshua. *Prescot*. End 18c. d.1802 Invented a pinion cutting engine.
R. *Fowey*. 1795. W.
George F., jun. *Marlborough*. 1795. C. & W.
HEWITTON, W. Kilshall. prob. *London*. an. 1773. Watch.
HEWKLEY—
John. *London*. CC.1732.
Squire. *London* (*Jewin St.*). a.1733, CC. 1741-78.
Squire, son. *Lonaon* (*Red Cross St.*). CC. 1764, d.1782.
John, bro. *London* (*Alfred Court*). a.1762, CC.1775, d.1819.
James Snelling, bro. *London*. a.1776, CC. 1788-1820.
John, son of John. *London*. a.1804.
HEWLETT—
Isaac. *Bristol*. 1743. d.1778. C. & W.
Andrew. *Bristol*. 1746. W.
Joshua. *Bristol*. 1749. d.1764. W. Partner with Isaac above.
Isaac. *Bristol*. 1779-93. W.
William. *Bristol*. 1781-1801. W.
HEWLINGS, Joseph. *London*. a.1794.
HEWSON, John. *London*. a.1683, CC.1699-1709.
HEYBACH, Nikolaus. *Nürnberg*. ca.1430. 'Oriogista.' Torquetum of 1434.
HEYDE, ——. *Cassel*. 1738. Court C.
HEYDEN, Christian. *Nürnberg*. b.1526, d. 1576. C. and mathematician. Celestial globe clock and sun- and moon-dial M.P.S. Dresden. Dial Old Ashmolean M. Made an astro. clock and several others for Maximilian II, and worked for the Dresden Court.
HEYDER, Jan. *Amsterdam*. ca.1760. Watch mt. S.K.M.
HEYDON, Samuel. *London*. an.1772. Watch.
HEYERN, ——. *Berlin*. 1785.
HEYLAND, Robert. prob. *London*. an.1787. Watch.
HEYLIN—
John. *London*. an.1771. Watch.
Isaac. *London*. a.1786, CC.1795.
HEYM, A. W. *Leipzig*. 1800-14.
HEYMAN, George. prob. *London*. an.1745. Watch.
HEYWOOD—
——. *London*. 1630. Subscriber to incorporation of CC.
Samuel. *Northwich*. 1784. l.c. clock.
William. *London*. 1817-40.

'H. N. HIBBARD.' Sig. on 1871-4 watches of the CORNELL WATCH Co.
HIBBEN, Andrew. *Charleston, U.S.A.* 1765. C. & W.
HICCOCK, Samuel. *Chester*. 1679. C.
HICCOX, John. *London*. a.1650, CC.1657-62. rep. watch.
HICHES, Thomas. *London*. a.1810.
HICK, Matthew. *York*. 1812. d.1834. W.
HICKMAN—
John. *London*. 1748. Watch.
Joseph. *London* (*Basinghall St.*). 1775-81.
HICKS—
Thomas. *London*. CC.1664-99.
Thomas. *London*. CC.1666.
John. *London*. a.1685.
John. *London*. a.1686, CC.1694-9.
David. *London*. a.1753.
John. *London*. a.1753-99.
Samuel. *London*. ca.1780. p.c. cyl. rep. watch G.M.
James. *Bristol*. 1781. C.
Willet. *New York*. 1790.
James. *London*. 1802-15.
Charles. *London*. 1809-24.
Thomas. *London*. a.1810.
J. *Midhurst*. an.1821. Watch.
Charles. *Liverpool*. 1824-9.
HICKSON—
Thomas. *London*. CC.1690-1706.
William. *London*. a.1708.
HIDE—
John. *London*. a.1637.
Samuel. *London*. a.1731.
Charles. *Banbury*. an.1759. Watch.
Ralph. *Sunderland*. ca.1770.
HIGDON—
Thomas. *East Pennard*. Mid. 18c.
John, bro. *Wells* (*Somerset*). Mid. 18c.
Panteness, bro. *Bruton*. Mid. 18c.
P. *Brewham*. ca.1760. l.c. clock.
HIGGINBOTHAM—
Henry. *Macclesfield*. ca.1780. l.c. clock.
John. *Macclesfield*. 1791. C. & W.
Joseph. *Wexford*. 1824.
HIGGINBOTTOM, William. *London*. a.1722.
HIGGINS—
Banger (Berenger). *London*. a.1715, CC. 1724, d.1748. Watch cap maker.
Thomas. *London*. a.1727, CC.1735-64. l.c. clock.
Thomas, son. *London*. a.1755, CC.1764.
Thomas. *London*. CC.1790.
Andrew. *London* (*Edmonton*). Early 19c.
HIGGINSON—
Nicholas. *London*. 1662.
Henry. *London*. CC.1662.
Henry. *Liverpool*. d.1694. W.
Nathaniel. *London*. 1692 CC.
Samuel. *London*. a.1688, CC.1698, d.an. 1736.
John. *London*. 1698 CC.
Samuel. *Chatham*. 1725. Insolvent. C.
George, son of Samuel. *London*. CC.1736-1758. Very fine mus. aut. clock Peiping M. Agate heart-shaped rep. watch set rubies and emeralds Wilsdorf coll.
Richard. *Fazakerley*. 1743. Watch Den. coll.
Joseph. *London* (*Shadwell*). 1744. W.
Matthew. *London*. 1st half 18c. Watch.
Robert. *Chester*. mar.1777-84. W.
John. *London*. 1785-1824. Succeeded by WILSON. Watch.
Thomas. *Liverpool*. 1805. W.
HIGGS—
John. *London*. CC.1661.
John. *London*. a.1681, CC.1688-1722.
Robert. *London*. a.1699, CC.1714-31. br. clock.
Thomas. *London*. a.1706, CC.1716, d.an. 1733.

HIGGS—*continued.*
James. *London.* a.1717.
Richard. *London.* 1730 CC.
John. *London.* a.1727.
Richard. *London.* a.1730.
Peter, son of Robert. *London.* a.1731, CC. 1740, m.CC. and d.1767.
Edward, son of Thomas. *London.* a.1733.
Richard. *Portsmouth.* 1749. Bankrupt.
Robert. *London* (*Sweetings Alley*). 1743. CC.1750-69. l.c. and br. clock and watch.
Robert & Peter. *London* (*Sweetings Alley*). 1770. Watch ca.1775 sd. 'Rob. & Pet. Higgs & Jas. Evans,' Ilbert coll. clock.
& EVANS. *London* (*Sweetings Alley* and later *R. Exchange*). 1775-1825. Firm of Rob. and Peter and Jas. EVANS. cyl. watch S.M.S.K. Watch mts. G.M. and Glasgow Art Gall. g. en. watch sd. 'Higg y Evens.' str. chiming mus. aut. br. clock ill. Cec. & Web. l.c. and br. clock ill. Britten. br. clock Virginia M. sd. 'Higgs y Diego Evans.'
William. *Oswestry.* 1778.
James. *Wallingford.* 1791. C.

HIGHAM, Thomas. *London.* a.1796, CC. 1803-24. W.

HIGHFIELD—
Josiah. *Liverpool.* 1761-73. W.
William. *Liverpool.* 1761. Later *Wrexham* and *Oswestry.* 1778. W.
Josiah. *London.* an.1781. Watch.
Samuel. *London.* 1802-04. W.

HIGHGATE, John. *London.* 1799. W.

HIGHLAND, Robert. *London.* an.1788. Watch.

HIGHMORE—
Edward. *London.* a.1680, CC.1687.
Lancaster. *London.* a.1685.
Richard. *London.* a.1714.
Jacob. *London.* 1790.

HIGHO—
John. *London* (*Shoreditch*). 1791. W.
John, son. *London.* a.1791.

HIGHT, Christian. *Philadelphia.* 1813-20. W.

HIGHTEM, Thomas. *London.* a.1796, CC. 1803.

HIGHTSMAN, George. *London* (*Norton Folgate*). 1817-24. C.

HIGMAN—
Jacob. *London.* CC.1788-1801.
Jacob. *St. Austell.* 1808-22 CC.

HIGNAR (HICNAR), Jean. *Copenhagen.* b. 1695 in *France.* 1750 in *Copenhagen.* d. 1762.

HIGNETT—
John. *London.* an.1751. Watch.
Richard. *London.* a.1795, CC.1805.

HILAR, ——. ——. 1556. Dial M.P.S. Dresden.

HILBERT, Bartholomäus. *Berlin.* 1794. Wooden C.

HILDEBRANDT, Johann Christian. *Nürnberg.* 1720. sil. rep. watch Den. coll. Watch Stuttgart M.

HILDEBURN—
Samuel. *Philadelphia.* 1811-24.
& WOODWORTH. *Philadelphia.* 1819.

HILDERSON, John. *London.* 1657.

HILDEYARD, Thomas. *Rotherwas* (*Hereford*) and *Liége.* b.1690, d.1747. Devised modified verge escapement for clock at Liége, which was desc. in a book pub. in Liége 1726 and in London 1727.

HILGER, ——. *Paris.* Late 18c.-1812. Mantel clock Petit Palais, Paris.

HILL—
John. *London.* 1630. Petitioner for incorporation of CC.
Thomas. *London.* CC.1632.
Benjamin. *London.* CC.1640, m.CC.1657, d.1670. A fine maker. sil. pomegranate watch G.M. g. filigree watch ill. Baillie and shagreen watch B.M. 16-lobed crys. watch S.K.M.
Abraham. ——. 1664. Patented the idea of using a pendulum clock at sea for finding the longitude.
Francis. *London.* a.1664, CC.1672.
John, son of Benjamin. *London.* CC.1670.
Francis. *London.* a.1672, CC.1679-1700.
William. *London.* a.1682.
Thomas. *London.* ca.1690. l.c. clock sd. 'Thomas Hill & Henry Harper,' Ironmongers Co.
Edward. *London.* a.1690, CC.1698-1718.
John. *London.* a.1692, CC.1703-15. l.c. clock.
Philip. *London.* a.1695.
John. *London.* CC.1705-30.
James. *London.* a.1702.
Thomas. *London.* a.1703.
John. *London* (*Seven Dials*). a.1712, CC. 1731-70.
Mark. *London.* a.1714.
Thomas. *London.* a.1715.
William. *Walsingham.* an.1743-64. Bankrupt. Watch.
Matthew. *London.* 1744-ca.1790. In 1777 moved from *Devonshire St.* to *Upper Charlotte St.* Watch.
Thomas. *London. Devonshire St.* in 1749, *Fleet St.* in 1762, d.1782.
Thomas, son. *London.* 1783, continues the business.
Thomas. *London.* a.1751.
Thomas. *London* (*Aldersgate St.*). ca.1760-1784. Watch mt. br. clock.
David. *Edinburgh.* 1761.
Edward. *London.* a.1759.
John. *Prescot.* ca.1770-95. W.
John. *Peterborough.* Went to *Wisbech* in 1771. C. & W.
Arthur. prob. *London.* an.1772. Watch.
Thomas. *Lambourn.* an.1776. Watch.
James. *London.* a.1765-1810.
Thomas. *London.* CC.1783.
Samuel. *Sheffield.* 1781-1811. l.c. clocks. Watch.
James Coysgarne. *London.* 1788.
Thomas. London. CC.1789.
Robert. *Stafford.* CC.1795. C. & W.
Sampson Coysgarne. *London.* CC.1795-1824.
Francis. *London.* 1799.
William Bewley. *Coventry.* 1802. W. Partnership of RYLEY, ROE & HILL dissolved 1807.
Ann. *London.* 1805-08.
Richard. *Liverpool.* 1807-14. W.
John. *London* (*Seven Dials*). 1817-24.
John. *London* (*Covent Gdn.*). 1820-4.
John Roe. *Clonmel.* 1824.
Robert. *Penrith.* Early 19c.

HILLCOAT, William. *London.* 1790.

HILLDOR, Daniel. *London.* a.1705.

HILLEFELT, Johan. *Bergen.* 1759 m.

HILLENBRAND, Joh. Joseph. *Augsburg.* ca. 1760. g. rep. watch M.P.S. Dresden.

HILLERY, John. *London.* a.1681.

HILLIAR—
Richard. *London.* a.1723, CC.1740.
Thomas. *Frome.* 1795. W.

HILLIARD—
James. *Charleston, U.S.A.* 1738. C. & W.
——. *London* (*Bunhill Row*). d.1767. W.
H. *London.* 1815.

HILLIER—
William. *London.* a.1669, CC.1679-1733. Also HILLYARD.
William. *London.* a.1760.
William. *London* (*Aldersgate*). a.1762, CC. 1769, d.1807.

HILLIER—*continued.*
Joseph. *London.* a.1780.
James. *London.* 1802-07.
George. *London* (*Cheapside*). CC.1807-20.
HILLINGS, Bernard. *London.* CC.1652. From *Antwerp.*
HILLIUS, Martin. *Dresden.* m.1668. One of the first four members of the clockmakers' guild. Watch and plate clock, set stones, M.P.S. Dresden.
HILLMANN, William. *Plymouth Dock.* 1770.
HILLS—
John. *London.* a.1712, CC.1728.
Mathew. *London.* a.1759.
Ralph. *Sunderland.* ca.1775-1820. W.
Benjamin. *Sudbury.* Early 19c. Watch.
'HILLSIDE.' Sig. on watches from 1882 of the AMERICAN WATCH Co., predecessor of the WALTHAM WATCH Co.
HILLSON, Richard. *Plympton.* 1795. C.
HILTEL, Christian. *Regensburg.* Early 19c. sil. p.c. rep. watch.
HILTON—
Thomas. *London.* a.1674.
John. *London.* a.1690 to TOMPION, CC.1698.
Emanuel. *Portsmouth.* ca.1775. l.c. clock ill. Cec. & Web.
Senai. *London.* an.1808. Watch sd. NOTLIH.
E. *London.* 1824.
HIMBERT, Louis. *Paris.* 1817-22.
HIMER, Jean Jacques. *Paris.* Juré 1779.
HIMLY—
——. *Paris.* Early 18c. Watch Feill coll.
——. *La Neuveville.* Early 18c. Watch.
Péterman. *La Sagne* and *La Neuveville.* a. 1707. Watch.
R. *Strasbourg.* 1735.
HIND, James. *London.* a.1814.
HINDE—
John. *London.* 1680 CC.
Joseph. *London.* a.1708.
John. *London.* 1767. With five sons, all Lancaster freemen, worked in London as math. inst. makers.
HINDHAUGH, Joseph. *S. Shields.* 1776. Watch. C.
HINDLE, James. *London.* a.1804.
HINDLEY—
——. *York.* ca.1700. Wall clock ill. Britten.
Henry. *York.* b.1701, d.1771. A very able maker of watches, clocks and turret clocks. Invented a wheel-cutting machine. Made clock for York Cathedral in 1750. Watch S.K.M. Regulator with pin-wheel escapement.
——. *Wigan.* ca.1760. l.c. clock Virginia M.
Joseph. *York.* 1754. d. at *Hull* 1774. Made clock for Trinity Church, Hull.
HINDON, William. prob. *London.* an.1766. Watch.
HINE—
Thomas. *London* (*Fleet St.*). an.1766. Watch. Watch mt.
John. *Watlington.* 1777. Sale of stock. C. & W.
John. *London.* 1790.
HINEMORE—
John. *London.* a.1733, CC.1741-71. d.an. 1777.
George, son. *London.* CC.1771-85.
John, bro. *London.* CC.1777.
HINES—
John. *Ipswich.* From 1774. From *Harwich.* C. & W.
John. *Needham Market.* 1784. cf. John HINDE.
HINKS, William. *Southampton.* an.1762. Watch.
HINKSMAN—
James. *Sutton Maddock.* 1760. C.
James. *Bridgnorth.* 1786-94. W.
HINMERS, Robert. *Edinburgh.* a.1779-1809.
HINSTOCK, William. *London.* 1799. W.
HINNOTT, Samuel. *London.* 1700.
HINTON—
James. *London.* an.1758. Watch.
John. *London.* a.1787-1835.
Josiah. *London.* 1805-08. W.
HINTSCHE, Matthis. *Strasbourg.* 1689.
HINTZCH—
Jacob Hans. *Göteborg.* b.1627, d.1697. Also HINSCH.
N. *Göteborg.* 1684. Perhaps same as above.
HINZE, Ulrich. *Brunswick.* 1594. From *Wolfenbüttel. Halberstadt* in 1600. The first W. in Brunswick.
HIORNE—
John. *London.* a.1699, CC.1707, m.CC. 1744-9.
William, son. *London.* CC.1741.
James, bro. *London.* CC.1748.
HIPP, Matthäus. *Ulm, Saint-Gallen, St. Aubin, Reutlingen, Berne and Neuchâtel.* b.1813, d.1893. Famous for work on electrical clocks.
HIRSCH, Carl Christian. *Copenhagen.* m. 1823.
HIRSCHAUER, ——. *Dresden.* ca.1770. g. en. watch, porcelain case watch.
HIRST, Samuel. *Leeds.* 1780-1807. W.
HIRT, Friedrich Christian. *Durlach.* 1685-1749. Painted landscapes having church towers fitted with going clocks.
HISETTE, ——. *Metz.* ca.1820. Clock in polished steel case.
HISLOP—
Adam. *Biggar.* b.1753, d.1827.
Richard. *London.* 1799-1803.
John. *Peebles.* b.1780, d.1856.
Richard, son of Richard. *London.* 1805-40.
William. *London.* 1820. d.1876.
Alexander. *Greenock.* 1821.
Alexander. *Liverpool.* 1825. W.
HITCHCOCK—
John. *London.* a.1697, CC.1718-22.
James. *London.* an.1773. Watch.
William. *Chard.* 1795. C. & W.
HITCHEN—
John. *London.* a.1707, CC.1720-49 Watch. Also HITCHINS.
Oliver. prob. *London.* an.1783. Watch.
HITCHILLS, Matthew. *Mansfield.* 1791. C.
HITCHIN, Joseph. *London.* an.1776-90. Watch.
HITCHMAN, Nicholas. *London.* a.1677.
HITTAS, John. prob. *London.* an.1778. Watch.
HITZINGER—
Jacob. *Vienna.* m.1779.
Joseph. *Vienna.* m.1808. Also HIETZINGER.
HJELMQVIST, N. Asa. *Hjälmaryd.* 18c. Clock. *v.* ELMQWIST, N. M.
HJERPE, Anders. *Stockholm.* 1818. d.an.1836. br. clock.
HOADLEY—
Benjamin. *London.* an.1777. Watch.
Samuel and Luther. *Winsted, U.S.A.* 1807. With Riley WHITING, made wooden clocks.
Silas. *Greystone, U.S.A.* b.1786, d.1870. In firm of TERRY, THOMAS & HOADLEY, 1809. THOMAS & HOADLEY, 1810-3, and then alone till 1849.
HOARE—
Charles. *London.* a.1711.
Joshua. *London.* a.1723.
HOBART—
George. *London.* CC.1717-37. Bankrupt.
Gabriel. *York.* 1750. W.
J. prob. *London.* an.1754. Watch.
William. *London* (*Borough*). 1805-08.
William. *London* (*Bermondsey*), 1809-24.
HOBBINS, Job. *London.* a.1695.

HOBBS—
William. *London.* a.1672.
Allin. *London.* a.1727, CC.1734-44.
William. *London.* a.1786.
HOBENS, Alphée. *Toulouse.* Mid. 17c. Watch.
HOBERG, Anders. *Stockholm.* b.1766, d. 1834. Verge and cyl. watches, one Nord. M.
HOBLER—
Paul. *London.* 1770. CC.1781-90. g. str. watch.
Francis. *London (Porter St.).* an.1761-90. Also sd. RELBOH. Watch Den. coll.
HOBRAN, Jean. *Paris.* 1609. Proposed as juré, but not elected.
HOBRICH (HOLRICH), Pierre. *Wissembourg.* b.1737, guillotined 1794.
HOBSON, John. *London.* 1630. Petitioner for incorporation of CC.
HOCHENADEL—
Andreas, sen. *Vienna.* m.1743. g. en. watch Stern. coll.
Benedetto. *Venice.* Mid. 18c. Watch, Turkish figures, Ilbert coll.
Franz, sen. *Vienna.* m.1775.
Johan. *Lintz-a.-D.* 2nd half 18c. Watch mt. Arts M. Prague.
Andre, jun. *Vienna.* m.1783. Also HOHENADL.
Adalbert. *Vienna* and *Venice.* m.1798. br. clock.
HOCHENALL, ——. *Vienna.* Late 18c. g. watch.
HOCHICORN, Isaac. *London.* a.1720, CC. 1728-32.
HOCKER—
John. *Reading.* 1682. Watch mt. G.M. Lantern clock.
John. *London.* a.1714, CC.1729-40.
John. *London.* a.1715.
John, son of John. *Reading.* CC.1729, d.1756. l.c. lacquer and gesso clock ill. Cec. & Web. Watch mt.
Joseph, bro. *Basingstoke.* 1730. *Reading* later. l.c. clocks.
HOCKERS, G. *Ephrata, Lancaster, U.S.A.* 1750. Tower clock for Ephrata cloister.
HOCKEY, Charles. *Stalbridge.* 1790. C.
HOCKLEY, ——. *Windsor.* an.1775. Sun and moon watch.
HOCKSON, John. *London.* Early 18c. Watch, tortoise-shell case.
HODDLE—
John. *Reading.* 1688. Lantern clocks.
John. *London.* a.1697, CC.1704, d.1751. Watch engraver. *v.* GRILLIAT.
Richard. *London.* a.1724.
HODGE—
Charles. *Edinburgh.* a.1752-9.
——. *Dartmouth.* 1791. W.
John. *Plymouth Dock.* 1795 CC.
H. *London.* End 18c. Watch.
HODGES—
Nathaniel. *London.* CC.1681-ca.1695. br. clock Weth. coll. Lantern clock and br. clock ill. Cec. & Web.
——. *Portsmouth.* an.1719. Watch.
William. *London.* a.1712, CC.1719-31.
John. *London.* 1729 in *Clements Lane.* 1738 in *Exchange Alley.* W.
William. *London.* a.1739.
Samuel. *London.* CC.1770.
James. *Dorking* and later *Shoreditch.* 1774. Insolvent.
John. *Dorchester.* 1790. C.
James. *London.* ca.1800. l.c. clock Weth. coll.
Frederick. *Dublin.* 1805-24. Rack lever watch mt. G.M.
HODGKINSON—
Sarah. *London.* CC.1700.
George. *London.* a.1811.
M. *Manchester.* Early 19c. Watch.
HODGSON—
Marcus. *York.* 1676, d.1709. W.
Jonathan. *Hexham.* 1784.
Henry. *Lancaster.* 1817. W.
William. *Lancaster.* 1820. l.c. clock.
Thomas. *Durham.* 1820-47.
Robert, & Son. *Annan.* 1820.
HODIERNE, John. *London.* a.1638.
HODMIN, James. *London.* a.1752.
HODSOLL, William. *London.* 1805-08.
HODSON—
John. *London.* a.1666.
Thomas. *Chorley.* d.1756. C.
George. *Bolton-le-Moors.* ca.1770-93. W.
William. *Bolton-le-Moors.* ca.1770-93. W.
Charles. *London.* a.1764.
HOE, Robert or Benjamin. *London.* a.1778.
HOED, F. *Rotterdam.* 1821-30.
HOEFMAN, Pieter. *Haarlem.* 1774. *Leiden.* 1784. sil. en. watch.
HOEVENAAR, Simon. *Holland.* ca.1650.
HOFER—
Stephan. *Soleure.* ca.1780.
Joh. Georg. ——. Early 19c. Watch.
HOFF—
George. *Lancaster City, U.S.A.* b.ca.1740 in *Germany.* Went to *U.S.A.* 1765. d. 1816. Good W. and C. Many l.c. clocks.
Friedrich Karl. *Frankfurt-a.-M.* b.1730, d. 1795. Made clock for Goethe's father. Town C.
Johann, son. *Frankfurt-a.-M.* 1795. Town C.
John, son. *Lancaster City.* d.1816. In business with his father.
HOFFMANN—
Hanns. *Germany.* 1566. Table clock.
Melchior. *Augsburg.* ca.1600. oct. watch. Spherical table clock Feill coll.
Ulrich. *Nürnberg.* 1620. aut. br. clock.
Caspar. *Augsburg.* 17c. Clock Cassel Landes-M.
Johann. *Tyrnau.* ca.1725. sil. trav. clock.
Michael. *Augsburg.* m.1763-70.
HOFFMEYER—
J. *Birmingham.* 1787-95. l.c. clocks.
——. *Berlin.* 1795. Wooden C.
HOFMANN, Konrath. *Vienna.* m.1791.
HOFMAYER, Leopold. *Neustadt.* 1787-91. Made brass wheels for Schwarzwald clocks.
HOG—
Thomas. *Edinburgh.* a.1698.
Charles. *Prestonpans.* 1788.
HOGAN—
——. *Ashwell Thorpe.* an.1756. Watch.
N. *London.* 1805-08. W.
HOGARTH, Thomas. *Berwick-on-Tweed.* 1806-22.
HÖGBERG, Lars Jacobsson. *Malmö.* 1775-1795. Watch mt. Nord. M.
HOGELAND, L. *Amsterdam.* 1822. W.
HOGG—
Jonathan. *Ipswich.* 1784.
Alexander. *Haddington.* 1790.
Alexander. *Salford.* 1804. W.
Robert. *Randalstown.* 1824.
HOGLATE, John. *London.* CC.1734.
HOGUET (HOQUET)—
Aimé. *Dieppe.* ca.1700. Watch.
Toussaint François. *Paris.* 1772. m.1779-89.
Jean Gatien. *Paris.* m.1773-89.
Augustus. *Philadelphia.* 1819-25.
HOHAUS, August. *Glatz.* 1843. Famous turret C. Made clock on Stephansturm, Vienna.
HÖHEER, Johann Christoph. ——. ca.1680. Clock Grüne Gewölbe, Dresden.
HOHENEGGER, Martin. *Vienna.* m.1786.

HOHMANN—
Johann. *Simmershausen*. m.1791. C.
Melchior. *Marktheidenfeld*. m.1793. C.
Johann. *Hilders*. m.1820. C.
HOHWII, Andreas. *Amsterdam*. b.1803, d. 1885. Famous maker of observatory clocks and chron.
HOIJENDIJK, ——. *Rotterdam*. ca.1730. Watch mt. cf. HOOGENDIJK.
HOIST, John. *London*. 1808. W.
HOL, ——. *Paris*. ca.1780. g. watch M.P.S. Dresden.
HOLBANK, George. *London*. ca.1800. Watch Den. coll.
HOLBECHE, Amilian. *Lichfield*. 1761. From *London*.
HOLBECK, John. *London*. a.1713.
HOLBORN, Robert. *Sheffield*. 1770-1813.
HOLBROOK—
Thomas. *Ipswich*. Early 18c. Watch mt.
Henry. *Liverpool*. ca.1770. Also HOWLBROOK.
HOLD, ——. *Stockholm*. 18c. Watch mt. Nord. M.
HOLDAM, Charles. *Southam*. 1795. C. & W.
HOLDCROFT, Henry. *London*. a.1678.
HOLDEN—
Onesiphorus. *v*. HELDEN.
George. *Sheffield*. 1825.
HOLDER—
William. F.R.S. *London*. 1694. Pub. 'A discourse concerning Time,' the first good exposition of the divisions of time and the calendar.
George. *London* (*Westminster*). 1765. Insolvent. W.
George Robert. *London* (*Soho*). 1769. Insolvent. W.
——. *Colchester*. d.1818. W.
Charles. *London*. an.1786-1824. Watch.
HOLDERICH, T. N. *Augsburg*. 18c. Sundial Fränkel coll.
HOLDERNESS, Samuel. *London*. a.1784.
HOLDERSTOCK, William. *London*. an. 1768. Watch.
HOLDFORD, ——. *London*. an.1721. Watch.
HOLDING, William Enoch. *London*. a.1824.
HOLDRED—
John. *London*. a.1778.
Theophilus. *London*. 1820-9.
HOLDSTOCK, *v*. HOLDERSTOCK.
HOLDWAY, George. *London*. a.1760-99. W.
HOLE, Henry. *London*. 1805-25.
HOLEYARD, Samuel. *London*. CC.1705.
HOLGATE, William. *Wigan*. ca.1780-1814. Watch.
HOLIDAY, Samuel. *London*. a.1753, CC.1765.
HÖLL, Andreas Ernst. *Nürnberg*. ca.1780. Table clock.
HOLLAND—
George. *London*. 1630-55. Petitioner for incorporation of CC.
Thomas. *London*. 1630. CC.1632, m.CC. 1656. Subscribed for incorporation of CC.
John. *London*. 1633. W.
Thomas. *London*. CC.1659-67.
Hugh. *London*. a.1660.
Lewis. *London*. a.1691, CC.1699. Watch mt. Buckley coll.
Alexander. prob. *London*. an.1711. Watch.
Henry. *Whiston*. 1744. W.
Richard. *Liverpool*. d.1747. W.
Joshuah. *London*. a.1717.
Robert. *London* (*Tower St.*). 1747-51.
Richard. *Coventry*. 1749-84. W.
Richard. *London*. an.1751. Watch.
Edward. prob. *London*. an.1756. Watch.
Matthew. *London* (*Borough*). an.1756-81. *Clapham*. 1799. W.
William. prob. *London*. an.1758. Watch.
John. *London*. a.1761-77.
Thomas. *Kidderminster*. ca.1760. C. & W.

HOLLAND—*continued*.
James. *Bury*. ca.1770-95.
William Toler. *London*. a.1764.
John. *London*. a.1771.
Henry. *Holywell*. mar.1789-95. C. & W.
George. *Louth*. 1791-5. W.
William. *Chester*. 1791-7. C.
Richard. *Chester*. 1797.
John. *London* (*Gray's Inn Lane*). 1799-1804. W.
Francis. *London*. 1802-08. C.
William. *London*. a.1803-08. C.
John. *Chester*. Early 19c. Watch.
Thomas. *Brighton*. 1822. C. & W.
HOLLANDSBRE, Charles. *London*. a.1772.
HOLLETZEK, Mattes. *Münnerstadt*. m.1816.
HOLLEY, James. *London*. an.1783. Watch. *v*. RICH & HOLLEY.
HOLLIDAIE, Edward. *London*. CC.1650-6.
HOLLIDAY, Nathaniel. *Cambridge*. d.1770. C. & W. His widow continued.
HOLLIER—
John. *Newington, Surrey*. an.1742. d.1769. Watch.
John. *London*. an.1768. Watch.
John. *London*. a.1769.
HOLLINGSWORTH—
Robert. *London*. a.1697.
J. *London*. 1817-24.
HOLLINSHEAD—
Jacob. *Philadelphia*. 1772. C. & W.
Morgan. *Morris Town* (*Philadelphia*). 1775. C. & W.
HOLLIS—
Thomas. *London*. a.1649, CC.1656-77.
Thomas. *London*. a.1682.
Samuel. *London*. a.1763.
John. *London*. 1784.
HOLLISONE, Alexander. *Liverpool*. d.(?) 1800. W.
HOLLIWELL—
William. *Liverpool*. 1767-73. C.
William. *Derby*. 1777. d.1802. Watch.
& HOLLIWELL, jun. *Derby*. ca.1790.
——. *Wirksworth*. Early 19c. Watch.
v. HALLIWELL.
HOLLOWAY—
John. *Lavington*. 1611. Iron br. clock Webster coll.
Robert. *London*. CC.1632.
Richard. *London*. a.1675.
William. *London* (*Cullum St.*). CC.1697-1723. Watch.
Arthur. *London*. a.1697-1712 CC.
——. *Stroud*. ca.1740. Clock.
John. *London*. a.1740.
Thomas. *Great Haseley*. d. or retired 1764. Succeeded by Thos. STOCKFORD.
Thomas. prob. *London*. an.1762. Watch.
HOLLSTEN, Hedvig. *Stockholm*. 1765.
HOLLYAR (HOLLIARD), Samuel. *London*. a.1693, CC.1705-18. Clock.
HOLLYER—
James. *London*. a.1698.
Samuel. *London*. an.1777. Watch.
HOLM—
Wolf Petersen. *Copenhagen*. 1778.
Boy Cornils. *Niebüll*. 1780. Wall clock.
John. *Lancaster*. 1783.
Jokum Henrik. *Aalborg*. m.1810.
Jacob. *Copenhagen*. m.1812.
Johan Petter. *Kristianstad*. 1814.
A. G. *Kungsbacka*. 1816-30. Wall clock.
O. *Falköping*. 1816-20.
I. P. *Göteborg*. 1820.
Johan. *Kristinehamn*. 1821.
J. P. *Halmstad*. 1824-40. Wall clocks.
HOLMAN—
Samuel. *London*. a.1696.
——. *Lewes*. 1787-1814 CC. W.
HOLMBERG, Johan. *Umeå*. 1822.

HOLMDEN, John George. *London.* a.1781, CC.1788, l.CC.1807-40. W.

HOLME—
Joseph. *Speke.* d.1726.
Thomas. *Liverpool.* 1767. W.
Lawrence. *Rochdale.* 1769.
John. *Cockermouth.* 1783. W. Lancaster freeman.
Lawrence. *Liverpool.* 1784. W.

HOLMES (HOLMS)—
Major. *London.* 1665. Pub. in Phil. Trans. Vol. V, an account of the trial of Huygens' pendulum clocks at sea.
Thomas. *London.* a.1686, CC.1697.
John. *London.* CC.1697.
Robert. *Belfast.* 1730. HOLMS.
Thomas. *London.* a.1723.
Isaac. *Keighley.* 1735.
John. *London.* a.1732.
John. *London.* a.1753.
John. *London (Strand, Somerset House).* 1762-1815. Maker of great repute. Supervised making by THWAITES of clock for Greenwich Hospital. MS. about the clock, ca.1779, in Library of CC. l.c. clock Weth. coll. in Chippendale 'Director' style case. g. watch F.W.M. p.c. watch G.M. cyl. p.c. watch S.M.S.K. Expert on Mudge's chron.
John. *London.* a.1760.
Robert. *Dublin.* an.1776. Watch.
Robert & Samuel. *Dublin.* an.1783. Watch.
John. *London (Strand).* 1784.
Thomas. *Cheadle.* 1784. C.
Joseph. *Wolverhampton.* 1790. l.c. clock.
Merritt. *London.* a.1785.
William, son of John. *London (Strand).* 1802-1824. ½ ¼ rep. duplex mt. G.M. br. clock ill. Cec. & Web.
Samuel. *Stourbridge.* Early 19c. Watch.
Matthew Steel. *London (Creed La.).* CC. 1817, l.CC.1825-42.
Thomas Ayscough. *London.* a.1813.

HOLMGREN—
Olof. *Stockholm.* 1808-12.
Jacob. *Stockholm.* 1811-35. br. clock.

HOLMQVIST, Nils. *Stockholm.* 1800.

HOLMSTEDT, Johan Peter. *Jönköping.* m. 1794-1810.

HOLMSTRÖM—
J. P. *Laholm.* 1816. d.an.1830.
——. *Skänninge.* 1821.

HOLNER, ——. *Prague.* Mid. 18c. Watch Nat. M. Prague.

HOLOWAY, John. *Newbury.* 1680. Watch with sun and moon hour indicators ill. Britten.

HOLROIDE, Richard. *London.* a.1780.

HOLROYD—
John. *Wakefield.* 1738-1814. C. & W.
Joseph. *Leeds.* 1758. W.

HOLT—
Henry. *London.* a.1694.
Thomas. *Lancaster.* 1747. d.1775. W.
William, son. *Lancaster.* 1767.
William. *Wigan.* an.1775. Watch.
Matthew. *Wigan.* 1775. d.1805. Watch Den. coll.
William. *Eastbourne.* 1803. Watch Ilbert coll.
Richard. *Newark.* 1804-45. l.c. clock.
John. *Rochdale.* ca.1820.
Valentine. *Rochdale.* ca.1820.

HOLTBY, A. *Driffield.* Early 19c. Watch.

HOLTHAM—
Thomas. *Canterbury.* 1729. C.
George. *London.* 1st half 18c. Watch mt.
Christopher. *Church Lawford.* an.1777. Table clock.

HOLTMAN, P. W. A. *Amsterdam.* 1822. W.

HOLTON—
Cob. *London.* a.1718. Watch.

HOLTON—*continued.*
——. *London.* an.1755. Watch.
Edward. *Bath.* 1773. W.

HÖLTZEL (HÖLZEL), Michael. *Cologne.* 1797-1813.

HOLTZMANN—
Johann. *Vienna.* m.1789. Watch with mt. separated from dial., ill. Britten.
Christian. *Vienna.* m.1791.
Johann. *Vienna.* m.1814.

HOLWORTHY, John. *London.* a.1772.

HOLYER, Richard. *London.* ca.1780. Watch Chamb. coll.

HOLZAPFEL—
Johann Georg. *Kulbach.* Early 17c. Table clock.
Martin. *Hannstetten.* Came to *Augsburg* 1733-51. Back in *Hannstetten* 1756.
——. *Westheim.* 1756.

HOLZMANN, Urban. *Winden.* Early 18c. Court C.

HOMAN, Robert. *Limerick.* 1824.

HOMANS, ——. *Nürnberg.* 1720. Pub. in sheet form a desc. of his Universal Geographical clock.

HOME, Paul. ——. ca.1600. Skull watch.

HOMER—
John. prob. *London.* an.1759. Watch.
Charles. *Nottingham.* 1798. Dissolves partnership with Wm. YOUNG.

'HOMER FOOT.' Sig. on 1870 watches of the NEW YORK WATCH CO.

HOMESBY, Thomas. *London.* 1755. C & W.

HOMMET, Jean. *Paris.* m.1690.

HOMO, Olivier. *Rouen.* 1410. 'Surrurier et horloger.' In charge of town clock.

HONALEINE, Alexandre. *Paris.* m.1789.

HONDERWOOD, James. *Ayr.* 1820.

HONE, Richard. *London.* an.1747-ca.1750. Watch Den. coll.

HONEFELT, Hans. *Wilten.* 1599. rect. table clock Spitzer coll.

HONEY—
Richard. *London.* a.1646.
Robert. *London.* an.1776. Watch.

HONEYBONE—
R. *Fairford.* ca.1690-1814 CC.
T. *Brentford.* Early 19c. Watch S.K.M.

HONEYCHURCH, ——. prob. *London.* an. 1766. Watch.

HONEYMAN, Thomas. prob. *London.* an. 1778. Watch.

HONNEY, George. *Haverfordwest.* 1796. Insolvent.

HÖNNIGER, C. *Morat.* ca.1800. rep. watch.

HONOR, William. *London.* a.1724.

HONWELL, Lee. *London.* an.1784. Watch.

HOOD—
Robert. *Blandford.* 1780. C.
James. *London.* a.1788-1805. Watch.
Francis. *New York.* 1805. W.

HOODHAMS, Thomas. *Peasemarsh.* an. 1797. Watch.

HOOGENBOOM, N. *Rotterdam.* ca.1800.

HOOGENDIJK—
Adriaan. *Rotterdam.* 1625-ca.1650. Large watch M.M.A. Watch mt. Stern. coll. trav. clock.
Steven. *Rotterdam.* ca.1720. g. repoussé watch Leeuwarden M. Watch Horstmann coll. Pedometer Old Ashmolean M. cf. HOIJENDIJK.

HOOGSTRAATE, P. *Rotterdam.* 1821-30.

HOOKE, Robert. *London.* b.1635, d.1703. Professor of Geometry and Secretary of the Roy. Soc. Prob. invented anchor escapement for clocks ca.1676 and a wheel-cutting engine with circular cutter and endless screw for division. Discovered the law of a spring, that the force is proportional to the extension. Claimed priority over HUYGENS in applying a balance spring

HOOKE—*continued.*
but did not publish what he had invented; it is clear from his diary that he did not have the idea of a spiral spring.

HOOKER—
John. *London.* CC.1698, d.1751. W.
Joseph. *London.* a.1758.
James. *London.* a.1762-91.
William. *London.* a.1794.

HOOKWAY, George. *Bristol.* 1818.

HOOLE, Samuel. *London.* 1758-ca.1770. l.c. clock.

HOOPER—
John. *Dorchester.* 1631. From *Wells.* C.
Humphrey. *Oakhampton.* 1748.
Giles. *London* (*Greville St.*). a.1749, CC. 1758-72.
Richard. *London.* a.1760.
George. *London.* ca.1760. Watch S.K.M.
Thomas. *London.* 1764.
Henry. *London.* 1780. d.ca.1800. Succeeded by J. C. LOWRIE.
& SON. *Winchester.* 1795.
John. *London* (*Islington*). Early 19c. Watch.

HOPCRAFT—
Edward. *London.* a.1714-25. Bankrupt. CC. 1734. W.
David. *London.* CC.1734.

HOPE—
Samuel. *London.* 1724. Watch.
Caleb. *London.* a.1732.
Hugh. *Dumfries.* b.1745, d.1828.
William. *London.* an.1778. Watch.
Thomas. *York.* an.1778. Watch.
Peter. *Liverpool.* 1795. Watch.
Charles. *London* (*Hollywell Mount*). 1799-1820.
S. *Marlborough.* Early 19c. Watch.

HOPETOWN, William. *London.* ca.1825. Watch.

HOPGOOD, T. B. *London.* 1807-23.

HOPKINS—
John. *London.* CC.1640. Watch.
Thomas. *London.* CC.1730. Engraver.
Thomas. *London* (*Oat Lane*). a.1738, CC. 1746-69.
William. *London.* a.1742, CC.1751-9.
Richard Thomas. *London* (*Foster La.*). CC. 1769, l.CC.1802. Watch S.K.M.
Henry. *Deptford.* an.1780. Watch.
William. *London.* an.1781. Watch.
Benjamin. *London.* an.1782. Watch.
Isaac. *London.* an.1786. Watch.
Edward. *Bradford* (*Yorks.*). 1787-95. Watch. l.c. clock.
Henry. *London.* a.1783.
——. *Tewkesbury.* d.1819. C. & W.
William. *Birmingham.* 1801. W.
Francis. *London.* a.1796.
Henry. *London* (*Deptford*). 1802-24. Watch.
P. ——. an.1810. Watch.
George. *London.* a.1805.
Edward. *London.* 1817-24.
Asa. *Northfield, U.S.A.* 1820. Wooden wall clocks.

HOPPER—
Christopher. prob. *London.* an.1772. Watch.
John M. *Philadelphia.* 1819. W.
Thomas. *Dublin.* 1824.

HOPPERT, Daniel. *Nürnberg.* ca.1810. l.c. clock.

HOPPERTON—
Emmanuel. *Leeds.* 1750-60. l.c. clocks.
Samuel. *Leeds.* 1770.

HOPPING, James. *London.* a.1774, CC.1781-1788.

HOPPS, George. *London.* a.1789, CC. 1798, l.CC.1812.

HOPSCH, Hubert. *Cologne.* 1797.

HOPSON, Thomas. prob. *London.* an.1762. Watch.

HOPTON—
Anthony and Matthew. *Edinburgh.* 1799-1817. Wooden clocks.
John, son of Anthony. *Edinburgh.* 1817-50. Wooden clocks.

HOPWOOD, William. *London.* a.1778.

HORDON, Joseph. *London.* an.1762. Watch.

HORIEUX, Charles. *Paris.* Juré 1692.

HÖRLE, Urban. *Mainz.* Early 17c. crys. cross watch.

HÖRMANN—
Stephan. *Augsburg.* 1728.
Joseph Carl. *Steppach.* 1756.

HORN—
Paulus. *Dantzig.* Mid. 17c. Fine hex. table clock Olivier coll.
Elisha. *London.* a.1715.
Johann Martin. *Augsburg.* m.1750-86.
Alexander. *Fyvie.* 1825. Clocks.

HORNBLOWER—
William. *London.* a.1694, CC.1714. l.c. clock.
William, son. *London.* a.1726, CC.1750.
William. *London.* a.1761, CC.1768-93.
Thomas. *London.* CC.1772.

HORNBY—
William. *Liverpool.* 1734.
Samuel. *London.* an.1767. Watch.
George. *Liverpool.* 1780-97.
Gerrard. *Liverpool.* 1780-1821. W.
John. *Liverpool.* 1784-1829. W.
Nehemiah. *Liverpool.* 1796. W.
James. *Liverpool.* 1803-29. W.
Thomas. *Liverpool.* 1805-21. W.
John. *Liverpool* (*Vernon St.*). 1807-14. W.
& SON. *Liverpool.* Early 19c. g. watch.
Richard. *Liverpool.* 1810-29. W. Two makers.
Henry. *Liverpool* (*Vernon St.*). 1810-4.
Henry. *Liverpool* (*Cunliffe St.*). 1818-21.
John. *Liverpool* (*Myrtle St.*). 1820-9. Watch.
James. *Liverpool.* ca.1820.

HORNE—
Samuel. *London.* CC.1654, m.CC.1673. d. 1685.
Edward. *London.* a.1696, CC.1704-33.
George Henry. *London* (*Moorfields*). a.1709, CC.1718, m.CC.1750. d.an.1775. g. watch Den. coll. prob. by him.
John, son. *London.* a.1744.
John. *London.* a.1772, CC.1788.
& ASH. *London* (*St. James St.*). an.1817. Watch.
Henry. *London.* a.1813, CC.1820.
William. *London.* Early 19c.-1842. Watch N.Y. Univ.

HORNER—
James. *Ripon.* ca.1720. Watch.
Thomas. *London.* 1805-08. W.
——. *Leipzig.* 1826. Pub. art. on the effect of magnetism on chrons. in Gehler's 'Physikalische Wörterbuch.'

HÖRNER, Christoffer. *Uppsala.* 1750. l.c. clock.

HORNIBLOW, James. *London.* a.1737.

HÖRNING, Sven Peter. *Stockholm.* 1785-1805. Two br. clocks.

HORNSBY—
Robert. *London.* a.1780, CC.1788.
v. HORNBY.

HORNSEY—
——. *Exeter.* an.1792. Watch.
Thomas Edward. *York.* 1826. W.

HORRIDGE, Robert. *Liverpool.* 1800-03. W.

HORROCKS, Christopher. *Warrington.* d. 1663. W.

HORSEHILL, Richard. *Hale.* an.1777. Watch. cf. HALSALL.

HORSEMAN—
Stephen. *London.* a.1702, CC.1709. Partner with QUARE. Bankrupt 1730. l.c. clock Virginia M.
Henry. *London.* an.1761. Watch.
John. *London.* a.1799.
HORSLEY—
Cornelius. *York.* 1656, d.1682. W.
Benjamin. *London.* a.1693.
HORSNAILE—
George. *Warfield.* 1st half 18c.
John. *Warfield.* Late 18c.
HORT, Josiah. *Bristol.* 1759. Dissolved partnership with J. JORDAN. W.
HORTLANDER, Hans. *Pitea.* 1816-35.
HORTON—
——. *London.* an.1757. Watch.
James. *London.* 1799. W.
'H. G. HORTON.' Sig. on 1870 watches of the NEW YORK WATCH CO.
HORWOOD—
Charles. *Bristol.* 1762. d.1787. Watch Stads M. Amsterdam.
& PAGE. *Bristol.* 1770. Dissolved partnership.
Moses. *London.* 1774. W.
& GREEN. *Bristol.* 1784-7.
HORY (ORY, HOURY)—
Georges. *Paris.* 1544-7. Founder member of Paris corporation.
Jacques. *Paris.* Juré 1674-84.
André. *Paris.* ca.1700-ca.1750. Fine Boulle-work br. clock Pal. de Pau, Paris. Watch with 6-hour dial Gélis coll. rep. watch Ilbert coll.
HOSEMAN, Stephen. *London.* a.1701.
HOSER—
Joh. Mich. *Vienna.* m.1786. Also HOSSER.
Georg. *Vienna.* m.1812. Also HOSSER.
Andreas. *Vienna.* m.1817.
Ferdinand. *Vienna.* m.1818.
HOSIER, T. *London.* an.1781. Watch.
HOSKEN, B. *London.* an.1793. Watch.
HOSKINS—
Daniel. ——. ca.1630. Lantern clock ill. Cec. & Web.
Joseph. *London.* CC.1819.
Jonah. *London.* 1822-4. Chron. maker.
& BIRD. *London.* 1825.
HOSMER, ——. *Tonbridge.* ca.1790 CC. Watch.
HOSSE, William. *Walton (Derby).* 1678.
HOSSELL, James. *Bewdley.* ca.1760. l.c. clock.
HOTHAM, Henry. *London.* a.1665, CC.1673.
HOTIRAH, ——. *London.* Late 18c. Sig. on g. rep. watch M.P.S. Dresden.
HOUBLIER, Jean. *Paris.* m.1757.
HOUBLIN—
Eustache François. *Paris.* m.1745, juré 1764-1772.
Veuve. *Paris.* 1789.
HOUDIN—
Nicolas. prob. *Paris.* ca.1780.
Jacques François, son. *Paris.* b.1783, d.1860. Eminent maker. Worked for Breguet. Made clock for C.A. & M.
Robert, son-in-law. *Paris.* ca.1800-58. The celebrated conjurer. Learnt watchmaking with his father, and made many automata. Mysterious clock Gélis coll. Box with al. and device for striking a light Ilbert coll.
Robert, son. *Paris.* Early 19c.-1863. Pub. 'L'art de connaître et de régler les montres et les pendules.'
v. OUDIN.
HOUET, ——. *Paris.* 1812.
HOUGH—
J. ——. an.1762. Watch.
William. *Birmingham.* 1808.
William. *Portsmouth.* Early 19c.
HOUGHAM, Charles. *London.* CC.1680-99. Also HOUGHMAN & HUFFAM.
HOUGHTON—
Richard. *London.* a.1653, CC.1690.
William. ——. 1695. Patented with Edw. BOOTH an esc. with 'a new sort of teeth made like tinterhooks.'
William. *Prescot.* End 17c. Devised pinion wire drawing.
Jasper. *London.* a.1722.
George. *London.* 1722.
Richard. *Liverpool.* 1734-61. W.
Charles. *London.* a.1734.
Jeffrey. *London.* a.1743.
John. *Chorley.* ca.1770-95.
Thomas. *Chorley.* 1780-1840. Clubfooted verge watch Chamb. coll.
James. *London.* 1790.
James. *Ormskirk.* 1800-20. Clubfooted verge mts. S.M.S.K. and G.M.
S. *Chorley.* ca.1820.
William. *London.* a.1817.
George. *London.* a.1819.
John. *Liverpool.* 1825. C.
HOUILLERE, Jonathan. *London.* 1725-63. Watch.
HOUISON, John. *London.* 1805-11.
HOULAHAN, Thomas. *Cashel.* 1824.
HOULBROOK, Henry. *Liverpool.* 1781-1814. W.
HOULGRAVE, Edward. *Liverpool.* 1764. Bankrupt. W.
HOULLGATT, W. *Ipswich.* ca.1640. Watch S.K.M.
HOUNSON, Thomas. *London.* a.1738, CC. 1746.
HOURIET, Jacques Frédéric. *Paris* to 1768 and then *Le Locle.* b.1743, d.1830. One of the ablest Swiss makers. Promoted precision horology at Le Locle. Started a factory with David COURVOISIER. Pub. an art. on the isochronism of spiral springs, 1814. Devised the spherical balance spring.
——. *St. Imier.* ca.1790.
HOURY (HORY, ORY, OURY, OURRY)—
Louis. *Paris.* 1675 m., juré 1693. Boulle br. clock. Watch ca.1680 with balance spring Ilbert coll.
Isaac. *Cassel.* ca.1710. Two clocks in Cassel Landes-M. OURRY.
Jean. *Paris.* m.1777-89.
——. *Paris.* 1821-5. Nephew and successor of TAVERNIER.
HOUSMAN—
Jacob. *Lancaster.* 1732. C.
——. *Kingston.* ca.1790 CC.
HOUSON, James. *York.* Early 19c. W.
HOUSTON—
Shean. *Dublin.* 1780-95. Watch.
John. *Dublin.* 1799. l.c. clock.
HOVELAC, Jacques. *Berlin.* In 1783 appointed manager of the Fabrique royale at *Berlin* and *Friedrichsthal.* d.1802.
HOVENSCHIÖLD—
Joachim. *Stockholm.* 1767. d.1800. Many watches, two Nord. M. br. and wall clocks.
Johan Eric, son. *Stockholm.* b.1782, d.1832. Table clock.
Joachim, bro. *Stockholm.* b.1784-1820.
HOVIL, John. *London (Horsleydown).* 1820.
HOVILL, John. *London (Borough).* 1799-1824.
HOW (HOWE)—
William. *London.* CC.1667-97. math. inst. maker.
Thomas. *London.* a.1670, CC.1677-89.
Daniel. *London.* a.1673.
Richard. *Dorchester.* b.1666, d.1713. l.c. clocks. Watch mt. S.K.M.
Benjamin. *London.* CC.1691-ca.1725. Watch mt. Ilbert coll.
John. *London.* a.1695.
Andrew. *Kilbarchan.* 1700.

HOW (HOWE)—*continued.*
Samuel. *London.* a.1704, CC.1712.
Richard, son of Rich. *Dorchester.* From 1713. Succeeded his father.
Ephraim. *London.* a.1716, CC.1729.
Samuel. *London.* a.1727, CC.1735.
Ephraim. *London.* a.1729.
Matthew. *London.* a.1730, CC.1747-53.
John. *Alresford.* ca.1800.
James. *London (Bromley).* 1802-24. W.
John. *London.* a.1796, CC.1811.
Peter. *Eltham.* Early 19c. Watch.
John. *Wigton.* 1820.
Allan. *v.* HOWIE.

HOWARD—
John. *London.* 1689. CC.1694. Watch.
Richard. *London.* a.1702, CC.1718. l.c. clock.
Jarvis. *London.* a.1725.
Thomas. *St. Albans.* an.1747. Watch.
Edmund. *London (Chelsea).* 1747-52. T.C.
John. *Bewdley.* an.1760. Watch.
William. *London.* a.1750.
William. ——. 1760. Repaired Exeter Cathedral clock.
William. *London (Kirby St.).* a.1759-77. g. repoussé watch S.K.M. Watches N.Y. Univ. and Ilbert coll.
James. *London.* an.1766. Watch.
Thomas. *Philadelphia.* 1775-83. C. & W.
Richard. *Brentford.* an.1777. Watch.
James. *Chorley.* 1777. C.
Edward. *London (Kirby St.).* 1780-1804. c.secs. watches S.M.S.K. and Den. coll. Two watches Ilbert coll.
——. *Lincoln.* an.1784. Watch.
Richard. *Yarmouth.* 18c. l.c. clock.
John Jarvis. *London (Aldersgate).* CC.1788-1810. Watch.
Wharton, son of Edward. *London (Hoxton and Shoreditch).* a.1780, CC.1787-1816. W.
Henry. *Liverpool.* 1796. W.
William. *Dublin.* 1796. Watch Ilbert coll.
William. *London.* a.1793.
John. *London (New Brentford).* 1802-08.
Reddish. *London.* 1805-08.
William. *Boston, U.S.A.* 1813-6. W.
Edward. *Hingham, Roxbury* and *Waltham, U.S.A.* b.1813, d.1904. Partner with D.P. Davis in clockmaking at Roxbury, 1842-9, then with A. L. Dennison started a factory for watches at Waltham, which failed in 1857. He then founded the Howard Watch and Clock Co.

HOWARTH, William. *Manchester.* 1804-13. C.

HOWDEN—
James. *Edinburgh.* a.1764, d.1810. Maker of repute. l.c. clocks.
James. *Edinburgh.* 1781-1842.
J. & W. *Edinburgh.* ca.1800. Watch mt. Ilbert coll.
John. *Edinburgh.* 1824-32.

HOWELL—
Daniel. *London.* CC.1637, d.1650.
Benjamin. *London.* a.1693, CC.1700-11.
Joseph. *London.* a.1713, CC.1721-52.
John. *London (Spitalfields* and later *Bishopsgate).* a.1717, CC.1724-78. Also HOWLE.
Richard. *London.* a.1731.
Thomas. *London.* a.1735.
Stephen. *London (Shoe Lane).* an.1749. Watch.
Richard. *Bristol.* 1781. W.
George. *London.* a.1814.
v. STOREY & HOWELL.

HOWELLS—
W. ——. 1724. In the Library of the CC. are 12 drawings of escapements with desc. by him.
William. *Bristol.* 1762-96. In 1796 entered into partnership with P. P. BARRAUD and G. JAMISON of Portsea to make Timekeepers on the principle of Mr. MUDGE.
John. *London.* 1765.
John, son. *London.* a.1765.
Thomas. *Hay.* 1776. W.
William. *London (Plumbtree St.).* a.1770, CC.1780, d.1814. Expert on Mudge's chron. Partner with PENNINGTON. Awarded prize by Soc. Arts for a detached escapement, desc. in Trans. Soc. Arts, 1792.
& PENNINGTON. *London.* 1790. Employed by MUDGE's son to make chrons. to his father's design. Remontoir chron. G.M.
jun. *Falmouth.* ca.1790 CC.
William Henry. *London (White Hart Row).* a.1794, CC.1820.
William Henry, son. *London.* a.1820.

HOWES (HOUSE)—
John. *London.* CC.1672-1710.
Joseph. *London.* a.1691, CC.1698-1714. Also HOWSE.
William. *London (Temple Bar).* a.1721, CC. 1730, l.CC.1766-73.
Charles. *v.* HOWSE.
John, son of William. *London.* l.CC.1780-1819.
Suckling. *Downham.* 1791. C. & W.
William. *London.* 1793 l.CC. Possibly same as William above.
John. *Tring.* ca.1800 CC.
Jesse John. *London.* a.1797, CC.1805. Also HOWSE.
John. *London.* a.1801.

HOWET, Nicholas. *London.* a.1699.

HOWGARTH, John. *N. Shields.* 1820.

HOWIE (HOW), Allan. *Irvine.* 1774.

HOWIESON—
George. *Edinburgh.* 1794.
John. *Perth.* 1808-22.

HOWLBROOK, *v.* HOLBROOK.

HOWLE, John. *v.* HOWELL.

HOWLETT—
Stephen. *London.* a.1657.
William. *Coventry.* 1754-84. Partner in VALE, HOWLETT & CARR.
G. *Birmingham.* 1768. From *London.* C. & W.
John. *Market Harborough.* 1775. C. & W.
Joseph. *Rothwell.* Went to *Northampton* in 1775. From *London.* W.
John. *London* and *Bath.* ca.1800. Watch Horstmann coll.

HOWSE (HOUSE)—
Thomas. *London.* CC.1632, w.CC.1642. sil. bud watch Mallett coll. Also HOUSE.
John. *Croydon.* CC.1687-1717.
Joseph. *London.* a.1691, CC.1698-1714. Also HOWES.
John. *London (Newington Gr.).* CC.1707-23. Bankrupt. W.
Matthew. *London.* CC.1730.
Charles. *London.* a.1720.
William. *London (Temple Bar).* CC.1731, m.CC.1777-80.
Charles. *London.* a.1750, CC.1761, m.CC. 1787-1804. br. clock. Also HOUSE and HOWES.
Robert. *London.* 1768-90. Watch.
Thomas. *Worcester.* 1774. W.
Jesse John. *London.* a.1797, CC.1805. Also HOWES.

HOWSON, John. *London.* CC.1699.

HOYER—
A. L. *Langenstrigis.* Early 19c. str. and mus. watch in snuff-box, M.P.S. Dresden. mus. aut. table clock.
Johann. *Vienna.* 1845. A clever maker. Devised a clock wound by generation of hydrogen.

HOYLE—
Thomas. *London.* Mid. 17c. sil. fritillary watch Mallett coll. The initial letter of the name is doubtful.
Henry. *London.* CC.1677.
Richard *London.* Late 18c. p.c. watch G.M.
William. *Rochdale.* 1820.
William. *Bolton-le-Moors.* ca.1820.
HOYSS, Leopold. *Bamberg.* 1713. d.1797. A C. of great repute. Made clocks with two pendulums swinging in opposite directions.
HOYT—
George R. *Albany City, U.S.A.* 1823.
Henry. *New York.* Early 19c.
'HOYT.' Sig. on 1870-5 watches of the ILLINOIS SPRINGFIELD WATCH CO.
HUART (HUAU), Alexis Louis Mathieu. *Paris.* m.1758-89.
HUAUD (HUAUT)—
Pierre. *Geneva.* m. goldsmith 1635. d.1680. Went to *Geneva* from *Châtellerault.* Enamel painter, but no work of his known.
Pierre, son. *Geneva.* b.1647. Went *Germany,* Court of Brandenberg, 1685. *Geneva,* 1686. Returned *Germany,* 1689. Appointed painter to Elector, 1691. d.ca.1698. The best enamel painter of the three brothers. Several sd. paintings; earliest known 1679. Sd. 'Huaud l'aisné' or 'P. Huaud primogenitus' or 'P. Huaud P.G.' or 'Huaud l'aîné de Genève' or 'Pierre Huaud' or 'Petrus Huaud major natus.' Watches Louvre, Musée d'art et d'histoire de Genève, Hohenzollern M. Berlin and Olivier coll.
Jean Pierre, bro. *Geneva.* b.1655, d.1723. Sd. 'Huaud le puisné.' Watch ill. Baillie. Watches B.M., S.K.M., Cluny M., Garnier and Olivier colls. *v.* LES FRÈRES, below.
Amy, bro. *Geneva.* b.1657, d.1729. *v.* LES FRÈRES, below.
LES FRÈRES (Jean, Pierre and Amy). *Geneva.* 1682. Appointed painters to the Court of Prussia, 1686, and went to *Berlin.* Returned *Geneva,* 1700. Sd. an.1686, 'Les deux frères Huaut les jeunes.' Sd. after 1686, 'Les Frères Huaud,' or 'Les deux frères Huaud,' with the addition of 'peintres de son A. E. à Berlin,' 'p.d. V. A. fct à Berlin.' Sd. after 1700, 'Les frères Huaut,' or 'Les deux frères Huaut,' or 'Peter et Amicus Huaut.' Also sd. 'Fratres Huault.' The name is spelt Huaud or Huaut and sometimes Huault. Watches B.M., S.K.M., Louvre, K.H.M., M.M.A., Hohenzollern M. Berlin, Königliche M. Berlin, Musée Condé, Musée de Dijon, Vienna Treasury.
HUBBARD—
John. *London.* a.1715, CC.1722.
William. *London.* a.1756.
John. *Louth.* 1776. C.
Samuel. *London.* a.1774.
Thomas. *Dorking.* Late 18c. Watch.
HÜBER—
Johann. *Vienna.* ca.1690. Watch Ilbert coll.
Mathias. *Friedberg.* 1795.
J. Hieronymus. *Fürth.* d.ca.1826.
HUBERT—
Noel. *Rouen.* 1612. juré 1650. Founder member of Rouen corporation. oct. watch B.M. oval watch S.K.M. oct. crys. watch M.M.A. Night-light clock.
Estienne. *Rouen.* ca.1620. Shell watch, crys. covers, Mallett coll., ill. Baillie.
Nicolas. *Rouen.* ca.1635.
Jean l'aîné. *Rouen.* 1645 m., juré 1664. A fine maker. Two watches G.M. Watch M.M.A.
Timothée. *Rouen.* m.1646. Melon watch Ashmolean M. crys. watch M.M.A.
Solomon. *Rouen.* 1646. Partner with Timothée.

HUBERT—*continued.*
Pascal. *Rouen.* m.1649, juré 1697-ca.1735. Sun and moon watch Ilbert coll.
Robert. *Rouen.* 1650 m. Went to *Amsterdam* 1689.
Jean le jeune. *Rouen.* 1652 m., juré 1701. g. watch Mallett coll.
Pierre, son of Nicolas. *Rouen.* m.1654, juré 1655.
Jacques. *Rouen.* m.1655, juré 1663-77.
Estienne. *Rouen.* m.1656-1702. A very fine maker. al. watch B.M. Watches G.M., S.K.M., Louvre, Cluny M., M.M.A., Stads M. Amsterdam. Two watch mts. G.M.
Timothée, son of Timothée. *Rouen.* ca.1660.
Noel. *Rouen.* a.1655.
Augustin. *Rouen.* an.1675. Watch.
Yves. *Richelieu.* ca.1685. Watch Ilbert coll.
Estienne l'aîné. *Amsterdam.* 1688. Watch Ilbert coll. There were two Huguenot refugees from *Rouen* of this name.
Jacques. *Rouen.* m.1694, juré 1696.
C. *France.* ca.1700. Watch Uhren M. Vienna.
Bernard. *Toulouse.* Went to *La Rochelle* in 1707. Watch.
Paul. *Kalmar.* Early 18c. br. clock.
R. *La Rochelle.* Early 18c. Watch M.M.A.
James. *London.* CC.1712-30. rep. watch Den. coll.
David. *London (Strand).* CC.1714, m.CC. 1743. An eminent maker. Succeeded by Joseph BARNES ca.1747. Watch G.M. rep. watches Den. and Buckley colls. c.secs. watch Ilbert coll. l.c. clock ill. Cec. & Web.
James, son of James. *London.* a.1721. g. and lapis lazuli watch Ilbert coll. ca. 1760, prob. by him.
Marte Charlotte. *London.* a.1725.
David, son of David. *London.* a.1727.
Oliver, bro. *London.* CC.1749.
Pascal. *Rouen.* 1749. en. watch ill. Britten.
John, jun. *London.* an.1759. Watch.
Philippe l'aîné. *Toulouse.* Late 18c. g. watch.
FRÈRES. *Geneva.* ca.1780. Painters on enamel.
——. *Liége.* 1782.
——. *Paris.* 1792-1812.
HUBICH, H. *Cologne.* 1813.
HUBNER, Friedrich. *Bremen.* Mid. 18c. Astro. watch Gotha M. Watch Gélis coll.
HÜBNER, Johann. *Vienna.* m.1793. trav. clock M.P.S. Dresden.
HÜBSCHER, J. *Basle.* 1st half 18c. Sig. on dial of watch by Emanuel GESSLER, Basle M.
HUCHASON (HUTCHASON)—
Richard. *London.* CC.1702-24.
James. *London.* CC.1718.
HUCKEL, Samuel. *Philadelphia.* 1819-25. W.
HUCKIN, William. *London.* a.1808.
HUDDERSICH, Job. *London.* a.1718.
HUDLESTON—
Charles. *London.* a.1673.
Richard. *London (Fleet St.* and later *Leadenhall St.).* a.1746 to George GRAHAM-1762. Also HUDSON.
Lawson. *London.* a.1757 to Thomas MUDGE-1773. Watch.
HUDSON—
John. *London.* a.1684.
William. *Edinburgh* and *London.* 1741-6. aut. and orreries.
Richard. *v.* HUDLESTON.
William. *London.* a.1753.
George. *London.* an.1770. Watch.
John. *Woolwich.* an.1775. Watch.
Jonathan. prob. *London.* an.1777. Watch.
Jarvis. *Manchester.* an.1785. Watch.
Thomas. *Nottingham.* ca.1790. Watch.

HUDSON—*continued.*
John. *Nottingham.* 1795-9. C. & W.
——. *London.* 1813. Watch Ilbert coll.
Thomas. *London.* a.1822.
HUE, Pierry. *London.* CC.1632. A Mr. Hewes, prob. the same, subscribed for incorporation of CC. cf. HUES and HUGHES.
HUES—
Peter. *Augsburg.* ca.1600. cf. HUE.
Peter. *London.* 1652 CC. cf. HUE.
Thomas. *London.* a.1662.
HUET—
Joseph. *Coventry.* an.1678. Watch.
——. *Rouen.* 1690 m.
Nicolas. *Rouen.* m.1694.
——. *Caen.* 18c. al. watch.
François. *Paris.* m.1767-91. Pub. 'Dissertation sur l'horlogerie.' Paris. 1791.
HUFFINGTON, John. prob. *London.* an. 1774. Watch.
HUGGEFORD—
Ignatius. *London* and *Florence* in 1686. CC. 1671-1710. Watch G.M. with ornamental jewel on balance cock, lantern clock.
Francis. *London.* a.1675.
Peter. *London.* a.1686 CC.
Cosmos Thomas. *Florence.* 1714. Dial-maker.
HUGGIN—
John. *Ashwell Thorp.* an.1752. Watch. l.c. clock.
William. *Ashwell Thorp.* an.1758. Watch.
HUGHES—
Peter. *London.* BC. 1628. 'english forrin.' cf. HUES.
John. *London.* a.1689.
Morris. *London.* a.1691, CC.1699.
John. *London.* a.1695, CC.1703-14. l.c. clock.
Thomas. *London (Broad St. Bdgs.).* a.1700, CC.1712, w.CC.1739, m.CC.1742, d.1753. Lacquer br. clock ill. Cec. & Web. rep. watch Den. coll.
Jacob. *London.* a.1705.
George. *London.* a.1712.
William. *London.* a.1721.
Richard. *Carnarvon.* 1730-48.
Robert. *Colchester.* 1738. Watch.
Thomas, son of Thomas. *London (New Broad St. Bdgs.).* a.1734, CC.1742, w.CC. 1762, m.CC.1765, d.1785.
J. *Maidstone.* 1st half 18c. Clock.
John. *Northampton.* an.1764. Watch.
Edward. *London.* a.1756.
William. *London (High Holborn).* 1766. CC. 1781-94. c.secs. watch G.M. Fine mus. aut. watch Webster coll. ill. Baillie. Watch in ring Feill coll. aut. clock. Made watches for China. Pair bloodstone boxes with watches and table mirror with watch, Peiping M. T.C.
Joseph. *London.* a.1777.
Richard. *Canterbury.* 1784. W.
Bartholomew. *Birmingham.* an.1787. l.c. clocks. Watch.
John. *Llanuwchllyn.* b.1767. Wooden clocks.
Joseph Henry. *London.* a.1785.
William. *London.* a.1787.
Hugh. *Carnarvon.* 1794-1806. Watch Den. coll.
William. *London.* a.1806.
H. E. *London (Goswell St.).* 1820.
Patrick. *Dublin.* 1824.
HUGHESDEN, Elles. *London.* a.1788.
HUGOT (HUGAULT), Gilles (Guillaume) Nicolas. *Paris.* m.1765-89.
HUGUELET—
Jean François. *Berne* and *Chaux-de-Fonds.* a.1737. C.
Abram. *Chaux-de-Fonds.* 1794-1822. C.
HUGUENIN—
Abram. *Le Locle.* 1643.
Daniel Jean. *Le Locle.* 1661.
Moïse. *Chaux-de-Fonds.* 1727. d.ca.1750. C. to the King of Prussia.
Abram, bro. and partner. *Chaux-de-Fonds,* with London branch. b.1702, d.1795. Very able maker. C. to the King of Prussia. Many clocks.
FRÈRES. *Chaux-de-Fonds.* Partnership of the two preceding.
Louis Frédéric, son of Abram (3). *Chaux-de-Fonds.* b.1713, d.1758. C. to the King of Prussia. Several clocks.
Jean Pierre. *Chaux-de-Fonds.* b.1718-86. Several clocks.
Frédéric Louis, son of L. Frédéric. *Chaux-de-Fonds.* 1764-1800. Several clocks.
Abram Louis, son of Moïse. *Neuchâtel.* b. 1733. Went to *Berlin* in 1765 as Director of the royal clock factory at Berlin. On its failure in 1770, went to *Courtelary* and in 1775 to *Porrentruy. Rastatt* in 1778 as C. to the Markgrave of Baden. At *Bienne* in 1792 and *Berlin* in 1804. d.1804.
Henri Charles. *Chaux-de-Fonds.* 1772-84. Worked on the Jaquet-Droz automata.
Friedrich. *Chaux-de-Fonds.* 1778.
David Guillaume. *La Brévine.* b.1765, d. 1841. W. & C.
Benjamin. *Chaux-de-Fonds.* 1782. C.
Isaac. *La Brévine.* a.1785-1820. g. rep. cyl. watch.
Charles Frédéric. *Chaux-de-Fonds.* 1792. Clock.
Charles F. *Philadelphia.* 1797-1825. prob. same as above.
Charles. *La Brévine.* 1806.
Aimé. *Liverpool.* ca.1820. W.
Sarah. *Liverpool.* 1825.
HUGUENIN-DIT-RICHARD—
Balthazard. *Le Locle.* an.1660.
Daniel, son. ——.
HUGUENIN-RICHARD, Jn. J. Hi. *Le Locle.* 1818. C.
HUILIER, Antoine Philippe. *Paris.* m.1746.
HUITINGA, J. P. *Leeuwarden.* 18c.
HULBERT—
William. *Bristol.* 1708. C.
Joel. *Dublin.* 1st half 18c. l.c. clock.
Robert. *Bristol.* an.1753. Clock.
HULCOP, Thomas. *London.* a.1739.
HULL—
Philip. *London.* a.1693.
Henry. *London.* a.1728 to Geo. GRAHAM, CC.1738.
William. *London.* a.1753 to Thos. MUDGE.
Charles. *Dublin.* 1774-80. W.
Francis. *Liverpool.* 1821. W.
John. *York.* a.1792-1822. W.
HULME—
John. *Stretford.* mar.1699. C.
James. *Stretford.* Early 19c. Watch mt. Platt Hall M. Manchester.
James. *London.* 1817.
HULOT, fils. *Paris.* 1760. Made wheel-cutting engines designed by his master TAILLEMARD. Wheel-cutting machine and fuzee-cutting machine C.A. & M.
HULSE—
Ralph. *Market Drayton.* 1791. C. & W.
Samuel. *Nottingham.* an.1799-1802. an. 1802 in partnership with Robert ORME.
Henry. *Manchester.* ca.1820.
HULSHOFF, J. C. *Purmerende.* ca.1800.
HULST, Jacob. *London.* CC.1646.
HULTERSTRÖM, Johan Fredric. *Linköping.* b.1797, d.1845.
HULTGREN—
Peter. *Kalmar.* 1790-5.
J. *Karlshamn.* 1794.
Albrecht. *Kalmar.* 1800-15.

HULTMAN—
Anders. *Örebro.* b.1756, d.1815.
Pehr And. *Örebro.* 1825.
HULTON, Ralph. *Chester.* 1670. W.
HULTQVIST, Nicl. Petter. *Stockholm.* 1798-1800. Watch.
HUMBER, Thomas. prob. *London.* an.1761. Watch.
HUMBERSTONE, Edward Gatward. *London.* a.1787.
HUMBERT—
Frères. ——. ca.1740. en. watch B.M.
J. B. *Paris.* 1786. Perhaps the following.
Joseph. *Paris.* 1789. *Geneva* and *Le Locle.* 1794. Started with Borel and Poterat the first watch factory in Geneva; it failed, and was taken over by the Republic. ca. 1800 made singing birds.
Jonas. *Savagnier.* End 18c. br. clock.
Veuve. *Fontainemelon.* 1812. Started an ébauche factory, taken over later by Robert, who built the existing factory.
——. *Langres.* Early 19c. g. c.secs. watch Gélis coll.
Ls. *Geneva.* Early 19c.
et Darier. *Geneva.* In 1820 founded a machine factory for watch parts, which failed.
Isaac. *v.* Humbert-Droz.
HUMBERT-DROZ—
Joseph. *Le Locle.* 1675. Made clock for the temple of Le Locle.
Louis. *Chaux-de-Fonds.* 1711. Clock.
Joseph. *Chaux-de-Fonds.* 1730-66. Able C. & W.
Jean Pierre. *Chaux-de-Fonds.* 1st half 18c. l.c. clock.
Frédéric. *Le Locle.* a.1753.
& Jacob Girard l'aîné. *Paris.* 1772.
Charles François. *Chaux-de-Fonds.* 1772-1779. C.
Alexandre. *Paris.* 1776 m. From *Le Locle.*
Isaïe (Isaac). *Paris.* m.1776-89. Also Humbert.
& Mairet. *Paris.* 1790.
——. *Philadelphia.* 1795.
David. ——. ca.1800. g. en. rep. watch.
Philibert. *Chaux-de-Fonds.* 1818. Associate in Courvoisier & Cie.
HUME—
Benjamin. *London.* a.1691.
John. *London.* Early 19c. Watch.
Peter. *Newcastle-o.-T.* an.1819. Watch.
HUMEL, Michael. *Vienna.* m.1791.
HUMFREYS—
Nicholas. *London.* a.1689.
William. *London.* a.1692.
HUMMEL, Matthäus. *Waldau* and *Glashütte.* 1740-80. Made watches all of boxwood. One of the first to make cuckoo clocks. Two wall clocks Furt. M.
HUMPHREYS—
Samuel. *London.* a.1720, CC.1728-33. d. an.1757.
Samuel. *London.* a.1727.
Jacob. *London.* a.1734.
William. ——. Mid. 18c. Watch.
John. *London.* 1756. W.
Thomas. *Guildford.* 1784-95. Also Humfry.
John. *Thrapston.* 1795.
George. *London.* 1799.
David. *Machynlleth.* ca.1800. l.c. clock.
Thomas. *Barnard Castle.* 1810-40.
William. *Hartlepool.* Early 19c. Watch.
HUMPHRIES—
——. *Southam.* an.1752. Watch.
Humphrey. *London.* a.1758.
John. *London.* a.1761.
Michael. *London.* a.1764.
Thomas. *London.* CC.1815.
HUMPHRYS, William. *London.* CC.1699.
HUNDON, John. *London.* an.1782. Watch.
HÜNELL (KÜNELL), Erik. *Malmö.* d.1709. Town C.
HUNGEY, Jehan. *Paris.* 1544-7. Founder member of Paris corporation.
HUNSDON—
Edward. *Maldon.* an.1761-84. W.
William. *London.* CC.1768.
H. *Chelmsford.* an.1775. Watch.
Thomas. *Chelmsford.* 1784.
HUNSTMAN (HUNTSMAN), Benjamin. *Doncaster.* b.1704, d.1774. Turret clocks. Improved steel-making and introduced 'Hunstman' steel. Watch Ashmolean M.
HUNT—
Robert. *London.* a.1661.
John. *London.* CC.1671.
Laurence. *London* (*Chelsea*). 1675. d.1681.
John. *London.* a.1676.
Edward. *London.* a.1677, CC.1684-1707. Watch mt. G.M. sd. 'Edw. Huntt.'
John. *London.* a.1685, CC.1699.
James. *London.* a.1699, CC.1708-23.
James. *Lichfield.* an.1758, d.1761. Watch.
Henry. *Salisbury.* ca.1760-ca.1800. br. clock and watch.
William. *Hatfield.* an.1777. Watch.
James. *London.* a.1768.
Abraham. *Yarmouth.* mar.1788-95 CC.
Thomas. *Amesbury.* ca.1790. Inn clock Virginia M.
——. *Yarmouth.* ca.1790 CC.
John. *Amesbury.* 1791. W.
James. *Overton.* 1791. C.
John. *Oxford.* 1795. C. & W.
Richard. *Manchester* (*Pendleton*). 1808-14.
James. *Bristol.* 1812.
Seth. *London.* 1818. From *U.S.A.* Patented an escapement.
James. *Fakenham.* an.1819. Watch.
Thomas. *Oxford.* Early 19c. Watch.
George. *Amesbury.* Early 19c.
Thomas. *London.* a.1812.
Thomas. *London* (*Tottenham Court Rd.*). 1822-35. Watch and chron. maker.
HUNTER—
William. *London.* an.1727. Watch.
Thomas. *London* (*Fenchurch St.*). 1744-99. p.c. watch G.M.
Andrew. *London.* d.1764. W.
John. *Bristol.* ca.1760-97. l.c. clock.
Thomas, jun. *London* (*Lombard St.*). 1770.
Thomas. *Liverpool* (*George St.*). 1774-1803. W.
John. *Bristol.* 1774-97. C. & W.
John. *London* (*Pear Tree St.*). d.an.1787.
Thomas. *Liverpool* (*Harrington St.*). 1781-1796. W.
John. *Bridlington.* 1775-1822. C. & W.
Peter. *Alloa.* 1786.
Thomas. *London* (*Fenchurch St.*). 1790-4.
Thomas. *London* (*Goswell St.*). 1790-4.
John. *Dunfermline.* 1790-1812.
John. *Deptford.* 1791. W.
Samuel. *London.* a.1787.
George William. *Perth.* a.1789.
W. H., & Co. *London* (*Cornhill*). Late 18c.
Peter. *Edinburgh.* 1794-1822.
John. *Clapham.* 1799-1815. Watch.
Robert. *London* (*Little Britain*). CC.1801.
Thomas and William. *London* (*Fenchurch St.*). 1802-04.
William. *London* (*Fenchurch St.*). 1802-04.
William. *Campbeltown.* 1803-34.
& Son. *London* (*Fenchurch St.*). 1805-24.
Thomas. *Clapham* and *London* (*Fleet St.*). 1805-08.
William. *Stirling.* 1807.
Samuel. *Clapham.* 1809-1824.
Andrew. ——. ca.1810. Duplex mt. Ilbert coll.
James. *Liverpool.* ca.1820. W.
Nathan. *Port Glasgow.* 1820.

HUNTER—*continued.*
Robert. *Girvan.* 1820.
William. *Dunfermline.* 1820-46.
HUNTLEY, John. *London.* a.1713.
HUNTSMAN, Ben. *Sheffield.* b.1704, d.1776.
HUNZIKER, ——. *Paris.* 1807-25. g. en. watch, set pearls, Fränkel coll.
HUON, Jacques. *Paris.* ca.1650. Fine en. watch S.K.M. ill. Baillie. Watch M.P.S. Dresden.
HÜPPE, Sigmund. *Breslau,* comp. 1745. *Augsburg,* 1763.
HURET—
——. *Paris.* 1692. 'Horloger du roi.'
Léopold. *Paris.* 1814.
HURLBURT, William. *London.* a.1785.
HURLEY, Isaac. *London.* a.1737, CC.1745-1790.
Jacob. *London.* a.1758, CC.1765.
Joseph. *Bristol* and *Bedminster.* 1775. d.1793.
HURSCH, ——. *Berlin.* 1792.
HURST—
Isaac. *London.* a.1668, CC.1677.
William. *London.* a.1752.
John. *London.* a.1764, CC.1771, l.CC.1792.
William. *Reading.* an.1777. Watch.
Timothy. *Datchet.* 1782. Bankrupt. C.
Stephen. *Liverpool.* 1805-13. Watch.
HURT—
Noe. *London.* a.1686, CC.1695.
Henry. *London* (*St. Paul's Churchyard* and in 1745 *Ludgate Hill*). a.1713, CC.1721-58.
William. *London.* a.1713.
Arthur. *Ashford.* d.1741. 'Clocksmith.'
Henry. *Bristol.* an.1770. Watch.
HURTER, Johann. *Schaffhausen.* Mid. 18c. Watch Geneva M.
HURTIN—
& Burgi. *New Jersey, U.S.A.* 1766. W.
William. *New York.* 1776. W.
HURTU, Jacques. ——. Early 17c. Made designs for eng. watches.
HUSBAND—
Thomas. *Hull.* 1760-95. l.c. clock. Watch.
David. *Kirkcaldy.* 1820-37. l.c. clock.
HUSBERG, Jonas. *Norrköping.* 1775. Watch.
HUSE, Joseph. *London.* a.1724.
HUSSAM, Charles. *London.* a.1672, CC. 1680.
HUSSEN, Lorentz. *Breslau.* 1st half 18c. Watch Ilbert coll.
HUSSEY—
Joseph. *London.* a.1676, CC.1685.
Benjamin. *London.* a.1717.
William. *London* (*Rotherhithe*). d.1763.
Henry *London.* a.1805.
HUTCHIN—
Joshua. *London.* 1670. CC.1683-1705. Apprenticed in *Liverpool.* Watch with sun and moon hour indicators. l.c. clock ill. Britten.
Francis. *London.* 1685 CC.
James. *London.* a.1685, CC.1698-1722.
Joseph. *London.* a.1696, CC.1703.
John. *London.* a.1696, CC.1703.
Henry. *London.* a.1711.
HUTCHINS—
Thomas. *London.* a.1737.
Abel. *Concord, U.S.A.* 1777-1809.
William. *Cullompton.* 2nd half 18c. l.c. clock.
HUTCHINSON—
John. *London.* 1622. a. to Corn. Mellin.
William. *London.* a.1688, CC.1706.
Richard. *London.* a.1694, CC.1702-36.
John. *London.* 1712. Patented watch wound without hole in case. MSS. in Library of CC. of the Petition for a patent and the Opposition by the CC.
Benjamin. prob. *London.* an.1716. Watch.
William. *London.* a.1706.
Richard. *London.* a.1719.

HUTCHINSON—*continued.*
Richard. *London.* a.1721.
Anthony. *Leeds.* 1st half 18c.-ca.1765. l.c. Chippendale clock.
Edward. *London.* ca.1750. Watch G.M.
John. *Durham.* 1752. C.
Thomas. *Colchester.* d.1764. W.
George. *Edinburgh.* a.1770-6.
George. *Stirling.* 1782.
John. *Kirkby Stephen.* 1784. C.
John. *Burnley.* 1790-1818.
William. *Retford.* 1795. C.
John. *Newcastle-o.-T.* ca.1800-17. Watch mt. Blackgate M. Newcastle.
John. *Kirkdale.* 1805-07.
Thomas. *Philadelphia.* 1817-20.
John. *Clitheroe.* ca.1820. l.c. clocks.
HUTIN, Jaques François. *Geneva.* ca.1770-91. From *Dardagny.*
HUTLY, Thomas. *Coggeshall.* ca.1720. Lantern clock.
HÜTTER, Marthin. a. in *Königsberg. Stockholm,* m.1697-1711.
HUTTLEY—
John. *London* (*Clerkenwell*). a.1769, CC. 1788-1802.
John Anthony, son. *London.* a.1803.
HUTTON—
James. *Edinburgh.* a.1685.
Richard. *London.* a.1691.
John. *London.* a.1716, CC.1724-7.
Barrett. *London.* a.1719, CC.1727-78.
Joseph. *London.* Mid. 18c. Watch mt.
William. *London* (*Gt. New St.*). a.1754, CC. 1762-99.
James. *Edinburgh.* 1764-79.
William. *Edinburgh.* a.1768-74.
George. *Perth.* a.1780-1800.
Patrick. *London.* an.1783-90. Watch.
G. F. *London.* 1823. Pub. art. in Phil. Trans. on a chron. trial at Greenwich.
HUVÉ, Le Fils. *Paris.* ca.1700. Watch Gélis coll.
HUVICARD, Nicolas. *Paris.* 1685 m.
HUX—
Thomas. *London* (*Old St.*). a.1772, CC.1785-1825. Watch.
Thomas. *London* (*Shoreditch*). 1799. W.
Thomas. *London* (*Hoxton*). 1804-14. W.
John. *London* (*City Rd.*). 1805-08.
William, son of Thos. *London* (*Shoreditch*). a.1799.
Thomas, son of Thos. *London* (*Hoxton*). a. 1804.
John, bro. *London.* a.1807.
HUXLEY, Thomas. *Lamberhurst.* 1790. W.
HUXTABLE, E. *S. Molton* and *Chittlehampton.* Late 18c. l.c. clock.
HUYGENS—
Christiaan. *The Hague* and *Paris.* b.1629, d.1695. A great geometrician, mathematician and astronomer; applied a pendulum to a clock in 1656 (pub. 1658), and a spiral spring to a watch in 1675 and a torsion spring for marine clocks in 1683. Was in *Paris* 1665-81. His pubs. on horology are: 'Horologium,' *The Hague,* 1658. 'Brevis Institutio de Usu Horologiorum ad inveniendas Longitudines,' The Hague, 1665. 'Lettre sur les horologes à Pendule,' Jl. des Sçavans, 1665. 'Horologium Oscillatorium,' Paris, 1673. 'Une nouvelle invention d'Horloges très justes et portatives,' Paris, 1675. 'Oeuvres complètes de Christiaan Huygens,' The Hague, Vol. XVII, pub. 1934.
——. *Louvain.* ca.1700. cal. and astrolabe clock.
Gt. *Haarlem.* 1792.
HUYSLAND, Hermanus. *Holland.* End 17c. Watch Ryks M. Amsterdam.
HVARFVÉN, Johan. *Skara.* 1816.

HYATT, ——. *W. Hampton.* 1798. Watch N.Y. Univ.

HYDE—

John. *London.* a.1637.

Thomas. *London.* a.1691.

Edward. *London.* a.1731, CC.1741-4.

Thomas, son of Thos. *London.* a.1731.

John E. *New York.* 1805.

HYETT, Giles. *London.* a.1648.

HYLAND, John. *London.* ca.1760. Watch mt.

HYLDE, Edward. *London.* a.1720.

HYLLIUS, Martinus. *Dresden.* 1677-97. Watch with pendulum on verge, in cardan suspension in a silver spherical case. Wall clock set stones. Both in M.P.S. Dresden.

HYLOP, Thomas. *Nunland.* an 1772. Watch Buckley coll.

HYMAN—

Samuel. *Philadelphia.* ca.1800. Watch.

Joseph. *Carnarvon* and *Bangor.* Early 19c. Watch. l.c. clock.

HYMONS, Thomas. *London.* a.1696.

HYNAM—

Robert. *London.* ca.1750. Went to *Petersburg* ca.1776-99, and became W. to the Russian Court. Fine watch and chatelaine entirely covered with diamonds, Winter Pal., Petersburg. Carillon clock.

Robert. *London* (*Clement's Lane*). 1770.

HYNES, William. *Grantham.* 1601.

HYORNS, Kite. *London.* a.1723.

HYPHOFF, Poul Christian. *Copenhagen.* m. 1780.

HYVER, *v.* YVER.

I

IACOPO DA NOVARA. *Genoa.* 1411. 'Magister orologii et organum.' Keeper of clock at Caffa.

IBELL—
Thomas. *London.* CC.1795, l.CC.1812, d. 1814. Watch-spring maker.
Thomas, son. *London.* a.1801.
John, bro. *London.* a.1802.

IBERY, ——. *London.* 1775. Watch.

IDELOT—
——. *Paris.* 1710-39. Opposed introduction of Geneva watches into France. Clock.
Laurent. *Paris.* m.1742.

IGGLESDEN, ——. *Chatham.* ca.1800. Watch.

IGNELL, Anders. *Stockholm.* 1811. d.1827. Also INGELL.

IGOIN, Pierre. *Paris.* Juré 1748.

IGOU, Pierre. *Paris.* Juré 1789.

IHLSTRÖM, Lars. *Stockholm.* b.1743, d. 1790. br. clock.

ILBURY (ILBERY)—
James. *London (Queen St.).* 1755. *Goswell St.* 1777. W.
John. *London.* a.1765.
William. *London.* 1780. d.1839. A fine maker. Made watches for the Chinese market, and appears to have introduced the style of watch known as 'la montre chinoise.' Two watches London M., two M.M.A., one Feill coll. and one Den. coll. g. en. duplex watch M.P.S. Dresden. Watch, jasper and set pearls, Fränkel coll.
——, son. *London, Fleurier* and *Canton.* b.ca.1805-43.

ILDERTON, ——. *York.* an.1714. Watch.

ILES, Thomas. *London.* an.1778-90. Watch. l.c. clock Weth. coll. br. clock.

ILIFF, Thomas. *London.* 1802-08. W.

ILLAIRE, Jean Henri. *Berlin.* 1769.

ILLIG, Moritz Friedrich. *Darmstadt.* b.1777, d.1845. Eminent maker. 3-wheel clock, showing hours, mins. and secs., Darmstadt M.; also str. rep. table clock and watch.

ILLING, Johann G. *Fürth.* d.ca.1820.

ILLINOIS SPRINGFIELD WATCH CO., *v.* SPRINGFIELD ILLINOIS WATCH CO. 'ILLINOIS WATCH CO.' Sig. on 1789 watches.

ILLMAR, André. *Innsbrück.* 1559. Made table clock for Philipp of Hesse.

IMBERT—
Jean Pierre. *Lyons.* 1698-1703. Also IMBARD.
Jean Gabriel l'aîné. *Paris.* 1772 m.-1789. Porcelain clock Munich Residenz. Mantel clock Pal. de Fontainebleau.

IMER, ——. *Paris.* 1786. g. en. watch Stern. coll.

IMISON—
John. *Lussley* an.1780. *Manchester* 1784. C. & W.
——. *London.* 1786. Watch S.M.S.K.

IMLAH—
Peter. *London.* CC.1786. W.
Peter. *London.* a.1785.

IMMISCH, Moritz. *London.* d.1903. Awarded prize for essay on the isochronism of the balance spring.

IMSS, Phil. *Tübingen.* 1554. circ. table clock with al. above, B.M.

INGALL, Robert. *London.* a.1774.

INGELMARK, Jöns. *Stockholm.* b.1759, d. 1834.

INGERSOLL—
Daniel, tertius. *Boston, U.S.A.* 1798-1800. W.
Daniel G. *Boston, U.S.A.* 1803-13.

INGLEBY—
——. *Liverpool.* d.(?)1770. W.
William. *Bristol.* 1769. From *Halkin.* W.

INGLIS—
William. *Edinburgh.* 1811.
Walter. *Glasgow.* 1813.

INGLISH—
James. *London (Watling St.).* a.1763, CC 1781-90.
James, son. *London.* a.1787.
James. *London.* a.1796.
David. *Manchester.* ca.1820.
Mary. *Manchester.* ca.1820.

INGOLD—
Michael. *Chaux-de-Fonds.* 1769. C.
Pierre Frédéric. *Paris, London, Chaux-de-Fonds.* b.1787, d.1878. A very able mechanician; devised many tools for watch factories, in particular a cutter for shaping the teeth of wheels. In *Strasbourg,* 1809-11. *Paris,* 1811-4. *London,* 1815, with RENTSCH. *Chaux-de-Fonds,* 1816. *Paris,* with BREGUET, 1817-24, and there learnt the working of jewels. He started this industry in *Chaux-de-Fonds* in 1825-7, and then returned to Paris. Repaired the Vaucanson aut. Made watch winding by turning the bottom of the case, about 1815. His watchmaking machines were opposed by the craft first in *Paris,* and then in 1839 in *London.* He went to *New York* in 1844, and returned to *Chaux-de-Fonds* ca.1855, where he introduced the Ingold cutters. Magnificent vase clock with singing birds ill. M. des Aut.

INGRAM (INGRAHAM)—
Thomas. *London.* a.1686, CC.1695-1730. Watch Den. coll.
William, son. *London.* CC.1730-42. Watch.

INGRAM (INGRAHAM)—*continued.*
J. *Bexley.* an.1733. Watch.
Moses. *London.* a.1744.
John. *Spalding.* an.1753. Watch.
Job. *London.* a.1746.
——. *Bridgin.* an.1760. Watch.
James. *Abergavenny.* 1791-5. W.
John. *Abergavenny.* 1822-30.
Richard. *London.* a.1787.
Richard. *Dumfries.* 1820-37.
——. *Gloucester.* Early 19c. W.
George. *Findon.* Early 19c. Watch.
INKSON, John. *London.* an.1764. Watch.
INMAN, James. *Colne* and *Burnley.* ca.1820.
INNES—
James. prob. *London.* an.1775. Watch.
Robert. *London.* an.1777. Watch.
John. *London.* a.1772.
Alexander. *Dalkeith.* b.1757, d.1824.
David. *Edinburgh.* a.1785.
William. *Dublin.* ca.1800. Watch.
George. *Aberdeen.* 1820. d.1842.
William. *Glasgow.* 1825.
INNEVER, John. *London.* a.1694.
INNOCENT, Franz. *Vienna.*
INSKIP, T. *Shefford.* Early 19c.
'INTER-OCEAN.' Sig. on watches of the ELGIN NATIONAL WATCH Co. from 1877.
INWOOD—
Samuel. *London.* a.1662. Watch.
James. *London.* a.1713. Pair agate caskets with watches Peiping M.
ION—
John. *London* (*Windmill Hill*). 1766.
Joseph, son. *London* (*Nightingale La.*). a. 1766, CC.1777, d.an.1803.
John, bro. *London.* a.1767.
John, son of Jos. *London.* a.1803, CC.1811.
IRELAND—
Henry. *London.* CC.1654-75. Lantern clocks.
William. *London* (*Lothbury*). 17c. Lantern clock.
John. *London.* a.1660, CC.1668.
Francis. *London.* CC.1668-84.
John. *London.* a.1699.
Daniel. *London.* a.1724.
John. *Shrewsbury.* ca.1760. Watch mt. Shrewsbury M.
John. *London* (*Maiden La.*). 1772-80. Watch mt.
IREVOT, L. *London.* d.1775. W.
IRISH—
James. *Steyning* and *Brighton.* an.1780-1800. Watch mt.
Joseph. *Havant.* 1784. W.
Joseph. *Portsmouth.* ca.1790-1820 CC. C. & W.
Charles. *New York.* 1822. W.
IRONS—
Thomas. *Alcester.* ca.1790.
Robert. *London.* a.1818.
IRVINE—
Alexander. *Edinburgh.* 1690. d.1717.
Alexander, son. *Edinburgh.* 1717.
William. *Monkscroft.* an.1768. Watch.
John. *Edinburgh.* 1799.
John. *London.* a.1806.
IRVING (**ERVIN**)—
Alexander. *London* (*Westminster*). a.1688, CC.1695. l.c. clock ill. Cec. & Web.
J. *Blackburn.* 2nd half 18c. Watch mt.
IRWIN—
Ormsby. *Ballina.* 1824.
John. *Boyle.* 1824.
ISAAC—
Sutton. *London.* a.1655, CC.1662-81.
Jack. *Portsmouth.* Late 18c. Watch for India, studded stones.
R. *Narberth.* ca.1790 CC.
James. *Carmarthen.* d.1820. l.c. clock.
Joel. *Portsmouth.* 1795. W.
——. *Llanelly.* 2nd half 18c.
ISAACS—
Jacob. *London.* ca.1775. Watch.
Lewis. *London* (*Bloomsbury*). Late 18c.
Ralph. *Liverpool.* 1814-29. W.
John. *Woolwich.* 1817-24.
M. *Woolwich.* 1817-24.
Lewis. *London* (*Houndsditch*). 1822-4.
ISDELL, ——. *London.* an.1748. Watch.
ISELIN, Basilius. *Basle.* b.1691, d.1731.
ISHERWOOD, Ellin. *London.* a.1789.
ISRAEL, Moses. *London.* a.1751-1812. Watch.
ISRAELS—
Israel. *London.* 1743. Insolvent.
Joseph. *London.* 1744-ca.1775. l.c. clock ill. Cec. & Web.
ITALIANO, Leonardo. *Genoa.* 1410. 'magister orologii.' Keeper of clock at Caffa.
IVE—
Matthew. *London.* ca.1610. Polish refugee. Watch M.M.A.
Thomas. *London.* CC.1634.
Francis, son of Matthew. *London.* ca.1640.
IVERS, Christopher. *Kilnesh.* 1824.
IVES—
Zacharia. *London.* CC.1682-9. Clock.
John. *London.* a.1693.
Francis. *London.* a.1700, CC.1709-27.
William. *London.* a.1747-83.
Joseph. *Bristol, U.S.A.* 1810-55. Wooden and, later, 8-day brass clocks. In 1818 made l.c. clocks with iron plates and brass wheels.
CHAUNCEY & LAWSON. *Bristol, U.S.A.* 1831-1836. 8-day brass clocks.
IVISON, John. *Carlisle.* 1810-29. l.c. clocks. Watch.
IVORY—
James. *Dundee.* 1762. d.1795. Maker of repute. Watch Stads M. Amsterdam.
Thomas, son. *Dundee.* 1795-1825.
IZOD, William. *London.* a.1641, CC.1649.
IZZARD, John. *London.* a.1800.

J

JACARD, Henry. *Vevey.* 1798 m.
JACCARD, David. *London.* 1820.
JACCOTTET, François. *Paris.* 1780 m.
JACKEMAN (JAKEMAN), Joseph. *London.* 1682-1716. Watches Ilbert and Den. colls. mt. G.M. l.c. clock S.K.M.
JÄCKLE—
Joseph. *Schwenningen.* b.1774, d.1851. Schwarzwald clocks.
Johannes, son. *Schwenningen.* b.1808, d.1875. Schwarzwald clocks.
JACKLER, John. *London.* a.1697.
JACKMAN—
John. *London.* a.1724. Watch.
Joseph. *London.* 1708-16. Watch.
JACKS, James. *Montego Bay (Jamaica).* 1777. *Charleston, U.S.A.* 1784. C. & W.
JACKSON—
Richard. *London.* CC.1632.
Joseph. *London.* a.1637, CC.1646.
Thomas. *London.* a.1646.
Sampson. *London.* a.1656.
Edward. *London.* CC.1669.
Edward. *London.* a.1672, CC.1680-9.
John. *London.* a.1675, CC.1682-1705.
Thomas. *London.* a.1680, CC.1688.
James. *London.* a.1681, CC.1689-1703.
David. *London.* a.1684.
Martin. *London.* CC.1697, m.CC.1721. br. clock.
Benjamin. *London.* a.1696.
Matthew. *London.* a.1698, CC.1715, d.an. 1735.
John. *London.* a.1705.
Catherine. *London.* a.1719.
Samuel. *London (Fleet St.).* 1727. W.
Samuel, son. *London.* 1736.
Matthew, son of Matthew. *London.* a.1723, CC.1730-6. Lantern clock.
William. *London.* a.1725, CC.1735, l.CC. and d.1776. br. clock Weth. coll.
John. *Liverpool.* 1734.
Obadiah. *London.* a.1727.
William. *London.* a.1728, CC.1736
William. *London.* a.1732, CC.1739.
Joseph. *London.* a.1737, CC.1746.
John. *London (Basinghall St.).* 1754-63.
John. *London (Bridgewater Sq.).* 1760. l.CC.1776, m.CC.1796-1825. The firm was John & John, 1781-94.
John. *London.* a.1753, CC.1778.
Richard. *York* to 1762. *Hexham* 1762-8. C. & W.
Owen. *Cranbrook* and *Tenterden.* 1767-83. In 1796 in partnership with his son John at *Tenterden.* W.
——. *Ashford.* d.1790. W.
James. *London.* a.1760, CC.1767.

JACKSON—*continued.*
William. *Easingwold.* ca.1770-1822. W.
William. *Thirsk.* 1772-5. l.c. clock. W.
John, jun. *London.* CC.1779, l.CC.1783-7.
Matthew. *London.* a.1773.
John, & Co. *London.* 1781.
John. *London.* a.1775.
John. *Henley-on-Thames.* 1783. W.
Thomas. *London (Clerkenwell).* 1783-1810. W.
——. *Gainsborough.* 1784. W.
Randal. *London.* 1785-1808.
Henry. *London (Clerkenwell).* 1790-1834.
Thomas. *London (E. Smithfield).* 1790.
Joseph H. *Mill Creek Hundred, Del., U.S.A.,* ca.1790. *Philadelphia,* ca.1803-17. l.c. clock.
John. *Boston.* 1791. C. & W.
Edward. *London (E. Smithfield).* a.1783, CC.1790-1808.
William. *Frodsham.* 1795-1801. C. Lancaster freeman.
William. *Maidstone.* From 1796-ca.1800 CC. W.
Joseph. *London.* CC.1797.
Jacob. *Bristol.* 1798-1818. an.1798 of DANIEL & JACKSON. W.
Thomas. *London (St. John St.).* 1802-08.
John. *London.* a.1799, CC.1806.
William. *London (Cow Cross St.).* a.1802, CC.1810-20. C.
John. *London (Bridgewater Sq.).* CC.1810, m.CC.1822-6.
William. *London (King St., Clerkenwell).* 1814. Watch case maker.
William Wilkinson. *Lancaster.* 1817. W. & C.
Edward. *York.* 1818. d.1858. W. & C.
Stephen. *London.* CC.1819.
Abraham. *Liverpool.* ca.1820-9. W.
John. *Liverpool.* ca.1820.
John. *Lancaster.* ca.1820.
John. *London.* CC.1824. W.
J., & Son. *Bristol.* 1825-30. chron. W. & C.
——. *Henley-on-Thames.* Early 19c.
JACOB—
Jacques. *Neuchâtel.* 1582. 'Horloger et Serrurier.'
von dem Wege. *Cologne.* 1596. Kleinuhrmacher.
Benjamin. *London.* a.1687, CC.1706.
John. *London.* a.1697.
Benjamin. *London.* a.1708, CC.1718.
——. *S. Germany.* 1741. Watch, case and mt. mainly of boxwood.
Isaac. *Moudon.* 1753. From *Valangin.*
Gottfried. *Bunzlau.* b.1738. astro. clock, desc. in pamphlet pub. ca.1783.
Charles & Abraham CLAUDE. *Annapolis, U.S.A.* 1773-5. From *London.* W. Part-

JACOB—*continued.*
nership dissolved in 1775 and Charles continued alone.
Lazarus. *Bristol.* ca.1780. Watch.
Jean Jacques. *Paris.* m.1783. l.c. year clock C.A. & M.
Herman. *Bunzlau.* 1784-97. A carpenter who made an aut. clock now in town M.
Jean Aimé. *Paris.* b.1793, d.1871. Able maker. Established a precision clock factory at *S. Nicholas d'Aliermont.* Made one-year regulators, chrons. and chronographs.
——. *Paris* (*Rue des Mathurins St. Jacques*). 1812-25. C.
——. *Paris* (*Rue St. Martin*). 1812-25. C.
JACOBELLI, ——. *Vienna.* Early 18c. br. clock.
JACOBI, John Henry. *London.* a.1799. From *Calcutta.*
JACOBS—
Jan. *Haarlem.* ca.1600. crys. oct. watch Gélis coll. cf. JACOBSEN.
Coenrad. *Leeuwarden.* ca.1610. Watch with astro. dials and compass and sundial B.M.
Johan. *Cologne.* m.1634. Kleinuhrmacher.
Solomon. *Norwich.* 1755. Insolvent.
Judah. *London.* 1760-ca.1770. br. clock.
Mark. *London.* an.1766. Watch.
Barent. *Norwich.* 1769. From *Ipswich.* W. Insolvent.
A. *Torquay.* Late 18c. l.c. clock.
Moses. *Redruth.* 1795. W.
H. *Nottingham.* 1818. C. & W.
Solomon. *Penzance.* Early 19c. Watch.
John. *London.* Early 19c. Watch.
& SON. *Hull.* Early 19c. Watch.
Ephraim. *London.* 1820-4.
Henry. *London* (*Whitechapel*). 1820.
Isaac. *London* (*Whitechapel*). 1824.
S. *Bristol.* 1825-30.
JACOBSEN—
Jan. *Haarlem.* Early 17c. oct. crys. watch Blot-Garnier coll. cf. JACOBS.
Jacob J. *Copenhagen.* m.1804.
Bernt. *Bergen.* m.1810.
JACOBZOON, Dirck. *Wormerveer.* 1698. br. clock.
JACOILLOT, ——. prob. *Paris.* 1st half 18c. Boulle clock Schloss M. Berlin.
JACOMBE, Samuel. *London.* 1760.
JACOPIN—
Abram. *Chaux-de-Fonds.* 1727-50.
Jean Jacques. *Paris.* m.1783-9.
Charles Henry. *La Brévine.* 1790.
Guillaume. *Fontaines.* 1791-1826. Several clocks.
David François. *La Brévine.* 1810. C.
——. *Paris.* 1813.
Henri Louis. *Fontaines.* 1819.
Le Capitaine. *La Brévine.* 1820. C.
JACOT—
A. Henri. *Le Locle.* 1760.
Guillaume. *Fontaines.* 1791-1826.
Charles Edouard. *Le Locle.* 1830. Said to have devised the Chinese duplex esc.
JACOTOT, ——. *Paris.* 1812.
JACQUARD, Antoine. *Blois.* 1652. Made designs for eng. watch-cases.
JACQUEMART, ——. *Lille.* 1422. 'Orlogeur et serrurier,' employed by the Duc de Bourgogne. Repaired Dijon clock.
JACQUEMET, Jaques Nicolas. *Geneva.* ca. 1775-91.
JACQUEMIN, ——. *Lyons.* 1443-5.
JACQUES—
——. *Lyons.* 1531-4.
Étienne François. *Paris.* m.1739.
François Étienne. *Paris.* m.1746-75.
Charles. *Chichester.* 1780-95. C. & W. From *London.*
Antony. *Grenoble.* Early 19c. Made clock with square and elliptical wheels.
JACQUET—
——. *London.* ca.1720. Watch M.M.A. Also JAQUET.
Joseph. *Paris.* m.1735, d.1797.
——. *Gray* (*Franche-Comté*). 1752. Invented a piston for pumps.
——. *Liége.* 2nd half 18c. C. to the Prince Eveque.
——. *Paris* (*Rue de Viarme*). 1812.
jeune. *Paris* (*Rue St. Eloy*). 1812.
JACQUIER, Pierre. *Avignon.* 1533. Keeper of town clock.
JACQUIN, A. *Paris.* 1807-25.
JACQUINS, Jean François. *Vevey.* 1798 m.
JACQUOT—
——. *Rouen.* 2nd half 18c. Watch.
——. *Paris.* 1812.
JACRET, ——. *Paris.* 1787-9.
JÄDERBERG, Olof. *Stockholm.* 1762-70.
JADWIN, Robert. *London.* a.1647.
JAFFRAY, John. *Stirling.* 1790.
JAGENAU, Peter. *Dresden.* 1576. Court C. From *Wismar.*
JAGER, Joseph. *London.* 1805-08.
JÄGER—
Johann Georg. *Augsburg.* m.1768-95.
Ignatz, son. *Augsburg.* m.ca.1805.
JAGGAR, Edward. *London.* CC.1702-35.
JAGGERS, John. *London* (*Westminster*). a. 1822, CC.1829.
JAGOE, John. *London.* 1809-11.
JAHN—
Franz. *Olmütz.* 1661. Repaired town clock.
——. *Olmütz.* 1733.
JAHNS, jun. *Berlin.* 1812.
JÄHNS, ——. *Berlin.* 1794.
JAHNSON, Jakob. *Copenhagen.* m.1777.
JALLI, André. *Grenoble.* 1550.
JALOUX, François. *Besançon.* 1551-75.
JAMBON, R. F. *Paris.* Made an orrery and pub. a treatise on astronomy based on it.
JAMES—
John. *London.* a.1653, CC.1661.
Francis. *London.* a.1655, CC.1662.
Joseph. *London.* a.1678, CC.1689-1723.
Moughan. *London.* a.1692.
John. *London.* a.1694.
William. *London.* a.1696.
William. *London.* a.1698.
Samuel. *London.* a.1705.
Thomas. *London* (*St. Anne's Churchyard, Soho*). an.1730. Watch.
Thomas. *London* (*Westminster*). d.1747.
Thomas. *London.* a.1738.
John. *London.* a.1762.
Joseph. *London.* an.1757. Watch.
Peter. *London.* an.1762. Watch.
Charles. *London* (*Gray's Inn*). 1762. W.
John. *London.* 1770. Watch N.Y. Univ.
George. *London.* CC.1771.
Francis. *London.* a.1767.
William. *Bath.* 2nd half 18c. Watch Den. coll.
Theophilus. *Gloucester.* 1774. Succeeded Rich. PEYTON W.
James. *Canton* (*China*). d.1791. W.
Richard. *London.* a.1775.
James. *London.* a.1781.
Thomas. *London.* a.1782.
Richard. *London* (*Red Lion Sq.*). 1791. W.
Isaac. *London.* a.1790.
P. *Edinburgh.* 1806. Watch Ilbert coll.
William. *London.* a.1805.
John. *Liverpool.* 1825. W.
Miles. *Liverpool.* 1825. W.
JAMESON, J. *London.* an.1772-96. Watch.
JAMET, Nicholas. *Blois.* 1587.
JAMIESON—
John. *Ayr.* 1798.
George. *Liverpool.* 1816-8. W.
James. *Newton-Stewart.* 1820.
JAMIN, Jacques. *Lyons.* 1665 m., d.1671.

JAMISON—
George. *London, Portsea* and *Portsmouth.* 1786-1810. Partner with Wm. HOWELLS and P. P. BARRAUD in making MUDGE'S Timekeepers up to 1799. Each partner continued his own business. Expert on Mudge's chron. 'Chron. maker to the High Commrs. of the Navy.' br. clock ill. Cec. & Web. Also JAMESON.
George. *Liverpool.* ca.1820.
Charles. *London.* Early 19c. Watch.
JAMMETT, Thomas. *London.* CC.1704.
JAMNITZER, Wenzel. *Augsburg.* 1550. d. 1585. math. inst. maker, goldsmith and C.
JAN, 'Kleynsmed.' *Göttingen.* 1441. Made the clock of St. Johann.
JANAWAY, William. *London.* a.1675.
JANIK, Johann. *Teschen.* Late 18c. sil. p.c. rep. watch, painted dial.
JANIN ET DELARUE. *Geneva.* Early 19c.
JANNOT, André. *Geneva.* ca.1755-71.
JANOVIUS, Georg Gottlob. *Bautzen.* 1757 finished his apprenticeship.
JANS, Franz. *Straubing.* 2nd half 18c. p.c. sil. watch.
JANSE. At. *Amsterdam.* ca.1750. br. clock.
JANSEN—
F. A. *Hamburg.* 1821.
v. JANZEN.
JANSON—
Martin. *London.* 1561. 'horologiarius.' Alien.
Joseph. *London.* CC.1820.
JANSSEN, Egbert. *Amsterdam.* Early 17c. sil. shell watch Gélis coll.
JANSSON, ——. *Eskilstuna.* 1822.
JANTZ, Josephus. *Augsburg.* ca.1670. Hex. table clock.
JANVIER—
Charles. *Blois.* a.1621-47.
Claude Étienne. *St. Claude.* 1750-69.
Jérémie, l'aîné. *Paris* (*Rue St. Honoré*). m. 1770-89.
Antide, son of C. Étienne. *Besançon.* b.1751-1769. *Morez,* 1771-2. *Paris,* 1775. *Verdun. Paris,* 1807. d.1835. C. to Louis XVI and Louis XVIII. An eminent horologist. Ruined by the Revolution. Wrote 'Étrennes Chronométriques' in 1810, which has passed through many later editions as 'Manuel Chronométrique.' Also, 'Essai sur les Horloges publiques,' Paris, 1811; 'Des Revolutions des Corps célestes par le Mécanisme des Rouages,' Paris, 1812. Several fine planetary clocks. Three fine clocks C.A. & M. A regulator with mounts by Gouthière sold in 1901 for £3,255. Regulator with ten dials showing Gregorian and Revolutionary calendars, Virginia M.
Joseph, bro. *St. Claude* and *Paris.* b.1754, d.1820. Went to *Paris* with his brother and returned *St. Claude* 1790.
Antoine, le jeune. *Paris* (*Rue Dauphine*). m. 1772-1815.
——. *Paris* (*Pavillon des Quatre-Nations*). 1812.
JANZEN—
Symen. *Haarlem.* 1658.
Anthony. *Amsterdam.* 2nd half 18c. cal. and aut. l.c. clock S.K.M.
JAPY—
Frédéric. *Beaucourt.* b.1749, d.1813. The first to manufacture watch ébauches by machine tools in 1776. His first machines were bought from J. J. JEANNERET-GRIS. Founded the watch factory of Japy Frères, and designed its machines. Started a factory for clock ébauches at *Baderel* in 1810. al. mt. S.M.S.K.
Adolphe. *Beaucourt.* b.1813, d.1897.
JAQUEMIN, ——. *Tour de Peilz* (*Vevey*). 1798 m.
JAQUES—
William. *London.* a.1679, CC.1687, m.CC. 1716.
James. *London.* a.1679.
William, son of Wm. *London.* a.1716, CC. 1724.
Robert. *London.* a.1717-31 CC. Also JACQUES.
Sarah. *London.* 1722.
JAQUEST, Edward. *London.* a.1715.
JAQUET—
——. *Neuveville.* 1652.
Guillaume. *St. Blaise.* 1668-80.
P. *London.* 1763. g. en. watch. Also JACQUET.
André. *Chaux-de-Fonds.* 1775. C.
——. *St. Imier.* ca.1790.
JAQUET-DROZ—
Jean. *Hüningen.* 1725.
Pierre. *Basle, Neuchâtel, Paris, Geneva* and *Madrid.* b.1721, d.1790. Celebrated clockmaker and mechanician. Made a number of famous aut. bought by Ferdinand VI of Spain. Made clock winding by the difference in expansion of two metals in 1755. Two l.c. clocks École d'horlogerie, Geneva. The aut. 'Le Berger' and a mus. clock exist in Madrid Pal. Fine clocks Kunst und Gewerbe M. Vienna, and École d'Horlogerie, Chaux-de-Fonds. g. en. cyl. mus. watch with barrel and 5 bells Wilsdorf coll.
Henri Louis, son. *Chaux-de-Fonds, Nancy* and *Geneva,* with branch in *London.* b. 1752, d.1791. Worked with his father. Associated with J. F. LESCHOT at Geneva from 1784. London branch in charge of Henri MAILLARDET from 1775. Celebrated clock, watch and automaton maker. Made many watches for China, sd. J‡D and, after 1784, J.L.-G. Carillon watch with 5 bells. Many watches in Swiss colls. Several singing birds and aut. ill. M. des Aut.
JAQUOT, ——. *Caen.* 1772.
JARDIN, John. *London* (*Bartholomew La.* in 1777, *Throgmorton St.* in 1800). 1740. CC.1781, l.CC.1796-1811.
JARDINE. John. *Glasgow.* 1765. d.1801.
JARED, George. *Oswestry.* 1791. C.
JARLE, Jean Antoine. *Paris.* m.1765-89. Mantel clock.
JARMAN—
John. *London.* a.1719, CC.1728-32.
Robert or Richard. *London.* a.1790.
John Bowkett. *London.* 1815. Watch G.M.
JAROSSAY, Urbain. *Paris.* m.1784-9. C. to the Comte d'Artois. Made clock for St. Germain-des-Prés in 1782. Cartel clock.
JAROUSSEAU, Claude. *Coivert-en-Saintonge.* Went to *La Rochelle* 1709. Watch.
JARRAD, William Thomas. *London.* a.1717.
JARRETT (JARRATT)—
Richard. *London.* CC.1632.
Richard. *London* (*Lothbury*). CC.1670, m. CC.1685-95. Watch ill. Britten. br. clock Weth. coll. Also JARRATT.
John. *London.* 1757.
William. *London* (*Peartree St.*). 1776-87.
John William. *London* (*Clerkenwell*). CC. 1783-1817. l.c. clock. Also JARRATT.
Barnard. *London* (*Pentonville*). a.1780, CC. 1787-1826.
George Lewis. *London.* a.1781, CC.1788.
William. *London.* 1806 CC.
Charles William. *London.* a.1808.
JARRY, Jean Pierre. *Berlin.* 1802-11. Last director of the Fabrique royale.
JARVIS—
Simon. *London.* a.1670.
Joseph. *London.* a.1670.
Abel. *London.* a.1696, CC.1704-40.
Samuel. *Birmingham.* ca.1710.

JARVIS—*continued.*
James. *London.* a.1719.
George, son of Abel. *London.* a.1720, CC. 1728.
William, bro. *London.* a.1730, d.an.1754.
Thomas. *London* (*St. James*). an.1753, d. 1778.
Stephen. *London.* a.1746.
William. *London.* a.1751.
John. *London* (*Quaker's Bdgs.*). a.1754, CC. 1762-90.
John. *Whitchurch.* Early 19c. Watch.
JAUNCEY, George. *London.* a.1783.
JAVELOT, ——. *Paris.* 1787-9.
JAVIN, Guillaume. *Avignon.* 1540-89. Town C. to 1553. Made aut. clock for Sorgue. Re-made clocks of Cavaillon and Mormoiron.
JAY—
Paul. *France.* Early 17c. Cross watch Pal. du Cinquantenaire, Brussels.
Jaques. *Moudon.* 1735.
Stephen. *London.* a.1784.
JAYNE, John. *London.* CC.1687.
JEAN—
l'orlogeur. *France.* 1405. Repaired clock of Château de Courville.
——. *Lyons.* 1408-12.
de Lycbourg. *Paris.* 1459. 'Maistre ouvrier d'Horloges.' Made five clocks for Charles VII.
de Paris. *Paris.* 1480. Made clock for Louis XI.
——. *Lyons.* 1558. 'fabro horologiorum.' Perhaps Jean ALBE or Jean NAZE.
de Lorrein. *Nancy.* 1620. Made moon mechanism for Beaune clock.
Adrien. *Paris.* Juré 1749.
——. *Paris* (*Rue des Francs-Bourgeois*). 1812-25.
JEANDEL, ——. *Paris.* 1795. Maker of mus. mechanism for clocks.
JEANGUENIN, Adam. *Courtelary.* ca.1780. Worked with his brother Jean David and sisters Catherine, Lydie, Suzon and Elisabeth.
JEANMAIRET, Sylvian. *Le Locle.* b.1805, d.1890. Spent five years in *London* an.1840. A fine precision watch and chron. maker. Most of his lever watches had all the lift on the esc. wheel teeth.
JEANNERET—
Charles François. *Chaux-de-Fonds* and *Val de Travers.* 1779-87.
P. *Val de Travers.* End 18c.-1802. Several clocks.
Lewis. *London.* a.1786.
Henri Ferdinand. *Couvet.* 1809-30.
——. *Paris.* 1812-22.
JEANNERET-GRIS—
P. *Lyons.* 1756.
Abram. *Chaux-de-Fonds.* 1784.
Jean Jacques. *Neuchâtel, Le Locle* and *Besançon.* End 18c. and early 19c. Devised many watchmaking machines, later sold to JAPY. l.c. clock.
Louis Frédéric, bro. *Neuchâtel.* 1770. Invented a pinion-cutting machine.
JEANNERET-GROSCLAUDE, Frédéric. *Le Locle.* b. end 18c., d. 1857.
JEANNERET-HERLEMÉE, ——. *Paris.* 1823.
JEANNERET-MATHEY, ——. *Paris.* 1819-1825.
JEANNIN, ——. *Paris.* 1812.
JEAN-PERRIN, ——. *Paris.* 1808-25.
JEAN-PETITMATILE, Jean Jacques. *Le Locle.* 1799.
JEANQUEMAIN, ——. *Paris.* 1822-5.
JEAN-RENAUD—
Daniel François. *Môtiers* and *Boveresse.* a. 1749. Several clocks.

JEAN-RENAUD—*continued.*
Pierre Henri. *Môtiers* and *Val de Travers.* 1777. C.
JEANRICHARD—
Abram. *La Sagne* and *Morat.* 1707-34.
Félix. *Chaux-de-Fonds.* 1756. C.
JEANRICHARD-DIT-BRESSEL—
Daniel. *La Sagne* and *Le Locle.* b.1665, d. 1741. Went to *Le Locle* ca.1700. One of the pioneers of horology in the Neuchâtel district. His five sons started a factory where many watches were made. Watch Le Locle M.
Daniel, son. *La Sagne.* 1741.
François Julien. *La Sagne.* b.1796, d.1879.
Louis. *Le Locle.* b.1812, d.1875. Very able maker of watches, chron. and regulators.
JEANS, Samuel. *London.* a.1702.
JEBOULT, H. *Salisbury.* 1793. W.
JEE, George. *Coventry.* 1770. Watch, skeleton mt., Ilbert coll.
JEEVES, Anthony. *Oxford.* 1774. l.c. clock.
JEFFARD, ——. *Newton Bushel.* 1795. W.
JEFFERSON—
Samuel. *London.* 1809-40. Clock Windsor Castle ill. Britten. W. to the Prince of Wales.
& GREGSON. *London.* 1815. Also GREGSON & JEFFERSON.
& Co. *London* (*Fetter La.*). 1820.
JEFFERYS (JEFFERY, JEFFERIES, JEFFERIS, JEFFREYS, JEFFRYS)—
John. *London.* CC.1639. (JEFFERIES.)
William Knight. *London.* a.1700, CC.1712-1723.
Edward. *London.* a.1710. (JEFFERY.)
John. *London.* a.1717, CC.1726. (JEFFERY.)
Joseph. *London.* a.1720. (JEFFERIES.)
John. *London.* CC.1726-35. (JEFFREYS.)
John. *London.* a.1734-42 CC.
William. *London.* a.1744.
Samuel. *London.* a.1753.
John. *Cirencester.* 1747. d. or retired 1757. Succeeded by John NORTH. Watch. (JEFFERIS.)
John. *Worcester.* From 1758. From *London* and *Cirencester.* Watch. C. (JEFFERIS.)
Isaac. *London.* a.1760, CC.1767.
Samuel. *Philadelphia.* 1771-7. C. & W.
Thomas. *London.* 1771. g. en. watch London M.
Nathaniel. *London.* ca.1780. Watch Ilbert coll.
Robert. *London.* a.1772.
John. *Bristol.* 1780. Partner with MCCARTHY.
George. *Chatham.* an.1783. l.c. clock. rep. watch.
Isaac. *London.* CC.1787. (JEFFERIES.)
William. *Maldon.* 1791-early 19c. W.
George. *London.* End 18c. l.c. clock.
Henry. *London* (*Salisbury Sq.*), 1799; (*Fleet St.*), 1804-29.
& JONES. *London* (*Cockspur St.*). an.1776-ca.1800. Well-known makers of richly decorated watches. en. watches F.W.M. and London M. g. en. watch set pearls Mallett coll. Regulator ill. Cec. & Web.
——. *London* (*Snow Hill*). 1800-20.
& HAM. *London* (*Salisbury Sq.*). 1810-25. cyl. watch Chamb. coll.
John. *London.* CC.1814. (JEFFREYS.)
John. *Biggleswade.* Early 19c. Watch.
JEFFS—
John. *London.* a.1689, CC.1697-1716.
James. *London.* CC.1700.
Benjamin. *London.* a.1693, CC.1702.
JEGER—
Hieronimus. *Basle.* m. 1518. In 1542 made a clock for Laufenberg-a.-R.
Johan Georg. *Augsburg.* 18c. rep. al. and cal. watch Stern. coll.

JEKYLL, Jonathan. *London.* a.1724, CC.1742.
JELF, William. *London.* a.1708, CC.1717-26.
JELLAND, ——. *London.* an.1781. Watch.
JELLISON, Robert. *London.* a.1725, CC. 1736-44.
JELLY (JELLES), Thomas. *London.* a.1701, CC.1720.
JEMIN, Isaac. *Dijon.* Early 17c. Watch Gélis coll.
JEMMETT—
Thomas. *London.* a.1697, CC.1704-16.
Thomas. *London.* a.1793, CC.1803.
JEMSON, ——. *London.* an.1719. Watch.
JENEWAY, William. *London.* a.1675.
JENKINS—
Thomas. *London.* a.1669, CC.1677-92.
Cornelius. *London.* a.1671, CC.1678-1709. Watch case maker.
James. *London (Strand).* a.1683, CC.1692-1708. l.c. clock Weth. coll.
John. *London.* a.1695-1704 CC.
Edward. *London (Holloway).* a.1699-1724. Insolvent.
Samuel. *London.* a.1712.
Edward. *Bristol.* 1724.
Henry. *London (Cheapside).* ca.1730-88. Pub. 1760 'A description of several Geographical and Astronomical clocks . . .' Fine astro. clock ill. Britten. Geographical l.c. and br. clocks ill. Cec. & Web.
M. *London.* ca.1750. Watch mt.
——. *Devizes.* an.1767. Watch.
& HIAM. *London (Cheapside).* 1762. Sold stock.
William. *London (E. Smithfield).* CC.1771-1780.
C. *London.* 1779. Watch Ilbert coll.
Thomas. *Rochester.* d.1789. *v.* following.
Mason. *Rochester.* d.1802. In partnership with Thos. till 1787.
J. & M. *Rochester.* 1784. W.
William Samuel. *London.* a.1805.
Emanuel. *London.* 1815.
Herman. *Albany, U.S.A.* 1817-23.
John. *Swansea.* Early 19c. Watch.
William. *Bandon.* 1824.
JENKINSON—
Edward. *London.* 1723. Insolvent.
Thomas. *London.* an.1740. Watch.
Thomas. *Sandwich.* d.1755. W.
Herbert. *London.* a.1737.
Morley. *Grantham.* an.1755. Watch.
S. *Sandwich.* ca.1760. Watch S.K.M.
John. *London.* an.1777. Watch.
Matthew. *London.* a.1767.
JENKSON, Joseph. *London.* an.1775. Watch.
JENNINGS—
Emanuel. *London.* a.1682.
Robert. *London.* a.1695, CC.1703-35, d.an. 1746. Engraver.
Thomas. *London.* a.1703, CC.1721.
Charles. *London.* a.1716, CC.1725.
Roger. *London.* a.1719.
William. *London.* a.1746.
Thomas. *Fritwell.* an.1776. Watch.
Benjamin. *London.* an.1781. Watch.
William. *London.* a.1775.
John. *London.* a.1794.
W. *Fritwell.* an.1823. Watch.
JENNION, William. *Chester.* 1602. 'Clocksmith.'
JENNYS, ——. *London.* an.1762. Watch.
JENSEN—
Peter. *Copenhagen.* 1798.
Lars. *Copenhagen.* m.1799.
Christen. *Copenhagen.* m.1813.
JENSON, Hans. *Copenhagen.* 1653. Court C.
JENTI, Josias. *Paris.* 1st half 17c. en. watch Mallett coll. ill. Baillie.
JEPHSON, J. *London.* 1782. Watch Ilbert coll.
JEPPS, William. *London.* CC.1772.
JEPSON—
William. *London.* a.1727.
George Andrew. *Nottingham.* 1811. Insolvent. C. & W.
JÉQUIER—
Jean Jacques. *Fleurier* and *Lausanne.* 1730-early 19c. g. en. watch Fränkel coll. aut. watches.
Charles Louis. *Fleurier.* 1783.
——. *Paris.* an.1795. Watch.
JERDAN, ——. *Glasgow.* 1754. Turret clock.
JEREY, A. *London.* ca.1780. g. en. watch.
JERMAN, ——. *London.* an.1774. Watch.
JERNEGAN, Edward. *London.* an.1750. Watch.
JEROME—
——. prob. *Geneva.* ca.1800. Watch with obscene en. paintings.
Chauncey. *Bristol* and *New Haven, U.S.A.* b.1793-1860. One of the pioneers of American clockmaking. In *New Jersey* with Lewis STEBBINS in 1812. Worked with Eli TERRY 1814-21. Started a wooden clock-case business in *Bristol* in 1821. In 1824 joined with his brother Noble and Elijah DARROW to make the whole clock, and produced the bronze looking-glass type of clock in 1825. Devised a wheel-cutting machine for mass production and in 1838 made the first 1-day br. clock, which had an enormous sale; consignments sent to England. Formed the Jerome Mfg. Co. in 1850, which failed in 1855, and was succeeded by the New Haven Clock Co. Pub. 'History of the American Clock Business,' New Haven, 1860.
Noble, bro *Bristol, U.S.A.* 1824-40, period of partnership with JEROME.
C. & N. *Bristol, U.S.A.* ca.1824. Wall clock Furt. M.
JERRARD—
Henry. *Hindon.* 2nd half 18c. l.c. clock.
John D. *London.* ca.1775. Watch Buckley coll.
JERSEY, Francis. *London.* CC.1770. br. clock. W.
JERVAIS, ——. *Falaise.* an.1777. Watch.
JERVIS, Francis. *London.* a.1656.
JESCH, Eric Emanuel. *Berlin.* 1785. C.
JESNER (JESSNER), Joseph. *Vienna.* m. 1815. l.c. clock Uhren M. Vienna.
JESSOP, Josias. *London.* 1780-94. g. en. watches M.M.A. and Stern. coll. c.secs. watch Ilbert coll.
JEVE, Richard. *London.* a.1771.
JEVON—
Henry. *London.* CC.1673-93.
Mary, daughter. *London.* CC.1706.
JEW—
James. *London.* CC.1814.
James. *Gloucester.* Early 19c.
JEWELL, ——. *London.* mar.1771. W.
JEWSON, Thomas. *London.* a.1698.
JEYES—
Samuel. *London.* a.1670.
James. *London.* a.1745, CC.1753.
JEZAPH, J. *London.* 1820.
JICKINSON, Joseph. *London.* an.1774. Watch.
JINERE, Jean Jacques. *Paris.* m.1756.
JOACHIM, ——. *Paris.* 1819-25. Wooden clocks.
JOB—
Robert. *London.* 1804-08.
John. *Philadelphia.* 1819.
JOBEZ, Philippe. *Bellefontaine.* 1743.
JOBON, ——. *Paris.* 1819-25.
JOBSON—
William. *London.* a.1702. Watch.
Thomas. *London.* 1815.

JODIN—
Jean. *St. Germain-en-Laye, Paris.* 1754. Pub. 'Les échappements à repos comparés aux échappements à recul,' Paris, 1754. 'Montre à deux balanciers,' Paris, 1759, and other arts. cyl. watch S.M.S.K.
Jean. *Paris.* m.1758.

JOEL, Isaac. *Preston.* ca.1820.

JOELL, John. *London.* a.1763.

JOERDE, Johann Ulrich. *Dresden.* m.1750.

JOFFROY, ——. *Besançon.* 2nd half 18c. Several good br. clocks.

JOGUIER, Jean. *Paris.* 1675 m.

JOHAN, ——. *Cologne.* 1418. 'Uireclockenmacher.' First known in Cologne.

JOHANN—
——. *Hagenau.* 1383. 'Orglocker.' Made clock for Frankfurt-a.-M.
Nicolaus Alexius. *Mainz.* b.1753, d.1826. Large astro. clock in the Stadtbibliothek, Mainz, desc. by Arentz in 1830.
Albert. *Chaux-de-Fonds* and *Aarau.* b.1822, d.1882. Pub. in 1879 'Traité générale d'Horlogerie.' A very fine maker.

JOHANNSEN, Nickolaus. *Germany.* Late 17c. hex. table clock Fränkel coll.

JOHANSEN, Christen. *Copenhagen.* comp. 1771.

JOHN—
Hans. *Königsberg-i.-Pr.* 1664. Acorn watch with pistol as alarum, B.M. ill. Baillie.
'JOHN EVANS.' Sig. on 1871-4 watches of the CORNELL WATCH CO.
'JOHN HANCOCK.' Sig. on 1871-5 watches of the NEW YORK WATCH CO.
'JOHN L. KING.' Sig. on 1870 watches of the NEW YORK WATCH CO.
'JOHN LEWIS.' Sig. on 1869-70 watches of the UNITED STATES WATCH CO.

JOHNLYNN, William. *London.* an.1753. Watch.

JOHNS—
Thomas. *London.* ca.1700-05. l.c. clock ill. Cec. & Web.
John. *Cerne.* 1740. C.

JOHNSON—
Leonard. *Nottingham.* 1541.
Roger. *London.* 1630. Petitioner for incorporation of CC.
George. *London.* a.1641, CC.1649.
Cornelius. *London.* a.1650.
Jeremy. *London.* a.1660, CC.1668-97, d.an. 1709. oct. watch, crys. cover. br. clock. Chiming l.c. clock.
William. *York.* 1665-1713. W.
John. *London.* CC.1678-99.
George. *London.* a.1668.
Thomas. *London.* ca.1680-1705. Two l.c. clocks, one with 1¼ secs. pendulum ill. Cec. & Web.
John. *London.* a.1673, CC.1680.
Michael. *London* and *Barnard Castle.* a. 1677, CC.1687-1704. Watch.
Benjamin. *London.* 1693-1720. l.c. clock.
Cornelius. *London.* a.1686, CC.1694-1715.
William. *London.* a.1690, CC.1702. br. clock.
Thomas. *London.* a.1692, CC.1700. l.c. clock.
John. *London (Fleet La.).* 1701. C.
John. *London.* CC.1701.
Jeremy, son of Jeremy. *London.* a.1697.
Isaac. *London.* a.1698, CC.1705-16.
James. *London.* CC.1706.
John. *London.* a.1701.
Thomas. *Richmond.* CC.1713. Watch S.K.M.
Thomas. *London.* a.1707, CC.1714-25. Bankrupt.
John. *London.* a.1710.
Williams. *London.* a.1711.

JOHNSON—*continued.*
John. *London.* a.1711.
Isaac. *London.* a.1713, CC.1723.
Thomas. *London (St. Giles, Cripplegate).* 1725. Insolvent. Cf. Thos. 2 & 4 above.
Thomas. *London.* a.1724.
John. *Morpeth.* b.ca.1710, d.ca.1778. W. From *Berwick.* Also JOHNSTON.
Charles Jacock. *London.* a.1727, CC.1750.
William. *London.* a.1734, CC.1741. Watch.
James. *London.* a.1740.
Thomas. *London (Gray's Inn Passage).* an. 1744, d.1775. Watch. Succeeded by his son John.
Samuel. *London.* an.1750. Watch.
Roland. *Liverpool.* 1758-1810. W.
James. *Kingston (Jamaica).* d.1784. W.
John. *Charleston, U.S.A.* 1763. Previously *London* and *Havana.* W.
John. *Walton-on-Thames.* an.1766. Watch.
David. *Dublin.* 1766. W.
James. *Liverpool.* 1768-1821. W. Also JOHNSTON.
Thomas. *London.* a.1760.
Joseph. *Dudley.* 1760-95. C. l.c. mus. clock and watch.
Richard. *London.* an.1773. Watch.
James. *London (New Road).* a.1763-94.
Richard. *Eccleston.* ca.1770. Watch Buckley coll.
Thomas. *London.* ca.1770. Watch mt. G.M.
Isaac. *Yarmouth.* 18c. l.c. clock.
John. *Halesworth* and *Yarmouth.* 1770. d. 1789. W. l.c. clock.
John. *London (Holborn).* 1770-99. br. clock Weth. coll. ill. Britten.
Christopher. *Knaresborough.* ca.1770-1807. l.c. clock.
John & Thomas. *Prescot.* ca.1770.
James. *Prescot.* ca.1770-95.
Richard. *Ripon.* ca.1770-1834.
Thomas. *Dublin.* 1774-80. W.
John. *London.* a.1766, CC.1775.
Thomas. *Halesworth.* mar.1775. W.
Edward. *London.* a.1768.
Roland, & Son. *Liverpool.* 1777.
Jeremiah. *London (Deptford).* a.1770-1808.
R. & J. *Liverpool.* 1781-1800. W.
William. *Cheshunt.* 1781. Bankrupt. From *London.*
Joseph. *Chesterfield.* d.1802. C. & W.
J. *York.* an.1785. Watch.
John. *London.* a.1775-1835.
James. *London (Islington).* 1787. W.
Richard. *London (Clerkenwell).* a.1787-1820.
Richard. *Kings Lynn.* 1791-5. C. & W.
John. *Petworth.* 1795. C.
John & Thomas. *Prescot.* 1795. C. & W.
Joseph. *Liverpool.* 1800-29. Lever watch Ilbert coll. Eleven watches N.Y. Univ.
Caleb. *Boston, U.S.A.* 1803-06. W.
George William. *London.* a.1800.
William. *Bristol.* 1812.
John F. *Dublin.* 1812-24. W.
& Co. *Bolton-le-Moors.* ca.1820.
Peter. *Liverpool.* 1816. W.
Richard. *London (Tottenham Ct. Rd.).* 1820
Eli. *Boston, U.S.A.* 1820. W.
Leonard. *London.* CC.1820-30. chron. W. & C. Watch mt. G.M.
C. *London.* ca.1820. Watch N.Y. Univ.
D. *Sheffield.* Early 19c. Watch.
Chauncey. *Albany, U.S.A.* 1823. W.
Francis Thomas. *Dublin.* 1824.
Robert. *Ballymoney.* 1824.
Michael. *Liverpool.* 1825. W.
William. *London.* 1825-40. l.c. clock.
Addison. *Wolcottville, U.S.A.* 1825.
Edward Daniel. *London.* b.1816, d.1889. Watch and chron. maker of great repute.
——. *Grantham.* Early 19c.

JOHNSTON (JOHNSTONE)—
Thomas. *Belfast.* ca.1757. C.
John. *London.* a.1750, CC.1769. Watch.
John. *Charleston, U.S.A.* 1764. a. in *London.* W.
John. *Quebec.* d.1783. W. From *London.*
John. *Edinburgh.* a.1757.
——. *Dublin.* an.1770. Watch.
John. *Ayr.* b.1755, d.1829.
Peter. *London.* a.1781.
James. *Edinburgh.* a.1785.
——. *Mitcham.* ca.1800 CC.
David. *Edinburgh.* 1800.
O. *London.* 1810-20. Watch N.Y. Univ.
J. F. *Dublin.* Early 19c. Watch.
James. *Portsoy.* Early 19c. Watch.
John. *Edinburgh.* a.1812.
Thomas. *Belfast.* 1819.
John. *Linlithgow.* 1820.
John. *London (Gray's Inn La.).* 1820.
Robert. *Philadelphia.* 1825.
v. JOHNSON.

JOHNSTOUN—
John. *Edinburgh.* a.1671.
Alexander. *Edinburgh.* a.1688.
James. *London.* a.1698, CC.1706.

JOHNSTOUNE, David. *Edinburgh.* a.1679.

JOLAGE (JOLLAGE), ——. *Paris.* 1807-10.

JOLE—
Robert. *London.* CC.1667-1701. math. inst. maker.
Thomas. *London.* a.1680.

JOLIN, ——. *Orléans.* an.1768. Watch.

JOLIT, Isaac. *London.* a.1807.

JOLLAIN, Pierre. *Paris.* m.1764-76.

JOLLAND, G. *London.* an.1751. Watch.

JOLLEY, John. *London.* 1809-11.

JOLLI, Louis. *Geneva.* End 17c.

JOLY (JOLLY)—
Josias. *Paris.* m.1609-40. Watches B.M., Louvre ill. Baillie, Olivier coll. Two watches with en. flowers K.H.M. All signatures have 'Paris.'
J. *Blois.* ca.1600. Watch Louvre. Prob. same as above.
Jacques. *Paris* or *Geneva.* 1st half 17c. Sig. never has name of place. Watch in form of dog, B.M. ill. Baillie. circ. sil. watch Mallett coll. 12-lobed watch, crys. cover.
Daniel. *London.* a.1637.
John. *London.* a.1732, CC.1739.
Ant. *London.* an.1747. Watch.
Noel. *Val de Travers.* a.1745. C.
François Antoine. *Paris.* m.1747.
Sigismond. *Moudon.* 1746 m.
Sigismond, son. *Moudon.* 1747 m.
——. *Moudon.* To 1754, then *Vevey.*
——. *Moudon.* 1758.
Joseph. *London (Holborn).* CC.1771-1800. Watch. JOLLY.
John. *London (Old Jewry).* a.1767, CC.1777-1794.
Quentin François. *Paris.* m.1781-9.
Arnold. *London.* 1784.
François Pierre Gaston. *Paris.* m.1784-9. g. en. watch, set pearls. g. rep. watch Den. coll. Decimal watch with Republican cal. Gélis coll.
Antoine. *Geneva.* an.1786. Watch.
——. *Paris (Rue du Faubourg St. Martin).* 1807-25.
William. *Leicester.* 1815-26. C. & W. JOLLY.
Richard. *London.* a.1802.

JON—
John. *London.* an.1747. Watch.
John. *London.* CC.1766-99. W.
Joseph, son. *London.* a.1766, CC.1777-97, d.an.1803.
John, bro. *London.* a.1767.
John, son of Joseph. *London.* a.1803, CC. 1811, l.CC.1812.

JONAS—
——. *London.* an.1761. Watch.
Samuel. *Exeter.* 1783. Watch.

JONES—
Evan. *London.* CC.1647-90. Watch.
William. *London.* a.1649.
Marmaduke. *London.* a.1652.
Henry. *London (Temple).* a.1654, CC.1663, m.CC.1691, d.1695. A very famous maker. g. en. watches B.M. and F.W.M ill. Baillie. Watches G.M., M.M.A. and Carnegie M. Oval watch with minute hand varying in length to follow the oval, Gélis coll. Clock Cassel Landes-M. l.c. clock. br. clocks ill. Britten.
William. *London.* a.1655, CC.1663.
Charles. *London.* a.1663.
Henry. *London.* a.1668-98.
Thomas. *London.* a.1671, CC.1679-1700. Watch Den. coll.
Daniel. *London.* a.1672.
Benjamin. *London.* a.1676.
Jonathan. *London.* a.1678, CC.1687-1701.
David. *London.* a.1680, CC.1687.
William. *London.* a.1682.
Edward. *London.* a.1686.
James. *London.* a.1687.
Samuel. *London.* a.1688.
Henry, son of Henry. *London.* a.1690, CC. 1698.
Hannah. *London.* 1697.
Henry. *London.* CC.1697.
Valentine. *London (St. Sepulchres).* a.1693, C.1704-25. Bankrupt.
Willliam. *London.* a.1695.
Charles. *London.* a.1700.
Edward. *London.* a.1703.
John. *London.* a.1700, CC.1716-26.
Robert. *London.* a.1714. Watch.
James. *London.* a.1715.
David. *London.* a.1719.
Robert. *Chester.* d.1747. W.
John. *Chester.* 1730. d.1764. W.
Robert. *Peterborough.* 1736. W.
John. *London.* a.1725, m.CC.1762. Watch en. Huaud le puisné Webster coll.
Thomas. *London.* a.1728.
George. *London.* a.1739.
Richard. *London.* ca.1750. g. en. watch M.P.S. Dresden.
William. *Brecon.* 1754. W.
John. *Abergavenny.* b.1718, d.1787. C. & W.
John. *Llannerch-coedlan, Brecknock.* an. 1755. Watch.
James. *Liverpool.* d.(?)1766. W.
Lewis. *Carmarthen.* 1760. d.1772.
John. *London.* a.1743, CC.1756.
William. *London.* a.1752, CC.1759.
Samuel. *London.* a.1752, CC.1761.
John. *London.* a.1753.
Gabriel. *London.* a.1753.
John. *Chester.* From 1761. C. & W.
Samuel. *Bath.* 1763.
James. *Brecon.* an.1767-94. Watch. Clock Nat. M. Cardiff.
Eli. *London.* 2nd half 18c. g. watch.
& BAMFORD. *Neath.* 2nd half 18c. l.c. clock.
Henry. *Dolwen (Colwyn Bay).* 1766. l.c. clock.
William. *London.* a.1760, CC.1768.
John. *London.* a.1764.
William. *Trebinshwn.* an.1770. Watch.
Samuel. *Worcester.* From 1769. C. & W.
John. *London (Islington).* 1769. Insolvent.
Jonathan. *London.* an.1771. Watch.
James. *Bristol.* 1771-81. Succeeded by Sarah.
Samuel. *London.* an.1773. Watch.
David. *Llangadog.* ca.1770-1810. br. clock.
William. *London (Southwark).* 1774. Insolvent.
James. *London (Hatton Wall).* 1774. Watch.

JONES—*continued.*
Gabriel. *London.* an.1775. Watch.
S. *Birmingham.* d.1803. Business continued by widow.
John. *Wrexham.* 1778. Watch Nat. M. Cardiff.
Owen. *London (Aldgate).* a.1767, CC.1779, l.CC.1787-1802.
James. *London (Bunhill Row).* a.1770-1824. Watch Den. coll.
John. *London.* a.1770.
William. *London (Barbican).* a.1770, CC. 1778, l.CC.1787-1810.
John. *London.* a.1773-1821.
Thomas. *London.* a.1774.
Thomas. *Merthyr Tydvil.* an.1783. Watch.
Joseph. *London.* a.1774, CC.1786.
Edward. *London.* 1788. Bankrupt.
Isaac. *London (Curtain Rd.).* 1788. W. Bankrupt.
Robert. *Liverpool.* 1788-96. W.
Theophilus, son of John. *Abergavenny.* 1791-1795. W.
Daniel. *Neath.* 1791. W.
Joshua. *Brecon.* 1791.
John. *Brecon.* 1792. C. & W.
Thomas. *Prescot.* 1795. Motion maker.
Samuel. *Kingston, Jamaica.* 1795-1830 CC. C. & W.
Sarah. *Bristol.* 1795-1830. Succeeded James.
William. *Llanfyllin.* 1796. W.
William. *London.* a.1775-1815.
Peter. *London.* a.1776.
Thomas. *Llannerch-y-medd.* Late 18c.-early 19c. l.c. clock.
David. *Merthyr Tydvil.* b.1763-1835. str. clock.
Henry James Alexander. *London.* a.1788.
Samuel. *London.* a.1789-1825. Watch.
Isaac. *London.* 1799.
Edward, son of Owen. *London.* a.1792. W.
John. *Liverpool (Crosshall St.).* 1800. W.
David. *Caeo, Monmouth.* ca.1800. l.c. clock.
Robert. *Ruthin.* ca.1800. Watch Nat. M. Cardiff.
John. *Stockport.* 1800.
Charles. *London.* 1800-19. Watch N.Y. Univ.
William. *Criccieth & Pwllheli.* b.1778, d. 1861. l.c. clock.
Peter. *Birmingham.* 1801.
Thomas. *London.* a.1798.
George. *Wilmington, U.S.A.* b.1782, d.1867. l.c. clock.
Thomas. *Liverpool.* 1810-29.
William Henry. *London.* CC.1811.
Ezekiel. *Boston, U.S.A.* 1813-25. W.
James. *London (Banner St.).* 1815.
John. *Bethesda.* 1803-79. l.c. clock.
Henry. *London.* a.1810.
Francis. *London.* CC.1817, l.CC.1824.
Edward. *Bristol.* 1818-30.
George. *London.* a.1809, CC.1820.
William. *Manchester.* ca.1820.
& FORRESTER. *Hull.* 1822.
John. *Liverpool (Gerard St.).* 1821-9. W.
Richard William. *London.* a.1818.
Richard. *London.* a.1819.
John. *Newtown, Wales.* 1822-35.
David. *Amlwch.* 1824. Watch Nat. M. Cardiff. l.c. clock.
Francis. *London.* CC.1825.
John. *Liverpool (Norfolk St.).* 1825. C.
Peter. *Liverpool.* 1825.
James. *London.* a.1820.
Humphrey. *Oswestry.* Early 19c. Watch.
John. *Mold.* Early 19c. Watch.
John. *Beaumaris.* Early 19c. Watch.
Daniel. *Chalford.* Early 19c.

JÖNS, ——. *Söderköping.* 1609. Made clock for Jönköping Castle.

JORDAINE, William. *London.* a.1646.

JORDAN—
F. Jacques. *Amsterdam.* Late 17c. en. watch.
Benjamin. *London.* a.1713.
John. *Bristol.* 1722, retired 1760. Partner with J. HORT. Watch Den. coll. and l.c. clock.
James. *Stadhampton.* Early 18c. l.c. clock.
Timothy. *London (Snow Hill).* 1770-80. l.c. clock.
William. *London (Spitalfields).* 1776-91.
Aaron. *London.* 1790. Watch Den. coll.

JORDEN & GORDON, ——. an.1744. Watch.

JORNOD (JONOD), David. *Ponts de Martel.* 1702.

JORNOT, Daniel. *Ponts de Martel.* 1701.

JORNS, Thomas. *Alcester.* 1791-5. l.c. clock. prob. IRONS.

JOSEL, T. *London.* an.1755. Watch.

JOSELIN (JOSSLIN), Edward. *London.* a. 1690, CC.1697-1728.

JOSEPH—
Isaac. *London.* an.1757. Watch.
Samuel. prob. *London.* 1769. Bankrupt. W.
Joseph. *London.* an.1775. Watch.
S. *Halifax.* 2nd half 18c. Watch mt.
Charles. *London.* a.1768.
Moses. *Randers, Aalborg* and *Copenhagen.* m.1785.
Symons, & Co. *Liverpool.* 1790. W.
Elias. *Liverpool.* 1790-6. W.
A. & SONS. *Plymouth.* 1791. W.
——. *Tavistock.* 1795. W.
J. *Bristol.* ca.1800. Watch G.M.
Gordon. *Ballymoney.* Early 19c. Watch.
David. *Liverpool.* 1825. W.

JOSEPHSON, John. *London.* an.1751-81. Watches N.Y. Univ. and Den. and Feill colls. and Oldham M. Pair agate caskets with watches Peiping M.

JOSSARD, ——. *Paris.* 1820.

JOSSELINE—
John. *London.* a.1761.
Edward. *London.* an.1776. Watch. JOSLIN.

JOST, Peter. *Burgdorf.* ca.1800. Watch.

JOSUÉ, Pierre. *Paris.* 1675 m.

JOUANIN, ——. *Paris.* 1786.

JOUANNEAU, Sébastien. *Blois.* mar.1611.

JOUARD (JOUAND), Louis. *Paris.* Juré 1741-69. Mantel clock Pal. de Versailles.

JOUASNAIR, François Mathieu. *Paris.* m. 1776.

JOUBERT, Joseph. *London.* ca.1720. g. repoussé watch.

JOURDAIN—
William. *London.* a.1646. Watch and mt. Clock in later case Breslau Schloss M.
David. *London.* an.1762. Watch.
Timothy. *London.* 1776.
Aaron. *London.* 1790-1811.

JOURDAN—
——. *Paris.* 1773.
——. *Geneva.* ca.1800. rep. aut. watch.

JOURJON, Jean. *St. Etienne.* 1717. Clock for Ste. Marie, Montbrison.

JOURLET, ——. *St. Quentin.* Early 17c. en. watch.

JOUSSET, Jacques. *Blois.* comp. 1617.

JOUVEL (JOVEL DIT MOUCHE)—
Gaspard. *Grenoble.* 1612-25.
Pierre. *Grenoble.* 1626.
Claude. *Grenoble.* 1663-82.

JOUVENCE, Jean. *France.* 1377-80. Maker of clock on the Château de Montargis. Bell founder.

JOVAT, ——. *London.* ca.1675.

JOY—
Julius. *Manchester.* 1808-14.
John. *Manchester.* 1808-11.

JOYCE—
George. *London.* a.1684, CC.1692.
William. *Cockshutt.* 1724. Prob. the founder in 1697 of J. B. JOYCE & Co. Sundial on church.
Peter. *London.* a.1700.
John, prob. son of Wm. *Cockshutt.* b.1717, d.1787.
John. *London.* a.1754.
Robert. *New York.* d.1811. W.
John. *Denbigh.* an.1774. Watch.
John. *Carmarthen.* 1761.
S. & C. *London* (*Lombard St.*). 1790-1825. g. 8-day watch Den. coll. Fine g. en. mus. watch Feill coll.
John. *Wisbech.* 1793-7.
John. *Ruthin.* 1791-1822. C. & W.
J. B., & Co. *Whitchurch* (*Salop*). ca.1800. Still making turret clocks. *v.* William.
James. *Whitchurch* (*Salop*). ca.1800. br. clock.
S., & Co. *London.* 1805-24.
Samuel. *London* (*Lombard St.*). CC.1810-1842. W.
Conway. *London* (*Lombard St.*). CC.1810-1837. W.
Conway. *London.* a.1811.
William. *Bristol.* 1818. W.
Thomas F. *Philadelphia.* 1820-5.
Samuel, son of Samuel. *London.* a.1821, CC. 1836-40.

JOYEUX—
Jacques. *Tour de Peilz* (*Vevey*). 1750.
——. *Rolle.* Went to *Vevey.* 1755.
Henry. *Vevey.* 1766. br. clock.
Pierre Louis. *Vevey.* 1798 m.

JOYNE—
John. *London.* a.1660, CC.1687.
John. *Paris.* ca.1700. sq. watch B.M.

JOYNSON, Richard. *Wrexham.* 1701. d.1711.

JUCKER, C. *Haigerlach.* Late 18c. g. en. watch.

JUDDEN, S. *London.* 1817-24.

JUDE, James. *London.* 1809-11.

JUDGE, T. *London.* 1828. Pub. art. on a 'Self-adjusting Pendulum' in Trans. Soc. Arts.

JUDGSON, Edward. *London.* a.1797.

JUGLE—
Pierre. *Tournai.* 1543. Added ½-hour str. train to town clock.
Jehan. *Mons.* 1638. Made a clock with 16-bell carillon.

JUHAN, A. *Dordrecht.* 1776. Watch, shagreen case, S.M.S.K.

JUHEL, jeune. *Paris.* 1812-25.

JUILLARD, Adam Louis. *Cortébert.* b.1790, d.1830.

JUILLERAT, Jean François. *Fournet Blancheroche.* Early 18c. Clock.

JUIN, Isaac. *Dijon.* 1624. cf. JEMIN.

JULER—
John. *N. Walsham.* 1753-73. C. & W. cf. JULES.
J. *Cambridge.* 1797. C. & W.

JULES, John. *N. Walsham.* 1770. cf. JULER.

JULIAN—
Gregory. *London.* a.1656, CC.1664.
John, & Co. *Brentford.* 1762. Watch.

JULIEN-LEROY, ——. *Paris* (*Rue de Vaugirard*). 1818-23. C. to the Chambre du Roi and the duc de Berry.

JULIMONT, Richart. *Cologne.* 1623. Kleinuhrmacher.

JULIN, Olof. *Arboga.* End 18c. l.c. clock.

JULLION—
John & SON. *New Brentford.* 1762. W. *v.* JULIAN.
Paul Aurelius. *London.* a.1812.

JULLIOTT, Solomon. *London.* 1738. Watch mt. G.M.

JUMEAU, Jean. *Blois.* a.1618-24.

JUMP—
Thomas. *Prescot.* 1803. W.
Richard, son. *London.* a.1803-25.
Richard Thomas. *London.* a.1825 to VULLIAMY.

JUNGBERG, Klas. *Sweden.* 1774. l.c. clock of rough work.

JUNGHANS, Erhard. *Schramberg.* 1861. d. 1870. In 1861 founded, with his brother Xaver, the important Junghanssche Uhrenfabrik.

JUNGNICK, ——. *Berlin.* Early 19c. sil. watch. Pub. an art. on oil for watches in 1828.

JUNN, ——. *London* (*Oxford Rd.*). 1767. W.

JUNOD—
Joseph. *Ste. Croix.* 1752. Started manufacture of repeaters. From *Vevey.*
James. *London.* 1783. Bankrupt. W.
FRÈRES. *Geneva.* Early 19c. g. eng. watch M.M.A.

JUNOR, Daniel. *Edinburgh.* 1797.

JUNTES—
Jan Marc. *Amsterdam.* Late 18c. l.c. clock. g. repoussé watch.
F. *Amsterdam.* 1822. W.

JUPP—
Arthur. *Croydon.* ca.1790. l.c. clock, painted panels.
& BARBER. *London.* 1820. mus. watches.

JÜRGENSEN—
Joergen. *Copenhagen.* b.1748, d.1811. Court C. Started a factory with LARPENT at *Röskilde* in 1780, where 1,500 watches were made.
Urban, son. *Copenhagen.* b.1776, d.1830. At *Le Locle* 1807-08. A very eminent maker of chronometers and observatory clocks. Pub. in 1805 'Principes généraux de l'exacte mesure du temps pour les horloges' (first edition in Danish in 1804), and several other works in Danish. These were pub. in French in 1832 by his son under the title, 'Mémoires sur l'Horlogerie exacte.'
Frédéric, bro. *Copenhagen.* 1811. Took charge of *Röskilde* factory.
Louis Urban, son of Urban. *Copenhagen.* b. 1806, d.1867. In charge of *Röskilde* factory. Wrote several arts. on horology.
Jules, bro. *Le Locle.* b.1808, d.1877. Founded the existing factory at *Le Locle,* which has always produced watches of the highest quality.

JURQUAND, Joh. *London.* Late 18c. Watch so sd. Fränkel coll.

JURY, William. *London.* a.1812.

JUST—
George. *Kirkcaldy.* 1761.
Leonard. *London.* 1790-1825. Watches for the Chinese market.
William. *London.* a.1797.

JUSTIS & CO. *London.* 1769.

K

KAAL, Rodolphe. *Paris.* m.1788.
KAALUND, Hans Vilhelm. *Copenhagen.* m. 1754.
KAEFFLIGER, ——. *Ferney.* 1775. Watch.
KAINE, Joseph. *Bristol.* 1812. W.
KALENDER, Orlando. *Exeter.* an.1781. Watch.
KALLE, Joseph Martin. *Marktbreit-am-Main.* m.1824.
KALTENBACH—
Georg. *Seelgut.* ca.1780. Wall clock Furt. M.
——. *Bristol* and *Bath.* 1794. Mus. C. from Germany. Advertised that he had a temporary shop in both towns.
KAM, Richard. *London.* 1762-91. W.
KAMBLY, Melchior. *Potsdam.* b.1710. Went *Potsdam* 1746. Cabinet-maker and bronze worker. Very large l.c. clock, tortoise-shell and ormolu mts. Schloss M. Berlin.
KAMEHL, *v.* CAMEEL.
KAMILOSCHI (KAMMLOSY)—
Sebastian. *Vienna.* m.ca.1720.
Karl. *Vienna.* m.1781.
KAMMERER—
Ambrosius. *Furtwangen.* 1770. Clock Furt. M.
Joseph. *Hirzwald.* 1770. mus. clock mt. Furt. M.
KAMPHUIS, H. *Oude Beierland.* ca.1800.
KANDEL, Joseph. *Augsburg.* 1786. mus. clocks with flutes and strings.
KÄNFF, Georg. *Basle.* 1769. From *Ruhland.*
KANTEL, Anthony. *London.* 1st half 18c. Watch Ilbert coll.
KÄPELI, Fl. Bastien. *Germany* (?). ca.1600. Oval eng. and pierced watch.
KAPPEL, ——. *Pouillerel.* Early 19c. Skeleton cyl. watch.
KAPPELIN, ——. *Switzerland.* 17c. 8-lobed crys. watch B.M.
KAPPLER (CAPPLER)—
J. *Vienna.* 1583. Oval crys. watch.
Jacob. *Vienna.* m.1685.
Paul. *Vienna.* m.1714.
KARBACH, Erhard. *Vienna.* m.1792.
KARKEEK, George. *Truro.* Early 19c.
KARL, G. *Germany.* 1598. Dial Old Ashmolean M.
KÄRLER—
Urban. *Memmingen.* 1566-83. Came to *Soleure* to repair town clock and was made town C.
Abraham, son. *Soleure.* 1576-ca.1600. Town C.
Daniel, bro. *Soleure.* 1576. Became burgher.
Matthäus, bro. *Soleure.* 1576. Became burgher.
Urban, son. *Soleure.* From 1605 at Vienna. C. to Ferdinand III.
KARMEYER, ——. *Marienburg.* Mid. 17c. Table clock with astrolabe above.
KARNER—
Caspar. *Nürnberg.* m.1564. inst. maker. Dial Old Ashmolean M.
Conrad. *Germany.* 1632. Dial maker.
Albrecht. *Germany.* 1655. Sundial Fränkel coll.
Melchior. *Germany.* 1690. Dial maker.
KÄSELAU, Asmus. *Hamburg.* 1801.
KÄSTELE, Joseph. *Augsburg.* m.ca.1805.
KÄSTNER, Abraham Gotthard. *Göttingen.* 1778. Pub. 'Ueber die Aenderung des Ganges der Pendeluhren in Sommer und in Winter.'
KATTERNS, Daniel. *Thrapston.* 1795. 'Clocksmith.'
KATZ, J. *Pforzheim.* ca.1800. cyl. watch Feill coll.
KATZBERGER, Joseph. *Vienna.* Early 19c. Watch Fränkel coll.
KAUFMANN—
Gottfried. b.1751 near *Chemnitz.* d.1818. *Frankfurt-a.-M.* mus. clockwork. Watch sd. 'Johann Gottfried Kaufmann a Dresde' Ilbert coll. perhaps by him.
Carolus. *Copenhagen.* comp. 1772.
Heinrich. *Vienna.* ca.1780. l.c. clock.
Friedrich, son of Gottfried. *Germany.* b. 1785, d.1866. mus. clockwork.
KAUS, James or John. *London.* a.1703, CC. 1712.
KAVANAGH, Charles. *Dublin.* 1795. W.
KAY—
David. *Dundee.* 1553-76. Made clock for St. Mary's Church.
John. *Aberdeen.* 1582. Made clock for town.
John. *Spilsby.* 1738. W.
F. *Cologne.* 1813.
Samuel. *Manchester.* ca.1820.
Thomas. *Warrington.* ca.1820.
KAYE—
John. *Liverpool.* 1773-1811. C.
William. *Liverpool.* 1781-1804. C.
William. *Liverpool.* 1805-10. W.
KAYNE, George. *London.* a.1777.
KAYSER, Ludwig. *Augsburg.* 1662. W.
KEARLY, James. *Peterborough.* 1795. W.
KEAT, Edward. *London.* 1822-40.
KEATE, Robert. *Wallingford.* 1795. W.
KEATES, William. *London.* 1783-1800. g. en. watch F.W.M.
KEATING, A. *London.* 1800-24. Watch N.Y. Univ.
KEATSBY, ——. *London.* an.1758. Watch.
KECKER, Jean Abram. *Chaux-de-Fonds.* 1778-1800. C.

KEDDON—
Daniel. *London.* CC.1717, d.1774. l.c. clock and watch.
Joshua, son. *London.* CC.1751.
KEEL, Charles. *London.* a.1810, CC.1818.
KEELE, Daniel. *Salisbury.* 1761-73. W.
KEELER, John. *Musselburgh.* 1814.
KEELEY—
Benjamin. *London.* an.1767. Watch.
Thomas. *London.* a.1761, CC.1784-1803.
James Howard. *London.* a.1803.
KEENE—
William. *London.* a.1730.
Joseph. *London.* a.1748, CC.1756.
James. *London.* an.1772. Watch.
John. *London.* a.1789.
Thomas. *London.* a.1792.
KEFFORD—
Thomas. *Royston.* Early 18c. Lantern and l.c. clocks and watch mt.
——. *London.* an.1744. Watch.
KEHLHOFF, Friederieck. *London.* 1761. Insolvent. In 1764 patented a centre-seconds watch with stackfreed. Watch with a kind of pin-wheel esc. Ilbert coll.
KEIGHLEY, Robert. *London.* a.1787.
KEIR—
Duncan. *Stirling.* 1706.
Peter. *Falkirk.* 1823.
KEITH—
George. *Strathaven.* d.1812. Watch mt. Glasgow Art Gall.
Robert. *Forfar.* 1819-37.
KELHAM—
Robert. *London (Redcross St.).* 1743. d.1762. 'Eminent W.'
Matthias. *London.* a.1732, CC.1745.
Joseph. *London.* CC.1766.
Robert. *London.* CC.1769-75. Watch.
Robert. *Chelmsford.* 1775-94. W.
KELL, Jonathan. *London.* a.1791.
KELLAWAY, William. *London.* a.1711.
KELLER—
I. Christ. *Linz.* ca.1590. Dial Old Ashmolean M.
Lorenz. *Steppach.* 1756-70.
Theodor. *Steppach.* 1770.
KELLET, Thomas. *London.* 1635.
KELLETT, ——. *Bredbury.* ca.1770. l.c. clock.
KELLEY, David. *Philadelphia.* 1808-13. W.
KELLNER, ——. *Cassel.* 1784.
KELLO, Simon. *London.* a.1715, CC.1723.
KELLOND—
Robert. *London (Fitzroy Sq.).* 1811.
Robert, son. *London.* a.1811.
KELLWAY, Ebenezer. *London.* a.1746.
KELLY—
Robert. *London.* a.1714.
John. *Hale.* d.1771. W.
Richard. *London (Long Acre).* 1755. W.
——. *London (Lincoln's Inn).* 1762. C. & W.
Patrick. *Dublin.* 1766. W.
Thomas. *Dublin.* an.1772. Watch.
Richard. *Dublin.* 1774. W.
John. *Liverpool.* 1813-29. g. watch.
Ezra. *New Bedford, U.S.A.* b.1798, d.1895. W. and maker of oils for clocks and watches.
Michael. *Drogheda.* 1824.
John. *Carrick-on-Suir.* 1824.
Matthew. *Carrick-on-Suir.* 1824.
KELTENBACK, D. *London.* 1825. Wooden C. *v.* KLEYSER & KELTENBACK.
KELVEY—
Robert. *Gainsborough.* 1772, retired 1796. W.
——. *Nottingham.* Early 19c. Watch.
KEMBER, Josiah. *Shaw.* an.1771-7. Watch G.M. l.c. clock. Also KIMBER.
KEMM, Samuel. *London.* a.1753, CC.1763, d.1810.

KEMP—
Henry. *London.* 1643. W.
Charles. *London.* a.1678, CC.1688, d.an. 1704.
Richard. *London.* a.1686, CC.1701.
James, son of Chas. *London.* a.1704.
William. *Lewes.* an.1756-84. Watch.
Henry. *London.* 1767-81. c.secs. jewelled watch Buckley coll.
Thomas. *London.* an.1769. Watch.
John. *London.* an.1776. Watch.
& BROWN. *Yoxford.* ca.1775. l.c. clock.
Matthew. *London.* a.1769.
James. *London.* CC.1780-1804.
William. *London (Highgate).* CC.1782, l.CC. 1787-1811. W.
& HOLMAN. *Lewes.* From 1787 to 1797. C. & W. Wm. K. & John H.
John. *Yoxford.* 1789. l.c. clock. W.
Joseph. *London.* 1790.
James. *London (Peckham).* 1799. l.CC.1812, d.1822.
William Henry, son. *London.* CC.1808.
William. *London (Hampstead).* 1824.
KEMPE—
Edward. *London.* a.1696.
Thomas. *London.* a.1726.
KEMPEN, Gert Gertsen. *Copenhagen.* m. 1789.
KEMPS, Matthew. *London.* a.1663, CC.1670.
KEMYES, Joshua. *London.* a.1673.
KEN, Samuel. *London.* a.1698.
KENDAL (KENDALL)—
John. *London.* Early 17c. oct. crys. watch Bernal sale.
Larcum. *London.* b.1721, d.1795. Appointed to make a duplicate of Harrison's timekeeper; made an improved timekeeper in 1771. Fine remontoire watch G.M. cyl. p.c. watch S.M.S.K.
James. *London. Walsall* from 1755. C. & W.
Benjamin. *London.* 1755 comp.
William. *London.* a.1753.
Thomas. *London.* an.1781. Watch.
Samuel. *Nottingham.* 1786. C. & W.
William. *London.* 1790.
Samuel. *Liverpool.* 1800-05.
KENDRICK—
John. *London.* a.1719, CC.1726.
——. *London (Lambeth St., Goodmans Fields).* an.1742-62. W.
Roger. *London.* a.1742, CC.1752.
John. *Liverpool.* 1800-10. W.
KENERDAL, Thomas. *Wigan.* ca.1770. Watch mt. Buckley coll. cf. KENNEDY.
KENEY, Vincent. *London.* 1530. Paid £19. 12*s*. 8*d*. by Henry VIII for 'xi clocks and dialls.'
KENFIELD, Richard. *Winchester.* 1750-90. l.c. clock.
KENN, Samuel. *London.* a.1700.
KENNEDY—
Thomas. *Wigan.* ca.1760-90. Watch Den. coll.
Alexander. *Edinburgh.* a.1753.
T. *London.* 1769. W.
John. *Dalmellington.* 1793.
Patrick. *Dublin.* 1795-1824. W.
Roger. *Dublin.* 1795-1824. W.
John. *Maybole.* 1820-37.
Mark. *Macclesfield.* Early 19c. Watch.
KENNERLEY, Thomas. *Liverpool.* 1825. W.
KENNEWELL, William. *London.* a.1715.
KENNEY, William. *London.* 1682.
KENNING, William. *London.* CC.1685-7. Maker of repute.
KENNINGTON, John. *Oxford.* 1772. C. & W. Succeeded ROSE.
KENNON—
William. *London.* a.1656, CC.1674-8.
William. *London.* 1685, not CC.
KENNY, Robert. *Ballyshannon.* 1824.

KENSALL, Francis. *London.* a.1752.
KENT—
Henry. *Westminster.* CC.1640-68. Watch.
William. *London.* CC.1681.
William. *London.* a.1681.
Henry. *London.* a.1699.
John. *London.* a.1723.
James. *Manchester.* 1759. Watch Den. coll.
John. *Saffron Walden.* mar.ca.1764-90.
John. *Manchester.* 1769-1813. Watch mt. Platt Hall M. Manchester.
Samuel. *London.* an.1774. Watch.
John. *Dudley.* 1776-8. W. l.c. clock.
William. *Lynton.* Late 18c. l.c. clock.
John, son of John. *Saffron Walden.* b.ca. 1765, d.1850. l.c. clocks.
Joseph. *London (Ratcliff Highway).* a.1772-1824.
John. *London (Bethnal Green).* ca.1800.
John. *Monmouth.* ca.1800-30. Watch.
John, jun. *Salford.* 1808-13. W.
John. *London.* 1809-35.
Jeph., jun. *London (Ratcliff Highway).* 1809-1811.
Joseph, jun. *London (St. George's, E.).* 1815-24.
Henry, son of John. *Saffron Walden.* b. 1809, d.1874.
KENTISH—
John, jun. *London.* 1758-74. Dissolved partnership with MANGAAR and ALLMAN in 1772. Bankrupt in 1774. rep. watch S.M.S.K.
& HAYNES. *London.* an.1793. Watch.
KENTON, Joseph. *London.* a.1679, CC.1686. p.c. tortoiseshell watch Ilbert coll.
KENWAY—
James. *London.* a.1779.
James. *Bridport.* 1790. C.
KENYON—
James. *Liverpool.* 1734. Bankrupt. C.
Richard. *Manchester.* 1796-1813. C.
Clayton. *Liverpool.* 1805-21. W.
KEPPEL, Anton. *Vienna.* m.1789.
KERBY—
Benjamin. *Bristol.* ca.1800, CC.1830.
Francis. *St. Helier, Jersey.* Early 19c. l.c. clock.
KERCKHELLEN, H. V. *Berlin.* 17c. g. watch Gélis coll. 5 mm. thick.
KERFOOT—
John. *W. Derby.* an.1744. Watch.
Robert. *Liverpool.* 1754. W.
Robert, jun. *Liverpool.* 1761. W.
KERFUTT, Walter. *Exeter.* 2nd half 18c. l.c. clock.
KERGXHAM, ——. *Paris.* 2nd half 18c. 3-case sil. watch.
KERIZER, Joh. Christoff. ——. ca.1670. str. trav. clock Mallett coll.
KERKELOO, Jacob. *Amsterdam.* ca.1750. l.c. clock.
KERMON, William. *London.* 1682 CC.
KERN, Krispin. *Schönwald.* 1770. Made several boxwood watches.
KERNER, Joseph. *Vienna.* m.1805.
KERNOR, E. P. *Poole.* 1800. C.
KERR—
John. *Glasgow.* 1783.
Joseph. *London.* a.1776.
Francis. *Jamaica.* 1789. C. & W.
Alexander. *Annan.* 1820.
KERRY—
Isaac. *Liverpool.* 1825. W.
John. *Liverpool.* 1825. W.
KERSHAW, George. *London.* an.1777-99. l.c. clock. Also KIRSHAW.
KERXHEIMER—
Antoni. *Oberhausen.* 1756.
Franz Xaver. *Günzberg.* 1760 comp.

KESSBORER—
Mathias. *Ulm.* Early 17c. oct. crys. watch M.M.A.
Johann, bro. *Ulm.* ca.1650. sil. watch S.K.M.
KESSELS (KESSELER), Heinrich Johann. *London, Copenhagen* and *Altona.* b.1781, d.1849. A most eminent maker of chronometers and observatory clocks. C. to the Danish Navy. Regulator mt. Furt. M.
KESSEN, ——. *Paris.* Early 18c. g. en. watch.
KESSLER, John, jun. *Philadelphia.* 1806-08.
KESSMANN, Heinrich. *Würzburg.* m.1761. From *Königsheim (Baden).*
KETCHEN, *v.* KITCHIN.
KETTERER, Franz Anton. *Schönwald.* b. 1676-1750. First maker of cuckoo clocks, and one of the first to start clockmaking in the Schwarzwald. Cuckoo clock Furt. M.
KETTLE, William. *Edinburgh.* a.1758, d. 1804.
KEVITT—
R. *London.* 2nd half 18c. Watch.
S. D. *London.* ca.1800. Watch N.Y. Univ.
KEWELL, Thomas. *London.* a.1685.
KEY—
Josiah. *London.* End 17c. Made locks for Hampton Court Palace. Watch(?) case Ashmolean M.
Daniel. *London.* 1799.
KEYES, Markham. *London.* a.1653.
KEYMAN, Mark. *London (Newington).* 1802-1808. W.
KEYMES, Joshua. *London.* a.1673.
KEYS, Joseph. *London.* 1805-08. C.
KEYSEN (CHEYSER, CAYSER), Christian. *Copenhagen.* m.1703. From *Saxony.* Turret C.
KHELLER, Johann Michael. ——. 1st half 17c. sq. watch B.M. ill. Baillie.
KHORNMAN, Johann Georg. *Austria(?).* Late 17c. and early 18c. Watch Fränkel coll. sq. table clock Feill coll. Perhaps same as KORMANN.
KIBLER, ——. *Paris.* 1812. C.
KIBLICH, Matthäus. *Pressburg.* Late 17c. Fine watch en. flowers on white ground, set stones, K.H.M.
KICKTUHN, ——. *Elbing.* 1780. Town C.
KIDD—
John. *London.* a.1655.
Joseph. *London.* 1778. Insolvent. W.
Gilbert. *Malton.* 1760-1807. Watch.
'C. L. KIDDER, San Francisco.' Sig. on 1875 watches of the CORNELL WATCH CO.
KIDGETT, Joseph. *London.* a.1751.
KIDMAN, John. *Saffron Walden.* mar.ca. 1735-45. Watch mt. G.M. Lacquer l.c. clocks.
KIDSON, William. *York.* 1614. C.
KIEFER, Joh. Th. *Fürth.* d.1826.
KIEHLBOCK (KIELBLOCK), ——. *Berlin.* Table clock Märkische M. Berlin.
KIELCKERT, A. *Potsdam.* ca.1770. Watch mt. Ilbert coll.
KIELSEN, Aage. *Copenhagen.* m.1806.
KIENING, Hans. *Füssen (Bavaria).* 1578. astro. clock in painted wood case K.H.M. Very fine book watch Mallett coll. prob. by him ill. Baillie.
KIENLING (KINNLING), Joseph. *Vienna.* m.1783.
KIENZLER, Sebastian. *Schwarzwald.* ca. 1780. Wall clock Furt. M.
KIER, Peder Basballe. *Copenhagen.* m.1792.
KIFER, J. P. *London.* an.1764. Watch. Also KISER.
KIHLBERG, Johan Abraham. *Stockholm.* b. 1783, d.1853. cyl. watch, two mantel clocks and mus. boxes.
KILBY, John. *London.* a.1714.

KILFORD, ——. *London.* an.1772. Watch.
KILGOUR—
Patrick. *Aberdeen.* 1672-92. Made town clock.
Patrick. *Edinburgh.* 1702.
William. *Glithnow.* 1775. d.1837.
KILIAN, Claud Seb. *Fürth.* d.1786.
KILMINSTER—
Henry. *London.* CC.1677-1710. Watch.
Richard. *London.* a.1721.
KILPATRICK, Gilbert. *Edinburgh.* a.1767.
KILPIN, George. *Portsea.* Early 19c. Watch.
KILSHAW, Richard. *Liverpool.* 1803. W.
KILVEY & WOOD. *London.* an.1783. Watch.
KIMBALL, John, jun. *Boston, U.S.A.* 1823.
KIMBER, ——. *London.* 1805-08.
KINABLE, ——. *Paris.* ca.1780-1825. Very fine lyre clock S.K.M.
KINDERMANN, Paul. *Bautzen.* Early 19c. cyl. watch M.P.S. Dresden.
KING—
Thomas. *London.* a.1657, CC.1669-90. l.c. clock.
Jonathan. *London.* a.1682, CC.1689.
John. *London.* a.1686.
Thomas. *London.* a.1692, CC.1699.
Robert. *London.* a.1698.
Robert. *London.* a.1700.
William. *London.* a.1704.
Thomas. *London.* a.1704.
William. *London.* a.1707, CC.1720.
R. ——. ca.1715. Watch mt. with glass on cock Buckley coll.
William. *London (Birchin La.).* an.1715. Watch.
Peter. *London (Gt. St. Andrew's St.).* CC. 1715-35. Year l.c. clock Virginia M.
John. *London (Fleet St.).* an.1718, d.1762.
John. *London.* CC.1715.
Elias. *London.* a.1709.
John. *London.* a.1711, CC.1729.
John. *London.* a.1712.
William. *London.* a.1713.
William John. *London (Camberwell).* CC. 1720-51. Watch B.M.
Henry. *London.* CC.1721, d.1754. Watch Den. coll.
Benjamin. *London.* a.1719.
James. *London.* a.1719.
William. *London.* a.1721.
John. *London.* a.1726.
Thomas. *London.* a.1731.
Horner. *London.* a.1733.
Henry. *London (Lincolns Inn).* an.1743. Watch.
Thomas. *London.* a.1735.
Henry Tudor, son of Henry. *London.* a. 1736, CC.1754.
John. *London.* a.1740-61.
——. *Woodford.* an.1751. Watch.
John. *London.* a.1744, CC.1753.
George, son of Henry. *London.* a.1745.
William. *London.* a.1746.
Daniel. *London (Bishopgate St.).* an.1755. Watch.
Joseph. *Shrewsbury.* an.1755. Watch.
——. *London (Princess Sq., Ratcliff Highway).* retired 1774. C. & W.
James. *London.* a.1754.
Thomas. *London.* a.1758.
Thomas. *Shrewsbury.* an.1763. Watch.
Thomas. *London (St. Anns, Blackfriars).* 1765. Insolvent. W.
James. *Shrewsbury.* an.1768. Watch.
Richard. *London.* an.1771-ca.1780. Watch.
Alexander. *Ringwood* and *Liverpool.* Insolvent in *Romsey* in 1772.
William. *Shrewsbury.* an.1774. Watch.
Thomas. *Alnwick.* 1773. Watch G.M. l.c. clocks.
Henry. *Bristol.* 1774-81.

KING—*continued.*
Samuel. *London.* an.1778. Watch. l.c. clock.
Robert. *London.* a.1769.
Andrew. *London.* a.1777.
John. *Aberdeen.* 1784.
Thomas. *London.* a.1783, CC.1827.
Edward. *Warwick.* 1795. W.
Stephen. *Chippenham.* 1795. C. & W.
Robert. *London.* a.1791.
Thomas William. *London.* a.1792, CC.1802-1840.
Benjamin. *London.* a.1792.
James Frederick. *London (Bridgewater Sq.).* a.1796, CC.1808.
Thomas & Benjamin. *London.* 1805-25. Sd. 'T. & B. King.' Watch.
R. *Scarborough.* 1808.
John. *Leeds.* b.1795, d.1863.
John. *Loughborough.* Early 19c. Watch.
Duncan. *Port Glasgow.* 1820.
David. *Montrose.* 1821-51.
Robert. *Bailiebofey.* 1824.
Carl. *Liverpool.* 1825. W.
KINGHAM, Caleb. *London.* a.1760.
KINGSBURY—
James. *London.* a.1749. Watch.
John. *Belfast.* 1824.
KINGSMILL, George. *London.* CC.1667.
KINGSNORTH, John. *London.* a.1688.
KINGSTON, Thomas. *London.* a.1737.
KINKEAD—
James. *Philadelphia.* 1774. C. & W.
Joseph. *Christiana, Del., U.S.A.* 1781. mar. 1820.
Joseph & Alexander. *Christiana.* ca.1790. l.c. clock.
KINLAN, Thomas. *Granard.* 1824.
KINNEIR, James. *Edinburgh.* a.1774.
KINNEMAN, Thom. *Stockholm.* ca.1660.
KINNER, Andrew. *London.* 1718 CC.
KINNING, John. *London.* a.1693, CC.1701-1730. Watch B.M.
KINSEY, Thomas. *London.* 1771.
KINTZING, Peter. *Neuwied.* b.1746, d.1816. C. Made the piano-playing automaton in C.A. & M. ill. M. des Aut. l.c. clock Schloss M. Berlin. Made mts. for several clocks for the case maker David RÖNTGEN.
KIPLING—
William. *London.* 1705-37. A fine maker. l.c. and br. clocks and three watches, one rep., G.M. p.c. watch S.M.S.K. Watch Liverpool M. str. and rep. watch Ilbert coll. Watch Den. coll. l.c. mus. clock Weth. coll. mus. br. clock Virginia M.
William & John. *London.* ca.1750.
G. *London.* an.1780. Watch.
William. *Stafford.* 1784. W.
John. *Stafford.* 1795.
KIPPIS, George. *London.* a.1687.
KIRBY—
Robert. *London.* a.1715, CC.1723.
John. *Bromley.* ca.1730. C.
Robert. *London.* a.1726, CC.1741.
John. *London.* a.1738.
Collins. *London.* a.1750, CC.1758.
Charles. *London.* an.1775. Watch.
Thomas. *London.* a.1771. Watch.
James. *St. Neots.* 1795. Watch.
KIRCHEL, Benno Joseph. *Dresden.* m.1811, d.1858.
KIRCHER, Athanasius. *Würzburg* and *Avignon.* b.1601, d.1680. Wrote several works dealing with dialling and water-clocks.
KIRCHHEIM, Thomas. *Mainz.* ca.1700. en. watch.
KIRCHMANN—
——. *Neisse.* ca.1700. hex. table clock.
Peter Christian. *Copenhagen.* m.1790.

KIRK—
John. *London.* a.1668, CC.1677.
Joseph. *Nottingham.* ca.1740. l.c. red lacquer clock ill. Cec. & Web.
Ann. *Nottingham.* ca.1750. Watch.
——. *London (Long Acre).* 1753.
William. *Stockport.* 1760-95.
William. *Manchester.* ca.1770-94. W.
Robert. *Ballymoney.* a.ca.1767.
Thomas. *London.* a.1794.
John. *Dalkeith.* 1800.
William. *Nottingham.* 1815. W.
Thomas, & Co. *Hull.* Early 19c. Watch.
Charles. *Bristol, U.S.A.* 1823.
v. PIGGOTT.
KIRKHALL, Thomas. *Bolton-le-Moors.* 1673. Made clock on Brindle (Lancs.) church.
KIRKHAM, Richard. *London.* 1805-08.
KIRKLAND—
James. *Glasgow.* 1775.
Richard. *Port Glasgow.* 1783.
KIRKPATRICK—
Martin. *Dublin.* 1720. d.1769.
Robert. *London.* a.1736.
KIRKUP, Matthew. *Newcastle-on-Tyne.* 1797-1811. C. & W.
KIRKWOOD—
Thomas. *London.* 1680 CC.
John. *Lauder.* 1734. Made town clock.
John. *Charleston, U.S.A.* 1761. C. & W.
Alexander. *Charleston, U.S.A.* 1768. C. & W.
James. *Perth.* 1771.
John. *Redpath.* 1798.
KIRNER (KÜRNER), Matthias. *Berlin.* 1794. Wooden C.
KIRSCH, Hans. *Copenhagen.* 1611. C. to Queen Sofie.
KIRTON—
John. *London.* a.1696, CC.1706.
William. *London.* a.1708.
K. *London.* an.1770. Watch.
KIRWOOD, Charles. *London.* a.1803.
KIRZINGER, Ignaz. *Vienna.* m.1780.
KISH, Henry. *London.* an.1775. Watch.
KISLER, Anthony. *Dublin.* 1795-1824. C.
KISSAR, Samuel. *London.* a.1700, CC.1712. *Canterbury* in 1732.
KITCHEN—
John. *Liverpool.* 1774. W.
James. *Whitehaven.* 1811.
KITCHIN—
& LLOYD. *Nantwich.* 1781-95. C.
Joseph. *London.* 1784.
John. *Nantwich.* 1795. C.
KITSON, Robert. *London.* a.1754. Watch.
KJÄRSTRÖM, B. O. *Trälleborg.* 18c. l.c. clock.
KJEDING—
Olof. *Landskrona.* b.1724, d.1805. l.c. clock. Also KIEDING.
——. *Ystad.* 1794.
KJELLSTRÖM—
Elias. *Linköping.* 1750.
Sven Christopher. *Göteborg.* b.1797, d.1839.
KLARENBEEK, Abraham. *Haarlem.* 1737.
KLAUS, ——. *Västervik.* an.1793.
KLEBUST, Lux. *Basle.* 1648-60. Kleinuhrmacher.
KLEEMAN, Joh. Mich. *Fürth.* d.1816.
KLEEMEYER, Christian Ernst. *Berlin.* 1766-1785. C. Table clock.
KLEIN—
Hans. *Dinkelsbühl.* 1456. Made clock for Würzburg Rathaus tower.
Michael. *Marienburg.* Late 17c. hex. table clock.
Christian. *Stettin.* 1693-1701. circ. table clock.
Johann Heinrich. *Copenhagen.* 1703-28. From *Silesia.* Table clock in ivory case Rosenborg Castle. rep. watch.

KLEIN—*continued.*
Halvor Iversen. *Copenhagen.* 1715.
Lorenz Henrik. *Copenhagen.* m.1735.
Johann. *Prague.* 1738. astro. clock M.P.S. Dresden.
Gotfred Henrik. *Copenhagen.* m.1741. Master of Corporation 1761-6.
——. *Paris.* 1812.
KLEINER, David. *Basle.* 1771. From *Lenzburg.*
KLEINHEMMEL, Melchior. *Annaberg.* 1543. Founder member of Corporation.
KLEININGER, J. P. *Germany.* 18c. Ivory dial M.M.A.
KLEINSCHMIDT—
Christian. *Vienna.* m.ca.1681.
Joh. Ant. *Vienna.* m.1691. Also KLAINSCHMIDT.
Johann Michael. *Landsberg.* 1728. Kleinuhrmacher.
KLENTSCHI—
Charles Frédéric. *Chaux-de-Fonds.* b.1774, d.1854. A very able W. & C.
Louis, son. *Chaux-de-Fonds.* b.1806, d.1881. A very able W. & C.; specialized in complex mts.
KLETTI, Christoffer. *Kronborg.* 1645. Court C.
KLEYSER—
John. *London (High Holborn).* 1790-1811. Wooden C.
George, & Co. *London (Borough).* 1790-1820. Wooden C.
George. *London (Borough).* 1805-08. Wooden C.
T. *London (High Holborn).* 1810-30. Wooden C.
& KELTENBACK. *London.* 1817-25. Wooden C.
Felix. *London (Commercial Rd.).* 1817-24. Wooden C.
J., & Co. *London (Oxford St.).* 1820.
John, & Son. *London (High Holborn).* 1820.
KLIEBER—
Ulrich. *Augsburg.* b.1487, d.1568. Famous math. inst. maker. Ivory dial of 1555 Old Ashmolean M. by him or his son.
Ulrich, son. *Augsburg.* 1554. d.1608. Watch-case Nat. M. Munich. Several pocket sundials.
Tobias. *Augsburg.* b.1545, d.1618. math. inst. maker. Dial B.M.
KLINCK, Michael. *Augsburg.* ca.1600. C.
KLINCKSPOR, Egidius. ——. End 17c. Table clock Cassel Landes-M.
KLINDWÖRTH, ——. *Göttingen.* 1770. Regulator Gotha M.
KLING, Lars. *Västergötland.* b.1790. Had eight sons who were clockmakers.
KLINGATSCH, Anton. *Vienna.* m.1813.
KLINGENBERG, J. B. *Amsterdam.* ca.1750. l.c. carillon clock.
KLINGLE, Joseph. *Philadelphia.* 1823-25.
KLOCKSPARGER, Johann. *Prague.* 2nd half 18c. math. inst. maker. Circ. scale giving comparative measures Nat. M. Prague.
KLOK—
Pieter. *Amsterdam.* 2nd half 18c. Many fine l.c. and br. clocks. Two en. watches M.M.A. Watch Stads M. Amsterdam.
Wietze Dooitzens. *Joure.* Late 18c.
KLOPFFER, Lorenz. *Strasbourg.* 1689.
KLOSE, Johann Gottlieb. *Potsdam.* 2nd half 18c. Very fine mus. l.c. clock Breslau Schloss M.
KLOTHEN, Konrad von. *Zürich.* 1366. Made clock for town.
KLSTRÖM, Nicolaus. *Danzig.* 2nd half 18c. Trav. clock.

KLYZOVICZ, Adam. *Cracow.* 1634. Table clock with straight balance spring ill. Britten.

KNAB, Paul. *Vevey.* 1795–8. Juré.

KNAPP—
Peter. *Karlshamn.* 1750-73.
William. *Annapolis, U.S.A.* 1764-7. W.
J. *Boston.* Early 19c.

KNAPTON, R. *Bognor.* Early 19c.

KNAUER, Leo. *Augsburg.* m.1750-86.

KNAUSS—
Johann Louis. *Darmstadt.* ca.1730-70. Court C. g. en. watch. Magnificent mus. aut. clock, with sil. mounts, known as the Maria Theresa clock, dated 1745, also br. mus. aut. clock, both Hofburg, Vienna. Watch N.Y. Univ.
v. VON KNAUSS.

KNETTLEFORD, William. *London.* 1696. W.

KNIBB—
Samuel. *Newport Pagnell* and, later, *London.* CC.1663, d.an.1674. l.c. ½ str. clock with short pendulum.
Joseph. *Oxford* and *London.* 1650. CC.1670. Prob. in *London* from 1677, and *Hanslop* from ca.1700. d.ca.1711. Worked with John while in Oxford. One of the finest makers of lantern, l.c. and br. clocks; many examples known. Eleven l.c. clocks in Weth. coll., one in Webster coll., and br. clock ill. Cec. & Web. Three br. and wall clocks Weth. coll. Four ill. Britten. Watches S.K.M. and Ilbert coll. Lantern clocks London M., Virginia M. and Weth. coll. Token farthing issued by him in B.M.
John, bro. *Oxford.* 1650. Mayor of Oxford in 1700. br. and l.c. clocks. Watch G.M. 30-hour wall clock ill. Cec. & Web. Wall, br. and l.c. clocks Weth. coll.
Peter. *London.* CC.1677.
Edward. *London.* a.1693 to Joseph.
Joseph. *London.* a.1710.

KNIBBS, Rebecca. *London.* 1773. Bankrupt. C.

KNIEWASSER, Johann H. *Fürth.* d.1830.

KNIFTON, Thomas. *London.* 1640-62 CC. Lantern clock Feill coll.

KNIGHT—
Michael. *London.* a.1673, CC.1681-1714. l.c. clock.
Richard. *London.* a.1674, CC.1682-95.
John. *London.* 1684. Made a watch for the King to give to Muley Hamet.
Charles. *London.* a.1678, CC.1685-97.
Thomas. *London.* a.1686.
James. *London.* a.1696.
Thomas. *London.* a.1712.
Henry. *London.* a.1713, CC.1723. Watch
Edward. *London* (*Wapping*). an.1762. Watch.
Thomas. *Thaxted.* b.1745, d.1812. W. & C. of repute. br. clock.
Joseph. *London.* an.1774. Watch.
John. *Halifax.* 1774. Bankrupt. W.
Benjamin. *Abingdon.* 1775. C. & W.
John, son of Thos. (3). *Thaxted.* d.1835.
Thomas. *Birmingham.* an.1785. Watch.
George. *London.* a.1770, CC.1780.
John. *Fareham.* 1784. W.
Benjamin. *London* (*Southwark*). 1784-90. W.
H. *Stafford.* ca.1790 CC. Watch.
Joseph. *Halstead.* ca.1790-early 19c. T. C. & W.
Hugh. *Stone.* 1795. C. & W.
William. *Farnham.* 1795. W.
William. *Thaxted.* 1795. W.
——, son of Thos. of Thaxted. *London.* 1799. Prob. John above.
Charles. *Dunmow.* ca.1800.
John. *Portsea.* From 1802-20. Watch.

KNIGHT—*continued.*
William. *London.* 1802-08.
Richard. *Bristol.* 1812. W.
William. *Bristol.* 1813-30. Watch.
Robert Millet. *London.* a.1806.
William. *London.* a.1813.
Thomas. *Manchester.* ca.1820.
Joshua. *Bristol.* 1825-30. W. & C.
& WITHERS. *Bristol.* Early 19c.

KNIP, Gerrit. *Amsterdam.* Mid. 18c.-ca.1780. Fine l.c. clock. rep. watch Ilbert coll.

KNITL, F. A. *Linz.* ca.1700. Dial maker.

KNIVETON, ——. *London.* d.1667. C.

KNOBLICH, Theodor. *Altona* and *Hamburg.* b.1827, d.1892. Fine chron. and observatory clockmaker.

KNODNOTT, ——. *London.* an.1752. Watch.

KNOLLYS, Francis. *London.* a.1669.

KNOOP, Johan Christian. *Stockholm.* 1769-1785. l.c. clock ill. Sidenbladh. Wall clock.

KNÖPLEN, Johannes. *Augsburg.* 1647. Made complex clock given by Frederick I of Prussia to the Czar.

KNOTT, Robert. *London.* a.1682.

KNOTTESFORD (KNOTSFORD)—
William. *London.* a.1656, CC.1663, m.CC. 1693-6. An able maker. rep. watch S.K.M. str. watch G.M. br. clock ill. Cec. & Web.
John, son. *London.* a.1680. l.c. clock Weth. coll.

KNOWLES—
Thomas. *Bolton.* d.1787. W.
William. *Liverpool.* 1774-81. Watch.
John. *Philadelphia.* 1784. W.
William. *Dublin.* an.1791. Watch.
Robert. *Liverpool.* 1800-29. W.
James. *London.* 1805-08.
John. *Liverpool.* 1825. W.

KNOX—
John. *Belfast.* 1729.
Robert. *Beith.* 1766. l.c. clocks.
John. *Larne.* 1769-83. A fine l.c. clockmaker.
Alexander. *Berwick-on-Tweed.* ca.1770-95. W.
William. *Paisley.* 1780.
William. *Beith.* 1785.
John. *London.* 1809-24. W.
James. *Paisley.* 1820-36.
Robert. *Paisley.* 1820-37.
James. *Tralee.* 1824.

KNUBLI, Lienhard. *Burgdorf.* 1505. Recommended for making clock at Lucerne.

KNUDSEN, Johan. *Stran.* Late 18c. Painted l.c. clock. Norsk Folke M. Oslo.

KOBB, William. *Montrose.* Early 19c. Watch.

KNÜPFER, Gottlieb Friedrich. *Dresden.* b. 1724, d.1773 m.

KÖBERLE (COEBERLE), Wilhelm. *Eichstätt.* 1680-1715. str. trav. clock S.K.M. Table clock, with canopy. Watch Fränkel. coll. trav. clock M.P.S. Dresden. hex. clock with temple canopy Stern. coll.

KOCH—
Johann. *Cologne,* 1654. *Stockholm,* 1665. d.1679. Court C. Watch Webster coll. Watch and circ. table clock sd. at Cologne. Two br. clocks and three sundials sd. at Stockholm.
Johann. *Lemberg.* Mid. 18c. br. clock Uhren M. Vienna.
J. A. *Berlin.* 1797. Pub. 'Ueber den Pendelschlag der astronomischen Uhren,' in Berliner astro. Jahrbuch.

KÖCHEL, Johann. *Erlangen.* 18c. sil. repoussé rep. watch.

KOCHENDÖRFFER—
Heinrich. *Cassel.* b.1769.
Heinrich, son. *Cassel.* 1828. Founded the existing firm of Heinrich KOCHENDÖRFFER.

KOCK—
Willem. *Haarlem.* 1758. g. en. watch.
Jacob. *Stockholm.* b.1737, d.1805. C. to Gustav III. A very fine maker. Watch-cocks sometimes sd. 'J.K.' Many watches; two Nat. M. Stockholm, one Nord. M. ill. Sidenbladh. Many wall, br. and l.c. clocks.
Pieter. *Haarlem.* 2nd half 18c. Watch mt.
KOGIES, *v.* KOOGIES.
KOHLER (KÖHLER)—
Johann Christoph. *Dresden.* Early 18c. Gilt sil. en. table clock, set stones, Grüne Gewölbe, Dresden.
Johann Gottfried. *Dresden.* 1745-1800. Observatory clocks.
Niklaus. *Basle* and *Chaux-de-Fonds.* 1784.
KOHLHAS, Johann. *Vienna.* m.1774.
KOHLI, Jakob. *Bienne.* 1738.
KOHLSCHITTER, Joseph. *Milan.* b.1813, d.1882. Maker to the Italian Navy and Milan Observatory.
KOLB—
Hans. *Lauf.* 1660. Clock Schramberg M.
Jacobus. *Augsburg.* 17c. Watch Gélis coll.
Andreas. *Strasbourg.* 1744.
——. ——. 1772-89. Wooden aut. clock Landesgewerbe M. Stuttgart. Prob. Andreas.
KOLBE, Friedrich August. *Dresden.* b.1754, m.1791, d.1838.
KÖLBEL, Nicolaus. *Buda Pesth.* 2nd half 18c. sil. trav. clock.
KOLLER—
Jakob. *Winterthur.* 1741. br. clock.
Jean Conrad. *Chaux-de-Fonds.* 1792-1806. C.
KÖLSCH, ——. *Göteborg.* 1681.
KÖLTZEL, Js. J. *Cocheim.* 18c.
KOMMAN, ——. ——. Early 17c. Very fine table clock.
KONAMBKE, Hans. *Dantzig.* 1637. Made a new clock for the Dammthür.
KÖNIG, Conrad. *Dresden.* 1576. Called to the Dresden Court from *Altenburg* with an automaton he had invented.
KONSTANZ, Johann von. *Basle.* 1475. Moved clock from St. Martin's church to the Münster and repaired it.
KOOGIES—
Jan. *Wormerveer.* Late 17c. Zaandam clock. Also KOGIES.
K. G. *Wormerveer.* 2nd half 18c. Clock.
KOOS, L. *Merthyr Tydvil.* Early 19c. Watch.
KOPP—
Joseph. *Vienna.* Early 17c. Table clock.
Franz Xaver. *Kriegshaber.* In 1797 came to *Augsburg.* Wooden C.
C. J. *Ystad.* Early 19c. Wall clock.
KOPPAUN, Christof. *Germany.* 1582. Large sq. table clock S.K.M.
KÖRBER, G. F. *Frankfurt-a.-M.* 1740. sil. watch B.M. g. watch Besançon M.
KORMANN, Johann Georg. *Friedberg.* 1722-1726. Perhaps same as KHORNMANN.
KÖRMANN, Hans Martin. *Strasbourg.* 1637.
KORN, Hartman. *Germany.* 1664. Dial Old Ashmolean M.
KÖRNER—
Leopold. *Vienna.* m.1779.
Johann. *Vienna.* m.1796.
Kilian. *Würzburg.* m.1806. From *Bischwind.* C.
KORNMANN, Anton. *Gratz.* ca.1720. Watch in snuff-box.
KORSCHEN, Jean. *Beraun.* Early 19c. c. secs. cal. watch Feill coll.
KOSTENBADER, Laurenz. *Strasbourg,* 1577. *Cologne,* 1587. Kleinuhrmacher.
KOSTER—
Samuel. *v.* COSTER.
Dirk. *Amsterdam.* Late 17c.-ca.1725. Watch with sun and moon hour indicators G.M.

KOSTER—*continued.*
Willem. *Amsterdam.* Mid. 18c. Watch Stads M. Amsterdam. rep. watch mt. École d'Horlogerie, Chaux-de-Fonds. Also COSTER.
Wed. *Rotterdam.* 1821-30.
KÖTL, Antoni, jun. *Vienna.* 18c. str. rep. br. clock Feill coll.
KOTTE, Jacob. *Frankfurt-a.-M.* 1666. sil. gilt circ. watch Basle M.
KOTZY (KOTZI), Anton. *Vienna.* m.1754.
KOVER, ——. *London.* ca.1720-ca.1760. Watch Den. coll.
KOZZI, Konrad. *Würzburg.* b.1729, m.1772, d.1809.
KRABBE, ——. *Paris.* 1789-1805.
KRACK, August. *Berlin.* 1785. C.
KRACKER, Joseph. *Vienna.* m.1765.
KRAIZERER, Conrad. crys. cross watch. Prob. same as KREIZER.
KRAMER, Tobias. *Augsburg.* 16c. gilt clock in form of elephant with castle K.H.M.
KRAMMER, Friederich. *Vienna.* m.1789.
KRAMP, Pelter. *Stjärnsund.* Early 18c. Large str. clock.
KRAMPE—
Johan Georg. *Basle.* b.1729, m.1764, d.1790.
Jakob, son. *Basle.* b.1795, d.1812. Clocks.
KRÄNKEL—
v. KRENCKEL.
Joseph. *Augsburg.* b.ca.1718-53.
KRANNER, Carl. *Prague.* Early 19c. g. watch.
KRANS, Andreas. *Schweidnitz.* 17c. hex. table clock Feill coll.
KRANTZ, A. *Warsaw.* End 18c. Watch mt. prob. Swiss made Ilbert coll.
KRANZ—
Kaspar. *Kitzingen-am-Main.* b.1743, m. 1794, d.1824. br. clock.
Georg. *Kitzingen-am-Main.* m.1802.
KRAPP, Joseph. *Mannheim. Munich,* 1777. Court C. 1788-1803. Table clock Bay. Nat. M.
KRATZ—
Michael. *Augsburg.* ca.1650. circ. sil. watch B.M. cal. watch Feill coll.
Jacob. *Munich.* 1799.
KRATZENSTEIN, Georg. *Copenhagen* and *Petersburg.* Wrote arts. in Jl. of the Acad. of Petersburg on heat expansion as driving power for clocks and chron. ca.1750 and 1751. In 1780 finished a talking head.
KRATZSCH, Carl. *Vienna.* Early 19c. Watch with sig. F. GERSTNER under cock Feill coll.
KRAUDY, Jacob. *Heidelberg.* ca.1630. 12-lobed crys. watch Marryat coll.
KRAUSE, Christian Friedrich C. *Hamburg.* 1804-21.
KRAUT, ——. *Ohlau.* ca.1700. Worked on the Rathaus clock.
KREBS, Matthäus. *Villingen.* ca.1750-80. Wall clocks Furt. M.
KREIS, Johann Christoph. *Basle.* 1764. From *Wetzlar.*
KREISBEUTEL (GREISBEUTEL, GREISSBÜTTEL)—
Hans. *Cassel.* Burgher in 1591. In 1602 repaired the Rathaus clock.
Martin, son. *Cassel.* 1631-59.
Johann Jost. *Cassel.* 1672-6.
KREITEMANN, Joseph. *Oberhausen.* 1756. Kleinuhrmacher.
KREITTMAIER (CREITMAYER)—
Johann. *Friedberg.* Court C. in *Munich* 1663-1713. astro. monstrance clock, gilt sil. en. and set stones, K.H.M. Watch Blot-Garnier coll.
Elias. *Friedberg.* ca.1700. Stand clock Arts M. Prague. Trav. clock Fitzwilliam M.

KREITTMAYR, Franz. *Prague.* Late 17c. en. watch Den. coll. repoussé watch Nat. M. Prague. Stand clock Fränkel coll.

KREIZER (KREISER, KREITZER and prob. **KRAIZERER),** Conrad. prob. *Strasbourg* or *Augsburg.* ca.1600. A very fine maker. Watches B.M. ill. Baillie, S.K.M. and Louvre. crys. cross and another watch M.M.A. crys. cross watch K.H.M. oct. crys. watch Cassel Landes-M. Oval watch, plates 9 and 11 mm. dia. held by figure on crys. cup, Grünes Gewölbe, Dresden. Prob. smallest early watch. g. en. pear watch Blot-Garnier coll. aut. clock Webster coll.

KREMBERGER, Joseph. ——. 2nd half 18c. br. clock Arts M. Prague.

KRENCKEL (KRAENKL, KROENKL), Petrus. *Eichstätt.* b.1687, d.1730. br.clock.

KRENEN, Gerrit. *Haarlem.* 1757.

KRES, Johann Georg. *Nürnberg.* 1780. Watch Damiano coll. Prob. same as KRESS.

KRESING, Carl. *Königsberg.* ca.1700. Table clock.

KRESS, Johann Georg. *Augsburg.* comp. 1783, m.1791-1800. From *Nürnberg.*

KRESSING, Abraham. *Danzig.* Early 18c. br. clock.

KRETZEL, Georg. *Strasbourg.* 1629.

KREUZ—

——. Near *Furtwangen.* ca.1660. Said to have made the first clock in the Schwarzwald.

Johann August Wilhelm. *Berlin.* 1805.

KREUZE, Gebrüder. *Waldau.* ca.1650.

KREUZER—

Johann Jakob. *Würzburg.* m.1804. Clock Luitprandt M.

Anton. *Würzburg.* m.1817. Clock Luitprandt M.

KREVET, Hans. *Bath.* 1645. Made clockwork for exploding gunpowder.

KRID, Johann Gottfried. *Bautzen.* Early 17c. oct. crys. watch. Prob. same as following.

KRIEDEL—

Johann Gottfried. *Bautzen.* b.1702, d. 1757. hex. table clock. Small br. clock M.P.S. Dresden.

Johann Gottfried, son. *Bautzen.* a.1738, m. 1751. *Cottbus* 1754.

Johann Gotthelf, bro. *Bautzen.* 1752 finished apprenticeship.

KRIEGK, Elias. *Annaberg.* Juré 1605.

KRIEGLEISSEN, Mathieu. *France.* Pub. desc. of equation clock in Gallon, 'Machines et Inventions,' Vol IV in 1726. Clock C.A. & M.

KRIN, Henri. *Montbéliard.* 1672.

KROESE—

J. Casper. *Amsterdam.* 2nd half 18c.

J. P. *Amsterdam.* 1742-ca.1775. l.c. clock. Watch S.K.M.

KROFITSCH, ——. *Leutschach.* b.1755. A parson. Complex cal. clock with 35 dials Uhren M. Vienna.

KROLLERUP, Lars. *Copenhagen.* m.1805.

KROLTZHAMER (KROITZHAMER), Joseph. *Vienna.* m.1791.

KRONAUER, Abraham. *Basle.* 1667. From *Winterthur.*

KROOK—

C. F. *Västervik.* 1821.

O. G. *Västervik.* 1822. d.1840.

KROON, Claas. *Leeuwarden.* 1743-55.

KROPLIN, Hinrich Wilhelm. *Hamburg.* 1801.

KROSSZ, J. G. *Warsaw.* Mid. 18c. C. to the King of Poland. p.c. trav. clock Ashmolean M.

KRUG—

Johann Christoph. *Basle.* 1763. d.1818. Kleinuhrmacher.

Paulus. *Fürth.* d.ca.1800.

KRÜGER—

Gottl. Friedrich. *Römhild.* 1699. Spherical clock falling down chain Gotha M.

Martin. *Berlin.* ——. Table clock Hessische Landes M. Kassel.

P. J. *Berlin.* Pub. 'Theoretischpraktischer Unterricht in der Uhrmacherkunst,' 1851.

KRUMHUBER, Joh. Michael. *Vorchdorf.* Late 18c.-early 19c. Watch mt. Arts M. Prague. sil. p.c. watch.

KRUMHUTER, Math. *Kremsmünster.* Early 19c. Watch.

KRUSE, ——. *Amsterdam.* ca.1750. l.c. clock. cf. KROESE.

KRÜTER, Hans Caspar. *Basle.* 1670.

KRUTMEIJER, Nils J. *Malmö.* b.1770, d. 1847.

KRYGER, Simon Peter. *Copenhagen.* m.1825.

KUHLBERG, A. M. *Stockholm.* 1805-10.

KUHN, J. D. *Carlsruhe.* ca.1780. l.c. clock Furt. M.

KÜHN, Johann Gottfried. *Dresden.* m.1802.

KÜHNAPFEL, ——. *Elbing.* 1785. d.1793. Town C.

KUHY, Jan Henrik. *Amsterdam.* End 18c. Four colour g. en. watch Feill coll.

KULLBERG—

Mathias. *Stockholm.* 1775-85. Watch Nord M. Two wall clocks.

Victor. *London.* b.1824, d.1890. A most eminent maker of chron. and precision watches.

KULLMAN, And. *Norrköping.* b.1780, d. 1824.

KULMANN—

Hindrich Evertsson. *Stockholm.* d.1678. Wall clock.

Karl Gustav, son. *Stockholm.* comp. 1698.

Henric Evert, bro. *Stockholm.* comp. 1698.

KÜLPER, Johann. *Brieg.* 1677-1746. Watch in snuff-box. rep. str. watch M.P.S. Dresden. trav. clock. Also CULPER.

KUMBEL, William. *New York.* 1776. W.

KUMLIN, Gustav Vilhelm. *Copenhagen.* 1796.

KUMLING, Carl Adolph. *Hudiksvall.* 1803-1846.

KÜPFER, ——. *Neuchâtel.* 1690. Clock in Neuchâtel.

KUPFERSCHMIEDS, Joseph. *Oberhausen.* 1756 comp.

KÜPPER, Carl. *Düren.* Early 19c. 'Mysterious' clock M.P.S. Dresden.

KURZ—

Heinrich. *Vienna.* m.1786.

Sebastian. *Brünn.* Early 19c. g. en. watch.

KURZROCKH, Hans. *Dresden.* 1587. Said to have made a clock showing minutes and seconds.

KUSTER, ——. *Paris.* 1824.

KUYPERS, ——. *Haarlem.* 1811.

KVIHNEL, ——. *Cottbus.* 17c. hex. table clock Feill coll.

KYDEREN, ——. *Paris.* Early 18c. Watch Besançon M.

KYFFIN, Edward. *London.* a.1682.

KYHL, Henrik. *Copenhagen.* m.1818. Master of Corporation 1832-6.

KYMER, Robert. *London.* an.1783. Watch.

KYNING, John. *London.* a.1693, CC.1701-11.

KYNSHAM, ——. *London.* an.1774. Watch.

L

LABAER, Jan. *Haarlem.* 1699.
LABAN, ——. *London.* an.1763. Watch.
LABBART, John W. *New York.* 1805.
LABDOUCHE, Joseph. *Paris.* m.1770-4.
LABÉ (L'ABBÉ), Claude. *Stuttgart.* b.1671, d.1717. Court C. Watch Uhren M. Vienna.
LABHARD, Johann. *Cassel.* 1738-95. Swiss. Designed clock for Observatory.
LABINGER, Georg. *Augsburg.* 1795. Turret C.
LABORIE, ——. *Paris.* 1807-25.
LABOSSIÈRE, ——. *Paris.* an.1773. Watch.
LABRY, Anibal. *Halberstadt.* Mid. 18c. sil. watch.
LACAILLE, ——. *Paris.* 1812-25.
LACAN—
Henry. *Paris.* m.1756, juré 1766. Perhaps same as following.
Henri Charles Jean. *Paris.* 1768, juré 1773.
Henri Charles Jean, son. *Paris.* m.1771.
——. *Paris.* 1789.
LACEY—
William. *London.* CC.1750.
Amos. *London.* a.1739.
Paul. *Bristol.* 1787-1830. Succeeded C. Horwood. W.
George. *Portsmouth.* 1795. W.
J. *London.* 1815. W.
John. *Philadelphia.* 1819-25.
LA CHAUMETTE, Jean. ——. ca.1685. Moving hour figure watch Ilbert coll.
LACHAUX, ——. *Paris.* 1807.
LACHÈRE, ——. *Paris.* 1812-24.
LACHÈVRE, ——. *Paris.* 1823.
LACHEZ, Simon. *Utrecht.* Early 18c. br. clock Holthuyzen M. Amsterdam.
LACHIS, Jean François. *Geneva.* m.1653. Watches Stern. and Gélis colls.
LACK—
James. *London.* a.1772.
Robert. *London.* a.1780.
LACKAM, John. *London.* an.1744. Watch.
LÅCKE, Gudmundus P. *Stockholm* and *Jönköping.* 1651-7. Made turret clocks for Stockholm, Göteborg, Växjö, Jönköping and other places.
LACON, Peter. *London.* Late 18c. Watch mt.
LACORDE, l'aisné. *France.* 1754. Water clock.
LA CROIX—
——. *Paris.* ca.1780. Clock ill. Britten. Watch N.Y. Univ.
——. *Paris (Rue St. Denis).* 1807-13.
——. *Paris (Rue neuve des Petits Champs).* 1807-09.
et Fils. *Geneva.* Early 19c. g. en. watch M.P.S. Dresden.

LA CROIX—*continued.*
Fils et Falconnet. *Geneva.* Early 19c. g. en. watch.
Pierre. *Geneva.* b.1804, d.1871. Started first watch-case machine factory ca.1855.
L. *Turin.* 1833. cyl. rep. watch S.M.S.K. g. en. watch M.M.A.
LACROY, P. *France.* 1st half 17c. oct. sil. watch eng. faceted covers.
LACY—
Solomon. *London.* a.1700.
John. *London.* a.1714, CC.1722-50.
John. *Portsmouth.* End 18c.
George. *Portsea.* 1795. W.
LAD, M. *Hannover.* an.1790. Watch.
LADBROOKE—
Henry. *London.* a.1705.
Thomas. *London.* a.1713.
LADD—
Samuel. *London.* a.1691, CC.1710.
Sir John. *London.* CC.1820-4. chron. maker.
Edward Wilds. *London.* a.1816.
LADE—
Michael. *Canterbury.* an.1744. Watch.
Joseph François. *Paris.* m.1786.
'LADIES STEM WIND.' Sig. on 1871-4 watches of the Cornell Watch Co.
LADOUSEUR, ——. *Paris (Faubourg St. Antoine).* Early 18c. Watch Ilbert coll.
LADTERER, Johann Georg. *Aichach.* 1738. Kleinuhrmacher.
'LADY ELGIN.' Sig. on 1869-75 watches of the National Watch Co. of Chicago.
'LADY WASHINGTON.' Sig. on watches of American Watch Co. from 1880.
LAEISZ, Johann Jacob. *Hamburg.* 1821.
LAFEUILLE—
Edouard. *Geneva.* 1668. From *Sédan.*
Daniel. *Amsterdam.* 1681. Huguenot refugee from France.
L'AFFILÉ (LAFFILLE)—
——. *Paris.* m.1588.
François. *Paris.* Sig. to Statuts of Paris Corporation of 1660. Table clock.
LAFOLIE, ——. *Paris.* 1812. C.
LAFOSSE, ——. *Paris.* 1817.
LAGEMANN, Hinrich. *Berne.* Early 19c. Watch.
LAGERLUND—
Erik. *Copenhagen.* m.1756.
Erik. *Norrköping.* 1780.
LAGERSTRAND—
Eric. *Uppsala.* b.1783, d.1833. Watch.
Nikl. *Hälsingfors.* b.1795, d.1849.
LAGERSTRÖM, Eric. *Uppsala.* ca.1800. br. clock.
LAGGAN, John. *London.* an.1780. Watch.

LAGIER ET BAUDIT. *Hamburg.* 1815. From *Geneva.*
LAGIS (LAGISSE)—
Pierre Didier. *Geneva.* d.1679. Went to *Ispahan* and became C. to the Shah. g. en. watches G.M. and Ilbert and Gélis colls. Watch Bernal sale.
François. *London.* ca.1700. sil. watch with cardinal's arms Ilbert coll.
LAGOE, John. *London.* a.1671.
LAGRANGE—
Joseph Louis. *Berlin* and *Paris.* b.1736. Went Paris 1787. Eminent mathematician. Pub. mem. on the mathematical theory of escapements 1777.
——. *Paris.* 1812-24. C.
LAGUESSE, L. J., ET FILS. *Paris.* 1810-13. C.
LÄHNE—
David Christian. *Leipzig.* 1798 m.-1801.
C. H. *Leipzig.* Late 18c.-1800. d.an.1814. g. en. watch M.P.S. Dresden. Maker of repute.
David C. *Leipzig.* 1800-14.
LAIDLAW—
Thomas. *London* (*Salisbury Ct.*). 1770. CC. 1781-94. en. watch London M.
William, son. *London.* a.1786.
Alexander. *Edinburgh.* a.1799.
Thomas. *Newcastle-o.-T.* 1820. Watch.
LAIDMAN—
Leonard. *London.* a.1726.
John. *London.* an.1765. Watch.
LAIGHT, John. *Birmingham.* 1730.
LAILLET, Jacques. *Evreux.* 1635. Called as expert on clock on St. Laurent, Rouen.
LAING—
David. *Perth.* 1767.
Robert. *London.* a.1771.
LAINY—
David. ——. ca.1680. Watch mt. G.M.
John. *London.* a.1711, CC.1720.
LAIRD, James. *Kilmalcolm.* 1770.
LAISNE (LASNE, LAINÉ)—
Nicolas. *Rouen.* 1617-21. Founder member of Rouen corporation.
Pierre. *Rouen.* 1st half 18c. g. en. watch.
——. *Paris.* 1820. Successor to DUBUC, aîné.
LAITHWAITE—
William. *Liverpool.* 1701. Watch case maker.
Robert. *Liverpool.* 1734.
R. *London.* an.1746. Watch.
John. *Liverpool.* 1754. W.
LAKE—
Bryan. *London.* a.1667, CC.1674.
Joseph. *London.* a.1707.
Thomas. *London.* a.1713.
Samuel. *Wexford.* Mid. 18c. Watch Stads M. Amsterdam.
Jonathan. *London* (*Fulham*). an.1776. Watch.
Robert. *London* (*Enfield*). CC.1770-1808.
James. *London.* a.1769.
Thomas. *Taunton.* 1795. W.
W. B. *London* (*Epping*). Early 19c.
LAKIN, John. *Tamworth.* ca.1760. Watch Ilbert coll.
LALANDE—
John. *London.* an.1776. Watch.
——. *Paris.* 1789.
v. DE LALANDE.
LALLEMAND (LALLEMAN, LALEMENT)—
Didier. *Paris.* m.1606. Fine crys. cross watch Mallett coll. ill. Baillie.
Henry. *Autun.* ca.1630, d.1670.
Henry, son. *Autun.* ca.1650.
Judith, sister. *Autun.* ca.1650. oct. watch M.M.A.
Louis. *Blois.* m.1667-1718. Made turret clock at Blois.

LALLEMAND (LALLEMAN, LALEMENT)—*continued.*
Didier. *Lyons,* 1672. *Paris,* 1686. Made a clockwork astro. globe, desc. in Phil. Trans. Vol. XII, Oxford, 1683.
Jean Jacques. *Neuchâtel.* 2nd half 17c.
Simon, son of Louis. *Blois.* m.1701.
Jean, bro. *Blois.* m.1715.
Jacques, bro. *Blois.* m.1718.
——. *Paris.* 1790-1813. cyl. rep. watch mt. C.A. & M.
LALLIER—
J. B. *Coblenz.* ca.1780. g. en. watch Nat. M. Stockholm.
Louis. *Paris.* m.1781.
——. *Paris.* 1823.
LALOE, ——. *Paris.* 1812. C.
LALOND, Pierre. *St. Lo.* an.1678. Watch.
LALOUEL, Pierre. *St. Lo.* an.1650. Watch Ilbert coll.
LA MARCHE-DIT-HENRY, Henry. *Blois.* m.1631-9.
LAMB (LAMBE)—
Thomas. *London.* 1630. CC.1632.
Abraham. *London.* a.1651.
Edmund. *London.* CC.1676.
Simon. *Rochester.* a.1669. l.c. clock.
Wright. *London.* a.1682.
Luke. *London.* a.1683.
Richard. *London.* a.1696.
William. *London.* a.1707.
John. *London.* a.1721.
Nicholas. *London.* a.1746.
James. *London* (*Christopher's Alley*). a.1751, CC.1759-83.
Benjamin. *London* (*Clerkenwell*). 1756. d.1784.
Edward. *London.* an.1763. Watch.
John. *London* (*Fetter La.*). 1775.
& WEBB. *London.* an.1774-95. Watch.
James. *London.* a.1775, CC.1798.
James. *London.* a.1783.
Thomas. *London.* 1790.
Samuel. *Northampton.* an.1796. Watch.
John. *Horncastle.* 1797. Watch. C. Succeeded James COATES.
Thomas. *Newcastle-o.-T.* 1820.
John. *London* (*Newman St.*). 1820.
John. *London* (*Cockspur St.*). ca.1830. Watch Ilbert coll.
LAMBDEN, Richard. *London.* a.1685.
LAMBERT—
Nicolas. *Rouen.* ca.1480. Keeper of town clock.
Jacques. *Rouen.* 1516. Keeper of town clock.
Guillaume. *Salins.* 1527. Made clock of Ste. Anatoile. Also LAMBART.
Robert. *England.* 1544. French. Worked on clock for Norwich.
Pierre. *Abbeville.* End 17c.-ca.1730. Watches Ilbert and Den. colls.
Thomas. *London.* a.1727.
William. *London.* a.1730, CC.1742.
Nicholas. *London.* 1750-70. l.c. clock Weth. coll. ill. Britten.
Edward. *London.* CC.1767.
Edward. *London* (*Bridgewater Sq.*). CC. 1773-87.
Benjamin. *Yarmouth.* 1777. d.1786. W.
George. *Blandford.* 1780. C.
John. *London* (*Shug La.*), 1784; (*Tichborne St.*), 1805-11. Watch.
——. *Naples.* 2nd half 18c. Watch.
——. *Besançon.* 2nd half 18c. Watch.
Thomas. *London.* a.1796.
John. *London.* a.1806.
jeune. *Paris* (*Rue de Vaugirard*). 1810-25. Succeeded L. P. BISSON.
——. *Paris* (*Rue Boucher*). 1812. C.
Harry. *London.* CC.1821.

LAMBERTIN—
——. *Paris.* ca.1755 m.
Pierre. *Paris.* m.1762.
LAMBFORD, Thomas. *London.* 1753. Watch mt. maker.
LAMBORN, John. *Cambridge.* an.1725. Watch.
LAMBREGHTS, ——. *Antwerp.* an.1751. aut. clock. Watch.
LAMER, Peter. *London.* 1568. Frenchman.
LAMERIS, W. H. *Amsterdam.* ca.1800.
LAMI—
——. *Paris.* 1786-9. Watch N.Y. Univ.
——. *Geneva.* ca.1800.
LAMIRAL, ——. *Paris.* Early 19c. Mantel clock. Two of this name, one in *Rue de la Vielle Monnaie,* the other in *Rue des Sts. Pères.*
LAMLEY, John. *Exeter.* mar.1700. C.
LAMONT, ——. *London.* an.1783. Watch.
LAMOTTE—
Frères. *Liége.* Early 19c. Mantel clock Stads M. Amsterdam.
——. *Paris.* 1825.
LAMPARD, Matthew. *London.* a.1697.
LAMPE, John. *London.* CC.1714-65. l.c. clock. Table clock. Watch mt. Ilbert coll.
John. *Baltimore, U.S.A.* 1780. From *Annapolis.* W.
LAMPÉN, Henric. *Åbo.* 1793-1805.
LAMPORT—
Daniel. *London.* a.1766-1810. Watch.
H. *Plymouth.* Early 19c. Watch.
LAMPRECHT, A. *Breslau.* 1828. Complex mus. aut. clock.
LAMSON, ——. *London.* 1772.
LAMUDE—
Peter. *London.* a.1684.
Reuben. *Chard.* an.1742-9. Watch.
John. *Chard.* a.1749-95. W.
John. *London.* a.1749.
LAMY—
Jeremiah. *London.* a.1733.
Valentin. *Couvet.* 1807-12. C.
——. *Paris.* 1812-25.
LAMY-GOUGE—
——. *Paris.* 1790. C. to the King.
——, son. *Paris.* 1807-25.
jeune. *Paris.* 1818-25.
LANCASTER—
Richard. *London.* a.1677.
Nicholas. *London.* a.1679.
Richard. *London.* a.1684.
James. *London.* an.1742. Watch.
——. *York.* an.1757. Watch.
& Lancaster, jun. *Plymouth Dock.* ca.1790. Also Lancaster & Son.
William. *Plymouth Dock.* 1795. Watch.
John. *Prescot.* 1795. W.
F. *Prescot.* 1809.
Francis. *Liverpool.* ca.1820.
Henry. *Liverpool.* 1825. Chron. maker.
James. *Liverpool.* 1825. Chron. maker.
LANCASTER, PA., WATCH CO. Issued watches ca.1878 with sigs.: 'New Era' and 'West End.'
LANCELOT, ——. *Paris.* an.1765. g. watch.
LANCOLAT, ——. *Paris.* m.1684.
LAND—
T. *Tiverton.* ca.1700. br. clock.
Richard. *Painswick.* an.1780. Watch.
William. *London.* an.1801. Watch.
LANDECK (LANDTECK)—
Andreas (Endres). *Nürnberg.* b.1589, d. 1663. Worked with Hanns Hagen at *Worms,* then with Abraham Habrecht at *Strasbourg,* then at *Nancy,* where he made a church clock; at *Windsheim* 1621, *Rothenburg-a.-d.-T.* 1630, *Nürnberg* 1636, where he was town C. Sundial dated 1647.
Johann Carl, son. *Nürnberg.* b.1636, d.1712. Went to *Amsterdam, Rotterdam, Copenhagen, Holstein.* At *Nürnberg* 1662, and in 1663 was town C. First to make pendulum clocks in Nürnberg. Clock for Rothenburg-a.-d.-T. br. clock.
Zacharias, son. *Nürnberg.* 1705. Town C. and well-known maker. l.c. clock. Geographic clock with J. B. Homann Feill coll.
Johann Adam, son. *Ansbach.* 1746. Court C.
Wolfgang Jacob Mathäus, bro. *Weimar.* b. 1715, d.1794. Court C.
Christian Achatius. *Nürnberg.* Mid. 18c. l.c. clock.
W. H. ——. 18c. l.c. clock.
Johann Caspar, son of W. J. M. *Nürnberg.* b.1752, d.1822. Watch Stuttgart M.
——. *London.* ca.1760. br. clock.
LANDIFIELD, Thomas. *London.* CC.1772. Retired 1777. Watch.
LANDLOVE, John. *London.* an.1777. Watch.
LANDO, ——. *London.* an.1780. rep. watch.
LANDRÉ—
Michel. *Blois* and *Rennes.* mar.1605, d.1623. Went *Rennes* 1610.
Pierre. *Blois.* m.1619-47. Also André.
Pierre, son. *Blois.* b.1627, d.1679. Also André.
P. *Brussels.* Mid. 17c. en. watch M.M.A.
Salomon, son. *Blois.* m.1672, d.an.1691. Also André.
LANDREAU, ——. *Amsterdam.* Mid. 17c. sil. watch in form of dog. Watch Ilbert coll.
LANDRICHTER, Johan Georg. *Gratz.* ca. 1760. Watch Ilbert coll.
LANDRIN, Louis. *Paris.* 1825. C.
LANDRU, Pierre. *Paris.* m.1784.
LANDRY, Jacques. *Chaux-de-Fonds.* 1813. Clock.
LANDSDOWN, Edward. *London.* Early 19c. Watch.
LANE—
Thomas. *Barnstaple.* 1611. Keeper of clock on Kay Hall.
John. *London.* a.1679. Watches Huddersfield M. and Buckley coll.
Wright. *London.* 1687 CC.
Thomas. *London.* an.1709. Watch.
Robert. *London.* a.1721.
Josiah. *London.* a.1729, CC.1736.
Stephen. *London.* an.1754. Watch.
William. *London.* a.1763.
J. *Parkham.* 18c. l.c. clock.
Joseph. *Moreton in Marsh.* 18c. l.c. clock.
Henry. *London (Mount Row)* and *Bristol.* 1775-97. W.
John. *London (Fetter La.).* CC.1809. Regulator ill. Cec. & Web.
——. *Evesham.* an.1818. Watch.
John. *London.* a.1805.
Edward. *Rathkeale.* 1824.
George. *Bristol.* 1825.
LANFROY, ——. *Paris.* 1812.
LANG—
Johann Christoph. *Augsburg.* Late 16c. Stand clock.
William. *Barnstaple.* 1614. Keeper of clock on Kay Hall.
Johann Georg. *Baden.* 17c. Fine pentagonal table clock.
A. *Augsburg.* 1726.
Samuel. *London.* an.1772. Watch.
Léopold. *Paris.* m.1776.
LANGCROFT (LONGCRAFT), Richard. *London.* a.1698, CC.1718.
LANGDEN, Elijah. *London.* a.1736.
LANGE—
Jakob. *Münster.* 1512. A smith who prob. made the original Dom clock.
Jean. *Lyons.* a.1647-64 m.
——. *Valenciennes.* Mid. 18c. g. en. watch.

LANGE—*continued.*
——. *Paris.* 1807.
Adolf Ferdinand. *Paris* and *Glashütte.* b. 1815, d.1875. An eminent W. Founder of the Glashütte watch industry in 1845.
LANGEL—
Jean Pierre. *Courtelary.* 1783
——, son. *Courtelary.* 1783.
LANGENBUCHER—
Achilles. *Augsburg.* 1610. Famous automaton maker; made a mus. work playing a whole vespers.
Caspar. *Augsburg.* Early 17c. A very able maker. Clock Brunswick M.
Gottlieb, son of Achilles. *Augsburg.* Mid. 17c.
LANGESTRAAT, H. *Rotterdam.* 2nd half 18c. Watch mt.
LANGEVIN, ——. *Paris.* 1811.
LANGFORD—
Gowen. *London.* a.1637, CC.1652-63.
Ellis. *London.* a.1663, CC.1672.
Benjamin. *London.* a.1715.
George. *London.* 1749. Watch.
George, son. *London.* a.1748.
William. *London.* a.1761, CC.1770. From *Ludlow.*
John. *London.* an.1771. Watch.
Thomas. *London.* CC.1781.
——. *Southampton.* Early 19c. Watch.
William. *Bristol.* 1825-30.
LANGGAARD, Jens Berthelsen. *Copenhagen.* m.1811.
LANGHAM—
William. *London.* CC.1751.
Samuel. *London.* an.1773. Watch.
William. *London.* a.1768.
LANGHAMMER—
Joseph. *Vienna.* m.1772.
Johann. *Vienna.* m.1800.
LANGHAUSS, Hanns Wolff. *Nürnberg.* Burgher 1687. Sand-glass maker.
LANGIN, Mathieu. *Basle.* 1685. From *Geneva.*
LANGLANDS—
& Co. *Newcastle-o.-T.* an.1780. Watch.
James. *Newcastle-o.-T.* an.1809. Watch.
John. *Newcastle-o.-T.* an.1816. Watch.
LANGLEY—
Thomas. *London.* a.1655, CC.1664.
Cornelius. *London.* a.1700, CC.1707-23. Bankrupt.
Harry. *Bristol.* an.1752. Watch.
LANGLOIS—
——. *Rouen.* 1591.
Pierre. *Paris.* m.1675-81. Watch Bourges M.
——. *Le Havre.* 17c. al. watch F.W.M.
Jacques. *Paris.* 1692 m.
Thimothée. *Paris.* 1693. Maker of water-clocks.
Charles François. *Paris.* 1730. d.1757. Watch Nat. M. Prague.
LANGSCHWERT, Johann Georg. *Würzburg.* m.1745. Table Clock Luitprandt M. l.c. clock and several br. clocks.
LANGSTON, John. *London.* 1822-4.
LÅNGSTRÖM, Hans. *Skellefteå.* Late 18c. l.c. clock.
LANGTHORNE, Joseph. *London.* a.1709.
LANGTON, John. *London.* a.1711.
LANGWITH—
James. *York.* b.1690, d.1723. C.
Samuel. *York.* 1770. C.
LANIELAY, John. *Sheffield.* 1774. W.
LANKESTER, Richard. *London.* a.1680.
LANLELME, Henry. *Geneva.* 1720. From *Dauphiné.*
LANNER, Josua. *Karlskrona.* 1773-93. Three l.c. clocks.
LANNÉR, Daniel. *Kalmar.* 1800-19.
LANNY, P. *London.* an.1764. Watch.
LANOIA, Guy. *Paris.* m.1776.
LA NOY, ——. *Paris.* 1772 m.
LANSDALE, ——. *London.* an.1777. Watch.
LANSDOWNE, John. *London.* a.1727.
LANTHEAUME, ——. *Madrid.* 1758.
LANY, John. *London.* CC.1720.
LANZ (LANTS), Niklaus. *Innsbruck.* Mid. 16c. small circ. table clock B.M. Clock K.H.M. Monogram 'N.L.'
LAPAIRIÈRE, Pierre. *Avignon.* 1723.
LAPEINE, ——. *Orange.* 1666.
LAPEU, Charles. *London.* a.1718.
LA PIERRE—
Jaques. *Vienna.* ca.1800. Guitar watch.
Bennet. *Baltimore, U.S.A.* 1802. W. & C.
——. *Paris.* 1812.
J. *Amsterdam (Kerk str.).* 1822.
J. *Amsterdam (Lange Leydeschedwar str.).* 1822.
LAPIERRE-MOUCHET, ——. *Paris.* 1812. C.
LAPLACE, Jean Baptiste Pierre. *Paris.* m. 1786.
LA PLANCHE, ——. *Naples.* Late 17c. Watch Miller coll.
LAPORTE, ——. *Vevey.* 1767 m. Also PORTE.
LAPOSTE, Louis. *La Brévine.* 1774. C.
LAPRET, Hippolyte. *Paris.* m.1786-9. Mantel clock.
LARARD, Edward. *Wirksworth.* 1795. W.
LARCÉ, J. François. *Paris.* ca.1690. Gilt watch.
LARCHER, Charles Henry. *Paris.* m.1770.
LARDENT, Benjamin. *London.* a.1792.
LARESCHE—
Jacques Antoine. *Besançon.* b.1700, d.1782. Several very fine br. clocks.
H. *Paris.* 1807-27. Wrote a mem. on the lubrication of pivots, Rouen, 1827. Many fine clocks. sil. rep. watch, painted dial.
LARGE—
Samuel. *London.* an.1772. Watch.
James. *Wymondham.* Early 19c. Watch.
LARK, William. *London.* a.1819.
LARKIN, Dennis. *Loughrea.* 1824.
LARKUM, Sarah. *London.* a.1719.
LAROCH, John. *London.* a.1785-1825. W. & C.
LARPENT—
James. *London.* a.1720.
Isaac. *Copenhagen.* b.1711, m.1745, d.1769. Started watch factory at *Röskilde* with Joergen JÜRGENSON. Watches F.W.M. and Chamb. coll. p.c. watch dated 1747 Feill coll.
LARRINGTON, ——. *London.* an.1756. Watch.
LARROQUE, Paul. *Lorreins.* 1759. Astronomer. Made new clock for Bordeaux.
LARRYMORE, Thomas. *London.* ca.1780. Pair mus. aut. clocks. Palace M. Pekin.
LARSÉ (LARCAY), L. *Paris.* 1724-33. Devised a single train str. and rep. mechanism, desc. in Gallon, 'Machines et Inventions,' Vol. VI.
LARSSON, And. *Sweden.* ca.1800.
LA RUE—
——. *Paris.* ca.1775. Bronze worker. Made clock-cases.
Carlos. *Madrid.* 1800. Sent by Spanish Navy to study chron. making in Paris, but died soon after his return.
LARWELL—
Abraham. *Frome.* 1774. C. & W.
Ebenezer. *London.* a.1796.
LASACKER, Alberten. *Cologne.* 1735.
LASALLE—
——. *Paris.* Mid. 18c. Ormolu clock.
Auguste. *Vevey.* 1795–8. Juré.

LASHBROOK—
Thomas. *London.* a.1661.
Thomas. *London.* a.1693, CC.1701-09.
Henry. *London (Clerkenwell).* a.1703, CC. 1715-28.
Thomas, son. *London.* a.1728.
LASHMAR, Richard Marchant. *Brighton.* 1822. C. & W.
LASHMORE, T. *Southampton.* Early 19c. Watch.
LASNIER, ——. *Paris.* 1740. Dial maker.
LASPOINTE, Estienne Martin. *Paris.* m. 1744.
LASSELL—
Thurston. *Liverpool.* ca.1750. l.c. clock.
William. *Liverpool.* 1770-1807. l.c. clock.
John. *London.* an.1773. Watch.
LASSIEUR, ——. *Paris.* Late 18c. Bro.-in-law of A. L. BREGUET and in charge of his business during the Revolution.
LAST, James. *Stalham.* 1796. W.
LATARD, Jean Philippe. *Geneva.* ca.1760-1774.
LATCH, Robert. *Limerick.* 2nd half 18c. l.c. clock.
LATHAM—
Henry. *London.* a.1655.
John. *London.* a.1693, CC.1700, d.1740. Watch S.K.M. g. rep. watch in eng. case sd. PARBURY, h.m. 1719 Ilbert coll. l.c. clock. Also LATHOM.
John. *Wigan.* 1751. C.
James. *London.* an.1778. Watch.
William. *Macclesfield.* 1793-7. C. & W.
LATIMER—
Henry. *Gateshead.* 1765. C. & W.
& MILLER. *Gateshead.* an.1773. Watch.
James. *Philadelphia.* 1813-20.
Henry. *Monaghan.* 1824.
Joseph. *Monaghan.* 1824.
LATOUR, René. *London.* a.1715, CC.1730.
LAUCH, Johann Friedrich. *Vienna.* ca.1695-1740. Pub. designs for br. clocks.
LAUCHER, Franz. *Vienna.* m.1772.
LAUD (LOD, LODE), John. *London.* 1662.
LAUDER—
John. *Prestonpans.* 1790.
James. *Prestonpans.* 1796.
LAUDERN, John. ——. an.1775. Watch.
LAUGHTON—
William. *London.* CC.1683-94.
William. *London.* a.1712.
William. *London (Leather La.).* 1731. W.
LAULTIER, Charles. *Paris.* m.1608.
LAUMOND, ——. *Amiens.* 1772.
LAUMUSSE (L'AULMUSSE, LOMMISSE, LOMUSSE)—
Jean. *Lyons.* mar.1595-1620. In charge of cathedral clocks.
Abraham. *Lyons.* 1611 m.-1626. Turret C.
LAUNAY—
René. *Paris.* m.1788.
David. *New York.* ca.1800.
——. *Paris.* 1812-24.
LAUNDY, John. *London.* 1692.
LAUNOIS, ——. *Paris.* Machinist to the Dauphin. Made aut.
LAURENCE—
——. *London.* 1576.
Henry. *London.* a.1691, CC.1704-25. Also LAWRENCE.
Thomas. *London.* a.1706.
Fifield. *London.* a.1715.
Benjamin. *London.* a.1730.
Thomas. *London.* a.1732-ca.1770. Watch.
Robert. *London.* a.1772.
LAURENT—
Peter. *London.* a.1700.
Félix. *Canton, China.* 1787-ca.1800. Firm of COX, BEALE & LAURENT from 1792.

LAURENT—*continued.*
——. *Paris.* 1793-1821. Two of this name, one in *Quai des Gèvres,* the other in *St. Jean de Latran.*
LAURIE, William. *London.* a.1768.
LAURIER—
François. *Blois.* 1654. d.1663. Watch mt. B.M. circ. en. watch Lincoln M.
Daniel. *Paris.* 1675 m.
LAURILLARD, ——. *Paris.* 1816-25.
LAUSSME, Esaius. *Edinburgh.* 1595.
LAUTIER, Benjamin. *Bath.* ca.1790-1848 CC. Watch N.Y. Univ.
LAVANCHY, Jean. *Vevey.* 1798 m.
LAVAUX—
——. *Paris.* ca.1750 m.
Claude, son. *Paris.* m.1756.
LAVENDER—
William. *London.* a.1720.
John. *Crediton.* 1795. C. & W.
LAVER, Benjamin. *London.* End 18c. br. clock.
LAVERGE, Philip. *London.* a.1717.
LAVESPEARE, William. *London.* 1662 CC.
LAVIER, ——. *Paris.* 1812.
LAVOYER, Pierre Cyprien. *Couvet.* a.1794.
LAW—
Isaac. *London.* 1632-76 CC.
Silvester. *London.* a.1689.
Timothy. *London.* a.1690.
Wasteneys. *London.* a.1698.
——. *Castle Douglas.* 1723.
John. *London.* a.1760, CC.1768.
Jeremiah. *Rochdale.* ca.1770-95.
Jean Jacques Philippe. *Paris.* m.1772.
William. *London.* an.1778. Watch.
James. *London.* an.1778-1811. Watch.
Thomas. *London (Southwark).* CC.1777-99.
James. *Aberdeen.* 1782.
John. *Beith.* 1784.
John. *Aberdeen.* ca.1790 CC.
Abraham. *Bedford.* 1791. W.
& SON. *Dublin.* ca.1800. l.c. clock. Watch.
John. *Edinburgh.* b.1770, d.1842.
George. *Peebles.* 1808.
Robert. *Castle Douglas.* 1818-30.
Samuel. *Rochdale.* ca.1820.
William. *Kirkcudbright.* 1820.
William. *Linlithgow.* 1820-37.
John. *Kirkcaldy.* 1821.
Anthony. *London.* Early 19c.
LAWELL, Paul. *London.* CC.1653.
LAWLESS, ——. *London.* 1778. Shagreen case maker.
LAWLEY—
Whitton. *London.* a.1715.
John. *Rugeley.* an.1776. Watch.
Andrew, & Co. *Bristol.* 1788. C.
William. *Rugeley.* 1795.
John. *Bristol.* 1825-30. C.
& SOLESMAN. *Liverpool.* 1825. C.
LAWORTHY, Mark Joseph. *London.* a.1703.
LAWRENCE—
Henry. *London.* a.1691, CC.1704-25. Also LAURENCE.
William. *Thame.* 1744-55. C.
Archibald. *v.* LAWRIE.
Richard. *Warminster.* 1752. C. & W. Prob. the following.
Richard. *Bath.* 1757. d.1773. Skeleton sil. watch G.M.
John. *Lancaster.* ca.1760-95. C.
John. *London.* 1762.
& WOOD. *Bath.* 1772. W.
Benjamin. *London (Shoe La.).* CC.1779-96.
William, son of John. *Stockport.* 1785. C. Lancaster freeman.
Harry, son of Benjamin. *London (Shoe La.).* a.1789, CC.1796-1809.
James. *London (Marylebone* and *Portugal St.).* a.1790-1824.
Robert. *London.* 1802-24.

LAWRENCE—*continued.*
Joseph. *London.* a.1805.
George. *London.* 1820.
James. *London* (*Rotherhithe*). 1820.
LAWRENSON, Francis. *Liverpool.* 1804. Watch Ilbert coll.
LAWRIE—
Archibald. *Edinburgh.* 1720.
Archibald. *Edinburgh.* a.1731.
Archibald. *Carlisle.* mar.ca.1748. Clock. Watch Ilbert coll. 'Eminent.'
John. *London* (*Stoke Newington*). 1799.
LAWSON—
John. *London.* an.1723. Watch with mt. under glass.
William. *Newton-le-Willows.* ca.1770. Watch mts. Grosvenor M. Chester and Buckley coll.
Richard. *London.* an.1778-1804. Watch.
Thomas. *Keighley.* 1765-95. C.
James. *Bristol.* 1784.
Robert. *Leigh.* an.1787. Watch and l.c. clock.
James. *London.* a.1778. Watch.
William. *Keighley.* 1780-1822. C. & W.
John Edward. *London* (*Bishopsgate St.*). a. 1790, CC.1798, l.CC.1812-24. cyl. mt. G.M.
Benjamin. *Manchester.* 1808-13. C.
John. *Warrington.* ca.1820.
William. *Todmorden.* ca.1820.
Christopher. *Edinburgh.* 1820. d.1837.
& Millar. *Edinburgh.* 1822-5.
LAXTON—
Thomas. *London.* a.1633, CC.1642.
Thomas. *London.* CC.1653.
LAY, Ambrose. *London.* a.1744.
LAYBOURN, Christopher. *Driffield.* ca.1770, d.1831. C. & W.
LAYFIELD, Robert. *Grindlestone Thorn.* 1785. W. Lancaster freeman.
LAYTON—
John. *London.* CC.1653-83.
William. *London.* 1703 CC. Also Laughton.
William, son. *London.* a.1703, CC.1710.
Francis. *London.* a.1719, CC.1726, d.1743. Spring maker.
Thomas. *London.* 1761-8. Livery Farriers Co.
Thomas. *London.* CC.1769, l.CC.1776-1823. Watch sd. Notyal.
LAZARUS—
David. *Portsea.* 1795. W.
Jacob. *London* (*Houndsditch*). 1805-08.
H. *London* (*E. Smithfield*). 1817-25. W.
Joseph, & Co. *London* (*Houndsditch*). 1820-4.
J. *London* (*Minories*). 1825. W.
& Lawrence. *London.* 1825. W. & C.
LAZENBY—
Robert. *London* (*Knightsbridge*). an.1776-1808. Clock. Watch.
John. *London* (*Knightsbridge*). 1809-11.
Richard. *London* (*Knightsbridge*). 1817-24.
LEA—
Joseph. *London.* an.1736. Watch.
Thomas. *London* (*Old Jewry*). CC.1764, l.CC.1766, m.CC.1782-93.
Thomas. *London.* a.1770.
John. *Liverpool.* 1810. W.
James. *Liverpool.* 1811-29. W.
LEABETTER, Charles. *Hindley.* ca.1780. Watch.
LEACH—
Samuel. *London.* a.1699.
William. *London.* a.1740, CC.1749. Also Leech.
Benjamin. *Winchester.* 1790-1803. Watch and l.c. clock.
John. *Romsey.* ca.1800. Clock.
John. *Liverpool.* 1803-05. W.
John. *Kirkham.* ca.1820.
Thomas Catteral. *London.* a.1819.
LEADBEATER, Charles. *Wigan.* ca.1818.
LEADBETTER—
Andrew. *Edinburgh.* a.1764.
William. *London.* 1790-1811.
Thomas. *Sandbach.* ca.1800. Watch.
LEADER, Thomas. *London.* an.1765. Watch.
'LEADER.' Sig. on watches of the Elgin National Watch Co. from 1877.
LEAF—
Leigh. *Prescot.* d.1785. W.
John. *London.* CC.1785.
LEAH, Samuel Henry. *London.* 1820-40.
LEAKE—
Faith. *London.* a.1677, CC.1685.
George. *London.* a.1685, CC.1693. Small lantern clock.
Daniel. *London.* a.1703.
LEAMAN, Thomas. *London.* a.1711.
LEAR, John. *London.* an.1744. Watch.
LÉAUTIER, Paul. *Paris.* m.1767-89. Watch N.Y. Univ. trav. clock Gélis coll.
LEAVENWORTH—
Mark. *Waterbury, U.S.A.* 1810-30.
William. *Waterbury, U.S.A.* 1810-15. Failed, and started with his son at *Albany.*
& Son. *Albany, U.S.A.* 1817-23. C.
LEAVER—
Nathaniel. *London.* a.1679. br. clock. Also Lever.
James. *London.* a.1710.
LEAY, James. *Liverpool.* 1813-6. W.
LEBALD, ——. *London.* an.1779. Watch.
LE BAS—
David. *London.* 1744. Watch.
David Peter, son. *London.* a.1744.
——. *Paris.* 1812. C.
LEBBY, Daniel. *Liskeard.* 1791-5. W.
LEBEAU, Jean. *Lyons.* a.1639.
LEBEL—
Joseph. *Paris.* m.1758.
——. *Paris.* 1822.
LE BEUF, Henry. *Geneva.* ca.1770. Watch Basle M.
LEBIHAN, ——. *Paris.* 1811-8. mus. clocks.
LE BLANC—
——. *Orléans.* 1644.
Joas. *Rouen.* m.1655.
——. *Paris.* 1811-24.
v. Blanc.
LE BLON, Michael. *Amsterdam.* b.1590, d. 1656. Engraver. Designs for watches. Example on watch by J. Spin Stern. coll.
LE BLOND—
P. *Paris.* 1st half 17c. oct. eng. watch. crys. watch and cloisonné en. watch.
Robert. *London.* 1760. Watch.
Pierre. *Paris* (*Rue St. Honoré*). m.1767-89.
Jean Nicolas. *Paris* (*Rue St. Paul*). m.1777-1810.
William. *London.* 1785.
l'aîné. *Paris* (*Rue St. Paul*). ca.1800-12. Fine mantel clock, case by Poisson.
Veuve. *Paris* (*Rue St. Paul*). 1813-9.
LE BLOND-DU-QUINTAUX, Nicolas. *Paris* (*Rue de la Vieille Boucherie*). m.1770-89.
LE BON—
Marc Antoine. *Rouen.* m.1695.
Joseph. *Basle.* 1705. From *Lyons.*
Alexander. *Paris.* 1714-50. Clock S.K.M. Watch mt. G.M. Experimented with anchor escapement for clocks. Said to have made, with Julien Le Roy, his pupil, the first equation clocks in France, desc. in Gallon, 'Machines et Inventions,' Vols. III & IV, 1714 & 1722. Devised a remontoir wound by the striking mechanism.
Charles. *Paris.* Mid. 18c. g. en. watch.
Frères. *Paris.* 1824.
LEBONVALLET, ——. *Paris.* 1809-25.
LE BOULLENGER, Pierre. *Rouen.* a.1702.

LE BOURN, Daniel. *London.* an.1764. Watch.
LE BRASSEUR, Nicolas. *Paris.* 1761 m.
LE BREM, ——. ——. ca.1800. Metal en. watch.
LE BRET, Robin. *Rouen.* 1470.
LE BRUN—
Jean. *Paris.* 1609. Juré.
Jacques. *Blois.* m.1664.
Jacques. *Paris.* m.1675. Prob. same as preceding.
Jacques. *Paris.* m.1788.
LE CAMU, ——. *Paris.* 1787-1807.
LE CAMUS, *v.* DE CAMUS.
LE CAS, Paul. *Paris.* Juré 1693.
LE CAUCHOIS, Nicolas. *Rouen.* 1617. Founder member of Rouen corporation.
LE CERF, ——. *Geneva.* 1779. Invented a proportion compass for wheel teeth, desc. in Phil. Trans. Vol. 68.
LECCINIEZ FRÈRES. *Joinville.* ca.1760. g. watch en. floral sprays Mallett coll.
LÉCHAUD—
Jean Jacques Thomas. *Petit-Saconnex.* Early 19c.
Antoine, son. *Geneva.* b.1812, d.1875. Worked with G. A. LESCHOT, and devised a very successful lever calibre.
Jean, bro. *Geneva.* b.1815, d.1884. A fine maker, specializing in lever escapements. Worked with his brother.
LÉCHET (LECHOT), Jean Henry Conrad. *Paris.* m.1788. g. en. watches S.K.M. and Fränkel coll.
LECHMAR (LECHMAYR), Joseph Arnold. *Vienna.* m.1747.
LECHNER, Marcus. *Vienna.* m.1781.
LÉCHOPIÉ—
Adam. *Paris.* m.1758, juré 1772-89. Table clock Blot-Garnier coll. Mantel clock Louvre.
Adam Auguste. *Paris.* 1807-25.
Philippe Adam. *Paris.* 1811-3
LECKEY & SON. *London.* 1781.
LECKIE—
T. *Newcastle-o.-T.* an.1759. Watch.
David. *Annan.* 1800-20. Watch.
LE CLERC (LE CLER, LECLERCQ)—
Jean. *Blois.* mar.1604-32.
Henry. *Cambrai.* 1618-25. Worked on clock of cathedral.
Daniel. *Paris.* ca.1630. Watch M.M.A.
——. *Avignon.* 1713.
Jean Pierre. *Vevey.* 1746 comp.
B. *Amsterdam.* Mid. 18c. Watch Stads M. Amsterdam.
——. *Rouen.* 1772.
Jean Jacques Henri. *Paris.* m.1787.
——. *Brussels.* Early 19c. Ormolu mantel clock.
——. *Paris.* 1817-24.
LE COEUR, ——. *Paris.* 1783-1808. g. en. watch S.K.M.
LE COING, l'aîné. *Paris.* 1786 m.
LE COIS, François. *Paris.* m.1776-89.
LE COMPTE (LE CONTE)—
René. *Paris.* 1772-7.
Charles. *Paris.* m.1785-9.
——. *Paris* (*Quai des Ormes*). 1807-23.
LECONTE—
Jehan. *Aix-en-Provence.* mar.an.1584.
Charles, son. *Lyons.* a.1598-1601
LECOQ, ——. *Paris.* 1812. C.
LECOULTRE—
Louis. *Geneva.* Early 19c.
Charles Antoine. *Le Sentier.* b.1803, d.1881. First to produce pinion cutting machines in 1823. In 1849 started the machine factory of LECOULTRE & CIE.
LE COUNT (LECOMTE)—
Daniel. *London.* CC.1676-93. Watch mt. G.M. Watch Den. coll. str. watches M.M.A., Ilbert and Feill colls.
James. *London.* CC.1687. W.
Peter. *London* (*Finsbury* and *City Rd.*). a. 1784, CC.1792, l.CC.1810-25. Watch.
Peter. *London* (*Shoreditch*). 1802-11.
Peter, R.N. ——. Wrote on the effect of magnetism on chrons. in Edinburgh Phil. Mag. Vol. VI, 1822.
Samuel. *London.* a.1799.
LE COUSTANCOIS (LE COUTANCOIS, LE CONSTANSSOIS)—
Nicollas. *Paris.* 1544-7. Petitioner for incorporation of Paris guild.
Nicolas. *Lyons.* 1562 m.
Jehan. *Geneva.* 1568.
LE COUSTURIER—
——. *Paris.* 1685 m.
Paul, son. *Paris.* m.1691.
LECRIMIER FRÈRES. *Joinville.* 1767. Two fine g. en. watches Stern. coll.
LE CROIX, Amy. *France.* ca.1800. br. clock.
LECRU, Isaac. *London.* a.1710.
LE DÉ, Nicolas *Paris.* 1775 comp.
LEDECK, Friederich. *Vienna.* m.1786.
LEDERTZ, Richard. *Strasbourg.* ca.1630. Oval al. watch Den. coll.
LE DESVÉ, Louis. *Rouen.* 1726-50.
LEDEUR, R. *London.* ca.1620. oct. crys. watch M.M.A.
LEDGARD, Joseph. *Newcastle-o.-T.* 1707-32. Watch mt. S.K.M.
LEDIEU—
Franciscus. *Leiden.* 2nd half 18c. mus. clock.
jeune. *Paris.* 1812-25.
LEDOUX—
Pierre. *Paris.* ca.1720-50 m. Vernis Martin br. clock.
Pierre Augustin. *Paris.* m.1755.
Pierre François. *Paris* (*Rue St. André des Arcs*). m.1758-89.
——. *Paris.* 1812.
LEDRU, ——. *London.* an.1760. Watch with two barrels connected by chain and one fuzee, going 8 days, Ilbert coll.
LEDUC, ——. *Paris.* 1812. C.
LEDUM, John. *Plymouth.* an.1785. Watch.
LEDUTAR, John. *Bristol.* 1722. C.
LEE—
Edward. *London.* a.1668.
Cuthbert. *London.* a.1668, CC.1676-1718. l.c. clock.
Samuel. *London.* a.1687, CC.1694-1719. l.c. clock Weth. coll.
Underwood. *London.* a.1688.
Christopher. *London.* a.1691.
Richard. *London.* a.1695.
John. *London.* a.1703, CC.1737.
George. *London.* a.1705-40.
Roger. *Leicester.* Early 18c. Watch mt.
John. *London.* a.1709, CC.1719-22.
Joshua. *London.* a.1712.
William. *Lancaster.* ca.1720. Watch mt. Buckley coll.
John. *London.* a.1719, CC.1737.
Thomas. *London.* a.1721, CC.1730-ca.1745. Watch mt. Buckley coll. Also LEIGH.
William. *London.* an.1744. Watch.
John. *London.* a.1734, CC.1745.
John. *Cookham.* a.1759-ca.1800 CC.
Samuel. *London.* a.1747.
Sarah. *London.* CC.1756.
Samuel. *Dover.* an.1765. Watch.
John. *High Wycombe.* 1767-78. W.
Richard. *Cookham.* 1768. C. & W.
William. *Charleston, U.S.A.* 1768. C. & W.
Richard. *Marlow.* 1770. C. & W.
William, bro. *Marlow.* 1771. W.
Thomas. *Leicester.* 1773. Bankrupt.

LEE—*continued.*
Sarah. *London.* a.1763.
——. *Pinkneys.* 1775-81. C. & W.
John. *London* (*Foster La.*). 1795. W.
Nicholas. *Liverpool.* 1796-1811. W.
Thomas. *Polton.* 1796. C. & W.
L. *Margate.* 1797. W.
Robert. *London.* a.1789.
James. *London.* a.1790, CC.1797.
Nicholson. *Liverpool.* 1807. W.
Richard. *London.* a.1792.
Benjamin. *Leicester.* 1815. C. & W.
James. *Liverpool* (*London Rd.*). 1818. W.
James. *Liverpool* (*Peter St.*). 1818. W.
John. *Liverpool.* ca.1820.
Edward. *London.* Early 19c. Watch.
Joseph. *Cheltenham.* Early 19c. Watch.
John. *Great Marlow.* Early 19c.
LEEB, Thomas. *London.* an.1778. Watch.
LEEFEVER, George. *Wisbech.* Early 19c.
LEEK, John. *London.* a.1753, CC.1760-69.
LEEKEY—
Gabriel. *London.* 1750-93. Livery Skinners Co. p.c. sil. watch G.M. Watch Den. coll.
George. *London.* CC.1778-1815.
& SON. *London.* 1784-99.
Gabriel. *London.* 1802-04.
Gabriel, & Son. *London.* 1805-08.
Samson. *London.* 1805. Watches Chamb. and Fränkel colls.
& CABRIER. *London.* 1809-19.
LEEMING—
Edward. *London.* a.1754, CC.1766, l.CC. 1787-1809. Watch case maker.
T. *Settle.* Early 19c. Watch.
LEES—
Peter. *Rochdale.* 1760. W.
Thomas. *Bury.* 1790-1814. Many l.c. clocks, one ill. Cec. & Web. Watch.
John. *Middleton.* ca.1790, d.1804. Watch mt. Oldham M.
Samuel. *Ashton-under-Lyne.* ca.1820.
William. *Haslingden.* ca.1820.
LEETE, Thomas. *London.* a.1764.
LE FAUCHEUR—
Alexandre. *Paris.* 1746-60. C. to Louis XV. Several fine clocks. Clock mt. C.A. & M.
Jean Jacques Ignace, son. *Paris.* 1773-89. C. to Louis XVI.
LEFEBVRE (LEFEVRE)—
Jacquart. *Cambrai.* 1390. Repaired town clock.
Colard. *Cambrai.* 1435-40. Keeper of cathedral clock.
Marin. *Lyons.* 1529. 'Faiseur d'orloges.'
Armand. *Paris.* m.1610.
E. *Blois.* comp. 1642. Watch.
Élie. *Rouen.* m.1653, juré 1660-1709. Keeper of cathedral clock. Watch.
Jacques. *Rouen.* 1675-83.
Fils, aîné. *Fontainebleau.* ca.1700.
D. *Haarlem.* ca.1700. l.c. clock.
Pierre. *Paris.* 1736-56.
Barthélemy Joseph. *Paris.* m.1739. Watch Besançon M.
——. *London.* 1748. W.
Thomas. *Paris.* Juré 1761.
Pierre François. *Paris.* m.1776.
Louis Joseph. *Paris.* 1781 m.-1789.
L. F. *Paris.* 1786 m.
——. *Paris* (*Rue St. Honoré*). 1807-25. Succeeded J. F. DEBELLE.
——. *Paris* (*Phélippeaux*). 1812. C.
——. *Paris* (*Quai des Grands Augustins*). 1812.
LE FERRE—
Daniel. *Haarlem.* 1746.
David. *Haarlem.* 1776.
LEFFEBURE (LE FEBURE)—
Charles. *London.* CC.1687.
Daniel. *London.* a.1686.
LEFFERTS—
& HALL. *Philadelphia.* 1819-20.
Charles. *Philadelphia.* 1820.
LEFFIN, Thomas. *London.* CC.1720.
LE FLET, Petrus de Dessus. *London.* 1562.
LEFO, Benjamin. *London.* a.1792.
LE FOL, *v.* FOL.
LEFORT—
Nicolas. *Rouen.* a.1655. Prob. same as following.
Nicolas. *Lyons.* 1671-82.
LEFOUNT, Margaret Sarah. *London.* CC. 1810.
LEFROY, George. *Wisbech.* ca.1785. br. clock ill. Cec. & Web.
LE GAGNEUR—
Aimé. *Paris.* 1590.
Pierre, son. *Blois.* a.1590.
Jean. *Paris.* 1639. Made clocks for Château de St. Germain-en-Laye and for Fontainebleau. Also LE GAIGNEUR.
L'ÉGARÉ, Gilles. *Paris.* 2nd half 17c. Engraver. Designs for watches.
LEGEAY, ——. *Paris.* 1812.
LEGEIPS, John. *London.* ca.1725. Large rep. watch B.M. str. al. trav. clock Fränkel coll.
LE GENTIL, Barthélemi. *Dijon.* 1398-1415. In charge of clock of Notre Dame. Made 'une orlaige de bois.'
LEGER—
Claude. *La Rochelle.* 1668-1701.
——. *Paris.* Late 18c. g. en. watch, set pearls, M.M.A.
LEGERTWOOD, George. *London.* Early 19c. Watch.
LEGG—
Michael. *v.* LÖGG.
John. *London* (*Holborn*). a.1717-24. Watch.
John. *Bletchingly.* 1787. Watch with figure at every third hour only S.M.S.K.
John. *London* (*St. Martin's La.*, from *Islington*). 1797. Insolvent. W.
LEGGET, John. *Dunse.* 1720.
LEGGETT, Thomas. *Beccles.* 18c. l.c. clock.
LEGNENT, ——. *Paris.* 1825.
LEGO, ——. *Lorient.* ca.1818. Marine chron. Ilbert coll.
LE GOIX DUNESME, Marie (or Maurice) Jean Claude. *Paris.* m.1762-89.
LE GRAND (LEGRANDE)—
Baptiste. *Lyons.* 1556.
François. *Rouen.* 1617. Founder member of Rouen corporation. Oval sil. watch Dumenil coll.
James. *London.* CC.1640-64.
Francis. *London.* CC.1646. Perhaps same as François of *Rouen.*
James. *London.* a.1656-64 CC.
Michel François. *Paris.* m.1765.
Peter. *London.* an.1772. Watch.
Antoine. *Paris.* 1812.
LEGRAS, ——. *Paris.* 1811-25.
LE GRAVE, ——. *London.* 1808. mus. C. Watch.
LE GROS—
Joseph. *London.* a.1784. From *Dunkirk.* br. clock.
——. *Paris.* 1807-10.
LEGUESSE, L. J. *Paris.* End 18c. Mantel clock ill. Britten.
LEHEIM, James. *London.* an.1783. Watch.
LEHMANN—
Christopher. *Pilestraede.* 1690. Table clock Rosenborg Castle. Watch Cassel Landes-M.
Jakob Philipp. *St. Georgen.* d.1829.
David. *Vattenwyl.* Early 19c. Watch.
LEHMANN-REINHART, J. A. *Germany.* ca.1750. Gilt trav. clock.

LEHNER—
Johann Martin. *Eger*. 1st half 18c. g. repoussé watch.
Andreas. *Munich*. 1st half 18c. rep. watch Ilbert coll.
Anselm Benedikt. *Augsburg*. m.1741, d.ca. 1759.
L. *Bautzen*. 2nd half 18c. Watch mt. Arts M. Prague.
Marcus. *Vienna*. Early 19c. g. watch.
LEHOUX, Nicolas Martin. *Paris*. m.1737.
LEHR, Sebastian. *Nürnberg*. 1525. d.1556. Town C. circ. table clock sd. 'Se: Le: Nor:' Webster coll. prob. by him.
LE HURAY—
Nicholas. *Guernsey*. ca.1780. *Philadelphia*, 1811-25. l.c. clock.
Nicholas, son. *Ogletown, Del., Philadelphia*. 1817. d.1834.
LEIBNITZ, Gottfried Wilhelm von. *Leipzig*. b.1646, d.1716. *Paris*, 1672. *Hannover*, 1676. Famous mathematician. Pub. in the Phil. Trans. of 1675 desc. of a watch with two alternately working remontoirs.
LEICESTER, James. *London*. ca.1710-29. Bankrupt. br. and l.c. clocks.
LEIGH—
——. *Shrewsbury*. 1768. W.
Thomas. *Bolton*. an.1781. Watch.
James. *London*. a.1793.
Joshua. *Liverpool*. 1825. W.
LEIGHTON, William. *London*. a.1789.
LEIGNES, Charles Peter. *London*. a.1741, CC.1749-94. Two watches London M.
LEIJON, Lars Joh. *Göteborg*. b.1775, d.1834.
LEINAR, P. *Bristol*. an.1801. Watch.
LEINBACH, Elias & John. *Reamstown, Lancaster, U.S.A*. 1788-1810. l.c. clocks.
LEINER, Johann. *Herrenstadt*. ca.1800. Watch.
LEINERT, ——. *Paris*. 1825.
LEISKY, C. B. *Goldberg*. ca.1810. trav. clock Ilbert coll.
LEISSAM, Renerus. *London*. a.1763.
LEISTER, Thomas. *Halifax*. 1784. W. Prob. LISTER.
LEITER, Carl. *Leipzig*. Mid. 18c. trav. clock Ashmolean M.
LEITERER, Christoph. *Geroldshofen*. m. 1798.
LEITHMER, Franz. *Dettelbach*. m.1798.
LEITHNER, Thomas. *Agram*. Mid. 18c. very fine trav. clock.
LEIVSLEY, George. *Shrewsbury*. 1720. Insolvent.
LEJEUNE—
Gille Prosper. *Paris*. Juré 1675.
Jean Baptiste. *Paris*. m.1786-1825. Keeper of the Bastille clock.
LEJONCQUE, G. J. *Malmedy*. 1786. Clock on Pfarrkirche with carillon.
'LEKCEH.' *London*. Early 18c. Sig. on watch, HECKEL reversed.
LELERNE—
——. *Paris*. 1684 m.
Jean. *Paris*. m.1684.
LELEU, ——. *Paris*. 1807-10.
LELIEVRE, ——. *Paris*. 1822.
LELLO, James. *London*. a.1648, CC.1656-64.
LELLYET—
John. *Havant*. 1768. Also LELLIOT. W.
William. *Havant*. 1795. W.
LELOUTRE, François. *Paris*. m.1741-80. Maker of repute. 'Fournisseur des Menus Plaisirs.' Urn clock ill. Britten. br. clock Pal. de Versailles.
LELOY, ——. *Paris*. 1823. Clock.
LE MAGE, Godfrey. *London*. a.1771.
LE MAIGRE, Nicholas. *Borgendael*. ca.1700. Clock.
LEMAINDRE—
Nicolas. *Blois*. 1598. d.1652. A famous maker; C. to Catherine and Marie de Médecis. Large watch, eng. dial and oval watch S.K.M. Oval watch B.M. ill. Baillie. Large oval watch with 4-wheel train Webster coll.
Nicolas, nephew. *Blois*. b.1600-60. *Paris* for 15 years an.1652. C. to duc d'Orléans 1624; to Louis XIV 1646. Exceptionally fine crys. watch with eng. crys. covers and g. en. frame and dial plate Wallace coll. Square watch Louvre ill. Baillie. Watch Basle M. en. watch Gotha M. g. en. watch Gélis coll.
Louis, son of Nicolas (1). *Blois*. b.1604-28. *Paris*, 1628-31. C. to Marie de Médecis.
Nicolas, bro. ——. 1653-1704.
Pierre, bro. *Blois*. 1653-60.
LEMAIRE—
P. *Blois*. ca.1610. hex. crys. watch Wallace coll. Watch Brunswick M.
Henry. *Paris*. 1675 m.
Pierre, son. *Paris*. 1675 m. A maker of this name went to *Amsterdam* from *Paris* in 1686.
Jérémie. *Amsterdam*. 1687. Huguenot refugee from *Meaux*.
——. *London*. ca.1700. Two watches G.M.
Jacques. *Paris*. 1740. Dial invented by Julien LE ROY, B.M.
Jean Pierre. *Copenhagen*. m.1774. Master of Corporation 1787.
Jean Alexandre. *Paris*. m.1778-89.
Nicholas Constant. *Paris*. b.1757, d.1832. Pupil of JAQUET-DROZ. Maker of singing birds. *v.* GLAESNER.
Jean Henri. *Copenhagen*. comp. 1801.
Jean Frederik. *Copenhagen*. m.1805.
cadet. *Paris* (*Rue Grenier St. Lazare*). 1812. C.
LE MAISTRE—
Nicolas. *Paris*. 1675 m.
——. *Dublin*. an.1743. Watch.
Henry. *Dublin*. 1795. W.
Peter. *Dublin*. 1795. W.
LEMAITRE—
——. *Bois*. ca.1750.
Paul Thomas. *London*. CC.1815-24. W.
LEMAN, Thomas. *London*. an.1744. Watch.
LEMASURIER, *v.* MAZURIER.
LE MAYRE, Estienne. *Geneva*. 1572. Refugee from *Paris*.
LE MAZURIER, *v.* MAZURIER.
LE MELAIS, Eléazar. *Geneva*. 1585. Refugee from *Paris*.
LEMELET, Gaspard. *Paris*. m.1588.
LE MIRE, Charles. *Paris*. 1675 m.-1699.
LEMIST, William K. *Dorchester, U.S.A*. 1812. d.1820.
LEMKE, Jacob. *Dantzig*. 1688. Remade clock on Dammthür.
LEMKES, J. G. *Cologne*. 1813.
LEMMON, Edward. *London*. an.1788. Watch. Also LEMON.
LEMOINE—
——. *Paris*. ca.1760 m.
Jean Louis. *Paris*. m.1767-79.
Claude. *Paris*. m.1776-89.
A. *Philadelphia*. 1813. W.
——. *Paris*. 1812-22. Two of this name, one in *Rue Geoffroi-Langevin*, the other in *Rue de la Verrerie*.
LEMON—
Thomas. *London*. a.1815.
v. LEMMON.
LE MONNIÈRE, Stephen. *London*. CC. 1712-19. Also LIMONIÈRE.
LE MONTJOYE, ——. *Paris*. ca.1770. Clock Wallace coll.
LEMPRIERE, Thomas. *London*. CC.1816.

LEMUDE, Reuben. *London.* ca.1715. l.c. clock.
LENARD, Isaak. ——. ca.1600. Watch S.K.M.
LENARDT, ——. *Stockholm.* 1567. Made clock for the Järntorg.
LENCKE, Johann Friedrich. *Berlin.* 1794.
LE NEPVEU—
Nicolas Antoine. *Paris.* m.1773-89.
jeune. *Paris.* 1812.
LENERD, Nicholas Aug. *London.* 1729. Insolvent.
LENFOIX, ——. *Paris.* 1819-23.
LENHAM, William. *London.* 1820. Watch N.Y. Univ.
LENIEL, Jacques Balthazar. *Paris.* m.1754.
LENK, Egidius. *Augsburg.* m.ca.1780-99. str. al. and rep. trav. clock Ilbert coll.
LENKER, Elias. *Nürnberg.* m.1562, d.1591. Goldsmith who made several very fine clock-cases. Clock M.P.S. Dresden.
LENNAN, James. *London.* CC.1789.
LENNEP, Johann Hartmann. *Cassel.* b.1685, d.1755. Kleinuhrmacher and Mechaniker.
LENNOX, Edward. *Perth.* a.1783.
LE NOIR (LENOIR)—
Jean Baptiste. *Paris.* m.1684.
——. *Rennes.* Early 18c. Watch G.M.
Timothy. *London.* a.1702.
Daniel. *London.* 1723. Insolvent.
Toussaints Marie. *Paris (Place du Pont St. Michel).* m.1730, juré 1789.
Étienne. *Paris.* ca.1740. A famous maker. Watch G.M. Watch Fränkel coll. winding at centre of dial. Clock ill. Britten. Clock with ormolu work by CAFFIERI sold for £850 in 1901. Two cartel clocks Pal. du Luxembourg. br. clock Nat. M. Stockholm.
——. *Lyons.* d.1751.
Augustin. *Paris.* d.1758.
Pierre Étienne. *Paris (Quai des Orfèvres).* m. 1743-89.
Marcel. *Paris.* Juré 1763.
Jean Baptiste Augustin. *Paris (Rue de l'Arbre Sec).* m.1764-89. al. watch M.M.A.
André Toussaint. *Paris.* m.1764, juré 1769. Clock.
Noel Nicholas. *Paris.* m.1764. Large p.c. sil. watch Ashmolean M.
——. *London.* 1768. W.
Julien. *Paris (Rue d'Argenteuil).* m.1783-9.
Étienne. *Paris (Quai des Orfèvres).* 1807-23.
——. *Paris (Rue St. Denis).* 1812.
LENORMAN (NORMAN), ——. *Cassel.* Appointed Court C. in 1686. Swiss.
LENORMAND—
Louis François. *Paris.* Juré 1754.
Louis Sébastien. *Paris.* 1830. Pub. 'Manuel de l'horloger,' which went through many editions to 1896, with the names of A. JANVIER and D. MAGNIER added.
LENS—
William. *London.* a.1704, CC.1712-28.
Mary. *London.* 1732-42.
Charles, son of Wm. *London.* CC.1750.
LENTZ, George K. *Philadelphia.* 1825.
LENWOOD, Samuel. *London.* a.1655.
LEO—
Christoph. *Augsburg.* 2nd half 17c. aut. maker.
D. L. *Rotterdam.* 1821-30.
LEONARD—
Thomas. *London.* a.1704.
Thomas Byles. *London.* a.1782.
LEONARDI, W. Vibrandi. prob. *Germany.* Early 17c. circ. watch pierced and eng. covers.
LEONHARD—
Joh. A. *Fürth.* d.1804.
F. *Berlin.* 1824. Founded a turret clock factory, now C. F. ROCHLITZ.
LEOPOL, Johan Hakiel. ——. 17c. sq. table clock Feill coll.
LEOPOLDT, A. *Golling.* 18c. Watch Besançon M.
LE PAGE, John. *Guernsey.* Early 19c.
LEPAUTE—
Jean André. *Paris.* b.1720, d.1787 or 1789. Came to *Paris* 1748 and started business with his bro. Retired 1774. An eminent maker. C. to the King. In 1752 made a clock with one wheel, showing hours, mins. and secs., and striking hours and quarters. In 1753 devised a pin-wheel escapement for clocks, with pins on both sides of the wheel, which has been widely used. Also a clock in which the pendulum made 60 swings for the escape of one tooth. He brought out the double virgule esc. (*v.* CARON). Pub. 'Traité d'Horlogerie,' Paris, 1755, 1760 and 1767. Made several public clocks in Paris; one on the École Royale Militaire still working. Clock S.K.M. with case of Vincennes porcelain. Four clocks Wallace coll. Year l.c. clock Buckingham Palace. Regulator and equation regulator C.A. & M. Three clocks Pal. de Fontainebleau. Fine vase clock Petit Palais.
Jean Baptiste (le jeune), bro. *Paris (Place du Palais Royal).* b.1727, d.1802. C. to the King. In partnership with Jean André, and when he retired in 1774 took into partnership his nephews Pierre HENRY and Pierre Basile LEPAUTE. Retired 1789.
Pierre Henry, nephew. *Paris.* b.1745, d. 1806. Entered his uncle's firm 1761; partner 1774.
Pierre Basile, nephew of J. A. *Paris.* b. 1750, d.1843. Entered his uncle's firm 1763; partner 1774 with Pierre HENRY, who retired 1798. P. B. then took as partner his nephew Jean Joseph LEPAUTE and, in 1811, formed the firm of LEPAUTE ET FILS with his son Pierre Michel, to whom he left the business in 1816.
Pierre Michel, son. *Paris.* 1803. d.1849. In his father's firm. Two regulators C.A. & M. g. ½ ¼ rep. duplex watch G.M. Made clock for the Bourse.
Gabriel Joseph, bro. *Paris.* Early 19c. In his father's firm.
Jean Joseph, grandnephew of J. A. *Paris (Rue St. Honoré).* b.1768, d.1846. Joined Pierre Basile in 1798. C. to Napoleon I. Made clocks for Pal. de Fontainebleau and the Château de St. Cloud. Many fine house clocks.
ET FILS. From 1811. *v.* Pierre Basile.
Henri. *Paris.* 1813. Lever rep. watch mt. Ilbert coll.
Augustin Michel HENRY, son of Pierre HENRY. In business as 'HENRY NEVEU LEPAUTE' and, in 1854, changed his name to LEPAUTE. *Paris.* b.1800, d.1885. C. to Louis Philippe and Napoleon III. Made clocks on Palais de Justice, Paris, and the Bourse, Marseilles.
Léon, son. *Paris.* b.1838, d.1909.
Paul, bro. *Paris.* b.1843, d.1897.
LE PAUTE DE BELLEFONTAINE, Jacques Joseph. *Paris.* 1779-ca.1830. In the Lepaute firm. Mantel clock, Pal. de Justice, Paris.
LEPECHETY & DECOURS. *Geneva.* Early 19c.
LEPELLETIER—
Charles. *Angers.* 1680. Fitted town clock with a pendulum.
——. *Paris.* b.ca.1732-1801. Mechanician. Made a flute-playing automaton.
LEPENNETIER, Renato. *Angers.* 1495. Made al. and str. clock for Chapter House.

LEPER, William. *London.* a.1768.
LEPERS, Jacques Mathieu. *Paris.* m.1737.
LEPETIT, Jehan. *Paris.* 1544-7. Founder member of Paris corporation.
LÉPINE (L'ÉPINE)—
Jean. *Paris.* Early 18c. Mechanician to the King. Calculating machine C.A. & M.
Philibert. *Challex.* ca.1720.
Jean Antoine, son of Jean. *Paris (Place Dauphine).* b.1720, d.1814. An eminent maker. mar. A. C. Caron's daughter in 1756, and worked as CARON ET LÉPINE till 1769. Left his business to his son-in-law RAGUET in 1783. W. to Louis XV, Louis XVI and Napoleon I. Introduced about 1760 the 'Lepine calibre,' in which separate bars were used instead of a single top plate. Introduced the use of a mainspring barrel supported at one end only, and other changes, leading, with cyl. escapement, to thin watches. Desc. a rep. mt. using rack in place of chain, in Mém. de l'Acad. des Sci. in 1766. Invented the virgule esc. and a keyless winding. Acted as agent for Voltaire's workshops at *Ferney* ca.1770. 4-colour g. watch S.K.M. en. watch and chatelaine F.W.M. ill. Baillie. Six watches G.M., two with virgule escapement. Watch Chamb. coll. 4-colour g. watch Fränkel coll. Lyre watch Basle M. g. en. watches M.P.S. Dresden. Watch Carnegie M. Two 4-colour g. watches Nat. M. Stockholm. Watch in porcelain case Gélis coll. Watch in ring Ilbert coll. Astro. clock and three mantel clocks Buckingham Palace. Two clocks Pal. de Compiègne, one made for Napoleon. Clock made for Joséphine, Mobilier National, Paris. Lépine's business was sold in 1810 to J. B. CHAPUY, who employed Jacques Lépine. It was sold in 1827 to DESCHAMP, who was succeeded in 1832 by FABRE. The business continued under the name LÉPINE till ca.1916.
Raguet. *v.* RAGUET-LÉPINE.
G. L. ——. ca.1800. 4-colour g. watch with en. and pearls Gélis coll.
Jacques. *Paris (Place des Victoires).* 1814-25. Court C. Nephew of J. A.
LEPLASTRIER—
John. *London (Wapping* and *Shadwell).* 1784-1825. W. & C.
William. *London.* a.1787.
Lewis. *London.* 1805-20.
——. *Deal.* Early 19c. W
Isaac. *London (Mark La.).* CC.1813-20. Chron. & W.
John. *London (Mark La.* and *Minories).* 1817-25.
& SON. *London.* 1820-5. W. & C.
William Louis, son of Isaac. *London.* a. 1821.
LE PLAT, Louis Antoine. *Paris.* 1751 m., d.1765. Clock wound by current of air. (Mém. de l'Acad. Paris, 1751.)
LEPP, James. *Liverpool.* 1821-9. W.
LEPPER, G. *Belfast.* 1778. Watch.
LEPPINGWELL, James. *London.* a.1752, CC.1769-74.
LEPRET, ——. *Paris.* 1788.
LE PRÉVOST—
Jérémie. *Rouen.* m.1649.
Étienne. *Rouen.* m.1658.
——. *Rouen.* 1775-7.
LE PRINCE—
Nicolas. *Lyons.* b.ca.1520-82. From *Cahors.*
David Louis. *Paris.* m.1776.
LE PROVENCAL, Guillaume. *Lyons.* 1493.
LE PROVOST, Gabriel. *Paris.* 1784.
LE QUEUX, Pierre. *France.* 1396. C. to the duc d'Orléans.
LEQUIN—
——. *Geneva.* 1730-50.
Antoine, son. *Fleurier.* 1750.
LEREBOURG, ——. *Paris.* 1812.
LERESCHE, J. L. *Paris.* 18c. al. clock.
LEROUX—
Alexander. *London (Dowgate Hill).* CC. 1707-30. Watch chain maker.
Robert, son. *London.* a.1707, CC.1745.
Jean. *Paris.* m.1745.
John. *London (Charing Cross).* 1744. CC. 1781-1808. An eminent maker. Made lever watches with all the lift on the esc. wheel teeth. Succeeded by James RIGBY. Fine watch with lever esc. of special form, conical balance spring and jewelled banking dated 1785, and ½ ¼ rep. cyl. mt. G.M. g. watch set brilliants. g. watch in earlier case en. Les Frères Huaud Stern. coll. br. clock ill. Cec. & Web. Also sd. LE ROUX.
Jean Furey. *Paris (Rue Guénégant).* m. 1755-89. Maker of repute. rep. watch.
Jean Louis. *Paris (Quai de la Mégisserie).* m.1778-89.
Veuve (of Jean Furey). *Paris (Rue Guénégant).* 1789.
Alexander. *London (Charing Cross).* ca. 1790. br. clock ill. Cec. & Web.
LEROW, Lewis. *Boston, U.S.A.* 1813-25. W.
LE ROY—
Pierre. *Geneva.* 1586.
Charles David. *Paris.* 1587-1635.
S. *Paris.* 1600. Sig. to Statuts of Paris corporation.
Pierre. *Blois.* mar.1628-32.
Grégoire. *Blois.* comp. 1635.
Pierre. *Amsterdam.* 1686. Huguenot refugee from *Meaux.*
Pierre. *Paris.* 1st half 18c. Devised a watch escapement with two escape wheels.
Julien, bro. *Paris (Rue de Harley).* b.1686, m.1713, juré 1735, d.1759. C. to the King in 1739. A celebrated maker, who raised the status of French watchmaking by the perfection of his work and design. Made an equation clock in 1717, desc. in Gallon, 'Machines et Inventions,' Vol. III. Devised the horizontal arrangement of parts in turret clocks, and gained a great reputation for his turret clocks. Devised a compensation pendulum in 1738 and an escapement for pendulum clocks. First made thin repeating watches by omitting the bell and allowing the hammers to strike on the case. About 1725 introduced the French form of potence with screw adjustment. Wrote several memoirs on horology. Four g. en. watches S.K.M. ill. Baillie. rep. watch and g. en. watch G.M. g. en. watch and porcelain case watch Feill coll. Watch in carved agate case Ilbert coll. Fine Boulle clock Pal. de Fontainebleau. sil. trav. clock and cartel clock Nat. M. Stockholm.
Pierre, son. *Paris.* b.1717, m.1737, juré 1748, d.1785. The most eminent horologist of France; pioneer, with BERTHOUD, of chronometer development in France; first to apply temperature compensation to the balance. Devised a duplex esc. with single balance. In 1748 showed the Acad. des Sci. a detent esc. It was applied to a chron. in 1766. His first marine chronometer tried 1763. Pub. 'Mém. pour les Horlogers de Paris,' 1750, and 'Étrennes chronométriques pour l'année 1760.' His inventions are desc. in Mém. de l'Acad. des Sci. 1742, 1751, 1752, 1755, 1763, 1769, and in Gallon, 'Machines et Inventions,' Vols. V and VII. He wrote a mem. on time measurement at sea, which gained the prize of the Acad. des Sci. in

LE ROY—*continued.*
1770, and other mem. on marine chronometers. Many fine watches and clocks.
Julien. *Paris.* b.ca.1738. Dumb rep. watch Ilbert coll.
Jean Joseph. *Paris* (*Rue St. Martin*). m. 1742-89.
Jean Baptiste Samson. *Paris* (*Rue Dauphine*). m.1753-89. Clock.
André Alexander. *Paris.* a.1748.
Abraham. *Lancaster City, U.S.A.* 1756-65. Swiss.
Étienne Augustin. *Paris* (*Rue St. Denis*). m.1758-89.
Pierre. *Paris* (*Rue St. Martin*). 1765-89.
Jacques Ignacius. *Paris.* ca.1770.
Charles. *Paris.* ca.1770-ca.1790. 4-colour g. watch M.P.S. Dresden. g. watch, set pearls, Nord. M., Feill and Ilbert colls. Porcelain and ormolu clock. Cartel clock.
Basile Charles. *Paris* (*Palais Royal*). m.1788-1825. C. to Napoleon, Mme Mère, the King of Westphalia, the Princess Pauline and the duc de Bourbon. Two mantel clocks Ministère de la Guerre, Paris.
Veuve (of J. Ignacius). *Paris* (*Rue St. Honoré*). 1789.
Gabriel. *Paris* (*Rue du Temple*). 1807-24.
Pierre. *Paris* (*Rue St. Médéric*). 1812-25.
Louis. *Paris* (*Rue du Bouloy*). 1812.
Toussaint Étienne. *Paris* (*Rue du fg. St. Antoine*). 1812-23.
Théodore. *Paris* (*Palais Royal*). 1815-25. Watch N.Y. Univ.
Fils. *Paris* (*Place Dauphine*). 1817-24.
J. H. *Paris* (*Rue St. Martin*). 1819-21.
——. *Paris* (*Rue St. Denis*). 1822-5.

LESAGE—
——. *Paris* (*Rue Dauphine*). 1814-24. C.
——. *Paris* (*Rue du fg. St. Martin*). 1822-5.

LESANDER, Pehr. *Stockholm.* comp. 1773, m.1783, d.1789. Watches and wall clock.

LESBOS, *v.* Bosley.

LE SCHEGS, Abraham. *Amsterdam.* ca. 1730. en. watch ill. Britten.

LESCHOT—
Frédéric. *Chaux-de-Fonds.* 1733-67. d.an. 1786. Clock.
Jean Frédéric, son. *Geneva, Chaux-de-Fonds* and *London.* b.1746, d.1824. W. and mechanician of great talent; associated with Jaquet-Droz until his death in 1791, and then worked on his own account. Singing birds and aut. watches.
Tite, bro. *Chaux-de-Fonds.* a.1781-1802 comp. C.
——. *Paris.* Early 19c. g. watch.
Georges Auguste, son of J. F. *Geneva.* b. 1800, d.1884. An eminent maker and designer of machines for Vacheron and Constantin. Developed the lever escapement and its manufacture by machine. Invented diamond drills for tunnelling.

LESEL, Michael. prob. *Germany.* 1629. Ivory dial B.M. Dial Old Ashmolean M.

LE SEYNE (LE SENNE), Jean. *Paris.* 1600-ca.1635. Sig. to Statuts of Paris corporation. Fine str. al. cal. trav. clock.

LE SIAMMOIS, ——. *Paris.* ca.1700. Watch Gélis coll.

LE SIEUR, ——. *Paris.* 1822-5. Mantel clock.

LE SIEURRE, Marin. *Lyons.* 1521-66. Repaired several town clocks.

LESIRE, Stephen. *London.* a.1725.

LESLIE—
Thomas. *Borrowstounness.* d.1788.
Thomas. *Edinburgh.* a.1775-90.
James. *London.* 1790. Watch.
Robert. *London.* 1793. Patented a torsional pendulum, pump-winding and a free escapement.

LESLIE—*continued.*
& Price. *Philadelphia.* 1796-1800.
J. & P. *Kirkcaldy.* 1815.
John. *Kirkcaldy.* 1821.

LESPINE, ——. *Paris.* 1786-9.

LESSELS, M. *Paris.* d.1849. German. Noted maker of observatory clocks. Worked with Breguet.

LESSENEY (LESNEY, LYSNEY, LE SENE), Sebastian. *London.* 1538-42. C. to Henry viii. Native of *Normandy.*

LESSER, T. *Paris.* ca.1790. en.watch S.K.M.

LESTER—
Thomas. *London.* CC.1698.
John. *London.* a.1731-74.
Robert. *Philadelphia.* 1795.

LESTOURGEON—
David. *Rouen.* m.1660. *London.* 1681.
David, son. *London.* 1681. CC.1698-1731. A fine maker. Watch and mt. G.M. Watches London M., M.M A. and C.A. & M. Watch Ilbert coll. Watch showing minutes ill. Britten.
David, son. *London.* a.1704, CC.1721-51. Watch sd. 'Bawcutt & David Lestourgeon.'
Jacob. *London.* an.1752. Watch.

LESTRANGE, Anthony. *Dublin.* 1795-1824. Watch.

LE SUEUR—
Louis. *Rouen.* a.1663.
——. *Paris.* 1819.

LETALL, James. *London.* a.1754, CC.1777.

LETANG—
——. *Nyon.* ca.1700. Watch Ilbert coll.
——. *Moudon.* 1735.

LE TAVERNIER, François. *Rouen.* m.1652.

LE TELIER, Pierre. *Cambrai.* 1380. Repaired Cathedral clock.

LETH, Johan Frederik. *Copenhagen.* m.1784.

LETHIER, Étienne *Paris.* m.1770.

LEUBA (LEUBAZ)—
Frères. *Buttes.* 1766.
——. *Vevey.* 1786 comp.
Élie. *Paris.* 1788.
Henry. *Basle.* 1823. From *Val de Travers.*

LEUDL, Johann. ——. ca.1650. Skull watch Blot-Garnier coll. ill. Britten.

LEUENBERGER, Johann. *Sumiswald.* 1826. In 1826 started the Neuchâtel type of clock in Sumiswald.

LEUKERT, Johann Gottlieb. *Dresden.* m. 1752, d.1795. From *Schweidnitz.* Watch, eng. jasper case, M.P.S. Dresden.

LEUPOLD, Jakob. *Schwarzwald.* b.1674, d. 1737. Devised a wheel-cutting machine for Schwarzwald clocks, desc. in 'Theatrum Machinarum,' Leipzig, 1724, which also contains methods of winding up clock weights and methods of making and hardening spiral springs and cutting fuzees.

LEURTIER, Pierre. *Paris.* ca.1750. Mantel clock.

LEUSCHNER, Christoph. ——. ca.1700. Crucifix clock with turning hour drum above Arts M. Prague.

LEUSSEL (LEVISSEL), ——. *London.* 1762.

LEUTMANN, Johann Georg. *Dabrun.* 1717-1721. A priest. Wrote 'Vollständige Nachricht von den Uhren,' Halle, 1717-21.

LE VACHER—
Gaspard. *La Rochelle.* 1634-48. C. to town of *Saintes* an.1634.
Jean Louis. *Paris.* m.1759-74.
André Louis, l'aîné. *Paris.* m.1759-89.
Jacques Jean, le cadet. *Paris.* m.1759-89.

LEVASSEUR—
Pierre. *Paris.* m.1748.
——. *Rouen.* Retired 1776. C. to the Cathedral.
Pierre. *Paris.* m.1778.
Antoine René. *Paris.* m.1783-9.

LEVASSEUR—*continued.*
Pierre Louis. *Paris* (*Rue de Sève*). m.1788.
——. *Paris* (*Rue St. Honoré*). 1807-25.
——. *Paris* (*Rue de Richelieu*). 1824.
LEVELY, George. *Baltimore, U.S.A.* 1774. From *Philadelphia.* C. & W.
LEVENS—
S. *London.* an.1751. Watch.
John. *London* (*Shoemakers Row*). a.1752, CC.1761-1807. W.
Thomas. *London.* a.1761, CC.1785.
S. *London.* 1809-11.
LÉVEQUE—
Michel. *Paris.* 1776. d.1786. Granted a privilege in 1776 to establish a large factory for watches at *Tours.* Removed to *Charenton* in 1786. *v.* COLIS.
——. *Paris* (*Rue du Jour*). 1817.
Michel. *Paris* (*Rue Montmartre*). 1822-5.
LEVER, Benjamin. *London.* 1792.
LEVERIDGE, ——. *Gloucestershire.* 1805. Repaired Westbury church clock.
LEVERSUCH, Joseph. *London.* a.1797.
L'EVESQUE, LES FRÈRES. *Geneva.* ca.1800. Painters on enamel.
LEVET—
Hugues. *Lyons.* mar.1591-1621, d.an.1627. Entrusted with the re-making of the aut. clock of St. Jean, and secured the assistance of Nicholas LIPPIUS.
François. *Lyons.* 1602-07.
LE VEULLE, Louis. *Blois.* 1587-1600.
LEVEY, ——. *Dover.* Early 19c.
LEVI—
Moses. *Leeds.* 1757-9.
Benjamin. *Witney.* From 1770. W.
Samuel. *Pembroke.* 1775-85. W.
Isaac. *Philadelphia.* 1780. W.
Benjamin. *Canterbury.* 1783-91. Then joined his bro. James in *Dover.*
Noah. *Ramsgate.* 1789. C. & W.
James & Benjamin. *Dover.* From 1791. C. & W.
Solomon. *Canterbury.* 1793. W.
Samuel. *London.* a.1787.
A. *Folkestone.* mar.1799. W.
E. *Margate.* 1804. C. & W.
Joseph. *Manchester.* 1813. W.
LEVIELLE, aîné. *Paris.* 1836. Regulator C.A. & M.
LE VIEZ (LE VIEFZ), Thomas. *Dole.* 1486-9. Made clock for town.
LE VILLAIN, Nicolas. *Rouen.* a.1651, m. 1658.
LEVIN—
Moses. *London.* 1790.
Mrs. *Staines.* 1795. Also LEWIS.
E. *Stockholm.* 1799.
John. *London.* 1808.
Simon, & SON. *London.* 1799, when Simon retired.
Lewin, son of Simon. *London* (*Aldersgate St.*). 1799-1824.
LEVINS—
John. *London* (*Blackfriars*). a.1752, CC. 1761-5.
Thomas. *London.* a.1761, CC.1785.
LEVITT—
John. *London.* a.1681.
L. *London.* 1825. Chron. W. & C.
LEVOL, ——. *Paris.* 1812.
LEVY—
——. *Aix-la-Chapelle.* ca.1620. sq. table clock S.K.M.
Hyam. *London* (*Whitechapel*). d.1792.
Michael. *Hull.* ca.1770-95. C. & W.
J. *Deptford.* an.1777. Watch.
Isaac Zacharias. *Horsens.* m.1784.
Michael & Isaac. *Baltimore, U.S.A.* 1785. From *London.* *v.* Michael below.
Moses & Moses. *Portsmouth.* 1788. Bankrupt.

LEVY—*continued.*
M., & Co. *London.* 1790.
& GODFREY. *Kidderminster.* 1795. Dissolved partnership. C. & W.
Barnet. *Kidderminster.* 1795. W.
Mark. *London.* an.1796. Watch.
Michael. *London* (*Princes St., Soho,* from *Northumberland St.*). 1797. Insolvent.
Jonas. *London* (*Bevis Marks*). 1802. CC. 1831-40. The first Jew admitted to the CC.
Michael. *Philadelphia.* 1802-17. W. Also LEVI. *v.* Michael & Isaac.
Joseph. *London* (*Whitechapel* and *Haymarket*). 1805-24.
John. *Liverpool.* 1805-11. W.
George. *Ipswich.* mar.1806.
Leo. *London.* 1808.
J. *London* (*Strand*). 1815-25.
Jonas. *London* (*Coventry St.*). 1815-24.
John. *London* (*Shadwell*). 1817-24.
Jonas. *London* (*Minories*). 1820.
B. *London.* 1820.
Lewis. *London.* 1820.
Alexander, & Co. *London.* 1822-24.
Abraham. *London.* 1822-40. Watch.
B. & A. *Plymouth.* Early 19c.
LEWIN—
William. *London.* a.1720, CC.1731.
Levin. *London* (*Goodman's Fields*). 1802-11.
LEWIS—
Winstanley. *London.* a.1632 under BC.
Peter. *Liverpool.* d.1699. W.
John. *London.* a.1697, CC.1705-12.
Charles. *London.* a.1714.
Ambrose. *London.* a.1717, CC.1725.
Nathaniel. *London.* a.1718.
John. *London.* a.1718.
John. *London.* a.1720.
Edmond. *London.* a.1727.
John. *Llanidloes.* 1736-1801. l.c. clocks.
Joseph. *Bristol.* 1739. C.
Rice. *London.* a.1736.
Thomas. *Chester.* d.1770. C.
Richard. *Wincanton.* an.1764. Watch.
Joseph. *London.* a.1756, CC.1768.
George. *London.* an.1772. Watch.
William. *London.* an.1773. Watch.
John. *London.* a.1761.
Peter Carteret. *London.* a.1766.
Christopher. *London.* an.1788. Watch.
William. *Sarum* (*Salisbury*). .1785. Bankrupt. Watch. Ilbert coll.
Daniel. *Edmonton.* 1793-7. W.
Mrs. *Staines.* 1795. Also LEVIN.
Evan. *Carmarthen.* mar.1790.
Henry. *Newcastle Emlyn.* d.1820. l.c. clocks.
William. *London* (*Clerkenwell*). a.1783, CC. 1796-1810.
——. *Philadelphia.* 1796. W.
David. *Egham.* ca.1800 CC.
George Samuel. *London.* a.1796.
Thomas. *London.* a.1799.
C. *London.* 1809-11.
Levi. *Bristol, U.S.A.* 1810-15. Wooden clocks.
& ALSTON. *London.* 1815-25. Duplex mt. G.M. Watch.
Rees. *Newbridge.* Early 19c. Watch.
——. *Chalford.* Early 19c. Watch.
George. *Manchester.* ca.1820.
LEWITT, Benjamin. *Leicester.* 1815-26. C. & W.
LEWNS, C. F. *Rye.* Early 19c. Watch.
LEWSE, John. *London.* 1662.
LEWTHWAITE, George. *Ulverstone.* ca. 1770-95.
LEWVY, Moe. *Bristol.* 1795-1830. W.
LEXANDER, Eric. *Uppsala* and *Viksta.* b. 1727, d.1806.

LEY—
William. *London.* a.1699, CC.1711-21.
William. *London.* a.1700, CC.1712.
Thomas. *London.* 1820.
LEYDEN, Thomas. *London.* an.1777. Watch.
LEYENDECKER, Malth. Jos. *Cologne.* 1797. Turret and house clocks.
LEYLAND (LAYLAND), Thomas. *Prescot.* 1820.
LEYRER, ——. *Karlstein a. d. Thaya.* Late 18c. Schwarzwald workshop with his tools Uhren M. Vienna.
LÉZÉ, ——. *Paris.* Late 18c. Very fine mantel clock, turning rings, astro. and cal. work below, ordered by Louis XVI for Tippoo Sahib, now Ministère des Affaires Étrangères, Paris.
LEZOUX, Jacques. *Paris.* 1674 juré.
LHARDY, François. *Paris.* End 18c. Watch with painted dial Horstmann coll.
LHERITIER, ——. *Avignon.* 1703.
LHOEST, L. *Paris.* 1822-5.
LHUILLIER—
Jacques. *Paris.* 1769-89.
——. *Paris.* 1822-4.
LIANNA, P. *London.* Early 18c. p.c. g. watch Feill coll.
LIARDET, Louis. *Paris.* m.1778, juré 1780-9. Monteur de boîtes.
LIBBERTZ—
Heinrich Quirin. *Hamburg.* 1804-21.
Johann Arnold. *Hamburg.* 1804-21.
LIBBEY—
John. *London.* 1799.
——. *Devonport.* Early 19c.
LIBIS, Andreas. *Augsburg.* comp. 1752, m. 1764-92. From *Alsace.*
LICHBODY, *v.* LIGHTBODY.
LICHTENAUER—
——. *Würzburg.* 1725. sil. p.c. watch.
Leonh. Friedr. *Cologne.* 1797-1813.
G. *Cologne.* 1813.
LICHTI, Ulrich. *Troppau.* 1703. Repaired Olmütz clock.
LIDDELL—
Joseph. *Old Swinford.* ca.1760.
James. *Stockton.* ca.1770.
John. *Morpeth.* 1791-1819. W. cf. LIDDLE.
Charles. *Stockton.* 1795. W.
Adam. *Newry.* Early 19c. Watch.
William. *Edinburgh.* 1819-22. l.c. clock.
& WOODHOUSE. *Newry.* 1824.
James. *Edinburgh.* 1825.
LIDDIARD—
Thomas. *London (Gutter La.).* a.1749, CC. 1757-86.
Thomas. *London.* a.1786.
LIDDLE, John. *Morpeth.* ca.1770-96. l.c. clocks. W. cf. LIDDELL.
LIDSEY, John. *London.* a.1790.
LIEB, Johann Wolfgang. *Munich.* 1721. Court C. Watch Feill coll.
LIEBERKUHN, Joseph David. ——. 1576. Made a clock desc. in a book of which no copy has been found.
LIEBHERR—
Xaver. *Immenstadt.* ca.1740-67. T.C.
Joseph, son. *Immenstadt* and *Munich.* b. 1767, d.1840. C. and eminent math. inst. maker.
LIEBOURC, Jehan. *Paris.* 1407.
LIECHTENSTERN (LICHTENSTERN)—
Ignatz. *Vienna.* m.1775.
Joseph. *Vienna.* m.1787.
LIECHTI, Laurent. *Wintherthur.* 1530-45. Made jacquemart clock for Thann, and re-made clock of Soleure.
LIEDER, Friedrich Wilhelm. *Berlin.* 1785. Astro. and mus. clock Märkisches M. Berlin.
LIEDERITZ, Joh. G. *Fürth.* d.ca.1800.
LIEF—
George. *Sheffield.* 1814-17.
G. T. *Sheffield.* 1825. W.
LIÈGE, David. *Vevey.* 1724.
LIENGME, ——. *Cormoret.* 1800-33. Was in Le Locle ca.1805-10. The only maker in Cormoret.
LIENHARD—
Melchior. *Nürnberg.* Burgher in 1598.
Jacob. *London.* 1769. Insolvent. W.
LIETUIJT, John. *Delft* and *London.* 1368. One of the three clockmakers invited to England by Edward III.
LIEUTAUD—
Honoré. *Marseilles.* ca.1750-70. en. watch ill. Britten. Watch Den. coll.
Jean Joseph. *Paris.* m.1764-89. g. en. rep. cyl. watch, set diamonds, F.W.M. Mantel clock Petit Palais, Paris.
——. *Aix.* rep. watch S.M.S.K.
B. *Paris.* ca.1770. Maker of case of fine l.c. clock by ROBIN, S.K.M.
LIÈVRE, François. *Geneva.* a.1602.
LIGHT—
John. *London.* CC.1646.
Benjamin. *London.* a.1687.
John. *London (Little Old Bailey).* CC.1730. Watch.
John. *London.* a.1736, CC.1744-59.
John. *Bristol.* 1825.
LIGHTBODY—
John. *Lanark.* 1799-1837.
James. *Lanark.* ca.1800-37.
LIGHTFOOT, Peter. *Glastonbury.* 1335. Has been credited with clocks at Glastonbury and Wimborne, but there is no evidence of his having made anything but sundials.
LIGHTMAN, ——. *London.* an.1777. Watch.
LIGIER, ——. *Besançon.* 1781. W.
LIGNOY, ——. *Paris.* m.1604.
LILJESTRÖM, A. *Hälsingborg.* 1825-35.
LILLE, Johan. *Marstrand.* 1816-25. Two watches.
LILLEY, ——. *London.* d.1765. Watch engraver.
LILLIENFELD, Nikolaus. *Stralsund.* 1394. Made clock in S. Nikolaikirche.
LILLIOTT, Richard. *London.* a.1733, CC. 1740.
LILLJEDAHL, J. *Stockholm.* ca.1790.
LILLY—
Edward. *London.* a.1748, CC.1762.
Thomas. *London.* an.1777. Watch.
LIMBERRY (LIMBRY), John. *Curry Mallet.* 1729. Insolvent. C.
LIMNELIUS, Nils. *Stockholm.* 1795.
LIMNELL, O. F. *Växjo.* 1789. Watch.
LIMOND, Robert. a.1790. From *India.*
LIMPARD, John. *London.* ca.1620. Oval watch B.M.
LINAKER (LINNAKER, LYNAKER)—
Samuel. *London.* ca.1610, d.1649. One of the original assistants of the CC. Oval watch M.M.A.
Henry. *Liverpool.* 1796-1829.
LINCK, Paul. *Falun.* 1816-35.
LINCKE—
Johan Jakob. *Copenhagen.* m.1741. Master of Corporation 1766-72.
Ephraim, bro. *Copenhagen.* m.1753.
H. F. C. *Hamburg.* 1801-04.
LINCKH, Hans Martin. *Strasbourg.* 1660. There was a Martin LINCKH in 1649.
'LINCOLN,' Sig. on watches of the AUBURNDALE WATCH Co. of 1789.
LIND—
John. *Philadelphia.* 1775. C. & W.
Nicholas. *London.* 1780-1825 CC. Watches N.Y. Univ. and Ilbert coll.
William, son of Nicholas. *London.* a.1785, CC.1796.

LINDBERG—
Anders. *Södertälje.* 1750.
Mathias. *Stockholm.* comp. 1754, m.1763-6. br. clock Nat. M. Stockholm.
Per. *Sweden.* 1789. Watch.
LINDBOM, A. P. *Umeå.* 1824.
LINDEMANN, Caspar. *Munich.* 18c.
LINDEROOTH, Niclas Knut. *Norrköping.* m.1700. Watch dial on English mt.
LINDEY, Thomas. *Bristol.* 1812-30. W.
LINDGREN—
Erik. *Stockholm.* a.1715, m.1725, d.1741.
Erik. *Stockholm.* b.1729, m.1754, d.1786. Court C. g. watch. Two watch mts. Nord. M. Three wall clocks, two ill. Sidenbladh, one Nord. M. br. clock ill. Sidenbladh. Watch F.W.M. g. en. watch Nat. M. Stockholm.
Johan. *Stockholm.* b.1730, m.1761, d.1762.
Andreas. *Hamburg.* 1801-04.
LINDGRÉN, Lars Johan. *Stockholm.* 1775. *Uppsala.* 1778-84. Clock.
LINDHART (LEENERT), Peter. *Copenhagen.* 1692.
LINDIAN, ——. *London.* an.1774. Watch.
LINDLEY—
Thomas. *London.* an.1758. Watch.
Thomas. *Leicester.* an.1775. Watch.
James. *London.* 1805-11.
LINDLÖF, Eric. *Stockholm.* 1785-8. d.an. 1790.
LINDMAN—
Jöns. *Harg.* b.1708-74. Turret clocks at Harg and Kristineholm. Two l.c. clocks.
Petter. *Arboga.* 1750.
LINDQVIST—
Johan. *Stockholm.* a.ca.1750 to Julien Le Roy. m.1754, d.1779. Court C. Nine g. and sil. watches, three in Nord. M. and ill. Sidenbladh. br. and wall clocks.
Bryngel. *Laholm.* 1787-94.
LINDSAY—
George. *London (Strand).* 1743. d.1776. W. to George III. rep. watch Den. coll. Watch mt. G.M. Watch Buckley coll. l.c. mus. clock Weth. coll. ill. Britten. Also Lindesey.
Luke. *Greenock.* 1823-38.
William. *Edinburgh.* 1825.
LINDSEY—
William. *London.* a.1759. Watch G.M.
Thomas. *London (Bridgewater Sq.).* 1793.
James. *London.* a.1793.
John. *London.* a.1806, CC.1828.
LINDSTRÖM—
Esbiörn. *Stockholm.* m.1733, d.1734.
J. E. *Stockholm.* Early 19c. l.c. clock.
——. *Falkenberg.* comp. 1819-24.
LINE—
J. *London.* an.1755. Watch.
v. Lyne.
LINEY, Thomas. *London.* 1764 CC. Perhaps same as Lyney.
LINFORD—
Henry. *London.* a.1691.
——. *Clapham.* ca.1790 CC.
I. T. *London.* Late 18c.
Edward. *Bristol.* 1794-7.
Edward. *London.* 1805-20. Watch.
LINGER, ——. *Paris.* 1823.
LINGFORD, John. *Nottingham.* ca.1800. Watch.
LINGOT-PIOLAINE, ——. *Paris.* 1816-24.
LINGWOOD, Samuel. *Halesworth.* d.1742. W. l.c. clock.
LINK, Henry. *Bristol.* 1777. C. Partner with T. Willshire.
LINLEY—
Thomas. *London.* CC.1732.
Thomas. *London.* a.1740, CC.1748-64.
LINMAN, Kenneth. *London.* an.1767. Watch.
LINNAKER, *v.* Linaker.
LINSEY, William. *London.* a.1763.
LINSLEY, James. *London.* an.1765. Watch.
LINTD, Henry. *Farnham (Kent).* Early 18c. Clock.
LINTER, Thomas. *London.* a.1728, CC.1737-1754.
LINTLAER, Jean. *Flanders.* 1612. Made clock for Hôtel de Ville, Paris, re-made by Lepaute in 1783.
LINTON, John. *Liverpool.* ca.1814.
LINTOTT, Henry. *Farnham.* an.1774. Watch.
LINTZKEN (LIZTKEN, LIETZKEN), Joseph. *Vienna.* m.1789.
LINZELER, ——. *Paris.* Early 19c. Watch Gélis coll.
LION—
Bau. *Namur.* ca.1760. Clock.
Englebert. *Hamburg.* 1801. From *Paris.*
LIONELL, James. *London.* 1662.
LIOTARD, Jean Étienne. *Geneva.* b.1702, d.1789. Painter on enamel. Watch-case.
LIOUTE, ——. *London.* an.1776. Watch.
LIOUVILLE, ——. *Paris.* 1823. C.
LIP, Peter. *London.* a.1794.
LIPPERT, Johann Gottlob. *Dresden.* m.1716.
LIPPIUS (LIPPE), Niklaus. *Basle.* b.ca. 1566-98. Repaired aut. clock in St. Jean, Lyons, with Hugues Levet.
LIPS, J. *Rotterdam.* 1821-30.
LIPSCOMBE—
Edmund. *London.* 1744-53. W.
George. *London.* d.1762. C. & W.
Benjamin, bro. *London.* Continues the business.
Edward. *London.* an.1779. Watch.
Benjamin. *Barnet.* 1784-91. l.c. clock. W.
LIPTROT—
William. *London.* an.1728. Watch.
Thomas. *Liverpool.* an.1787. Watch.
LISCOMBE, Richard. *Kingsteignton.* 2nd half 18c. l.c. clock.
LISSETT, Richard. *London.* a.1785.
LISSIGNOL, Abraham. *Geneva.* b.1749, d. 1819. Painter on enamel.
LISSIMAN, Christopher. *London.* a.1701.
LIST—
Johann. *Augsburg.* m.1782-95. Watch Chamb. coll. From *Pfullingen.*
Anton. *Vienna.* ca.1825. g. en. watch.
LISTER—
Thomas. *Luddendon.* b.1718, d.1779.
John. *London.* a.1731, CC.1746.
Elizabeth. *London.* 1749.
Thomas, son of Thomas. *Halifax.* b.1745, d.1814. Made clocks for Halifax and Illingworth and an orrery in University M. Glasgow.
William. *Halifax.* ca.1770. l.c. clocks.
Samuel. *Bolton-le-Moors.* ca.1770-95.
Nicholas. *Sheffield.* 1797. W.
William. *Newcastle-o.-T.* 1815-20. Advertised chrons. on 'Earnshaw's plan' for £55.
LITCHFIELD, Paul. *London.* an.1794. Watch.
LITHERLAND—
Peter. *Liverpool.* 1790. d.1805. Patented the rack-lever escapement in 1792, a watch beating seconds, and keyless winding work. Rack-lever watch G.M. Succeeded by
Whiteside & Co. *Liverpool.* 1800-16. Succeeded by Davies & Co.
& Co. *Liverpool.* Watch hm. 1799 Ilbert coll.
John. *Liverpool.* 1800-24. W.
Davies & Co. *Liverpool.* 1818-37. These three firms made many watches with rack-lever escapements. Lever mt. Ilbert coll.
Richard. *Liverpool.* 1817-29. Patented an escapement.
Ann. *Liverpool.* 1825.
LITOT, ——. *Paris.* 1809-21.

LITTLE—
John. *London.* a.1726, CC.1733.
James. *Annan.* b.1775, d.1831.
Peter. *Baltimore, U.S.A.* 1799-1807. W. & C.
James. *Sligo.* 1824.
LITTLEFORD, John. *London.* 1817-24.
LITTLEJOHN, James. *London.* ca.1750. *Charleston, U.S.A.* from 1761. C. & W.
LITTLEMORE—
Whitestone. *London.* CC.1698-1704. a. to TOMPION.
Jacob. *Ruabon.* 1728. Bankrupt. C. br. clock.
LITTLETON—
Thomas. *London (Gt. Arthur St.).* a.1752, CC.1769-74.
William. *London.* a.1752.
James. *London.* 1773. rep. watch Den. coll.
John. *London.* 1774. Insolvent. W.
George. *London.* 1817-24.
LITTLEWORT, George. *London.* a.1789, CC.1822. Timepiece maker to the G.P.O.
LIURDET—
——. *Paris (Rue St. Louis du Palais 65).* 1789.
——. *Paris (Rue St. Louis du Palais 82).* 1789.
LIVERMORE—
Ezra. *London.* a.1765, CC.1773, d.an.1821.
Ezra, son of Ezra. *London.* CC.1821.
LIVINGSTONE—
George. *Edinburgh.* 1769.
James. *London.* ca.1775. Watch S.K.M.
Edward. *Dundee.* 1790.
LIVSLEY & BLIGH. *London.* 1800. Watch case makers.
LJUNGDAHL—
Olof. *Stockholm.* 1775. d.an.1780. Two watches, one Nord. M. Three wall and one br. clock.
Eric. *Köping.* comp. 1793.
LJUNGSTEDT—
Daniel. *Växjö.* 1787. l.c. clock.
Samuel. *Stockholm.* Late 18c. Clock.
Samuel. *Örebro.* 1790. Prob. same as above.
LLOYD—
William. *London.* CC.1668-1707.
David. *London.* a.1657, CC.1677-87.
William. *London.* a.1658, CC.1671.
Edward. *London.* a.1662, CC.1670.
Joseph. *London.* a.1664, CC.1673.
Richard. *London.* a.1670, CC.1681.
Lewis. *London.* a.1673.
Nathaniel. *London.* a.1673.
Charles. *London.* a.1683, CC.1691-1707.
James. *London.* a.1691, CC.1700, d.1721.
James, son. *London (West Smithfield).* a. 1713, CC.1722, d.1764. Watch.
Daniel. *London.* a.1713.
Thomas, son of James. *London.* a.1721, CC. 1733.
William, bro. *London.* CC.1740-65.
Edward. *London.* a.1741, CC.1763-76.
Thomas. *London.* a.1745.
William. *London.* CC.1760.
William. *London (Newcastle St.).* 1761. Insolvent. C. Watch.
William. *Walsall.* 1768. l.c. clock.
Robert. *London.* CC.1770.
& NORTHLEIGH. *London (Islington).* an. 1771-85. Watch.
George. *London.* an.1776. Watch.
Philip. *Bristol.* 1775. l.c. clock. W.
Joseph. *London.* a.1765.
John. *London (Aldgate).* CC.1774, l.CC. 1795.
John. *London (Minories).* 1781.
P. *Llanhaden.* ca.1806. l.c. clocks.
John. *Brecon.* Early 19c. Watch.
Owen. *London.* 1815.
Joseph. *Wigan.* 1816-24.

LLOYD—*continued.*
William John. *London.* CC.1825.
Joseph. *London.* a.1819.
LOADER, James. *London.* a.1735.
LOAT—
Henry. *Liverpool.* 1796.
Henry. *Wrexham.* 1822-35.
LOBENIGK, Egidius. ——. 1589. Fine mus. clock, ivory column, bronze base, Grüne Gewölbe, Dresden.
LOCHARD—
Robert. *London.* a.1647, CC.1655. g. en. watch.
John. *London.* CC.1655-70. Watch.
LOCHART, William. *Edinburgh.* 1813-22.
LOCK—
Edward. *Oxford.* an.1764. Watch.
T. *London.* an.1775. Watch.
James. *Bristol.* 1774-87.
James. *Bath.* 1780.
Samuel. *London.* a.1778.
Benjamin. *London.* a.1787.
Robert. *Edinburgh.* 1825.
LOCKE & MULTON. *Dunfermline.* 1825.
LOCKHART, Robert. *Portsmouth Point.* ca. 1790 CC.
LOCKIN, William. *London.* a.1687.
LOCKWOOD—
Robert. *London.* a.1647.
Benjamin. *Swaffham.* an.1749-95. l.c. clock and watch.
David. *Swaffham.* 1752. C. & W.
Joshua. *Charleston, U.S.A.* From 1757-81. W.
Jeremiah. *Mansfield.* 1791-5. W.
——. *London.* 1822. Duplex watch mt. Ilbert coll.
LOCKYER—
John. *London.* a.1759.
Robert. *Portsmouth.* Early 19c.
LOCQUET, Jean. *Blois.* 1639-64. C. to the duc d'Orléans.
LODDINGTON—
Isaac. *London.* CC.1720-34. Watch.
James. *London.* an.1769. Watch.
LODE, ——. *London.* ca.1800. chron. watch.
LODEREAU, Espafras. *Geneva.* 1644. From *Nérac.*
LODERER, Johann Eusebius. *Augsburg.* m. ca.1770-6, d.an.1793.
LODGE, Thomas. *London.* an.1725. Watch.
LODOWICK, Peter. *London.* a.1681, CC. 1689-91.
LODWICK, Abraham. *London.* a.1695.
LÖFBERG, Simon Peter. *Uppsala.* b.1777, d.1810. Two watches.
LÖFFLER—
Mathias. *Gütenbach.* b.1689-1720. Introduced wheel-cutting machines into the Schwarzwald in 1720.
Simon. *Neustadt.* ca.1770. Three wall clocks Furt. M.
Alois. *Vienna.* 1848. Made clocks with two wheels of 60 and 240, and one pinion of 8, showing hours, mins. and secs.
LÖFGREN, Abraham. *Varberg.*1752. *Växjö.* 1753. l.c. clock.
LOFT—
Nicholas. *London.* a.1717.
William. *London (Goodman's Fields).* a.1747, CC.1759-73.
John. *London.* a.1773.
LOFTUS—
Thomas. *Wisbech.* 1718. C. Watch.
John. *London.* a.1726.
John. *Liverpool.* 1734.
LÖFVALL, ——. *Jakobsstad.* 1794.
LOGAN—
——. *London.* an.1779. Watch.
Thomas. *Dorchester.* 1795-early 19c. Watch.
Adam. *New York.* 1805. W.

LOGAREC, François. *Paris.* 1675 m.
LOGEAT FRÈRES. *Paris.* 1812.
LÖGG, Michael. *Vienna.* ca.1725. Watch with wandering hour-figure.
LOGGE, Johannes. *Amsterdam.* Early 18c. Watch mt. S.K.M.
LOGGEN, Pieter. *Amsterdam.* Late 17c. g. watch en. Huaud le puisné Stern. coll.
LOGGIN, John. *Halifax.* 1781. Bankrupt.
LOGIE, Robert. *Edinburgh.* a.1784-1827.
LOHMAN, Johan. *Växjö.* ca.1790. Two watches.
LOHMANN, Johan Fredrik. *Copenhagen.* 1728.
LÖHR, ——. ——. Watch with pedometer winding Chamb. coll.
LÖHRER, Johannes. *Basle.* 1613. From *Bischofszell.* Kleinuhrmacher.
LOHRTÏOIS, H. *Amsterdam.* 1822. W.
LOIAL, Barthélemy. *Avignon.* 1613. Restored Avignon clock, with NICOLAS & BAL.
LOISEL, Jean. *Amiens.* 1409. 'Maistre de l'orloge du beffroy.'
LOLL, G. *Berlin.* ca.1820. Jump c.secs. watch mt. Ilbert coll.
LOMAS—
Samuel. *Poulton.* 18c. l.c. clock.
James. *Blackburn.* ca.1770.
Thomas. *Sheffield.* 1817. C.
Joseph. *Sheffield.* 1821. C. & W.
LOMAX—
George. *Brecon.* ca.1730-55. l.c. clock. Watch mt. Nat. M. Cardiff.
Samuel. *London.* an.1760. Watch.
LOMBARD—
Jacques. *Geneva.* a.1684.
——. *Chaux-de-Fonds.* 1781-1804.
Nathaniel & Daniel. *Boston, U.S.A.* 1825. W.
LOMBART—
Pierret. *Mons.* 1430-6. C. to Philip the Good of Burgundy. Supposed maker of a Gothic spring and fuzee table clock Marfels coll.
——. *Paris.* m.1605.
Claude. *Liége. Avignon* in 1736. Re-made town clock.
LOMER, Charles. *Paris.* m.1743.
LOMET—
Pierre. *Paris.* d.1788.
——. *Paris.* 1789.
LOMIER, John. *London.* an.1770. Watch.
LOMMEL, Johann Leonhardt. *Nürnberg.* 17c. Large tower clock, astrolabe dial, 12 and 24 hour str. Old Ashmolean M.
LONDERFIELD, Thomas. *London.* 1773.
LONDIVERTON, ——. *London.* an.1771. Watch.
LONDON—
Anthony. *London.* a.1702.
James. *London.* 1820.
William. *London.* 1820-40.
James. *London.* a.1813.
LONG—
Thomas. *London.* a.1646, CC.1654-73.
John. *London.* CC.1677-1717.
John. *London.* a.1690, CC.1698-1725. Watch.
Edward. *London.* a.1698.
Henry. *London (Little Britain).* 1762-80. p.c. g. rep. watch Ilbert coll.
John, son. *London.* a.1767.
Joseph Ambrose. *London.* CC.1774.
Thomas. *London.* a.1769.
——. *Cullompton.* 18c. l.c. clock.
Richard. *Deal.* 1784. W.
John. *Moreton Hampstead.* 1791-5. C.
Leonard John. *Dublin.* 1795.
Charles. *London.* an.1796. Watch.
William. *Sandwich.* Early 19c. Watch.
LONGCHAMPS, Élie, Frères. *Geneva.* Early 19c.
LONGCRAFT (LONGCROFT)—
Richard. *London.* a.1698, CC.1718.
Thomas. *London.* a.1775.
LONGHURST—
William. *London.* a.1770.
Richard. *Steyning.* an.1777-95 CC. W.
——. *Chatham.* ca.1790 CC.
Henry. *Kingston (Surrey).* 1791-1808.
John. *Kingston (Surrey).* 1795-1808.
LONGLAND—
Francis. *London.* a.1671.
John. *London.* CC.1677-95. Maker of repute. l.c. clock.
LONGSTAFF—
Joseph. *London.* a.1766.
Thomas. *London.* a.1817.
LONGWORTH—
Peter. *Liverpool.* 1824-9. W.
Thomas. *Liverpool.* 1825. W.
LÖNNGREN, Johan. *Marstrand.* 1793-1820.
LONSDALL, John. *London.* a.1706.
LOOF, William. *Tunbridge Wells.* Early 19c. Watch.
LOOKER, William. *London.* a.1797.
LOOMES (LOUMES), Thomas. *London.* CC.1649-74. A maker of great repute. Lantern clock G.M. Chiming br. clock.
LOON, William. *Dordrecht.* 1720. mt. G.M.
LOOR, Thomas. *Amsterdam.* 1st half 18c. Watch mt.
LOOSLEY, John. *London.* CC.1781-99.
LOPIN, ——. *Paris.* 1811-25.
LORAINE, James. *Newcastle-o.-T.* 1820.
LORD—
Richard. *London.* CC.1632.
Joseph. *London.* a.1684.
John. *Farington.* 1784-97. W. l.c. clock. Watch Exeter M.
LORENZ—
Johann Norbert. *Vienna.* m.1768.
Gottlob. *Schwartzenberg.* ca.1800. Large sil. watch Feill coll.
LORIMER—
John. *London.* an.1767. Watch.
James. *London.* ca.1780. l.c. mus. clock ill. Britten. Watch.
& EDWARDS. *London.* 1805-25. W. & C.
David. *London.* 1815-20.
LORIMIER—
LES FRÈRES (David François and Jean Jacques). *Fontaines* and *Paris.* 1760-1805.
François Louis, son of J. Jacques. *Fontaines, Geneva* and *Paris.* 1782-1810. At *Besançon* ca.1805.
Th. *Chaux-de-Fonds.* 1826.
LORION—
Jacques. *Blois.* m.1670, d.an.1696.
Jacques, son. *Blois.* m.1676.
LORITZ, Xaver. *Vienna.* m.1788.
LORKING, Abraham. *London.* a.1732.
LORMET, Jacques. *Lyons.* 1657. d.1670.
LORMIER, Salomon. *Groningen.* ca.1700. Wandering hour-figure watch. rep. watch mt. Ilbert coll.
LORMOY, Jean François. *Paris.* m.1743.
LORON (LAURON), Jean. *Blois.* comp. 1619-25.
LORRY—
——. *Paris.* 1730 m. cf. LORY.
Claude. *Paris.* m.1737. cf. LORY.
——. *Paris.* 1816.
LORY—
Marc Antoine. *Paris.* m.1742.
Claude, l'aîné. *Paris (Rue de Berry).* m. 1767-89. cf. LORRY. Made and repaired clocks at Châteaux de St. Germain, des Gobelins, de la Savonnerie, des Capucines, Meudon, Marly, de la Ste. Chapelle and de Vincennes.

LORY—*continued.*
Germain Claude, le jeune. *Paris* (*Rue Phélypeaux*). m.1778-89.
——. *Paris* (*Rue Montorgeuil*). 1807-13. Designed fine astro. clocks.
LOSCH, Christopher. *Copenhagen* and *Bergen.* m.1782.
LOSEBY—
John. *London.* a.1750.
Edward Thomas. *London* (*Islington*), ca. 1830-53. *Leicester,* 1853. d.1890. Eminent chron. maker. Devised a successful balance with mercury auxiliary compensation. Wrote in Naut. Mag. 1845 on chrons. He failed to obtain orders for chrons. from the Admiralty and turned his attention to turret clocks.
LOSELEY, Edward. *Shifnal.* ca.1790.
LOSSIER—
——. *London.* 2nd half 18c. Watch mt.
——. *Paris.* Late 18c. g. en. watch.
Louis. *Besançon.* b.1847, d.1893. An eminent horologist. Director of Besançon school. Pub. a standard work on springing and adjusting.
LOTHER, ——. *London.* an.1755. Watch.
LOTHERINGTON, ——. *Hull.* Early 19c. Watch.
LOTTER, Tobias. *Augsburg.* 1726 m., juré 1736-48.
LOTTIN, Joseph. *Paris.* m.1771-89.
LOUARTH, Jasper. *London.* CC.1641.
LOUBET, Félix. *Paris.* 2nd half 16c. circ. table clock S.K.M. eng. after Étienne Delaune.
LOUCH, Charles. *St. Albans.* 1784. W. Succeeded ca.1800 by George HATCH.
LOUDAN, William. *London.* 1825-40.
LOUDEREAU, *v.* LODEREAU.
LOUDON—
J. *London.* an.1769. Watch.
John. *Irvine.* 1820.
LOUEST, ——. *Paris.* 1817.
LOUGH—
Thomas. *London.* a.1680.
Hugh. *Penrith.* 1740-91.
Robert. *Penrith.* ca.1770-95. l.c. clock.
LOUGHBOROUGH, John. *Durham.* 1820. l.c. clock. Watch.
LOUGHTON, William. *London.* 1689 CC.
LOUIS—
Pierre. *Nimes.* 1410. Made clock for Montpellier with PETIT.
Simon. *London.* an.1764. Watch.
Marie. *London.* an.1774. Watch.
——. *Paris.* 1810-13.
Jean Baptiste. *Leipzig.* 1814.
J. *Amsterdam.* 1822. W.
LOUMAND, Lorens. *Copenhagen.* 1689. d. 1728.
LOUNDES (LOWNDES)—
Jonathan. *London* (*Pall Mall*). CC.1680-1710. A famous maker. br. and l.c. clocks Weth. coll. Watches. Three br. clocks ill. Cec. & Web. Miniature lantern clock.
Charles. *London* (*Pall Mall*). a.1674, CC. 1682-1724. br. and l.c. clock.
Isaac. *London* (*Pall Mall*). CC.1682-1702. l.c. clocks Weth. coll. br. clock. Also W.
Samuel. *London.* 1695.
William. *London.* a.1691.
Isaac. *London.* a.1695.
& KNIBB. *London.* an.1727. Watch.
Jennis. *London.* an.1766. Watch.
LOUP—
——. *Vevey.* 1764 comp.
——. *Ripon.* 1774. C. & W.
Henry. *Vevey.* 1798 m.
LOUTEAU, Pierre. *Lyons.* 1604. m.1607-1628. crys. cross watch M.M.A. Watches Gélis coll. and Spitzer sale. Fine eng. cross watch Marryat coll.

LOUVET—
——. *Amsterdam.* 1822. W.
——. *Paris.* 1825.
LOUYS, George. ——. ca.1630. Watches in form of a fleur-de-lys S.K.M. and Mallett coll.
LOVAGE, ——. *London.* 1747.
LOVE—
John. *London.* a.1697, CC.1707. Watch case maker.
James. *Elgin.* 1712.
Neilson. *Port Glasgow.* 1770.
James. *London.* Late 18c. en. watch, set pearls, S.K.M.
James. *Edinburgh.* 1774.
John. *Edinburgh.* 1779.
James. *London.* a.1799.
John. *Baltimore, U.S.A.* 1802. W.
Christopher. *London.* 1816-25.
LOVEDAY—
James. *London.* a.1715. Watch.
Edward. *London* (*Peartree St.*). d.an.1818.
George. *London.* a.1818.
LOVEJOY—
John. *London.* a.1732, CC.1741.
Peter. *London* (*Finsbury Sq.*). a.1787, CC. 1794-1810.
LOVELACE—
Jacob. *Exeter.* b.1706, d.1766. Very complex cal. aut. and mus. clock in Liverpool M. destroyed 1941. Watch.
Robert. *London.* a.1725.
William. *London.* 1799. Watch S.M.S.K.
LOVELAND—
William. *London.* a.1753. Watch.
J. *London.* an.1776. Watch.
LOVELL—
Paul. *v.* LOWELL.
Paul. *London.* a.1646, CC.1653-62.
Nathan. *London.* a.1655.
George. *London.* 1793 l.CC.
LOVETT—
Jonathan. *London.* a.1692.
William. *London.* a.1694, CC.1702-14. W.
Leonard. *London.* a.1784.
LOVISELL, ——. *London.* 1762. Watch.
LOW—
John. *London.* CC.1692.
John. *Winwick.* mar.1694. W.
James. *Edinburgh.* a.1755-61.
Alexander. *Edinburgh.* 1799.
Alexander. *Errol.* 1815-37.
John. *London.* a.1809.
George. *London.* a.1814.
LOWCOCKE, John. *London.* an.1744. Watch.
LOWDEN, James. *Edinburgh.* ca.1760. Watch.
LOWDER, Charles. *London.* a.1699.
LOWDIN, Thomas. *Bristol.* 1774-81.
LOWE—
John. *London.* a.1653-1728 CC. Watch.
Joseph. *London.* CC.1709-30.
William. *London.* a.1707.
Richard. *London.* an.1752. Watch.
Thomas. *Worcester* and *Gloucester.* 1761. Bankrupt.
Edward. *Liverpool.* 1761. W.
John. *London.* a.1768-1818.
——. *Arbroath.* 1784.
——. *Dartford.* ca.1790 CC.
Edward. *Chester.* 1793. C. & W.
Richard. *Ware.* ca.1800 CC.
George. *Gloucester.* Early 19c. Watch.
George. *Chester.* Early 19c. Watch mts. Glasgow Art Gall. and Grosvenor M. Chester.
T. *London.* Early 19c. Watch.
Gavin. ——. 1819. Art. in Phil. Mag. on mercurial pendulums.

LOWELL (LOVELL), Paul. *London.* BC. 1628-54, d.an.1672. Subscribed for incorporation of CC. 'High German.'
LOWFORD, Alexander. *London.* a.1730.
LOWLEY, William. *Ballymoney.* 1824.
LOWMAN, J. *Ramsgate.* ca.1810. From *London.*
LOWNES, David. *Philadelphia.* 1802-08. W.
LOWRIE—
John Clavering. *London (Botolph Alley).* a. 1780, CC.1804-14. Watch.
Ebenezer, son. *London (Clerkenwell).* a.1814, CC.1825.
LOWRY—
Morgan. *Leeds.* 1720-50. Year clock.
John Uffington. *London.* a.1785.
George Henry. *Drogheda.* 1824.
LOYACE-DIT-PÉRONNET. *Lyons.* 1379. C. Keeper of clock of St. Jean.
LOYSEAU, Philippe. *Blois.* 1622.
LOYSET, Philippe. *Dole.* 1584. Made clock for Poligny.
LOZANO, Thomas. *London.* Early 18c. Watch.
LUANS, Jean de. *Paris.* ca.1430-9. Keeper of the clock on the Palais de Justice.
LUBERT, Florens G. *Amsterdam.* ca.1730. Fine l.c. clock Gemeente M., The Hague.
LUCAS—
William. *London.* CC.1669.
Jaques. *Amsterdam.* 1681. Huguenot refugee from *La Rochelle.* en. watch S.K.M.
Edward. *London.* a.1715, CC.1727. W.
Henry. *London.* a.1722, CC.1731.
John. *London.* a.1725.
——. *Newbury.* an.1748. Watch.
Anthony. *London.* a.1751.
Nathaniel. *London.* a.1757.
Richard. *London.* a.1765, CC.1772-97. W.
Joseph. *London.* 1777. Watch.
James. *London.* an.1784. Watch.
Joel, son. *London.* a.1792.
John. *London.* 1802-11. mt. maker.
Richard. *London.* 1802-08 CC.
William. *Liverpool.* 1825. W.
LUCE—
David. *Rouen.* ca.1620. Watch Ilbert coll.
Pierre. *Rouen.* 1626 m.
Pierre. *Blois.* 1663-9. Native of *England.*
LUCIE, John. *London.* a.1655, CC.1663.
LUCIN, ——. *Paris.* 1817-25.
LUCK—
Richard. *London.* a.1704.
Robert. *London.* an.1773. Watch.
LUCKHURST—
Edward. *London.* a.1734.
W. *Dover.* Early 19c. Watch.
LUCKMAN, John. *Bickenhill.* ca.1765.
LUCY, Solomon. *London.* an.1711. Watch.
LÜDEMANN, ——. *Lüneburg.* 1821.
LUDEWIG, ——. *Dresden.* 1st half 18c. Compass dial M.M.A.
LUDFORD, Ralph. *London.* a.1656.
LUDLAM, ——. *Cambridge.* Prof. of astronomy. In 1769 pub. a work containing the description of a clock with wooden pendulum.
LUDLOW—
Samuel. *London.* a.1695, CC.1707.
Benjamin. *Yarmouth.* From *London.* 1780. Clock. rep. watch mt.
LUDWIG, ——. *Nürnberg.* 1483. Made str. work for the clock of the Sebaldus Kirche.
LUEB, Michael. *London.* a.1655.
LUFFMAN, Daniel. *London.* 1766.
LUGNBECK, Nils. *Kristinehamn.* 1773.
LUGRIN, Adolphe. *Geneva.* Early 19c.
LUKE, John. *London.* 1820.
LUKENS, J. ——. 1827. Art. on hardening chron. balance springs in Gill's Tech. Repository, Vol. I.
LUKJE, J. J. *Hoogezand.* ca.1800.
LULHAM, Curtis. *London.* a.1762.
LULLIN, Paul. *London.* Early 18c. Watches Stads M. Amsterdam and Carnegie M. Watch with moving hour-figures Hist. M. Chaux-de-Fonds.
LÜLMANN, J. D. *Hamburg.* 1815-21.
LUM, Joseph. *London.* an.1745. Watch.
LUMB, John. *London.* 1790.
LUMBER—
James. *Chester.* 1762-95. W.
Henry. *Bristol.* 1797-1812. W.
Jacob. *Bristol.* 1801. W.
LUMLEY—
George. *London.* 1737. W.
George, son. *London* and *Bury St. Edmunds.* a.1737, CC.1745, d.1784. l.c. clock. 3-case watch.
Mary, widow. *Bury St. Edmunds.* b.1724, d.1800. 'Eminent W.'
& GUDGEON. *Bury St. Edmunds.* ca.1790.
LUMPKIN—
Thomas. *London.* 1689. CC.1694-1715. l.c. clock.
Thomas, son. *London.* a.1709.
——. *London (Fleet St.).* 1726. C.
LUMSDANE—
Walter. *Cupar-Fife.* 1740-92.
Walter. *Cupar-Fife.* 1792.
LUMSDEN—
John. *Aberdeen.* 1735-57.
George. *Pittenweem.* 1818-49.
LUN, George. *London.* 1801.
LUNAN, Charles. *Aberdeen.* 1760-1816.
LUND—
Christopher Larsen. *Christiania.* 1779 m.
Rasmus. *Copenhagen.* m.1798.
Laurits. *Copenhagen.* m.1800.
Jürgen Jacob. *Hamburg.* 1821.
LUNDBÄCK, Olof. *Gäfle* and *Stockholm.* 1752. l.c. clock.
LUNDBERG—
Joh. *Norrköping.* b.1770, d.1811.
Johan Eric. *Hedemora.* 1802-40.
Anders. *Stockholm.* 1822-35. br. clock.
Johan Gustaf. *Stockholm.* 1822-64.
LUNDER, William. *London.* an.1782. Watch.
LUNDGREN—
Andr. *Karlskrona.* a.1774-8. Watch.
Johan. *Uppsala.* 1789.
Abraham. *Umeå.* 1822.
LUNDIE—
John. *Elgin.* a.1743.
William. *Inverurie.* b.1743, d.1816.
John. *Dundee.* 1809-37.
LUNDIN, Carl Detloff. *Stockholm.* 1821-25.
LUNDMARK—
Petter. *Stockholm.* mar.1769. Wall clock.
Jonas. *Skellefteå.* 18c. trav. clock Nord. M.
LUNDSTEDT—
Anders. *Stockholm.* 1786-1820. sil. cyl. watch. Wall and br. clock ill. Sidenbladh.
Carl Otto. *Stockholm.* 1822-45.
LUNDSTRÖM, Johan Eric. *Stockholm.* 1810. d.1827. Two watches Nord. M.
LUNDVALL, And. *Köping.* 1819-26.
LUNDVIK—
Olof. *Uppsala.* b.1781, d.1820.
Georg. *Stockholm.* 1820. d.an.1828.
LUNGDELIUS, Olof. *Örebro.* b.1724, d.1791.
LUNLEY, James. *London.* an.1755. Watch.
LUNTLEY, Thomas. *London.* a.1684.
LUPTON—
William. *York.* 1645. d.1680. C.
William, son. *York.* 1681. C.
John. *Altrincham.* 1765.
George. *Altrincham.* 1772-95. C.
LURASCO FRÈRES. *Amsterdam.* Late 18c. g. en. watch.
LUSH, John. *London.* a.1737. Watch.
LUSUERG—
Dominicus. *Rome.* 1668-ca.1700. Dial and compass Old Ashmolean M.
Jakob. *Rome.* 2nd half 18c. inst. maker.

LUTERER (LUTHER), Hans. *Zürich.* 1516-1538. Made second clock on St. Peter's tower. From *Waldshut.*
LÜTGE, ——. *Zerbst.* 1775. hex. str. al. table clock Ilbert coll.
LUTTEROU (LUTHER), Jürgen. *Copenhagen.* 1725 m. From *Mecklenburg.* Turret C.
LUTTMAN, William. *London.* a.1708, CC. 1720-7, d.an.1735.
LUTWICHE (LUTWYCHE)—
John. *London.* a.1764.
Thomas. *Worcester.* 1774-95. W.
LUTZ—
Aloysius. *Copenhagen.* 1803. From *Nürnberg.*
Jean Célanis. *Geneva.* b.1800, d.1863. In 1846 started the production of hardened balance springs.
LÜTZELKIRCHER, Johann. *Westheim.* 1756. *Kriegshaber.* 1770.
LUYA, Edouard. *Geneva.* Left in 1770.
LUZURIER, ——. *Paris.* 1812. C.
LYDDIATT, Thomas. *London.* End 17c. Watch.
LYE, William. *London.* 1716 CC.
LYFORD, Richard. *London.* CC.1779.
LYKELL, G. *London.* an.1776. Watch.
LYNAM, Philip. *London.* a.1682.
LYNCH—
Robert. *London.* a.1651, CC.1670-92. Also LINCH.
Robert. *London.* a.1654.
Anthony. *Newbury.* an.1781. Watch.
John. *Newbury.* 1795. W.
John. *Baltimore, U.S.A.* 1802-32. C.
Timothy. *New Ross.* 1824.
LYNDE, John. *London.* a.1725.
LYNDSAY, Alexander. *Aberdeen.* 1537.
LYNE—
William. *London.* CC.1703.
John. *London.* a.1747, CC.1769.
John. *London.* 1815. d.1820.
LYNES—
Thomas. *London.* a.1700, CC.1721-6.
Henry John. *London (St. Giles, Cripplegate).* a.1775, CC.1792-8.
William John. *London.* a.1798.
LYNEY—
Thomas. *London.* a.1718.
Thomas. *London.* a.1719.
LYNGAGER, Oluf. *Copenhagen.* m.1753. Master of Corporation 1770-87.
LYNN—
——. *Deptford.* an.1745. Watch. Also LYNE.
Michael. *Parsonstown.* 1824.
LYNNAKER, *v.* LINAKER.
LYON—
John. *Warrington.* 1685 CC.
Samuel. *London.* 1720. Insolvent.
Thomas. *London (Foster La.).* 1744-62. Bankrupt. W.
Gabriel. *London.* a.1737, CC.1745.
Matthew. *Lanark.* 1770.
Henry. *London.* an.1774. Watch.
Andrew. *Port Glasgow,* 1783-99.
Thomas George. *London (St. Martin's-le-Grand).* 1790.
Francis. *Bideford.* 1795. W.
William. *Liverpool.* 1796.
Aaron. *London.* 1799.
J. *Ramsgate.* 1807. sq. watch mt. Stads M. Amsterdam.
——. *Bathgate.* 1810.
Edward. *Manchester.* ca.1820.
Charles. *Lanark.* 1820.
Morris. *Liverpool.* 1825. W.
LYONS—
Richard. *London.* a.1649, CC.1656, m.CC. 1683-96. Watch. l.c. clock ill. Cec. & Web.
Timothy. *Athlone.* 1824.
LYSLE (LISLE), Benjamin. *Rotterdam.* ca. 1640-58. circ. cast sil. watch S.K.M. Watch B.M.
LYTHAM, Thomas. *London.* a.1745.

M

MABB, William. *London.* a.1688.
MABERLEY—
John. *London.* a.1698, CC.1705, m.CC.1738-1755. Made the springs for HARRISON'S chrons. g. rep. watch Den. coll. Also MABBERLEY.
Benjamin. *London.* a.1700.
MABILLE—
Jean Mathieu. *Paris.* 1773 comp.
Charles. *Paris.* 1773 m.-1785. rep. watch. Rack clock.
MABIT, ——. *Nottingham.* an.1750. Watch.
MACADAM—
Walter. *Glasgow.* 1800.
Robert. *Dumfries.* 1820-45.
MACAIRE—
Louis Benjamin. *Geneva.* 1689-1733.
F. *London.* 1732. p.c. al. watch.
Antoine. *Paris.* ca.1770. Watch Den. coll.
MACARA, Robert. *Dunfermline.* 1796-1820.
MACAULEY, George Lionel Augustus. *London.* a.1778.
MACBETH, Daniel. *Glasgow.* 1818-46.
McBRIDE, John. *Ballymena.* 1824.
McCABE—
Patrick. *Lurgan.* an.1766. Watch.
Thomas. *Belfast.* ca.1770. C.
John. *Baltimore, U.S.A.* 1774. From *Dublin.* C. & W.
James. *London* (*Cheapside* and *Royal Exchange*). 1778. CC.1781, w.CC. and d. 1811. A very fine maker. His business was continued under the same name by his sons and Robt. Jeremy until 1883. McCabe's best watches were sd. 'James McCabe,' the second quality 'McCabe,' and the third quality 'Beatson.' Many watches and clocks.
William. *Newry.* 1798. Watch Belfast M.
William. *London* (*Borough*). 1805-11.
Thomas, son of James. *London.* CC.1815-9.
& Co. (William). *London* (*Poplar*). 1815-24.
& SON. *London* (*R. Exchange*). 1817-24. Also *Cornhill.*
John. *London.* 1817. Watch G.M.
Robert, son of James. *London.* CC.1821-4.
James, son of James. *London* (*Cornhill*). CC. 1822-38.
& STRACHAN. *London.* 1825.
McCARDLE, James. *Strabane.* 1824.
McCARTER, Richard. *London.* a.1765.
McCARTHEY, Charles. *Bristol.* 1780-9. W. Of McCARTHEY & JEFFRY.
McCARTNEY, William. *Portarlington.* 1824.
MACAULAY, George Lionel Augustus. *London.* a.1778.
MACCERI, Faustin. *Augsburg.* 1786-91. Allowed to work without essay.

McCLARY—
Thomas. *London.* a.1752.
Samuel. *Wilmington, U.S.A.* b.1788, d.1859. l.c. clocks.
Samuel & Thomas, sons. *Wilmington.* 19c. Both C.
McCLELLAN—
——. *London.* an.1789. Watch.
——. *Deptford.* Early 19c.
McCLENNAN, Kenneth. *v.* MACLENNAN.
McCLURE, John. *Boston, U.S.A.* 1823-25.
McCLYMONT, James. *Ayr.* 1761.
McCOLGAN, John. *Londonderry.* 1824.
McCOLLIN, Thomas. *Philadelphia.* 1825.
McCONCHY, James. *London.* a.1772.
McCORMACK, Andrew. *Dundalk.* 1824.
McCRACKEN, Francis. *Portaferry.* 1824.
McCREADY, John. *Westport.* 1824.
McCREARY, James. *London.* an.1778. Watch.
McCREASY, Edward. *London.* 1820.
McDANIEL, William H. *Philadelphia.* 1819-1825.
MACDONALD—
Andrew. *London.* a.1747.
John. *Inverness.* an.1760, d.1790. Watch.
Joseph. *Liverpool.* 1776-1821.
Peter. *Inverness.* 1780-1801 CC.
H. F. *Quinton.* ca.1785.
Peter. *London.* 1790-9. p.c. g. and en. rep. watch Carnegie M.
Duncan. *Edinburgh.* a.1787.
Donald. *Inverness.* 1801.
William. *Edinburgh* 1819.
David. *Edinburgh.* 1822-35.
MacDOWALL, James. *Philadelphia.* 1796-1825. W.
MacDOWELL—
John. *Belfast.* ca.1770. C.
BROS. *Dublin.* Early 19c. Watch sd. 'Gontard, Paris, and M'Dowell Bros., Dublin.'
James. *Sligo.* 1824.
McDUFF, J. *Maybole.* 1830.
MACÉ—
Barthélemy. *Blois.* a.1624, m.1630, d.1662. Fine en. watch ill. Britten.
Barthélemy, son. *Blois.* b.1638, d.1668.
Michel, bro. ——. b.1639. Left *France.*
Michel. *Paris.* Juré 1736. Watch Besançon M.
MACE—
Laurence. *London.* a.1732, CC.1742-52.
Nathaniel. *London.* a.1734.
McELWEE, James. *Philadelphia.* 1813.
McENTIRE, James. *Enniskillen.* 1824.
MACEY—
——. *London.* an.1751. Watch. cf. MACY.
Robert. *Plymouth.* 1795.

MACFARLANE—
James. *London.* a.1749.
Patrick. *Glasgow.* 1781.
Patrick. *Perth.* a.1790.
Alexander. *Perth.* 1789-1808.
John *Boston, U.S.A.* 1796-1813. W.
Peter. *London.* ca.1800. W.
Duncan. *Glasgow.* 1818.
MACFIE, Brice. *Greenock.* 1820.
MacGEORGE, ——. *Dumfries.* 1755.
MacGILCHRIST, J. *Kirkintilloch.* 1818.
MacGILL, G. & W. *Paisley.* 1820.
McGLUE, E. *London.* an.1777. Watch.
McGRAW, Donald. *Annapolis, U.S.A.* 1767. W. From *Edinburgh.*
MacGREGOR—
Alexander. *Dunse.* 1808.
John. *Edinburgh.* 1811.
James. *Edinburgh.* 1825-36.
MACHAM, Samuel. *London.* 1700-15. Two l.c. clocks ill. Cec. & Web. sil. watch with royal coat of arms on cock and trav. clock Ilbert coll.
McHARG, Aexander. *Albany, U.S.A.* 1817-1823. W.
McHINCH, William. *Donaghadee.* 1824.
McILHENNEY—
& West. *Philadelphia.* 1819.
Joseph E. *Philadelphia.* 1820-5. W.
MacILWAIN, James. *Rathfryland.* 1824.
MacILWRAITH, J. C. *London.* 1808.
MACK, Joseph. *Holt.* 1795. W. cf. Mask.
MACKARSIE (MACKARTHY), *v.* Muckarsie.
MACKAY—
Alexander. *London.* d.1763. W.
Alexander. *Banff.* 1774.
Crafts. *London.* a.1770, CC.1781.
Crafts. *Boston, U.S.A.* 1789. Prob. same as above.
Alexander. *Peterhead.* 1798-1807.
John. *Edinburgh.* ca.1825. Partner in Forrest & Co.
McKEAN, George. *London.* an.1763. Watch.
McKEEN, Henry. *Philadelphia.* 1823.
MACKENZIE—
Kenneth. *Edinburgh.* a.1737.
Francis. *Edinburgh.* a.1753.
William. *London.* an.1776. Watch.
Dunkin. *London.* a.1771.
Colin. *London.* 1784-91. *Inverness.* 1800.
Alexander. *Edinburgh.* a.1787.
Murdoch. *Edinburgh.* a.1787-94.
Lewis. *Edinburgh.* a.1797.
——. *London.* 1800. cyl. watch Chamb. coll.
McKEOWN, James. *Coleraine.* 1824.
McKERRILL, William. *London.* a.1776.
MACKERSON, David. *Edinburgh.* a.1704-12.
MACKGLASHEN, Charles. *London.* a.1779.
MACKIE—
George. *London (Helmet Row, City Rd.).* 1784-1811.
James. *London (Whitecross St.).* 1799-1824.
George, & Son. *London.* 1809-25. Chron. W. & C.
James. *London (Bunhill Row).* 1810-40. Watch.
MACKINLEY, Edward. *Philadelphia.* Early 19c. From *Dublin.* W.
MACKLIN, James. *London.* CC.1767, l.CC. 1812-5. Watch-case maker.
McKNIGHT, P. *London.* Early 19c. Watch.
MACKY, George. *Londonderry.* 1824.
McLACHLAN—
John. *London.* CC.1791.
William. *Kingston, Jamaica.* ca.1795 CC.
Hugh, son of John. *London.* 1810-40. Succeeded his father. Marine chron. G.M.
John. *Dumfries.* 1820.
MACLAREN—
James. *Glasgow.* 1779.
James. *Kingston, Jamaica.* ca.1790 CC.

MACLEAN—
George. *Edinburgh.* 1776.
John. *Dublin.* 1780. W.
Andrew. *Edinburgh.* a.1783-1812.
McLELLAND, James. *Kingston, Jamaica.* Early 19c.
MACLENNAN—
Henry. *London.* an.1774. Watch.
Kenneth. *London.* 1776-1825. Made a planetarium for the R. Institution. l.c. lacquer clock. br. clock Weth. coll. g. watch.
Kenneth & William. *London.* 1817-24. Same firm as preceding.
MacMARTIN, Samuel. *Ballymena.* 1824.
MacMASTER—
William John. *London.* 1817-24.
William. *Greenock.* 1820.
M. *Dublin.* 1824.
MACMILLAN, Angus. *London.* a.1778.
McMILLAR, Douglas. *London.* an.1771. Watch.
McMURDE, Thomas. *Liverpool.* 1803. W.
McMURRAY, Thomas. *Liverpool.* 1800. W.
MacNAB—
Robert. *Perth.* 1800.
John. *Perth.* 1820.
John. *Perth.* 1824-42.
MacNALLY, Charles. *Omagh.* 1824.
MacNAUGHTON—
Donald. *Perth.* 1768.
Alexander. *Edinburgh.* 1814. Duplex watch mt. Ilbert coll.
MacNEILLY, Alexander. *Antrim.* 1824.
MacNIESH, John. *Falkirk.* 1805.
MACORS, André. *Paris.* m.1776-89.
McPHAIL, Thomas. *London.* a.1765.
MACPHERSON—
Normand. *Edinburgh.* a.1749, d.1783. Maker of repute. l.c. clock. g. cyl. watch Ilbert coll.
John, son. *Edinburgh.* a.1773, d.1785.
& Leslie. *Edinburgh.* 1785-8.
MacQUEEN, Alexander. *Edinburgh.* a.1788-1834.
MACQUART—
——. *Paris.* 1726-42. Dial maker.
& Cadot. *Paris.* 1730.
MACQUET, Isaac. *Berlin.* 1792-4.
MACREDIE, William. *London.* a.1784.
MacROBERT, Thomas. *Stranraer.* 1820.
MACROU, ——. *Amsterdam.* Late 18c. sil. p.c. watch Horstmann coll.
MacSWEENY—
Denis. *Tralee.* 1824.
Eugene. *Tralee.* 1824.
MACUNE—
William. *London.* 1769. W.
Thomas, son. *London.* a.1769, CC.1783. Watch.
MacWALTER, James. *Paisley.* 1784.
MacWHINNIE, Robert. *Ayr.* 1820-38.
MACY, Benjamin. *London.* CC.1713-28.
MADDEN—
Thomas. *London.* a.1647.
Matthew. *Bath.* an.1776. Watch.
Benjamin. *London.* a.1773.
MADDINS, George. *London.* a.1697.
MADDISON, Joseph. *London.* CC.1780,d.1821.
MADDOCK—
William. *London.* 1763-70.
W. *Waterford.* Late 18c. Watch.
& Murphy. *Waterford.* ca.1790 CC.
Patrick. *Waterford.* 1824.
MADDOX—
Daniel. *London.* an.1751. Watch.
Edward. *London (Bull and Mouth St.).* 1769-1796. c.secs. cyl. watch Den. coll.
William. *London.* a.1764.
John, son of Edward. *London.* a.1789-1804.
Charles. *Liverpool.* 1818-21. W.
William. *Liverpool.* 1825. W.

MADEL, ainy. *Paris.* ca.1730. br. clock Uhren M. Vienna.
MADELONG, ——. *London.* an.1757. Watch.
MADGWICK, Edward. prob. *London.* an. 1776. Watch.
MADRIP, William. *London.* an.1794. Watch.
MADS, ——. *Frederiksborg* and *Faurholm.* 1559-62. Court C. Made clock for palace.
MADSEN—
Hans, son of Mads. *Odensegaard.* 1586. Court C.
Hans. *Copenhagen.* m.1760.
Johan Andreas Frederik. *Copenhagen.* m. 1806.
MAERK, Jean. *Aarau.* Early 19c. g. watch.
MAGE, ——. *Paris.* 1824.
MAGELLAN, L. H. *Paris.* His collected arts. on watches and astro. clocks pub. 1780.
MAGGE, ——. *London.* a.1704.
MAGGER, Ralph. *London.* a.1702.
MAGGS, William. *London.* 1740.
MAGILL, William. *Dublin.* 1795.
MAGITOT, Jean Baptiste. *Paris.* m.1771-89. Turret clock.
MAGNAC, ——. *Paris.* 1819.
MAGNEN, Michel. *Paris.* m.1770-89.
MAGNENAT, Henry. *Geneva.* Early 19c.
MAGNETTE, Frédéric Élie. *Geneva.* ca. 1760-87.
MAGNIÈRE, ——. *Paris.* 1807-12.
MAGNIEUX, ——. *Paris.* 1787-9.
MAGNIN—
J. S. *London.* ca.1760. Watch, Debaufre escapement, S.M.S.K.
Jacque Etienne. *Copenhagen.* 1800. Refused permission to start a factory for chron. and clocks in Copenhagen. Joined JÜRGENSEN in 1801.
——. *Geneva.* ca.1800. Associated with DEMOLE.
MAGNUS—
Moses. *London.* 1802-08.
Edward James. *London.* 1820.
MAGRATH, ——. *London.* Early 19c. Watch.
MAGSON—
John. *London.* a.1697, CC.1704-16. Watch mt. G.M. l.c. clock. In firm of MAGSON & WELLER.
& WELLER. *London.* an.1716. Watch.
MAHOY, Daniel. prob. *London.* an.1806. Watch.
MAHVE, Matthew. *Philadelphia.* 1761. Watch finisher from *London.*
MAIDSTONE, N. *London.* an.1784. Watch.
MAIERIS, Jacques. ——. Early 18c. al. watch Den. coll.
MAILAND, Henri. *Paris.* m.1764-89.
MAILES, Thomas. *London.* a.1738.
MAILLARD—
Jean Jacques. *Dole.* mar.1637.
——. *Paris.* a.1692.
——. *Paris.* 1733. Made two elaborate automata.
MAILLARDET—
Jean. *Fontaines.* 1662. Repaired clock at Corcelles.
Jacques Rodolphe. *Fontaines.* b.1743, d. 1828. C. Made watches for China.
Henri, bro. *Fontaines* and *London.* b.1745. 1768 in *Berlin* with Jean David. 1784-ca.1815 in *London,* where he managed the branch of JAQUET-DROZ & LESCHOT. Worked on his own account after the death of JAQUET-DROZ in 1791, and later with PHILIPSTRAL, with whom he exhibited a number of aut. Watches sd. 'Henri Maillardet, London,' and singing birds, for which he devised the single whistle with moving piston.
Jean David, bro. *Chaux-de-Fonds* and *Fontaines.* b.1748, d.1834. Famous clock-

MAILLARDET—*continued.*
maker and mechanician; made many remarkable automata. Also watches for China.
Jean Daniel, son of J. R. *Fontaines* and *London.* b.1768, d.1851.
Victor, son of J. D. *Fontaines* and *London.* b.1775. *London* in 1792.
Julien Auguste, bro. *Chaux-de-Fonds* and *Fontaines.* b.1779, d.1852. Very clever clockmaker and mechanician.
——. *Val de Ruz* (*Neuchâtel*). Early 19c. Watch.
——. *Geneva.* Early 19c. Four-colour g. watch M.M.A.
PÈRE ET FILS. *Fontaines.* Firm of Jean David and J. Auguste. Two 'Magician' aut. clocks M. d'Horlogerie, Chaux-de-Fonds.
Henri Louis, son of J. D. *Chaux-de-Fonds.* b.1790, d.1842. Several clocks.
MAILLARD-SALINS, ——. *Hérimoncourt.* ca.1820. Started factory for watch pinions.
MAILLEFAUD, Featherston John. *London.* a.1734.
MAILLEFER, ——. *Paris.* 1825.
MAILLET, ——. *Morbier.* Early 18c. Devised a modified verge esc.
MAILLETT, Henry. *London.* 1790. C.
MAILLOT—
François. *Paris.* m.1750.
Jean George. *Chaux-de-Fonds.* 1784.
MAINADIE, Estienne. *Magdeburg.* Early 18c. Watch.
MAINCOURT—
——. *Paris.* ca.1380. Keeper of Henri de Vic's clock.
Jean de. *Paris.* 1439. Keeper of clock on the Palais de Justice. *Montargis.* 1451. Keeper of clock on Château.
MAINE, Francis. *London.* 1696.
MAINGOT—
Étienne. *Paris.* 1607 juré.
Jean. *Paris.* m.1606.
'MAINSPRING,' Caleb. ——. Pub. two arts. in Phil. Mag. 1829 and 1830 on the system of trying chrons. at Greenwich.
MAINWARING, Thomas. *London.* a.1686, CC.1694. Also MANWARING.
MAIR, Simon. *Neuburg.* Early 18c. Watch Feill coll. *v.* MAYR.
MAIRE—
——. *Nancy.* Mid. 18c. 'Horloger de la Reine.'
Abram Jean. *Chaux-de-Fonds.* 1784.
MAIRESSE, Nicolas Antoine. *Paris* m.1755.
MAIRET—
Jean Henri. *Ponts de Martel, Paris* and *London.* Left *Ponts de Martel* ca.1760. d.ca.1772. W. & C. and mechanician of repute.
Charles. *Chaux-de-Fonds.* 1760. Clock. Watch N.Y. Univ.
Sylvain. *v.* JEANMAIRET.
MAIRON, Jean Baptiste. *Paris.* 1695-1751. Table clock Damiano coll.
MAISTRE, ——. *Paris.* 1822.
MAITLAND, John. *Glasgow.* 1818.
MAJOR—
John. *London.* a.1637.
Nathaniel. *London.* a.1686.
MAJOT, LES. *Neuchâtel.* 1664-1723. Keepers of the Neuchâtel clocks.
MALACRIDA, ——. *Berne.* ca.1680. g. watch Ilbert coll.
MALCHAIRE, Joh. Corn. *Cologne.* 1797.
MALE, Thomas. *London.* a.1805.
MALET, Jean. *Paris.* 1764-90. Clock. en. str. watch.
MALIGNON, ——. *Geneva.* Early 19c. g. en. watch Fränkel coll.

MALLET—
Michel. *Périgueux*. 1476. 'Reloggier.'
Pierre. *Amsterdam*. 1686. Huguenot refugee from *Dieppe*.
François. *Rouen*. a.1694.
Peter. ——. an.1727. Watch.
Pierre Henry. *Paris*. m.1757-89.
Louis. *Paris*. End 18c.-1824. C. to duc d'Orléans. g. en. watches Lincoln M. and M.P.S. Dresden. g. en. watch set pearls and stones Feill coll.
J. *Paris*. ca.1790. Ormolu clock.

MALLETT—
Stephen. *London*. a.1689.
Peter. *Barnstaple*. 1705. l.c. clock.
John. *London* (*Clerkenwell*). 1764. Carries on the business of his late partner George SANDERSON.
John. *Barnstaple*. 1840.

MALLEY, John. *Lancaster*. 1800-23.
MALLINGER, ——. *Berlin*. 1792.
MALLINGLEY, Robert. *London*. 1790.
MALLOCH, David. *Kingston, Jamaica*. Early 19c.
MALLORY, Daniel. *London*. a.1729.

MALLOT—
Samuel. *Blois*. 1633-40.
Samuel. *Paris*. 1675 m.
Samuel, son of Samuel of Blois, prob. the same as Samuel of Paris. *Blois*. 1689.

MALLOWES, John. *London*. a.1697.
MALM, Petter. *Stockholm*. b.1744, m.1766, d.1796. br. clock Nord. M. Two watches.
MALMGREN, Lars. *Copenhagen*. m.1816.
MALMSTRÖM, ——. *Stora Malm*. 18c. l.c. clock.
MALSON, John. *London*. a.1707.
MALTBY, Henry. *York*. 1812. W.
MALTET, Jean. *Montbéliard*. 1568.
MALVEZIN, Girard. *Avignon*. 1518. Repaired clock on the Augustins.
MÄLZEL, Leonhard. *Munich* and *Vienna*. b.1776, d.1855. Invented the metronome. Mechanician to the Austrian Court. Made a talking head and a trombone-playing aut.
MAMMELL, ——. *London*. an.1762. Watch.
MANASIERE, ——. *London*. 1774-82.
MANCEAU (MANOREAU), Jean. *Lyons*. a.1591-1606. *Paris*, 1606-07. d.1629 at *Lyons*. C. to the Queen.
MANCHENER, William. *London*. a.1744.

MANCHESTER—
John. *London*. a.1691, CC.1700-16.
Richard. *London*. d.1749. W.
Richard, son. *London*. a.1749.

MANCOR, ——. *Bolton*. Early 19c.
MANCOT, Claude. *Poligny*. 1558.
MANDELBERG, Petter. *Lilla Malma*. 1781. Two l.c. clocks.

MANDER—
Richard. *London*. a.1708-49.
John Henry. *London*. a.1765.

MANDERN, *v.* VON MANDERN.
MANDEVILLE, J. prob. *London*. an.1769. Watch.
MANDEY, Ven. *London*. 1698-1709. Pub. 'Mechanic Powers,' treating of clocks. First pub. by MANDEY and J. MOXON.
MANELLI, Ludovico. *Bologna*. ca.1680. Night-light wandering hour-figure, br. clock.
MANFER, T. *London*. an.1791. Watch.
MANFIELD, John. *v.* MANSFIELD.
MANFREDI, Bartolommeo. *Mantova*. 1478. Astronomer. Made town clock.
MANGAAR, John Adam. *London*. a.1763-99. Dissolved partnership with KENTISH & ALLMAN in 1772. T.C.

MANGAN—
William. *London*. 1805-08.
James. *Cork*. 1824.

MANGEANT, ——. *Paris*. 1772.
MANGER, Adam. *Würzburg*. m.1807. From *Marktsteinach*. C.
MANGIE, Edward. *York*. 1659. W.
MANGIN, Thomas. *London*. Mid. 18c. Watch, Turkish figures.
MANGMEISTER, Vitus. *Augsburg*. 1753. m.1756. In 1770 went to *Nürnberg*.
MANGUILLITON, Jean. *Lyons*. 1494.

MANIÈRE—
——. *Lavaur*. 1678. Repaired clock on St. Alain.
Jean Pierre. *Paris*. m.1765.
Charles Guillaume. *Paris*. m.1778-1810. Also bronze worker. Clock Windsor Castle ill. Britten. Lyre and mantel clock, Pal. de Fontainebleau. Clock with turning rings on globe, Mobilier Nat. Paris.

MANIGOT, Pierre. *Paris*. 1600. Sig. to Statuts of Paris corporation.
MANION, James. *Tuam*. 1824.
MANKIN, George. prob. *London*. an.1761. Watch.

MANLEY (MANLY)—
Daniel. *London*. a.1650, CC.1660. l.c. clock Virginia M.
John. *Bury St. Edmunds*. an.1697. Watch.
H. *London*. 1695-1730. Celebrated maker of repoussé watch-cases—examples S.K.M., G.M. and B.M.
Cornelius. *Norwich*. ca.1700. l.c. lacquer clock.
John. *Chatham*. an.1782-ca.1790 CC. Watch.
Edward. *London*. Early 19c. Watch.

MANLOVE—
Richard. *London*. a.1728.
Richard. *London*. a.1732.

MANN—
Joseph. *London*. a.1687.
Edward. *London*. an.1722. Watch.
Percival. *London* (*Lincolns Inn Fields*). 1754-1790. Devised a small 8-day watch.
Thomas. *London*. an.1768. Watch.
Francis. *London*. a.1756, CC.1768.
Thomas. *Coventry*. ca.1775.
Edward. *Coventry*. 1787. Enters into partnership with WALL.
& WALL. *Coventry*. From 1787. C. & W.
Jean Geoffrey. *Strasbourg*. 1789.
James. *London*. Late 18c. Watch Ilbert coll.
Robert. *Norwich*. 1795. l.c. clock.
James. *Norwich*. d.1821. Succeeded by Wm. MITCHELL.
Robert. *Reading*. To 1817.

MANNER, John. *Exeter*. ca.1780.

MANNERS—
Thomas. *London*. a.1784.
James. *Berwick-on-Tweed*. 1820.
Robert. *London*. Early 19c. Watch London M.

MANNEVILLE, ——. *Paris*. 1810-13.
MANNHARDT, Johann. *Miesbach*. b.1798, went *Munich* 1827, d.1878. A fine turret C. Invented new str. work, a pin escapement, and a partially free pendulum. Made many clocks.

MANNING—
Charles. *London*. a.1720.
J. *London*. an.1741. Watch.
William. *London*. an.1745. Watch.
Thomas. prob. *London*. an.1776. Watch.
William. *London*. a.1784.
——. *Chichester*. 1800. W.

MANNINTON, Samuel. *London*. 2nd half 18c. Watch Horstmann coll.

MANSELL—
Edward. *London*. CC.1769.
William. *London*. a.1790, CC.1800-13.
William. *London*. a.1816.

MANSER—
William. *London (Islington)*. 1795. W.
John, son. *London*. a.1795.
& ASHLEY. *London*. 1820. Escapement makers.
MANSFIELD—
William. *London*. a.1699.
Joseph. *London*. a.1709.
Charles. *London*. a.1734. Watch.
John. *London*. ca.1760. Watch. l.c. clock.
Thomas. *London*. a.1787.
William. *London*. a.1791, CC.1800-05.
MANSIR, Robert. *London*. a.1808.
MANSON, David. *Dundee*. 1806.
MANSUY—
——. *Paris*. ca.1760 m.
Jean Louis, son. *Paris*. m.1770.
MANTON—
Samuel. *London*. an.1761. Watch.
Joseph. *London*. 1807. Devised a vacuum case for timepieces.
MANTS, ——. *London*. 2nd half 18c. Watch.
MANUFACTURE ROYALE DE FERNEY. *Ferney*. 1770. Managed by DUFOUR ET CERET. Watch mt. Ilbert coll.
MAPLE, Joseph. *London*. a.1765.
MAPPLE, Henry. ——. Pub. two arts. in Trans. Soc. Arts, 1838 and 1839 on clock springs and an esc.
MAR, Andrea. *Germany*. 1589. Dial Old Ashmolean M.
MARA—
Francis. *London*. a.1756, CC.1768-76. W.
William, son. *London*. a.1780.
MARANDET, François Ferdinand. *Morbier*. 1770.
MARBOTIN, Isaac. *London*. an.1752. Watch.
MARC, Henry. *Paris*. ca.1800. Clock in porcelain case Virginia M.
MARCEAUX, Jean Charles. *Paris*. m.1761.
MARCELL, ——. *Stockholm*. 1767-70.
MARCH, William. *London*. an.1705. Watch. l.c. clock.
MARCHAIX, ——. *Paris*. 1823.
MARCHAND—
F. *Geneva*. ca.1687. Watch en. by Huaud l'aisné.
Amedée. *Geneva*. mar.ca.1695-1726. Watches Horstmann and Gélis colls. and Geneva M. Clock.
David. *Sonvilier*. d.1761.
Charles Frédéric. *Paris*. m.1777.
FILS. *Paris*. Late 18c. Watch, tortoise-shell case, G.M. g. en. watch.
Frédéric Auguste. *Convers*. ca.1800. Went to *Renan* in 1810.
——. *Paris*. 1816-25. g. rep. watch.
MARCHANT—
Richard. *London*. a.1664.
Samuel. *London*. a.1670, CC.1677.
Samuel. *London*. CC.1689, w.CC.1704. l.c. clocks.
Samuel. *London*. a.1692, CC.1700.
John. *London*. a.1729.
Peter. *London*. 1742. W.
Andrew. *London (Gerrard St.)*. an.1762. rep. watch Den. coll.
MARCHE, ——. *Rouen*. ca.1730. Watch. B.M.
MARCHET—
Daniel. *London*. a.1748.
Joseph. *London*. a.1754.
MARCHINVILLE—
Morin. prob. *Paris*. ca.1685-ca.1725. Watch en. LES FRÈRES HUAUD. p.c. str. watch G.M. Watch Ilbert coll.
FRÈRES. *Geneva*. ca.1750. g. en. watch. sil. rep. watch.
MARCKLIN, ——. *Stockholm*. 18c. Wall clock.
MARCON, ——. *Paris*. 1812.
MARCOU, M. *Amsterdam*. ca.1700. p.c. repoussé watch. Watch with sun and moon dial G.M.
MARDER, Joseph. *London*. a.1759, CC.1767. Watch.
MARE—
Peter. *London*. 1544. French. Worked on clock for Norwich.
Claude François. *Rouen*. 1701.
Michel. *Paris*. Juré 1736.
Charles. *Paris*. m.1777.
MARECHAL, Don Pedro. *Madrid*. 1767. Pub. book on horology in Spanish.
MARÉCHAL—
Henri. *Blois*. mar.1661-7.
J. E. *Comanster*. 18c. l.c. clock.
——. *Paris*. 1825.
MARELIUS, Nils. *Stockholm*. b.1707, d. 1791.
MARESCHAL—
Jacques. *Lyons*. mar.1654, d.1679.
Hugues. *Lyons*. b.1636-1707.
MARET, Jean. *Blois*. m.1618-26.
MARFIELD, William. ——. ca.1750. Watch.
MARGAS, Jacob. *London*. an.1718. Watch.
MARGETTS—
George. *London (Cheapside)*. CC.1779, l.CC. 1799-1808. A famous maker of complex astro. watches—examples B.M. ill. Baillie, G.M., Schloss M. Berlin and Stern. coll. Fine mus. aut. watch F.W.M. mus. watch Carnegie M. Marine chron. G. M. chron. with helical spring and lever watch Den. coll.
& HATTON. *London*. 1805-11. Marine chron.
George. *London (Hatton Gdn.)*. 1805-08.
MARGOLLIER (MARGOILLET), Jacques. *Lyons*. 1658-61.
MARGOTIN—
Clément. *Blois*. 1634-76. Oval eng. watch with compass and dial M.P.S. Dresden.
Pierre. *Paris*. Juré 1681. Watch Glasgow Art Gall. Clock.
Michel, son of Clément. *Blois*. m.1684.
MARGRAM, John. *London*. a.1787.
MARGUAN, Jean. *Paris*. 1675 m.
MARGUERAT—
Jean François. *Luthy (Vevey)*. m.1785-98.
A. *Geneva*. 1837. Pub. 'Guide des Horlogers.'
MARGUERITE, ——. *Paris*. Late 18c. Watch mt. S.K.M.
MARGUERITTE, Mathurin. *Paris*. 1675 m.
MARIE—
Philippe. *Blainville*. 1521-6. Worked on clock of St. Maclou, Rouen.
Nicolas. *Paris*. 1679 m.
Charles François. *Paris*. m.1759-89. Elected master without essay on the ground of his having married one of the 100 orphan girls of the Hôpital de la Miséricorde.
David. *London (St. Martin's La.)*. 1762. Patented a watch calibre.
John. *London (New Bond St.)*. 1771. Bankrupt.
Jean. *Paris*. 1771-7 comp.
Nicolas. *Paris*. m.1777-89.
MARIN, le Sucreur. *Lyons*. 1545.
MARION—
Philippe. *Nevers*. 1490. 'Faiseur d'Arreloge.
Antoine Auguste. *Paris*. m.1776.
——. *Paris (Rue St. Denis)*. 1812.
MARIT, Joseph. *Metz*. 1547. Repaired cathedral clock.
MARITON, Robert. *London*. a.1733.
MARK—
John. *London*. CC.1667-74. math. inst. maker.
& Co. *Peterborough*. Early 19c. Watch.

MARKHAM—
James. *London.* 1697. Watch B.M. and mt. G.M.
Robert. *London.* ca.1725-80. Son-in-law of, and partner with, James (2) MARKWICK, and succeeded him in 1730. Used the trade name MARKWICK-MARKHAM (q.v.), but traded also under his own name, and also with that of Fras. PERIGAL. Watch sd. 'Robert Markham. Fras. Perigal' Ilbert coll. br. clock. g. watch Den. coll.
John. *London.* 1769. Watch M.M.A. made for Holland. Watch Den. coll. p.c. g. and onyx watch set stones Stern. coll.
C. *London.* an.1774. Watch.
MARKLAND, William. *Liverpool.* 1796. W.
MARKS—
Isaac. *Chippenham.* 1730, retired 1790.
John. prob. *London.* an.1776. Watch.
Michael. *Cardiff.* 1822.
Solomon. *Cardiff.* 1822-75.
Lewis. *London.* ca.1825. Watch.
MARKUS, Gerrit. *Amsterdam.* Early 19c. l.c. clock.
MARKWICK—
James (1). *London.* a.1656, CC.1666-98. sil. p.c. watch with min. hand and turning hour circle S.K.M. Watches Den. and Buckley colls. br. clock Weth. coll. l.c. clock. sil. watch Nat. M. Stockholm. Also MARQUET.
James (2), son. *London.* CC.1692, m.CC. 1720, d.1730. An eminent maker. Partner with Robert MARKHAM, and succeeded by him. Watches B.M. and M.P.S. Dresden. str. watches G.M. and Den. coll. l.c. clock.
MARKHAM. *London.* ca.1725-ca.1805. See preceding. Specialized in clocks and watches for Turkey. Lacquer l.c. clock ill. Cec. and Web. Watches in S.K.M., G.M., M.M.A., K.H.M. and Fränkel coll. Watches are found with this name and that of another maker added, e.g. 'Markwick Markham, Perigal' in B.M., G.M., M.M.A., Feill and Fränkel colls.; 'Markwick Markham, Story' and 'Markwick Markham, Borrell' in London M.; 'Markwick Markham, Roger' Den. coll. Markwick Markham Recordon, g. en. str. watch. Watches with the name Story are known to 1780, with Borrell to 1813 and with Perigal to 1825.
MARKWITH, James. *London.* 1699 CC. Perhaps MARKWICK.
MARLEY, David. *London.* an.1773. Watch.
MARLIER, ——. *Paris.* 1812-24.
MARLOW—
Joseph. *London.* a.1728.
——. *Cranbrook.* 2nd half 18c. Watch mt.
MARMOCHIUS, Carolus. *Florence.* an.1500. Keeper of clock in Piazza dei Signori up to 1500.
MAROT, Daniel. *Paris.* b.1660. *Holland* 1685. Celebrated designer. Became architect to William of Orange. Many designs for clock-cases and watch-cocks in a book by him pub. Amsterdam, 1712.
MAROTTE, ——. *Paris.* 1807-11.
MARQTIN, ——. *Paris.* 1646. Sig. to Statuts of Paris corporation.
MARQUARD, ——. *Brunswick.* 1386-1409. Made two clocks for Brunswick and one for Dorstadt.
MARQUART—
Benedikt. *Augsburg.* Mid. 16c.
Jacob, son. *Augsburg.* Late 16c.
Baltzer. *Berlin.* 1577.
Johann. *Augsburg.* Early 18c. Turret C.
Antony. *Prague.* 2nd half 18c. Watch mt. Arts M. Prague.
MARQUIS—
Thomas. *Paris.* 1675 m.
—— *Paris.* Late 18c. Clock.
MARR—
William. *London* (*Moorfields* and *Bishopsgate St.*). a.1752, CC.1769-75.
James. *London.* a.1785-99.
Jonathan. *Retford.* 1795.
MARRINOW, Baltazar. *Paris.* 2nd half 17c. Watch.
MARRIOTT—
John. *London.* a.1641.
John. *London.* a.1690, CC.1715.
Erasmus. *London.* a.1696.
——. *Oundle.* d.1788. W.
John. *London* (*Fetter La.*). CC.1768, l.CC. 1776, m.CC.1799, d.1824. mus. C. mus. br. clock Weth. coll. Elaborate en. mus. clock Palace M. Pekin.
T. *Edinburgh.* ca.1770. Watch.
William. *London.* a.1769.
John Thomas. *London.* a.1787.
& SON. *London.* Late 18c. Watch mt. G.M.
——. *Cambridge.* Early 19c.
W. & J. *London* (*Fenchurch St.*). ca.1825. Watch.
MARRIS, Charles. *Hull.* Early 19c. Watch.
MARROW, Richard. *Liverpool.* d.(?)1796. W.
MARRYATT, ——. *London* (*Hammersmith*). an.1775. Watch.
MARS, ——. *London* (*Bishopsgate*). 1773. W.
MARSCHALL, Felix. *Hamburg.* 1801.
MARSDEN—
John. *London* (*St. John's Sq.*). CC.1698, m.CC.1731-41. W. Specialized in rep. work.
John. *London.* a.1806.
Samuel. *London.* 1820.
MARSÉ, Claude. *Paris.* m.1738.
MARSEILLES, M. *Tours.* ca.1640. sil. eng. al. watch Mallett coll.
MARSH—
Ricardus. *Ipswich.* 17c. Watch Liverpool M.
John. *London.* a.1676. Watch Stads M. Amsterdam.
Jonathan. *London.* a.1691, CC.1698. l.c. clock. Also MARCH.
Ono. *Highworth.* d.1733. Business carried on by his widow Jane.
Anthony. *London* (*Threadneedle St.*). a. 1714, CC.1724, d.1775.
William. *London.* a.1725. Watch.
Samuel. *Liverpool.* 1754. W.
Edmund. *London.* 1756. Watches Den. coll. and Stads M. Amsterdam.
Samuel. *London* (*Ratcliffe Cross, Stepney* and *Limehouse*). a.1761, CC.1770-1820. Partner with John DECKA. Rack lever watch Ilbert coll.
John. *Shrewsbury.* an.1773. Watch.
Esau. *London.* an.1777. Watch.
John. *Eastry.* d.1788. C. & W.
Thomas, son of Anthony. *London.* a.1770-1811. Watch with his escapement S.M.S.K., patented in 1811.
William. *London.* a.1773, CC.1787-91.
Robert John. *London* (*Bunhill Row*). a.1785, CC.1795-1810. Watch engraver.
Thomas. *London.* a.1789.
Samuel. *London.* a.1791, CC.1804.
William. *London* (*Nicholas La.*). l.CC.1811. l.c. clock.
Joseph, son of Samuel (1). *London.* a.1804, CC.1814.
Joseph John Edward, son of Rob. John. *London.* a.1808.
MARSHALL—
Benjamin. *London.* a.1672, CC.1680-1732.
Matthew. *London.* a.1677, CC.1689.
John. *London.* a.1682, CC.1689-1716. l.c. clock Weth. coll. Inventor of the 'Magic night watch.'
Samuel. *London.* a.1682, CC.1689-1718.
Christopher. *Halifax.* 1694-1716.
Thomas. *London.* an.1708. Watch.

MARSHALL—*continued.*
——. *Dublin.* Early 18c. Red tortoise-shell br. clock.
Samuel. *London.* CC.1718, d.1750.
William, son. *London.* a.1719, CC.1733-40.
William. *Newark.* 1730-70. l.c. clocks.
John. *Newark.* ca.1730. l.c. clocks.
George. *London.* a.1723, CC.1733-78.
Joseph. *London.* a.1725.
Jonathan. *London.* a.1725.
Mary. *London.* 1736. d.1742.
George. *London.* d.1779.
Richard. *Wolsingham.* 1745. d.1796. l.c. clocks.
Joseph. *Leicester.* 1751. C. & W.
William. *Leicester.* an.1766. Watch.
Francis. *Durham.* ca.1770-95.
John. *London.* a.1769, CC.1777.
Thomas. *London.* an.1785. Watch.
Thomas. *Lincoln.* 1791-5. W.
John. *Leicester.* 1794. W.
John. *Newcastle-o.-T.* From 1813-20.
James. *Wishaw.* 1815-53.
James, & WALLER. *Edinburgh.* 1816.
Francis, & Sons. *Edinburgh.* 1816.
William. *London* (*Gt. Portland St.* and *Percival St.*). 1817-25. Watch.
W. W. *London* (*New Cavendish St.*). 1820.
Charles Potkin. *London.* a.1818.

MARSTON—
Robert. *London.* a.1649.
William. *London.* a.1659, CC.1669-85.
——. *Shrewsbury.* 1761-91. C. l.c. clock.
William. *Bishops Castle.* 1781. Insolvent. C. & W.

MARTEAU—
Joseph, sen. ——. 1721. g. en. watch Bernal sale.
Étienne. *Rouen.* 1726.
Père. *Rouen.* 1st half 18c. g. en. watch Gélis coll.

MARTEMANN, ——. *Paris.* 1807.

MARTENET, Josué. *Neuchâtel.* 1646. C. to the town from 1646.

MARTI, ——. *Berne.* 1565. C. to the town. Made clock for Burgdorf.

MARTIN—
Marx. *Frankfurt-a.-M.* 1642.
Johann, son. *Augsburg.* b.1642, d.1720. al. watch Den. coll. astro. clock Nat. M. Munich. Several sundials.
Edward. *London.* a.1662. Watch.
John. *London.* a.1672, CC.1679-1701. al. watch S.K.S.M. br. clocks S.K.M. and Weth. coll.
Thomas. *Wigan.* ca.1680, d.1716. One-hand watch mt. with outer circle divided into 144 Ilbert coll.
Abraham. *London.* CC.1682-9. Engraver.
Jeremiah. *London.* a.1680, CC.1687-1704. Watches G.M. and S.M.S.K.
William. *London.* a.1682.
Francis. *London.* a.1683.
John. *London.* a.1684.
Thomas. *London.* a.1685.
Pierre. prob. *France.* ca.1695. Watch with en. painting sd. 'André Père et Fils' Ilbert coll.
William. *London.* a.1685, CC.1702. l.c. clock.
William. *Bristol.* 1703-39. Watch Liverpool M. C.
Thomas. *London* (*Royal Exchange*). a.1692, CC.1699-1714. br. clock Weth. coll. l.c. clock.
William. *London.* a.1698, CC.1709.
William. *London.* a.1699, CC.1710.
John. *London.* a.1705, CC.1714.
John. *Bristol.* 1722-34. W.
William. *London.* a.1716.
Benjamin. *London* (*Fleet St.*). b.1704, d. 1782. Made globes, planetariums and a clock invented by him. Pub. 'Institutiones horologicae, or a Physico-mathematical theory of clockwork,' in 1764, and other works.
Robert. *Paris.* b.1706, d.1765. Varnisher to the King in 1733. Invented 'Vernis Martin.'
William. *Compton Dando.* 1722. W.
B. *Paris.* 1738-63.
William. *Glasgow.* 1739.
Johann. *Fürth.* d.1773.
Robert. *Perth,* 1745. *Glasgow,* 1764.
Jean. *Paris.* m.1746.
Edmund. *Puddletown.* 1750. C.
William. *London.* a.1744, CC.1751.
George. *Birmingham.* 1756. From *London.* W. l.c. clocks.
Thomas. *London.* a.1750.
John. *Coventry.* a.1751.
Charles. *Paris.* m.1758.
Edmund. *London* (*Cheapside*). 1760-95. A good maker. l.c. mus. and aut. clock Webster coll. l.c. mus. clock Virginia M. Also W.
John. *Spalding.* 1763-ca.1775. Pub. 'Mechanicus and Flaven,' a sententious dialogue on religion and clocks.
Thomas. *Baltimore, U.S.A.* 1764. From *Philadelphia.* W.
David. prob. *London.* an.1770. Watch.
Michael. *London.* an.1773. Watch.
——. *Liverpool.* ca.1770.
Thomas. *London* (*Cornhill* and *R.Exchange*). CC.1771, l.CC.1780-94, d.1811. Pocket chron. and watches G.M. Clock Peiping M.
Edward. *London.* an.1775. Watch.
& BATH. prob. *London.* an.1775. Watch.
Pierre. *Paris.* m.1773. Clock Bernal sale.
Vincent. *Brest.* ca.1775. C. to the King and to the Marine. a. to Ferd. Berthoud. Fine regulator clock.
John. *London.* a.1767.
Augustin. *Chaux-de-Fonds.* 1779.
Thomas. *Dublin.* 1780-95. W.
Young. *Dublin.* 1780-95. W.
Robert. *Glasgow* and *Grahamston.* 1782-99.
Jonathan. *Durham.* an.1786. Watch.
Dunsford. *Ashburton.* 1787.
Louis Desfontaines. *Paris.* m.1788.
Antoine Thomas. *Paris.* m.1788.
Jean. *Paris.* b.1773. Worked for P. L. BERTHOUD for nine years. Had his own business from ca.1802.
Edmund, son of Edmund. *London.* a.1788, CC.1795.
& JORDAN. *London.* 1795. Submitted design for a complex astro. marine timepiece to Board of Longitude.
William. *Liverpool.* 1795-1829. W.
——. *Beaumont-le-Roger.* 1796-1826. Made new clock for St. Nicolas church.
Bilcliffe. *London.* a.1790.
Joseph. *Kippen.* 1798.
George. *London* (*Westminster*). 1802-04.
Jeremiah. *London.* 1802-04.
William. *London* (*Westminster*). 1802-40.
Samuel. *New York.* 1805.
William. *Manchester.* 1808-13. W.
——. *Paris.* 1810-3.
William. *Darlington.* 1812. W.
Thomas. ——. 1813. Pub. in London 'The circle of the Mechanical Arts,' with chapter on Watch and Clock making.
A. *Brighton.* Early 19c. Watch.
——. *Maidstone.* Early 19c. Watch.
James. *London* (*Piccadilly*). 1815.
James. *London.* a.1814, CC.1833.
Edward Horatio. *London.* a.1821.
——. *Quebec.* Early 19c.

MARTINA, ——. *Prague.* Early 19c. Devised a ¼ rep. mechanism.

MARTINEAU—
Joseph, sen. *London* (*Orange St.* and later *St. Martin's Ct.*). 1744-94. rep. watches M.M.A. and M.P.S. Dresden. Watches Ilbert and Chamb. colls.
James. *London.* an.1767. Watch.
Joseph, and Son. *London.* 1784. g. en. watch, set opals and diamonds, Carnegie M.
MARTINELLI, Domenico. *Spoleto* and *Rome.* b.1650, d.1718. Architect and painter. Pub. 'Horologi Elementari,' Venice, 1669, 1680 and 1696.
MARTINET—
James. *London.* 1700. cal. clock C.A. & M.
Hubert. *Paris.* 1780.
MARTINOT (MARTINEAU)—
——. ——. 1564. 'Aorlogeur.' Perhaps the following.
Gilbert. *Paris.* 1572-80. C. to Charles IX, Henry III and the City of Paris. sq. table clock Gélis coll.
Denis, son. *Paris.* 1581-1631. Succeeded his father in 1581 as C. to the City of Paris. C. to the King and Valet de Chambre. Kept the 'gros orloge du Palays.' Two Martinots sd. Statuts of Paris corporation in 1600. Oval sil. watch, sundial in cover, Louvre. oct. watch Mallett coll. Table clock, oval gilt watch, Webster coll. Oval watch Marfels coll.
——. *Paris.* m.1603. Prob. Barnaby or Zacharie.
Barnaby. *London.* 1618-62. Born in *Paris.*
Zacharie. *Paris.* 1637-1659. C. to Louis XIII and XIV.
Balthazar. *Paris.* 1637-95. Juré in 1678. C. to Louis XIV. One of the principal Paris makers. A very beautiful sq. watch, with g. ornament on blued steel, Louvre ill. Baillie. Large watch Cluny M. sq. watch, steel, sil. and g., Olivier coll. Boulle br. clock S.K.M. Fine Boulle clock Pal. de Pau, Paris.
Gilles, bro. *Paris.* 1640-72. C. to Louis XIV. Watch B.M., with min. circle divided into 144. Large watches Louvre and Chamb. coll. Fine Boulle br. clock Pal. de Pau, Paris.
Balthazar. *Rouen.* Juré 1649.
Balthazar. *Rouen.* m.1649. Juré 1659. Prob. same as Balthazar of Paris.
Jean. *Paris.* 1659. d.1669. C. to Louis XIV.
Louis Henry, son of Gilles. *Paris.* b.1646, d.1725. Succeeded his father in 1669 as C. to Louis XIV. Made several complex astro. clocks. Prob. author of 'La sphère mobile présentée au Roi par Martinot et Haye,' Paris, 1701.
Jean Henri, son. *Paris.* 1679-1708. d.an. 1712. C. to Louis XIV. Complex br. clock Virginia M.
B. *Rouen.* ca.1680. Watch B.M. sil. str. watch Blot-Garnier coll.
M. *Avignon.* End 17c.-1709. Watch G.M. Tried unsuccessfully to repair the town clock.
Zacharie. *Paris.* m.1692.
Jérôme, son of Jean. *Paris.* 1697-1732. d.an. 1749. C. to Louis XIV. Thiout describes a very complex astro. clock by him.
Claude, son of Louis Henry. *Paris.* 1707-32. d.an.1749. C. to Louis XV.
Jacques, son of Louis Henry. *Paris.* 1718-32. C. to Louis XV.
Jean, son of Jérôme. *Paris.* 1727-49. C. to Louis XV.
Jérôme. *Paris.* 1740-60. Bronze and ormolu elephant clock, with case by CAFFIERI, S.K.M.
Honoré. *Paris.* m.1747.
Ludwig. *Berlin.* 1786.
August. *Berlin.* 1786.

MARTINS, ——. *Cheltenham* and *Bath.* Early 19c. T.C.
MARTMOTT, William. *London.* 1622. Alien. Perhaps MARTINOT.
MARTOREL, Pierre. *Lyons.* 1642 m.
MARTORELLI, Luigi. *Rome.* 1812. Pub. 'Dissertazione sull'orologio.'
MARTY, Benedict. *Le Locle.* 1779.
MARTYN—
Richard. *Northampton.* ca.1700. Lantern clock.
——. *Falmouth.* Early 19c.
'MARTYN SQUARE.' Sig. on watches of the AMERICAN WATCH CO. from 1882.
MARUM, John. *London.* an.1783. Watch.
MARX—
Johan Tilman. *Cologne.* 1723-30. W.
Philipp. *Cologne.* 1797-1813.
MARZOLFF, ——. *Strasbourg.* 1797.
MASCARONE, Gio. Batt. *Milan.* Early 17c. Padlock-shaped crys. watch Bernal sale, ill. Britten. eng. cross watch M.P.S. Dresden.
MASCON, Jean. *Arbois.* 1433-52. Repaired Poligny clock.
MASEL, Rémy. *Blois.* 1524.
MASEY, Thomas. *Oxford.* 1550. Repaired clock on St. Mary's Church.
MASIG, P. *Germany.* ca.1730. Sundial.
MASK, Joseph. *Holt.* 1784. W. cf. MACK.
MASKELYNE, Rev. Nevil, F.R.S. *London.* b.1732, d.1811. Astronomer Royal. Wrote several pamphlets in connection with the trials of Harrison's and Mudge's marine watches.
MASLAND, Henry. *Paris.* m.1764.
MASMEJAN, ——. *Lausanne.* Mid. 18c. Watch mt. Geneva M.
MASON—
Richard. *London.* BC.1615, CC.1632.
Henry. *London.* a.1647.
Robert. *London.* a.1658.
William. *London.* a.1680, CC.1688-1713.
Timothy. *Gainsborough.* ca.1700.
John. *London.* a.1696-1706 CC.
Samuel. *London.* a.1699.
John. *London.* a.1703.
Samuel. *London.* a.1704, CC.1712.
John. *London.* a.1705, CC.1712. Clock.
Henry. *London.* a.1708, CC.1715. cf. MAYSON.
John. *London.* a.1710, CC.1719-30. l.c. clocks.
John. *Doncaster.* 1720-40.
Henry. *London.* a.1713.
James. *London.* a.1715. Watch.
William. *London.* a.1716.
William. *London* (*Southwark*). a.1734-87.
Charles. *London.* an.1743. Watch.
William. *London* (*Rotherhithe*). 1750-74.
John. *Halifax.* ca.1750.
Robert. *London.* a.1749-90.
Thomas. *Bilston.* 1761. l.c. clock.
Richard. *London.* a.1752.
Thomas. *London.* a.1759-ca.1790. Watch.
——. *Bedford.* Mid. 18c. Watch.
——. *Bexley.* an.1762. Watch.
Charles. *London.* 1762-8. Pub. art. in Phil. Trans. 1762, on the going of Ellicott's clock.
Francis. *London.* an.1763-71. Watch.
William. *London* (*Dockhead*). 1763-87. W.
Samuel. *Bedford.* 1765. Watch.
William. *Prescot.* 1769. W.
Alexander. *Liverpool.* d.(?)1792. W.
Thomas. *Bawtrey.* ca.1770-93. l.c. clock.
Edward. *London.* an.1775. Watch.
Richard. *St. Albans.* an.1777-95 CC. Watch.
Timothy. *Chesterfield.* ca.1780-91. Watch mt. Buckley coll.
William. *Southwark.* 1781.
Hudson. *London.* 1784-8. W.
Richard. *St. Albans.* 1784. W.

MASON—*continued.*
Peter. *London.* 1787. W.
Peter, son. *London.* a.1787.
John. *Kington* (*Hereford*) and *Hereford.* 1794. Insolvent.
& JENKINS. *Rochester.* 1795.
John. *Kelso.* 1809.
Jonathan. *London.* a.1808.
——. *Colchester.* Early 19c. Watch.
C. *Canterbury.* Early 19c. Watch.
Robert. *Worksop.* Early 19c. Watch.
John. *London* (*Old St.*). 1820.
Samuel. *Philadelphia.* 1820-5.
John. *Rotherham.* 1825.
J. & E. *Worcester.* Early 19c. T.C. Watch.
'MASON.' Sig. on 1870-5 watches of the ILLINOIS SPRINGFIELD WATCH CO.

MASPOLI, MONTI & CO. *Sandwich.* Early 19c. Watch.

MASQUERIER—
Lewis. *London.* 1753-83. Watch.
& PERIGAL. *London* (*Coventry St.*). 1772-83. Partnership with Lewis, dissolved 1783.
William. *London* (*Sherrard St.*). 1778-95.

MASSE-DIT-LAROCHE, Jean Pierre. *Grenoble.* 1654. From *Blois.*

MASSEY—
Edmund. *London.* a.1674, CC.1682-90.
Benjamin. *London.* an.1744. Watch.
John. *London* (*Lambeth*). an.1776-1825. Watch. C.
Edward. *Newcastle-under-Lyme.* 1778-95. C. & W.
Henry. *Chester.* 1784. W.
Thomas. *London.* an.1785. Watch.
John. *Wenlock.* 1791. W.
Laurence. *Eccleshall.* 1795. C.
Edward. *Hanley.* 1804.
Edward. *London. Coventry* in 1814. b.1772, d.1852. A well-known maker. Invented the crank-roller lever escapement, and patented a pump-winding. Watch with his escapement Chamb. coll. Watch beating seconds Marryat coll. Watch with secs. hand turning once in 2½ secs. Ilbert coll. Pub. arts. in Trans. Soc. Arts, Vol. 21 and Phil. Mag. 1804 on clocks.
Francis. *Liverpool.* ca.1820.

MASSINGHAM—
J. *Fakenham.* ca.1770-91. br. and l.c. clock.
John. *Wells* (*Norfolk*). 1791. W.

MASSMANN, ——. *Berlin.* 1794.

MASSON—
P. Aimé. *London.* ca.1700. Watch.
Denis. *Paris.* m.1746. Ormolu mantel clock S.K.M.
——. *Paris.* 1767. Spring-maker.
Charles François. *Paris.* m.1784-9.

MASSOT—
Jacques Paul. *Geneva* and *Montbéliard.* 1765.
André. *Geneva* and *Montbéliard.* 1765.

MASSOTEAU, Sieur de St. Vincent. *Paris.* 1734. C. to the King. Pub. 'Instruction pour bien régler les montres.'

MASSY—
Nicholas. *Blois.* mar.1623. d. between 1646 and 1658. Maker of repute.
Nicholas, son. *Blois.* mar.1661-76. Went to *London* (*Cranbourn St.*) a few years later. CC.1682, d.1698. al. watch M.M.A. Small g. en. watch Mallett coll. ill. Baillie.
Henry, son. *London* (*Charles St.*). CC.1692-1745. Fine watch G.M. rep. watch S.M.S.K. Watch Den. coll. rep. watch Feill coll. ca.1720. l.c. and br. clocks ill. Cec. & Web.
Nicholas, bro. *London* (*Cranbourn St.*). CC.1693-1723. Watch mt. G.M. Watch Den. coll. Watch ill. Britten. Also C.
Jacob. *London* (*Cranbourn St.*). 1689. CC. 1715-25. br. clock.

MASSY—*continued.*
——. *Amsterdam.* 1722. Gained prize of Paris Acad. des Sciences for memoir on timekeeping at sea.

MASTER—
W. Henshaw. *London.* 1689 CC.
W. J. *London.* 1823. Watch.

MASTERMAN—
Richard. *London.* BC.1628. 'english forrin.'
J. *London.* 1770-95. Watch Feill coll.

MASTERS—
William. *London.* a.1672, CC.1701.
John. *Bristol.* 1707-39. W.
John. *Shepton Mallet.* 1722. W.
John. *London.* a.1783.
John. *Newfoundland.* Late 18c. Watch mt. Buckley coll.
Thomas. *Southampton.* 1795.
James. *London.* CC.1809, l.CC.1810-12.
Richard. *Bristol.* 1812-8. W.

MASTERSON—
Richard. *London.* 1630. CC.1633, m.CC. 1642, d.1653. Subscriber for incorporation of CC. Cockle-shell and another watch G.M. Watches M.M.A. and Ilbert coll.
John. *London.* a.1648-1703.

MASTON—
John. *Westminster.* 1662.
Thomas. *London.* an.1777. Watch.

MATCHAM & GILBERT. *Southampton.* 1790. Thos. M. & Wm. G. dissolved partnership.

MATCHETT—
John. *London* (*Bedford St.*). CC.1647, w.CC.1674-89. Watch en. in relief. Watch Ilbert coll.
George. *London.* a.1651.

MATHÉ, ——. *Paris* (*Quai de la Megisserie*). 1812. cf. MATHEY.

MATHER—
Samuel. *London.* CC.1691-1712.
Samuel. *Petersham.* Early 18c. Watch.
John. *London* (*Cold Bath Fields*). 1769.
William. *Nottingham.* 1818. C. & W.

MATHEWS (MATHEW, MATTHEW)—
Francis. *London.* a.1647, CC.1656.
William. *London.* a.1686-1720. **Bankrupt.**
Samuel. *London.* a.1694.
Thomas. *London.* a.1714.
Humphrey. *London.* a.1716. Watch.
Thomas. *Hadleigh.* d.1747. W.
William. *London* (*Fleet St.*). a.1723, CC. 1731, l.CC.1766, d. or retired 1776. Expert on Harrison's No. 4 timepiece. cyl. rep. mt. G.M.
David. *London.* a.1723.
John. *London.* a.1723, CC.1731. l.c. clock.
David. *London.* a.1728.
James. *London.* a.1735.
William. *London.* a.1736, CC.1744-68. *v.* Wm. below.
Samuel. *London.* a.1743.
Thomas. *Woodbridge.* 18c. l.c. clock.
Nathaniel. *London.* an.1760. Watch.
Henry. *Highworth.* an.1772-84.
——. *Dorchester.* 1772. W.
William. *Leighton Buzzard.* 1785.
William. *London.* ca.1795. Watch mt. Ilbert coll. Perhaps Wm. above.
Charles. *London.* a.1795-1815.
John. *Leighton Buzzard.* ca.1800. l.c. clock. Watch.
Daniel Dering. *London.* 1808. Patented an escapement.
James Andrew. *London.* a.1806.
Edward. *Welshpool.* 1820. W.
Edward. *Coleraine.* 1824.
William. *Penrith.* Early 19c. Succeeded the PORTHOUSES.
R. *Oswestry.* Early 19c. Watch.
'MATTHEW LAFLIN.' Sig. on 1868-75 watches of the NATIONAL WATCH CO. OF CHICAGO.

MATHEWSON (MATTHEWSON)—
John. *Anstruther.* 1755.
Andrew. *Kilconquhar.* 1795-1830.
William, bro. *Kilconquhar.* In 1830 went to *America.*

MATHEY—
l'aîné. *Moudon.* 1735.
Widow & Son. *London.* 1762. Shagreen case maker.
Simon. *Paris.* m.1789.
Pierre Frédéric. *Paris.* 1789.
Charles Lewis. *Paris.* 1824.

MATHIAS, John Baptist. *London.* an.1774. Watch.

MATHIESON—
Peter. *Copenhagen.* m.1724. Master of Corporation 1758. d.1769. l.c. clock ill. Liisberg.
Robert. *Edinburgh.* a.1738.
Christian, son of Peter. *Röskilde.* 1760. d.ca. 1773.
Henrik August. *Copenhagen.* 1770.
John. *Edinburgh.* a.1774.

MATHIEU—
Claude (Charles), l'aîné. *Paris.* m.1754-89.
Edme, le jeune. *Paris.* m.1769-89.
Léonard. *Geneva.* 2nd half 18c. g. rep. watch.
Veuve. *Paris.* 1807-13. Successor to Edme.
Alexandre. *Paris (Rue St. Honoré).* 1812.

MATHION, Oled Louis. *France.* b.1620, d. 1700. Franciscan and Benedictine monk. Pub. 1676, 'Nouvelle montre minutale. . . .'

MATHON, Pierre François. *Paris.* 1774.

MATHURIN—
Jean. *Lyons.* 1591.
Maurice Jacques. *Paris.* 1775.

MATIGNON, ——. *Paris.* 1812.

MATLACK—
White. *New York,* 1773-5. *Philadelphia,* 1777. C. & W.
White & William. *Philadelphia.* 1780.

MATSON, Richard. *London.* a.1649.

MATTHEY—
Isaac. *La Brévine.* 1670. Repaired clock at Môtiers.
Abram. *Le Locle.* 1711. Also MATEY-PIERRET.
Jean Jacques, son of Isaac. *La Brévine.* 1740-1767. Turret and house C. Several small clocks.
Frédéric. *Chaux-de-Fonds.* 1750. d.1767. C.
——. *Paris.* 18c. g. en. watches Lazarus coll. and Fränkel coll.
Louis. *Fontaines.* 1779 m. W.
& COMP. *London.* ca.1780. Two g. en. watches F.W.M. g. en. watch Feill coll.
Henri François, son of Abram. *La Brévine.* a.1774-86. C.
——. *Geneva.* 1793. Commissionaire over the Geneva watchmakers.
Félix. *Chaux-de-Fonds.* 1799. C.
& CIE. *Switzerland.* ca.1800. g. en. watch S.K.M.
Jacques Henri. *Chaux-de-Fonds.* 1804. C.
Jacques, fils. *La Brévine.* 1815-20. C.
Eugène. *Chaux-de-Fonds.* 1816-27. C. of repute.

MATTHEY-CLAUDET—
Moïse Élie. *La Brévine.* 1781. Several clocks.
——. *Chaux-de-Fonds.* End 18c. Devised an engine turning lathe.
Abram. *La Brévine.* 1796-1821. C.

MATTHEY-DORET, Abram. *La Brévine, Donaueschingen* and *Besançon.* a.1786-1819. C. Silver medal at Paris Exhibition of 1819.

MATTHEY-DUPRAT—
Isaac Henri. *Chaux-de-Fonds.* 1801. C.
David Henri. *La Brévine.* 1807-24. C.
David Henri, son. *La Brévine.* 1838-41. C. of repute.

MATTHEY-GUENET, Pierre. *La Brévine* ca.1700-40. Made clock for La Brévine.

MATTHEY-JOUAIS, Jacques. *La Brévine.* 1728-40. Clock dated 1728 in Chaux-de-Fonds M.

MATTINGLEY, Robert. *Reading.* From 1782. C. & W.

MATTOCKS—
John. *London.* a.1738, CC.1747.
John, son. *London.* CC.1784, l.CC.1787, d.1810.
William, son. *London.* a.1793.

MAUBAG, Paulus. *Utrecht.* 1676.

MAUBERT—
——. *Paris.* m.1606.
Peter. *London.* a.1679.

MAUCOMBRE, ——. *Paris.* 1812.

MAUCUY, Jean Louis. *Paris.* m.1770-1812.

MAUD—
Halstead. *London.* a.1767, CC.1786-94. Watch-cap and spring maker.
Edward. *Daventry.* 1791-5. W.

MAUDE—
Benjamin. *London.* an.1760, CC.1782, d. 1819. Watches London M. and Chamb. and Ilbert colls. Also MAUD.
Edward. *London.* 1784-95.
J. *London.* Succeeded Benjamin.
M. *London.* 1809-11.

MAUDSLEY—
Thomas. *London.* 1753. Watch.
George. *Wakefield.* 1770. Watch.
George. *Leeds.* To 1785.

MAUDUIT, Isaac. *London.* a.1717, CC.1724.

MAUGER, Gabriel. *Paris.* m.1757.

MAUGRAY, ——. *Vienna.* ca.1800. en. drum watch.

MAUL—
P. *London.* 2nd half 18c. Watch mt.
Thomas. prob. *London.* an.1796. Watch.

MAULL, James. *London.* a.1782.

MAUPAS—
Abel. *Blois.* 1621-30.
Daniel, bro. *Blois.* a.1615, comp. at *Lyons,* 1619. *Autun,* 1625. *Blois* to 1653.
Charles. *Blois.* 1644. d.1668.

MAUR, Jean. *Blois.* d.1630.

MAURER—
Johann. *Füssen.* ca.1660. Skull watch B.M. ill. Baillie.
Johan. *Prague.* ca.1735. Watch Ilbert coll.
J. *Berlin.* an.1780. Watch.

MAUREY, Pierre Denis. *Paris.* m.1742.

MAURHOF, Georg Friderich. *Hannover.* 18c. trav. clock shagreen case Feill coll.

MAURICE—
FRÈRES. *Geneva.* Mid. 18c. Watch.
John. *v.* MORRIS.
——. *Paris.* 1807-12.

MAURIN, Paul. *Rome.* ca.1660. Watch with steel dial, g. inlaid figures and steel inner case Ilbert coll.

MAURIS—
——. *London.* Early 18c. sil. eng. watch with en. on cock Feill coll., bears the sig. on the upper plate. Other watches bear it on the case. Prob. a case maker.
Henri. *Geneva.* ca.1775-ca.1810. Watch.
Jean Antoine. *Paris.* m.1781-9. Watch.

MAURY, Louis Jean Baptiste. *Paris.* m.1755.

MAUS, Jacob. *Trenton, U.S.A.* 1780-4. C. & W.

MAUSSION, ——. *Verdun.* 18c. Watch Besançon M.

MAUVAIS, Jean Baptiste. *Bois.* ca.1750.

MAUVOISIN, Philibert. *Chartres.* 1392. C. of the Cathedral.

MAVAIS, Daniel. ——. Mid. 18c. sil. al. watch.
MAVINE, Daniel. *Edinburgh.* a.1681.
MAWKES—
T. *Derby.* ca.1770. Watch Derby M.
Thomas. *Chesterfield.* 1791. C.
MAWLEY—
Robert. *London.* 1st half 18c. br. clock and shagreen watch.
Thomas. prob. *London.* an.1774. Watch.
MAWTASS, Nicholas. *London.* CC.1768.
MAXEY—
——. *Wallingford.* 1766. W.
Charles. *Woodstock.* 1795.
Charles. *Witney.* 1795.
MAXWELL—
William. *Edinburgh.* a.1748.
Robert. *Wigtown.* 1770.
Robert. *London.* CC.1778.
A. *Philadelphia.* 1805-11. C.
MAY—
William. *London.* a.1671, CC.1679-84. d. an.1699.
John. *London.* CC.1692, d.1738. Watches M.M.A. and Den. and Feill colls. Watch mts. G.M. and S.M.S.K.
May Joanna, widow of Wm. *London.* 1699-1712.
Michael. *London* (*Plumtree St.*). an.1724. Watch.
John. *Witney.* ca.1725. cf. John below.
John. *London.* 1750-88. Watch G.M. sil. p.c. repoussé watch. Watch hm. 1788 Ilbert coll.
Boys Err. *London* (*Bridgewater Sq.*). a.1746, CC.1753, d.1796.
Edward. *Henley-o.-T.* 1755-95. C. & W.
David. *Prescot.* ca.1770.
Frederick. *Dublin.* 1770-96. W.
John. *Southampton.* 1773. d.1791. C. & W.
John. *Witney.* 1795. C. & W. cf. John above.
Frederick & Son. *Dublin.* 1800. Watch.
Samuel. *London.* a.1800, CC.1810.
William. *Portadown.* 1824.
Robert. *Deptford.* 1828. Award from Soc. Arts for a detached escapement, desc. Trans. Soc. Arts, Vol. 46.
MAYBAUM, Johann Philipp. *Strasbourg.* 1783. With his son made a very large clock for the cathedral tower, which never went well. Watch sd. 'MEYBAUM, Strasbourg' Besançon M.
MAYER—
Jacob. *v.* MAYR.
Johann Leonhard. *Vienna.* m.1772. Also MEYER.
Franz. *Vienna.* m.1786.
Franz. *Kremsir.* Early 19c. g. watch set stones Feill coll. Prob. same as preceding.
Joseph. *Vienna.* m.1805.
MAYERS—
John. *Richmond* (*Yorks*). 1770.
Walter. *London.* a.1767.
Walter. *Gloucester.* 1782-1802. C. & W.
——. *Liverpool.* 1813.
MAYET—
Jacques. *Blois.* 1562. C. to the duc de Nemours.
Les frères. *Morbier.* 1647-60.
Pierre Claude. *Morbier.* 1687-1729. Made clocks for St. Just d'Arbois in 1687, the Ursules de Nozeroy in 1699 and St. Anatoile de Salins in 1729.
Pierre François, son. *Morbier.* 1729-63. With his son made clock for Bourg-en-Bresse in 1733.
Jean Baptiste, son. *Morbier.* 1733.
Jean Baptiste. *Foncine.* 1735. Clock for Trévoux.
Augustin. *Morbier.* 1770.

MAYET—*continued.*
François Pierre Ignace. *Paris.* m.1770-89.
Nicolas Joseph. *Morbier.* 1773.
MAYFIELD—
John. *London.* a.1768.
Edward. *London* (*Little Minories*). a.1784, CC.1798, l.CC. and d.1812.
MAYHEW—
William. *Parham.* 1750. C.
James. prob. *London.* an.1775. Watch.
William. *Woodbridge.* 1784. l.c. clock. W.
MAYLAND (MAYLARD)—
Thomas. *London.* a.1682, CC.1698.
John. *London.* a.1695.
Thomas. *London.* a.1733.
MAYNARD—
Christopher. *London* (*R. Exchange*). a.1660, CC.1667-92.
George, son. *London* (*St. Martin in Fields*). a.1692-1723. Insolvent.
George. *New York.* 1702-25.
George. *Melford.* 2nd half 18c. Watch and l.c. clock.
MAYNE, Thomas. *Cootehill.* 1824.
MAYNER, G. prob. *London.* an.1771. Watch.
MAYO—
William. *London.* a.1676.
William. *Coventry.* 1817.
& SON. *Manchester.* Early 19c. Watch.
MAYOR—
John. *London.* 1702. Bell founder.
Barnabas. *London.* a.1760.
MAYOWE, John. *Uxbridge.* 1467. C.
MAYR—
Johann Hans Georg. *Munich.* ca.1650, d. 1684. Court C. 1663-71. sq. table clock Spitzer coll. astro. table clock, tortoise-shell and silver with armillary sphere Nat. M. Munich. Magnificent astro. mus. clock K.H.M. Vienna. Small str. al. br. clock M.P.S. Dresden.
Jacob. *Augsburg.* 1672. d.1714. sil. trav. clock, sq. table clock Gélis coll., magnificent sil., tortoise-shell and en. clock of 1712, in Altenburg Residenzschloss. Tortoise-shell and sil. astro. clock Buckingham Pal. Hanging ball clock Ilbert coll. Also MAIR.
Simon. *Heidelberg.* ca.1690. Gilt watch with en. portrait of Philipp Wilhelm von der Pfalz.
Jacob. *Augsburg.* 1720 m.-ca.1750. Clock Grüne Gewölbe, Dresden. Watch Feill coll. prob. by him.
Johann Peter. *Augsburg.* m.ca.1740, juré 1745-58. sil repoussé watch. g. onyx watch. g. and porcelain watch Fränkel coll. sil. rep. watch Feill coll. rep. trav. clock Ilbert coll. Also MEYR.
Rupert. *Nördlingen.* Mid. 18c. C. of repute.
Johann. *Dillingen.* ca.1750. Watch.
Carl. *Pfersen.* 1784-91. Kleinuhrmacher.
MAYSMOR—
Humphrey. *London.* 1692 CC. Also MAYSMAR.
William. *London.* a.1693.
William. *Wrexham.* Early 18c. Watch mt. G.M.
MAYSON, Henry. prob. *London.* 1712. mus. clock. Prob. MASON.
MAYSTRE, Jean Jacques. *Geneva.* ca.1775-1791.
MAYUS, Johannes. *Berlin.* 17c. Oval hanging plate clock Feill coll.
MAZE, ——. *Paris.* 1780.
MAZIÈRE, ——. *La Rochelle.* 1665.
MAZURIER (LEMASURIER)—
Jacques. *Paris.* 1738 m., juré 1750-89. Presented a clock with seconds pendulum to Louis xv. In 1754 made a clock with one wheel in going and one in str. train, desc. in Mém. de l'Acad. des Sci. 1755.
Jean (or Jacques) Denis. *Paris.* m.1774-89.

MAZZOLENI, Giuseppe. *Padua.* *Venice* from 1551. d.1577. Keeper of clock of S. Marco.
MEACHER, Joseph. *London.* a.1792.
MEADE—
Garrett. *London.* CC.1703.
Garrett. *London.* a.1704.
MEADER, Thomas. *London.* a.1762.
MEADES—
Thomas. *London.* a.1679, CC.1687-1721.
Matthew. *London.* a.1735.
MEADHURST, William. *London.* 1753. Watch case maker.
MEADLOW, James. *London.* an.1776. Watch.
MEADOWS—
Matthew. *London.* a.1715.
Charles. *London.* 1719. p.c. sil. watch, painting under tortoise-shell, Carnegie M.
James. *London.* an.1793. Watch.
MEAK (MEEK), John. *London.* 1815-24. mus. clocks and watches.
MEAKINS, George. *Witney.* From 1767. From *London.*
MEAN—
William. *London* (*Albemarle St.*). CC.1789, l.CC.1813. W.
William. *London.* CC.1810-7.
MEAR, Thomas. *Dursley.* 1789-93. C. & W.
MEARNS, Ernest. *Banff.* 1749.
MEARS—
Isaac. *London.* a.1661.
William. *London.* a.1738.
Henry. *London.* an.1775. Watch.
MEASURE (MESURE), Anthony. *London.* 1799-1824. chron. maker.
MECHEM, Samuel. ——. an.1744. Watch.
MECK, Conrad. *Fürth.* d.ca.1820.
MEDCALF—
William. *Liverpool.* ca.1770.
Cuthbert. *Liverpool.* 1777-1805. W.
John. *Liverpool.* 1790. W. Prob. same as METCALF.
William. *Liverpool.* 1795. W.
——. *Woodstock.* ca.1800.
Townley.. *Liverpool.* 1805. W.
William. *London.* 1809-11. W.
Thomas. *Liverpool.* 1825. W.
MEDDON, Richard. *London.* a.1824.
MEDHURST, Richard. *Croydon.* CC.1687-1724. W.
MEDLEY, Joseph. *Boston.* an.1743. Watch.
MEDLYCOTT, John. *London.* a.1773.
MEDNALL, ——. *London.* 1636. cf. MIDNALL.
MEDOX, Michel. *Moscow.* 1776-93. Made mus. aut. clock in Kremlin M. for Catherine II.
MEDSGER (METSCHER), Hans. *Helsingör.* 1626-38. Court C. Made clock for Kronborg. Prob. a relation of Jeremias METZGER.
MEEBERRY, Elizabeth. *London.* a.1680.
MEEKING, Thomas. *Dublin.* 1682. d.1709.
MEEKS—
Edward. prob. *London.* an.1758. Watch.
Edward. *New York.* 1796.
MEGAN, John. *Stewartstown.* 1824.
MÉGEVAND—
Jean Estienne. *Amsterdam.* 1686. From *Cologne.*
Laurent. *Le Locle* and *Besançon.* b.1754, d.1814. Went Besançon in 1790 and started the watch industry there in 1793, under the Government.
FRÈRES. *Geneva* and *Besançon.* 1793.
MEGIER, Joseph. *London.* 2nd half 18c. Watch mt. S.K.M.
MEGRET, ——. *Paris.* 1822.
MEGROS—
Frédéric. *Luthy* (*Vevey*). 1783-98 m.
Jean Benjamin. *Vevey.* 1798 m.
MEHRWALD, Balthazar. *Fürth.* d.ca.1800.
MEIER—
Bernhard. *Berlin.* 1794. Wooden C.
Joseph Anton. *Augsburg.* 1795. Wooden C.
MEIFIELD—
James. *London.* CC.1818.
William, son. *London.* a.1818, CC.1825.
John, bro. *London.* a.1818.
MEIGH, Moses. *London.* a.1706, CC.1714-61. Bankrupt.
MEIJER, Lor. *Åbo.* 1648.
MEIN, William. *Newcastle-o.-T.* 1801. C. & W.
MEIREDAY, John. *London.* 1662.
MEISSNER, Franz. *Leitershofen.* 1770.
MEISSONNIER, Juste Aurèle. *Paris.* b. 1675, d.1750. Architect and bronze worker; designed clock-cases. Pub. 'Livre d'Ornament.'
MEISTER, Michael. *Vienna.* m.1785.
MELCHER, ——. *Stockholm.* 1646-55.
MELET, Jean Jacques. *Dole.* 1638.
MELIN, Nils. *Bårsta.* 18c. Watch mt. Nord. M.
MELL, David. *London.* CC.1655-9.
MELLET, Jean Samuel. *Moudon.* 1762 m.-1798. *Vevey* from 1762.
MELLIE, J. *Châtellerault.* Late 17c. en. watch Gélis coll.
MELLIN—
Gui. *London.* Early 17c. Oval watch Ilbert coll.
Cornelius. *London.* 1622. Alien. Oval gilt watch.
MELLING, John. *Chester.* 1719. d.1733. W.
MELLIS—
John. *Edinburgh.* a.1749.
A. prob. *London.* an.1775. Watch.
MELLNS, John. *Edinburgh.* 1711.
MELLOR—
John. *Manchester.* ca.1820.
John. *Liverpool.* ca.1820.
MELLY—
Ami. *Geneva.* 1778-85. Director of watch factory of ROMAN, MELLY & ROUX at *Constance.* g. watch M.M.A. Geographical watch Stern. coll.
Étienne. *Geneva.* ca.1780. g. en. lyre watch.
Jacob. *Paris.* Late 18c. g. en. watch Stern. coll.
FRÈRES (Ruel & Ferdinand). *Geneva* and *Paris.* Late 18c.-1829. 8-day cyl. watch and two g. en. watches Feill coll. Made a lever esc. with 9-tooth esc. wheel and 4 pallets.
Antoine. ——. ca.1790. g. en. watch.
v. BLONDEL ET MELLY.
MELMOUTH, George. *London.* a.1707.
MELOR, Louis Claude. *Paris.* m.1740.
MELSOM, John. *London.* a.1709.
MELTON—
John. prob. *London.* an.1755. Watch.
——. *Lausanne.* 1760 comp.
MELVILL, Robert. *Stirling.* 1736-67.
MELVILLE—
James. *London* (*Saffron Hill*). 1774.
John. *London* (*Chelsea* and *Clerkenwell*). CC.1781-1806.
John. *London* (*Pentonville*). 1791. W.
& STODDART. *London.* 1799-1824.
Frederick, son of John (1). *London.* a.1811.
MELVIN, James. prob. *London.* an.1773. Watch.
MEMES, James. *Berwick-on-Tweed.* ca.1770-1811. W.
MEMESS—
James. *Garnock.* ca.1730.
John. *Johnshaven.* ca.1730.
Robert. *London.* 1817. CC.1825.
——. *Woolwich.* Early 19c. Watch.
MEMIS, William. *Aberdeen.* 1787.
MENANT, T. *Paris.* 1743. Sundial G.M.
MENARD, F. D. *Paris.* 1805-25. Pub. book on adjusting watches.

MENAT—
Gilbert. *Paris.* m.1786-9.
——. *Paris.* 1807-21.
MENDENHALL, Thomas. *Philadelphia.* 1775. C. & W.
MENDHAM, S. *London.* 1807. Awarded medal by Soc. Arts for a remontoire, desc. Trans. Soc. Arts, Vol. 25.
MENG (MENGIS, MENGS), Hans. *Basle.* 1612-32. From *Hesse.*
MENKEL, Johann Georg. *Mannheim.* 1747. Kleinuhrmacher.
MENNESDÖRFER—
Joh. *Fürth.* d.ca.1803.
J. A. S. *Fürth.* d.1825.
MENOUSE, ——. *Paris.* ca.1640. cf. following. sil. watch Miller coll.
MENOUST, Léonard. *Blois.* comp. 1643.
MENS, Benjamin. *Philadelphia.* 1796.
MENT, Georg. *Nürnberg.* m.1557, d.1605. Town C. Also MENND.
MENTI, Mattis. *Lübeck.* Early 17c. crys. oct. watch.
MENU—
Simon. *Paris.* 1685 m.
Daniel. *Geneva.* b.1734-69.
Jean Nicolas. *Geneva.* ca.1800. en. watch.
MENZIES—
Robert. *Coupar Angus.* 1800.
Robert. *Perth.* 1804.
Thomas. *Philadelphia.* 1806-25.
MENZINGER, Veith. *Munich.* 1670. Court C.
MENZON & CO. ——. Early 19c. Metal cal. watch.
MEOK, Samuel. *London.* a.1738.
MERANDA, Peter. *London.* a.1726.
MERCER—
Edward. *London.* a.1690, CC.1699.
Samuel. *London* a.1695.
William. *Liverpool.* 1734-54. Watch case maker.
John. *Sutton (Liverpool).* 1734.
John. *Hythe.* 1st half 18c. br. and l.c. clocks and watch. cf. John below.
John. *Manchester.* d.1759. W.
Thomas. *Folkestone.* 1760-71. C. & W.
William. *Folkestone.* From 1761. C. & W.
James. prob. *London.* an.1775. Watch.
Thomas. *London.* a.1767.
John. *Hythe.* 1793-7. C. & W. cf. John above.
Robert. *London.* an.1801. Watch.
John. *Liverpool (Sir Thomas Bdgs.).* 1805-1821.
John. *Liverpool (Dickson St.).* 1818-29.
John. *Liverpool (Scotland Rd.).* 1825. W.
Thomas. *London* and *St. Albans.*. b.1822, d. 1900. A fine chron. maker and springer and founder of the firm of Thos. MERCER & SON.
MERCERIUS, Franciscus. ——. 17c. al. watch Fränkel coll.
MERCHIE (MURCHI, MARKIE)—
Johan. *Copenhagen.* 1695-1717. Swiss. Turret C. Made existing clock for Our Saviour's Church, Christianshavn, ill. Liisberg.
Jørgen. *Copenhagen.* a.1717.
Christian Karl. *Copenhagen.* a.1726.
MERCIER—
François. *Paris.* Late 17c. g. watch en. Huaud frères. sil. watch Carnegie M.
Pierre. *Amsterdam.* 1687. Huguenot refugee from *Meaux.*
Jacques. *Amsterdam.* 1687. Huguenot refugee from *Paris.* Perhaps the same as the following.
James. *London.* 1697. French. Watch.
Louis. *Geneva.* Mid. 18c. p.c. watch.
Emmanuel. *La Sagne.* 1752. C.
——. *London.* 1753. Shagreen case maker.

MERCIER—*continued.*
Jean Baptiste. *Paris.* m.1781-9.
Pierre. *Paris.* m.1785.
Paul. *Paris.* 1788.
Antoine. *Vevey.* 1798 m.
——. *Paris.* 1818-25.
MERCINER, Theodore. *London.* an.1752. Watch.
MÉRÉAUX, Jean Charles. *Paris.* m.1671-89.
MEREDITH—
Lancelot. *London.* CC.1637-64.
John, son. *London.* a.1654, CC.1664.
John. *London.* an.1751-5. p.c. watch.
William. prob. *London.* an.1777. Watch.
William. *Chepstow.* 1791. C. & W. l.c. clock.
MEREY, John. *Hertford.* an.1755. Watch.
MERFELDEN, Gert. *Flensborg.* 1551. C. and bell-founder.
MERFIELD—
James. *London.* CC.1818.
John. *London.* a.1818.
William. *London.* a.1818, CC.1825.
MERGET, Johann Ludwig Carl. *Berlin.* 1821-47.
MERI, Jacob Louis. *Geneva.* ca.1775-91.
MÉRIENNE—
Jean René. *Geneva.* ca.1775-92. Awarded prize for watch by Soc. des Arts.
——. *Paris.* 1812.
MERIFIELD, ——. *Falmouth.* Early 19c.
MERIGEOT—
John. *London (Spitalfields).* 1742.
John, son. *London.* a.1742, CC.1750, l.CC. 1766. Sig. on clock in Buckingham Pal. made by MOXON.
Peter. *London.* a.1750. Vernis Martin l.c. clock.
MERITON, Charles. *London.* a.1735.
MERKEL, Martin. *Bamberg.* 1766.
MERKELL, Georgius. *Dantzig.* Mid. 17c. g. en. watch Den. coll.
MERKES, P. *Rotterdam.* ca.1800.
MERKLE (MERCKLE), Anton Joseph. *Vienna.* 1st half 18c. Table clock.
MERKLEIN (MERCKLEIN), Friedrich Wilhelm. *Augsburg.* m.ca.1805.
MERLIN (MESLIN), Pierre. *Poitiers.* 1388. *Paris,* 1390-1409. C. to the duc de Berry.
MERMILLIOD, Guillaume. *Paris.* m.1777-1825.
MERMILLON, ——. *Geneva.* Late 18c. Watch.
MERMOD FRÈRES. *Sainte Croix.* 1815-89. Makers of mus. mechanism. Devised rep. work operated by going train mainspring.
MERN, William. *Oxford* and *Bristol.* 1774.
MEROZ, Abram Louis. *Sonvilier.* 1788.
MERRA, Pierre Martin. *Paris.* m.1773-89. Vase clock Bernal sale.
MERRELL, John. *London (Richmond).* 1799. en. watch.
MERRET, Richard. *Stroud.* an.1768. Watch.
MERRIAM, Silas. *Connecticut, U.S.A.* 1790.
MERRICK—
Joseph. *Bristol.* 1734. W.
Richard. *London.* 1817-24. W.
MERRILL—
Charles. *London (Moorfields).* a.1748, CC. 1757-96.
John. *London.* a.1767, CC.1777.
Charles, son of Chas. *London (Pudding La., Cumberland St.* and *Richmond).* CC.1782, l.CC.1810.
James, son. *London (Richmond).* CC.1797.
T. *London (New Brentford).* 1802-24.
Josiah, son of Chas.(2). *London.* a.1808.
MERRIMAN—
Butler. *London.* Late 18c. Watch mt.
Titus & Butler. *Bristol, U.S.A.* 1810-5. Wooden wall clocks.

MERRITT—
John. *London.* an.1760. Watch.
Charles. *London.* 1808 CC., l.CC.1810.
Josiah, son. *London.* a.1808.
MERRY—
Charles. *London.* a.1726, CC.1735, m.CC. 1768-93. l.c. clock.
Edward. *London.* CC.1749.
John. *London.* a.1744.
James Owen, son of Charles. *London.* CC. 1771.
MERRYLEES, Charles. *Edinburgh.* 1806-25.
MERRYMAN—
Henry. *London.* a.1667, CC.1674-1707. Watch. Also MERRIMAN.
Benjamin. *London.* CC.1682-1734. Watch. Also MERRIMAN.
Thomas. *London.* a.1692.
John. *London.* a.1697, CC.1711.
MERRYWEATHER, Francis Isaac. *London, Birmingham* and *Bristol.* a.1750-65. Bankrupt.
MERTTINS, George. *London.* a.1680, CC. 1688, m.CC. and knighted 1713, Lord Mayor 1724, d.1727.
MERZ (MÄRTZ)—
Georg Anton. *Augsburg.* b.1716, m.1756-70.
Johann Anton. *Augsburg.* 1756-85. Prob. same as preceding.
Joseph. *Augsburg.* comp. 1784, m.1802.
MESIN—
——. *Paris.* 1685 m.
Estienne, son. *Paris.* m.1691.
MESLIER DIT DE BEAUVAIS, Anthoine. *Paris.* 1544-7. Founder member of Paris corporation.
MESNARD, Jean Claude. *Paris.* 1773.
MESNIEL, James. *London.* CC.1682. Frenchman.
MESNIELL, James. *London.* a.1699.
MESNIER, Ursin. *Blois.* comp. 1630.
MESNIL—
Jacques. *Blois* and *Mer.* 1676. Made clock at Vendôme. br. clock.
Jacques. *The Hague.* Early 18c. p.c. sil. watch Feill coll. Also MENIL. Perhaps the preceding.
——. *Paris.* 1808-55. Clock made for Joséphine, bronze by Ravrio, Pal. de l'Élysée.
MESPLAIN, Claude. prob. *Autun.* mar. 1576. 'Orologeur, serrurier et hacquebutier.'
MESSELINK, L. *Leyden.* ca.1800.
MESSER, ——. *Southampton.* an.1756. Watch.
MESSIER, Joh. Christoph. *Fürth.* d.ca. 1820.
MESSNER, Gallus. prob. *Augsburg.* ca.1560. Small clock M.P.S. Dresden.
MESTAYER—
Henry. *London.* a.1705, CC.1713-5.
——, son. *London.* CC.1744. rep. watch.
MESTIVIER, Jacob. *London.* an.1723. Watch.
MESTRAL—
P. *Ferney.* 1775. Watch mt.
——. *Paris.* 1822.
MESTREGENT—
François. *Besançon.* 1685. d.1722. Called to Besançon to make clock for Monastère du Refuge.
Jean Philippe, son. *Besançon.* 1749.
MESTREZAT—
Moïse. *Grenoble.* 1651. From *Geneva.*
Pierre. *Grenoble.* 1670.
MESURE (MEASURE), Anthony. *London.* 1799-1851. chron. maker. Pocket chron. Ilbert coll.
MÉTARE (MEYTARE), ——. *St. Etienne* (*Loire*). 1700-02.
METCALF—
Edward. *London.* a.1684.
Mark. *Askrigg.* 1710-76. Watch.
Augustine. *Liverpool.* 1761. W.
George Marmaduke. *London.* CC.1781, l.CC.1787-1825. Watch mt.
John. *Liverpool.* 1790-1818. W.
Richard. *Louth.* 1791-5. W.
METHVEN, David. *St. Andrews.* 1768-73.
MÉTRAL—
Abram David. *Payerne,* then *Chaux-de-Fonds* 1766.
——. *Paris* and *Cambrai.* 1811-8. en. watch.
METTLER—
Hans. *Basle.* 1634-43. Kleinuhrmacher.
Johann. *Basle.* 1643-8. Kleinuhrmacher.
METZ—
Johann Anton. *Würzburg.* m.1704. C.
Andreas. *Kissingen.* m.1791. C.
METZE (METZCKE)—
Augustin. *Sorau.* Early 18c. trav. clock Ashmolean M. sq. table clock Feill coll.
Carl Benjamin. *Berlin.* 1816.
METZKER (METZGER), Jeremias. *Augsburg.* 1564-88. Gilt eng. clock K.H.M. Stand clock Arts M. Prague. Oval watch sd. 'I. M.' Fränkel coll. prob. by him. Made clock for Frederik II of Denmark.
METZNER, George. *Neusohlii.* Late 17c. Table clock Virginia M.
MEUGNOT, ——. *Paris.* 1813.
MEURAND, ——. *Paris.* 1780. Dial maker.
MEUREUS, G. *Rome.* ca.1590-1620. Dial maker.
MEURON—
——. *Neuchâtel.* 1775-83.
SILLIMAN & CIE. *Chaux-de-Fonds.* Late 18c. g. rep. watch.
——. *Paris.* Late 18c. and early 19c. g. rep. watch. g. en. watch Damiano coll.
& CIE. *Paris.* ca.1790. str. and rep. watch G.M. al. watch S.M.S.K. rep. watch M.M.A.
Guglielmo. ——. ca.1795. Pedometer watch Ilbert coll.
MEUSNIER (MEUNIER)—
Claude. *Paris.* 1772.
Claude François. *Paris.* m.1781-1812. C.
MEVYN, Jean. *Nevers.* 1548. 'Orrelogeur.'
MEW—
Joseph. *Blandford.* 1725.
James. *London.* 1760. Watch Cardiff M.
Samuel. *Shrewsbury.* an.1773. Watch.
William. *Blandford.* 1780.
MEYBOM (MAYBON), F. L. *Paris* (*St. Germain*). ca.1650. sq. watch B.M. sd. 'Maybon.' sq. watches, g. on blued steel, F.W.M. ill. Baillie and M.M.A.
MEYENBERG, J. H. W. *Hamburg.* 1801-04.
MEYER—
Appollinaris. *Basle.* 1583-1610.
——. *Paris.* 17c. circ. sil. eng. watch Spitzer coll.
Jakob. *Basle.* b.1677, d.1737.
Wilhelm. *Cologne.* m.1707. Kleinuhrmacher.
Jacob. *Copenhagen.* m.1735.
——. *Elbing.* 1746. Town C.
Dietrich, son of Jakob. *Basle.* b.1745, d.1807. Watch mt. sd. 'Diet. Meye' M.M.A. Two watches Basle M.
François. *Paris.* 1771 m.-1789. g. en. watch.
Christian Vilhelm. *Copenhagen.* m.1792.
C. G. *St. Petersburg.* End 18c. cyl. watch mt. Ilbert coll.
Anthony. *Bristol.* 1817-30.
——. *Paris.* 1817-25.
MEYERS, John. *London.* 1799.
MEYLAN—
Samuel Olivier. *Vallée de Joux.* b.ca.1725. Started watchmaking in the Vallée.
Abraham Samuel. *Fleurier.* a.1742. Went to *Vallée de Joux.*

MEYLAN—*continued.*
Henry. *Lausanne.* Mid. 18c. Watch mt.
——. *Vevey.* m.1766.
Philippe Samuel. *Brassus* and *Geneva.* b. 1770-1829. Eminent maker of automata and complex watches. First to make mus. watches with reeds and disc and later with barrel. Invented the ring alarm with pin to prick finger. Went to *Geneva* in 1811. In firm with L. AUDEMARS and Isaac Daniel PIGUET, 1811-28.
Pierre Abram. *Vevey.* 1798 m.
MEYLIN, ——. *Zürich.* ca.1720. p.c. sil. watch S.K.M.
MEYNADIER, Philippe. *Geneva.* ca.1780-early 19c. g. en. lyre watch and two g. en. watches M.M.A.
MEYNIER (MOYNIER)—
——. *France.* 1724. Devised planisphere, desc. Gallon, 'Machines et Inventions,' Vol. IV, and pedometer.
——. *Paris.* 1811.
MEYRAT—
Jean Pierre. *Courtelary.* b.1738.
Jean François. *St. Imier.* 1781. d.1800. Started an important business, continued by his widow and daughter.
MEYRAT-LANGEL, François, son. *St. Imier.* 1817. Took over the firm of RAIGUEL JEUNE & CIE. Watch.
MEYRENNE, Alexandre. *Geneva.* ca.1690. Huguenot refugee from *Serres* in *Dauphiné.*
MEYRICKE, Charles or William. *London.* a.1763.
MEYS, Jean. *Nivelles.* 1694. Repaired town clock.
MÉZERAY, ——. *Paris.* 1821.
MEZIÈRES - DIT - LABAUME, Jacques. *Lyons(?).* Late 17c. Fine aut. clock, M. d'Art, Geneva.
MEZIS, William. *London.* 1774. Insolvent.
MICABIUS, John. *London.* 1632. Promised to subscribe for incorporation of CC.
MICAL, l'Abbé. *Paris.* b.1730, d.1789. Very able mechanician. Made an aut. flute-player and, in 1783, the first talking head, ill. M. des Aut.
MICALLEF—
Salvatore E GIGLIO. *Malta.* End 18c. Watch mt. Ilbert coll.
Salvatore. *Malta.* Early 19c. Virgule watch, prob. English, Fränkel coll.
MICHAEL—
W. prob. *London.* an.1782. Watch.
David. *Swansea.* 1785.
D., & Sons. *Swansea.* Late 18c. and early 19c. Watch Den. coll.
C. *London.* Early 19c. Watch.
MICHAU—
——. *Paris.* ca.1750. g. en. watch Blot-Garnier coll. Prob. MICHAUD.
Étienne. *Paris.* m.1782-9.
MICHAUD—
P. *Paris.* ca.1760. Watch G.M.
Pierre. *Geneva.* 1771. From *Orléans.*
Veuve. *Paris.* 1792. g. en. rep. watch M.M.A.
——. *Paris.* 1812-23.
MICHAUT—
Daniel. *London.* 1794.
& PETITPIERRE. *London (Greek St.).* Early 19c.
MICHÉ—
Stanislas Elizabeth. *Paris.* m.1780-89.
Charles Léon. *Paris.* m.1785-9.
MICHEL—
Adam. *Lyons.* 1593-1609.
Jaques. *Paris.* Mid. 17c. Lantern clock Feill coll.
——. *Angers.* 1666. Serrurier. Restored Cathedral clock.
Jacob. *Paris.* 1678 m.

MICHEL—*continued.*
——. *Dijon.* Early 18c. Boulle br. clock.
John. *London.* 1753 CC. Prob. same as MITCHELL.
Jean. *Paris.* 1770-99. Petitioned for an award for improvements in clocks without success.
Nicolas. *Paris.* m.1778-89.
Michel. *Paris.* m.1781-9.
Nicolas Louis. *Paris.* m.1786.
——. *Paris.* 1808-25.
Jean François. *Chaux-de-Fonds* and *Strasbourg.* m.1814.
Edward Eccott. *London.* a.1813, CC.1831.
MICHELE, frate, da Pisa. *Caffa.* 1446. Keeper of clock at Caffa.
MICHELEZ, ——. *Paris.* 1811-25. Pupil of BREGUET. g. watch.
MICHELI, Pietro Adamo. *Mantua.* 1547. Pub. a desc. of the clock of Mantua, the earliest book on horology.
MICHELIN, Samuel. *Langres.* ca.1680. Fine cal. trav. clock ill. Britten.
MICHELL—
Peter. *London.* 1622. a. to Corn. MELLIN.
John. *Chardstock.* 1670-ca.1700. Lantern clock.
J. *Penzance.* Early 19c.
v. MITCHELL.
MICHELSON, *v.* MITCHELSON.
MICHELZOON, Kornelis. *Wormerveer.* 1678. Zaandam clock.
MICHIEL, Pierre. *Mons.* 1469. Repaired Cambrai Cathedral clock.
MICHINALE, William. *London.* a.1693 CC. 1702-16. Also MICHINALLE.
MICHOD—
Jean Philippe. *Vevey.* m.1728.
Abram Louis. *Vevey.* a.1727, m.1742, d. an.1773.
Jean Baptiste. *Vevey* and *Berne.* a.1730-1770 m. Took over ADOR's factory at Berne in 1762 and moved it to Vevey. Watch mt.
Jean Philippe. *Vevey.* 1798 m.
MICKLEWRIGHT—
Erasmus. *London.* a.1666, CC.1673-99.
Erasmus James. *London.* a.1700, CC.1708.
MICOUIN, ——. *Auxerre.* 1722. Applied a pendulum to the town clock.
MIDDLETON—
Timothy. *London.* a.1680, CC.1687.
Thomas. *London.* a.1718-81 CC.
C. *London.* 1793. Watch.
Robert. *London.* 1809. Watch Furt. M.
Henry. *Liverpool.* 1816-8. W.
MIDGLEY—
Richard. *Halifax.* 1720-40. l.c. clocks.
Richard. *Exeter.* 1771. l.c. clock.
MIDHURST, George. *London (Pentonville).* 1791. C.
MIDNALL, John. *London.* ca.1620, CC.1632, w.CC.1635. One of the first assistants of the CC. Plain sil. oval watch B.M. Marrow-shaped watch F.W.M. ill. Baillie. Oval watch M.M.A.
MIDRÉ ET CIE. *Paris.* 1823.
MIDWINTER—
——. *Oxford.* an.1767. Watch.
Thomas. *London (Bridgewater Gdns.).* CC. 1774-1810.
William. *London.* CC.1774-94.
MIEFUNDT, Conrad. *Riga.* Early 18c. Table clock.
MIÈGE, Philip. *Geneva.* b.1702, d.1785. Watch G.M.
MIERS, ——. ——. 1762. Watch.
MIES, Jo. ——. 17c. Sig. on table clock Garnier coll. cf. following.
MIESSLIN, Johan Jacob. *Zug.* 1685. Falling ball clock in glass sphere Webster coll.
MIGNARDET, ——. *Paris.* 1821-5.

MIGOLET (MIGNONNET)—
Joseph. *Paris.* m.1786-9. g. en. rep. watch Blot-Garnier coll.
——. *Paris.* 1812-25. C. to the King.
MIGNOT, Martin. *Blois.* 1560.
MIKKELSON, Niels Tygesen. *W. Ballum.* 1802. Wall clock.
MILBORNE (MYLBOURNE)—
John. *London (Clerkenwell).* CC.1698-1722. d.an.1735. W.
James. *London (Cow Cross).* 1747-61. W.
MILDE, G. W. *Östersund.* 1820-46.
MILES—
Jonathan. *London.* a.1701.
William. *London.* a.1711.
Stephen. *Kidderminster.* 1753-72. C. & W.
Samuel. *Halesowen.* ca.1765.
Thomas. *London (St. James' Walk, Clerkenwell).* CC.1768-99.
John. *Stroud.* 1775-95. Watch. Repaired Westbury Church clock.
William. *Dudley.* 1770. Watch. l.c. clock.
& MORGAN. *London.* 1790.
Joseph. *Shaftesbury.* 1795. c.secs. l.c. clock.
Septimus. *London.* 1795. CC.1797, l.CC. 1810-40. Rack-lever watch mt. G.M. Chiming br. clock. br. clock ill. Cec. & Web.
James. *Shaftesbury.* 1795.
T. *Hereford.* 1798. C. & W.
George. *London.* 1799-1824.
John. *Liverpool.* 1800. W.
Thomas. *Bath.* 1825.
MILL, John. *Montrose.* 1776. C. & W.
MILLAR—
John. *London.* a.1719.
Benjamin. prob. *London.* an.1755. Watch.
Alexander. *Edinburgh.* a.1766-82.
John. *Edinburgh.* a.1771-90. Orrery.
David. *Bathgate.* 1790.
Peter. *Alloa.* 1798.
Richard. *Edinburgh.* 1814. d.1860.
Thomas. *Philadelphia.* 1819-25.
MILLARD—
D. *Paris.* Late 17c. al. watch S.K.M. Table clock.
John. *Tewkesbury.* 1771. W.
MILLBANK, Joseph. *London.* 1820.
MILLENER, ——. *Paris.* m.1617.
MILLENET—
Daniel. *Geneva.* 1712. str. and al. watch. Large circ. table clock with c.secs. and year cal. Geneva M.
André. *Geneva.* mar.ca.1735-62.
Jacob. *Geneva.* ca.1755-74.
MILLER—
Leonhard. *Augsburg.* 1622-51. math. inst. maker. Dials B.M. and Old Ashmolean M.
Nicolaus. *Germany.* 1646-51. Sundials B.M. and Fränkel coll.
Ferdinant. *Germany.* Mid. 17c. hex. table clock Gélis coll.
John. *London.* a.1667, CC.1674-99. Lantern clock. br. clock Virginia M.
Peter. *London.* a.1673, CC.1681, d.1733.
Ralph. *London.* a.1690, CC.1697.
Joseph. *London.* a.1718, CC.1728-41. Very fine g. en. and repoussé p.c. watch. g. repoussé watch.
Christoph. *Augsburg.* 1st half 18c. Large sq. table clock Arts M. Prague.
Edward, son of Peter. *London.* CC.1724-55.
Reinhard. *London.* an.1743. Watch.
William. *London.* a.1735, CC.1743-6.
Aaron. *New Jersey, U.S.A.* 1748. C.
Johann Conrad. *Kriegshaber.* 1755.
James. *London (Lombard St.).* 1758. Watch.
William & James. prob. *London.* an.1762. Watch.
William, son of Ed. *London.* a.1755.
Philip. *New York.* 1763. W.
Thomas. *London.* 1767. Watches Den. coll., Arts M. Prague, Oldham M. and Ilbert coll.

MILLER—*continued.*
James. *Alloa.* 1768. Made church clock. *v.* LATIMER & MILLER.
Jos. Ignatius. *Augsburg.* ca.1780. Gilt en. watch.
Ramus Larsen. *Paris.* m.1780-9.
Archibald. *Glasgow.* 1781.
George. *Gateshead.* 1782-7. l.c. clock.
John. *Ware.* 1784. C.
T. *Lancaster.* an.1787. Watch.
James. *London.* a.1778.
John. *London.* a.1784. From *Schenectady.*
Thomas. *London.* a.1787.
Frederick. *London.* 1795-9.
J. *London (Gerrard St.).* 1799. W.
Robert *London (St. John's Sq.).* 1799. W.
Thomas. *London.* a.1796.
Robert. *London (Tottenham).* 1802-24.
George. *Perth.* 1811.
James. *Port Glasgow.* 1820-38.
Archibald. *Kirkcudbright.* 1820.
David. *Omagh.* 1824.
'MILLER.' Sig. on 1870-5 watches of the ILLINOIS SPRINGFIELD WATCH CO.
MILLERET—
——. *Geneva.* 1805. mus. aut. watch.
& TISSOT. *Geneva.* Early 19c. Very small g. cyl. 8-day watch G.M. Specialized in small watches.
MILLES, David. *London.* a.1766.
MILLETT—
Edward. *London.* a.1672, CC.1680-2.
John. *London.* a.1677.
Thomas. *London.* a.1695-1734 CC.
William. *London.* a.1703, CC.1715.
MILLIGAN—
Andrew. *Ayr.* an.1769-1801. Watch.
——. *Edinburgh.* 1791. W.
MILLIKIN (MILLIKEN), Robert. *Cork.* 1824.
MILLING, ——. ——. an.1764. Watch.
MILLINGTON—
John. *London.* an.1756-72. Watch.
Thomas. *London.* an.1758. g. watch.
John. *London.* 1762.
& Co. *Shrewsbury.* an.1773. Watch.
Thomas. *London (Wapping).* 1790.
MILLION—
William. *London.* CC.1671. C. of repute.
Joseph. *London.* a.1704.
MILLIS—
Michael. *London.* a.1727, CC.1736-52.
Joseph. *London.* an.1760-5. Watch.
MILLISON, Joseph. *London.* a.1699.
MILLÖGG—
Marcus Antonius. *Vienna.* m.1691. sil. watch Carnegie M. Also MILLEGG.
Leopoldus Antonius. *Vienna.* m.1723.
Ignatius Dominicus. *Vienna.* m.1729.
MILLON—
Daniel. *London.* CC.1712-31.
——. *Paris.* 1807.
MILLOT—
Pierre. *Paris.* m.1754-72. C. to the King. Vase clock. Elaborate cal. clock approved by the Acad. des Sci. Made a jump half-secs. clock and an astro. clock desc. Mém. de l'Acad. des Sci. 1762.
Jean Pierre Nicolas. m.1785.
MILLS—
Thomas. *London.* 1648. CC.1652-60. Lantern clock.
Richard. *Edinburgh.* m.1678, d.1705.
Jeremiah. *London.* a.1676.
Humphrey. *v.* MILNE.
Ralph. *London.* a.1690, CC.1697-1715.
John. *London.* a.1713.
William. *London (Cock La.).* d.an.1761. W.
George. *Ripon.* 1750.
Thomas. *London.* a.1758, CC.1766. Watch.
Richard. *London.* an.1769. Watch.
William. *Tetbury.* 1770. W.

MILLS—*continued.*
Robert. *London (Ratcliffe Highway).* a.1761, CC.1772, l.CC.1782-93.
Daniel. *London (E. Smithfield).* 1776. Sale of stock.
John. *Monmouth.* From 1791. C. & W.
Daniel. *London.* CC.1796.
Edward. *Liverpool.* 1796-1829. W.
James. *Liverpool.* 1796. W.
William. *London.* 1799-1824.
& WEBB. *London.* 1809-11.
Jonathan. *Liverpool.* 1810-21. W.
Thomas, & Son. *London.* 1817-24.
Richard. *London.* a.1809.
Robert. *London.* a.1809, CC.1838.
John. *London.* 1820.
Frederick. *Liverpool.* 1821. W.
——. *Calcutta.* Early 19c.
MILNE—
John. *Edinburgh.* 1647-50.
Humphrey. *Edinburgh.* 1660. d.1692. A fine maker. Lantern and l.c. clock. Lantern clock Glasgow Art Gall. Also MILLS and MYLNE.
Richard. *Edinburgh.* a.1661, d.1710.
Gideon. *Edinburgh.* a.1676.
George. *Edinburgh.* 1725-54.
John. *Edinburgh.* 1753.
James. *St. Ninians.* 1761-84.
Thomas. *Huntly.* 1780.
Joseph. *Huntly.* 1797.
Alexander. *Aberdeen.* 1820-37.
Robert. *Aberdeen.* 1821.
MILNER—
Lenhart. *Nürnberg.* 1626. Dial maker.
Thomas. *London.* a.1726, CC.1739, d.an. 1763. l.c. clock.
Thomas. *York.* 1740. C.
James Hugh. *London.* a.1737.
Thomas, son of Thos. (1). *London.* a.1754, CC.1763-72.
Henry. *London.* 1815-24.
MILNES, G. *Nottingham.* From 1802. C. & W.
MILON, Vincent. *Paris.* m.1778.
MILROY, James. *Stockton-o.-T.* d.1802.
MILSON, ——. *Newbury.* 1808. W.
MILSTED, Thomas. *Bristol.* 1825.
MILTON—
Thomas. *London.* a.1767, CC.1777-1804.
M. *London.* 1790. Watch Ilbert coll.
John Dryden. *Coventry* and *London.* 1794. Insolvent.
Thomas. *London.* a.1797.
G. D. *London (Marylebone).* 1805-08.
——. *London (Stepney).* 1817-24.
MILVIUS, Johann. *Neureusch.* Early 19c. rep. mantel clock.
MILWARD—
William. *London.* 1729. Watch case maker.
——. *Hammersmith.* ca.1790, CC.1824.
George. *London.* ca.1800. mus. C. & W.
John. *London.* 1805-20. Also MILLWARD.
MINAIZE, ——. *Salins.* 1646. Remade clock of Ste. Anatoile.
MINAUT (MINART), ——. *Paris.* 1812-21.
MINCE—
Francis. *London.* a.1787-early 19c. Watch.
J. *London.* 1799-1824.
MINCHENER, William. *London.* a.1744.
MINCHIN, John. *London.* a.1767, CC.1789.
MINET, ——. *Paris.* 1807-25. Mantel clock.
MINEUR, Carl Henric. *Stockholm.* 1805-15. Watch mt. Nord. M.
MINGO, Jonathan. *London.* a.1717.
MINIFEE, John. *Tiverton.* 1619.
MINNS, Samuel. *London.* a.1762.
MINOCHE—
Jullien. *Paris.* Juré 1681.
Nicolas, son. *Paris.* m.1684.
Jean. *Paris.* m.1693.
John. *London.* an.1784. Watch.
MINORY—
Cyprien. *Lyons.* d.1616.
Jacques. *Lyons.* 1615 comp.
MINOT, Jullien. *Paris.* Juré 1673.
MINSHULL—
William. *London.* a.1666.
William. *London.* a.1731. Also MINSHALL.
John, sen. & jun. *Denbigh.* 1764.
John. *Ashton-under-Lyne.* ca.1820.
MINTERN—
John. *Beaminster.* 1650. Lantern clock.
Charles. *London.* a.1728.
John. *London.* an.1753. Watch.
Daniel. *London.* a.1752.
MINTO, John. *Newcastle-o.-T.* 1809-11.
MINUEL—
David. *London.* CC.1683-1701.
Daniel. *London.* 1686 CC. Engraver.
MINUTTI, Joseph. *Munich.* Early 17c. sil. skull watch.
MIOL, ——. *Lausanne.* 1760.
MIRET, Nicollas. *Paris.* 1544-7. Petitioner for incorporation of Paris guild.
MIREY, Adam. *Rouen.* a.1659.
MIRFIELD—
Robert. *London* and, later, *Dublin.* CC.1749-1764.
Robert, son. *London.* a.1764.
MIROGLIO, Denis. *Geneva.* a.1697. Watch with en. portraits Drexel coll.
MIROIR—
J. *London.* Mid. 18c. sil. al. trav. clock formerly in Shandon coll.
——. *Paris.* 1823.
MIROLI, Denis. *Geneva.* Early 18c. Watch. Prob. same as, or son of, MIROGLIO.
MIRON, Gauthier. *Paris.* d. between 1544 and 1547. Founder member of Paris corporation.
MISKIN, William Scammell. *London.* CC. 1819.
MISON, Jeremiah. *London.* a.1688, CC.1698.
MITCHELL—
Myles. *London.* CC.1640.
John. *v.* MICHELL.
Stephen. *London.* a.1674.
Joseph. *London.* a.1674.
John. *London.* a.1705, CC.1713-42.
Thomas. *London.* a.1712-44.
Arthur. *Dorchester.* b.1701, d.1761. C. In partnership with Mariane VIET.
John. *London.* a.1735.
William. *London.* an.1744. Watch.
John. *London.* a.1742, CC.1751.
James. *London.* 1755-81. Also MICHELL.
Robert. *London (Gray's Inn La.).* 1750. l.CC.1766.
Walter. *Edinburgh.* a.1749.
George. *London.* a.1767.
D. prob. *London.* an.1781. Watch.
John. *London (Oxford Rd.).* 1784.
T. & W. *Glasgow.* Late 18c. and early 19c. g. watch, set stones, Den. coll.
James. *London.* a.1785.
Alexander, & Son. *Glasgow.* 1798-1837. Watch Den. coll.
William. *Glasgow.* 1798-1838. Partner in above firm.
William. *London.* 1799.
Henry George. *London.* a.1793.
John. *London (Bloomsbury).* 1802-04.
& RUSSELL. *Glasgow.* 1803-41. Watch mt. Glasgow Art Gall.
William. *Liverpool.* 1805. W.
James. *Saltcoats.* 1810.
Barwise. *Cockermouth.* Early 19c.
Phineas and Moses WHITNEY. *Boston, U.S.A.* 1813-21. W.
William. *Aberdeen.* 1820.
William. *Norwich.* In 1821 succeeded James MANN.
Phineas. *Boston, U.S.A.* 1822-5. W.

MITCHELL—*continued.*
George, & Rollin ATKINS. *Bristol, U.S.A.* 1825-37. Looking-glass clocks.
James Edward. *London.* a.1819, CC.1829.
& SON. *Glasgow.* Early 19c. W. to the King.
MITCHELSON—
John. *Edinburgh.* 1749-56.
James. *Edinburgh.* d.1755.
Alexander. *Edinburgh.* a.1752-61.
Alexander. *London.* 1769-75.
Walter. *London (Helmet Row).* 1781-1800. Watch N.Y. Univ.
David. *Kingston (Jamaica).* 1795. W.
John. *London.* a.1790.
W. *London (Old St.).* 1799-1824.
MITCHENER, John. *Arundel.* 1784-95. W.
MITENDERO, ——. *Cadiz.* 1817. Watch N.Y. Univ.
MITFORD—
John. *London.* a.1703, CC.1710-6.
John. *London.* CC.1717-58.
Robert. *London.* CC.1738, l.CC.1766. d.an. 1775.
Robert, son. *London.* CC.1773-8.
Robert, son. *London.* a.1794.
MITTGKE, Frederica. *Vienna.* 18c. Oval watch, crys. covers, M.M.A.
MITTON, P. *London.* 1817-24. W.
MITZELL, John. *London.* 1697. Watch, tortoise-shell outer case, M.M.A. Watch ill. Britten.
MOBBS, John. *London.* a.1718.
MOBERG, ——. *Stockholm.* End 18c. br. clock.
MOBERSTEG, Barthélemy. *Paris.* 1772 m.
MOCHELLE & ROQUERBE. *Paris.* 1824.
MODÉN, Nils. *Jämtland.* Early 18c. Carved wood wall clocks and watches.
MODEST, Johan Gotfred. *Copenhagen.* 1787.
MODEVEG—
Joachim Carl. *Malmö.* 1750. d.ca.1787.
Elias. *Hälsingborg.* 1773-1824.
D. *Malmö.* 1793-1826. Wall clocks.
MODEWEG, Thomas. *Copenhagen.* m.1782.
MODGE, ——. *France* or *Switzerland.* Early 19c. g. filigree and en. watch, set pearls and diamonds, M.M.A.
MOFFAT, Alexander. *Musselburgh.* 1790-1831.
MÖGELE, Ignatius. *Augsburg.* m.1771.
MOGINIE, Samuel. *London (Pimlico).* 1820-1842. Succeeded GLOVER. A fine C. & W. Regulator and br. clock ill. Cec. & Web.
MOHLER, Jacob. *Baltimore, U.S.A.* Late 18c. C. & W.
MOIDER, Joseph. prob. *London.* an.1782. Watch.
MOILLETTE, Jean Jacques. *Paris.* 1789.
MOILLIET—
John. ——. Early 18c. al. watch Den. coll.
Fils. ——. Mid. 18c. en. watch Ilbert coll.
Daniel. *Geneva.* 2nd half 18c. Watch mt.
D., ET VIRGINIO. *Geneva.* Late 18c. sil. p.c. repoussé watch.
A., & CIE. *Geneva.* ca.1800. Apple watch.
Jean. *Geneva.* Early 19c.
MOINET, Louis. *Paris.* b.1758, d.1853. Pub. 'Nouveau Traité Général Astronomique et Civil d'Horlogerie Théorique et Pratique,' Paris, 1848, 1853, 1875 and 1877. An eminent maker. Worked with BREGUET.
MOISAN—
Guillaume. *Blois.* mar.1606, d.1645.
Pierre. *Blois.* m.1618-28.
MOÏSE, Alais. *Blois.* m.1630, d.ca.1632. Native of *Autun.* sil. eng. skull watch.
MOISY, Jean. *Paris.* m.1753. C. & W. of repute. Ormolu clock. Fine Vernis Martin br. clock, Ministère des Finances, Paris.
MOJON, A. L. *Chaux-de-Fonds.* ca.1760.
MOLANTZIA, Jacques. *Chaux-de-Fonds.* a. an.1764.
MOLARD, ——. *Paris.* 1709. Devised a bad method of operating distant dials, desc. Gallon, 'Machines et Inventions.'
MOLE (MOULE)—
John. *London.* a.1679.
James. *Birmingham.* ca.1760. l.c. clock.
MOLIN, ——. *London (Fleet St.).* an.1717. Watch.
MOLINA, Antonio. *Madrid.* 1800. Sent by Spanish Navy to study chron. making in Paris; died soon after return.
MOLINEAUX—
——. *Prescot.* an.1762. Watch.
Thomas. *Derby.* an.1763. Watch.
Thomas. *Rochdale.* ca.1770-95.
William. *Rochdale.* ca.1820. Watch mt. Oldham M.
MOLITHOR, Karl. *Vienna.* m.1790.
MOLITOR, J. C. *Germany.* 1753. Pub. in Frankfort and Leipzig, 'Gründl. Anweisung wie die Geh-, Schlag- und Repetir- Uhren können berechnet und zusammengesetzt werden.'
MOLLARD, Jacques. *Grenoble.* 1693-1717.
MÖLLER—
Hans Jonas. *Hälsingborg.* 1816-25.
Nils. *Landskrona.* 1820-5.
MOLLER—
P. *Mols.* ca.1750.
Ole Olsen. *Bergen.* 1759 m.
Mads Ratken. *Copenhagen.* m.1790.
Knud. *Copenhagen.* m.1796.
MOLLETT, William. *London.* a.1709.
MOLLIEN, ——. *Paris.* 1812.
MÖLLINGER, Christian. *Berlin.* 1754-1826. Complex astro. clock. astro. and mus. clock Schloss M. Berlin. Pub. desc. of a clock in the Akademie, showing true and mean time, Berlin, 1787, and 'Kleiner Uhrenkatechismus,' Berlin, 1817.
MOLLISON, Charles. *Edinburgh.* 1770-87.
MOLLOY—
James. prob. *London.* an.1761. Watch.
Charles. *London* and *Woolwich.* 1778-84. W.
MOLONY, James. *Ennis.* 1824.
MOLPUS, ——. *Hereford.* an.1679. Watch.
MOLSWORTH, G. prob. *London.* an.1780. Watch.
MOLTENI, C. *London.* Early 19c. Watch.
MOLTON—
Edward. *London.* a.1766, CC.1773, d.1802. Also MOULTON.
William, son. *London.* CC.1802.
MÖLTZER (MELZER), Antonius. *Vienna.* m.1740.
MOLYNEUX (MOLINEUX, MOLLINEUX, MULLINEUX)—
Thomas. *London.* a.1693.
John. *Liverpool.* 1734.
Thomas. *Derby.* an.1763. Watch.
William. *Liverpool.* 1775.
——. *Coventry.* an.1785. Watch.
Thomas. *Rochdale.* ca.1770-95. W.
Robert. *London.* ca.1800-40. A good chron. maker. Patented an auxiliary compensation in 1840. Marine chron. and duplex mt. G.M. cyl. mt. S.M.S.K. Regulator Bristol M.
——. *Inniskillen.* ca.1800. l.c. clock.
William. *Blackheath.* 1802-08.
Thomas. *Dublin.* 1824.
William. *Sligo.* 1824.
& ATKINSON. *Drogheda.* Early 19c. Watch.
R. & H. *London (Southampton Row).* Early 19c. Pocket chron. Ilbert coll.
Robert, & Sons. *London.* Early 19c. br. clock.
MOLYNS (MOLINS, MOLLINS), Charles. *London.* a.1696, CC.1709-37. Bankrupt.
MONASCH, L. E. *Oude Beierland.* ca.1800.
MONCAS, John Francis. *Liverpool* ca.1820. Lever watch Ilbert coll.

MONCEAUD, ——. *Paris.* Mid. 18c. g. en. watch.
MONCER, Peter. *London.* an.1781. Watch.
MONCK & SON. *Stamford.* 1809. C. & W.
MONCRIEF, John. *London.* a.1688. Watch.
MONDAY—
Joseph. *London.* a.1647, CC.1654-61.
Francis. *London.* CC.1653. Also MUNDEN.
Benjamin or Harvey. *London.* a.1661. Also MUNDAY.
MONGER, Stephen. *London.* 1759.
MONGIN, David. *Charleston, U.S.A.* 1743-7. W.
MONGINOT—
Giovanni. *Florence.* ca.1660. Watch mt. in base of crucifix clock Ilbert coll.
——. *Paris.* ca.1680-1720. C. to the Court of Versailles.
MONIER & FILS. *Geneva.* Early 19c. Watch M.P.S. Dresden.
MONIN, Pierre Louis. *Sonvilier.* 1788.
MONK—
William. *Berwick St. John.* b.1690, d.1753. Made clock for town 1740.
John. *London.* a.1762. Sig. on clock in Buckingham Pal. made by MOXON.
MONKES, George. *Prescot.* ca.1770. cf. MONKS.
MONKHOUSE—
John. *London.* 1756-71. 'Grandmother' clock. Watch.
James. *Carlisle.* ca.1770-95.
James, & Son. *Carlisle.* 1785-1810.
John. *Carlisle.* 1790.
John. *Darlington.* 1820. d.1840. l.c. clocks.
MONKS—
Charles. *Prescot.* ca.1820. l.c. clock.
George. *Prescot.* ca.1820. cf. MONKES.
MONLEY, Robert. prob. *London.* an.1768. Watch.
MONNÉE, ——. *Vienne* (prob. *Vienna*). ca. 1770. Tulip watch M.M.A.
MONNEY, ——. *Paris.* 1820-5.
MONNIER—
Alexandre Ami. *Geneva.* ca.1750-61. Four-colour g. rep. watch en. by Soiron.
ET MUSSARD. ——. Mid. 18c. g. en. watch.
ET ROCHAT. ——. Late 18c. g. en. watch.
——. *Paris.* Late 18c. en. watch.
John. *London.* 1806-25.
John, son. *London.* a.1806.
Daniel. *Philadelphia.* 1825.
MONNIN, ——. *Lyons.* 1638 m. Perhaps same as Pierre MONTMAIN-BLACHON.
MONNIS, François. *Paris.* m.1674.
MONNOT, Jean Louis, l'aîné. *Paris.* m.1770-1789.
MONPAS, Abell. *London.* 1622. Alien.
MONRO—
George. *Edinburgh.* b.1724, d.1804. g. cyl. watch S.K.M. l.c. clock. Maker of repute. Also MUNRO.
Hunter. *Edinburgh.* a.1804.
MONTAGUE, James. *London.* an.1772. Watch.
MONTAN, Jacob. *Nyköping.* 1753.
MONTANARI, Geminiano. *Bologna* and *Padua.* b.1633-1727. Mathematician. Designed a complex planisphere clock, made by Bernardo FACCINI, for the Duchessa di Parma, now in the Vatican, desc. in Horological Jl., 1941.
MONTANDON—
David. *Paris.* m.1770.
Jean Henri. *La Brévine.* b.1751. C. Clock signed 'J. H M.'
Abram. *Chaux-de-Fonds.* 1780-97. C.
Daniel Louis. *La Brévine.* 1793. C.
Abram Louis. *Couvet.* 1795. C.
Abram. *La Brévine.* 1815-20. C.
Abram. *Le Locle.* 1815-22. Possibly the same as Abram above.

MONTANDON—*continued.*
Henri Louis. *Copenhagen.* m.1817.
——. *Paris.* 1820-4.
P. Jonas. *La Brévine.* 1825. C.
FRÈRES. *Paris.* 1825.
MONTANDON-JACOT, Henri François. *Le Locle.* 1764-1850. C.
MONTASSIER, ——. *Paris.* 1812-24. C.
MONTBARON, David. *Tramelan.* Early 19c. Made cheap and bad watches.
MONTEITH, James. *Edinburgh.* 1781.
MONTENY, ——. *Paris.* 1773.
MONTI, P. *Sandwich.* Early 19c. Watch.
MONTGOMERY, John. *London.* 1726-49.
MONTILLET, Pierre François. *Hermance.* 1811.
MONTJOYE—
Louis. *Paris.* m.1748-89.
Adrien. *Paris.* m.1764.
Adrien Nicolas. *Paris.* m.1766.
Louis. *Paris.* m.1766.
Joseph Bernard, son. *Paris.* m.1775-89.
Philippe Gabriel. *Fontaines.* 1781-5. C.
MONTLOW (MOUNTLOW, MOWTLOW, MOWLTON)—
Henry. *London.* a.1678, CC.1685-1710. l.c. clock.
Conan. *London.* a.1691, CC.1700.
Henry. *London.* a.1707, CC.1715.
Henry, son. *London.* CC.1749.
MONTMAIN—
Pierre. *Lyons.* b.ca.1576, d.1666 m. Also MONTMAIN-BLACHON.
Pierre. *Lyons.* 1640. d.1651. Also MONTMAIN-GOBY & L'AISNÉ.
Pierre. *Lyons.* b.1612, d.1684. Also MONTMAIN-PEYRETIER & LE JEUNE.
Pierre, son of Pierre (1). *Lyons.* b.1624, d. 1651 m.
Pierre, bro. *Lyons.* b.ca.1632, d.1669. Also MONTMAIN-GUIGAIR.
Alexandre, bro. *Lyons.* 1651. d.1660.
MOODY—
David. *London.* CC.1649-51. Also MOODIE.
John. *London.* a.1758-69.
William. *London.* a.1760.
Alexander. *Newtownlimavady.* 1824.
MOON—
John. *Bristol.* ca.1740. Watch.
Christopher. *London* (*Holborn*). CC.1768. Watch. Succeeded Wm. EDWARDS.
William. *London.* an.1766-ca.1780. Watch Den. coll.
Edward. *London.* 1784.
& Co. *London.* 1790.
Charles. *London.* 1803. g. en. watch.
William, son of Chris. *London.* a.1799, CC. 1808, l.CC.1820-42. W.
MOONE—
Robert. *London.* a.1663.
Robert. *London.* a.1745.
MOOR—
Johannes. *Herzogenbusch.* 1560. Made Dantzig Rathaus clock.
——. *Paris.* an.1752. Watch.
MOORE—
Sir Jonas. *London.* 'A Mathematical Compendium,' containing a chapter on Watches and Clocks was pub. in 1674 and 1693 from his papers.
Joseph. *London.* a.1683, CC.1690-2.
Daniel. *London.* a.1689, CC.1697.
William. *London.* a.1693, CC.1701-19. l.c. clock.
Peter. *London.* a.1704.
Robert. *London.* ca.1720. Fine g. chased watch Mallett coll. ill. Baillie.
Thomas. *London* (*Upper Moorfields*). d. 1785. C. & W.
Thomas. *Ipswich.* 1720-89. Heir of Thos. of London. str. and rep. br. clock Weth. coll.

MOORE—*continued.*
l.c. clock. Watch G.M. Watch mt. Ipswich M. Devised a fuzee winding both ways.
L. ——. 1st half 18c. Watch for Dutch market Den. coll.
Edward. *London.* a.1723, CC.1732.
William. *London.* a.1727.
John. *London.* a.1736, CC.1742.
John. *London (Fleet St.).* a.1736, CC.1744-1775. Turret clock.
Thomas. *London.* a.1736.
Thomas. *Melford.* 1746. l.c. clock.
Thomas. *London.* a.1739. Watch S.K.M.
Peter. *London (Sweetings Alley).* an.1756-1811. Watches G.M. and Horstmann coll.
William. *London.* a.1749, CC.1759.
William. *Woodbridge.* 18c. l.c. clock.
Joseph. *Lichfield.* 1760. l.c. clock and watch.
George. *London.* an.1765. Watch.
James. *Tewkesbury.* an.1766. Watch.
Hatley. *Ipswich.* d.1796. W.
Benjamin. prob. *London.* an.1772. Watch.
F. *London.* an.1775. Watch.
Francis. *Ferrybridge (Yorks).* 1775.
Edward. *Oxford.* 1776. W.
Ambrose. *Dublin.* 1780-95. W.
James. *Salisbury.* ca.1780. l.c. clock Weth. coll. ill. Britten. Watch.
Edmund Thomas. *London (Lombard St. and Kingsland Rd.).* a.1772, CC.1781-1835.
Michael. *London.* a.1775.
Richard. *London.* a.1777.
& GEARING. *London.* 1783.
——. *Ipswich.* 1784. W.
John. *Maidstone.* 1784. W.
William. *Warrington.* an.1786. Watch.
C. *London.* an.1791. Watch.
John. *London.* a.1785.
& EDWARDS. *London.* 1793.
John C. *West Tarring.* 1794. From *London.*
John. *Warminster.* 1795. W.
Robert. *Dublin.* 1795. W.
James. *London.* ca.1800. trav. clock.
James. *Warminster.* ca.1800. l.c. clock. Watch.
Patrick. *London.* CC.1806-11.
John. *London.* 1809-40. Turret and house C.
James. *Belfast.* 1819-24.
Thomas. *London (Clement's La.).* 1820.
Joseph, son of Edmund. *London.* a.1813.
& STARKEY. *London.* 1823.
& SON. *London.* Early 19c. Turret C.
Peter, M.P. *London.* CC.1823.
George. *Kilrea.* 1824.
David. *Randalstown.* 1824.

MOP, John. *Rochdale.* ca.1820.

MOQUIN, Christien. *Geneva.* ca.1775-91.

MORALEY, William. *London.* a.1680, CC. 1688-1704. Watch mt.

MORAN—
Andrew. *London (St. Marylebone).* 1731.
——. *London (Vere St.).* 1738.

MORAND—
Antoine. *Pont-de-Vaux* and *Lyons.* b.1674, d.1757. C. to Louis XIV. Made clock for Pont-de-Vaux in 1730. Magnificent mus. aut. clock Versailles.
——. *Geneva.* 1773. Made watches in rings, knobs of sticks, etc.
Pierre. *Paris.* m.1782-9. p.c. g. en. watch with carillon Feill coll.

MORCOMBE, John. *Barnstaple.* 1622-58. Made town clock of Hartland.

MORDAN, T. *Birmingham.* 1781.

MORDECAI, Solomon. *Rochester.* an.1786. Watch.

MORDSTEIN, Aloys. *Augsburg.* m.ca.1805.

MORE—
Joseph. *Lichfield.* 1760. l.c. clock and watch.
William. *London.* a.1739. Watch. Pair agate caskets with rep. watches Peiping M.

MORÉ—
Augustin. ——. Mid. 18c. g. astro. watch Gélis coll.
Jean Pierre. *Geneva.* 1755-71.
André. *Geneva.* 1768.
Jean Louis. *Geneva.* Late 18c.-1829. g. en. watch, set pearls. mus. rep. watch.
Jacob. *Geneva.* Late 18c. Watch N.Y. Univ.
——. *Paris.* 1812.

MOREAU, ——. Banished from *England,* 1813. *Paris,* 1821. Partner with BOUQUET, W. to Napoleon, 1814.

MORECOCK—
John. *London.* a.1734-64.
& PITNEY. *London.* 1764. Bankrupt. Partnership with John.
Daniel. *Birmingham.* 1785-1801. W.

MOREL—
Claude. *Geneva.* a.1598.
David. *Rouen.* a.1649.
Camille. *Morez.* ca.1700. Boulle mantel clock.
Jean. *Rouen.* a.1694.
Jean Baptiste. *Morbier* and *Sail-sous-Couzan.* mar.1754.
Samuel. *Neuchâtel.* 1755. C.
Jean Samuel. *Geneva.* ca.1775-91.
Jean François. *Paris.* 1777. g. en. watch.
Pierre. *Geneva.* ca.1780-ca.1835. 4-colour g. watches M.M.A. and Fränkel coll.
——. *Gisors.* ca.1800. Watch.
Joseph Aimé, son of J. B. *Sail-sous-Couzan.* mar.1789, d.1837.
Jean Marie, son. *Montbrizon.* b.ca.1796, d.ca.1874.
——. *Paris.* 1812-24. C.

MORELAND—
——. *London (Soho Sq.).* b.1703, d.1788. Watch case maker.
John. *London.* a.1727, CC.1738-45.
John. *London.* a.1747, CC.1766.

MORELL, James. *London.* a.1676.

MOREMAN, James. prob. *London.* an.1777. Watch.

MORER, ——. *Paris.* 1764.

MORERO, ——. *Paris.* 1810.

MORET—
Jean Baptiste. *Morbier.* 1770. cf. MOREL.
Pierre Claude. *Morbier.* 1776.

MORETON—
Ralph. *London.* a.1696.
Thomas. *London.* a.1734-43.
E. *London.* 1783. Watch Ilbert coll. cf. MORTON.

MOREZ, Pierre François. *Le Locle.* 1820. C.

MORF, C. *Berlin.* 1780. C.

MORGAN—
Richard. *London.* 1630-49. Petitioner for incorporation of CC. Very fine watch Louvre.
Robert. *London.* a.1638, CC.1647.
Jude. *London.* CC.1654.
William. *London.* a.1650, CC.1658.
Thomas. *London.* CC.1659-94.
Roger. *London.* a.1658.
Henry. *London.* CC.1677-82. Keymaker.
William, son of Thos. *London.* a.1689-96.
John. *London (Chancery La.).* a.1692, CC. 1706-15. l.c. clock.
Elizabeth. *London.* a.1694.
William. *London.* a.1695, CC.1704.
Edward. *London.* a.1703, CC.1735. d.an. 1754. In *Southwark* 1724. In *Clerkenwell* 1752. In *Holborn* 1754.
Walter. *Hereford.* 1743. Insolvent. C. & W.
Thomas. *Swansea.* 1744-91. l.c. clock.
John. *London (Aldersgate St.).* d.1773.
Charles. *London.* a.1734-42 CC.
Charles. *London.* a.1742.
Anthony. *London.* a.1745.
John. *Monmouth.* 1753-7. C. & W.
William. *London.* a.1747.

MORGAN—*continued.*
George. *London.* a.1753.
William, son of Ed. *London.* a.1754.
William. *London.* a.1758.
Thomas. *Baltimore, U.S.A.* 1772-82. From *Philadelphia.* C. & W.
Thomas. *Leominster.* an.1773. Watch.
James. *London.* an.1774. Watch.
John. *Bristol (Broad Ware).* 1775-1815. W.
Thomas. *Edinburgh.* a.1767-1803.
John, sen. *Wotton-under-Edge.* 1778. From *Gloucester.* Insolvent.
S. & Co. *London (Ludgate St.).* ca.1780. T.C.
John, jun. *Thornbury.* 1784. From *Gloucester.*
Thomas. *Bristol.* 1787. d.1838.
John. *London.* a.1783, CC.1790.
& MILES. *London (Ludgate St.).* 1790.
Lewis. *Llandilo.* 1791. C. & W.
Morgan. *Llandilo.* 1791.
Thomas. *Newport (Mon.).* mar.1791.
John. *Bristol (High St.).* 1792-7. C. & W.
John. *Aberystwith.* Early 19c. Watch.
William. *London.* Early 19c. Watch S.K.M.
John, & Son. *Bristol.* 1815-8.
John. *London.* a.1816.
William. *Dublin.* an.1822-4.
George. *Parsonstown.* 1824.
John, jun. *Bristol.* 1825-30.

MORICAND—
——. *Geneva.* 1794. Director, with PAUL, of the State factory. Watches M.M.A. and N.Y. Univ. Watch in form of scent flagon, en. and set stones, Feill coll.
Ch. ——. ca.1795. Watch mt. Ilbert coll. Perhaps the above or MORICANT.
& DE GRANGE. *Geneva.* 1800-29. Fine g. en. very thin verge watch Chamb. coll. g. en. watch M.M.A.
ET COMP. *Geneva.* Early 19c. en. watch, set pearls.

MORICANT, Cht. *Geneva.* ca.1800. en. apple watch in en. snuff-box. 4-colour g. watch M.M.A. Watch N.Y. Univ.

MORICE—
Thomas. *London.* a.1653.
David. *London (Fenchurch St.).* CC.1796, l.CC.1810-9. W.
David, & Son. *London.* 1804-25. Duplex watch Chamb. coll. br. clock.
David & William. *London.* 1805-25. Same firm as preceding.
William. *London.* a.1808.
——. *Paris.* 1824.

MORIEL, ——. *Paris.* 1602 juré.

MORIER (MORI)—
G. S. *Vevey.* 1750-66 comp.
Moyse. *Vevey.* 1769. Watch mt.
In. P. Aîné. *Vevey.* Early 19c. Watch.

MORIJET, Charles Peter. *London.* a.1739.

MORIN—
Jehan. *Autun.* 1656. Repaired cathedral clock.
Pierre. *Amsterdam.* ca.1700. sil. en. watch.
Francis & Alexander. prob. *London.* an.1773. Watch.

MORIN-MARCHINVILLE—
Luc. *Switzerland.* b.1659, d.1739. al. watch.
Pierre, son. *Switzerland.* ca.1700.

MORISON, Thomas. *London.* Early 19c. Watch.

MORISSET, R. and C. LUKINS. *London.* ca. 1780. g. en. watch.

MORITZ, Andreas. *Sulzfeld-am-Main.* m. 1825.

MORIZE, ——. *Paris.* 1810-25.

MORIZOT, ——. *Paris.* ca.1824. Watch.

MORLAND—
John. *London.* CC.1734.
William. *London.* 1790.

MORLAND—*continued.*
——. *London.* 1790-4.
——. *Ripon.* 1820.

MORLET, David. *Paris.* 1739. *Val de Travers,* 1739-49. C. to the King of Poland.

MORLEY—
William. *London.* a.1691.
William. *London.* a.1694, CC.1703-08.
Hassell. *London.* a.1700.
William. *London.* a.1718.
William. *Newcastle-o.-T.* 1729. Bankrupt. C.
Robert. *York.* 1732. C.
Hildebrand. *London.* 1782. Patented a water-clock.
John. *Liverpool.* 1790-6. W.
Robert. *Hursley.* 1808. Made church clock.

MORLIÈRE, Christophe. *Blois.* b. *Orléans* 1604, went to *Blois* 1628, d.1643. One of the first painters on enamel. Goldsmith and engraver to Monsieur le frère du roi, to whom the town of Blois presented a watch en. by him in 1643. En. flower painting on g. watch K.H.M., by his brother-in-law Jacques POETE, attributed to him ill. Baillie.

MORNAND—
I. *Paris.* End 17c. Watch ill. Britten.
N. *Paris.* 1st half 18c. 8-day watch Feill coll.

MORPETH—
Thomas. *Hexham.* 1725-1815. Watch. l.c. clocks. Two makers.
Robert. *London.* a.1728.

MORPIE, Thomas. *Dublin.* Early 19c. Watch Dublin M.

MORQUAIN, Jean. *Paris.* m.1674.

MORRELL—
John. *London.* a.1699.
Edward. *London.* a.1777.
James. *Richmond (Surrey).* 1791. C. & W.
J. C. *Middleburg.* ca.1800.

MORRICE, Sampson. *London.* 1802-11.

MORRIS—
Edward. *London.* a.1664, CC.1672-77. Lantern clock.
Edward Thomas. *Bala.* b.1712. Clock.
William. *London.* a.1712.
William. *London (Charles St.).* a.1713. Retired 1773. Watch.
Thomas. *London.* a.1717. Watch.
Henry. *London.* 1733-75. g. watch Den. coll.
John. *London.* a.1741.
George. *Swaffham.* 1754. C. & W.
David. *London.* a.1748.
John. *London.* a.1751.
John. *London (Gravesend).* 1761. Bankrupt. From *Dover.*
Tobias. *London (Wapping)* and *Liverpool.* 1794-1812. Gaudy gilt aut. mus. table clock made for India, S.K.M. Rack lever watch mt. Ilbert coll. Patented a sea clock.
John. *Haverfordwest.* 1795 CC. l.c. clock and watch. Also MAURICE.
Bartholomew. *London.* 1805-11.
George. *Liverpool.* 1813. W.
George. *London.* 1815. W.
Robert. *Shrewsbury.* Early 19c. Watch.
Mary. *Bolton-le-Moors.* ca.1820.

MORRISON—
Christopher. *London.* a.1706.
Theodore. *London (St. Swithin's La.).* d. 1766.
Samuel. *London.* a.1736.
John. *Edinburgh.* a.1787-94.
George. *Aberdeen.* 1792.
George. *Auchtermuchty.* 1795.
Mary. *Gosport.* 1795. W.
Caleb Hyde. *London.* a.1803.
Alexander. *London.* a.1806.
William. *Glasgow.* 1820.
v. MORISON.

MORRITT, William. *London.* a.1752, CC. 1769-74.
MORRY, George. *London.* an.1769. Watch.
MORSE—
Justinian. *Barnet.* 1752. Sale of stock. C.
John. *West Cowes.* 1809. C. & W.
——. *Malmesbury.* Early 19c. Watch.
& MOSELY. *Albany, U.S.A.* 1823. W.
MORSON, William. *London.* an.1758-67. Watch.
MORT—
Richard. *London.* CC.1693.
John. *London.* a.1738, CC.1762.
MORTEL, Louis Martin (or Nicolas). *Paris.* m.1774-89.
MORTENSEN, Jürgen P. *Rodenäs.* 1721. Wall clock.
MORTIMORE, ——. *Dartmouth.* 1825. Watch.
MORTON—
Joseph. *Aberford.* 1700-50.
Thomas. *London (Gt. Tower St.).* 1742-7. W.
William. *London.* a.1743.
J. *Sheerness.* an.1773. Watch.
E. *London.* 1779. Watch Ilbert coll. cf. MORETON.
Thomas. *St. Helens.* ca.1820.
MOSBRUCKER, ——. *Saverne.* 2nd half 18c. Rack clock.
MOSEL, Edward. *Chatham.* an.1778. Watch.
MOSELEY (MOSELY, MOSLEY, MOZLEY)—
William. *London.* CC.1680.
Elinor. *London (Gracechurch St.).* a.1718, CC.1726-38. MOSELY.
Charles. *London.* a.1728. Late 18c. Watch.
Catherine. *London.* a.1727.
Lewis. *Liverpool.* ca.1770-1803. W.
Moses. *London (Whitechapel).* 1799-1824. Previously with Sander RUSELSHEIM.
Martin. *London.* 1804-25. W.
Moses. *London (Bevis Marks).* 1805-40.
Moses. *London (Aldgate).* 1805-08.
Robert. *London.* CC.1818. W.
Richard, son. *London.* a.1818.
v. MORSE & MOSELY.
M. *Glasgow.* 1825.
T. *Swansea.* Early 19c.
MOSER—
Hensilly, alias Trinquevin. *Neuchâtel.* 1451. Locksmith. Re-made the clock of the Collegiale.
George Michael. *London.* b.1705, d.1783. Fine worker in repoussé and enamel. Watch cases Stern coll. and G.M.
Johannes. *Schaffhausen.* b.1731, d.1820. T.C. C. to the town.
Erhard, son. *Schaffhausen.* b.1760, d.1820. C. to the town.
Anton. *Augsburg.* m.1768-99. Also MOSSER.
Érard. *Chaux-de-Fonds.* 1789.
Henri, son of Erhard. *St. Petersburg* and *Schaffhausen.* b.1805. Went to *St. Petersburg* 1827 and to *Schaffhausen* 1848. d. 1874.
Henry, & Co. *Le Locle. Paris,* 1825. Founded 1826, and still in business. Supplied watches to Russia.
MOSES—
Henry. *London.* a.1722.
Moses. *London.* 1784. W.
Ephraim. *London.* 1785-90.
Lewis. *Portsea.* 1791. C. & W.
Messrs. *Dover.* 1801.
——. *Brighton.* 1822. C. & W.
MOSMANN, Jonny. *Colmar.* 2nd half 18c. 4-colour g. watch.
MOSNIER, Claude. *Paris.* m.1684.
MOSS—
Thomas. *Frodsham.* 1740. d.1784. His widow Mary carried on. br. and l.c. clock dial ill. Britten.

MOSS—*continued.*
Thomas. *London.* 1775. CC.1786, l.CC. 1801, d.1827. W. & C. en. watch. br. clock.
——. *Nottingham.* 1814. W.
John. *Rochdale.* 1814.
George. *Carlisle.* 1814-20.
Robert. *Liverpool.* 1816. W.
William S. *Manchester.* ca.1820.
John Dennett. *Liverpool.* 1825. W.
MOTE, Garrett. *London.* 1655.
MOTEL, Jean François Henri. *Paris.* b.1786, d.1859. Horloger de la Marine. Eminent maker of chrons. and observatory clocks. Used Houriet's spherical spring, and devised cylindrical spring with conical ends. One of the first to employ heart cams in chronographs. Succeeded by DUMAS. Marine chron. Ilbert coll.
MOTIN DE MATAZ, ——. *La Rochelle.* 1423.
MOTLEY—
Richard. *London (Wapping).* CC.1682. l.c. clock.
Robert. prob. *London.* an.1767. Watch.
Richard, son of Rich. *London (Whitecross St.).* mar.1771.
MOTT—
Thomas. *London.* a.1648, CC.1656. Also MOTH.
Henry (Henricus). *London.* a.1655-75. Watch.
& MORNE. *New York.* 1805. W.
William. *London.* ca.1825. Watch.
MOTTE, Jacobus. *Augsburg.* 1640. Watch mt. B.M.
MOTTEUX, Samuel. *London.* a.1686, CC. 1697.
MOTTRAM, John. *London.* 1790-1808. C. mus. clock.
MOTTU, Adolphe L. *Geneva.* Early 19c.
MOUCHE, Claude. *Grenoble.* 1662.
MOUCHIE, John de. *London.* 1622. Alien.
MOUCHOTTE, Nicolas. *Avignon.* 1742-78. Town C. Made clocks for Orange and Caderousse.
MOUCHY, Jean. *La Rochelle.* 1662.
MOUDE (MONDE), David. *London.* 1662 CC.
MOULAM, G. *Bath.* 1819.
MOULD, William. *London (Moorfields).* 1760-1771. Watch.
MOULE, John. *London.* a.1679. Also MOLE.
MOULIN, jeune. *Paris.* 1812-19.
MOULINIÉ—
——. *Geneva.* To ca.1795.
ET BAUTTE. *Geneva.* ca.1795-1810.
BAUTTE & MOYNIER. *Geneva* and *Paris.* ca. 1810-25. g. and turquoise cyl. watch S.M.S.K. Four-colour g. watch set rubies M.M.A.
Aîné et Cie. *Geneva.* 1829. g. cyl. rep. watch.
MOULTON—
Benjamin. *London.* 1738.
Edward. *London.* 1780-1802 CC.
Thomas. *London (Orchard St.).* a.1788, CC. 1796-1814.
Edward, son. *London.* CC.1802.
MOUN, Jean Baptiste. *Paris.* Mid. 18c. g. en. rep. watch.
MOUND, Theophilus. *London.* a.1693.
MOUNIEZ, Pierre. *Lyons.* 1631.
MOUNT—
William. *London.* a.1682, CC.1692.
Edward. *London (Coleman St.).* CC.1731.
MOUNTAGE, John. *London.* a.1646.
MOUNTFORD—
Zachariah. *St. Albans* and *South Mimms.* a.1676, CC.1684-1723. Watch. l.c. clock.
John. *London.* a.1729.
William. *London.* ca.1770. Watch mt. Buckley coll.

MOUNTFORT, Joseph. *London.* a.1700-28.
MOUNTJOY—
Thomas. *Bandon.* 1824.
Zebulon. *Charleville.* 1824.
John D. *Cork.* 1824.
MOURGUE, Peter. *Charleston, U.S.A.* 1735. W.
MOURIER FRÈRES. *Geneva.* ca.1765-70. Ring watch Feill coll. *v.* TRUITTE.
MOURROUX, ——. *Paris.* 1822.
MOUSE—
Richard. *London.* 1760. W.
Richard, son. *London.* a.1774.
MOUSLEY, Arthur. *London.* a.1671.
MOUTIER, D. *Geneva.* Early 19c. g. en. watch M.P.S. Dresden.
MOUTON, ——. *Paris.* 1823.
MOWATT, George. *Richmond (Yorks.).* an. 1767. Watch.
MOWBRAY, William. *Doncaster.* ca.1770-95.
MOWRAY—
Anthony. *London.* CC.1766-70.
& ELLIS. *London.* an.1778. Watch.
MOXON—
Richard. *Birmingham.* an.1774. Watch.
J. *London.* Late 18c. Skeleton clock designed by Wm. CONGREVE, Buckingham Palace. *v.* MANDEY.
James. *Bradford (Wilts.).* 1795. C.
Joseph. *Bradford (Wilts.).* 1795. C.
Walter Christy. *London.* a.1798.
MOY, Matthew. *London.* a.1661.
MOYLE—
Thomas. *Nantwich.* ca.1750. Watch with glass on cock.
George. *Chester.* 1791-7. W.
MOYNIER—
——. *Geneva.* ca.1790. Watch. *v.* BAUTTE ET MOYNIER.
ET FILS. *Geneva.* ca.1825. rep. cyl. watch. g. en. watch M.M.A.
MOYS, John. *Brumle.* Mid. 18c. Watch Stads M. Amsterdam.
MOYSAN, Jean. *Blois.* mar.1569-89.
MOYSER, Thomas. *London.* a.1653.
MOYSSET, ——. *Toulouse.* Mid. 18c. g. en. watch.
MOZART, Don J. *New York.* b.1820, d.1877. Started in 1863 in *Bristol* to make year clocks, but failed. Started NEW YORK WATCH Co. and directed MOZART WATCH Co. in *Ann Arbor, Mich.* from 1866-70, when it failed; invented a 3-wheeled lever watch, with special escapement; example in Chamb. coll.
MOZART WATCH CO. *Ann Arbor, Mich.* 1866-70. Failed, and succeeded by FREEPORT WATCH Co., 1874.
MOZE, Henry. *London.* 1743. Insolvent.
MOZLEY, Morris Lewin. *Liverpool.* 1796-1803. W.
MUCKARSIE (MACKARSIE)—
James. *London (Holborn).* CC.1784, d.1801.
George James, son. *London (Gt. Queen St.).* a.1801, CC.1814, l.CC.1824. chron. maker.
MUCKLE (MUKLE), Benedikt. *Furtwangen* and *Neukirch.* b.1771, d.1857. mus. C. of repute. mus. clock Furt. M.
MUCKLESTONE, ——. *London.* an.1730. Watch.
MUDDISON, Joseph. *London.* 1794.
MUDDLE—
Edward. *Chatham.* an.1760. Watch.
Nicholas. *Tonbridge.* an.1775. Watch.
MUDGE—
Thomas. *London* and *Plymouth.* b.1715, CC.1738, l.CC.1766, d.1794. Apprenticed to, and worked for, GRAHAM. He started in business in Fleet St. after Graham's death in 1751. One of the most eminent makers. Invented the lever escapement about 1757, and made a lever watch for Queen Charlotte, but made few others. Was the first to use stones for pallets and impulse pins. From 1771 worked on the development of the chron.; sent his first for trial in 1774, ill. Gould; eventually was awarded £3,000 by a Committee of the House of Commons. W. to George III in 1776. Entered into partnership with DUTTON in 1755, and went to *Plymouth* in 1771. Said to have made a minute rep. watch ca. 1750. Pub. 'Thoughts on the Means of Improving Watches, particularly those for use at sea.' London, 1765. l.c. clock. Remontoir c.secs. verge watch made for King of Spain in 1755, G.M. rep. watch Art M. Boston. Watch S.M.S.K. br. clock with lever esc. Ilbert coll. A rough guide to the dates corresponding to watch Nos. is: 1742, No. 51. 1755, No. 250. 1758, No. 460. 1759, No. 600.
Thomas, and William DUTTON. *London.* 1755-90. (See above.) Watches not sd. Mudge & Dutton till 1765. p.c. cyl watch S.M.S.K. Duplex ½ ¼ rep. watch and cyl. watch G.M. br. and l.c. clock Weth. coll. l.c. clock ill. Cec. & Web. al. cyl. watch Chamb. coll. g. rep. watch Marryat coll. rep. watch Den. coll. Watch sd. 'MUDGE & Co.'
J. B. prob. *London.* 1756.
Thomas, son of Thos. *London.* CC.1800. Not a maker, but employed HOWELLS & PENNINGTON to make chrons. to his father's design. l.c. clock Weth. coll. with his name. In 1792 pub. 'A Narrative of Facts relating to some Timekeepers constructed by Thomas Mudge' and 'Description with plates of the Timekeeper invented by the late Mr. Thos. Mudge,' London, 1799.
Thomas. *Bath.* ca.1800 CC.
John. *London.* ca.1800. l.c. clock Weth. coll.
MUGERIDGE, Samuel. *London.* a.1767.
MUGNIER—
Benjamin. *Geneva.* a.1599.
Charles. *Paris (Rue neuve des Petits-Champs).* 1807-23. W. to Napoleon and Louis XVIII. Copied Breguet's 'souscription' watches. Pedometer watch Feill coll.
jeune. *Paris (Rue de Richelieu).* 1812-24.
MÜHLHAUSEN, Andreas August. *Dresden.* m.1808.
MUILES, Thomas. *London.* 1747. C. & W.
MUIR—
Katherine. prob. *London.* an.1773. Watch.
James. *Glasgow.* 1792.
MUIRHEAD, James. *Glasgow.* 1817-41. W. to the Queen. Duplex c.secs. mt. Ilbert coll.
MUISARD, ——. ——. Late 17c. Enameller of watch by GRIBELIN, B.M. Prob. Jean MUSSARD.
MUKLÉ, Anthon. *Stockholm.* 1784-1815. Wooden C. l.c. clock. Cuckoo clock Nord. M.
MULCASTER, George. *London.* a.1793.
MULFORD—
William. *London.* a.1682.
John. *London.* CC.1716-29.
John. *London.* CC.1735, w.CC. and d.1748. g. watch Den. coll.
John, son. *London.* a.1736, CC.1748-54.
MULLAN, Thomas. *Duncannon.* 1824.
MULLART, Frederick. *London.* a.1752.
MULLEN—
James. *Mountmelick.* 1824.
Henry. *Aughnacloy.* 1824.

MÜLLER—
Michel. *Lucerne*. 1557. From *Winterthur*.
Michael. *Strasbourg*. 1579. comp. to Isaac HABRECHT. Went with him to finish Heilbronn clock.
Jost. *Strasbourg*. 1606.
Christopher. *Nürnberg*. Early 17c. Table clock Den. coll.
Andreas. *Dresden*. 1638. d.1653. Court C. Clock M.M.A.
Hans Jacob. *Strasbourg*. 1664.
Johann Georg. *Dresden*. m.1670. str. trav. clock Hohenzollern M. Berlin.
Alexander Andreas. *Dresden*. m.1703.
Johann Heinrich. *Cassel*. 1672. d.1738. Court C. Dial Old Ashmolean M.
Ludovicus Theodor. *Augsburg*. ca.1740. Sundials B.M. and Fränkel coll. Compass.
——. *Kriegshaber*. 1756. Two brothers. cf. MILLER.
Georg. *Basle*. 1763. *Paris*, 1793-5. Kleinuhrmacher.
Johann. *Basle*. 1768.
Ferdinand. ——. 2nd half 18c. 'Kayserliche Hoffbefreiter.' Wall clock Furt. M.
Martin. *Ellingen*. 1776.
F. C. *Germany*. 1778. Pub. in Berlin and Leipzig 'Von Gebrauch der Taschenuhren zu geometrischen Messungen.'
Johann Gottlieb. *Vienna*. m.1787. rep. br. clocks M.P.S. Dresden. g. en. shell watch M.M.A.
Sebastian. *Günzberg*. a.ca.1784. *Augsburg*, 1795-1801. Kleinuhrmacher.
Paulus. *Fürth*. 1793.
Samuel Carl. *Dresden*. m.1800.
Johann Gotthilf. *Hamburg*. 1801-04.
Mathias. *Vienna*. m.1803. Also MULLNER.
In. Pre. *Bienne*. Early 19c. Watch.
R. *Paris*. 1824.

MULLIKEN—
Samuel. *Newburyport, U.S.A.* b.1720, d. 1756. C.
Jonathan, son. *Newburyport, U.S.A.* Carried on his father's business from 1756.

MULLINER, Abraham. *London*. a.1712.
MULLINS, ——. *London*. b.ca.1713-65. Watch case maker.
MULOTIN, ——. *Paris*. 1807-25.
MUMMERY, ——. *Dover*. Early 19c. Watch.

MUNCASTER—
John. *Kendal*. 1790-1820.
William. *Whitehaven*. ca.1790-1820. Lancaster freeman. Watch Den. coll.
John, son. *Lancaster, Liverpool* and *Ulverstone*. 1806-24. C.
Thomas. *Lancaster*. ca.1820.

MÜNCH—
Nikolaus. *Nürnberg*. 1640.
Joachim Heinrich. *Münster*. 1696.
Karl. *Münster*. 1818. Fitted deadbeat escapement to Dom clock.

MUNDAY—
Thomas. *London*. a.1685, CC.1692-1708.
Thomas. *London*. a.1688.
William. *London*. 1734-57 CC.
William. *London*. a.1740, CC.1747.
David. *Bridgend*. 1769.

MUNDEN—
Francis. *London*. CC.1653-87.
Francis. *London*. a.1663, CC.1670.
Richard. *London*. 1695.

MUNDY—
Hugh. *London*. a.1706.
James. *London*. a.1758.

MUNGER, A. *Auburn, U.S.A.* 1825.
MÜNHOFIN, Christoph. *Prague*. ca.1675. Watch Ilbert coll.

MUNIER—
Benjamin. *Lyons*. 1609 comp.
Nicolas. *Paris*. m.1741.
Philippe François. *Geneva*. ca.1775-91

MUNKERSON, David. *Edinburgh*. m.1712
MUNOZ, Blas. *Madrid*. 1806-23. C. to the King. Sent by Spanish Navy to study chron. making in Paris.

MUNRO—
John. *Edinburgh*. 1783. cyl. watch.
John. *Charleston, U.S.A.* 1785. Previously *Edinburgh* and *London*.
Nathaniel. *Boston, U.S.A.* ca.1810.
Benjamin. *London*. 1820.

MUNROE, Daniel, jun. *Boston, U.S.A.* 1813-1825. W.
MUNSEY, William. *London*. a.1766.

MUNSHALL—
Hugh. *London*. a.1749-62.
& BEALES. *London* (*New Bond St.*). an.1776. Watch.

MUNSLOW, John. *London*. a.1792, CC.1799.

MURCH—
Richard. *Honiton*. 2nd half 18c. l.c. clock. Also MARCH.
John. *Honiton*. 1817. Made clock for Sidbury Church. l.c. clock.
Matthew. *Honiton*. Early 19c. Watch.

MURDEN, Thomas. *Birmingham*. 1790. l.c. clock.

MURDOCH—
John. *Edinburgh*. a.1752-75.
John. *Edinburgh*. a.1767.
James, & Son. *Ayr*. 1820-50.
James. *London*. Early 19c. Lever watch with two mainsprings to run for 8 days Chamb. coll.

MURE, Peter. *England*. 1544. French.
MURET, John. *London*. 1761. cyl. watch Ilbert coll.

MURGATROYD—
George. *London*. 1710. Watch.
Frederick. *London*. a.1809, CC.1821.

MURPHY—
Peter. *Bristol*. 1739. W.
J. *Norfolk*. ca.1800.
P. *Dublin*. ca.1800. Watch.
& CULLINAN. *Dublin*. ca.1800. Watch N.Y. Univ.
James. *Boston, U.S.A.* 1803-06. W.
Andrew. *Mullingar*. 1824.
John. *Cork*. 1824.
Patrick. *Waterford*. 1824.

MURRAY—
Charles. *London*. 1702. W.
William. *Edinburgh*. a.1706-12.
James. *London*. a.1713.
William. *Kings Lynn*. 18c. l.c. clock.
William. *Chelmsford*. an.1755. Watch.
John. *Lymercleugh*. an.1765. Watch.
T. *London*. ca.1780. Watch.
David. *Edinburgh*. b.1755, d.1832.
John. *Lanark*. 1790.
James. *Perth*. a.1790.
George. *Doune*. 1798.
James. *London*. 1810. CC.1815, l.CC.1817-1840. Watch and chron. maker of great repute; in partnership with STRACHAN. g. repoussé watch Den. coll.
John. *Liverpool*. 1816-18. W.
W. *London*. Early 19c. Watch.
& STRACHAN. *London*. 1820-4.

MURRELL, William. *London*. an.1777-99. W.
MURRETT, John. *London*. 1737. Insolvent.
MURTAIN, Edward. *London*. an.1777. Watch.
MUSCATT, George. *London*. a.1726.
MUSENBERG, Johan Henrik. *Copenhagen*. m.1735.

MUSGRAVE—
George. *Taunton*. 1760-90. Watch mt.
William. *Leeds*. d.1791. C.
William, son. *Leeds*. From 1791.
Richard. *Wigton*. 1800-42.

MUSGROVE, Richard. *London*. CC.1818.

MUSHIN (MUSHAM), John. *London.* CC. 1768.

MUSKET, John. *Prescot.* ca.1770-95.

MUSSARD—

Daniel. *London.* CC.1686-9. From *Geneva.* rep. watch. l.c. clock.

Isaac. *Geneva.* 1698.

Jean. *Geneva.* b.1681, d.1754. Famous painter on enamel. Watches B.M. and Olivier coll.

Jean, et Fils. *Geneva.* 1743.

D. F. *St. Petersburg.* ca.1820. rep. watch Ilbert coll.

MUSSELWHITE, William. *Bicester.* 1791. C. & W.

MUSSEY, William. *Nantwich.* Early 19c. Watch mt. Grosvenor M. Chester.

MUSSON—

——. *Paris.* ca.1760 m. g. rep. watch.

Pierre François, son. *Paris.* m.1767.

Pierre Marie. *Paris.* m.1772.

——. *Orléans.* 2nd half 18c. Watch.

Louis. *Paris.* 1783-90.

B. *Louth.* Early 19c. Watch mt. Buckley coll.

MUSY, ——. *Paris.* 1762. Devised a clock for invalids with candle and alarum and illuminated dial, acting as night-light and heater for potions.

MUT (MUTH), Gerard. *Frankfurt-a.-M.* ca. 1670. Made watches with polygonal wheels, examples in K.H.M. and M.P.S. Dresden. Clock on inclined plane Cassel Landes-M.

MUYS, Joannes. *Mosam.* 1653. Clock Ilbert coll.

MUYTER, Jan de. *Haarlem.* 1755-82. *Amsterdam.* 1785.

MUZZALL—

John. *Horsham.* 1784. W.

John. *Southampton.* 1792. C. & W.

Cornelius. *Horsham.* 1793-7. 'Clocksmith.'

MYERS—

John. *York.* 1778. *London* (*Southwark*), 1783-1808. l.c. clock S.K.M. W.

Henry. *London.* 1804. Watch.

Mary. *London.* 1809-11.

MYLES, George. *Edinburgh.* a.1676.

MYLNE—

J. A. *Montrose.* 1740.

John. *London.* an.1775. Watch.

Jacob. prob. *London.* an.1784. Watch.

James. *Edinburgh.* 1793.

MYNUEL, ——. *Paris.* 1693-ca.1750. Ormolu cartel clock S.K.M. Very fine clock Wallace coll. br. clock Louvre. Gilt watch dated 1693.

MYON, Pierre. *Lyons.* 1603.

MYSON, Jeremiah. *London.* CC.1698-1708.

N

NABER, Joseph. *Vienna.* m.1796.
NACHBAR, Mathias. *Vienna.* m.1799.
NADAULD—
William. *London (Houndsditch).* a.1788, CC. 1801, l.CC.1812-20.
Thomas. *London.* a.1789.
John. *London.* 1809-11.
W. E. *London.* 1820.
NADWYD, ——. *London.* an.1779. Watch.
NAFTELS, ——. *Guernsey.* ca.1800.
NAGEL, ——. *Strasbourg.* 1535.
NAGL, Andreas. *Vienna.* m.ca.1667.
NANCE, Antoine. *Salins.* 1472. Repaired clock of Ste. Anatoile.
NANGLE, Nathaniel. *Bristol.* 1761. d.1793. W.
NANSTOOLS, J. J. *Rotterdam.* ca.1800.
NAPIER—
John. *London.* a.1752. Watch.
& Dunn. *Glasgow.* 1783.
Thomas. *Edinburgh.* 1789-1803.
NAPJUS (NAPPIS), H. *Sneek.* ca.1790. br. clock.
NAPPER, Edward. *London.* a.1754.
NAPTON, William. *London.* a.1688, CC.1695.
NARDIN, Ulysse. *Neuchâtel* and *Le Locle.* b. 1823, d.1876. Famous maker of precision watches and chrons.
NARNEY, Joseph. *Charleston, U.S.A.* 1753-1761. W.
NASH—
William. prob. *London.* ca.1605. Oval watch Marryat coll.
William. *London.* a.1663.
John. *London.* CC.1667-89. inst. maker.
James. *London.* a.1697.
John. *London.* a.1709.
Thomas. *London (Red Cross Sq.).* CC.1717, l.CC.1769-71.
——. *Dublin.* an.1750. Watch.
Samuel. *London (Blackfriars).* a.1753, CC. 1761-90. Watch.
William. *Bridge (Canterbury).* 1762. d.1794. Watch mt. Ilbert coll.
John, bro. *Breakesbourn.* 1769. Previously working with his bro.
Thomas, son of Thomas. *London (Jewin St.).* CC.1768.
Francis. *London.* a.1774.
Levy. *Bath.* an.1780. Watch.
William Strudwick, son of Samuel. *London.* a.1789, CC.1810. W.
George, bro. *London.* a.1794, CC.1810. W.
Henry Richard. *London.* a.1803, CC.1826.
NATAL, ——. *Nyon.* 1st half 18c.
NATHAN—
P. E. *Birmingham.* ca.1800 CC.
Isaac. *London.* 1809-11. W.

NATHAN—*continued.*
Mary. *London.* 1817-24.
John. *Liverpool.* 1824-9. W.
Philip. *Liverpool.* 1824-9. W.
NATHEY, ——. *Nyon.* 2nd half 18c.
NATIONAL WATCH CO. OF CHICAGO, *v.* Elgin National Watch Co.
NATSON, ——. *London.* an.1753. Watch.
NATTLE—
Richard. *Launceston.* 1791-5. C. & W.
George. *Holdsworthy.* 1795. C. & W.
NAU—
Richard. *London.* a.1653, CC.1661.
George. *London.* CC.1675-95. d.an.1702.
Margaret, widow. *London.* 1702.
NAUDIN, ——. *Paris.* 1812-25.
NAUGHAN, Charles. *London.* Early 19c. Watch.
NAUMANN—
Johann Heinrich. *Dresden.* m.1730. Court C. from *Hainichen.* Table clock M.P.S. Dresden.
Johann Friedrich. *Dresden.* m.1744. Fine g. watch set cornelians.
Carl Heinrich. *Dresden.* m.1773, d.1795.
NAUNDORFF, Carl Wilhelm. *Potsdam.* b. 1785, d.1845. Claimed to be the son of Louis xvi.
NAUSITER, Edward. *London.* Early 19c. Watch.
NAUTA—
Jacobus. *Leeuwarden.* 1685. Maker of repute. Table clock. Fine p.c. g. eng. watch Ilbert coll.
Jan Jacobus. *Leeuwarden.* 1714 m.
Gysbartus J. *Leeuwarden.* 1718. d.an.1757. l.c. clock.
NAVET, ——. *Versailles.* Early 19c. Watch Ilbert coll.
NAWE, François (Francoy). *London.* Late 16c. Two oval watches Webster coll. ill. Baillie. Prob. same as Noway, *q.v.*
NAYLOR—
William. *Liverpool.* m.1697. W.
J. *Nantwich* and *London (King St., Covent Garden).* ca.1725, d.1752. astro. clock Cluny M.
Michael. *London.* a.1719.
Joshua. *London (King St.).* d.1752. W.
Thomas. *London.* an.1771. Watch.
Charles. *Liverpool.* 1790-1813. W.
NAZE, Jean. *Lyons.* a.ca.1545, d.1581. Maker of repute. hex. table clock Petit Palais, and square table clock. *v.* Jean.
NEAL—
John. *Dublin.* 1780. W.
Daniel. *Philadelphia.* 1825.

NEALE—
George. *London.* 1721. W.
George. *London.* a.1726.
John. *London* (*Leadenhall St.*). 1743-58. Patented a 'Quadrantal planetarian' watch. Watch with Turkish figures.
George. *Gloucester.* an.1776. Watch.
Michael. *London.* a.1810, CC.1825.
James. *London.* a.1816.
William. *Brighton.* Early 19c. Watch.
William. *Lindfield.* Early 19c. Watch.
John. *Kirkdale.* 1825. W.
William. *Liverpool.* 1825. W.

NEALL—
James. *Edinburgh.* a.1775.
James. *London.* 1820.

NEAP, Edward. prob. *London.* an.1776. Watch.

NEATE, George. *London.* a.1773.

NEATH, Henry. prob. *London.* an.1751. Watch.

NEATON, John. *London.* an.1770. Watch.

NECKER, Joseph. *Wasserburg.* Early 19c. g. watch.

NEEDHAM—
John. *London.* a.1691.
Benjamin. *London.* a.1700, CC.1709.
James. *London* (*Lambeth Hill*). a.1735, CC. 1746-73.
John. *London.* a.1745.
Thomas. *London.* a.1745, CC.1756.
George, son of James. *London.* CC.1790.

NEEDS—
Amos. *Minehead.* an.1783. Watch.
John. *London.* a.1787.

NEESE, John. prob. *London.* an.1762. Watch.

NEEVE, John. *Hingham.* 1795. W.

NEFF, Joh. Theo. *Fürth.* d.1819.

NEGELEIN, ——. *Nürnberg.* Early 18c. Dial Old Ashmolean M.

NEGRO, Bartolomeo. *Caffa* (*Genoa*). 1456. 'Clavonerius magister orologii.' Keeper of clock at Caffa.

NEGUS—
William. *London.* a.1780, CC.1787, d.1807.
Charles. *Huntingdon.* 1795. C. & W.

NEHMZOW, Johann Andreas. *Hamburg.* 1821.

NEIDLAIS, ——. *Blois.* Late 18c. g. watch g. piqué skin case, formerly in Shandon coll.

NEIDTHARDT, L. *Fürth.* d.1807.

NEIGHBOUR—
William. *London.* a.1677, CC.1685-93.
Joseph. *Bristol.* 1743-75. C. & W.

NEILE, John. *London.* a.1657.

NEILL—
John. *Glasgow.* 1627-49.
Robert. *Belfast.* a.1791, d.1857. Partner with R. L. GARDNER, 1809-18. Watch.
Robert, & Sons. *Belfast.* 1818.

NEILSON—
John. *Glasgow.* 1810-17.
George. *Dumfries.* 1820.

NEIMEIER, J. ——. 1st half 18c. Fine g. p.c. watch, both cases en.

NEISSER, Augustine. *Philadelphia.* 1770-8. W.

NELLIS, J. *London.* an.1771. Watch.

NELLSON, James. *v.* NELSON.

NELMES, Robert. *London.* CC.1717.

NELSON—
James. *London.* a.1638-45. astro. watch G.M. Also NELLSON.
Robert. *London.* a.1684, CC.1698. Watch Den. coll.
John. *London.* a.1689, CC.1697. Also NOLSON.
Robert. *Amsterdam.* 1st half 18c. sil. tortoise-shell watch.
William. *Liverpool.* 1777-1818. W.

NELSON—*continued.*
Thomas. *London.* a.1764, CC.1779.
Paul. *London.* an.1785. Watch.
Thomas. *Nottingham.* 1785. C.
John. *Dublin.* 1786-1813.
Richard. *Liverpool.* 1796-1811. W.
H. *London.* 1799. Watch N.Y. Univ.
Thomas. *Liverpool.* 1807-29. W.
John. *Liverpool.* Early 19c. Watch.
T. *Market Deeping.* 1811. C. & W.
Gerard. *Liverpool.* 1824-9. W.
Henry. *Liverpool.* 1825. W.

NELTHROPP, Rev. Henry Leonard. b.1820, d.1901. Collector of watches. His collection was given to the CC. and is now in the G.M. Pub. 1873, 'A treatise on watch-work, past and present.'

NEMES—
Robert. *London.* a.1669, CC.1677-1717. d.an.1735.
Robert, son. *London.* a.1702, CC.1717-45.
John, bro. *London.* a.1710, CC.1724-53. Dial Old Ashmolean M.

NEPVEU, Nicolas Antoine. *Paris.* 1773 m.

NERIAULT, Jean Auguste. *Paris.* Juré 1748.

NERRY, John. *London.* ca.1740. Watch mt. G.M.

NESBITT, George. *Sunderland.* 1820.

NESL, Johan Georg. *Gratz.* 17c. Fine trav. clock.

NESSELIUS, Israel. *Örebro.* 1800. *Linköping,* 1816-46. Watch and trav. clock.

NESTFELL (**NESFEL**), Johann George. *Würzburg, Wiesentheid* and *Alsfeld.* 1753-1761. Planetaria in K.H.M. and Luitprandt M.

NETHERCOTTE—
——. *Chipping Norton.* Mid. 18c.
George. *Fifield.* 18c. l.c. clock.

NETHERWOOD, Job. *London.* a.1686.

NETTER, Robert. *London.* a.1681.

NETTLETON, F. *London.* 1788. Watch Oldham M.

NETTMANN—
Dietrich Heinrich. *Cassel.* 1767-84. Court C. Clock Cassel Landes-M.
——. *Cassel.* 1817. Court C.

NETTO, J. *London.* 1820.

NETZLIN, Jacob. *Berne.* 1523. Made clock for Berne.

NEUHAUS—
Vincent. *Couvet.* a.1745-62.
Rodolphe, son. *Couvet.* a.1763.
L. *Arbourg.* Early 19c.

NEUHENS, ——. *Paris.* 1825.

NEUWENHOF, ——. *Amsterdam.* 2nd half 17c. Watch. cf. NIEUWENHOFF.

NEUWERS, Michael. *v.* NOUWEN.

NEVE (**NEUE**), Henry. *London* (*Strand*). ca. 1700-52. br. clock ill. Cec. & Web. g. repoussé watch.

NEVEREN (**NEUREN** or **NEWEREN**), D. B. D. *London.* 1784. Watches S.M.S.K., Glasgow Art Gall. and Ilbert coll.

NEVEU, Jean Baptiste. *Paris.* m.1787-9.

NEVILL—
George. *London.* a.1653.
William. *Bristol.* ca.1765.
Thomas, son. *Bristol.* 1781-1818.
John. *London* (*Clerkenwell*). a.1774, CC. 1783-1812.
John. *Norwich.* 1784-95. l.c. clock.
John. *London.* CC.1818.

NEVINSON, ——. *Kendal.* an.1774. Watch.

NÉVIR, Georg. *Berlin.* 1763. d.ca.1815.

NEWARK WATCH CO. *Newark, U.S.A.* 1867-9. Watches sd. 'The Newark Watch,' 'Robert Fellows,' 'Edward Bevin,' 'The Arthur Wadsworth.'

NEWBALD, James. *York.* 1825. W.

NEWBERRY—
Robert. *London.* a.1713.
James. *Annapolis, U.S.A.* 1748. W.
John. *London.* a.1746.
James W. *Philadelphia.* 1819-25.
NEWBOLT, ——. *London.* d.1744. W.
NEWBROUGH, John. *London.* an.1743. Watch.
NEWBURY, John. *London.* a.1695.
NEWBY—
William. *Kendal.* ca.1770-97. l.c. clock.
James. *Kendal.* ca.1770-97. W.
Richard. *Liverpool.* 1825. W.
NEWCOMB—
Joseph. *London.* a.1798, CC.1807, l.CC. 1810.
George. *Bristol.* 1817. W.
NEWELL—
John. *London.* a.1681.
John. *Wrexham.* an.1771. Watch.
William. *London.* a.1747, CC.1754.
William, son. *London* (*Wood St.* and *Newgate St.*). CC.1779, l.CC.1810-19.
Joseph, son. *London.* a.1797.
N. *Leicester.* 1815. C. & W. Also NEWILL.
'NEW ERA.' Sig. on watches of the LANCASTER, PA., WATCH CO. ca.1878.
NEWEY, John. *London.* a.1707.
NEWLANDS—
John. *London.* an.1775. Watch.
L. F. *Glasgow.* 1816.
James & Luke. *Glasgow.* 1823.
NEWLOVE, John. *York.* 1823-30. l.c. clock. W. & C.
NEWMAN—
Elizabeth. *London.* a.1694.
Nathaniel. *London.* a.1694, CC.1703-34.
John. *London.* a.1704.
Thomas. *London.* a.1705, CC.1713.
Robert. *London.* a.1721. Clock.
John. *Norwich.* an.1743. Watch.
William. *London.* a.1737, CC.1755.
William. *Norwich.* 18c. l.c. clock. Watch mt.
Joseph. *London* (*Ayliffe St.*). 1767-79. W.
Charles. *Norwich.* 1772. W.
George. *Topsham.* mar.1774. W.
Richard. *Kings Lynn.* 1784. Watch.
Joseph. *London.* a.1779-90.
Thomas. *London.* a.1782, CC.1790.
Charles. *London.* a.1783, CC.1794.
John Addison. *London* (*Bartholomew Close*). CC.1790, l.CC.1808, d.1820.
William. *Rye.* 1791. W.
Richard. *Kings Lynn.* 1791-5. W.
William. *Romsey.* 1795.
——. *Kingston.* Late 18c.
Robert. *London* (*Clerkenwell*). a.1792, CC. 1800.
Edward. *London* (*Clerkenwell*). 1800-11. br. clock ill. Cec. & Web.
George. *London* (*Kensington*). 1808.
Thomas. *London.* a.1803.
John. *London.* a.1804, l.CC.1810-25.
William. *London.* 1817-20.
John. *Charlton, Kent.* 1821.
Thomas. *Cavan.* 1824.
James. *London.* a.1819.
NEWNES, Samuel. *Whitchurch.* 1795. Watch.
NEWNHAM—
Nathaniel. *London.* CC.1703 (?), d.1793.
James. *London.* a.1769.
NEWSAM—
Bartholomew. *London.* 1568. d.1593. C. to Queen Elizabeth from 1572. Table clocks B.M. and M.M.A., latter sd. 'Nusam.' Large watch M.M.A., sd. 'B×N' ill. Britten prob. by him. Also NEWSHAM.
John. *York.* 1568-98. Repaired Ousebridge clock. Also NEWSOME.
NEWSHAM—
Richard. *Liverpool.* 1791. c.secs. cal. watch.
John. *Liverpool.* 1796. W.
NEWSOM, Thomas. *London.* ca.1800. T.C.
NEWSON—
John. *London* (*Basinghall St.*). a.1722, CC. 1734-84.
George. *London.* a.1737.
John. *London.* a.1796, CC.1805-14.
N. W. *Halesworth.* Early 19c. Watch.
NEWSTEAD, Christopher. *York.* 1755. d. 1801. C.
NEWTON—
Thomas. *London.* 1664 CC.
Herbert. *London.* a.1663.
William. *London.* a.1673.
William. *London.* a.1676, CC.1685.
John. *Stoke.* 2nd half 17c. Lantern clock.
Richard. *London.* a.1684, CC.1695-1706.
Jonathan. *London.* a.1708.
Elizabeth. *London.* a.1725.
John. *London.* CC.1732.
Thomas. *London.* a.1728-56.
James. ——. ca.1760. Fine tortoise-shell and ormolu br. clock Buckingham Pal.
Mary. *London.* a.1732.
James. *Guernsey.* an.1774. Watch.
George. *London.* a.1762.
Joseph. *Liverpool.* 1781-1829. W.
Charles. *London.* an.1784. Watch.
Andrew. *London.* 1783. Watch Ilbert coll.
Jonathan. *London* (*Red Lion St., Clerkenwell*). CC.1784.
John. *London* (*Lamb's Conduit St.*). 1790-1815. Succeeded Wm. DEVIS.
Joseph. *London.* a.1784-1811. Watch.
John. *London* (*Gt. Ormond St.*). 1815-24.
John. *Leeds.* 1817. C.
NEWTONHED, James. *London.* ca.1780. sil. mounted br. clock.
NEW YORK WATCH CO. *Springfield, Mass.* Issued the following watches with sigs.: 'Springfield,' 'John L. King,' 'Homer Foot,' 'No. 5,' 'J. A. Briggs,' 'H. G. Norton,' 'Albert Clark' in 1870, and 'Frederick Billings,' 'George Walker,' 'New York Watch Co.,' 'John Hancock,' 'Geo. Sance Rice,' 'Chas. E. Howard,' 'Chester Woolworth' in 1871-5.
NEWZAM, John. *Newark.* 1786. W.
NEYTON, Claude. *Chambéry.* 1486. Locksmith. Repaired table clocks, one 'en argent en façon d'un tambourin.'
NIBLETT—
Harry. *Dorking.* 1791. W.
Henry Joseph. *London.* CC.1825. W.
NICASIUS, John. *London.* CC.1632, m.CC. 1653-79. oct. crys. watch G.M. sil. watch Gélis coll. oval crys. watch.
NICHOL, Isaac. *London.* a.1674, CC.1681-1712.
NICHOLAS—
C. *London.* 1685-1705. l.c. clock ill. Cec. & Web.
Benjamin. *London.* a.1682. Also NICKLIS.
William. *Birmingham.* 1785-1825. Watch N.Y. Univ. l.c. clocks.
Caleb. *Birmingham.* 1787-1808. l.c. clocks.
W. & C. *Birmingham.* an.1793. Watch.
Joshua. *Birmingham.* 1797-1801. l.c. clocks.
——. *Daventry.* Early 19c. Watch.
William. *London.* 1820-5.
NICHOLLS—
Roger. *London.* a.1659, CC.1667-1708.
Isaac. *London.* 1697.
Thomas. *London.* a.1698, CC.1707-18.
George. *New York.* 1728-50.
William. *London.* an.1751. Watch.
James. *Wells* (*Norfolk*). an.1755. Watch.
William. *Wells* (*Norfolk*). an.1759. Watch.
John. *London.* CC.1771-88.
P. *Oundle.* Late 18c. l.c. clock.

NICHOLLS—*continued.*
William. *London* (*Gt. Portland St.*). 1790-1825. br. clock ill. Cec. & Web. Also NICOL and NICOLL.
& SON. *Newport* (*I. of Wight*). 1795. C. & W. cf. NICHOLS.
John. *London.* a.1788.
William. *London* (*Hoxton*). 1802-08. W.
Samuel. *London.* a.1797.
John. *London* (*Hoxton*). 1808. W.
John. *London* (*Clerkenwell*). 1809. C.
Hammond. *Canterbury.* 1810. C. & W.
James. *Newport* (*I. of Wight*). 1814. W. cf. NICHOLS.
Robert. *London.* 1815-20. W.

NICHOLS—
Thomas. *London.* a.1708, CC.1720.
John. *London.* a.1738.
Peter. *Newport.* ca.1770. Sheeps head clock. cf. NICHOLLS.
Henry. *Mold.* 2nd half 18c. Watch Nat. M. Cardiff.
Thomas. *London.* a.1766, CC.1781-99.

NICHOLSON—
John. *London.* a.1718.
James. *London.* a.1726, CC.1733-7.
Richard. *London.* a.1739, CC.1747-55.
John. *Durham.* From 1768. d.1803. Succeeded Joseph GREY. C. & W.
——. *West Cowes.* ca.1790 CC.
W. *London.* 1797. Clock, gravity esc. Ilbert coll.
Henry. *London.* a.1796.
Richard. *Berwick-on-Tweed.* 1806-22. Watch.
Charles. *Brighton.* 1822. C. & W.
Nicholas. *Cork.* 1824.

NICKALLS, Job. *London.* a.1762, CC.1769.

NICKALS, Isaac. *Wells* (*Norfolk*). ca.1750. l.c. c.secs. clock Weth. coll. ill. Britten. cf. NICHOLLS.

NICKISSON—
William. *Newcastle-under-Lyme.* 1804. C. & W.
Sampson. *London.* 1808-40. Watch mt. Ilbert coll.
John. *Newcastle-under-Lyme.* Early 19c. Watch.

NICKLIN—
William. *Liverpool.* d.(?)1773. W.
William. *Birmingham.* 1755-74. l.c. clock and watch.

NICOD (NICOT)—
——. *London.* ca.1750. Watch Chamb. coll.
Philippe. *Moudon.* Mid. 18c.
Samuel. *Moudon.* Mid. 18c.
——. *Moudon.* Went to *Vevey* 1754.
Denis Joseph. *Paris.* m.1770-89.
Aîné. *Paris* (*Rue du Bac*). 1807-14.
Jeune. *Paris* (*Rue des Sts. Pères*). 1812-25.
Auguste. *Cortébert.* Early 19c.

NICOL—
David. ——. 17c. str. and al. watch.
Joseph. *Coupar Angus.* 1801-37.
James. *Midcalder.* Early 19c. Watch.

NICOLAS LE RELOGIER—
——. *Lyons.* 1561. Perhaps Nicolas GAILLARD or Nicolas ODET.
Annibal. *Avignon.* 1613. Restored belfry clock with LOIAL & BAL.

NICOLAUS—
——. *Copenhagen.* 1587. C.
M. C. *Dantzig.* ca.1700. Table clock.

NICOLAYSON, Lars. *Kirkerup.* m.1817.

NICOLE—
John. *London.* 1371. Keeper of clock in Palace of Westminster.
——. *Geneva.* 1820. Watch G.M.
FRÈRES. *Geneva.* Early 19c.
ET CAPT. *Solliat* (*Vallée de Joux*). In 1862 showed first chronograph with returning hand at the Exhibition in London. *v.* PIGUET, H.F.

NICOLET (NICOLLET)—
Abraham Louis. *La Ferrière.* 1766.
Jacob Louis. *St. Imier.* b.1751.
Jacob Pierre. *Geneva.* ca.1775-91.
Marie Joseph. *Paris.* m.1784-92. *Philadelphia,* 1793-9. g. en. watch sd. at Paris.
C. L. F. *Chaux-de-Fonds.* ca.1800. Developed engine-turning.
Auguste. *Renan.* ca.1810.

NICOLL (NICOLLS)—
James. *Edinburgh.* a.1721-60. l.c. clock.
William. *Edinburgh.* a.1740-75.
Samuel. *London.* an.1769. Watch.
Henry. *St. Austell.* 1795. C. & W.

NIEBERG, J. L. *Hamburg.* 1846. chron. maker. Patented a constant force free escapement for clocks.

NIEDERMAYR—
Christoph. *Salzburg.* 1640. Watch in form of tulip.
Johann Franz. *Salzburg.* 1666.
Johann Christoph. *Salzburg.* 1673.
Adam. *Salzburg.* 1694.
Franz Jacob. *Salzburg.* m.1708-ca.1730. p.c. sil. and tortoise-shell watch Feill coll.
Joseph. *Salzburg.* 1739.

NIELSEN, N. ——. 2nd half 18c. Hanging rack clock Feill coll.

NIEUWENHOFF, N. *Amsterdam.* Early 18c. Watch, cast sil. case, Ilbert coll. cf. NEUWENHOF.

NIGG, Joseph. *Salzburg.* Late 18c. sil. en. watch.

NIGGL, Vital. *Austria.* Late 18c. sil. p.c. watch, painted dial.

NIGHTINGALE—
John. *London.* a.1655.
Matthew. *London.* a.1686.
Thomas. *London.* a.1714.
Thomas. *London.* a.1733.
William. *London.* 1747-70. On spring of aut. carriage. Watch mt. Buckley coll.

NILOE, Hans. *London.* 1609. 'The clerk of the signet to prepare a warrant to pay 300 li to Hans Niloe a Dutchman, for a clock with music and motions.'

NIMMO—
J. *Leith.* 1806.
Alexander. *Leith.* 1819.
Alexander. *Kirkcaldy.* 1820.

NINDE, James. *Baltimore.* 1799-1807. W. & C.

NINOCHE, Jacques. *Gien.* 1619.

NIOUX, Étienne. *Paris.* m.1765. A dead secs. watch approved by the Acad. des Sci.

NISBET, James. *Edinburgh.* a.1760.

NISBETT, James. *London.* a.1793.

NITSCHNER—
Franz. *Vienna.* m.1778.
Leopold. *Vienna.* m.1797.

NIVERT (NIVARD), Henry Nicolas. *Paris.* m.1786-9.

NIVIANNE, Jean Auguste. *Paris.* Juré 1743.

NIXON—
Thomas. ——. ca.1610. Oval watch G.M.
——. *Lincoln.* an.1767. Watch.
John. *New York.* 1773. Called himself 'Musical, Repeating and Plain Clock and Watch-Maker, Periodical Titivator, the only regular Watch-Maker (Not of the London Company though).' *v.* SIMNET.
Samuel. *Newcastle-under-Lyme.* 1795. C. & W.

'NO. 5.' Sig. on 1870 watches of the NEW YORK WATCH CO.

NOADE, ——. *Dublin.* an.1770. Watch.

NOAKES—
James. *London* (*Bishopsgate St.*). an.1755-1824. Watch.
James. *London* (*Charterhouse Sq.*). 1755-90. W.
——. *Peterborough.* 1764-73. C. & W.

NOAKES—*continued.*
William. *London.* CC.1783.
James. *London (Houndsditch).* CC.1789, l.CC.1794, d.1818. p.c. g. repoussé watch Carnegie M.
James. *London (Stoke Newington).* CC.1796-1804.
James. *London.* a.1795.
George, son of James (1). *London.* a.1808.
J. *Burwash.* Early 19c. Watch.
John. *London.* 1817-24. C.
NOBBS, Thomas. *London.* a.1714.
NOBLE—
Phineas. *London.* a.1693.
James. *London.* a.1710.
Edward. *London.* 1794. Watch Ilbert coll.
William. *London (Cowcross St.).* 1799-1804.
John. *Perth.* a.1791.
Thomas. *London.* 1808.
NOBLET—
Pierre. *Lyons.* 1610-19. Cast sil. chiselled watch in form of a walnut Marryat coll.
——. ——. 1817. Began new clock for Auxerre.
NOD, Richard. *London.* 1662.
NODES—
——. *London.* retired 1774. Succeeded by WILLIAMS & SHARP.
William. *London.* an.1781.
NÖDING, C. W. *Cassel.* 1774. Astro. clock Cassel Landes-M.
NOEL—
Aymé. ——. ca.1640. crys. watch, sil. outer case, B.M. ill. Baillie.
Étienne. *Rouen.* m.1660.
——. *Paris.* 1789.
Samuel. *London.* ca.1800. Watch.
Père. *Paris (Rue St. Avoye).* 1812. C.
Fils. *Paris (Rue Ste. Croix de la Bretonnière).* 1812-24. C.
NOHRDAL, J. Prob. same as NORDAHL, Johan. Watch.
NOHRIN, ——. *Falun.* 18c. Wall clock Nord. M.
NOHRMAN, Eric. *Stockholm.* m.1763. *Norrköping.* 1773. d.1780. Five watches and three trav. clocks, one in Nord. M.
NOLAN, John. *Loughrea.* 1824.
NOLDA—
Hamm. ——. ca.1690. Watch en. by Huaud le puisné.
J. A. *London.* ca.1740. Watch.
NOLEN—
Spencer. *Boston, U.S.A.* 1813. C.
Spencer, & Samuel CURTIS. *Boston.* 1816-18.
NOLLANT, ——. *Paris.* 1600. Sig. to Statuts of Paris corporation.
NOLLATH, Hornsby. *London.* a.1801.
NOLLORTH, Charles. *Yarmouth.* 1775. Watch mt. G.M.
NOLY, ——. *Paris.* Early 19c. g. en. spherical watch Fränkel coll.
NOON—
John. *London.* a.1655.
Manton. *London.* a.1716.
Thomas. *Ashby-de-la-Zouche.* an.1773. Watch.
Thomas. prob. *London.* an.1785. Watch.
William. *Ashby-de-la-Zouche.* 1791-5.
James. *London.* 1802-25. W. & C.
NORBECK, Johan Fredric. *Stockholm* and *Nora.* 1751-66.
NORBERG, Daniel. *Stockholm* and *Sundsvall.* comp. 1766-94.
NORBLIN, ——. *Paris.* 1815. C.
NORCELL, John. *London.* Late 17c. str. watch Den. coll.
NORCOTT—
John. *London.* CC.1681-91. Watches London M. and Ilbert coll.
Samuel. *London.* an.1781. Watch.
NORDAHL, Johan. *Skara.* b.1710, d.1784. Turret and other clocks. *v.* NOHRDAL.
NORDBERG, Johan. *Lilla Malma.* b.1730, m.1766, d.1807. l.c. lacquer clock.
NORDLANDER, Alexander. *Härnösand.* 1816-46.
NORDLAW, John. prob. *London.* an.1772. Watch.
NORDLUND, Eric. *Östersund.* 1819-35.
NORDMAN, Olof. *Stockholm.* b.1717, d. 1782.
NORDOT, Jean. *Paris.* 1675 m.
NORDSTÉEN, Peter. *Petersburg,* 1760. *Stockholm,* 1764. *Moscow,* ca.1785. Watch mt. Ilbert coll.
NORDTSEN, Pet. *Åbo.* b.1740, d.1807.
NORDVALL—
Eric. *Sundsvall.* b.1756, d.1808.
Joh. M. *Sundsvall.* 1816-35.
NOREL, Claude Joseph. ——. 1815. mus. rep. cyl. watch mt. C.A. & M.
NORGAN, William. *London.* a.1803.
NORGATE, John. *London.* a.1700, CC.1712-1730.
NORGREN, Daniel. *Stockholm.* 1811-20.
NORLING—
Johan. *Stockholm.* b.1747, m.1777, d.1799. Court C.
Georg. *Stockholm.* b.ca.1762. *Uppsala,* 1795. d.1829.
NORMAN—
Anders. *Stockholm.* 1695-1710.
Ralph. *Poole.* an.1726. Watch.
James. *Poole.* an.1755. Watch.
John. *Preston.* an.1756. Watch.
John. *London.* an.1779. Watch.
Jonathan. *Sherborne.* 1780. C.
Simon. *Lowestoft.* 1784-95. W.
John. *Toxteth Park.* 1787. W.
B. *Dudley.* ca.1790.
James. *Charminster.* 1800. C.
John. *Liverpool.* 1805-11. W.
Charles. *London.* 1808. Watch N.Y. Univ.
Ebenezer. *London.* a.1802.
NORMAND—
François. *Paris.* 1749 m. Watch.
Louis François. *Paris.* 1789-1812 juré.
NORRBY, Jakob. *Visby.* b.1798, d.1883.
NORRIE, David. *Leith.* 1787-1811.
NORRIS—
Edward. *London (Dove Ct.).* a.1650, CC. 1658, m.CC.1686-1705. Lantern clock.
John. *Childen.* 1687. Watch spring maker.
Joseph. *London.* a.1662, CC.1670-96.
Charles, son of Edward. *London.* CC.1687.
William. *London.* Late 17c. Watch Webster coll.
Josephus. *Amsterdam.* ca.1700. Two g. watches Stern. coll. en. Huaud le puisné. br. clock. str. watch Den. coll.
Edward, son of Edward. *London.* a.1694, CC.1702.
Thomas. *London.* a.1715. Watch.
Daniel. *London.* 1723. W.
Charles. *London.* a.1726-94.
John. *London.* a.1744.
John. *London.* a.1752.
Hugh. prob. *London.* an.1774. Watch.
William. *Birmingham.* 1774. W. l.c. clocks.
George. *London.* an.1776. Watch.
Richard. *London.* an.1777. Watch.
Patrick. *Liverpool.* 1781-1829. Pocket chron. mt. Ilbert coll.
William. *Liverpool.* 1781-1829. W.
T. *Albrighton.* Late 18c. Wall clock.
James. *London.* a.1784.
William. *London.* a.1788.

NORRIS—*continued.*
Samuel. *London.* 1808. W.
Henry. *Liverpool.* 1814-29. W.
NORSELL, Peter. *Visby.* b.1728, d.1789. l.c. clock and watch.
NORTH—
William. *London (St. Paul's Churchyard).* CC.1639. C. & W. astro. watch ill. Britten.
John. *London.* a.1641, CC.1650-96.
Lancelot. *York.* 1623. *London,* 1639-64.
John. *London.* CC.1720-5.
John. *London.* a.1725, CC.1747.
Robert. *London.* an.1753. Watch.
John. *Cirencester.* 1757. From *Highworth (Wilts.).* C. & W. Succeeded John JEFFERIS.
Richard. *London.* a.1754, CC.1767-1800.
Richard. *Driffield.* ca.1770-91. C. & W.
William. *London.* 1790.
Joseph. *London.* 1809-11. W.
William. *York.* 1816. Later *Leconfield.*
Thomas. *London.* 1817-24.
Thomas. *Drogheda.* 1824.
NORTHAM—
Simon. *London.* a.1794, CC.1802.
Samuel. *London.* 1809 CC.
George. *London.* 1809-25. mus. C. & W.
NORTHCOTE—
John. *London.* CC.1681-1706.
——. *Plymouth.* an.1747. Watch.
Samuel. *Plymouth.* 1766-95. Watch mt. G.M.
NORTHEN, Richard. *Hull.* ca.1790-1820. Rack lever watch Ilbert coll.
NORTHEY, John. *London.* a.1765-1804. Watch Den. coll.
NORTHGRAVES, Denton. *Hull.* 1806-22.
NORTHLEIGH & CO. *London.* 1799. *v.* LLOYD & NORTHLEIGH.
NORTHROPP, William. *Wakefield.* 1751. C.
NORTHWOOD, John. *London.* a.1752.
NORTON—
Edward. *Warwick.* 1640-ca.1700. Clock with 48 instead of 60 divisions on hour circle. Watch.
Thomas. *London (St. Brides).* a.1707, CC. 1720-9. Bankrupt. g. p.c. rep. watch.
Joseph or Thomas. *London.* a.1743.
Eardley. *London (St. John St.).* 1762. CC. 1770-94. A maker of great repute of watches and complex clocks. Patented in 1771 a str. mech. for clocks and rep. work for watches. Astro. clock Buckingham Palace ill. Britten. Many watches. Very small cartel clock Nat. M. Stockholm. Clock Cassel Landes-M. Elaborate aut. clock with organ Palace M. Pekin. br. clock Virginia M. Marine chron. Ilbert coll.
Samuel. *London.* an.1773-92. Watch.
John. *London.* a.1766, CC.1770.
John. *London.* a.1777.
William. *London.* a.1778.
Samuel. *Yarmouth.* 1784. W.
G. *Ipswich.* 1790-4. C. & W.
Eardley. *Stanmore.* 1795. W. prob. the above.
Graham. *London.* Late 18c. Watch and clock.
NORTONS. *London.* ca.1780. Watch set stones Ilbert coll.
NORWOOD, Thomas. *London.* a.1695.
NOT, Jean Jacques. *Geneva.* ca.1775-91.
NOTLIH, *v.* HILTON.
NOTRON, Yeldaye. *London.* An anagram of Eardley NORTON mentioned by Britten as sig. on a br. clock.
NOTTAGE, John. *London.* a.1770.
NOTTESTAD, Jeder. *Oslo.* ca.1760. Painted l.c. clock Novsk Folke M. Oslo.
NOTTON, Samuel. *London.* 1775.
NOUET, Nicolas. *Paris.* 1685 m.
NOURRISSON—
Guillaume. *Lyons.* 1656 m., d.1700. From *Ambert.* Made astro. aut. clock at Brioude an.1645. Remade astro. aut. clock in St. Jean, Lyons (*v.* Hugues LEVET). Town C. 1664. Juré in 1678. Made new clock for Hôtel de Ville in 1684. sil. al. watch Côte coll. ill. Vial & Côte. g. al. watch Gélis coll. crys. watch in form of mussel shell. l.c. cal. clock.
Antoine, bro. *Lyons.* b.ca.1629, d.1715. Town C. with his brother.
Guillaume, son of Guillaume. *Lyons.* b. 1660-1731. Town C. in 1706.
Pierre, bro. *Lyons.* b.1670, d.1708.
Guillaume, son of Guillaume (2). *Lyons.* mar.1699-1716.
Jean Baptiste, son of Guillaume (2). b.1705. Town C. in 1731.
Claude, son. *Lyons.* b.1738.
NOURRY—
Pierre. *Lyons.* b.ca.1587, d.1672. br. clock by him or Jean.
Nicolas. *Gisors.* 1626-35. C. to the Queen. Also DE NOURRY and NORRY.
Pierre. *Gisors.* 1645. Trav. clock Gélis coll.
Pierre. *Paris.* 1650. C. to Louis XIV.
Jean, son of Pierre (1). *Lyons.* b.ca.1637-84.
Pierre. *Rouen.* a.1656. Also NORRY.
NOURSE—
Thomas. *London (Beech La.).* CC.1740, l.CC.1766-70. Watch.
William, son. *London.* a.1767, CC.1774.
Thomas, bro. *London (Hoxton).* a.1772, CC. 1784, d.1801.
NOUWEN (NOWE, NOWAN, NEUWERS), Michael. *London.* 1582-1613. An exceptionally fine maker. Fine crys. watch B.M. ill. Baillie. str. watch G.M. Oval watch Ashmolean M. al. watch dated 1600 Mallett coll. Watch ill. Britten. Prob. son of Andrewe NOWAY of Flanders, who came to London 1571.
NOVELLO, ——. *Padua.* 1437. Made clock on Tower of Piazza dei Signori.
NOWAY—
Andrewe (Andris NOWETHE). *London.* 1571. Born in *Flanders.*
Francis. *London.* 1580-3. Born in *Brabant.* *v.* NAWE.
NOWELL, Mathew. *London.* a.1628 under BC.
NOWETHE, Andris. *v.* NOWAY.
NOWLAN, John. *Waterford.* 1824.
NOWLAND—
Thomas. *Philadelphia.* 1806-08. W.
John. *Liverpool.* 1825. W.
NOYES—
William. *London.* a.1707.
Samuel. *London.* a.1719.
NOYL, Charles. prob. *London.* an.1771. Watch.
NOYON, Claude. *Geneva.* 1469. 'Serralious et magistro horologii.'
NOYTOLON—
Christophe. *Lyons.* b.1558, d.1607. Clock with armillary sphere Côte coll. ill. Vial & Côte.
Pierre, son. *Lyons.* b.1588-1630. d.an.1646. Clock.
Christophe, bro. *Lyons.* b.1589-1626. d.an. 1654.
NUER, Jean. *Saintes.* ca.1600. Oval watch ill. Britten.

NUMAN, I. *Amsterdam.* 1822. W.

NUNN—

Robert. ——. Early 19c. Watch mt. Ilbert coll.

Simon. *Lowestoft.* 1821. W.

NURÉ, ——. *Paris.* 1793.

NURSE, John. *London.* a.1710, CC.1718.

NUSSBAUM, Georg. *Marktbreit-am-Main.* m.1825.

NUTT, William Robert. *London.* a.1778.

NUTTALL, Robert. *London.* a.1741.

NYBERG—

Johan. *Stockholm.* b.1713, d.1768. l.c. lacquer clock.

NYBERG—*continued.*

Johan. *Stockholm.* b.1740, d.1801. br. and l.c. and four wall clocks.

Johan Ad. *Stockholm.* mar.1802. Wall clock.

And. *Stockholm.* 1805.

NYE, John. *Hurst.* Early 19c. Watch.

NYLANDER, Gustaf. *Stockholm.* b.1707, d.1751. Three l.c. and two br. clocks.

NYMAN, Johan Israel. *Stockholm.* b.1726, m. 1753, d.1780. Watch.

NYQVIST—

Nils. *Åmal.* 1750-4.

Carl Gustaf. *Örebro.* 1780.

Carl Pet. *Örebro.* 1785-90.

NYS, ——. *Paris.* 1812.

O

OAKE, John. *London.* 1776. W.
OAKES, John. *Oldham.* ca.1820.
OAKEY—
John. *London.* a.1683.
John. *London.* a.1685.
OAKHAM—
Thomas. *London.* a.1798.
William Henry. *London.* a.1802.
OAKLEY—
John. *London.* a.1685.
James. *London.* a.1716.
James. *Oxford.* an.1767. Watch.
William. *London (E. Harding St.).* 1757. W.
John. *London.* ca.1760. g. repoussé watch Feill coll.
William, son of William. *London.* a.1769, CC.1776.
William. *London.* 1804. CC.1813, d.1821.
OAKMAN—
James. *London.* a.1793.
Thomas. *London.* a.1798, CC.1809.
William Henry. *London.* a.1802.
John. *London.* a.1806.
ÖBERG—
——. *Uppsala.* 1792.
C. A. *Sigtuna.* 1819-21.
OBERLÄNDER, ——. *Grüne Eiche.* ca.1730. Watch.
OBERY, John. *London.* an.1801. Watch.
O'BRIEN—
Francis. *Cork.* 1824.
——. *Dublin.* Early 19c. Watch.
OBRYANT—
Benjamin. *London.* 1805. Hour glass maker.
Joseph, son. *London.* a.1805.
OBY MANUFABRIQUE. *Oby.* 1741. br. clock Nord. M.
OBYE, Stephen. *Harleston.* 1749. C. & W.
OCHILTREE, James. *Newcastle-o.-T.* 1801. C. & W.
ÖCHSNER, Georg. *Strüth.* m.1815.
OCLEE, James. *Ramsgate.* ca.1790 CC.
O'CONNOR—
David. *Horsham.* 1795. 'Clocksmith.'
Samuel. *Dublin.* 1824.
ODDIN, Peter. *London.* 1729. Insolvent.
ODELEM, A. *Brunswick.* 18c. Dial maker.
ODELL—
Jacob. *St. Albans.* Early 18c. l.c. clock.
Thomas. *London.* a.1744.
ODET—
Nicolas. *Lyons.* 1557-63.
Michel. *Lyons.* 1561.
ODRY, Estienne. *Amsterdam.* 1685. Huguenot refugee from *Meaux.*
OFARD, ——. *Gex.* ca.1700. en. watch ill. Britten.
OFFINGTON, Samuel. *London.* a.1732, CC. 1740.
OGBORN, Samuel. *London.* CC.1698-1722. W.
OGDEN—
Thomas. *London.* a.1651, CC.1659.
John. *Bowbrigge.* 1681. d.1741. l.c. clock ill. Britten.
Samuel. *Halifax.* b.1669-1701.
John. *Alnwick.* 1720. l.c. clock.
Thomas. *Halifax.* b.1692, d.1769. l.c. clock dial ill. Britten.
John. *Darlington.* ca.1730. Watch.
Bernard. *Darlington.* ca.1740. Watch.
John. *Sunderland.* 1751. d.1753. cyl. watch. C.
Jane, widow. *Sunderland.* From 1753.
Samuel. *Newcastle-o.-T.* ca.1760.
junior. *Halifax.* an.1765. Watch.
Mary. *Darlington.* an.1766. Watch.
Samuel. *Alnwick.* an.1779. Watch.
'M. D. OGDEN.' Sig. on watches of the ELGIN NATIONAL WATCH Co. from 1876.
OGER, ——. *Paris.* 1812. C.
OGG—
Hendrie. *Dunfermline.* 1820.
Daniel. *Dublin.* 1824.
OGILVIE, Thomas. *London.* a.1751.
OGLE—
Edward. *London.* 1697.
John. *Amsterdam.* Insolvent at *Lavenham* in 1771. W.
Niels. *Elverum.* Late 18c. l.c. clock Norsk Folke M. Oslo.
Cuthbert. *London.* 1805-08.
OGLETON, John. *London.* a.1763.
OGSTON, James. *London.* 1826. Patented, with J. T. BELL, watches with two barrels. *v.* DWERRIHOUSE.
O'HAGAN, Lawrence. *Limerick.* 1824. rep. watch mt.
O'HAMLEY, ——. *London.* an.1776. Watch.
OHLSSON—
Åke. *Lund.* b.1724, d.1819.
Olof, son. *Lund.* b.1773, d.1844.
Per, bro. *Lund.* b.1776, d.1852.
ÖHMAN—
And. *Stockholm.* 1757.
Eric Pettersson. *Stockholm.* m.1759-78. Court C. Made mus. clock playing on strings and pipes. Wall and three trav. clocks. Watch mt. Nord. M.
Carl. *Stockholm.* 1818. Watch.
ÖHRMAN—
Carl. *Västerås.* 1749. d.ca.1767.
Anna Brita, widow. *Västerås.* 1769-75.
OKEHAM, Edward. *London.* CC.1632.
OKESHOT, Robert. *London.* a.1664.
OLANDER, Joh. *Kalmar.* b.1788, d.1870.
OLDBERG, Olof. *Stockholm.* 1769-80. l.c. clock.

OLDENBURG, ——. *Wismar*. Early 19c.
OLDENZIJL, ——. *Haarlem*. 2nd half 17c. g. en. watch Mallett coll.
OLDFIELD—
T. *London*. an.1743. Watch.
John. *Manchester*. 1800. C. & W.
OLDHAM—
Charles. *Southam*. an.1776. Watch.
Joseph. *Liverpool*. 1813-24. W.
John. *Liverpool*. 1821. W.
OLDIS, John. *Dorchester*. 1760-80. Watches Dorchester M.
OLDMEADOW, Thomas. *Kings Lynn*. 1784-1795. W.
OLDSWORTH, Stephen. *London*. a.1712.
OLEAR, John. prob. *London*. an.1739. Watch.
OLEGNIK, ——. *Vienna*. Early 19c. Large en. cross watch, set crys. and lapis lazuli, M.M.A.
OLIÉE, ——. *Paris*. 1812.
OLIN, Jacques Charles. *Paris*. 1776 m., juré 1778-89.
OLIPHANT—
Robert. *London*. 1790 CC., l.CC.1811, d. 1818. cf. OLLIPHANT.
Alexander. *Anstruther*. b.1784-1818.
Thomas. *London*. 1805-08. W.
Alexander. *Pittenweem*. 1815-40.
OLIVE—
Thomas. *London*. a.1756.
Samuel. *Tonbridge*. 1773-94. 'Makes clocks upon an invention of his own: they go 8 days and repeat and cost £2. 5*s*.'
Thomas. *Penryn*. 1784.
OLIVER—
John. *London*. a.1704.
John. *Manchester*. Early 18c.-1749, when he sold his stock.
Richard. *York*. 1743. Bankrupt.
Bernard. *Geneva*. ca.1750-70.
Henry, bro. *Geneva*. ca.1750-70.
John. *Manchester* and *Huddersfield*. 1755. Bankrupt.
John. *Charleston, U.S.A.* 1764. From *London*. W.
John, jun. *Charleston, U.S.A.* 1765. From *London*. W.
Thomas. *London* (*New Bond St.*). 1780-99. In partnership with Jos. WEST till 1785. mus. C. Watch.
& WEST. *London*. To 1785. Partnership with Thos.
Thomas. *Hitchin*. an.1785. Watch.
——. *St. Columb*. 1795. C.
John. *London*. a.1795.
David. *Reading*. Early 19c.
OLIVET, ——. *Paris*. 1812-17.
OLIVIER—
Lenard. *Venice*. 1550. Mechanic to the Cardinal de Tournon.
——. *Paris*. 1819.
OLLENBERG, Carl. *Stockholm*. comp. 1740, m.1752, d.1754. Made watch with secs. hands as master's essay.
OLLIPHANT, Robert. *London*. CC.1776. cf. OLIPHANT.
OLLIVANT—
John & Son. *Manchester*. 1788-1800. John d.1795. Watch.
T. *Manchester*. ca.1815. c.secs. stop watch Platt Hall M. Manchester.
& MORTON. *Manchester*. ca.1820.
OLLIVE—
Thomas. *Tenterden* and *Cranbrook*. mar. 1777-95. W.
——. *Lewes*. 1780. C. & W.
& READER. *Cranbrook*. Early 19c. l.c. mus. clock.
OLLIVIER, Denis. *Caen*. 1537. Serrurier. Repaired town clock.
ÖLLSNER, Joseph. *Langenbielau*. ca.1700. sq. table clock.
OLLYFFE, Thomas. *London*. a.1761.
OLSEN, Anders. *Copenhagen*. m.1697. Turret C.
OLTRAMARE—
Estienne. *Geneva*. 1643. d.1693. Large en. watch M.M.A.
David (OULTREMER). *Rouen*. 1649 m.-1654. *v.* OSTRAMARE.
Jean François. *Berne*. 1674-7. Then *Lausanne*.
Jaques. *Bordeaux*. 1777-ca.1800. Watch, virgule escapement and jump secs. with independent train, Chamb. coll.
Pierre François, son. *La Rochelle*. b.1777, d. 1851.
Benjamin. *Geneva*. Early 19c. Wrote 'Mém. sur un Tour aux Balanciers,' Geneva, 1837.
ÖMAN, Anders. *Raumo*. 1792.
OMENT, William. *London*. a.1799.
O'NEAL, William. *Liverpool*. 1800-05. Prob. same as following.
O'NEILL—
William. *Liverpool*. ca.1790 CC.
& ROSKELL. *Liverpool*. To 1798.
Arthur. *Dublin*. 1795. W.
ONION—
Thomas. *London*. a.1702.
John Clarkson. *London*. a.1762.
John. *Stockport*. 1785. Watch.
John. *Manchester*. 1794-1800. W.
ONORI, Dominicus. *Rome*. 1726. Clock.
OORTKRAS, Barend. *The Hague*. Early 18c. Watch Stads M. Amsterdam. l.c. clock.
OORTWIJN, Johannes. *Appingadam*. 2nd half 18c. str. watch Stads M. Amsterdam.
OOSTERWIJK—
Severijn. *Holland*. 1665. C. employed by HUYGENS after COSTER's death.
Jacobus. *Rotterdam*. Early 18c. br. clock.
Abraham. *Middelburg*. ca.1710. l.c. clock Weth. coll. ill. Cec. & Web. Watch with secs. hand.
Joh. *Amsterdam*. Mid. 18c. g. eng. watch formerly in Shandon coll.
OPPENORD, Gilles Marie. *Paris*. b.1672, d.1742. Designed cartel clock cases.
OPPERMANN, Adolf. *Berlin*. Early 19c. Tortoise-shell br. clock.
ORAM—
Morris. *London*. a.1684.
James. *Somerton*. End 18c. l.c. clock.
ORANGE, ——. *Versailles* and *Paris*. Late 18c.-1815. Watch.
ORBIN, Carl Erick. *Stockholm*. 1774. d.ca. 1800. Four watches, one Chicago M. Wall clock.
ORCHARD, Robert. *London*. a.1794. CC. 1801.
ORD, John. *London*. a.1696.
ORDAC, François. *Paris*. an.1795. Watch.
ORDSON, William. *London*. Early 18c. Watch G.M.
ORE—
Thomas. *Wolverhampton* and *Tong*. 1763-79, then *Birmingham* to 1788. Clock in Birmingham cathedral. l.c. clocks and watch.
Thomas. *Philadelphia*. 1813. W.
O'REILLY—
R. prob. *Paris*. 1802. Pub. mem. on the effect of magnetism on watches, and another on a new chron., Paris, 1803.
Charles. *Dublin*. an.1820. Watch.
ORFORD, Robert. *London*. 1795-1805.
ORGAN, W. *Bideford*. 18c. l.c. clock.
ORGANI, Giovanni degli. *Milan* and *Genoa*. 1354. Made the first clock for Genoa on the Duomo San Lorenzo.

ORIANI, B. ——. 1782. Pub. 'De motu duorum horologiorum effectum caloris per se corrigentibus instructorum,' Milan, 1782 and 1787.

ORME—

John. *Preston.* 1712. W. Lancaster freeman. Watch Belfast M.

William. *Dinting Vale.* Late 18c. Watch.

Robert. *Nottingham.* Till 1802 partner with Sam. HULSE.

Thomas. *Oldham.* ca.1820.

ORMEROD, Thomas. *Liverpool.* 1825. W.

ORMOND, John. *London.* a.1713.

ÖRNSTEDT, Jacob. *Sweden.* 18c. Watch.

ORPION, J. *London.* Mid. 18c. Watch.

ORPWOOD—

William. *Woodbridge.* From 1789. *Ipswich,* ca.1800. Watch. *v.* DAIMES.

——. *Harwich.* 1790-8. C. & W.

Richard. *London.* a.1797-1824.

George. *London.* 1810-40. Lancet br. clock ill. Britten.

Edward. *London.* Early 19c. Watch Glasgow Art Gall.

ORR—

Thomas. *Philadelphia.* 1811.

James. *Greenock.* 1817.

James. *Bandon.* 1824.

ORRELL—

John. *Preston.* ca.1820.

Peter. *Liverpool.* 1825. W.

ORRY, Julian. *Blois.* comp. 1624.

ORSON, J. prob. *London.* an.1751. Watch.

ÖRTEL, Adolph Ferdinand. *Dresden.* m.1765.

ORTON—

Edward. *London.* a.1680, CC.1687-1709.

John. *Manchester.* ca.1820.

Rasin. *Grantham.* an.1822. Watch.

OSAKA WATCH CO., *v.* OTAY.

OSBITON, James. *London.* a.1749.

OSBORNE (OSBORN, OSBOURNE)—

Humphry. *London.* BC.1617. Lantern clock.

William. *London.* a.1693, CC.1700-21.

Robert. *London.* a.1698.

Richard. *London.* a.1721.

Thomas. *London (Ironmonger Row).* CC. 1767.

John. *Colchester.* 18c. l.c. clock.

& WILSON. *Birmingham.* 1772. Partnership of Thos. O. and Jas. W. dissolved in 1777.

Edward. *Cleeve Prior.* 2nd half 18c. l.c. clock.

John. *Fenny Stratford.* 1793-7. C. & W.

John Thomas. *London.* a.1793.

Thomas. *Birmingham.* 1801. astro. and mus. C.

OSELL, William. *Hexham.* an.1779. Watch.

OSGOOD, John. *Boston, U.S.A.* 1823. W.

O'SHAUGHNESSY—

Mark. *Cork.* Late 18c.-1824. l.c. clock.

Robert. *Limerick.* 1824.

OSMAN—

Richard. *London (Southwark).* a.1793, CC. 1812, l.CC.1817.

William. *London.* a.1805.

OSMOND—

Henry. *London.* a.1681.

James. *London.* a.1681.

James. *London.* a.1687.

Thomas. *London.* a.1700.

James. *London (Whitecross St. & Union St.).* CC.1774-99.

James. *London.* a.1789.

OST, Matthias von. *Lübeck.* 1561-5. Made clock on the Marienkirche.

OSTENFELDT, Nicolai. *Assen.* m.1812.

OSTER, Johann. *Basle.* 1776.

OSTERBERGER, Endres. *Nürnberg.* 1528.

ÖSTMAN, Olof. *Nyköping.* 1734-52. l.c. clock.

OSTRAMARE, D. ——. 1st half 17c. Prob. David OLTRAMARE. Watch Mallett coll.

OSWALD, Robert. *Durham.* 1820-60.

OSWELL, ——. *Shrewsbury.* 1780. Watch.

OTAY WATCH CO. *Otay, Cal.* Started 1888, plant moved in 1891 to *Alviso,* and from there to *Osaka, Japan,* where the OSAKA WATCH Co. started in 1893. Otay watches inscribed, 'Golden Gate,' 'Overland Mail,' 'Native Son,' 'F. A. Kimball,' 'R. D. Perry.'

OTERCEY, John. *Torrington.* 2nd half 18c. l.c. clock.

OTERIDGE, Gideon. *London.* a.1737.

OTGHER, Beauchamp. *London.* a.1699.

OTHENIN-GIRARD—

Abraham. *Chaux-de-Fonds.* 1743-78. Made elaborately ornamented clocks.

Moïse. *Switzerland.* 1754.

F. J. *Chaux-de-Fonds.* b.1780, d.1846. Developed engine-turning.

OTTE (OTH)—

Johan Caspar. *Copenhagen.* m.1720-8. Turret C.

Christian Vilhelm. *Copenhagen.* a.1743.

OTTERGREN, Daniel. *Ystrad.* 1816-46. Watch.

OTWAY, John. *Torrington.* an.1791-5. Watch. l.c. clock.

OUDET, Jean Joseph. *Pontarlier.* 1781.

OUDIN—

Charles. *Paris (Palais Royal).* 1807-25. A fine W. g. en. watches M.M.A. and M.P.S. Dresden. g. rep. repoussé watch. Pupil of BREGUET and copied his 'souscription' watches. g. watch sd. 'Élève de Breguet' Ilbert coll.

Pierre. *Paris (Palais Royal).* 1807.

——. *Paris (Rue Vivienne).* 1807.

——. *Paris (Rue Feydeau).* 1812. Also HOUDIN.

J. F. *Paris (Rue Harlai du Palais).* 1823-5. Also HOUDIN.

OUGHTON—

Samuel. *London.* a.1747. Also ORTON.

Thomas. *London.* an.1755. Watch.

OUGHTRED—

Benjamin. *London.* CC.1639.

William. *Oxford.* 1677. Mathematician. Pub. method of finding ratios of wheel teeth.

OURRY, ——. *Cassel.* 1760. Court C.

OURSEL, Jean. *Amsterdam.* 1687. Huguenot refugee from *Le Havre.*

OUTHIER, L'Abbé. *France.* 1727-31. Designed a clockwork celestial globe made by J. B. CATIN, desc. in Gallon, 'Machines et Inventions,' Vol. v.

OUTHWAITE, Thomas, & Co. *Liverpool.* ca. 1820.

OVER, Ellis. *London.* a.1752.

OVERALL—

——. *Wellingborough.* an.1755. Watch.

Henry. *Dover.* 1778-95. W.

Henry. *Romsey.* ca.1780. l.c. lacquer clock. Watch.

Joseph. *Wellingborough.* 1784.

OVERBURY—

Thomas. *London.* 1667. CC.1688. W.

Henry, son. *London.* a.1687.

Henry. *Rotterdam.* ca.1705. Pendulum watch G.M.

OVERSTALL, John. *London.* a.1764.

OVERTON—

John. *London.* a.1748.

Henry. *London.* 1761.

OVERY—

John. *London.* b.1675, d.1767. Tortoise-shell watch case maker.

John. *London.* a.1797.

OVERZEE—
Gerard. *Isleworth.* CC.1678-90. Lantern clock. Watch.
Timothy. *London.* a.1693.

OVINGHAM—
Thomas. *London.* an.1770. Watch.
Robert. *London.* an.1775. Watch.
Richard. *London.* an.1776. Watch.
Samuel. *London.* an.1776. Watch.

OVINGTON, ——. *London.* an.1780. Watch.

OWEN—
Benjamin. *London.* a.1687, m.1694-1740. l.c. clocks.
Richard. *London.* a.1696.
Samuel. *London.* a.1700.
Robert. *London.* a.1707.
Watkin. *Llanrwst.* ca.1700.
John. *Denbigh.* ca.1700.
Thomas. *Birmingham.* 1753. l.c. clock.
John. *Llanrwst.* 1755-ca.1780. l.c. clock. Made town clock.
Watkin. *Llanrwst.* 1761-1809. Three watches Nat. M. Cardiff.

OWEN—*continued.*
Thomas. *Llanfrothen.* 1769-early 19c. .c. clock.
William. *London (Limehouse).* CC.1775.
Thomas. *London.* a.1771, CC.1789.
William. *Copenhagen.* 1781.
J. *London (Helmet Row).* ca.1800. br. clock.
Griffith. *Philadelphia.* 1802-13.
Joseph. *London (Old St.).* 1805-08.
Joseph. *London (Holborn Hill).* 1805-11. br. clock.
John. *Philadelphia.* 1819. C.
William. *Oswestry.* Early 19c. Watch.

OWENS—
Henry. *London.* a.1702.
——. *Worksop.* an.1788. Watch.
Evan. *London.* a.1793.

OWTTRIM, Thomas. *London.* a.1791.

OXLEY, Joseph. *Norwich.* Early 17c. l.c. clock.

OYENS—
Peter. *London (Wapping).* 1756-78. Bankrupt.
Peter. *Plymouth* and *Plymouth Dock.* 1797. W.

P

PACE—
Thomas. *London*. 1630-62 CC. Lantern clocks.
John. *London*. a.1720.
Thomas. *London (Whitechapel)*. 1784-1825. br. and l.c. clocks. Lever watch G.M.
John. *London*. 1790.
Henry. *London (Whitechapel)*. Early 19c.
John. *Bury*. Early 19c. Watch.
PACHER, Karl. *Vienna*. m.1797.
PACHIS, Jean François. ——. 2nd half 17c. Agate and en. watch.
PACK—
Robert. *London*. a.1701.
Richard. *London*. a.1705, CC.1712.
Thomas. *London*. a.1721.
John. *Harleston*. 1788. W.
PACKER—
Thomas. *Reading*. an.1796. Watch.
Charles. *Reading*. 1795-1803. C. & W.
John. *Buckingham*. an.1800.
PADBURY—
Andrew. *Bishop's Waltham*. 1730-75. Two l.c. clocks ill. Britten.
——. *Cirencester*. ca.1790 CC.
PADEVAL, Henry. *Paris*. ca.1740. Wooden Louis xv clock Peiping M.
PAGE—
Joseph. *London*. a.1674, CC.1683.
Luke. *London*. a.1683.
Henry. *London*. a.1699, CC.1714-47.
Robert. *London*. Early 18c. Watch G.M.
Henry. *London*. a.1722.
William. *London*. a.1725.
Henry. *Upper Broughton*. Early 18c. Clock.
John. *Ipswich*. ca.1740. Also *Harwich* from 1760. d.1773. l.c. and br. clocks.
Thomas. *Norwich*. 1750. d.1784. Watch Ilbert coll. and l.c. clock.
Charles. *London (R. Exchange)*. 1759. W.
Robert. *Harwich*. an.1763. Watch.
Isaac. *Bristol*. 1769. *Chippenham*. 1774. *Bath*. 1781. C. & W.
John. *London*. an.1773. Watch.
——. *Salisbury*. an.1778. Watch.
& Christian. *Norwich* and *Aylsham*. From 1777. Partnership of Thos. P. and John C. succeeded by Geo. Barwick in 1788. C. & W.
John. *London*. a.1776-94.
Isaac. *Cheltenham*. ca.1790 CC. l.c. clock.
William. *Hadleigh*. an.1791. Watch.
Richard. *London*. a.1793.
Robert. *Yarmouth*. mar.1817.
PAGENT, Philip. *London*. 1776. Watch Horstmann coll.
PAGET—
Ambrose. *London*. a.1716, CC.1729.
William. *Burford*. an.1771. Watch.
PAGETT, William. *Chiswick*. an.1775. Watch.
PAILLARD (PALIARD, PAELLARD)—
Pierre. *Besançon*. 1722-35. Town C. Several fine Boulle-work br. clocks. Watch Besançon M.
Frères (Pierre Antoine and Claude Antoine, sons). *Besançon*. 1735-ca.1770. Watch and several fine br. clocks Vuillemot M. Besançon.
Jean Baptiste Charles. *Paris*. m.1750. Watch.
Claude François. *Paris*. m.1770.
Jean Jaques. *Geneva*. ca.1775-92.
Antoine. *Paris*. m.1776, juré 1782-9.
Thomas. *Rouen*. 1786. (Paliard.)
——. *Paris (Quai des Orfèvres)*. 1786. (Paliard.)
——. *Paris (Rue Boucher)*. 1786. (Paliard.)
——. *Paris (Rue de Seine)*. 1787. (Paliard.)
——. *Paris (Rue de Sève)*. 1788. (Paellard.)
Claude Antoine. *Besançon*. 1791.
——. *Paris (Rue des Fossés St. Germain des Prés)*. 1807-11. Succeeded Petite.
E., & Cie. *Sainte-Croix*. Founded ca.1814. Makers of mus. mechanism.
H. *Paris (Rue St. Honoré)*. 1824.
Charles Auguste. *Geneva*. b.1840, d.1895. Invented palladium alloy balance-springs.
PAILLET—
Daniel. *London (Soho)*. 1754. W.
Paul. *London*. an.1773. Watch.
PAILLION, ——. *Paris*. ca.1740. en. watch G.M. g. en. watch Fränkel coll.
PAIN—
Benjamin. *London*. a.1672.
Thomas. *London*. a.1709. Watch.
William. *London*. CC.1729. l.c. clock. Also Payne.
Peter. *London*. CC.1729.
John Terrill. *London*. CC.1768.
William. *Trowbridge*. ca.1790. l.c. clock ill. Cec. & Web. Also Paine.
PAINE—
David. *London (Spitalfield Mkt.)*. 1721. Watch.
Edward. *London*. a.1755.
Richard. *London*. an.1763. Watch.
Francis. *London (Mile End)*. a.1752, CC. 1770. Watch. Also Payne.
George. *London*. a.1787.
J. P. *London*. 1825-40. Chron., W. & C. Wrote arts. in Trans. Soc. Arts 1827 and 1838 on a self-illuminating clock and an esc. wheel.
PAINTER, Richard. *London*. a.1795.
PAJON, ——. *Paris*. ca.1775. Bronze worker. Made clock-cases.
PAJOU, ——. *Paris*. 1812.

PALAY, Louis. *Geneva.* ca.1750-71.
PALFREY—
John. *London.* a.1646, CC.1654-64.
Charles. *London.* a.1712.
PALING, W. *Clapham.* 1817-24.
PALLIER, ——. *Valence.* 1451. Made clock for Montélimart.
PALLISON, John. *London.* End 18c. Watch.
PALMER—
David. *Barnstaple.* 1563. Keeper of clock on Kay Hall.
John. *London.* a.1647.
Thomas. *London.* 1672. BC.
John. *London.* a.1693.
Henry. *London.* a.1693.
William. *London.* a.1699. A Wm. PALMER was watch finisher to Wm. WEBSTER.
Philip. *London.* a.1709.
William. *York.* 1716. Pub. 'A great improvement in watchwork directed to finding the Longitude.'
William. *Northampton.* 1723. Insolvent. Watch mt. S.K.M.
Thomas. *London* (*St. John St.* and later *Fetter La.*). 1737-62. W.
Thomas. *Sheffield.* 1740.
Richard. *London.* 1752-99. W.
William. *Worcester.* ca.1760. l.c. clock.
John. *London.* a.1761, CC.1769.
Edward. *London.* an.1773. Watch.
Thomas. *London.* a.1764.
Francis. *London.* a.1765.
Robert. *London.* 1776.
Thomas. *London* (*Fetter La.*). 1776.
Henry. *London.* a.1771.
Thomas. *London* (*Holborn*). a.1773-1800.
Robert. *London* (*Kennington La.*). Late 18c. and early 19c.
& SAFFELL. *London.* 1791. Watch case makers. Dissolved partnership.
John. *Philadelphia.* 1796. W.
John. *London* (*Clerkenwell*). a.1790-1811.
——. *Chiswick.* an.1798. Watch.
John. *East Grinstead.* ca.1800. l.c. clock.
John. *London.* a.1796.
Joseph Gunn. *London* (*London Wall* and *Whitechapel*). a.1801, CC.1809-25.
William. *Bristol.* 1810-18.
H. W. *Margate.* an.1713. Watch.
Joseph. *London* (*Whitechapel*). 1815-25.
Thomas. *Liverpool.* 1816. W.
Robert. *London* (*Kennington*). 1820-4. Watch.
Robert. *Limerick.* 1824.
Charles. *Bristol.* 1825.
PALMGRÉN, Mathias. *Stockholm.* 1800.
PALMLÖF, ——. *Sala.* b.1755, d.1815.
PALOUEL, Pierre. *St. Lo.* ca.1650. Watch mt. Ilbert coll. Perhaps LALOUEL.
PAMER, Edward. *London.* ca.1800. Watches G.M. and Den. coll.
PAMPE, Frederick. *London.* a.1767.
PAMPHILLON, William. *London.* a.1714, CC.1725.
PANCHAUD—
Abel. *London.* an.1764-84. Watch Den. coll. Watch sd. DUANCHAP. br. clock.
François. *Geneva.* ca.1780. Partner with PIOT.
David. *London.* a.1779-90.
& CUMMING. *London.* 1799-1824.
David. *London.* a.1794, CC.1802-25.
PANCK, Ralph. *London.* a.1677.
PANCOST—
Isaac. *London.* a.1724.
Richard. *London.* a.1727.
PANETIER, René. *Angers.* 1492. Remade cathedral clock.
PANIER (PANIÉ, PANNIER)—
Samuel. *Paris.* 1678 juré.
Josué. *Paris.* Early 18c. Fine Boulle br. clock S.K.M. Watch B.M.

PANIER (PANIÉ, PANNIER)—*continued.*
Jacques. *Paris.* ca.1710. rep. watch Ilbert coll.
Louis Jacques. *Paris.* m.1743. Boulle clock, École Nat. des Mines, Paris.
Louis César. *Paris.* m.1743.
Jacques Charles. *Paris* (*Rue de la Verrerie*). 1759 juré-1789. rep. watch.
Georges Charles. *Paris.* Juré 1766.
Jean. *Paris.* m.1778.
J. B. *Paris.* 1786 m.
Jacques Antoine, son of J. C. *Paris* (*Rue St. Martin*). m.1787.
PANNELL—
Robert. *London.* a.1653.
Joshua. *Northallerton.* 1770-90. l.c. clock.
Hugh. *Northallerton.* 1775.
PANRIER, ——. *Ferney.* 1770. Director of watch factory.
PANTER, William. *Henley-on-Thames.* 1787. C. & W.
PANTHER, ——. *London.* a.1790. Watch.
PANTIN—
Nicholas. *London.* a.1651.
Robert. *London.* a.1674. l.c. clock.
Lewis. *London.* 1775.
PANTON—
James. *Edinburgh.* a.1750-65.
Robert. *Edinburgh.* 1825.
PAPAVOINE, Isaac. *London.* CC.1687-1710. l.c. clock Weth. coll.
PAPE, Thomas. *Rothbury.* 1808. W.
PAPENGUTH, Johann Friedrich. *Berlin.* 1783. C.
PAPILLION, Francesco. *Florence.* ca.1700. al. watch F.W.M. p.c. watch Ilbert coll.
PAPILLON, Jean François. *Geneva.* ca.1770-1791.
PAPIN—
Henri. *Blois.* a.1604, d.1658.
——. *St. Nicolas d'Aliermont* (near *Dieppe*). End 17c. Said to have started the clock industry there with CROUTTE.
PAPLETT, Robert. *Mitcham.* ca.1750. Watch Ilbert coll.
PAPON—
Léonard. *Gien.* ca.1630. Watch B.M.
Paul. *Paris.* 1654. Registered a private punch mark.
PAPUS, François. *Rennes.* 2nd half 17c.
PAPWORTH—
John. *London.* a.1678, CC.1688-98.
John. *London.* a.1717.
PAQUIN, Mathieu. *Paris.* 1804.
PARADISE, John. *London.* a.1709, CC.1718-1727. Watch.
PARAITRE, Jean Pierre. *Paris.* Juré 1760.
PARATTE, ——. *Paris.* 1812. C.
PARBURY, ——. ——. 1719. Fine worker in repoussé.
PARDOUX, Annel. *Vice-le-Comte.* d.1834. Made a very elaborate clock shown in Paris in 1867.
PARENT—
Pierre. *Amiens.* 1508. Locksmith. 'Conducteur de l'orloge du beffroy.'
Jean, son. *Amiens.* 1536. Succeeded his father as keeper.
PARÈS, Jacques Louis. *Paris.* m.1790.
PARESY, Jean. *Amsterdam.* 1686. Huguenot refugee from *Dieppe.*
PARIS—
Huguenin. *Dijon.* 1480. In charge of clock on Notre Dame.
M. *Rennes.* ca.1620. Oval watch B.M.
Pierre. *Nantes.* 2nd half 17c. circ. sil. watch S.K.M.
Jacques Louis. *Paris.* 1738 m. Retired 1790.
——. *Nyon.* 1751 juré.
Charles. *Pekin.* b.1738-93. Clocks and a writing automaton.

PARIS—*continued.*
James. *London.* a.1768, CC. 1778-1814.
——. *Paris.* 1807-12.
BRANDE & CIE. *Paris.* 1810-13.
Edmond Thomas. *London.* a.1808.

PARISH—
Simon. *London.* a.1696, CC.1723.
Simon, son. *London.* a.1738.
Robert. *London.* a.1738.
Edward. *London.* a.1740.

PARISSET, Pierre. *Lyons,* a.1612.

PARKE (PARK, PARKES)—
Nicholas. *London.* CC.1640-59. PARK.
John. *London.* a.1659. PARK.
J. *London* (*Cheapside*). 1728.
John. *London.* a.1724, CC.1733. PARK.
Joseph. *Liverpool.* 1734-66. Clock Liverpool M. PARKS.
Benjamin. *London.* a.1728, CC.1735.
John. *London* (*Cornhill*). Wife d.1744. W.
J., & KING. *London.* an.1744. Watch.
William. *Wolverhampton.* an.1766-75. C. & W.
Thomas Josias. *London.* a.1764. PARK.
Solomon. *Southampton, U.S.A.* 1782. *Philadelphia.* 1791-1820. C. & W.
John. *London.* ca.1800. circ. wall lever clock ill. Cec. & Web.
James. *Kilmacolm.* 1802. PARK.
Solomon, & Son. *Philadelphia.* 1806. C.
Charles B. *Philadelphia.* 1806. W.
Solomon, & Co. *Philadelphia.* 1808. C.
Augustus W. *Philadelphia.* 1819.
James. *Preston.* ca.1826. PARK.

PARKER—
John. *York.* Mid. 17c. sil. cal. watch Webster coll.
John. *London.* a.1656, CC.1674-97.
Thomas. *London.* a.1658, CC.1669-84. Lantern clock ill. Britten.
Robert. *London.* a.1659-76 CC.
Cuthbert. *London.* a.1659.
John. *London.* a.1670, CC.1678.
John. *London.* a.1672.
Edward. *London.* a.1683.
Daniel. *London* (*Fleet St.*). ca.1690. l.c. clock. Weth. coll. ill. Britten.
John. *London.* a.1684.
Robert. *London.* a.1690, CC.1698.
John. *London.* a.1691, CC.1706.
John. *London.* a.1695.
Christopher. *London.* a.1697.
Christopher. *London.* a.1701.
William. *London.* a.1703, CC.1710. Watch.
Thomas. *Dublin.* ca.1710-52. Watches G.M. Ilbert and Den. colls.
Thomas. *London.* a.1705.
Thomas. *London.* a.1713.
James. *London.* a.1730.
John. *London.* a.1739, CC.1747-ca.1775.
Thomas. *Dublin.* ca.1750. Watches G.M. and Den. coll.
Isaac. *Salisbury.* an.1759. Watch.
John. *Liverpool.* 1763-96. W.
George. *Dublin.* 1766. Watch mt.
James. *Cambridge.* 1767. d.1787. W.
George. *London.* an.1774. Watch.
Peter. *London.* an.1776. Watch.
Francis. *Knaresborough.* 1773, retired. C. & W.
& WAKELIN. *London.* an.1778. min. rep. watch.
Joseph or Jasper. *Greenwich.* an.1780.
William. *London.* a.1774, CC.1782.
John. *Cambridge.* 1784. W.
Thomas. *Philadelphia.* 1785-1819.
Thomas. *London.* 1786-1817. Watch Den. coll.
Matthew. *Dunfermline.* 1786-1830. mus. cal. clock.
Samuel. *Greenwich.* an.1786.

PARKER—*continued.*
Thomas. *London.* an.1791. Case maker.
John. *Louth.* 1791-5. W.
P. *London.* an.1792. Watch.
William. *London.* a.1783.
George. *Wisbech.* 1795. Watch.
Charles. *London.* an.1798. Watch.
John. *London.* a.1790-1804.
Benoni. *London.* a.1800.
James. *London.* 1811-24. W.
James. *Horncastle.* 1812. W.
John. *Lindfield.* 1813. Night and day watch Chamb. coll.
James. *Dudley.* Early 19c. Watch.
George. *Ulverstone.* Early 19c. Watch.
Thomas, & Co. *Philadelphia.* 1817-19.
Thomas, jun. *Philadelphia.* 1819-25.
Isaac. *Philadelphia.* 1819-25.
William. *Philadelphia.* 1823.

PARKHURST (PARKHOUSE)—
Michael. *London.* a.1683.
James. *London.* a.1716, CC.1734-8.
Roger. *Richmond* (*Yorks.*). 1750, d.1790.
William, son. *London.* a.1751, CC.1763-91.
William, son. *London.* CC.1791.

PARKINS—
Anios. prob. *London.* an.1766. Watch.
John. prob. *London.* an.1778. Watch.

PARKINSON—
Robert. *London.* CC.1637. Watch.
Matthew. *London.* a.1712, CC.1719.
Robert. *Lancaster.* 1732. d.1760. C.
Roger. *Edinburgh.* 1745-61. Made Haddington clock.
William, son of Robert. *Lancaster.* 1758.
William. *Lancaster.* ca.1770, d.1799.
Edward. *Settle.* ca.1770-1822. W.
Francis. *London.* an.1788. Watch.
William, son of Wm. *Prescot.* 1789. Lancaster freeman.
Edward. *London.* Late 18c. Watch.
William. *London.* CC.1802-42. W. In partnership with W. J. FRODSHAM. rep. pocket chron. sd. 'Parkinson' Ilbert coll.
& FRODSHAM. *London.* 1800-50. Pub. reports on trials of their chron. in 1832 and 1833, and an art. in Naut. Mag. 1834 on 'The change of rates in chrons.' Marine chron. G.M. rep. br. clock.
James. *Liverpool.* 1816. W.
Thomas. *Bury.* ca.1820.
Nathaniel. *Kendal.* 1820.
James. *London.* 1820.
William. *Liverpool.* 1825. W.

PARLIAMENT, Richard. *London.* 1799. W.

PARMAN, Thomas. *London.* an.1762. Watch.

PARMEE, William. *London.* a.1753.

PARMELEE, Ebenezer. *Guildford, Conn., U.S.A.* 1706-41. In 1706 made a wooden turret clock for the church, said to be the first public clock in U.S.A.

PARMENTIER, Abraham. *Rouen.* m.1654.

PARMER, Robert. *London.* Mid. 18c. Watch Feill coll.

PARNELL—
Thomas. *Canterbury.* mar.1785-1801. C. & W.
Thomas. *London.* 1815-24.

PARNHAM, Thomas. *London.* a.1746, CC. 1758.

PARQUOT (PARQUAIT)—
Peter. *London.* 1723. Bankrupt. Watch.
——. *Canterbury.* an.1750. Watch.

PARR—
John. *London.* a.1693.
William. *London* (*opposite Guy's Hosp.*). a. 1713-44.
R. *London.* ca.1750.
William Glover. *London.* an.1773. Watch.
William. *Liverpool.* 1781-1810. C.
Thomas. *Prescot.* an.1787. Watch.
William. *Farnworth-within-Widnes.* 1796.

PARR—*continued.*
William. ——. 1804. Pub. in London 'A Treatise on pocket Watches.'
John. *Liverpool.* 1805-29.
James. *Liverpool.* 1813.
Peter. *Liverpool.* 1816.
PARRATT—
Thomas. *London.* a.1667.
Henry. *London.* a.1678.
John. *London.* a.1691.
Samuel. *London.* a.1715, CC.1736-48.
PARROTT—
Richard. *London.* End 17c. Watch.
Thomas. *London.* CC.1702.
PARRS, Joshua. *London.* a.1697.
PARRY (PARREY)—
David. *London.* CC.1646-57. Small sil. watch Ashmolean M.
Francis. *London.* a.1646.
Jonathan. *London.* a.1659.
John. *London.* a.1706.
David. *Carmarthen.* ca.1775. l.c. clock.
John. *London.* a.1778.
John. *Philadelphia.* 1796.
John I. *Philadelphia.* 1796-1825.
PARSÉ, Mathieu. *Paris.* m.1745.
PARSON—
John. *London.* a.1685.
Samuel. *London.* a.1762, CC.1770.
PARSONS—
Richard. *London.* a.1682, CC.1690-1730. br. and l.c. clocks.
John. *London (Basinghall St.).* CC.1696-1729. Watch Stads M. Amsterdam.
John. *London.* a.1695.
George. *London.* a.1718. Watch.
John Wootton. *London.* a.1729-75.
F. E. J. *London.* 1755. Chiming br. clock.
Charles. *London.* a.1754.
Thomas. *Worcester.* 1768. C. & W.
Mark. *Norwich.* 1773. Watch.
T. *London.* an.1793. Watch.
Richard. *London.* a.1796.
& SAVILL. *London.* 1815. g. watch.
PÄRSSON, A. *Klingsbo.* 18c. Watch mt. Nord. M.
PARTEN, William. *London.* CC.1720-9. Prob. same as PARTON.
PARTER—
William. *London.* CC.1692.
Francis. *London.* CC.1730.
PARTINGTON—
Puleston. *Chester.* 1671-88. W.
Thomas. *London.* a.1713, CC.1720.
John. *London.* 1790.
Samuel. *London.* 1808-24.
M. *London.* 1808.
Thomas. *Salford.* 1813. W.
William. *London.* 1815-24.
C. F. *London.* 1826. Pub. 'Clock and Watchmaker's Complete Guide.'
S. *London.* Early 19c.
C. *London.* Early 19c.
PARTON—
William. *London.* a.1712, CC.1720, d.an. 1757.
William. *Sunderland.* 1820.
PARTRIDGE—
William. *London.* CC.1640-60. C. to the King.
John. *London.* a.1700-53.
Walter. prob. *London.* an.1743. Watch.
Samuel. *London.* a.1783.
William. *London (W. Smithfield).* 1813.
PASCAL, Claude. *The Hague.* ca.1650. Watch with very fine painted enamel S.K.M. ill. Baillie. Fine watch with g. pierced work on green en. back S.K.M. Watch crys. covers Feill coll.
PASCALL, James. *London.* a.1800, d.1863.
PASCO, William. *Penzance.* 1758. sil. p.c. watch.
PASEY (PACEY), Thomas. *London.* 1646. C. & W.
PASHLER, Edward. *London.* 1766. W.
PASSEMENT, Admiral. *Paris.* 1750. Designed a very complex astro. clock, made by DAUTHIAU for Louis XV ill. Britten. Designed an equation clock in 1760. Made a telescope driving clock with uniform motion desc. Mém. de l'Acad. des Sci. 1746.
PASSEY, Abraham. ——. ca.1690. sil. p.c. cal. watch M.M.A.
PASSION, Henry. *London.* a.1646.
PASSMORE, R. *Barnstaple.* 2nd half 18c. l.c. clock. Watch.
PASTA, Laurent. *Chaux-de-Fonds.* 1784.
PASTEUR—
Jacques. *Geneva* and *London.* ca.1750. en. watch M.P.S. Dresden. Watch Hist. M. Chaux-de-Fonds.
Horace Benedict. *Paris.* m.1751. g. en. watch Gélis coll.
PASTILAKI, Johann. *Dresden.* m.1696. From *Hamburg.*
PATCHING, Elisha. *London.* CC.1728.
PATEK, Antoine Norbert de. *Geneva.* 1839. A Pole. Started business with CZAPEK. In 1845 entered into partnership with Adrien PHILIPPE and Gostkowski, starting the firm of PATEK, PHILIPPE & CIE, which still exists.
PATELING—
John. *London.* a.1722.
——. *Lincoln* an.1757. Watch.
PATEMAN—
William. *London.* ca.1730. l.c. clock.
William. *Bedford.* 1785.
PATEN, Archibald. *Edinburgh.* 1722.
PATENOSTE, Jean. *Geneva.* ca.1775-92.
PATERSON—
Patrick. *Edinburgh.* a.1728. *London.* 1747. W.
R. prob. *London.* an.1768. Watch.
James. *Banff.* b.1757, d.1829.
William. *Edinburgh.* a.1768-74.
James. *Edinburgh.* a.1789-1825.
John. *N. Leith.* 1807.
Alexander. *Leith.* 1814.
——. *Glasgow.* 1824.
PATIENT, William. *London.* a.1753.
PATIN—
Jehan. *Paris.* 1544. Petitioner for incorporation of Paris guild.
——. *Paris.* 1821-5.
PATMORE, Peter. *London.* CC.1813-15. W.
PATON—
James. *Edinburgh.* 1773.
David. *Dunfermline.* 1824.
PATRICK—
John. *London.* CC.1712.
Edward. *London.* 1760. l.c. clock.
Thomas. *London (Haberdashers Sq. & Moorfields).* a.1756, CC.1765-78.
Thomas. *Market Weighton.* ca.17750-9. C. & W.
William. *Dublin.* ca.1790. Watch Horstmann coll.
Miles. *Greenwich.* 1795. rep. watch mt.
German. *Long Melford.* 1792. C. & W.
G. *Greenwich.* Early 19c. Also G. & W.
PATRIE, Abraham. *Geneva.* a.1611.
PATRON—
Daniel. *Paris.* b.1723, d.1792. g. en. watch.
& ARNAUD. *Geneva.* an.1756. Watch.
& Co. *Geneva.* Mid. 18c. g. repoussé p.c. watch.
Jean. *Geneva.* Mid. 18c. Single hand watch Ilbert coll.
Jacques. *Geneva.* 1770. g. en. mandoline watch F.W.M. g. en. spherical watch M.M.A. str. watch Bernal sale. 4-colour g. watch in lorgnette.

PATRON—*continued.*
J. L. *Paris* ca.1800. c.secs. pedometer watch Ilbert coll.
J. S. *Geneva.* Early 19c. g. watch Feill coll.
PATRY—
Alex. *Paris.* Late 18c. en. watch. Watch, set pearls, Gotha M.
ET CHENEVIÈRE. prob. *Geneva,* ca.1800. Small en. balloon watch Bernal sale. en. pear watch.
ET CHAUDOIR. *Geneva.* ca.1800. g. en. watch, set pearls, Carnegie M.
PATTEE, Thomas. *London.* a.1785, CC.1793, l.CC.1810.
PATTEN—
Joseph. *London.* a.1783.
Robert. *Liverpool.* 1816-29. W.
Anthony. *Liverpool.* 1818. W.
PATTENDEN, John. *London.* a.1711.
PATTENSON, Robert. *London* a.1661, CC. 1668.
PATTERSON—
John. *London.* a.1726-52.
Peter. *London.* an.1743. Watch.
David. *Sunderland.* 1763-6. l.c. clocks.
Alexander. *Fermoy.* 1824.
Richard. *Kells.* 1824.
PATTEY, ——. *London.* ca.1710. sil. watch.
PATTIER, ——. *Paris.* 1771. Devised a dividing engine.
PATTINSON, John. *Burnley.* ca.1820.
PATTISON—
Robert. *London.* a.1661, CC.1668.
Robert. *London.* a.1676, CC.1688.
Joseph. *Chester.* 1767. W.
John. *Halifax.* ca.1780-1801. l.c. clocks.
J., jun. *Coventry.* 1799. Bankrupt. W.
James. *Edinburgh.* 1824.
PATTON—
& JONES. *Baltimore, U.S.A.* 1798-1807. Also *Philadelphia* from 1805. W. & C.
Abraham. *Philadelphia.* 1800-17.
James. *Clones.* 1824.
PATTRU, ——. ——. ca.1620. oct. crys. watch B.M.
PATY, William. *London.* a.1710. Watch mt. G.M.
PATZELT, Joseph. *Reichenberg.* Late 18c. Crucifix clock M.P.S. Dresden.
PAUL—
Thomas. *London.* a.1663, CC.1670.
Edward. *London.* a.1696.
Jacques. *Geneva* and *Montbéliard.* 1765.
William. *London.* a.1759, CC.1766.
Keene. *London.* 1799.
John. *London.* a.1793.
Philip. *London.* 1802-25. Also PAULL.
'Paul Cornell.' Sig. on 1871-4 watches of the CORNELL WATCH CO.
PAULET—
L. *London.* Late 17c. and early 18c. sil. gilt table clock S.K.M. str. watch Den. coll.
Joseph. prob. *London.* an.1711. Watch.
John. *London.* a.1728, CC.1740. Watch S.K.M. rep. watch mt. G.M. l.c. clock Weth. coll.
PAULI—
——. *Leitomischel.* 1544. Made aut. clock for Mahrisch-Trübau.
Wilhelm. *Stockholm.* 1795-1810. Watch, br. and wall clocks.
PAULSEN & JÜRGENS. *Hamburg.* 1801-1804.
PAULUS—
Hans. *Heilbronn.* 1525 began town clock, finished by Isaac HABRECHT in 1580.
Pieter. *Amsterdam.* Late 17c. Watch en. by Huaud l'aîné Ilbert coll.
PAUMIER, Nicolas. *Rouen.* a.1695.
PAUPARD, Peter. prob. *London.* an.1758. Watch.
PAUPIN, Léonard. *Autun.* a.ca.1565.
PAUTER, Josué. *Paris.* ca.1720. Watch Feill coll.
PAUTEX, Moïse. *Geneva.* 1792. Awarded prize for watch by Soc. des Arts.
PAVIS, Pierre. *Angers.* 1569. Keeper of cathedral clock.
PAWSEY, Ralph. *London.* 1820.
PAWSON, William. *Lewes.* an.1820. Watch.
PAXTON—
Joseph. *Higham Ferrars.* an.1770. Watch.
——. *Cheltenham.* 1777. W.
John. *St. Neots.* 1784-95. Watch.
Frances. *London.* a.1777.
PAY, C. *London.* ca.1730. g. rep. watch Den. coll.
PAYEN, ——. *Paris.* 1771. Made a writing automaton.
PAYER, Johann. *Vienna.* m.1703.
PAYNE (PAYN)—
John. *Southwold.* 1495. A smith. Made a clock for Walberswick, Suffolk.
William. *London.* 1618. Lantern clock ill. Cec. & Web. Webster coll.
Nicholas. *London.* a.1641, CC.1648, d.1676.
François. *Rouen.* a.1652.
Sarah, widow of Nich. *London.* 1676-1707.
George. *London.* a.1687.
Humpfrey. *London.* 1703.
——. *Hadleigh.* ca.1720. Hood clock.
Richard. *London* (*Wood St.*). a.1717, CC. 1725-64. Watch.
George. *Ludlow.* 1743-95. Watch.
Richard. *London* (*Carthusian St.*). 1747. Watch-case maker.
Southern, son of Rich. *London.* a.1743. CC. 1750, m.CC.1778.
Richard, bro. *London.* CC.1755-62. Watch sd. 'Richard Payne Junior.'
John. *Lenham.* b.1731-95. C. & W.
v. DAWSON & PAYNE.
Robert. *London* (*Bridgewater Sq.*). 1770. Bankrupt.
William. *Godstone.* an.1777. Watch.
——. *Harwich.* an.1787. Watch.
James. *London* (*Foster La.*). 1794-1825.
John. *London* (*St. Ann's La.*). 1795-1825.
William. *Hadleigh.* 1795-1900. W.
William. *Deal.* 1796. C. & W.
Robert. *Walthamstow.* 1813. Watch, Enderlin escapement, G.M.
William. *London.* 1820-40. mus. watch mt. C.A. & M.
PAYNE'S. *London.* ca.1760. Watch mt. Buckley coll. Prob. partnership of Southern and Richard.
PAYNES, ——. *Abingdon.* Early 19c.
PAYRAS (PAIRAS, PEIRAS, PERRAS, PEZAR, PEZAS, PLAIRAS)—
Pasquier. *Blois.* 1594. d.1632. Watch Louvre. Oval watch with fine eng. Mallett coll. ill. Develle. oct. gilt watch with very fine pierced and chiselled covers Arts M. Prague.
Charles. *Blois.* 1597. d.1616. oct. watch S.K.M. Watch Louvre.
Jacques, son. *Gien.* 1628.
Salomon, son of Charles. *Blois.* b.1605, d. 1684. Fine painted en. watch by him or his son Stern. coll.
Salomon, son. *Blois.* mar.1657-97.
Charles. *Amsterdam.* 1688. Huguenot refugee from *Blois.*
Jacques. *Amsterdam.* 1688. Hugeunot refugee from *Blois.*
PAYTON—
H. *Bromsgrove.* 1765. Watch.
R. *London.* an.1778. Watch.
D. *London.* an.1787. Watch.
William. *London.* 1790.
PEACE—
Mathew. *Beaminster.* d.1750. C.
Henry. *Beaminster.* d.1817. C.

PEACHEY—
William. *London.* CC.1728-53.
Newman, son. *London* (*Dean St.*). a.1742, CC.1749, d.1802.
William, bro. *London.* CC.1754-9.
John, bro. *London* (*New St. Hill*). a.1747, CC.1755-68.
Joseph. *London.* mar.1764. W.
James. *London.* a.1776, CC.1783, l.CC.1811.

PEACOCK—
George. *London* (*Threadneedle St.*). 1770-1785.
George. *London* (*R. Exchange*). an.1771. c.secs. watch Ilbert coll. g. p.c. watch.
Francis. *London.* an.1776. Watch.
William. *Kimbolton.* an.1778-ca.1790 CC.
Samuel. *Kimbolton.* Late 18c. Watch.
George. *London* (*Cornhill*). 1784.
William. *York.* 1789-1832. W.
John. *Lincoln.* 1791-5. W.
Samuel. *Lincoln.* 1812. C. & W.
John. *Penrith.* 1820.

PEADLE, John. *London.* a.1765.
PEAKE, Henry. *London.* a.1759.
PEAL, Lowther. *London.* an.1776. Watch. Also PEEL.

PEALE—
Charles Wilson. *Annapolis, U.S.A.* 1764. C. & W.
Thomas. *London.* an.1770. Watch.

PEARCE (PEARSE)—
Jonas. *London.* a.1717. g. watch Den. coll. Also PEARSE.
——. *Stratford-on-Avon.* 1st half 18c. l.c. clock.
Thomas. *London.* 1740. Watch.
John. *London.* 1740-60.
Henry. *London.* a.1739, CC.1749.
H. F. prob. *London.* an.1776. Watch.
William. *London.* a.1765.
John. *London.* a.1771.
Samuel. *Honiton.* an.1781. Watch. l.c. clock.
William. *London.* a.1777, CC.1786, m.CC. 1804, d.1824.
William. *Plymouth.* 1795.
J. *London* (*Lambeth*). Early 19c. Watch.
John. *Tavistock.* 1822.

PEARKES, F. *London.* 1820-5. W.
PEARL, J. *London.* 1825. W.
PEARMAN, William. *London.* a.1823.
PEARSALL, Thomas. *New York.* ca.1780 CC.

PEARSON—
Richard. *London.* a.1747.
Matthew. *London* (*St. Catherine's*). 1761-1782.
Henry Strangeways. *London.* a.1766.
& GREY. *George Town* (*S. Carolina*). 1768. C. & W.
William. *New York.* 1768-75. C. & W.
Joseph & Thomas. *New York.* 1770-3. W.
Thomas. *Berwick-on-Tweed.* ca.1770-1820. l.c. clock.
William. *Blackburn.* ca.1770-1814.
Joseph. *New York.* 1773-5. W.
Thomas. *New York.* 1773. W.
George. *London.* an.1777. Watch Feill coll.
Thomas. *Newcastle-o.-T.* 1778-1827. C. & W.
Samuel. *Halifax.* 1790-1814. l.c. clock-maker.
Amos. *Peterborough.* In 1795 succeeded by Eliz. DAVIE.
Thomas. *Berwick-on-Tweed.* 1795. W.
R. *Oxford.* 1796. Exhibition of his mechanical microcosm.
J. *Towcester.* From 1797.
Charles. *London.* a.1793.
The Rev. W. *East Sheen* and *S. Kilworth.* b.1767, d.1847. Pub. in 1791 in 'Rees' Cyclopaedia' a treatise on horology.
B. *Oxford.* 1810. Watch.

PEARSON—*continued.*
Henry. *Bedale.* ca.1800-22.
——. *Worcester.* Early 19c. Watch.
——. *Manchester.* an.1820. Watch.
John. *Whitehaven.* 1820.
Thomas. *London.* 1820.

PEAT—
John. *Crieff.* 1782. Made clock for Kenmore Church.
Thomas. *Crieff.* 1784.
Thomas. *Stirling.* 1818.

PEAVEY, William. *London.* a.1761.
PECHLIN, Henrik Jacob. *Aarhus.* m.1737.

PECK—
George. *London.* a.1718, CC.1725-52.
George, son. *London.* CC.1755. d.an.1792.
Elijah. *Boston, U.S.A.* 1789. W.
Moses. *Boston, U.S.A.* 1789-1800. W.
Floyd Clay. *London.* CC.1792.
John. *Wellingborough.* 1795. W.
George, bro. *London.* CC.1800.
Benjamin. *Montego Bay, Jamaica.* ca.1800 CC.

PECKETT, John. *London.* a.1683, CC.1691-1712.

PECKHAM—
John. *Ashford.* 1741. C. & W.
Clark. *Burwash.* 1791. C. & W.
John Randall. *London.* 1798. Patented a watch with compass.
William. *London.* 1805.

PECKOVER—
Richard. *London* (*Change Alley* in 1735, *R. Exchange* in 1751). a.1700-54. Prob. took over QUARE & HORSEMAN's business in 1733. The Nos. of watches sd. by him are known from 6480 to 7377, the series apparently continuing from Quare & Horseman's. rep. watch mt. G.M. Watch M.M.A. with Turkish figures. Small br. clock Weth. coll. Gilt metal case br. clock Prestige coll.
Richard. *London.* 1791. g. watch G.M.

PEDACCHIA, Domenico da. *Rome.* 1543. C. to the Pope.
PEDDELL, John. *London.* a.1721. Also PEDDLE.

PEDDIE—
James. *Stirling.* 1786.
James. *Stirling.* 1801-50.
Andrew. *Stirling.* 1806-32.

PEDERSEN, Anders. *Copenhagen.* 1575 Court C.
PEELE, Edmund. *London.* a.1730.
PEER, Joseph. *Vienna.* m.1797.
PEERES, Thomas. *London.* a.1698.

PEERS—
John. *London.* a.1676.
Benjamin. *Chester.* 1773-84. l.c. clock.

PEFFENHAUSER (PEFFINHAUSS, PFEFFENHAUSER, BEPFFEN-HAUSER)—
Wilhelm. *Augsburg.* mar.1647-76. crys. helix watch B.M. ill. Baillie. Oval watch M.M.A. Agate watch, cover with cameo and set rubies. Tower clock Gotha M.
Philipp Heinrich. *Augsburg.* mar.1683. sil. table clock, en. and set stones, K.H.M. p.c. rep. sil. watch. Dial B.M.

PEGG—
John. *London.* 1725. Insolvent.
William. *London.* a.1759.
Charles. *London.* a.1762.
Robert. *Ashby-de-la-Zouche.* Early 19c. Watch.

PEGLER—
Daniel. *Trowbridge.* 1779. C. & W.
Daniel. *Southampton.* 1795. W.

PEIGNAT, Gabriel Pierre. *Paris.* 1764-77.

PEIRCE—
William. *London.* a.1717.
H. *London.* an.1777. Watch.
L. J. *London.* Early 19c. Watch.

PEIRSON, William. *Kirby Moorside.* ca.1770-1795. C.
PEJON (PEJOCT, POUGHON), Damien. *Lyons.* 1567-72. C. to St. Jean.
PELEAT, ——. *Pont Audemer.* 1772.
PELHAM, Samuel. prob. *London.* an.1790. Watch.
PELICIER, François. *Avignon.* 1684.
PÉLISSIER, Michel. *Paris.* m.1777-89.
PELLATON, Ami. *Chaux-de-Fonds.* Early 19c. Famous for minute lettering on dials.
PELLATON-FAVRE, Albert. *Le Locle.* b. 1832, d.1914. Eminent maker of tourbillon watches. His son James made one 23 mm. dia. in 1923.
PELLET—
Samuel. *Geneva.* b.1737-68.
——. *Paris.* 1812.
PELLETIER—
——. *Paris.* d.1742.
Jacques. *Paris.* 1736 m.-1789. C. to Louis XVI.
Jean Baptiste. *Paris.* m.1743.
Antoine. *Paris.* 1749. C. to Louis XV.
Jacques. *Paris.* m.1770.
——. *Paris (Rue Grenetat).* 1812. Succeeded COUTURIER.
PELLIÈRE (PILLIÈRE), Collin. *Avignon.* 1444. Made clock for Carpentras. Remade clock at Orange in 1446.
PELLING, Edward. *London.* a.1700.
PELLITIER (LE PELLETIER), Peter. *London.* a.1729, CC.1736.
PELOT, François Armand. *Paris.* m.1780.
PELOUX, Antoine. *Geneva.* ca.1770-91.
PELSING (PELTSING), Andreas. *Haarlem.* 1751.
PELTIER, ——. *Paris.* 1810-17.
PELTON, Thomas. *London.* an.1752. Watch.
PEMBERTON—
James. *Whitchurch.* an.1767. Watch.
George. *London.* an.1791. Watch.
PEMBROKE, George. *London.* ca.1740. en. watch Peiping M.
PEMMELL, John. *London.* a.1696.
PEN—
William. *Scotland.* a.1696.
Edward. *London.* a.1722.
PENARD, Isaac. ——. ca.1600. Watch M.M.A.
PENARICK, Peter. *London.* an.1774. Watch.
PENAVOYRE, Benjamin. *London.* a.1721.
PENCINO, Raffaele. *Venice.* 1531-9. From *Padua.* Keeper of clock of S. Marco.
PENDLETON—
Samuel. *Farnworth-within-Widnes.* d.1778. W.
Richard. *London.* an.1780-1808. Lever watch Ilbert coll.
Samuel. *Ditton (Lancs.).* an.1784. Watch.
Pennington. prob. *London.* Late 18c. Marine chron. M.P.S. Dresden.
John. *Liverpool.* 1821. W.
PENEFIELD, William Weston. *London.* an. 1762.
PENEL, Guillaume. *Beauvais.* 1580. 'Horloger, Serrurier et Arquebusier.' Made clock for L'Abbaye de St. Symphorien.
PENFOLD (PENFORD)—
Joshua. *London.* a.1684, CC.1695.
——. *Middleton Cheney.* 1765. W.
Thomas. *Banbury.* 1771-95. C. & W. Also PINFOLD.
PENHAM, D. *London.* an.1801. Watch.
PENKETHMAN, Thomas. *London.* a.1682, CC.1692.
PENLEAZE, David. *London.* 1743. W.
PENLINGTON—
Thomas. *Sheffield.* 1780-1817. Watch.
John. *Liverpool.* ca.1820.
Joseph. *Liverpool.* 1825. W.
PENMAN, Robert. *Dunfermline.* 1820.
PENN—
Thomas. *London.* a.1700. W.
Richard. *London.* an.1732-ca.1750. Watch mt. G.M.
John. *London (Barbican).* a.1756, CC.1764-1776. W.
Thomas, son of Thomas. *London.* a.1769, CC.1776.
PENNECUIK, James. *Glasgow.* 1791.
PENNINGTON—
John. *Ince.* d.1764. C.
Robert. *London.* 1780-1824. chron. maker. Partner with Wm. HOWELLS. Watch G.M.
Christopher. *Kendal.* 1790-1820. Watch. l.c. clock.
Thomas. *Liverpool.* 1805-11. W.
Joseph. *Liverpool.* ca.1818.
John. *Liverpool.* 1818-29. W.
——. *London (Camberwell).* Early 19c.
PENNOCK—
John. *London.* mar.an.1630, CC.1638, m. CC.1664-79. Lantern clock B.M.
William. *London.* 1637. C.
PENNSÉ, Jean. *Neuchâtel.* 1598. Town C.
PENNY—
Richard. *London.* a.1698-1715. Watch.
James. *London.* a.1699.
Charles. *Wells (Somerset).* an.1743. Watch.
Francis. *London.* an.1774. Watch.
John. *London (Aldersgate St.).* a.1763, CC. 1770 l.CC.1790, d.1818.
Charles. *Bristol.* 1781-1801. W.
John. *Portsea (Hants).* ca.1790 CC.
George. *Wells (Somerset).* Late 18c.
Charles. *Bristol.* 1781-1801. C. & W.
John. *London.* a.1787, CC.1804, l.CC.1813.
John. *London.* a.1814.
PENROSE, ——. *Redruth.* 1795. C. & W.
PENSOTH, Joshua. *Dudley.* Early 19c. Watch.
PENTINEAU, I. *Geneva.* End 17c. Watch Den. coll.
PENTON, Charles. *London.* an.1774-8. Watch.
PENTY, William. *York.* 1831.
PEPIN, ——. *Paris.* 1772. Turret C. of repute. Made clocks for St. Sauveur and St. Sulpice.
PEPPER—
Samuel. *London.* a.1655.
John. *London.* a.1684.
Thomas. *London (Stayning La.).* a.1757, CC.1764, l.CC.1787-94.
James. *Biggleswade.* an.1768. Watch.
EPYS—
Richard. *London.* a.1667, CC.1674-88.
John. *London.* a.1672, CC.1680, m.CC.1707-1715. Watch B.M. l.c. clock Weth. coll.
Peter. *London.* a.1680.
John, son of John. *London (Fleet St.).* a.1708, CC.1715, m.CC.1739-48. Watch mt. S.K.M.
Samuel, bro. *London.* a.1713.
William, bro. *London.* a.1715, CC.1723-40.
Richard. *London.* a.1736.
Thomas. *London.* a.1740. Watch.
PÉRACHE, ——. *Paris.* ca.1800. Mantel clock.
PERARD—
Marc Alexis. *Bellefontaine.* 1757-62. Made clock for cathedral of Embrun.
Pierre Louis. Worked with Marc Alexis.
PERCEVAL, Carblet. *Besançon.* 1599.
PERCHARD, James. *London.* a.1764.
PERCHE (PORCHER), ——. *Paris.* 1807-1825.
PERCIVAL—
James. *Chester.* 1742. W.
Philip. *London (Strand).* 1757. Watch.
John. *Woolwich.* Late 18c.-1811. Clock. Watch.
Thomas. *London.* 1802-08. Pocket chron. Ilbert coll.

PERCIVAL—*continued.*
D. *London.* 1809-11.
Mary and Thomas James. *Woolwich.* 1817-1824.
William Chennel. *London.* a.1814, CC.1822.
PERCIVELL, William. *London.* Early 19c. Watch.
PERCY—
James. *Stradbroke.* ca.1800.
Charles. *London.* 1800. Watch N.Y. Univ.
PERDONNET—
François Auguste. *Vevey.* m.1736-49.
——. *Vevey.* 1768. Established a factory with ROUSSATIER.
Jean Denis Alexandre. *Vevey.* 1798 m.
PERDUE (PERDIE), William. *London.* a. 1702.
PEREAM, George. *Axminster.* mar.1742. C.
PERES—
Mark. *London.* CC.1680. Lantern clock.
Jan. *Haarlem.* 1765.
PERETTON (PERRETON), ——. *Paris.* 1807.
PEREY, Étienne Louis Henri. *Geneva.* ca. 1775-92.
PERGAUD, Louis Charles. *Geneva.* ca.1770-1791.
PERICHON, Pierre Noel. *Paris.* m.1749.
PERIER, Henry. *London.* ca.1730. Watches S.K.M. and Den. coll. *v.* REIREP.
PERIGAL—
Gideon. *London.* a.1710-50. Watch in jasper case.
Claude. *London* (*Rose St.*). d.1749. 'One of the most eminent men in England for making motions for rep. watches.'
Francis. *London* (*Threadneedle St.* and *R. Exchange*). CC.1741, m.CC.1756.
Claude. *London* (*Rose St.*). From 1749.
Francis, son of Francis. *London* (*Threadneedle St.* and *R. Exchange*). a.1748, CC. 1756, m.CC.1775. Watch G.M. g. watch en. by MOSER Stern. coll. prob. by him. g. watch set amethysts Ilbert coll.
Francis, & Son. *London* (*R. Exchange*). 1763-1805.
Francis, son of Francis (2). *London* (*R. Exchange*). a.1778, CC.1786, l.CC.1787-1793. Watch mt. G.M.
Francis S. *London* (*New Bond St.*). 1770. CC.1781, m.CC.1806, d.1824. W. to the King. Watch S.K.M. rep. p.c. watch and chatelaine F.W.M. rep. watch, Turkish figures, M.M.A. g. watch Den. coll. *v.* MARKWICK MARKHAM. In firm of Francis & Son.
John. *London* (*Coventry St.*). 1770. CC. 1781-1800. Partner with MASQUERIER 1772 to 1782, then with BROWNE. g. rep. watch.
BROTHERS. *London.* 1772. g. en. cyl. watch.
Thomas. *London* (*Coventry St.*). 1784.
& BROWNE. *London* (*Coventry St.*). From 1782 to 1799. Partnership with John above. Pocket chron. Ilbert coll.
Francis. *London* (*Finsbury Sq.*). 1805-11.
John. *London* (*Leicester Sq.*). 1805-15.
& DUTERRAU. *London* (*New Bond St.*). 1803-1840. W. to the King. cyl. rep. mt. Ilbert coll. g. watch M.M.A.
PÉRISCEL—
Pierre. *Lyons.* mar.1623-65 m.
Vincent, son. *Lyons.* b.1624-59. *Geneva,* 1668.
PERISSE, Jaques Laurent. *Geneva.* ca.1755-1772.
PERISTA, Jean. *Paris.* m.1759.
PERKINS—
John. *London.* a.1661.
Eysam. *London.* a.1670-82.
Richard. *Dover.* 1726. 'Maketh good watches.'
James. *London.* CC.1730.

PERKINS—*continued.*
James. *London.* a.1730.
James. *London.* a.1734.
Thomas. *Evesham.* 1757. d.1785. l.c. clock. Watch.
& SPENCER. *London.* 1765-1806. ½ ¼ rep. and str. g. watch Den. coll. Also SPENCER & PERKINS.
William. *London.* an.1781. Watch.
Thomas. *Philadelphia.* 1785. C. & W.
John. *Leominster.* 1797. C.
John. *London.* 1820. W.
PERLINGER, Ignaz. *Vienna.* m.1802.
PERNELL, Thomas. *London.* a.1756. l.c. clock.
PERNETTI, F. *Switzerland.* Early 19c. Watch Carnegie M. Two g. en. watches M.M.A.
PERNOT, J. *Dunkerque.* 1785. Dial Old Ashmolean M.
PERONE, Isack. *London.* 1622. Alien.
PEROT—
Pasque. *London.* 1664 CC.
Estienne. *Geneva.* a.1657.
PEROWNE, ——. *Margate.* Early 19c. W.
PERPIGNAN, Peter. *Philadelphia.* 1819-23. W.
PERRACHE, ——. *Paris.* 1752.
PERRAD, Julien. *Morbier.* 1774.
PERRARD, PETIT ET VALET, ——. *Jura.* 1765. W.
PERRAULT, Claude. ——. b.1613, d.1688. Pendulum clock driven by water C.A. & M. desc. in Gallon, 'Machines et Inventions,' Vol. I.
PERREGAUX—
Henri. *Le Locle.* ca.1825. W.
Girard, *v.* GIRARD.
PERRELET—
Jean Jacques. *Le Locle.* 1656-66.
Abram Louis. *Le Locle.* b.1729, d.1826. Eminent maker of precision watches. One of the first to make pedometer watches. Invented several watchmaking tools. A. L. BREGUET was his apprentice.
Abram Robert. *Le Locle.* ca.1750-66. W. and tool-maker.
Daniel. *Le Locle.* ca.1750-66. Able tool-maker.
Abram Louis, son of A. L. *Chaux-de-Fonds.* 1760-97. Turret C.
Louis Frédéric, grandson of Abram. *Paris.* b.1781, d.1854. Worked with BREGUET. An eminent maker of observatory clocks and chrons. Clock C.A. & M. with 5 alternative escapements.
——. *Paris.* 1824.
PERRENOD—
David. *Môtiers.* 1670.
Frédéric. *Ponts-de-Martel.* 1712-16.
Daniel. *Ponts-de-Martel, La Brévine* and *Môtiers.* 1712.
Moïse. *Ponts-de-Martel.* 1765. Mentioned as 'artiste universel.' Turret and house C.
PERRENOUD—
Jean Jacques. *Valangin.* 1771. C.
Frédéric Louis. *Ponts-de-Martel* and *La Brévine.* 1761-1801.
Jean Frédéric. *La Brévine.* Made complex clocks.
David Benguerel. *Fontainemelon.* 1793. Started a factory with Julien and François HUMBERT-DROZ. Factory re-organized in 1821 by Jacob Robert TISSOT.
Francis. *London.* 1802-11. W.
PERRET—
Alexander. *La Ferrière.* 1766. Able W.
Daniel Henry. *La Brévine.* 1776. C.
Jean Jacques. *Switzerland.* 1778. Awarded prize for essay on steel in watchmaking. Prob. same as PERRET-GENTIL.

PERRET—*continued.*
Jean Jacques Henri. *La Brévine.* b.1772-1816. C.
Humbert, et Cie. *Paris.* 1780.
——. *Paris (Place Maubert).* 1813-25.
FILS. *Paris (Rue Ste. Avoie).* 1822.

PERRET-DIT-TORNARE, Abram. *Le Locle, La Sagne* and *Neuchâtel.* 1630-72. Made church clock at Le Locle.

PERRET-GENTIL—
Pierre. *Le Locle.* 1st half 18c. Watch.
Moïse. *Chaux-de-Fonds.* 1749-69. Clock.
Jean Jacques. *Le Locle.* 1750-75. 'Expert horloger en pendules.' Several clocks. *v.* PERRET.
Abram Louis, bro. and partner. *Le Locle.* 1751-61.
Théodore. *Le Locle.* a.1748. C. to the King of Prussia. Several clocks.
Moïse. *Chaux-de-Fonds.* a.1753. Carillon clocks.
Moïse, son of Moïse (1). *Chaux-de-Fonds.* 1769.
Charles François, bro. *Chaux-de-Fonds.* 1769-83. Partner with his brother.
LES FILS. *Le Locle.* ca.1770. Louis xv clock sd. 'Les Fils de Perret-Gentil au Locle.'

PERRET-JEANNERET—
Jonas. *Le Locle.* 1766. W. of repute. g. en. watch Gélis coll.
David. *La Brévine.* 1774-1807. C.
Jean Jacques. *La Brévine.* 1785-91. A fine maker.
Phinée, nephew. *La Brévine, Le Locle* and *Chaux-de-Fonds.* b.1777, d.1851. A fine maker of clocks and regulators.
Jules Frédéric, bro. *La Brévine.* b.1783-1826. A fine C.
Isaac Henri, bro. *La Brévine, Le Locle* and *Couvet.* b.1794, d.1873. Fine maker. Several clocks.

PERREY, ——. *Morteau.* ca.1800. Watch mt. Ilbert coll.

PERREZ, ——. *Paris.* 1825.

PERRIER—
——. *'arl' (Arles?).* ca.1700. sil. repoussé al. watch M.P.S. Dresden.
——. *Moudon.* 1739.
Honoré. *Rolle.* ca.1740.
H. *London.* ca.1750. Watch.
Gabriel. *Vevey.* 1798 m.
——. *Paris.* 1812.

PERRIN (PERIN)—
Pierre. *Dole.* 1634.
Jean. *Paris.* 1675 m.-1685.
Edme. *Paris.* m.1746.
David. *Lausanne.* m.1749. Went *Vevey* 1753.
William. *London.* a.1759.
Charles. *Le Locle.* 1772-9. C.
Jean Baptiste. *Paris.* m.1784-9.
Jean. *Paris.* 1807-24.
——. *Noiraigue.* 1814.
FRÈRES. *Neuchâtel.* Early 19c. rep. c.secs. watch.

PERRINGHAM, Francis. *London.* 1790.

PERRINS, John. *London.* an.1755-90. Watch.

PERROCHOT, ——. *Paris.* 1811.

PERRON—
Richard. *London.* 1790.
L. *Besançon.* b.1779, d.1836. A very fine maker of watches and clocks. Designed in 1798 the pin-lever escapement with pin pallets. Pub. 1834 'Essai de l'histoire abregée de l'horlogerie.' In 1819 made the first chron. in Besançon.

PERROT—
Isaac. *Geneva.* 1674. Watch.
Guillaume. *Paris.* m.1770.
Henry. *Besançon.* 1780. br. clock in Vernis Martin.

PERRY—
Richard. *London.* a.1656.
George. *London.* d.1691. W.
John, son. *London.* CC.1691-1725.
Henry, bro. *London (Soho).* 1689. CC.1691-1721. br. and l.c. clock. Watch.
& PRICE. *London.* an.1734. Watch.
Martin. *London.* a.1725.
Thomas. *London.* a.1726.
Samuel. *London.* a.1728.
Thomas. *London.* a.1742-90. Watch G.M.
Edward. *England.* Early 18c. sil. p.c. watch.
Henry. *London (Westminster).* 1751. Watch.
Richard. *London.* a.1751. Watch.
Peter. *London (Rosemary La.).* a.1754, CC. 1763-71.
Thomas. *New York.* 1749. d.1774. C. & W. From *London.*
Thomas. *London.* 1765. Watch case maker.
Thomas & Mervin. *New York.* 1767. W. Partnership of Thomas with his son Mervin.
Mervin. *New York.* 1768-80. W.
Peter, son of Peter. *London (Aldgate).* a. 1777, CC.1784, l.CC.1812. W.
Joseph. *London.* a.1787, CC.1814.
John Addington, son of Peter. *London.* a. 1798, CC.1807, m.CC.1850.
George Levi. *London.* a.1810.
'PERRY.' Sig. on watches of the HAMPDEN WATCH Co. ca.1880.

PERRYMAN—
Thomas. *London.* ca.1770. g. en. rep. watch.
James. *Almondsbury.* 1774. W.
John. *Barnstaple.* Early 19c. Watch.

PERSA, Giambattista. *Genoa.* 1670-4. Keeper of clock on Palazzo delle Compere.

PERSE, Henry. *London.* a.1659.

PERTHOLLINGER, Jac. Reichard. *Vienna.* m.ca.1665.

PERUCHOT, ——. *Paris.* 1812.

PERY, Pierre. *Geneva.* Early 19c. rep. watch.

PERYER, John. *London.* a.1664.

PESCHEL—
Adam Friedrich. *Dresden.* b.1711, d.1785 m.
Carl August. *Dresden.* b.1750, d.1812 m.
Johann Friedrich. *Dresden.* m.1787, d.1831.
FRÈRES. *Dresden.* 18c. g. en. watch Fränkel coll.

PESCHOT (PÉCHOT)—
André. *Paris.* m.1786-9.
——. *Paris (Rue neuve St. Eustache).* 1807-1824.
Jeune. *Paris (Rue St. Honoré).* 1810-25.

PESNE, François. *Paris.* 1678 m.

PESTA (PESCHKA, PESTKA), Ignaz. *Vienna.* m.1808.

PESTRE, Jean. *Geneva.* 1811.

PETER, ——. *Basle.* 1436. Made clock for St. Niklaus Kapelle.

PETER ASTRONOMEN (Peter the Astronomer). *Vadstena.* 1506. A monk of Vadstena monastery. *Uppsala,* 1513, where he made a planetary clock for the church, and then went to *Rome.*

PETER (PETTER, PEDER) SEGERMAKARE (Peter the Clockmaker). *Vadstena,* 1587. *Ålesten,* 1599.

PETER UHRMAKARE (Peter the Clockmaker). *Stockholm.* 1637.

PETER—
François. *Le Locle.* a.1740. From *Vevey.*
& Co. *Dublin.* 1824. Watch.

PETERKIN, John. *London.* 1811-40. Watch.

PETERMANN, ——. *Chaux-de-Fonds.* 1784. trav. clocks.

PETERS—
John. *London.* a.1699.
Samuel. *London.* a.1728.
E. *Sheffield.* 1746. Watch.
André Jaques Étienne. *Geneva.* ca.1750-71.

PETERS—*continued.*
Paul Christian. *Berlin.* 1785. C.
Edward. *Sheffield (Fargate).* 1790-1817. W.
Edward. *Sheffield (Chapel Walk).* 1817. W.
James. *Cambridge.* Early 19c. Watch.

PETERSEN—
Paul. *Frederiksborg.* 1746.
Johannes. *Copenhagen.* m.1770. Court C.
Caspar Valfast. *Copenhagen.* m.1799.
Franz Nicholaus. *Hamburg.* 1801-21.
Johann G. *Hamburg.* 1801-21.
Peter Erik. *Copenhagen.* m.1803. From *Strasbourg.*
Jens Christ. *Göteborg.* 1813-15.
Joh. *Göteborg.* 1813-15.
Joh. *Göteborg.* 1818. Also PEDERSSON.

PETERSON—
Peter. prob. *London.* an.1775. Watch.
James. *London.* an.1776. Watch.

PETERSSON—
Haqvin. *Örebro.* 1805.
Jonas. *Ystad.* 1816-26.

PETHOUD, Abram. *Couvet.* 1807. C.

PETINEAU, ——. *London.* ca.1770. Watch mt. London M.

PETIT—
Gérardin. *Avignon.* 1410. Made clock for Montpellier with Pierre LOUIS.
Jean. *Paris.* ca.1550. C. to Henri II.
Guillaume. *Rouen.* 1559. d.1578. C. to Charles IX in 1573.
Guillaume. *London.* 1630-56. Petitioner for incorporation of CC. Watch.
FRÈRES. *Paris.* 1st half 18c. Watch Stads M. Amsterdam.
François. *Paris (Rue St. Denis).* m.1768-89.
Edward. prob. *London.* an.1777. Watch.
William. *London.* a.1764.
J., l'aîné. *Amsterdam.* ca.1780. Mantel clock.
Antoine. *Paris (Rue du Bout du Monde).* m. 1780-9.
Jean Baptiste. *Paris (Quai des Orfèvres).* m. 1781-1825.
Jacob. *Paris.* Late 18c. Clock.
——. *Paris. (Rue de Harlay).* 1812.
——. *Paris (Rue des Fossés St. Germain).* 1814-25.
B. L. *Paris (Rue St. Honoré).* 1814-25.
Gédéon. *Geneva.* Early 19c. Skeleton rep. watch Ilbert coll.

PETITDANT, Jean Nicolas. *Paris.* m.1782-9. Mantel clock.

PETITE, Jacques. *Paris.* m.1785-9.

PETIT-JEAN, Jacques. *Charlieu.* 16c. Keeper of town clock.

PETITMAITRE—
Théodore. *Neuveville.* d.1700.
Jean Jaques. *Le Locle.* Mid. 18c. C.

PETITOT—
Jean. b. *Geneva,* 1607. *England,* ca.1637. *France,* ca.1644-86. *Vevey,* d.1691. Celebrated painter on enamel. The invention of this painting is often wrongly attributed to him.
André. *Paris.* m.1786.

PETITPIERRE—
Samuel. *Couvet.* 1722-53.
David, son. *Môtiers, Neuchâtel* and *Couvet.* a.1735, d.1771. C.
Jean Henri. *Couvet,* 1741-56. 'Très expert horloger.' Many fine clocks.
Jean Pierre. *Neuchâtel.* 1749-55. C.
Henri. *Couvet.* ca.1770. *Geneva* 1780, d. 1825. Invented many improvements in watchmaking tools.
Pierre David. *Couvet.* 1775-98. C.
J. H. J. *Chaux-de-Fonds* and *Valenvron.* 1793. Clock.
Louis. *Couvet.* 1794. *Neuchâtel.* 1800-30. C.
F. *London.* 1809-11. W.

PETITPIERRE-BOY-DE-LA-TOUR—
Pierre David. *Couvet.* 1679-76. C.
Charles Henry, son. *Pekin, Macao, Manilla* and *Batavia.* b.1769. In 1792 went to *Pekin* with Lord Macartney's mission in charge of the clocks and automata taken as presents.

PETRE, James. *London.* a.1763, CC.1770.

PÉTREMAND—
Jacob. *Neuchâtel.* 1680-1700.
Abram, son. *Neuchâtel.* 1684. d.1747. Turret and other clocks. Made clock for the Tour de Diesse in 1715.
David François. *Neuchâtel.* d.1757.

PETRI, Johann Heinrich. *Basle.* a.1686, m. 1689-1701. A watch by J. H. Petri of *Heidelberg* Den. coll.; prob. the same maker.

PETRITSCH, W. Conrad. *Fürth.* d.1750.

PETT, Samuel. *London.* an.1760. Watch. cf. PETTY.

PETTAU, Karolos Nachber. *Steiermarck.* ca. 1800. Table clock.

PETTER, Christopher. *London.* CC.1730.

PETTERSSON—
Johan Gabr. *Göteborg.* b.1788, d.1851. l.c. clock.
——. *Malmö.* 1816.
J. *Alingsås.* 1819-30.

PETTEY, William. *London.* a.1760.

PETTIGREW (PETTYGREW), John. *Edinburgh.* 1780-1804. Watch.

PETTITT—
William. *London.* a.1764.
John. *Epping.* 1791. C. & W.
John. *London.* a.1785-1824.

PETTO, James. *London (Edgware* and *Stanmore).* 1799-1808.

PETTRE, ——. *Paris.* 1772.

PETTY—
William. *London.* a.1638, CC.1646-65.
Samuel. *London.* a.1716. cf. PETT.
Richard. *Gloucester.* 1763. W.
Peter. *Bradford (Yorks.).* 1795. W.

PETZ, Casimir. *Augsburg* and *Aichach.* 1738 comp.

PETZOLD, Henry. *London.* a.1785.

PEUPIN, Henry Alexandre. *Paris.* b.1809, d. 1872.

PEUZEL, DUPLEIX ET CIE. prob. *Geneva.* Early 19c. Complicated clocks.

PEVERELLO, ——. *Milan.* Late 17c. Watch mt. Ilbert coll.

PEW—
Edward Phillips. *London.* a.1735, CC.1778. Watch.
Richard Griffith, son. *London.* a.1766.

PEYTLING—
Thomas. *London.* a.1675, CC.1682.
J. *Boston.* 1796. C. & W. PEATLING.

PEYTON—
Robert. *Gloucester.* an.1740. Watch.
Richard or Richardson. *Gloucester.* 1743. d.1774. Succeeded by Theophilus JAMES. p.c. g. watch.
Thomas. *London.* a.1777.

PEZIERES, Dominique. *Paris.* 1737-57.

PFABE (PFAB), Andreas. *Dresden.* m.1732. From *Elterlein.* br. clock and trav. clock Uhren M. Vienna. Dial M.P.S. Dresden.

PFAFF—
Jereme. *Augsburg.* End 17c. Table clock with figure of Madonna ill. Britten. Table clock Webster coll.
Daniel. *Basle.* 1769. From *Liestal.*

PFAFFIUS, ——. *Wesel.* 1804. Made clock with conical pendulum.

PFALMER, Ludwig. *Elbing.* 1823-8. Town C.

PFALTY, John William. *Baltimore, U.S.A.* 1802. W. & C.

PFEFFER—
Johann Batist. *Germany.* ca.1760. Wall clock.
Leonhard. *Würzburg.* m.1796. Fine mantel clock Kunstgeschichtliche M. Würzburg.
PFEIFFER—
J. A. *Coburg.* ca.1717. Dial maker.
——. *Oberhausen.* 1756 comp.
PFEILSCHMIDT, Heinrich August. *Dresden.* m.1802. Went to *Grossenhain.*
PFENNINGER—
I. C. *Zürich.* ca.1750. Steel, g. and sil. watch Blot-Garnier coll.
J. C. *Cassel.* 1764. Clock and Sundials Cassel Landes-M.
PFLEGE, Johan Paul. *Augsburg.* Late 16c. Clock Brescia M.
PFLOCKS, Michael. *Geroldshofen.* m.1791.
PFLUGER, ——. *Soleure.* Several of this name were town C. from 1600-1850.
PFLÜGER, ——. *Berlin.* 1816.
PFLÜGRITTER, Hans. *Nürnberg.* Burgher in 1556. Kleinuhrmacher.
PHAREZ—
John. *London.* a.1767, CC.1774.
Ebenezer Richard, son. *London.* a.1796.
PHELIZOT—
C. *Dijon.* ca.1620. 6-lobed gilt watch, set crys., Mallett coll. ill. Baillie. crys. cross watch Louvre ill. Baillie.
Jacques. *Dijon.* 17c. Watch Gélis coll.
PHELP, John. *Brighton.* ca.1790 CC.
PHILBERT—
Daniel. *Paris.* 1675 m.
Daniel. *London.* 1695.
PHILIBERT—
——. *Visan (Avignon).* 1721.
Antoine. *Paris.* m.1776-1825. Clock.
PHILIP (PHILP)—
Robert. *London.* an.1776-88. mus. clocks and watches. br. clock ill. Cec. & Web. mus. astro. clock Peiping M.
Joshua E. *Brighton.* ca.1790 CC.
John. *Brighton.* Early 19c. C. & W.
PHILIPPAUT (PHILIPPUS), Isac. *Copenhagen.* 1714. From *France.*
PHILIPPE—
——. *Basoche-Gouet.* 1815.
Adrien, son. *Geneva.* b.1815, d.1894. Partner with A. N. de Patek and Gostowski in PATEK, PHILIPPE & Co. from 1845. Invented keyless winding by shifting-sleeve in 1842. Pub., 1863, 'Les Montres sans Clef.'
PHILIPPINI, Francesco. *Escorial.* 1688. Rack clock Cassel Landes-M.
PHILIPPON (PHILIPPSON, PHELIPPSON)—
Isaac. *London.* ca.1735. g. watch Mallett coll. p.c. g. and agate rep. watch Stern. coll.
James. *London.* an.1783. Watch.
PHILIPSON—
Henry. *Ulverstone.* ca.1814.
Henry, jun. *Ulverstone.* ca.1824.
PHILIPSTHAL, ——. *London.* 1811. Mechanician, associated with Henri MAILLARDET.
PHILLIMORE, ——. *London.* ca.1825. Watch.
PHILLIP—
William. *Chester.* 1640. C.
William. *Edinburgh.* a.1796-1846. Also PHILIP.
Alexander. *Glasgow.* 1803.
Alexander. *Edinburgh.* 1814-37.
PHILLIPS—
Samuel. *London.* a.1671.
John. *Tewkesbury.* 1737. C. & W.
John. *London.* a.1729.
Richard. *London.* a.1735.
David. *Llantrisant.* 2nd half 18c. l.c. clock.

PHILLIPS—*continued.*
Joseph. *London (Hoxton).* 1761. Insolvent.
Jonas. *London.* a.1750, CC.1771, d.1797.
James Thomas. *London.* CC.1772.
Samuel. *Oswestry.* 1771. C.
——. *Plymouth.* an.1775. Watch.
Philip. *London (St. John Sq.).* CC.1777, l.CC.1790-1840. sil. p.c. watch Carnegie M.
Thomas. *London.* an.1779. Watch.
Joseph. *Somersham.* Retired 1785. C. & W.
Richard. *W. Bromwich.* 1783. C. & W.
Levi. *Haverfordwest.* 1785. W.
Philip. *London (Aldersgate St.).* From 1785. Previously DERRICK & PHILLIPS.
Thomas. *Ludlow.* 1791-5. W.
Philip. *Haverfordwest.* 1790-1800. C.
Michael. *London.* a.1784.
William, son of Jonas. *London (Aldersgate St.).* CC.1797-1805.
John. *London (City Rd.).* 1799-1808.
Sanders. *London.* 1802-24.
Charles Thomas. *Kingston.* a.1798, CC.1819.
Samuel Hood, son of Philip. *London.* a.1800.
Joseph. *London.* 1817-24.
Joel. *London (Norton Folgate).* 1820.
——. *Reading.* an.1822. Watch.
Eduard. *Paris.* b.1821, d.1899. Prof. of mechanics. Evolved the theory of the isochronous balance-spring in memoir pub. 1860. Several later publications bearing on the balance and spring. His work was the foundation of modern springing.
PHILP, John. *London.* Early 19c. Watch.
PHILPIN, François Joseph. *Chaux-de-Fonds.* a.1774.
PHILPOT—
——. *London (Southwark).* d.1763. Watch case maker.
John, jun. *Thaxted.* 1795. C. & W.
William. *London.* a.1801.
PHIPPARD—
Thomas. *London.* a.1738.
Thomas. *Poole.* 1751. d. or retired 1761. C. & W.
George. *Poole.* 1791-1800. C. & W.
PHIPPS—
Joseph. *London.* a.1713.
James. *London.* a.1759, CC.1767.
PHITHIAN (PHYTHIAN)—
John. *Prescot.* d.1785. W.
Joseph. *(Liverpool* and *W. Derby).* 1767. W.
PHYFE, Duncan. *New York.* 1768-1854. Case maker. l.c. clock case M.M.A.
PHYSON, Joseph. prob. *London.* an.1764. Watch.
PIAGET—
Auguste. *Yverdon.* Mid. 18c. Watch.
Jean Pierre. *Verrières.* 1797. C.
François. *Berne.* Early 19c. Watch.
PICARD, ——. *Autun.* 1666-87. In charge of cathedral clock.
PICAUD, Jean. *Paris.* 1675 juré.
PICCARD, Jean. ——. b.1620, d.1682. First observed in 1666 the variation of period of a pendulum with temperature.
PICHART, ——. *Paris.* ca.1640. circ. str. and al. trav. clock Webster coll.
PICHAT, Loys. *Geneva.* 1561. Repaired clock of St. Pierre.
PICHON—
André. *Lyons.* mar.1637-58. Watch.
——. *Paris.* 1813.
——. *Geneva.* 1820. Made lever watches with pin pallets.
PICK, J. *London.* ca.1740. Very small watch Ilbert coll.
PICKELMANN (PICKLMANN)—
Wolff. *Nürnberg.* Burgher 1638.
Joseph Antoni. *Augsburg.* Early 18c. Turret C.

PICKER (PICKEN)—
Charles. *Edinburgh.* a.1794-1800.
John. *Edinburgh.* a.1796-1850.
Thomas. *Edinburgh.* a.1813-50.
John. *Leith.* 1822-30.
PICKERING—
John. *London.* a.1686.
George. *London.* a.1700.
James. *Dublin.* 1737. d.1771. W.
John. *Newcastle-o.-T.* an.1806. W.
Joseph. *Philadelphia.* 1817-25.
PICKES, Hannah. *London.* a.1702.
PICKETT—
John. *London.* 1693 CC.
William. *London.* Mid. 18c. Partner with THEED.
& RUNDELL. *London.* 1775-83. en. watch London M.
John. *Marlborough.* 1790-5 CC. l.c. clock dial ill. Britten.
& Co. *London.* an.1816. Watch.
PICKFORD, John. *Liverpool.* 1814-29. W.
PICKMAN—
William. *London.* 1811-24. Watch mt. Ilbert coll.
R. *London.* 1822-4.
PICKNETT, Joseph. *London.* CC.1771.
PICOT, Nicolas. *Paris.* m.1738.
PICQUERET, ——. *Paris.* Late 18c. Cartel clock, Ministère des Finances, Paris.
PIDER, H. J. *Augsburg.* ca.1580. Clock with astrolabe and calendar, M.P.S. Dresden.
PIDGEON, Thomas. *London.* a.1660.
PIERARD, DE GAND. *Dijon.* 1383. Installed the clock on Notre Dame.
PIERCE—
Humphrey. *London.* a.1646, CC. 1653, d. 1680.
Richard. *London.* a.1646, CC.1657, d.1668.
T. *Carnarvon.* ca.1680.
Sarah, widow of Humphrey. *London.* 1680-1691.
John. *London.* a.1680.
John. *London.* a.1688.
Thomas. *London.* 1724-47. Watch. Also PEIRCE.
Joseph. *London.* a.1729.
Thomas. *Bristol.* 1739. d.1793.
Thomas, son. *Bristol.* 1771-92. Bankrupt.
Zacharias. *London.* a.1770, CC.1788.
PIERINOUX, Philippe. *Paris.* m.1737.
PIERPOINT (PIERREPOINT)—
Thomas. *Liverpool.* 1781-4. W.
John. *Liverpool.* ca.1820.
PIERRE—
Pasquier. *London.* CC.1648.
——. *Paris.* ca.1800. aut. maker.
PIERREFORT, François. *Lyons.* 1626 m.
PIERRET, Victor Athanase. *Paris.* b.1806, d.1893. Maker of repute of complex watches. In 1863 invented lamp clocks with turning globe marked with hour figures.
PIERROT—
Joseph. *Basle.* 1687. W. of *Langres.*
Maurice. *Geneva,* 1714. *Neuchâtel,* 1723. d.1738.
PIERSSENE, Stephen. *London.* 1751-61. W.
PIET, ——. *Paris.* 1812.
PIGALLE, ——. *Paris.* ca.1775. Bronze worker. Made clock-cases.
PIGEON, ——. *Paris.* 1825.
PIGG, Robert. *London.* a.1674.
PIGGIN, John. *Norwich.* Early 19c. Watch.
PIGNET, père et fils. *Paris.* 1825.
PIGNEY, ——. *London.* 1743. W.
PIGOTT (PIGGOTT)—
Henry. *London.* a.1671, CC.1687-92.
Mrs., dau. of Joseph KIRK. *Nottingham.* 1736. d.1786. W.
——, son. *Nottingham.* From 1787-99. Appears to have taken the name of Piggott KIRK.

PIGUET—
Abel. *Piguet-Dessus.* 1775. Established a small watch factory with his son.
David, son. *Piguet-Dessus.* 1775.
Charles Auguste. *Le Sentier.* 1790. Established an ébauche factory.
Isaac Daniel. *Geneva.* b.1775, d.1841. One of the finest makers of complex watches.
Isaac Del, et Co. *Geneva.* 1802-11. Firm with Henri Daniel CAPT.
ET MEYLAN. *Geneva.* 1811-28. Firm with Philippe Samuel MEYLAN. Very fine makers. Often sd. 'PM.'
Père. *Paris.* 1812.
Auguste, son of Isaac Daniel. *Geneva.* b.ca. 1800.
ET FILS. *Geneva.* 1829. Firm with Auguste.
ET CIE. *Geneva.* Early 19c. g. eng. watch M.M.A.
Louis Elisée. *Brassus.* b.1836, d.1924. Devised improvements in repeaters and first perpetual calendar mechanism in 1853.
Henri Féréol. *London.* 1861. Invented the modern chronograph mech. In business of NICOLE & CAPT.
PIKE—
Robert. ——. End 17c. l.c. clock Mallett coll.
James. *Newton Abbot.* an.1775-84. Watch.
William. *Totnes.* Late 18c. l.c. clock.
——. *Newton Bushel.* 1795. W.
H. *Wellington (Somerset).* 1796. C. & W.
Benjamin. *London.* an.1797. Watch.
James. *Eltham.* 1805-08.
& GREEN. *London.* 1806.
William. *Cirencester.* Early 19c.
PILE—
——. *Newport.* an.1747. Watch.
Francis. *Honiton.* an.1762. Watch.
Jonathan. ——. an.1777. Watch.
John. *Newcastle-o.-T.* 1791. C. & W.
PILKINGTON—
Thomas. *Dublin.* 1795-1824. W.
F. *Woolwich.* 1808-11.
PILLETT, Peter. *London.* a.1771.
PILLIÈRE, *v.* PELLIÈRE.
PILLING, John. *Boothfold.* ca.1800. l.c. clock ill. Cec. & Web.
PILLIOT, Jehan. *Geneva.* a.1568.
PILLON—
Jacques. *Blois.* m.1632.
——. *Paris.* ca.1720. str. watch Fränkel coll. Watch Den. coll.
PILSON, Abraham. *Plymouth.* ca.1700. Watch.
PIMBLOT, W. *London.* an.1758. Watch.
PIN, Charles Frédéric. *Le Locle.* 1786. C.
PINART, Charles. *Paris.* 1611. Proposed as juré, but not elected.
PINAULT, Marc Fabry. *Geneva.* 1759. Fine g. astro. watch, bloodstone outer case, F.W.M. ill. Baillie.
PINCHBECK—
Christopher. *London (Fleet St.).* b.1670, d. 1732. A celebrated maker of astro. and musical clocks, and inventor of a zinc-copper alloy resembling gold and called 'Pinchbeck.' Astro. clock Buckingham Palace. Pinchbeck watch Marryat coll. rep. watch Den. coll.
Christopher, son. *London (Fleet St.).* b.1710, CC.1781, d.1783. Called himself 'Senior.' C. to the King. Left his father's shop in Fleet St. in 1738. Was in Edinburgh in 1745. Watch and mt. G.M. with early example of engine-turning, 1779.
John, bro. *London (Cheapside).* From 1738. W. & Toyman
Edward, bro. *London (Fleet St.).* b.1713-1766. Succeeded to his father's business and sold the Pinchbeck metal. Advertised

PINCHBECK—*continued.*
that he reduced large watches to a fashionable size. br. aut. clock made for George III.

PINCON, ——. *Paris.* 1812.

PINDAR, Joseph. *London.* a.1692.

PINE—
Philip. *London.* a.1768, CC.1775-82.
John. *Bridgewater.* 1795. W.

PINELL—
William. *London.* a.1723, CC.1735.
James. *London.* a.1781.

PINET, Nicolas & Gabriel. *L'Isle* and *Avignon.* 1703-25. Made clock for Flassan and rerepaired Avignon clock. Town C. of Avignon.

PINGEON, François. *Besançon.* 1581. Repaired clocks of the Madeleine and St. Pierre.

PINGO, John. *London.* a.1684.

PINK—
George. *London.* an.1775. Watch.
William. *London.* an.1777. Watch.
Tirrey. *London.* 1776. Watch for China.

PINKART, John. *London.* a.1663.

PINKERTON, John. *Haddington.* 1804-50. Watch.

PINKSTON (PINGSTON), Charles. *London.* 1726-44. Watch.

PINN, Richard. *Sidmouth.* an.1786. Watch.

PINNEY—
Richard. *Beaminster.* d.1696. C.
Francis. *London.* 1757-63. p.c. sil. watch G.M. and Wakefield M. Watch mt. Buckley coll.

PINNINGTON, Thomas. *Liverpool.* 1810-29. Rack lever watch mt. Ilbert coll.

PINNIVELL, William. *London.* a.1723, CC. 1735.

PINNOCK, G. *London.* Mid. 18c.

PINON, ——. *Paris.* 1765-89. C. to Louis XV and Louis XVI. br. clock Pal. de l'Élysée, Paris.

PINSON—
John. *London.* a.1675.
——. *Paris.* 1819-25.

PINTA, aîné. *Paris* (*Bde. Montmartre*). 1812.

PINTE, ——. *Paris* (*Rue de la Calandre*). 1812.

PIOCHON—
Jean. *Blois.* d.1678.
——. *Blois.* 1680.

PIOLAINE—
Michel François. *Paris.* m.1787-9. Mantel clock, Hôtel de la Monnaie, Paris.
& Co. *London.* 1802-24. mus. C.
——. *Paris.* 1807-11. Ormolu clock.
Veuve. *Paris.* 1812-15.
Fils. *Paris.* 1825.

PIOT—
Jean Étienne. *Geneva.* ca.1770-91. Watch Feill coll.
J. E., et Fr. PANCHAUD. *Geneva.* ca.1780.

PIOU, ——. *Paris.* 1811.

PIPER—
William. *London.* a.1713.
Thomas. *London.* a.1745, CC.1752-61.

PIPPS, John. *London.* ca.1790. Watch, shagreen outer case, G.M.

PIQUENOT, ——. *Paris.* 1821-5.

PIQUERÉ, Jos. *St. Ursanne* (near *Neuchâtel*). Early 19c. Watch.

PIQUET—
Guillaume. *Rouen.* 1554.
——. *Rennes.* ca.1700. al. watch B.M. Watch Gélis coll.
——. *Paris.* 1818-21.

PIRANESI, Giovanni Battista. *Rome* and *Venice.* b.1720, d.1778. Engraver. Designed some clock-cases.

PIRON—
Christophe. *Blois.* mar.1597, d.1630. 'Orlogeur et géoumetricien.' A maker of repute. Oval astro. watch Gélis coll.
Isaac, son. *Blois.* 1617.
Abraham, bro. *Blois.* mar.1620, d.1633.
Benjamin. *London.* 1752. Watch case maker.

PIRORDY, Christian. *Basle.* 1685. From *Stettin.*

PIRY, Pierre. *Blois.* m.1652.

PISTOR—
Matthäus Conrad. *Cassel.* 1720.
Edward. *London* (*Prescot St.*). 1755-77. C. & W.
Edward. *London* (*Leadenhall St.*). a.1767, CC.1777-94. Clock and Watch. Clock and organ maker.
Edward & John. *London.* 1782-98. Watch and mus. clockmakers.
Henry. *London* (*Holborn*). 1799. W. Watch by him or the following.
Henry. *London* (*Fleet St.*). 1799. W.

PITCHER—
Robert. *London.* a.1662.
John. *London.* CC.1689-97. W.
Edward. *London* (*Dean St.*). 1745. W.

PITCHFORD, William. *London.* a.1792.

'H & J. F. PITKIN.' Sig. on watches by Pitkin Bros., Hartford, Conn., U.S.A., 1838-42.

PITMAN, John. *London.* a.1701, CC.1714.

PITNEY, Thomas. *London.* a.1752, CC.1759-1780. W. Also PITTNEY.

PITON—
James. *London.* a.1702, CC.1711-51. Also PITAN and PITTAN.
James, son. *London.* CC.1748.

PITT—
Francis. *London.* a.1757. Watch.
William. *London.* CC.1775, l.CC.1787-93.
Thyar. *London.* CC.1784, l.CC.1787, d.1811. mus. clock. sil. rep. watch and trav. clock London M.
Caleb. *London.* 1790-1825. W. g. p.c. watch London M.
John. *London* ca.1790. Watch.
& GOATER. *London.* 1815.

PITTARD, Thomas. *Sherborne.* 1750. C.

PITTET, Jean. *Geneva.* 1722 comp.

PITTON, Charles. *Ferney.* 1775. Watch.

PITTS—
Samuel. *London.* a.1689.
John. *London.* 1737. Insolvent.
J. *London* (*Nassau St.*). ca.1810. T.C.

PITTUM, Mimi. *Italy.* 1553. Dial Old Ashmolean M.

PIX, John. *London.* Left in 1776. W.

PIXLEY—
John. *London.* an.1744. Watch.
John. *Gravesend.* Early 19c. Watch.

PIZZI & CETTI. *Buckingham.* Early 19c. Watch.

PLACE, James. *Preston.* ca.1820.

PLAN—
David. *Geneva.* 1734.
Jean Philippe. *Paris.* 1766 m.-1780. g. en. watch. Watch Besançon M.
——. *Geneva.* 1794. Director of State factory with COULIN.
LES FRÈRES. prob. *Paris.* 18c. 4-colour g. watch Fränkel coll.

PLANBERG, Axel. *Stockholm.* comp. 1750, m.1755-78.

PLANCHET ET CIE: *Paris.* 1807.

PLANCK, Johann. *Gratz.* ca.1685. al. watch Ilbert coll.

PLANKH, Nikolaus. *Augsburg.* End 16c. Very fine large monstrance clock Neue Hofburg, Vienna.

PLANNER—
Thomas. *London.* a.1694, CC.1701-30. l.c. clock. Also PLUMER.
Thomas. *London.* CC.1730. l.c. clock.

PLANT—
Edward. *London*. a.1655, CC.1664.
William. *Walsall*. 1771-95. W.
Thomas. *Newport* (*Salop*). 1795. C.

PLANTARD (PLANTART), Nicolas. *Blois*. comp. 1619. From *Abbeville*. Table clocks S.K.M. and Gélis coll. Table clock ill. Britten. sq. table clock Feill coll. made at Abbeville.

PLASKETT—
Peter. *London*. a.1794.
Reuben. *Bath*. 1812-26.

PLATIER, ——. *Paris*. Mid. 18c.-1773. C. to the Prince de Conti. Devised a detent esc. desc. in Rozier, 'Observations sur la Physique, Paris, 1774.

PLATT—
Thomas. *London*. CC.1637-52.
William. *London*. 1755. Watch case maker.
Matthew. *London*. an.1785. Watch.
William. *Stockport*. 1791. C.
William. *Manchester*. 1800-13.
Samuel. *Boston, U.S.A.* 1825. C.

PLATTEL (PLATEL), Daniel Samuel. *Paris*. m.1766-89.

PLATTES, Robert. *York*. 1590. C.

PLATZER, L. *Carlsbad*. 18c. Equinoctial dial Old Ashmolean M.

PLAYER—
Thomas. *London*. a.1664, CC.1672-1718. Also PLAIRE.
Simon. *London*. a.1671.
Robert. *London*. CC.1678-92. Clock-case maker.
Robert, son. *London*. a.1691, CC.1700-42. l.c. clock. Watch Stads M. Amsterdam.
John. *Reading*. Early 19c.
H. J. *London*. 1820-4.

PLAYTERS, Lionell. *London*. a.1680.

PLEACE, William. *London*. To 1796 partner with Sam. CLEGHORN, and then with Edw. BRACEBRIDGE to 1799.

PLEIG, Christoph. *Ulm*. 1625. aut. wall clock Feill coll.

PLESKES—
Wilhelm. *Cologne*. 1797.
G. *Cologne*. 1813.

PLETTERL (PLÖTTERL, BLÖDERL, BLETERL), Ambrosy. *Vienna*. m.1787.

PLEUVIER (PLAEVIER, PLEVIER, PLUIER, PLOVIER)—
Isaac. *London*. 1641. CC.1652, d.1665. Dutchman. Shell watch with amber cover and back Ilbert coll.
Jacobus. *Haarlem*. 1781.

PLEY, George. *London*. a.1691.

PLEYDELL, John. *London*. a.1666. l.c. clock. Watch.

PLIMMER—
N. *Wellington* (*Salop*). an.1783. Watch.
Abraham. *Wellington* (*Salop*). 1792. C. &. W.

PLÖEN, Christian. *Christiania*. 1785 m.

PLÖNINGER, J. G. *Munich*. 1720. Dial maker.

PLOWMAN—
Thomas. *Lancaster*. ca.1820.
William. *Athy*. 1824.
Thomas. *Athy*. Early 19c.
J. *Chichester*. Early 19c. Watch.

PLUETT, Anthony. *London*. a.1688, CC. 1697-1704.

PLUIJM, J. J. *Rotterdam*. ca.1800-30.

PLUMB (PLUMBE)—
John. *Wavertree*. d.1729. W.
Matthew. *Liverpool*. 1767. C.
William. *Liverpool*. 1790-6. W.

PLUMBER, ——. *London* (*Bartholomew Close*). 1769. W.

PLUMBLY—
James. *London*. 1820. Watch.
& TUPMAN. *London*. 1825. W.

PLUMBTREE, ——. *London* (*Petty France*). 1749. W.

PLUMER, Thomas. *London*. a.1694.

PLUMIERE, Isaac. *London*. 1662.

PLUMLEIGH—
Thomas. *London*. a.1687.
Thomas. *Exeter*. 1725. Bankrupt. W.

PLUMLEY—
Edward. *London*. a.1682. Also PLYMLEY.
William. *London* (*Cheapside* to 1769, then *Ludgate Hill*). a.1749, CC.1756, m.CC. 1779. Watch mt. Buckley coll.
William, son. *London* (*Ludgate Hill*). a.1773, CC.1780, l.CC.1786, m.CC.1801-18. Watch G.M.
William, & Son. *London*. 1784. Firm of two preceding.
Charles, bro. of Wm. (2). *London*. a.1777.
William Dawson, bro. *London*. a.1802.
Charles, bro. *London*. a.1806, CC.1819, l.CC.1825.
John, bro. *London*. CC.1819.
Charles & John. *London* (*Ludgate Hill*). 1820-24. Firm of two preceding, successors to William & Son. T.C.

PLUMMER—
Joseph. *London*. a.1669.
Thomas. *London* (*Little Britain*). an.1747-ca.1780. Watch Den. coll.
——. *London* (*Whitechapel*). 1755. W.
Charles. *London*. ca.1760. mus. aut. clock Palace M. Pekin.
John. *London*. ca.1770. Watch.

PLUMPTON—
Samuel. prob. *London*. an.1740. Watch.
James. *London*. a.1751, CC.1763.
John. *Liverpool*. 1781-90. W.

PLUNKELD, Richard. *London*. 1820.

PLUNKETT, Christopher. *Portsmouth*. 1763.

PLUYÈRES, ——. *Valenciennes*. d.1773. Made ca.1750 aut. clock for the town.

PLYE, George. *London*. an.1762. Watch.

POARSON, Emmanuel. *Edinburgh*. 1700.

POCHET, Annet. *Lyons*. comp. 1638.

POCOCK, Joseph. *London*. a.1773.

PODNEAU, ——. *Paris*. an.1751. Advertisement of engine-turned g. watch.

POESTD, Johann. prob. *Germany*. ca.1600. Oval eng. watch. cf. PÖSTDORFFER.

POETE—
Hector. *Blois*. 1600. d.1609.
Claude, bro. *Blois*. 1603-19.
Jacques, son of Hector. *Blois*. 1635. d.1662. g. en. watch K.H.M., en. flowers prob. by Christophe MORLIÈRE ill. Baillie.
Jacques. *Blois*. m.1667-72.

POHL—
Anton. *Saxony*. 1419-22. Made Rathaus clock in Olmütz; that in Prague attributed to him, but prob. made by HANUSH.
Hanns. *Oels* (*Silesia*). 1572. d.1584. Repaired Olmütz clock.

POHLACK, Wilhelm. *Hamburg*. 1821.

POHLMANN—
Mark. *London*. a.1741.
Peter. *London* (*Drury La.*). 1762. l.c. clock. Watch.
——. *London*. In 1764 moved from *Holloway St.* to *Leadenhall St.* mus. C.
Christoph Joachim Peter. *Berlin*. 1786. Court C.

POHNDORFF, C. G. C. *Hamburg*. 1801-05.

POINTEAU, E. L. Auguste. *Paris*. b.1809, d.1885. Able maker of clocks with esc. devised by him.

POIRÉE, Pierre. *Paris*. m.1760-89.

POIRET, Jean Baptiste Charles. *Paris*. 1768-1774. cf. POIROT.

POIRIÉ, Pierre. *Paris*. m.1760.

POIRIER, ——. *Paris*. m.1588.

POIROT—
Jean Baptiste. *Paris.* m.1759. cf. POIRET.
Jean Christophe. *Paris.* ca.1760.
Veuve (of preceding). *Paris.* 1789. Also POIREAU.

POISSON, Henry. *London.* ca.1695-1720. l.c. clock S.K.M. Watch.

POITEVIN, Isaac. *Montpellier.* 1598-1600.

POLACK (PORLACK), Benjamin. *Sheffield.* 1805-17. W.

POLETNICK—
——. *Paris.* ca.1755 m.
Joseph Michel. *Paris.* m.1764-89.
H. *Bonn.* ca.1770. Table clock.

POLEY, ——. ——. an.1732. Watch.

POLHAMMER, Anders. *Stockholm* and *Stjärnsund.* b.1705, d.1767. Nephew of POLHEM. In charge of Stjärnsund works. l.c. clock Nat. M. Stockholm.

POLHEM, Christoffer. *Stockholm, Stjärnsund* and *Kopparsberg.* b.1661, d.1751. Famous engineer and C. Started Stjärnsund works ca.1711.

POLINGUE (POLINQUE or POULINGUE)—
John. *London* (*Cock La.*). a.1734, CC.1743-1777.
Jacob, son. *London* (*Drapers Ct.*). a.1768, CC.1781.
John, bro. *London.* a.1777.

POLL, Robert. *Wissett* and *Harleston.* To 1771. Watch. l.c. clock.

POLLARD—
——. *Crediton.* 1760.
Thomas. *Exeter.* 1795. l.c. clock.
John. *Plymouth Dock.* 1795.

POLLECKE, Andreas. *Lübeck.* 1605-28. aut. clocks for Petrikirche and Dom.

PÖLLER (PELLER), Martin. *Vienna.* m. 1719. Fine str. and al. trav. clock.

POLLEY, George. *London.* a.1772.

POLLINGER, Johann Wolfgang. *Friedberg.* 1741. 3-case sil. and shagreen trav. clock S.K.M.

POLLISCOTT (POLLYCOTT), Thomas. *London.* a.1684.

POLLIT, Thomas. *London.* a.1792.

POLSON, Henry. prob. *London.* an.1722. Watch.

POLTON, ——. *London* (*Bloomsbury*). an. 1731-51.

POLWARTH, William. *Dunse.* 1825.

POMEROY—
Joseph. *London.* a.1717, CC.1728-53. Watch.
Joseph, son. *London.* a.1746, CC.1757-72.

POMFRET, ——. *Saffron Walden.* 1693.

PONCELIN, Thomas. *Gray.* 1561-1625. circ. table clock Feill coll. with T. PONCELIN on case and H.G.B. and S.B. on mt.

PONCET—
François. *Lyons.* a.1595.
Jean François. *Warsaw* and later *Dresden.* b. 1714, d.1804. Swiss. Director of Grüne Gewölbe. rep. watch, porcelain case. Watch, jasper case. Two rep. al. trav. clocks M.P.S. Dresden. g. en. rep. watch Feill coll.
C. *Dresden.* Late 18c. g. and jasper watch Fränkel coll.

PONCHET—
Jacob. *Blois.* 1586-8.
——. *Clermont.* Early 17c. Oval watch B.M. Or POUCHET.

PONCY—
Jean Pierre Esaïe. *Geneva.* ca.1775-92.
Abram. *Geneva.* Early 19c.

POND (POUND)—
John. *London.* a.1673.
——. *Abingdon.* Late 18c.

PONS—
Denis. *Paris.* 1544-7. Founder member of Paris corporation.
David. ——. ca.1770. g. equation cyl. watch Ilbert coll.

PONS DE PAUL, ——. *Paris.* Early 19c. Awarded gold medal by Soc. d'encouragement for his work in the manufacture of good cheap watches. Went to *St. Nicolas d'Aliermont* (near *Dieppe*) to organize the clock industry there in 1806. *v.* DELÉPINE. chron. C.A. & M.

PONSON, Peter. *Philadelphia.* 1796. W.

POOLE—
George. *London.* CC.1654.
Edmund. *London.* a.1713, CC.1722-7.
John. *London* (*Strand*). a.1720, CC.1743-53. Watch.
Robert, son of Edm. *London* (*Aldersgate St.*). CC.1754, m.CC.1781-6.
Francis. *London.* a.1749.
Francis. *London.* a.1752.
James. *London.* 1767.
T. *London.* an.1778. Watch.
William. *London.* CC.1777.
James. *London.* CC.1778.
E. *London.* an.1791. Watch.
Robert. *Pershore.* 1793 CC.
Matthew. *London.* a.1786, CC.1794.
John. *London* (*Red Cross St.*). 1805-07.
James. *Liverpool.* 1825. W.

POOLEY—
Thomas. *Ashby.* 2nd half 18c.
John. *Stoke*(?). Early 19c. Watch mt. S.K.M.

POORE—
Richard. *London.* a.1752.
James. *London.* a.1758.

POPE—
Nicholas. *London.* a.1678.
John. *Canterbury.* From 1766. W.
John. *Margate.* 1769. 'Eminent W.'
Robert. *Boston, U.S.A.* 1786.
Joseph. *Boston, U.S.A.* 1788-1803. W.
Thomas. *London.* 1793.

POPLUS—
Pierre. *Fontaines, Cerney* and *Vevey.* 1782-1820. C. Three br. clocks.
Charles Henri Benjamin. *Le Locle.* 1822. C.

POPP—
Conrad. *Fürth.* d.1794.
G. M. G. *Hamburg.* 1821.

POPPE, Johann Heinrich Moritz. *Göttingen* and *Tübingen.* b.1776, d.1854. Prof. of mechanics. Pub. 'Versuch einer Geschichte . . . der Uhrmacherkunst,' Göttingen, 1797. 'Wörterbuch der Uhrmacherkunst,' Leipzig, 1799. 'Ausführliche Geschichte der . . . Uhrmacherkunst,' Leipzig, 1801. 'Die Verfertigung der Uhren,' Frankfurt, 1806. 'Praktisches Handbuch für Uhrmacher,' Leipzig, 1810. 'Der Wecker für Jedermann,' Heidelberg, 1810. 'Die Englische Uhrmacherkunst,' Pesth, 1819. 'Die Uhren und die Uhrmacherkunst,' 1829. Die Wand, Stand und Taschenuhren,' Frankfurt, 1818.

POPPLEWELL—
——. ——. an.1753. Watch.
John. *Bridlington.* 1770-91. Watch.

PORCH, William Henry. *London.* a.1784.

PORCHER—
Jacques. *Blois.* m.1669.

PORCHER-DUPRÉ, Pierre. *Paris.* m.1788.

PORCHEZ (PORCHÉ)—
——. *Paris* (*Rue Trainée*). 1812. Mantel clocks, bronzes by RAVRIO, Pal. de Compiègne and Fontainebleau. Clock made for Joséphine, Pal. de la Légion d'honneur.
——. *Paris* (*Rue du Mail*). 1812.

PORKER, ——. *London.* 1820.

PORNETTI, Félix. *Geneva*. Early 19c. mus. watch Fränkel coll.

PORSDORFER, Peter. *Dresden*. m.1668. One of the first four members of the clockmakers' guild.

PORTALEZ, Jean André. *St. Imier*. 1791.

PORTE, François. *Rouen*. 1740-56. Repaired clock of St. Laurent.

PORTÉ, Jean Jacques. *Paris*. 1763.

PORTELLO, William Forrester. *London*. a. 1816.

PORTER—
John. *London*. a.1680. Table clock.
Sebastian. *London*. a.1680.
Matthew. *London*. a.1682, CC.1692.
Robert. *London*. a.1687.
Thomas. *London*. a.1704.
George. *Coventry*. 1727-53. W. Mayor of Coventry.
Francis. *London*. a.1717, CC.1730-44.
Samuel, son. *London*. a.1743, CC.1756.
William. *Penrith*. an.1771. Watch.
William. *London* (*Hosier La.*). CC.1771-83.
Mark. *Oakingham*. an.1775-95. cf. Mark below.
Jonathan. *London* (*Southwark*). 1778.
John. *London*. CC.1779.
Francis Crumpton. *London*. a.1778.
A. *Oakingham*. ca.1790 CC.-early 19c.
William. *Tutbury*. 1795. C. & W.
William. *Williamstown, Mass., U.S.A.* 1800. Joined with Daniel Clark and Zenas Cook in 1810 at *Waterbury*. The firm failed ca.1815. l.c. clock ill. Milham.
Mark. *London*. 1805-08. cf. Mark above.
Charles. *Dartford*. Early 19c. Watch.

PORTEUS (PORTEOUS)—
William. *London*. a.1797.
Robert. *Manchester*. 1808-20.

PORTHOUSE—
William. *Penrith*. 1706-95. Prob. two makers. l.c. clocks. Small l.c. clock mt. Glasgow Art Gall. Watch Den. coll. *v.* Posthouse.
George. *Penrith*. b.1743, d.1817. l.c. clock. W.
William. *Barnard Castle*. ca.1770-1810. l.c. clocks.
John. *Penrith*. 1771. l.c. clock.
Thomas. *London*. 1820. d.1860. T.C. Maker to the Admiralty. g. pump winding watch, hm. 1829 Ilbert coll.

PORTIER, Pierre. *Hannover*. Early 17c. crys. cross watch Blot-Garnier coll.

PORTLOCK, William. *London*. a.1794.

PORTSMOUTH, John. *London*. a.1660.

POSCH, ——. *Berlin*. In 1807 made a talking head.

PÖSCH, Rupert. *Vienna*. m.1776.

POSE, Joseph. *London*. an.1773. Watch.

POST—
William. *London* (*London Br.*). an.1727, l.CC.1766. l.c. clock. Watch mt. S.K.M.
Richard. *London*. CC.1771.

PÖSTDORFFER, Johann. *Dresden*. ca. 1600-40. Came to *Dresden* from *Prague* ca.1600. oct. crys. watch Grünes Gewölbe, Dresden. Watch M.M.A. Oval watch sd. 'Johann Poestd.'

POSTEN, Edward Joseph. *London*. an.1773. Watch.

POSTHOUSE, William. *Penrith*. 1820. Prob. Porthouse.

POTDEFER, ——. *Paris*. 1788.

POTER, Guillemet. *Neuchâtel*. 1380. Engaged in the construction of the clock for the Collégiale.

POTERAT, ——. *Geneva*. 1794. Started with Borel & Humbert the first watch factory in *Geneva*; it failed and was taken over by the Republic.

POTHENOT, ——. *Paris*. 1710. Boulle br clock.

POTHIER—
Michel. *Paris*. 1544. Petitioner for incorporation of Paris guild.
René. *Blois*. m.1618.

POTIER, Charles Thomas. *Paris*. m.1776-1789.

POTIQUET, ——. *Valegue*. ca.1780. g. en. watch.

POTTECARY, Edmond. *London*. a.1738.

POTTEN, Henry. *London*. 1750.

POTTER—
John. *London*. BC.1628. 'English Forrin.
George. *Coventry*. 1727.
Christopher. *London*. a.1719, CC.1730-60.
Francis. *London*. CC.1730.
John. *London*. an.1743. Watch. Table clock.
Edward. *Liverpool*. d.1754. W.
William. *London*. a.1731, CC.1738.
William. *Bristol*. 1774-81. C.
Ephraim. *Concord, U.S.A.* 1775-90.
Harry, senior. *London* (*Walworth*). a.1761, CC.1778, m.CC.1795-1803. 3-case watch M.M.A. p.c. g. repoussé watch Carnegie M.
William. *London*. a.1772.
Harry, junior. *London*. w.CC.1792, m.CC. 1812, d.1813.
John. *London*. a.1787.
——. *Wotton-under-Edge*. ca.1800. In firm of Shepherd & Potter.
James. *London* (*Bishopsgate St. Without*). CC.1809, l.CC.1810-23.
Fergus. *Kilkenny*. 1824.

POTTIER, René. *La Rochelle*. 1474.

POTTINGER, John. *London*. a.1716.

POTTS—
Josiah. *Goldbourne*. 1721. g. watch with en. panels Mallett coll.
Thomas. *London* (*St. James' St.*). a.1713-51 CC. Watch.
John. *Partington*. ca.1770.
Charles. *London*. a.1796.
James. *Berwick-on-Tweed*. 1806. l.c. clock.
Joshua. *York*. 1810-33. mus. clocks. Also W.

POTZ, Herb. *Grosse-Glogau*. End 17c. l.c. clock.

POUCHOULIN—
J. L. *Geneva*. 1750. Watch Geneva M.
Auguste. *Geneva*. Early 19c.
et Pautex. *Geneva*. Early 19c.

POUDRA—
Pierre. *Paris*. m.1777-89.
Veuve. *Paris*. 1807-15.

POUGNEAU, Gabriel. *London*. a.1734.

POUILLET, Jacob. *Clermont*. ca.1700. Watch.

POUILLY, ——. *Paris*. 1691. math. inst. maker. Designed clock made by Henri Martinot ill. Britten in Virginia M.

POULAIN—
Gilles. *Blois*. m.1666-82.
Michel. *Besançon*. 17c. 'Serrurierhorloger.' Restored clock on St. Pierre.

POULIN, ——. *Paris*. 1825.

POULSON—
William. *London*. a.1786, CC.1801.
Edward. *Newtown*. Early 19c. Watch.

POULTER—
Thomas. *London*. a.1761.
James. *London*. a.1781.

POULTIER, ——. *Paris*. 1812-15.

POULTON—
Thomas. *London*. an.1752. Watch.
William. *London*. an.1773. Watch.

POUND, Isaac. *Charleston, U.S.A.* From 1746. C. & W.

POUNDALL, ——. *Northwich*. 1783. C.

POUPART, Jean. *Montbéliard*. 1726.

POURIE, Henry. *Perth.* 1820.
POURPRY, Jean Chrétien. *Paris.* a.1747.
POURQUIÉS, ——. *Paris.* 1820.
POURROY, Jacques. *Geneva.* 1698.
POUZAIT—
Ami. *Geneva.* ca.1770-88.
Louis Philippe. *Geneva.* 1770. Went to *Versoix.*
David François. *Geneva.* 1770. Went to *Versoix.*
——. *Paris.* Late 18c. g. watch. c.secs. watch Schloss M. Berlin.
Jean Moïse. *Geneva.* b.1743, d.1793. A very able maker. In charge of the first school of horology at Geneva in 1788. Worked at the improvement of the lever escapement. Gave a model escapement in 1786 to the Soc. des Arts of Geneva, which may be the first with divided impulse faces. Invented in 1776 an independent sweep secs. mechanism, with auxiliary train and mainspring. It was largely used till late 19c.
& GODEMAR. *Geneva.* ca.1780-1800. Watch with virgule escapement. Made Lepine cyl. watches with sweep secs., example in Feill coll.
POVEY, James. *Salisbury.* 1791. C.
POVL, ——. *Copenhagen.* d.1585. Court C.
POWELL—
Bartholomew. *London.* a.1650, CC.1668-73.
John. *London.* a.1665.
Robert. *London.* CC.1710-44.
John. *London.* a.1739-63. Watch.
William. *London.* a.1752, CC.1763.
Edward. *London.* a.1753, CC.1777.
Richard. *London.* a.1765.
Thomas. *Fenny Stratford.* 1785. C.
Thomas. *Gainsborough.* an.1791-5. Watch.
Thomas. *Dunstable.* 1791. W.
Edward. *Bristol.* 1795-1818. W.
James. *Worcester.* 1804-08. W. to the Prince of Wales. Watch Horstmann coll.
& DAVIES. Merthyr Tydvil. Early 19c. l.c. clock.
William. *London.* a.1803.
John. *London.* 1820.
POWER, Anne. *London.* a.1714, CC.1722.
POWIS, Richard. *London.* 1820-5. W.
POWLEY—
I. *Ashby* (*Westmorland*). 1730. l.c. clocks. sd. 'I.P.'
Robert. *Appleby.* ca.1770-95. W.
POWNALL, Nathaniel. *London.* a.1649.
POWRIE, Henry. *Edinburgh* and *Glasgow.* 1822-37.
POY—
Godfrie. *London.* 1718-50. A fine maker. br. clock. Magnificent rep. watch, set large emeralds and diamonds, Winter Pal. Petrograd. rep. watch Den. coll. g. repoussé watch. g. rep. watch Damiano coll. p.c. g. watch Feill coll. Watch N.Y. Univ.
Godfrey. *London* (*Pall Mall,* 1742-7. *Haymarket* in 1753). Watch. l.c. clock dial Stads M. Amsterdam.
POYER, l'aîné. *Dieppe.* Late 17c. al. watch.
POYRIER, Philibert, dit le Sergent Sans-Souci. *Grenoble.* 1613.
POZZIE, Joseph. *Elgin.* 1820.
PRACHT, Anton. *Würzburg.* m.1792. Fine astro. clock.
PRADEL, Jean. *Lyons.* d.an.1659.
PRADEZ, Pierre Louis. *Vevey.* 1798 m.
PRAETORIUS (PRIGTORI), Daniel Emanuel. *Copenhagen.* m.1712.
PRANDOUL, Guilquin. *Paris.* 1401. Made a clock for the Queen.
PRAND-STETTER, Paulus. *Deggendorf.* 1654. Clock.
PRASSE, J. G. *Zittau.* 1792. Town C. Made clock on St. Peter and Paul church.
PRATT—
Charles. *Saffron Walden.* b.1735, d.1829.
Matthew. prob. *London.* an.1772. Watch.
——. *Towcester.* d.1797.
John. *Saffron Walden.* 1779.
John. *Epsom.* 1795. W.
John. *London.* End 18c. br. clock.
Thomas. *Canterbury.* ca.1800. Trav. clock Virginia M.
Charles. *London.* 1817-24. Watch.
PRATTIN—
J. W. *London.* an.1774. Watch.
William. *London.* a.1773.
PRAUN, Hanns. *Nürnberg.* m.1565. Kleinuhrmacher. Petitioned in 1565 with Esias VOGEL and Marx STEPPINGER for a separate Guild for Kleinuhrmacher.
PRAY, B. *France.* ca.1790. Devised a form of cyl. esc.
PREDDY, William. *Langport.* ca.1780. l.c. clock.
PREDHAUER, ——. *Vienna.* 2nd half 18c. l.c. clock Uhren M. Vienna.
PREECE—
Rodolphus. *Hereford.* 1753-92. Succeeded Wm. WINSTON.
William. *Bristol.* Early 19c. W. Prob. PREIST.
PREIL, Adrianus. *Zittau.* ca.1670. sil. str. watch M.P.S. Dresden.
PREIST, William. *Bristol.* 1812-18. W. cf. PRIEST.
PRENOT, Henry. *New York.* 1805.
PRENTICE (PRENTIS)—
Philip. *London.* a.1742, CC.1749.
Joseph. *London.* 1760-9.
v. WELCHMAN & PRENTICE.
Daniel. *London.* 1795.
& SON. *London.* 1802-11. Successors.
John. *London.* 1815-24. Successor.
Richard. *London.* 1815-25.
PRESBURY—
William. *London.* a.1703.
William. *Coventry.* 1795.
PRESCIOT, Peter. *London.* 1790. Table clock.
PREST—
Edward. *Prescot.* an.1764-84. Watch.
Thomas, son. *London.* a.1784.
Thomas. *Chigwell.* 1820. Patented a keyless device.
PRESTIGE—
Bartholomew. *London.* CC.1703.
Walter. *Towcester.* an.1806. Watch.
PRESTO, Jugato. ——. Mid. 18c. Watch N.Y. Univ.
PRESTON—
Josias. *London.* a.1640.
Edward. *Chorley.* mar.1696. *Pownall Fee,* 1716. W.
Clark. *London* (*St. Nicholas La.*). 1711. W.
Edward. *London.* a.1713, CC.1721.
Daniel. *London.* an.1764. Watch.
J. D. *London.* an.1764.
Robert. *Liverpool.* 1781. In 1783 also in *Chester.* 1796 Bankrupt. W.
N. *London.* an.1808. Watch N.Y. Univ.
William. *Kendal.* 1809. Stock sold. C. & W.
William. *Lancaster* and *Ulverstone.* ca.1820. From *London.*
PRESTRIDGE, Richard. *London.* a.1699.
PRESTWOOD—
George. *London.* a.1693.
Joseph. *London.* CC.1703-10. l.c. clock.
PRETLOVE, Nathaniel. *London.* a.1771.
PRETTY, John. *London* (*Deptford*). a.1796, CC.1807.
PREUDHOMME—
——. *Rolle.* ca.1630-ca.1650. en. watch.
Alexandre Jean. *Geneva.* mar.an.1711.
Paul Michel. *Geneva.* 1723. Fine watch mt. G.M.

PREUDHOMME—*continued.*
Louis Baptiste. *Paris.* 1778-82. Partner with GLAESNER. In 1782 tried to start a French factory with workmen from Geneva. Watch. Pub. mém. 'Considérations pratiques sur les engrenages.'
PRÉVAUX, Jean. *Paris.* Mid. 18c. Enameller to Louis xv. Watch ill. Britten.
PREVOST—
Nicholas. *London.* ca.1710. p.c. sil. watch Feill coll. l.c. clock and watch mt. Name on dial of br. clock by Jas. STEVENS.
L. N. *London.* ca.1750. Watch G.M.
William. prob. *London.* an.1759. Watch.
PRÉVOST—
——. *Lille.* 1545.
Pierre. *Blois.* 1629-51. Also PRÉVOT and PROUVOST.
Pierre. *Saumur.* ca.1660 m.
Louis. *Saumur.* a. to Pierre ca.1660. From *Geneva.*
Joseph. *Blois.* m.1667-79. Also PRÉVAULT, PROVOST and PROUVOST.
Marc. *Geneva.* a.1670. g. en. watch Blot-Garnier coll.
F. *Amiens.* ca.1720. sil. watch. Also PRÉVOT.
Pierre. *Geneva.* Juré 1723. Watch.
Jean François Lucien. *Paris.* m.1760.
PREW, Richard. *Tewkesbury.* 1791. C.
PREYER, ——. *London.* ca.1780. Box with watch Peiping M.
PRIAUD, George. *London.* an.1773. Watch.
PRICE—
John. *London.* a.1678.
Charles. *London.* a.1680.
Thomas. *London.* a.1686.
Elizabeth. *London.* a.1701.
Humphrey. *London.* a.1713.
E. *Llanfyllin.* b.ca.1713-1805.
W. *London.* ca.1725. p.c. shagreen watch Ilbert coll.
Richard. *London.* 1729. Insolvent.
v. PERRY & PRICE.
John. *London.* a.1731, CC.1744.
James. *London.* an.1748. Watch.
John. *London.* a.1751.
Obadiah. *London.* a.1752.
Thomas. *London.* a.1752.
Thomas. *London.* a.1754.
Samuel. *London.* a.1760.
George. *London.* a.1765, CC.1772-1806.
David. *London.* CC.1770.
Richard. *London.* CC.1772.
John. *London.* a.1768.
Edward. *Liverpool.* 1777-96. W.
Francis. *London.* a.1774, CC.1786, l.CC. 1787-93.
Thomas. *London.* a.1778.
John. *Chichester.* 1784. W.
William. *Worcester.* 1784. W.
H. *London.* an.1786. Watch.
J. *Deptford.* 1791. W.
William. *Pembroke.* 1791-1830. W. l.c. clock.
Charles. *Wellington (Somerset).* 1795. W.
Isaac. *Philadelphia.* 1796. W.
Griffith. *Ashford.* 1799. C. & W.
Joseph. *Baltimore.* 1799.
William. *Birmingham.* 1801. W.
William. *Liverpool.* 1810-16. W.
Philip. *Philadelphia.* 1817-25.
John. *London.* a.1812.
James Joseph. *London.* a.1813.
Joseph. *London.* a.1816.
PRICHARD—
John. *London.* 1805-08.
——. *Ewell.* Early 19c. Watch.
PRICKLOVE, John. *London.* a.1728.
PRIDDITH, Thomas. *London.* CC.1639.
PRIDE, ——. *Salisbury.* an.1762. Watch.
PRIDEAUX, Edmund. *London.* 1743-90. Made fine cyl. watches. Watch mt. Buckley coll.
PRIDGEN, William. *Hull.* ca.1755. Watch. br. clock.
PRIDGRIN, William. *York.* 1778. Dissolved partnership with J. B. CARLILL in 1800. W.
PRIDHAM—
William. *London.* an.1742-63. Watch.
Noah. *London.* a.1752.
PRIEST—
Thomas. *London.* a.1716, CC.1729-44.
John. *London (Aldersgate St.).* Partner with COLLEY (q.v.) in 1762. a.1739, CC.1746.
William. *Bristol.* 1772-93. W. cf. PREIST.
Richard. prob. *London.* an.1777. Watch.
George. *Norwich.* 1796-1854. Watch.
John. *Liverpool.* 1825. W.
PRIGG—
John. *London.* a.1725, CC.1732, l.CC.1776.
Richard, son. *London.* a.1750.
PRIGGIN, John. *London.* a.1646.
PRIGNAN, Jean. *Paris.* m.1778-1812.
PRIMATE, Thomas. *London.* a.1756. Watch.
PRIME—
Andrew. *London.* CC.1646-82. Lantern clock S.K.M. l.c. clock dial ill. Britten.
Abraham, son. *London.* a.1665, CC.1672-86.
Andrew. *London.* a.1727, CC.1736.
PRINCE—
Richard. *London.* a.1659, CC.1680-2.
Thomas. *London.* a.1674.
Isaac. *Grove.* 18c. l.c. clock.
David Louis. *Paris.* m.1776-89.
& Co. *York.* an.1781. Watch.
v. HAMPTON.
William. *London.* a.1799.
——. *Paris.* 1811-25.
PRING, Robert. *Bristol.* 1781. C.
PRINGLE—
James. *Dalkeith.* 1763-70. W.
Adam. *Edinburgh.* 1794-1820.
George. *Edinburgh.* a.1793-1822.
Thomas. *Edinburgh.* d.1825.
William. *Monk Wearmouth.* Early 19c. Watch.
George, & Son. *Edinburgh.* 1822. Wooden clocks.
William. *Edinburgh.* 1825-36.
PRINS, Willem. *Rotterdam.* Late 17c.-ca. 1725. Large sq. table clock M.M.A. Watch Ilbert coll.
PRINSEN, I. *Amsterdam.* 1822. W.
PRINT, Richard. *London.* a.1681, CC.1698. Watch.
PRINTZ, Pehr. *Stockholm.* 1769-80. Court C. Pub. in 1769 'Försök Til en Historisk Beskrifning Om Wägg och Byxsäcks-Uhr.' l.c. br. and wall clocks and three watches.
PRIOR—
Thomas. *London (Prescot St.).* d.1763. Watch.
William. *London.* a.1724.
William. *Nessfield.* b.an.1727-82.
John. *London.* a.1750.
George. *London (Prescot St.).* 1765-1810. Watch Chamb. coll. Watch Den. coll.
John, son of Wm. *Nessfield.* b.1747-1820. Received six awards from Soc. Arts for an esc., alarum and str. work. Pub. arts. in Trans. Soc. Arts Vols. 16, 21, 23, 29 and 35.
G. *Otley.* Late 18c.
George, son of John. *Nessfield.* b.1782. *London* after 1822. 1793-1830. Maker of repute, especially in watches for Turkey; received two awards from Soc. Arts. 3-case watch S.M.S.K. Tortoise-shell and ormolu br. clock S.K.M. 3-case watch, with outer case of wood inlaid silver. g. watch, with oriental chased case, S.K.M. g. 3-case

PRIOR—*continued.*
en. rep. watch M.M.A. Watch with pierced steel outer case eng. excerpts from the Koran Ilbert coll. Watch Fränkel coll. Associated with the following.
Edward. *London.* 1800-68. Maker of repute, especially in watches for Turkey. Watches B.M., M.M.A., Fränkel, Feill, Ilbert and Den. colls.
George. *Leeds.* 1817-26. Chron., W. & C.
J. W. *London* (*Newington Causeway*). Early 19c. Watch.
PRITCHARD—
Bariah. *London.* a.1674.
Thomas. *London.* a.1722.
Griffith. *Llanbedrog.* ca.1770. l.c. clock.
Thomas. *Shrewsbury.* an.1774. Watch.
George. *Madeley Wood.* ca.1795. Watch Shrewsbury M.
Thomas. *London.* a.1787.
Samuel. *London.* a.1797.
William. *London.* a.1802.
PRITTY, William *London.* a.1708.
PROBERT, James. *Wigan.* ca.1820.
PROBIN, Thomas. *London.* 1820.
PROCTOR—
Goodham or Goodday. *Chelmsford.* 1723. Bankrupt. l.c. clock.
Carden. *New York.* 1734-68. W.
William. *London* (*Covent Gdn.*). an.1785. Watch.
Charles. *Sheffield.* ca.1780. Dial maker.
William. *London* (*Whitecross St.*). a.1790, CC.1797, l.CC.1810-22.
PRODHOMME, J. B. G. *Paris.* 1812-21. C.
PRON, ——. *London.* an.1753. Watch.
PROQUATE, ——. *London.* an.1743. Watch.
PROSPER—
——. *Besançon.* 1599.
Le Comte. *Paris.* 1729. Invented a sand clock desc. Gallon, 'Machines et Inventions,' Vol v.
Père, de S. Joan Hep. ——. Mid. 18c. Fine astro. br. clock Feill coll.
PROSSER—
Edward. *London.* a.1655.
Thomas. *Hereford.* 1764. W.
Richard. *London.* an.1785. Watch.
John, & PROSSER, jun. *Clonmel.* ca.1790.
Simon. *Clonmel.* 1824.
Joseph. *Tipperary.* 1824.
PROT (PROUST), Pierre. *Pau.* 1580. 'Relodgier.'
PROTAT, ——. *Paris.* b.1821, d.1898. Famous maker of aut. clocks.
PROUVARELLE, ——. *Paris.* 1807-25.
PROVAUX, ——. *Charleston, U.S.A.,* from 1775. W.
PROVOST, William. *Newcastle-o.-T.* 1698. *v.* THIRKELD.
PROY, ——. *London.* an.1743. Watch.
PRUJEAN, John. *England.* ca.1670. Paper astrolabe Old Ashmolean M.
PRYOR—
Thomas. *London.* 1st half 18c. Sheepshead clock with Turkish figures.
James. *London.* an.1775. Watch.
John. *London.* a.1771.
Nathaniel. *Leeds.* 1798. W.
PRYTZ, Johan. *Stockholm.* a.1655.
PUCKRIDGE—
Moses. *London.* a.1758.
Thomas. *London* (*Cow La.*). 1766-1808. W.
Charles. *London* (*Goldsmith St.*). a.1763, CC.1776-1805. l.c. clock ill. Cec. & Web. prob. by him. Also W.
John, son of Thomas. *London.* a.1780, CC. 1788, l.CC.1814-25. W. & C.
Charles, son of Charles. *London.* CC.1808-1824.
James, bro. *London.* a.1805.
H. *London.* 1820.
PUGH—
Thomas. *London.* a.1715.
Ellis. *London.* 2nd half 18c. br. clock.
Benjamin. *London* (*Jewin St.* and later *Whitecross St.*). CC.1777-1800.
George. *London.* a.1794.
John Sankey. *London.* CC.1808.
PUHKAW, Georg. *Plauen* (*Saxony*). 1548. Made aut. clock for town, now in M.
PULBROOK, Joseph Zachariah. *London.* CC. 1822.
PULLAN—
Benjamin. *Leeds.* an.1767, d.1787. Watch.
John. *London.* an.1773. Watch.
PULLEN—
James. *London.* a.1669.
David. *London* (*Coleman St.*). a.1738, CC. 1745-69.
David, son. *London.* a.1763, CC.1773.
PULLER, Jonathan. *London.* a.1676, CC. 1683-1706. l.c. clock Weth. coll. g. watch Ilbert coll.
PULLIN, Charles. *London.* a.1738, CC.1745-1772.
PULMAN, ——. *Axminster.* 18c. l.c. clock.
PUNCHARD, William. *London.* a.1676.
PUNCHEARD, Isaac. *London.* a.1785.
PUNG—
John. *London.* a.1780.
J. *Hastings.* Early 19c.
PUNY, John. *London.* a.1780.
PUPLETT (PAPLETT, PUPPETT), Robert. *Mitcham.* an.1748. Watch Ilbert coll.
PURBACH, M. *Germany.* 1561-97. Dial Old Ashmolean M.
PURCELL, John. *Limerick.* 1824.
PURDEN—
——. *London* (*St. Martin's Ct.*). 1743. Watch.
John. *London* (*Dean St.*). 1752-ca.1790. Watch. l.c. clock ill. Cec. & Web.
Charles. *London.* CC.1777.
George. *London.* CC.1820.
PURDOX, ——. *London* (*Hatton Gdn.*). an. 1776. Watch.
PURMAN, Marcus. *Munich.* 1601. Dial Old Ashmolean M.
PURNELL—
John. *London.* a.1697.
Richard Smith. *London.* a.1748. Watch.
T. *London.* an.1774. Watch.
PURRIER—
Richard. *London.* a.1697, CC.1705.
Thomas. *London.* a.1763.
PURSE—
George. *London.* 1804-15. Watch N.Y. Univ.
Thomas. *Baltimore, U.S.A.* 1807. W. & C.
H. *Newtownards.* Early 19c. l.c. clock.
PURSER—
Matthew. *London* (*Shoe La.*). 1755. W.
John. prob. *London.* an.1774. Watch.
William. *London* (*Lambeth & Holborn*). 1778.
PURSFORD, Frederick. *London.* a.1812.
PURVES, William. *Edinburgh.* 1539-48. Church clocks.
PURVIS, Alexander. *London.* Early 19c. Watch.
PUSCH, Balthazar. *Elbing.* 2nd half 17c. Falling ball clock Webster coll.
PÜSCHL, Joseph. *Prague.* ca.1800. g. en. watch set pearls Feill coll.
PUTLEY—
Francis. *London.* a.1779, CC.1804, l.CC. 1812-40. W. & C. cyl. mt. G.M.
Francis, son. *London.* a.1819.
PUTTENHAM, Peter. *London.* a.1753.
PUZELAT—
Antoine. *Blois.* mar.1600-50.
Nicolas. *Blois.* mar.1616-39.
PUZY, Isaac. *London.* a.1651, CC.1658-85. Lantern clock.

PY—
Daniel. *Chaux-de-Fonds.* 1763.
David. *Chaux-de-Fonds.* 1781-94. C.
PYBUS, William. *London.* CC.1788-94. c.secs. watch Ilbert coll.
PYE—
Charles. *Birmingham.* 1774-80. Stock sold. l.c. clocks.
John. *Manchester.* 1804. C.
——. *Paris.* 1807. d.1808.
Veuve. *Paris* (*Rue du fbg. St. Denis*). 1809-1812.
John Elliott. *Exeter.* Early 19c.
PYKE—
John. *London* (*Holborn & Bedford Row*). a. 1710, CC.1720, d.1762. 'Eminent' C. & W. 'That great artist.' l.c. lacquer clock ill.

PYKE—*continued.*
Cec. & Web. mus. br. clock Nat. M. Stockholm. Also PIKE.
George, son. *London.* a.1739, CC.1753-63. mus. aut. clock Peiping M.
Thomas. *London.* Mid. 18c. Watch.
John. *London* (*Grays Inn*). 1747-ca.1780. C. & W. to the Prince of Wales. Watch mt. G.M. br. clock ill. Cec. & Web.
PYM, Thomas. *London.* a.1713, CC.1721.
PYNE, Nathaniel. *London.* a.1667, CC.1677-1706. l.c. clock.
PYOT, James. *Edinburgh* and *Leith.* 1796.
PYSING, John. *Canterbury.* an.1756. Watch.
PYTTERS, Hannes. *Bolsward.* 1609. 'Meyster Slotmaker en Uhrwerckmaecker.'

Q

QUACKELSTYN, Pieter. *The Hague.* ca. 1730. Watch mt. Ilbert coll.
QUANDALE, Lewis. *Philadelphia.* 1813-25.
QUARE—
Daniel. *London.* b.1649, CC.1671, m.CC. 1708, d.1724. A very celebrated maker of watches and clocks; invented repeating work for watches about 1680; rep. watch submitted to James II for patent, in competition with Barlow, Mallett coll. Made several one-year l.c. clocks, one in Hampton Court, another Weth. coll., both ill. Britten, and one Ilbert coll.; devised a motion work enabling hour and minute hands to be set together. Very large l.c. clock showing solar time, Mercers Co. Seven l.c. and br. clocks Weth. coll. Magnificent Boulle work l.c. clock Hofburg, Vienna. Lantern clock and table clock B.M. Clock Cassel Landes-M. ¼ rep. watch S.K.M. Fine astro. watch and rep. watch B.M. Two watches and mt. G.M. Early rep. watch F.W.M. rep. watches G.M. and R. Scottish M. 3-case watch S.M.S.K. Three watches M.M.A., one ill. Britten. Watch with turning hour circle under a minute hand Webster coll. ill. Baillie. str. watch Den. coll. Watches Carnegie M. and Bourges M. and many in private colls. The Nos. of watches sd. Quare are known from 233 to 4989. No. 4600 is about 1716. Rep. watches had a separate series known from 109 to 857.
& HORSEMAN. *London.* 1718-33. Partnership with Daniel QUARE, the style continuing after Quare's death until bankrupt in 1733, when the business was prob. taken over by PECKOVER. p.c. g. rep. watch and rep. mt. G.M. g. rep. repoussé watch, set topazes and diamonds, Winter Palace, Petrograd. The Nos. of watches sd. Quare & Horseman are known from 4677 to 5503, and of repeaters from 843 to 1129.
Daniel. *London.* a.1707 to Daniel.
QUARI, Jean. *London.* ca.1700. Table clock S.K.M. sd. 'De Jean Quari, London.'
QUARMAN—
Samuel. *Temple Cloud.* ca.1770. l.c. clock and watch.
Joseph. *Temple Cloud.* ca.1780. l.c. clock ill. Cec. & Web.
George. *Temple Cloud.* ca.1780.
QUARREL—
Richard. *London.* a.1691.
Jonathan. *London.* a.1716.
QUARTERMAINE—
Joseph. *Aylesbury.* Mid. 18c. Watch.
Stephen. *London.* a.1770.
W. *Aylesbury.* 1791. W.
QUARTIER—
David François. *Chaux-de-Fonds,* 1742. *Les Brenets,* 1750.

QUARTIER—*continued.*
Olivier. *Le Locle* and *Paris.* b.1776, d.1852. Awarded prize in 1825 for a wheel cutting and rounding machine, and in 1836 a prize for making balance springs. Watch N.Y. Univ. Watch with dead-beat verge and two escape wheels and a watch for Chinese market, both Chamb. coll.
QUASH, Joseph. *London.* a.1637, CC.1646-1664. Watch S.K.M. Watch mt. G.M.
QUELCH—
Richard. *Oxford.* ca.1650. oct. watch Ashmolean M.
John. *London.* d.1699. W.
Jeremiah. *London.* an.1758. Watch.
QUENOVAULT, Charles. *London.* an.1743-ca.1760. rep. watch Den. coll.
QUESNEL, ——. *Jersey.* an.1774. Watch.
QUESNOY (**QUESNAY**)—
Vincent. *Rouen,* 1524. *Hampton Court* or *London,* 1532. *Rouen,* 1532-63. There was paid to him from the Privy Purse 11 li. 8*s.* 8*d.* Keeper of Rouen town clock. Remade Rouen Cathedral clock 1540.
Jean. *Rouen.* 1553-65. In charge of town clock.
Claude. *Rouen.* 1575-92. In charge of town clock, and repaired several others.
Nicolas. *Amsterdam.* 1688. Huguenot refugee from *Dieppe.*
QUESTED—
Henry. *London.* a.1752.
Thomas. *Wye.* 1780-7. W.
QUICK—
Thomas. *London.* 2nd half 18c. Watch mt.
William. *Bristol.* 1825-30. W.
QUIERY (**QUERY**), François. *Paris.* m.1787.
QUILLET, ——. *Paris.* 1764. d.an.1776. Made clock for the Bastille.
QUILLIAM, Samuel. *Liverpool.* 1825. W.
QUIN—
John. *London.* an.1766. Watch.
Edward. *London* (*Blackfriars Rd.*). l.CC. 1805, d.1825.
Edward, son. *London.* a.1812.
Patrick, bro. *London.* a.1812.
QUINCHE, Pierre. *Neuchâtel.* 1650.
QUINETTE, ——. *Paris.* 1760. Clock with double pendulum for compensation approved by Acad. des Sci.
QUINN, John. *London.* a.1785.
QUINSON, Aymé. *Lyons.* 1670. From *Valence.*
QUINTON—
William Brett. *London.* a.1761, CC.1769-1806.
William, son. *London.* a.1785.
QUONIAM—
Joseph. *Paris.* m.1740, d.1779.
François Joseph. *Paris.* m.1752.
QUOSIG, ——. *Mannheim.* Early 19c. Watch Horstmann coll.

R

RABBY, ——. *Paris.* 1745. Watch G.M.
RABE, Ab. *Hamburg.* an.1678. Watch. cf. Raeb.
RABERT, Johann Conrad. *Berlin.* 1785-1816. C.
RABINOT, Jacques. *Strasbourg.* 1729.
RABIQEAU, ——. *Paris.* ca.1750. Made automata.
RABOUIS, Joseph. *Paris.* m.1616.
RABY—
Étienne. *Paris.* m.1784-9.
Louis. *Paris.* ca.1810. Watch.
RACINE—
David. *Tramelan.* 1708 m.
Charles Frédéric. *Chaux-de-Fonds.* d.1832. Enameller of great repute. sd. watch-case M.M.A. Famous for minute lettering on dials.
——. *Paris.* ca.1800. g. en. watch Carnegie M.
RACLE, Barthélemy. *Paris.* m.1770-80.
RADANT—
Georges Louis. *Paris.* m.1783-9.
Fils. *Paris.* 1807-12.
RADCLIFFE—
Charles. *Liverpool.* 1677. Watch Den. coll.
Samuel. *London.* a.1714.
John. *London.* a.1727.
RADCLOFF, Nicolaus. *Schleswig.* 1654. Clock with balls running down spiral, Nat. M. Copenhagen, ill. Liisberg.
RADFORD (REDFORD)—
Henry. *London.* a.1714, CC.1721-30.
Richard. *London.* a.1723.
Thomas. *London* (*Grays Inn La.*). a.1732, CC.1749, d.1774.
Thomas. *Leeds.* ca.1759, d.1793. Watch Ilbert coll.
John. *London.* an.1766. Watch.
James. *London.* 1790.
William, bro. of Thos. *Leeds.* 1793-1826. In partnership with his bro. in 1792 and continued the business. Watch mt.
Mary. *London.* 1805-08.
RADI, F. Archangelo. *Rome.* Pub. 'Nuova scienza di Horlogi a Polvere,' Rome, 1655 and 1665.
RADISH, Francis. *London.* 1729. Insolvent.
RADLEY, Charles. *London.* a.1751.
RADSMA—
Tjeerd Jacobs. *Harlingen.* 1731. d.ca.1790. l.c. astro. and several br. clocks.
Martin Tjeerds, son. *Harlingen.* b.1761, d. 1836.
RAE—
The Rev. Peter. *Kirkconnel.* 1703-48. astro. clock.
Alexander. *Tunbridge Wells.* ca.1810. br. clock.
Charles. *London.* CC.1816.
RAEB, Andreas. *Hamburg.* 1639. Oval cal. watch Pal. du Cinquantenaire, Brussels.
RAFE, Thomas. *England.* 1661. Lantern clock.
RAFFARD—
F. L. *Geneva.* 1789. Watch.
Daniel. *Geneva.* 1811.
——. *Paris.* 1812-25.
RAFIN, Ferrier. *Avignon.* 1496. Made new clock for belfry with Granja.
RAFQUIST, Anders. *Landskrona.* 1820-40. Wall clocks.
RAGER, James. *London.* a.1755, CC.1769.
RAGG, James. *London.* a.1712. Watch.
RAGGEN, Louis Antoine. *Paris.* m.1784-9.
RAGNET, ——. *Paris.* 1822-5. Successor to Sauvage.
RAGOT—
Claude. *Paris.* m.1785, d.1790.
——. *Paris* (*Rue du fbg. du Temple*). 1807-1812.
RAGUET-LÉPINE, Claude Pierre. *Dôle* and later *Paris.* b.1753, d.1810. Son-in-law of and succeeded Jean Antoine Lépine in 1783. Watch sd. Raguet, N.Y. Univ.
RAHN, Franz Hinrich. *Hamburg.* 1801-15.
RAIGUEL—
Jonas. *Corgémont.* 1780.
Jean Pierre, son. *St. Imier* and *Paris.* ca.1790.
Jean Henri, bro. *St. Imier* and *Paris.* ca.1790-1808.
Les Frères. *St. Imier* and *Paris.* ca.1800. Firm of the two preceding. Watch Stads M. Amsterdam.
Jeune. *Paris.* ca.1800. Watch with auxiliary decimal dials Ilbert coll.
Jeune & Cie. *St. Imier.* Early 19c. Taken over by François Meyrat-Langel in 1817. Watch.
RAILLARD (RAILLART)—
Claude. *Paris.* 1646. Juré 1675. Signatory to Statuts of Paris corporation. *v.* Rallart.
Claude, son. *Paris.* m.1676, juré 1692. Fine Boulle br. clock Pal. de Pau, Paris.
Jacques. *Bourges.* 17c. Watch Bourges M.
Claude. *Paris.* m.1691, d.1762.
Claude. *Paris.* 1739-89. Juré 1745. Pub. 'Extraits des principaux Statuts des Horlogers de Paris.'
RAIMOND, Charles Eugène. *Paris.* 1780.
RAIMONDO, Annibale. *Venice.* 1550.
RAINE—
John. *London.* a.1741.
Nathaniel. *Durham.* an.1756. Watch.
David. *London.* an.1761. Watch. Also Rayne.
Joseph. *Durham.* 1804-20. l.c. clock.
John. *Durham.* 1816. W.

RAINERI—
Bartolommeo. *Parma.* ca.1450. Given special privileges by the Duke of Milan.
Gian Paolo, prob. son. *Reggio.* 1481-1522. From *Parma.* Made aut. clock of Reggio Modenese. *v.* Gian Carlo.
Gian Carlo, son. *Venice.* 1493. d.1529. Worked with his father on the clock erected in the Piazza San Marco. 'Uomo famoso nelle mathematiche che è di molta esperienza in così fatti magisteri, fu . . . dalla Republica . . . rimunerato cortesemente.' He and his heirs were made keepers of the clock in perpetuity, in lieu of payment for the clock.
Gian Ludovico, bro. *Italy.* ca.1500-36.
Gian Lionello, bro. *Italy.* ca.1500-36. With his bro. replaced the clock of Reggio. With DA PONTE made a clock for Ferrara.
Girolamo, son of Gian Carlo. *Venice.* 1529. d.1551. Keeper of clock of S. Marco. Discharged in 1531 because unable to keep it going.
RAINES (RAYNES), William. *London.* a. 1653, CC.1660-7. Lantern clocks.
RAINFORD, William. *Liverpool.* 1800-03. W.
RAINGO, M. *Paris.* Orrery clocks Windsor Castle and Soane M., Glasgow Art Gallery, and Palais du Cinquantenaire, Brussels. Planetarium and planetary clock C.A. & M. Pub. 'Description d'une pendule à sphère mouvante.'
RAINIER—
John. *London.* CC.1786, l.CC.1787, d.1814.
Daniel, son. *London.* a.1800, l.CC.1806.
RAINSFORD—
Bernard. *London.* a.1667, CC.1677-95. Also RANCEFORD.
Francis. *London.* a.1681, CC.1689-1709. Table clock.
John. *London* (*New St. Sq.*). a.1714, CC. 1721-57. Bankrupt. l.c. clock, br. clock, regulator Weth. coll.
Benjamin. *London.* CC.1708-15.
Benjamin. *London.* a.1722.
RAIT, D. C. *Glasgow.* Early 19c. Watch.
RAKE, John. *London.* CC.1780-96.
RALLART, ——. *Paris.* p.c. watch, shagreen case, Den. coll. Prob. RAILLARD.
RALPH—
Richard. *London.* a.1736.
James. *London.* a.1796.
RAM, Hewett. *London.* a.1691.
RAMAGE, James. *Edinburgh.* a.1780-1820.
RAMBLEY, William. *London.* 1790.
RAMERY, John. *London.* 1st half 18c. Watch Horstmann coll.
RAMIANO, Antonio. *Parma.* 1463-93. Keeper of city clock.
RAMSAY—
Patrick. *Dundee.* 1588-1612.
David. *Dundee, France* and *London.* ca.1590, d.ca.1654. One of the finest of the early makers. Came to *London* from *France* about 1610. King's clockmaker in 1613, when he was granted a pension; in 1618 received grant of office of Chief C. to the King; in 1619 received grant of denization, because born in Scotland. First master of CC. in 1632. Oval watch, fine eng. case, B.M., sd. 'David Remsey Scotus me fecit' ill. Baillie. oct. watch S.K.M. Oval cal. watch in Limoges en. case M.M.A. Exceptionally fine domed table clock S.K.M.
John, son of Patrick. *Dundee.* 1610-46.
Silvester, bro. *Dundee.* 1610-46.
John. *London.* CC.1637-54. Oval watch M.M.A. This maker may be the same as John above. Also RAMSEY.

RAMSAY—*continued.*
Robert. *Dumfries.* 1816-25.
——. *Cork.* Early 19c.
Barbara. *London.* Early 19c. Watch.
RAMSBOTHAM, Richard. *Bury* (*Lancs.*). d. 1734. C.
RAMSDEN—
Thomas. *London.* CC.1648.
John. *London.* a.1654.
John. *Hall Green.* ca.1785.
RAMSEY—
Robert. *London.* a.1753.
William. *Letterkenny.* 1824.
RAMSOE, Jon Jonsen. *Copenhagen.* m.1779. Master of Corporation 1789-93.
RAMSTEDT—
Petter. *Stockholm.* 1770-1816. Watch mt. Nord. M.
D. *Stockholm.* 1790. Prob. same as preceding.
——. *Eksjö.* 1821-4.
RAMU—
Jean. *Geneva.* 1670 m. g. watch.
Jérémie. *Geneva.* mar.ca.1786-91.
——. *Paris.* 1810-25.
RAMUSAT, Jean Louis. *Geneva.* ca.1755-70.
RANALS, William. *London.* Early 18c. Watch.
RANCE, Henry. *London.* a.1786.
RAND—
Henry. *London.* a.1736.
Benjamin. *London.* an.1765. Watch.
William. *London.* an.1779. Watch.
R. *London.* an.1785. Watch.
Daniel. *Boston, U.S.A.* 1825. W.
RANDALL—
Henry. *London.* a.1660. Also RANDOLPH and RANDLOE.
Richard. *London.* a.1665.
Morris. *London.* a.1680.
Timothy. *London.* a.1683.
Thomas. *London.* a.1721.
William. *London.* a.1753.
——. *Warrington.* an.1767. Watch.
James. *London.* an.1772. Watch.
John. *London.* an.1775-90.
Thomas. *London* (*Whitecross St.*). 1781 Insolvent.
W. *Reading.* End 18c. l.c. clock.
v. SMALLPAGE & RANDALL.
William. *Wareham.* 1795. W.
William. *Newbury.* 1795-1812. C. & W Church clock with Cumming's esc.
John. *Holt.* Early 19c. Watch.
RANDE, Thomas. *France.* 2nd half 17c. g. en. tulip watch.
RANDELL & BRIDGE. ——. ca.1800. g. en. watch Den. coll.
RANGEN—
W. *London.* 1809-11. W.
M. *London* (*Gt. Chesterfield St.*). 1817-24.
RANGER—
——. *Chipsted.* an.1773. Watch.
Michael. *London* (*Marylebone*). 1774-1820. Table clock. W.
——. *London* (*Tottenham Ct. Rd.*). 1774. Insolvent.
RANKEN, James. *Edinburgh.* a.1791.
RANKIN (RANKINE)—
——. *London.* 2nd half 18c. Watch.
John. *Edinburgh.* a.1761.
John. *Old Cumnock.* 1789.
J. & W. *Sorn.* 1798.
Alexander. *Greenock.* ca.1800.
James. *Alnwick.* an.1817. Watch.
John. *Belfast.* 1819. W.
RANNA, Michael. *Vienna.* Early 19c. en. lyre watch. g. watch, set pearls.
RANNER, Joseph. *Vienna.* Early 19c. en. lyre watch.

RANSOM—
Edward. *London*. d.1612. C.
William. *London*. ca.1760. Watch S.K.M.
George. *London*. an.1781. Watch.
RANSON—
Robert Hill. *London*. a.1769, CC.1777.
Richard. *London*. an.1785. Watch.
M. *London*. an.1789. Watch.
RANT—
John. *London*. a.1676, CC.1687-1708.
Jonathan. *London*. a.1680, CC.1687-1725. rep. br. clock Weth. coll.
Joshua. *London*. an.1731. Watch.
Edward. *London*. a.1726.
William. *London*. a.1737.
RANTEY, ——. *London*. an.1722. Watch.
RANZONET, ——. *Nancy*. 1770. Watch 'which plays an air en duo.'
RAPHARD, ——. *London*. Mid. 18c. en. watch ill. Britten.
RAPSON—
W. *London* (*Oat La.*). 1748. Watch.
William. *London* (*Little Moorfields*). a.1711-1777.
Richard. *London*. an.1772. Watch.
Robert. *London*. 1802-20.
RAPTON—
William. *London*. a.1711.
John Stewart. *London*. CC.1773.
RASETTI, Paul. *St. Nicolas d'Aliermont*. Early 19c. Worked with PONS DE PAUL at his clock factory.
RASHER, John. *London*. a.1695, CC.1703-21.
RASMUSSON, Hans. *Simrisham*. b.1792, d.1870. l.c. clock.
RASON, George. *Boston*. Early 19c.
RASTIN, William. *London*. a.1770.
RATCLIFFE—
Charles. *Liverpool*. d.1700. W.
John. *Chester*. 1763-97 CC.
John. *Wrexham*. ca.1735-63. l.c. clock.
Benjamin. *Welshpool*. 1743-59. Sundial and clock.
John. *London*. 1776. Had a factory for watches selling at 18*s*. upwards.
Owen, son of Benj. *Welshpool*. 1780.
RATHBONE—
Joseph. *Middlewich*. an.1756. Watch.
Samuel. *Sandbach*. an.1775. Watch.
RATHBORN, John. *Deptford*. Early 19c. Watch.
RATZENHOFER (RAZENHOFER), Mathias. *Vienna*. m.1799. l.c. clock of 1827 Uhren M. Vienna.
RAU—
Johann. *Vienna*. m.1785.
Nikolaus. *Vienna*. m.1805.
RAUCH—
Antoni. *Zisserstorff*. Early 18c. str. rep. br. clock Feill coll.
Johann Georg. *Vienna*. m.1770.
RAUENECKER, Martin. *Augsburg*. comp. 1727, m.1736, juré 1740-70.
RAULET, Samuel. *Monmouth, U.S.A.* ca. 1800.
RAUPACH, ——. ——. Pub. desc. of a clock showing true time, in Ann. der Physik. Halle, 1819.
RAUSCHENPLATT, H. *Göttingen*. Early 19c. mus. clocks with harp and flute.
RAUWERDINK, W. *Rotterdam*. 1821-30.
RAVEN—
Samuel. *London*. a.1760, CC.1768-ca.1795. l.c. clock ill. Cec. & Web.
William. *Sheffield*. 1817-40.
RAVENAT, ——. *Paris*. 1807-25. Succeeded GRAVEREAU.
RAVENÉ, ——. *Berlin*. 1794. g. watch.
RAVENECK, J. *Rotterdam*. 1821-30.
RAVENHILL, James. *Gloucestershire*. 1771. Repaired Westbury church clock.
RAVES, Charles. *London*. CC.1768.
RAVIZZA, Amicino. *Cremona*. 1788. Pub. desc. of the astro. clock of Cremona.
RAVRIO ET CIE. *Paris*. ca.1790-1820. Celebrated bronze workers of the first Empire. Made many clock-cases.
RAWDEN—
Samuel. *London*. a.1722.
Samuel. *London*. a.1744.
RAWLEY, Joseph Anderson. *London*. a.1810.
RAWLINGS—
Edward. *Canterbury*. d.1751. C.
Charles. *London* (*Holborn*). CC.1818, l.CC. 1826, d.1864. W.
RAWLINS—
Henry. *London*. a.1696, CC.1706-23.
William. *London*. an.1768. Watch.
James. *London* (*Wilderness Row*). a.1766, CC.1775, l.CC.1792. Went to *Liverpool* in 1833.
Nathaniel. *London*. a.1776.
James, son of Jas. *London*. a.1790.
George Spencer. *London*. a.1820.
RAWLINSON—
Samuel. *London*. a.1752.
John. *London*. an.1783. Watch.
RAWORTH (RAWWORTH)—
John. *London*. a.1771.
Samuel. *Plymouth*. 18c. l.c. clock. rep. watch.
Henry. *Plymouth*. 1795. C. & W.
RAWSON—
Peter. *London*. a.1700.
Thomas. *Penrith*. b.1718, d.1811. C. & W.
John. *Penrith*. ca.1770-1820. C. & W.
John. *Newcastle-o.-T*. 1787-90. W.
William. *Newcastle-o.-T*. 1790. C. & W.
——. *London*. an.1794. Watch.
John. *Morpeth*. 1808-20.
RAXHALL, Christopher. *London*. a.1657.
RAY—
Daniel. *Sudbury*. Early 18c. l.c. clock.
Daniel. *Manningtree*. d.1755. Watch.
William. *Sudbury*. 1762-90 CC. W.
William Redmore, son. *London*. a.1776.
Daniel. *Battle*. ca.1790.
J. *Dumbarton*. 1791. Clock.
William. *Battle*. Early 19c. Watch.
Samuel. *London*. Early 19c. Watch.
RAYMANN, Georg. *Nürnberg*. m.1555. inst. maker.
RAYMENT (RAIMENT)—
Richard. *Bury St. Edmunds*. 1743. W. Lantern and l.c. clock. Also RAYMOND.
Thomas. *London* (*Old Jewry*). a.1708, CC. 1719-68. Watch. Vase with watch Palace M. Pekin.
John. *Huntingdon*. 1751-95. W. Also RAYMOND. circ. wall clock.
Thomas. *Stamford* (*Lincs.*). 1760-84. l.c. clock. W.
Griffin. *Bury St. Edmunds*. 1754-64. l.c. clock.
John. *Stamford*. 1795. W.
RAYMOND—
Henry. *London*. a.ca.1746. Watch.
George. *Manningtree*. 1760. C. & W.
John. *London* (*Change Alley*). 1762-84. Watch.
Charles Eugène. *Paris*. 1765-74.
William. *Dublin*. 1774-95. W.
Lazare Toussaint. *Geneva*. ca.1775-91.
William. *Calne*. 1795. C.
Joseph. *London*. 1805-08.
Charles. *Lydeway* (*Devizes*). Early 19c.
'B. W. RAYMOND.' Sig. on 1867-75 watches of the NATIONAL WATCH CO. OF CHICAGO.
v. DE MONTFERRAT.
RAYNER—
Stephen. *London*. 1689. CC.1691-1701. g. watches S.K.M. and Ilbert coll. l.c. clock.

RAYNER—*continued.*
John. *London.* a.1687, CC.1697-1727. Watch Den. coll.
Dove. *London (Little Old Bailey).* a.1693, CC.1701-65. Bankrupt.
Isaac. *London.* 1754. Watch.
REA & CO. *Walton-upon-Trent.* 1784. W.
READ (READE)—
Thomas. *London.* a.1751.
Robert. *London.* an.1771-99. Watch.
Thomas. *Wootton Bassett.* 1784. W.
Thomas. *Manchester.* 1790-1804. C.
W. *Grantham.* ca.1790 CC.
Matthew. *Aylsham.* 1791-5. W.
William. *Buntingford.* 1791. W.
William. *Grantham.* 1795. W.
Lewis. *London.* 1799-1807.
Mark. *Aylsham.* ca.1800.
George. *London.* 1805-25.
William Henry. *London.* a.1803.
Isaac. *Philadelphia.* 1819-25.
READER—
William. *Hull.* 1743. Watch.
William & Nathaniel. *Hull.* an.1783. Watch.
READING—
Andrew. *London.* a.1705.
Daniel. *London.* a.1735, CC.1743, d.1777.
Robert. *London (Shoe La. & New St).* a.1754, CC.1761-70. Watch.
Philip. *London.* an.1775. Watch.
Richard. *London.* a.1790.
REASEY, James. *London.* a.1748.
REASON—
John. *London.* a.1702.
G. *London.* ca.1775. Cartel clock ill. Cec. & Web.
REAY, John. prob. *London.* an.1767. Watch.
REBOUL, Daniel Antoine. *Geneva.* ca.1775-1791.
RECH, Wolff. *Nürnberg.* Burgher 1649. Sand-glass maker.
RECKLESS, Joseph. *London.* a.1702.
RECORDON—
Louis. *London (Soho).* 1778-1824. Succeeded EMERY in Cockspur St. Partner with DUPONT. Retired 1796, but firm continued. Succeeded by DES GRANGES. Patented pedometer winding in 1780. Made watches for China. Mantel clock sd. 'Recordon late Emery.'
& DUPONT. *London (Tottenham Court Rd.).* To 1796. g. en. watch. c.secs. watch with large diamond on case Wilsdorf coll.
RECOUZ, Joseph. *Saint-Julien.* 1811.
RECTOR, S. A. *Stockholm.* 1762. Invented a secs. mt.
REDARD—
Jacques Henri. *Verrières.* Early 19c. Chiming clock.
——. *Buttes.* 1817. C.
REDIER, Antoine. *Paris.* b.1817, d.1892. An eminent maker of clocks and registering instruments. Pub. several memoirs. Successor of DUCHEMIN of Paris. Used aluminium in gridiron pendulums and for escape wheels.
REDKNAP—
Enos. *London.* a.1785, CC.1792-1817.
Enos, son. *London.* a.1817.
Henry Stevens, bro. *London.* a.1820.
REDLEFSEN, Jakob Detlef. *Klanxbüll.* 1807. Wall clock.
REDOUTÉ, Marc. *Geneva,* b.1747. *Lyons,* 1768-72.
REDPATH, Henry. *Stirling.* 1787-1820.
REDRICH, Joseph. *London.* an.1797-1808. Watch.
REDSHAW, Daniel. *Newcastle-under-Lyme.* 1791. C. & W.
REDSTALL—
John. *Tiverton.* 1726. C.
Francis. *Overton.* 1726. C.
REDWOOD, Thomas. *London.* a.1701.
REEAD, Thomas. *London.* CC.1632.
REED—
Alexander. *London.* CC.1707. str. watch.
Richard. *Chelmsford.* d.1772. Succeeded by his son Rich. C. & W.
James. *London.* an.1743. Watch.
Andrew. *London.* ca.1750. Watch.
William. *London.* a.1760.
William, son of Rich. *Chelmsford.* 1770-84. W.
Richard, bro. *Chelmsford.* 1772-87. C. & W.
Benjamin. *Bristol.* 1775-97. C. & W.
George. *Barnstaple.* 1784.
William. *Bristol.* 1787. W.
George. *Bristol.* 1792. W.
B. *Plymouth.* 1795.
Andrew. *Sanquhar.* 1798.
George Jeremiah. *London.* a.1794, CC.1816, l.CC.1819-23.
William. *Montrose* and *Whitehaven.* d.1815.
Stephen. *New York.* 1805.
——. *Newcastle-o.-T.* an.1816. Watch.
Frederick. *Philadelphia.* 1817-20.
William, jun. *London.* CC.1824.
George P. *Boston, U.S.A.* b.1827, d.1908. Only maker of chronometers in quantity in U.S.A. Example Chamb. coll.
'G. A. REED.' Sig. on the 1869-70 watches of the UNITED STATES WATCH CO.
REES, Hildebrand. *Wolfenbüttel.* ca.1550-84. In *Brunswick* 1562-3. C. to Duke Heinrich d. J. zu Wolfenbüttel.
REEVE—
Thomas. *London.* 1630. CC.1632-56. Subscribed for incorporation of CC. Fine sil. watch, eng. dial, red figures, Webster coll.
Robert. *York.* 1660. W.
Thomas, son of Thos. *London.* a.1656.
Henry. *London.* a.1658, CC.1682-98.
John. *London.* a.1702, CC.1712.
Samuel. *Chatham.* 1725. Insolvent. C.
Gervais. *London.* a.1716, CC.1730-61. Watch mt.
Jarvis. *London (Fleet St.).* a.1716, CC.1731-1774. Watch. Also REEVES.
Joseph. *London.* a.1754.
Charles. *London.* an.1769. Watch.
John, jun. *Leicester.* 1791. C. & W.
R. *Philadelphia.* 1805-08. W.
John. *London.* 1817-24.
REEVES—
William. *Rye.* an.1729. Watch.
Benjamin. *Lamberhurst.* an.1774, d.1790. W. l.c. clock.
& COTTON. prob. *London.* an.1774. Watch.
William. *London.* a.1775.
James. *London.* 1805-08. Watch.
Richard. *London (City Rd.).* 1809-19. C.
Richard. *London (Shoreditch).* 1820-40. Watch.
& EDGE. *London.* 1820.
William. *London (Newington Causeway).* ca. 1825. Watch.
REGARD, Reymond. *London.* CC.1677-93.
REGAVELLY—
Pierre. *Neuchâtel.* 1575. Town C.
Jean, son. *Neuchâtel.* 1580-2. Town C.
REGEM, Thomas. *London.* an.1755. Watch.
REGNARD FRÈRES. *Sens.* Water-clock C.A. & M.
REGNAULT—
Claude. *Paris.* 1675 m.
——. *Chalons.* Early 18c. Devised a fuzee-cutting engine, a clock escapement, a striking mechanism, and experimented with rolling suspension for pendulums. Rack clock C.A. & M.
Pierre. *Paris (Rue vielle du Temple).* Juré 1752.

REGNAULT—*continued.*
Jerosme François. *Paris.* m.1747-89.
Pierre Antoine. *Paris.* m.1754, juré 1768-89. Took down the clock of the Bastille in 1789.
REGNELL—
Carl Axel. *Vrigstad.* b.1776, d.1841.
G. A. *Jönköping.* 1811-25.
RÉGNIER—
——. ——. 1597. Repaired Caen clock.
J. *Paris.* 1605. oct. crys. watches Louvre and Blot-Garnier coll.
REGTER, O. C. *Roermond.* ca.1800.
REGUEUX (REGEUX)—
Jacques Samuel. *Nyon.* 1st half 18c.
J. P. *Nyon.* 2nd half 18c.
RÉGUEX, Alexandre. *Paris.* m.1781-9.
REGUILLON—
ET BERGER. *Geneva.* Mid. 18c. Watch.
——. *London.* Mid. 18c. rep. trav. clock Ilbert coll.
P. *Geneva.* 2nd half 18c. g. en. watch.
REHFUS, Lorenz. *Breslau.* ca.1640. str. al. cal. clock.
REHKEUR, ——. *Nab* (prob. *Nabburg*). Early 17c. Watch, in Meissen porcelain case, B.M.
REHLE, Johann. *Freiburg.* 1690. Table clock.
REHR, Christian. *Brunswick.* 1600. From *Leipzig.* W.
REICH, Lorenz. *Augsburg.* m.ca.1740, juré 1745-57.
REICHEL—
Tobias. *Dresden.* 1603-10. Court C. str. and plain watches in hilts of a rapier and dagger in Johanneum, Dresden ill. Baillie. aut. table clock and aut. spider Grünes Gewölbe, Dresden. Monogram of TR.
C. G. *Leipzig.* 1800-14 juré.
J. C. *Leipzig.* 1814. Court C.
REICHENBACH, Jos. *Unterglottertal.* ca. 1750. Wall clock Furt. M.
REICHENEDER—
Leopold. *Burghausen.* 2nd half 16c. Drum watch M.M.A.
——. *Burghausen.* 1742-7.
Leopold. *Friedberg.* 1750.
REICHENMANN, Leonhard. *Friedberg.* 1795.
REICHERT, Ferdinand. *Montbéliard.* 1737. From *Württemberg.*
REICHOL, Melchior. ——. 1569. Cross watch S.K.M.
REID—
Alexander. *London.* a.1698, CC.1707.
John. *Banff.* 1721-4.
Thomas. *Edinburgh.* b.1746, CC.1825, d. 1831. A celebrated maker. Partner with AULD from 1806. Pub. 'Treatise on Clock and Watchmaking,' in 1826 and six later editions to 1859, and the art. 'Horology' in the Edinburgh Encyclopaedia, 1816 and 1830, and several other arts. on horology, in the Phil. Mag. and Nicholson's Jl. Devised a modified form of Flamenville esc. with double esc. wheel. cyl. watch S.M.S.K.
James. *London* (*Ball Alley*). an.1789-1824. Watch Ilbert coll.
Thomas. *London.* ca.1780. br. clock ill. Cec. & Web.
Thomas. *Montrose.* 1788.
William. *Edinburgh.* a.1781-1819.
Francis. *Glasgow.* 1789-1806. Also Francis & Sons.
William. *London.* 1795-1820. Watch.
Alexander. *Edinburgh.* a.1790.
Andrew. *Biggar.* b.1767, d.1860.
James. *Edinburgh.* 1798.
John. *Edinburgh.* 1798-1806.
Thomas, & Co. *Edinburgh.* ca.1800-06. Style of firm before partnership with AULD.
James. *Edinburgh.* 1804.
David. *Glasgow.* 1805-18.
Robert. *Glasgow.* 1806.

REID—*continued.*
& AULD. *Edinburgh.* 1806-23. Partnership with Thomas, above. A very famous firm. Regulator in Horological Inst.
& Co. *London.* 1807. g. pocket chron. G.M.
Adam. ——. Pub. arts. on a compensation pendulum in Trans. Soc. Arts, 1811 and 1827.
& SON. *Newcastle-o.-T.* Early 19c. Watch Den. coll. min. rep. watch.
Francis, & Sons. *Edinburgh.* 1812-25.
John. *Edinburgh.* 1814.
John. *Edinburgh.* 1819-36.
& HALBERT. *Glasgow.* 1823.
William, junior. *London.* CC.1824. W.
& TOD. *Glasgow.* 1828.
REIJER, George Abraham. *Dantzig.* Mid. 18c. sil. trav. rep. clock, formerly in Shandon coll.
REIJNDERS, Hermanus. *Arnhem.* 18c. Watch.
REILLY—
Richard. *London.* a.1743.
John. *Dublin.* 1753-80. Watch N.Y. Univ.
John. *Philadelphia.* 1785-97.
Philip. *Dublin.* Early 19c. Watch.
REIMANN (REINMANN)—
Georgius. *Nürnberg.* 1555. Dial Old Ashmolean M.
Ieronimus. *Nürnberg.* 1558-63. Ivory dial Old Ashmolean M.
Paulus. *Nürnberg.* 1588. d.1608. math. inst. maker. Three dials B.M. Dials Old Ashmolean M., M.M.A. and M.P.S. Dresden.
Hans. *Nürnberg.* m.1567. inst. maker. Dial Old Ashmolean M.
T. D. *Nürnberg.* 1588. inst. maker.
REIMER, Jørgen. *Christiania.* 1748 m.
REINBOLDT—
Hans. *Strasbourg.* 1594. Also REINBOLT.
Hans Georg. *Strasbourg.* 1643. Clock.
REINDINGER, Joh. Th. *Fürth.* d.ca.1820.
REINERDES, Richard. *Brunswick.* 1574. Kleinuhrmacher.
REINHARDT, Carl Gotthelf. *Dresden.* m. 1764, d.1800.
REINHOLD—
Johan Georg. *Augsburg.* 1584. d.an.1600. str. clock in S.K.M. by him and Georgius ROLL, dated 1584. Celestial globe clock by him and G. ROLL, dated 1586, M.P.S. Dresden. Large oct. crys. watch M.M.A. Clockwork globe C.A. & M.
Hans. *Augsburg.* b.1587, d.ca.1640. cal. watch Fränkel coll.
Janus. ——. Early 17c. rect. table clock Spitzer coll.
'REIREP MK.' *London.* an.1767. Sig. on watch. PERIER reversed.
REISBYE (RISBIE), Anthony. *London.* 1622. Oval watches F.W.M. and Webster coll.
REISCHACKER, Joseph. *Montbéliard.* 2nd half 18c.
REISNER, Michael. *Cologne.* 1797-1813.
REISSIG, Christ. *Cassel.* 1794. Water clock in form of lyre.
REISSMANN—
Adam Andreas. *Fürth.* d.1738.
J. A. *Fürth.* d.1798.
REITER, F. W. *Hamburg.* 1801.
REITH—
James. *Versailles* and *London* (*Strand*). a. 1698, CC.1705-36. rep. watch S.K.M. l.c. clock. trav. clock Ilbert coll.
——. *London* (*Fleet St.*). 1711. W.
Jarvis. *London.* a.1736.
REITHMANN, Christian. *Schwabing* and *Munich.* b.1818, d.1909. Devised a free escapement and a wheel-cutting machine and a four-cycle gas engine in 1873.

REITMEYR, Joseph Anton. *Augsburg.* m. 1794.
REIWICH, ——. *Amberg.* 1751. C. Was credited with having made a perpetual motion clock.
REJETON, Timothy. prob. *London.* an.1762. Watch.
'RELBOH.' HOBLER reversed.
REMCHING, Edmund. *London.* a.1659.
REMLASS, Thomas. prob. *London.* an.1773. Watch.
REMMEN, Cornellis. *Wel.* 1736. Turret clock Stads M. Amsterdam.
REMON, ——. *Geneva.* ca.1800. Worked for JAQUET-DROZ ET LESCHOT.
REMOND—
Jn. G. *Geneva.* ca.1800. Watch mt. pin wheel esc. Ilbert coll.
LAMY & CIE. prob. *Geneva.* 1802.
——. *Paris.* 1822.
REMY, ——. *Chaux-de-Fonds.* 1784.
RENAR, ——. *La Rochelle.* 1695.
RENARD—
Armand (Amand). *Paris.* m.1751-89.
Jean. *Paris.* m.1778-89.
——. *Rheims.* Early 19c. Watch.
——. *Paris.* 1817-25. C.
RENAUD—
Jean. *Lyons.* 1653-60. Also REGNAULD.
François. *Geneva.* a.1688.
Alexandre. *La Brévine* and *Corcelles.* b. 1711-53. br. clocks.
Jean. *Môtiers.* 1766.
——. *Lyons.* Late 18c. g. rep. watch.
RENAULT, ——. *Paris.* 1775. Prob. same as REGNAULT.
RENAUT, ——. *Paris.* 1780. Prob. same as RENAULT and REGNAULT.
RENDELL—
James. *Wiveliscombe.* mar.1775. W.
Henry. *Tiverton.* 1795. W.
RENDU, Jean Pierre. *Paris.* m.1787. Monteur de boîtes.
RENER, Michael F. *Kronstadt.* ca.1590. Table clock.
RENEVIER, ——. *Paris.* 1823.
RENGGER, Samuel. *Bienne.* 1718.
RÉNIER, Jean. *Lyons.* 1610. Also REYNIER.
RENKRIW, ——. *Paris.* ca.1740. str. and rep. trav. clock Virginia M.
RENISH, ——. *Geneva.* an.1776. Watch.
RENNARD, Thomas. *London.* a.1785.
RENNEZ, Nowell. prob. *London.* Late 16c. C. The Earl of Rutland paid for a 'watch and ij compas dialles iij li.'
RENNIE, James. *Carlisle.* 1820-36. Watch.
RENOU—
Jacob. *London.* a.1655.
Claude. *London.* a.1710.
Peter. *London.* 1802-04. W.
Philip. *London.* 1805-08. W.
RENOUARD, Johan. *Copenhagen.* m.1804. From *Calmar.*
RENOUX, ——. *Paris.* 1749 m.
RENSMAN, Gerrit. *Zwol.* Early 18c. Watch mt. G.M.
RENSTRÖM, Johan Gustaf. *Stockholm.* 1824-1859.
RENTNOW. WONTNER reversed.
RENTON, John. *London.* an.1805. Watch.
RENTZSCH—
W. *London.* 1809-11.
Sigismund. *London.* 1813-40. Patented a water-clock and devised a chron. escapement. Fine duplex mt. G.M. g. keyless watch repeating hours on turning the bezel in one direction and quarters on turning it back Ilbert coll.
RENVORSE, G. *London.* Early 19c. Watch.
RENZSEA ,——. *Constance.* 1750.
RÉPOUX (RÉPOND)—
Pierre Joseph. *Paris.* m.1778-89.
——. *Paris.* 1807.
Veuve. *Paris* (*Rue Montmartre*). 1809-18.
RERXOLL. *Liverpool.* an.1817. Sig. on watch.
RESDON, T. prob. *London.* an.1773. Watch.
RESEN, Focke Etje. *Enkhuizen.* 1679.
RESLER, Nicolaus. *Prague.* Early 17c. Fine circ. table clock, with al. mechanism fitting over it. circ. table clock Feill coll.
RETLAND, Walter. prob. *London.* an.1777. Watch.
RETSREFF. *London.* Late 18c. Sig. on p.c. g. en. and jasper watch.
RETTICH, Anton. *Vienna.* m.1800.
REUBEN—
——. *London.* 18c. trav. clock Fränkel coll.
& LYON. *Liverpool.* 1825. W.
REUMANN, Jheronimus. *Nürnberg.* m.1556. inst. maker.
REUSILLE, David de la. *Tramelan.* ca.1800.
REUTTER, Ciprianus. *Augsburg.* Early 17c. crys. cross watch M.P.S. Dresden.
REUTTI, Nicolaus Fridl zu. ——. ca.1700. Book watch.
REVEL—
Joseph. *Paris.* 1775 m.-1789. Mantel clock. rep. cyl. watch mt. C.A. & M. Marble column clock Petit Palais. Clock Nat. M. Stockholm.
——. *Paris.* 1807-18. Succeeded by VENAULT.
REVELL, Samuel. *London.* a.1664.
REVERONY, ——. *Paris.* 1824. C.
REVETT, J. *Eye.* 1790. C. & W.
REVILLE, Jean Baptiste. *Paris.* b.1780.
REVOLLON, ——. *Lyons.* Early 19c. cyl. mus. watch G.M.
REW—
Joseph. *Wyveliscombe.* 2nd half 18c. l.c. clock.
Robert. *London.* an.1780. Watch.
REWALLING, Thomas. *London.* a.1704, CC. 1715. *Ipswich* in 1751. Watch.
REWIS, Stephen. *London.* a.1698.
REY—
Hugues. *Lyons.* 1659 m.-1703.
Antoine. *Geneva.* 1690. From *Dardagny.*
Jean François. *Geneva.* mar.1712, d.1748.
Jean Antoine. *Geneva.* b.1682, d.1787.
LES FRÈRES. *Geneva.* 1712. Firm of the two preceding. Watch Geneva M.
Jacob. *London* (*St. Giles in Fields*). 1720. W.
Thomas. *London.* an.1753. Watch.
Jean Louis. *Geneva.* 18c. Watch Besançon M.
——. *Coppet.* 1750. Watch Den. coll.
Isaac. *London.* ca.1770.
John Anthony. *London.* ca.1770.
Charles. *Paris.* m.1770, juré 1786-9.
Jean Samuel Charles Gabriel. *Geneva.* ca. 1775-91.
Jn. Ant. et fils. *Paris.* Late 18c.-early 19c. Fine 3-case g. en. watch.
Jules. *Paris.* Juré 1788.
Isaac & J. J. ——. Late 18c. Watch.
——. *Paris.* 1825.
ET FLOURNOY. prob. *Paris.* Early 19c. Fine g. en. watch in form of nut.
FRÈRES. *Geneva.* Early 19c. Two g. en. watches M.M.A.
REYBAZ, ——. *Vevey.* 1757 comp.
REYMANN, Benedikt. *Nürnberg.* m.1564. inst. maker.
REYMOND—
Jean. *Lyons.* 1610.
Mathieu. *Rolle.* ca.1740.
Claude. *Montbrison.* 1745. Clock for Priory of St. Romain-le-Puy.

REYMOND—*continued.*
——. *Charleston, U.S.A.* 1785. From *Paris.* C. & W.
——. *Bienne.* Early 19c. Copper en. watch Fränkel coll.
S. *Geneva.* ca.1825. Very thin g. watch M.M.A.

REYMOND-BERTRAND, F. *Paris.* ca. 1835. From *Le Chenit.* Devised a keyless winding and setting mech.

REYMONDET, César. *St. Claude.* 1771.

REYNIER, François Xavier. *Chaux-de-Fonds.* 1784.

REYNOLDS—
George. *York.* 1641-80. W.
Alban. *London.* a.1670.
Joseph. *London.* a.1683, CC.1691.
Thomas. *London (Noble St.* and later *St. Martin's-le-Grand).* a.1696, CC.1706-1737. br. clock.
Francis. *London.* a.1697.
& EARLE. *Oxford.* 1720-95. C.
William. *Sombourne.* an.1727. Watch.
James. *London.* a.1715.
Robert. *London.* a.1717.
Thomas, son of Thos. *London (St. Martin's-le-Grand).* CC.1736. Watch and mt. G.M.
John. *Hagburn.* 1732.
Charles. *London.* an.1758. Watch.
Anthony. *London.* a.1738.
Thomas. *Warwick.* an.1759-95. Watch Den. coll.
Thomas. *Oxford.* 1758-70. C.
William. *Warwick.* 1759-95. l.c. clock.
John. *Leeds.* 1761. Bankrupt.
John. *London.* a.1753.
Henry. *London.* a.1753.
John. *London.* a.1754.
James. *London (Fleet Mkt. & Holborn Hill).* CC. 1766, l.CC.1767, d.1799.
Francis. *London.* 1776.
Joshua. *Coventry.* an.1781-95. Watch.
John. *St. Ives (Hunts.).* 1795.
Thomas. *London.* 1817-24. W.
Michael. *Longford.* 1824.
Joseph. *Liverpool.* 1825. W.

RHEINSTEIN, Caspar. *Neustadt-a.-d.-Saale.* m.1791.

RHEITA, Antonius Maria. *Schirlei.* 1642. astro. clock.

RHETORICK, Walter. *London.* a.1651.

RHODENHURST, William. *London.* a.1768, CC.1776-1820.

RHODES—
William. *London.* a.1755, CC.1762.
Manoah. *Bradford.* Early 19c. Watch.

RHYNE, ——. *Strasbourg.* an.1821. Watch.

RIACH, Hugh. *London.* ca.1790-1808. br. clock ill. Cec. & Web.

RIALZ, George. *Geneva.* ca.1800. Worked for JAQUET-DROZ ET LESCHOT.

RIAM, ——. *London.* Mid. 18c. Watch.

'RIAULDIEZ.' *London.* ca.1750. Sig. on g. repoussé watch.

RIAULT, ——. *Rouen.* 1740. Expert on clock of St. Maclou.

RIBARD (RIBAR, RIBARS)—
Thomas. *Blois.* mar.1603-33. Very fine en. watch Louvre. en. watch Blot-Garnier coll.
T. *Paris.* 1st half 17c. Perhaps same as preceding. Oval watch Pal. du Cinquantenaire, Brussels.
Antoine, son of Thomas. *Blois.* b.1608-37.
Jean. *Avignon.* 1689-93. Keeper of town clock.

RIBARDO, ——. prob. *London.* an.1726. Watch.

RIBOULEAU, Lason. *London.* a.1736, CC. 1746-62.

RICAUD, Isaac. *France.* Mid. 17c. oval crys. watch.

RICCARD, Richard. *London.* 1675. Watch.

RICE—
James. *London.* a.1738. Watch.
John. *Prescot.* 1765. W.
Joseph. *Baltimore.* 1784. C. & W. Entered into partnership with Standish BARRY in 1785.
Benjamin. *Neath.* b.1757, d.1813. W.
Thomas. *London.* a.1792, CC.1800.
Joseph T. *Albany, U.S.A.* 1813-23.
William. *London.* 1820.

RICH—
William. *London (Gt. Wild St.).* 1727-77.
John. *London.* 1735-75. Watch M.M.A. g. en. watches Den. and Fränkel colls.
Thomas. *London.* 1st half 18c. Watch.
William, son of Wm. *London (Gt. Wild St.).* 1770.
William, son. *London.* a.1770.
Thomas. *London.* a.1770.
& HOLLEY. *London.* an.1780. Watch.
T. *Cheltenham.* 1788-1810. br. clock.
Charles. *London.* a.1787.
Edward. *London.* a.1792.
John. *Bristol, U.S.A.* ca.1800. Wooden clocks.
Abraham. *Bridgewater.* Early 19c. Watch.

RICHARD—
Robert. *Vufflens-le-Château* (near *Morges*). 1595. From *Paris.*
——. *Paris.* m.1616.
David. *Neuchâtel.* 1660-7. Repaired town clocks.
Peter. *London.* CC.1679. French. W.
Js. *Le Locle.* 1st half 18c. Watch.
Jean Jacques. *Le Locle.* 1740-66. W. of repute.
FRÈRES. *Le Locle.* 1742.
F. *Paris.* 2nd half 18c. g. en. watch.
Christophe. *Paris.* 1750 m.-1789. Repaired clock on La Samaritaine.
François. *Vevey.* 1761-1798.
Jean Louis. *Geneva.* ca.1775-91.
François. *Hamburg.* ca.1780. Watches S.K.M. and Fränkel coll.
Samuel Théophile. *Vevey.* m.1786.
Louis. *Le Locle.* 1812-75.
——. *Paris.* 1812.
Etienne. *Berlin.* 1812. Clock.
Auguste. *Rouen.* ca.1830. Watch M.M.A., with letters of owner's name instead of hour figures.
v. JEANRICHARD-DIT-BRESSEL.

RICHARDET, ——. *Luneville.* 1736. aut. with singing birds.

RICHARDS—
Luke. *London.* CC.1646-62.
Richard. *London.* CC.1652. Watch.
John. *London.* a.1654-62 CC.
Henry. *London.* a.1688, CC.1699-1703. Watch.
Robert. *London.* a.1691.
Hugh. *London.* a.1701, CC.1709, m.CC. 1735-48. Also RICHARDSON.
John. *London.* a.1733, CC.1770-99. Watches G.M., Wakefield M. and Den. coll.
——. *Wisbech.* an.1752. Watch.
Frederick. *London.* a.1749-69. Insolvent. Watch.
John. *Worcester.* In 1761 went to *Monmouth.* W.
Thomas. *Clapham.* 2nd half 18c. Watch.
James. *London.* a.1752.
James. *London.* a.1763, CC.1770.
Thomas. *London.* a.1764-72.
Edward. *Dolgelly.* prob. mar.1786. l.c. clocks.
Charles. ——. ca.1790. Watch Den. coll.
E. *Guernsey.* ca.1790 CC.
William. *London (Old St.).* a.1773-99.
Isaac. *Birmingham.* 1801-08. W. & C.

RICHARDS—*continued.*
Thomas. *London* (*Bridgewater Sq.*). 1802-1825. W. br. clock by him or Thomas, below, ill. Cec. & Web.
John Frederick. *London* (*Chiswick*). 1805-1808.
Thomas. *New York.* 1805. W.
James. *London.* 1806.
Thomas. *London* (*City Rd.*). 1809-11. W.
W. & S.R. *Philadelphia.* 1819-25. W.
Thomas, jun. *London* (*Bridgewater Sq.* and, later, *Shoreditch*). 1820-35.

RICHARDSON—
William. *London.* a.1647.
Richard. *London.* a.1667, CC.1675.
Richard. *London.* a.1677.
Hugh. *London.* a.1691.
Henry. *London.* ca.1700. l.c. lacquer clock ill. Cec. & Web.
Moses. *London.* ca.1700.
Hugh. *v.* RICHARDS.
John. *Hexham.* 1710. l.c. clock.
Thomas. *London.* 1723. Insolvent.
Josiah. *Chester.* 1732. W.
Charles. *London.* CC.1739.
John. *London* (*Bell Yd.*). a.1731, CC.1738, d.1774.
Richard. *Aston.* 1756. C.
Charles. *London.* a.1749, CC.1760.
——. *Dublin.* an.1764. Watch.
William. *Alloa.* 1769-90.
——. *Brampton.* ca.1770.
James. *Helmsley.* ca.1770.
James. *Luton* and *London.* CC.1770, m.CC. 1788, d.1808.
Thomas Kelly. *London* (*Fore St.*). a.1767, CC.1775-82.
William. *London.* an.1778. Watch.
Richard. *Liverpool.* ca.1780-1803. l.c. clock. W.
T. *Darlington.* 1783. Watch. C.
——. *Howden.* Late 18c. Watch.
Thomas. *Weaverham.* 1795. C.
John. *London.* 1798. CC.1807.
Henry. *London.* a.1793.
William. *Paisley.* 1801.
George. *Edinburgh.* 1802.
Thomas. *Manchester.* 1804. C.
B. *London.* an.1808. Watch.
Henry. *London.* CC.1813.
Thomas. *Brampton.* 1815. W.
William. *Nottingham.* 1818. C. & W.

RICHE, John. *Frampton.* 1524-44.
RICHELET, ——. *Paris.* 1820-5.
RICHER, Jean. *Paris.* 1672, mém. Acad. des Sciences. Found secs. pendulum had to be 5/4 ligne shorter in Cayenne than in Paris.

RICHMOND—
John. *London.* a.1711.
James. *Bradford.* ca.1770-95.
Thomas. *London.* an.1784. Watch.
Joseph. *York.* 1810-23. C.
Robert. *Lancaster.* 1817. W.

RICHMORY, T. *London.* an.1784. Watch.

RICHOT—
——. *Paris.* ca.1745 m.
Merlin Perron. *Paris.* m.1754.

RICHSON, John. prob. *London.* an.1778. Watch.

RICHTER—
Felix Jacob. *Nürnberg.* Late 17c. Gilt en. rep. watch. Wall clock Feill coll. sd. RICHTER prob. by him.
——. *Geneva.* b.1766, d.1841. Famous painter on enamel.
C. W. *Hamburg.* 1821.

RICKABEY, Robert Pemmel. *London.* a.1759.

RICKARD—
John. *London.* a.1649, CC.1657.
John. *Exeter.* ca.1760-95. Watch Exeter M.

RICKEL, Richard. *Augsburg.* a.1776.

RICKETTS—
James. *Pershore.* ca.1750. Sheepshead clock.
Thomas. *High Wycombe.* 1757. W.
John. *London.* a.1761.
William. *London.* 1820.

RICKMAN, William. *London.* 1820.
RICORD, Richard. *London.* CC.1649-64.
RIDDEL, Charles. *Old Meldrum.* 1800-37.

RIDDLESDON—
William. *London.* an.1765. Watch.
Samuel. *London.* CC.1766-77.

RIDEL (RIDELLE), ——. *Paris.* ca.1800. Mantel clocks Pal. de Fontainebleau and Gemeente M., The Hague. Clock in cabinet Virginia M.

RIDER—
Thomas. *London.* a.1691, CC.1698-1717.
Benjamin. *London.* a.1731.
Richard. *London.* a.1735.
Job. *Belfast.* 1791-1808. Watch. Partner with R. L. GARDNER 1805-07, and with William BOYD after 1807.
W. *Welshpool.* 1792. l.c. clocks.
William. *Liverpool.* 1800-03. W.
Peter. *Weidhofen-a.-d.-Thaya.* Early 19c. g. watch.

RIDEREAU, Simon. *Paris.* m.1737-70. Clock str. hours and quarters and rep. all with the same train, approved by the Acad. des Sci. Planetary clock going a year. Turret clocks. Pub. a pamphlet on equation clocks, Paris, 1770.
RIDGDALE, N. ——. ca.1610. Oval watch S.K.M.
RIDGEWAY, John. *London.* a.1752.
RIDIER, ——. *Paris.* ca.1800. Clock.

RIDLEY—
Josiah. *London.* a.1677, CC.1685-93. l.c. clock.
Joseph. ——. 1788. Pub. art. in Trans. Soc. Arts, Vol. 6, on a sector depthing tool.
Thomas. *London.* a.1790.

RIDOU, ——. *Paris.* 1812.
RIEBE, ——. *Ohlau.* 1718. Completed the Rathaus clock.
RIED, Jacob von. *Berne.* b.1560-87. C. to the town.
RIÉDER, Alexandre. *Vevey.* 1798 m.
RIEDIG, ——. *Leipzig.* Early 19c. Watch M.P.S. Dresden.

RIEDL—
——. *Vienna.* 1680.
Philipp. *Vienna.* m.1759.
Joseph. *Vienna.* m.1765. g. rep. watch Den. coll. Also RIDL.
Joseph. *Linz-a.-D.* 1810-30.

RIEFF, Franz Antoni. *Passau.* 2nd half 18c. br. clocks Stuttgart and Furt. M.
RIEFLER, Sigmund. *Munich.* b.1847. Famous maker of observatory clocks with special escapement. Devised a lever esc. for watches, with the lever attached to one end of the balance spring. Many publications.
RIEGE, Georg. *Nürnberg.* d.1700. inst. maker.
RIEL, Johan. *Stadtamhof.* 1st half 18c. p.c. sil. and tortoise-shell rep. watch Feill coll.
RIEPPOLT (RIEBOLD), Johann S. *Regensburg.* m. in *Augsburg* 1727, juré 1735-59, d.an.1770. g. en. watch. Fine watch Rijks M. Amsterdam.
RIEUSSEC, ——. *Paris.* 1807-25. Well-known maker. Invented chronograph making ink mark on dial. chron. C.A. & M.
RIFAUT, ——. *Paris.* 1809-25.

RIGAUD—
Gedeon. *London.* ca.1700. Watch.
Pierre. *Geneva.* ca.1780. g. en. watch, set diamonds.
Gédéon. *Paris.* End 18c. 4-colour g. watch Fränkel coll.

RIGAULT—
Thomas. *La Rochelle.* mar.1617. *Blois,* 1619. d.1627.
Paul. *Blois.* comp. 1619, d.ca.1638. C. to the duc d'Orléans.
Paul, son. *Blois.* 1661-92. C. to the duc d'Orléans.

RIGBY—
Nicholas. *Ormskirk.* 1754. W.
Joshua. *London.* 1765. CC.1781-1820.
Henry. *Liverpool.* 1774. d.1787. W.
Edward. *London.* an.1778. Watch.
Thomas Gillingham. *London.* a.1775.
Elizabeth, & Son. *London.* 1799.
Thomas. *London* (*Pentonville*). 1791-1815.
James. *London* (*Pentonville*). 1791. C. & W.
James. *London* (*Clerkenwell*). 1795-1808. Succeeded LEROUX in 1808 at Charing Cross -1830. g. en. watch, set diamonds and pearls, Lincoln M. g. rep. str. duplex watch.
James. *Liverpool.* 1813-29. W.
Joseph. *Liverpool.* 1821-9. W.

RIGG—
William. *London.* a.1711. Watch.
John. *London.* a.1732.
John. *Guisborough.* ca.1750. Watch mt. Buckley coll.

RIGGS, William H. C. *Philadelphia.* 1819-25.

RIGHTON, James. *Rochdale.* ca.1820.

RIGOULE, fils. *Paris.* 1772.

RIHER, Anton. *Vienna.* m.1790.

RIHLL, William. *Moreton.* 18c. l.c. clock.

RIIS, Ole. *Christiania.* 1776 m.

RILEY—
George. *London* (*Clerkenwell*). a.1715-59.
James. *London.* CC.1752.
Patrick. prob. *London.* an.1769. Watch.
John. *Philadelphia.* 1783-1808. C. & W.
Gillingham. *Halifax.* 1797. Insolvent. From *Skircoat.*
Riley. *New York.* 1805. W.
Robert. *Philadelphia.* 1806-08. W.
G. O. *Dublin.* Early 19c. Watch Dublin M.
J. *Leicester.* 1815. C. & W.

RILLIET, ——. *Strasbourg.* ca.1760.

RIMAUD, Jean Pierre. *Paris.* m.1778.

RIMBAULT—
John Stephen. *London* (*Gt. St. Andrew's St.*). 1744-85. mus. clock Ashmolean M. Clock Brunswick M. br. clock ill. Britten. l.c. clock, Adam case, for Spain. br. clock of French type. br. clock Feill coll. rep. clock Peiping M.
Paul. *London* (*Denmark St.*). 1770-85. mus. clock Peiping M.

RIMES, William. *London.* a.1708.

RIMMER, Robert. *Liverpool.* 1825. W.

RIMOND, Charles. *Geneva.* ca.1755-72.

RINDERLE, Thaddäus. *Freiburg-i.-Br.* b. 1748, d.1834. Prof. of Mathematics. Devoted himself to furthering the clockmaking industry in the Schwarzwald. astro. clock Furt. M.

RING, John. *London.* a.1686, CC.1693.

RINGIUS—
Andr. *Karlskrona.* b.1785, d.1811.
D. E. *Karlskrona.* 1820. Watch.

RINGLER, ——. *Antwerp.* ca.1715. Watch Ilbert coll.

RINNDUD, *v.* RUMDUD.

RINSES, Sipke. *Grouw.* 1792. d.1830. aut. clock.

RIPERT—
Bernard. *Paris.* ca.1760.
Veuve. *Paris.* 1789.

RIPLEY—
John. *York.* 1471.
William. *London.* an.1773. Watch.

RIPON, Martin. *Blois.* comp. 1619.

RIPPON—
Richard. *London* (*King St., Seven Dials*). 1810-24. Teacher of E. J. DENT. Made rep. mechanisms. Watch mt. G.M.
William Frederick, son. *London.* a.1822, CC.1831. Experimented with glass springs for chrons.

RISBRIDGER, William. *Dorking.* ca.1700. Lantern clock and l.c. clock Virginia M.

RISDON, Francis. *London.* an.1744. Watch.

RISING—
Olof. *Stockholm,* a.1732. *Göteborg,* 1747. d. 1783. Watch and l.c. clock.
Nils. *Stockholm,* b.1722. *Göteborg,* 1756. d. 1784. l.c. lacquer clock.

RISLEY, William. *London.* a.1790.

RISOAN, Valentine. *London.* a.1748.

RISOLIERE, Isaac. *London.* a.1749, CC. 1756-64. d.an.1795.

RITCHIE—
Peter. *Edinburgh.* 1749.
John. *Edinburgh.* a.1765.
Samuel. *Cupar-Fife.* 1800-37.
James. *Edinburgh.* 1805-42.
David. *London.* 1812. Devised a compensation pendulum.

RITHE, John. *London.* a.1654.

RITHERDON, George. *London.* 1753-83. sil. watch Horstmann coll.

RITTELMEYER, ——. *Berlin.* 1769.

RITTENHOUSE, David. *Norristown, U.S.A.,* 1751-70. *Philadelphia,* 1770-7. Complex astro. clock Univ. of Pennsylvania. Pub. art. in Trans. American Phil. Soc., Vol. IV, on the improvement of timekeepers, 1801.

RITTER, J. Louis. *Geneva.* 1754-ca.1790. 4-colour g. watch.

RITTERBAND, H. *Bristol.* 1825-30.

RIVAL—
David. *Geneva.* b.1696, d.an.1770.
Jean Pierre, son. *Geneva.* ca.1750. Went to *Versoix,* 1770.
Jean Jaques Antoine Louis. *Geneva.* ca.1775-1791.
Ct. *Geneva.* Early 19c. g. en. rep. watch with pearls Gélis coll.

RIVAZ—
Pierre Joseph de. *Paris.* 1748. d.ca.1770. An eminent mechanician, but not actually a clockmaker, though he wrote a memoir on clocks, attacking Pierre Le Roy (Paris, 1750). Designed a clock remontoir and many clocks, including year clocks. Granted a privilege by the King for his discoveries, which was opposed by the Paris Corporation. Went to London to try for the prize for marine chrons. without success. They were tried in France after his death. Three clocks C.A. & M.
——. *Vevey.* 1757 comp.

RIVERS—
David. *London* (*Bridgewater Sq.*). a.1745, CC.1753-75.
David, son. *London* (*Sweetings Alley*). l.CC. 1766, m.CC.1773, d.1815. Watch.
Jacob John. *London* (*Holborn*). 1764-75 CC. W.
Thomas. *London.* an.1769. Watch.
William. *London.* CC.1770, m.CC.1794, d. 1820. br. clock. 3-case g. watch M.M.A. p.c. g. watch Fränkel coll.
David. *London* (*Lombard St.*). 1775. Sale of stock.
David. *London.* a.1769.
William. *London.* CC.1776, m.CC.1801-20.
John. *London.* an.1774-85. Watch.
Thomas, son of J. J. *London.* a.1775, CC. 1784.
James. *London.* a.1777.
& SON. *London* (*Cornhill*). 1782-1815. Succeeded DE ST. LEU.

RIVERS—*continued.*
Samuel. *London.* CC.1785.
David, & Son. *London.* 1785-99.
David. *London.* CC.1789-95.
'RIVERSIDE.' Sig. on watches of the AMERICAN WATCH Co. from 1877.
RIVIER, Willem Janze. *Haarlem.* 1697.
RIVIÈRE—
Lubin. *Blois.* m.1670, d.1694.
Jean. *Blois.* m.1670.
Daniel. *London.* a.1732.
Jacob. *London (Marylebone).* a.1746, CC. 1756, d.1815.
& William SMITH. *London (Cavendish Sq.).* ca.1770. T.C. Firm with Jacob.
Samuel Newton. *London (New Bond St.).* an.1784-1811. W.
Charles. *London.* CC.1815.
RIVOIRE, Henri. *Geneva.* ca.1775-90.
RIVONNEAU, Joseph. *Paris.* Juré 1784.
RIX, ——. *London.* ca.1750. Clock and watch.
RIZIO, ——. *Florence.* 1500-03. Repaired Lugano clock. Locksmith.
ROACH—
——. *Bristol.* an.1753. Watch.
William. *New York.* 1783. Watch.
ROAST, John. *London.* a.1805.
ROBART, Achilles. *London.* 1610. C.
ROBB, William. *Montrose.* 1776. l.c. clock.
ROBBINS, ——. *Canterbury.* Early 19c. Watch.
ROBERDEAU, ——. *London.* 1712. W.
ROBERT—
Abram. *Le Locle.* 1666.
Josué. *Chaux-de-Fonds.* b.1691, d.1771. A famous C. C. to the King of Prussia from 1725. Founder of firm J. ROBERT ET FILS. Many clocks.
Jacques. *Cortaillod.* 1716-22.
David, son of Josué. *Chaux-de-Fonds.* b. 1717, d.1769. 'Très expert horloger'; made 'Toutes sortes de pendules curieuses.' Many clocks signed 'Robert l'aîné.'
Louis Benjamin, bro. *Chaux-de-Fonds.* b. 1732, d.1781. C. of repute.
Abel. *La Brévine.* 1740-2.
Théodore. *Chaux-de-Fonds.* 1745. d.1775. Able C.
Abram. *Chaux-de-Fonds.* 1750-4. *Basle,* 1759.
Abram Louis. *Chaux-de-Fonds.* 1756-87. C. Said to have invented the depth tool.
Antoine. *Paris.* m.1763.
Frédéric. *Chaux-de-Fonds.* a.1757-86. C.
Aimé, son of Louis B. *Chaux-de-Fonds.* b. 1758, d.1834. Member of firm J. ROBERT ET FILS, *Chaux-de-Fonds.*
Claude Alexandre. *Paris.* m.1767-89.
Nicolas. *Paris.* m.1769-89.
Jean Pierre. *Chaux-de-Fonds.* 1781. Associate of J. ROBERT ET FILS.
le justicier. *Chaux-de-Fonds.* 1782. mus. clocks.
J., ET FILS, COURVOISIER ET CIE. Name taken by firm of J. ROBERT ET FILS in 1787 by association with Louis COURVOISIER. Changed to ROBERT, COURVOISIER ET CIE in 1805 and to COURVOISIER ET CIE in 1811.
& COURVOISIER. *Geneva.* 1790-1800. g. en. shell watch. c.secs. watch Den. coll. Watch Feill coll. with the arms of a figure indicating hours and mins. on pressing a knob.
François. *Switzerland* and *Besançon.* 1798-1815. A maker of repute.
Amadeus. *Chaux-de-Fonds.* 1798.
& COMP. *Paris.* ca.1800. cal. watch Feill coll. Watch, virgule esc. Ilbert coll.
& COURVOISIER. *Paris.* ca.1800. Watch Glasgow Art Gall. Also *Chaux-de-Fonds.* 1805-16. en. rep. watch.

ROBERT—*continued.*
Benjamin. *Paris.* 1819-25.
Veuve Amiet. *Paris.* 1821-5.
J. L. *Geneva.* ca.1825. g. en. cyl. watch.
Louis. *Switzerland.* 1824-30. C. Several chiming clocks.
Sylvain. *Ponts de Martel.* b.1798. Enameller. Famous for minute lettering on dials.
Henri. *Paris.* b.1794, d.1874. An eminent maker. Pub. 'L'Art de connaître les pendules et les montres,' Paris, 1841, 1849 and 1867, and 'Études sur diverses questions d'horlogerie,' Paris, 1852, and many mem. in the Revue Chronométrique and elsewhere. cal. watch Ilbert coll.
ROBERT-HOUDIN, *v.* HOUDIN.
ROBERTS—
John. *Dorchester.* 1639-50. Keeper of town clock.
William. *London.* 1637. Watch. Small lantern clock.
Richard. *London.* a.1653.
Hugh. *London.* a.1657, CC.1664-1716. astro. watch B.M. Also ROBARTES.
William. *London.* a.1692.
John. *London.* a.1712.
Edward. *London.* a.1719.
John. *Chester.* 1732. W.
James. *London.* a.1733.
John. *Derby.* From 1751. C. & W.
Henry. prob. *London.* an.1755. Watch.
Samuel. *Llanfair Caereinion.* 1755, d.1800. Many l.c. clocks.
John. *London (St. James's Mkt.).* 1756-90. Watch.
Isaac. *London (Compton St.).* 1762. d.1774. Watch Den. coll.
Timothy. *Otley.* ca.1770-95. l.c. clocks. Watch.
John. *London (Mays Bdgs.).* a.1764, CC. 1771.
Samuel. *London.* an.1767-76. Watch.
F. prob. *London.* an.1774. Watch.
Jacob. *London.* an.1776. Watch.
John. *Trawsfynydd.* 1774-1845.
John, son of Sam. (2). *London.* CC.1776.
William. *London.* a.1771.
Ellis. *London.* a.1771.
Gideon. *Bristol, U.S.A.* b.1749, d.1813. Wooden clocks.
B. *London.* an.1781. Watch.
William. *London (St. James's Mkt.).* 1784-1825.
John. *Bristol.* 1787. W.
John. *Ruabon.* 1760. *Wrexham* from 1764. l.c. clock.
John. *Carnarvon.* b.1763.
John. *Holyhead.* 1791. l.c. clock.
John. *Bury St. Edmunds.* 1791. W.
John. *Dartmouth.* 1791-5. W.
John. *London.* a.1785.
Edward. *London.* a.1785.
Josiah. *London.* 1793. g. watch F.W.M.
John. *Philadelphia.* 1799.
Noah. *London.* a.1794.
John. *London (Clerkenwell).* CC.1805-20.
Robert. *Liverpool.* 1805-10. W.
James. *London (Adelphi).* 1805-08.
James. *London (Leicester Sq.).* 1809-11.
Jacob. *Easton, U.S.A.* 1810-30.
Piercy. *London (Blackfriars).* CC.1816.
George. *London.* 1820.
James. *London (Borough).* 1820.
John. *Burnley.* ca.1820.
William. *Bath.* 1825.
Piercy Price Hart, son of Piercy. *London.* a. 1818.
S. *Kingston (Surrey).* Early 19c.
R. *Bangor.* Early 19c. Watch.
S. *London.* Early 19c. Watch. Perhaps Sam. above.

ROBERTSON—
John. *Chester*. 1712. W.
David. *Edinburgh*. a.1741.
William. *London*. an.1755. Watch
William. *Edinburgh*. a.1749.
James. *Edinburgh*. a.1752-8.
George. prob. *London*. an.1764. Watch.
William. *Edinburgh*. 1764-80.
Patrick. *Perth*. 1765.
Thomas. *London*. an.1769. Watch.
Robert. *London*. an.1776. Watch.
James. *Perth*. a.1770.
John. *Edinburgh*. 1783-1821.
James. *Dundee*. 1785.
——. *London*. ca.1790.
W. *Edinburgh*. 1791.
Ebenezer. *Glasgow*. 1801.
Robert. *Glasgow*. 1802-28.
William. *Dundee*. 1803.
George. *Dundee*. 1806.
George. *Edinburgh*. a.1802.
James. *Dundee*. 1811-28.
James. *Edinburgh*. a.1806.
Charles. *Coupar-Angus*. 1814-37.
James. *Leith*. 1818-36.
Robert. *Perth*. 1825-37.
George. *London*. a.1823.
Charles. *London*. a.1823.
James. *Sydney*. Early 19c.

ROBERT-THEURER, Édouard. *Chaux-de-Fonds*. b.1793, d.1877. Great grandson of Josué ROBERT.

ROBERT-TISSOT, Abram. *Le Locle* and *Chaux-de-Fonds*. 1630. d.1668.

ROBESON, William. *Newcastle-o.-T*. ca. 1800.

ROBILIÈRE, ——. *Paris*. 1812.

ROBILLARD, ——. *Paris*. 1822-5. C.

ROBIN—
Robert. *Paris*. b.1742, d.1809. A famous maker. C. to Louis XV and XVI, to the Queen, and, in 1795, to the République. Devised a pin wheel lever esc. for watches. Watch G.M. g. cyl. watch M.M.A. br. and l.c. clocks S.K.M. Clock Wallace coll. Regulator mean and solar time C.A. & M. Decimal watch of 1794 and lever rep. watch C.A. & M. Watch Ilbert coll. with esc. invented by him in 1791 and desc. in a pamphlet pub. Paris, 1794. Very fine geographical mantel clock, with gridiron pendulum, Louvre. Mantel clock made for Marie Antoinette, Palais de Trianon. Mantel clock Palais de Fontainebleau. Skeleton clock Louvre. Turret clock Palais de Trianon going a week. Wrote several memoirs on remontoirs, turret clocks and an observatory decimal clock.
——. *Paris* (*Rue de Richelieu*). ca.1790-1825. C. to Louis XVIII. Mantel clock Mobilier National, Paris.
Joseph. *Paris* (*Rue St. Honoré*). 1807-17.
Fils aîné. Paris (*Rue St. Honoré*). 1812.

ROBINET—
Charles. *Paris*. 1640.
Pierre. *Paris*. 1776 m., juré 1778-1812.

ROBINS—
Fabian. *London*. End 17c. l.c. clock New York University. Chiming br. clock. Watch. Also ROBBIN.
Joseph. *London*. a.1694.
Thomas. *London*. a.1723.
Thomas. *London* (*Aldermanbury*). a.1763, CC.1774. Watch.
William. *London*. CC.1779, m.CC.1815, d.1816.
& UNDERWOOD. *London*. 1795. Dissolved partnership.
John. *London* (*Leicester Sq.*). 1795-9. Partner in the preceding.
Joshua. *London* (*Bow*). a.1791, CC.1808-20. W.

ROBINS—*continued.*
John. *London* (*Charing Cross*). 1814-24. cyl. watch Ilbert coll.
John. *London* (*Frith St.*). 1825.

ROBINSON—
George. *London*. a.1631.
Robert. *London*. a.1645, CC.1652-6. Lantern clock.
William. *London*. a.1655, CC.1667-88.
Francis. *London*. a.1672.
Daniel. *London*. a.1681-ca.1710. l.c. clock ill. Cec. & Web.
John, son of Wm. *London*. a.1682.
Francis. *London* (*Inner Temple La.*). a.1685, CC.1707, m.CC.1725-47. rep. watch G.M. Watch Den. coll. br. clock. W. to the Prince of Wales.
Thomas. *London*. a.1691, CC.1703-16.
John. *London*. a.1698.
Ruhamer. *London* (*Gracechurch St.*). CC. 1713-59. str. watch Ilbert coll.
William. *London*. a.1709, CC.1720-45.
Oliver. *London*. a.1720, CC.1727.
Thomas, son of Thos. *London*. a.1721.
James. *London* (*Grace's Alley*). 1730-70. T.C. Watch Den. coll.
John. *London* (*Westminster*). 1730-55. Advertised that he had invented a watch that will go much truer than any other, upon account the friction is 3 parts in 4 taken away. Gold watches 21 guineas, jewelled 24 guineas.
Israel. *London*. 1731. W.
——. *Gosport*. an.1744. Watch.
Henry. *London*. a.1724, CC.1733-9.
William. *London*. a.1739.
Thomas, son of Wm. *London*. a.1745-80. Watch S.K.M.
George. *London*. an.1760. Watch. cf. Geo. below.
Samuel. *Malmesbury*. To 1766. comp. C.
& VENABLES. *London* (*Westminster*). an. 1769. Watch.
Joseph. *London* (*Holborn* and *Old St.*). a. 1750, CC.1769-96.
William. *London*. a.1758.
Dolly. *Sheffield*. an.1777. Watch.
Owen. *London* (*Lambeth*). 1780-1810. Escapement maker.
John. *Lancaster*. 1783-95.
Samuel. *London*. CC.1785.
Thomas. *Bath*. 1787.
Thomas. *Liverpool*. 1790-1829. W.
Matthew. *London*. 1790. mt. maker.
Joseph. *Dewsbury*. 1791. C. & W.
Thomas. *Staines*. 1795. W.
William. *Liverpool*. 1795-1824. Lever watch Chamb. coll. Watch N.Y. Univ.
Charles. *Liverpool*. 1796. W.
William. *Huddersfield*. ca.1800. Watch mt. Huddersfield M.
J. *London*. ca.1800.
Benjamin. *Manchester*. 1800-14 W.
George. *London*. 1806. Watch Chamb. coll. cf. Geo. above.
Thomas, son of Owen. *London*. a.1800, CC. 1812. Watch.
Martin. *London*. CC.1812.
James. *Warrington*. ca.1820.
Thomas R. *Liverpool*. ca.1820.
Thomas. *Sheffield*. 1821. C. & W.
Andrew. *Galway*. 1824.
Joseph. *Clones*. 1824.
——. *Brigg*. Early 19c.

ROBISON, John. ——. 1822. Pub. 'A System of Mechanical Philosophy,' Edinburgh, containing a treatise on Watch work.

ROBOTHAM—
Francis Jonathan. *Hampstead*. ca.1790 CC.-1824.
Charles. *Leicester*. 1791. C. & W.

ROBOTTOM, William. *Tarporley*. 1770. C.

ROBSON—
William. *London* (*Red Cross St.* and *Bridgewater Sq.*). a.1771, CC.1787, m.CC.1817 and 1819, d.1823. mus. C. Watch mt.
Samuel. *N. Shields.* 1784. Watch.
James. *London* (*New St., Covent Gdn.*). ca. 1785. Clock.
W. *Linton.* 1787.
Michael. *Chester-le-Street.* mar.1803-12. C. & W.
William. *N. Shields.* 1807-20.

ROCHAT—
Jacques, *Brassus.* ca.1760.
LES FRÈRES, sons. *Brassus.* 1773.
Jean Marc David. *Geneva.* ca.1775-91.
Jacob. *London.* 1777-91. Watch.
Jacob Henry, son. *London.* a.1792.
D., et Fils. *Brassus.* 1802-13. Maker of singing birds.
James. *Newcastle-o.-T.* 1804. C. & W.
LES FRÈRES. *Geneva.* 1810-25. Singing birds. Fine makers. sd. 'FR' in a circle. Singing bird snuff-box ill. M. des Aut.
E. *Geneva.* Early 19c.
ET JOSSEAUME. *Geneva.* Early 19c.
Louis. *Brassus.* 1825. Maker of automata. Very fine mus. aut. clock Palace M. Pekin.
——. *Paris.* 1825. mus. clocks.

ROCHE—
Cas. Philippe. *Collonges.* Late 17c. Watch en. Huaut Frères.
E. *Paris.* 1819-25.

ROCHÉ, ——. *Berlin.* 1794.

ROCHLITZ, C. F. *Berlin.* b.1813, d.1891. Fine turret C.

ROCK—
Richard. *Dublin.* 1763. Watch.
William. *Dublin.* an.1768. Watch.
William. *Prescot.* an.1774. Watch.
Patrick. *London.* an.1784. Watch.

ROCKWELL, E. & S. S. *New York.* 1822. W.

ROCQUET—
Dominique. *Paris.* m.1756.
Jacques Martin. *Paris.* m.1759-89.
——. *Paris* (*Rue de Grenelle St. Honoré*). 1807-17. Mantel Clock. Also ROQUET.
Veuve. *Paris.* 1818-20.

RODANET, Julien Hilaire. *Paris.* b.1810, d. 1884. *Paris* 1826-37, and then *Rochefort.* An eminent watch and chron. maker.

RODEN, John. *London.* a.1716.

RODET—
Jacob. *London.* an.1721. Watch.
Isa. *London.* ca.1740. Very fine rep. g. watch M.M.A. Watch, en. portrait on cock, Fränkel coll.

RODGERS—
Benjamin. *Chesterfield.* 1729. Insolvent. C.
William. *Norwich.* 1787. C. & W.

RODIER, Fils. *Paris.* 1812. C.

RODIN ET CIE. ——. Watch with a combination of a lever and Chinese duplex escapement Chamb. coll.

RODY, H. *Limburg.* ca.1800. l.c. clock Furt. M.

ROE—
Joshua. *London.* a.1687.
Nathaniel. *Norwich.* ca.1740.
John. *London.* a.1766.
Richard. *Haslemere.* ca.1780. l.c. clock.
John. *Coventry.* b.1776. In firm of RYLEY, ROE & HILL.
Richard. *Midhurst.* 1791-5. W.
William. *Alton.* 1791-5. C. & W.
James. *Haslemere.* 1797. C. & W.
William. *Midhurst.* an.1821. Watch.

ROEMER—
——. *Alkmaar.* 1498-1536. Keeper of Alkmaar clock.
Olow (Olaf). *Aarhus.* b.1644, d.1710. astro. clocks. Recommended the epicycloid for spur and the cycloid for crown wheels. Made planetarium on Copernican system and another showing eclipses, both in Copenhagen M.

ROFFEL, ——. *Môtiers.* 1766.

ROGER—
——. *Barnstaple.* 1424. Repaired Exeter Cathedral clock.
François. *Rouen.* 1592. Keeper of town clock.
Pierre. *Angers.* ca.1600-26. Re-made cathedral clock in 1626. Oval watch Bourges M.
Jacques. *Lyons.* mar.1643-83 juré. Also ROGIER and ROUGIER.
Charles. *Paris.* m.1760-8.
William. *Stonehaven.* 1820.
v. Markwick MARKHAM.

ROGERET, Thinoman. *France.* 1396. Made clock of Châteauneuf for the duc d'Orléans.

ROGERS—
William. *London.* CC.1640-62.
Charles. *London.* a.1649, CC.1657-78.
Charles, son. *London.* a.1677.
William. *London.* a.1682.
William Christopher. *London.* a.1713 to Edw. EAST.
John. *London.* a.1715, CC.1732.
Thomas. *Bath.* 1742. d.1781. C. & W.
Isaac. *London.* 1748-76. g. repoussé watch B.M.
John. *London.* a.1747. Watch.
Thomas. *London.* a.1754, CC.1763.
Thomas. *Bristol.* d.1781.
Stephen. *London* (*Fenchurch St.*). 1765.
John. *Leominster.* an.1767, d.1778. Watch.
Robert. *Bristol.* 1767-90.
Isaac, son of Isaac. *London* (*Gracechurch St.*). b.1754, CC.1776, m.CC.1813, d.1839. A maker of great repute. Watch S.M.S.K. Two watches M.M.A. rep. watch Den. coll. br. clock with aut.
Thomas, & SON. *Bath.* 1776.
Lawrence. *Llanhilleth.* 1776. W.
William. *Bristol.* 1778-81.
James, bro. of John. *Leominster.* 1778-95.
Mary, widow of John. *Leominster.* 1778-95. Carried on John's business with James.
David. *Saffron Walden.* b.1757, d.1827.
Robert. *London.* an.1782. Watch.
Thomas. *Jamaica.* 1784. From *London.*
Henry. *Dudley.* ca.1790. l.c. clock.
Thomas. *Devizes.* 1791-5. C. & W.
Allen. *London.* a.1787.
Thomas. *London* (*Dockhead*). 1799-1804.
Thomas. *London* (*Horsleydown*). 1799.
Thomas. *London* (*Charing Cross*). CC.1800, l.CC.1810, d.1816.
Samuel. *London.* a.1792.
William. *London.* a.1793.
J. *London* (*Strand*). 1805-11.
James. *London* (*Dockhead*). 1805-11.
J. *London* (*Charing Cross*). 1808-24.
James. *London* (*Borough*). 1809-11.
James. *London* (*Goswell St.*). 1809-11.
Thomas. *London.* a.1802, CC.1820.
Richard. *Dudley.* Early 19c. Watch.
John. *Alderton.* Early 19c. Watch.
& CLARK. *London.* 1825. Chron., W. & C.
J, & R. *Dudley.* Early 19c.

ROGERSON—
William. *London* (*R. Exchange*). a.1747, CC. 1754, m.CC.1774-8.
Henry. *London* (*Swithin's La.*). 1762. d. 1772. C. & W.
Joshua. *London.* a.1766, CC.1773, l.CC. 1779, d.1782.

ROGET—
Jaques. *Geneva.* b.1728-68.
——. *London.* ca.1750. Dutch type watch Glasgow Art Gall.
——. *Paris.* ca.1770. g. en. watch Stern. coll.

ROGEUX, Alexandre. *Paris.* m.1781.
ROGGEN, Louis Antoine. *Paris.* m.1784-9.
ROGIER, Jean Baptiste. *Paris.* 1746 juré.
ROHR, John A. *Philadelphia.* 1808-13.
ROIAN, Francis. *London.* 1577-83. Born in *France.*
ROIZIN, ——. *Paris.* 1772. C. and maker of jacks.
ROJARD, Jean Daniel. ——. ca.1750-70.
ROLAND, ——. *Lausanne.* Juré 1751.
ROLDT, Gabriel. *Copenhagen.* 1661. Court C.
ROLFE—
Samuel. *London.* 17c. Dial Old Ashmolean M.
James. *London.* a.1719.
Joseph, & SON. prob. *London.* an.1796. Watch.
ROLITT, John. ——. 1812. Watch Oldham M.
ROLL, Georg. *Friedberg* and *Augsburg.* 1566. d.1592. Came from *Liegnitz.* Clockwork globe K.H.M. dated 1588. Clocks in celestial spheres S.K.M. and M.P.S. Dresden by him and J. REINHOLD. Made clocks for Rudolf II and the Dresden Court.
ROLLAND, Jean Joseph. *Geneva.* ca.1775-91.
ROLLE, Isaac Simon. prob. *London.* an.1775.
ROLLET, Veuve. *Paris.* 1822.
ROLLISON, D. *Sheffield.* ca.1790. Watch.
ROLOFF, Friedrich Andreas. *Hamburg.* 1801.
ROLUFF, Erik, *Kristianstad.* d.1724.
ROLYAT, Thomas. prob. *London.* an.1763.
ROMAIN—
Claude. *Carpentras (Avignon).* 1707. Repaired clock of Sorgue.
Pierre Étienne. *Paris.* 1807-11. Bronze worker. Magnificent astro. and mus. bronze mantel clock, Ministère des Affaires étrangères, Paris.
——. *La Brévine.* 1815-20. C.
ROMAN—
François. *Geneva* and *Constance.* In 1785 director of the watch factory at Constance.
MELLY ET ROUX. *Constance.* Late 18c. g. en. watches S.K.M. and Fränkel coll. Watch Feill coll.
BORDIER ET CIE. *Geneva.* Early 19c.
ROMBACH, Johannes. *Glashütte.* ca.1770. Wall clock Furt. M.
ROMBERG, Johann Georg. *Hamburg.* 1801.
ROMEAU, Isaac. *London.* CC.1635-41.
ROMER—
Isaac. *London.* CC.1661.
Thomas. *London* and *Paris.* 1816-24.
ROMETT, William. *London.* a.1650.
ROMEY, ——. *Moudon.* 1735.
ROMIER, Isaac. *London.* 1622. Alien. Prob. ROUMIEU.
ROMIEU, L. *Rouen.* Mid. 17c. sil. watch M.M.A. g. en. watch ill. Britten. Prob. ROUMIEU.
ROMILLY—
Jean. *Paris (Place Dauphine).* b.1714, m. 1752, d.1794. Native of Geneva. A very able watchmaker. Made 8-day and equation watches and in 1755 watches beating seconds. In 1768 made a marine timekeeper, damaged during trial. Made a watch going for a year at a winding. Wrote the technical part of the article on Horlogerie in the 'Encyclopédie Méthodique.' Two watches G.M. rep. watch S.M.S.K. Watch Ashmolean M. 4-colour g. watch S.K.M. Two g. en. watches M.M.A. Watches Chamb. coll., N.Y. Univ., Gotha M. and Fränkel coll. g. en. watches Lincoln M., Den. coll. and M.P.S. Dresden. Carved bloodstone watch Stern. coll. en. watch with engine turning Feill coll. Mantel clock Hofburg, Vienna.

ROMILLY—*continued.*
Peter. *London.* 1769-75. Watch, set stones.
——. *Geneva.* 1823.
ROMLEY, Christopher. *London.* a.1747, CC. 1754.
ROMNEY, Joseph. *London.* a.1657, CC.1664.
RONALDS, Sir Francis. ——. 1815. Wrote two arts. in Phil. Mag. on electric clocks.
RONE, John. *London.* a.1775.
RÖNTGEN, David. *Germany.* b.1743, d.1807. Fine maker of clock cases. Often worked with Peter KINTZING of *Neuwied* as mt. maker. l.c. clock Schloss M. Berlin.
RONTREE, Ralph. *York.* Late 17c. br. clock. Perhaps ROWNTREE.
ROOF, Daniel. *London.* CC.1676-91.
ROOKE—
Joseph. *London.* an.1749. Watch.
John. *London.* 1765. CC.1781-94.
ROOKER—
Richard. *London (W. Smithfield).* a.1685, CC.1694-1735. Watch Ilbert coll.
Richard, son. *London (Chelsea).* CC.1729-1759. Watch. br. clock ill. Cec. & Web.
ROOKES, Barlow. *London.* a.1656, CC.1665, d.an.1680.
ROOKESBY, Robert. *London.* 1684 CC.
ROOKSBY—
John. *York.* 1647. *Hull* an.1691. W. cf. ROUSBY.
——. *Hull.* an.1691. Watch Feill coll. early 18c. sd. ROOKSBY.
ROOTS, Edward. *London.* a.1728.
ROPER—
William. *Lavenham.* In 1766 went to *Hadleigh.* From *London.* C. & W.
——. *Lewes.* an.1769. Watch.
William. *Harwich.* 1783. W. Absconded with watches.
P. R. *London.* ca.1800. br. clock. Watch.
Martin. *Penrith.* 1820-9. Watch.
ROPRAT, Jacques. *Paris.* m.1788.
ROQUE, Jean (Joseph) Léonard. *Paris.* m. 1770-89. Mantel clock C.A. & M. Made turning globes for the King.
RORE, ——. *Vevey.* 1746 comp.
RORMAN, Anton. *Gratz.* 1720.
ROSAT, Frédéric Honoré. *Le Locle,* 1816. *Paris,* 1817. C.
ROSBOTHAM, Daniel. *London.* a.1719.
ROSCOW, Robert. *Liverpool.* 1813-29. Watch N.Y. Univ.
ROSE—
Michael. *London.* a.1663, CC.1676. l.c. clock.
Christopher. *London.* a.1663.
Daniel. *London.* 1685-9 CC.
William. *London.* a.1705. Watch.
Thomas. prob. *London.* an.1731. Watch.
James. *Lichfield.* d.1750.
John. *London.* a.1736, CC.1748. g. watch.
William. *West Derby.* 1747. Watch case maker.
Joseph. *London (Aldersgate).* an.1752-95. Livery Dyers Co. Clock. Watch.
Robert. *Dublin.* an.1752-69. Watch.
& SON. *London.* Mid. 18c. Watch, prob. foreign, Ilbert coll. Clock with Hebrew numerals and watch works Virginia M.
——. *Oxford.* d.1772.
William. *London (Bloomsbury).* a.1752, CC. 1767-1806.
Joseph, & Son. *London (Foster La.).* 1765-1784. T.C. Watch Ilbert coll.
Joseph, jun. *London.* 1775-93. Livery Goldsmiths Co.
Joseph, Son, & PAYNE. *London.* 1790.
William. *Dublin.* Late 18c.
Henry. *Wigan.* ca.1820. Watch.
Thomas. *Wigan.* ca.1820.
Thomas, jun. *Wigan.* ca.1820.

ROSÉ, ——. *Soleure*. 2nd half 18c. Watch with very large balance S.M.S.K.
ROSEDALE, George. *Liverpool*. 1825. W.
ROSÉE—
Christian. *Nürnberg*. 1790. en. watch.
Johann Christoffle. *Nürnberg*. 1790. Watch Stuttgart M.
ROSENBERG, Christian. *Eskilstuna*. 1793. l.c. clock.
ROSENBUSCH, Adolph. *Ansbach*. 1733. Made burgher. From *Barby* (*Magdeburg*).
ROSENTRETER, Paulus. *Nürnberg*. m. 1566. Kleinuhrmacher. Clock K.H.M. ca. 1600 sd. 'P. R.,' possibly by him.
ROSET—
Jean Étienne. *Couvet*. 1759. *Grenoble*, 1803. Several clocks.
Jean Henri, son. *Couvet*. 1792-5. C.
ROSEVEAR, John. *St. Austell*. 1795. C. & W.
ROSEWELL, ——. *London*. an.1747. Watch.
ROSFELD, P. *Cologne*. 1813.
ROSIER, Jean. *Geneva*. 1770-1815. Watch.
ROSINCRAFT, ——. *London*. an.1727. Watch.
ROSKELL—
Robert. *Liverpool* and *London*. 1798-1830. Partner with O'NEILL to 1798. l.c. clocks and many watches. Used Litherland's rack-lever escapement.
John. *Liverpool*. 1805-21. W.
Robert & John. *Liverpool*. 1805-21.
James. *Liverpool*. 1816. W.
Robert, & Son. *Liverpool*. 1825.
Nicholas. *Liverpool*. 1825. W.
ROSKOPF, Georges Frédéric. *Chaux-de-Fonds*. b.1813, d.1889. German naturalized Swiss. A most eminent maker. Produced in 1868 the Roskopf watch selling at 20 francs, the first cheap yet good watch.
ROSLOF, Hans Frederik. *Copenhagen*. m. 1782.
ROSOMANS, ——. *London*. 2nd half 18c. p.c. en. watch G.M.
ROSS—
——. *London*. an.1755. Watch.
William. *Cork*. 1764-1817. p.c. sil. cyl. watch G.M. g. rep. watch Den. coll.
Thomas. *Hull*. ca.1770-95. C. & W.
James. *Glasgow*. 1790-1800.
Robert. *London*. a.1793.
William. *Montrose*. 1820.
John Thomas. *London*. a.1813.
——. *Exeter*. Early 19c. Watch.
Alexander. *Dublin*. 1824.
ROSSBACH, Adam. *Cologne*. m.1662. Kleinuhrmacher. Watch Giersberg coll.
ROSSE—
Samuel. *London*. a.1664, CC.1672-89.
Daniel. *London*. 1688 CC.
William. *London*. a.1683, CC.1691.
Christoph. *Nürnberg*. ca.1750.
Jeune. *Paris*. 1825.
ROSSEL—
Pierre Louis. *Môtiers*. 1755-65. l.c. clock.
ET CIE. *v.* SANDOZ ET TROT.
——. *Rouen*. Late 18c. Watch.
ROSSELET, David Louis. *Les Verrières*. 1808.
ROSSIGNON, ——. *Paris*. 1812. C.
ROSSIUS—
Henri. *Liége*. ca.1730. br. clock.
Mathieu. *Liége*. 2nd half 18c.
Henry Joseph. *Liége*. 2nd half 18c.
ROST—
Johann. *Fürth*. d.1815.
Nikolaus. *Fürth*. d.1818.
Heinrich. *Salzburg*. End 18c. en. watch.
Johann Gottlieb. *Dresden*. b.1786, m.1815, d.1818. From *Zeitz*.
ROTA, Angelo. *Rome*. ca.1600. circ. German type watch sd. by him Carnegie M.
ROTH—
Franz Anton. *Augsburg*. m.1759-90. 4-colour g. watch. trav. clock Carnegie M.
Johann Jakob. *Basle*. 1767. From *Potsdam*.
——. *Elberfeld*. 18c. en. watch.
Michael. *London*. an.1773. Watch. br. clock.
ROTHEA, Franz Georg. *Strasbourg*. 1737. g. eng. watch M.M.A.
ROTHERHAM—
Thomas. *London*. a.1654, CC.1662-66.
Richard Kevitt. *Coventry*. ca.1760-1832. *v.* VALE.
J. *Coventry*. 1787. C. & W.
William. *London*. a.1784.
T. *London*. Early 19c. Watch.
ROTHERY, Samuel. *London*. an.1778. Watch.
ROTHKNECHT, J. C. *Salzburg*. ca.1720. Dial maker.
ROTHMUND, Ignaz. *Vienna*. ca.1825. Watch.
ROTHWELL—
James. *Bolton*. d.1796. C.
John. *Ormskirk*. ca.1820.
ROTHWOOD—
Robert. *London*. CC.1632.
Robert. *London*. CC.1646.
RÖTIG—
Johann Anton. *Hachenburg*. d.1805. A very able maker of large mus. clocks.
Emil. *Hachenburg*. b.1814. Specialized in thin watches.
ROTTI—
Georg Leopold. *Augsburg*. comp. ca.1746, m.1755, d.1791.
Georg Leopold. *Augsburg*. m.1788-1800.
Caspar Leopold, bro. *Augsburg*. m.1788.
Georg Ignatz, bro. *Augsburg*. b.1758, comp. 1774, m.1791-5.
ROU (LEROUX)—
Pierre. *Blois*. 1623. d.1662. Large str. watch N.Y. Univ.
Pierre. *Blois*. 1652-89.
Martin. *Blois*. 1653-72.
Jean. *Blois*. 1654-84.
Gilles, son of Pierre (1). *Blois*. b.1630-81.
ROUBEL, John. *Bath*. 1774-81. W.
ROUCHER, ——. *Paris*. 1820-5.
ROUCLIFFE, John. *Bridgewater*. an.1765. Watch. l.c. clock.
ROUENNIER, Paul. *Rouen*. m.1654.
ROUGEAU, Antoine. *Lyons*. 1561.
ROUGEMONT—
Florimond. *Blois*. 1636.
Frères et Soeurs. *Paris*. 1807-25.
ROUGH—
David. *Dundee*. 1820.
Robert. prob. *London*. 1824.
ROUGHLEIGH, George. *Launceston*. 1791-1795. C. & W.
ROUGHLEY, Jonathan. *London*. 1743. In firm of SMITH, DE LA BALLE & ROUGHLEY.
ROUGHSEDGE, R. *Twickenham*. an.1770. Watch.
ROULEAU, Benjamin. *London*. a.1765, CC. 1777.
ROULET, Les. *La Sagne*. Early 19c. Clock ébauches makers.
ROULLET—
Gabriel. *London*. a.1742, CC.1753.
James, son. *London*. a.1766.
ROULSTONE, John. *Boston, U.S.A*. 1789-1803. W.
ROUMA—
G. *Liége*. End 17c. Watch en. Huaut Frères K.H.M. Wall clock.
——. *Liége*. Early 19c. rep. mus. lever watch.
Grégoire. *Paris*. 1821-5.

ROUMIEU (ROMMIEU)—
Pierre. *Rouen.* m.1645. Fine en. watch G.M. p.c. watch M.M.A.
Paul. *Rouen,* 1652 m. *Edinburgh,* 1677. d.1693. A famous C. & W.
Anthony. *Rouen.* 17c.
Adam. *London.* a.1657, CC.1687. Watch case maker. Case marked A.R.
Paul, son of Paul. *Edinburgh.* m.1682, d. 1710.
James. *London.* 1689. CC.1692-1707. Also ROUMYEU.
Adam. *London.* 1689. CC.1695-1707.
Lewis de. *London.* a.1700, CC.1707. Also ROMIEU.
John. *London.* a.1711, CC.1720-38. d.an. 1742.
Adam, son of Adam. *London.* a.1719, CC. 1727.
Jane. *London.* 1742.
John, son of John. *London.* a.1742.
ROUND, George. *London.* a.1819.
ROUNDELL, Thomas. *London.* a.1729, CC. 1749.
ROUNEAU DIT PONTHY, Jehan. *Paris.* 1544-7. Founder member of Paris corporation.
ROURKE—
Patrick. *London.* an.1774. Watch.
Thomas. *Dublin.* 1795.
ROURS, Ch. *Paris.* Early 19c. Clock of papier maché with mainspring in form of a spiral spring in tension.
ROUSBY, John. *York.* 1683. W. cf. ROOKSBY.
ROUSE, Robert. *London.* a.1683.
ROUSSATIER—
Abraham Louis. *Nyon.* 1761 m. Then *Vevey* and *Geneva.* 1792. Established a factory with PERDONNET.
François Emmanuel. *Vevey.* 1798 m.
ROUSSEAU—
Antoine. *Lyons.* 1561.
Jean. *Paris.* 1575. C. to the city.
Jean. *London* and *Geneva.* b.1606, d.1684. A fine maker. Watches in B.M., S.K.M., Louvre, Petit Palais, M.M.A., M.P.S. Dresden and Schloss M. Berlin. Skull watches Cluny M. and Spitzer sale. crys. cross watch and oval crys. watch Blot-Garnier sale.
Noé, son. *Geneva.* d.1695. 'Marchand horloger.'
Jacques, bro. *Geneva.* d.1712. 'Marchand horloger.'
David, bro. *Geneva.* b.1641, d.1738. crys. cross watch B.M. g. en. watch 9 mm. dia. M.P.S. Dresden.
Michel. *La Rochelle.* 1664. C. to the town.
Antoine. *Lyons.* 1664-86. Small lantern clock, dated 1664, Webster coll.
Jacob, son of Jean. Went to *London* ca.1670, to represent his father.
André, bro. *Hamburg.* ca.1670.
Jean. *Orléans.* End 17c.
Jacques. *Orléans.* 1713.
Isaac, grandson of Jean. *Geneva.* b.1672, d.1747. In *Constantinople* an.1711. Went to *Nyon* 1722. Father of Jean Jacques Rousseau. Made watches for Turkey.
Jean François, son of Noé. *Geneva.* b.1685, d.1763.
H. *London.* ca.1735. Watch Ilbert coll.
Jacques Nicolas. *Paris.* m.1737.
Pierre. *Paris.* m.1739.
James. *London.* 1743-61. Watch.
v. FERRAL & ROUSSEAU.
——. *Paris.* 1823.
ROUSSEL—
A. *The Hague.* ca.1640. oct. watch, crys. mounts, B.M.
Jean Michel. *Paris.* Juré 1736-41, d.an.1760.
Nicolas Martin. *Paris.* m.1741.

ROUSSEL—*continued.*
Gilles Edme, son of J. M. *Paris.* m.1749-79.
——. *Paris.* 1772. Maker of repute. Made several public clocks of Paris.
——. *Paris.* 1810-17. C.
Veuve et Fils. *Paris.* 1823.
ROUSSELL, J. *London.* ca.1700. Watch Horstmann coll.
ROUSSELOT (ROUSSELET)—
Estienne. *Paris.* 1675 m.
Jean Étienne. *Paris.* m.1743.
ROUSSEY, Richard. *Twickenham.* an.1780. Watch.
ROUT, William. *Enfield.* an.1765. Watch.
ROUTH—
Samuel. *London.* 1682 CC. Clock.
Samuel. *London.* a.1740.
George. *Bristol.* an.1776. Watch.
ROUTLEDGE—
George. *Lydford.* b.1745, d.1802. Also ROUTLEIGH.
Adam. *Carlisle.* Early 19c. Watch.
ROUVIÈRE—
——. *Rolle,* 1749. *Vevey,* 1760 m. Went to *London.*
Jean Louis. *Paris.* m.1781-9.
——. *Paris.* 1807.
ROUVITRE, Jean Christian. *Vevey.* 1798 m.
ROUWERDINK, J. W. *Rotterdam.* 1821-30.
ROUX—
P. *Sarlat.* ca.1700. Watch with bal. spring Gélis coll.
Alexander. *London.* a.1700-10 CC.
Père et Fils. *Geneva.* ca.1770. Painters on enamel.
ET DASSIER. *Geneva.* 1783.
Gabriel. *Paris.* m.1787.
Abram. *Vevey.* 1798 m.
ET BORDIER. *Geneva.* Late 18c. g. en. watch Lincoln M.
BORDIER ET CIE. *Geneva.* Late 18c. g. en. watch S.K.M. g. aut. watch Gélis coll.
BORDIER ET ROMAN. *Geneva.* Early 19c. g. en. rep. watch, set pearls. aut. watch M.P.S. Dresden.
——. *Paris.* 1810-16.
ROUZIER & MELLY. *Geneva* and *Paris.* Late 18c. g. watch, showing on back the time in different places, M.M.A. Small en. watch B.M. 4-colour g. watch set stones Feill coll.
ROVENIER, Adam. *Paris.* 1675 m.
ROVER, P. prob. *London.* an.1771. Watch.
ROWARTH, William. *Southampton.* a.1789.
ROWDEN, John. *London.* a.1683, CC.1691. Watch.
ROWE—
Thomas. *London.* a.1691, CC.1699.
Benjamin. *London.* a.1698, CC.1708-39.
John. *London (Gutter La.).* a.1714-27.
George, son of Benj. *London.* CC.1739.
James. *London.* 1758. p.c. g. watch F.W.M.
ROWELL—
Edward. *London.* a.1745.
George. *Oxford.* ca.1790-1813 CC. Watch mt. Ashmolean M.
T. *Brighton.* 1822. C. & W.
ROWETTER, ——. *Amsterdam.* Mid. 18c. Watch Ilbert coll.
ROWLAND (ROWLANDS)—
William. *London.* a.1712.
John. *London.* a.1718.
John. *London.* a.1752.
T. *Berwick-on-Tweed.* 1760.
Jonathan. *Berwick-on-Tweed.* 1766. W.
John. *Berwick-on-Tweed.* an.1772-1830. l.c. clock.
David. *Aberystwith.* 1779. W. l.c. clocks.
David. *Llanuwchllyn.* ca.1780-1850.
John. *Manchester.* 1788-97. W.
Walter. *Berwick-on-Tweed.* 1790-1820.

ROWLAND (**ROWLANDS**)—*continued.*
James. *Bristol.* 1801-18. W.
Christopher. *London* (*City Rd.*). a.1803, CC.1810-24. W.
William. *London.* CC.1820-4.
ROWLEY—
Eliza. *London.* a.1694.
James. *London.* a.1714, CC.1721, d.1788.
John. *London.* 1716. Made an orrery with GRAHAM. Four orreries Old Ashmolean M.
Thomas. *London.* a.1734.
C. prob. *London.* an.1764. Watch.
John. *London.* a.1780, CC.1793.
ROWLINGSON, Tom. *Worcester.* 1813. p.c. watch Ilbert coll.
ROWNING—
John. *Cambridge.* 1732. Patented a clock with a single train for str. and rep.
William. *Brandon.* To 1737. l.c. clock.
——. *London.* an.1743. Watch.
J. *Newmarket.* d.1771. C. & W.
Bartholomew. *Cambridge.* In 1752 takes a shop at *St. Ives.* Watch.
George. *Newmarket.* an.1776-84. W.
ROWNTREE, Robert. *York.* 1823. W. & C.
ROWORTH, William. *London.* a.1789.
ROWSON, Philip. *London.* a.1739.
ROWTE, John. *London.* a.1737.
ROXBOROUGH, William Simon. *London.* a.1806. From *Edinburgh.*
ROXBURGH, John. prob. *London.* an.1769. Watch.
ROY (**ROI**)—
Jean. *Neuchâtel.* 1574.
David. *London.* CC.1682-9.
Samuel. *Fontaines* and *Chaux-de-Fonds.* b.1746, d.1822. A famous maker. Founded the firm of Samuel ROY ET FILS, which was a large exporter of watches. Many watches and clocks. One-wheel regulator with hour hand tip describing a spiral over 12 hours. str. mech. also with one wheel.
James. *Edinburgh.* a.1759.
François, et Frères. *Chaux-de-Fonds.* To 1785.
François, et Cie. *Chaux-de-Fonds.* From 1785.
William. *Dunfermline.* 1786-1811.
William. *Edinburgh.* 1787.
Simon. *Paris.* m.1787.
FRÈRES ET CIE. *Paris.* 1789.
Henri Louis, son of Samuel. *Chaux-de-Fonds.* b.1770, d.1843. Succeeded his father as head of S. ROY ET FILS in 1804.
Jacques Louis, bro. *Chaux-de-Fonds.* b. 1782, d.1808. In the firm of S. ROY ET FILS.
François. *Chaux-de-Fonds* and *Trieste.* b. 1785-1818. Head of COURVOISIER ET CIE at Trieste.
Samuel, bro. *Chaux-de-Fonds.* 1820. In the firm of S. ROY ET FILS.
——. *Paris.* 1807.
v. also LE ROY.
'ROYAL.' Sig. on watches of the AMERICAN WATCH Co. from 1889.
ROYALSON, ——. *London.* an.1750. Watch.
ROYCE, James. *London.* a.1783. en. watch.
ROYCROFT—
Thomas. *London.* a.1681, CC.1699-1717. Watch mt. Ilbert coll.
Arthur, son. *London.* a.1701.
ROYD (**ROYDE**), Stephen Joseph. *London.* a.1760, CC.1767-80. *Hertford* in 1790.
ROYDEN, James. prob. *London.* an.1802. Watch.
ROYER—
Lewis. *London.* a.1730.
S. *London.* an.1753. Watch.
Georges. *Paris.* 1767.
Peter. *Paris.* 1791. Made Chevé watch-glasses.

ROYER—*continued.*
William. *London.* 1805-24.
——. *Paris.* 1812. C.
ROYLAND, John. *Liverpool.* 1785. W.
ROYLANDS, William. *London.* 1790. mt. maker.
ROYLE—
John. *Bolton.* 1738. C.
Ralph. *Manchester.* d.1760. W.
Thomas. *Liverpool.* 1754. W.
ROYSTON, W. *London.* an.1769, Watch.
ROZÉ, Auguste C. *Paris.* b.1812, d.1862. Eminent maker. Used cylindrical chron. spring with reversal in middle. Made a planetarium exhibited 1844. Worked with PHILLIPS on terminal curves of balance springs.
ROZESTRATEN, A. *Schiedam.* ca.1800.
ROZETTE, Pierre. *Paris.* ca.1400. Keeper of clock on Palais de Justice.
RUARD, Jehan. *Geneva.* 1602.
RUBOTTOM, William. *Liverpool.* 1790-6. W.
RUCHET, ——. *Vevey.* 1765 comp.
RÜCKEN, Hindrick. *Stockholm.* 1694. m. 1696-1723.
RÜCKERT, Thomas. *Augsburg.* 1574-1606. Went to the Dresden Court ca.1580, and later to the Court of Prague. Maker of pedometers.
RUDD—
John. *London.* a.1745.
Tillam. *Warminster.* an.1760. T.C. Watch.
Edward. *Melksham.* 1774. C. & W.
Henry Phillips. *London.* a.1783, CC.1791.
RUDER, Henrik Christian. *Copenhagen.* 1792.
RUDKIN—
Thomas. *London.* a.1673, CC.1683.
——. *Amsterdam.* Early 18c. Watch.
RUDOLPHI, Johan Traugott. *Copenhagen.* m.1778.
RUE, Jacob de. *Bienne.* 1st half 18c.
RUEGGER—
——. ——. ca.1790. Watch mt. Ilbert coll.
E. M. *Geneva.* Early 19c. Fine maker. Lever watch. g. en. watch. g. cyl. rep. watch.
S. M. *Paris.* 1823. mus. clocks.
RUEL—
Samuel. *Rotterdam.* 1675-1705. Watch mt. G.M. Watch Den. coll.
Samuel. *Rotterdam.* 1788. Fine cal. watch ill. Britten. Watches Stads M. Amsterdam and Den. coll.
RUEMPOL—
Goslink. *Laren.* 1736-49. Wall clock Stads M. Amsterdam.
Hendrick, son. *Laren.* 1st half 18c. Wall clock.
H. J. *Amsterdam.* 1822. W.
RUEP, Leopold. *Stadt Bergen* (*Augsburg*). 1756.
RUF, Joseph. *Seelgut.* ca.1780. Wall clock Furt. M.
RUFF—
Joseph. *Vienna.* m.1783.
Franz. *Vienna.* m.1789. Also RUEFF.
RUFFET, ——. *Paris.* 1816-25.
RUGELEY, George. *London.* a.1749.
RUGENDAS—
Nicolaus. *Augsburg.* b.1585, m.1610, d.1658. Usual sig. 'N.R.' Fine watch B.M. ill. Baillie. crys. cross watch S.K.M. Oval watches Webster coll. and Den. coll. crys. watch Ilbert coll.
Nicolaus, son. *Augsburg.* mar.1662, d.1694. Fine table clock Neue Hofburg, Vienna.
Nicolaus, son. *Augsburg.* m.1699, d.1745. Sundial. Stuttgart M.
RUGLESS—
Samuel. *London.* 1820.
G. *London.* 1820.

RUISMAN, R. *Joure.* ca.1800.
RULAND (RUHLAND)—
Johann Christoph. *Dresden.* b.1764, m.1792, d.1813.
Johann Georg. *Dresden.* m.1800, d.1840.
RULE—
Walter. *Edinburgh.* 1733.
John. prob. *London.* an.1774. Watch.
James. *Portsmouth.* an.1778. Watch.
James. *York.* 1776-97. W.
John. *Kelso.* 1791-1836.
RÜLKE, Georg. *Görlitz.* ca.1730. Monstrance clock.
RUMAULT, G. *Abbeville.* Late 17c. Oval str. watch Stern. coll.
RUMBALL, John. *London.* a.1749.
RUMDUD (or **RINNDUD**), Isaac. *London.* 1662.
RUMEL, Matthias. *Salzburg.* 1725. Dial of watch Fränkel coll. sd. 'Rumel.'
RUMFORD, John. *Bishop Auckland.* ca.1770-1795. W.
RUMMEL, Joseph. *Oberhausen.* 1756-70. Kleinuhrmacher.
RUMPELSBERGER, Georg Joseph. *Würzburg.* a.1747, m.1760-94. Court W.
RUMSEY—
John. *Woolwich.* 1723. Insolvent.
Thomas. prob. *London.* an.1772. Watch.
John William. *London.* a.1801.
RUNCHEL, Peder Christian. *Aalborg.* m. 1811.
RUNCHMAN, Samuel John. *London.* a. 1824.
RUNCHORNE, Richard. *Liverpool.* 1777. W.
RUNCORN—
Richard. *Manchester.* 1782-95. Bought Thos. BARTON's business in 1782. Bankrupt 1793. Went *Stockport* in 1795. 'The most eminent maker in Manchester.' Watch.
Richard & John. *Manchester.* 1782.
Richard & Robert. *Manchester.* To 1791. cyl. watch mt. Platt Hall M. Manchester.
Richard & Co. *Manchester.* Late 18c. Watch Platt Hall M.
John & Robert. *Manchester.* Late 18c.
RUNDBERG, Carl. *Stockholm.* 1787-90. d. an.1795.
RUNDELIUS—
Anders. *Stockholm.* 1783-1805. Wall and l.c. clock.
Eric. *Stockholm.* 1790-5. Wall clock.
Carl Peder, son of Anders. *Stockholm.* b. 1785-1804.
RUNDELL—
Philip. *London.* 1770. en. watch.
Joseph. *Plymouth.* an.1788. Watch.
——. *London* (*Fleet St.*). an.1788. Watch.
& BRIDGE. *London.* ca.1772-1825. W. to the King. g. en. watch, set diamonds, Carnegie M. g. en. rep. watch, set diamonds, Wilsdorf coll.
BRIDGE & RUNDELL. *London.* Early 19c. Watch mt. Ilbert coll.
RUNEMARK, P. *Kalmar.* 1819-26.
RUNGEL, ——. *Augsburg.* 1660. aut. clock M.P.S. Dresden.
RUNICLES, J. F. *London.* Early 19c. Watch.
RUNSTEN, Erich. *Stockholm.* 2nd half 18c. l.c. clock.
RUPANO, Carlo. *Venice.* 2nd half 18c. g. en. str. watch.
RUPE, ——. *Plymouth.* ca.1720. Watch Liverpool M.
RUPERT—
C. R. *Amsterdam.* 1822. W.
Wed. *Amsterdam.* 1822. W.
RUPT DE COURTMONT, Nicolas de. *Montbéliard.* 1585.
RUSBACKS (RASBOCKS), Hans. *Copenhagen.* 1674. Court C.
RUSELSHEIM & MOSELEY. *London.* In 1800 dissolve partnership.
RUSH—
Thomas. *Saffron Walden.* 1651-61.
Goodman. *Saffron Walden.* 1651.
Samuel. *London.* an.1758. Watch.
RUSHMAN, John. prob. *London.* an.1773. Watch.
RUSHTON, James. *Liverpool.* 1816.
RUSSELL—
John. *London.* a.1655.
Nicasius. *London.* a.1656, CC.1663, m.1692, d.1701.
John. *London.* 1682 CC.
Cornelius, son of Nicasius. *London.* a.1686-1701.
William. *London.* a.1698.
John. *London.* a.1711.
G. *London.* Mid. 18c. Watch mt. G.M.
Samuel. *Selkirk.* 1773.
Robert. *Moffat.* 1774.
John. *Falkirk.* 1783. d.1817. W. to the Prince Regent. A well-known maker of mus. clocks.
Isaac. *London.* a.1781.
William. *London.* a.1785.
J. *London.* ca.1790.
John. *Dublin.* 1795. W.
Edward. *Norwich.* 1795. Watch.
Thomas. *Lancaster.* 1797 m.-1832. Watch.
Mitchell. *Glasgow.* 1801. g. watch.
John. *Bridport.* 1800. C.
William. *Glasgow.* 1802. d.1816.
Edward. *Buxton.* Wife died 1818. C. & W.
William. *Falkirk.* 1820.
Joseph. *London.* a.1813.
Robert. *Navan.* 1824.
Robert. *Belfast.* 1824.
John. *Sheffield.* 1825.
RUST—
Stephen. *London.* a.1701.
William. *Bury St. Edmunds.* 1769. Succeeds Thos. WATTS.
Thomas. *Hull.* 1770.
William. *Hull.* 1780.
Daniel. *London.* CC.1782-8.
Wilhelm Joachim. *Hamburg.* 1804-21.
William. *Hull.* 1822. Partner with John Shipham as RUST & SHIPHAM.
RUTH—
Andreas. *Hälsingborg.* d.an.1773.
Anders. *Norrköping.* 1784.
John. *London.* a.1777.
Carl Ad. *Norrköping.* b.1770, d.1819. Watches and clocks.
John. *Hemel Hempstead.* 1795. W.
N. *Västervik.* comp. 1793.
RUTHERFORD—
William. *Hawick.* ca.1800. br. clock.
Robert. *London.* a.1818.
RUTHIN, Owen William. prob. *London.* an. 1763. Watch.
RUTLAND—
D. *London.* an.1783. Watch.
William. *Dublin.* an.1785. Watch.
RUTSCHMANN—
David. The lay name of SAN CAJETANO, *q.v.*
Joseph. *Vienna.* m.1786. Complex astro. clock.
RUTTER, Moses. *Baltimore, U.S.A.* 1802-07.
RUUTH, Laurentz. *Norrköping.* b.1704, d. 1759. Two l.c. clocks.
RUXTON, Henry. *Bailieborough.* 1824.
RYALL, George. *Parsonstown.* 1824.
RYCROFT—
Thomas. *London.* 1756. Watch.
George. *Dublin.* an.1769. Watch.
RYDBERG—
Peter. *Stockholm.* 1808-20. Watch Nord. M. Wall clock.
Joh. *Stockholm.* Early 19c. Wall and br. clock.
And. Joh. *Karlskrona.* b.1789, d.1845. cyl. watch.

RYDELIUS, ——. *Askersund.* 1778. Watch.

RYDER—

Thomas. *London.* CC.1712.

Joseph. *London.* a.1747.

——. *Welshpool.* 1792. W.

Richard. *London.* a.1802.

'J. T. RYERSON.' Sig. on 1867-75 watches of the NATIONAL WATCH CO. OF CHICAGO.

RYLAND (RYLANDS)—

Benjamin. *Lancashire.* 1747. W.

Samuel. *London.* a.1741. *Hornsey* in 1751, *Ironmongers Row* in 1755, *Old St.* in 1761. W.

——. *London* (*Hoxton*). d.1775.

John. *London.* an.1769-ca.1800. sil. repoussé watch Ilbert coll.

Robert. *London.* an.1793. Watch.

James. *Ormskirk.* 1795. d.1803. Watch mt. G.M. Club-footed verge watch S.M.S.K.

Joshua. *Ormskirk.* Late 18c. Watch mt. G.M.

John. *Ormskirk.* ca.1820.

RYLANDER, N. Gustaf. *Jönköping.* b.1777 m.1805, d.1832. Watch.

RYLER, William. *London.* CC.1712.

RYLEY—

Laurence. *London.* a.1662. Also RILLEY.

George. *London.* a.1683. Also RILY.

Thomas. *London.* a.1697, CC.1705-52. Also RILEY.

William. *London.* a.1733. Watch.

Erastus, son of Thos. *London.* CC.1741-53.

John. *Coventry.* 1799. Partner in RYLEY, BRADSHAW & RYLEY, and then in BRADSHAW & RYLEY.

Thomas. *Coventry.* 1799. Partner in BRADSHAW & RYLEY. Partnership dissolved and business continued by BRADSHAW & John RYLEY.

ROE & HILL. *Coventry.* 1799. Partnership with Thos. RYLEY dissolved in 1807.

——. *Liverpool.* Early 19c. Watch.

RYLY, William. *London.* a.1700, CC.1712.

RYMER, Henry. *London.* 1817.

RYPPLAY (RIPLEY), John. *York.* 1471. C.

S

SABEROWSKY, Johann Gottlieb. *Hamburg.* 1801-21.
SABERTY, J. *London.* 2nd half 18c. Watch.
SABOURIN, ——. *London.* ca.1730. Watch Chamb. coll.
SABROFFSKY, Johann Gottfried. *Basle.* 1755.
SACHEVERELL, Benassir. *London.* a.1680, CC.1687. Watch.
SACHS—
Johann. *Vienna.* m.1765.
Leonhard. *Rippberg.* m.1791.
SACHWELL, Joseph. *London.* a.1717.
SACK, Solomon. *Augsburg.* m.ca.1735, juré 1740, d.1751.
SACKER, William. *London.* 1805-08. W.
SACRÉ—
le jeune. *Paris* (*Rue du Martrois*). 1792-1825. Made watches and clocks 'à l'ivrogne,' winding whichever way the key was turned.
——. *Paris* (*Rue de Malthe-Tuileries*). 1812.
SADDLETON, ——. *Kings Lynn.* ca.1820-1830. br. clock ill. Cec. & Web.
SADLEIR—
Samuel. *London.* a.1687, CC.1694, w.CC. 1723. l.c. clock. Also SADLER.
Samuel. *London.* CC.1735-47.
SADLER—
Hatton. *London.* a.1676.
Robert. *London* (*Bedford Row*). a.1701-37. Bankrupt. l.c. clock. br. clock ill. Cec. & Web.
John. *London.* a.1709.
Thomas. *Berkhamsted.* Mid. 18c.
Thomas. *Norwich.* an.1752-84. Watch mt. Buckley coll. l.c. clock.
Richard. *London.* a.1781.
Edward. *London.* a.1802, CC.1817.
SADTLER, Philip B. *Baltimore, U.S.A.* 1802-1807. W.
SAER, Joseph. *London.* CC.1687. Clock.
SAFELY (SAFLEY), John. *Edinburgh.* 1764. d.1803. l.c. clock.
SAFFELL—
Charles Wilson. *London.* CC.1773, l.CC. 1803, d.1816.
Charles Wilson. *London.* CC.1816.
SAFFORD, Thomas Jeffrey. *Bristol.* 1767-87. W.
SAFLY (SAIFLOY), John. *Lanark.* 1790.
SAGAR—
Edmund. *Skipton.* 1769. d.1805.
M. *Colne.* 1802. C. & W.
Robert. *Blackburn.* 1818.
Robert Holgate. *Blackburn.* 1824.
SAGE, R. H. *London.* Early 19c. Watch.
SAGER (SAAGER), Martin. *Vienna.* m. 1816.
SÄGER, ——. *Berlin.* 1806.
SAGNE—
Jean Jacques. *La Sagne.* 1713. Clock.
Tite. *Chaux-de-Fonds.* 1754. C.
Pierre Ésaïe. *Val de Travers.* 1762-71. C Chiming clock.
SAGNIER, François. *Geneva.* ca.1775-91.
SAIGLER, Johan. *Ulm.* End 16c. cf. SAYLLER.
SAILER, ——. *Landsberg.* 1728. Kleinuhrmacher.
SAILLER, Johann. *Vienna.* 1575. circ. drum watch Spitzer coll. sd. 'Sailler. Jo. Mic. Bren.' cf. SAYLLER.
SAILOR, Washington. *Philadelphia.* 1825.
SAINSBURY—
Robert. *Bristol.* 1682.
——. *Chippenham.* an.1732. Watch.
Richard. *Bridgewater.* 2nd half 18c. l.c. clock. Watch mt.
ST. AUBIN, ——. *France.* an.1776. Watch.
ST. CANNON, ——. *London.* an.1776. Watch.
ST. GEORGE, John. *London.* a.1674.
ST. JOHN, George. *London* (*Westminster*). 1808.
SAINTPER, ——. *Paris.* m.1690.
SAINT-PREUIL, ——. *Paris.* 1767 m.
SALBIE, Thomas. *Nottingham.* 1615.
SALCHOV, ——. *Berlin.* 1769.
SALE, Francis. *London.* a.1734.
SALÉN, Johan Fredric. *Stockholm.* 1821. d.1859.
SALIGAN, Louis. *Blois.* m.1663.
SALISBURY—
William. *London* (*Temple Bar*). 1716. Watch mt.
Edward. *London.* a.1789.
SALKIN, ——. *Paris.* 1812.
SALLAT, ——. *Ohlau.* ca.1700 worked on the Rathaus clock.
SALLES, ——. *Caen.* ca.1700. Fine Boulle br. clock S.K.M.
SALMON—
John. *London.* a.1648, CC.1654. Also SAMON.
John. *Bristol.* 1734-54. W.
Pierre. *Paris.* 1780.
John. *London.* a.1776, CC.1784.
Robert. *London* (*Strand*). an.1780-95.
Peter. *Stockholm.* 1785. d.1800.
William Henry. *London.* a.1788.
Edward. *London.* CC.1798.
George. *London.* a.1797.
William. *London* (*Low Leyton*). 1802-11.
Colin. *Dundee.* 1811.
William. *London* (*Spitalfields*). 1817-24.
Amos James. *London.* a.1810.
Charles. *London.* CC.1821.

SALMOON—
Jacob. *Stockholm.* 1720-54.
Gideon Abraham, son. *Kalmar.* b.1724, d. 1791.
Joh. Nath., son. *Kalmar.* b.1765, d.1822.
SALOMON, Jean. *Blois.* mar.1578.
SALOP, Edward. *London.* 1778.
SALTER—
Samuel. *London.* a.1713.
Joseph. *Oswestry.* an.1783. Watch.
Robert. *Oswestry.* 1795. W.
Cleaveland. *Portsea.* 1795. C. & W.
——. *London.* an.1801. Watch.
John. *London.* a.1796.
SALTWELL, George. *London.* a.1801.
SALVIS, Franc. de. *Rome.* 1695. Dial maker.
SAMBIN, Jacques. *Blois.* 1587. d.1602.
SAMBROOK, John. *London.* a.1668, CC. 1680.
SAMMER, Joseph Anton. *Augsburg.* a.1752, m.1770-98.
SAMON, John. *London.* a.1648, CC.1654. Also SALMON.
SAMPSON—
Charles. *London.* a.1715.
Umfrevil. *London.* a.1728, CC.1735.
Robert. *London (Westminster).* 1779-93. Award from Soc. Arts for a chiming mechanism, desc. Trans. Soc. Arts, Vol. 4.
Robert. *Liskeard.* 1791-5. C. & W.
Henry. *Penzance.* 1795 CC. W.
Samuel. *London (Goodman's Fields).* 1808.
Robert. *Liverpool.* 1825.
SAMSON—
——. *London.* ca.1770. Watches G.M., Glasgow Art Gall., London M., M.M.A. and Fränkel coll.
Samuel. *London (Westminster).* 1780-1800. Watch B.M. 3-case watch G.M. br. and l.c. clock.
J. *London.* Late 18c. and early 19c. Watches Den. coll. and N.Y. Univ.
F. *London.* 1800. Watch.
& GRANDIN. *London.* 1810.
SAMUEL—
John. *England.* 1665. Lantern clock.
Thomas. *London.* an.1770. Watch.
S. *Lincoln.* an.1772. Watch.
Samuel. *London.* an.1772-1810. Watch mt. Buckley coll.
Hugh. *London.* an.1777. Watch.
Hart. *Sunderland.* 1777. W.
Abraham. *Market Harborough.* 1782-1800. W.
Humphrey. *London.* 1790.
Israel. *London.* an.1796. Watch.
Abraham. *London.* 1809-25.
SIMPSON & Co. *Liverpool.* 1811-ca.1820.
Lewis. *Liverpool.* 1813-29. W.
Solomon. *Liverpool.* ca.1818. Watch N.Y. Univ.
David. *York.* a.1809-20. W.
LEWIS & Co. *Liverpool.* 1821. Rack lever watch.
BROS & Co. *Liverpool.* 1821-9.
S. H., & Co. *Liverpool.* 1824.
Flora, & Co. *Liverpool.* 1824-9. W.
Moses. *Liverpool.* 1824-9. W.
Philip. *N. Shields.* Early 19c. Watch.
S. *Chichester.* Early 19c. Watch.
'SAMUEL CURTIS MFG. CO.' Sig. on 1853 watches of one of the predecessors of the WALTHAM WATCH CO.
SAMY, ——. *Paris.* Early 19c. Watch Feill coll.
SAN CAJETANO, David. *Vienna.* b.1726, d.1796. Lay brother in Marienbrunn monastery. Lay name David RUTSCHMANN. Able maker of complex astro. clocks; one at Zwettl, one in Uhren M. Vienna and another Hofburg, Vienna. Pub. 1793 and 1794 'Neues Rädergebäude.'
SANCELE, ——. *Paris.* Early 19c. crys. star watch M.M.A.
SANCHEZ, Cayetano. *Madrid.* 1789. d.1800. Sent by Spanish Navy in 1789 to learn chron. making with BERTHOUD & EMERY.
SANCY, Jean Baptiste. *Paris.* m.1770.
SANDBERG, ——. *Stockholm.* End 18c. br. clock.
SANDBERGER, Daniel. *Olmütz.* 1579. In charge of the town clocks.
SANDBLOM, Lars. *Uddevalla.* 1794-1840.
SANDE, Thomas. ——. ca.1620. Fritillary watch B.M. ill. Baillie.
SANDER & MACK. *Mittenberg.* ca.1780. Watch Gemeente M., The Hague.
SANDERHOLM, Lars Fredrik. *Stockholm.* 1823-45. Wall clock.
SANDERLIN, John. *London.* a.1699.
SANDERS—
Daniel. *London.* 1622. CC.1632. Also SAUNDERS.
Alexander. *London.* a.1665.
Charles. *London.* a.1672. Also SAUNDERS.
John. *London.* a.1714, CC.1721. Also SAUNDERS.
Joseph. *London (Long Acre).* a.1746, CC. 1753-68.
B. *London.* ca.1765. Fine bloodstone watch.
Nathaniel. *Manchester.* 1772-1800. C.
Thomas. *London.* a.1769.
John. *London (Holborn Hill).* a.1763, CC. 1777-1819. *(Aldermanbury)*, 1820.
Richard. *London.* an.1774, CC.1780. cf. SAUNDERS.
James. *London.* 1790.
William. *Wallingford.* 1795. C.
Joseph. *Bristol.* 1801. W.
Charles. *Banbury.* 1805. Bankrupt. W.
SANDERSON (SAUNDERSON)—
John. *Wigton,* 1680. *Edinburgh,* 1715. *Carlisle,* 1730. Many l.c. clocks.
Francis. *London.* a.1694.
Robert. *London.* a.1695, CC.1704-31. Watch M.M.A.
Richard. *London.* a.1701.
——. *Liverpool.* d.(?)1771. W.
George. *Exeter.* 1751. d.1764 in *London,* where he was partner with John MALLETT. Patented in 1761 watch tools and a calendar watch-key in 1762.
Henry. *London.* an.1772-83. Watch.
J. *Newcastle-o.-T.* an.1776. Watch.
C. *London.* 1784.
W. *Doncaster.* 1795 CC. C. & W.
Thomas. *London (Shoreditch, Moorfields* and *Bishopsgate St.).* a.1784, CC.1792-1825. W.
Alexander. *Dunblane.* 1798.
George. *London.* a.1800.
William. *London.* 1815.
Benjamin, son of Thos. *London.* a.1812.
SANDFORD (SANFORD), William. *London.* 1802-25.
SANDIALY, ——. *Paris.* 1823.
SANDIFORD, James. *Salford.* 1772-81. C.
SANDLER, John. *Feckenham.* ca.1790.
SANDOT, ——. *Paris.* 1768-75.
SANDOZ—
Jacques. *Les Planchettes* and *Chaux-de-Fonds.* b.1664, d.1738. Sundials and clocks.
David (1). *Chaux-de-Fonds.* 1697. Made a clock for the town.
Henry. *Le Locle.* 1711. Restored the town clock.
Abram. *Chaux-de-Fonds.* b.1719-39.
Abraham. *Chaux-de-Fonds.* b.1723-44. C.
Jacques. *Les Planchettes* and *Chaux-de-Fonds.* 1733-57. Several clocks. Watch.
David (2). *Chaux-de-Fonds.* d. or retired 1758. C.

SANDOZ—*continued.*
Jean Jacques. *Les Planchettes.* 1740. Small clock.
Louis. *Basle.* 1750. From *Neuenstadt.*
Jacques. *Chaux-de-Fonds.* 1753. trav. clocks.
Felix, son of David (2). *Chaux-de-Fonds.* 1758.
Florian. *Chaux-de-Fonds.* 1781. In firm of J. Robert et Fils.
et Trot. *Besançon.* 1792. *Geneva.* 1804-16. Then called Sandoz et Rossel and, in 1821, Rossel et Cie.
Aîné, et Cie. *Paris.* 1808-25.
Louis. *Switzerland.* 1818. Clock.
Ami, et Fils. *Switzerland.* Early 19c. g. en. watches. Watch mt. sd. 'Ami Sandoz & Son' Ilbert coll.
Henri Frédéric. *Tavannes.* b.1815, d.1913. Started Tavannes Watch Co.
SANDRA, Georg Joseph. *Augsburg.* m.1793. From *Würzburg.*
SANDRIE, Louis. *Paris.* Late 17c. Fine Boulle br. clock Pal. de Pau, Paris.
SANDRIN, Daniel. *London.* CC.1692. French. Engraver.
SANDS—
John. *London.* a.1668.
Stephen. *New York.* 1772-86.
John. *London.* CC.1772-98.
SANDYS—
William. *London.* a.1659.
Richard. *London (Old St.).* d.1775. W.
James. *London (Beech La.).* a.1761, CC. 1768-1811. Watch.
SÄNGER—
Johannes. *Basle.* m.1653. Turret C. from *Langnau.*
——. *Augsburg.* Early 18c.
Jakob. *Cassel.* 1794. Court C.
SANGSTER—
John Trower. *Bradwell.* CC.1803, l.CC. 1812-40.
James. *Youghal.* 1824.
SANGUINEDE—
Jean. *Paris.* m.1777-89.
——. *Paris.* 1810-16.
SANIER, Jean. *Avignon.* 1500-02. Keeper of town clock.
SANSOM, John. *Hemel Hempstead.* an.1769. Watch.
SANSOY, Jacques. *Paris.* m.1675.
SAPHIN, ——. prob. *London.* an.1755. Watch.
SAPKIN, Thomas. *London.* 1820.
SARAZIN, ——. *Paris.* 1812-25.
SARGENT—
Robert. *London (Foster La.).* a.1707, CC. 1720-56.
William, son. *London.* CC.1756.
Nathaniel. *London.* CC.1769, m.CC.1783. l.c. clock.
John. *London.* a.1769-99.
Hammond. *Boston.* an.1772-91. Watch. C.
William. *Boston.* 1791. C.
Lewis. *London.* a.1780.
Joseph. *London.* 1794-1820. W. to the Princess of Wales. Succeeded by Wm. Watch mt. G.M. Also Sarjent.
William, jun. *London (Jermyn St.).* 1817-24.
SARJENT, William. *London (Golden Sq.).* 1820.
SARLITT, ——. *London.* 1778. W.
SARRABAT, T. *Paris.* a.1632, m.1675. Clock.
SARRASIN, Vincent. *Avignon.* 1726-48. Town C.
SARREBOURG, ——. *Nancy.* 1753. Proposed clock winding by change in barometric pressure.
SARTES, ——. *Hastings.* Early 19c. Watch.
SARTON—
——. *Paris.* an.1776. Watch.
Hubert. *Liége.* Late 18c. Maker of repute. C. to the Prince Eveque. Fine cal. mantel clock. Lever watch mt. S.M.S.K. dup. rep. c.secs. watch mt. Ilbert coll. Clock Uhren M. Vienna.
SARTOR, Johann Thomas. *Tölz.* End 18c. en. watch.
SARTORI—
Johann Martin. *Bamberg.* Mid. 18c. astro. str. rep. table clock.
Johann Georg. *Kronach.* 1794.
SARTORIUS, Georg. *Hassfurt.* m.1798.
SATCHELL, Edward. *London.* 1728-48. 'Eminent' W.
SATCHER—
Thomas. *London.* a.1759, CC.1775-86.
Thomas, son. *London.* a.1786, CC.1798.
SATLER, Johann. ——. Early 18c. sil. str. watch with sundial, formerly in Shandon coll.
SATZMANN, Jacob. *Couvet.* an.1773. C.
SAUER, ——. *Olmütz.* 1733.
SAULET, ——. *Paris.* 1822-5.
SAULNIER—
——. *Paris.* 1823.
Aîné. *Paris.* 1824.
SAUNDERS—
Daniel. *London.* 1622. CC.1632. Also Sanders.
Charles. *London.* a.1672. Also Sanders.
Robert. *London.* a.1675.
William. *London.* a.1696. W.
John. *London.* a.1714, CC.1721. Also Sanders.
Samuel. *London.* a.1723, CC.1730.
Isaac. *London (Little Arthur St.).* a.1755, CC.1768.
Peter. prob. *London.* an.1778. Watch.
Richard. prob. *London.* an.1778. Watch. cf. Sanders.
Joseph, son of Isaac. *London (Chick La.).* CC.1792-1810.
William. *London (Mile End).* 1792.
Joseph. *Bristol.* 1794.
Thomas, son of Wm. *London.* a.1792-1824. Watch.
Daniel. *London.* 1802-24. Watch.
John. *London.* Early 19c. Watch.
Thomas. *Dorchester.* Early 19c.
SAUNIER, Claudius. *Paris.* b.1816, d.1896. Well-known horologist. Founded in 1859 and edited the 'Revue Chronométrique.' Pub. 'Traité des échappements . . . ,' Paris, 1855. 'Le Temps,' Paris, 1858. 'Traité d'horlogerie moderne,' Paris, 1870. 'Guide-Manuel de l'Horloger,' which passed through many editions, and many mems. and arts.
SAUNOIS, ——. *Dijon.* 1714. Repaired clock on Notre Dame.
SAURER, Lorenz. *Augsburg.* m.1758-70.
SAURIN, ——. *Paris.* 1720. Wrote Mém. on 'Les Horloges à Pendule' for l'Acad. Roy. des Sci.
SAURON, Dominique. *Paris.* m.1777.
SAURWEIN, Balthasar. *Strasbourg.* 1583.
SAUTER—
J. *Strasbourg.* 1800.
Fr. J. *Stockholm.* 1808. Three br. clocks, one ill. Sidenbladh.
SAUTTER, Adam. *Switzerland* and *Würtemberg.* b.1820, d.1902. A leading maker in Germany. Started a factory in *Würtemberg.*
SAUVAGE—
Thomas. *Paris.* m.1779-89.
——. *Paris.* 1807-24. Succeeded by Raffart.
SAUVAGE DE SAINT-PREUIL, François. *Paris.* m.1764.

SAUVAISTRE, Mathieu. *Paris.* m.1770.
SAUVAJOT, ——. *Paris.* Late 18c. Fine ormolu clock.
SAUZER—
Abram. *Chaux-de-Fonds.* 1786-1806. C.
David Louis. *La Brévine.* 1793. C.
SAVAGE—
John. *Exeter.* 1613. cf. SAVIDGE.
John, son. *London.* a.1613 in BC.
Abraham. *London.* a.1648.
Thomas. *London (E. Smithfield).* a.1659-1721. Insolvent.
Joshua. *London.* ca.1720-ca.1770. l.c. clock. Watch Ilbert coll.
Thomas. *Clifton (Cumberland).* 1730. l.c. clock.
——. *Dublin.* an.1747. Watch.
Francis. *London.* a.1739.
——. *Ormskirk.* Mid. 18c. l.c. clock Virginia M.
Henry. *Canterbury.* an.1766. Watch.
——. *Appleby.* ca.1770-95.
James. *Howden (Yorks.).* 1784.
Thomas. *London (Red Lion St.).* a.1788, CC.1797-1825. Watch, ruby cyl., S.M.S.K.
William. *London (Goswell St.).* 1802-08.
George. *Huddersfield* and *London.* 1808-23. Went to Canada and d.1855. A very able watchmaker. Patented a remontoir in 1808, and gained award of Soc. Arts for a detached escapement for watches, desc. in Trans. Soc. Arts, Vol. 40, 1823.
& Co. *London.* 1815.
William. *London (Bedford Row).* 1820.
Thomas, son of Thomas. *London.* CC.1825. Watch Chamb. coll.
SAVAGLIO & COMPANY. ——. Early 19c. g. en. watch M.M.A.
SAVARIN, ——. *Bourg.* ca.1772. Became manager of Castel Frères' factory after their failure.
SAVIDGE, John. *Exeter.* d.1627. cf. SAVAGE.
SAVIGNY, Charles Henry. *London.* a.1804.
SAVILLE—
John. *London.* CC.1653, d.1679. 3-case watch. Watch Ilbert coll. Also SAVILE.
John, son. *London.* a.1671, CC.1678-90. Lantern clock.
William. *London.* a.1686.
George Hugh. *Richmond (Surrey).* 1791. C.
SAVOIE, Henry. *Le Locle* and *Besançon.* Early 19c. Nephew of A. L. BREGUET. Made a pin lever esc. with pins barrel-shaped to retain oil.
SAVORY—
Andrew. *London.* a.1669, CC.1676-93. Lantern and br. clocks.
William. *London.* a.1770, CC.1777-94.
Joseph. *London.* an.1795. Lever watch.
FARRAUD & Co. *London.* an.1795. Lever watch Buckley coll.
Adey B. *London.* 1815-25.
SAVYON, C. C. *London.* ca.1760. g. repoussé watch. Also SAVION.
SAWIN & DYER. *Boston, U.S.A.* 1800-25. Lyre clock M.M.A. ill. Milham.
SAWTELL, James White. *London.* a.1802.
SAWYER—
Paul. *London.* a.1711, CC.1718.
Charles. *Bristol.* 1754. W.
Edward. *London.* a.1757.
John. *Leeds.* 1770-98.
William. *London (Peckham).* an.1776-ca. 1800. Watch.
Samuel. *Huntingdon.* Late 18c. Watch.
SAXBY—
Thomas. *London.* a.1729.
Christopher. *London.* a.1731, CC.1749-57, d.an.1760.
Jane. *London (St. John St.).* 1762-77.
Richard. *London.* an.1799. Watch.
SAXON, Thomas. *Liverpool.* ca.1790.
SAXTON, John. *London.* a.1726.
SAY—
Nehemiah. *London.* CC.1656.
Richard. *London.* a.1688.
Richard. *London.* a.1813.
SAYER—
Matthew. *Exeter.* 1763. l.c. clock and watch Exeter M.
William. *Devizes.* an.1765. Watch.
Ralph. *London.* a.1749.
SAYERS, Thomas. *London.* a.1748.
SAYES, Nehemiah. *London.* a.1648, CC.1656.
SAYLES, Samuel. *Sheffield.* 1821. C. & W.
SAYLLER, Johann. *Ulm.* b.1597, m.1646, d. 1668. Oval sil. watch K.H.M. sil. oval cal. watch and crys. watch M.P.S. Dresden. Oval watch Gélis coll. Steel watch Ilbert coll. Table clock Virginia M. Table clock going for three months. cf. SAILLER and SAIGLER.
SAYRE—
I. & R. *New York.* 1805. W.
& RICHARDS. *New York.* 1805.
SCADDING, James. *Sidmouth.* mar.1728. C.
SCAFE—
William. *London (King St., Guildhall).* CC. 1721, m.CC.1749-64. A maker of repute. Chased watch ill. Britten.
Joseph. *London.* 1729 CC.
——. *London (Milk St.).* an.1751. Watch.
SCAGULLER, Stefano. *Venice.* End 16c. rect. table clock of German type Fränkel coll.
SCALE, Peter Bernard. *London.* a.1750.
SCALES—
John. *London.* a.1710.
Edward. *London (Strand).* an.1772. Watch.
Edward. *Manchester.* ca.1800. Table clock Virginia M. eng. 'Patent detached lever.'
William. *Kendal.* 1820.
SCALI, ——. *Amsterdam.* 2nd half 18c. Watch.
SCANAVINO, David. *Genoa.* 17c. Watch.
SCANDER—
Martial. *Toulouse.* ca.1600.
Pierre. *Blois.* m.1633-54. C. to the duc d'Orléans from 1641. Also SCANDE and SCANDRE.
SCANDRETT, John. *Worcester.* mar.1782-1816. W.
SCARBOROUGH, John. *London.* a.1819.
SCARDEVILE, John. *London.* a.1663.
SCARF, George. *Beccles.* Early 19c. Watch.
SCARFE, Thomas. *Ingatestone.* an.1711. Watch.
SCARLETT, John. *London.* a.1815.
SCARRETT, T. C. *Kington.* 1790. C.
SCATLISS, Simon. *London.* a.1683.
SCETTOT, ——. *Paris.* 1812-15.
SCHADE, Ferdinand. *Breslau.* 1828. d.1857. An able maker. In 1828 made a clock with helicoidal gearing, and wrote a pamphlet on the gearing, Breslau, 1847. Pub. 'Uhrmacher Lexicon,' Weimar, 1855.
SCHAFFER, Conrad. ——. End 17c. Gilt sil. watch Nat. M. Stockholm.
SCHAFFRATH, Bernard. *Cologne.* 1689.
SCHAFFT, Christian Ferdinand. *Hamburg.* 1821.
SCHAGER, Robert R. *Uddevalla.* 1819-35.
SCHALIN, Michael. *Lilla Malma.* b.1738, d. 1782. l.c. clock.
SCHALLER, Johann Georg. *Hannstetten.* 1770-83.
SCHAPPE, John. *London.* 1799. W.
SCHARDEES, Thomas. *London.* ca.1715. Watch G.M.
SCHARFFENSTEIN, Léopold Henri. *Paris.* m.1782-9.
SCHARP (SCHARFF), Joh. Erik. *Kristinehamn.* b.1765, d.1825.

SCHATZ—
——. *Feuchtwangen.* ca.1660.
Johann Heinrich, son. *Altdorf.* ca.1685. Great-grandfather of Schiller.

SCHAUDT—
Philipp Gottfried. *Onstmettingen.* 1769. Fine astro. clock.
Philipp Matthäus. *Onstmettingen.* b.1766, d.1855. br. clock Furt. M.

SCHAUFEL, Veyt. *Munich.* 1554. Very fine astro. stand clock with 10 dials and sundial, made as masterpiece, Feill coll.

SCHÄZLER, Fr. Aug. *Fürth.* d.ca.1820.

SCHECKS (SCHECX, SCHEGS), Abraham. *Nürnberg.* Burgher 1656. Watch B.M. str. al. watch Den. coll. Watch in cast chiselled case Stern. coll. g. en. watch Gélis coll. Watch eng. dial Mallett coll.

SCHEER, Johann Hinrich. *Ritzebüttel.* 1821.

SCHEFFER—
Hans. *Fritzlar.* 1517. From *Homberg.*
Hans. *Cassel.* 1531. The first C. in the book of burghers. Prob. same as preceding.
——. *Paris.* 1818-21.

SCHEFFLER, Joseph. *Vienna.* m.ca.1682.

SCHEIBLER, Jörg. *Germany.* ca.1580. oct. watch Fränkel coll. prob. by him.

SCHEIER, Johan. *Augsburg.* Early 17c. circ. watch Feill coll. cf. SCHEIRER.

SCHEIKEL, Jos. *Vienna.* ca.1690. str. and rep. br. clock.

SCHEILIN, Jacob. *Dresden.* 1614-28. Court C.

SCHEIRER—
Johan. ——. ca.1620. hex. table clock ill. Britten. cf. SCHEIER.
Daniel. *Vienna.* 1st half 17c. Oval astro. watch. Oval crys. watch.

SCHELHORN, Andreas. *Schneeberg.* 1571. astro. clock Grünes Gewölbe, Dresden.

SCHELIN, Zacharias. *Uddevalla.* 1815-26.

SCHELLE, Elias. *Biberach.* a.1779.

SCHELLENBERG, Johann Jacob. *Löhningen.* 1626. Made wooden chiming and cal. clocks.

SCHENK—
Ferdinand. *Augsburg.* m.1758-70.
Alois. *Vienna.* ca.1800-ca.1840. g. en. harp watch. Skeleton clock Uhren M. Vienna.

SCHEPKE, Daniel. *Warsaw.* ca.1740. C. to the King. sil. trav. clock.

SCHERER—
Andreas. *Dresden.* 1570. Court C. From *Leipzig.*
J. C. *Geneva.* Late 18c. en. watch M.M.A.

SCHERIDAM, ——. *London.* 1799. cyl. watch. Ilbert coll.

SCHERMER (SCHIRMER)—
Erik. *Stockholm.* m.1712, d.1725.
Johan, son. *Stockholm.* b.1714, m.1741, d. 1747.

SCHERRER—
Der Aeltere. *Oberhausen.* 1756. Kleinuhrmacher.
Christoph. *Oberhausen.* 1756.
Johann. *Oberhausen.* 1756. Turret C.

SCHERZENBERGER, Joseph Anton. *Augsburg.* m.1786-99.

SCHERZINGER, Salomon. *Furtwangen.* 1770. mus. clocks with pipes.

SCHETTER, A. N. *Cologne.* 1813.

SCHEUBLEIN, W. V. *Gorichem.* Mid. 18c. l.c. clock Stads M. Amsterdam.

SCHEULT, Pierre. *Paris.* 1654. crys. cross watch M.M.A.

SCHIBANI, Martin. *Würzburg.* m.1727, d. 1759. A good maker. Stand and wall clock Würzburg M.

SCHIESSEL—
Benedict. *Vienna.* m.1786. br. clock Uhren M. Vienna.
Franz. *Vienna.* m.1788.
Benedict, jun. *Vienna.* m.1800.

SCHIETZEL, Friedrich August. *Dresden.* 1779, m.1806, d.1847.

SCHIFFERDÖCKER (SCHIEFERDÖCKER), Johann. *Vienna.* m.1709.

SCHILLER—
Bernhard. ——. ca.1600. Oval crys. watch.
Paullus. ——. End 17c. aut. table clock.

SCHILTER, Ignaz. *Vienna.* m.1789.

SCHINDLER—
Carl Christian. *Halle.* 1704-16. Compass. Altitude dial Old Ashmolean M.
Fidel. *Rohrbach.* 1760. Wall clock Furt. M.
——. *Prague.* 2nd half 18c. Inst. maker. Scale Nat. M. Prague.
J. *Nijmegen.* ca.1800.

SCHIOLBERG, Christian. *Christiania.* 1781 m.

SCHIOTT, Jens Jørgen. *Christiania.* 1787 m.

SCHIOTTZ, Sigvardt Mathiesen. *Bergen.* 1753 m.

SCHIRCK, Johann. *Berlin.* 1794. Wooden C.

SCHIRLEI DE RHEITA, Antonius Maria. *Cologne.* 1642. astro. clock.

SCHISSLER—
Christoph. *Augsburg.* 1554. d.1609. The greatest math. inst. maker of his time. Very fine dial and astrolabe M.M.A. Dial Old Ashmolean M. Quadrate dial Bodleian.
Hans Christoph. *Augsburg.* mar.1580. *Prague* and *Vienna,* 1591-1610. C. to Rudolph II and math. inst. maker.

SCHIWE—
Peter. *Copenhagen.* m.1791. Master of Corporation 1808-22.
Jacob. *Copenhagen.* m.1822.

SCHLATTER, Johann. *Basle.* 1790. From *Eydingen.*

SCHLEIDER, aîné. *Paris.* 1825.

SCHLEINVOIGT, Johan Jacob. *Göteborg.* mar.1667-74.

SCHLEUER, Jacob Philipp. *Cologne.* 1701.

SCHLICKER, Joh. Georg. *Neustadt.* Late 18c. g. en. cal. watch.

SCHLOER—
Johann Sigmund. *Regensburg.* 1st half 17c. Fine watch Louvre ill. Baillie. Fine sil. gilt sq. watch Fränkel coll. sq. iron and brass watch Carnegie M.
Joan Philipp. *Cologne.* 1730.
Arnold. *Cologne.* 1797.
Peter. *Cologne.* 1813.

SCHLOSS—
Sebastian. *S. Germany.* ca.1635. sil. cross watch.
Philipp. *Würzburg.* m.1673.

SCHLOSSER, ——. *Paris.* 1812-15.

SCHLOTT, Hanns. *Augsburg.* 1581. Magnificent sil. ship with clock and aut. B.M.

SCHLOTTHEIM, Hanns. *Augsburg.* b.1547, d.1625. In *Prague* 1585, and *Dresden* 1592. Made the famous Tower of Babel clock with rolling ball in the Grünes Gewölbe, Dresden. aut. clock M.P.S. Dresden. Made clocks and aut. for Rudolph II. Worked for some time at the Dresden Court.

SCHMALS (SCHMALZ)—
——. *Cologne.* ca.1700.
Franz, son. *Cologne.* m.1716-30.

SCHMAUTZ, Martin. *Partenkirchen.* 1715. Repaired Ansbach church clock.

SCHMELZER, F. Adam. *Fürth.* d.1795.

SCHMID, ——. *London.* ca.1760. g. and agate watch Stern. coll.

SCHMIDT—
Hanns. *Nürnberg.* Burgher 1553.
Georg. *Würzburg.* 1573. Court and town C. Made second clock for Dom, still existing.
Carl or Carol. prob. *Germany.* ca.1600. Stand clock B.M. Clock in crys. sphere Nat. M. Copenhagen. aut. clock Feill coll. Oval str. watch M.M.A. crys. crucifix watch Ilbert coll. Also SCHMIED.

SCHMIDT—*continued.*
Terentius. *Cassel.* 1612, became burgher. From *Saarbrücken.* Later master of the mint.
Georg. *v.* SCHMIT.
Nicolaus. *Augsburg.* mar.1620. Ring watch Gotha M. Table clock with aut. of the flagellation, ill. Britten, sd. 'Nicolaus Schmidt der Junger.'
Johan Ulrich, son. *Augsburg.* mar.1648. circ. watch en. flowers M.M.A.
Jørgen. *Copenhagen.* 1691. Kleinuhrmacher.
Johann Jakob. *Basle.* m.1697. From *Brügg.* Watch.
Johann. *Bamberg.* Early 18c. Table clock G.M.
Johann Heinrich. *Mannheim.* 1747-60. Watch.
Johann Jacob. *Stettin.* 1765. Pupil of George GRAHAM.
Thomas. *Günzburg.* 1770.
Michael. *Vienna.* m.1776.
Johan Andreas. *Copenhagen.* m.1783. *London,* 1801. In 1808 patented a mysterious clock with watch mt. in a pivoted hand. Agate watch M.M.A.
Friedrich August. *Silesia.* 1795. Pub. 'Belehrungen über Taschenuhren.' In 1797 pub. 'Beitrag zur Zeitmesskunst für Freunde und Liebhaber von Uhrwerken aller Art.'
Ferdinand. *Prague.* ca.1800. Regulator.
Christ. *Neuchâtel.* 1800.
Der Aeltere. *Stettin.* ca.1800. Made clocks attached to mirrors.
Andreas Jørgensen. *Odense.* m.1811.
Aîné. *Trèves.* Early 19c. g. en. watch.
——. *Paris.* 1807-17.
Veuve. *Paris.* 1818.

SCHMIDTBAUER, Johann. *Bamberg.* ca. 1750. Clock.

SCHMIED—
Carol. prob. *Germany.* ca.1600. Clock in crys. sphere Nat. M. Cop. Prob. same as Carl SCHMIDT.
——. *Friedberg.* Early 18c.
Maria Johanna. *Friedberg.* 1778. Made cocks and hands for Nürnberg makers.

SCHMIEDHANS, Martin. *Oberhausen.* 1756 comp.

SCHMIT (SCHMITT)—
Georg. *Augsburg.* 1st half 17c. Also SCHMIDT. aut. work and watch K.H.M. Clock Cassel Landes-M. crys. globe clock Webster coll.
Christinn Klein. *Vienna.* ca.1675. al. watch mt. G.M.
Urban. *Würzburg.* m.1738-44. C.
Jean Nicolas. *Paris.* m.1781-9. Mantel clock Pal. de Compiègne.
C. *Bödelfeld.* 1793. br. clocks.
Martin. *Ochsenfurt.* 1794 comp., m.1801.
——. *Paris* (*Rue de la Tixéranderie*). Early 19c. Mantel clock. Prob. Jean Nicolas.
Thomas. *Ochsenfurt.* m.1808. C.
——. *Paris* (*Rue St. Marc*). 1812.

SCHMITS, Joseph. *Aix-la-Chapelle.* Late 18c. Fine astro. l.c. clock with 24 hour dial Feill coll.

SCHMUTZER, Johann Georg. *Vienna.* ca. 1740. Fine astro. stand clock.

SCHNABL, Andreas Antonius. *Dresden.* m. 1815. From *Warsaw.*

SCHNACK (SNACK)—
Petter. *Stockholm.* b.ca.1705, d.1742. A famous maker. Made turret clock for Åbo and large mus. clock for the King. Started 'Stockholms Manufabrique,' by which his clocks were sd. Six l.c. clocks, one Nord. M. Eight br. clocks, two ill. Sidenbladh.
Johan Erland, bro. *Stockholm.* b.1710-62.

SCHNEIDER—
Johannes. *Augsburg.* 1625. Table clock.
Baltzer. *Basle.* 1670. From *Landsberg.*
Josua. *Augsburg.* 1680. mus. str. astro. clock Nat. M. Munich.
J. Paulus. *Fürth.* d.1759.
Christian. *Fürth.* d.ca.1760.
Johann Friedrich. *Basle.* m.1741-46. Town C.
Johann Heinrich, son. *Basle.* 1763-98. Turret and other clocks.
Johann Jakob, bro. *Basle.* 1770.
J. *Vienna.* 2nd half 18c. Watch mt. Arts M. Prague.
Ch. Michael. *Fürth.* d.1793.
Friedrich. *Fürth.* d.ca.1800.
Ignatz. *Ochsenfurt.* 1794.
Johann David. *Leipzig.* 1800-14 juré.
Carl Christian. *Hamburg.* 1821.

SCHNIEP—
Ulrich. *Munich.* 1555-88. Court C. Famous math. inst. maker. Dials B.M. and Old Ashmolean M.
Alexius, son. *Vienna.* 1583. d.1613. Kleinuhrmacher. Sundial Uppsala M. and Old Ashmolean M.
Hans. *Speyer.* 1583. Book watch Webster coll. circ. clock with stackfreed Ilbert coll. Prob. maker of book watch sd. 'H. S.' in M.M.A.

SCHOENY, Abram. *Chaux-de-Fonds.* 1807-1826. C.

SCHOFIELD (SCHOLFIELD)—
John. *Halifax.* 1720.
Major. *Manchester, Salford* and *Rochdale.* b. 1707, d.1783. l.c. clocks. The firm continued till 1804.
James. *London* (*Strand*). an.1747-ca.1760. (SCHOLEFIELD). l.c. clock ill. Cec. & Web. Watch.
Jonathan. *Ogden.* 1747. C.
John. *London.* an.1776. Watch.
William. *London.* an.1778. Watch.
Edmund. *Rochdale.* d.1792. C.
Robert. ——. Late 18c. l.c. clock.
Francis. *Dewsbury.* ca.1800-40. Watch.
Joseph. *Manchester.* 1808.
John. *London.* a.1807.
William. *London* (*Chelsea*). 1820. l.c. clocks.
W. *London* (*Battersea*). 1822-4. C.

SCHOL (SKULT, SCHIOLD), Daniel. *Copenhagen.* m.1705, d.ca.1708. From *Breslau.*

SCHOLLET, John Baptist. *Boston, U.S.A.* 1796-1803. W.

SCHOLTEN, H. *Amsterdam.* 1822. W.

SCHOLTZ, Wilhelm. *Amsterdam.* Early 19c. sil. watch.

SCHONBERG, Nils. *Linköping.* comp. 1758, d.1772. Watch mt. Nord. M.

SCHONBERG, Andreas. *Copenhagen.* m. 1797.

SCHÖNER (SCHÖNNER, SCHONER)—
Christoph. *Augsburg.* mar.1681-1710. Magnificent table clock and astro. clock Nat. M. Munich.
Jacopo. ——. ca.1700. Made an astro. clock desc. in a pamphlet by VULPERT.
Joseph Anton. *Augsburg.* 1703-29. astro. clock. Stand clock Feill coll.
Rochus Anthoni. *Stadtamhof.* ca.1720. sil. watch. rep. watch Fränkel coll.

SCHÖNMANN, Johann. *Constance.* 1584. aut. astro. br. clock K.H.M.

SCHONNE, Johan Daniel. *Copenhagen.* m. 1788.

SCHOOLMAN, M. *London.* an.1778. Watch.

SCHOONBEEK, Henry. *Amsterdam.* ca. 1700, l.c. clock.

SCHORN (SCHOR), Aloysius. *Vienna.* m. 1783

SCHORRER, Joseph Xaver. *Augsburg.* m. 1765-70, d.an.1790.
SCHOT, P. *Rotterdam.* ca.1800.
SCHOTT—
Gaspar. ——. Pub. Würzburg, 1657, 'Mechanica Hidraulico-Pneumatica,' showing many water clocks, and 'Tecnica Curiosa,' Nürnberg, 1664, showing many clocks.
Joseph. *Schwarzwald.* ca.1750.
SCHOULT—
Abraham. *Paris.* 1675 m.
Guillaume. *Paris.* 1675 m.
Jean. *Paris.* 1675 m.
SCHOUTEN, H. *Amsterdam.* Early 18c. l.c. clock Webster coll.
SCHPEKE, Daniel. *Warsaw.* ca.1700. C. to the King. Trav. clock.
SCHRADER, Hans. *Hildesheim.* 1589. Made clock for church of Basse (Hannover).
SCHRADI, Georgius. *Germany.* ca.1660. sq. cal. table clock Ilbert coll.
SCHRAMM, Heinrich Ferdinand. *Berlin.* 1775-1840. C.
SCHREIBELMAYER—
Joseph. *Vienna.* m.1771.
Anton. *Vienna.* m.1781.
SCHREINER—
Martin. *Lancaster, U.S.A.* b.1767-1830. Large number of fine l.c. clocks.
Charles W. *Philadelphia.* 1813-25.
Martin, son of Martin. *Lancaster.* 1830-6. Continued his father's business.
Philip, bro. *Lancaster.* 1830-6. Worked with his brother.
SCHRETTEGGER, Johann. *Augsburg.* ca. 1700. Sundials Fränkel coll., G.M., Ashmolean M., M.M.A. and Carnegie M.
SCHREUDER, H. *Amsterdam.* 1822. W.
SCHROEDEL, Christoph. *Fürth.* d.ca.1800.
SCHROEDER—
Michael. *Copenhagen.* 1714.
Johann. *Emden.* 1750-80. Fine l.c. clock.
Alexander. *Danzig.* 18c. Table clock.
Jørgen Otto. *Skien.* 1771 m.
Christen Jensen. *Copenhagen.* comp. 1772, m.1781. Master of Corporation 1800-08.
F. H. *Lüneberg.* 1821.
SCHROEL, Johann. *Germany.* 1st half 17c. Oval watch Feill coll.
SCHROETER—
Davidt. *Elbing.* ca.1680. Falling ball clock National M. Cracow.
——. *Lilienthal.* 1789. Used varnished wood pendulum rod.
Charles. *Baltimore, U.S.A.* 1807-17. C.
SCHUBARDT, Carl. *Nürnberg.* b.1631, d. 1693. Town C.
SCHUBERT, Friedrich Theodor. ——. Long art. on clocks and watches in his 'Vermischte Schriften,' Vol. 4, Stuttgart and Tübingen, 1823-6.
SCHUBLER, Johann Jakob. *Germany.* 1732. Combined a clock dial with a magic lantern whereby an image of the dial was thrown on wall or ceiling. Pub. 'Perspectivische Belustung . . .,' Nürnberg, 1732.
SCHUELER, ——. *Paris.* 1824.
SCHUETZE (SCHIOTZ, SCHOTTE), Josias. *Copenhagen.* 1636. d.1676. trav. clock Nat. M. Copenhagen, ill. Liisberg.
SCHUHMANN, Johann Friedrich. *Dresden.* m.1784, d.1817. Court C. 1808. Chron. M.P.S. Dresden.
SCHULER, Josef. *Germany.* 1830. Wrote MS. on 'Uhrenmacherkunst.'
SCHULLER, ——. *Paris.* 1812. C.
SCHULLT, Mickel. *Stockholm.* comp. 1655. German.
SCHULTENBERGER (SCHULLENBERGER), Benno. *Augsburg.* Went *Fürth.* 1751 comp.
SCHULTHESS, Heinrich. *Basle.* 1732. From *Zürich.*
SCHULTZ—
——. *Augsburg.* ca.1570. Cross watch.
N. D. *Hamburg.* 1801.
T. *Copenhagen.* m.1822.
SCHULTZE—
Johann Wilhelm. *Cassel.* 1689. sil. sundial.
Matthew. *Cassel.* 1708. l.c. clock.
——. ——. Pub. arts. on pendulum clocks in Mém. de l'Acad. des Sci. de Berlin, 1780 and 1782.
SCHULZ—
Michael. *Dantzig.* ca.1640. hex. table clock Ilbert coll.
Vincent. *Stockholm.* 1728 m.-1737. d.ca. 1762. br. and two l.c. clocks and watch.
David. *London.* 1753. From *Breslau.* Prepared jewels for watches.
Carl, son of Vincent. b.1752, a.1771.
SCHUMO (SCUMMO), Thomas. *Philadelphia.* 1823-5.
SCHÜPBACH, Christian. *Diesbach.* ca.1800. Watch.
SCHUPPE, John. *London.* a.1770.
SCHUPPERLE & TRITSCHLER. *Amsterdam.* Early 19c.
SCHUR, Joh. Martin. *Ulm.* ca.1790. Watch.
SCHURER, Martin. *Augsburg.* 1795 comp. Turret C.
SCHURICHT—
Theoph. Christian. *Dresden.* m.1728.
August Christian. *Dresden.* b.1726, m.1756, d.1793.
Friedrich Christian. *Dresden.* b.1728, m. 1756, d.1792.
Christian Traugott. *Dresden.* m.1784, d. 1808. Court C.
SCHUSTER—
Hanns. *Nürnberg.* Burgher 1545. d.1601.
Caspar. *Nürnberg.* ca.1550. 'CA×SCH' on watch Munich M. prob. by him.
Paulus. *Nürnberg.* 1591. d.1634. Complex clock, with 11 dials and aut. and enamel plaques, ill. Britten. aut. clock with astrolabe M.P.S. Dresden. Watch Gélis coll. Made clocks for the Dresden Court.
Johann Christoph. *Westheim* and *Echterdingen.* b.ca.1770. Brother-in-law of P. M. HAHN. astro. clock M.P.S. Dresden.
SCHÜSTER, Franz. *Vienna.* m.1818. Four-colour g. watch set stones Feill coll.
SCHUTE, Jasper. *London.* CC.1647.
SCHÜTZ—
Joseph. *Oberhausen.* 1756.
S. *Karlshamn.* 1816-40.
SCHUYLER, Peter C. *New York.* 1802-06. C. & W.
SCHWANDER, Pierre. *Schwarzbourg* (prob. *Schwartzenberg*). ca.1800. Watch.
SCHWARZ—
Sebald. *Nürnberg.* 1580.
Sebald. *Augsburg.* Early 17c. sil. cross watch.
SCHWARZFRIED, S. *Fürth.* ca.1750.
SCHWEIGERT, Anton. *Schlipsen,* 1756. *Steppach,* 1770.
SCHWELBELIN, ——. *Breslau.* 1368. Maker of Breslau clock.
SCHWENSEN, Christian Ludvig. *Copenhagen.* m.1755.
SCHWERER—
Matthew. *Hull.* 1814-34.
Laurence. *Sheffield.* 1818-36. C. & W.
Joseph. *Hull.* 1822-6.
SCHWILGUÉ—
Jean Baptiste. *Strasbourg.* b.1776, d.1856. Mathematician and turret C. of exceptional ability. In 1838-42 he, with his pupils Albert and Théodore UNGERER, made the existing Strasbourg clock, which surpassed

SCHWILGUÉ—*continued.*
by far, in its performance, any other clock, until J. & A. UNGERER made the clock for Messina.
Charles, son. *Strasbourg.* 1856-8. Succeeded his father, and the firm became UNGERER FRÈRES in 1858, and J. & A. UNGERER from 1900. Pub. several pamphlets on turret clocks, and three on the Strasbourg clock.

SCHWINZBERGER—
A. *Fürth.* ca.1750.
Joh. Carl. *Fürth.* d.1772.
Joh. Georg. *Fürth.* d.1776.
P. K. *Fürth.* d.ca.1800.
Joh. Carl. *Fürth.* d.1830.

SCIENCE, John. *London.* a.1716, CC.1724. Watch.

SCOBLE, John S. *Colyton.* 2nd half 18c. l.c. clock.

SCOLDING, John. *London.* 1795-1811.

SCOLSON, Joseph. *Liverpool.* 1784. C.

SCOOPE, Richard. *London.* a.1709. Watch.

SCORESBY, Capt. W., jun. ——. Pub. art. on the effect of magnetism on chrons. in Trans. Roy. Soc., Edinburgh, 1823.

SCOT, James. *Dalkeith.* 1760.

SCOTLAND, Hawke. *London.* a.1752.

SCOTSON—
Isaac. *Liverpool.* 1766-77. C.
Joseph. *Liverpool.* 1781.

SCOTT—
Edward. *London.* d.1654. W.
Simon. *London.* a.1647.
Edward. *London.* a.1650.
Joshua. *London.* a.1674.
Daniel. *London.* a.1697.
Caleb. *London.* a.1699.
George. *Edinburgh.* 1716-55.
Stephen. *Elham.* b.1725, d.1798.
David. *Edinburgh.* 1750.
David. *London.* an.1764. Watch.
John. *London (Gracechurch St.).* an.1767-76. Insolvent. Watch.
James. *London (Holborn).* CC.1766.
James. *Selkirk.* ca.1770.
John. *Tamworth.* 1771-84. Watch.
William. *London (Westminster), Falkirk* and *Aberdeen).* an.1773, d. in London 1798.
Andrew. *Edinburgh.* a.1764-76.
John. *London.* CC.1772.
James. *Leith.* 1774-91.
John. *London (Red Lion Sq.).* 1775. CC. 1781-94. br. clock Weth. coll.
Andrew. *Dundee.* 1776.
R. *London.* an.1780. Watch.
John. *London.* CC.1777.
John. *Edinburgh.* a.1770-1802.
Robert. *Virginia, U.S.A.* 1779.
Walter. *Lauder.* 1780.
John. *London (Lombard St.).* 1781. Watch.
John. *London (Gloucester St.).* an.1784. Watch.
William. *Newcastle-o.-T.* 1782-4.
John. *Newcastle-o.-T.* 1782-1811. l.c. clocks.
John. *Edinburgh.* a.1779, d.1798. Maker to the Prince of Wales.
& STEELE. *Edinburgh.* 1790.
Nicholas. *Maidstone.* 1791-5. W.
Thomas. *Gainsborough.* 1795. C. & W.
John. *London (Corporation Row).* 1799.
& GILES. *Maidstone.* ca.1800.
T. *London (City Road).* ca.1800.
& COUTTS. *London.* an.1806. Watch.
Robert. *London.* 1805-20. Watch.
James. *Dublin.* 1806-20. 'Longitudinal watchmaker.' Proposed platinum for balance-springs.
James Amos. *London (Clerkenwell).* CC. 1809-16. W.
William, son. *London.* a.1816.
James. *Kendal.* Early 19c. Watch.

SCOTT—*continued.*
Thomas. *London (Charing Cross).* 1816-24.
John. *London (Goswell St.).* 1817-24. chron. maker.
William. *Dundee.* 1820.
——. *Rochester.* Early 19c.
& SONS. *Dublin.* 1824.
James. *Ballynahinch.* 1824.
William. *London.* a.1816.

SCRATCHLEY, Thomas. *London.* a.1765.

SCRIVENER—
Richard. *London.* CC.1639-68. l.c. clock.
Richard. *London.* a.1697. l.c. clock ill. Cec. & Web. ca.1710 prob. by him.
Edward. *London.* a.1727.
——. *Guildford.* an.1754. Watch.
P. *Stowmarket.* Early 19c. Watch.

SCROGIE, Charles James. *London.* a.1821.

SCRUTTON, Joseph. *London.* a.1801.

SCRYMGEOUR, James. *Glasgow.* 1816-37. chron. maker.

SCURR—
Richard. *Thirsk.* b.1761, d.1827. C.
Jonah, bro. and partner. *Thirsk.* 1790.

SEABOURNE—
James. *London.* a.1642, CC.1649-91.
Thomas. *London.* 1649 CC.
William. *London.* a.1651, CC.1659.

SEAFIELD, James. prob. *London.* an.1760. Watch.

SEAGER—
George. *London.* 1805-08. W.
John. *Liverpool.* ca.1820.

SEAGRAVE—
Matthew. *London (Snow Hill).* a.1720, CC. 1731-50. Alleged to be mad.
Robert. *London.* an.1773-1811.

SEAICH, Edward. *London.* a.1748.

SEALE—
William Richard. *London.* a.1753.
Richard. *London.* a.1766, CC.1780-98.

SEALL—
Frederick. *London.* a.1776, CC.1789-1810.
& STOREY. *London.* 1802-04.
F. A. *London.* 1809-11.

SEALY, James Milbank. *London.* a.1795.

SEAMAN—
William. *London.* CC.1659. Watch.
John. *London.* a.1789.

SEAMER (SEAMOUR, SEYMOUR)—
William. *York.* 1627. W. cf. SEMOR.
Peter, son. *York.* 1636. W.
Abel, bro. *York.* 1649-1710. W.
Joseph, bro. *York.* 1649. W.
W. *London.* Mid. 18c. Watch Feill coll. (SEAMOURE.)

SEARCH, J. *London.* 18c. Compass Old Ashmolean M.

SEARGEANT, John. *London.* a.1737.

SEARLE—
William. *London.* a.1673.
George. *Chudleigh.* 1791. C. & W.

SEARS, Samuel. *London.* a.1762.

'SEASIDE.' Sig. on watches of the AMERICAN WATCH Co. from 1886.

SEATON, ——. *London (Pall Mall).* 1714. W.

SÉBASTIEN—
Le Père. *Paris.* b.1667, d.1729. Carmelite monk of name Jean TRUCHET. Made a very elaborate aut. theatre for Louis XIV. He opened and repaired the first repeater, sent by Charles II to Louis XIV. Martinot, to whom it was given for repair, could not discover its secret opening, and said that Sébastien, then 19 years old, was the only man capable of doing it. He became member of the Académie des Sciences. Made several artificial arms.
Philippe. *Lyons.* a.1686-9.

SEBERT, Henry. *Strasbourg.* Early 17c. Fine watch in sil. sphere eng. with map of the world with compass and dial Stads M. Amsterdam ill. Baillie.
SEBILLE, ——. *Paris.* ca.1700. Watch Gélis coll.
SEBIRE, John. *London.* an.1744. Watch.
SECHAYE, Jean. *Geneva.* ca.1755-70.
SÈCHEHAYE, Jean Marc. ——. b.1724-68.
SECHTING, Johann Gottfried. ——. 1749-1814. Pupil of P. M. HAHN.
SECRETAN, Frederick. *London.* a.1802.
SEDAN, Nathan. *London.* 1727. Prob. SEDDON.
SEDDON—
James. *London.* a.1655, CC.1662.
Nathaniel. *London.* CC.1691, d.1739. *Pall Mall* in 1700, *St. James* in 1729. 'Noted' W. Watch.
John. *London (St. James St.).* 1743-52. W.
Samuel. *Liverpool.* 1767. W.
John. *Frodsham.* 1784-95.
William. *Liverpool.* 1816. W.
S. D. *Liverpool.* Early 19c. Watch.
SEDERSTRÖM, Gustaf. *Åbo.* 1797-1805.
SEDGWICK—
Samuel. *London.* a.1692. Watch.
Henry. *London (Bartholomew Close).* 1766.
SEDLEY—
John. *London.* a.1686, CC.1701-32. Watch mt.
Andrew. *Dundalk.* 1824.
SEDMAN, Johan. *Filipstad,* 1750. *Kristinehamn,* 1753. l.c. and br. clocks. Two trav. clocks, one Nord. M.
SEDWELL (SIDWELL), Edward. *London.* a.1656, CC.1664.
SEEBECK, Henry. *London.* a.1767.
SEED—
Edward. *Southampton.* 1771. W.
Richard. *Dublin.* 1824.
SEEDALL, Frederick. *London.* an.1783. Watch. cf. SEALL.
SEFFIN, Thomas. *London.* CC.1720.
SEFTON, Edward. *Tadcaster.* 1775.
SEGAR—
Thomas. *Liverpool.* 1810. W.
John. *Liverpool.* 1813-29.
SÉGAUD, Claude Benoît. *Paris.* m.1783-9.
SEGNER, George. *London.* CC.1689-1707.
SEGOND, Pierre. *Geneva.* ca.1770-87.
SEGUY-MARECHAUX, ——. *Paris.* 1812. C.
SÉHEUT, Pierre. *Paris.* 1654 m. Registered a private punch mark.
SEHR, Christoph. *Vienna.* m.1783.
SEIGNEURET, Pierre. *Paris.* m.1771-80. C. to the comte d'Artois. Hanging clock S.K.M.
SEIGNIOR, Robert. *London.* CC.1667-85. d.an.1692. A watch and clockmaker of great repute. l.c. and br. clocks Weth. coll. Clock C.A. and M. g. p.c. filigree watch F.W.M. g. str. watch Webster coll. with balance-spring. Accused by Henry JONES in 1673 of putting his name on a clock by JONES when sent for repair.
SEITENGLANZ, Johann. *Oberhausen.* 1756. Turret C.
SEITZ, Franz Xaver. *Munich.* 1720. Boulle-work clock.
SELBY—
Thomas. *London.* a.1716, CC.1745.
G. J. *Deventer.* Mid. 18c. 8-day watch Stads M. Amsterdam.
Peter. *Wareham.* 1760-95. l.c. clock.
Thomas. *London* and *Leeds.* Went *Knaresborough* 1765-95.
John. *Stratford (Essex).* 1766. W.
John, & SON. *Cirencester.* Two generations to 1793, when son d.

SELBY—*continued.*
Edward. *London.* 1799-1808.
J. *Wakefield.* 1814.
Richard. *Huddersfield.* 1814.
SELDON, ——. *London.* d.1746. W.
SELF, Robert. *London.* a.1760.
SELLAR, John. *Elgin.* 1820-37.
SELLARS—
John. *London.* CC.1667, w.CC.1692, elected m.CC.1696-9.
Bezer. *London.* a.1758, CC.1765-73. d.an. 1788.
Bezer, son. *London.* CC.1801.
Diton, bro. *London.* CC.1814.
SELLBERG—
Mag. *Fäderstad.* 1791. g. watch.
——. *Stockholm.* ca.1820.
SELLERS—
William. *London.* a.1682, CC.1691-1740. Watch Den. coll.
Robert. *London.* an.1748-ca.1755. mus. clock in agate case Palace M. Pekin.
SELLIARD—
Jeune. *Paris.* 1807-25.
Aîné. *Paris.* 1812-25. rep. aut. watch Ilbert coll.
SELLIER & CO. *Leipzig.* ca.1780. Mantel clock.
SELLIÈRE (SELLIER), François. *Paris.* m. 1782-9.
SELLON—
Humphery. *London (Southwark).* 1764-9. Partner in WRIGHT & SELLON. Inn clock S.K.M. Watch.
R. prob. *London.* an.1778. Watch.
SELLS, John. *London.* a.1756.
SELLSTRÖM, ——. *Falköping.* 1819.
SELSON, Charles. *London.* a.1795, CC.1802.
SELWOOD (SELLWOOD)—
William. *London.* CC.1633-52. Lantern clock Glasgow Art Gall.
John. *London.* CC.1640, d.1651. Lantern clock dated 1642 Feill coll.
SEMAUR, ——. *Paris.* 1822.
SEMLERO, Christoph. ——. 1723. Pub. pamphlet on methods of finding the Longitude, Magdeburg.
SEMOR—
W. *York.* ca.1640. p.c. oval cal. sil. watch Mallett coll. ill. Baillie. cf. SEAMER.
Robert. *London.* an.1682. Watch.
SENÉ, Jean. *Geneva.* ca.1800. *Myes.* ca. 1825. sil. rep. watch.
SENEBIER, A. *Geneva.* ca.1630. crys. cross watch and sil. bud watch, with 3 crys. covers, S.K.M. crys. watch G.M.
SENECE & CO. *London.* ca.1800. g. en. watch, set pearls.
SENEGAL, Jaques. *Dieppe.* Early 18c. Ivory dials B.M. and M.M.A.
SENESSE, John. *London.* a.1744.
SENESTRE, Guillaume. *Rouen.* a.1630. Oval crys. watch.
SENEY (SENEZ)—
Guillaume. *Rouen.* 1617-26. Founder member of Rouen corporation. C. to the King. crys. fleur-de-lys watch S.K.M.
SENKSTARKEN, Peter. *Basle.* 1775.
SENS, William. *London.* CC.1711.
SENSIGNET, ——. *Paris.* 1812. C.
SENWOOD, John. *London.* an.1770. Watch.
SEPHTON, Daniel. *Whiston.* 1767. Insolvent. W.
SERES, Joseph. *London.* 1695.
SERGANT, John. *London.* a.1769.
SERGEANT—
Prettyman. *London.* a.1664, CC.1671-88.
Nathaniel. *London.* CC.1763, m.CC.1783-6. Traded as an auctioneer.
Nathaniel. *London (Cannon St.).* CC.1768-1790. Watch G.M.
Nathaniel. *London.* CC.1823.

SERMAND—
J. *Paris.* 1st half 17c. Two watches Louvre, with crys. covers, in forms of shell and almond, sd. 'Sermand.' crys. cross watch.
Jaques. *Geneva.* b.1636, d.1667. Oval lobed cal. watch, crys. cover, Louvre. Watches M.M.A. and Cluny M. Watches B.M.: (1) jasper and en. gold, (2) 8-lobed crys., (3) crys. star ill. Baillie, (4) sil. tulip. Oval cal. watch Mallett coll. ill. Baillie. Large oct. astro. crys. watch Nat. M. Stockholm. crys. en. watch Ilbert coll. Sig. always 'J. Sermand.'
F. ——. ca.1640. Watch G.M., tulip form, crys. sides.
SERMET, ——. *Geneva.* 1566. Repaired the clock of St. Pierre.
SERMON, Joseph. *London.* a.1675.
SERNER, J. J. *Lübeck.* 2nd half 17c. Watch.
SERRE—
Antoine. *Grenoble.* 1561. From *Valence.*
Étienne. *Geneva.* Mid. 18c. Watch.
SERRÉ, ——. *London.* ca.1750. Fine en. watch, set diamonds and rubies, Winter Pal. Petrograd.
SERVANIER, ——. *London.* an.1744. Watch.
SERVANT ET BOURSAULT. *Ferney.* 1770.
SERVAUD, Pierre. *Avignon.* 1629. From *Lyons.*
SERVEL, César. *Geneva.* 1673-6.
SESSFORD, Joseph. *Newcastle-o.-T.* 1816-1824. W.
SETON, Joseph. *Portsmouth.* an.1752. Watch.
SETTOT, ——. *Paris.* 1819.
SEVERBERG, Christian. *New York.* 1755-1775. cf. SYBERBERG.
SEVERN, Luke. *London.* a.1754.
SEVILLE, ——. *London.* Late 18c. Watch.
SEWELL—
Anthony. *London (Holborn).* b.1686, d.1768. C. & W.
John. *London (Fleet St.).* a.1734-72.
Jonathan. *London.* an.1771. Watch.
George. *London (Camberwell).* an.1771-1804. Watch.
Thomas Wilson. *London.* a.1771.
Gregory. *London.* an.1776. Watch.
James. *London.* 1799.
Jeremiah. *London.* 1799.
Christopher. *Bradford.* 1814-40.
Ebenezer. *Liverpool.* 1816. W.
William, jun. *London.* CC.1825.
SEXTON, John. *London.* a.1726.
SEYDELL—
Georg. *Cöllen-a.-d.-Spree.* ca.1640. cal. watch B.M. Globe clock in Cassel Landes-M.
——. *London (Catherine St.).* 1731.
Frederick. *London.* an.1745. Watch. l.c. clock.
SEYDOUX, Georges. *Paris.* m.1777.
SEYFFERT—
Heinrich. *Dresden.* b.1751, d.1818. chron. and precision C. chron. and cyl. watches M.P.S. Dresden.
Frederick William. *London.* 1818. Patented a repeating work.
SEYMOUR (SEYMORE)—
Henry. *Wantage.* 1525. Made clock for E. Hendred Church, still in use.
John. *London.* a.1703, CC.1711-48. g. repoussé p.c. watch.
John, son of John. *London (Little Old Bailey* in 1744, *Aldersgate St.* in 1748). CC.1744-1766. Watch G.M.
John. *Wantage.* d.1760. Watch.
William, son of John (2). *London (Hoxton* and *Chelsea).* CC.1766-1825. Watch and br. clock.
John, son. *London.* a.1766.
William, bro. *London.* a.1770, CC.1789.
James, bro. *London.* CC.1789.

SEYMOUR (SEYMORE)—*continued.*
Edmund. *London.* a.1788.
William. *London.* There was a Wm. of *Holborn* in 1801-13, and one of *Johnson's Ct., Fleet St.,* in 1816.
William Henry, son of Wm. *London.* a.1801.
Thomas. *Manchester.* 1804. C.
John. *London.* a.1806.
Robert. *Waterbury, U.S.A.* 1814.
SEZILLE, ——. *Paris.* 1818-25. g. en. watch M. des Arts, Geneva.
SHADLEY, John. *London.* a.1734. Watch.
SHACKLOCK, Godfrey. *Bolsover.* 1795. C. & W.
SHACKWELL, Richard. *Pershore.* 1795. W.
SHAKESHAFT—
William. *Preston.* 1800-24. Watch N.Y. Univ.
Lawrence. *Preston.* 1818-21. C. & W.
Joseph. *Preston.* ca.1820.
SHAKESPEAR, T. *Burton.* Early 19c. Watch.
SHALLCROSS, William. *London.* 1758. Watch.
SHALLER, Nicholas. *London.* a.1672.
SHANNAN, Samuel. *Castleblayney.* 1824.
SHAPP, George. *London.* 1817-24. W.
SHARENBECK, ——. *prob. London.* an. 1767. Watch.
SHARGELL, Samuel. *Sheffield.* an.1776. Watch.
SHARMAN, ——. *Melton Mowbray.* 1807. C. & W.
SHARP (SHARPE)—
John. *London.* a.1647.
Thomas. *London.* a.1667.
William. *London.* a.1672, CC.1681-99. Watch.
Thomas. *Stratford-on-Avon.* 1762-95. l.c. clock in Shakespeare's house.
——. *Romford.* an.1771. Watch.
——. *Leighton.* an.1772. Watch.
Thomas. *London.* 1777. Watch.
——. *Feversham.* ca.1780. br. clock.
& WILLIAMS. *London (Strand).* 1781. Partnership dissolved.
John. *London (Little Tower St.).* a.1785, CC. 1793-1811.
Peter. *Coldstream.* ca.1800.
Robert. *Snaith.* 1800-22.
John. *London (Fish St. Hill).* CC.1806, m. CC.1833-5.
George Paul, son. *London.* a.1803, CC.1815-1825. Watch.
James. *Northampton.* From 1812. C. & W.
Christopher. *Dublin.* 1824. Regulator. Also SHARPE.
John Vidion. *London (London Bridge).* a. 1812-40. Watch.
William. *Retford.* Early 19c. Watch.
& SON. *London (London Bridge).* Early 19c.
SHARPELEIN, William. *London.* a.1749-72. Bankrupt.
SHARPLES, James. *Liverpool.* 1790-1829. W.
SHARPREY—
Stephen. *London.* an.1775-late 18c. Watch Den. coll.
Thomas. *London.* an.1781. Watch.
SHARRATT, Isaac. *Manchester.* 1797-1804. C.
SHATTON, ——. *Malmesbury.* 1793. W.
SHATWELL, ——. *Leek.* ca.1700. Watch.
SHAW—
John. *London (Holborn).* a.1672, CC.1682, m.CC.1712-15. l.c. clocks. Watch Ilbert coll.
William. *Diss.* 1680.
John. *London.* a.1675.
John. *London.* a.1675, CC.1682.
John. *London.* a.1683.
Edward. *London.* a.1689.

SHAW—*continued.*
John. *London.* a.1700.
John. *London.* a.1707. Watch.
Samuel. *London.* a.1712. Watch.
John. *Sandbach.* 1728. C.
Anna Maria. *London.* a.1738.
George. *London.* an.1764. Watch.
Thomas. *Lancaster.* 1766-95. C.
Joseph. *London.* a.1767.
William. *Botesdale.* 1760-90. C. & W. l.c. clock.
Joseph Kember. *London.* an.1773-7. Watch G.M.
Joshua. *Billingborough.* 1782. C. & W.
William. *London.* an.1784. Watch.
Robert. *Hatton.* 1789. C. Lancaster freeman.
James F. *Halifax.* 1790-1830.
Thomas. *Doncaster.* 1790.
George. *Botesdale.* 1791. W.
Nathaniel. *Sleaford.* Late 18c. l.c. mus. clock.
Aaron. *London.* a.1799.
Robert. *London.* 1813. Watch.
William. *London.* a.1810.
John. *Philadelphia.* 1819. W.
Robert. *Belfast.* 1824.
Joseph. *Liverpool.* 1825. W.
David. *Leicester.* ca.1825. Watch.

SHEAFE—
Thomas. *London* (*College Hill*). a.1737, CC. 1749-81. Also SHEAF.
William. *London.* an.1768-90. rep. watch mt.

SHEARER—
Michael. *Edinburgh.* 1786-1825.
James. *London.* 1825-40. astro. clock showing mean and sidereal time.

SHEARMAN—
——. *London.* 1745. C.
Robert. *Wilmington, U.S.A.* 1768-70. *Philadelphia,* 1799. l.c. clock.
Thomas. *Bristol.* 1818. C.

SHEARSMITH, R. *London.* 1817-24. W.

SHEARWOOD, James. *London.* 1759-80. cal. watch S.M.S.K. Watch Den. coll. sil. p.c. repoussé watch.

SHEDDEN, Charles. *Perth.* 1813-71.

SHEERER, Charles. *London.* 1799-1808.

SHEFFIELD—
James. *London.* a.1701.
John. *London.* a.1737.

SHEILL, James. *Earlston.* 1730.

SHELBURY, John. *London.* a.1725.

SHELLEY—
John. *London.* 1660. Lantern clock.
Joseph. *London.* a.1708, CC.1717. l.c. clock ill. Cec. & Web.
Charles. *London.* a.1716-34 CC.

SHELTON—
Samson. *London.* 1623. w.CC.1632, d.1649. Took part in the incorporation of the CC. Fine str. watch B.M.
John. *London.* a.1662. Watch. Also SKELTON.
William. *London.* a.1695.
John. *London.* a.1695, CC.1702.
John. *London.* a.1711, CC.1720, l.CC.1766. astro. clocks. br. and l.c. clock Weth. coll. Clock presented to Göttingen Observatory by the King.
John. *London* (*Shoe La.*). a.1737, CC.1745.
John, son. *London.* a.1777.

SHENOON, ——. *London.* 1662. French.

SHEPHERD (SHEPARD, SHEPPARD, SHEPPERD)—
Thomas. *London.* CC.1632. Oval watch Webster coll. Also SHEPPERD.
Thomas. *London.* a.1655.
John. *London.* a.1674.
Thomas. *London.* a.1689.
Matthew. *London.* a.1713.

SHEPHERD (SHEPARD, SHEPPARD, SHEPPERD)—*continued.*
William. *London.* a.1724. Also SHEPPARD.
Robert. *Eye.* 18c. l.c. clock.
John. *London.* a.1752.
William. *Liverpool.* 1763-84. W.
John. *Whitehaven.* ca.1770.
Thomas. *Liverpool.* ca.1770.
Matthew. *Charleston, U.S.A.* From 1774. *New York* from 1760. From *London.* W.
John. *London.* an.1778. Watch.
Thomas. *Wotton-under-Edge.* 1782-93 CC.
John. *Whitehaven.* 1791. W.
——. *Reading.* 1794. W.
& POTTER. *Wotton-under-Edge.* ca.1800.
William Robert. *Pontefract.* 1822-40. SHEPPARD.

SHEPHERDSON, J. *London.* an.1774. Watch.

SHEPLEY—
John. *Stockport.* d.1750. W.
William. *Stockport.* To 1784. Prob. went *Liverpool.*
Edward. *Manchester.* 1790-1800. l.c. clocks S.K.M. and Manchester Art Gall.

SHEPPERLEY, Anthony. *Nottingham.* 1814-1818. Watch Nottingham M. Later SHEPPERLEY & PEARCE.

SHERBIRD, J. *London.* 1820.

SHERMAN—
William. *Chester.* 1732. W.
Thomas. *Bristol.* 1812.

SHERMER, John. *Philadelphia.* 1805-13.

SHERRAT, Ralph. *London.* a.1700.

SHERRIFF, William. *Edinburgh.* a.1727.

SHERRING, Stephen. *London.* 1817-24.

SHERVEY—
William. *London.* a.1736.
William. *London.* a.1737.

SHERWIN, J. J. *Whitehaven.* Early 19c. Watch.

SHERWOOD—
William. *London.* a.1686, CC.1695-1722.
John. *London.* a.1690.
William, son of William. *London.* CC.1720, m.CC.1740-4. Watch.
John. *London.* a.1714, CC.1721-44.
Benjamin. *London* (*Clerkenwell*). d.1773.
Joseph. *London.* ca.1750-75.
Jeremiah. *London.* a.1764.
Thomas. *Yarm.* 1775-91. C. & W. Also SHURWOOD.
Thomas. *Doncaster.* 1784. W.
Thomas. *Leeds.* From 1801-34. W.
James. *Yarm.* 1816-34.
Thomas. *Yarm.* 1822-40.

SHEVILL, John Randall. *London.* a.1802.

SHEW, George. *Weymouth.* 1795. C. & W.

SHICK, William. *London.* 1805-20.

SHIELD—
John. *London.* a.1691.
Thomas. *London.* a.1692.
Alexander. *London.* a.1736.
Alexander. *London.* a.1779.

SHIELDS—
Michael. ——. End 17c. Sun and moon watch Ilbert coll.
William. *London.* an.1711. Watch.
Tobias. *London.* a.1733.
John. *London.* a.1753.
James. *Woolwich.* 1784. W.

SHILLING—
James. *Boughton.* 18c. Watch Chamb. coll.
Thomas. *Selling.* an.1767. Watch.

SHINDLER—
Thomas. *Canterbury.* ca.1720, d.1797. Watch Stads M. Amsterdam.
Robert. *London.* a.1765.

SHIPHAM, John. *Hull.* 1822-40. In RUST & SHIPHAM.

SHIPLEY, James. *Derby.* 1809. Watch.

SHIPMAN, John. *Newcastle-o.-T.* 1787-1801. C. & W.
SHIPPEN—
Christopher. *London.* an.1765. Watch.
William. *Philadelphia.* 1819-24. W.
SHIPPY, John. *London.* a.1706.
SHIPTON—
——. *London.* 1748. W.
——. *Andover.* an.1755. Watch.
SHIPWAY, John. *London.* CC.1813.
SHIRLEY—
James. *London.* a.1680.
John (or James). *London.* a.1705, CC.1720-4.
SHIRT—
John. *London.* a.1700.
William. *London.* a.1784-1835.
SHOLE, Robert. *Truro.* 1795. C. & W.
SHON, Shenkyn. *S. Wales.* 1714. l.c. clock.
SHORROCK, Thurston. *Preston.* ca.1770-1795. W.
SHORT—
Joshua. *London.* a.1656, CC.1665-82.
James, F.R.S. ——. Wrote art. in Phil. Trans. 1762 on the going of ELLICOTT's clock, and a pamphlet in 1763 on the controversy about HARRISON's timekeeper.
William. *London.* a.1758.
Ramsay. *Edinburgh.* a.1781.
SHORTALL, Thomas. *London.* CC.1718.
SHORTEN, James. *London.* a.1709.
SHORTER—
William. *London.* a.1707.
Thomas. *London.* a.1717.
SHORTGRAVE, Robert. *Northampton.* 1734. d.1751. W.
SHORTLAND, Thomas. *London.* a.1745, CC.1764.
SHORTMAN—
S. *Penzance.* Early 19c.
Samuel. *Newnham.* Early 19c. Watch.
SHOVELL—
John. *London.* a.1691.
James. *London.* a.1691-ca.1720. Watch Ilbert coll.
Thomas. *London.* a.1773.
SHOYWELL, Henry. *London.* a.1660.
SHRAPNELL, James. *London.* 1761-75. g. en. watch, set diamonds and pearls, and chatelaine F.W.M.
SHREWSBRIDGE—
John. *London.* 1802.
James, son. *London.* a.1800.
SHRIMPS, William. *London.* a.1722.
SHRIVELL, Richard. *Brighton.* 1822. C. & W.
SHRUBB—
Thomas. *London.* a.1689.
John. *London.* a.1700.
SHRUBSALL, Thomas. *London.* a.1751.
SHUCKBURG, Charles. *London.* a.1706, CC.1719-29. Insolvent.
SHUCKFORD (SHUCKFORTH)—
John. *Diss.* an.1743. Watch. l.c. clock.
Benjamin. *Diss.* an.1754, d.1760. Watch. l.c. clock.
SHUFFLEBOTTOM, William. *London.* a. 1764.
SHUTE, James. *London.* a.1729.
SHUTTER, William. *London.* ca.1755. Two mus. clocks in agate cases Palace M. Pekin and Peiping M.
SHUTTLEWORTH—
Henry. *London.* a.1662, CC.1669.
Francis. *London (Barbican).* 1802-11.
Francis. *London (Duke St.).* 1805-15.
SHUTZ, Gustavus. *Philadelphia.* 1825.
SHWERER, Lawrence. *Sheffield.* 1818-36.
SIBBALD, William. *London.* 1817-30.
SIBBERN, Jørgen. *Nyborg.* b.1615, d.1700.
SIBE, Johan. *Copenhagen.* 1547-58. Fleming. Goldsmith, clockmaker and mathematician

SIBE—*continued.*
to Christian III. Magnificent astro. clock in form of tower made by him and Steffen BRENNER, now destroyed; ill. Liisberg.
SIBELIN—
Josué. *Neuchâtel.* a.1684, d.1738. Watch.
Laisné. *Neuchâtel.* Early 18c. rep. watch.
Jean. *Neuchâtel* district. a.1706, d.1742. Some sd. sundials. W. & C.
Emer Louis. *Neuchâtel.* b.1702-46.
SIBLEY—
John. *London.* an.1759. Watch.
James. prob. *London.* an.1778. Watch.
SIBON—
Jacques. *Paris.* mar.ca.1650.
——. *Paris.* 1822-5.
SICH (SYCH), Joseph. *Vienna.* m.1734. Table clock with tinder lighter Feill coll.
SIDEBOTHAM, Peter. *Sunderland.* 1701. l.c. clock.
SIDEY—
Benjamin. *London (Moorfields).* a.1701, CC. 1711, m.CC.1761 and 1789, d.ca.1790. A good maker. rep. cyl. watch G.M. Watch Den. coll.
Benjamin, jun. *London (Moorfields).* a.1731, CC.1738-95. Watch.
SIDLEY—
John. *London.* CC.1701-32.
Benjamin. *London.* CC.1710. Watch.
SIDRAC (SIDERACQUE, SANDERACQUE), ——. *Paris.* 1818-25.
SIEBENHAER, Nicolaus. *Lübeck* . ca.1600. Fine sq. cal. table clock Nat. M. Stockholm.
SIEBER, P. M. *Moravia.* Early 19c. Dial Nat. M. Prague.
SIEDLE—
Johann. *Neukirch.* ca.1750. Introduced metal wheels and pinions into the Schwarzwald clocks.
Mathias. *Gütenbach.* Late 18c. mus. C.
& Co. *London.* Early 19c. Watch.
SIEGFRIED—
Sebald. *Basle.* 1649-61.
Johannes, bro. *Basle.* 1649-61.
SIEGMUND, Johann. *Regensburg.* Early 17c. sq. sil. watch.
SIEGRIST, John, & Cie. *Chaux-de-Fonds.* Late 18c.-early 19c. Watch for Turkey, M.M.A. aut. rep. watch Arch. M. Geneva.
SIEHGER, Johann Georg. 'Em Ney Offing.' Prob. *Offingen,* near *Günzburg.* Early 18c. Boulle-work clock, Hofburg, Vienna.
SIEMERS—
Franz Hinrich. *Hamburg.* 1851-21.
H. J. (widow). *Hamburg.* 1821.
SIEVERT, F. *S. Germany.* Late 17c. Watch Basle M.
SIGG—
Jakob. *Basle.* b.1620-61. From *Schaffhausen.*
Hanns Jakob, son. *Basle.* b.1644, a.1663-99.
SIGNAC, Pierre. *Blois* and *Sweden.* b.ca.1624, d.1684. *Sweden* from 1646. Painter on enamel. Pupil of the TOUTINS. Watch Stockholm.
SIGNOL—
——. *Paris (Rue de la Poterie).* 1812-20.
Aîné. *Paris (Bd. Poissonnière).* 1817-21.
——. *Paris (Rue Chenet).* 1823.
SIGNORÉ, ——. *Paris.* 1812.
SIKMAN, Johannes. *Haarlem.* 1779.
SILBEREN, Arndt. *Ottense.* sq. table clock.
SILESBY, Thomas. *Northampton.* 1658. W.
SILK—
Robert. *London.* a.1729.
John. *Stouting.* an.1779. Watch.
John. *Hythe.* 1795. C. & W.
SILKE, John & Co. *Elmstead.* In 1780 went to *Cheriton.* C. & W.
SILLEMAN, Joost. *Leeuwarden.* ca.1610. Two very fine watches Louvre.

SILLIMAN, ——. *Neuchâtel.* ca.1650. crys. watch.
SILLITO, Thomas. *Uttoxeter.* an.1757. Watch.
SILVER—
Joseph. *London.* 1672.
John. *London.* a.1754, CC.1762. Watch N.Y. Univ.
Joseph. *London.* ca.1800. en. box with watch Peiping M.
Benjamin. *London.* 1805.
Frederick. *London.* CC.1810-25.
F. & F. *London.* ca.1825. Watch.
SILVESTER—
John. *London.* a.1686, CC.1693-8.
Philip. *London.* a.1695.
John. *Stafford.* Early 18c. Watch N.Y. Univ.
SILVESTRE, Joseph. *Paris.* m.1755.
SIMCOCK—
Henry. *Daventry.* 1714. l.c. clock S.K.M. Watch.
Henry. *London.* CC.1787.
Thomas. *Warrington.* ca.1820.
SIMCOX—
William. *London.* a.1674, CC.1682-94.
Josiah. *London.* a.1675.
Joshua. *London.* a.1693.
Samuel. *London.* a.1700, CC.1708-10.
SIME, Robert. *Edinburgh.* a.1768.
SIMERY, Jaques. *Geneva.* ca.1775-91.
SIMINS, Thomas. *London.* 2nd half 18c. sil. 3-case watch.
SIMISTER—
Richard. *Birmingham* and *Wolverhampton.* 1762-1801. l.c. clock. Watches.
Richard. *Wolverhampton.* an.1766-70. Watch.
SIMKIN, Benjamin. *London.* 1781-1807. C.
SIMKINS—
Thomas. *London* (*Trinity La.*). a.1694, CC. 1711-29. Insolvent.
Robert. *London.* a.1695, CC.1709-21.
Thomas. *London.* a.1723, CC.1733.
Robert. *London.* a.1727.
SIMMELKJAER, Christian. *Copenhagen.* m. 1777.
SIMMONDS—
John. *London* (*Fleet St.*). 1747. Watch case maker.
Thomas. *London* (*Clerkenwell*). d.1778. W.
John. *London.* an.1766. Watch.
Thomas. *Birmingham.* Left in 1770. W.
John. *Henley-in-Arden.* ca.1790. Clock in church. l.c. clock.
Edward. prob. *London.* an.1796. Watch.
John. *Coventry.* 1809. C. & W.
——. *Fareham.* Early 19c. Watch.
SIMMONS, Ebenezer L. *London.* 1815-25.
SIMMS—
Andrew. *London.* a.1711.
Joseph. *London* (*Clerkenwell Gr.*). 1747. W.
Thomas. *London.* a.1772.
SIMNEL, ——. *Dublin.* an.1778. Watch.
SIMNER—
Francis. prob. *London.* an.1759. Watch.
Richard. *London* (*Roebuck Ct., Old St.*). a.1751, CC.1760-95. Watch.
Richard, son. *London.* a.1792.
James. *Liverpool.* 1796-1816.
SIMNET, John. *New York.* 1770-5. W. and 'Periodical Titivator.' From *London.* Cleaned watches for two shillings. *v.* Nixon.
SIMON—
mit dem lahmen Hand. *Nürnberg.* 16c. Sculptor, goldsmith, clockmaker, painter, 'und in Summa aller künstlichen Ding fast mehr Vortheil denn andere Verständig.'
Blaise. *Paris.* b.1667, m.1689.
Julien. *Paris.* m.1754.
François. *Paris.* m.1759.
——. *Paris* (*Pont Marie*). 1786-9.

SIMON—*continued.*
——. *Delfshaven.* 18c. l.c. clock.
Frères (Philippe and Isaac). *Paris.* 1809-1825.
Frères. *La Brévine.* 1815-20. C.
Charles H. *La Brévine.* Partner in preceding.
SIMOND, François. *La Brévine.* 1815-20. C.
SIMONDS, John. *London.* 1752. Watch case maker.
SIMONDSON, William. *Liverpool.* 1825. W.
SIMONIN—
——. *Paris.* 1777.
——. *Paris* (*Rue Hautefeuille*). 1810-25.
——. *Paris* (*Rue de la Vannerie*). 1812.
SIMONS—
G. *Breda.* ca.1680. Watch en. Huand le puisné B.M.
M. J. ——. ca.1690. Dutch type watch.
William. *London.* a.1726. Watch.
John. *London.* an.1778. Watch.
Arnoud. *Paris.* m.1780-9.
A. *Bideford.* 2nd half 18c. l.c. clock. Watch Exeter M.
X. *Paris.* ca.1800. Clock with mt. in pendulum.
SIMPER, Georg. *Vienna.* m.1781.
SIMPKIN—
John. *Rillington.* b.1767, d.1834.
John. *Leeds.* 1817. W.
SIMPKINS—
Thomas. *London.* CC.1710-24.
John. *London.* a.1701, CC.1710.
George. *London* (*Gt. Turnstile, Holborn*). a.1731, CC.1766. Also Simpson.
William. *London.* a.1741, CC.1749.
John. *London.* a.1759.
Thomas. *London.* a.1764, CC.1772.
Lancelot, son of Geo. *London.* a.1766. Also Simpson.
William. *London.* a.1771.
SIMPKINSON, Roger. *London.* 1758-75.
SIMPSON—
William. *London.* a.1681, CC.1700.
John. *London.* a.1701, CC.1710.
Thomas. *London.* a.1710.
John. *London* (*Glasshouse St.* in 1732, later *Brewer St.*). a.1715, CC.1723, d.1743.
George. *London* (*Gt. Turnstile, Holborn*). a. 1731, CC.1766. Also Simpkins.
William. *London.* a.1741, CC.1749. Watch.
John. *London.* a.1759.
Richard. *Yarmouth.* 18c. l.c. clock.
John. *Edinburgh.* a.1761.
Robert. *Edinburgh.* a.1761-8.
John. *Wigton.* 1770-1820. l.c. clock dial ill. Britten.
Stephen. *Greta Bridge.* 1770-82.
Lancelot, son of Geo. *London.* a.1766. Also Simpkins.
Thomas. *London.* a.1766, CC.1772. *Hertford,* 1775-95. Watch. Also Simson.
John. *Reading.* From 1775. C. & W.
Benjamin. *Halifax.* 1775.
William. *London.* a.1771.
James. *Lincoln.* ca.1780-95. Watch.
William Ellison. *London.* CC.1781.
Hector. *London. Hanover Sq.* from 1782, *Old Bond St.* from 1784-90. C. Watch.
Robert. *London.* an.1782-1811. Watch.
Robert. *Halifax.* 1785.
Benjamin. *London.* 1787. C.
Stephen. *Gibraltar.* ca.1790 CC.
Archibald. *London.* 1790-1808.
Robert. *Wirksworth.* 1791. C.
& Son. *Yarmouth.* 1791. W.
Margaret Jane. *London.* a.1784.
George. *London.* a.1785.
John. *Oakham.* 1795. C. & W. Also Simson.
Robert. *Liverpool.* 1796-1803. W.
Stephen. *London.* 1799-1804.
Richard. *London.* 1802-11.
Joseph. *London.* 1805-08.

SIMPSON—*continued.*
William. *London.* a.1799.
Thomas. *London.* a.1803.
Daniel. *Workington.* 1810-20.
Anthony. *Cockermouth.* 1811.
William. *Southwell.* Early 19c. l.c. clocks.
William. *Reading.* Early 19c.
——. *Congleton.* 1814 CC.
Samuel. *London.* 1817-24.
Stephen. *Preston.* 1818. C. & W.
William. *Bingley.* 1820-42.
Isaac. *Chorley.* ca.1820.
John. *Garstang.* ca.1820.
Jonathan. *Preston.* ca.1820.
Robert. *Poulton-in-the-Fylde.* ca.1820. Watch.
Joshua. *Preston.* 1821. C. & W.
S. *Oakham.* Early 19c.
SIMPTEN, ——. *London.* 1757. Watch Ilbert coll.
SIMS—
William. *London.* a.1693.
Andrew. *London.* a.1711.
v. FINCH & SIMS.
George. *London.* a.1723, CC.1732-44.
George, son. *London.* CC.1761.
George. *Canterbury.* 1750. W.
Henry. *London (Harp La.).* an.1760, CC. 1771-92. Watch.
Henry. *Canterbury.* 1760. d.an.1792. W.
——. *Alderbury.* an.1764. Watch.
Francis. *Edinburgh.* 1767.
John. *London (Lombard St.).* 1775.
George. *Prescot.* ca.1770.
Thomas. *London.* a.1772.
Richard. *Walford.* 1795. C. & W.
James. *London.* 1805-08. W.
James. *Stockport.* Early 19c. Watch.
SIMSON—
Lars (Laurent). *Göteborg.* b.1733, m.1763, d.1794. Turret clocks.
Gustaf. *Göteborg.* b.1776, d.1833. Watch.
SINATEAU-VERDURE, Jacques. *Paris.* b. 1767, guillotined 1794.
SINCLAIR—
Alexander. *Edinburgh.* a.1764.
Alexander. *Edinburgh.* a.1767.
SINCLARE—
W. & Gordon D. *Dublin.* ca.1725. Watch Dublin M.
Gordon D. *Dublin.* ca.1740-80. Watch, moving hour figures, G.M.
William. *Dublin.* an.1753. Watch.
SINDERBY—
William. *London.* an.1775. Watch.
Francis. *London (Newgate St.).* an.1778-1808. Watch.
Francis Hayward, son. *London (Bull and Mouth St.).* a.1793, CC.1800, l.CC.1810-1840. Watch.
Francis. *Lewes.* Left in 1823. From *London.*
SINDRY, Lawrence. *London.* a.1649, CC. 1661-1705.
SINFIELD, T. *Oxford.* an.1777. Watch.
SING—
Johann Michael. *Augsburg.* b.1684, m.1723, juré, d.1767.
Severinus. *Cracow.* 1st half 18c. rep. trav. clock Den. coll.
Moritz. *Augsburg.* m.1732, d.1772.
Joseph. *Grätz.* 2nd half 18c. 4-colour g. rep. watch.
SINGER—
B. prob. *London.* an.1752. Watch.
J. W. *Frome.* Early 19c. Watch.
SINGLETON—
John. *London.* 1770. W.
John, son. *London.* a.1782.
John. *Manchester.* 1800-11. W.
John. *London.* 1806. W. Lancaster freeman.
& HOLDEN. *London.* 1820.
& WRIGHT. *London.* 1820.
Leigh Charles. *London.* 1820.
SINKINSON—
Joseph. *Bury St. Edmunds.* 1796, enters into partnership with Bilby DORLING.
John. *Doncaster.* an.1817. Watch.
SION, ——. *London.* an.1773. Watch.
SIROT (SIROST), M. *Paris.* 1803-24. C. Lever watch Ilbert coll.
SIROUVAL—
——. *Paris (Palais Royal).* 1822-5. Watch set pearls.
Jeune. *Paris (Rue de Bussi).* 1823-5.
SISSON, Jonathan. *London.* a.1720-69. Watch Bernal sale. Dial M.M.A.
SITHERWOOD—
John. *Portadown.* 1824.
William. *Tanderagee.* 1824.
SITTLE—
Johann Michael. *Steppach.* 1756-70. Also SIEDLE.
Johann Michael. *Vienna.* m.1776. Prob. same as preceding. g. en. watch. g. rep. cal. watch. Also SITLE.
SIVAD (SIVED)—
Theophilus. *London.* an.1744. Watch.
William. prob. *London.* an.1756. Watch.
In. *London.* Mid. 18c. Watch given by Geo. III to the Emperor of China.
SIVERS, ——. *Copenhagen.* 1786. Repaired HABRECHT's clock in Rosenborg Castle.
SIVERTSEN—
Joen. *Copenhagen.* m.1762.
John Frederick. *Copenhagen.* m.1812.
SIVIL, E. *London.* an.1777. Watch.
SIX, Hironymus. *Augsburg.* 1712 m. d. soon after 1726.
SJÖBERG, S. *Stockholm.* 18c. br. clock.
SKARRAT (SKARRETT)—
Carleton. *London.* a.1768.
Thomas. *London.* a.1772, CC.1782.
John. *London.* a.1777.
Charles. *Worcester.* 1793. Bankrupt. W.
John. *Worcester.* 1794 CC. Watch.
SKEETES, Robert. *London.* a.1714.
SKEGGS—
William. *London (Rotherhithe).* 1756. d. 1771.
William. *London.* 1795-1824. l.c. clock.
S. *London.* 1795.
SKELTON—
Samuel. *London.* a.1662.
Robert. *New Malton.* 1752-75. C.
George. *Edinburgh.* a.1773, d.1834. Partner in, and successor in 1787 to, BROWN & SKELTON.
Coultas. *New Malton.* 1822-41.
SKEPPER, Thomas. *London.* a.1675.
SKERRETT, ——. *Devonport.* ca.1800. Watch. l.c. clock.
SKIKELTHORPE, William. prob. *London.* an.1751. Watch.
SKINNER—
Peter. *London.* a.1694.
Matthew. *London.* CC.1713, m.CC.1746. Watch mt. G.M.
John. *Exeter.* an.1780, d.1818. W.
Robert. *London (Moorfields).* a.1783, CC. 1792, d.1821.
Thomas. *Exeter.* 1792. l.c. clock.
Mark. prob. *London.* an.1793. Watch.
John, son of John. *Exeter.* From 1818. W.
William, son of Thos. *London.* CC.1821.
Alvah. *Boston, U.S.A.* Early 19c.
SKIORSAK, Lorents. *Copenhagen.* 1589-96. From *Göttingen.* Court C. Made clock for Nykøbing Castle.
SKIPTON, J. F. *Cirencester.* 1820.
SKIPWORTH, Francis. *London.* a.1670-85, not CC.
SKIRROW—
James. *Lancaster* and *Wigan.* 1783-1814. C.
Robert. *Halifax.* Early 19c.-1848.
SKIRVING, John. *Edinburgh.* 1771-81.

SKOWING—
John. *London.* a.1779.
John. *London.* a.1795.
SLACK, Joseph. *London.* a.1716, CC.1723.
SLADE—
J. prob. *London.* an.1755. Watch.
——. *Camelford.* 1795. C. & W.
SLADER, Samuel. *London.* a.1735.
SLANGE, Jakob. *Helsingor.* 1643. Fine monstrance clock Nat. M. Copenhagen ill. Liisberg.
SLANN, Daniel. *London.* a.1735.
SLARK, ——. *London.* an.1793. Watch.
SLATER—
John. *London.* 1729-74. Insolvent.
Robert. *London.* CC.1775-85.
George. *Burslem.* Early 19c. Watch.
SLATFORD, John. *London.* a.1802, CC.1810.
SLAUGHTER, William. *London.* an.1764. Watch.
SLAYTER, John. *Steyning.* Early 19c. Watch.
SLEATH—
Thomas. *London.* a.1683.
Stephen or Joseph. *London.* a.1716.
Gabriel. *London.* a.1733.
John. *London.* a.1747, CC.1758.
SLEEMAN—
John Francis Cundy. *London,* a.1779.
Henry. *Penzance.* Early 19c. Watch.
SLEIGH, William. *Stockton-on-Tees.* mar. 1818. W.
SLINDON, Robert Lance. prob. *London.* an. 1773. Watch.
SLIPPER (SLOPER), Jeremiah. *London.* a.1714, CC. 1726.
SLOCOMB, Samuel. *Cork.* 1735-50.
SLOSSER, Hans. *Nürnberg.* 1471. Made a clock for Frederick IV.
SLOTBOOM, J. *Elst.* ca.1800.
SLOUGH—
William. *London.* a.1676, CC.1687-96.
William. *London.* a.1699.
SLOW, ——. ——. an.1755. Watch.
SLUCE, John. *London.* a.1804.
SLY—
Robert. *London.* a.1707, CC.1720.
Thomas. *Norwich.* 1784. W.
Samuel. *Norwich.* 1795. C. & W.
——. *Weymouth.* ca.1800.
SMALE, William. *Bristol.* d.1782. W.
SMALL—
William. *London.* a.1684-1705. Pendulum watch G.M. of Dutch type.
Thomas. *Dundee.* 1722.
——. *Lichfield.* an.1767. Watch.
William. *Birmingham.* 1773. Patented a timepiece of a vague kind.
William. *Edinburgh.* a.1769-75.
SMALLEY—
Thomas. *London.* CC.1687-1700. Clock at Battle Abbey.
John. *Blackburn.* 1721. C. Lancaster freeman.
SMALLMAN, ——. *London.* 1749. W.
SMALLPAGE—
——. *Halifax.* 1721.
——. *Wakefield.* an.1750. Watch.
& RANDALL. *Leeds.* 1794. W.
——. *Norton.* Early 19c. Watch.
John. *Leeds.* 1825. W.
SMALLPIECE, John. *London.* a.1699.
SMALLWOOD—
——. *London (Lothbury).* d.1653. C.
John. *Macclesfield.* d.1715. W.
Joseph. *London.* a.1698.
John. *Lichfield.* 1730. Sale of stock in 1741. br. clock ill. Cec. & Web.
Joseph. *Sandbach.* an.1744, d.1757. C.
SMARLEY, Thomas. *Chester.* d.1770. Watch case maker.
SMART—
John. *London.* a.1674, CC.1682-96.
William. *London.* a.1718.
R. ——. Mid. 18c. Watch Den. coll.
Thomas. *London.* a.1781.
James. *London.* a.1800.
Walter. *London.* a.1801.
Thomas. *London.* 1815-20. Watch.
William. *London.* Early 19c. Watch.
SMEATON—
John. *York.* 1646. Large sil. watch B.M. Clock York M.
Tobias. *London.* a.1664.
John, grandson of John. *York.* 1779. d.1792. MS. letters on Turret clocks Library of CC.
SMEDBYE, Poul Andreas. *Christiania.* 1787 m.
SMEITON, Charles. *Dundee.* d.1791.
SMELLIE, Thomas. *London.* a.1809, CC. 1816.
SMELT, Robert. *London.* CC.1785-94.
SMERDON, ——. *Newton Abbot.* Early 19c. Watch.
SMID BLUIS, Jean. *Augsburg.* ca.1660. g. en. ring watch, made for Johann Friedrich der Grossmüthigen. Indicated the hours by a needle which protruded to touch the finger, Gotha M.
SMILEY, John. *Larne.* 1824.
SMINT, ——. *London.* ca.1775. p.c. cal. watch M.M.A.
SMIT (SMITT)—
Hermanus. *Amsterdam.* ca.1740. l.c. clock.
Anthony. *Haarlem.* 1751.
J. L. *Groningen.* ca.1800, d.1825. Pub. posthumously 'Horologie en Uurwerkmakers Handboek.'
J. *Rotterdam.* 1821-30.
SMITH—
George. *London.* ca.1600, CC.1632. circ. sil. eng. watch Webster coll.
John. *London.* 1622. m.CC.1638-49. Petitioner for incorporation of CC. Also SMYTH.
James. *Edinburgh.* 1629. d.1660.
Gersen. *London.* 1630. Petitioner for incorporation of CC. sd. 'Ssmidt.' Oval eng. watch.
Robert. *London (Pope's Head Alley).* 1630. CC.1640, m.CC.1650, d.1654. Watch M.M.A.
Walter. *London.* CC.1640.
Robert. *Edinburgh.* 1647-60.
Aurther. *Wrexham.* Mid. 17c. T.C.
Robert. *London.* CC.1659.
Nathaniel. *London (Pope's Head Alley).* a.1647-59.
John. *London.* a.1647, CC.1654.
Thomas. *London.* a.1647.
John. *London.* a.1648, CC.1656.
Henry. *London.* a.1650, CC.1658.
John. *London (Lombard St.).* 1660. W.
Stephen. *London.* a.1651, CC.1658.
David. *London.* a.1654, CC.1661.
William. *London.* a.1654, CC.1661.
John. *London.* a.1654.
William. *Dundee.* 1668.
Robert. *London.* CC.1668.
William. *London.* a.1663.
Thomas. *London.* a.1664.
John. *London.* CC.1674, d.an.1730. Pub. 'Horological Dialogues' in 1675, the earliest horological book published in England. Pub. 'Horological Disquisitions,' 1694 and 1708, and 'On the Unequality of Natural Time,' London, 1686.
Benjamin. *London.* a.1669.
Henry. *London.* a.1670.
John. *Edinburgh.* 1680.
John. *Macclesfield.* 1680. cf. John below.
Ruth. *London.* a.1674.
William. *London.* a.1678.

SMITH—*continued.*
Nathaniel. *London.* a.1680, CC.1689-1719.
William. *London.* a.1681.
Thomas. *London.* a.1682.
Henry. *London.* a.1683.
John. *London.* a.1687.
John. *London.* a.1688.
Thomas. *London.* a.1690.
Thomas. *London.* a.1691, CC.1700. l.c. clock Weth. coll.
Robert. *London.* CC.1697.
William. *London.* a.1692.
Benjamin. *London.* a.1693.
——. *Hogsden.* 1697. W.
Thomas. *London.* a.1693.
Edward. *Richmond.* ca.1700. Fine l.c. clock. Watch.
Francis. *London* (*Cornhill*). 1705. sil. watch Ilbert coll.
Morris. *London* (*near the Exchange*). a.1693, CC.1702. Watch.
——. *Blois.* 1701.
John. *London.* 1701. W. Asked CC. for money to take him to Carolina.
John. *London*. a.1693, CC.1703-30. Made clock at Westminster Abbey; replaced in 1860.
Maurice. *London* (*R. Exchange*). a.1694, CC.1702. Sale of stock in 1732. Watch mt. S.K.M.
Robert. *London.* a.1695.
Richard. *London.* a.1695.
Henry. *London.* a.1696, CC.1703-18. Partner in SMITH & FREEMAN. Clock.
John. *London.* a.1702.
Samuel Henry. *London* (*Swan Alley*). a. 1708, CC.1715, d.an.1774.
Tudor. *London* (*St. Clement Dane*). a.1708, CC.1717-42. C.
Thomas. *London.* a.1709, CC.1718.
Edward. *London.* a.1709.
& FREEMAN. *London* (*Grays Inn*). 1718-26. Partnership with Henry S. and Geo. F.
Alexander. *Dundee.* 1718-42.
Thomas. *London.* a.1712.
John. *London.* a.1714.
John. *London.* a.1715.
Richard. *London.* a.1715.
Thomas. *London.* a.1716.
Obadiah. *London.* a.1718, CC.1725.
Joseph. *London.* a.1718, CC.1742.
John. *London* (*New St., Cloth Fair*). 1729. Insolvent. W.
Roger. *London.* a.1721.
James. *London.* a.1722.
James. *London.* a.1723.
John. *London.* a.1727, CC.1738.
William. *London.* a.1728, CC.1768.
George. *London.* a.1728, CC.1735. Watch Webster coll.
Edward. *Bury St. Edmunds.* 1730. From *London.* Clock.
Joseph. *Bristol.* 1730. d.1778. Watch mt. G.M. l.c. clock.
Walter. *London.* a.1732. Watch.
Benjamin. *London.* a.1734, CC.1742-78. Watch.
James. *Dundee.* 1742.
Jude. *London.* a.1736.
——. *Sandbach.* an.1743. Watch.
DE LA BALLE & ROUGHLEY. *London* (*Seven Dials*). 1743. W.
Samuel. *London.* 1744. Shagreen case maker.
Richard. *Newport.* an.1745. Watch.
Samuel. *Richmond.* an.1746. Watch.
Richard. *Portsmouth.* an.1748. Watch. C.
——. *Tideswell.* an.1748. Watch.
Richard. *Harleston.* an.1749. Watch.
Thomas. *Bristol.* d.1750. W.
Richard. *Plymouth.* 1748.

SMITH—*continued.*
William. *London* (*Upper Moorfields*). 1749. Church clock.
Laurence. *London.* a.1738.
Robert. *London* (*Nixon Sq.*). CC.1750.
John. *York.* 1750-4. Made clock for St. Martin's Church.
James. *London* (*Chiswell St.*). a.1743, CC. 1751-62. Watch.
Anthony. prob. *London.* an.1754. Watch.
James. *London* (*Upper Moorfields*). mar. 1754.
John. *Charleston, U.S.A.* 1754.
Peter. *London.* an.1755. Watch.
Charles. *London.* d.1774.
Joseph. *London.* a.1746.
Gabriel. *Chester.* 1752-97. W.
Suzanna. *London.* a.1747.
William. *London.* a.1748.
Joshua. *Bristol.* an.1757. Watch.
John. *Macclesfield.* 1756.
John. *London* (*Seven Dials*). 1757. W.
Joseph. *Skipton.* b.1742, d.1795.
Samuel. *Newcastle-under-Lyme.* an.1759. Watch.
William. *London.* mar.1764. W. 'Eminent.'
John. *London.* a.1749, CC.1764.
William. *London* (*Cheapside*). 1759-80. C. Lancaster freeman.
Benjamin. *Alfreton.* 1765-1803.
Samuel. *London.* a.1752.
James. *London* (*Bunhill Row*). 1760-90. Watch.
William. *London.* a.1759.
William. *Bristol.* 1768. d.1778. C. & W.
Thomas. *Norwich.* an.1769. Watch.
Richard. *Wolverhampton.* an.1769. Watch.
Benjamin. *Canterbury.* From 1768-81. C. & W.
John, son of Benj. *London.* CC.1768.
John. *London* (*Houndsditch*). ca.1770-90. Prob. same as preceding. br. clock ill. Cec. & Web.
John. *London.* a.1762.
George. *Beaminster.* d.1798. C.
Edward. *Richmond* (*Surrey*). an.1770. Watch.
Edward. *London.* an.1770. Watch.
Thomas. *London* (*Princes St., Aldgate*). a.1763, CC.1770.
Edward. *Newark.* 1770-90. l.c. clocks. Watch.
John, son of John, York. *Thirsk.* a.1758-1807.
John. *Pittenweem.* 1770. d.1814. Magnificent mus. l.c. clock.
——. *Bardfield.* an.1771. Watch.
Charles. *London.* an.1771. Watch.
William. *Perth.* 1772.
Robert. *Chelmsford.* an.1773. Watch.
James. *Saxmundham.* an.1773. Watch. Also SMYTH.
Walter. *Cuckfield.* 1773-91. C. & W.
Thomas. *London* (*Kirby St.*). 1774.
Thomas. *Sheffield.* 1774. C.
Charles. *Dublin.* an.1775. Watch.
John. *Dublin.* an.1775. Watch.
Edmund. *Bury St. Edmunds.* 1772. From *London.* l.c. clock.
James. *London* (*Fleet St.*). ca.1775-1800. l.c. and br. clocks ill. Cec. & Web.
James. *Norwich.* 18c. l.c. clock.
Joseph. *Bristol.* 1775. W.
Isaac. *London.* an.1777. Watch.
Samuel. *Holywell.* an.1777. Watch.
Joseph. *Wrexham.* d.1799. Watch mt. Nat. M. Cardiff.
Charles. *London* (*Lombard St.*). a.1766, CC. 1783.
Philip. *London* (*Red Cross St.*). CC.1776-87.
James. *London* (*Jermyn St.*). 1776. CC. 1781-94. C. to George III.
Thomas. *London.* a.1770.

SMITH—*continued.*
William. *London.* a.1770.
William. *London.* a.1771.
Frederick. *London.* a.1771. Watch.
Samuel. *London.* a.1772.
William. *London.* a.1773.
Samuel, son of Sam. *London.* a.1774.
Charles. *London (Bunhill Row).* CC.1779-1820.
William. *Keighley.* 1780-1810.
James. *London (Oxford St.).* 1781-1824.
Abraham. *Dublin.* an.1783. Watch.
John. *Glasgow.* 1783-1806.
John. *Chester.* 1784. l.c. clock ill. Britten.
William. *London (Old St.).* 1784.
Thomas. *London (Houndsditch).* 1784-90.
Owen. *Broad Oak.* Left 1784. C. & W.
John. *Norwich.* an.1785. Watch.
W., & Son. *London.* an.1791. Watch.
John. *Kings Lynn.* an.1792. Watch.
James, & Son. *London (Bunhill Row).* 1785-1790.
Jabez. *London.* CC.1786-95.
John. *Scarborough.* Late 18c. l.c. clock.
James. *London.* a.1780.
Joseph. *London.* CC.1788.
Joseph Samuel. *London.* a.1780.
Charles. *Liskeard.* ca.1790 CC.
James. *Edinburgh.* 1790-1806.
& Wareham. *London.* 1790.
John and James. *London (Bunhill Row).* 1790-4.
Abraham. *Manchester.* 1790-4. Wooden C.
William. *Pentonville.* 1791. W.
Charles. *London (Shoemaker Row, Blackfriars).* 1791.
John. *London.* a.1783.
Nathaniel. *London.* a.1783.
James. *London.* a.1783.
John. *Perth.* 1791.
John. *London.* a.1784.
William. *London.* a.1785.
Thomas. *London.* a.1786.
John. *London (Fenchurch St.).* 1794.
Henry. *Reading.* 1794-1803 CC. Watch Ilbert coll.
Joseph. *Taunton.* 1795.
John. *Coventry.* 1795. C. & W.
George. *March.* mar.1795. C. & W.
Joseph. *Taunton.* 1795. W.
Joshua. *Walsham.* 1795. W.
Joseph. *St. Albans.* 1795. C. & W.
John. *Thirsk.* 1795. C. & W.
John. *Stanmore.* 1795. C.
John. *Dublin.* 1795.
Walter. *London.* 1795.
John. *London (Poultry).* 1795.
Charles. *London (Coleman St.).* 1796.
John. *Wrexham.* b.1777, d.1830. Watch Nat. M. Cardiff. l.c. clock.
Alfred Charles. *London.* a.1791.
Frederick. *London.* a.1791, CC.1807.
John Garden. *London.* a.1791.
Walter. *Aberdeen.* 1799.
William. *London (Wapping).* 1799-1811.
& Upjohn. *London.* 1799.
John. *London.* a.1793.
Samuel. *Coventry.* ca.1800. Watch beating secs.
George. *Haverfordwest.* ca.1800. l.c. clock.
Jesse. *Concord, U.S.A.* ca.1800.
John. *London (Aldersgate).* 1802-04.
Benjamin. *London.* 1802-04.
Alwin William. *London.* a.1796.
William. *London (Bridgewater Sq.).* 1805-11.
William. *Inverness.* 1805-53.
William. *London.* CC.1805.
Joseph. *London (Hoxton).* 1805-08.
Samuel. *London (Old St.).* 1805-08.
Thomas. *London (Goswell St.).* 1805-08.
William. *London (St. Luke's).* 1805-08.
B., & Cherry. *London.* 1805-08.

SMITH—*continued.*
John. *Liverpool.* 1805.
Guy. *Burton-in-Lonsdale.* 1806.
Frederick. *London.* CC.1807.
Mercer & Piercy. *Coventry.* 1808. Partnership with Samuel S.
J. J. *London.* ca.1810. Duplex mt. Ilbert coll.
E. *Newcastle-o.-T.* 1811. C. & W.
Henry & Edward. *Reading.* Early 19c.
John. *London.* a.1803.
David. *London.* a.1804.
William James. *London.* a.1804.
Joseph. *London.* a.1805.
Samuel. *London* and *Coventry.* 1812. Patented the use of stone pallets. Pirouette watch Ilbert coll.
James. *Bristol.* 1812.
William, son of Rich. *London.* a.1807.
William Thody. *London.* a.1808.
Henry C. *Waterbury, U.S.A.* 1814.
James. *Liverpool.* 1815. Pub. 'Panorama of Science and Art,' containing 30 arts. on horology, and, in London, 1824, 'The Mechanic,' also containing many arts. on horology.
William. *London (Old Compton St.).* 1815-1824.
George. *London (Horsleydown).* 1817-24.
Thomas. *Liverpool.* 1818. W.
John. *Edinburgh.* 1819-22.
Thomas William. *London.* CC.1819. W.
William. *Philadelphia.* 1819-25. W.
Robert. *Philadelphia.* 1819.
John. *Newcastle-o.-T.* 1820.
J. H. *London (Rotherhithe).* 1820.
George. *London (New Cut).* 1820.
Thomas. *Newcastle-o.-T.* 1820.
Thomas. *London.* a.1812, CC.1829.
Robert. *Irvine.* 1820.
William Charles. *London.* a.1814.
William. *London.* a.1814.
William. *Irvine.* 1821-50.
Samuel. *Sheffield.* 1822-36.
Horatio. *York.* 1822-32. W.
Baker. *Dublin.* 1824.
Edward. *Dublin.* 1824. l.c. clock.
George. *London (St. Martin's Churchyard).* 1825.
James. *London (John St.).* 1825.
William. *Leith.* 1825.
T. W. *London.* 1825.
Samuel. *Newcastle-o.-T.* 1825. C.
William Sellars. *Bristol.* 1825.
John. *Leek.* ca.1825. Watch.

SMITHER, William. *London.* l.CC.1823-40.

SMITHERS—
George. *London.* an.1752-98. Watch N.Y. Univ.
C. E. *Portsea.* Early 19c. Watch.

SMITHFIELD, William. *Romford.* a.1730.

SMITHIES (SMITHYES)—
George. *London.* 1748-56. W.
Draper John. *London.* a.1756.
v. Smythies.

SMITSON, G. ——. 1825. Pub. 'Hülfsbuchlein für Uhren-Besitzer,' Leipzig.

SMITTON, Peter. *London.* 1820.

SMOD, ——. *Geissheim.* ca.1640. Watch with long bristle as balance-spring ill. Britten.

SMORTHWAITE, ——. *Colchester.* Early 18c. Lantern and l.c. clock. Watch.

SMOULT—
Thomas. *Lancaster.* 1708. d.1749. W. Mayor of Lancaster.
James. *Lancaster.* 1739. d.1768. Watch mt.
James. *Newcastle-o.-T.* 1745. d.1749. C. & W.
& Gilbertson. *Newcastle-o.-T.* 1745-7. Partnership of James above.
James. *Newcastle-o.-T.* and *Lancaster.* 1749. d.1758. At *Lancaster,* 1749-50. C. & W.

SMOULT—*continued.*
Eleanor, widow. *Newcastle-o.-T.* 1758, retired 1759.
Thomas. *Newcastle-o.-T.* 1787, retired 1791. l.c. clocks.
SMYTH, James. *Woodbridge.* 1784. W.
SMYTHE—
James. *Salisbury.* 1697. Clock.
Philemon. *Edinburgh.* 1800.
SMYTHIES—
James. *London.* a.1679.
James. *London.* a.1680.
SNARL, William. *London.* an.1777. Watch.
SNEAD, Ralph. *London.* a.1783.
SNEBERGER, Michael. *Prague.* 1606. Gilt sil. table clock, set stones and en., K.H.M.
SNEEWINS—
H. *Leyden.* 1660. Dial maker.
W. *Delft.* 1709. Dial Old Ashmolean M.
SNELL—
George. *London.* a.1679, CC.1688-1700. l.c. clocks.
E. *Barnstaple.* 2nd half 18c. l.c. clock.
Frederick. *London.* a.1786-1820.
SNELLING—
Thomas. *London.* a.1672, CC.1680-2.
James. *London* (*Poultry*). a.1703, CC.1712, m.CC.1736, d.1751. 'Eminent' W. Watches B.M., S.K.M., G.M. and Glasgow Art Gall.
Reuben. *London.* a.1727.
John. *Alton.* 1761-95. C. & W.
John. *London.* an.1771. Watch.
Henry. *London.* 1770-5. *Philadelphia,* 1776. W. & C.
——. *Newton Abbot.* 18c. l.c. clock.
James. *Alton.* Early 19c. Watch.
'SNEVETS.' *London.* Sig. on a watch, early 19c. STEVENS reversed. Perhaps Joseph.
SNEYD, P. prob. *London.* an.1762. Watch.
SNIDALL—
James. *Sheffield.* 1770-1814. His second quality watches were sd. 'Dalsni.'
Samuel. *Sheffield.* 1814-40. W.
SNOSWELL, William. *London.* a.1803, CC. 1818-20.
SNOW—
John. *London.* 1630. Lantern clock.
Nicholas. *Salisbury.* Lantern clock dated 1636 Salisbury M. SNOWE.
——. *Lavington.* 1660. Watch.
Daniel. *Otley.* 1664.
William. *Otley.* ca.1710. cf. Wm. below.
John. *London.* a.1716.
Richard. *London.* a.1750, CC.1758-63.
William. *Padside* (*Nidderdale*). 1763.
Thomas. *London* (*Fetter La.* and *Coldbath Fields*). a.1763, CC.1773-8.
William. *Otley.* 1780.
Thomas, son. *London.* a.1778.
Thomas. *Otley.* 1780-1822.
L. *Bradford* (*Yorks*). 1814.
Thomas. *Bradford* (*Yorks*). 1822-30.
Thomas. *Birstwith.* 1822.
Richard. *Pateley Bridge.* 1822-41.
SNOWDEN—
Thomas. *London.* a.1766.
John. *Grimsby.* 1795. C. & W. and Barrel organ maker.
SOAN, William. *London.* a.1780.
SOAR, James. *London.* a.1823.
SOCTERIJK, Daniel. *Dordrecht.* Mid. 18c. Watch.
SÖDERBERG, Victor. *Visby.* 1825-40.
SÖDERDAHL, I. *Visby.* 18c. Watch mt. Nord. M.
SÖDERLING, Carl. *Göteborg.* b.1745, d. 1807.
SÖDERMAN, Petter. *Stockholm.* 1769-1810. Watch, l.c. clock, two br. clocks, two wall clocks ill. Sidenbladh.
SÖDERSTRÖM—
Anders. *Stockholm.* 1792-1805. Wall clock.
Anders. *Uppsala.* 1823.
SOFFLEUR, Thomas. *London.* an.1681. Watch.
SOILLAT, Pierre. *Paris.* 1675 m.
SOIRON—
Jean François. *Geneva.* b.1756, d.1812. Painter on en. of repute. One of the few watch enamellers who signed his work.
——, son. *Geneva.* ca.1800. Painter on enamel.
SOLDANO, ——. *London* (*Jermyn St.*). 1772. W.
SOLET, Friedrich. *Basle.* 1687. From *Geneva.*
SOLEY, Joseph. *London.* an.1781. Watch.
SOLIANS, ——. *Paris.* ca.1790. Mantel clock Windsor Castle ill. Britten.
SOLLINGER, Jacob. *Vienna.* ca.1770. aut. and carillon clock.
SOLMAN, Hans. *Basle.* 1455. 'Orlimacher.' Made clock for St. Martin's Church.
SOLOMON—
Nathaniel. *Margate.* an.1783-95. Watch.
Emanuel. *Canterbury.* 1785-91. W.
A. *Birmingham.* ca.1790. Watch Birmingham M. l.c. clock.
S. C. *London.* 1794-1808.
Isaac. *London.* 1799.
E. *Margate.* ca.1800. Watch.
Simon. *Manchester.* 1804.
Moses. *London.* 1817-25.
P. *London.* 1820.
L. T. *St. John's, Newfoundland.* Early 19c.
S. *Lewes.* 1815-30. Watch.
SOLOT, François Armand. *Paris.* m.1780-9.
SOLTIN, Adam. *Björneborg.* 1769-1807.
SOMELLIER, François. *Geneva.* 1555. From *Dieppe.* 'Fayseur de reloges.'
SOMERS—
John. *London.* a.1697.
William. prob. *London.* 1st half 18c. Watch.
SOMERSALL—
Mandeville. *London.* CC.1685. Lantern clock.
John. *London.* CC.1708.
George. *London* (*Grub St.*). a.1701, CC. 1708-52.
Mandeville. *London* (*Wood St.*). a.1726, CC. 1735-56. W. and clock engraver.
Henry. *London.* an.1748. Watch.
John, son of George. *London* (*Barbican*). CC.1743-68.
George, bro. *London* (*Finsbury*). CC.1752-1773.
Richard. *London* (*City Rd.* and *Moorfields*). CC.1769, l.CC.1787-1811.
John, son of John. *London.* a.1768.
Frederick. *London.* CC.1781.
George, son of Richard. *London.* a.1796-ca. 1825.
SOMERSGILL, Robert. *Preston.* ca.1820.
SOMERSON, G. *London.* Early 18c. Lantern clock and watch.
SOMERTON, John Andrew. *England.* End 18c. l.c. astro. clock with 8 dials.
SOMERVELL, James. *Gt. Boughton.* 1746. C.
SOMERVILLE—
Robert. *Glasgow.* 1798-1804.
David. *St. Ninians.* 1805-20.
SOMILLIER, John. *London.* a.1649.
SOMMELLIER (SOMMELIER)—
François. *Lyons.* d.ca.1564. cf. SOMELLIER.
Pierre. *Rouen.* 1617. Founder member of Rouen corporation.
Barthélemy Le. *Rouen.* Juré 1650-2.
SOMMER—
Hans. *Nürnberg.* 1579.
C. P. J. *Fürth.* d.ca.1820.
SONES, ——. *London.* 1751. Watch case maker.

SONLEY (SOULEY), Richard. *London.* a. 1740.
SONN, Fredrich. *Ystad.* 1750-4.
SONNATOT, Louis. *Autun.* 1st half 17c. 10-sided watch, faceted covers.
SONNE, Niels. *Bornholm* and *Copenhagen.* Late 18c.
SONNENBURG, Paul Jan van. *Copenhagen.* m.1708. From *Holland.* Kleinuhrmacher.
SONNENLEITNER, H. *Dresden.* ca.1780. Small br. clock.
SONNTAG, Hans Jørgen. *Copenhagen.* 1692. From *Alsace.* Turret C.
SOPER, Robert. *Twickenham.* 1805-08.
SORBITT, John. *London.* 1774. Insolvent. W.
SORDET, Étienne Marc. *Geneva.* ca.1775-91.
SOREN, ——. *Copenhagen.* 1581. Court C.
SORENSEN—
Mathias. *Copenhagen.* 1678.
Mogens. *Aastrup.* m.1765.
Christian. *Copenhagen.* m.1779.
SORET—
Louis. *Paris.* ca.1650. Clock in wood case.
Pierre. *Lyons.* 1667. en. watch ill. Britten.
Barthélemy. *Geneva.* 1668. From *Blois.*
Jacques. ——. Late 17c. Watch with en. portraits of Louis XIV and Mme. de Maintenon given by Louis XIV to William III Lincoln M. Watch with balance spring Gélis coll.
Jean Robert. *Geneva.* 1740-80. aut. rep. watch G.M. 4-colour g. watch, en. and set stones, Fränkel coll. Similar watch Gemeente M., The Hague. g. en. watch.
Isaac. *Geneva.* b.1673, d.1760. p.c. sil. rep. trav. clock Feill coll. Watch Geneva M.
David, son. *Geneva.* b.1705, d.1780. Watch.
Isaac, et Fils. *Geneva.* 1765. Watch S.M.S.K. 4-colour g. watch S.K.M. g. jewelled watch M.M.A. Watch with 12 and 24 hour dials on the two sides.
Jean Robert, son of David. *Geneva.* b.1731, d.1799. Watch.
Edouard. *Geneva.* b.1826, d.1909. About 1865 made three watches 9 mm. dia.
SORGENFREY, Henning. *Copenhagen.* m. 1816.
SÖRLING—
Johan. *Norrköping.* 1774.
Carl Mag. *Nyköping.* 1794-1813. Two watch mts. Nord. M.
SORTHOUSE, T. *London.* 1822-4.
SOTIAU (SORIAU), Nicolas. *Paris.* m.1782, d.1791. Mantel clocks Windsor Castle and Ministère des Affaires étrangères, Paris, and Pal. de Versailles.
SOUBEYRAN, Barthélemi. *Geneva.* ca.1755-1771. Watch. Associated with ROMILLY in writing the article on Horlogerie in the 'Encyclopédie Méthodique.'
SOUEFVE, Jacques. *Blois.* comp. 1664.
SOULTER ——. *Paris.* 1813-16.
SOUMILLE, L'Abbé. *France.* 1746. Devised pendulum escapement with crank.
SOUND—
Edward. *London.* an.1763. Watch.
Joseph. *London.* an.1776. Watch.
SOUNDY (SOUNDS), Thomas. *London.* CC. 1752. Watch.
SOURDEN, ——. *Paris.* End 17c. str. and al. watch Den. coll.
SOURIAU, ——. *Paris.* 1825. Watch mt. Ilbert coll.
SOURIT, ——. *Neuchâtel.* 1723.
SOUTH—
Joseph. *London.* a.1702, CC.1709-30.
Henry. *Rotherham.* 1710.
John. *London.* a.1747, CC.1767-1808. mt. maker.
SOUTHALL, Thomas. *Old Hill, Stafford.* ca. 1795. l.c. clock.
SOUTHAM—
——. *London.* an.1737. Watch.
Samuel. *London.* 1790-1808.
SOUTHCOTE, Josiah. *London.* a.1681.
SOUTHEN, Thomas. *London.* a.1681.
SOUTHEY, ——. *Rochester.* ca.1790 CC.
SOUTHWOOD, Samuel. *London.* a.1663.
SOUTHWORTH—
Peter. *London.* a.1656, CC.1664-92.
John. *London.* a.1668, CC.1689-1701
Thomas. *London.* a.1677.
SOUTTER, ——. *Geneva.* ca.1800. Painter on enamel.
SOUZA, Samuel. *Philadelphia.* 1819.
SOWERBY ——. *Carlisle.* an.1777. Watch.
SOWERS, Thomas. *St. Albans.* ca.1750. Watch.
SOWTER—
John. *London.* a.1671, CC.1683-94.
John. *Oxford.* From 1818. br. clock Furt. M.
SOYER, Jacques. *Rouen.* a.1660.
SPACHETT, Robert. *London.* a.1729.
SPACKMAN—
Edward. *London.* a.1673.
John. *London.* a.1711.
Thomas. *Bristol.* 1754. Watch.
George. *Philadelphia.* 1825. W.
SPALDIN—
William. *Liverpool.* 2nd half 18c. Watch.
William. *Gainsborough.* From 1755. From *Caistor* and *London.* C. & W.
SPARCK, Peter. *Philadelphia.* 1796-1806.
SPARK (SPARKE)—
Angel. *Plymouth.* ca.1770-95. Watch.
William. *Aberdeen.* 1820.
SPARKES, Thomas. *Liverpool.* 1796. W.
SPARKS—
Thomas. *London.* a.1689-1732. Watch.
William. prob. *London.* an.1776. Watch.
SPARREVOGN—
Søren Andersen. *Copenhagen.* 1761. m. 1773.
Anders Christian. *Copenhagen.* m.1781.
SPARROW—
——. *London.* an.1749. Watch.
Thomas. *London.* a.1772, CC.1787.
John. *London.* a.1779, CC.1787-1824.
SPATCHETT, Robert. *London.* a.1729.
SPATEMAN—
Samuel. *London.* a.1740.
John. *London.* an.1755-90. Watch.
SPATZ, Johannes. *Augsburg.* comp. ca.1766, m.1772.
SPEAKMAN—
William. *London.* a.1654, CC.1661, m.CC. 1701-17. l.c. marqueterie clock, Vintners Co.
Thomas, son. *London.* a.1675, CC.1685-1714. l.c. clock.
Edward, bro. *London* (*Newgate St.*). a.1682, CC.1691-1712. l.c. marqueterie clock. cf. SPEAKMETT.
William. *London.* a.1688.
John. *London.* a.1692, CC.1707-12.
Richard. *London.* a.1692.
——. *London* (*Hatton Wall*). 1709. C.
John. *London.* CC.1707.
William, son. *London.* a.1725.
John. *London.* a.1729.
Francis. *Berkhamsted.* 1791. C.
SPEAKMETT, E. *London.* ca.1700. l.c. clock ill. Cec. & Web. cf. SPEAKMAN.
SPEAR, James. *London.* a.1786.
SPEARING, William. *London.* a.1701, CC. 1719.
SPEARMAN—
Leonard. *London.* a.1750.
Thomas. *London.* a.1756.
SPEDDING, Richard. *Eastby.* 1794.
SPEED—
Francis. *London.* a.1707.
George. *Dundee.* 1749.

SPEEDWELL, G. *London.* an.1775. Watch.
SPEER, Samuel. *Newton Stewart.* 1824.
SPEERS—
James. *Liverpool.* 1818. W.
Robert. *Liverpool.* 1821. W.
Charles. *Liverpool.* 1825. W.
SPEIGHT—
James. *Skipton.* mar.1713, d.1721.
James. *Tong.* 1750-85.
SPENCE—
Henry. *London.* a.1763.
John. *Market Harborough.* 1778. d.1783. C. & W. His widow, Catherine, continues the business.
John. *London.* an.1779. Watch.
Robert. *Dysart.* 1780.
Thomas. *Dysart.* 1780.
James. *London.* an.1782. Watch.
John. *Boston, U.S.A.* 1821-5. W.
SPENCER—
Thomas. *London.* a.1671, CC.1685. l.c. clock.
Jonathan. *London.* a.1696, CC.1704-14.
Thomas. *London.* a.1700.
John. *London.* a.1702.
John. *Colne.* ca.1770.
Richard. *Dublin.* 1725. Watch Den. coll.
Arthur. *London* and *Dublin.* a.1724, CC. 1732. Watch.
Charles. *Liverpool.* 1734.
John. *London.* a.1766.
& PERKINS. *London* (*Snow Hill*). 1765-1806. Pedometer G.M. Watch London M. Also PERKINS & SPENCER.
Emanuel. *London* (*Snow Hill*). 1774-93.
W. *London.* 2nd half 18c. Watch mt.
John. *London.* CC.1787.
John. *Billericay.* 1791. W.
T. *Chelmsford.* ca.1800.
Eli. *Bolton-le-Moors.* ca.1820.
Thomas. *Manchester.* ca.1820.
SPENDLOVE—
——. *Cambridge.* 1770. W. Also SPENDELOW.
John Simpson. *Thetford.* an.1775-1818. Wall clock ill. Cec. & Web. Watch.
James. *Brandon.* 1784-91. C. & W.
SPENGLER, Jakob. *Nürnberg.* m.1468. 'Orelmacher.'
SPENS, James. *Edinburgh.* a.1808.
SPICER—
William. *London.* a.1750.
Charles. *Haverhill.* an.1768. Watch.
SPICHT, F. V. *Amsterdam.* ca.1700. Watch.
SPIES, Lucas. ——. 1627. Table clock Colmar M. which came from the neighbouring village of Selestat.
SPIEGELHALDER—
Adam. *Waldau.* Early 18c. Said to have devised wheel-cutting machines for Schwarzwald clocks.
Anton. *Waldau.* ca.1760. Wall clock Furt. M.
SPILLER—
Henry. *Exeter.* 18c. l.c. clock.
Nathaniel William. *London* (*Friern Barnet* and *Whetstone*). an.1791-1808. Watch.
John. *Wellington* (*Somerset*). 1791. C.
Henry. *Bideford.* 1795. W.
SPILSBY, W. W. ——. ca.1760. Watch.
SPIN, Jacob. *Amsterdam.* Early 17c. sil. oct. watch Stern. coll.
SPINAY, William. prob. *London.* an.1774. Watch.
SPINDLER, ——. *Berlin* and *Potsdam.* 1765-1793. Two brothers, cabinet-makers. Several clock-cases.
SPINDLES, John. *London.* a.1752.
SPINK, Marshall. *London.* 2nd half 18c. Watch.
SPINNEY, John. *Stickland.* 1750. C.
SPIRLS, ——. *Dublin.* 1757. Fine l.c. clock.
SPITTAL, James. *Glasgow.* 1793.
SPITTEL, William. *London.* a.1739.
SPITTLE, Richard. *London.* a.1691, CC.1699-1701. l.c. clock.
SPITZ, Kaspar. *Schwaz.* ca.1550. sq. clock and aut. work K.H.M.
SPIVEY, ——. *London* (*Westminster*). Late 18c.
SPLEIS—
G. M. *Schaffhausen.* Early 18c. Sig. on watch Feill coll. 'G. M. Spleis/Rector. fil. a Schafhaus.'
Sal. *Schaffhausen.* Mid. 18c. Watch Geneva M.
SPORER—
Andreas. *Dresden.* ca.1575. Court C. From *Torgau.*
Martin. *Nürnberg.* 1581 comp.
SPÖRLICH, Melchior. *Annaberg.* 1543.
SPRADBURY, John. *London* (*Brixton*). Early 19c. Watch.
SPRAECKEL, Jr. *Zutphen.* 1685.
SPRAKEL (SPRAACKEL)—
William. *Haarlem.* 1665.
William. *Haarlem.* 1744.
SPRANGER, ——. *Berlin.* 1812.
SPRATLEY, Richard. *London.* a.1772, CC. 1780.
SPRATNELL, Samuel. *London.* ca.1800. br. clock.
SPRATT—
Peter. *Bristol.* 1784.
William. *Saintfield.* 1824.
SPRENGEL, P. N. ——. Pub. Berlin, 1711, a work on crafts, containing treatises on clock and watchmaking.
SPRENGELIN, J. S. *Berlin.* 1794.
SPRIGG—
Henry. *London.* a.1637.
——. *London* (*Moorfields*). dau. mar.1758. W.
SPRING, John. *London.* a.1694.
SPRINGFIELD ILLINOIS WATCH CO., successor of the ILLINOIS SPRINGFIELD WATCH CO., which issued watches with sigs.:—'Hoyt,' 'Stuart,' 'Mason,' 'Miller,' 'Currier' in 1870-5, and 'Bunn' 1870-82, and 'Illinois Watch Co.,' 1879.
'SPRINGFIELD.' Sig. on 1870 watches of the NEW YORK WATCH CO.
SPRINGHAM, John. *London.* a.1729.
SPROGELL—
John. *Annapolis.* From 1764.
John, jun. *Philadelphia.* 1771-9.
SPRUYT, A. *Gorinchem.* ca.1800.
SPURRIER—
John. *London.* a.1677, CC.1684-6.
John. *Poole.* 1710. C.
John. *Poole.* 1795. C. & W.
SPYER, John. *London.* 1825.
SQUIRE—
C. *Buckland Brewer.* 18c. l.c. clock.
Robert. *Buckland Brewer.* 18c. l.c. clock.
Thomas. *London.* a.1804. Pub. in Phil. Mag. 1827 an art. on a clock with dead-beat esc.
STABLE—
Joseph. *London.* an.1755. Watch.
John. *London.* an.1774. Watch.
STACEY—
John. *London.* a.1675, CC.1683.
William. *London* (*Fleet St.*). a.1749, CC. 1760-84. br. clock. Watch.
Thomas. *Farnsfield,* mar.1774, then *Southwell,* 1795. l.c. clock.
Jonathan. *London.* a.1773.
George. *Worksop.* Early 19c. Watch Nottingham M.
STÄCKEL, Reinhold. *Berlin.* b.1823, d.1897. Founded the *Deutsche Uhrmacher Zeitung.*

STACY—
John. *London.* a.1734.
John. *London.* a.1763.
STADLER—
Rodolphe. *Zürich.* b.1611. Went to *Ispahan.* Executed 1639.
Sebastian. *Friedberg.* b.1734-94.
STADLIN, Franz Louis. *Pekin.* b.1658. Went to *Pekin* 1707. d.1740. C. to K'ang-hi.
STAFFORD—
John. *London.* a.1699, CC.1708, m.CC.1741. Watch engraver. *v.* GRILLIAT.
James. prob. *London.* an.1755. Watch.
Samuel Ward. *London.* a.1758.
William. *Dublin.* 1766-80. W.
——. *Bristol.* 1775. Partner in TRAPP & STAFFORD.
M. A. *Dublin.* 1795. W.
STAHL, Andreas. *Augsburg.* Early 17c. Watches Louvre, K.H.M. and M.P.S. Dresden sd. 'A. S.' possibly by him. Watch Feill coll.
STAINE, Roger. prob. *London.* an.1791. Watch.
STAINES—
Jeffery. *London.* 1700-12 CC.
John. *London.* a.1795.
STAINROD—
Thomas. *Barnsley.* 1814-22.
G. *Barnsley.* 1816-22.
STAINSBY, Matthew. *London.* a.1766.
STAINTON—
Henry. *London.* a.1727.
John. prob. *London.* an.1759. Watch.
STALP (STALPP)—
Daniel Georg. *Coburg.* a.1705, m.1711-36. a. in *Ansbach.* Court C.
Nicolaus. *Fürth.* d.1755.
Johann Friedrich. *Dresden.* m.1767, d.1789. g. en. jasper watch. g. repoussé rep. watch M.P.S. Dresden.
Johann Gottfried. *Dresden.* m.1795, d.1803.
STAMFORD—
——. *London.* 1640 CC.
Richard. *London.* a.1652.
& Co. *Liverpool.* Early 19c. Lever watch mt. S.M.S.K.
STAMM, Fideli. *Boll.* ca.1800. aut. with organ.
STAMP, Samuel. *London.* b.1689, d.1770. mus. C.
STAMPER—
Francis. *London.* a.1675, CC.1682-1700. p.c. watch, with sun and moon hour indicator, S.K.M. Watch with balance spring. A good maker.
John. *London.* 1745.
STANBOROUGH, Joseph. *London.* a.1720, CC.1722.
STANBURY—
Henry. *London (Holborn).* a.1701, CC.1709-1732. l.c. clock.
James, son. *London.* a.1732.
William. *London.* Mid. 18c. Watch Stads M. Amsterdam.
——. *Bath.* Early 19c. Watch.
STANCLIFFE—
John. *Halifax.* 1720-60.
Joshua. *Sheffield, Halifax* and *London.* 1776. Bankrupt.
John. *Barkisland.* ca.1780. l.c. clocks.
Joshua. *Woodhead (near Barkisland).* 1785. C.
John. *Askrigg.* ca.1785-1840.
Joseph. *Barkisland.* 1807.
John. *Burnley.* ca.1820.
STANDISH—
William. *London.* a.1660, CC.1668-87.
Benjamin. *London.* an.1779. Watch.
STANDLEY, Miles. *London.* a.1810, CC. 1818.
STANDRING—
James. *Rochdale.* ca.1770-95. C.
Jeremiah. *Bolton.* ca.1780. l.c. clock.
STANES, Jeffery. *London.* CC.1686.
STANET, ——. *London.* an.1746. Watch.
STANFORD—
John. *London.* CC.1718.
William. *Yarmouth.* 1795 CC. W.
STANG, ——. *London.* an.1743. Watch.
STANGE, C. *High Wycombe.*
STANILAND, John. *Malton.* Early 19c. Watch.
STANLEY—
John. *London.* a.1704.
Samuel. *London.* a.1706.
Patrick. *London.* a.1723.
John. *London.* a.1725, CC.1732-56.
George. *London.* an.1759. Watch.
Joseph. *N. Shields.* 1761. C. & W.
Thomas. *Liverpool.* 1769-77. W.
Richard. *Liverpool.* 1773. W.
Thomas François. *Paris.* m.1776-99.
John. *London.* a.1792.
——. *Paris.* 1807-12.
George. *Liverpool.* 1825. W.
STANNIER, John. *Chester.* 1790. C.
STANSBURY, Thomas. *Hereford.* an.1756-1765. Watch.
STANSELL, Edward. *Bristol.* 1813.
STANTON (STAUNTON)—
Edward. *London.* a.1655, CC.1662, m.CC. 1696-1707. br. clock Weth. coll. ill. Britten. l.c. clock ill. Cec. & Web. Watch.
Originall. *London.* 1662.
Reginald. *London.* Left CC.1669.
Samuel. *London.* 1688 CC.
John. *London.* a.1684, CC.1692-1725. br. clock.
Samuel. *London.* a.1692, CC.1719-33.
Joseph. *London.* a.1696, CC.1703-32.
Samuel. *London.* a.1703, CC.1715. Lantern clock.
Richard. *London.* a.1716.
Mary. *London.* a.1716.
William, son of Jos. *London.* a.1725, CC. 1732.
John, son of Sam. *London.* a.1733.
Job. *New York.* 1810.
John. *London.* a.1821.
STANYER, John. *Nantwich.* 1795. C.
STAPFF, Johann August Samuel. *Dresden.* m.1803, d.1808. Watch, Meissen china, g. mounts, Stern. coll.
STAPLE, Joseph. *London.* a.1725.
STAPLES—
Richard. *London.* a.1684.
James. *Odiham.* 1757-95. C. & W.
William. *London.* ca.1790. p.c. g. str. rep. watch. mus. trav. clock.
James. *London.* 1790. g. en. watch Den. coll.
STAPLETON—
George. *London.* 1689 CC.
Thomas. *London.* a.1686, CC.1694-1723. Watch.
William. *London (Hanover Sq.).* Early 18c.-1747. Watch Den. coll. Lantern clock.
Thomas. *London (Golden Sq.).* 1751. W.
——. *London (Conduit St.).* 1755. W.
——. *Sutton (Lancs.).* an 1777. Watch.
Charles. *Liverpool.* Early 19c. Watch.
STAPLYTON, ——. *Middleham (Yorks).* ca.1750.
STARCK—
Thomas. *Germany.* 17c. Watch Louvre.
Hans Gottfried. *Reval.* d. between 1698 and 1715.
David Hindrich, son. *Hälsingfors.* 1713. m. 1716. *Stockholm,* 1734. d.1748. Watch.
STAREY, John. *London.* 1770. CC.1785, l.CC.1787, d.1800. l.c. clock. c.secs. watch mt. G.M.
STARGE, Joseph. *London.* a.1739.

STARK—
——. *London (Cockspur St.).* 1776. W.
Henry. *Ennis.* 1824.
STARKEY, Joseph. *London.* a.1697, CC. 1706.
STARLING—
Charles. *London (Ironmonger Row* and *Chequer Alley).* CC.1776-1809.
Joseph. *London (Aldersgate St.).* a.1786, CC.1795-9.
STARNILL, James. *London.* 1660 CC.
STARR, Robert. *London.* CC.1667-86. math. inst. maker.
START, John. *London.* a.1760.
STARTRIDGE—
John. *Lymington.* an.1776. Watch.
Joseph. *West Cowes.* 1795. W.
STARZAKER—
William. *London.* a.1757, d.an.1791. C. Also STIRZACKER.
John, son. *London.* a.1791.
STASINON—
P. J. *Gand.* Early 18c. Watch with mother-of-pearl bas-relief on cock Stads M. Amsterdam.
——. *Tournai.* Early 18c. Prob. same as preceding. Watch Carnegie M.
STASLEY, John. *London.* 1690.
'STATE STREET.' Sig. on watches of the HAMPDEN WATCH Co. ca.1881.
STATMO, Johan Hansen. *Copenhagen.* m. 1813.
STAUFFER—
Abram. *Chaux-de-Fonds.* 1788-97. C.
ET SANDOZ. *Chaux-de-Fonds.* 1788-early 19c. Watches and clocks.
Abram, ET FILS. ——. ca.1800. Large sil. c.secs. watch Arts M. Prague.
Fils. *Geneva.* Early 19c. cyl. watch S.M.S.K.
Samuel C. *Manheim, Lancaster, U.S.A.* Early 19c. A good maker. Many l.c. clocks.
& EBY. *Manheim, U.S.A.* Partnership of Sam. STAUFFER and Christian EBY.
STAWTON, William. *London.* a.1798.
STAYNE, Thomas. *London.* CC.1654-8. Also SAYNOE.
STAYNER, Anthony. *London.* a.1722. Watch.
STAYNES, Jeffrey. *London.* CC.1686.
STEAD—
Thomas. *London.* a.1668, CC.1678-86.
Thomas. *London.* a.1720.
Joseph. *London (Knightsbridge).* 1745-55. W.
John, son. *London (Fetter La.).* a.1740, CC. 1747-75.
STEARN, Joseph. *London.* a.1781.
STEBBING—
Thomas. *London.* a.1749.
William Joseph. *London.* a.1792.
STEBER, D. *Dover.* Early 19c. Watch.
STEDMAN—
James. *London.* 1690 CC.
Richard. *Godalming.* an.1773-early 19c. Watch Ilbert coll.
J. *London.* 1790.
Thomas James. *London.* a.1798.
William. *London.* 1805-08.
& VARDON. *London.* Early 19c. g. watch with en. and pearls Gélis coll.
STEEDMAN, William. *London.* a.1766.
STEEL—
Benjamin. *London (Old Southampton Bdgs.).* 1744. Watch.
Thomas. *Edinburgh.* a.1784.
Peter. *Perth.* a.1792.
James. *London (Clerkenwell).* CC.1801, d. 1825.
John. *Edinburgh.* a.1810.
William. *Glasgow.* 1818.

STEELE—
Edward. *Whitehaven.* an.1768. Watch.
William. *London.* an.1781. Watch.
Alexander. *Edinburgh.* 1785-99.
John. *London.* 1799. mus. W. & C.
James. *London (Clerkenwell Close).* a.1793, CC.1801-40.
John. *Edinburgh.* a.1802.
I. *Oxford.* Early 19c.
STEENBERG, Knud Magnus. *Copenhagen.* m.1816.
STEENBERGEN, ——. *Amsterdam.* 1st half 18c. Watch Stads M. Amsterdam.
STEENHOLT, Ketel Boy. *Lindholm.* 1706. Wall clock.
STEERS—
Barnard. *London.* CC.1769.
William. *London.* CC.1769, d.1816.
STEEVERT, F. *Amsterdam.* 1822. W.
STEFFENONI, ——. *Paris.* Early 19c. Mantel clock. Clock with mus. box.
STEFFENS, Jacop. *Bolsward.* 1730. Watch Stads M. Amsterdam.
STEGAR, John. *London.* CC.1699-1729. Watch.
STEGER, Joh. Matt. *Fürth.* d.1791.
STEGMANN, Franz. *Basle.* 1725. From *Strasbourg.*
STEHELIN, Hans Konrad. *Basle.* 1670. From *Rheinfelden.*
STEIB, Andreas. *Würzburg.* m.1792.
STEIGHT, Thomas. *Pershore.* ca.1750. l.c. clock.
STEILL, John. *Edinburgh.* 1741-55. Watch.
STEIN—
Abraham. *Philadelphia.* 1796-1825. Prob. only a dealer.
Diedrich Daniel. *Hamburg.* 1821.
STEINER—
Philipp Jacob. *Augsburg.* comp. ca.1721, m. 1745-70.
L. *Zürich.* Mid. 18c. Watch Basle M.
Philipp Jacob. *Augsburg.* comp. 1746, m. 1787.
Jean. *Couvet.* b.1726, d.1807. C. & W. Maker of repute.
Johann Baptist. *Würzburg.* m.1772, d.1795.
Jean Louis. *Convers* and *Chaux-de-Fonds.* 1777-96.
Maurice. *Chaux-de-Fonds.* 1781.
Jacob. *Burgdorf.* ca.1800. Watch.
Philipp Jacob. *Augsburg.* m.1803.
Lorenz Adam. *Augsburg.* m.ca.1805.
Anton. *Kitzingen-am-Main.* m.1806.
Joseph. *Würzburg.* m.1817. Clock Würzburg M.
STEINHART—
Martin. *Munich.* Court C. 1772.
——. *London.* Early 19c. Watch.
STEINMETZ, Carl Ludvig. *Copenhagen.* m. 1823.
STEINMILLER, Johann. *Germany.* Late 18c. sil. en. watch Fränkel coll.
STEINMÜLLER—
Lienhart der ältere. *Basle.* m.1521-55.
Urban. *Basle.* 1550.
Lienhart der Jüngere. *Basle.* 1556-80.
Ludwig. *Basle.* m.1588-1620.
Melchior. *Basle.* 1588.
Lienhart. *Basle.* 1588.
Johann Melchior. *Gera.* ca.1725-75. astro. clock Furt. M. trav. rep. clock M.P.S. Dresden. Watch.
STEINSONE, Robert. *Glasgow.* 1690.
STEIR, D. *Germany.* 1614. Watch mt. B.M.
STELL, Jonathan. prob. *London.* an.1769. Watch.
STELLAS, John. *London.* an.1785. Watch.
STELLEVEGE, Christianus. *Uppsala.* 1607-1610.
STELZER, ——. *Altwasser.* 1834. Devised a str. and rep. mechanism.

STEM, Richard. *London.* an.1778. Watch.
STEMS, Edward. prob. *London.* an.1769. Watch.
STENBERG—
Ingebricht Larsen. *Trondhjem.* 1759 m.
C. T. *Copenhagen.* m.1821.
A. *Falkenberg.* 1822.
STENBUCH, Hans. *Copenhagen* and *Kronberg.* 1620-47. Court C.
STENDER, Franz. *Hamburg.* 1801-04.
STENNETT—
William. *London.* a.1773, CC.1784.
Robert. *Bath.* 1784-95 CC. W.
William. *London.* 1808 CC., d.1821.
Benjamin Franthem, son. *London.* CC.1808.
William, bro. *London.* CC.1821-40.
STENSPROTT, Gregorie. *London.* Early 17c. Oval crys. watch.
STENVOIGT, Paul Ludvig. *Copenhagen.* 1691. Kleinuhrmacher.
STEPHANUS, Laurentii. *Vadstena.* 1395. d.1448. Keeper of monastery clock.
STEPHENS—
Francis. *London.* CC.1632-58.
Edward. *London.* a.1693.
Richard. *London.* a.1695, CC.1715. Watch.
Thomas. *London.* CC.1702.
Joseph. *London* (*Aldgate* to 1742, later *Whitechapel.* a.1713, CC.1721, m.CC. 1752. Also STEVENS.
John. *Bristol.* 1739. W.
Joseph, son. *London* (*Aldgate, High St.*). a.1739, CC.1748, m.CC.1776-84.
Philip, bro. *London* (*Minories*). a.1741, CC. 1748-52. Watch.
Samuel, son of Jos. *London* (*Whitechapel*). CC.1752-1808.
John. *London* (*Coleman St.*). a.1746, CC. 1755-72. Watch S.K.M.
Joseph. *London.* a.1754.
Samuel. *London.* a.1761, CC.1774.
Samuel. *London.* a.1786.
Richard. *London.* a.1788.
William. *Godalming.* End 18c. l.c. clock.
William. *London* (*Lombard St.*). 1799.
A. *London.* 1799-1804.
William. *London.* a.1803.
J. M. *Portsmouth.* Early 19c. Watch.
STEPHENSON—
Oliver. *London.* a.1714.
Andrew. *London.* a.1714.
John. *Cleveland.* mar.1776. W.
Henry. *Dorchester.* ca.1790 CC. Watch.
William. *London.* CC.1794-1820. Watch N.Y. Univ. Also STEVENSON.
Thomas Samuel. *London.* a.1787, CC.1799, l.CC.1810.
Daniel Weston. *London* (*Lombard St.*). CC. 1820-30.
& Co. *London* (*Lombard St.*). 1820-4.
D. W., & FARROW. *London* (*Lombard St.*). 1820. Pocket chron. mt. Ilbert coll.
Robert. *Pickering* (*Yorks*). 1822-41.
Robert. *Stokesley.* 1822.
STEPNEY—
James. *London.* a.1796.
Henry. *London.* CC.1807.
STEPPINGER (STOPINGER), Marx. *Nürnberg.* 1565-70. 'Uhrleinmacher.' Petitioned in 1565 with Hanns PRAUN and Esias VOGEL for a separate guild for Kleinuhrmacher.
STEPSTOW (STEPTOE, STAPTOE), William. *London.* a.1695, CC.1703-09.
STERCK, William. *London.* an.1762-90. Watch.
STERKY, ——. *Lausanne.* 1760 m.
STERLAND, John. *Nottingham.* an.1767-88. W.
STERLING, William. *Dublin.* 1795. W.
STERRY Thomas. *London.* a.1713.

STEUER, ——. *Guben.* Late 17c. hex. table clock Fränkel coll.
STEVENS—
Francis. *London.* 1650. Also STEEVENS.
Francis, son. *London.* a.1648. Also STEEVENS.
John. *London.* a.1648, CC.1655. Also STEEVENS.
Daniel. *London.* a.1653, CC.1661, d.1703. Also STEEVENS.
George. *London.* CC.1673-93. A George STEVENS, 'servant' to Daniel QUARE, d.1702.
Giles. *London.* a.1670. Also STEPHENS.
Samuel. *London.* a.1672, CC.1680-1706.
Benjamin. *London.* a.1673.
John. *London.* a.1684, CC.1691-1708. Also STEEPHENS and STEEVENS.
Ralph. *London.* a.1688.
Thomas. *London.* a.1692, CC.1700-24. Watch. Also STEEVENS.
Samuel, son of Sam. *London.* a.1699, CC. 1706-18. Lantern clock.
James. *London.* ca.1710. br. clock.
Nathaniel. *London.* a.1700, CC.1712-28.
Benjamin. *London.* a.1701.
George. *London.* a.1706.
William. *London.* a.1707.
Richard. *London.* CC.1715.
Richard. *London.* a.1718.
Richard. *London.* a.1720.
Thomas. *Leicester.* 1729. Insolvent. C.
Joseph. *London.* CC.1745, m.CC.1752-94.
Richard. *Bridgnorth.* an.1751-5. Watch.
John. *London.* a.1751.
Joseph. *London.* a.1753.
John. *Prescot.* an.1769. Watch.
George. *Hindon.* an.1770-95. Watch.
William. *Gloucester* and *Cirencester.* 1775-1812 CC. C. & W.
Robert. *London.* a.1771.
Samuel. *London.* 1790-3 l.CC.
Robert. *Milton.* 1781-95 CC. C. & W.
Edward. *Boston.* an.1786. Watch.
Richard. *Leicester.* 1791. W.
Thomas. *London.* a.1785.
Thomas. *Plymouth.* 1795.
John. *London.* Early 19c. Watch.
H. *Stoke Newington.* Early 19c. Watch.
Thomas. *London* (*Aldgate*). 1824.
William. *London.* a.1817.
STEVENSEN, Jacob. *Germany.* Late 16c. Clock.
STEVENSON—
Adam. *Dunfermline.* 1698-1752.
Benjamin. *London.* a.1715.
Edward. *London.* a.1722.
N. *London.* an.1743. Watch.
John. *Stafford.* an.1749. Watch.
William. *Maidstone.* 1756. W.
David. *Kilmarnock.* d.1786.
Charles. *Congleton.* 1768. d.1796. C. & W.
William Hart. *Edinburgh.* a.1766-81.
Robert. *Stafford.* an.1785. Watch.
Adam. *London* (*Holborn. Theobald's Row* in 1786). CC.1774, l.CC.1787.
Alexander. *Edinburgh.* a.1779-86.
Robert Slater. *London.* a.1785. *Worcester,* 1795.
William. *London.* CC.1794.
Alexander. *Jamaica.* 1795. W.
John. *Liverpool.* 1796. W.
v. HALLAM & STEVENSON.
STEWARD—
Henry. *York.* 1816. d.1870. W. Also STEWART.
Frederick. *London.* a.1811.
Robert. *Helmsley.* 1822.
Charles Samuel Dale. *London.* a.1816.
STEWART—
Elizabeth. *London.* a.1708.
Alexander. *Edinburgh.* a.1722.
——. *Newport Pagnell.* an.1743. Watch.
William. *London.* a.1756.

STEWART—*continued.*
Alexander. *Dublin.* 1766-74. W.
James. *London.* a.1763.
Charles Mannant. *London.* a.1764.
George. *Perth.* a.1765.
Charles. *Edinburgh.* a.1766.
John. *Edinburgh.* a.1771.
John. *Edinburgh.* a.1772.
James. *Glasgow.* 1778-99.
James. *London.* 1790. W.
John. *Dunbar.* 1792.
Thomas. *Auchterarder.* 1798.
& Co. *Dublin.* Early 19c. Watch.
Peter. *Tanderagee.* 1824.
STEYER, C. F. *Leipzig.* 1800-14.
STEYERER, Christian. *Eisenbach.* ca.1720.
STEYRER, F. *Germany.* 1796. Pub. 'Geschichte der Schwarzwälder Uhrmacherkunst.'
STIBBS, Christopher. *London.* ca.1765. Watch.
STICHES, Gabriel. *Metz.* 1660. Repaired cathedral clock.
STICKLAND—
Sarah. *Bristol.* 1812-15. W.
John. *Bristol.* 1815-18. W.
STICKLER, William. *Bristol.* 1787. C. & W.
STIEBEL, B. *London.* 1825.
STIEBER, Johann Georg. *Vienna.* Mid. 18c. br. clock Uhren M. Vienna.
STIEBLER, C. G. *Paris.* 1824.
STIELER, Franz. *Berlin.* 18c. Watches with en. portraits.
STIENNON, ——. *Paris.* 1812-25.
STIETZ, J. *Cassel.* 1747-72. Clock Cassel Landes-M.
STIFF, William. *London.* a.1676.
STIFTER, Christian. *Vienna.* m.1783.
STILEMAN, John. *London.* CC.1640.
STILES—
John. *London.* a.1697, CC.1704-27. l.c. clock Brewers Co. Watch M.M.A.
Nathaniel. *London.* a.1716, CC.1725, m.CC. 1751-70. Watch.
STILL—
Francis. *London.* a.1691, CC.1699-1710. Watch.
Stephen. *London.* an.1744. Watch.
STILLARD, George. *London.* an.1803. Watch.
STILLAS, John. *Philadelphia.* 1783. C. & W.
STILLES, David. prob. *London.* an.1777. Watch.
STILLETTO, Samuel. *London.* a.1686 CC.
STILLINS, John. *London.* a.1722.
STILLMAN, James. *London.* a.1807.
STILTON—
William. *London.* a.1745.
——. *London (Old Bailey).* 1768. W.
STILWELL, Thomas. *London.* a.1755, CC. 1762.
STIMMETZ, Frederick. *Haarlem.* 1766.
STIMSON—
Henry. *Sleaford.* 1756. C. & W.
Henry. *Bath.* 1763. d.1766. mus. C.
Henry. *London.* 2nd half 18c. Watch.
——. *Newport.* an.1778. Watch.
Richard. *Cambridge.* 1793. d.1797. W.
STINT, ——. ——. an.1781. Watch.
STIRLE, Konrad. *Nürnberg.* Burgher 1612.
STIRLING—
John. *London.* 1784-94. W.
Robert. *Stirling.* 1820-60.
STITZ, Christian Friedrich. *Augsburg.* comp. ca.1783, m.1792.
STJÄRNSUNDS URFABRIK. 1711-67. Many l.c. clocks, two in Nord. M. ill. Sidenbladh.
STOAKES, ——. *London.* 1779. Watch London M. Perhaps John STOKES.
STOCK—
Joseph Nikolaus. *Hannstetten.* 1770.
James. *Liverpool.* 1800-03.
STOCKAR, Henry. *London (Change Alley).* 1708-31.
STOCKDALE, Samuel. *London.* an.1773. Watch.
STOCKDON, Mathew. *London.* CC.1717.
STÖCKEL—
H. F. A. *Nürnberg.* 1802. Pub. 'Anweisung für Liebhaber des Uhrenbaues.'
Johann Matthias. *Möschlitz.* 1820. Pub. 'Praktische Lehre . . . über den Uhrenbau'
STOCKELL (STOCKWELL & STOKELL)—
——. *Lincoln.* an.1755. Watch.
Hugh. *Newcastle-o.-T.* b.1751, d.1816. l.c. clock.
& STUART. *Newcastle-o.-T.* 1795. l.c. clock. Watch.
STOCKER—
——. *Honiton.* 2nd half 18c. l.c. clock.
——. *London (Threadneedle St.).* 1772. W.
STOCKERT, E. C. *Nürnberg.* Early 18c.-ca. 1780. Dials M.M.A. and Old Ashmolean M.
STOCKFORD—
Thomas. *Great Haseley.* From 1764.
Joseph. *Thame.* 1770. Made Ewelme church clock.
Thomas. *Thame.* 1778. C.
STOCKHEYNE (STOKHEYN), Albert. *Haarlem.* 1760.
STOCKHOLMS MANUFABRIQUE, *v.* Petter SCHNACK.
STOCKINGS, G. *London.* an.1773. Watch.
STOCKS, Thomas Fletcher. *London.* a.1802.
STOCKTON—
Peter. *Liverpool.* 1734-61. W.
Henry. *London.* an.1743. Watch.
Thomas. *Yarmouth.* 1784. W.
George. *S. Shields.* Early 19c. Watch.
Samuel. *Philadelphia.* 1823-5.
STOCKWELL, Richard. *Pershore.* ca.1790.
STODDART—
James. *Edinburgh.* 1750.
John. *Edinburgh.* 1761.
James. *London.* an.1775. Watch.
Charles. *Morpeth.* an.1782. Watch.
Babington. *Newcastle-o.-T.* 1782-4.
Robert. *Edinburgh.* 1787.
George. *Edinburgh.* 1793.
William. *London.* 1799.
Robert. *London (Red Lion St.).* 1817-25.
Robert, son. *London.* a.1817, CC.1825.
James, bro. *London.* b.1806, a.1821, CC. 1829, d.1886.
Benjamin. *S. Cave (Yorks).* 1822-34.
STOE, Harry. *London.* a.1767.
STOGDEN—
Matthew. *London.* 1st half 18c. Devised a repeating mechanism much used in England.
Thomas. *London.* a.1775.
STOKES—
John. *Saffron Walden.* ca.1660. Lantern clock.
Samuel. *London.* 1699. l.c. clock. Watch Horstmann coll.
John. *Saffron Walden.* 1725. Perhaps same as John above. l.c. clock S.K.M.
Stephen. *London. W. Smithfield* in 1744, d. 1764 in *Clerkenwell.*
John. *Bewdley.* an.1751. Watch. l.c. clock.
John. *Coventry.* an.1753-67. Watch. l.c. clock.
John. *Bridgnorth.* ca.1765.
John. *St. Ives.* an.1766.
James. *Stourbridge.* 1767.
John. *London.* ca.1770-87. Watches Ilbert and Den. colls.
Benjamin. *London.* a.1772.
Thomas. *London.* a.1789.

STOLLE, Johann Georg. *Fürth.* d.ca.1820.
STOLLEWERCK—
——. *Paris.* ca.1740-70. Clock S.K.M. Two clocks Wallace coll. Clock showing solar and mean time and planetary motions.
P. M. *Philadelphia.* 1813.
STONE—
Henry. *London.* 1623. C
Thomas. *London.* 1689 CC.-1712.
Andrew. *London.* CC.1699.
James. *London.* a.1692.
William. *London.* a.1692, CC.1700-03. g. en. watch.
Roger. *London.* a.1703, CC.1710-21.
William. *London.* a.1718.
William. *London.* an.1768. cyl. watch.
John. *Aylesbury.* 1760-1830. T.C.
John. *Thame.* 1764. C. & W.
Robert. *London.* a.1759.
Thomas. *London.* an.1771. Watch.
Richard. *Thame.* a.1761-82. Watch.
George. *London.* a.1765, CC.1774.
Samuel. *Shrewsbury.* an.1784. Watch.
Charles. *London.* an.1785. Watch.
Richard. *Reading.* an.1786-95. Watch.
Francis. *Bristol.* 1787-93. W.
James. *London.* a.1779.
John. *Reading.* ca.1790 CC.
John. *Henley-on-Thames.* 1795. W.
Thomas. *Thame.* Late 18c. Watch mt. Ashmolean M.
——. *Windsor.* ca.1800.
James. *Bristol.* 1812. W.
David. *Hull.* 1818-22.
STONEHOUSE—
Richard. *Whitby.* 1715-1809. W. l.c. clock. Perhaps two makers.
Jonathan. *Leeds.* 1798-1817. C.
Ann & Sons. *Leeds.* 1818.
Robert, son of Ann. *Leeds.* 1822-41.
John, bro. *Leeds.* 1822-34.
STONER, ——. *Brighton.* 1822. C. & W.
STONES—
Simon. *Sheffield.* 1654. Made clock for Marston church.
Thomas. *London.* a.1684, CC.1692, m.CC. 1730-47. l.c. clock Fishmongers Co. Watch. Also SCOLES.
George. *Blackburn.* ca.1820.
STOOSS, Gottfried. *Elbing.* 1804. d.1823. Town C.
STOPES—
Thomas. *London.* ca.1710. l.c. clock.
Elias Aylmer. *London.* ca.1740. l.c. clock ill. Cec. & Web. Also STOPPES.
STOPFORTH, Edward. *London.* 1691.
STORE, John. *Chester.* 1747. C. & W.
STORER—
Charles. *London* (*Berkeley Ct.* and later *Islington Rd.*). mar.1772, d.1810.
Robert. *London* (*Berkeley Ct.*). b.1746, CC. 1781-1820.
Robert. *London* (*Berkeley Ct.*). CC.1782.
Robert, & Son. *London* (*Berkeley Ct.*). Late 18c. and early 19c.
Robert. *London* (*Berkeley Ct.*). a.1787-1840.
Robert & Charles. *London* (*Islington Rd.*). 1799-1811.
James, son of Chas. *London.* a.1810-23. Watch N.Y. Univ.
A. & J. *London* (*St. John's Sq.*). 1815.
William. *Nottingham.* 1818. C. & W.
STOREY (STORY)—
James. *London.* a.1695, CC.1703. l.c. clock.
John. *London.* b.1688, d.1763. 'Eminent' W.
William. *London* (*Red Lion St.*). 1737. d. 1784. g. watch. mus. br. clock.
John. *London.* a.1738.
& HOWELL. *Yarmouth.* an.1778. Watch.
William, son of Wm. *London* (*Cornhill*). a. 1775-84.

STOREY (STORY)—*continued.*
Charles. *London.* an.1788. Watch.
Henry, bro. of Wm.(2). *London.* a.1789-1820.
James & William. *London.* 1820.
STORK, Johann. *Vienna.* m.1792.
STORLAND, John. *Nottingham.* 1784. W.
STORM, Gerrit. *Amsterdam.* 2nd half 18c. l.c. clock ill. Cec. & Web.
STORR—
Marmaduke. *London* (*Lombard St.*). a.1724-1775. l.c. clock. 'Eminent W.' Watch.
Batty. *York.* b.1710, d.1793. Watch.
& GIBBS. *London* (*Lombard St.*). 1752. W.
Jonathan, son of Marmaduke. *York.* b.1739, d.1795. W. & C.
William. *London.* CC.1781-95. Watch mt. S.M.S.K.
William. *York.* 1784. W.
——. *Tadcaster.* dau. mar.1804. C. & W.
STORRS, N. *Utica, N.Y.* Early 19c. l.c. maple clock M.M.A.
STORT, Charles. *London.* an.1776. Watch.
STOS—
Valentin. *Ulm.* b.1709, d.1785. trav. clock Ulm M.
Theodorus Augustus. *Ulm.* Early 18c. Watch Besançon M.
STOTESBURY, George. *Cork.* Early 19c. Watch.
STOTT—
Ely. *Wakefield.* ca.1770-95. C.
Mark. *Skipton.* 1804-22.
STOTZER, Hans. *Zürich.* 1594. C. to the town.
STOUF, Nicolas. *Paris.* m.1773-89.
STOWE, Rowland. *London.* a.1768.
STOWELL, John. *London.* a.1731.
STRACEY, John. *London.* 1787-90.
STRACHAN (STRAHAN)—
Andrew. *London.* 1691.
Archibald. *Newcastle-o.-T.* ca.1740, d.1808. l.c. clock. Watch.
John. *London* (*Ratcliffe Row*). 1770. W.
Thomas. *London* (*Threadneedle St.*). CC. 1771.
John. *Hull.* ca.1790 CC.-1822. br. clock.
Charles. *London.* CC.1815, l.CC.1819.
STRADLING, Lewis. *Caerphilly.* 1791. C. & W.
STRAHM, Charles Louis. *Sonvilier.* 1782.
STRAIN, Charles. *London.* an.1798. Watch.
STRAINGER, John Snooke. *London.* BC. 1610 m.
STRAITON—
Archibald. *Edinburgh.* 1726-59.
David. *Montrose.* 1820. Watch.
Alexander. *London.* CC.1823, d.1873.
STRAND, Petter. *Stockholm.* 1791-1815. mus. clock Nord. M. ill. Sidenbladh.
STRANGE—
Robert. *London.* an.1771. Watch.
Thomas. *Kingston* (*Surrey*). 1791-1824. Watch. l.c. clock.
Thomas. *Banbury.* Early 19c.
STRANGFELLOW, Thomas. *London.* a.1681, CC.1691.
STRASSER—
Bendicht. *Basle.* m.1675.
J. P. *St. Petersburg.* Early 18c. trav. clock.
Ludwig. *Glashütte.* b.1853. A fine maker of precision clocks for observatories. Firm of STRASSER & ROHDE.
STRÄSSLER, Rochus. *Augsburg.* d.an.1681.
STRATER, Daniel. *London.* a.1699.
STRATFORD—
George. *London.* a.1695, CC.1704-16.
Sarah. *London.* a.1696.
William. *London.* a.1705.
John. *London.* a.1800.

STRATTON—
Richard. *London.* a.1710, CC.1720-47.
James. *Minchinhampton.* 1781. W.
John. *London* (*London Wall*). 1787. W.
John, son. *London* (*Bunhill Row* and *Whitecross St.*). a.1791, CC.1800-25. Chron. & W.

STRAUBHAR—
Johann Jacob. *Strasbourg.* 1721-32. Repaired the Strasbourg clock.
Franz Joseph. *Strasbourg.* ca.1750. Boulle br. clock by him or preceding.

STRAUCHAN, Thomas. *Edinburgh.* 1701.
STRAUGHAM, John. *London.* 1687 CC.
STRAUNE, Charles. *London.* an.1791. Watch.
STRAUSS, Simon. *Vienna.* m.1743.
STREATE, William. *London.* 1799.

STREELIN (STREETIN)—
Richard. *London* (*Cursitor St.* and *Holborn*). a.1738, CC.1745-76. Watch.
Richard, son. *London.* a.1762.
Henry, bro. *London.* a.1776.

STREET—
Edward. *London.* a.1633 under BC.
Henry. *London.* a.1673.
John. *London.* 1685, not CC.
Richard. *London* (*Fleet St.*). CC.1687, w. CC.1715-22. W. l.c. clock Weth. coll. Watch with minute hand making 4 turns per hour G.M. Watch Art M. Boston.
George. *London.* a.1687 CC.
William. *London.* an.1752. Watch.
James. *London.* an.1766. Watch.
Richard. *London.* an.1766. Watch.
Richard. *Bridgnorth.* an.1768. Watch.
& Pyke. prob. *Bridgnorth.* an.1778. Watch.
William Henry. *London.* a.1807.
George. *London.* a.1811.

STREIBEL (STREBELL), Christoph. *Augsburg.* Early 17c. Gilt clock with dome, and watch with crys. cover, K.H.M.
STREK, Jabez. *London.* an.1747. Watch.
STRELLER, Jacob. *Nürnberg.* ca.1700. Falling ball clock Grünes Gewolbe, Dresden.

STRELLY—
——. *Windsor.* an.1660. Watch.
Francis. *London.* CC.1666-91.
John. *Greenwich.* an.1684. Table clock.

STRENGBERG, Peter. *Stockholm.* 1807-25. Four br. clocks, two watch mts. Nord. M.

STRETCH—
Samuel. *Bristol.* b.1657, d.1743. 'Eminent W.' Watches Ilbert and Den. colls.
Peter. *Philadelphia.* 1717. Repaired town clock.
Samuel. *Philadelphia.* 1717. Freeman of town. W.
Joseph. *Birmingham.* 1724. W.
——. *Wolverhampton.* an.1726. Watch.
Samuel. *Keynsham.* 1734. W.
Benjamin. *Bristol.* 1734-54. Watch.
Christopher. *London.* a.1731.
James. *Birmingham.* 1735. d.1770. Watch mt. Birmingham M. l.c. clock.
Samuel, son. *Birmingham.* 1770-81. Succeeds his father.
Thomas. *Philadelphia.* an.1782. Watch.

STRETCHAM, ——. *Lichfield.* an.1772. Watch.
STRETTON, Sarah. *London.* a.1704, CC.1716.
STRICK, William. *London.* 1784.

STRICKLAND—
George. *Bath* and *Daw Green.* 1770-6. Bankrupt. Left Bath 1770.
Sarah. *Bristol.* ca.1790.
——. *Tenterden.* ca.1800.
James. *Manchester.* 1813. C.
William Stokes. *London.* a.1813.

STRIGEL—
George Philip. *London* (*Pimlico*). b.1718, CC.1781, d.1798. W. to the Queen. cyl. watch with secs. and quarter secs. dials Ilbert coll.
Brothers. *London.* an.1753. Prob. the two following. Watch.
William Frederick. *London.* an.1759. Watch.
John Christian. *London.* an.1759. Watch.
& Co. *London* (*Buckingham Gate*). an.1772. Watch.
Nathaniel. *London.* an.1773. Watch.

STRIGELLUS, Thomas Christopher. *London.* Early 18c. Watch.
STRIGG, Henry. *London.* a.1637.
STRIGNER, ——. ——. ca.1687. Watch with carnelian outer case, made for James II.

STRINGFELLOW—
John. *London.* a.1681, CC.1691. Also Strangfellow.
Richard. *Liverpool.* 1810-29.

STRINGHAM, George. *London.* 1820.

STRIPLING—
Thomas. *Barwell.* ca.1710. l.c. clock in carved oak case ill. Britten.
Thomas. *Lichfield.* From 1761, d.1775. From *Coventry.* Succeeds John Hunt.
& Gilbert. *Lichfield.* From 1775. Firm of Hannah, widow of Thos., and Thos. Gilbert, nephew. Clocks sd. Thos. Stripling up to 1817 prob. by this firm.
T. & J. *Lichfield.* 1825. Watch.

STRIXNER—
Johann Jakob. *Friedberg.* 1741 juré.
——. *London.* Mid. 18c. Watch mt.
Joseph. *Vienna.* m.1785.

STROEBER, Bastian. *Montbéliard.* 1567. Repaired Château clock.
STRÖM, Sven. *Stockholm.* 1820-6.
STRÖMBECK, Joh. C. *Stockholm.* 1785-90.

STRONG—
T. *London.* 1st half 18c. Watch.
James. *London.* an.1771. Watch.
Andrew. *Dublin.* an.1780. Watch.
T. *London.* ca.1800-29. Watches Fränkel coll. and N.Y. Univ.
G. *London.* ca.1800. Watch with black dial S.M.S.K.

STROPP, Gottlob Wilhelm. *Berlin.* 1785-1804.

STROUD—
S. *London.* an.1750. Watch.
John. *London.* an.1774. Watch.
Robert. *London.* an.1775-1822. Ten watches N.Y. Univ. br. clock.
Joseph or John. *London.* a.1771.
Benjamin. *Ware.* 1784 CC. W.
v. Evill, Naish & Stroud.
Thomas. *London.* an.1791. Watch.
George. *London.* a.1808.
Joseph. *London.* 1817-24. Watch.

STROWBRIDGE, ——. *Dawlish.* ca.1805. br. clock. Watch Exeter M.
STROY, Joseph. *Amsterdam.* 1686. Huguenot refugee from *Paris.*
STRUBEL, ——. *Schorndorf.* ca.1770. mar. P. M. Hahn's sister.
STRÜBIN, Johann. *Basle.* 1816. From *St. Gall.*
STRUGGLE, Christopher. *London.* a.1671.

STRUTT—
Samuel. *London.* a.1748.
Jonathan Dennis. *London.* CC.1803-08. Watch.

STRUTTON, Archibald. *Edinburgh.* an.1770. Watch.

STUART—
Bernard. *Regensburg* and *Salzburg.* b.1706, d.1755. A Scotsman. Made the movement of a Boulle-work astro. clock with celestial sphere in 1731, in K.H.M.
Robert. *London.* a.1745.
George. *London.* a.1749.

STUART—*continued.*
William. *London.* an.1774. Watch.
George. *Newcastle-o.-T.* 1790-1820. l.c. clock. Watch.
Henry. *Liverpool.* 1825. Watch N.Y. Univ.
'STUART.' Sig. on 1870-5 watches of the ILLINOIS SPRINGFIELD WATCH CO.
STUBBE—
N. B. *Geneva.* Early 19c. cyl. rep. mus. watch Feill coll.
N. G. *Hamburg.* 1821.
STUBBS—
Gabriel. *London* (*Westminster*). a.1670, CC. 1675-7. From *York.* W. & C. of repute.
Thomas. *London.* CC.1685-1726. l.c. clock ill. Cec. & Web. Prob. the Stubbs who was keeper of St. Paul's clock to 1738, when he died.
John. *London* (*Gt. Arthur St.*). a.1747, CC. 1758, d.1794.
& Co. *London.* 2nd half 18c. Watch mt.
——. *Kegworth.* ca.1800.
Joseph. *Manchester.* 1813. C.
STUBLEY, Joseph. *Manchester.* 1808. C.
STUCE, John. *London.* a.1804.
STUDART, Joseph. prob. *London.* an.1761. Watch.
STUFFLER, Hans George. *Vienna.* m.1689.
STUK, William. *London.* 1781.
STUMBELS (STUMBLES)—
William. *Totnes.* 1754. Watch Glasgow Art Gall. and Ilbert coll. l.c. chiming clock.
——. *London.* 1762. W.
STUMP, Richard. *Oldham.* ca.1820.
STUNT, Charles. *London.* Early 19c. Watch.
STUNTZL, Johan. *Brünn.* 2nd half 18c. Watch mt. Arts M. Prague.
STURGIS, Edmund. *Dublin.* an.1729. W.
STURMBERGER, Michael. *Vienna.* m.1774.
STURZENBAUM, W. C. L. H. *Fürth.* d.1785.
STYCH, Edmund. *London.* a.1807.
STYLE—
Nathaniel. *London* (*Wood St., Cheapside*). CC.1725, m.CC.1751, retired 1773. l.c. clock. Watches Ilbert and Den. colls. Watch F.W.M. sd. 'N. Styles.'
Richard, nephew. *London* (*Cheapside*). a. 1742, CC.1750, l.CC.1766, m.CC.1790-4. Succeeds his uncle. Watch.
John, son of Nathaniel. *London.* CC.1772-99.
Senior. *London.* Early 19c. Watch.
STYLES, Richard or Robert. *London.* a.1696.
SUDBURY—
John. *London.* a.1675, CC.1686.
John. *London.* ca.1760. Watch mt. S.K.M.
SUDELL—
William. *London.* a.1683.
John. *London.* a.1683.
SUDGER, Charles. *London.* a.1739.
SUDLOW, ——. *Yarmouth.* 1764. W.
SUDMORE, John. *London.* 1st half 18c. Watch.
SUÈS, Jean Jacques. *Geneva.* b.1726, d.1802. Painter on enamel, specialized in flower subjects.
SUFF, Thomas. prob. *London.* an.1745. Watch.
SUFRY, A. *Geneva.* ca.1800. en. cyl. watch.
SUGAR, George. *London* (*Strand*). an.1743. Watch.
SUGGATE (SOUTHGATE)—
George. *Halesworth.* 1764-early 19c. Lantern and l.c. clock and watch.
William. *Sotherton.* 1817. Watch.
SUGNOT, ——. *Paris.* 1812.
SUHR—
Andreas. *Jauer.* 1st half 18c. sq. table clock M.P.S. Dresden.
Johann Hinrich. *Hamburg.* 1801.
SULLEY, ——. *Nottingham.* Early 19c
SULLY, Henry. *London* and *Paris.* b.1680, CC.1705, d.1728. In *Leiden* 1708-11, *Frankfurt-a.-M.* 1711, then *Vienna.* Went to *Paris* 1715. An eminent maker; directed a factory at Versailles in 1718, and another at St. Germain; devised a marine timepiece in 1724, tried at Bordeaux 1726; in 1721 made a modified Debaufre esc. with one esc. wheel and two diamond pallets on the verge, used in his marine timepiece; claimed to have been the first to apply equation work to a watch, ca.1706; pub. 'Règle Artificielle du Temps,' Vienna 1714 and Paris 1717, which passed through many editions and translations, 'Méthode pour régler les montres et les pendules,' Paris 1717, and 'Description Abrégée d'une Horologe . . . pour la juste mesure du temps sur mer,' 1726, describing his marine timepieces, ill. Gould; his marine timepiece G.M.
SULMAN, Thomas. *London.* a.1796-1820. Spring-maker.
SULZBERGER, Benedict. *Fürth.* d.1785.
SUMART, Joseph. *London.* an.1774. Watch.
SUMERS, John. *London.* a.1696.
SÜMMERER, Hanss. *Nürnberg.* Burgher 1564, m.1566.
SUMMERHAYES, R. *Ilminster* and *Taunton.* d.1857. l.c. clocks, watch.
SUMMERS—
John. *London.* a.1695.
Charles. *London.* an.1781-1800. g. en. watch.
E. *London.* an.1801. Watch.
SUMNER—
William. *London.* a.1654, CC.1661.
Joseph. *London.* a.1663.
James. *Liverpool.* 1700. C. & W.
Francis. *London.* 1784.
William. *London.* a.1793.
SUNDBERG—
Erik. *Stockholm.* 1743-65. Court C. Six watches, one Nord. M. Two br. and wall clocks.
A. *Stockholm.* 1790.
Johan Larsson. *Stockholm.* 1799-1810. Wall and br. clock.
SUNDELL—
Jonas. *Vadstena.* 18c. l.c. clock.
Olof. *Torneå.* 1808.
SUNDQVIST, And. *Mariestad.* 1815.
SUNDWALL, Pehr. *Norrköping.* 1810-40.
SUNNER, James. *Liverpool.* ca.1820.
SUPER, William. *Shrewsbury.* an.1761. Watch.
SUPPLE, John. *London.* an.1760. Watch.
SURMOICE, John. *London.* 1640 CC.
SURRIDGE, James. *London.* CC.1786.
SÜSSBAUER, Joseph. *Kitzingen-am-Main.* m.1803.
SÜSSNER, Caspar. *Vienna.* Mid. 18c. Clock.
SUTHERLAND—
Thomas. *London.* a.1767.
David. *Leith.* 1775. Clock.
George. *Elgin.* 1803-37.
David. *Keith.* 1805.
George. *Elgin.* 1820.
SUTLER, William. prob. *London.* an.1768. Watch.
SUTOR, William. *Edinburgh.* a.1704-18.
SUTTER, Emile. *Geneva.* 1760-1800. en. watch.
SUTTON—
H. *England.* 1659. Planisphere Old Ashmolean M.
Isaac. *London.* CC.1662-4.
John. *London.* a.1661.
John. *London.* a.1698.
Thomas. *London.* a.1698, CC.1705.
Edward. *London.* a.1701.
Robert. *Skipton.* b.1701, d.1761.
John. Late of *Dunkirk.* 1737. Insolvent. W.

SUTTON—*continued.*
Joseph. *London.* Mid. 18c.
John. *London.* 1751. CC.1760.
Alexander. *London.* 1766.
William. *Liverpool.* ca.1770.
Robert. *Stafford.* an.1774-95. Watch.
Thomas. *Maidstone.* 1790-9. C. & W.
James. *London.* a.1795, CC.1828.
William. *Liverpool.* 1803-05.
Thomas. *Liverpool.* 1811-29.
SVANBERG, Peter. *Linköping.* 1792-1821.
SVANHOLM, Anders. *Söderköping.* 1754.
SVENZON, S. *Torönsborg.* 1807. l.c. clock.
SWAAN, Pieter. *Amsterdam.* 1690. Watch mt. G.M. Watch Fränkel coll. Clock.
SWAAYEN (SWAAYER, SWAYERS), ——. *Haarlem.* 1744.
SWABY, Jacob. *Romney.* 1795. C.
SWADLING, Charles or William. *London.* a. 1793.
SWAINE—
William. *Ipswich.* 1776. Insolvent. W.
William. *Woodbridge.* 1795. d.an.1824.
SWALE, Robert. *London.* a.1735.
SWAN (SWANN)—
Edward. *London.* a.1650.
William. *London.* a.1692, CC.1703. Also SWANN.
——. *Margate.* an.1754. Watch.
Robert. *Bridlington.* 1760-70. SWANN.
George. *Edinburgh.* 1786.
SWANELL & CO. *London.* 1790. W.
SWANES, James. prob. *London.* an.1777. Watch.
SWANSON—
Robert. *London.* a.1722, CC.1730, d.an.1752.
William. *London.* 1790. Watch.
SWANWICK, G. *London.* 1820.
SWART, Bauke. *Joure.* Late 18c.
SWAY, Daniel. *Dublin.* an.1788. Watch.
SWAYNE, John. *London.* 1724. Watch.
SWEARER—
John. *London.* 1799-1808. Wooden C.
& SONS. *London.* 1820. Wooden clocks.
SWEBY, Thomas. *London.* a.1805.
SWEEBY, John. *London.* a.1662, CC.1671-98. l.c. clock.
SWEENY, Patrick. *Clonmel.* 1824.
SWEEPER, ——. *Romsey.* Late 18c.
SWEET, William. *London.* a.1725.
SWETMAN—
Isaac. *London.* 1723. Insolvent.
Thomas. *London.* ca.1750. p.c. watches S.M.S.K. and Den. coll.
SWIFT—
Hugh. *London.* a.1707.
Anthony. *London.* a.1754.
A. *Northampton.* 1771. W.
Anthony. *Haverfordwest.* an.1777-95. Watch.
William. *London.* 1790.
Richard. *Coltishall.* 1791. W.
Richard. *Yarmouth.* mar.1812, d.an.1824. W.
SWINBURNE (SWINBURN, SWINBOURNE—
John. *Hexham.* 1700. d.1748. l.c. clocks.
John. *Sunderland.* 1761-95. C. & W. From *Bishop Auckland.*
John. *Hexham.* 1770-84. l.c. clocks.
Thomas. *London.* a.1801.
SWINDELLS, Jasper. *London.* 1806. Watch case maker.
SWINDEN—
Francis. *Brentford.* 1782-1802. W.
James. *London (Rotherhithe St.).* 1784.
Henry, son of Francis. *Brentford.* a.1797-1808.
Francis, & Son. *Brentford.* 1802-04.
SWINDLE, John. *Macclesfield.* 1791-5. W.
SWINNEY, Henry. *London.* a.1761, CC.1773.
SWINTON, David. *London.* an.1780. Watch.
SWORDEN, Thomas. *London.* a.1721.
SWYGART—
John. *London.* a.1785.
Joseph. *London.* CC.1816. math. inst. maker.
SYBERBERG—
Christian. *New York.* 1756. From *London.* W. cf. SEVERBERG.
Christopher. *Charleston, U.S.A.* 1768. C. & W.
SYCHER, Hans. *Ochsenfurt.* an.1560 made the fine clock on the Rathaus.
SYDENHAM, H. & J. *London.* 1800-04. Watch Horstmann coll.
SYERS, Richard. *Manchester.* 1804. C.
SYKES—
Thomas. *London.* an.1793. Watch.
William. *Leeds.* 1798. C.
Thomas. *Leeds.* 1817.
Joseph, jun. *Ackworth.* Early 19c. Watch.
SYLVANDER—
Jacob. *Åbo.* 1778-1805. Wall clocks and watches.
Mich. *Uppsala.* 1790. d.1820.
SYLVER, John. *Dublin.* 1795. W.
SYLVESTER, John. *London.* a.1686, CC. 1693.
SYM, ——. *Edinburgh.* a.1773.
SYMMS (SYMM, SYMIS, SIMMS, SIMES)—
Isaac. *London.* 1615-28. Watches B.M., Taunton M. and M.M.A.
Andrew. *London.* a.1711. SIMMS.
Joseph. *London (Clerkenwell Green).* 1747. W. SIMMS.
Thomas. *London.* a.1772. SIMMS.
SYMONDS—
Richard. *London.* a.1669, CC.1691-8.
Elizabeth. *London.* a.1699.
Joseph, & Co. *Liverpool.* ca.1770.
John. *Rupham.* 1784. W.
Thomas. *London.* a.1778-88.
SYMONS, Thomas. *London.* a.1655, CC.1661. Lantern clock.
SYMSONE, James. *Dunfermline.* 1773. Firm of TURNBULL & SYMSONE.

T

TAAFFE, Tobias. *London.* a.1728.
TABOR, Bartholomew. *London.* a.1744.
TABORSKY, Johann. *Prague.* 1566. Repaired the aut. clock.
TABUIS, Hermanos. *Cadiz.* Early 19c. g. en. rep. watch Feill coll.
TAILLEMARD, ——. *Paris.* 1st half 18c. Designed a wheel-cutting machine desc. by Berthoud. His pupil HULOT continued to make them.
TAILLOT, ——. *Paris.* 1824. C.
TAILOR, Edward. *London.* a.1629 under BC.
TAINSH, David. *Crieff.* 1816.
TAIT—
David. *Edinburgh.* 1798.
William. *Wigtown.* 1820-37.
TALBAY, Joshua. *London.* 1710. W.
TALBERT, ——. *Paris.* 1819-24.
TALBOT—
Thomas. *Nantwich.* d.1717. C.
John. *Portsea.* 1795. C. & W.
Charles. *London.* a.1802.
TALBOYS, Jacob. *London.* a.1756, CC.1763.
TALÉN, Carl Adolph. *Stockholm.* 1809. d. between 1815 and 1820. Wall clock and watch.
TALLANS—
J. *Delft.* ca.1700. Sq. lapis lazuli watch Ilbert coll.
Gabriel. *Lausanne.* 1705. Watch M.M.A.
TALLERY, Nicolas. *Paris.* 1788 m.
TALLET, ——. *Paris.* 1768.
TALLIS, Aaron. *London.* a.1710, CC.1722.
TALON (TALAN, TALLON)—
——. *Paris.* 1737 m. Watches Den. coll. and Miller coll.
Alexandre Louis. *Paris.* m.1743.
Claude Olivier. *Paris.* m.1766.
TANAUER, Carl. *Warsaw.* comp. 1745.
TANDER, Eric. *Stockholm.* 1750-60.
TANFORD, ——. *London.* 1822-4. W.
TANNER—
Joseph. *London.* CC.1682-98.
——. *London (St. James).* 1733. W.
Edward. *Llancarfan.* a.1791.
James. *London.* a.1814.
TANQUERAY, James. *London.* an.1752. Watch.
TANSLEY, Thomas. *Birmingham.* 1808. C.
TANSPET—
Joseph Michael. *Augsburg.* comp. 1750, m. 1763-70. Austrian.
Joseph Xaver, son. *Augsburg.* 1778. m.1786-1799.
TANTAU, Hans Peter. *Hamburg.* 1801-04.
TAPERNON, ——. *Vevey.* 1764. comp. Perhaps the following.
TAPERNOUX, Jacques Louis. *Vevey.* 1798 m.
TAPLEY—
Thomas. *London.* d.an.1778. math. inst. maker.
Thomas. *London.* a.1779.
TAPP, George. *London.* a.1691.
TAPPAN, William B. *Philadelphia.* 1819. C.
TAPPIN, Samuel. *London.* a.1736
TARAULT—
Aîné. *Paris (Rue St. Honoré).* 1807-25.
Jeune. *Paris (Rue St. Denis).* 1807-26.
TARBUCK, Robert. *London.* a.1686.
TARDIF, Guillaume. *Rouen.* m.1653, juré 1657.
TARGE, Jean Baptiste. 1739. Juré 1743.
TARLESS—
John. *London.* CC.1690-1715. Engraver.
William. *London.* a.1710.
TARLETON—
Jeremiah. *London.* a.1690.
William. *Liverpool.* 1763-1807. A watchmaker of repute. Watch mt. with centre cal. hand Liverpool M.
Richard. *Liverpool.* 1790-6. W.
Philip. *Liverpool.* 1805. W.
TARON, Jean François. *Laroche.* 1811.
TARRANT, William. *London.* a.1813, CC. 1821.
TARRY—
William. *Saffron Walden.* m.1702, d.1729. Maker of repute.
John. *London.* a.1764.
TARTS, J. *London.* 2nd half 18c. Sig. on many watches for Dutch market, prob. a fictitious name.
TARTY, ——. *Paris.* 1812.
TARVES, Robert. prob. *London.* an.1785. Watch.
TASKER, Thomas. prob. *London.* an.1717. W.
TASMA, Douwe Jelles. *Grouw* and *Gorredijk.* b.1753, d.1845. br. clock.
TASMAN, John. *London.* a.1787.
TASSEL—
Jean. *Rouen.* m.1653.
André. *Rouen.* 1663 m.
Louis. *Rouen.* m.1691.
Pierre. *Rouen.* Juré 1696.
TATE—
George. *Belford.* 1810. W.
Robert. *Manchester.* ca.1820.
Thomas. *Alnwick.* 1820.
TATET FRÈRES. *Verrières.* 1766. Also *Paris.*
TATHAM—
A. *London.* an.1790. Watch.
C. *London.* an.1795. Watch.
——. *Cockermouth.* Early 19c.
TATLER, George. *London.* 1744. Insolvent.

TATTET, ——. *Côte-aux-Fées (Jura)*. 1730. *v.* TATET.

TAVAN, Antoine. *Geneva*. b.1749, d.1836. An eminent maker of watches and chrons. Made 10 large scale models of escapements about 1805, to the order of MELLY Frères, now in M. of École d'Horlogerie, Geneva. They included the verge, virgule, duplex, lever, 'Arnold' with spring and pivoted detent and three of his own invention. Watch with ordinary secs. hand and independent sweep c.secs. hand Geneva M. Devised a chron. escapement in 1819, and a lever esc. called 'échappement anchor' with pointed teeth.

TAVERNER—
Jacob. *London (Lombard St.)*. an.1762. Watch.
Joseph. *London*. a.1764.
William. *Coleshill*. 1774. l.c. clock.

TAVERNIER—
Jean Pierre. *Paris*. m.1743, d.1793. Maker of repute. Specialized in small watches for rings, etc.
Louis, son. *Paris*. b.1754, d.1840. A maker of great repute. Worked for BREGUET. Fine cal. watch, dials both sides, Marryat coll. cal. keys Blot-Garnier coll. and Arch. M. Geneva.
Étienne, bro. *Paris*. b.1756, d.1839.

TAVEY, Albert Francis. *London*. a.1789. rep. watch.

TAWNEY—
Peter (Pepe). *London*. ca.1700-ca.1750. rep. watch S.M.S.K. l.c. clock. Watch Den. coll.
Peregrine. *London*. an.1730. Watch. Prob. same as preceding.
James. *London*. a.1751, CC.1759.
Robert. *London*. an.1776. Watch.

TAWS, Richard. prob. *London*. an.1785. Watch.

TAYLER, Charles Foot. *London*. a.1811.

TAYLOR—
Edward. *London*. a.1637, CC.1645.
Thomas. *London (Strand)*. a.1638, CC.1646, m.CC.1687, d.an.1692. Watch and mt. G.M. Watch M.M.A. Watch Den. coll.
George. *London*. a.1648.
Richard. *London (St. Giles in Fields)*. a. 1648, CC.1655-1719.
Thomas. *London (By St. Paul's and Holborn)*. CC.1659-94.
Abraham. *London*. CC.1668.
William. *London*. a.1662.
William. *London*. a.1674, CC.1682.
Thomas. *London (Holborn)*. a.1678, CC. 1685, m.CC.1710-23. Watches G.M., S.M.S.K., M.M.A. and Den. coll. l.c. and br. clock Weth. coll.
John. *London*. CC.1687. Clock. Watch ca. 1700 Ilbert coll
Charles. *London*. a.1679.
John. *London*. a.1680.
Jasper. *London (Gray's Inn)*. a.1685, CC. 1695-1714. Watch.
Jacob. *London*. a.1688.
George. *London*. CC.1699.
Robert. *London*. a.1693, CC.1703, d.1716.
John. *London*. a.1694, CC.1702.
George. *Liverpool*. 1705. d.1722. Watch.
Charles. *London*. a.1698.
Jeremiah. prob. *London*. an.1708. Watch.
Thomas. *London*. a.1700.
Thomas. *London*. a.1705.
Montague. *London*. a.1707.
John. *London*. a.1708.
Joseph. *London (Wood St.)*. a.1709-23. Bankrupt.
Richard. *London*. a.1711.
Charles. *London*. a.1712, CC.1723.
Richard. *London*. a.1713, CC.1724.

TAYLOR—*continued*.
Joseph. *London*. a.1714.
Joseph. *Ashton-under-Lyne* and *Dukinfield*. d.1744.
Robert, son of Rob. *London*. a.1716.
Jasper. *London (Holborn)*. CC.1729, m.CC. 1754, d.1770. g. repoussé watch Den. coll.
Josiah. *London*. 1st half 18c. Watch.
Joseph. *London*. a.1722.
William. *London*. a.1725.
Joseph. *London*. a.1730.
George. *Preston*. 1738. C.
John. *Masham (Yorks)*. 1740.
William. *Bridgnorth*. 1743. d.1781. C. & W.
Henry Cleaver. *London*. a.1737, CC.1746.
William. *London*. a.1743, CC.1753.
George. *Bath*. 1748-51.
John. *Manchester*. 1750-81. C.
James. *Ashton-under-Lyne*. b.1724, d.1813.
Peter. *London*. an.1757. Watch.
Henry. *London*. 1761.
Edward. *London*. a.1760.
John. *Bath*. 1730-ca.1770. Watch Den. coll.
Samuel. *London (Holborn)*. CC.1770, m. CC.1807, d.1824.
Jonathan. *London*. an.1773. Watch.
Josiah. *London*. an.1774. Watch.
John. *Wigan*. 1772-80. C. Lancaster freeman.
Benjamin. *London (Lombard St.)*. CC.1773, d.1800.
William. *Whitehaven*. ca.1775-91. l.c. clock of bad design.
John. *London (Gloucester St.)*. ca.1780. br. clock.
John. *Kirkby Stephen*. 1784. C.
William. *Petworth*. 1784-90. C. & W.
John. *London (Upper Moorfields)*. 1784.
& SON. *London (Red Lion Sq.)*. 1784.
Joshua. *Congleton*. 1784. W.
John. *Petworth*. an.1790.
John. *Ormskirk*. ca.1790.
John. *Wolverhampton*. 1790. l.c. clock.
John. *Deptford*. 1791. W.
Elliott. *London (Holborn Hill)*. CC.1795, l.CC.1800-40.
George. *Shepton Mallet*. 1795. C. & W.
Richard. *Reading*. From 1797. Previously partner with Chas. PACKER.
Samuel. *Philadelphia*. 1799.
James. *London (Bloomsbury)*. 1799.
Edward. *London (Moorfields)*. 1799.
James. *Strichen*. 1799-1840. l.c. clocks.
Edward. *London*. a.1793, CC.1800, l.CC. 1810-30. Watch.
William. *Dumfries*. 1800-23 CC.
James. *Liverpool*. 1800-24.
Samuel. *Framlingham*. 1800. W.
John, & WOOD. *London*. 1802-04. C.
& SON. *London (Leadenhall St.)*. 1802-04.
James. *London*. CC.1802, l.CC.1811, d.1821. W.
John. *London*. a.1796.
J. & T. *London*. 1805-08. C.
John. *London (Clerkenwell)*. 1805-24.
William. *Newcastle-o.-T*. an.1811. Watch.
Edward. *London (Leadenhall St.)*. CC.1811-1825.
George. *London*. a.1802.
John. *Liverpool*. 1813-16. W.
Charles. *London (Cannon St. Rd.)*. 1813. Shagreen case maker.
Thomas. *Darlington*. 1818. W. Insolvent.
Thomas. ——. 1819. Pub. art. in Trans. Soc. Arts on a 'Repeating alarum.'
William. *Liverpool (Soho St.)*. ca.1820.
Thomas. *Manchester*. ca.1820.
M. J. Tobias, & Co. *Liverpool*. ca.1820.
W. T. *Liverpool*. ca.1820. Watch.
J. & S. *Liverpool*. ca.1820.
Charles Foot. *London*. a.1811.
John. *London*. a.1813.

TAYLOR—*continued.*
G. R. *Sunderland.* 1820.
Mark. *Staithes (Yorks).* 1822.
Luther. *Philadelphia.* 1823-5.
William. *Liverpool (Clare St.).* 1825. W.
William. *Liverpool (Whitechapel).* 1825. W.
William. *Liverpool (Lionel St.).* 1825. W.
Henry. *Liverpool.* 1825. W.
J. D. *Liverpool.* 1825. W.
'H. H. TAYLOR.' Sig. on 1867-75 watches of the NATIONAL WATCH CO. OF CHICAGO.
TEAGUE, Henry. *London.* a.1728.
TEAMS, John. *London.* 1790.
TEBBATT, Benoni. *London.* a.1676, CC. 1683-1700. W.
TECKNAU, Carl Ferd. *Jönköping.* 1778-85.
TEDMAN, James. *London.* 1688. W.
TEFLER, Marco. *Florence.* 1653-8. C. to the Grand Duke Ferdinando II. Incorrect name for Joh. Phil. TREFFLER, *q.v.*
TEGELBERGH, Johannes. *The Hague.* 1670. Clock with cycloidal cheeks.
TEICHMANN, Thomas. ——. 1513. aut. clock Nat. M. Munich.
TEIRS, Daniel. *Dromore.* 1824.
TELFER—
Samuel. *Glasgow.* 1720.
John. *Glasgow.* 1752.
Alexander. *Glasgow.* 1770.
Alexander. *Aberdeen.* 1805.
TELFORD—
John. *Wigton.* 1820.
Edward. *Carlisle.* Early 19c. Watch.
TELFORTH, Isaac. *London.* a.1715. Watch.
TEMPEL—
Gottfried. *Basle.* 1767. From *Potsdam.*
Klaas Johannes. *Grouw.* Early 19c.
TEMPERA, Antonio. *Rome.* 1668. Pub. 'L'Orivolo Giusto, utilissimo a' naviganti.'
TEMPEST, Henry. *London.* a.1638
TEMPLE, Thomas. *London.* a.1695, CC.1720. Watch.
TEMPLER—
Charles. *London.* a.1665, CC.1673.
Richard. *London.* 1766-81. Bankrupt. W.
TEMPLETON, James. *Glasgow.* 1818.
TENAILLON, ——. *Paris.* 1812-24. C.
TENCH, John. *London.* a.1702.
TENNANT—
Thomas. *London.* a.1660, CC.1668-92.
Thomas. *Childwall.* an.1759. Watch.
TENNUL, J. *London.* 1778 Watch Ilbert coll.
TENWAY, Robert. prob. *London.* an.1779. Watch.
TEQUIN, ——. *Fleurier.* Early 19c. g. en. watch M.M.A. Prob. LEQUIN.
TEROLD, Henry. *Ipswich* and *Bury St. Edmunds.* ca.1640. Fine eng. cross watch Mallett coll.
TÉROND—
FRÈRES *Geneva.* Early 19c. *v.* ALLIEZ.
ALLIEZ ET BACHELARD. *Geneva.* Early 19c. 4-colour g. watch M.M.A.
ET RAVIER. *Geneva.* Early 19c. Two eng. watches M.M.A.
TERRETT, Thomas. *London.* a.1739.
TERRIEN FRÈRES. *Paris.* 1812. C.
TERRIER—
James. *London.* a.1685, CC.1694-1706.
Thomas. *London.* a.1687, CC.1694-1722. Watch.
David. *Paris.* 1700. Registered a private punch mark. Watch M.M.A.
Mary. *London.* a.1706, CC.1714.
TERROT—
Philippe. *Geneva.* b.1697-1743. From *Dauphiné.*
Philippe. *Geneva.* ca.1750-80. Cockleshell watch G.M. Watch Glasgow Art Gall. en. watch, set zircons, Carnegie M. Watch Schloss M. Berlin

TERROT—*continued.*
ET THUILLIER. *Geneva.* Mid. 18c. Watch with chiselled steel on gold Gélis coll.
Ph., & FAZY. *Geneva.* 1770. g. watch G.M. g. en. watches Blot-Garnier and Wilsdorf colls.
cf. THERROT.
TERROUX—
François. *Geneva.* ca.1700-ca.1720. Watches Geneva M. and Ilbert coll.
——. *Paris.* 1st half 18c. g. en. watch Gélis coll.
Elizabeth. *Geneva.* ca.1760-90. Painter on enamel.
l'aîné. *Geneva.* 1772-89. Engine-turned watch ill. Britten. g. en. cyl. rep. watch. p.c. g. al. watch. al. watch Geneva M.
Abraham. *Geneva.* an.1788. Watch.
TERRY—
John. *York.* 1705, d.1757. Watch. In 1706 made clock for cupola in Thursday Market. cf. TIRRY.
John. *York.* b.1696, d.1783. 'An eminent watchmaker.' Made clock for York Castle.
Reuben. *York.* 1725.
Thomas, son of John (1). *York.* a.1733. C.
Charles. *London.* 1760.
John. *London.* an 1766. Watch.
Christopher. *London.* 1768.
William. *Bedale.* 1770.
William, son. *Richmond (Yorks).* b.1774, d.1848.
Eli. *Plymouth, U.S.A.* In *Northbury* to 1810. b.1772, d.1853. Retired 1826. Initiated the manufacture of clocks in quantity in America, making first clocks with brass movements and, in 1809, formed a company with Seth THOMAS and Silas HOADLEY to make wooden clocks. He left the firm in 1810 and went to Plymouth. Terry's clocks were at first wall clocks, but from 1814 bracket or shelf clocks known as Pillar Scroll Top clocks. br. clocks ill. Milham.
THOMAS & HOADLEY. *Greystone, U.S.A.* 1809. Firm which started making wooden clocks, but lasted only one year, becoming THOMAS & HOADLEY.
Thomas. *Boston, U.S.A.* 1810-25. W.
Eli, son of Eli. *Plymouth Hollow* (now *Thomaston*), *U.S.A.* b.1799, d.1841.
Thomas. *Nottingham.* 1818. C. & W.
Silas Burnham, bro. of Eli (2). *Thomaston, U.S.A.* b. ca.1801, d.1876. Made clocks with torsion pendulums.
Henry, bro. *Plymouth, U S.A.* b.ca.1802, d.1877. Retired from clockmaking ca.1830.
Samuel, bro. of Eli (1). *Bristol, U.S.A.* 1825-1835. Wooden clocks and looking-glass clocks.
Eli & Samuel. *U.S.A.* Early 19c. Shelf clock M.M.A.
William. *London.* Early 19c. Watch.
Isaac. *Richmond (Yorks).* 1820-50.
Leonard. *York.* 1822. C.
William. *Hull.* 1822-40.
William. *Masham (Yorks.).* 1822-40.
TERVEEN—
Gerrit. *Haarlem.* 1700.
Joost. *Haarlem.* 1728.
TERVOOREN, Gerrit. *Amsterdam.* ca.1750. l.c. mus. clock.
TESCH, Ernst Emanuel. *Berlin.* 1800.
TESSEYMAN—
George. *Northallerton.* b.1794, d.1871.
John. *Northallerton.* 1823.
TESSIER, Thomas. *London.* a.1804.
TETLEY, James. *London.* a.1784, CC.1794.
TEULON, William. *Cork.* Early 19c. Watch.
TEW, Thomas. *London.* a.1674.
TEXTOR, Joh. Mart. ——. ca.1725. Dial M.P.S. Dresden.

TEY, Henry. *London.* a.1688.
TEYSSON, Jean. *Lyons.* 1527. Turret C.
TEZZANO, Antonio. *Cremona.* 1471. Made clock for the Torrazzo tower.
THACKE—
Philip. *London.* a.1676, CC.1685-1701. l.c. clock.
Robert. *London.* a.1681, CC.1689-1706.
THACKER, Jeremy. *Beverley (Yorks).* 1714. Pub. 'The Longitudes Examined,' and made a marine timepiece desc. Gould. First used word 'chronometer,' and invented maintaining device.
THACKWELL—
Paul. *Ross.* 1774-84. W.
John. *Cardiff.* 1788-95. C. & W. l.c. clock.
Richard. *Pershore.* ca.1790. l.c. clock.
Thomas. *London.* 1812-30. W.
Thomas. *Monmouth.* 1822-30.
THAL, ——. ——. End 18c. 8-day rep. watch Ilbert coll.
THARLES, John. *London.* a.1686.
THATCHE, Robert. *London.* a.1684, CC. 1689-1706.
THATCHER—
George. *Cranbrook.* 1716. d.1773. C. Watch mt. G.M.
James *Bury St. Edmunds.* 1737. Insolvent. C.
W. *Wantage.* 18c.
——. *Tenterden.* an.1772. Watch.
THEED—
William. *London.* a.1742. en. watch.
& Pickett. *London.* Mid. 18c. Watch.
THELOTT, Philipp Jacob. *Uppsala.* 1679-1703. Swiss. Sundial Nord. M.
THEMAN, David. *Aberdeen.* 1493.
THEMER (DEMER), Ignatius. *Vienna.* m. 1720. trav. clock Den. coll.
THEOBALD, Thomas. *Bromley (Kent).* Early 19c. Watch.
THEOBALDS, Peter. *London.* a.1709, d. 1764. W.
THEODRICKE, Henry. *London.* a.1679 CC.
THERASBY (THORESBY), Peter. *York.* 1666. W.
THERROT, Phil. *Paris.* 1735. cf. Terrot.
THETFORD, John. *London.* a.1736.
THÉVENOT—
——. *Paris.* m.1607.
Achille René. *Paris.* m.1756-73.
Charles. *Paris.* m.1758.
Antoine. *Paris.* m.1777-89.
THEW—
George. *London.* 1805-08.
John. *Newton-on-the-Moor.* 1811. Watch.
THIBAUD, Jean. *Sedan.* 1607. Went to *Egypt.* Returned *Lyons* 1610.
THIBAUT, Pierre Barthélemy. *Paris.* m.1758-1789.
THIBOU, Jacques. *Edinburgh.* 1695.
THIÉBAULT (THIBAULT)—
Sébastian. *Dreux.* 1588. Dial maker.
——. *Paris.* 1812-25.
THIELL, Johann Georg. *London.* 1768. Watch with temperature compensation by brass rods on steel base.
THIEMECKE (THÜMCKE), ——. *Berlin.* 1812.
THIER, Johannis. *Regensburg.* Late 16c. Book watch Feill coll.
THIERIOT (THIRIOT, TIRIOT), François. *Lyons.* mar.1655-82.
THIERRY—
——. *Caen.* 1690. Watch with very large balance S.M.S.K.
Jean B. *Paris.* 1774-1812.
THIEVES, Joes. Cornelius. *Cologne.* 1730-44. g. rep. watch. sil. al. watch M.P.S. Dresden.
THIJMEN, Pieter. *Goude.* Mid. 18c. Watch S.M.S.K.
THIL—
Charles Louis. *Geneva.* Early 19c.
et Mottu. *Paris.* 1825.
THING, Elder. *Wrentham.* 1801. W.
THIOUST, Nicolas. *France.* ca.1730. Clock Designed a day-of-the-month mechanism.
THIOUT (THIOUST)—
Antoine, l'aîné. *Paris (Quai Pelletier).* b. 1692, juré 1743, d.1767. A very famous maker. C. to the duc d'Orléans and the Dowager Queen of Spain. Devised a turret clock esc. with esc. wheel in a plane at right angles to the plane of the pallets. Pub. 'Traité d'horlogerie,' 1741, and several arts. on equation clocks and rep. mechanism. br. clock Garde Meuble, Paris.
Charles. *Paris.* m.1746.
Pierre Nicolas. *Paris.* m.1773.
le jeune. *Paris.* 1780. br. clock.
THIRKELD (THRELKELD)—
Deodatus. *Newcastle-o.-T.* 1657. mar.1699-1732. Challenged in 1698 by Wm. Provost, a French C., that the maker of the best clock should have both, Ed. Burgis and Sam. Watson to decide. Thirkeld won. Watch.
——. *London.* an.1759. Watch.
THIRY, Gilles. *Namur.* 1677. 'Maître harquebusier et horlogier.' Repaired town clock with Leonard Évrard.
THISTLETHWAITE, Miles. *London.* a. 1696.
THOM—
William. *London.* a.1806.
J. *London.* Early 19c. Watch.
THOMACQUE, Abraham. *London.* CC. 1675-7.
THOMAS—
Jean. *Blois.* mar.1602, d.an.1617.
Daniel, son. *Blois.* comp. 1618. *Orléans,* 1628-48.
François. *Nantes.* ca.1640. sil. gilt sea urchin watch Mallett coll.
Louis. *La Rochelle.* 1647. d.ca.1660.
Pierre. *Nantes.* 1665.
Daniel. *London (Minories).* a.1675, CC. 1682-1711.
Hugh. *London.* a.1686.
Thomas Jacob. *London.* a.1698.
John. *London.* a.1701-43. Watch G.M.
Evan. *London.* a.1703.
Patrick. *Pen-y-clawdd, Denbigh.* 1719-21.
John. *Swansea.* mar.1735.
Jacob. *London (Westminster).* 1723. Insolvent.
John. *Crewkerne.* 1723. C. & W.
Owen. *Birmingham.* 1753. C.
John. *Edinburgh.* an.1757. Watch.
Richard. *London.* an.1758. Watch.
Josiah. *Bristol.* 1760.
Lewis. *London.* 1768-77. Worked as C. for George Graham.
Richard. *Clydey, Pembroke.* 2nd half 18c. l.c. clocks.
Morris. *Carnarvon.* 1769-94. l.c. clocks.
Rees. *Bridgend, Glamorgan.* a.1769.
William. *London.* a.1762, CC.1772. br. clock.
James. *Chester.* 1777-85. C. & W.
Lucy. *London.* an.1774. Watch.
Joseph. *Chester.* 1773. C.
Nicolas. *Paris.* m.1778-89. Mantel clock Pal. de l'Élysée by him or following.
Philippes. *Paris (Rue des Vieux Augustins).* m.1779-1825. C.
Henry. *London.* an.1782. Watch.
Olive. *Penrith.* 1781. Insolvent. C. & W.
François. *Paris.* m.1780-9.
Hugh. *Birmingham.* 1781. Watch and l.c. clock.
George. *London.* a 1780.
Richard. *Helston.* ca.1790 CC.

THOMAS—*continued.*
Robert. *Carnarvon.* 1788. d.1827. l.c. clocks.
Griffith. *Carnarvon.* 1789-95. W.
Griffith. *Amlwch.* 1790. W.
John. *Worcester.* 1790-6 CC. Watch mt. Worcester M.
John. *London* (*St. James St.*). 1792. Watch.
William. *Polton.* 1792. Insolvent. C. & W.
Samuel. *Swansea.* 1791-5. C. & W.
James. *London.* 1799.
Seth. *Plymouth Hollow* (now *Thomaston*), *U.S.A.* b.1774, d.1859. Partner with Eli TERRY and Silas HOADLEY at *Greystone* for one year to 1810. The firm was then THOMAS & HOADLEY till 1813, when Thomas left it and went to *Plymouth.* He was originally a case maker and made many l.c. clock cases. Made a fortune by making first wooden and then brass clocks. Shelf clocks ill. Milham.
——. *Paris* (*Rue de Grétry*). 1807-10.
Richard. *Manchester.* 1808-13. C.
& HOADLEY. *Greystone.* 1810-13. Successors to TFRRY, THOMAS & HOADLEY. After 1813 the business was carried on by HOADLEY alone till 1849. l.c. clock ill. Milham.
——. *Paris* (*Rue des Vieux Augustins*). 1812. C.
——. *Paris* (*Pavé des Italiens*). 1812.
J. *N. Shields.* 1815. Watch N.Y. Univ.
W. *London.* 1817-24.
——. *Paris* (*Rue J.-J. Rousseau*). 1817-24.
& HUNSLEY. *Doncaster.* 1818.
James. *Doncaster.* 1822.
THOMASEN, Ts. *Amsterdam.* ca.1760. l.c. clock ill. Britten.
THOMASON—
John. *London.* Mid. 18c.
John. *Sutton* (*Lancs.*). 1786. W.
THOMBET, Jean Pierre. *Geneva.* 1668.
THOMÉ—
——. *Versailles.* 2nd half 18c. en. watch.
——. *Paris.* 1814.
THOMEGAY, Marc. *London.* ca.1725-ca. 1770. Watches Feill and Den. colls.
THOMEGUEX—
Jean. *France* or *Geneva.* ca.1675. Small g. en. watch.
Claude. *Geneva.* b.1685, d.1730. Watch Geneva M.
Jaques. *Geneva.* ca.1755-70.
THOMEYER, ——. *Cassel.* 1775. Court C.
THOMINGS, D. *Halesowen.* 1777. C.
THOMIRE, DUTERME ET CIE. *Paris.* ca. 1790-1820. Celebrated bronze workers of the first Empire. Made many clock cases.
THOMLINSON, Richard. *London.* a.1669.
THOMPSON—
John. *York.* 1633. d.1692. Fine sil. watch, filigree outer case, champlevé sil. dial.
John. *London.* a.1655, CC.1662.
Robert. *London.* a.1666, CC.1681-4.
Rowland. *London.* a.1674.
George. *London.* a.1676. TOMPSON.
Isaac. *London.* 1689 CC.
Isaac, son. *London.* a.1689, CC.1699.
John, son of John of York. *York.* Chamberlain of York, 1698.
William. *London.* a.1698, CC.1708.
Ambrose. *London.* a.1708.
William. *London.* a.1708-32.
John. *London.* a.1713, CC.1720.
John. *London.* a.1717.
Troughton. *London.* a.1717, CC.1732.
James. *Liverpool.* 1734.
John. *Liverpool.* 1734-73. W.
Charles. *London.* a.1729-ca.1760. Watch.
William. *Chester.* 1743-ca.1767. Watch G.M.
Henry. *London* (*St. Martin's-le-Grand*). CC. 1748-59.

THOMPSON—*continued.*
Thomas. *Lancaster* and *Liverpool.* 1748-66. Watch M.M.A. prob. by him.
Francis. *London* (*St. Martin's-le-Grand*). 1748-59. W.
John. *Uxbridge.* 1750-6. W.
Thomas. *London.* a.1752.
William. *Annapolis, U.S.A.* 1762. C. & W.
Thomas. *Shrewsbury.* an.1768. Watch.
James. *London* (*Walworth*). an.1771. Watch.
John. *London* (*Clerkenwell*). 1770-94.
Jeremiah. *London.* CC.1770-83.
William. *London.* a.1775.
W. *Newcastle-o.-T.* 1782-4.
William. *London.* a.1780.
William. *New York.* 1775. C. & W. 'Lately arrived from Britain.' cf. Wm. *Baltimore* below.
——. *Chester.* ca.1780. l.c. clock. cf. Wm. above.
William. *Wolverhampton.* 1780-1805. C. & W.
James. *Darlington.* 1786, d.1825. W.
Samuel. *London* (*Aldgate*). CC.1789.
Ann, & Son. *London.* 1790.
J. *London* (*Laurence Lane*). ca.1790.
Joseph. *London* (*Fleet St.*). 1790. br. clock Weth. coll.
William. *London* (*Clerkenwell*). 1790-1811. C.
Charles. *London.* a.1788.
Benjamin. *London.* 1799-1804.
William. *Baltimore, U.S.A.* 1799-1807. W. & C. cf. Wm. *New York* above.
John Little. *London.* a.1795, CC.1812.
John. *London* (*Lewisham*). 1805-08.
John. *London* (*Walworth*). 1805-08.
Thomas. *London.* a.1800.
Philip. *Woodbridge.* 1815. Watch.
John. *Hexham.* mar.1817. W.
R. *London.* Early 19c. Watch Ilbert coll.
C. *Bath.* Early 19c. Watch.
Rowland. *Wigton.* Early 19c. Watch.
James. *London.* Early 19c. Watch.
John P. *Philadelphia.* 1819-24.
Joseph. *Whitehaven.* 1820.
Edward. *Liverpool.* 1825.
THOMSEN, Christian. *Copenhagen.* m.1740.
THOMSON—
James. *Edinburgh.* a.1696.
John. *Perth.* 1706-37.
William. *London* (*Bishopsgate St.*). 1725-55. g. watch.
George. *London.* a.1722.
David. *Perth.* a.1733-44.
George. *Edinburgh.* a.1734.
Philip. *London.* an.1743. Watch.
Alexander. *Edinburgh.* a.1736.
Robert. *Bo'ness.* 1760-88.
James. *Bristol.* an.1765. Watch.
Robert. *Edinburgh.* 1764. W.
Peter Neilus. *Edinburgh.* a.1756.
John. *Leith.* 1768.
Philip, & Son. *London.* 1770-81.
William. *Edinburgh.* a.1766, d.1784.
William. *Perth.* 1772.
John. *London.* an.1781. br. clock.
Olive. *Penrith.* 1781. Insolvent.
Robert. *Glasgow.* 1788-1801.
John. *Leslie.* 1789.
John. *Edinburgh.* 1794-1814.
Archibald. *Edinburgh.* 1794-1836. Watch.
Alexander. *Keith.* 1807.
John. *Edinburgh.* a.1811.
George. *Kilmarnock.* 1820-37.
James. *Leslie.* 1825.
Adam. *London.* 1830-50. Pub. 'Time and Timekeepers,' London, 1842. br. clock.
THONISSEN, ——. *Paris.* 1812. C.
THORALD, ——. *Ipswich.* an.1683. Watch.

THORELET—
David. *London,* 1626. *Rouen,* 1630-1661. Called himself 'Premier orloger reçu par chef d'oeuvre à Rouen.' Pub. description of the clock of the Hôtel des Consuls made by him in 1657.
Jacques. *Rouen.* m.1646.
Jean, son. *Rouen.* m.1694. oct. watch, émail en resille sur verre.
Jonas. *Rouen.* 1695 m. Watch M.M.A. l.c. clock.
THORKEIN, William. *Edinburgh.* 1695.
THORN—
Hans Lucas. ——. 1680. sq. table clock Nat. M. Munich.
Michael. *S. Molton.* 1795. W. l.c. clock.
James. *Colchester.* an.1769-late 18c. Wall clock. Watch.
John. *Weymouth.* 1795. C. & W.
Richard. *London,* a.1816.
THORNBURGH—
George. *London.* an.1724. Watch Stads M. Amsterdam.
John. *London.* 1743. Watch Ilbert coll. hm. 1740.
THORNBURY, Jane. *London.* a.1730.
THORNDELL, Richard. *Bampton.* 1768. C.
THORNDIKE—
Samuel. *Ipswich.* Mid. 18c.-ca.1800. Watch.
Samuel, jun. *Ipswich.* mar.1781. Watch.
THORNE—
Simon. *Tiverton.* To 1720. Insolvent. C.
Samuel. *London.* a.1722. Watch.
Abraham, son of Simon. *Tiverton.* 1750-9.
——. *Weymouth.* Mid. 18c. Watch.
William. *London.* an.1753. Watch.
Thomas, prob. *London.* an.1756. Watch.
Robert. *London.* 1754-70. p.c. rep. watch M.M.A. Watch Den. coll.
Richard. *London (Hoxton).* 1775-94. W.
Richard, son. *London.* a.1789.
John, & Son. *London.* 1820.
James. *London.* 1820.
THORNHAM, George. *Hull.* 1806-34.
THORNHILL—
Bryan. *London.* a.1683.
John. *London.* a.1714.
D. *London.* an.1766. Watch.
James. *London.* an.1778. Watch.
T. D. *London.* an.1808. Watch.
THORNLEY, ——. *London (Borough).* d. 1771. W.
THORNTON—
Henry. *London (Basing La.* in 1723, *R. Exchange* in 1730). a.1692, CC.1699-1732. A maker of repute. l.c. clock. Two g. repoussé watches Winter Pal. Petrograd. str. en. watch.
John, son. *London (Lambeth).* a.1716, CC. 1731-60. Watch.
William. *York.* a.1741. C.
James. *London.* 1771. Watch B.M. Very fine g. en. and repoussé p.c. watch.
William. *London.* an.1778. Watch.
William. *London.* a.1783, CC.1792.
Samuel. *London.* l.CC.1812.
Joseph. *Philadelphia.* 1819.
THOROGOOD (THOROWGOOD)—
John. *London.* a.1652, CC.1660.
William. *London.* a.1652, CC.1660-87.
James. *London.* a.1660.
Edward. *London.* CC.1668. math. inst. maker.
Luke. *London.* a.1761, CC.1768-1810. l.c. clock.
Richard. *London.* 1783-90.
Joseph. *London.* 1792. Watch N.Y. Univ.
Frederick, son of Luke. *London (Wood St., Cheapside).* CC.1810, l.CC.1813-23.
William, bro. *London.* CC.1820.

THORP—
Edward. *London (Cornhill).* CC.1780-90.
Thomas. *Colchester.* an.1785-95. Watch. C.
Thomas. *London.* an.1786. Watch.
E. *London (Stockwell).* ca.1790.
Edward. *Colchester.* 1795. W.
Samuel. *Abberly.* Early 19c.
——. *Bath.* Early 19c.
Richard. *Hull.* 1814.
Richard. *Market Weighton.* 1822-41.
THORPE—
John. *London.* a.1641, CC.1657-79.
William. *London.* 1817-19. Wooden C.
Thomas. *London (Clerkenwell).* a.1811, CC. 1820.
THOURON, J. *Geneva.* b.1749, d.1789. Famous painter on enamel.
THOUVEROT (THOUVEREZ), Louis. *Paris.* m.1788-1825. Equation and cal. clock. *v.* TOUVEREZ.
THRELKELD—
William. *London (Strand).* an.1701-27. Clock Soane M. Watch N.Y. Univ.
R. ——. an.1722. Watch mt. G.M.
William. *London (Minories).* 1743.
THRESHER, Henry. *London.* a.1821.
THRIP, Benjamin. *London.* a.1698.
THRISTLE, ——. *Williton.* ca.1730. Clock.
THRISTRAM, William. *Salford.* 1813. W.
THROUGHTON, Joseph. *London.* 1799. W.
THUILET, ——. *London.* ca.1740. Fine rep. p.c. watch, with panels of amethyst and olivine, F.W.M.
THUILIER, ——. *Paris.* ca.1750. Repaired clock on la Samaritaine.
THUILLIER—
Nicolas Pierre. *Paris.* ca.1760. Boulle-work br. clock St. James's Pal.
——. *Geneva.* ca.1780. Watch B.M.
Veuve. *Paris.* 1789.
v. TERROT.
THUNMARK (TUNMARCK), Carl Olof. *Stockholm.* 1805-10.
THURBIN, Langford. *London.* a.1719.
THURET (TURET)—
Isaac. *Paris.* 1669. d.1700. C. to Louis XIV and to the Observatory. Claimed invention of spiral balance spring, but denied it in letter to Huygens in 1675, saying that the invention claimed was the use of a flat spring for pendulum support. Made watches with balance spring for Huygens, and a clock for Leiden Observatory to Huygens' order. Watch Louvre. Fine clock with Caffiéri bronzes C.A. & M. Watch M.P.S. Dresden.
Jacques, son. *Paris.* 1694-1712. In 1694 was granted his father's appointments. Boulle-work clock S.K.M. Wall clock Wallace coll. Very fine l.c. clock with turning globe C.A. & M. Watch Gélis coll.
——. *Paris.* 1819-25.
THURIGNY, Michel. *Lyons.* 1690-9.
THURNER, Johannes. *Prague.* 1659. Compass and dial Old Ashmolean M.
THUYER, ——. *Lisieux.* ca.1700. Watch Ilbert coll.
THWAITES—
Ainsworth. *London (Rosoman Row).* a.1735, CC.1751-80. Made the Horse Guards clock. Very fine pair l.c. clocks in India Office ill. Cec. & Web. br. clock.
James. *London (Ratcliff Highway).* an.1766. Watch.
Benjamin, son of Ainsworth. *London.* a.1762, CC.1770.
Thomas. *Mitcham.* an.1778-81. Insolvent.
John, bro. of Ben. *London.* a.1772, CC.1782, m.CC.1815-20. Made clock of St. Paul's Chapel, New York. br. clock ill. Cec. & Web.
James. *London.* ca.1780. mus. br. clock.

THWAITES—*continued.*
Joseph. *London.* a.1783.
A. & J. *London.* 1795.
& Reed. *London.* 1808-40.
J. & W. *London.* 1815.
THWING, James. *London.* a.1679, CC.1707-1712. Watch.
TIBBOT, John. *Newtown, Wales.* b.1757, d. 1820. Worked from 1777-97. Sent a clock to Soc. Arts giving impulse to pendulum once a minute, with cycloidal cheeks. Several clocks.
TICHBOURNE, John. *London.* a.1750, CC. 1771.
TICKLE (TICKELL)—
John. *Crediton.* ca.1730. l.c. clock.
William, senior. *Newcastle-o.-T.* 1763. d. 1801. l.c. clocks. Watch.
William, junior. *Newcastle-o.-T.* 1790-5.
Mary. *Newcastle-o.-T.* 1805-11. W.
TIDBLAD, Olof. *Stockholm.* 1795. l.c. and wall clocks.
TIDDEMAN—
& Co. *Canterbury.* To 1789. C. & W.
Edward. *Canterbury.* From 1789-1801. W. From the preceding firm.
TIDSTRAND, ——. *Falun.* 1780.
TIEDE, Christian Friedrich. *Berlin.* b.1794, d.1877. A fine maker of chron. and observatory clocks. Royal astro. and Court C. in 1838.
TIERBUCK, William. *London.* a.1727.
TIFFIN, John. *London.* a.1713.
TIGHT—
Samuel. *London* (*Whitecross St.*). d.1788. W. Also Tite.
George. *London.* a.1767.
William. *London.* a.1780.
Thomas. *Daventry.* 1791-5. Also Tite.
George, son of Geo. *London* (*Islington*). a. 1798, CC.1791-1811.
George. *Reading.* Early 19c.
George. *Deptford.* 1822-4. Watch.
TIHLE, Georg. *Hamburg.* 17c. Monstrance clock.
TILBURY, Robert. *London.* a.1767.
TILBY, John. *London.* ca.1780. br. clock.
TILLBROOKE, John. *Bury.* 1785. Watch Den. coll.
TILLEY—
William. *London.* 1770-7.
John Austin. *Bristol.* 1825-30. W.
TILLIER, John. *London.* an.1761-99. Watch.
TILLINGHART, Stephen. *Liverpool.* 1763-1777. W.
TILLY—
Joseph. *London.* a.1696, CC.1703-40. l.c. clock.
Nathaniel. *London.* a.1710. Watch by him or following.
Nathaniel. *London.* a.1714.
Simon François. *Paris.* m.1767.
TILS, Richard. *London.* Late 17c. Watch Webster coll.
TIMBRELL, Thomas. *London.* a.1709.
TIMEWELL, John. prob. *London.* 1773.
TIMMIS, William. *Alfreton.* 1791-5. W.
TIMMONS, James. *Liverpool.* 1816-21. W.
TINDALL, Samuel. *Leeds* 1817. *Keighley* 1830-40.
TINDELL, Joseph. *London.* a.1715.
TINELLY, C. *Aix* ca.1630. g. repoussé cross watch B.M. ill. Baillie.
TINGES, Charles. *Baltimore, U.S.A.* 1799-1807. W.
TINGLEY—
Thomas. *London.* a.1682.
Thomas. *London.* a.1686.
TINK, William. *London.* a.1772.
TINKER, Samuel. *Leeds.* 1817-26. Watch.
TINKLER, Strachan. *Gateshead* 1811. *Newcastle-o.-T.* 1820. l.c. clocks.
TINSWOD, ——. *Preston.* Mid. 18c. l.c. clock.
TINTRELIN, Jean Baptiste. *Paris.* m.1747-1789.
TION—
——. *Paris.* ca.1745 m.
Nicolas, jun. *Paris.* m.1755.
TIPHESNE (TIFENE), Jean. *Paris.* m.1743.
TIPLING, William. *Leeds.* ca.1720.
TIPPETTS, Timothy. *London.* a.1754.
TIPPING, George. *London.* a.1664, CC. 1674-80.
TIPTON—
Thomas. prob. *London.* an.1762. Watch.
Benjamin. *Ludlow.* 1776. l.c. clock.
TIPTOP, Edward. *London.* an.1771. Watch.
TIRRY, John. *York.* ca.1680. l.c. clock. cf. Terry.
TISOT, Alexander. *New York.* 1805. W.
TISSIB, James. *London.* 18c. Clock mt. G.M.
TISSON, E. L. *Paris.* 1822-5.
TISSOT—
David. *Chaux-de-Fonds.* 1701. C.
Abram Louis. *La Sagne.* 1783. C.
Jean Daniel. *Copenhagen.* m.1791.
Eugène. *Renan.* ca.1810. Exported cheap watches in large numbers to America.
Jacob Robert. *Fontainemelon.* Re-organized factory in 1821. *v.* Perrenoud.
Aîné. *Paris.* 1822-5.
TISSOT-DAGUETTE, Abram. *Neuchâtel* district. 1727-54.
TITCHENER—
Benjamin. *London.* a.1747, CC.1763, d.an. 1771.
James. *London.* 1799. W.
William. *London.* 1808. W.
TITFORD, John. *London.* CC.1723.
TITT & GORTER. *London.* 1817-24.
TITTER, Thomas. *London.* a.1699.
TITTERTON, Thomas. *London.* 1814.
TOBIAS—
Joseph. *Oberhausen.* 1756 comp.
Morris. *London* (*Wapping*). 1794-1840. chron. G.M. Patented a clock to show time by ship's bells, example Ilbert coll.
Morris, & Co. *London* (*Wapping*). 1802-08.
Michael Isaac. *Liverpool.* 1805-29.
Michael Isaac, & Co. *Liverpool.* 1810-29. Watch mt. London M. Rack lever watch with secs. hand turning 4 times a min. Chamb. coll.
Samuel Isaac. *Liverpool.* 1811-13.
Esau. *Llandilo.* 1818-35.
Morris, & Levitt. *London* (*Wapping* and *Minories*). 1817-24. g. rep. watch.
TOCQUEVILLE, Jean. *Rouen.* m.1658.
TODD—
John. *York.* 1665. C.
Samuel. *York.* 1686. W.
Robert. *London.* a.1684.
John. *London.* a.1696, CC.1707-56. Watch.
Benjamin. *London.* a.1709, CC.1747.
John. *Bradford.* 1757. W.
R. *Scarborough.* 1765.
Michael. *Hull.* an.1781. Watch.
Jonathan. *London.* a.1777.
James. *Bradford.* 1784. d.1788. Clock. W.
Joseph. *Hull.* 1806-41.
John. *Hull.* 1814.
John. *Dumfries.* Early 19c. Watch.
John. *Glasgow.* 1823-37.
TOLBY, Charles. *London.* CC.1720.
TOLDERVY, William. *London.* a.1807.
TOLEMAN, William. *Carnarvon.* 1795-ca. 1840. Watch Nat. M. Cardiff.
TOLKIEN—
T. B. *London.* 1802-04.
Benjamin. *London.* 1805-08.

TOLKIEN—*continued.*
George. *London.* 1809-11. mt. maker.
& GRAVELL. *London.* Early 19c. mus. br. clock. cyl. watch mt. Ilbert coll.
TOLLÉ, ——. *Paris.* 1600. Sig. to Statuts of Paris corporation.
TOLLER—
Thomas. *London.* a.1734, CC.1741.
Bostock. *London.* a.1742, CC.1766. Watch mt.
TOLLEY—
Charles. *London.* a.1676, CC.1683-1719, d. an.1730. l.c. clock.
Charles, son. *London.* CC.1720-6.
TOLLODAY, Thomas. *London.* a.1788.
TOLLOT, Pierre. *France.* b.1671, d.1742. Watches Schloss M. Berlin and Geneva M.
TOLLY, ——. *Paris.* an.1766. Very large watch.
TOLMAN, J., & SON. *Colyton* and *Seaton.* 18c. l.c. clock.
TOLSON (TOLESON, TOLLISON)—
Ralph. *London* (*Phillip La.*). a.1693, CC. 1701-16. Watch Den. coll.
John. *London* (*Bishopsgate*). a.1708, CC. 1715. W.
TOMBES (TOMBS)—
John. *London.* 1761. BC.
Savery. *London* (*Kentish Town*). 1765.
Thomas. prob. *London.* an.1769. Watch.
Edmund. prob. *London.* an.1776. Watch.
John Savery, son of Savery. *London.* a.1780.
TOMBET, ——. *Genoa.* ca.1680. en. watch Ilbert coll.
TOMES, James. *London.* a.1678.
TOMEY, Joshua. *Dublin.* 1774-80. W.
TOMKINS (TOMPKINS)—
William. *London* (*Winchester St.*). a.1750. CC.1762-75. Watch.
John. *London.* a.1758.
T. prob. *London.* an.1771. Watch.
William. *London.* a.1789, CC.1819.
TOMLIN (TOMLYN)—
T. *London.* an.1752. Watch.
Edward. *London* (*Bartholomew La.* and *R. Exchange*). CC.1768-98. br. clock ill. Cec. & Web. Pair mus. clocks Peiping M. en. cyl. watch S.M.S.K.
Robert. *London.* ca.1790-early 19c. W. to the King. Watch Ilbert coll.
TOMLINS—
Nicholas. *London.* a.1639, CC.1646, d.an. 1658. Also TOMLYNS.
William. *London.* 1650 CC.
TOMLINSON—
Thomas. *London.* a.1646-64 CC.
George or Richard. *London.* a.1669, CC. 1673-80.
William. *London* (*Birchin La.* to 1719, then *White Hart Ct.*). CC.1699, m.CC.1733-41. br. clock Weth. coll. l.c. clock M.M.A. Watch S.K.M. Watch mt. G.M. Fine rep. watch Chamb. coll. g. p.c. watch hm. 1702 Ilbert coll.
John. *London* (*Thames St.*). 1744-55. W.
——. *Bicester.* 1790.
TOMO—
Thomas. *London* (*Shoreditch*). 1799-1808.
Thomas E. *London* (*Minories*). 1820-4.
TOMPION—
Thomas. *London.* b.1639, CC.1671, m.CC. 1704, d.1713. One of the greatest clock and watchmakers; to his work is due the supremacy of English horology in the 18c.; he made some of the first watches with balance-springs. He took Edward BANGER into partnership about 1701, then, apparently, worked alone, and took Geo. GRAHAM into partnership about 1711. On his death, in 1713, Graham continued alone. The watches were numbered in three series, for plain, repeating and special watches, the numbering being continued from Tompion to Graham. Approximate dates and numbers are: with sig. Thos. Tompion to 1701 (No. 3292 plain, No. 203 rep.); Tho. Tompion Edwd. Banger from 1701-8 (No. 3252-4119 plain, No. 196-290 rep.); Thos. Tompion 1709-13 (No. 4265-4312 plain, No. 359-392 rep.); T. Tompion & G. Graham 1711-13 (No. 4369-4543 plain); Geo. Graham from 1713 (No. 4669 plain, 393 rep.). Examples of his watches and clocks in most collections. Several one-year clocks (two in Buckingham Pal.), including a spring clock striking hours and quarters ill. Britten. Many watches, l.c. and br. clocks ill. Cec. & Web. and Britten. Thirteen l.c., nine br. and lantern clocks Weth. coll. g. en. watch and small lantern clock B.M. l.c. four-month and lantern clocks and watches G.M. and London M. Watch and clock Cassel Landes-M. Six watches M.M.A. g. eng. watch Mallett coll. ill. Baillie. Early watch Chamb. coll. en. watch Carnegie M. Very early rep. watch No. 63, ca.1690, Ilbert coll.
Thomas, junior, nephew. *London.* a.1694, CC.1702. Imprisoned for theft in 1720. Heir to his uncle and prob. retired in 1713.
& E. BANGER. *London.* ca.1701-8. Banger was nephew, apprentice and assistant of Tompion, senior. *v.* Thomas (1). l.c. clock Weth. coll. Fine g. watch B.M. str. and rep. watch mt. G.M. p.c. watch S.M.S.K. g. rep. watch Den. coll. br. clock ill. Cec. & Web.
& GRAHAM. *London.* ca.1711-13. Nephew and, from 1696, pupil of TOMPION, senior, and succeeded him in his business. Watches Ilbert and Webster colls. and mt. G.M. l.c. clock Virginia M. sd. 'Thomas Tompion and George Graham.' *v.* Thomas (1).
G. *London.* ca.1715. rep. watch.
Charles. prob. *London.* an.1764. Watch.
Richard. *Liverpool.* Late 18c. Watch.
TOMPTON, William. *Wolverhampton.* 1779. l.c. clock.
TOMSON—
S. *London.* ca.1760. Watches M.M.A. and Stern. coll.
Thomas. *London.* an.1776. rep. watch Den. coll.
J. *London.* 1821. Watch Ilbert coll.
TON—
J. *London.* 1st half 18c. Lantern clock.
& MAXFIELD. prob. *London.* an.1754. Watch
TONCKHURE, Francis. *Baltimore, U.S.A.* Early 19c. W. & C.
TONKIN, Nicholas. *London.* a.1739.
TONYCLIFFE, Robert. *London.* a.1703.
TOOKE, William. *Kings Lynn.* Late 18c. Watch.
TOOKEY, Charles. *London.* a.1735.
TOOKIE, Daniel. *London.* a.1695.
TOONE—
Thomas. *London.* a.1751.
John. *London.* a.1756.
TOOTELL, William. *Chorley.* 1790-1824.
TOPFFLER, ——. *Augsburg* an.1682. Projected a clock dial optically.
TOPHAM—
Christopher. *London.* a.1728.
R. *London.* an.1777. Watch.
Thomas. *London.* an.1777. Watch.
J. *London.* 1790-9.
Edward. *Castlebar.* 1790-1824.
TOPP, ——. *Hull.* ca.1800.
TOPPING—
John. *London.* a.1691, d.1747. l.c. month clock. Desc. himself as 'Memory Master.'
Richard. *Antigua.* an.1770. Watch.

TORADO—
Francis. *London.* CC.1633, d.1683. Oval watch G.M.
Francis, son. *London.* 1662.
TORBECK, Johan. *Copenhagen.* 1702-05. From *Lübeck.* Kleinuhrmacher. Watch mt.
TORBORCH, Gottfried. *Munich.* ca.1710. Oval sil. watch. g. and tortoiseshell watch Feill coll.
TORENSTRAND, Magnus Lorentz. *Mariestad* and *Varberg.* 1820-30.
TORIN—
Daniel. *London* (*Moorfields*). a.1721-63. l.c. clock S.K.M. Watch Miller coll. mts. sd. 'Torin, London,' Ilbert and Fränkel colls. aut. watch for Turkey Carnegie M.
Berchere Abraham, son. *London.* a.1744.
v. FONTAINE & TORIN.
TORKIN, Thomas. *Pentonville.* 1791. C. & W.
TORKINGTON—
——. *Newcastle-under-Lyme.* 1769. C. & W.
Jeffrey. *Whitchurch* (*Salop*). 1795. C.
TORKLER, Peter. *London.* 1782-90.
TORN, Abraham. *Sheffield.* an.1749. Watch.
TORPORLEY, Nathaniell. *England.* 1593. Dial Old Ashmolean M.
TORRIANO, Giovanni. *Cremona, Toledo* and *San Yuste.* 1529. d.1585. One of the greatest early clockmakers. Brought by Charles v in 1529 to repair Giovanni de Dondi's planetarium clock of 1364; he largely re-made it; Torriano and the clock were taken to Spain by Charles v, who retained him in his service in the Cloister of San Yuste in 1556. Torriano's works are known only from descriptions. Bust in Toledo M. Account of his life in von Bassermann-Jordan's 'Alte Uhren und ihre Meister.' Called by Cardan, Jannellus Turrianus, and by Sacco, Giovanni Janellus or Gianello.
TORSELL, Anders. *Husby.* End 18c. l.c. clock.
TORSLUND, Lars. *Stockholm.* b.1720, d. 1764. l.c. and br. clocks.
TORTEL—
François. *Paris.* m.1786-9.
——. *Paris.* 1815.
TORY—
Sarah. *London.* a.1660.
William. *Market Deeping.* 1795. C.
TOSCHI, Marchionne. *Brescello.* 1421-37. Made clock for Torre pubblico of Parma, and for the Certosa of Pavia.
TOSEMBACH, ——. *Paris.* 1769. str. and rep. watch with combined trains, approved by Acad. des Sci.
TOSHACH—
——. *London.* an.1775. Watch.
Patrick. *Perth.* 1778-85. mus. clocks.
TOTEN, Joseph. *London.* a.1760.
TOTHAKER, William. *London.* a.1696, CC. 1703.
TOULEMONDE—
François. *Paris.* m.1788.
——. *Paris.* 1807-25.
TOULMIN, Samuel. *London* (*Strand*). an. 1757-83. p.c. g. en. watch. c.secs. cyl. pirouette watch mt. G.M. al. rep. watch S.M.S.K. Watch for China Gélis coll. br. clock Virginia M.
TOURBIER, ——. *Paris.* 1825.
TOURET, ——. *Paris.* Early 18c. Copper en. watch.
TOURLE, William. *London.* a.1748, CC. 1776-1805.
TOURNARRE, Claude. *Neuchâtel.* 1517-50. T.C.
TOURNEL, ——. *Rouen.* 1731.
TOUSSAINT—
Marie. *Paris.* 1767. Officer of the Paris corporation.
——. *Paris.* 1825. C.
TOUTIN—
Jean. *Châteaudun, Blois* and *Paris.* b.1578, d.1644. Went to *Paris* ca.1632. Discovered the technique of painting on enamel. No work known.
Henry, son. b. *Châteaudun,* 1614. Went to *Paris,* 1636. d. after 1683. Painter on enamel. Example on watch dated 1641 Rijks M. Amsterdam.
Jean, bro. b. *Châteaudun,* 1619. *Sweden,* 1645. d. after 1660. Painter on enamel to Queen Christina. Fine paintings on watches B.M. and Louvre ill. Baillie.
TOUVEREZ, ——. *Paris.* Late 18c. Mantel clock Pal. de Fontainebleau. Prob. THOUVEREZ.
TOVEY, William. *London.* a.1655.
TOWAN, James. *Edinburgh.* Late 18c. g. en. watch.
TOWELL, Nicholas. *London.* a.1669.
TOWERS—
John. *Farnworth.* d.1747. C.
William. *London.* an.1763. Watch.
W. *Wincanton.* Late 18c. l.c. clock.
TOWLE, Edward. *London.* a.1753, CC.1760.
TOWLER, William. *London.* an.1782. Watch.
TOWN, Jeffrey. *London.* a.1762.
TOWNELL, T. prob. *London.* an.1767. Watch.
TOWNESON—
Samuel. *London.* a.1695, CC.1702-38.
William. *London.* a.1708, CC.1716-60.
TOWNLEY—
Henry. *London.* 1710. W.
Thomas, & Son. *Liverpool.* 1824-9. W.
Edward. *Dundalk.* 1820-4.
John. *Liverpool.* 1825. W.
TOWNSEND—
Joseph. *Helmdon.* ca.1700. l.c. clock with very narrow trunk.
Gray. *London.* a.1728.
George. *London* (*Haymarket*). 1750.
John. *London.* an.1769. Watch.
John. *Newport, R.I., U.S.A.* 1769. On case of l.c. clock M.M.A.
Robert. *Greenock.* 1770-90. l.c. clock.
R. *London.* an.1780. Watch.
William. *Greenock.* an.1786-91. Watch.
David. *Boston, U.S.A.* 1789-1806. W.
Isaac. *Boston, U.S.A.* 1789-1806. W.
W. *London* (*Fleet St.*). an.1794. Watch.
Thomas. *Bath.* Late 18c. Watch Horstmann coll.
Charles. *Philadelphia.* 1800-25.
John. *Philadelphia.* 1813-25.
TOWSON—
John. *Plymouth Dock.* 1795.
J. T. *Devonport.* 1825. Award from Soc. Arts for a chronometer banking.
TOY, John James. *London.* a.1811.
TOYE, John. *London.* a.1797.
TOZER, Abraham. *Exeter.* ca.1770. Watch.
TRACY—
Richard. *London.* a.1660.
Steven. *Rotterdam.* 1683. Planetarium in Leiden M. Watch B.M. en. Huaud ill. Baillie.
Stephen. *London.* ca.1700-ca.1720. Watch Den. coll. Watch mt. Buckley coll.
TRAFFORD, Thomas. *London.* ca.1665. Lantern clock ill. Cec. & Web. Bird-cage clock.
TRAIL, William. *London.* 1802-24.
TRAMIERI, J. *Turin.* ca.1600. oct. crys. watch M.M.A.
TRANCHANT, G. *Châlon-sur-Saône.* Early 18c. Watch Besançon M.

TRANCHEPAIN, Jacques Sulpice. *Paris.* m. 1780-9.
TRAND, William. prob. *London.* an.1780. Watch.
TRÅNG, Daniel. *Stjärnsund.* ca.1750.
TRANSPET—
Joseph Michael. *Augsburg.* 1763.
Joseph Xaver. *Augsburg.* 1780.
TRANTER—
G. G. *London.* ca.1770. Watch.
——. *Shrewsbury.* 1771. W.
TRAP (TRAPP)—
Richard. *London.* an.1760. Watch.
Edward. *Bristol.* 1765. d.1784. Watch.
& STAFFORD. *Bristol.* 1775.
TRASER, ——. *Worcester.* an.1714. Watch.
TRASILLION, Ant. *Hampton Court.* 1528-1534. C. Paid wages from the Privy Purse.
TRATTLE, Joseph. *London.* a.1733.
TRAUNER, Johann. *Würzburg.* m.1749, d. 1772. A good maker. Partner with his father-in-law, Johann HENNER, 1753-6. p.c. repoussé watch Würzburg M.
TRAVERS—
John. *London.* Mid. 18c. Watch.
Adam. *Liverpool,* 1769-77. *London,* 1781-1799. W.
William. *London.* 1781-1811. p.c. rep. c. secs. watch, en. and set pearls, M.M.A.
TRAVIEZ, F. *Berlin.* Early 19c. virgule watch mt. Ilbert coll.
TRAVIS—
T. *Newcastle-o.-T.* 1710.
Thomas. *Sheffield.* ca.1710-29. Watch.
Joshua. *Manchester.* 1748. Bankrupt. W.
James. *Rotherham.* ca.1770-95.
George. *Thorne.* ca.1770-1822. W.
William. *Oldham.* an.1783. Watch.
George. *Rotherham.* 1770-95. W.
J. *Thorne.* 1780.
Thomas. *Thorne.* 1795.
Edward. *Manchester.* 1788. C. & W.
TRAYS, ——. *Dartmouth.* 1791-5. W.
TREACHER, Thomas. *London.* a.1795.
TREBOR, James. *London.* an.1744. Watch. ROBERT reversed.
TREBUH, John. prob. *London.* an.1753. Watch. HUBERT reversed.
TRECHSLER—
Christoph. *Dresden.* mar.1571, d.ca.1624. math. inst. maker.
Christoph, son. *Dresden.* ca.1600. math. inst. maker.
TREFFLER, Sebastian. *Prague.* Mid. 18c. Two watches Nat. M. Prague. sil. chased trav. clock K.H.M.
TREFLER—
Johann Phil. *Augsburg.* 17c. C. to Grand Duke Ferdinando II, 1653-8. Clock by him alleged to have been made with pendulum an.1657. Clock Cassel Landes-M.
Christoph. *Augsburg.* Late 17c.
Caspar. ——. 1st half 18c. p.c. sil. watch.
TREGAYLE, Nathaniel. *London.* a.1724.
TREGENT—
James. *Newcastle-o.-T.* 1st half 18c. Watch.
James. *London.* 1759. CC.1781-1808. A famous maker. W. to the Prince of Wales. br. clock Weth. coll. ill. Britten. br. clock S.K.M. Watch and chatelaine B.M. Watch G.M. cyl. mt. and cyl. rep. watch G.M. cyl. c.secs., cyl. rep. and duplex watches S.M.S.K. g. rep. watch Den. coll.
TREGIDGEON, William. *London.* 1757-68. Watch.
TREGOE, Timothy. *Marlow.* 1795. W.
TREIBLER—
Johann. *Friedberg.* 17c. aut. clock.
Johann Christian. *Germany.* End 17c. Prob. same as above. Watch Feill coll.
TREMBLAY—
Johannes de. *Vincennes.* 1390. 'Horelogiator.'
Pierre. *Blois.* m.1676-94.
TREMBLEAU, ——. *Paris.* 1812-25.
TREMBLEY—
Jean Louis. *Geneva.* b.1681, d.1756. Watch M. des Arts déc. Geneva.
David. *Geneva.* ca.1750. p.c. g. en. rep. watch M. des Arts déc. Geneva. Watch sd. 'Trembley London' perhaps by him.
TREMLETT, Rev. John. *Hopton.* CC.1805.
TRENCHANT—
Guillaume. *Lyons.* 1603 m. cf. TRANCHANT.
Pierre. *Lyons.* 1673-6 m. From *Châlon-sur-Saône,* and returned there in 1676.
TRENDELL, James. *Reading.* 1819. C. & W.
TRENGROUSE, Lewis. *London.* a.1728.
TRENHOLME, William. *London.* a.1721, CC.1728-35.
TRENT, William. *London.* an.1767. Watch.
TRENTHAM, Thomas. *Shrewsbury.* an.1779. Watch.
TREU—
Isaac. *Basle.* 1620-50.
Jakob. *Basle.* 1650. d.1690.
Rudolf. *Basle.* 1690.
TREVAN, ——. *Marseilles.* 2nd half 18c. Watch.
TREVEEN, Jarrett. *London.* CC.1688. W. Also TERVEEN and TURVEEN.
TREVENA, William, jun. *Redruth.* 1775. Bankrupt. C. & W.
TREVERTON, James. *Plymouth.* 2nd half 18c. l.c. clock.
TREVIS, ——. *Worcester.* 1755.
TREVOR—
Thomas. *London.* a.1654.
Thomas. *London.* a.1696.
Richard. *Topsham.* mar.1790. W.
TREWERY, John. *Redruth.* Early 19c.
TREWINNARD—
Joshua. *London (Bermondsey).* 1790-5.
Joshua & James. *London (Bermondsey).* 1805-40.
Joshua. *London (Strand).* 1805-10.
Edward. *London.* 1820-5.
TRIBE, George. *Thackenham.* an.1746. Watch.
TRIBER, John. prob. *London.* an.1770. Watch.
TRIBOLET—
Maurice. *Neuchâtel.* b.1663, d.1704.
Jean Ferdinand. *Neuchâtel.* d.1722.
TRIBOULET, S. *Geneva.* Late 18c. Watch with escapement visible at back Carnegie M.
TRICK—
William. *London.* a.1718.
William. *Bideford.* 18c. l.c. clock.
John. *Merthyr Tydvil.* 1791.
TRICKLER, R. *London.* an.1786. Watch.
TRIGG—
Thomas. *London (Bread St.).* a.1692, CC. 1701-18. Watch.
William Matthew. *London.* a.1800.
TRIGGS—
Thomas. *London.* a.1695, CC.1708.
——. *Guildford.* ca.1800.
TRIMBLE & KEAN. *Newry.* 1824.
TRIMNELL, ——. *Canterbury.* Early 19c. Watch.
TRIMOLET, François Louis. *Geneva.* ca. 1775-91.
TRINALL, Richard. *London.* 1744. W.
TRINGHAM—
T. *London.* an.1770. Watch.
John. *London.* an.1772. Watch.
George. *London.* 1799-1824.
TRINITE, J. G. *Rotterdam.* 1821-30.
TRINQUAND—
Isaac. *London.* 1780. W.
William, son. *London.* a.1784.

TRIPONEZ, François Xavier. *La Brévine.* 1815-20. C.

TRIPP—
Thomas. *London.* 1708. Watch Horstmann coll.
Job. *London* (*Westminster*). 1775. Watch Ilbert coll.

TRIPPETT—
Thomas. *London.* a.1654-82.
John. *Kingston* (*Surrey*). CC.1668-71. l.c. clock.
Robert. *London* (*Wapping*). a.1688, CC. 1700-23. Insolvent. l.c. clock.
William. *London* (*Hatton Gdn.*). a.1699, CC. 1706-42. Watch.
Robert, son of Robert. *London.* a.1715.

TRIST, Joseph. *Exeter.* d.ca.1832. C.

TRISTRAM, James. *Liverpool.* 1825. W.

TRITTLÄW, Andreas. *Augsburg.* m.1758-60.

TROCHE, *v.* DIETSCHI.

TROCKENBRODT, ——. *Strasbourg.* ca. 1700.

TRÖGER, J. Pet. *Asch.* 18c. Ivory watch Pal. du Cinquantenaire, Brussels.

TROIS, Guillaume. *Dijon.* 1383-98. Dutch. In charge of clock on Notre Dame. Discharged because he stopped the clock when not paid.

TROSCHEL—
Hanns. *Nürnberg.* b.1549, d.1612. math. inst. maker. Dial B.M.
Hanns. *Nürnberg.* 1620-3. Ivory dials B.M., M.M.A. and Old Ashmolean M.

TROSILLION, ——. prob. *London.* an.1711. Watch.

TROSSEY, Bartholomew. *London.* a.1744.

TROT, ——. *Besançon* and *Geneva.* 1792. Associated with MÉGEVAND FRÈRES. *v.* SANDOZ ET TROT.

TROTMAN—
Alexander. *London.* an.1782. Watch.
Charles. *Harsfield.* Early 19c. Watch.

TROTT—
Peter. *Boston, U.S.A.* 1800-05. W.
Andrew C. *Boston, U.S.A.* 1806-09. W.

TROTTER—
Alexander. *Jedburgh.* 1788-1815. l.c. clocks. Watch.
Joseph. *Newcastle-o.-T.* 1820-33. l.c. clock.
Robert. *Leith.* 1822-36.
William. *Blackwatertown.* 1824.
Thomas. *Sunderland.* Early 19c.

TROUGHTON—
Joseph. *London.* 1779. Lancaster freeman. W.
Edward. *London.* b.1754, CC.1823, d.1835. Invented a wheel-cutting engine and a compensation pendulum.
Thomas. *London.* a.1782, CC.1796-1809.

TROUP—
& Co. *London.* 1815. W.
James. *London.* CC.1825.

TROUT—
Edward. *London.* an.1747-ca.1753. Watch.
Edward. *London.* a.1753.

TROUTBECK, John. *London.* Partner with Jos. DODDS to 1793.

TROUVÉ, Pierre François. *Paris.* m.1777-89.

TROVEY—
Charles. *London.* a.1754, CC.1776-99. W.
Charles, son. *London.* a.1782.

TROWE—
John. *London.* a.1685.
Thomas. *London* (*St. Brides*). a.1685-1729. Insolvent.
Gilbert. *London* (*Salisbury Ct.*). a.1715, CC. 1722-40, d.an.1757. Watch.
Gilbert, son. *London.* a.1745.

TROYS, Jean de. *Avignon.* 1405. Made clock for Pertuis, going 24 hours.

TRUBSHAW, John. *London.* a.1679, CC. 1686, w.CC.1714. br. clock Weth. coll. rep. watch S.K.M. g. rep. watch Den. coll.

TRUCHET, Jean. *v.* SÉBASTIEN LE PÈRE.

TRUGARD, Moses. *Dartmouth.* 1795. W.

TRUITTE—
MOURIER ET CIE. *Geneva* up to ca.1765. The firm was DAN, TRUITTE ET MOURIER to 1770. 4-colour g. watch.
Louis. *Berlin.* In 1770 went to Berlin with DAN as managers of the Fabrique royale d'horlogerie. DAN left in 1775. In 1782 was manager also of the Fabrique at Friedrichsthal. The Fabriques failed in 1783 and TRUITTE died. p.c. watch M.P.S. Dresden.

TRUMAN—
Thomas. *London.* a.1740.
P. *London.* an.1798. Watch.

TRUMP, Philipp. *Crailsheim.* ca.1700. aut. maker. aut. table clock Feill coll.

TRUNDLE, John. *Enfield.* 1795. W.

TRURY, ——. *Geneva.* Early 19c. g. watch M.M.A.

TRUSCOTT—
Lewis. *Mevagessey.* Late 18c. l.c. clock.
Lewis. *Haverfordwest.* 1822-44.
& MICHAEL. *Haverfordwest.* ca.1820. l.c. clock.

TRUSTED, Charles. *Oversley.* 1796. Patented a 'Timepeater' or rep. clock.

TRUSTY, Stephen. *London.* CC.1770-8.

TRYBOM, Isac. *Stockholm.* 1763-70.

TRYGESSON, Olof. *Stockholm.* 1752.

TRYGG—
Olof. *Sala.* 1750-4. l.c. clock.
Petter. *Falun.* 1750-94. l.c. clock.

TSCHUMY, Johannes. *Basle.* 1763. From *Berne.*

TUBALDINI, Gasparo. *Siena.* 1394. Made clock for campanile of S. Jacopo di Rialto.

TUBB—
Daniel. *London.* a.1778.
Thomas. *Chester.* an.1785. Watch.

TUCHER—
Hanns. *Augsburg.* m.1537. math. inst. maker.
Hanns. *Augsburg.* m.1557. math. inst. maker.
Hans. *Nürnberg.* 1567-1621. Dials M.P.S. Dresden and Old Ashmolean M.
Hanns. *Augsburg.* m.1570. math. inst. maker.
Christoph. *Augsburg.* d.1632. math. inst. maker.
Joseph. *Augsburg.* d.1644. math. inst. maker.
Thomas. *Augsburg.* d.1645. math. inst. maker.

TUCKER—
John. *Tiverton.* 1710. Watch Exeter M.
Christopher. prob. *London.* an.1726. Watch.
James. *Portsmouth.* To 1759. W.
John. *Portsmouth.* an.1776-95. Watch.
R. *Bideford.* 2nd half 18c. l.c. clock.
John. *Exeter.* 1789-1800. Succeeded Rob. BATES.
John. *Tiverton.* 1795-1810. Bankrupt. W.
Walter. *Exeter.* Early 19c. Watch.

TUCKEY—
Thomas. *London.* CC.1646.
Edward. *London.* a.1681.
Giles. *Manningtree.* 1759. Decamped with watches. W.
Giles. *London.* ca.1770. Watch and l.c. clock.

TUDMAN, James. *London.* 1688. l.c. and br. clock.

TULL, Jethro. *London.* a.1739.

TUNNELL, John. *London.* CC.1814, l.CC. 1826-30. Watch. Succeeded FLASHMAN.

TUNSTALL, Stephen. *Skipton.* 1725, d.1748.

TUOSMAIS, Stanislaw. *Lublin.* Late 17c. Table clock Feill coll.
TUPLING, B. *London.* 1820.
TUPMAN—
William. *Rowell.* 1775. C. & W.
George. *London* (*Charles St., Hanover Sq.*). 1794-1820. en. watch.
William, son. *London.* a.1806.
James. *London.* 1817-24.
TUQUOY, Martin. *Parthenay.* a.1641-57.
TURATTE, ——. *Paris.* ca.1700. Watch Gélis coll.
TURBANT, Joseph. *Taninge.* 1811.
TURBET, Cuthbert. *London.* a.1716.
TURBUTT, Francis. *London.* a.1692.
TURCQ, ——. *Paris.* 1819-25.
TURGES—
James. *London.* a.1660.
Josiah. *London* (*St. Sepulchre*). a.1752, CC. 1764-70. p.c. watch London M.
TURGY, John. *Manchester.* 1804. C.
TURLES—
Richard. *London.* a.1723.
James. *London.* a.1731. *Windsor.* 1791.
TURLINGTON, Robert. prob. *London.* an. 1775. Watch.
TURLL, James. *London.* 1742. Watch.
TURMEAU, Michel. *Blois.* m.1661, d.1667.
TURNBULL—
William. *Edinburgh.* 1758-82.
William. *Darlington* and *Newcastle-o.-T.* 1761-80. Watch.
& AITCHISON. *Edinburgh.* 1768-80.
John. *Edinburgh.* a.1765-72.
& SYMSONE. *Dunfermline.* 1776.
John. *Dunfermline.* 1780.
Robert. *Greenock.* 1790-1832.
William. *Inverkeithing.* 1795.
Peter. *Glasgow.* 1812.
Thomas. *Whitby.* 1818-40.
William. *Whitby.* 1822-40.
——. *Kingston, Jamaica.* Early 19c.
TURNELL, William. *London.* a.1821, CC. 1828.
TURNER—
Henry. *London.* a.1694.
Joseph. *London* (*Fleet St.* and later *Clerkenwell*). a.1709, CC.1717-61. Bankrupt.
Richard. *Lewes.* 1720.
William. *Bristol.* 1725. Bankrupt. C.
R. *London.* 1st half 18c. Watch.
Thomas. *London.* a.1714, CC.1735.
William. *London* (*Spitalfields*). a.1734-75. Watch.
William. *London* (*Cornhill*). an.1760. Watch.
Charles, son of Jos. *London* (*Goswell St.*). a.1752-1804.
Thomas. *London.* a.1753.
Edward. *London.* CC.1769.
Thomas. *London.* a.1768.
John. prob. *London.* an.1782. Watch.
Thomas. *London.* a.1776.
Charles. *London.* a.1777, CC.1786.
William. *London.* a.1785.
William. *Gloucester.* 1795. W.
Daniel. *Kings Lynn.* From 1795.
James. *London.* a.1792, CC.1801.
James. *London* (*Old St.*). 1799. W.
Charles Thomas. *London* (*Old St.* and *Goswell St. Rd.*). a.1793, CC.1811-22.
Matthew. *London.* a.1795.
Francis. *Rochford* (*Essex*). ca.1800 CC.
——. *Honiton.* 18c. l.c. clock.
James. *London* (*Aldersgate St.*). 1805-08.
John. *Hull.* 1806.
James. *Edinburgh.* 1811.
Charles. *London.* a.1808.
John. *London* (*Poplar*). 1820.
William. *London.* CC.1821.
William Hart. *London.* a.1818.

TURNER—*continued.*
James. *Larne.* 1824.
William. *London* (*Fenchurch St.*). 1825-40 Chron. & W.
TURNEY, James. *London.* a.1727.
TURNHAM, Richard. *London.* an.1786. Watch.
TURNISH, Samuel. *London.* a.1738.
TURNLEY, Samuel. *London.* a.1791.
TURPAIN, Jacques. *La Rochelle.* 1679-90.
TURPIE, Jacob. *London.* 1817-24. W.
TURPIN—
Jacques. *Paris.* 1777.
William. *London.* a.1809.
Benjamin. *London.* 1817-24.
TURQUAND, ——. prob. *London.* an.1751. Watch.
TURRELL, Samuel. *Boston, U.S.A.* 1789-1800. W.
TURTON—
Nathaniel. *Manchester.* 1804-14. C.
William. *Sheffield.* 1817. C. & W.
TUSSINGHAM, John. *London.* a.1682.
TUSTIAN, Joseph. *Tewkesbury.* an.1757. Watch.
TUTET—
Edward. *London.* a.1754, CC.1765, m.CC. 1786, d.1792. br. clock Weth. coll. l.c. clock. Watch.
Edward, son. *London.* CC.1792-1811. Abroad in 1813.
TUTIN, William Anthony. *London.* a.1777.
TUTING, William. *Newmarket.* 1780. Bankrupt. W.
TUTTLE, Thomas. *London.* a.1688, CC.1695-1699. Analemmatic dial Old Ashmolean M.
TUTTON, C. *Bath.* 1825.
TUVET, Edouard. *Fleurier.* Early 19c. g. watch.
TWAITES, John. *London.* a.1781.
TWELL, George. *London.* a.1685.
TWELLS, William. *Birmingham.* 1770-5. C. & W. Watches Birmingham M. and Buckley coll.
TWEMLOW, William. *Chester.* Early 19c. Watch.
TWENTYMAN, L. *Cape Town.* Early 19c.
TWHING, James. *London.* a.1679, CC.1688.
TWIGG, Thomas. *Sheldon.* 1791. C.
TWISS—
Ira. *Montreal.* Late 18c. l.c. clock.
Alexander. *Mallow.* 1824.
TWYCROSS, Stephen, & SON. *London.* Early 19c. Watch.
TWYFORD—
William. *Timperley.* d.1781. W.
Robert. *London* (*Strand*). 1770. CC.1781-1819. c.secs. pocket chron.
Robert. *Timperley.* an.1782. Watch.
Robert, & Co. *London.* 1787-1819.
John. *Manchester.* 1788-1800. W.
William. *Manchester.* 1790-4.
Josiah. *Manchester.* 1790-1818. C. Watch Platt Hall M. Manchester.
John. *London.* 1802-04.
William. *London.* 1805-11.
TYAS—
William. *London.* a.1785.
William Thomas. *London.* CC.1820-5. Watch.
TYLER—
John. *London.* a.1667.
George. *London* (*Pope's Head Alley, Lombard St.*). a.1692, CC.1699-1723. br. clock Weth. coll. l.c. clock. rep. watch Den. coll.
John. *London.* a.1701. str. watch.
Richard. *Wallingford.* 1740-82. W.
William. *London.* a.1745.
Thomas. *London* (*Gt. Prescot St.*). an.1777. Bankrupt in 1778. Watch.

TYLER—*continued.*
Thomas. *London.* a.1768.
Nathaniel. *London.* a.1783.
H. *London.* an.1798. Watch.
William. *Bristol.* 1801. W.
Charles. *London.* a.1808.
R. *Melton Mowbray.* an.1822. Watch.

TYMMS—
John. *London.* a.1656.
H. J. *London* (*Vauxhall, Lambeth*). an. 1795-1811. Also TIMMS.
A. *London.* 1820.
M. *London.* 1820.

TYRELL—
Thomas. *London.* a.1730.
Walter. *London* (*Shoe La.*). a.1732, CC.1740, d.1789.
John, son. *London.* a.1775.

TYRELL—*continued.*
Walter, bro. *London.* a.1782.
H. *London.* 1799. W.
Thomas. *London.* 1805-08. W.

TYRER—
Edward. *Chester.* 1638. C.
Thomas. *London.* 1782. Patented an escapement.
Henry. *London* (*Clerkenwell*). an.1784-6. Watch.
William. *Knowsley.* 1787. W.
James Henry, son of H. *London.* a.1801-24.

TYSELL, Carl Joh. *Lund.* 1821-5.

TYSON—
William George. *London.* a.1771.
Leech. *Philadelphia.* 1823-5.

TYTE, Samuel. *Warminster.* Early 19c. Watch.

TZOEFY, Stephanus. *Rotterdam.* 1679.

U

UBALDINO, DA FIRENZE. *Caffa* (*Genoa*). 1446. Keeper of town clock.
UBEE, Charles. prob. *London.* an.1763. Watch.
UDALL—
Thomas. *London* (*Shoe La.*). CC.1789-1814.
& BALDWIN. *London.* 1802-04.
Richard. *London.* 1805-08.
J. *London.* 1820.
UFFINGTON—
John. *London.* a.1695, CC.1702-67.
Daniel. *London* (*St. Swithin's La.*). d.1746. 'W. of considerable business.'
George. *London.* CC.1728.
John, son of John. *London.* a.1727, CC.1739. C.
Samuel. *London.* CC.1740.
UFFORD—
J. *London.* an.1772. Watch.
Robert. *London.* a.1771.
UGLOW, George. *Stratton.* 1795. C.
UHLIG, Friedrich Eduard. *Dresden.* m.1822, d.1871.
UHRSTRÖM, Peter. *Kristianstad.* b.1769, d.1842.
UIJTERVEER (OIJTERWEER)—
S. *Rotterdam.* ca.1700-10. sil. p.c. watch.
Cornelis. *Rotterdam.* ca.1705. Watch mt. G.M. Watch Stads M. Amsterdam. p.c. sil. watch with sil. dust cover and p.c. sil. watch repoussé by COCHIN, both Feill coll.
P. *Rotterdam.* 1821-30.
ULLGREN, ——. *Falköping.* 1821.
ULLMEYER, Christoph. *Augsburg.* ca.1680. aut. cal. filigree clock Grüne Gewölbe.
ULRICH—
Johann. *Bürglen.* ca.1600. crys. mussel-shell watch.
Joh. Gott. *Hamburg.* Late 17c. g. watch en. Huaut, formerly in Shandon coll.
Anders. *Copenhagen.* 1692. Turret C.
Johann Gottlieb. *London.* b.1795, d.1875. An eminent chron. maker; devised many improvements.
ULYATE—
William. *London* (*Bartlett's Bdgs.*). CC. 1773-99.
William Phillipps, son. *London.* a.1779.
Henry, bro. *London.* CC.1807.
UNDEN, Gustaf Michael. *Stockholm.* b.1778, d.1829. Three watches, br. and four wall clocks.
UNDERHILL—
Cave. *London.* a.1647, CC.1655-69.
Benjamin. *London.* a.1762, CC.1785.
——. *Newport.* Late 18c. Watch.
UNDERWOOD—
William. *London* (*Westminster*). ca.1720, d. 1754. l.c. clock ill. Cec. & Web.

UNDERWOOD—*continued.*
William. *London* (*R. Exchange*). Went to *Reading* 1756.
John. *London.* a.1751.
William. *London. Highworth* in 1773. a.1752, CC.1759-73.
Robert. *London* (*Noble St.*). mar.1769-1808. Livery Fishmongers Co.
Caesar. *London.* 1795-1820. *v.* ROBINS.
Ebenezer. *Bristol.* 1818.
UNEMAN, John & William. *England.* 1368. Two of the three Delft clockmakers invited to England by Edward III.
UNETT, William. *London.* a.1692.
UNGARUS, Aegidius. *Budapest.* 1592. Drum watch.
UNITED STATES WATCH CO. *Marion, N.J.* Made watches with the following sigs.: 'Frederick Atherton,' 1867; 'Fayette Stratton,' 'Geo. Channing,' 'Edwin Rollo,' 1868; 'United States,' 'S. M. Beard,' 'A. H. Wallace,' 'John Lewis,' 'Alexander,' 'Henry Randel,' 'G. A. Reed,' 'J. W. Deacon,' 'Chas. G. Knapp,' 'Asa Fuller,' 1869-70.
UNSWORTH, John. *Farnworth.* d.1810. W.
UNTHANK, George. *Guisborough.* 1822-34.
UNVERUS, Ad. *Stockholm.* ca.1750. Wall clock.
UNWIN—
John. *London.* a.1736.
William. *Newark.* 1780-1805. l.c. clock. W.
& HOLT. *Newark.* 1805-10. l.c. clocks.
UPHAM, Richard. *Ottery St. Mary.* 1774. Insolvent.
UPJOHN—
Henry. *v.* APIOHN.
Richard. *Exeter.* ca.1730, d.1778. l.c. clock.
William. *Exeter.* 1741-87. Watch.
Peter. *Bideford.* a.1740, d.1785. Succeeded by Rob. BATES. Watch Exeter M.
Thomas. *Exeter.* ca.1760-95. Lacquer br. clock ill. Cec. & Web.
Edward. *Exeter.* ca.1760. g. repoussé watch.
Richard. *Exeter.* d.1778. W. Business taken over by James, from London.
James. *London* (*Threadneedle St.* moved to *Lombard St.* in 1765, also at *Red Lion St.*). an.1752-79. In partnership with eldest son Francis till 1773. Then gave up a branch to him and carried on as James U. & Co. in Red Lion St. g. en. watches S.K.M. and Den. coll.
Francis, eldest son. *London* (*Bridgewater Sq.*). In 1773 left his father. CC.1781, l.CC.1787-93.
James, & Co. *London* (*Red Lion St.*). From 1773-95. *v.* James above. c.secs. watch G.M.
John. *London.* an.1775. Watch.

UPJOHN—*continued.*
John, & Co. *London* (12 *Red Lion St.*). 1777.
——. *Plymouth.* an.1779. Watch.
James, sen. and jun. *London* (12 *Red Lion St.*). 1781-93.
James. *London.* a.1766, CC.1781, l.CC.1790. Went to *U.S.A.* 1802.
Peter. *London* (58 *Red Lion St.*). To 1791 partner with Richard BAYLEY, then alone to 1825. Watch sd. 'NATHAN JOSEPH, PLYMOUTH. Fecit PETER UPJOHN.'
Edward. *London.* a.1768.
James. *London* (*Bridgewater Sq.*). 1795.
William. *London.* ca.1800 CC.
——. *London* (*Brentford*). ca.1800 CC. Watch.
James. *London.* a.1795.
Henry. *Bideford.* ca.1800.
T. & J. *London* (*Chandos St.*). ca.1805. Regulator ill. Cec. & Web. Watch.
William John. *London.* 1815-24. Verge watch Chamb. coll. Very fine en. dup. watch set pearls with 4-colour g. dial Wilsdorf coll.
James. *London* (*New Brentford*). 1817-24. Watch.

UPTON—
Nathaniel. *London.* a.1674.
John. *London.* b.ca.1757. In 1792 suspected of arson. W.

URDALE, ——. *London.* an.1764. Watch.

URINGS, Burross Robert. *London.* a.1758.

URNIKA, Jaronimus. *Stockholm.* 1644-59.

URQUHART—
& HART. *London.* 1799.
John. *Perth.* 1805-37.
William. *London.* a.1817.

URSEAU—
Nicholas. *London.* 1531-68. At *Hampton Court* 1538-42, and *Westminster* in 1568. C. to Edward VI. A native of France. Received payments from the Privy Purse and wages for keeping the clock at Hampton Court over the above period. His name takes the following forms in the different records: Urican, Oursian, Wourston, Worston, Orshawe, Curceau and Nicholas the Astronomer.
Nicholas. *London.* 1572-90. C. to Queen Elizabeth. Britten thinks it probable that this was a second Nicholas, prob. son of the former.

USHERWOOD, J. *Picehurst.* Early 19c.

USMAR, George. *London.* a.1822.

USWALD, Johs. *Amsterdam.* Mid. 18c. l.c. aut. clock.

UTTER, Anders. *Eksjö.* 1743-50. l.c. clock.

UTTING, Thomas. *Yarmouth.* 1743. Watch. l.c. clock.

V

VACHERON—
Abraham. *Geneva.* b.1760, d.1843. Started in 1785. mar. a GIROD in 1786 and took the name of VACHERON-GIROD.
Jacques Barthélemy, son. *Geneva.* b.1787, retired 1844, d.1864. Associated with his uncle Barthélemy GIROD in representing the firm of VACHERON in Paris till 1816, and in 1819 with François CONSTANTIN. Virgule mus. watches. g. en. watches sd. VACHERON & GIROD M.M.A. and Carnegie M.
CHOSSAT CIE. *Geneva.* Title of the firm 1810-1819.
& CONSTANTIN. *Geneva.* Title of the firm 1819-67. Sig. 'Abraham Vacheron' used in 1822 for second quality watches. Other sigs. were: 'Vacheron & Constantin à Genève,' 'Chossat & Comp. à Genève.' In 1839, the firm engaged Georges LESCHOT to make machine tools for watches; he remained in the firm till 1882. Two eng. watches M.M.A.
Charles César, son of Jacques B. *Geneva.* b. 1812, d.1868. In 1844 took his father's place in VACHERON & CONSTANTIN.
Charles, son of Ch. César. *Geneva.* b.1846, d.1870.
Charles, & CIE. *Geneva.* Title of the firm from 1867-70, then Vve César & CIE to 1877 and ANCIENNE FABRIQUE VACHERON & CONSTANTIN. S.A. to the present day.
VACHET, Jacques. *Paris.* m.1691.
VACHEZ, ——. *Paris.* ca.1785. p.c. g. watch, both cases en., F.W.M. Perhaps VAUCHEZ.
VAGNARELLI, Lorenzo. *Urbino.* 1639. inst. maker.
VAILLANT—
——. *Paris.* 1730 m. cf. VALLANT.
Jacques François. *Paris.* m.1750, juré 1770, d.1786. Clock.
——. *Arras.* 2nd half 18c. g. en. watch.
Louis Jacques. *Paris.* m.1787-1821.
VAIOLA, Pre. *Geneva.* an.1790. Watch.
VAJE, François. *Paris.* m.1741.
VALADIER, Luigi. *Rome.* ca.1770. Made clock on model of Trajan's column, with a ball running down the spiral every minute.
VALE—
Samuel. *Coventry.* 1747-1814.
HOWLETT & CARR. *Coventry.* 1754.
CARR & ROTHERHAM. *Coventry.* ca.1760-1840.
William. *Birmingham* and *Coleshill.* ca. 1760-75.
William. *Walsall.* ca.1765.
Joseph. *Walsall.* 1760-72. l.c. clock and watch.
William Randall. *London.* a.1773,
John. *Walsall* 1781. C,

VALE—*continued.*
William. *London (Bunhill Row).* 1784-90. Watch.
John. *London.* ca.1790. Pair of very elaborate mus. aut. clocks Peiping M.
Joseph. *Coventry.* 1795. C. & W.
& Co. *Coventry.* 1802. Watch.
William. *London (Finsbury).* 1805-24. mus. clocks.
VALEN, John. *London.* 1586. Fleming.
VALENGIN, ——. *Mâcon.* Early 19c. Head of school of horology. Directed a colony at *Les Gras.* Emigrated after Neuchâtel insurrection of 1831.
VALENTIN—
Guillaume Henri. *Geneva.* Left in 1770. g. watch.
& CIE. *Ferney.* 1770. Prob. G. H. Valentin.
Peter Johannes. *Copenhagen.* m.1799. Court C. Master of Corporation 1822-32.
VALENTINE—
Richard. *Middle Hulton.* d.1753. C.
William. *Royston.* 1770. C. & W.
John. *London.* a.1762, CC.1771-1811.
James. *London.* an.1776-1820. Watch.
Bartholomew. *London.* 1787-1800. Watch.
Charles Davis Frederick, son. *London (Clerkenwell).* CC.1809-24.
M. *Newcastle-o.-T.* Early 19c. Watch.
VALÈRE, ——. *Paris.* 1780. g. en. watch Fränkel coll. Watch N.Y. Univ.
VALERIUS, ——. *Coburg.* ca.1565. Planetarium and calendar M.P.S. Dresden.
VALIN, Jean. *San Yuste.* 1556-8. C. to Charles v in his Cloister. Assistant to Giovanni TORRIANO.
VALLAIRE, ——. *Paris.* 1786-9.
VALLANCE, Thomas. *Liverpool.* 1816.
VALLANT—
N. *Paris.* an.1681. Watch. cf. VAILLANT.
——. *London.* an.1755. Watch.
VALLÉ—
Jean. *Lyons.* Late 16c. Oval watch Spitzer coll. Prob. the same as VALLIER.
N. *France.* Early 17c. Watch.
Thomas. *Paris.* m.1783-9.
VALLERAN, Fleurent. *Paris.* 1544. Petitioner for incorporation of Paris guild.
VALLERY, Nicolas. *Paris.* 1767 m.-1789.
VALLET—
——. *Dijon.* 1694. Fitted pendulum and pin-wheel esc. to clock on Notre Dame.
——. *Paris (Rue des Fossés St. Germain).* 1819-21.
Claude Joseph. *Paris (Rue du fg. du Temple).* 1819-25.
Auguste. *Paris (Rue du Marché aux Poirées).* 1825.
VALLETTE, Léonard. *Geneva.* ca.1755-71.

VALLIER—
F. *Lyons.* 1561-4.
Jean Baptiste, son. *Lyons.* 1596. m.1602, d.1649. One of the finest makers of his time. His chef d'oeuvre is the magnificent astro. str. and al. watch in the B.M. ill. Baillie. Three watches Louvre. crys. star watch K.H.M. trav. clock B.M. Oval watch F.W.M. ill. Baillie. g. en. tulip watch M.M.A. Finely pierced and chiselled watch Stern. coll. str. watch Lyons M. crys. watch Museo Nazionale, Florence.
Antoine. *Nancy.* 1606.
Jean. *Lyons.* a.1619.
Marius. *Nancy.* 1628.
Claude. *Nancy.* 1721-6.
VALLIN, N. prob. *London.* 1598-1640. Very small oval watch, with St. George and dragon in enamel, M.M.A. Chiming clock dated 1598 and al. watch Ilbert coll.
VALLION, père. *Paris.* 1822.
VALOIS, ——. *Paris.* 1825. sq. table clock B.M.
VAN, J. *Middlesex.* an.1763. Watch.
VANACKRON, Abraham. *London.* 1655.
VAN ALEURS, H. *Amsterdam.* ca.1775. Watch.
VAN ALLER, Carels. *Rotterdam.* Early 18c. Watch.
VAN BAGHIJN, Adrian. *Amsterdam.* 1750. A maker of repute.
VAN BLADA, Laurens. *The Hague.* ca.1690. br. clock Gemeente M., The Hague.
VANBROFF, James. ——. ca.1605. Watch.
VAN BURGH, J. *West Bromwich.* Early 19c. Watch.
VAN BUSSEL, A. *Eindhoven.* Late 18c. Clock.
VAN CALL, Peter. *Nijmegen.* 1647-71. Made clock and carillon for Darmstadt. Dial maker.
VANCE, James. *Magherafelt.* 1824.
VAN CEULE (CEULEN)—
T., le jeune. *The Hague.* ca.1650. Watch. M.M.A.
Johannes. *The Hague.* 1677. d.1715. Made several watches and clocks with balance spring for HUYGENS. Large en. watch M.M.A. p.c. g. watch Feill coll. A famous maker. Velvet dial br. clock Webster coll.
Phillipus. *The Hague.* ca.1700. en. watch B.M.
Jean, le jeune, son of Johannes. *The Hague.* ca.1700-ca.1725. 3-case trav. clock Ashmolean M. l.c. clock Gemeente M., The Hague. g. en. watch, en. by les deux frères Huaud, Blot-Garnier coll. Watch Feill coll. Small circ. clock Arts M. Prague.
H. *Utrecht.* Early 18c. g. watch.
VANCOURT, Timothy. *London.* a.1695.
VAN DEN BERGH (BERG)—
Wilhelm. *Haarlem.* Late 17c. Velvet dial clock, with sil. fittings.
Adriaen. *The Hague.* Late 17c. sil. filigree clock S.K.M.
A. J. *Rotterdam.* 1821-30.
P. *Rotterdam.* 1821-30.
VAN DEN BRINK, J. *Utrecht.* Early 18c. g. equation watch.
VAN DEN BRÜEL, ——. *Lille.* Late 18c. Watch.
VAN DEN CRUIJCEN, L. *Holland.* 1770. Engraver. Made designs for watches.
VAN DEN EECKHOUT, ——. *Middelburg.* 1782-7. Made an orrery.
VANDENHOVE, ——. *Amsterdam.* ca.1730. en. watch ill. Britten.
VAN DEN NAATEN, E. *Amsterdam.* 1822. W.
VAN DER BILDT, Jan Pieters. *Leeuwarden.* 1754. Clock and inst. maker.
VAN DER BREMT, Jan. *Haarlem.* 1687.
VAN DER CLOESEN, Bernard. *The Hague.* 1688-1719. A maker of repute, who worked for HUYGENS. Oval watch with hand varying in length to follow the oval Ilbert coll.
VANDERCRUSE DE LACROIX, Jean François. *Paris.* m.1778.
VAN DER ELST, J. F. *Haarlem.* 1794.
VAN DER GIESSEN, Pieter. *Haarlem.* 1773.
VAN DER HEGGE, Jacobus. *The Hague.* ca. 1750. l.c. mus. and cal. clock.
VAN DER HULST—
Cornelius. *Haarlem.* 1651.
Hendrik. *Haarlem.* 1718.
VAN DER MEER, M. *Krommenie.* 18c. Watch.
VAN DER MEULEN, Marten Hijlkes. *Joure.* Late 18c.
VANDERMULEN—
Laurence. *London.* 1771. W.
William, son. *London.* a.1786.
VAN DER SMISSEN, ——. *Mülheim-a -Rh.* 1778. g. repoussé watch in London case
VANDERSTEEN—
——. *Mons.* ca.1800. g. en. watch.
——. *Paris.* 1811-24.
VAN DER THOORN, Johannes. *Rotterdam.* 1658.
VAN DER VELDE—
Rosardus. *Haarlem.* 1787.
S. *Krommenie.* ca.1800.
VAN DER VEN, ——. *Rotterdam.* ca.1800.
VAN DER WHERF, Theunis. *Joure.* Late 18c.
VAN DE SANDT, ——. *Nymegen.* End c.17. Watch Ilbert coll.
VAN DIK, ——. *Holland* (?). 18c. Watch Fränkel coll.
VANDOOGANE, Awdryan. *London.* 1570. Dutchman. 'Came for religion.'
VAN DORT, Pieter. *Haarlem.* 1718.
VAN DRONGELEN, Willem. *Haarlem.* 1716.
VAN EEDEN—
Pieter. *Amsterdam.* ca.1750. l.c. aut. clock.
Arie. *Haarlem.* 1772.
VANETTI, ——. *Brighton.* 1822. C. & W.
VANGALAND (VANGALE, VANGANDE, Gyles), Giles. *London.* 1565-85. 'Clockmaker borne under the obedyence of the King of Spaine, payeth tribute to no companye & is of the Dutche Church.'
VAN GHEELE (VAN GHELLE), Ghijlis. *Holland.* 1589. Large oval watch B.M. circ. table clock Webster coll. Oval watch Miller coll. eng. watch Mallett coll. dated 1589, mt. held in case by pin on top plate passing through case.
VAN GRUISEN, ——. *Leeuwarden.* Early 19c.
VAN HAARST, Dirk H. *Amsterdam.* 2nd half 18c. l.c. clock.
VANHESON, Charles. *London.* a.1795.
VAN HOOF—
J., et fils. *Antwerp.* 1790. Fine mus. clock C.A. & M.
J. D. *Amsterdam.* 1822. W.
VAN HULSEN, ——. *Middleburg.* 1606-17. Designed watch cases.
VANIER, Joseph. *Paris.* m.1778-89.
VANIÈRE—
Pierre. *Geneva.* b.1737-71.
Piramé, son. *Geneva.* a.ca.1770.
VAN LAAR, Barend. *Haarlem.* 1774.
VAN LEENMAN, Frans. *Haarlem.* 1714.
VAN LEEUWARDEN, J. *Amsterdam* and *Utrecht.* 1663-ca.1700. Mantel clock. Watch Ilbert coll.
VAN LEEUWEN—
Simeon. *Amsterdam.* 1742. g. en. watch Bernal sale. Watch Stads M. Amsterdam.
Frans. *Haarlem.* ca.1750. l.c. clock Gemeente M., The Hague. Watch. Also LEEWES
Dirk. *Amsterdam.* 18c. l.c. clock.

VAN LENNEP, H. *Cassel.* 1693. Finished globe begun in 1583 by Just BURGI in Cassel Landes-M.
VAN LIMMEN, Adriaan. *Alkmaar.* 1740.
VAN LOO, Jacobus. *Haarlem.* 1703.
VAN LOON—
Hendrik. *Haarlem.* 1691.
Paulus. *Haarlem.* 1698.
Barend. *Haarlem.* 1714.
VANLOVE (VANLOÜÉ, VAULOVE)—
Matthew (Mathieu). *London* (*St. Martin's La.*). 1689-1708. CC.1692. French. W.
Peter. *London* (*Panton St.*). 1706. W.
James. *London.* an.1743. Watch.
Francis. *London.* an.1748. Watch.
VAN MEURS—
Otto. *Amsterdam.* ca.1730-80. l.c. clock. Watch mt. mus. table clock.
Rutgerus. *Amsterdam.* ca.1770. l.c. astro. clock.
J. L. *Amsterdam.* 1822. W.
VAN NIEUWENBOURGH, J. *St. Trond.* br. clock.
VAN NOOIJEN, Isaac. *Middelburg.* Mid. 18c. Watch mt. S.K.M.
VAN OORSCHOT, Pieter. *Haarlem.* 1724.
VAN OOSTROM, ——. *Amsterdam.* ca.1750. l.c. clock.
VAN OSS (OST), Mathias. *Lübeck.* 1561. Clock in Marienkirche, now in Kunstgewerbe M.
VAN OVERKLIFT, H. *Dordrecht.* ca.1720. Watch mt. G.M.
VAN PELDEN, P. *Rotterdam.* 1821-30.
VAN PILCOM, Daniel. *Amsterdam.* 1640. Fritillary watch B.M.
VAN PRENG, Gerrit. *Haarlem.* 1762.
VAN ROSMALEN, J. *Amsterdam.* 1822. W.
VAN ROSSEN (ROSSUM), Cornelius. *Koog.* Late 17c. Zaandam clock.
VAN RUYVEN, Levynias. *London.* 1743. Insolvent.
VANS—
Patrick. *London.* a.1672-80. Fine p.c. watch.
Charles. *London.* a.1682.
VAN SCHILFGAARDEN (SCHLIFGAARDE), Andries. *Gouda.* 1734. d.1802. From *Rotterdam.* Watch.
VANSCOLINAR—
Jeremiah. *London.* a.1769, CC.1776, d.1816.
Jeremiah, son. *London.* a.1791-1820.
VANSELOW, Daniel Friedrich. *East Prussia.* 1794. Appointed town C. of *Elbing,* but did not take up the post.
VAN SPREKEN, Hermanus. *The Hague.* 1665.
VAN SWINDEN, H. *Franeker.* 1780. Prof. of Philosophy. Pub. work on HUYGENS as inventor of pendulum clocks and desc. of a planetarium clock.
VANTACK, Albert. *London.* a.1723.
VAN VECHELEN, Jacobus Dieles. *Breda.* 1670.
VAN VLIJMAN—
Hijn. *Amsterdam.* ca.1800.
R. *Amsterdam.* 1822.
VAN VOOST, Hendrik. *Holland.* ca.1730. Watch.
VAN VUYVEN, John. *London.* 1759.
VAN WAGENINGE, B. *Dorderege* (prob. *Dordrecht*). Early 18c. Watch Den. coll.
VAN WELSEM, J. W. *Deventer.* ca.1800.
VAN WIJCK—
Johannis. *Amsterdam.* ca.1700. Hood clock.
Stephen. *New York.* 1805. W.
I. A. *Amsterdam.* 1822.
VAN WOERKOM, M. *Druten.* ca.1800.
VAN WUDENBERG, Cornelius. *Haarlem.* 1696.
VAN ZWIERINGEN, Pieter. *Haarlem.* 1731.
VARDY Thomas. *Alnwick.* 1774. W.
VARIER—
George. *Pont Nedd Fechan.* 1673.
Samuel. *Pont Nedd Fechan.* 1731-54. Clocks.
George, bro. *Pont Nedd Fechan.* 1749. d. 1782. Clock.
VARIGNON, L'Abbé. *Paris.* b.1654, d.1722. Geometrician. Art. on the form of the fuzee in Hist. de l'Acad. des Sci. Paris, 1704.
VARIN (VOIRIN, VUARIN), Jacques. *Lyons.* mar.1642, d.1681. From *Varenne.*
VARLEY—
John. *Huddersfield.* ca.1750. Clocks.
William, son. *Huddersfield.* 2nd half 18c. Succeeded his father.
Samuel. *Thorne.* 1775.
Samuel. ——. Pub. art. on the effect of magnetism on timekeepers, in Phil. Mag. 1798.
VARNAN, Samuel. *London.* 1656.
VARNEAUX, François. *Paris.* Juré 1760. cf. VERNEAUX.
VARNISH, John. *Rochdale.* ca.1770.
VARNOD, Henriette. ——. ca.1800. Watch.
VAROQUIER, J. M. *Paris.* ca.1800. g. watch Gélis coll.
VASEY, John. *London.* CC.1766.
VASLET, Andrew. *London.* a.1710, CC.1717.
VASSAL, ——. *Paris.* 1812-22. Succeeded by WALTRIN.
VASSALIEU (VASSELY), Humbert. *Lyons.* 1523-57.
VASSART, ——. *Paris.* 1813-25.
VASSE, David. *Paris.* m.1782-1824.
VASSIERE, Thomas. *London.* CC.1698.
VATRIN, ——. *Paris.* 1788. cf. VAUTRAIN and WATRIN.
VATU, Samuel. *London.* 1746-62. W.
VAUCANSON, Jacques de. *Grenoble* and *Paris.* b.1709, d.1782. Famous engineer. Made a number of automaton figures which obtained great celebrity, desc. and ill. M. des Aut. and in pamphlet pub. Paris, 1738.
VAUCHER—
David Jean Jacques Henri. *Fleurier.* 1734-1749. Introduced watchmaking into Fleurier.
Jean Henri, bro. *Plancemont.* 1745. Master of Ferd. BERTHOUD.
Pierre, bro. *Fleurier.* 1749.
Antoine. *Môtiers.* a.1741.
Claude Jean Pierre. *Fleurier.* b. 1752.
Daniel. *Paris.* m.1767-86. An eminent maker. Watches in most museums ill. Baillie. Fine 4-colour g. en. rep. watch F.W.M. sd. 'VAUCHÉ À LA CITÉ.' Watch mt. Ilbert coll. sd. 'VAUCHEZ EN LA CITÉ.' g. en. rep. watch set diamonds Lincoln M. A Vaucher, prob. Daniel, was granted in 1778 by the Govt. a premium for a file-cutting machine. Also VAUCHEZ and VAUCHÉ.
Jean Henri David, son. *Paris.* m.1779, juré 1780-9.
Louis Théodore. *Paris.* b.1775, d.1806.
FRÈRES. *Geneva.* ca.1780-1830. Fine ruby cyl. parachute c.secs. watch G.M. Many watches and small clocks. mus. watch Chamb. coll.
FRÈRES. *Fleurier* and *Canton.* 1800-66. A different firm from that of Geneva, composed of Claude and César. g. en. c.secs. watch.
Claude. *Fleurier.* 1800-20. Introduced train of 18,000.
César. *Fleurier.* 1800-20.
——. *Paris* (*Rue St. Pierre aux Boeufs*). 1812.
——. *Paris* (*Rue de Glatigny*). 1824.
Fils. *Paris* (*Place de l'Hôtel de Ville*). 1824.
VAUCHET ET BOUET. *Paris.* 1825.

VAUDE, ——. *Lyons.* 1772-8. Tried to start a French factory with workmen from Geneva.

VAUDET, Louis. *Paris.* m.1785-9.

VAUDRY, Charles François. *Paris.* 1776.

VAUGHAN—

Robert. *London.* a.1655.

Richard. *London.* a.1704.

Edward. *London.* a.1706, CC.1715-23. Also VAUGHTON.

——. *Brainton.* 1st half 18c. Watch.

Thomas. *London.* a.1748.

Charles. *Pontypool.* ca.1730-ca.1780. l c. clock Nat. M. Cardiff.

George. *London.* 1802-20. rep. watches.

VAUGUE, ——. *Paris.* ca.1620. Oval watch Ilbert coll.

VAULX, Nicolas. *Montbéliard.* 1568 m.

VAUS, Patrick. *London.* 1680.

VAUSON, ——. *Paris.* m.1607.

VAUTIER (VAUQUER)—

Gilles. *Blois.* mar.1558, d.ca.1576. Also VAUTHIER and VAULTHYER.

Louis (Loys). *Blois.* mar.1589, d.1623.

Abraham. *Blois.* 1578. d.an.1600.

Loys, son. *Blois.* b.1591, d.1638. A very fine maker. Fine en. watch B.M. ill. Baillie. Watch Louvre.

Michel, son of Louis. *Blois.* 1617. d.1630. C. and engraver.

Jacques. *Blois.* b.1621. Engraver. Many designs for watches, especially for en. paintings.

Robert, son of Michel. *Blois.* b.1625, d. 1670. A celebrated painter on enamel. Watches Louvre and Bernal sale.

Daniel, son of Loys. *Blois.* 1654-86.

Jean. *Blois.* 2nd half 17c. Engraver. Designs for cocks.

VAUTRAIN, Alexandre. *Paris.* m.1764-1772.

VAUTRAVERS, Théophile. *Vevey.* 1764 m.-1772.

VAUTREMER, Adrien Modeste. *Paris.* m. 1782.

VAUTRIER, Gilles. *Beauvais.* 1599. 'Arologeur.'

VAUTROILLIER, P. *France* (?). Watch Louvre.

VAUTROLLIER (VAULTROLLIER). James. *London.* 1622. CC.1632. One of the first assistants CC. Watches G.M., M.M.A., Mallett and Blot-Garnier colls.

VAUVERT, Frederick. *London.* a.1725.

VEALE, William. *Harwich.* From 1774. C. & W.

VEBER, Jacob Benoît. *Vevey.* 1798 m.

VECUE, Thomas. *London.* CC.1632.

VÉDIE, Louis. *Rouen.* Juré 1691.

VEDTER, Philip. *Vienna.* 17c. Table clock.

VÉGÉAS, René. *Paris.* m.1782-9.

VEIGNEUR—

FRÈRES. *Geneva.* 1770-1800. Made Lepine cyl. watches with sweep secs. Fine aut. watch. Watch Den. coll. g. en. vase watch. Decimal watch Gélis coll.

FRÈRES ET CORET. *Geneva.* ca.1800. Watch.

VEINIER, François. *Geneva.* 1768.

VEIRAS, Jean Jaques. *Geneva.* ca.1755-70.

VEIT, Anders August. *Stockholm.* comp.1760, m.1764, d.1772.

VEITCH—

William. *Haddington.* 1754-81.

Robert. *Edinburgh.* a.1774-82.

William. *Edinburgh.* a.1778.

VELIN, ——. *Geneva.* ca.1800. Painter on enamel.

VELLAUER, Johann. *Vienna.* m.1776. br. clock.

VELLUM, James. prob. *London.* 1779. Watch.

VELTMAN—

De Wed. *Rotterdam.* ca.1800.

A. *Rotterdam.* 1821-30.

VENABLES—

A. *London* (*Westminster*). an.1771. Watch.

George. *London.* a.1762, CC.1769.

George. *London.* a.1768, CC.1795-1805.

VENAT, Jean. *St. Claude.* 1655. Repaired clock of the Chapter.

VENAULT, ——. *Paris.* 1790-1818. Successor to REVEL. Watch.

VENET, ——. *Paris.* 1821.

VENN, Thomas. *London.* a.1752, CC.1772-5. Watch.

VENTROSSI, J. *Florence.* ——.

VENTURI, Antonius. ——. 1738. br. clock Furt. M.

VERBACK, William. *London.* a.1681.

VERDELET, Jean. *Paris.* 1685 m.

VERDIER—

——. *Paris.* 1730 m.

Jean Jacques. *Paris.* m.1737, juré 1773-89. g. en. watch.

George. *London.* an.1769. Watch.

——. *Paris.* 1813-25. Succeeded STANLEY.

VERDON, Charles. *Galway.* 1824.

VERGER, François. *Paris.* 1770 m.

VERGO, ——. *France.* ca.1730. Devised a clock escapement with two pin wheels geared together and a 'fusée à l'yvrogne,' winding both ways.

VERIDET, ——. prob. *France.* Early 19c. g. watch Ilbert coll.

VERIEUX, ——. *Paris.* 1770-9.

VÉRITÉ—

——. *Paris.* 1825.

August Lucien. *Beauvais.* b.1806, d.1887. An able engineer and C. Devised a constant force clock esc. in which impulse was given by suspended balls. Made very complex astro. monumental clocks in Besançon and Beauvais Cathedrals.

VERMEULEN (VERMEULE)—

Nicolas. *Rotterdam* and *Amsterdam.* ca.1720. Watch Den. coll.

Andries. *Amsterdam.* Mid. 18c. Watch mt. S.K.M.

VERMONT, ——. *London.* an.1791. Watch.

VERNEACE, ——. *London.* an.1782. Watch.

VERNEAUX, Henry François. *Paris.* m.1757, juré 1767-89. en. watch F.W.M. cf. VARNEAUX.

VERNEDE—

J. *Agen.* ca.1650. Watch, crys. covers, M.M.A.

G. *Agen.* ca.1700. Watch Gélis coll.

Pierre. *Agen.* Early 18c. Watch Gélis coll.

Jean. *Agen.* 1740.

VERNET, Jean. *Cassel.* ca.1690. Sundial.

VERNEY, ——. *Dublin.* an.1777. Watch.

VERNEZOBRE DE LAURIEUX—

Jean Baptiste Louis. *Paris.* m.1769-89.

——. *Paris.* 1812.

VERNIER, Timothy. *England.* Mid. 18c. br. clock.

VERNOD, H. *Paris.* End 18c.

VERNON—

Samuel. *London.* CC.1648, m.CC.1679. d. an.1685. Watch.

Samuel, son. *London.* a.1677, CC.1685-1705.

Daniel. *Nantwich.* mar.1695. C.

Thomas. *London* (*Fleet St.*). a.1701, CC. 1708-40. Watch and br. clock.

Richard. *London.* ca.1720. Watch 12 hour circle and 120 minute circle Ilbert coll.

J. *London.* Early 18c. Fine g. en. and repoussé p.c. rep. watch.

Thomas. *Liverpool.* 1734-66. W.

Thomas. *Ludlow.* d.an.1740. l.c. clock.

James. *Liverpool.* 1754. W.

& EDEN. *Liverpool.* 1767. W.

& SHEPHERD. *Liverpool.* an.1790. Watch.

VERON—
——. *St. Imier.* ca.1790.
——. *Paris.* 1808.
VEROW, John. *Hinckley.* 1795. C.
VERPORT, ——. *Paris.* 1819-25.
VERRE—
Henri. *Geneva.* Came to the Versailles factory in 1795, prob. returned to Geneva ca.1797.
——, son. *Geneva.* Came to the Versailles factory in 1795 and in 1797 established himself in Paris.
VERSEN, Charles. *Paris.* an.1780. Watch.
VESEY, Agmondesham. *London.* a.1692.
VESPER—
William. *London.* a.1763-1824. Watch.
J. *London.* 1820.
VETTINER, Jean Daniel. *Geneva.* b.1736-71.
VEUVE—
André. *Neuchâtel.* 1600. Keeper of the clock on the Tour de Diesse.
Jean Jacques. *Chaux-de-Fonds.* a.1747.
VEVERS, William. *Hemel Hempstead.* 1795. W.
VEY, John. *Wimborne.* Early 19c.
VEYRASSAT—
Paul Louis. *Vevey* from 1774-98. m. in *Gex.*
——. *Geneva.* 1794. Started the third machine factory, which failed.
VEYRAT, Mme. ——. 1824. cyl. watch Gélis coll.
VEYRIN, Jean Antoine. *Paris.* m.1773-92.
VEZIT, ——. *Paris.* Late 18c. g. en. watch Stern. coll.
VIAL, ——. *Walsingham.* an.1787. Watch.
VIALA—
——. *Pforzheim.* 1765.
P. *Geneva.* ca.1780. en. watch set jargoons Ilbert coll.
FRÈRES. *Switzerland.* ca.1800. en. watch Basle M.
VIBERT, J. P. *Penzance.* 1780. Watch and l.c. clock.
VICAIRE DE ST. CYR, ——. *France.* 1725. Devised an equation clock desc. in Gallon, 'Machines et Inventions,' Vol. 4.
VICARY—
George. *London.* a.1682.
George. *London.* a.1685.
Thomas. *Bristol.* 1797. C.
VICCARIDGE—
Charles. *London.* a.1699.
Charles. *London.* a.1700.
VICK—
Richard. *London (Strand).* a.1692, CC.1702, m.CC.1729, d.1750. Keeper of clocks in the King's palace. Boulle-work clock St. James's Pal. Made rep. watch for the King. l.c. clock Windsor Castle ill. Britten. rep. watch mt. Ilbert coll.
Philip. *London.* a.1694-1733. cal. br. clock.
James. *London (St. Mary le Strand).* rep. watch Horstmann coll.
Philip. *Leiden.* 18c. Table clock.
VIDAL, Jacques Augustin, fils. *Paris.* 1772 m.-1789. Cartel clock.
VIDER, Pierre. *Le Locle.* 1820. C.
VIDION, John. *Faversham.* 1774-1801. W.
VIDMER, Dieshelm. *Chaux-de-Fonds.* 1783-1790.
VIÉ, Paul. *Geneva.* 1626. Comp. from *Blois.* cf. VIET.
VIEDENMANN, Jacques. *Vienna.* Late 18c. g. watch.
VIEL—
Richard. *London.* a.1651.
Charles. *London.* a.1678, CC.1686-9. Also VIELL.
VIENOUF, Edouard. *Jelsey.* 18c. l.c. clock.
VIERLEIN, Johann. *Heugrumbach.* m.1791.
VIET—
Paul. *Blois.* a.1616, d.1656. Fine watch B.M., with enamel by Henri TOUTIN. cf. VIÉ.
Charlemagne, son of Paul. *Blois.* m.1673, d. 1695.
Claude. *London (Cornhill).* CC.1698, d. 1734. W. to the Queen. rep. watch Den. coll. Watch with end stone Horstmann coll. Watch with scenes, changing on pressing the pendant, Gélis coll.
Ch. *London.* 1699.
Charlemagne, son of Charlemagne. *Blois.* 1703.
——. *Rotterdam.* Early 18c. Watch S.M.S.K.
Mariane, dau. of Claude. *London.* a.1714-38 CC. In partnership with Thomas MITCHELL.
VIEUSSEUX—
Jean et Mt. *Geneva.* Mid. 18c. Watch.
& RAMERU. ——. ca.1735-ca.1775. Watches Ilbert and Feill colls.
VIEUX, Michel. ——. Late 18c. g. en. watch set pearls.
VIEVAR, George. *London.* a.1693.
VIGIER (VIGER)—
François. *Paris.* m.1744, juré 1769. mus. clock.
Abraham. *Paris.* m.1783.
Étienne Philippe. *Paris.* m.1784-9.
——. *Paris (Bd. St. Denis).* 1812.
VIGNE—
——. *London (Charing Cross).* d.1763. Watch.
Ferdinando. *London.* an.1759. Watch onyx case, set diamonds, formerly in Shandon coll.
Francis. *London.* an.1764. Watch.
James. *London (Strand).* 1770. CC.1781-90. p.c. watch.
——. *London (Charing Cross* and, later, *Westminster).* Late 18c. and early 19c.
Peter. *Bath.* ca.1800, CC.1812.
VIGNEAU—
Daniel. *London.* a.1691.
Peter. *London.* CC.1709.
VIGNET, Joseph. *Paris.* m.1786-9.
VIGNIAUT, ——. *Paris.* 1821.
VIGNIAUX, P. *Toulouse.* Pub. 'Horlogerie Pratique,' 1788 and 1802, and 'Traité élémentaire d'horlogerie,' 1800.
VIGNIER—
Isaac. *Montreuil.* 1698. C.
Pierre, bro. *Neuchâtel.* 1702. Huguenot refugee. C.
Abraham. *Geneva.* 1798. Juré.
VIGNON—
François. *Paris.* Juré 1609-16.
Gilles. *Paris.* 1675 m.
Jean Gabriel. *Paris.* m.1758.
VIJFEEKEN, ——. *Haarlem.* 1752.
VIJLSTRA, Jurgen Jeltes. *Joure.* Late 18c.
VIJT, ——. *Holland.* ca.1550. Made clocks for Groningen and Aduard.
VILE, ——. *Deal.* Early 19c. Watch.
VILLACROCE, Giovanni Battista. *Rome.* Mid. 18c. br. clock.
VILLE, ——. *Paris.* Early 19c. Mantel clock.
VILLEREUX (VILLECEUX), François. *Paris.* m.1758-89.
VILLERME, Isaac. *Lyons.* 1636-49. From *Geneva.*
VILLER-SELLIARD—
——. *Paris.* 1817-23.
Veuve. *Paris.* 1824.
VILLET, Oudard. *Amsterdam.* 1681. Huguenot refugee from *France.*
VILLETTE—
Philippe Emmanuel. *Lyons.* b.ca.1614, d. 1694.
Joachim. *Lyons.* 1658-60.
——. *Lyons.* 1707 juré.

VILLINGER, Lorenz. *Ibental.* ca.1780. Wall clock Furt. M.
VIMARD, ——. *Bayeux.* 1772.
VIMONS, Pierre André. *Paris.* m.1743.
VINCAR, ——. *Zug.* ca.1700. Small watches.
VINCENT—
Jacques. *Lyons.* 1683. mar.1686.
Peter. *London.* Mid. 18c. Watch.
William. *York.* b.1761, d.1797. W.
Samuel. *London.* a.1775.
Jean Gédeon. *Paris.* m.1773-86. Associated with BRALLE FRÈRES, *q.v.*
Aimé. *Paris.* an.1787. Watch.
A. *Bath.* 1819-26.
Charles. *London.* 1805-20. Watch mt. with double wheel duplex escapement S.M.S.K.
——. *Paris.* 1812. C.
VINCENTI, ——. *Montbéliard.* 1822. d.1834. Started factory for ébauches with machines of his design.
VINE, James. *London.* 1790-1825. g. p.c. rep. al. watch.
VINER—
Charles Edward. *London.* a.1802, CC.1813, l.CC.1819-40. al. watch, duplex mt. and pump-winding cyl. mt. G.M. Two watches S.M.S.K. rep. al. ruby cyl. watch Den. coll.
& HOSKINS. *London.* 1825.
VINES—
James. *London.* CC.1708.
Robert. *London.* an.1784. Watch.
VINESON—
James. prob. *London.* an.1772. Watch.
Samuel. prob. *London.* an.1784. Watch.
VIOLLIER, Jacques. *France.* 1st half 17c. Watch Louvre.
VIPONT, John. *London.* a.1682.
VIRET, ——. *Paris.* 1820-4. C.
VIRGOE, Thomas. *London.* a.1674, CC.1682.
VIRIDET—
Marc François Emanuel. *Geneva.* ca.1775-1791.
ET CIE. *Geneva.* Early 19c. g. rep. watch.
VISBACH, Pieter. *The Hague.* 1690-ca.1700. A famous maker, who worked for HUYGENS. en. watch S.K.M. ill. Baillie. Spring clock G.M. l.c. clock.
VISCHER, Georg Adam. *Basle.* 1653. From *Leuttershausen.*
VISE—
John. *Wisbech.* 1740-50. Watch.
William. *Wisbech.* 1758. Watch.
VISSER, T. *Amsterdam.* 1822. W.
VISSIÈRE—
——. *Argenteuil.* End 18c. Marine chron. G.M.
Simon. *Le Havre.* b.1822, d.1887. Eminent chron. maker. One of the first to use non-magnetic balances and springs.
VISTEURRE, ——. *France.* 1380. Repaired clock of Rouvre.
VITROLLE, ——. *Paris.* ca.1650. br. clock.
VITU, ——. *London.* ca.1700. Succeeded by GAUCHERON.
VIVANT, L. *Dijon.* Mid. 18c. Watch mt. Arts M. Prague.
VIVIEN—
Noël. *Geneva.* 1668. From *Paris.*
John Baptiste. prob. *London.* an.1781. Watch.
ET DE CHOUDENS. *Geneva.* Early 19c.
VIVIENNE, ——. *Paris.* Early 19c. Sundial.
VIVIER, l'aîné. *Rouen.* ca.1700. Watch Ilbert coll.
VIZER—
Barnaby, senior. *Dublin* (*Gt. George St.*), 1784-8; (*The Combe*), 1789-90. Watch S.K.M.
Barnaby, junior. *Dublin* (*Golden Lane*), 1789-95; (*Meath St.*), 1796-1824.
VOGEL—
Esias. *Nürnberg.* 1553-65. Petitioned in 1565 with Hanns PRAUN and Marx STEPPINGER for a separate Guild for Kleinuhrmacher.
Joh. Jacob. *Cologne.* 1690-3. Town C. Watch Miller coll. Sundial Giersberg coll. Also VOGELIN.
Hilgerus. *Cologne.* Late 17c. Watch Carnegie M.
Nicolaus. *Stockholm.* m.1695, d.1723. trav. clock.
Niclas, son. *Göteborg.* 1705-54. Watch Nord. M.
Jos. Theodorus. *Cologne.* m.1703.
C. F. ——. Pub. 'Praktischer Unterricht von Taschenuhren,' Leipzig, 1774, and another book on watches, Meissen, 1790.
Johann Abraham. *Dresden.* m.1798. Went to *Görlitz.*
Johann. *Trèves.* In 1804 was granted burghership in Augsburg. Turret C. to the Court in Trèves.
VOGELSANG, Henrik Christian. *Copenhagen.* m.1769.
VOGLER—
Johann Georg. *Augsburg.* mar.1754, d.1765. inst. maker. Sundial B.M. and M.P.S. Dresden.
Andreas, bro. *Augsburg.* 1766. d.1808. inst. maker. Several sundials.
VOGT—
Johann Peter. *Vienna.* m.1730.
John. *New York.* 1758. W.
Mathias. *Vienna.* m.1764.
Joseph. *Vienna.* m.1770.
VOGTIECK, ——. *Vienna.* Late 18c. Small br. clock Uhren M. Vienna.
VOGUIER, J. B. *Paris.* m.1615.
VÖHRENDORFF, M. K. ——. Early 19c. sil. p.c. watch.
VOICE, William Henry. *London.* a.1801.
VOIGHT—
Henry. *Philadelphia.* 1775. d.1817.
Thomas, son. *Philadelphia.* 1813-25.
Thomas H. *Philadelphia.* 1820-5.
VOIGT, ——. *Rudolstadt.* 2nd half 18c. Watch London M.
VOILEAU, Jean. *Leiden.* Mid. 18c. Watch mt. S.K.M.
VOISIER, René. *La Rochelle.* 1624.
VOISIN—
Charles. *Paris.* ca.1695-ca.1730. Porcelain clock Munich Residenz. Lantern clock. Watch Ilbert coll.
Antoine l'aîné. *Paris* (*Rue Hyacinthe St. Michel*). 1740. m.1743, juré 1754-89.
Antoine Henry. *Paris* (*Rue Dauphine*). m. 1755, juré 1765-89. Fine mantel clock.
Henry. *Paris* (*Rue de Thionville*). an.1773-1807. Watch.
Charles. *Paris* (*Rue de Vaugirard*). 1807-12.
François Joseph. *Paris* (*Rue de Vaugirard*). 1809-25.
VOLANT—
Fritz. *Nürnberg.* 1456. 'Orelmeister.' Prob. the same as a Volant who became m. locksmith in 1432.
——. *Paris.* 1612 m. Prob. same as following.
Elias (Eliè). *London.* 1622. BC.1628, CC. 1632-4. Frenchman. Also VOLUNT and VOLLANT. Oval sil. watch ca.1640 Ilbert coll.
VOLCHAMER (VOLCKMER)—
Tobias. *Brunswick.* 1584-1626. Goldsmith and math. inst. maker. Complex dial B.M. Dial Old Ashmolean M.
J. M. *Brunswick.* 1647. Dial Old Ashmolean M.
VÖLCKERS, J. G. *Hamburg.* 1821.

VOLET, ——. *France.* 1745. Devised a watch esc., desc. in Gallon, 'Machines et Inventions,' Vol. 7.

VOLLAND, N. *Paris.* Late 17c. Oval jasper watch.

VOLLENHAUSS (VALINGHAUSS, WOLLINHAUSS), Carl Andreas Friedrich. *Berlin.* 1785-1800. C.

VOLLERT, Christian. *Colberg.* ca.1660. str. and al. hex. table clock.

VOLLRATH, Christopher. prob. *London.* an. 1758. Watch.

VOLON—
Louis. *Paris.* 1736 m.
François. *Paris.* m.1744.

VOLPAIA, Lorenzo della. *Florence.* 1500. 'Eccellentissimo maestro d'oriuoli e ottimo astrologo.' Made a clock for Lorenzo de' Medici, showing motions of sun, moon and planets and eclipses, now in Museo fisico, Florence. Keeper of clock in Piazza dei Signori. Portrait by Alessio Baldovinetti in chapel of San Gilio in S. Maria la Nuova.

VOLPARIAE, Camillo della. *Florence.* 1542-1554. Dial maker.

VOLPERT, Joannes Jacobus. ——. Pub. in 1703 a desc. of an astro. clock made by Jacopo SCHONER.

VOLTAIRE, ——. *London.* an.1781-97. Watch Ilbert coll.

VOLTMERS, Herman Andreas. *Copenhagen.* m.1756.

VON AESCH, Auguste. *Chaux-de-Fonds.* In 1827 went to *St. Poelter, Austria.* C. and engraver.

VON DER HEID, Johann Paulus. *Nürnberg.* 1790. Watch Stuttgart M.

VONDERHEIT, Valentin. *Vienna.* m.1800.

VON DER PLATZ, Gilius. *Stockholm.* 1602. Made clock for the Stor Church, having head with moving eyes and tongue moving in and out.

VON GUERICKE, Otto. *Magdeburg.* b.1602-1680. Inventor of the vacuum pump. l.c. clock made by him Magdeburg Stadtbibliothek.

VON KAPFF, Christoff. *Bremen.* Late 17c. sq. table clock Feill coll.

VON HALTERN, Joh. Melch. *Elberfeld.* Early 18c. Watch Horstmann coll.

VON KEMPELEN, Baron Wolfgang. *Vienna.* b.1734, d.1804. Made a talking head in Deutsche M. Munich ill. M. des Aut., and several automata.

VON KNAUSS, Friedrich. *Brussels* and *Vienna.* b.1724, d.1789. Eminent mechanician. Court mechanician to Charles of Lorraine and the Emperor of Austria. Made a writing automaton now in the Technisches M. Vienna ill. M. des Aut.

VON MANDERN, Carl. *Copenhagen.* End 17c. sq. table clock with attached alarum Ilbert coll.

VON MELLEN, Reinhold. *Ystad.* b.1768, d. 1805. br. clock.

VON OSEDE, Gerdt. *Flensborg.* 1595. Watch.

VON RENARD, Andreas Gr. *Germany.* 1731. Sundial.

VON REYEK (VONREICH), Antoine. *Avignon.* 1714.

VON SCHÄUFLE, Josephus. ——. 1792.

VON SCHNEIDAU, Carl Anton. *Stockholm.* b.1751, d.1817. Watch.

VON STEIN, ——. *Switzerland.* 1518. Repaired clocks of Berne and Soleure.

VONTIER, Garret. *London.* a.1721.

VOORHELM, Cornelius. *Haarlem.* 1712.

VOORHOUT, Adriaen. *Haarlem.* 1684.

VOPEL, Caspar. *Medebach (Cologne).* b.1511, d.1561. astro. inst. maker. Dial B.M. Nocturnal Old Ashmolean M.

VORE, Abel. *Paris.* m.1609.

VORENBACH, Konrad. *Neustadt.* Early 19c. Two wooden aut. wall clocks ill. M. des Aut.

VORET, Salomon. *Paris.* 1675 m.

VOS—
H. C. *Appingadam.* ca.1800.
G. *Amsterdam.* 1822.

VOSMERE, Samuel. *London.* a.1697.

VOSPER, ——. *London.* Early 19c. Watch.

VOSS, Johann Gottfried Heinrich Carl. *Berlin.* 1808.

VOSSELER, Jak. *Schwenningen.* 1767. Schwarzwald clocks.

VOTIER, John. *England.* 1532-44. French, prob. VAUTIER.

VOTTE, ——. *London.* an.1723. Watch.

VÖTTER—
Philipp. *Vienna.* m.1731-63. Maker of repute. Fine sil. trav. clock Carnegie M. Fine miniature watch with 3 cases of g., tortoiseshell and outer of jasper. Also VOTER.
Franz. *Vienna.* m.1758.

VOUANTZ, Simon. *Geneva.* Early 19c.

VOULSTACKER, William Robert. *London.* a.1813.

VOUMARD—
J. H. *Le Locle.* 1801-15. g. en. watch Fränkel coll.
Lucien. *Renan.* ca.1810.
H. L. *Hamburg.* 1815.

VOUTREMER, ——. *Paris.* 1813-25. C.

VOWELL, Ambrose. *London.* a.1714, d.1776. l.c. clock.

VOYCE—
Gamaliel. *London.* a.1687, CC.1694-1740. br. clock.
Richard. *London.* a.1693.
George. *Monmouth.* Early 18c.
Nathaniel. *Gloucestershire.* 1759. Repaired Westbury Church clock.
George. *Dean.* 1791. C.

VREVEN, A. *Almolo.* ca.1800.

VRIJTHOFF—
J. le jeune. *Maestricht.* 2nd half 17c. en. watch.
Jan Bernardus. *The Hague.* Early 18c. Large watch Stads M. Amsterdam. l.c. clock. mus. br. clock. en. watch ill. Britten.
J. le jeune. *Hüningen.* Early 18c. From *Holland.* Clock Stuttgart M. Watch mt. Also VRITHOFF.
John Herman. *The Hague.* mar.1776 at *Bath.*

VUAGNIÈRE, Charles. *Geneva.* Early 19c. g. en. watch M. des Arts déc. Geneva.

VUAILLIET, Philibert. *Amsterdam.* 1690. Huguenot refugee from *Gex.*

VUER, Abraham. *Angouleme.* ca.1700. Watch.

VUICCART, J. B. *Zug.* ca.1630. Small circ. sil. watch B.M.

VUIDEPOT, ——. *Paris.* 1812. C.

VUILLE—
Jean Jacques. *La Sagne.* 1713.
Jean Pierre. *La Ferrière.* 1766. Devised winding by a push button.

VUILLEMIN, Louis. *Lausanne.* Mid. 18c. Watch mt.

VUILLEUMIER—
Moïse. *Tramelan.* ca.1730-60.
——, bro. *Tramelan.* ca.1730.
Élie. *La Reussille.* a.ca.1772.
Jean Pierre, bro. *La Reussille.* a.ca.1772.
David Louis, bro. *Tramelan.* ca.1780.
Abram, bro. *Tramelan.* ca.1780.
——. *Switzerland* and *Besançon.* Early 19c.

VULLIAMY—
Justin. *London (Pall Mall).* 1730-ca.1790. From *Switzerland.* Partner with, and son-in-law of Benjamin GRAY. A very fine

VULLIAMY—*continued.*
maker. Watch G.M. p.c. cyl. watch S.M.S.K. Two l.c. clocks Weth. coll. g. rep. watches Ilbert and Den. colls.
Benjamin, son. *London.* 1775. CC.1781-1820. C. to George III. Regulator with Harrison's escapement and gridiron pendulum, and whole train on friction rollers, made for the King in 1785.
Benjamin Lewis. *London.* b.1780, CC.1809, w.CC.1821-5, d.1854. An eminent maker. C. to the King. Many fine clocks in Windsor Castle, several ill. Britten.

VULLIAMY—*continued.*
Justin Theodore. *London.* l.CC.1813, w.CC. 1820-3. Duplex watches G.M. and S.M.S.K.
& Son. *London.* 1784-1824. C. to the King.

VULLIEMOS, François. *Geneva.* Early 19c.

VULPARIA, Girolamo. *Florence.* 1592. Boxwood dial Miller coll.

VULTERS, ——. *Cornwall.* an.1774. Watch.

VUOLF, J. C. ——. ca.1620. Skull watch B.M.

VURLEY, Thomas. *Wisbech.* 1791. W.

VUY, Étienne de. *Geneva.* 'Recteur de l'horloge' of Cathedrale, 1419.

W

WACHTER, Fra. *Brünn.* Late 18c. en. cal. watch.
WACKERHAGEN, Carl. *Vienna.* Early 19c. Devised watchmaking machines with WIEBEL.
WADDELL, John. *Glasgow.* 1825.
WADE—
John. *London.* 1680 CC., d.1693.
Henry. *London.* a.1719, CC.1728-44.
William. *London.* a.1752.
——. *Burton* (*Westmoreland*). 1766. W.
John. *London.* a.1756. Watch.
Burtt. *London.* a.1757, CC.1764-ca.1800. l.c. clock.
Henry. *London.* CC.1768.
Thomas. *London.* an.1777. Watch.
Michael. *Wakefield.* 1795. C. & W.
Walter. *London.* 1805-08.
William. *London* (*Curtain Rd.*). 1809-11.
S. *Moulsham.* Early 19c. Watch.
WADGE—
Agrippa. *Callington.* 1795. C. & W.
R. Dodge. *Callington.* 1795. C. & W.
WADSWORTH, Eli. *Halifax.* b.1780, d.1861.
WADY—
John. *London.* 1724-9. Insolvent. Watch. br. clock Virginia M.
William. *Bristol.* 1763-1801. Partner with T. CHILETT till 1772. W.
WAGDON, Stephen. *London.* CC.1724.
WAGER, Charles. *London.* a.1751.
WAGGITT—
Michael. *Richmond* (*Yorks*). 1753.
Michael. *York.* 1804-23.
Charles. *York.* a.1804-40. W. & C.
John. *London.* a.1819.
WAGNER—
Ulrich. *Fribourg.* 1476. 'Maistre facteur dez reloges.' Made an artificial arm.
Johann. *Nürnberg.* 1538. Inst. maker. Astrolabe Old Ashmolean M.
Gottfried. *Dresden.* m.1668. One of the first four members of the clockmakers' guild.
H. *Breslau.* 17c. circ. table clock Fränkel coll.
Wolfgang. *Wolfenbüttel.* End 17c. Made watches with moving hour figures.
Michael. *Breslau.* mar.1681, d. after 1704. Made watches with moving hour figures. Stand clock. Watch mt. Arts M. Prague.
Johann Georg. ——. Mid. 18c. gilt metal repoussé watch.
Johann Heinrich. *Pirna.* Mid. 18c. Table clock.
E. M. *Berne.* ca.1760. Watch.
Fred. Ab. *Niesky* (*Liegnitz*). ca.1770. g. en. watch.
Bernard Henri. *Paris.* End 18c.-1836. Able maker of Turret clocks. Invented gear shaping machine.

WAGNER—*continued.*
Jean. *Paris.* b.1800, d.1875. Cousin and pupil of Bernard H. and manager. Maker of great repute. Devised many improvements in turret clocks and various instruments. Perfected the pin wheel esc. and devised several free escs. for clocks, remontoirs and compensation pendulums. Pub. books on escs. and the pendulum.
WÄGNER, Christian. *Stettin.* Early 18c. br. clock.
WAGNON, Jean Pierre. *Geneva.* ca.1775-92.
WAGRENEST, Edouard. *Paris.* 1675 m.
WAGSTAFFE (WAGSTAFF)—
Edward. *London.* a.1650.
Samuel. *London.* a.1697.
Thomas. *London* (*Carey St.* and *Gracechurch St.*). 1756-93. Livery Merchant Taylors Co. Watches M.M.A. and Den. coll. cyl. watches Ilbert coll. l.c. clock Virginia M. and br. clock.
George. prob. *London.* an.1792. Watch.
WAHLSTRÖM—
Jakob. *Stockholm.* b.1745, d.1815. Watch. Court C.
P. G. *Ulricehamn.* d.1804.
WAIGHT—
William. *Birmingham.* 1790-1808. W. & C. Watch mt. Ilbert coll. Watch Birmingham M.
William. *Burslem.* Early 19c. Watch.
WAINE, James. *London.* 1766-74.
WAINMAN, W. *Howden.* ca.1785.
WAINWRIGHT—
John. *London.* a.1671, CC.1679.
Henry. *London.* 1713. W. Broke gaol.
John. *Wellingborough.* 1738-51. Also at *Northampton* from 1751. Watch Ilbert coll.
John. *Liverpool.* 1761. W.
Samuel. *Wellingborough.* an.1763. Watch.
Samuel. *Northampton.* an.1763-95. Watch.
William. *Peterborough.* d.1768. C. & W.
George. *London.* 1769. Insolvent. Watch.
John. *Nottingham.* 1780-99. l.c. clock. Watch.
& SON. *Nottingham.* 1798. C. & W.
Robert. *Rochdale.* an.1803. Watch.
William. *Nottingham.* 1814-18. C. & W.
Timothy. *Wolverhampton.* 1781.
——. *Warrington.* Late 18c. Watch mt.
John. *Manchester.* 1790-1809. C.
Humphrey. *Bunny.* Late 18c. mus. l.c. clock.
John or Humphrey. *Nottingham.* 1797. l.c. clock. Watch.
WAITE—
John. *London* (*Wapping*). 1745. W.
John, & Son. *London* (*Wapping*). 1747-70.
Abraham James. *London.* a.1785.
Thomas. *Cheltenham.* Early 19c. Watch.

WAKEFIELD—
William. *Lancaster*. 1790-1814. W.
——. *Ayton Banks*. 1804. C. & W.
Timothy, son of Wm. *Lancaster*. 1811. W.
Thomas. *Harlow Green*. an.1815. Watch.
WAKEFORD, Hawkes. *Alton*. an.1762. Watch.
WAKELEY, George. *Liverpool*. 1816. W.
WAKELING, Samuel. *London*. CC.1767-86.
WAKEMAN, Edward. *London*. a.1716.
WAKER—
Peter. *London*. a.1656, CC.1663.
Joseph. *London*. a.1736.
WALBANK, William. *London*. a.1759, CC. 1767, d.1806.
WALBERG, And. *Vaxholm*. 1745.
WALBOURN, W. ——. Watch N.Y. Univ.
WALDECK, Johann Heinrich. *Strasbourg*. 1714. Judge of essays for mastership.
WALDEN, Thomas. *Dorchester*. 1620-39. Keeper of town clock.
WALDEGRAVE, Thomas. *London*. a.1654.
WALDMAN, Johan. *Stockholm*. 18c. Watch.
WALDOE, John. *London*. CC.1677.
WALDRAM, John. *London*. a.1704.
WALDRON—
John. *Tiverton*. 1737. Insolvent. l.c. clock.
John. *London* (*Cornhill*). d.1770. W.
John. *London*. a.1756, CC.1763-88. Watch.
WALE—
John. *London*. a.1704.
Charles. *London* (*Ratcliff Cross*). 1723. Insolvent. W.
John. *London*. a.1726.
Francis. *Reading*. Early 19c.
WALES, William, F.R.S. ——. Pub. London, 1794, 'Method of finding the longitude at Sea by Timekeepers.'
WALESBY, Thomas. *Horncastle*. 1795. C. & W.
WALEY, John. *London*. a.1791.
WALFORD—
Thomas. *London*. CC.1690-1716. Engraver and W.
John. *London*. a.1704, CC.1717-28.
James. *London*. a.1718.
Richard. *London*. an.1732. Watch.
Charles. *Warrington*. an.1775. Watch.
H., & Son. *Oxford* and *Banbury*. ca.1775.
Peter. *Flixton*. an.1789. Watch.
W. *Brackley*. Late 18c. l.c. clock.
John George. *Banbury*. 1790-1832.
WALHAUPTER, John. *New York*. 1805. W.
WALKDEN, Thomas. *London*. a.1682, CC. 1694-1719.
WALKER—
John. *London*. CC.1632. Lantern clock.
James. *London*. Late 17c. Lantern clock.
George. *London*. a.1675.
George. *London*. a.1676, CC.1683.
Jonadab. *London*. a.1678, CC.1687-1729. Watch mt. B.M.
John. *Saffron Walden*. 1687.
Peter. *Holland*. a. in *London*. 1681-1730. l.c. clocks.
Walter. *London*. a.1681. Watch.
Thomas. *London*. 1689 CC.
George. *London*. a.1684.
Samuel. *London*. 1699 CC.
Matthew. *London*. a.1694.
John. *London*. a.1694.
William. *London*. a.1700. Watch.
John. *London*. a.1709, CC.1717-30. Invented a lamp clock.
Benjamin. prob. *London*. an.1724. Watch.
Jonah. *London*. a.1727, CC.1734.
John. *London*. a.1731.
James. *London*. a.1733.
William. *Lewes*. an.1744. Watch.
John. *Newcastle-o.-T*. an.1754, d.1773. From *London*. Watches and clocks. Made clock for St. Nicholas Church. Skeleton watch Ilbert coll.

WALKER—*continued.*
Richard. *London*. Mid. 18c. Watch Glasgow Art Gall.
D. *London*. an.1756. Watch.
William. *London*. a.1752, CC.1759.
John. *London*. a.1754.
William. *London* (*Fetter La.*). a.1757, CC. 1764-95.
Samuel. *London*. CC.1766. Two agate watches Winter Pal. Petrograd.
Robert. prob. *London*. an.1769. Watch.
James. *Newcastle-o.-T*. Bankrupt 1769. C.
——. *Cubberley*. 2nd half 18c. Watch.
Samuel. *London*. a.1763.
John. *London*. a.1764, CC.1771.
John. *York*. 1772.
George. *London*. a.1770.
Jane, widow of John of Newcastle. *Newcastle-o.-T*. 1773-84.
George. *Dublin*. 1774-95. W.
Levi. prob. *London*. an.1777. Watch.
Joseph. *Nantwich*. 1781-95. Watch.
William. *London*. a.1776.
Allen. *London*. Mid. 18c.-1783. Watches London M., Wilsdorf, Den. and Gélis colls.
James. *Dumnow*. 1785-91. C. & W.
Richard. *London*. a.1778.
Joseph. *London* (*Warwick Ct., Holborn*). CC. 1787-99.
John. *Newcastle-o.-T*. 1787-95. g. en. watch.
John, son of Wm. *London*. CC.1788-93.
George. *Edinburgh*. 1789-92.
Joseph. *Workington*. ca.1790-1847. Watch mt. Buckley coll.
Charles. *Ludlow*. 1791-5. l.c. clock Virginia M. W.
William. *London*. a.1784.
Robert. *Montrose*. 1795. Watch.
Michael. *Chester-le-Street*. 1795. C. & W.
——. *Ottery St. Mary*. 1795. C. & W.
John. *London* (*Bloomsbury*). 1802-11.
E. ——. Pub. 1802, 'Methods of diminishing the irregularities of timepieces, arising from differences in the arc of vibration of the pendulum,' and, in Phil. Mag. 1812, 'On variations in the vibrations of a pendulum.'
Thomas. *London*. a.1796, CC.1803.
Thomas. *London* (*Oxford Market*). 1805-19.
J. *London* (*Clerkenwell*). 1805-15.
John. *Liverpool*. 1805-16.
Francis. *Maryport*. 1811-30.
John. *London*. a.1806.
Thomas. *London* (*Castle St.*). CC.1814-24.
John. *London* (*Queen St.*). 1815-20.
William. *Liverpool*. 1816-29. W.
James. *Leeds*. 1817. C.
Michael. *Bolton-le-Moors*. ca.1820.
Robert. *York*. 1820. W.
James. *Montrose*. 1820-37.
John. *Howden*. 1822.
George. *Hull*. 1822.
John. *London* (*Gloucester St.*). Early 19c. br. clock.
Robert. *Beverley*. Early 19c. Watch.
Robert. *Maghera*. 1824.
Samuel. *London*. a.1819.
Thomas, & Son. *London* (*Castle St.*). 1825.
WALKING, A. prob. *London*. an.1755. Watch.
WALKWOOD, Samuel. *London*. an.1774. Watch.
WALL—
Andrew. *London*. a.1664.
John. *London*. a.1676.
Charles. *London*. a.1702.
Peter. *Västerås*. 1758-88.
William. *Richmond* (*Surrey*). an.1772. Watch.

WALL—*continued.*
v. MANN & WALL.
Carl Gottfried, son of Peter. *Danzig.* b.1757-1775.
Thomas. *Stourbridge.* ca.1785.
William. *Putney.* 1791. C. & W.
William, & SONS. *Richmond (Surrey).* 1791. C. & W.
Thomas. *Birmingham.* ca.1795. l.c. clock.
John. *Coventry.* 1796. W.
William. *Putney* and *Wandsworth.* 1796-1817. Patented an esc. with two esc. wheels.
B. *Richmond (Surrey).* Late 18c.
& WALL. *Richmond (Surrey).* ca.1800 CC.
John. *London.* a.1798, CC.1809, l.CC.1812.
John, & Co. *Coventry.* Early 19c. Watch.
Charles Frederick. *London.* a.1811.
——. *Hull.* an.1822. Watch.

WALLACE—
William. *Aberdeen.* 1533.
John. *Paisley.* 1603.
George. *Prestonpans.* 1646.
Charles. *London.* a.1702.
Blackett. *Brampton.* Mid. 18c. l.c. clocks.
Thomas. *Brampton.* ca.1760. l.c. clocks.
John. *Leven.* b.1766, d.1835.
Robert. *Forfar.* 1789.
Andrew. *Ayr.* 1816.
John. *Belfast.* 1810-24. Watch Ilbert coll.
William. *London.* Early 19c. Watch.
Robert. *Newtownards.* 1824.
'A. H. WALLACE.' Sig. on the 1869-70 watches of the UNITED STATES WATCH Co.

WALLBANK—
William. *London (Phillip La.).* an.1758-93.
William, son. *London.* a.1786, CC.1796.

WALLBAUM, Matth. *Augsburg.* 17c. aut. clock K.H.M.; richly ornamented. Renaissance stand clock Fränkel coll. attributed to him.

WALLDEN, William. *London.* an.1759. Watch.

WALLEN—
William. *Henley-on-Thames.* 1725. Also *Reading.* 1756. Watch Ashmolean M.
William. *London.* a.1728, CC.1738.
J. *Henley-on-Thames.* 1790. Watch.

WALLÉN, Johan. *Stockholm.* b.1752, d.1816. Watch.

WALLER—
James. *London.* a.1735.
John. *London.* a.1757-90.
——. *Wokingham.* an.1772. Watch.
Thomas. *Preston.* Late 18c. l.c. clock.
Thomas. *London.* 1793. Livery Masons Co.
Robert. *London (Covent Gdn.).* Early 19c. T.C.

WALLERAND, Florent. *Paris.* 1544-7. Founder member of Paris corporation.

WALLERIUS, E. *Norrköping.* 1794. Three watches.

WALLEY—
Richard. *Liverpool.* 1734.
Samuel. *Manchester.* 1768-88. l.c. clock.
Joseph. *Liverpool.* ca.1770. Later took his son-in-law Rob. JONES as partner.
& JONES. *Liverpool.* 1785. W. Jos. WHALLEY retired in 1787 and was replaced by Joseph, jun.

WALLFO, J. *London.* an.1775. Watch.

WALLGREN, Olaus. *Laholm.* 1822. d.ca. 1837.

WALLINGFORD (WALINGFORD), Richard. *St. Albans.* d.1335. Abbot of St. Albans. Devised an astro. inst. desc. in MS. in Bodleian and called 'Albion.' Started the erection of a horologium in the Abbey, finished ca.1395 by Thomas De la Mare.

WALLINGTON, Samuel. *London.* a.1689.

WALLIS—
Richard. *London.* a.1686.
Thomas. *London (Gracechurch St.).* a.1695-1743.
William. *London.* CC.1715.
Richard. *Truro.* ca.1725. Watch.
Henry. *London (Clerkenwell).* d.1768. 'Eminent W.'
J. *London.* an.1767. Watch.
Charles. *London.* an.1776. Watch.
John. *London.* a.1778.
Jeremiah. *London.* a.1798.
——. *London (Finsbury).* ca.1800.

WALLITT—
Richard. *London.* a.1686, CC.1693, d.an. 1709.
Katherine, widow. *London.* 1709-16.
Samuel. *London.* a.1716.

WALLO, Johan Gotfred. *Copenhagen.* comp. 1772.

WALLS, Richard. prob. *London.* an.1769. Watch.

WALMERSLEY, Joseph. *London.* an.1768. Watch.

WALPOLE—
William. *London.* 1743. Bankrupt. Watch finisher.
Henry. *London.* 1751. d.1776. C. & W.

WALRAVEN, Anthony. *London.* a.1699 to Thos. TOMPION.

WALSH, ——. *London (Newgate St.).* an. 1744. Watch.

WALSHAM, William. *London.* a.1753.

WALSHAW, John. *London.* a.1761.

WALTER—
Nicholas. *London.* 1622-30. Subscriber to incorporation of CC. Oval watches B.M. and Fränkel coll. Also WALTERS.
John. *London.* a.1638, CC.1645-97. Also WALTERS.
Peter. *London.* a.1681.
——. *London.* Late 17c. 3-case watch, Dutch painted dial, M.M.A.
Samuel or William. *London.* a.1699.
Joseph. *Paris.* m.1746.
Redfern. *London.* a.1751.
W. J. *Woolwich.* Early 19c. Watch.
Friedrich. *Mitau.* Early 19c. Fine wall clock.
Henry. *London.* a.1814.
John. *Liverpool.* ca.1820.
James. *Godstone.* Early 19c.

WALTERS—
Henry. *Charleston, U.S.A.* 1757. From *London.* C. & W.
Richard. *Carlow.* 1824.

WALTHALL, John. *London.* a.1684.

WALTHAM WATCH COMPANY. Sigs. on watches of its predecessors: 'The Warren Mfg. Co.,' 'Samuel Curtis Mfg. Co.,' 'Boston Watch Co.,' made in 1853 at Roxbury. 'Dennison, Howard & Davis,' made 1854-1856 at Roxbury. 'Appleton, Tracy & Co.,' made 1857-69 at Waltham. The following were all made by the American Watch Co. at Waltham: 'American Watch Co.,' 1860-72. 'P. S. Bartlett,' 1861-78. 'Wm. Ellery,' 1861-79. 'Crescent Street,' 1869. 'Broadway,' 1872. 'Crescent Garden,' 1877. 'Riverside,' from 1877. 'Adams St.,' from 1878. 'A. W. Co. Waltham' and 'Lady Washington,' from 1880. 'Martyn Square' and 'Hillside,' from 1882. 'Seaside' and 'Bond St.,' from 1886. 'Royal,' from 1889.

WALTHELM, Nicolaus. *Fürth.* d.ca.1820.

WALTHER, Søren Christian. *Copenhagen.* m.1762.

WALTON—
Philip. *London.* a.1707.
John. *London.* a.1713.
Isaac. *London.* ca.1725. l.c. lacquer clock.

WALTON—*continued.*
John. *London.* a.1757-95. Watch Ilbert coll.
Thomas. prob. *London.* an.1771. Watch.
John. *Alston.* Early 19c. Watch mt. Buckley coll.
Thomas Robert. *London.* a.1814.
WALTRIN—
Charles Henry. *Paris.* 1762-77. 'Horloger ordinaire du Roy.'
Charles Henry, son. *Paris.* m.1767-89.
Joseph. *Paris.* Juré 1773.
Louis René. *Paris.* m.1771-89.
——. *Paris.* 1823. Successor to VASSAL.
WALYNG, Robert. *London (Westminster).* 1537.
WANACKRON, Abraham. *London.* a.1655.
WANDESFORD, Miles. *London.* 1633.
WANDT, Friedrich. *Berne.* 1785.
WANFIELD, Edmund. *London.* a.1655. cf. WANSELL.
WANFORD, John. *London.* a.1686.
WANGERIN—
Johan Gottlieb. *Stockholm,* 1759. *Linköping* and *Falun,* 1773-94.
Carl Friedrich. *Berlin.* 1785-1801. C.
Johan Olof. *Gäfle.* 1797-1805.
Carl Ludwig. *Berlin.* 1799.
WANNEMACHER, Franz. *Oberhausen.* 1756 comp.
WANNER, Johann Georg. *Augsburg.* comp. 1733, m.1746-70.
WANOSTROCHT (WONOSTROCHT), Vincent. *London.* a.1796, l.CC.1812.
WANSELL, Edmund. *London.* a.1655. cf. WANFIELD.
WANSEY, Henry. *London.* a.1662.
WANSON, ——. *London.* 1801.
WAPLES—
——. *London.* an.1765. Watch.
Nathaniel. *Philadelphia.* 1817-19.
WARBURTON—
William. *London.* a.1685, CC.1693-1701.
Henry. *Liverpool.* 1734.
Henry. *Wolverhampton.* 1760-72. l.c. clock.
John. *Liverpool.* 1824-9. W.
WARD—
Thomas. *London.* CC.1632.
Edward. *London.* CC.1638.
John. *London.* a.1659. Lantern clock dated 1699.
John. *Richmond (Yorks).* ca.1700.
Joseph. *London.* a.1697.
Anthony. *Philadelphia.* Freeman in 1717. *New York.* 1724-50.
Richard. *London.* 1729. Insolvent.
John. *London.* a.1721, CC.1730.
John. *London.* a.1722, CC.1731.
Edward. *London.* a.1723, CC.1732.
Joseph. *New York.* 1735-60.
Robert. *London.* 1751.
Henry. *Blandford.* 1755-1820. Watch. Awards from Soc. Arts for equation work and for a compensation pendulum. Pubs. in Trans. Soc. Arts, 1805, 1807 and 1814.
Francis. *London.* an.1762. Watch.
William. *Horncastle.* From 1761. From *Spilsby.* W.
Benjamin. *London (Norton Folgate).* ca. 1765-90. Two mus. aut. clocks Peiping M.
William, son of Edw. *London (Holborn Hill).* CC.1767-94. Watch S.M.S.K.
Walter Stacy. *London.* a.1760.
Robert. *London (Abchurch La.).* a.1768, CC.1779-1808. mus. clocks. Watch for Turkey Marryat coll. Watches N.Y. Univ. and Ilbert coll.
John. *Ipswich.* To 1770. W.
George. *Helmsley.* ca.1770.
C. *London.* an.1773. Watch.
Gilbert. *London.* a.1767.
John. *London (Cripplegate).* CC.1772, l.CC. 1774, m.CC.1797, d.1813.

WARD—*continued.*
Richard. *Bath* to 1776. *Dublin,* 1776-95.
Thomas. *Baltimore, U.S.A.* 1777. C. & W.
John. *London (Fore St.).* 1784-99.
John. *London (Greek St.).* 1790.
Richard. *Liverpool.* 1790-1818. W.
Richard. *London (Tower St.).* 1790.
James. *Birmingham.* 1790. Watch. br. clock.
William. *London.* a.1785.
James. *London.* a.1786.
Richard. *Winchester.* 1795.
William H. *Liverpool.* 1796-1829. W.
Benjamin. *London (St. George's Fields).* 1799-1808.
William. *London.* a.1793, CC.1800.
Joshua. *Newcastle-o.-T.* 1801. C. & W.
B. *Newcastle-o.-T.* 1805-11.
W. *Grimsby.* ca.1810. Watch mt. Ilbert coll.
Daniel. *Nottingham.* 1811. Insolvent. C.
Isaac. *Philadelphia.* 1811.
& GOVETT. *Philadelphia.* 1813.
Jehu. *Philadelphia.* 1813-25.
Joseph. *London.* a.1810.
Richard. *London (Bunhill Row).* 1817-40.
William. *Helmsley.* 1822.
John. *Liverpool.* 1825. W.
WARDEN—
William. *London.* a.ca.1665.
Thomas. *London.* CC.1672-91.
Thomas. *London.* a.1705.
Robert. *London.* ca.1720. g. en. p.c. watch.
Samuel. *London* and *Lewes.* a.1763, CC. 1785.
WARDLAW, James. *Perth.* 1768.
WARDLOW, Henry. *Liverpool.* 1805-29.
WARE—
Robert. *London.* a.1693, CC.1701-12.
Joseph. *London (Bishopsgate St.).* d.1764.
WAREHAM—
William. *London.* a.1699.
John. *London.* 1802-25.
WAREING—
Richard. *Chester.* 1752. W.
James. *Liverpool.* 1800-14.
WARFIELD—
John. *London.* a.1629 under BC.-1662.
Alexander. *London.* 1690 BC.
Alexander, son. *London.* a.1683, CC.1692-1719. Watch Den. coll.
John. *London.* 1726 CC.
William. *London.* an.1780. Watch.
WARHAM, William. *London.* a.1765, CC. 1773.
WARING—
William. prob. *London.* an.1771. Watch.
Thomas. prob. *London.* an.1777. Watch.
WARLOCK, Samuel. *Killarney.* 1824.
WARNE—
Nicholas. *London.* a.1680.
James. *London.* 1763-75. rep. watch M.M.A.
John. *London (Carey St.).* 1776. C. & W.
WARNER—
John. *London.* a.1672.
John. *London.* a.1675, CC.1682-92.
John. *Draycott.* ca.1690.
John. *London.* a.1689, CC.1696-1716.
John. *London.* a.1712.
Samuel. *London.* a.1717.
& HINDS. *Dublin.* Late 18c.-1824.
William. *Northampton.* 1792. W.
John. *Evesham.* 1795. Watch.
George. *Dublin.* 1795-Early 19c. Watch.
George T. *New York.* 1795-1806. W.
Cuthbert. *Baltimore, U.S.A.* 1799-1807. W.
WARNIER, Jehan. *Cambrai.* 1408. Repaired cathedral clock.
WARNITZER, Carl Friedrich. *Berlin.* 1816-1847.
WARNOCK, John. *London.* a.1814.
WARR, Robert. *London.* 1713 CC.

WARREN—
Richard. *London.* a.1659, CC.1668, d.1702. Watch.
Thomas. *London.* a.1667.
John. *London.* a.1693.
Elizabeth, widow of Rich. *London.* 1702-15.
Jeremiah. *London.* a.1706.
John. *London.* a.1706.
Thomas. *London.* a.1720.
William. *London* (*Shoreditch*). 1743-52. Watch.
William. *Royston.* 1753 CC. C. & W.
George. *London.* a.1750.
Richard. *London.* a.1752.
S. *Liverpool.* d.(?)1772. W.
James. *Canterbury.* 1778-98. Watch.
Eleazer. *Dublin.* 1780-95. W.
James. *Dublin.* 1795.
Thomas. *London.* a.1788, CC.1803.
J. *Windsor.* ca.1800.
John. *London.* 1805-07.
——. *Stamford.* Early 19c. Watch.
& SON. *Canterbury.* Early 19c. Watch.
J. *Ixworth.* Early 19c. Watch.
J. *Eton.* 1813. C. & W.
Eleazer. *Arklow.* 1824.
'THE WARREN MFG. CO.' Sig. on 1853 watches. Predecessor of the WALTHAM WATCH CO.
WARRINGTON—
John. *Chester.* 1743. W.
John. *Philadelphia.* 1811-20.
J. & S. R. *Philadelphia.* 1823-5.
WARRY, John. *Bristol.* 1812-30. Watch.
WARSON, William. *London.* an.1787. Watch.
WARTON, Richard. prob. *London.* an.1771. Watch.
WARWICK—
James. *London.* a.1656.
William. *London.* 1793. Watch Den. coll.
Thomas. *London.* a.1796.
Thomas. *Birmingham.* Early 19c. Watch.
WASBERG—
Johannes. *Lilla Malma.* b.1696, d.1774. Two l.c. clocks.
Eric, son. *Eskilstuna.* b.1727, d.ca.1790. l.c. clock.
Petrus, bro. *Lilla Malma.* b.1738-68.
WASBROUGH—
William. *Bristol.* 1766.
Matthew. *Bristol.* 1778.
Richard. *Bristol.* 1792. C.
Rice. *Bristol.* 1819.
WASHBOURN—
John. *Gloucester.* 1741. T.C.
George. *Gloucester.* an.1742-92. Clock. Watch.
Thomas. *London.* an.1744, d.1756. Watch.
Ann. *Gloucester.* Retired 1750.
& ILBURY. prob. *London.* an.1763. Watch.
WASHBROOK, Joseph. *London.* an.1765. Watch.
WASHINGTON, Mark. *London.* a.1687-99. Watch.
WASS—
John. *Hull.* an.1753. Watch.
Benjamin. *London.* a.1803.
WASSE, Thomas. *London.* a.1682. Watch.
WASSON, Solomon. *Bristol.* ca.1659.
WASTNESSE, Francis. *London.* a.1671.
WATERER, George. *London.* a.1694.
WATERFALL & HOWELL. *Coventry.* Early 19c. Watch.
WATERMAN, William. *London.* a.1682.
WATERS—
John. *London.* a.1674, CC.1682-1705. Watch.
Jonathan. *London.* a.1686.
Daniel. *London.* a.1704.
Thomas. *London.* a.1724, CC.1732.
Robert. *London.* a.1729, CC.1767. *Cheshunt* in 1793.

WATERS—*continued.*
Francis. prob. *London.* an.1756. Watch.
Joseph. *London* (*Bethnal Gr.*). 1778. Insolvent. C.
Henderson. *Dublin.* 1824.
WATERTON, William. *London.* a.1685.
WATHEN, Thomas. *Bristol.* 1780.
WATIES, Thomas. *London.* a.1705.
WATKINS—
George. *London.* a.1703, CC.1716.
Anne. *London.* 1724.
Eustace. *London.* a.1724.
Thomas. *Merthyr Tydvil.* 1761. C.
John Lake. *London.* a.1752-62. Watch.
Richard. *Merthyr Tydvil.* ca.1780. l.c. clock Nat. M. Cardiff.
Joseph. *London* (*Clerkenwell*). CC.1787-1824. Expert on EARNSHAW's chronometers.
John. *London* (*Wilderness Row*). CC.1787, l.CC.1820-38. Award from Soc. Arts for a spring detent escapement. Pub. 'Improvements in Timekeepers,' Jl. Soc. Arts, Vol. 23.
Thomas. *London* (*Stratford*). 1809-24.
John. *London.* a.1801, CC.1810.
James. *London.* a.1810.
WATMORE, William. *London.* 1672 CC.
WATRELO, Anthoine. *Cambrai.* 1569. Repaired Palace clock.
WATRIN, Joseph. *Paris.* 1768 juré. cf. VATRIN.
WATSES (WATSE). *Heerenveen.* 1686. Wall clock.
WATSON—
Thomas. *London.* a.1662.
Samuel. *Coventry* and *London* (*Long Acre*). CC.1687-ca.1710. Called 'Mathematician in Ordinary to His Majesty.' l.c. clock and br. clock Weth. coll. Elaborate astro. and cal. clock in Windsor Castle made for Charles II ca.1680, mentioned by Derham and J. Smith. Astro. and cal. clock made for Isaac Newton G.M.
William. *London.* CC.1691. l.c. clock.
Robert. *London.* a.1689.
Edward. *London.* a.1696, CC.1704.
Henry. *London.* a.1709.
Walter. *London.* a.1711, CC.1719.
John. *London.* a.1712.
John. *London.* a.1734.
John. *London* (*Cornhill*). a.1737, CC.1744-1785.
Alexander. *London.* a.1735, CC.1742-45.
David. *Dundee.* 1748.
Thomas. *London* (*Clerkenwell*). 1748. Insolvent.
Joshua. *London.* an.1770. Watch.
John. *Pocklington.* 1770-1823. W.
Thomas. *Blackburn.* ca.1770-95. C.
John. *Kirby Moorside.* ca.1770-95. C. & W.
John. *London* (*St. Martin's-le-Grand*). 1773 Watch.
Christopher. *Kirby Moorside.* 1775. C. & W. cf. Christopher below.
John. *London.* CC.1781-5. Watch mt. S.K.M.
James. *London.* an.1785. Watch.
Thomas. *London* (*Aldersgate St.*). a.1776-94.
William. *Glasgow.* 1785.
B. *Wangford.* From 1789. C. & W.
William. *Blackburn.* 1790-1814. C.
Thomas. *Newcastle-o.-T.* an.1801. W.
John. *Newcastle-o.-T.* 1805-11. W.
& MARSHALL. *Edinburgh.* 1810. Rack lever mt. Ilbert coll.
Christopher. *York.* 1810-22. W. cf. Christopher above.
Michael. *Newcastle-o.-T.* 1811-20. l.c. clock.
William. *London* (*Clerkenwell*). CC.1813-24. W.

WATSON—*continued.*
George. *Edinburgh.* 1814.
William. *York.* a.1808-40.
Edward. *London* (*Cheapside*). CC.1815, l.CC.1820-40. W. T.C.
John. *Blackburn.* ca.1820.
James. *Philadelphia.* 1820-5.
Francis. *Beverley.* 1822-41.
William. *Elland* (*Yorks*). 1822-40.
George. *London* (*Southwark*). l.CC.1822.
John. *Liverpool.* 1825. W.
G. *Nassau, New Providence, U.S.A.* Early 19c.
J. *Cambridge.* Early 19c. Watch.
WATT—
James. *Edinburgh.* 1787.
Thomas, & Co. *Edinburgh.* 1823.
& McAlpine. *Edinburgh.* 1825-37.
WATTNALL, Thomas. ——. 1730. Watch with Chester hm.
WATTS—
John. *London.* a.1651.
John. *London.* CC.1664.
Richard. *London.* a.1673, CC.1680-98. Watch.
Thomas. *London.* a.1681.
Brouncker. *London* (*Fleet St.*). a.1684, CC. 1693, d.1719. rep. watch G.M. l.c. and mus. l.c. clocks.
Walter. *London.* a.1688, CC.1695-8.
John. *London.* a.1698, CC.1712, d.1775. W.
James. *London.* a.1703, CC.1720.
Edward. *London.* a.1712.
Thomas. *Lavenham.* 1st half 18c. l.c. clock. Watch.
——. *Bristol.* an.1745. Watch.
John. *Canterbury.* an.1751, d.1775. Watch.
John. *London.* d.1775. W.
Thomas. *Hadleigh.* an.1753.
Stewart. *Holbeach.* 1755. W.
William. *Wotton-under-Edge.* 1761-95. C. & W.
Thomas. *Bury St. Edmunds.* From 1766, d.1769. From *Hadleigh.* Invented an engine to finish clock wheels. l.c. clock.
John. *Guernsey* and *London.* 1772. Bankrupt.
Robert. *London.* a.1764, CC.1785.
William. *London.* a.1767-75.
John. *London* (*York St.*). an.1782. Watch.
Frances. *Lavenham.* 1791-5. C. & W.
John. *London.* a.1783.
WAUGH—
George. *London.* a.1773.
John. *London.* a.1795, CC.1804.
William. *Liverpool.* ca.1820.
John. *Wigton.* 1820-41.
WAVRE—
——. *Neuchâtel.* 1755.
Jean Jacques André, son. *Neuchâtel.* 1755-1828.
WAWEN, Gervas. *London.* a.1689.
WAY—
James. *London.* a.1681.
George. *Wincanton.* 1796-1805. Attended the town clock.
WAYCOTT—
Peter. *Ashburton.* 1799. Also at *Holne, Staverton* and *Totnes.* Many l.c. clocks.
Robert, son. *Paignton* and *Torquay.* ca. 1820-45. l.c. clocks.
WAYD, John. *London.* a.1659.
WAYLAND, Henry. *Stratford* (*Essex*). Early 19c. Later H. & J.
WAYLETT—
James. *London.* a.1755, CC.1769-99. Watch.
John, son. *London.* CC.1794, l.CC.1799, d. 1813.
WAYND, Richard. *York.* 1667. W.
WAYTE, ——. *London.* an.1743. Watch.
WEARE, Joseph. *Wincanton.* ca.1800. l.c. clock.
WEATHERALL, Thomas. *Hexham.* 1796-Early 19c. Watch.
WEATHERBURN, Robert. *Berwick-on-Tweed.* 1820.
WEATHERBY—
Thomas. *Berwick-on-Tweed.* ca.1770-95. W. Also Weatherly.
David. *Philadelphia.* 1806-25.
WEATHERHILT (WEATHERILL)—
Daniel. *London.* a.1696.
Richard. *London.* a.1698.
Samuel. *Liverpool.* ca.1770-1818. Watch, crank roller lever escapement for Turkey S.M.S.K. Watch N.Y. Univ.
John. *Liverpool.* ca.1780-1829. l.c. clock.
Samuel, jun. *Liverpool.* 1821-9. W.
John Grace. *Liverpool.* 1825. W.
William. *Liverpool.* 1825. W.
WEATHERLEY—
Joseph. *London.* Early 19c. Watch.
Philip. *Ipswich.* 1819. Hanged himself. C.
WEATHERSTON—
William. *Morpeth.* 1784. C.
John. *Morpeth.* 1778. Foreman to Normand McPherson of Edinburgh. C. & W.
John. *Newcastle-o.-T.* 1787-1801. C. & W.
WEAVER—
Cuthbert. *London.* CC.1682.
Simon. *London.* a.1684.
George. *London.* CC.1740.
Francis. *London.* a.1733, CC.1748.
Benjamin. *London.* a.1752.
James. *London.* a.1753.
WEBB—
Joseph. *London.* a.1650.
Isaac. *London.* CC.1668-95. math. inst. maker.
Thomas. *London.* 1660 CC. d.an.1672.
Elizabeth, widow. *London.* 1672.
Daniel. *London.* a.1692.
Isaac. *London.* a.1696.
James. *Bristol.* 1711. C.
——. *Shepton Mallet.* an.1713. Clock.
William. *London.* a.1708.
Ambrose. *London.* a.1712, CC.1721.
Thomas. *Birmingham.* ca.1730. Watch Birmingham M.
Edward. *Bristol.* 1734. d.1761. W.
Abraham. *Ashford.* From 1741. From *Wye.*
Thomas. *London.* a.1738.
William. *Wellington.* ca.1750. Watch mt. Buckley coll.
Henry. *London.* a.1744.
William. *London.* a.1745.
Marmaduke. *Bath.* 1756-67. W.
Mary, dau. of Edw. *Bristol.* 1761.
William. *London.* a.1761. Watch.
Richard. *London.* an.1769. Watch.
Lanham. *London.* an.1774. Watch.
Benjamin. *London.* an.1775, CC.1781-1810. Maker to the King. c.secs. watch G.M.
Thomas. *London* (*Gt. Arthur St.*). 1776. W.
——. *Bampton.* 1776. W.
Edward. *London* (*Oxford St.*). an.1776-84. Watch.
Thomas. *London.* a.1776, CC.1789, l.CC. 1802.
Thomas. *London.* 1794 CC.
James. *Frome.* 1795. W.
James. *London* (*St. John's Sq.*). 1799. C. & W. Advertized 'Patent polar watches.'
Edward. *London* (*Manchester Sq.*). 1799.
William. *London.* a.1791.
Benjamin. *London.* a.1792.
Edward. *London* (*Tottenham Ct. Rd.*). 1805-1820.
William. *London.* 1805-40.
——. *Frome.* 1814. Watch N.Y. Univ.
Robert. *London* (*St. John's Sq.*). 1815-25.
Thomas, son of Thos. *London.* a.1808.
R. *London* (*Cornhill*). ca.1820. Lever watch mt. Ilbert coll.

WEBB—*continued*
——. *Tarnworth.* Early 19c. Watch.
& SON. *Newbury.* Early 19c. Watch.
WEBBER—
Richard. *Pilton (Barnstaple).* 1713. Made clock on church.
P. *London.* an.1778. Watch.
John. *St. Columb.* 1795. C. & W.
John. *Woolwich.* ca.1800.
WEBDEN, Richard. *London.* an.1759. Watch.
WEBER—
David. *Augsburg.* 1685. Juré 1702, d.ca. 1726.
C. F. *Dresden.* ca.1740. str. rep. al. trav. clock M.P.S. Dresden.
F. J. *Pirna.* 18c. Stand clock Feill coll.
FRÈRES. *Paris.* 1824.
WEBSTER—
Robert. *London.* CC.1675, m.CC.1704. str. table clock G.M.
John. *London.* a.1676 to TOMPION.
Thomas. *Dundee.* 1689.
John. *London.* a.1686, CC.1695-1700.
Sarah. *London.* a.1688.
George, son of Robt. *London.* a.1696, CC. 1703-11.
Anne, sister. *London.* a.1698.
Mary, sister. *London.* a.1698.
Thomas. *London.* CC.1709.
Henry. *London.* a.1700, CC.1710-37.
William. *London (Exchange Alley).* CC. 1710, w.CC. and d.1734. a. to and journeyman with Thos. TOMPION. br. clock. l.c. Chinese lacquer clock ill. Cec. & Web. g. rep. watch Den. coll. rep. watch G.M. p.c. eng. watch Ilbert coll., ca.1710. l.c. clock Virginia M.
Edmund or Edward. *London.* a.1701.
Margaret. *London.* CC.1711.
William, son of Wm. *London (Change Alley).* a.1727, CC.1734, m.CC.1755, l.CC.1766-1776. An eminent maker. br. clocks ill. Cec. & Web. g. c.secs. watch Ilbert coll.
William, son of Hy. *London.* a.1730.
Henry, bro. *London.* CC.1742.
Samuel, son of Hy. *London.* CC.1756, l.CC. 1766.
William. *London.* a.1756, CC.1763. rep. watch and str. watch M.M.A.
William, & Son. *London (Change Alley).* 1770-1800.
Robert. *Whitby.* 1772. mar.1790. Patented a rep. mechanism.
John. *Shrewsbury.* 1772. C.
Robert. *Shifnal.* 1777. C. & W.
Robert, jun. *Whitby.* d.1800. W.
Richard. *London.* l.CC.1787-1808.
Lawrence. *Liverpool.* 1790-6. W.
Robert. *Shrewsbury.* 1792-1800. C. & W.
William Bennet. *London.* a.1792.
——. *London (Stoke Newington).* ca.1800.
John. *Liverpool.* 1800-16. W.
Philip Thomas. *London.* a.1797.
Benjamin. *London.* a.1797.
Richard. *London.* a.1800, CC.1807, l.CC. 1810-40.
George. *Nottingham.* 1814-18. W.
WECKHERLIN, Elias. *Augsburg.* 1646-88. al. watch B.M. Oval watch Fränkel coll. oct. crys. watch. Watch mt. Ilbert coll. Clock mt. Damiano coll. sil. gilt repoussé watch formerly in Shandon coll.
WEDDERBURN, ——. *Berwick-on-Tweed.* 1823.
WEDRED, M. *Kirkby Lonsdale.* Early 18c. Wall clock. br. clock.
WEED, Henry. *London.* a.1704.
WEEDON, William. *London.* a.1686, CC. 1695.
WEEKES—
Thomas. *London.* CC.1654-7. d.an.1688.
Thomas, son. *London.* CC.1688-1710.

WEEKES—*continued.*
Thomas, son. *London.* a.1703.
Charles. *London.* CC.1713. Also WEEKS.
John. *London.* a.1708.
Richard. *London.* a.1717.
WEEKS—
Johnson. *London.* a.1671, CC.1683-90.
Thomas. *London.* 1820.
James & William. *Haslemere.* Early 19c. Watch.
WEELAND, William. *London.* 1817-24.
WEGE, Jacob von dem. *Cologne.* 1596. Kleinuhrmacher.
WEGELIN—
G. Josua. *Augsburg.* ca.1670-1700. Fine sq. table clock. rep. clock. Clock Cassel Landes-M. Gilt metal case br. clock Prestige coll.
Johann Georg. *Augsburg.* 1726. Wall clock.
WEGNER—
Johann. *Simonswald.* 1763. Made the first mus. clock with glass bells. cf. WEHRLE.
Christian, son. *Neukirch.* ca.1775. Clocks with glass bells and strings. mus. clock Furt. M.
WEHRLE, Johann. *Simonswald.* 1768. Made mus. clocks with glass bells. cf. WEGNER.
WEIDEMAN—
——. *Norrköping.* b.1723, d.1807.
Claes Hinric. *Stockholm,* comp. 1760. *Linköping,* m.1770-80.
WEIDENHEIMER, Joseph. *Mainz.* 1794. Astro. watch, desc. in pamphlet pub. in Rovereto in 1862.
WEIFISCHER, T. H. *Copenhagen.* m.1821.
WEIGEL, ——. *Nürnberg.* d.1746. Engraver; designed watch-cases.
WEIHERMANN, Niklaus. *Basle.* 1776. From *St. Gallen.*
WEIJBRANDT—
Nicolas. *Amsterdam.* ca.1700. Fine tortoiseshell br. clock Rijks M. Amsterdam.
Nicolas. *Amsterdam.* ca.1770. Watch mt. S.K.M. Perhaps same as preceding.
WEIJDOGEN, Jan. *Haarlem.* 1783.
WEIJGEL, J. M. *Amsterdam.* Early 19c.
WEINGART, Georg. *Sulzthal.* m.1825.
WEINHARDT, Anton. *Vienna.* m.1781.
WEINMEISTER, Johann. *Würzburg.* m. 1741. From *Vienna.* br. clock.
WEIR—
David. *Glasgow.* 1690.
Robert. *Lanark.* 1798.
WEIS, ——. *Nürnberg.* 1608. Stand clock.
WEISCHER, Jakob Friedthoff. *Copenhagen.* m.1789.
WEISHAUPT, Joseph. *Prague.* ca.1750. sil. repoussé watch. Watch mt. Nat. M. Prague.
WEISKOPF, Franz. *Vienna.* m.1798.
WEISS, Carl. *Stockholm.* 1791-1805.
WEISSE (WEISE)—
Carl Heinrich. *Dresden.* b.1722, m.1756, d. 1784. Gilt en. watch.
Christian Heinrich. *Dresden.* m.1775, d. 1793.
Christian Ehregott. *Dresden.* m.1788, d.1818.
Christian Heinrich, son of Chr. H. *Dresden.* b.1768, m.1803, d.1842. Court C. 1820.
Carl August, bro. *Dresden.* m.1814, d.1860. Balanced hand with watchwork for mysterious clock M.P.S. Dresden.
Joh. Conrad Salomo, bro. *Dresden.* m. 1814, d.1855. Court C. 1845.
WEITNAUER, Hans Jakob. *Basle.* 1679.
WEITZE, Johann Gottlieb. *Berlin.* 1785-1801. C.
WEIZ, ——. ——. Mentioned by Dubois as a 16c. maker, prob. WEIS.
WELAMSON, Eric. *Stockholm.* End 18c. Wall clock.

WELBECK, William. *London.* an.1758. Watch.
WELBORNE, William. *London.* a.1772, CC. 1783-1810.
WELCH—
Jeremiah. prob. *London.* an.1777. Watch.
William. *Plymouth Dock.* an.1781. Watch.
William. *London (Skinner St.).* a.1802, CC. 1811, l.CC.1824.
George. *London.* a.1805.
David. *London.* a.1806.
Elisha N. *Bristol, U.S.A.* b.1809-54.
WELCHER—
Fredric. *Eskilstuna.* 1788-1824. l.c. clock.
G. H. *Eskilstuna.* cà.1800. Three l.c. clocks.
WELCHMAN—
Matthew. *London.* a.1737. Watch.
& PRENTICE. *London.* an.1757. Watch.
WELCOME, John. *London.* a.1697 CC.1705.
WELDON—
Samuel. *London.* ca.1740-80. Watch G.M. g. repoussé watches Carnegie M., Fränkel coll. and M.P.S. Dresden.
John. prob. *London.* an.1762. Watch.
George. *London.* an.1782. Watch.
Joseph Thomas. *London.* a.1792.
WELL, C. *London.* an.1770. Watch.
WELLBRIGHT, W. *London.* 2nd half 18c. Watch.
WELLDON—
I. *London.* ca.1730. Watch mt. A str. rep. al. table clock sd. Weldon, Feill coll. perhaps by him.
W. ——. ca.1780. 3-case watch, Dutch style, M.M.A. p.c. watch.
WELLENIUS, Eric. *Norrköping.* b.1731, d. 1802. Watch with crown and monogram of Gustavus III on cock Chamb. coll. Watches Nord. M. and Nat. M. Stockholm.
WELLER—
John. *London.* a.1694, CC.1713-22. Partner in WELLER & MAGSON.
& MAGSON. *London (Essex St.).* 1710. C.
Henry. *Eastbourne.* an.1760. Watch.
Francis. *Philadelphia.* 1777. From *London.* W.
George. *Exeter.* 18c. l.c. clock.
Thomas. *Croydon.* 1802-24.
Richard. *Croydon.* 1808-11.
WELLINGTON—
John. *London.* a.1717, CC.1726-44.
James. *London.* 1778. Watch Den. coll.
William. *London.* an.1794. Watch.
WELLS—
Joseph. *London.* CC.1668. math. inst. maker.
John. *London.* a.1672, CC.1682-8. l.c. clock.
Jonathan. *London.* a.1676.
William. *London.* CC.1689. Keymaker.
Neddy. *Shipley (Yorks).* 1700.
John. *London.* 1734-ca.1775. Watch mt. Buckley coll.
Charles Penny. *London.* an.1743. Watch.
Francis Gregory. *London (Wood St.).* ca. 1760-73. br. clock. l.c. clock.
Henry. *London.* an.1773. Watch.
John. *Shipston-on-Stour.* d.1810. C. & W. Traded as John WELLS & Co.
Alfred. *Boston, U.S.A.* 1803-05 CC. W.
A. & G. *Boston, U.S.A.* 1806. W.
George. *London.* a.1806, CC.1832.
Thomas. *Banbury.* Early 19c.
J. *London (Goswell St.).* 1817-24.
William. *London.* 1817-24.
Matthew. *Lurgan.* 1824.
WELLSON, R. *London.* an. 1776. Watch.
WELSH—
Edward. *London (Newgate St.).* 1744. d. 1762. Watch. Also WELCH.
Robert. *Dalkeith.* 1768-77. W.

WELSH—*continued*
William. *New York.* 1805. W.
George. *Dalkeith.* 1820.
John. *Glasgow.* 1825.
WELSTEAD, Andrew. prob. *London.* an. 1773. Watch.
WELTIN, Melchior. *Vienna.* 1720-44. Sundial maker.
WELTZIEN, Daniel. *Hamburg.* 1754. d.1771. W. & C. and inst. maker.
WELZ—
Johann. *Fürth.* d.1777.
Joh. F. *Fürth.* d.1826. Pedometer winding watch Nürnberg M.
Joseph. *Vienna.* m.1791.
WENANT, Benjamin. *London.* 1791. Bankrupt. W.
WENDAY, Anne. *London.* a.1685.
WENDEL, Jacob. *Hamburg.* 1821.
WENDELL—
Hyeronimus. *Cologne.* m.1719. Kleinuhrmacher.
Johannes, son. *Cologne.* m.1730.
WENDEROTH, G. F. W. *Eisenbach.* 1804. Pub. Kurze und fassliche Anweisung zu einer zweckmässigen Behandlung der Taschenuhren.'
WENDT, Ernst. *Copenhagen.* m.1791.
WENHAM—
John. *East Dereham.* Mid. 18c.-1795. Watch. l.c. clock ill. Cec. & Web. Wall clock S.K.M.
——. *Bury St. Edmunds.* d.1816. W.
William. *London.* 1799.
A. S. T. *St. Petersburg.* Early 19c. Ruby cyl. rep. watch M.P.S. Dresden.
——. *Paris.* 1812.
William. *Watton.* Early 19c. Watch.
WENKE, G. *Rotterdam.* 1821-30.
WENN, Charles. *Salisbury.* 1795. C.
WENSHIPP, George. *London.* a.1725.
WENSLEY, Edward. *London.* an.1777. Watch.
WENT, Daniel. *London.* a.1693.
WENTRYDGE, Robert. prob. *London.* an. 1772. Watch.
WENTWORTH—
Wombwell. *London.* a.1656.
Thomas. *Salisbury.* an.1707. Watch.
George. *London (Fleet Market).* a.1729, CC. 1738-56.
William. *London.* an.1774. Watch.
George. prob. *London.* an.1774. Watch.
WENTZ, Hilary. *Philadelphia.* 1823.
WENZEL—
Balthazar. *Strasbourg.* 1585.
Matthis. *Strasbourg.* 1636.
A. *Strasbourg.* ca.1660. en. watch Gotha M.
WEPF, Gottlieb. *Basle.* 1760. From *Berne.*
WERDER, Chevalier de. *Berlin.* 1793. mus. clock.
WERGENROTH, Christian. *Frankfurt-a.-M.* Late 18c. l.c. mus. clock Goethe House, Frankfurt.
WERLANDT, Nicolas. *Amsterdam.* 18c. cal. and mus. br. clock.
WERNER—
Caspar. *Nürnberg.* 1528-57. Dopplmayr says he died in 1545. If this be not an error, there was a second maker of the same name in 1557. A locksmith who gained great repute by his small watches (kleine Uhren).
Georg. *Annaberg.* 1599-1605. Made a clock for Leipzig.
——. *Colmar.* 2nd half 18c. mus. clock Colmar M.
WERRLE, Bartholomäus. *Friedberg.* 1732.
WESER, ——. *Prague.* 1581.
WESLAKE (WESTLAKE)—
John. *London.* 1820-40.
Robert. *Plymouth.* Early 19c. Watch N.Y. Univ.

WESSMAN, Hans. *Stockholm.* b.1736, d. 1805. Four br. clocks.
WEST—
Thomas. *London.* a.1687, CC.1695, d.1723.
Thomas. *London.* a.1688, m.1698. l.c. clock Weth. coll. and one ill. Cec. & Web, and watch Den. coll. by him or preceding. Also WEAST and WESTT.
William. *London.* a.1697.
William. *London (Aldermansbury).* CC.1698. Watch.
Thomas. *Reading.* End 17c. Lantern clock N.Y. Univ.
Thomas. *London.* a.1711.
John. *London.* a.1721.
William. *London.* a.1723-76. Bankrupt.
James. *London.* a.1732, CC.1741-65. Watch mt. Ilbert coll.
James. *Sidbury.* ca.1750. C.
Samuel. *Bath.* an.1758. Watch.
Jacob. *London (Ludgate St.).* a.1749, CC. 1757-71.
Samuel. *London (R. Exchange).* l.CC.1766. br. clock. Watch.
——. *Chester.* an.1775. Watch.
William. *London.* a.1774, CC.1782.
Thomas. *Reading.* an.1762-ca.1780. Watch and l.c. clock.
Samuel. *N. Shields.* d.1794. W.
Joseph. *London (New Bond St.).* 1785. W. Left partnership of OLIVER & WEST.
Thomas. *London.* a.1788-1842.
William. *London.* a.1796.
John Gray. *London.* a.1809.
& SON. *Dublin.* Early 19c. g. en. watch.
Thomas G. *Philadelphia.* 1819.
James. *Bolton-le-Moors.* ca.1820.
'WEST END.' Sig. on watches of the LANCASTER, PA., WATCH CO. ca.1878.
WESTBEECH, John. *London.* a.1817.
WESTBERG, Claes. *Västerås.* 1816-46.
WESTBROOK, William. *London.* Early 18c. Watch Den. coll. l.c. clock.
WESTBURY, Edward. *London.* a.1702.
WESTCOTT—
John. *London.* a.1691, CC.1703.
John. *London.* a.1726. l.c. clock.
WESTEN, Robert. *London.* CC.1721.
WESTER, Lorents Adamson. *Stockholm.* 1780-95. Four br. clocks, one in Nord. M.
WESTERMAN—
Jan. *Leeuwarden.* 1743 comp.
Andreas. *Laholm.* 1750-70.
Carl M. *Hälsingborg.* 18c. l.c. clock.
WESTERMANN, E. C. *Rotterdam.* ca.1800.
WESTFIELD—
R. *Louth.* 1796. C. & W.
Robert. *London.* 1813. Patented a cylinder escape wheel with teeth of unequal height to distribute the wear.
WESTIN, William. *London.* a.1776.
WESTLIN, E. *Nätra.* End 18c. Watch.
WESTMAN, Hans. *Stockholm.* 1798. Two wall clocks.
WESTMANN, Christian August. *Dresden.* b. 1773, m.1808, d.1813.
WESTMORE—
Thomas. *Lancaster.* 1708-27.
Robert, son. *Fazakerley* and *W. Derby.* 1761. W. Lancaster freeman.
Daniel. *Macclesfield.* 1763. W.
Robert, son of Rob. *Fazakerley* and *W. Derby.* 1785. W. Lancaster freeman.
Robert. *Preston.* 1821. Watch.
WESTOBY, John. *London.* a.1669, CC.1677-1697. str. chiming clock mt. Watch.
WESTON—
Samuel. *London.* a.1698.
Francis. *London.* a.1732.
Thomas. *Stratford (Essex).* an.1742. Watch.
William. *London (Limehouse).* Mid. 18c. l.c. lacquer clock. Watch.

WESTON—*continued.*
Edward. prob. *London.* an.1755. Watch.
James & Abraham. *Lewes.* 1779. C. & W.
Abraham. *Lewes.* 1783. W.
William. *Newark.* 1790-1820. l.c. clocks.
Robert. *Hastings.* Early 19c. Watch.
John. *London.* 1805-08.
James, son. *Newark.* 1825-40. l.c. clocks.
William. *Sowerby (Yorks).* b.1789, d.1859.
John. *Hastings.* an.1827. Watch.
WESTPHALL, Ferdinand. *Philadelphia.* 1819. W.
WESTRÖM, Eric. *Uppsala.* b.1794, d.1864.
WESTWOOD—
Richard. *London.* a.1684, CC.1691-1710. Lantern clocks. Watch London M.
James. *London.* a.1771.
Robert. *London.* 1820-9. Patented and made 8-day watches.
WETENHALL, Richard. *London.* a.1807-20. Escapement maker.
WETHERED, George. *London.* a.1677.
WETHERELL—
Thomas. *London.* a.1664. Also WETHELL.
& JANAWAY. *London.* 1785-94. g. en. watch, set pearls, M.M.A.
Samuel. *Liverpool.* 1790-6. W. Perhaps same as WEATHERHILT.
WETHERILL, Robert. *London.* a.1698.
WETHERLEY, Henry. *Liverpool.* 1790. W.
WETHERSPON, Alexander. *Haddington.* 1796-1803.
WETTSTRÖM, And. Gust. *Hedemora.* m. 1817-20.
WEYDMANN, Lucas. *Cracow.* 1648. Fine stand clock B.M.
WEYERMAN, J. H. *Ronsdorff.* 1747. Dial maker.
WEYLAND, Nicolaas. *Amsterdam.* 1756. Watch.
WHALEY, Barnaby. *London.* a.1675.
WHALLEY, John. *London.* 1805-08.
WHAM, W. *London.* 1820.
WHARTON—
John. *London.* a.1687.
——. *London (Wardour St.).* d.1772. W.
WHATLEY—
Robert. *London.* 1800-14. W.
Robert, son. *London.* a.1814, CC.1821.
WHEATLEY—
John. *London.* a.1657, CC.1668.
William. *London.* a.1690, CC.1698-1700.
John. *London.* a.1707.
Alexander. *Dublin.* ca.1800.
Charles. *London.* CC.1819.
WHEELER—
Thomas. *London.* a.1647, CC.1655, m.CC. 1684, d.1694. Lantern clock ill. Britten and Cec. & Web.
Vincent. *London.* a.1653.
John, son of Thos. *London.* CC.1680.
Rev. Maurice. ——. Pub. in Phil. Trans. 1684, a desc. of 'A clock descendant on an inclined plane.'
Thomas. *London.* ca.1700. l.c. clock ill. Cec. & Web.
James. *London.* a.1690.
George. *London.* a.1730.
John. *London (Cheapside).* an.1771. Watch.
John. *London (Norton Folgate).* 1772. W.
James. *London.* a.1760.
William. *London.* a.1767, CC.1774. Watch.
Thomas. *London (Oxford St.).* Late 18c.
John. *London.* a.1772-94. Watch Ilbert coll.
Joseph Mort. *London.* a.1783.
'G. M. WHEELER.' Sig. on 1867-75 watches of the NATIONAL WATCH CO. OF CHICAGO.
WHEELHOUSE—
Francis. *Sheffield.* ca.1760. Watch mt. Buckley coll.
——. *London.* an.1772. Watch.

WHEELS, Francis. *Sheffield.* End 18c. Watch Ilbert coll.
WHEELWRIGHT, Oxford. *London.* 1701 CC. Watch.
WHELAN—
Samuel. *Glasgow.* 1810.
Thomas. *Maryborough.* 1824.
WHETHALL, Thomas. *London.* a.1664.
WHEYNARD, Edward. *London.* an.1787. Watch.
WHICHCORD—
William. *Ingatestone.* 1787. C. & W.
J. *Ingatestone (Essex).* Early 19c.
WHICHCOTE—
Samuel. *London (Fleet St.).* a.1716, CC. 1724, m.CC.1748. He, or the following, d.1775. Watch Den. coll.
Samuel. *London.* m.CC.1764, l.CC.1766-9, d.1775.
WHICHELLO, Abiel. *London.* a.1698.
WHILESON, Christopher. ——. Early 18c. Watch Den. coll.
WHINFIELD, Philip. *London.* a.1651.
WHIPHAM, Thomas. *London.* a.1719-75.
WHITAKER—
Edward. *London.* CC.1712. Watch.
Thomas. *London.* a.1748.
Charles. *London.* 1789. W.
Charles, son. *London.* a.1793.
John. *London.* 1799.
William. *London (Camberwell).* 1805-24. Watch.
WHITBREAD, J. *Ampthill.* ca.1800.
WHITBY—
Thomas. *London.* a.1695.
Robert. *London.* a.1771.
John. *Ipswich.* 1789. C. & W.
William. *Cullompton.* 1791-5 CC. l.c. clock.
WHITCHURCH—
Samuel. *Kingswood.* ca.1765. l.c. clock ill. Cec. & Web.
Thomas. prob. *London.* an.1786. Watch.
WHITE—
John. *London.* CC.1646.
Edward. *London.* a.1647.
John. *London.* a.1663, CC.1670-85.
John. *London.* a.1668.
Thomas. *London.* CC.1683-ca.1700. Watch mt. Buckley coll.
John. *London.* a.1684, CC.1692.
Caesar. *London.* a.1684, CC.1692. Cross watch in ivory case, mounted sil., Fränkel coll.
William. *London.* a.1697.
Robert. *London.* a.1701.
Joseph. *London.* CC.1714, d.1766. g. p.c. watch.
Amos. *London.* a.1733, CC.1741-51.
Arthur. *London.* a.1734.
Edward. *Morpeth.* 1751. W.
Thomas. *London.* 1759-71. Watches S.K.M., Carnegie M. and Schloss M. Berlin.
Samuel. *London.* an.1771. Watch.
James. *London.* an.1776-88. Patented the use of an escapement instead of a fly for striking work. Watch.
Joseph. *London.* a.1770.
Thomas Seabrook. *London.* a.1772.
Francis. *Chesterfield.* 1791. C. & W.
Samuel. *Torrington.* 1795. W.
Richard. *London.* a.1788.
Sebastian. *Philadelphia.* 1796. W.
Robert. *Edinburgh.* a.1791-1804.
George. *Bristol.* 1781-1801. C. & W.
Charles. *England.* ca.1805. br. clock.
James. *Paisley.* 1809.
Joseph. *Philadelphia.* 1811-17.
Joseph, junior. *Philadelphia.* 1811-17.
J. *New York.* Early 19c. l.c. clock M.M.A.
——. *Bideford.* Early 19c.
George. *Glasgow.* 1824-49. Watch. N.Y. Univ.
WHITEAR & RAVES. *London.* 1790.
WHITEAVES, Richard. *London.* a.1768, CC. 1788, l.CC.1812-40. Prob. father and son. Watch.
WHITEBREAD, William. *London.* a.1711, CC.1728-53. Watch.
WHITEHALL, Thomas. *Nottingham.* 1814-1818. W.
WHITEHEAD—
Richard. *Reading.* 1648. Lantern clock.
Charles. *London.* a.1663.
Richard. *London.* a.1663, CC.1671-93.
Simon. *London.* a.1677.
Samuel, jun. *Braintree.* ca.1690. Watch.
Charles, son of Rich. *London.* a.1693.
Samuel. *London.* a.1703.
Thomas. *London.* 1695-1725. Insolvent.
Edward. *Wetherby.* ca.1770-91. l.c. clock. Watch.
Robert. *Edinburgh.* a.1770.
William. *Stratford-on-Avon.* 1795. C. & W.
Joseph. *Liverpool.* 1796-1829. W.
Thomas. *Warley (Yorks).* mar.1802.
Robert. *London.* 1809-25.
Thomas. *Wetherby.* Early 19c. Watch.
WHITEHEAR, Richard. *London* and *Reading.* CC.1648. Lantern clock.
WHITEHOUSE, Joshua. *London.* d.1773. W.
WHITEHURST—
John. *Derby* and *London.* b.1713, d.1788. F.R.S. An eminent maker of turret and other clocks. l.c. clock M.M.A. Wall clock ill. Cec. & Web.
Egerton. *Congleton.* 1791. C. & W.
& SON. *Derby.* 1805-46. Invited to tender for Big Ben clock, Westminster. Lever watch mt. Ilbert coll.
WHITELAW—
James. *Edinburgh.* b.1776, d.1846.
David. *Edinburgh.* 1815-25. A maker of repute. Pub. in Edinburgh Phil. Jl. 1823 'An account of a new escapement.'
Alexander. *Edinburgh.* 1824.
& FLETCHER. *Edinburgh.* 1824.
WHITEMAN, Thomas. *London.* 1706-32 CC. Watch.
WHITERNE, Johnson. *Abingdon.* 1791. Inn clock.
WHITESIDE—
Thomas. *Liverpool.* 1777-1805. W.
James. *Ormskirk.* ca.1820.
WHITEWAY, John. *Killyshandra.* 1824.
WHITFIELD—
Edward. *London.* a.1655, CC.1663-1700. Also WHITEFIELD.
Robert. *West Derby.* 1704. W.
James. *Liverpool.* 1734.
Jonathan. *London.* an.1770. Watch.
WHITFORD—
Samuel. *London.* 1760.
Thomas. *London.* a.1756, CC.1768-1808.
——. *Haverfordwest.* an.1788. Watch.
& SON. *London.* 1809-24.
George, son of Thos. *London (Smithfield Bars).* CC.1810-40. Watch.
Samuel. *London (Soho).* CC.1819-25.
WHITHAM, Jonathan. *Sheffield.* 1770-90. Watch.
WHITHORNE, Gordon & William. *Dublin.* 1780. W.
WHITING, Riley. *Winchester* and *Winsted, U.S.A.* 1800-41. With Luther and Samuel HOADLEY at first. In 1841 sold the business to the Clark and Gilbert Co., now the Gilbert Manufacturing Co. Wooden wall clocks and looking-glass clocks.
WHITLATCH, John. *London.* CC.1637-52.
WHITLEY—
Richard. *London.* b.ca.1725-73. Watch case maker.
William. *London.* 1799.

WHITLOCK (WHITTLOCK)—
James. *London.* a.1697, CC.1704.
George. *London.* a.1703-29. Bankrupt.
James, son of James. *London.* CC.1744.
William. *London.* a.1739. Watch.
WHITLOW, Searle. *London.* a.1819, CC. 1826.
WHITMORE, Samuel. *Daventry.* From 1771. C. & W.
WHITNER, Thomas. *Manchester.* 1800. C.
WHITNEY—
Asa. *New York.* 1805. W.
A. *Enniscorthy.* Early 19c. Watch.
Moses. *Boston, U.S.A.* 1822-5. W.
Ebenezer. *New York.* 1822.
Andrew. *New Ross.* 1824.
WHITTAKER—
Edward. *London.* a.1696, CC.1711.
Samuel. *Middleton (Lancs.).* d.1746. C.
Christopher. *Skipton.* mar.1726, d.1754.
Thomas. *Thorne.* 1750.
James. *London.* an.1775. Watch.
William. *London.* an.1785. Watch.
WHITTHORNE, James. *Dublin.* From 1725. W.
WHITTINGHAM—
William. *London.* 1685. Not CC.
Thomas. *London.* a.1699.
Edward. *London (Oxford St.).* 1761-84. Watch.
John. *London.* 1805-08.
WHITTINGTON, William. *Bristol.* 1812.
WHITTLE—
Thomas. *London.* a.1671, CC.1683-91. Watch.
Angil. *London.* an.1688. Watch.
Peter. prob. *London.* an.1759. Watch.
WHITTON—
Clay. *London.* a.1690, CC.1698-1709.
Corbett. *London.* a.1725.
Richard. *London.* a.1731, CC.1740-8.
WHITWELL—
Car. *London.* 1593-1606. Universal dial Old Ashmolean M.
Robert. *London.* a.1642, CC.1649-73. Britten illustrates a very early minute-hand watch by him, now in Marryat coll.
William. *London.* a.1649.
WHITWICK, John. *London.* an.1783. Watch.
WHITWORTH—
Samuel. *Crankshaw.* d.1711. C.
James. *Lussley.* ca.1775. l.c. clock dial ill. Britten.
WHOLEY, Jonathan. *London.* CC.1825.
WHOOD, Isaac. *London.* a.1680.
WHYATTE, Thomas. *London.* an.1774. Watch.
WIBEL, Johann Friedrich. *Berlin.* 1785-98. C.
WIBERG—
Jonas. *Enköping.* 1787. d.1791. Watch.
Johan. *Norrköping.* 1787-91. Watch.
J. A. *Norrköping.* b.1770, d.1820.
Nils. *Ystad.* b.1781, d.1826.
Carl Gustaf. *Ekenäs.* 1803. Wall clocks.
Anders Petter. *Falun.* 1824-46.
WICHELL, Samuel. *London.* a.1697, CC. 1705-27. l.c. clock. Watch.
WICHENS, John. *London.* a.1749, CC.1755.
WICHERS—
'LUEDER WICHERS,' sig. on German watch, early 18c., Feill coll.
Liebs. *Amsterdam.* 18c. l.c. clock.
WICHMANN, J. C. *Ritzebüttel.* 1821.
WICKERS, John. prob. *London.* an.1796. Watch.
WICKES—
Joseph. *London.* d.an.1786.
John. *London (Cannon St.).* a.1771, l.CC. 1784, d.1807.
Joseph. *London (Islington Rd.).* a.1786, CC.1794.

WICKES—*continued.*
John. *London (Eastcheap).* 1799.
John Haughton, son. *London (Clement's La.).* a.1798, CC.1807, l.CC.1810-40. Watch.
Alfred Nelson, son. *London (Clement's La.).* a.1821, CC.1833.
William Gibson. *London (Bermondsey).* CC. 1814-25.
WICKLANDER, Jonas. *Gränna.* b.1753, d. 1813. Watch.
WICKLIFFE, William. *Liverpool.* 1734.
WICKMAN—
Anders. *Stockholm.* b.1746, d.1796.
Erik. *Stockholm.* 1784.
L. J. *Södertälje.* 1820-30.
WICKS—
William. *London.* an.1762, CC.1771. l.c. clock. Watch.
Thomas. *London (Walthamstow).* 1805-20.
WICKSTEAD (WICKSTED)—
Edward. *London.* 1763-95. g. watch. str., chiming and mus. br. clock ill. Cec. & Web.
H. *London.* an.1788. Watch.
WICKSTEED, Edward. *Wolverhampton* and *Walsall.* 1752.
WICKSTRÖM, Petter. *Stockholm,* b.1776 *Göteborg,* 1808. d.1828.
WIDDOWSON, James. *London.* a.1815.
WIDEMAN (WIDTENMAN)—
Mathias. *Vienna.* m.1657. Trav. clock Feill coll.
Josua. *Basle.* 1670. From *Winterthur.*
Johan. *Stockholm.* 1675. d.1717. German. C. to the King. Three l.c. clocks, one Nat. M. Stockholm. Wall clock Nord. M. ill. Sidenbladh. Six watches. Also WIDMAN. *v.* WIEDEMANN.
Johan, son. *Stockholm.* 1686. m.1716-20.
WIDENHAM, R. *London.* 1824. Gained prize in chron. trial.
WIDMAN (WIDENMANN or WYNMAN)—
Jacob. *Antwerp* and *Mantua.* ca.1570. An ironworker and goldsmith. An exceptionally fine ring watch with enamels in M.M.A. is attributed to him by Dr. Williamson.
Jacob. *Augsburg.* b.1583-1621. In *Mantua* 1608-15.
Jacob, son. *Augsburg.* 1662. d.1664. A leading W. 12-sided watch Nat. M. Stockholm.
Jacob. *Vienna.* m.1762.
Johann. *Vienna.* m.1800.
WIDMARK, Olof. *Umeå.* ca.1800. l.c. clock.
WIEBEL, Friedrich. *Vienna.* Early 19c. Devised watchmaking machines with WACKERHAGEN.
WIEDBERG, Hans. *Copenhagen.* m.1781.
WIEDEKING, Johann Hendrik. *Utrecht.* Came from *Germany* in 1750.
WIEDEMANN—
Johann. ——. ca.1700. Drum watch Adelmann coll. Prob. by WIDEMAN.
Theodor. *Vienna.* ca.1700. Watch with 3 balances geared together Copenhagen M.
WIEGELS, D. *Amsterdam.* 1822.
WIEGERS G. F. *Leens.* ca.1800.
WIELAND—
Johann Georg. *Salem, U.S.A.* ca.1780. br. clock Furt. M.
Edward. prob. *London.* an.1775. Watch.
John. *London.* 1799-1820.
William. *London.* 1817-24.
WIELANDY, Abraham. *Paris.* m.1767-89.
WIER—
Douglas. *London.* 1774. Insolvent. W.
Thomas. *London.* d.an.1809.
Thomas. *London.* a.1809.
WIESE, C. F. *Stockholm.* 1790.
WIET, ——. *London.* ca.1740. en. watch Ilbert coll.
WIFE, John. *London.* Late 17c. Lantern clock Feill coll.

WIGAN, Thomas. *Bristol.* 1760. d.1790. W.
WIGG, William. *Halesworth.* Early 19c. Watch.
WIGGIN, Robert. *Skipton.* 1806. *Colne.* ca. 1820. WIGGAN.
WIGGINS, Francis Smith. *London.* a.1805.
WIGGINTON—
John. *London.* a.1663.
William. *London.* a.1783-1824.
WIGHT—
James. *London.* a.1726.
Thomas. prob. *London.* an.1776. Watch.
James. *London.* 1815-24.
WIGHTMAN—
James. *London.* a.1663, CC.1670-84.
William. *London.* a.1686, CC.1696, d.1744. l.c. clock.
John. *London.* a.1688-1717.
Thomas. *London* (*Lombard St.*). a.1692, CC.1701, m.CC.1737-45. p.c. sil. str. watch G.M. str. watch Ilbert coll.
Samuel. *London.* a.1727.
George, son of Thos. *London.* CC.1738.
John. *London* (*Tower St.*). 1744. W.
Thomas. *London.* 1799-1820. l.c. clock ill. Cec. & Web.
J. *London.* 1817-24.
WIGHTWICK—
John. *London.* 1775. CC.1781-1805. Partner with Moss. Watch Den. coll.
& Co. *London.* 1780. en. watch London M.
& Moss. *London.* 1788-1836. Watches G.M. and N.Y. Univ.
WIGNALL (WIGNELL), John *Ormskirk.* ca.1770-95. l.c. clock.
WIGSON—
William. *London.* CC.1781, l.CC.1792.
William. *Colchester.* 1792-1825 CC.
WIJBRANDTS (WIBRANTS, WILBRANDT, VIBRANDI)—
Wijbe. *Leeuwarden* 1601. 'Cleyn Uurwerckmaker.' Fine eng. astro. watch Willet-Holthuizen M. Amsterdam.
Jacob. *Leeuwarden.* 1640. crys. oct. watch B.M. Watch M.M.A.
WIJERS, Jan. *Haarlem.* 1786.
WIJLANT, ——. *Amsterdam.* ca.1750. l.c. clock.
WIJNGAARDEN—
——. *Leeuwarden.* 1777.
Folkert. *Sneek.* Late 18c. A maker of the same name at *Franeker.* Watches.
WIKELMAN, James. *London.* Mid. 18c. p.c. g. repoussé watch Wilsdorf coll.
WIKLANDER, B. *Stockholm.* 1756. Watch.
WILCKY, Daniell. *Basle.* 1769. From *Greiffenberg.*
WILCOCKS (WILCOCK, WILCOX)—
Thomas. *London.* a.1716-48 CC.
Daniel, son. *London* (*Aldersgate St.*). a.1748, CC.1757-72.
James. *London* (*Fleet Market*). 1818.
WILCOCKSON—
Henry. *Liverpool.* 1821-9. W.
James. *Liverpool.* 1821. C.
WILD (WILDE)—
——. *Augsburg.* 2nd half 17c.
Hans Jakob. *Basle.* 1687. From *Berne.* al. watch Ilbert coll.
Stephen. *London.* a.1732.
George. *London.* a.1755.
Thomas. *London* (*Borough Market*). a.1755, C.C.1766. Watch.
Michael. *Wakefield.* ca.1770-90.
Thomas. *Reading.* From 1775-99. Lacquer inn clock.
Joseph. *Macclesfield.* 1782-1814. Watch mt. Glasgow Art Gall.
James William. *London.* 1790-1808.
Samuel. *London.* ca.1800-40. Watch. Horstmann coll.
J. *Ghent.* Early 19c. Wooden aut. clock ill. M. des Aut.

WILDER—
Richard. *London* (*Conduit St.*). l.CC.1776. Partnership of FLADGATE & WILDER dissolved 1775. Watch.
William. *London.* an.1760-88. Watch.
Joshua. *Hingham, U.S.A.* 1780-1800. l.c. clock M. of Fine Arts, Boston, ill. Milham.
John, son of William. *London* (*Seward St.*). a.1782, CC.1790. cf. WYLDER.
WILDERS, J. *London.* ca.1780. Perhaps a fictitious name. Many Dutch style watches G.M., Den. coll., Chamb. coll. l.c. clock and watch Stads M. Amsterdam.
WILDMAN, William. *London.* 1804-09. C.
WILDT, Georg. *Frankfurt.* 1589. Small sq. stand clock Arts M. Prague.
WILEY (WILLEY)—
John. *London* (*Islington*). an.1752-78. Watch.
D. *London.* an.1773. Watch.
——. *London* (*Edmonton*). ca.1800.
Alexander. *Lisburn.* 1824.
WILFORD, Joseph. *London.* a.1792.
WILFRED, Gil. *Winster.* 1795. W.
WILHELM DER WERKMEISTER. *Basle.* 1500-25. Renewed clock in St. Martin's Church.
WILKES—
Elias. *London.* a.1715.
Thomas. *London.* an.1766. Watch. C.
John. *London* (*Grub St.*). 1772. W.
Thomas. *Stratford-on-Avon.* 1789. C.
——. *Evesham.* 1795. C. & W.
Charles. *London.* 1802-08.
Henry. *Bristol.* 1812.
WILKIE—
Robert. *Cupar-Fife.* 1792-1830.
Robert. *London.* CC.1819.
WILKIESON, John. *Kendal.* 1771.
WILKINS—
Robert. *London* (*R. Exchange*). a.1660, CC.1670, d.1706. Watch Liverpool M.
John. *Leicester.* an.1689-1729. Insolvent. C.
Thomas. *London.* a.1693.
Speed. *London.* a.1694, CC.1704.
——. *Devizes.* Early 18c. Watch.
Jeremiah. *London.* a.1721.
——. *Yoel.* 1731. W.
James. *London* (*Islington*). 1744. W.
Jonathan. *London* (*Plumbtree Ct., Holborn*). a.1744, CC.1753-65.
Joseph. *London.* a.1750.
John. *London* (*Islington*). 1773. Watch.
John. *London.* a.1773.
William. *London.* CC.1784, l.CC.1794-1840.
George. *Oxford.* From 1786-98. C & W.
George. *London.* 1809-24.
WILKINSON—
Edward. *London.* a.1655.
John. *Leeds.* 1695.
Joseph. *Newcastle-o.-T.* an.1717. Watch.
William. *London.* CC.1718-23. sil. p.c. watch S.M.S.K.
Robert. *London.* a.1732.
William. *London.* CC.1749.
Thomas. *York.* 1750. d.1776. C.
William. *Congleton.* d.1780. C.
Martine de. *London.* an.1767. Watch.
William. *Wigton.* an.1786. Watch.
William. *Penrith.* ca.1790 CC.
S. *Coventry.* 1795. C. & W.
Timothy. *London.* Late 18c. and early 19c. str. watch London M.
J. *Pontypool.* ca.1800.
Joseph. *Hexham.* mar.1809. W.
William. *Leeds.* 1809.
Joseph. *London.* Early 19c. Watch.
John. *Leicester.* 1815-26. C. & W.
James. *London* (*Castle St., Holborn*). CC. 1816-22.
John. *Leeds.* Early 19c.-1836. Watch.

WILKINSON—*continued.*
Joseph. *Penrith.* 1820.
Thomas. *Liverpool.* 1825 W.
William. *Liverpool.* 1825. W.
John Nettleship. *London.* a1819.

WILL—
Johannes. *Heidelberg.* Early 17c. Clock.
LES FRÈRES. *Heidelberg.* ca.1700. Watch, en. portrait on cock, Fränkel coll.
Johann. *Heidelberg.* Early 18c. Fine watch Cassel Landes-M.
Alexander. *Huntly.* 1822.

WILLANS—
Joseph. *London.* 1785-1807 CC.
William. *London.* 1792 l.CC., d.1810.
William, son of Jos. *London* (*City Rd.*). a. 1800, CC.1807, l.CC.1810.
William, son. *London.* a.1807.

WILLARD—
Alexander. *London.* a.1717.
Benjamin. *Grafton, Lexington* and *Roxbury, U.S.A.* b.1743, d.1803. l.c. clocks and mus. clocks. Also WILLIARD.
Simon, bro. *Grafton* and *Roxbury.* b.1753, d.1848. Made l.c. clocks and in 1801 invented the 8-day banjo clock and discontinued l.c. clocks. Made turret clock for the University of Virginia at Charlottsville.
Aaron, bro. *Roxbury* and *Boston, U.S.A.* b.1757, d.1844. *Boston* in 1800. Simon was the most important maker of the three brothers, who were famous in Massachusetts. They made a few l.c. clocks and high mantel or shelf clocks, but mainly 'banjo' clocks, with a circular top, narrow trunk, and wide rectangular base. Many ill. Milham. Succeeding members of the family are among the following.
——. *Philadelphia.* 1778. W. Also WILLAR.
Ephraim. *Medford, Roxbury* and *New York.* b.1755-1805. l.c. clocks.
John. *Boston, U.S.A.* 1803. W.
& NOLAN. *Boston.* 1806. C.
Simon, son of Simon. *Boston.* b.1795. W. In Boston from 1828.
Benjamin, son of Simon (1). ——. ca.1825.
Aaron, son of Aaron. *Roxbury* and *Boston.* 1816-63. C. Continued his father's business.

WILLATS, John. *London.* 1759. d.1762. Watch Ilbert coll.

WILLCOCKS—
John. *London* (*Old St. Sq.*). 1760-73.
Daniel. *London* (*Clerkenwell*). an.1774. Watch.
Richard, son of John. *London* (*Clerkenwell*). CC.1782, d.1822. C.
Charles, son. *London.* a.1797.
Thomas. *London* (*St. Martin's La.*). 1805.
Thomas. *London* (*Goswell St.*). CC.1819-24.
Thomas. *London* (*Holborn*). 1820.

WILLEBRAND, Johann Martin. *Augsburg.* 1682. d.1726. Dials B.M., M.M.A., Old Ashmolean M. and Stuttgart M. Pedometer Old Ashmolean M.

WILLER—
Caspar. *Augsburg.* 1704.
Caspar. *Augsburg.* m.ca.1805.

WILLETT—
James. *London.* 1730. l.c. clock. Watch Den. coll.
John. prob. *London.* an.1766. Watch.
Humphrey. *London.* a.1766.

WILLEUMIER FRÈRES. *Tramelan.* 1801. 8-day watch G.M.

WILLIAMS—
Peter. *London.* 1662.
John. *Leeds.* 1700.
Thomas. *London.* a.1689.
Thomas. *London.* a.1699.
Charles. *London.* a.1713.
Lewis. *London.* a.1715.

WILLIAMS—*continued.*
Samuel. *London.* a.1739.
Rees. *Cwmwysg, Brecknock.* 1737-1827. l.c. clock.
Thomas. *Chepstow.* 1750-85. From *Bristol.*
Thomas. *Llancarfan.* Mid. 18c. br. clock.
John. *London.* a.1746, CC.1753-63.
Thomas. *Haverfordwest.* 1756-ca.1810. Watches and l.c. clocks Nat. M. Cardiff.
Abraham. *Winchester.* an.1758. Watch.
Thomas. *London.* a.1754.
Grismond. *Carmarthen.* 1763. d.an.1784.
P. *London.* an.1767. Watch.
Edward. *London.* an.1768. Watch.
Peter. *Dunfermline.* b.1745, d.1768.
David. *Enfield.* a.1759-74.
Robert. *London* (*Strand*). a.1760-84. W.
John. *London.* CC.1768-1802.
John. *London* (*Unicorn Ct.*). 1770.
David. *Neath.* 1770-82.
Benjamin. prob. *London.* an.1771. Watch.
H. prob. *London.* an.1772. Watch.
Henry. *Llancarfan.* 2nd half 18c. l.c. clocks.
Charles. *London* (*Aldersgate St., Silver St.* and *Monkwell St.*). a.1763, CC.1771-8, d.an.1787 W.
Letitia. *London.* a.1763.
William. *Cwmwysg, Brecknock.* 1774-1825.
& SHARP. *London.* 1774. Succeeded NODES.
Evan. *Neath.* 1775.
William. *Liverpool.* 1775. W.
Gresham. *London.* a.1767.
John. *London.* a.1768.
James. *Bristol.* an.1776. Watch.
William. *Dublin.* 1777. Watch N.Y. Univ.
M. *Dublin.* an.1778. Watch.
George. prob. *London.* an.1780. Watch.
Evan. *Newport, Wales.* ca.1780-1830. l.c. clocks.
George. *Bristol.* 1782-1830.
Thomas. *London.* 1780-96. Watch London M.
John. *London.* a.1773.
John Abraham. *London.* a.1777.
William. *London* (*Strand*). 1781-90.
Thomas. *London.* a.1781.
John. *Liverpool.* 1790. C.
Thomas. *Axbridge.* 1791. W.
George. *Axbridge.* 1791-5. W.
J. *Kings Lynn.* 1791-5. W.
Robert. *Bristol.* 1792. C. & W.
John. *London.* a.1782, CC.1792.
Alexander. *Chichester.* CC.1790, l.CC.1798, d.1811.
Griffith. *Newport, Wales.* 1793-5. l.c. clock.
Thomas. *Beaumaris.* Late 18c. l.c. clock.
John. *London.* a.1784, CC.1796.
James. *London.* a.1785.
James. *London* (*Goodge St.*). 1794. Watch Den. coll.
John. *London* (*Charles St.*). 1799.
John. *London* (*Shoreditch*). 1799-1804.
John. *London* (*St. Pancras*). 1800.
George. *Bristol.* 1801-30.
Charles, son of Charles. *London.* a.1790.
George, bro. *London* (*Monkwell St.*). a. 1793, CC.1801, l.CC.1813.
William. *Carmarthen.* ca.1800-47. l.c. clock. Watch Nat. M. Cardiff.
John. *London* (*Goodge St.*). 1802-08.
George. *London.* a.1797.
John James. *London.* a.1800.
William. *London* (*Islington*). 1805-08.
William. *London* (*Paradise La.*). 1805-08.
Thomas. *London* (*Hoxton*). 1805-07.
William. *London* (*Hoxton*). 1808.
Owen. *Penrhyn-dendraeth.* 1809. l.c. clock.
Richard. *Bristol.* 1813-18. C.
John. *London.* a.1808, CC.1815.
R. *Liverpool.* 1815. Watch N.Y. Univ.
Robert. *Wrexham.* Early 19c. Watch.
'E. S. WILLIAMS.' Sig. on 1871-4 watches of the CORNELL WATCH CO.

WILLIAMSON—
William. *London.* a.1655, CC.1663, d.an. 1679.
Robert. *London* (*near R. Exchange*). a.1658, CC.1666, m.CC.1698-1714. Watch, shagreen case, B.M. Watch, white agate, M.M.A. Watch Den. coll.
Thomas. *London.* CC.1668-84. Watch en. by Huaud le puisné Wilsdorf coll.
John. *London.* CC.1682. l.c. clock.
Joseph. *London* (*Clements La.*). a.1686, m. CC.1724, d.1725. W. to the King of Spain. An eminent maker; claimed the invention of equation mechanism in a paper to the Roy. Soc. Two l.c. clocks and l.c. equation and cal. clock Weth coll. g. repoussé watch Fränkel coll. Pair en. watches Palace M. Pekin.
William. *London.* CC.1689-ca.1710. Watch Glasgow Art Gall.
Samuel. *Cronton.* d.1726. W.
John. *Leeds.* ca.1700. Watch S.K.M. l.c. clock.
Edward. *London.* a.1687. l.c. clock.
John. *London.* a.1692.
Thomas. *London.* a.1695.
Michael, son of Robert. *London.* CC.1714.
William. *London.* a.1717.
Ralph. *London.* 1723. Insolvent.
J. W. *London.* ca.1730. l.c. clock.
John. *Liverpool.* 1st half 18c. Watch, sun and moon hour indicators, Den. coll.
Christopher. *London.* a.1729.
Dom. *Cadiz.* Mid. 18c. sil. al. watch, shagreen case, formerly in Shandon coll.
Rice. *London.* ca.1740.
A. prob. *London.* an.1754. Watch.
Thomas. *London.* a.1746.
John. *Edinburgh.* a.1750.
——. *Ulverstone.* 1762. W.
J. *London.* 1763. g. shagreen p.c. watch Ilbert coll.
John. *Bold.* 1765. W.
Timothy. *London.* 1769-88. Fine sil. p.c. en. mus. c.secs. watch made for Emperor of China Carnegie M Pair agate flasks with watches Peiping M. Four mus. aut. clocks and a mus. clock with aut. figure writing in Chinese characters Palace M. Pekin.
William. *Whitehaven.* an.1775. Watch.
James. prob. *London.* an.1775. Watch.
Shaw. *Dublin.* an.1777-95. Watch Ilbert coll.
George. *London.* 1780-1819. W.
John. *Edinburgh.* a.1778-1825.
Charles James. *London.* a.1795.
W. Williamson. *Penrith.* ca.1800.
Anthony. *London.* a.1811.
George. *Leith.* 1819.
John. *Warrington.* ca.1820.
Christopher. *London.* CC.1821. W.
James. *Dundee.* 1824.
Robert. *Falkirk.* 1825-37.

WILLIAMSTON, Ralph. *London.* a.1699, CC.1706-49. Watch S.K.M.

WILLIARME, Pierre. *London.* 1623. CC. 1648. Native of *Geneva.* Also WIELLERME.

WILLIEUMIER ET AMEZ-DROZ. *Geneva* or *London.* Early 19c.

WILLIN, William. *London.* 1800. CC.1807, l.CC.1810.

WILLINGHAM, John. *London.* 1809-11.

WILLINGTON—
& Co. prob. *London.* an.1769. Watch.
J. prob. *London.* an.1791. Watch.

WILLIS—
Ambrose. *London.* a.1687.
William. *London.* 1716 CC.
George. *London.* a.1716.
Richard Ockshut. *London.* a.1752, CC.1760.
James. *Brighthampton.* an.1775. Watch.
John. *Brighthampton.* an.1775. Watch.

WILLIS—*continued.*
Jacob. *Frome.* 1795. W.
Edward. *Liverpool.* 1825. W.

WILLMAN—
Georg. *Neustadt.* 1740.
Gallus. *Cologne.* 1797.

WILLMORE, William. prob. *London.* an. 1772. Watch.

WILLOUGHBY—
John. *London.* a.1676.
Benjamin. *London.* a.1676.
John. *London.* a.1679, CC.1686-1710.
John. *London.* a.1704, CC.1711-28.
Benjamin. *Bristol.* 1700-65. Watches Ilbert and Den. colls.
John. *Norwich.* 1st half 18c. Watch.
——. *Windsor.* Early 19c. Watch.

WILLOWE (WELLOWE)—
Christopher. *Leominster.* ca.1600. C.
John, son. *London.* a.1609, BC.1617, w.CC. 1632, m.CC.1635. Scallop-shell watch B.M. Oval watch Blot-Garnier coll.

WILLS—
John. *London.* a.1682.
William. *London.* a.1702.
Edmund. *Salisbury.* ca.1730. Wall clock.
Edward. *London.* a.1755.
John. *London* (*St. John's La.*). a.1758, CC. 1770, d.1824.
Ann. prob. *London.* an.1774. Watch.
Richard. *Truro.* an.1777-95. Watch. l.c. clock ill. Cec. & Web.
Robert. *Carrick-on-Shannon.* 1824.

WILLSHIRE—
James. *London.* a.1750-81. l.c. clock.
Thomas. *Bristol.* 1777. Dissolved partnership with T. LINK.

WILLSTEAD, Edward. prob. *London.* an. 1778. Watch.

WILMEAU, Antonio. *Cambrai.* 1696. In charge of cathedral clock.

WILMOT—
George. *London.* a.1651, CC.1670.
Thomas. *London.* a.1653.
Isaac. *London.* a.1662.
Stephen. *London.* a.1667, CC.1674-1713. l.c. clock. Watch.
John. *London.* 1679. W.
John. *London.* a.1676.
Thomas. *London.* CC.1715-24.
——. *London* (*Upper Rosoman St.*). ca.1810. br. clock ill. Cec. & Web.
Richard Frederick. *London.* 1820.

WILMSHURST (WILMHURST)—
Thomas. *London.* a.1713.
Thomas. *Deal.* Retired 1764.
Stephen. *Odiham.* Went to *Reading.* 1755.
& SON. *Brighton.* 2nd half 18c. Watch mt.
——. *Chichester.* ca.1790 CC.
Stephen. *Basingstoke.* 1791. W.
Stephen. *Burwash.* 1797. W.
Thomas. *Brighton.* 1799. C. & W.
Joseph. *Brighton.* 1822. C. & W.

WILMURT, Stephen. *New York.* 1805. W.

WILS, Pieter. *Haarlem.* 1661.

WILSMAN—
J. *London.* an.1742. Watch.
Thomas. *London.* 1729-Mid. 18c. sil. watch en. scenes inside and outside case.

WILSON—
Richard. *York.* 1586. C.
William, son. *York.* 1607. C.
John. *London.* Mid. 17c. Oval sil. eng. watch.
Thomas. *London* (*R. Exchange*). a.1651, CC.1659-94. Watch.
Nathaniel. *London.* a.1658.
Edward. *London.* a.1663, CC.1670-82.
Joseph, bro. of Thos. *London.* 1686 CC.
George. *London.* a.1681, CC.1692-1700.
William. *London.* a.1686, CC.1693-1712.
Thomas. *Warwick.* 1709.

WILSON—*continued.*
Joshua. *London* (*Lombard St.* in 1712, *Clement's La.* in 1720). a.1688-1733 CC. l.c. clock Weth. coll. and one ill. Cec. & Web. Lantern clock. Watch S.M.S.K. Also WILLSON.
Laurence. *London.* a.1700.
——. *Warwick.* 1709.
John. *London.* a.1707, CC.1714-32. Watch Den. coll.
James. *London* (*Guildhall*). a.1707, CC. 1723-59.
John. *Edinburgh.* a.1708-14.
John. *Dublin.* 1st half 18c. p.c. watch.
John. *London.* a.1720.
George. *London* (*Strand*). a.1721, CC.1730, d.1774.
Robert, son of Josh. *London.* CC.1733. Watch.
William. *London.* a.1732.
John. *London.* a.1733-72. Watch.
James. *Nuneaton.* 1742.
James. *London* (*Cateaton St.*). 1743. Watch.
Charles. *London.* a.1734.
Robert. *Moorhouse* (*Yorks*). 1750.
James. *Askrigg.* d.1786.
Thomas. *Edinburgh.* a.1742.
Richard. *London* (*Cheapside*). an.1751, d. 1764. Watch.
Henry. prob. *London.* an.1753. Watch.
James. *Belfast.* 1755. mus. clock.
John. *Belfast.* ca.1757.
William. *Kendal.* 1759. C.
S. prob. *London.* an.1762. Watch.
Alexander. *Cardiff.* 1761-80.
George. *Edinburgh.* a.1760.
Nicholas. *Kendal.* ca.1770-95. W.
John. *Ulverstone.* ca.1770-95. C.
Benjamin. *London.* ca.1770. l.c. clock. Watch.
Alexander. *London* (*Drury La.*). an.1772, CC.1781-94. g. watch.
E. *London.* an.1773. Watch.
Christopher. *London* (*Clerkenwell*). 1775. Bankrupt. W.
James. *Hawick.* 1775. Bankrupt. W.
James. *Norwich.* an.1778. Watch.
Nicholas. *Askrigg.* mar.1778. 'Eminent C.'
Charles. *Dublin.* an.1780. Watch.
James. *Ettrick.* b.1748, d.1821.
Hugh. *Edinburgh.* a.1772-80.
John. *Newcastle-o.-T.* 1778-90.
Titus. *Kendal* and *Leeds.* 1779-96. C. Lancaster freeman.
Christian. *London.* a.1773.
James. *London* (*Westminster*). CC.1781-1824.
James. *Newcastle-o.-T.* 1782-4.
William. *Cambridge.* 1784.
William. *Jamaica.* From 1784-9. From *London.*
James. *Stamford.* 1786-95. C. & W.
William. *London.* End 18c. l.c. chiming clock.
Thomas. *Guisborough.* 1790-1825. l.c. clock. Later T. & J.
John. *London.* a.1787.
Thomas. *London.* a.1787, CC.1807.
Robert. *London.* a.1788.
John. *Peterborough.* 1795. W.
Ralph. *Stamford.* 1795. W.
William. *Cardiff.* 1795. C. & W.
Thomas. *Grantham.* 1795. W.
James. *Liverpool.* 1796. W.
Richard. *Liverpool* (*Oldhall St.*). 1796. W.
Richard. *Liverpool* (*Dale St.*). 1796. W.
James. *London* (*Drury La.*). 1799.
Richard. *Liverpool.* 1800-29.
James. *London* (*Threadneedle St.*) CC.1802-1809. W.
——. *Cambridge.* 1802. W.
Edward. *London.* a.1798.

WILSON—*continued.*
William. *London.* 1805-11.
James. *London.* a.1800.
William. *London.* CC.1809. W.
James. *London* (*Sweeting's Alley*). 1809-11.
J. T. *Stamford.* Early 19c.
H. *London.* Early 19c.
Joseph. *Chichester.* Early 19c.
——. *London* (*Stoke Newington*). Early 19c.
William. *Falmouth, Jamaica.* Early 19c.
Titus. *Manchester.* 1813. C.
Charles. *London.* a.1811, CC.1824.
Thomas. *Dublin.* 1824.
Robert. *Belturbet.* 1824.
Richard. *Lincoln.* ca.1825. Watch.
Edmund. *Sheffield.* 1825.
Gustavus. *Liverpool.* 1825. C.

WILTER, John. *London.* ca.1775. Many Dutch-type watches G.M., London M., Den. coll., Marryat coll., Carnegie M. Perhaps a fictitious name.
WILTON, John. *London.* an.1775. Watch.
WILTSHIRE—
William. *London.* an.1787. Watch.
Thomas. *London.* a.1780.
WIMBLE, George. *Ashford.* From 1740. From *Faversham.*
WIMEN, George. *Philadelphia.* 1820. W.
WIMER, Andrew. *Philadelphia.* 1819. W.
WINCH—
Amos. *London.* a.1670, CC.1677-90.
John. *Reading.* From 1772. Also at *Wokingham.* From *London.* Watch.
Richard. *Reading.* From 1817.
WINCKLES, John. *London.* 1782. Watch Den. coll.
WINDEMAKER, Nikolaus. *Münster.* 1540. Made Dom clock to design of the monk Joannes Aquensis.
WINDER—
——. *Stroud.* 1733. Also WINDOW.
Thomas. *Lancaster* and *Garstang.* 1784-1814.
——. *Canterbury.* Early 19c.
Stephen. *Lancaster.* 1823. W.
Thomas, son of Thos. *Lancaster.* 1825.
WINDING, J. L. *Göteborg.* b.1790, d.1833.
WINDISCH, Joh. Paulus. *Fürth.* d.1750.
WINDLE—
Thomas. *London.* an.1777. Watch.
G. *London.* an.1782. Watch.
WINDMILLS—
Joseph. *London* (*Tower St.*). CC 1671, m. CC.1702-23. A very fine maker of clocks and watches. Watches generally sd. 'Joseph Windmills' to late 17c. Entered into partnership with his son Thos. about 1700, watches then being generally sd. 'Windmills.' Three l.c. clocks Weth. coll. Watch with sun and moon hour indicator B.M. str. watches G.M. and Den. coll. Watch Ilbert coll. with arms of William III. l.c. clock M.M.A. Lantern clock Feill coll. br. clock ill. Cec. & Web. Fine crys. and sil. crucifix clock with turning hour globe above. l.c. clock M.M.A.
Thomas, son. *London* (*Tower St.*). a.1686, CC.1695, m.CC.1719-32. Worked alone for a short time and then entered into partnership with BENNETT. Fine niello rep. watch and mt. G.M. p.c. watch S.M.S.K. Watches M.M.A. and Feill coll.
& BENNETT. *London* (*Tower St.*). ca.1725-1729. l.c. clock ill. Cec. & Web. Watch with mt. under glass.
& WIGHTMAN. *London.* ca.1725. l.c. clock ill. Cec. & Web.
& ELKINS. *London.* ca.1730. l.c. lacquer clock ill. Cec. & Web.
Tiger. *London.* an.1766. Watch.
John. *London.* an.1775. Watch.
——. ——. 1789. Watch Den. coll.

WINDON, Daniel. *London.* a.1707, CC.1718-1734. Also WINTON.
WINDOW, David. *London.* CC.1718. Watch.
WINDSOR—
Robert. *Lymington.* an.1753. Watch
James. *London.* a.1778, CC.1787-96. Watch.
WINEROW, William. *London.* CC.1718-38. Watch mt.
WING, Mark. *London.* CC.1811-24. W.
WINGATE, Paine. *Boston, U.S.A.* 1789. *Newburyport,* 1803.
WINGFIELD, Mary. *London.* a.1746.
WINGHAM—
John. *London.* CC.1785-1800.
John. *London.* a.1800.
WINHURST, Joseph. *London.* a.1695.
WINK, John. *London.* an.1762. Watch.
WINKLER (WINCKLER)—
Johann Wolfgang. *Vienna.* m.1682. Also WINKHLER.
Joh. Georg. *Augsburg.* 1760 comp., m.1768.
Johann Michael. *Augsburg.* comp. ca.1775, m.1781. Left *Augsburg* 1786.
WINNELL, ——. prob. *London.* an.1731. Watch.
WINNERL, Joseph Thaddeus. *Paris.* b.1799, d.1886. Came to *Paris* 1829. An eminent maker of watches and chronometers. Invented a split-seconds mechanism for chronographs. Astro. clock Paris Observatory. Marine chron. C.A. & M.
WINNOCK—
Joshua. *London.* a.1664, CC.1672-1723.
Daniel, son. *London.* a.1695, CC.1707.
Joshua. *London.* a.1716.
WINQVIST, Johann N. *St. Petersburg.* 2nd half 18c. cyl. watch Ilbert coll.
WINROWE—
William. *London.* CC.1718-34. Watch. Fine br. clock.
Stephen. *London.* a.1719.
WINSMORE—
William. *London.* a.1699, CC.1712.
John. *London.* CC.1712-28. Watch mt. Buckley coll.
WINSON, Thomas. *London.* an.1772. Watch.
WINSTANLEY—
James. *London.* a.1687.
Joseph. *Barnstaple.* 1709.
Jeremiah. *Holywell.* Mid. 18c. l.c. clock.
Henry. prob. *London.* an.1771. Watch.
Peter. *Huyton.* ca.1775. Watch.
Edward. *Liverpool.* 1790-1803.
Alexander. *Wigan.* 1790-1814. l.c. clock.
William. *Mold.* 1790-early 19c. Watch.
Thomas. *Holywell.* 1791-1844. C.
John. *Holywell.* 1791-1835. C. & W.
John. *Liverpool.* 1805. C.
William. *Liverpool.* 1818-29. W.
Edward. *Wigan.* ca.1820.
Robert. *Ormskirk.* ca.1820.
William. *Preston.* 1820. C. & W.
Edward. *Preston.* 1821. C. & W.
WINSTON, William. *Hereford.* 1770. d.1785. W. Succeeded by R. PREECE.
WINT—
Daniel. *London.* a.1693.
Daniel. *London* (*Holborn*). a.1720-53.
George. *London.* a.1732.
A. *London.* an.1755. Watch.
John. *London.* a.1774.
WINTER—
Samuel. *London.* a.1683.
William. *London.* a.1686.
John. *London.* 1728. C.
Thomas. prob. *London.* an.1745. Watch.
Francis. *London.* a.1742.
John. *London.* a.1777.
F. *London* (*Bloomsbury*). 1799. Prob. Francis. Wooden C.
Abraham. *Hereford.* 1800. C. & W.
——. *London* (*Mile End Green*). ca.1800.

WINTER—*continued.*
J., & Co. *London* (*Bloomsbury*). 1802-24. Wooden C.
Georg Ernst Gotthelf. *Dresden.* m.1808, d. 1856. Town C.
Robert. *London.* 1820.
Vitus, & Co. *London* (*Bloomsbury*). 1820-5. Wooden C.
Thomas. *Liverpool.* 1825. W.
WINTERBOTHAM, ——. *Stockport.* 1791. W.
WINTERBOURN, Thomas. *London.* 1805-1808. C.
WINTERHALDER, Martin. *Schwarzwald.* ca.1750.
WINTHER, P. F. *Copenhagen.* m.1811.
WINTWORTH, Thomas. *Salisbury.* ca.1780. br. clock.
WIRGMAN, G. *London.* 1790-1825. g. en. watch.
WIRRALL, Copley. *London.* a.1657, CC.1647. Also WYRALL.
WIRTH—
Heinrich. *Nürnberg.* Burgher 1560. 'Ormacher.'
Franz Bernhard. *Würzburg.* 1772m.-1780. C.
WIRTZ (WIRZ, WÜRZ), Johann Jakob. *Augsburg.* b.1725, m.1753, d.1771. From *Zürich.* aut. maker.
WISDEN, Edward. *Brighton.* 1822. C. & W.
WISE (WYSE)—
John. *London.* a.1638, CC.1646, d.an.1694.
William. *Wantage.* 1660-1703. Lantern clock.
John. *London.* CC.1669-1718. Clock.
Richard, son of John (1). *London.* a.1671, CC.1679, d.an.1690.
John, bro. *London.* a.1675, CC.1683-1723. Two l.c. clocks ill. Cec. & Web.
Luke. *Reading.* 1686-ca.1710. Watch and l.c. clocks.
Thomas, son of John. *London.* a.1678, CC. 1686-1704. l.c. clock. Watch.
Joseph, bro. *London.* a.1678, CC.1687.
Cadwallader. *London.* a.1679.
Peter. *London* (*Cheapside*). CC.1693, m.CC. 1725-41. br. clock ill. Britten. Watch Stads M. Amsterdam.
Luke, son of John. *London.* CC.1694-98.
Robert, bro. *London.* a.1680, CC.1695-1705. Watch.
John. *London.* a.1698, CC.1710.
Luke, son of Luke. *London.* a.1698.
Mark, bro. *London.* a.1703, CC.1719.
Matthew. *Daventry.* 1786. C. Watch.
William. *Wantage.* 1791. W.
Richard. *Stanford.* an.1799. Watch.
Featherstone. *Hull.* 1822-41.
WISEMAN—
John. *London.* CC.1646.
——. *St. Ives.* an.1752. Watch.
WISENPAINDNER, Georg Ignatz. *Eichstätt.* 1782. Court C.
WISHART, ——. *London.* an.1747. Watch.
WISS—
G. *Geneva.* 1750.
FRÈRES. *Geneva.* ca.1775. g. en. rep. and metal rep. watches Stern. coll. g. rep. watch Den. coll.
ET AMALRIC. prob. *Geneva.* Late 18c. 4-colour g. watch.
Gebrüder. *Geneva.* Early 19c. sil. p.c. watch, painted dial.
F., ET MENU. *Geneva.* Early 19c. Two g. en. watches M.M.A.
WISTHOFF, ——. *Hall.* 1665. Inclined plane clock M.P.S. Dresden.
WISTRAND, Lars. *Sweden.* 18c. Watch.
WISWALL, Thomas. *London.* an.1778-99. Watch.

WITCHELL—
Robert. *London* (*Hatton Garden*). a.1735, CC.1744, l.CC.1766-72.
E. prob. *London*. an.1776. Watch.
WITCHFIELD, John. prob. *London*. an.1782. Watch.
WITGENS, Joan. *Cologne*. m.1702.
WITHAM, Jonathan. *Sheffield*. 1774-97. W.
WITHER—
James. *London*. a.1637.
Richard. *London*. a.1681.
Richard. *London*. a.1682.
John. *London*. CC.1699-1720. l.c. clocks and watch.
WITHERELL, Richard. *London*. a.1699.
WITHERS—
Timothy. *London*. a.1750.
William. *London*. ca.1760. l.c. clock. Watch Glasgow Art Gall.
John. *Greenwich*. 1778. Bankrupt. W.
John. *London* (*Blackfriars*). CC.1790-1816.
W. *Bristol*. Early 19c. Watch.
WITMER, Able. *Ephrata*, *Lancaster*, *U.S.A.* End 18c. Good maker. l.c. clocks.
WITNESS, Francis. *London*. a.1653.
WITNEY, R. *London*. an.1775. Watch.
WITT—
Richard. *London*. 1662.
Abraham. *Thorne*. 2nd half 17c. Table clock Feill coll.
WITTE—
Samuel. *London* (*Westminster*). a.1651, CC. 1660.
Hans. *Copenhagen*. m.1698. Also VIET, VEIT and HUEIT.
Jacob Nicolai. *Copenhagen*. m.1699, d.an. 1741. sil. watch Nat. M. Copenhagen, ill. Liisberg. Also VIET, VEIT and HUEIT.
Johann. *Breslau*. Mid. 18c. Sq. table clock.
Alexander. *Copenhagen*. a.1754.
WITTENBÖCK (WIDENBÖCK), Karl. *Vienna*. m.1817.
WITTINGHAM, William. *London*. a.1721. Watch.
WITTIT, James. *London*. ca.1750-63. Bankrupt. Watch mt. G.M.
WITZ, ——. *Bienne*. Early 19c. Watch.
WIWEL, Christian Henry. *London*. CC.1823.
WIX, William. *London*. a.1705.
WIXHAM, J. B. prob. *London*. an.1763. Watch.
'WM. ELLERY.' Sig. on 1861-79 watches of the AMERICAN WATCH CO.
WOGAN, George, *v.* KINGSMILL.
WOGDEN, Stephen. *Greenwich*. a.1713, CC. 1724. Clock.
WOLBRECHT, Georg. Pub. Leipzig, 1828, 'Die Uhrmacherkunst,' a large work.
WOLF—
C. *Paris*. Early 17c. circ. table clock Bernal sale.
Jeremias. *Vienna*. b.1663, d.1724. aut. maker. Book watch. Clock on pillar Bernal sale. Table clock Webster coll.
Hans Heinrich. *Dresden*. m.1721. From *Hamburg*.
William. *London*. 1784. W.
Daniel. *Basle*. 1790.
WOLFE—
John. *London*. a.1721, CC.1728-55.
Samuel. *London*. a.1762.
WÖLFEL, Johannes. *Vienna*. m.1749.
WOLFERT, ——. *By*. 1st half 18c.
WOLFF—
Franz. *Stadt Bergen* (*Augsburg*). 1756.
Christian. *Pfersee*. 1756. Watch.
August. *Kriegshaber*. 1756-70.
Daniel. *Brünn*. 2nd half 18c. l.c. clock.
Andreas. *Pfersee*. 1770.
Étienne Auguste. *Geneva*. ca.1775-91.
Peter Heinrich. *Berlin*. 1785-1801. C.

WOLFF—*continued.*
Johann Jacob. *Hamburg*. 1801-04.
Peter Hansen. *Denmark*. m.1805.
——. *Paris*. 1822.
WOLFFENBERG, ——. *Habersleben*. 17c. Clock.
WOLFGANG, Johann. *Friedberg*. 1st half 18c. Watch S.K.M.
WOLFORNE, Robert. *London*. 1662.
WOLKENSTEIN, David. *Strasbourg*. 1590. Mathematician. Collaborator with DASYPODIUS. Wrote 'Descriptio astronomici horologii,' in Trin. Coll. Library, Cambridge, about a clock made by Isaac (1) HABRECHT for Fugger.
WOLLASTON, ——. ——. Pub. in Phil. Trans. 1771, 'An account of the going of an Astronomical Clock.'
WOLLER, Matthew. *Birmingham*. 1801-08. C.
WÖLLMER—
Joh. P. *Fürth*. d.1793.
Joh. Mic. *Fürth*. d.ca.1820.
WOLMERSLEY, John. *Huddersfield*. 1787. C.
WOLTERS, Clawes. *Brunswick*. 1535.
WOLVERSTONE—
Thomas. *London*. a.1643, CC.1650, d.an. 1690.
Benjamin. *London*. a.1649, CC.1656-68. al. watch G.M. Watch Gélis coll.
Thomas. *London*. a.1667, CC.1670.
James. *London*. CC.1670-97. Engraver. Also WOLFRESTON.
James. *London*. CC.1690.
Benjamin. *London*. a.1693.
WOMBELL, ——. *London*. Early 19c. Watch.
WOMERSLEY, Masterman. *London*. a.1752.
WONTNER—
John. *London* (*Minories*). CC.1770, l.CC. 1792-6, d.an.1807. A maker of repute. Sd. JNO. RENTOW and JOHN WONTNER. Watches Glasgow Art Gall. and Ilbert coll.
& ANNESS. *London* (*Minories*). 1795.
& KING. *London* (*Shoreditch*). 1799-1804.
John, & Son. *London* (*Minories*). 1805-12.
John, son of John. *London*. a.1798, CC.1807, l.CC.1810.
George, bro. *London*. a.1802.
WOOBORN, George. *London*. 1798. Watch Den. coll.
WOOD—
Richard. *London*. a.1651.
James. *London*. a.1668.
Robert. *London* (*St. Dunstan's*). CC.1670, mar.1674-82. Watch.
Thomas. *London*. a.1682, CC.1691-1707.
Samuel. *Sutton* (*Salop*). mar.1698. W.
George. *Shrewsbury*. ca.1700. Clock.
John. *London*. a.1689, CC.1701-43.
William. *London*. a.1700.
Henry. *London*. a.1704.
Daniel. *London* (*Haymarket*). a.1707-45. Watch.
Henry. *London*. a.1712, CC.1720.
John. *London*. a.1713.
John. *London*. a.1717.
Thomas. *London* (*Aldersgate St.* in 1761). a. 1720, CC.1727-61. Watch Ilbert coll.
Charles. *London*. a.1722.
Charles. *London*. a.1724.
Joseph. *London*. a.1724.
George. *Nailsworth*. 1740-66. W.
George. *Romford*. an.1745. Watch.
Richard. *Shrewsbury*. an.1745, d.1752. Watch.
James. *London* (*Norman St.*). a.1734, CC. 1745-70. Watches G.M., Ilbert and Den. colls.
Mary, widow of Rich. *Shrewsbury*. From 1752.

WOOD—*continued.*
John. *Grantham.* 1753-97. Watch Ilbert coll.
Richard. *London.* a.1745.
William, son of Thos. *London.* a.1746, CC. 1754. Watch mt. G.M. of Dutch type.
John. *Philadelphia.* 1755-85. l.c. clock M.M.A.
James. *Dorchester.* 1760. C.
Joseph. *Stratford (Essex).* ca.1760.
Joseph. *Scarborough.* ca.1760-90. l.c. lacquer clock.
F. *Scarborough.* 1760.
Francis. *London.* 1762. BC.
David. *Newburyport, U.S.A.* 1765-90. br. clock ill. Milham. Made small l.c. clocks called 'Massachusetts pattern.'
J. *Exeter.* 18c. l.c. clock.
Thomas. *Tetbury.* an.1767. Watch.
John. *Stroud.* 1769-92. W.
Benjamin. *London.* an.1769. Watch.
Joseph. *Bath.* mar.1769. W.
Charles. *London.* an.1774. Watch.
Charles. *Stratford (Essex).* an.1774. Watch.
John. *New York.* 1775. W.
Joseph. *Bristol.* 1775. d.1791. W.
v. KILVEY & WOOD.
Peter. *London.* an.1780. Watch.
Bartholomew. *London (Barbican).* a.1773, CC.1780-92.
William. *Bristol.* 1785. C. & W.
William. *Birmingham.* 1785. C.
George. *Bath.* 1787. W.
James. *Brighton.* 1799 CC.
J. *Shrewsbury.* 1795. W.
Robert. *London.* a.1789. br. clock.
John. *Liverpool.* 1796-1824 CC. W.
James. *London (St. Luke's).* 1799.
Robert. *London (Borough).* 1799-1811.
Thomas. *Dorchester.* 1800. C.
William. *Manchester.* 1804-13. C.
Robert. *London (Finsbury Sq.).* 1808-11. C.
Robert. *Workington.* 1811-29.
——. *Bath.* 1812.
John. *London (Golden Sq.).* 1817-24.
William. *Liverpool.* ca.1820. Watch N.Y. Univ.
Robert. *London (Kent Rd.).* 1820.
J. *London (Wapping).* Early 19c.
W. H. *Staines.* Early 19c. Watch.

WOODALL—
Thomas. *London (Birchin La.).* a.1787, CC. 1796, l.CC.1804, d.1817.
T. J. *London.* 1802-24.
Edward. *London.* a.1800, CC.1807.

WOODCOCK, ——. *Kings Lynn.* an.1765. Watch.

WOODDEN—
Charles. *London.* a.1743, CC.1755-78.
John. *London (Skinner St.).* 1778. W.

WOODFIELD, Charles. *London.* an.1767. Watch.

WOODFINE, Robert. *Liverpool.* 1805-18. W.

WOODFORD, Jonathan. *London.* a.1684. Watch.

WOODGATE, James. *London.* 1767. Watch Ilbert coll.

WOODHAM—
James. *London.* a.1761.
James. *Hungerford.* 1795. W.

WOODHAMS, Samuel. *London.* a.1696.

WOODHOUSE—
John. *Carnarvon.* 1720. Insolvent. C.
William. *London.* mar.1766. W.
Robert. *Bristol.* 1774.

WOODING—
John. *London.* 1784. W.
Thomas. *London.* a.1803.

WOODINGTON, William. *London.* a.1638.

WOODLAND—
Elizabeth. *London.* a.1717.
Philip. *London.* a.1792.

WOODLES, John. *London.* an.1785. Watch.

WOODMAN—
John. *London.* ca.1760. br. clock ill. Cec. & Web.
William. *London.* a.1786-early 19c. Watch.

WOODRUFF—
James. *Shrewsbury.* 1762. C. & W.
Thomas. *Shropshire.* Late 18c. br. clock.
——. *Margate.* Early 19c. Watch.
& SON. *London.* 1822.

WOODS—
Thomas. *London (Cripplegate).* a.1706, CC. 1714-20.
John. *Liverpool.* ca.1770.
John. *Manchester.* 1804. W.

WOODWARD—
John. *London.* a.1656.
Thomas. *London.* a.1671.
Samuel. *London.* a.1734.
James. prob. *London.* an.1762. Watch.
John. *London.* an.1764. Watch.
William. *Greenwich.* an.1767. Watch.
William. *London.* an.1772. Watch.
Charles. *London.* ca.1800. l.c. clock.
Joseph. *London.* a.1803, CC.1820.

WOODWORTH—
James. *London.* an.1773. Watch.
Nathaniel. *London.* a.1767.

WOOLER—
John. *London.* a.1778.
Richard. *London.* a.1786.

WOOLF, Daniel. *Brighton.* ca.1800-22.

WOOLFE, James. *London.* 1747 CC.

WOOLFENDEN, John. *Manchester.* d.1711. C.

WOOLHEAD, Major. *London.* 1735-47 CC. Watch.

WOOLLARD, Edward. *London.* a.1699.

WOOLLERTON, Thomas. prob. *London.* an. 1755. Watch.

WOOLLETT, John. *Maidstone.* ca.1790 CC.

WOOLLEY—
——. *Codnor.* d. when old, 1786. C. & W.
v WRAIGHT & WOOLEY.
George. *Bristol.* 1825-30. W.

WOOLRICH, ——. *Prescot.* ca.1590. Huguenot refugee who started making watch mts. in Prescot.

WOOLRIDGE, Stephen. *London.* a.1652.

WOOLSAY—
J. *London.* an.1775. Watch.
John. *London.* a.1808.

WOOTTON—
Joseph. *London.* a.1703.
Batson. *London.* a.1723.
Thomas. *Colchester.* 1795. C. & W.

WORCESTER—
William. *London.* an.1779. Watch.
Paul. *London.* an.1781. Watch.

WORGAN—
John. *London.* 1696. Compass and Plane table Old Ashmolean M.
Matthew. *Bristol.* 1754-94 CC. C. & W.
James. *Bristol.* 1792-1808. C. & W.

WORKE, John. *London.* 1760-85. p.c. watch F.W.M. Dutch-style watch mt. G.M. Watch Stads M. Amsterdam.

WORKMAN, ——. *London.* an.1781. Watch.

WORLIDGE, Daniel. *London.* a.1661.

WORM, Claus. *Aalborg.* 1825 m.

WORRELL—
Peter. *London.* 1764.
John. *London.* a.1796.

WORSFOLD—
John. *Dorking.* b.1704. Watch. C.
Thomas. *Hampton Wick.* 1775-90 CC. Watch.

WORSLEY, Thomas. *Liverpool.* 1785. Watch presented to Robert Burns.

WORSWICK, Thomas. *Lancaster.* 1753, d.1801 Watch mt. maker. Succeeded by H. BELL.

WORTHINGTON—
Edward. *London*. a.1655.
John. *London*. a.1713, CC.1721-45. Watch mt.
John, son. *London*. CC.1746.
Basil, bro. *London*. CC.1752-5.
Thomas. *London*. 1753. Watch.
Daniel. *London*. a.1752.
John. *London*. a.1785.
Thomas. *Grantham*. Early 19c. Watch.
WORTHEY, John. *London*. an.1770. Watch.
WORTLEY, Humphrey. *London*. a.1653.
WORTON—
John. *Coventry*. d.1799. T.C.
William, nephew. *Coventry*. From 1799. Succeeded his uncle.
WOSTER, William. *London*. a.1697.
WRAGG—
John. *London*. a.1698.
Houblon. *London*. a.1716, CC.1724. l.c. clocks. small g. p.c. watch, ca.1730, Ilbert coll.
WRAIGHT—
——. *Tenterden*. b.1745, d.1793. C.
& Wooley. *Tenterden*. an.1803. Watch.
WRANGLE, Thomas. *Scarborough*. 1807.
WRAPSON—
J. *Chichester*. 1795. W.
H. *Havant*. Early 19c. Watch.
WRAY, Hilton. *London*. a.1752, CC.1769, m. CC.1785, d.1812.
WRAYPIERE, William. *London*. 1622.
WREGHIT, John. *Patrington* (*Yorks*). 1822-1841.
WREN, George. *London*. a.1766.
WRENCH—
John. *Chester*. 1690-1717. W.
Edward. *Chester*. mar.1694. sil. p.c. watch S.M.S.K.
William. *Chester*. 1717. d.1763. Watch.
William. *London* (*Vere St.* to 1720, then *Holborn*). 1720-8. W.
John (2). *Chester*. 1732. W.
William. *Chester*. 1746-61. W.
John. *London*. an.1773. Watch.
——. *London* (*Borough*). an.1775. Watch.
Charles. *London* (*Spitalfields* and *Bishopsgate St.*). a.1769, CC.1785-1820.
Charles James, son. *London*. CC.1814, l.CC. 1815.
WRESSELL, Robert. *London*. CC.1795.
WRICHAS, ——. *Namur*. ca.1800. Bronze mantel clock Feill coll.
WRIGHT—
Robert. *London*. CC.1634.
John. *London*. a.1653, CC.1661. Watches B.M. and M.M.A. mt. G.M.
John. *London*. CC.1671.
John. *Norwich*. an.1679.
Richard. *London*. a.1667, CC.1696.
Benjamin. *London*. a.1678, CC.1685, d.1709.
Edmund. *London*. a.1682.
William. *London* (*Crown Ct., Southwark*). a.1684, d.1758. l.c. clock Weth. coll. g. watch.
John. *London*. a.1691, CC.1700.
Benjamin. *London*. a.1693.
John. *London*. a.1693, CC.1715.
Thomas. *London*. a.1700. Dial Old Ashmolean M. dated 1740, perhaps by him.
Mary, widow of Benj. *London*. 1709-20.
John. *New York*. 1712-53, d.1768. W.
Thomas. *London*. 1st half 18c. Inst. maker to the King. Dial with geared minute dial M.M.A. Watch. Dial Old Ashmolean M.
Thomas. *Chester*. 1714-37. C.
John. *London*. CC.1715.
George. *London*. a.1709.
George. *London*. a.1712.
Francis. *London*. a.1715.
Edward. *London*. a.1721-5. Watch.
John. *London*. a.1724.

WRIGHT—*continued.*
Susannah. *London*. 1733. d.1741.
James. *London*. CC.1733.
Hugh. *London*. a.1729.
John. *Whalley*. d.1755. C.
Samuel. *Northwich*. d.1757. C.
——. *Chelmsford*. ca.1740. Prob. Rich. below. Lantern clock Virginia M.
Luke. *London*. an.1743. Watch.
& Sellon. *London* (*Borough*). 1743-9. Watch.
Thomas. *Wellington*. 1744. C.
Henry. *London*. a.1742.
Stedman. *London*. a.1756.
Samuel. *London* (*Bunhill* and *Featherstone St.*). 1759. W.
James. *Knowle*. ca.1760.
Jeremiah. *Stratford-on-Avon*. ca.1760.
Charles. *Jamaica*. d.1786. W.
John. *Chesterfield*. 1767. Watch.
Jeremiah. *Stratford-on-Avon*. an.1770.
Thomas. *London* (*Poultry*). CC.1770, d. 1792. W. to the King. Patented a bimetallic strip for varying the length of a pendulum in 1783. Watch G.M. br. clock.
& Sellon. *London*. 2nd half 18c. Watch.
Joseph. *Warwick*. 1771-95. W.
Thomas. *London*. a.1766.
Charles. *London*. a.1768-90.
Nathaniel. *London*. a.1769.
Robert. *London*. a.1773.
Paul. *London*. ca.1775.
Richard. *Chelmsford*. 1776. d.1816. W.
& Thorp. *London* (*Poultry*). 1777.
William. *London*. 1778. Watch.
Richard. *Witham*. an.1779-86. Watch.
John. *London*. CC.1781. Watch S.K.M.
James. *Derby*. an.1783-91. Watch.
John. *London*. a.1776.
Matthew. *London*. a.1779.
William. *Birmingham*. ca.1790. Watch Birmingham M.
John. *Dorking*. 1791. C.
Thomas. *London*. a.1783.
John. *London*. a.1784.
George William. a.1785.
Charles. *London*. a.1789.
John. *Long Melford*. ca.1800.
Thomas. *Dorking*. ca.1800. br. clock ill. Cec. & Web.
James. *London*. a.1796.
William. *Baltimore, U.S.A.* 1802. W.
William. *London*. a.1801.
William. *London* (*Brixton*). CC.1817.
John Heely. *London*. a.1810.
Richard. *Manchester*. ca.1820.
S. *London*. 1820.
James. *London* (*Borough*). 1820-30.
James. *Rotherham*. 1825.
John. *Liverpool*. 1825. W.
Walter. *Ecclefechan*. Early 19c.
WRIGHTSON, Thomas. *London*. 1724. m. CC.1737.
WRIGLEY, James. *Manchester*. d.1697. C.
WRIGSTEDT, Johann. *Åbo*. 1750.
WRITS, Willem. *Amsterdam* 1767. Watch, shagreen outer case, G.M.
WROTH, Edward. *London*. a.1778, CC.1797.
WUILLY, Philippe. *Rolle*. 1728.
WUNSCHHORN, Bartholomaeus. *Copenhagen*. m.1783.
WURM, Carl. *Vienna*. m.1795. g. watch, set pearls.
WURTH—
Ferdinand. *Donaueschingen*. b.1775, d.1872. Wall clock Furt. M. by him or his son.
Ferdinand, son. *Donaueschingen*. b.1808, d.1876.
WÜRTL, Jos. ——. Early 19c. Watch with case, wheels, balance and cocks of mother-of-pearl.

WÜST, ——. *Amorbach.* 1792.
WÜSTHOFF, Christoph. *Hamburg.* 1693.
WUTKY, Johann. *Breslau.* ca.1690. Watch M.M.A.
WYATT—
John. *Saffron Walden.* 1710.
Richard. *Dublin.* 1731. d.1755.
Thomas. *London.* an.1765. Watch.
Thomas. *Woodstock.* an.1772. Watch.
——. *Plymouth.* Late 18c.
John. *Altrincham.* an.1799. Watch.
Anthony. *London.* 1799-1824.
Robert. *London.* a.1811.
William. *Liverpool.* 1825. W.
——. *Romsey.* Early 19c.
WYCH—
John. *London.* a.1677. Watch. Also WEYCH.
David. *London (Strand).* a.1686, CC.1694-1717. Watch. Also WYCHE.
WYCHERLEY, John. *Prescot.* b.1817, d.1891. Founded the INTERCHANGEABLE LEVER WATCH Co. of *Birmingham.*
WYER, Joseph. *London.* a.1760, CC.1770-91.
WYETH—
George. *London.* CC.1646.
John. *London.* CC.1655-64.
WYKE—
Arthur. *London.* a.1691.
James. *London.* a.1704.
John. *Prescot.* b.1720, d.1787. C. Invented a wheel cutting engine.
Nehemiah. *Liverpool.* 1758. d.1787. Famous for watch and clockmaking tools.
John. *Liverpool.* 1766-81. l.c. clock. Also W.
& GREEN. *Liverpool.* 1781-1805. l.c. clock.
WYLD—
John. *Nottingham.* ca.1780. l.c. clock.
James. *London.* a.1715.
WYLDER—
John. *London (Bishopsgate St.).* 1790-9. cf. WILDER.
& HALL. *London.* 1795. Bankrupt in 1796. Partnership of John W. and Nathaniel H.
WYLIE—
William. *Edinburgh.* a.1756.
David. *Greenock.* 1783.
George. *Dumfries.* 1796.
James. *Thirsk.* 1822-40.
WYLLIE—
Alexander. *Edinburgh.* a.1721.
Alexander. *Dumfries.* 1746.
Alfred. *Dumfries.* 1753.
WYMARK—
Philip. *Brighton.* ca.1800-22.
Mark. *London.* 1816-24. Watch finisher.
WYNCH, David. *London.* an.1754. Watch.
WYNN—
Edward. prob. *London.* ca.1630. Oval watch.
George. *Wokingham.* 1750-64. C.
George. *London.* an.1774. Watch.
Richard, son of Geo. (1). *London.* a.1764, CC.1773-1800. Also WYNNE.
William. *Farnham* and *London.* 1810-35. Gold medal and two awards from Soc. Arts for improvements in clocks, desc. in Trans. Soc. Arts 1818, 1823 and 1827. Church clock at Boston (Lincs.).
Joseph. *Windsor.* 1795. W.
John Lawrence. *Alresford.* 1795. br. clock.
WYNNE—
Robert. *London.* a.1641.
Henry. *London.* a.1654, CC.1662, m.CC. 1690-1708. Made a pendulum watch, with shagreen case, for the King.
John. *London.* a.1670, CC.1678-98.
Walter. *London.* a.1723.
WYTH—
Thomas. *London.* a.1653.
John. *London (Holborn).* 1662. W.
——. *Cambridge.* an.1685. Watch.
WYTHE—
Lionel. *London.* a.1638, CC.1645-62, d.an. 1674. Also WYETHE.
Joan. *London.* 1678.
Richard. *London.* a.1682.

Y

YADIS, B. *London.* an.1762. Watch.
YALDEN, Benjamin. *London.* a.1777.
YAPP, S. *London.* ca.1825. Watch.
YARDLEY—
James. *Bishop's Stortford.* 1690. br. clock.
W. *Bishop's Stortford.* ca.1790.
James. *Bishop's Stortford.* an.1796. Watch.
W. & P. *Bishop's Stortford.* Early 19c.
YATE—
William. *London.* 1622. Oval watches Ilbert and Mallett colls.
Cornelius. *London.* 1622.
YATES—
Samuel. *London.* CC.1647.
Michael. *London.* a.1664.
Samuel. *London.* CC.1685.
John. *Culcheth.* d.1729. C.
George. *Malden.* 1746. Watch G.M.
John. *London.* a.1750. Watch Oldham M.
Richard. *London.* an.1762. Watch. Clock.
Thomas. *Prescot.* 1766. W.
William. prob. *London.* an.1771. Watch.
John. *Bootle.* an.1788. Watch.
Joseph. *Burton-on-Trent.* 1791. C. & W.
John. *Liverpool.* 1766. W.
Robert. *London.* a.1791.
John. *Wandsworth.* ca.1800. Watch.
Samuel. *Kingston, Jamaica.* ca.1800 CC.
Samuel. *Liverpool.* ca.1820. W.
& Hess. *Liverpool.* 1824-9. W.
Thomas. *Preston.* ca.1825. Lever watch, beating seconds, Marryat and Ilbert colls.
Ellis, Samuel & Co. *Liverpool.* 1825. W.
YEADEN, Richard. *Charleston, U.S.A.* 1771. C. & W.
YEADON, William. *Stourbridge.* 1755-67. W.
YEAMAN—
John. *Edinburgh.* 1734-49.
James. *Edinburgh.* a.1791.
YEATES—
Robert. *Maldon.* 1782. Watch. Also Yeats.
John. *London (Wandsworth).* 1809-11.
Thomas. *Penrith.* Early 19c.
YEATMAN, Andrew. *London.* a.1684, CC. 1692-1703. Watch G.M., with hall-mark 1739.
YELAH. Haley reversed, *q.v.*
YEO, Bevis. *London.* a.1697.
YEOMANS—
——. *Guisborough.* 1690-1700.
Ralph. *London.* a.1713, CC.1722-44.
John, son. *London.* a.1737.
James. *Birmingham.* 1767. W. In *New York* and partner with John Collins, 1769. Alone in 1771. d.1773. l.c. clock.
Joseph. *London.* a.1769.
Edward. *Stockport.* Late 18c. Watch.

YERIAF. Fairey reversed, *q.v.*
YERSIN—
Abram. *Fleurier.* 1759.
Jonas. *Fleurier.* 1766.
David Louis. *La Brévine.* b.1755-93. Able C.
Jonas Louis. *Paris.* m.1778-89.
YEURY, Louis Pierre Jean Chrysostome. *Paris.* m.1788.
YEWDALL, John. *Bradford.* ca.1800. Watch.
YOAKLEY, Thomas. *Jamaica.* d.1782.
YOCKSON, Joshua. *Chester.* 1704. W.
YOLENS, Jacquemart. *Lille.* 1393. C. and locksmith.
YONGE—
George. *London.* 1776-1815. Fine maker. l.c. clock. p.c. cyl. al. watch G.M.
——. *Andover.* 1795. C. & W.
George, & Son. *London.* 1820-5. C. to the Lord High Admiral.
George & Walter. *London.* Early 19c. Successors. Duplex bar watch mt. S.M.S.K.
YONNER, Charles Auguste. *Verrières.* b.1809, d.1883. Made a clock with 40 dials giving time in different places.
YORKE (YORK)—
Thomas. *London.* a.1709, CC.1716-52.
Joseph Wadham, son. *London.* a.1735, CC. 1742-62, d.an.1769.
Thomas, son. *London.* a.1770. Watch.
Thomas. *London (Shoe La.).* CC.1799-1804.
William, son. *London.* a.1799.
YOUDALL, William. *London.* a.1732.
YOUELL, Robert. *London.* a.1691.
YOUL, George. *Edinburgh.* a.1773.
YOULE, George. *Jamaica.* mar.1789, d.1793. W.
YOUNG (YOUNGE)—
William. *London.* a.1656, CC.1668, w.CC. 1695. l.c. clock.
Henry. *London.* a.1659, CC.1672-ca.1700. Watch.
Richard. *London.* a.1669.
William. *London (Charing Cross).* a.1674, CC.1682-1703. l.c. clock.
G. *London (Charing Cross).* ca.1685. Watch mt. Ilbert coll. cf. George below.
Francis. *London.* a.1680.
Thomas. *Croydon.* a.1689, CC.1699. Shutter watch.
Samuel. *Baddiley.* 1722. C.
Thomas. *Edinburgh.* a.1713.
George. *London.* 1723. Insolvent.
Robert. *London.* a.1740, CC.1747.
James. *Edinburgh.* a.1752.
James. *Edinburgh.* a.1757.
William. *Perth.* 1763-5.
James. *Perth.* 1764-92.
Isaac. *Liverpool.* 1766. W. l.c. clock.

YOUNG (YOUNGE)—*continued.*
Francis. *Philadelphia.* 1777. Previously *London.*
James & Wm. Bluck. *London.* 1779. Partnership dissolved. Perhaps James below.
Malcolm. *Edinburgh.* a.1772.
John. *London* (*Bloomsbury*). 1778. CC. 1787-1811. br. clock.
Malcolm. *Perth.* 1781. Watch.
Samuel. *Perth.* 1781. cyl. mt. G.M.
Isaac. *Hale.* an.1784. Watch.
James. *London.* CC.1786, l.CC.1789-1814.
James. *London.* a.1785.
Patrick. *Forfar.* d.1811.
Richard. *Newcastle-o.-T.* b.1773, d.1815. C. & W.
William. *Stirling.* d.1824.
James. *Portsmouth.* ca.1790 CC.
James. *London.* a.1785.
Thomas. *Perth.* a.1789-1848.
John. *Dublin.* 1795.
Charles. *Perth.* 1795.
Henry. *Swaffham.* 1795. Inn clock. Watch.
John. *Liverpool.* 1796-1810. W.
William. *Nottingham.* 1798. Dissolved partnership with Chas. Homer.
William, son of John. *London* (*Abchurch La.*). a.1793, CC.1801-25.
W. ——. ca.1800. Wall clock ill. Cec. & Web.
James. *Liverpool.* 1800-18. W.
William. *Dundee.* 1805-43.

YOUNG (YOUNGE)—*continued.*
Mary. *London.* 1805-08.
Stephen. *New York.* 1805.
John. *London.* a.1800-20.
George. *Liverpool.* 1810-21. C.
Robert. *Newcastle-o.-T.* Early 19c.
James. *Portsmouth.* Early 19c.
William. *Nottingham.* Early 19c. Watch Nottingham M.
John. *London* (*Wapping*). 1820.
William. *London.* 1820.
Charles. *London.* ca.1820. Marine chron. G.M.
Thomas. *Edinburgh.* 1823-50.
Robert. *Ballymena.* 1824.

YOUNGER, R., & Co. *London.* 1813. Watch N.Y. Univ.

YVER (HYVER)—
——. *Angouleme.* ca.1670.
Abraham. *Angouleme.* 1689. Watch M.M.A.
N., son of the first mentioned. *Angouleme.* ca.1700. His watches had a great reputation.
Élie. *Angouleme.* b.1661, d.1744.
Isaac. *Angouleme.* m. and d.1702.
François. *Angouleme.* m.1726.
Pierre. *Angouleme.* ca.1760.
Marc. *Angouleme.* ca.1760.
Jean. *Angouleme.* m.1783.

YVERT, Pierre. *Paris.* m.1780.

YXBERG, Johan. *Stockholm.* End 18c. br. clock.

Z

ZACH—
J. J. *Fürth.* d.1804.
Alex. C. *Fürth.* d.1815.
F. X. von. ——. Pub. in Berliner Astronomisches Jahrbuch, 1796, an account of the going of a Mudge Timekeeper.
ZACHARIAS, Christian Frederich. *Leipzig.* 1814. sil. trav. clock formerly in Shandon coll.
ZACHARIE—
Guillaume. *Lyons.* 1663. C. to the town.
Antoine. *Lyons.* 1672. mar.1674, dead in 1702.
François. *Lyons.* 1761. d.1768. Fine g. watch en. flowers.
ZACHARY, John. *London.* a.1687, CC.1694-1713.
ZACHAU, Friedrich. *Dresden.* m.1806, d. 1820. Court C. 1817.
ZADEMACH, C. *Leipzig.* 1814.
ZANCHI, Giorgio de'. *Polcevera.* 1547. 'Maestro d'oriuoli.' Made clock for Serra.
ZANKER, ——. *Oggersheim.* 18c. Clock.
ZANTNER, Joh. *Fürth.* 1777. d.1810.
ZANTZIG, Joh. Melchior. *Munich.* ca.1760. Large table clock.
ZAPPECK, F. *Germany.* Early 19c. Dials M.M.A. and Nat. M. Prague.
ZAUG, Jacob. *Sumiswald.* ca.1800. Watch.
ZECH (the Czech)—
Jakob. *Prague.* 1518. d.1540. Generally, but incorrectly, credited with the invention of the fuzee. Table clock, with fuzee, dated 1525, Soc. Antiquaries.
——. *Aichach.* d.an.1738.
Johann Ignatz. *Augsburg.* a.ca.1764, m. 1783-95.
ZEHNG, Ferdinandus. *Hamburg.* ca.1660. Astro. watch, ill. Britten, Ilbert coll.
ZEITELMEIER—
——. *Hanstetten* (*Augsburg*). 1756.
Johann. *Augsburg.* m.ca.1758-70.
ZEITZ, Johann Georg. *Munich.* 1765. Court C. 1797-1803. Son-in-law of ARZT.
ZELANDER, ——. *Nyköping.* 1794.
ZELANDINO, Guglielmo. *Pavia.* 1402. Made clock for city.
ZELLER—
Johann Jakob. *Basle.* b.1701, d.1778. A maker of repute. Veilleuse clock in Basle Hist. M.
Christofle. *Zürich.* 18c. Watch Besançon M.
ZELLING, Andreas. *Hamburg.* Late 17c. en. watch.
ZELWEGER, ——. *Besançon.* 1823. Started first dial factory in France.
ZERELLA Y ICOAGA, Don Manuel. *Madrid.* 1789. C. to Ferdinand VI. Pub. a treatise on horology.
ZETTERSTRÖM, Pehr. *Gäfle,* 1819-30.
ZIEGENBEIN, Christian Gottlieb. *Leipzig.* 1800. d.an.1814. Master of Corporation.
ZIEGENHIRT (ZIEGELHART), Ernst Nicolai. *Copenhagen.* m.1724. First master of Copenhagen Corporation 1755. d.1756. Made l.c. clock with carillon for Hørsholm castle ill. Liisberg.
ZIEGER, Urbanus. *Fürth.* d.ca.1820.
ZIEGLER—
Zacharias. *Annaberg.* 1605.
Joh. Jonas. *Fürth.* d.ca.1820.
Joseph. *Fleurier.* 1753. From *Mühlhausen.*
Michael. *Königshofen-im-Grabfeld.* m.1791.
Friedrich. *Fleurier.* 1795. From *Mühlhausen.*
Jonas Henri. *Fleurier.* 1795. From *Mühlhausen.*
Daniel. *Königshofen-im-Grabfeld.* m.1818.
ZIERBÖCK, Georg Sigmund. *Vienna.* m. 1661.
ZILLZER, Joachim. *Althofen.* 1802. rep. br. clock.
ZIMMER, Joh. Mich. *Fürth.* d.1802.
ZINNG, Melchior. *Germany.* 16c. rect. table clock Spitzer coll.
ZINZANTH, Henry. *London.* a.1656.
ZÖGNER, Johann. *Vienna.* m.1783.
ZOLL, Benjamin. *Dantzig.* Late 17c. Trav. clock. Fine br. clock.
ZOLLEN, Elias. *Augsburg.* Late 16c. Repaired aut. on Perlachthurm.
ZOLLER—
Martinus. *Augsburg.* 1590-1633. Table clock Neue Hofburg, Vienna.
Wilhelm David. *Nürnberg.* ca.1730. g. repoussé watch Feill coll.
ZOLLING—
Ferdinand. *Frankfurt-a-M.* 1750. Watch Chamb. coll. and mt. Arts M. Prague.
Peter. *London* and *Hamburg.* Mid. 18c. g. rep. watch.
ZÖRY, Friedrich. *Vienna.* m.1662.
ZOUCH, William. prob. *London.* an.1755. Watch.
ZURBUN (SUHRBOM, TURBOM), Caspar. *Stockholm.* 1651-65. Dane. Table clock Nord. M. ill. Sidenbladh.
ZUURMOND, R. *Rotterdam.* ca.1800.
ZWALIS, Henry. ——. 1427. Made a clock for the duc de Bourgogne.
ZWECKER, Anton. *Vienna.* m.1804.
ZWIEBLER, Theodor Hendrik. *Copenhagen.* m.1806.
ZWOLLIS, ——. ——. 1459. Made an Oroiloige. Perhaps Zwalis.

LIST OF INITIALS AND MONOGRAMS FOUND ON CLOCKS AND WATCHES

Arranged in alphabetical order of the last initial

UNDER the initials are given the names and particulars of makers who might possibly be the signatories. When more than one name appears under a set of initials, the names are arranged in order of probability.

Early German clocks and watches sometimes indicated the place of making by the following signs:

Augsburg, A pineapple.
Berne, A bear.
Mainz, A wheel.
Nürnberg, Nor. or N.

B.G.A. On German stand clock, tower shape. End 16c.
A.B. Antoni BRADL. *Augsburg.* m.1739-70.
C.B. On oval watch. Prob. German. Early 17c.—
Also, with shield between letters and, on case, M with K through it; stackfreed mt. brass wheels, in crucifix, Ilbert coll. *v.* M.K.—
Caspar BUSCHMANN. *Augsburg.* 1590-1611.
Chasparus BOHEMUS. *Vienna.* 1568. Table clock.
Also, with crown between letters, on oval watch, prob. French or Swiss—
Claud BIDAULT. *Paris.* 1628. d.1652. C. to Louis XIII and XIV.
Claude BERGIER. *Geneva.* 1559.
H.G.B. and S.B. with shield between, on circ. table clock. *v.* PONCELIN.
I.B. On oval stackfreed watch, Ilbert coll.—
Johannes BUZ. *Augsburg.* ca.1625.
Johann BOCK. *Frankfurt-a.-M.* 1640. Several watches.
Joseph BONHÖFER. *Hagen (Brunswick).* 1593.
Johannes BENNER. ——. ca.1650. Table clock.
I.B. On cases. Sig. of John BETTS. *London.* 1720.
J.B. Zug. On oval watch. 2nd half 17c.—
Possibly a relation of Paulus BENGG. *Zug.* 17c. Crys. heart watch.
M.B. in shield. On German oct. watch. ca.1600—
Matthäus BUSCHMANN. *Augsburg.* d.1636. Oval watch.
Moritz BEHAM. *Vienna.* 1559. Rect. table clock.
Michel BUMEL. *Nürnberg.* 1601.
Martin BAYER. *Annaberg.* Juré 1605.
M.H.B. On table clock. Prob. German. Late 16c.
N.B. On German watch with stackfreed, Ilbert coll. Late 16c.—
Niclaus BRUN. *Basle.* 1550-71.
Nb. On German watch, going train only with stackfreed, all steel, no screws, Ilbert coll. ca.1560. May indicate Nürnberg.
F.C. On book watch, Stern coll. German. 16c.
P.C. *v.* C.P.
J.P.C. On wall clock, Neuchâtel district. Early 18c.
D.R.D. On hex. table clock. Prob. S. German. Early 17c.
H.D. Monogram in shield. On German watch. Late 16c.—
Hans DIEBOLDER. *Basle.* 1598. d.1630.
Hans DUCHER. *Nürnberg.* ca.1580. Dial B.M.
I.D. With I through D. On German stackfreed al. watch, Ilbert coll. ca.1575.
I.E. Over P. Stand clock, Feill coll. 17c.—
Johann ENGELSCHALK. *Prague.* ca.1650-1700. Watch and clock.
Johann EICHSTEL. *Germany.* ca.1600. Table clock and tower clock.
Jerg ERNST. *Germany.* ca.1620. Two watches.
Isaac EBNER. *Steyer.* 1617-mid. 17c.

I.E. Jakob ECHSTEDT. *Elbing*. ca.1640.
Jakob ENDERLIN. *Basle* and *Breslau*. b.1628, d.1699.
G.F. With G in shield. Very fine astro. table clock, Cassel Landes-M. ca.1600.
J.F. On table clock. *Augsburg*. Early 17c.
S.F. On g. en. repoussé watch. *London*. Late 18c.—
Samuel FENN. *London*. CC.1776, m.CC.1793, d.1821.
W.F. On trav. clock. ca.1800.
H.G. In shield containing crossed spades. Sig. of Hans GRUBER. *Nürnberg*. m.1552, d.1597.
H.G. On circ. table clock. S. German. 2nd half 16c.—
Hans GOBE (GEBE, GEEB). *Dresden*. 1558. d.1574. Court C.
Hans GRIMM. *Nurnberg*. m.1563.
Hans GASTEIGER. *Munich*. 1562. Stand clock.
I.S.G. and G with P through it in shield. On circ. table clock dated 1576, Ilbert coll.—
Paulus GRIMM. ——. 1619.
M.G. On two circ. German watches, with dates 1554 and 1574—
Michael GRUBER. *Nürnberg*. Burgher 1607. Str. watches.
Marc GIRARD. *Blois*. d.ca.1616. Of German origin.
Melchior GEMBE. *Basle*. m.1600. From *Württemberg*.
M.H. On drum watch. German. End 16c.—
Melchior HOFFMANN. *Augsburg*. ca.1600. Oct. watch.
Martin HAIMMERT. *Nürnberg*. Burgher in 1582.
Me.Ho. On oval watch. *Augsburg*. ca.1600. Melchior HOFFMANN.
Sa.Ha. On square table clock. *Dresden*. Early 17c.
On tower table clock with *Augsburg* mark. Early 17c.
A.K. On watch. German. Late 16c.—
Adam KLYZOVICZ. *Cracow*. 1634. Clock with straight balance spring.
Andreas KRANTZ. *Schweidnitz*. 17c. Hex. table clock.
C.K. On watch. Late 16c.
C.K. in shield with jumping horse. German. Late 16c.—
Conrad KREIZER. *Strasbourg* or *Augsburg*. ca.1600. Several watches.
Christoph KOPPAUN. *Germany*. 1582. Sq. table clock.
Conrad KÖNIG. *Dresden*. 1576.
D.K. On oval str. watch. 1st half 17c.—
Dirk KOSTER. *Amsterdam*. Late 17c. Watch.
F.K. On circular watch. German. ca.1600.
H.K. On rect. gilt box, Ilbert coll. ca.1620—
H.K. with profile head. On book watch. German. Late 16c.—
Hans KIENING. *Füssen* (*Bavaria*). 1578. Astro. clock.
Hans KIRSCH. *Copenhagen*. 1611. C. to Queen Sofie.
J.K. Initials engraved on the balance-cock of watches by Jacob KOCK. *Stockholm*. b.1737, d.1805.
M.K. On tower table clock and watch. German. Early 17c.
M.K. Monogram. On oct. crys. watch. German. ca.1580—
Mathias KESSBORER. *Ulm*. Early 17c. Oct. crys. watch.
Melchior KLEINHEMMEL. *Annaberg*. 1543.
Michael KLINCK. *Augsburg*. ca.1600.
Michael KRATZ. *Augsburg*. ca.1650. Circ. sil. watch.
I.B.L. a Zug (B & L together as monogram). On oval str. watch, Ilbert coll. ca.1615.
C.K.L. On circ. table clock. German. ca.1560.
M.L. Monogram. On circ. German watch. 2nd half 16c.—
Melchior LIENHARD. *Würzburg*. 1598.
N.L. Monogram. On table clock. Mid. 16c.—
Niklaus LANZ. *Innsbruck*. Mid. 16c. Table clocks.
Se : Le : Nor : On circ. table clock—
Sebastian LEHR. *Nürnberg*. 1525. d.1556. Town C.

M. with mark above like ? and three vertical strokes below.
A.M. *v.* A.M.W.
C.M. On table clock. *Augsburg*. Late 17c.
G.M. On French watch. 1599—
Gilbert MARTINEAU. *Paris*. 1572-80. C. to Charles IX, Henry III and the City of Paris.
Guillaume MOISAN. *Blois*. mar.1606, d.1645.
On German trav. clock. Mid. 17c.—
Georgius MERKELL. *Dantzig*. Mid. 17c. g. en. watch.
G.V.M. On drum watch. *Brussels*. ca.1600.
H.M. Augsburg. On clock with carillon. Mid. 17c.
I.M. On oval watches and aut. table clock. German. 2nd half 16c.—
Jeremias METZKER. *Augsburg*. 1564-88. Clock.
Jacob MARQUART. *Augsburg*. Late 16c.
Jost MULLER. *Strasbourg*. 1606.
Jacobus MOTTE. *Augsburg*. 1600. Watch.
J.H.M. Initials used by Jean Henri MONTANDON. *La Brévine*. b.1751. C.
P.M. Initials used by PIGUET ET MEYLAN. *Geneva*. Early 19c.
V.M. Augsburg. On table clock and stand clock. German. Late 16c.
A.H. with N. below. On str. watch with stackfreed, Ilbert coll. ca.1550.
I.P. Initials used on clocks by I. POWLEY. *Ashby*. 1730.
I.E.P. *v.* I.E.
C.P. (C encircling P, in shield). On German book watch with stackfreed. End 16c.—
Christoph PLEIG. *Ulm*. 1625. Aut. wall clock.
J.P. On en. flagon watch. *Vienna*. ca.1800.
M.P. Initials used by Marcus PURMAN. *Munich*. 1601. Dial.
A.R. Monogram in shield. On German oval watch with stackfreed. Late 16c.
A.R. with pineapple (Augsburg). On very fine astro. table clock. Late 16c.
C.I.R. On sil. mussel-shell watch. Prob. French. Mid. 17c.
F.R. in a circle. Initials used by ROCHAT FRERES. *Geneva*. 1810-25. Singing birds.
N.R. Initials used by Nicolaus RUGENDAS. *Augsburg*. b.1585, d.1658.
N.R. in shield. On table clock. German. 17c.—
Nicolaus RADCLOFF. *Schleswig*. 1654. Clock with balls running down a spiral.
Nicolaus RESLER. *Prague*. Early 17c. Table clock.
Nicolaus REUTTI. ca.1700. Book watch.
P.R. On clock. German. ca.1600—
Paulus ROSENTRETER. *Nürnberg*. m.1566.
Paulus REIMANN. *Nürnberg*. d.1608. Math. inst. maker.
T.R. Monogram used by Tobias REICHEL. *Dresden*. 1603-10. Court C.
A.S. On German watches, ca.1600, in Louvre, K.H.M., M.P.S. Dresden and Feill coll.—
Andreas STAHL. *Augsburg*. Early 17c.
Alexius SCHNIEP. *Vienna*. 1583. d.1613.
Abraham SCHECKS. *Nürnberg*. Burgher in 1656. Watch B.M.
Andreas SCHELHORN. *Schneeberg*. 1571. Astro. clock Grünes Gewolbe.
Andreas SCHERER. *Dresden*. 1570. Court C.
Andreas SPORER. *Dresden*. ca.1575. Court C.
B.S. in shield. On trav. clock with stackfreed, Ilbert coll. ca.1590—
Baltazar SAURWEIN. *Strasbourg*. 1583.
Bernhard SCHILLER. ca.1600.
Bluis SMID. *Augsburg*. ca.1660.
E.S. On oct. crys. watch. Early 17c.
G.S. On fine clock with turning hour globe. German. 17c.—
Georg SCHMIT. *Augsburg*. 1st half 17c. Watch and crys. globe clock.

H.S. On book watch. German. Late 16c.—
Hans SCHNIEP. *Speyer*. 1583. Book watch Webster coll.
Hanns SCHLOTT. *Augsburg*. 1581. Aut. ship with clock.
Hanns SCHLOTTHEIM. *Augsburg*. b.1547, d.1625. Tower of Babel clock and others.
Hanns SCHMIDT. *Nürnberg*. 1553.
Hanns SCHUSTER. *Nürnberg*. Burgher 1545, d.1601.

H.S. Hans SOMMER. *Nürnberg*. 1579.
HANS SÜMMERER. *Nürnberg*. m.1566.

J.S. On fine circ. table clock. German. ca.1600—
Johann SAILLER. *Vienna*. 1575. Drum watch.
Johann SCHEIRER. *Augsburg*. Early 17c. Hex. table clock and watch.
Jorg SCHEIBLER. *Germany*. 1580. Oct. watch.
Johannes SCHNEIDER. *Augsburg*. 1625. Table clock.
Johann SCHONMANN. *Constance*. 1584. Aut. astro. br. clock.
Jacob SCHEILIN. *Dresden*. 1614-28. Court C.

N.S. in shield. German. Late 16c.—
Nicolaus SCHMIDT. *Augsburg*. mar.1620. Ring watch and table clock.
Nicolaus SIEBENHAER. *Lübeck*. ca.1600. Cal. table clock.

V.S. On circ. watch. German. 2nd half 16c.—
Ulrich SCHNIEP. *Munich*. 1558-88. Court C.
Veyt SCHAUFEL. *Munich*. 1554. Astro. stand clock.
Urban STEINMULLER. *Basle*. 1550.

CA. SCH. On watch. German. 2nd half 16c.—
Caspar SCHUSTER. *Nürnberg*. ca.1550. Watch.
Carl SCHMIDT or Carol SCHMIED. ca.1600. Watch and crystal globe clock.

CT. On watch. German. Dated 1572—
Christoph TRECHSLER. *Dresden*. mar.1571, d.1624.

G.K.V. On watch with stackfreed. Also on sil. pillar dial with watch. ca.1600.

M.V. On sq. table clock. German. Late 16c.

A.M.W. W under A.M. in shield. On circ. German watch, Ilbert coll. ca.1625.

G.W. with engraving of a foliot. On large table clock. ca.1600—
Georg WERNER. *Augsburg*. 1599-1605.
Georg WILDT. *Frankfurt-a.-M*. 1589. Small sq. stand clock.

I.W. Augsburg. On watch on en. ring. Late 16c. Strikes up to 6—
Jacob WIDMAN. *Augsburg*. b.1583-1621. *Mantua*. 1608-15.

J.W. On watch with hours I-VI, minutes and seconds. English. Early 18c.—
There are many possible makers; two famous makers are:
Joseph WILLIAMSON. *London*. a.1686, m.CC.1724.
Joseph WINDMILLS. *London*. CC.1671, m.CC.1702-23.

H.Z. On astro. monstrance clock. *Augsburg*. End 18c.

M.Z. On cal. watch. German—
Melchior ZINNG. *Germany*. 16c. Rect. table clock.
Martinus ZOLLER. *Augsburg*. 1590-1633.

LIST OF PLACE NAMES AND MAPS

MAPS

THE towns and villages included in the List of Place Names are, with some exceptions, shown in the maps following the List.

America, Spain, Norway, Finland and Russia are not included. Some villages close to large towns have been omitted. Some places have not been found, probably because their names have been changed.

The six maps of England, Scotland and Wales are to the same scale. The map of Ireland is to a smaller scale, and the six maps of Europe to a still smaller scale.

Map No. 9 including Germany and Switzerland shows three dotted rectangles which include areas shown in maps 10, 11A and 11B to a much larger scale. These areas are, respectively, Switzerland, the Black Forest and the Nürnberg and Würzburg district.

LIST OF MAPS

1. Scotland
2. NW. England
3. NE. England
4. SW. England
5. S. England
6. SE. England
7. Ireland
8. W. France
9. E. France, S. Belgium, Switzerland, NW. Italy, SW. Germany,
10. Switzerland

11A. Black Forest

11B. Nürnberg and Würzburg district

12. Holland, NW. Germany, Denmark, SW. Sweden
13. Czechoslovakia, Austria, NE. Italy
14. NE. Germany, SE. Sweden

LIST OF PLACE NAMES MENTIONED IN THE LIST OF MAKERS

ABBREVIATIONS

T.	Town	Sub.	Suburb
t.	Small town	adj.	adjoining
Vil.	Village	m.	miles
Beds	Bedfordshire	Leics	Leicestershire
Berks	Berkshire	Lincs	Lincolnshire
Brecon	Brecknockshire	Mon	Monmouthshire
Bucks	Buckinghamshire	Northants	Northamptonshire
Cambs	Cambridgeshire	Notts	Nottinghamshire
Glam	Glamorganshire	Oxon	Oxfordshire
Glos	Gloucestershire	Salop	Shropshire
Hants	Hampshire	Staffs	Staffordshire
Herts	Hertfordshire	Wilts	Wiltshire
Hunts	Huntingdonshire	Worcs	Worcestershire
Lancs	Lancashire	Yorks	Yorkshire

Distances are as the crow flies.

	Map No.
Aalborg. T. NE. Jutland, Denmark	12
Aalten. Vil. Holland on German frontier	12
Aarau. t. 23 m. W. of Zürich	9
Aarberg, Arbourg. Vil. 10 m. NW. of Berne	10
Aarhus. t. E. coast of Jutland, Denmark	12
Aarstrup. Vil. Jutland, Denmark	12
Abberley. Vil. 9 m. NNW. of Worcester	5
Abbeville. T. 25 m. WNW. of Amiens	8
Abbots Leigh. Vil. adj. Bristol	
Aberdare. T. Glam	4
Aberdeen	1
Aberford. Vil. Yorks, 8 m. E. of Leeds	3
Abergavenny. T. 18 m. W. of Monmouth	5
Aberystwyth. T. W. coast of Cardigan	4
Abingdon. T. Berks, 6 m. SW. of Oxford	5
Abingdon, U.S.A. T. W. Virginia	
Åbo. T. SW. coast of Finland	
Åby. Vil. SE. Sweden	
Ackworth. t. Yorks, 13 m. SE. of Leeds	3
Adderbury. Vil. 18 m. N. of Oxford	5
Agen. T. France, 60 m. NW. of Toulouse	8
Agram, Zagreb. T. NW. Yugoslavia	
Aichach. t. 15 m. NE. of Augsburg	9
Aix, Aix-en-Provence. T. 17 m. NE. of Marseilles	9
Aix-la-Chapelle. T. Germany, near Belgium	9
Albany, U.S.A. T. 135 m. N. of New York	
Albrighton. t. 18 m. NW. of Birmingham	5
Alcester. t. 17 m. S. of Birmingham	5
Aldeburgh. t. E. coast of Suffolk	6
Alderbury. t. 3 m. SE. of Salisbury	5
Alderton. Vil. 11 m. E. of Ipswich	6
Alençon. T. 110 m. WSW. of Paris	8
Alessandria. T. 50 m. E. of Turin	9
Ålesten. t. in Sweden	
Alford. t. 29 m. E. of Lincoln	3
Alfreton. t. 12 m. N. of Derby	3
Alingsås. T. Sweden, 50 m. NE. of Göteborg	12
Alisay. Vil. 10 m. S. of Rouen	8
Alkmaar. T. 18 m. NNW. of Amsterdam	12
Alloa. T. 6. m. E. of Stirling	1
Almolo. T. 74 m. E. of Amsterdam	12
Almondsbury. t. Glos, 17 m. N. of Bristol	5
Almwych, Amlwch. t. N. coast of Anglesey	2
Alnwick. T. Northumberland near E. coast	3
Alresford. T. 7 m. NNE. of Winchester	5
Alsfeld. t. 50 m. NNE. of Frankfurt-am-Main	9
Alston. t. 20 m. E. of Carlisle	2
Altdorf. t. 13 m. ESE. of Nürnberg	9
Altenburg. T. 24 m. S. of Leipzig	14
Althofen. Vil. 50 m. WSW. of Gratz, Austria	13
Althorp. Vil. 6 m. NW. of Northampton	5
Alton. t. 15 m. ENE. of Winchester	5
Altona. T. adj. Hamburg	
Altrincham. T. 8 m. S. of Manchester	3
Altwasser. t. 40 m. WSW. of Breslau	14

	Map. No.
Alverton. Vil. 14 m. E. of Nottingham	6
Alviso. T. California	
Åmal. t. on Lake Wener, Sweden	12
Amberg. T. 34 m. E. of Nürnberg	9
Ambert. t. 45 m. WSW. of Lyons	
Amersham. T. Bucks, 23 m. WNW. of London	6
Amesbury. Vil. 6 m. N. of Salisbury	5
Amiens. T. NE. France	8
Amorbach. t. 40 m. SSE. of Frankfurt-am-Main	9 and 11B
Ampthill. T. 8 m. S. of Bedford	6
Andover. T. 12 m. NNW. of Winchester	5
Angelholm. T. S. Sweden	12
Angers. T. on the Loir, France	8
Angouleme. T. 70 m. NNE. of Bordeaux	8
Annaberg. T. 65 m. SE. of Leipzig	13
Annan. T. S. coast of Dumfriesshire	2
Annapolis, U.S.A. T. Maryland	
Ann Arbor, U.S.A. T. Michigan	
Annonay. T. 40 m. S. of Lyons	9
Ansbach. T. 23 m. SW. of Nürnberg	11B
Anstruther. T. E. coast of Fife	1
Antigua. West Indies	
Antrim. T. 11 m. NE. of Belfast	7
Antwerp	12
Appingadam. T. NE. Holland	12
Appleby. County town Westmorland	2
Appleton. Vil. near Warrington, Lancs	
Appoquinemonk, U.S.A. T. near Delaware Bay	
Arad. t. Hungary	
Arboga. t. 80 m. W. of Stockholm	
Arbois. T. 26 m. SW. of Besançon	9
Arborfield. Vil. 13 m. SW. of Windsor	6
Arbroath. T. on Forfarshire coast	1
Ardee. t. 28 m. N. of Dublin	7
Argenteuil. Sub. N. of Paris	
Arklow. T. 30 m. S. of Dublin	7
Arles. T. 40 m. NW. of Marseilles	9
Armagh. T. 27 m. SW. of Belfast	7
Arnhem. T. 66 m. E. of The Hague	12
Arnstein. Vil. 12 m. N. of Würzburg	11B
Arras. T. NE. France	8
Arundel. T. 18 m. W. of Brighton	6
Asa. Vil. central Sweden	
Asch. T. NE. Belgium	9
Aschach. Vil. 115 m. W. of Vienna	13
Ashbourne. T. 13 m. NW. of Derby	3
Ashbrook. Vil. E. Glos	
Ashburnham. t. 25 m. E. of Brighton	6
Ashburton. T. 16 m. SW. of Exeter	4
Ashby. Vil. Westmorland	
Ashby-de-la-Zouche. t. Leics, 12 m. S. of Derby	5
Ashford. T. 12 m. SW. of Canterbury	6
Ashton, Ashton-under-Lyne, and *over-Lyne*. T. 6 m. E. of Manchester	3 inset
Ashton (*Devon*). Vil. 5 m. S. of Exeter	4
Ashwell Thorp. Vil. 10 m. SW. of Norwich	6
Askersund. t. N. end of Lake Wetter, Sweden	14
Askrigg. Vil. NW. Yorks	3
Assens. t. W. of Fyen, Denmark	12
Asten. t. 64 m. ESE. of Rotterdam	12
Asti. t. 29 m. ESE. of Turin	9
Aston. Vil. 7 m. W. of Chester	2
Ath. t. 30 m. SW. of Brussels	9
Atherstone. t. 20 m. N. of Warwick	5
Athlone. T. 55 m. W. of Dublin	7
Athy. T. 30 m. SW. of Dublin	7
Attleborough. t. 15 m. WSW. of Norwich	6
Auburn, U.S.A. T. Pennsylvania	
Auburndale, U.S.A. t. near Toledo	
Auch. T. 42 m. W. of Toulouse	8
Auchterarder. T. 12 m. SW. of Perth	1
Auchtermuchty. T. in Fife 10 m. SE. of Perth	1
Aughnacloy. t. 35 m. W. of Belfast	
Aughton. Vil. 10 m. N. of Liverpool	2
Augsburg. T. in Bavaria	9
Autun. T. 44 m. SW. of Dijon	9
Aux Breuleux. Vil. 12 m. N.E. of Chaux-de-Fonds	10
Auxerre. T. 90 m. SE. of Paris	9
Avignon. T. 47 m. NW. of Marseilles	9
Avranches. T. 70 m. S. of Cherbourg	8
Axbridge. t. 15 m. SW. of Bristol	5
Axminster. T. 23 m. E. of Exeter	5
Aylesbury. T. Bucks, 36 m. NW. of London	6
Aylsham. t. 12 m. N. of Norwich	6
Ayton Banks. Vil. near Gateshead, Durham	
Ayr	2
Baddeley. Vil. 16 m. SE. of Chester	2
Baden. T. 40 m. W. of Stuttgart	9
Baderel. Vil. Switzerland	
Bagshot. t. Surrey, 10 m. S. of Windsor	6
Baileybofey, Ballybofey. Vil. Donegal	7
Bailieborough. Vil. 30 m. NW. of Dublin	7
Bala. t. Merioneth	4
Baldock. t. Herts, 32 m. N. of London	6
Ballibay. t. Monaghan, Eire	7
Ballina. t. Mayo, Eire	7
Ballinsloe. t. Galway, 80 m. W. of Dublin	7
Ballycastle. t. Antrim, 35 m. N. of Belfast	7
Ballymena. t. Antrim, 18 m. NW. of Belfast	7
Ballymoney. t. Antrim, 40 m. NW. of Belfast	7
Ballynahinch. t. 14 m. S. of Belfast	
Ballyshannon. t. Donegal, Ireland	7
Baltimore. T. Maryland	
Bamberg. T. 30 m. N. of Nürnberg	9 and 11B
Bampton. Vil. 12 m. W. of Oxford	
Banbury. T. 21 m. N. of Oxford	5
Bandon. t. 17 m. SW. of Cork	7
Banff. T. 38 m. NNW. of Aberdeen	1
Bangor. T. NW. coast of Wales	2
Barbadoes. West Indies	
Bardfield. Vil. N. Essex	
Barkisland. Vil. 18 m. NE. of Manchester	3
Barnard Castle. T. 20 m. SW. of Durham	3
Barnet. T. 10 m. N. of London	6
Barnsley. T. 11 m. N. of Sheffield	3
Barnstable. T. N. Devon	4
Barrow. Coast T. 19 m. W. of Lancaster	2
Bårsta. Sweden	
Barton-in-the-Beans. Vil. 11 m. W. of Leicester	5
Barton-on-Humber. T. opposite Hull	3
Barwell. t. 10 m. WSW. of Leicester	5
Basingstoke. T. 17 m. NNE. of Winchester	5
Basle, Basel. T. Switzerland on the Rhine	9, 10 and 11A
Basoche-Gouet. Prob. Vil. near Geneva	
Bassano. T. Italy 40 m. WNW. of Venice	13
Batavia. Java	
Bath. T. 11 m. WSW. of Bristol	5
Bathgate. t. 17 m. W. of Edinburgh	1
Battle. t. 27 m. ENE. of Brighton	6
Bautzen (old form *Budissin*). T. 31 m. ENE. of Dresden	14
Bawtry. t. 18 m. E. of Sheffield	3
Bayeux. T. near N. coast of Normandy	8
Bayreuth. T. 40 m. NNE. of Nürnberg	9
Beaminster. t. 14 m. WNW. of Dorchester	5
Beaucourt. Vil. 11 m. S. of Belfort, France	9 and 10
Beaugency. t. 20 m. N.E. of Blois	8
Beaulieu. t. 8 m. S. of Southampton	5
Beaumaris. t. Anglesey	5
Beaumont-le-Roger. t. 30 m. SSW. of Rouen	8
Beaune. T. 90 m. N. of Lyons	9
Beauvais. T. 42 m. N. of Paris	8
Beccles. T. 16 m. SE. of Norwich	6
Bedale. t. 29 m. NW. of York	3
Bedford	6
Bedminster. T. adj. Bristol	5
Beeston. T. near Nottingham	5
Beith. T. 16 m. SW. of Glasgow	1
Belfast	
Belford. Vil. 14 m. SSE. of Berwick-on-Tweed	3
Belfort. T. 50 m. NE. of Besançon	9 and 10
Bellefontaine. Vil. France, 27 m. N. of Geneva	10
Bellingham. t. 28 m. WNW. of Newcastle-o.-T.	3
Belp. t. near Berne	10

Map No.

Belturbet. t. 55 m. NW. of Dublin 7
Beraun. T. 17 m. SW. of Prague 13
Bergamo. t. 30 m. NE. of Milan 9
Bergen. T. W. coast of Norway
Bergzabern. t. 30 m. W. of Carlsruhe 9
Berkhamsted. t. Herts, 30 m. NW. of London 6
Berlin 14
Bermondsey. SE. London
Berne 9 and 10
Berwick-on-Tweed. T. E. coast border of England and Scotland 1
Berwick St. John. Vil. 14 m. WSW. of Salisbury 5
Berwick, U.S.A. T. 100 m. NW. of Philadelphia
Besançon. T. France, 70 m. N. of Geneva 9 and 10
Bethesda. t. N. Carnarvon 2
Beverley. T. 8 m. NNW. of Hull 3
Bewdley. t. 12 m. N. of Worcester 5
Bexley. T. Kent, 14 m. ESE. of London 6
Biberach. t. 23 m. SSW. of Ulm 9
Bicester. T. 11 m. N. of Oxford 5
Bickenhall. Vil. 5 m. SE. of Taunton 5
Bickerstaffe. t. 9 m. N. of Liverpool 2
Bideford. T. N. Devon 4
Bielefeld. t. 55 m. SW. of Hanover 12
Bienne. T. 17 m. NW. of Berne 10
Biggar. T. 25 m. SSW. of Edinburgh 1 and 2
Biggleswade. t. 9 m. E. of Bedford 6
Billericay. Vil. 7 m. S. of Chelmsford 6
Billin. t. 43 m. NW. of Prague 13
Billingborough. t. S. Lincs, near Grantham 6
Bilston. t. 9 m. NW. of Birmingham 5
Birmingham 5
Bischofszell. t. 36 m. ENE. of Zürich 9
Bischwind. Vil. near Würzburg
Bishop Auckland. t. 9 m. S. of Durham 3
Bishop's Castle. t. 18 m. SSW. of Shrewsbury 5
Bishop's Lydeard. t. near Taunton 5
Bishop's Nympton. Vil. 22 m. NNW. of Exeter 4
Bishop's Stortford. t. 11 m. NE. of Hertford 6
Bishop's Waltham. t. 10 m. SE. of Winchester 5
Björneborg. t. W. coast of Finland
Blackburn. T. 21 m. NNW. of Manchester 2
Blackheath. SE. Sub. of London
Blackwatertown. Vil. 28 m. WSW. of Belfast 7
Blainville. Vil. near St. Malo
Blandford. t. 17 m. NE. of Dorchester 5
Bletchingley. Vil. 17 m. S. of London 6
Blewbury. Vil. 12 m. S. of Oxford 5
Blois. T. 100 m. SSW. of Paris 8
Blyth. Coast t. 12 m. N. of Newcastle-o.-T. 3
Bodelfeld, Bodefeld, Vil. 38 m. ESE. of Dortmund 12
Bodmin. T. 16 m. WNW. of Plymouth 4
Bognor. Coast t. W. Sussex 6
Bold. Vil. adj. Farnworth, near Widnes
Boll. Vil. 22 m. ESE. of Freiburg-in-Br. 11A
Bologna. T. 50 m. N. of Florence 13
Bolsover. t. 22 m. N. of Derby 3
Bolsward. t. in Friesland, Holland
Bolton, Bolton-le-Moors. T. 11 m. NW. of Manchester 2
Bombay. T. W. Coast of India
Bo'ness. *v. Borrowstounness*
Bonn. T. 15 m. SSE. of Cologne 9
Boothfold. Vil. E. Lancs
Bootle. T. adj. Liverpool 2
Borås. t. 30 m. E. of Göteborg, Sweden 12
Bordeaux. T. SW. France 8
Borgendael. Vil. Belgium or Holland
Bornholm. Danish Island off S. coast of Sweden 14
Borrowstounness, Bo'ness. T. on Firth of Forth 1
Boscowen, U.S.A. T. 70 m. NNW. of Boston
Boston. T. Lincs on The Wash 6
Boston, U.S.A. T. Massachusetts
Bosworth. t. 11 m. W. of Leicester 5
Bottisdale, Botesdale. Vil. 21 m. NNW. of Ipswich 6

Map No.

Boudevilliers. Vil. near Neuchâtel
Boudry. t. 6 m. SW. of Neuchâtel 10
Boughton. t. 18 m. NNE. of Nottingham 3
Boulogne 8
Bourg, Bourg-en-Bresse. T. 35 m. NNE. of Lyons 9
Bourges. T. 120 m. S. of Paris 8
Bourne. Vil. 14 m. NNW. of Peterborough 6
Boveresse. Vil. 16 m. WSW. of Neuchâtel
Bowbrigge. Prob. *Bowbridge*. Vil. NW. Yorks 3
Boyle. t. Roscommon, Eire 7
Brackley. t. 20 m. N. of Oxford 5
Bradbury. adj. Stockport, Cheshire
Bradford (Wilts). t. 16 m. ESE. of Bristol 5
Bradford (Yorks). T. 8 m. W. of Leeds 3
Bradwell. t. 9 m. ENE. of Buckingham 6
Braintree. t. 11 m. N. of Chelmsford 6
Brampton. t. 8 m. ENE of Carlisle 2
Brandon. t. 35 m. NW. of Ipswich 6
Brassus. Vil. 20 m. W. of Lausanne 10
Bray. T. 15 m. S. of Dublin 7
Brechin. T. E. Forfar 1
Brecknock 5
Bredbury. Vil. 6 m. SE. of Manchester 3 inset
Breda. T. 28 m. SSE. of Rotterdam 12
Bregenz. T. Austria, near Swiss-German frontier 9
Bremen. T. NW. Germany 12
Brentford. Sub. W. London 6
Brentwood. t. 20 m. ENE. of London 6
Brescello. t. 11 m. NE. of Parma 9
Brescia. T. 50 m. E. of Milan 9
Breslau. T. SE. Germany 14
Brest. T. extreme NW. of France 8
Brewham. Vil. 23 m. SSE. of Bristol 5
Bridge. Vil. near Canterbury 6
Bridgend. T. S. Glam 4
Bridgewater. T. 28 m. SW. of Bristol 5
Bridgewater, U.S.A. T. E. Massachusetts
Bridgin. Prob. *Bridgen*. Vil. near Bexley, Kent
Bridgnorth. t. 22 m. W. of Birmingham 5
Bridlington. Coast t. E. of York 3
Bridport. t. 14 m. W. of Dorchester 5
Brieg. T. Silesia, 26 m. ESE. of Breslau 14
Brigg. t. 15 m. S. of Hull 3
Brighthampton. Vil. 8 m. W. of Oxford 5
Brighton. T. Sussex coast 6
Bristol 5
Bristol, U.S.A. T. Connecticut
Broad Oak. Prob. Vil. 15 m. WNW. of Plymouth 4
Bromley (Kent). T. 11 m. SE. of London 6
Bromley (Midd). Sub. E. London
Bromsgrove. t. 12 m. SW. of Birmingham 5
Broseley. t. 12 m. SE. of Shrewsbury 5
Broughton. Prob. Sub. W. Manchester
Bruges. T. NW. Belgium 8
Brügg. T. 27 m. E. of Basle 9
Brülon. t. 80 m. WNW. of Blois 8
Brün, Brünn. T. 115 m. ESE. of Prague 13
Brunswick. T. 34 m. E. of Hanover 12
Brunswick, U.S.A. Coast T. Maine
Brussels 9
Bruton. t. 24 m. SSE. of Bristol 5
Buckingham 5
Buckland Brewer. Vil. 34 m. WNW. of Exeter 4
Bucks County. In Pennsylvania
Budapest 13
Budissin. Old form of *Bautzen*
Builth. t. N. Brecon 5
Bungay. t. 13 m. SSE. of Norwich 6
Bunny. Vil. 7 m. S. of Nottingham 5
Buntingford. t. 10 m. N. of Hertford 6
Bunzlau. T. 60 m. W. of Breslau 14
Büren. Vil. 13 m. NNW. of Berne 10
Burford. t. 17 m. W. of Oxford 5
Burgau. t. 24 m. W. of Augsburg 9
Burgdorf. t. 12 m. NE. of Berne 9
Burghausen, Burckhausen. t. 58 m. E. of Munich 13
Bürglen. Vil. near Altdorf, Switzerland

Map No.

Burlington. Same as *Bridlington*
Burnley. T. 21 m. N. of Manchester 3
Burntisland. T. in Fife on Firth of Forth 1
Burslem. T. Staffs, 30 m. S. of Manchester 3
Burton. t. S. Westmorland 2
Burton-on-Trent. T. 10 m. S. of Derby 5
Burwash. Vil. 26 m. ENE. of Brighton 6
Bury. T. 8 m. N. of Manchester 2 and 3
Bury St. Edmunds. T. 22 m. NW. of Ipswich 6
Buttes. Vil. 18 m. WSW. of Neuchâtel 10
Buxton. T. Derby, 20 m. SE. of Manchester 3
By. t. near Trondhjem, Norway

Cadiz. T. S. coast of Spain
Caen. T. Normandy 8
Caerphilly. T. 7 m. N. of Cardiff 5
Caffa. Vil. adj. Genoa
Cahors. T. 100 m. ESE. of Bordeaux 8
Caistor. t. 16 m. S. of Hull 3
Calais 8
Calcutta. Capital of Bengal
Callington. Vil. 12 m. NW. of Plymouth
Calmar. *v. Kalmar*
Calne. t. 25 m. E. of Bristol 5
Cambrai. t. NE. France 8
Cambridge 6
Cambusnethan. t. 15 m. ESE. of Glasgow 1
Camelford. t. N. Cornwall 4
Camerton. Vil. 11 m. SE. of Bristol 5
Campbeltown. t. in Kintyre, Scotland
Cannock. T. 10 m. SSE. of Stafford 5
Cannstatt. T. 2 m. NE. of Stuttgart 9
Canterbury 6
Canton, U.S.A. T. NE. Ohio
Cardiff. T. Glam on Severn 5
Cardigan 4
Carlisle. County T. Cumberland 2
Carlow. T. 43 m. SW. of Dublin 7
Carlsbad. T. 65 m. W. of Prague 13
Carlsruhe. T. 32 m. S. of Mannheim 9
Carmarthen. County T. SW. Wales 4
Carnarvon. Coast T. NW. Wales 2
Carnwath. T. 22 m. SW. of Edinburgh 1
Carouge. Sub. of Geneva 10
Carrickfergus. T. 7 m. NNE. of Belfast 7
Carrickmacross. t. 38 m. N. of Dublin 7
Carrick-on-Shannon. t. Leitrim, Eire 7
Carrick-on-Suir. t. Tipperary, Eire 7
Cartigny. t. 32 m. E. of Amiens 8
Cartmel, Cartmel Fell. t. 12 m. NW. of Lancaster 2
Cashel. t. 25 m. ESE. of Limerick 7
Cassel. T. 74 m. S. of Hanover 12
Castlebar. t. Mayo, Eire 7
Castleblayney. t. 36 m. SW. of Belfast 7
Castle Donnington. Vil. 8 m. S. of Derby 5
Castle Douglas. t. 13 m. SW. of Dumfries 2
Castres. T. 40 m. E. of Toulouse 8
Caton. Vil. near Lancaster 2
Cavan. County T. Eire 7
Cerne, Cerne Abbas. Vil. 7 m. NNW. of Dorchester 5
Cerney. Vil. 18 m. SE. of Gloucester 5
Cernier. Vil. 5 m. N. of Neuchâtel 10
Chalford. Vil. 10 m. S. of Gloucester 5
Challex. Vil. in France near Geneva
Challock. Vil. 10 m. SW. of Canterbury 6
Chalons. Prob. *Chalons-sur-Marne*. T. 95 m. E. of Paris 9
Chalon-sur-Saône. T. 70 m. N. of Lyons 9
Chambery. T. France, 42 m. S. of Geneva 9
Chapel-en-le-Frith. t. 17 m. SE. of Manchester 3
Chard. T. 25 m. NE. of Exeter 5
Chardstock. Vil. 4 m. S. of Chard 5
Charenton. Sub. E. Paris
Charing. Vil. 12 m. SW. of Canterbury 6
Charleston, U.S.A. T. W. Virginia
Charleville. t. 21 m. S. of Limerick 7
Charlieu. t. 40 m. NNW. of Lyons 9
Charlton. Sub. SE. London

Map No.

Charminster. Vil. near Dorchester 5
Chartres. T. 50 m. SW. of Paris 8
Châteaudun. T. 37 m. N. of Blois 8
Châtellerault. T. 70 m. SW. of Blois 8
Chatham. T. 28 m. ESE. of London 6
Chatteris. t. 18 m. N. of Cambridge 6
Chaux-de-Fonds. T. 30 m. WNW. of Berne 9 and 10
Cheadle. t. 6 m. S. of Manchester 3
Cheltenham. T. 7 m. ENE. of Gloucester 5
Chemnitz. T. 40 m. SE. of Leipzig 14
Chepstow. t. 11 m. S. of Monmouth 5
Cherbourg. Coast T. N. France 8
Cheriton. Vil. 2 m. W. of Folkestone 6
Chertsey. t. 20 m. WSW. of London 6
Cheshunt. t. Herts, 14 m. N. of London 6
Chester 2
Chesterfield. T. 11 m. S. of Sheffield 3
Chester-le-Street. t. 6 m. N. of Durham 3
Chewstoke. Vil. 7 m. SSW. of Bristol 5
Chiavari. t. 20 m. E. of Genoa 9
Chichester. T. 27 m. W. of Brighton 6
Chigwell. t. Essex, 12 m. NE. of London 6
Childwell. Vil. near Liverpool 2 inset
Chippenham. t. 20 m. E. of Bristol 5
Chipping Norton. t. 18 m. NW. of Oxford 5
Chipping Ongar. t. Essex, 20 m. NE. of London 6
Chipstead. Vil. 5 m. SW. of Croydon 6
Chiswick. Sub. W. London 6
Chittlehampton. Vil. 27 m. NW. of Exeter 4
Chorley. T. 20 m. NW. of Manchester 2
Christchurch. t. 20 m. SW. of Southampton 5
Christiania. Now *Oslo*, capital of Norway
Christiania, U.S.A. t. S. Tennessee
Chudleigh. t. 9 m. S. of Exeter 4
Chur. T. E. Switzerland 9
Church Lawford. Vil. near Rugby 5
Cirencester. T. 15 m. SE. of Gloucester 5
Clapham. Sub. S. London 6
Clapton. Sub. E. London
Clare. Vil. Suffolk, 24 m. W. of Ipswich 6
Cleeve Prior. Vil. 23 m. S. of Birmingham 5
Cleobury. Vil. 25 m. SSE. of Shrewsbury 5
Clermont, Clermont Ferrand. T. 80 m. W. of Lyons 8
Cleve. t. Germany near Dutch frontier 12
Cleveland. Prob. *Cleveland Port*. Vil. on Tees mouth, Yorks 3
Clifton (Cumb). Vil. near Penrith 2
Clifton. T. adj. Bristol 5
Clitheroe. t. 27 m. N. of Manchester 2
Clones. t. 60 m. SW. of Belfast 7
Clonmel. T. 45 m. NE. of Cork 7
Cluses. t. France, 27 m. ESE. of Geneva 9
Coblenz. T. 48 m. SSE. of Cologne 9
Coburg. T. 56 m. N. of Nürnberg 9 and 11
Cocheim. t. 55 m. S. of Cologne 9
Cockermouth. t. 23 m. SW. of Carlisle 2
Cockshutt. Vil. 12 m. NW. of Shrewsbury 5
Codnor. Vil. 9 m. NNE. of Derby 3
Coffrane. Vil. 7 m. NW. of Neuchâtel
Coggeshall. t. 13 m. NE. of Chelmsford 6
Coivert-en-Saintonge. Vil. near Rochefort, France
Colberg, Kolberg. T. Germany on Baltic 14
Colchester. T. NE. Essex 6
Coldstream. t. in Berwick 1
Coleraine. t. N. coast of Ireland 7
Coleshill. t. 8 m. E. of Birmingham 5
Cöllen-an-der-Spree. Sub. SE. Berlin
Collingham. Vil. 14 m. WSW. of York 3
Collonges. t. France, 4 m. S. of Geneva 10
Colmar. T. 40 m. SSW. of Strasbourg 9
Colne. T. 25 m. N. of Manchester 3
Cologne 9
Colombier. t. 4 m. SW. of Neuchâtel or 8 m. W. of Lausanne 10
Coltishall. Vil. 8 m. N. of Norwich 6
Colyford. Vil. 20 m. E. of Exeter 5
Colyton. Vil. adj. Colyford

Map No.

Comber. t. 8 m. SE. of Belfast 7
Como. T. 25 m. N. of Milan 9
Compiègne. t. 45 m. NNW. of Paris 8
Compton Dando. Vil. 6 m. SSE. of Bristol 5
Concord, U.S.A. T. 70 m. NNW. of Boston
Conflans. t. 20 m. E. of Verdun 9
Congleton. T. 22 m. S. of Manchester 3
Coningsby. t. 17 m. ESE. of Lincoln 3
Constance. T. 32 m. NE. of Zürich 9
Convers. t. 8 m. NW. of Neuchâtel
Cookham. t. 7 m. NW. of Windsor 6
Cookstown. t. 33 m. W. of Belfast 7
Cootehill. Vil. 60 m. SW. of Belfast 7
Copenhagen 12
Coppet. Vil. 8 m. N. of Geneva 10
Corcelles. t. 4 m. W. of Neuchâtel 10
Corgémont. Vil. 17 m. NNE. of Neuchâtel 10
Cormoret. Vil. 25 m. NNE. of Neuchâtel
Corscombe. Vil. W. Dorset
Corsley. Vil. 22 m. WNW. of Salisbury 5
Cortaillod. Vil. on Lake of Neuchâtel 10
Cortébert. Vil. 16 m. NNE. of Neuchâtel 10
Côte-aux-Fées. 30 m. SW. of Neuchâtel
Côte-Bertin. Vil. Switzerland
Cottbus. T. 65 m. SE. of Berlin 14
Coulommiers. t. 38 m. E. of Paris 8
Coupar-Angus. t. 12 m. NE. of Perth 1
Courtelary. t. 15 m. NNE. of Neuchâtel 10
Courtrai. t. Belgium, 60 m. E. of Calais 8
Couvet. t. 14 m. WSW. of Neuchâtel 10
Cowes. t. Isle of Wight 5
Cracow 14
Crailsheim. t. 50 m. WSW. of Nürnberg 9 and 11B
Cranborne. Vil. NE. Dorset 5
Cranbrook. t. 12 m. S. of Maidstone 6
Crawley. Vil. 26 m. S. of London 6
Crediton. t. 7 m. NW. of Exeter 4
Cremona. T. 48 m. SE. of Milan 9
Crewkerne. t. S. Somerset 5
Criccieth. Vil. S. coast of Carnarvon 4
Crieff. t. 15 m. W. of Perth 1
Cronton. Vil. 6 m. E. of Liverpool 2 inset
Croydon. T. 13 m. S. of London 6
Cubberley. Vil. 8 m. E. of Gloucester 5
Cuckfield. t. 13 m. N. of Brighton 6
Culchett. Vil. 8 m. W. of Manchester 2 inset
Cullompton. t. 11 m. NNE. of Exeter 5
Cupar-Angus. *v. Coupar-Angus* 1
Cupar-Fife. T. 10 m. S. of Dundee 1
Curry-Mallet. Vil. S. Somerset 5
Cwmwysg. Vil. Carmarthen 4

Dabrun. Vil. 40 m. NNE. of Leipzig 14
Dalarne. Province in Central Sweden, now *Kopparberg*
Dalkeith. t. 6 m. SE. of Edinburgh 1
Dalmellington. t. 13 m. SE. of Ayr 2
Dalry. t. Ayr, 20 m. SW. of Glasgow 1
Danvers, U.S.A. T. 23 m. NW. of Boston
Danzig 14
Dardagny. Vil. 8 m. W. of Geneva 10
Darlaston. T. Staffs, 8 m. NW. of Birmingham 5
Darlington. T. 17 m. S. of Durham 3
Darmstadt. T. 25 m. S. of Frankfurt-am-Main 9 and 11B
Dartford. T. 14 m. E. of London 6
Dartmouth. t. on SE. Devon coast 4
Datchet. Vil. near Windsor 6
Daventry. T. 12 m. W. of Northampton 5
Daw Green. Vil. 6 m. S. of Leeds 3
Dawlish. t. 10 m. S. of Exeter 4
Deal. t. 8 m. NE. of Dover 6
Dean. Prob. *Deane*. Vil. SE. Lancs
Deddington. Vil. 18 m. N. of Oxford 5
Dedham. Vil. 6 m. NE. of Colchester 6
Deggendorf. t. 80 m. NE. of Munich 13
Délémont. Vil. 19 m. SSW. of Basle 10
Delfshaven. Part of Rotterdam
Delft. T. 5 m. SE. of The Hague 12
Demerara. British Guiana

Map No.

Denbigh. County T. N. Wales 2
Deptford. Sub. SE. London
Derby 5
Dereham. t. 15 m. NW. of Norwich 6
Detmold. T. 47 m. SW. of Hanover 12
Dettelbach. t. 8 m. E. of Würzburg 11B
Deventer. T. E. Holland 12
Devizes. T. 26 m. E. of Bristol 5
Devonport. T. adj. Plymouth 4
Dewsbury. T. 9 m. S. of Leeds 3
Didsbury. Sub. S. Manchester
Dieppe. T. N. coast of France 8
Dijon. T. 165 m. SE. of Paris 9
Dillingen. t. 23 m. NW. of Augsburg 9
Dinkelsbühl. t. 43 m. SW. of Nürnberg 11B
Dinting Vale. Vil. 10 m. E. of Manchester 3 inset
Diss. t. 30 m. SW. of Norwich 6
Ditton. t. 10 m. E. of Liverpool 2 inset
Dole. T. 27 m. WSW. of Besançon 9
Dolgelly. T. Merioneth, W. Wales 4
Dolwen. Vil. near Llanidloes, Montgomery 4
Dollar. t. 11 m. ENE. of Stirling 1
Dombresson. Vil. 6 m. N. of Neuchâtel 10
Donaghadee. t. 16 m. E. of Belfast
Donaueschingen. t. S. of Black Forest 9 and 11A
Doncaster. T. 16 m. NE. of Sheffield 3
Dorchester. County t. Dorset 5
Dorchester, U.S.A. Part of Boston
Dordrecht. T. 10 m. SE. of Rotterdam 12
Dorking. t. Surrey, 26 m. SW. of London 6
Dortmund. T. 115 m. SW. of Hanover 12
Douai. t. 18 m. S. of Lille 8
Douanne. Vil. 20 m. NE. of Neuchâtel
Douglas. T. Isle of Man 2
Doune. Vil. Perth, 6 m. NNW. of Stirling 1
Dover 6
Downham, Downham Market. Vil. 39 m. W. of Norwich 6
Downpatrick. t. 21 m. SSE. of Belfast 7
Draycott. Prob. Vil. 6 m. E. of Derby 5
Dresden 14
Dreux. T. 80 m. WSW. of Paris 8
Driffield. t. 25 m. E. of York 3
Drogheda. T. 26 m. N. of Dublin 7
Droitwich. t. 6 m. NE. of Worcester 5
Dromore. t. 60 m. W. of Belfast 7
Druten. t. 48 m. E. of Rotterdam 12
Dublin 7
Dudley. T. 8 m. W. of Birmingham 5
Duffield. Vil. 5 m. N. of Derby 5
Dufftown. Vil. 43 m. NW. of Aberdeen 1
Dukinfield. T. 8 m. E. of Manchester 3 inset
Dumbarton. T. on the Clyde 1
Dumfries 2
Dunbar. t. 27 m. E. of Edinburgh 1
Dunblane. Vil. 9 m. N. of Stirling 1
Duncannon. Vil. near Waterford, Eire 7
Dundalk. T. 45 m. N. of Dublin 7
Dundee 1
Dunfermline. T. 14 m. WNW. of Edinburgh 1
Dunkirk, Dunkerque. T. French coast near Belgium 8
Dunmow. Vil. 11 m. NW. of Chelmsford 6
Dunse. County T. of Berwick 1
Dunstable. T. 33 m. NNW. of London in Beds 6
Düren. T. 22 m. WSW. of Cologne 9
Durham 3
Durlach. t. near Carlsruhe 9
Dursley. Vil. 15 m. SSW. of Gloucester 5
Düsseldorf. T. Germany near Dutch frontier 12
Dutton. Vil. 11 m. NE. of Chester 2
Dysart. t. Fife on Firth of Forth 1

Eamont Bridge. Vil. 18 m. SSE. of Carlisle 2
Earlston. Vil. 29 m. SE. of Edinburgh 1 and 2
Easingwold. Vil. 12 m. NNW. of York 3
Eastbourne. T. Sussex coast 6
East Dereham. *v. Dereham*
East Grinstead. t. 26 m. S. of London 6

	Map No.
East Hartford, U.S.A. t. in Connecticut	
Easton, U.S.A. T. 50 m. N. of Philadelphia	
East Pennard. Vil. 19 m. S. of Bristol	5
Eastry. Vil. 9 m. N. of Dover	6
East Sheen. t. 8 m. W. of London	
Ecclefechan. Vil. 12 m. E. of Dumfries	2
Eccles. T. adj. Manchester	2 and 3 inset
Eccleshall. t. 7 m. NW. of Stafford	5
Eccleston. t. 10 m. E. of Liverpool	2 inset
Echterdingen. Vil. near Stuttgart	
Edinburgh	1
Edinton, U.S.A. t. N. Carolina	
Edmonton. Sub. N. London	
Eger. T. Czechoslovakia, 75 m. NE. of Nürnberg	
Egham. T. 21 m. W. of London in Surrey	6
Eichstätt. T. 40 m. S. of Nürnberg	9
Eindhoven. T. 53 m. SE. of Rotterdam	12
Eisenbach. Vil. 15 m. E. of Freiburg-in-Br.	11A
Ekenäs. Coast t. on Gulf of Finland	
Eksjö. t. 25 m. S. of Jönköping, Sweden	14
Elberfeldt. T. 15 m. E. of Düsseldorf	12
Elbing. T. 32 m. E. of Dantzig	14
Elburton. Vil. near Plymouth	4
Elgin. T. 35 m. E. of Inverness	1
Elgin, U.S.A. T. 35 m. NW. of Chicago	
Elham. Vil. 9 m. WNW. of Dover	6
Ellesmere. t. 20 m. NNW. of Shrewsbury	5
Ellingen. Vil. 29 m. S. of Nürnberg	9 and 11B
Elmstead. Vil. near Bromley, Kent	
Elterlein. t. 16 m. S. of Chemnitz	13
Eltham. Sub. SE. London	6
Elverfeldt. Prob. *Elberfeldt*	
Elverum. t. E. Norway	
Emden. Coast T. NW. Germany	12
Emsworth. Vil. 8 m. NE. of Portsmouth	5
Enfield. t. 10 m. N. of London	6
Enkhuisen. t. 28 m. N. of Amsterdam	12
Enköping. t. 40 m. WNW. of Stockholm	
Ennis. t. 20 m. NW. of Limerick	7
Enniscorthy. t. 57 m. S. of Dublin	7
Enniskillen. County T. of Fermanagh	7
Ephrata, U.S.A. t. SE. Pennsylvania	
Epping. t. 15 m. NNW. of London	6
Epsom. T. Surrey, 17 m. SSW. of London	6
Erfurth. T. 13 m. W. of Weimar	12
Erith. T. Kent, 14 m. E. of London	6
Erlangen. T. 12 m. N. of Nürnberg	9 and 11B
Errol. Vil. 8 m. E. of Perth	1
Escorial. t. 25 m. NW. of Madrid	
Eskilstuna. t. 58 m. W. of Stockholm	
Essington. t. 12 m. NNW. of Birmingham	
Etchells. t. 8 m. S. of Manchester	
Eton. t. near Windsor	6
Ettrick. Vil. 34 m. S. of Edinburgh	2
Evesham. t. 13 m. ESE. of Worcester	5
Evreux. T. 30 m. S. of Rouen	8
Ewell. t. 16 m. SSW. of London in Surrey	6
Ewhurst. Vil. Sussex, 32 m. SSW. of London	6
Exeter	4
Eye. t. 19 m. N. of Ipswich	6
Fabiano. Prob. *Fabriano.* t. 90 m. NE. of Rome	
Fairford. Vil. Glos, 25 m. WSW. of Oxford	5
Fakenham. t. 23 m. NW. of Norwich	6
Falaise. T. Normandy	8
Falkenberg. Vil. 15 m. NE. of Chaux-de-Fonds	
Falkirk. T. 22 m. W. of Edinburgh	1
Falköping. t. 75 m. ESE. of Göteoorg, Sweden	
Falmouth. T. W. Cornwall	4 inset
Falun. t. 125 m. NW. of Stockholm	
Fareham. T. 6 m. NW. of Portsmouth	5
Faringdon. Vil. Berks, 15 m. WSW. of Oxford	5
Farington. Vil. near Preston	2
Farnham. T. Surrey, 38 m. SW. of London	6
Farnsfield. Vil. mid. Notts	
Farnworth, Farnworth-within-Widnes. T. near Widnes	
Farringdon. Vil. 15 m. E. of Winchester.	
Fauville. t. 27 m. NW. of Rouen	8
Faversham. T. 8 m. WNW. of Canterbury	6
Fazackerley. Sub. N. Liverpool	2 inset
Fenny Stratford. t. Bucks, 17 m. SW. of Bedford	6
Fermoy. t. 19 m. NE. of Cork	7
Ferney. t. France near Geneva	9 and 10
Feuchtwangen. t. 38 m. WSW. of Nürnberg	11B
Feurs. t. 30 m. W. of Lyons	9
Feversham. Prob. *Faversham*	
Fifield. Vil. 18 m. WNW. of Oxford	5
Filipstad. t. in Wermland, Sweden	
Fiume. T. N. end of Adriatic	13
Flensborg. T. N. Schleswig-Holstein	12
Fleurier. t. 17 m. WSW. of Neuchâtel	10
Flixton. t. 6 m. SW. of Manchester	3 inset
Florence	13
Flushing. T. SW. coast of Holland	12
Folkestone	6
Foligno. t. 20 m. ESE. of Perugia	13
Foncine. Vil. 30 m. N. of Geneva	
Fontainebleau. T. 38 m. S. of Paris	8
Fontainemelon. Vil. near Chaux-de-Fonds	
Fontaines. Vil. near Neuchâtel	
Fordingbridge. Vil. 9 m. S. of Salisbury	5
Forfar	1
Forli. T. 50 m. NE. of Florence	13
Fort-du-Plane. Vil. Franche-Comté in Jura	
Fournet-Blancheroche. Vil. France, 4 m. N. of Chaux-de-Fonds	10
Framlingham. Vil. 13 m. NNE. of Ipswich	6
Frampton. Vil. Lincs on The Wash	6
or 5 m. NW. of Dorchester	5
Franche. Vil. near Kidderminster	
Franeker. t. in Friesland, Holland	12
Frankfurt-am-Main	9 and 11B
Frankfurt-an-der-Oder. T. 47 m. ESE. of Berlin	14
Frant. Vil. Sussex near Tunbridge Wells	6
Fraserburg. T. on coast 47 m. N. of Aberdeen	1
Fredericia. T. SE. coast of Jutland, Denmark	12
Frederiksborg. Sub. of Copenhagen	
Freeport, U.S.A. T. Illinois.	
Freiburg, Fribourg. T. 17 m. WSW. of Berne	10
Freiburg. t. 33 m. WSW. of Breslau	14
Freiburg-in-Br. T. SW. Black Forest, Germany	9 and 11A
Friedberg. t. adj. Augsburg	
Friesland. N. Province of Holland	12
Fritwell. Vil. 13 m. N. of Oxford	5
Fritzlar. t. 75 m. NNW. of Frankfurt-am-Main	12
Frodsham. t. 10 m. NE. of Chester	2
Frome. T. 19 m. SSE. of Bristol	5
Fürth. Sub. of Nürnberg	11B
Furtwangen. t. S. Black Forest, Germany	11A
Füssen. T. 55 m. S. of Augsburg	9
Fyvie. Vil. 22 m. NNW. of Aberdeen	1
Gäfle. T. 100 m. W. of Stockholm	
Gainsborough. T. 15 m. NW. of Lincoln	3
Galway. County T. Eire	7
Gand, Ghent. T. 30 m. WNW. of Brussels	9
Garnock. Vil. near Glasgow	
Garstang. Vil. 10 m. S. of Lancaster	2
Garston. Sub. SE. Liverpool	2 inset
Gateshead. T. adj. Newcastle-o.-T.	3
Gedau. Vil. 20 m. SW. of Königsberg, E. Prussia	14
Gee Cross. Vil. E. Cheshire	
Geneva	9
Genoa	9
George Town, U.S.A. T. S. Carolina	
Gera. T. 32 m. E. of Weimar	12
Geroldshofen. t. 42 m. NW. of Nürnberg	11B
Gex. t. France, 12 m. NNW. of Geneva	9 and 10
Ghent. *v.* *Gand*	
Giebelstadt. Vil. 10 m. S. of Würzburg	9 and 11B

Map No.

Gien. t. 80 m. S. of Paris 8
Giessen (old form *Gissa*). T. 32 m. N. of Frankfurt-am-Main 9
Girvan. t. 17 m. SW. of Ayr 2
Gisors. T. 32 m. E. of Rouen 8
Glasgow 1
Glashütte. T. 15 m. S. of Dresden 14
Glastonbury. t. 22 m. S. of Bristol 5
Glatz. T. 47 m. SSW. of Breslau 14
Gleresse. Vil. 20 m. NE. of Neuchâtel
Glogau. t. 55 m. WNW. of Breslau 14
Glotterthal. Vil. near Freiburg-in-Br. 11A
Gloucester 5
Gloverstone. Sub. of Chester
Godalming. T. Surrey, 34 m. SW. of London 6
Godstone. Vil. Surrey 26 m. S. of London 6
Göggingen. Vil. near Augsburg
Goldberg. t. 35 m. S. of Rostock 12
Goldbourne. Prob. *Golborne*. Vil. 6 m. N. of Warrington
Golling. t. 15 m. SE. of Salzburg 13
Gorinchem. T. 22 m. E. of Rotterdam 12
Görlitz. T. 55 m. E. of Dresden 14
Gorredijk. t. in Friesland, Holland 12
Goshen, U.S.A. T. 50 m. N. of New York
Gosport. T. adj. Portsmouth 5
Göteborg, Gothenberg. T. SW. coast of Sweden 12
Gotha. T. 103 m. NE. of Frankfurt-am-Main 9 and 12
Göttingen. T. 50 m. S. of Hanover 12
Gouda, Gouden. T. 10 m. ENE. of Rotterdam 12
Gourock. t. on mouth of Clyde 1
Grafton, U.S.A. t. 30 m. W. of Boston
Grahamston. t. near Falkirk 1
Granada. T. S. Spain
Granard. t. in Longford, Eire 7
Grand Saconnex. Vil. near Geneva 10
Gränna. t. on Lake Wetter, Sweden 14
Grantham. T. 22 m. S. of Lincoln 6
Gratz. T. 90 m. S. of Vienna 13
Gravesend. T. Kent, 22 m. E. of London 6
Gray. T. 25 m. NW. of Besançon 9
Great Boughton. Sub. of Chester
Great Haseley. Vil. 7 m. ESE. of Oxford 5
Great Marlow. *v. Marlow*
Great Missenden. t. Bucks, 25 m. WNW. of London 6
Greenock. T. on mouth of Clyde 1
Greiffenberg. t. 120 m. NE. of Berlin 14
Greiffswald. T. 110 m. N. of Berlin 14
Grenoble. T. 57 m. SE. of Lyons 9
Greystone, U.S.A. T. Connecticut
Griesbach. t. 26 m. ESE. of Strasbourg 11A
Grimsby. T. on mouth of Humber 3
Groningen. t. NE. Holland 12
Grosse Glogau. t. 55 m. WNW. of Breslau 14
Grossenhain. t. 18 m. NW. of Dresden 14
Grouw. t. 10 m. S. of Leeuwarden, Holland 12
Grove. Vil. Berks, 12 m. SW. of Oxford 5
Grüne Eiche. Vil. 42 m. SW. of Berlin 14
Gruyères. t. 32 m. SW. of Berne 10
Guildford. T. 26 m. SW. of London in Surrey 6
Guildford, U.S.A. Vil. Connecticut
Guisborough. t. 27 m. SE. of Durham 3
Günzburg. T. 28 m. W. of Augsburg 9
Gutenbach. Vil. S. Black Forest, Germany 11A

Haarlem. T. 12 m. W. of Amsterdam 12
Hachenburg. Vil. 46 m. ESE. of Cologne 9
Haddington. t. 18 m. S. of Edinburgh 1
Haderslev. T. N. Schleswig-Holstein 14
Hadleigh. t. 8 m. W. of Ipswich 6
Hagburn. Vil. Bucks, 11 m. S. of Oxford 5
Hagenau. T. 25 m. N. of Strasbourg 9
Hague 12
Haigerlach. Vil. 36 m. SSW. of Stuttgart 9
Hainichen. t. 40 m. W. of Dresden 14
Halberstadt. T. 34 m. SE. of Brunswick 12
Hale. t. 7 m. ESE. of Liverpool 2 inset
Halesowen. t. near Birmingham 5
Halesworth. t. 25 m. NE. of Ipswich 6
Halewood. t. 8 m. SE. of Liverpool 2 inset
Halifax. T. 22 m. NE. of Manchester 3
Halkin. Vil. 12 m. W. of Chester 2
Hall. T. 24 m. NE. of Stuttgart 9
Halle. T. 80 m. SE. of Brunswick 12
Hall Green. Sub. of Birmingham
Halmstad. Coast t. 75 m. S. of Göteborg 12
Hälsingborg. Coast T. Sweden facing Denmark 12
Hälsingfors. Capital of Finland
Halstead. Vil. 15 m. SE. of London in Kent 6
Halton. Vil. 10 m. NNE. of Chester 2
Hamburg 12
Hamilton. T. 11 m. SE. of Glasgow 1
Hamilton. Bermuda
Hampton Court. Sub. W. London
Hampton Wick. t. adj. Kingston, Surrey
Hanau. T. near Frankfurt-am-Main 9 and 11B
Hanover. T. NW. Germany 12
Hanover, U.S.A. t. Pennsylvania
Hanslop. Vil. 9 m. S. of Nottingham
Harbledown. Vil. adj. Canterbury 6
Harg. Vil. 60 m. NE. of Stockholm
Harleston. Vil. 15 m. S. of Norwich 6
Harlingen. t. NW. coast of Friesland, Holland 12
Harlow Green. Vil. 10 m. W. of Newcastle-o.-T. 3
Härnösand. t. Sweden on Gulf of Bothnia
Harrington. t. Cumberland on coast 2
Harringworth. Vil. 16 m. N. of Peterborough 6
Harsfield. Vil. 5 m. S. of Gloucester 5
Hartland. Vil. N. Devon 4
Hartlepool. T. 17 m. SE. of Durham 3
Harwich. Coast T. Essex 6
Harwinton, U.S.A. Vil. in Connecticut
Haseley. *v. Great Haseley*
Hasenried. Vil. 30 m. E. of Nürnberg
Haslemere. t. Surrey, 43 m. SW. of London 6
Haslingden. T. 14 m. N. of Manchester 2 and 3
Hassfurt. t. 45 m. NW. of Nürnberg 9 and 11B
Hastings. Coast t. E. Sussex 6
Hatfield. T. Herts, 18 m. N. of London 6
Hatherleigh. Vil. 23 m. WNW. of Exeter 4
Hatton. Vil. near Warwick 5
Hauts Geneveys. Vil. near Neuchâtel
Havant. t. 7 m. NE. of Portsmouth 5
Haverfordwest. t. 9 m. N. of Pembroke 4
Haverhill. Vil. Suffolk, 16 m. ESE. of Cambridge 6
Hawick. T. 50 m. SSE. of Edinburgh 2
Hawkshead. Vil. 12 m. W. of Kendal 2
Hay. Vil. 13 m. NE. of Brecknock 5
Hedemora. Vil. in Kopparberg, Sweden
Heerenveen. t. Friesland, Holland 12
Heidelberg. T. 52 m. S. of Frankfurt-am-Main 9 and 11B
Heidenheim. Vil. 47 m. E. of Stuttgart 9
Heilbronn. T. 25 m. N. of Stuttgart 9 and 11B
Helmdon. Vil. 14 m. SW. of Northampton 5
Helmsley. Vil. 20 m. N. of York 3
Helsingør, Elsinore. T. 25 m. N. of Copenhagen 12
Helston. t. SW. Cornwall 4 inset
Hemel Hempsted. t. Herts, 23 m. NW. of London 6
Henley-in-Arden. Vil. 8 m. W. of Warwick 5
Henley-on-Thames. t. 13 m. W. of Windsor 6
Hereford 5
Herimoncourt. t. France near Swiss frontier 10
Hermance. Vil. near Geneva
Hertford 6
Herzogenbusch. T. 40 m. ESE. of Rotterdam 12
Hesdin. t. 40 m. S. of Calais 8
Hesse Cassel. *v. Cassel*
Heugrumbach. Vil. 12 m. N. of Würzburg 11B
Hexham. t. 19 m. W. of Newcastle-o.-T. 3
Higham Ferrars. Vil. 13 m. ENE. of Northampton 6
Highworth. Vil. Wilts, 21 m. WSW. of Oxford 5

Map No.

High Wycombe. T. Bucks, 34 m. NW. of London 6
Hilders. Vil. 90 m. SSE. of Cassel
Hildesheim. t. 18 m. SSE. of Hanover 12
Hinckley. T. 14 m. SW. of Leicester 5
Hindley. T. near Wigan 2 inset
Hindon. Vil. 15 m. W. of Salisbury 5
Hingham. Vil. 11 m. W. of Norwich 6
Hingham, U.S.A. Vil. 12 m. SE. of Boston
Hinterzarten. Vil. in Black Forest, Germany 11A
Hitchin. T. 13 m. NW. of Hertford 6
Hjälmaryd. t. 80 m. W. of Stockholm
Hoddesdon. t. near Hertford 6
Hogsden. Prob. *Hogston*. Vil. 9 m. SE. of Buckingham 5
Holbeach. t. Lincs near The Wash 6
Holbeck. T. adj. Leeds
Holdsworthy. Vil. 35 m. W. of Exeter 4
Holmes. Prob. Sub. of Rotherham
Holne. Vil. 19 m. SW. of Exeter 4
Holstein, Schleswig-Holstein. Province of Holland till 1866 12
Holt. Vil. 20 m. NNW. of Norwich 6
Holyhead. T. NW. Anglesey 2
Holywell. Vil. Flint, 14 m. WNW. of Chester 2
Honfleur. T. on the mouth of the Seine 8
Honiton. t. 16 m. ENE. of Exeter 5
Hoogezand. t. NE. Holland 12
Hoorn. t. 20 m. N. of Amsterdam 12
Hopton. Vil. near Yarmouth 6
Horncastle. t. 17 m. E. of Lincoln 3
Horsens. T. SE. coast of Jutland, Denmark 12
Horsham. T. Sussex, 32 m. SSW. of London 6
Hoveton. Vil. 4 m. NE. of Norwich 6
Howden. Vil. 17 m. SSE. of York 3
Hoxton. Sub. NE. London
Huddersfield. T. 14 m. SW. of Leeds 3
Hudiksvall. t. on Gulf of Bothnia, Sweden
Hungerford. Vil. Berks, 9 m. E. of Marlborough 5
Hüningen, Huningue. t. France near Basle 9, 10 and 11A
Huntley. Vil. 7 m. W. of Gloucester 5
Hurley. Vil. 10 m. WNW. of Windsor 6
Hursley. Vil. 5 m. SW. of Winchester 5
Hurst. Vil. SE. Lancs or E. Berks or SE. Kent
Husby. t. 100 m. NW. of Stockholm
Huxley. Vil. 7 m. SE. of Chester 2
Huy. T. 17 m. SW. of Liége 9
Huyton. t. 5 m. E. of Liverpool 2 inset
Hythe. t. S. Kent coast 6

Ibenthal. Vil. 2 m. W. of Freiburg-in-Br. 11A
Ilkeston. T. 7 m. ENE. of Derby 5
Illingworth. t. 5 m. WSW. of Leeds 3
Ilminster. Vil. 10 m. SE. of Taunton 5
Immenstadt. t. Germany near Swiss-Austrian frontier 9
Ince. T. Lancs, 7 m. NE. of Chester 2
Ingatestone. Vil. Essex, 23 m. NE. of London 6
Ingolstadt. T. 45 m. NW. of Munich 9
Inniskillen. *v. Enniskillen*
Innsbrück. T. 60 m. S. of Munich 9
Inverkeithing. t. Fife on Firth of Forth 1
Inverness 1
Inverurie. t. 14 m. NW. of Aberdeen 1
Irvine. t. 10 m. N. of Ayr 1 and 2
Isleworth. Sub. W. London
Ixworth. Vil. 21 m. NW. of Ipswich 6

Jakobstad. t. Finland
Jämtland. Province NW. Sweden
Jauer. T. 35 m. W. of Breslau 14
Jedburgh. County t. of Roxburgh 2
Jelsey. Prob. *Jersey*
Jena. T. 12 m. ESE. of Weimar 12
Johnshaven. Coast vil. 26 m. SSW. of Aberdeen 1
Joinville. t. 110 m. ESE. of Paris 9

Map No.

Jönköping. T. S. end of Lake Wetter, Sweden 14
Joure. t. in Friesland, Holland 12

Kaiserswerth. t. near Düsseldorf 12
Kaisheim, Kaisersheim. Vil. 30 m. N. of Augsburg 9
Kalmar. T. SE. coast of Sweden 14
Karlshamn. t. S. coast of Sweden 14
Karlskrona. T. SE. extremity of Sweden 14
Karlstad. t. N. end of Lake Wener, Sweden
Karlstadt-am-Main. t. 50 m. E. of Frankfurt-am-Main 11B
Karlstein-an-der-Thayer. Vil. N. Austria
Karstorp. t. in Jönköping Land, Sweden
Kegworth. t. NW. Leics 5
Keighley. T. 15 m. W. of Leeds 3
Keith. t. Banff, 42 m. NW. of Aberdeen 1
Kells. t. 37 m. NW. of Dublin 7
Kelso. t. 37 m. SE. of Edinburgh 2
Kendal. County T. of Westmorland 2
Keswick. t. 21 m. SSW. of Carlisle 2
Kettering. T. 13 m. NE. of Northampton 6
Kettle. Vil. Fife, 15 m. S. of Dundee 1
Keynsham. t. 5 m. SE. of Bristol 5
Kidderminster. T. Worcs, 16 m. WSW. of Birmingham 5
Kilbarchan. t. 12 m. W. of Glasgow 1
Kilburnie, Kilbirnie. t. 20 m. SW. of Glasgow 1
Kilconquhar. Vil. Fife, 18 m. S. of Dundee 1
Kilkenny. T. 60 m. SW. of Dublin 7
Killarney. t. 43 m. W. of Cork 7
Kilmacolm. t. 14 m. W. of Glasgow 1
Kilmarnock. T. 11 m. NNE. of Ayr 1 and 2
Kilmaurs. t. 13 m. NNE. of Ayr 1 and 2
Kilrea. Vil. 35 m. NW. of Belfast 7
Kilsyth. T. 11 m. NE. of Glasgow 1
Kimbolton. Vil. 9 m. W. of Huntingdon 6
Kingsbridge. Vil. 17 m. SE. of Plymouth
Kings Lynn. T. 37 m. W. of Norwich 6
Kingsteignton. Vil. 12 m. S. of Exeter 4
Kingston (Kent). Vil. 5 m. SE. of Canterbury 6
Kingston (Surrey). T. 12 m. SW. of London 6
Kingswood. Sub. E. Bristol
Kington. Vil. NW. Herefordshire
Kinnoul. Sub. of Perth
Kinross. Vil. 13 m. S. of Perth 1
Kinsale. t. 13 m. S. of Cork 7
Kippen. Vil. 9 m. W. of Stirling 1
Kirby Kendal. *v. Kendal*
Kirby Moorside. Vil. 22 m. N. of York 3
Kirkburton. t. 15 m. S. of Leeds 3
Kirkby Lonsdale. Vil. S. Westmorland 2
Kirkby Stephen. Vil. E. Westmorland 2
Kirkcaldy. T. Fife on Firth of Forth 1
Kirkconnel. Vil. 24 m. E. of Ayr 2
Kirkcudbright. t. S. coast of Scotland 2
Kirkdale. t. adj. Liverpool
Kirkham. t. 25 m. N. of Liverpool 2
Kirkintilloch. T. 7 m. NE. of Glasgow 1
Kirkwall. t. in Orkney
Kirriemuir. t. 14 m. N. of Dundee 1
Kirton. Vil. 17 m. N. of Lincoln 3
Kissingen. t. 30 m. N. of Würzburg 9 and 11B
Kitzingen-am-Main. t. 11 m. ESE. of Würzburg 11B
Klanxbüll. Vil. N. Friesland, Holland
Knaresborough. t. 15 m. W. of York 3
Knowle. Vil. 9 m. SE. of Birmingham 5
Knowsley. Vil. 7 m. NE. of Liverpool 2 inset
Knutsford. t. Cheshire, 13 m. SSW. of Manchester 2
Kolding. T. SE. coast of Jutland, Holland 12
Königsberg. T. E. Prussia on Baltic 14
Königsheim. Vil. in Black Forest, Germany
Königshofen-in-Grabfeld. Vil. 45 m. NNE. of Würzburg 11B
Könitz. T. 63 m. SW. of Dantzig 14
Koog. Vil. on Texel Island, Holland
Köping. Vil. 75 m. W. of Stockholm
Kopparsberg. Province NW. of Stockholm

Map No.

Kornwestheim. t. 9 m. N. of Stuttgart 9
Krems. T. 40 m. WNW. of Vienna 13
Kremsir. T. Czechoslovakia, 60 m. E. of Brünn
Kremsmünster. T. 90 m. W. of Vienna 13
Kriegshaber. Vil. near Augsburg
Kristianstad. T. S. coast of Sweden 14
Kristinehamn. Vil. on Lake Wener, Sweden
Krommenie. t. 10 m. NW. of Amsterdam 12
Kronach. T. 55 m. N. of Nürnberg 9 and 11B
Kronborg. Part of Helsingør, Denmark
Kronstad. T. SE. Transylvania
Kungsbacka. Vil. 15 m. S. of Göteborg 12

Laaland. Island SE. Denmark 12
L'Abbaye. Vil. 30 m. WNW. of Lausanne 10
La Brevine. Vil. 15 m. W. of Neuchâtel 10
La Ferrière. Vil. 12 m. W. of Neuchâtel
Lagfors. t. NE. Sweden
Laholm. Vil. SW. coast of Sweden 12
Lamberhurst. Vil. 12 m. SSW. of Maidstone 6
Lambourn. Vil. 10 m. NE. of Marlborough 5
Lancaster, U.S.A. T. 25 m. W. of Philadelphia
Landsberg. T. 23 m. S. of Augsburg 9
Landskrona. T. SW. coast of Sweden 12
La Neuveville. t. 9 m. NE. of Neuchâtel 10
Langenbielau. t. 35 m. SSW. of Breslau 14
Langensalza. T. 95 m. SE. of Hanover 12
Langenstrigis. Vil. 45 m. SE. of Leipzig 14
Langholm. Vil. 25 m. ENE. of Dumfries 2
Langnau. t. 17 m. E. of Berne 9
Langport. Vil. 12 m. E. of Taunton 5
Langres. T. 55 m. NW. of Besançon 9
Languedoc. French province on Gulf of Lions
Laren. t. E. Holland
La Reussille. Vil. 18 m. NNE. of Neuchätel
Larne. T. 18 m. N. of Belfast 7
Laroche. Vil. near Geneva
La Rochelle. T. W. coast of France 8
La Sagne. t. 7 m. NW. of Neuchâtel 10
Lauder. Vil. 23 m. SE. of Edinburgh 1
Lauf. t. 10 m. ENE. of Nürnberg 11B
Lauffen. t. 20 m. N. of Stuttgart 9
Launceston. t. NE. Cornwall 4
Laurencekirk. Vil. 25 m. SSW. of Aberdeen 1
Lausanne. T. N. side of Lake of Geneva 9
Lavour. t. 22 m. ENE. of Toulouse 8
Lavenham. Vil. 16 m. W. of Ipswich
Lavington. Vil. 17 m. N. of Salisbury 5
Leamington Spa. T. near Warwick 5
Leatherhead. t. 18 m. SW. of London in Surrey 6
Le Chenit. t. 20 m. NW. of Lausanne
Ledbury. Vil. 13 m. E. of Hereford 5
Leeds 3
Leek. T. Staffs, 27 m. SSE. of Manchester 3
Leens. Vil. near Groningen, Holland
Leeuwarden. T. in Friesland, Holland 12
Le Havre. Coast T. N. France 8
Leicester 5
Leiden. T. 10 m. NE. of The Hague 12
Leigh. T. 21 m. NE. of Liverpool 2 inset
Leighton, Leighton Buzzard. t. Beds, 37 m. NW. of London 6
Leipzig 14
Leitershofen. Vil. near Augsburg
Leith. T. adj. Edinburgh 1
Leitomischel. t. 97 m. E. of Prague 13
Le Locle. T. 10 m. WNW. of Neuchâtel 9 and 10
Lemberg, now *Lwow.* T. SE. Poland
Lenham. Vil. 8 m. E. of Maidstone 6
Lenzburg. t. 20 m. W. of Zürich 9
Lenzkirch. t. S. Black Forest, Germany 9 and 11A
Leominster. t. 12 m. N. of Hereford 5
Le Puy. T. 70 m. SW. of Lyons 9
Les Bois. Vil. 23 m. N. of Neuchâtel 10
Les Brenets. Vil. 12 m. WNW. of Neuchâtel 10
Le Sentier. t. 12 m. WNW. of Lausanne 10
Les Eplatures. Vil. S. of Chaux-de-Fonds
Les Geneveys. Vil. 18 m. NNE. of Neuchâtel

Map No.

Les Gras. Vil. France, 18 m. W. of Neuchätel 10
Leslie. t. Fife, 18 m. N. of Edinburgh 1
Les Montagnes Neuchâteloises. W. border of Canton Neuchâtel
Les Planchettes. Vil. 10 m. W. of Neuchâtel
Les Verrières. Vil. 23 m. WSW. of Neuchâtel 10
Letterkenny. t. 16 m. WSW. of Londonderry 7
Leutschach. Vil. N. Bosnia
Leutershausen. Vil. near Ansbach 11B
Leven. t. Fife on Firth of Forth 1
Lewes. T. 7 m. ENE. of Brighton 6
Lewisham. Sub. SE. London
Lexington, U.S.A. T. 10 m. WNW of Boston
Leyden. v. *Leiden*
Leyton. Sub. NE. London
Liancourt. t. 34 m. N. of Paris 8
Lichfield. t. 14 m. SE. of Stafford 5
Lichfield, U.S.A. t. in Connecticut
Lidköping. t. S. end of Lake Wener, Sweden 12
Liége. T. E. Belgium 9
Liegnitz. T. 35 m. W. of Breslau 14
Liestal. t. 10 m. ESE. of Basle 9
Lilienthal. Vil. near Bremen
Lilla Malma. Vil. 60 m. WSW. of Stockholm
Limburg. t. 20 m. E. of Coblenz 9
Limerick. County T. Eire 7
Limoges. t. 87 m. W. of Clermont 8
Limpsfield. t. Surrey, 18 m. S. of London 6
Lindau. t. Germany on Lake of Constance 9
Lindesberg. Vil. 85 m. W. of Stockholm
Lindfield. Vil. 14 m. N. of Brighton 6
Lindholm. Vil. W. coast of Schleswig-Holstein, Denmark 12
Linköping. T. 110 m. SW. of Stockholm 14
Linlithgow. t. 5 m. W. of Edinburgh 1
Lintz, Linz-an-Donau. T. 95 m. W. of Vienna 13
Lisburn. T. 8 m. SW. of Belfast 7
Liskeard. t. 15 m. W. of Plymouth 4
Lissa. T. 50 m. NNW. of Breslau 14
Liverpool 2
Lizy-sur-Ourcq. Vil. 35 m. ENE. of Paris 8
Llanbedrog. Vil. Carnarvonshire 5
Llancarfan. Vil. 8 m. WSW. of Cardiff 5
Llandilo. Vil. 14 m. E. of Carmarthen 4
Llanelly. T. 10 m. WNW. of Swansea 4
Llanfair-Caereinion. Vil. 9 m. NW. of Montgomery 5
Llanfrothen. Vil. NW. Merionethshire
Llanfyllin. Vil. N. Montgomeryshire 5
Llangadog. Vil. E. Carmarthenshire 4
Llangollen. Vil. Denbighshire 5
Llanhilleth. Vil. 16 m. N. of Cardiff
Llanidloes. Vil. S. Montgomeryshire 4
Llanerch-Coedlan. Vil. NE. Denbighshire
Llanerch-y-Medd. Vil. Anglesey 2
Llanrwst. Vil. 16 m. W. of Denbigh 2
Loches. t. 35 m. SSW. of Blois 8
Lochwinnoch. t. 14 m. WSW. of Glasgow 1
Lögdö. t. Sweden on Gulf of Bothnia
Lohningen. Vil. in Baden or N. Switzerland
Loich. Vil. 75 m. WSW. of Vienna 13
Londonderry. T. N. Ireland 7
Long Buckby. Vil. 10 m. NW. of Northampton 5
Longford. t. 70 m. WNW. of Dublin 7
Long Melford. Vil. 18 m. W. of Ipswich 6
Longtown. t. 9 m. N. of Carlisle 2
Lons-le-Saunier. T. France, 42 m. NW. of Geneva 9
Lorient. T. S. coast of Brittany 8
Loughborough. T. 10 m. NW. of Leicester 5
Loughrea. t. S. Galway 7
Louth. t. 24 m. ENE. of Lincoln 3
Louvain. T. 15 m. E. of Brussels 9
Lowestoft. T. Norfolk coast 6
Lübeck. T. 35 m. NW. of Hamburg on Baltic 12
Lüblin. T. 95 m. SE. of Warsaw
Lucca. t. 40 m. W. of Florence 9
Lucerne. T. 45 m. E. of Berne 9
Luddendon. t. 20 m. NE. of Manchester 3
Ludlow. t. Salop, 35 m. W. of Birmingham 5

Map No.

Ludwigsberg. T. 8 m. N. of Stuttgart 9
Luleå. t. Sweden, N. end of Gulf of Bothnia
Lund. T. SW. extremity of Sweden 14
Lüneberg. T. 26 m. SSE. of Hamburg 12
Lunéville. T. 52 m. W. of Strasbourg 9
Lurgan. T. 20 m. SW. of Belfast 7
Lussley. Prob. *Lustleigh*. Vil. 10 m. SW. of Exeter 4
Luton. T. 28 m. NNW. of London in Beds 6
Lutterworth. Vil. 6 m. N. of Rugby 5
Luxembourg 9
Lydford. Vil. 19 m. N. of Plymouth 4
Lymington. t. 12 m. SW. of Southampton 5
Lynn. *v. Kings Lynn*
Lynton. Vil. N. coast of Devon 4
Lyons

Macao. S. China
Macclesfield. T. 17 m. SSE. of Manchester 3
Mâcon. T. 28 m. N. of Lyons 9
Madeley Wood. t. 13 m. ESE. of Shrewsbury 5
Maestricht. T. 55 m. E. of Brussels 8
Magdeburg. T. 80 m. E. of Hanover 12
Maghera. t. 35 m. NW. of Belfast 7
Magherafelt. t. 29 m. NW. of Belfast 7
Maidenhead. T. Berks, 24 m. W. of London 6
Maidstone. T. Kent, 41 m. SE. of London 6
Mainz. T. 20 m. WSW. of Frankfurt-am-Main 9
Malden. T. Surrey, 10 m. SW. of London 6
Maldon. t. Essex, 9 m. E. of Chelmsford 6
Malling. t. near Maidstone 6
Mallow. t. 18 m. N. of Cork 7
Malmedy. T. 20 m. ESE. of Liége 9
Malmesbury. t. N. Wilts 5
Malmö. T. Sweden, facing Copenhagen 12
Malton, New Malton. t. 17 m. NE. of York 3
Malvilliers. Vil. near Neuchâtel
Manchester 2 and 3
Manheim, U.S.A. t. 68 m. W. of Philadelphia
Mannheim. T. 45 m. S. of Frankfurt-am-Main 9
Manningtree. Vil. 8 m. NE. of Colchester 6
Mansfield. T. 14 m. N. of Nottingham 3
Mantua. T. 85 m. ESE. of Milan 9
Marburg. T. 47 m. N. of Frankfurt-am-Main 9
March. T. Cambs, 14 m. E. of Peterborough 6
Margate. Coast T. NE. Kent 6
Mariefred. Vil. 30 m. W. of Stockholm
Marienburg. T. 30 m. SE. of Dantzig 14
Mariestad. t. E. side of Lake Wener, Sweden 14
Marietta, U.S.A. t. 65 m. W. of Philadelphia
Market Deeping. Vil. 8 m. NW. of Peterborough 6
Market Drayton. t. 18 m. NE. of Shrewsbury 5
Market Harborough. t. 16 m. SE. of Leicester 5
Market Weighton. Vil. 17 m. ESE. of York 3
Marksteinach. Vil. near Würzburg
Markbreit-am-Main. t. 24 m. ESE. of Würzburg 11B
Marktheidenfeld. Vil. 15 m. W. of Würzburg 11B
Marlborough. t. 24 m. N. of Salisbury 5
Marlow. t. Bucks, 32 m. W. of London 6
Marseilles 9
Marville. Vil. 35 m. N. of Verdun 9
Maryborough. t. 50 m. WSW. of Dublin 7
Maryport. T. Cumberland coast 2
Matlock. t. 13 m. N. of Derby 3
Maubeuge. t. France near Belgian frontier 9
Maybole. t. 8 m. SW. of Ayr 3
Meaux. T. 25 m. E. of Paris 8
Mecklenburg. German state on Baltic
Medford, U.S.A. T. near Boston
Meiningen. T. 82 m. ENE. of Frankfurt-am-Main 9
Melford. *v. Long Melford*
Melksham. t. W. Wilts 5
Melrose. t. 30 m. SE. of Edinburgh 2
Melton Mowbray. T. 14 m. NE. of Leicester 5
Membury. Vil. 22 m. ENE. of Exeter 5
Memmingen. t. 45 m. SW. of Augsburg 9

Map No.

Menars. Vil. near Blois 8
Mer. t. 20 m. NE. of Blois 8
Mergentheim. t. 22 m. S. of Würzburg 11B
Merthyr Tydvil. T. 24 m. NNW. of Cardiff 5
Merville. t. 19 m. W. of Lille 8
Metz. T. 165 m. E. of Paris 9
Mevagessy. Vil. S. Cornwall 4 inset
Mid Calder. Vil. 11 m. W. of Edinburgh 1
Middelburg. T. SW. corner of Holland 12
Middle Hulton. Vil. 7 m. NW. of Manchester 3 inset
Middleton. Sub. of Manchester
Middleton Cheney. Vil. 11 m. N. of Oxford 5
Middlewich. t. 18 m. E. of Chester 2
Midhurst. Vil. 10 m. N. of Chichester 6
Miesbach. t. 29 m. ESE. of Munich 13
Milan 9
Milnthorpe. Vil. 13 m. N. of Lancaster 2
Milton. Part of Gravesend
Minchinhampton. t. 12 m. S. of Gloucester 5
Minehead. t. 33 m. N. of Exeter 4
Missenden. *v. Great Missenden*
Mitcham. T. Surrey, 9 m. S. of London 6
Mittenberg. Prob. *Miltenberg*. Vil. 30 m. W. of Würzburg 11B
Modbury. Vil. 12 m. E. of Plymouth
Moffat. Vil. 19 m. NNE. of Dumfries 2
Mold. t. Flint 10 m. W. of Chester 2
Mols. Vil. 30 m. SE. of Zürich 9
Monk Wearmouth. t. adj. Sunderland 3
Monmouth 5
Mons. T. 33 m. SSW. of Brussels 9
Montargis. t. 70 m. S. of Paris 8
Montbéliard. t. 40 m. ENE. of Besançon 9
Montbrison. t. 35 m. WSW. of Lyons 9
Montfaucon. Vil. 21 m. N. of Neuchâtel or near Besançon 10
Montgomery 5
Montpellier. T. 75 m. W. of Marseilles 9
Montreuil. t. 20 m. S. of Boulogne 8
Montreux. t. E. end of Lake of Geneva 10
Montrose. T. Forfarshire coast 1
Monza. t. 11 m. N. of Milan 9
Morat. t. 15 m. W. of Berne 10
Morbier. Vil. 23 m. N. of Geneva
Moreton. Vil. 7 m. E. of Dorchester or in Staffs 5
or in Cheshire on NW. coast 2
Moreton Hampstead. Vil. 10 m. WSW. of Exeter 4
Moreton-in-Marsh. Vil. 25 m. NW. of Oxford 5
Morez. t. France, 23 m. N. of Geneva 10
Morges. Vil. 7 m. W. of Lausanne 10
Morley. T. 5 m. SW. of Leeds 3
Morpeth. t. 15 m. N. of Newcastle-o.-T. 3
Morteau. t. France, 16 m. W. of Neuchâtel 10
Mortimer. Vil. 7 m. S. of Reading 5
Möschlitz. Vil. 100 m. SSW. of Leipzig
Môtiers. Vil. 16 m. WSW. of Neuchâtel 10
Mottram. t. 12 m. E. of Manchester 3 inset
Moudon. Vil. 13 m. NNE. of Lausanne 10
Moulins. T. 170 m. S. of Paris 8
Mountmelick. t. 45 m. WSW. of Dublin 7
Moutier. Vil. 21 m. SSW. of Basle 10
Mühlhausen. T. 83 m. SSE. of Hanover 10
Mühlheim-am-Rh. T. near Cologne 9
Mullingar. t. 45 m. WNW. of Dublin 7
Munich 9
Münnerstadt. t. 50 m. WNW. of Nürnberg 11B
Münster. T. 93 m. WSW. of Hanover 12
Musselburgh. T. 5 m. E. of Edinburgh 1
Myes. Vil. 20 m. N. of Geneva

Naas. t. 18 m. WSW. of Dublin 7
Nabburg. t. 50 m. E. of Nürnberg 13
Nailsworth. Vil. 14 m. S. of Gloucester 5
Nakskov. t. W. coast of Laaland, Denmark 12
Namur. T. 36 m. SE. of Brussels 9
Nancy. T. 170 m. E. of Paris 9
Nantes. T. mouth of the Loire 8
Nantwich. t. 17 m. ESE. of Chester 2
Narberth. Vil. 11 m. NNE. of Pembroke 4

Map No.

Nassau. T. 57 m. SE. of Cologne 9
Nassau, U.S.A. t. in New Providence
Nätra. Vil. Sweden on Gulf of Bothnia
Navan. t. 27 m. NW. of Dublin 7
Neath. T. 8 m. NE. of Swansea 4
Needham Market. Vil. 16 m. NW. of Ipswich 6
Neisse. T. 46 m. SSE. of Breslau 14
Nenagh. t. 68 m. N. of Cork 7
Nerac. t. 65 m. SE. of Bordeaux 8
Nessfield. Vil. 15 m. NW. of Leeds 3
Nether Alderley. Vil. 14 m. S. of Manchester 3
Neuburg. t. 50 m. S. of Nürnberg
Neuchâtel. T. 22 m. W. of Berne 9 and 10
Neuenstadt. v. La Neuveville
Neukirch. Vil. in Black Forest, Germany 11A
Neumünster. T. 36 m. N. of Hamburg 12
Neunkirchen. Vil. 58 m. WSW. of Mannheim 9
Neureusch. Prob. *Neureisch.* Vil. in Czechoslovakia
Neustadt. t. 22 m. WNW. of Nürnberg 11B
or 19 m. ESE. of Freiburg-in-Br. 11A
or 16 m. SW. of Mannheim 9
Neustadt-an-der-Saale. T. 40 m. N. of Würzburg 11B
Neuveville. v. La Neuveville
Neuwied. T. 43 m. SE. of Cologne 9
Nevers. T. 130 m. S. of Paris 8
Newark. T. 17 m. NE. of Nottingham 3
New Bedford, U.S.A. T. 50 m. S. of Boston
Newbridge. t. 26 m. S. of Dublin 7
Newbury. T. Berks, 25 m. S. of Oxford 5
Newburyport, U.S.A. T. 35 m. N. of Boston
Newcastle-on-Tyne 3
Newcastle County, U.S.A. In Pennsylvania
Newcastle (Munster). t. 27 m. S. of Limerick 7
Newcastle Emlyn. Vil. 26 m. NW. of Carmarthen 4
Newcastle-under-Lyme. T. 14 m. NNW. of Stafford 3 and 5
New Haven, U.S.A. T. 65 m. NE. of New York
New Holland, U.S.A. t. 40 m. NW. of Philadelphia
Newington. Sub. S. London
Newmarket. t. 15 m. E. of Cambridge 6
Newnham. Vil. 11 m. SW. of Gloucester 5
Newport (Mon). T. 10 m. NE. of Cardiff 5
Newport (Salop). t. 17 m. ENE. of Shrewsbury 5
Newport, U.S.A. T. in Rhode Island
Newport Pagnell. t. Bucks, 12 m. SE. of Northampton 6
New Romney. v. Romney
New Ross. t. W. Wexford, Eire 7
Newry. T. 35 m. SSW. of Belfast 7
Newton Abbot. T. 20 m. S. of Exeter 4
Newton Bushel. Part of Newton Abbot
Newton-le-Willows. t. 5 m. N. of Warrington 2 inset
Newton-on-the-Moor. Vil. E. Northumberland 3
Newton Stewart. Vil. Wigtonshire 2
Newtown. T. 7 m. SW. of Montgomery 5
or one of many small villages
Newtownards. t. 9 m. E. of Belfast 7
Newtownlimavady. t. 16 m. E. of Londonderry 7
Niebüll. Vil. SW. coast of Holland
Nieuwe Pekela. t. near Groningen, Holland 12
Nijmegen. T. 58 m. E. of Rotterdam 12
Nimes. T. 60 m. NW. of Marseilles 8
Niort. T. 105 m. N. of Bordeaux 8
Nivelles. T. 18 m. S. of Brussels 9
Nogent, Nogent-le-Roi. t. 60 m. NW. of Besançon 9
Noiraigue. Vil. in Val de Travers, Switzerland
Noirmont. Vil. 20 m. N. of Geneva 10
Nora. t. 103 m. W. or 75 m. NNW. of Stockholm
Nordheim-v.-d.-Rhön. Vil. 58 m. N. of Würzburg 9
Nördlingen. t. 37 m. NNW. of Augsburg 9
Norfolk, U.S.A. T. Virginia
Normanton. Vil. 9 m. SE. of Leeds 3

Map No.

Norristown, U.S.A. T. 18 m. NNW. of Philadelphia
Norrköping. T. 85 m. SW. of Stockholm 14
Norrtälje. t. 35 m. NE. of Stockholm
Northallerton. t. 29 m. NNW. of York 3
Northampton 5 and 6
Northfield, U.S.A. t. E. Minnesota
Northiam. Vil. 29 m. S. of Maidstone 6
North Leith. v. Leith
North Shields. T. on mouth of the Tyne 3
North Walsham. t. 16 m. N. of Norwich 6
Northwich. t. 16 m. E. of Chester 2
Northwood. Vil. NW. Salop 5
Norton. Many villages of this name
Nottingham 5
Nottingham, U.S.A. t. in Maryland
Norwich 6
Nuneaton. T. 17 m. E. of Birmingham 5
Nunland. Perhaps Vil. in N. Berwickshire
Nürnberg 9 and 11B
Nyborg. t. E. coast of Fyen, Denmark 12
Nykøbing. t. on Falster, Denmark 12
Nyköping. t. 55 m. SW. of Stockholm 14
Nymegen. v. Nijmegen
Nyon. T. 14 m. N. of Geneva 10

Oakhampton, Okehampton. t. 25 m. W. of Exeter 4
Oakingham. Perhaps *Wokingham.* t. near Reading 6
Oberhausen. Sub. of Augsburg
Ochsenfurt. t. 10 m. SSE. of Würzburg 12
Odense. T. on Fyen, Denmark 12
Odensegaard. t. on Fyen, Denmark
Odiham. t. 20 m. NE. of Winchester 5 and 6
Oels. T. 13 m. NE. of Breslau 14
Ogden. Vil. 4 m. N. of Halifax 3
Oggersheim. t. 10 m. W. of Mannheim 9
Ogletown, U.S.A. t. near Philadelphia
Ohlau. T. 18 m. SE. of Breslau 14
Okehampton. v. Oakhampton
Old Cumnock. t. 15 m. E. of Ayr 2
Oldenburg. t. 25 m. W. of Bremen 12
Oldham. T. 7 m. NE. of Manchester 3
Old Meldrum. Vil. 15 m. NNW. of Aberdeen 1
Old Swinford. Vil. adj. Stourbridge
Olmütz. T. 100 m. NNE. of Vienna 13
Olney. Vil. Bucks, 11 m. SE. of Northampton 6
Omagh. t. 55 m. W. of Belfast 7
Önnestad. Vil. in Kristianstad Land, Sweden
Onolzbach. Old form of Ansbach
Onstmettingen. Vil. 30 m. S. of Stuttgart
Orange. T. 63 m. NNW. of Marseilles 9
Örebro. T. 100 m. W. of Stockholm
Orléans. T. 70 m. S. of Paris 8
Ormskirk. T. 11 m. N. of Liverpool 2
Osch. t. 28 m. ESE. of Rotterdam 12
Osnabrück. T. 72 m. WSW. of Hanover 12
Ostend. T. on Belgian coast 8
Ostersund. t. in Jämtland, Sweden
Oswestry. t. 17 m. NW. of Shrewsbury 5
Otley. T. 9 m. NW. of Leeds 3
Ottense. Sub. of Altona and Hamburg
Ottery St. Mary. Vil. 12 m. NE. of Exeter 5
Oude Beierland. t. 6 m. S. of Rotterdam 12
Oundle. t. 13 m. SW. of Peterborough 6
Ousebridge. Prob. *Ouseburn.* Vil. 11 m. WNW. of York 3
Oversley. Vil. 24 m. S. of Birmingham
Overton. Vil. 13 m. N. of Winchester 5
Oxbridge. Vil. W. Devon

Padstow. Vil. W. coast of Cornwall 4
Padua. T. 22 m. W. of Venice 13
Paignton. T. 20 m. S. of Exeter 4
Painswick. Vil. 6 m. SE. of Gloucester 5
Pangbourne. Vil. 5 m. NW. of Reading 5
Parham. Vil. 13 m. NE. of Chichester 6
Paris 8
Parkham. Vil. 30 m. WNW. of Exeter 4
Parma. T. 74 m. SE. of Milan 9

Map No.

Parsonstown. Vil. 70 m. W. of Dublin 7
Partenkirchen. Vil. 50 m. SSW. of Munich 9
Parthenay. t. 125 m. N. of Bordeaux 8
Partington. Vil. Cheshire, 10 m. WSW. of Manchester 3 inset
Passau. T. 90 m. ENE. of Munich 13
Pateley Bridge. t. 22 m. NNW. of Leeds 3
Pau. t. 105 m. S. of Bordeaux 8
Pavia. T. 20 m. S. of Milan 9
Payerne. Vil. 12 m. S. of Neuchâtel 10
Peasley Cross. Vil. adj. St. Helens
Peasemarsh. Vil. E. Sussex 6
Peckham. Sub. S. London
Peebles. T. 22 m. S. of Edinburgh 1 and 2
Pembridge. Vil. 12 m. NW. of Hereford 5
Pembroke 4
Pengelly. Vil. W. Cornwall 4
Penrith. t. 17 m. SSE. of Carlisle 2
Penrhyndeudraeth. Vil. NW. Merionethshire 4
Pentonville. Part of N. London
Penzance. T. extreme W. of Cornwall 4 inset
Perigueux. t. 70 m. ENE. of Bordeaux 8
Perpignan. t. France on Gulf of Lions
Pershore. t. 7 m. SE. of Worcester 5
Perth 1
Perugia. T. 70 m. ESE. of Florence 13
Péry. Vil. 14 m. NNE. of Neuchâtel
Pesaro. t. on Adriatic E. of Florence 13
Pesth. Part of Budapesth
Peterborough 6
Peterhead. Coast T. 32 m. NNE. of Aberdeen 1
Petersfield. t. 16 m. NNE. of Portsmouth 5
Petersham. adj. Richmond, Surrey
Petit Saconnex. Vil. near Geneva
Petworth. Vil. 12 m. NNE. of Chichester 6
Pfersee. t. adj. Augsburg
Pfersen. Prob. *Pfersee*
Pforzheim. T. 20 m. WNW. of Stuttgart 9
Pfullingen. t. 20 m. S. of Stuttgart 9
Philipstown. Vil. 42 m. W. of Dublin 7
Piacenza. T. 40 m. SE. of Milan 9
Picehurst. Perhaps *Ticehurst*
Piguet-Dessus. Vil. 20 m. NE. of Lausanne
Pinkneys. Vil. near Maidenhead 6
Pirmasens. Vil. 43 m. SW. of Mannheim
Pirna. T. 12 m. SE. of Dresden 14
Piteå. t. N. end of Gulf of Bothnia, Sweden
Pittenween. Vil. Fife on Firth of Forth 1
Plancemont. Vil. 15 m. WSW. of Neuchâtel
Plauen. T. 60 m. S. of Leipzig 9
Plymouth 4
Plymouth, U.S.A. T. 35 m. SE. of Boston
Plymouth Hollow, U.S.A. Now *Thomaston*. Sub. of New York
Plympton. t. 4 m. E. of Plymouth 4
Pocklington. t. 12 m. E. of York 3
Poitiers. T. 85 m. SW. of Blois 8
Poitou. Province of France on W. coast 8
Polcevera. t. near Genoa
Poligny. t. 34 m. SSW. of Besançon 9
Polmont. t. 19 m. W. of Edinburgh 1
Polton. Vil. 7 m. S. of Edinburgh 1
Pontarlier. t. France, 27 m. WSW. of Neuchâtel 10
Pont Audemer. t. 27 m. W. of Rouen 8
Pont de Vaux. t. France, 48 m. W. of Geneva 9
Pontefract. T. 21 m. SSW. of York 3
Pont Nedd Fechan. Vil. Brecon near Aberdare 4
Ponts-de-Martel. Vil. 8 m. W. of Neuchâtel 10
Pontypool. T. 15 m. SW. of Monmouth 5
Poole. T. SE. Dorset coast 5
Poplar. Part of E. London
Porrentruy. t. 32 m. N. of Neuchâtel 10
Portadown. t. 25 m. SW. of Belfast 7
Portaferry. Vil. 22 m. SE. of Belfast 7
Portarlington. t. 40 m. SSW. of Dublin 7
Port Glasgow. T. 20 m. W. of Glasgow 1
Portsea. Part of Portsmouth
Portsmouth 5
Portsoy. Vil. N. coast of Banffshire 1
***Potsdam*. T. 15 m. SW. of Berlin 14**

Map No.

Potton. Vil. 11 m. E. of Bedford 6
Pouillerel. Mountain region W. of Chaux-de-Fonds
Poulton. Vil. 17 m. SSW. of Lancaster 2
Prague 14
Prescot. T. 7 m. E. of Liverpool 2
Pressburg. T. Hungary, 35 m. E. of Vienna 13
Preston. T. 27 m. NW. of Manchester 2
Preston, U.S.A. t. SE. Connecticut
Prestonpans. t. 8 m. E. of Edinburgh 1
Prestwich. T. 4 m. N. of Manchester 3 inset
Providence, U.S.A. T. in Rhode Island
Puddletown. Vil. 5 m. NE. of Dorchester 5
Pudsey. T. 5 m. W. of Leeds 3
Purmerende. t. 9 m. N. of Amsterdam 12
Pwllheli. Vil. 20 m. SW. of Carnarvon 4

Quernmore. Vil. 3 m. SE. of Lancaster 2
Quinton. Vil. near Stratford-on-Avon 5

Rainhill. Vil. 9 m. E. of Liverpool 2 inset
Ramsey. t. Isle of Man 2
Ramsgate. T. 15 m. N. of Dover 6
Randalstown. Vil. 19 m. NW. of Belfast 7
Randers. T. E. coast of Jutland, Denmark 12
Rastatt. T. 43 m. W. of Stuttgart 9
Rathfryland. Vil. 17 m. S. of Belfast 7
Rathkeale. t. 18 m. SW. of Limerick 7
Ratisbonne. *v. Regensburg*
Raumo. t. Finland
Reading. T. Berks 5
Reading Penna. T. 47 m. N. of Philadelphia
Reconvilliers. t. 22 m. NE. of Neuchâtel 10
Redbourn. Vil. 14 m. W. of Hertford 6
Redmile. Vil. 24 m. NNE. of Leicester 5 and 6
Redpath. Vil. near Melrose 2
Redruth. t. W. Cornwall 4 inset
Regensburg. T. 55 m. SE. of Nürnberg 13
Reggio. T. 70 m. NNW. of Florence 9
Reichenberg. T. 55 m. NNE. of Prague 14
Reims. T. NE. France 9
Reigate. T. Surrey, 24 m. S. of London 6
Remorey. Vil. France, 40 m. N. of Geneva 10
Renan. Vil. 17 m. N. of Neuchâtel 10
Remnes. T. mid Brittany 8
Retford. T. Notts, 21 m. E. of Sheffield 3
Reus. Vil. in Aargau, Switzerland
Reutlingen. T. 20 m. S. of Stuttgart 9
Reval. T. in U.S.S.R. on Gulf of Finland
Rheinfelden. t. 9 m. E. of Basle 9
Richelieu. t. 22 m. WSW. of Tours 8
Richmond (Surrey). T. 10 m. WSW. of London 6
Richmond (Yorks). T. 38 m. NW. of York 3
Riga. T. in Latvia on Baltic
Ringwood. t. 16 m. WSW. of Southampton 5
Riom. T. near Clermont 8
Ripley. Vil. Derbyshire or Yorks or vil. Surrey 3
Ripon. t. 21 m. NW. of York 3
Rippberg. Vil. 44 m. SE. of Frankfurt-am-Main
Ritzebüttel. t. mouth of the Elbe
Roby-within-Huyton. Vil. 5 m. E. of Liverpool 2 inset
Rochdale. T. 10 m. N. of Manchester 3
Rochefort. T. on Bay of Biscay 8
Rochester. T. Kent, 27 m. E. of London 6
Rochford. Vil. 24 m. SE. of Chelmsford 6
Rodenäs. Vil. in province of Christiania
Roermond. T. SE. corner of Holland 12
Rohrbach. t. 25 m. WNW. of Stuttgart
Rolle. t. on Lake of Geneva 10
Romainmôtier. Vil. 15 m. NW. of Lausanne 10
Romans. T. 50 m. S. of Lyons 9
Romford. T. Essex, 13 m. E. of London 6
Römhild. t. 68 m. NNE. of Nürnberg
Romney, New Romney. t. S. coast of Kent 6
Romont. t. 18 m. NE. of Lausanne 10
Romorantin. t. 27 m. SE. of Blois 8
Romsey. t. 7 m. NW. of Southampton 5

Map No.

Ronsdorff. Vil. 22 m. E. of Düsseldorf 12
Roscommon. County t. Eire 7
Roscrae. t. 70 m. WSW. of Dublin 7
Röskilde. t. 20 m. W. of Copenhagen 12
Ross. t. 12 m. SE. of Hereford 5
Rostock. T. on Baltic, 95 m. E. of Hamburg 12
Rothbury. Vil. 25 m. NNW. of Newcastle-o.-T. 3
Rothenburg-a.-d.-T. t. 40 m. W. of Nürnberg 9 and 11B
Rotherham. T. 6 m. NE. of Sheffield 3
Rotherhithe. Sub. E. London
Rotherwas. Vil. near Hereford 5
Rothweill. Vil. 50 m. SW. of Stuttgart 9 and 11A
Rothweill. T. 4 m. SE. of Leeds 3
or t. 12 m. N. of Northampton 5 and 6
Rotterdam 12
Roubaix. t. near Lille 8
Rouen. T. N. France 8
Rowell. v. *Rothwell*
Royston. t. 12 m. SSW. of Cambridge in Herts 6
Roxbury, U.S.A. Part of Boston
Ruabon. t. Denbigh, 15 m. SSW. of Chester 5
Rudolstadt. T. 63 m. SW. of Leipzig 9
Rugby. T. Warwick 5
Rugeley. t. 8 m. SE. of Stafford 5
Ruhland. t. 30 m. N. of Dresden 14
Rushbury. Vil. 13 m. S. of Shrewsbury 5
Ruthin. Vil. 8 m. SE. of Denbigh 2
Rye. t. E. Sussex coast 6

Saarbrück. T. 67 m. WSW. of Mannheim 9
Sadsburyville, U.S.A. t. 40 m. W. of Philadelphia
Saffron Walden. t. 24 m. NNW. of Chelmsford 6
Sail-sous-Couzan. Vil. 33 m. W. of Lyons 9
St. Albans. T. Herts, 21 m. N. of London 6
St. Andrews. t. E. coast of Fifeshire 1
St. Aubin. Vil. in Jersey
St. Austell. t. 28 m. W. of Plymouth 4
St. Blaize. Vil. 3 m. NE. of Neuchâtel 10
St. Claude. t. France, 19 m. NW. of Geneva 9 and 10
St. Columb. t. 35 m. W. of Plymouth 4
Ste. Croix. t. 23 m. SW. of Neuchâtel 10
St. Eloy. t. 25 m. NNW. of Clermont 8
Saintes. T. 65 m. N. of Bordeaux 8
St. Etienne. T. 32 m. SW. of Lyons 9
Saintfield. t. 11 m. SSE. of Belfast 7
St. Gall, St. Gallen. T. 40 m. E. of Zürich 9
St. Georgen. t. 60 m. SW. of Stuttgart 9 and 11A
St. Germain-en-Laye. Sub. NW. Paris
St. Helens. T. 12 m. ENE. of Liverpool 2
St. Helier. Vil. Surrey, 13 m. SW. of London
St. Imier. t. 12 m. N. of Neuchâtel 10
St. Ives. Coast t. extreme W. Cornwall 4 inset
St. Ives (Hunts). Vil. near Huntingdon 6
St. Julien. Vil. France, 5 m. S. of Geneva 9 and 10
St. Léonard de Corbigny. Vil. 90 m. W. of Dijon
St. Lo. T. 40 m. SSE. of Cherbourg 8
St. Malo. T. N. coast of Brittany 8
St. Märgen. Vil. 11 m. E. of Freiburg-in-Br. 11A
St. Neots. t. Hunts, 16 m. W. of Cambridge 6
St. Nicholas D'Aliermont. t. near Dieppe 8
St. Ninians. Sub. of Stirling
St. Pierre-en-Grandvaux Vil. near Lausanne
St. Poelten. T. 60 m. W. of Vienna 13
St. Quentin. T. 85 m. NE. of Paris 8
St. Sulpice. Vil. 18 m. WSW. of Neuchâtel 10
St. Trond. T. 21 m. WNW. of Liége 9
Sala. t. 65 m. NW. of Stockholm
Salem, U.S.A. T. 30 m. NE. of Boston
Salford. T. adj. Manchester 3 inset
Salins. t. 28 m. SSW. of Besançon 9
Salling. Vil. NW. of Jutland, Denmark 12
Saltcoats. T. 13 m. N. of Ayr 2

Map No.

Salzburg. T. SW. Austria near German frontier 13
Sandbach. t. 23 m. E. of Chester 2
Sandwich. t. 10 m. N. of Dover 6
Sanquhar. t. 35 m. S. of Glasgow 2
San Yste. Vil. N. Spain
Sarlat. T. 85 m. E. of Bordeaux 8
Saumur. T. 70 m. WSW. of Blois 8
Savagnier. Vil. near Neuchâtel
Saverne. Vil. near Strasbourg
Saxmundham. Vil. 18 m. NE. of Ipswich 6
Scarborough. T. on Yorks coast 3
Schaffhausen. T. 22 m. N. of Zürich 9 and 11A
Scharnstein. Vil. 65 m. WNW. of Vienna
Schellenbach. Vil. 23 m. WNW. of Mannheim 9 and 11B
Schenectady, U.S.A. T. 155 m. N. of New York
Schiedam. T. 4 m. W. of Rotterdam 12
Schio. T. 50 m. WNW. of Venice 13
Schlipsen. Prob. *Schlipsheim.* Vil. near Augsburg
Schneeberg. t. 50 m. S. of Leipzig 13
Schollenbach. Vil. 30 m. ENE. of Mannheim
Schönwald. Vil. in Black Forest, Germany 11A
Schorndorf. t. 17 m. E. of Stuttgart 9
Schramberg. t. in Black Forest, Germany 9 and 11A
Schwabing. Part of Munich
Schwartzenberg. t. 12 m. SSW. of Berne 10
Schwarzenberck. t. 55 m. S. of Leipzig 13
Schwarzwald. Black Forest, Germany
Schwaz. t. Austria S. of Munich 13
Schweidnitz. T. 30 m. SW. of Breslau 14
Schweinfurt. Vil. 22 m. NE. of Würzburg 11B
Schwenningen. t. in Black Forest, Germany 11A
Schwerin. T. 58 m. E. of Hamburg 12
Seagrave. Vil. 6 m. N. of Leicester 5
Seaton. Vil. near Axminster 5
Sedan. T. 50 m. NE. of Reims 9
Sedberg. t. Yorks, 9 m. E. of Kendal 2
Sedgefield. t. 9 m. SSE. of Durham 3
Seeberg. Vil. in Canton Berne
Seelgut. Vil. 2 m. WNW. of Freiburg-in-Br. 11A
Selby. T. 14 m. S. of York 3
Selkirk. t. 30 m. SSE. of Edinburgh 2
Selling. Vil. 7 m. W. of Canterbury 6
Seloncourt. t. 42 m. WNW. of Besançon
Senlis. t. 28 m. NNE. of Paris 8
Sens. T. 60 m. SE. of Paris 8
Septmoncel. Vil. France, 16 m. NW. of Geneva 10
Serrières. Vil. 30 m. S. of Lyons 9
Settle. Vil. 21 m. E. of Lancaster 2
Sevenoaks. T. Kent, 21 m. SE. of London 6
Shaftesbury. t. 18 m. W. of Salisbury 5
Shaw. t. 9 m. NE. of Manchester 3
Sheerness. T. on mouth of Thames 6
Sheffield 3
Shefford. Vil. 10 m. SE. of Bedford 6
Sheldon. Vil. Derbyshire 3
Shepton Mallet. t. 18 m. S. of Bristol 5
Sherborne. t. 18 m. N. of Dorchester 5
Shifnal. t. 17 m. ESE. of Shrewsbury 5
Shipton. Vil. 5 m. NW. of York 3
or 11 m. E. of Gloucester 5
Shipston-on-Stour. Vil. Worcs, 14 m. S. of Warwick 5
Shoreditch. Part of NE. London
Shrewsbury. County T. of Salop 5
Shrewsbury, U.S.A. t. 30 m. W. of Boston
Sidbury. Vil. 14 m. E. of Exeter 5
Sidmouth. t. on coast 14 m. ESE. of Exeter 5
Siena. T. 35 m. S. of Florence 13
Sigtuna. Vil. 22 m. N. of Stockholm
Silchester. Vil. 28 m. S. of Oxford 5
Simmershausen. Vil. 45 m. N. of Würzburg 9
Simonswald. Vil. in Black Forest, Germany 11A
Sinrisham. t. S. extremity of Sweden 14
Sittingbourne. T. Kent, 38 m. E. of London 6

Map No.

Skanderborg. t. E. coast of Jutland, Denmark 12
Skänninge. t. 120 m. SW. of Stockholm
Skara. t. 80 m. NE. of Göteborg 12
Skellefteå. Vil. NE. Sweden
Skien. t. 65 m. SW. of Oslo
Skipton, Skipton-cum-Craven. T. 26 m. NW. of Leeds
Skirbeck. Part of Boston
Skircoat. Part of Halifax
Sleaford. t. 17 m. S. of Lincoln 3 and 6
Sligo. T. NW. coast of Eire 7
Snaith. Vil. 18 m. S. of York 3
Sneek. T. in Friesland, Holland 12
Söderhamn. t. 140 m. N. of Stockholm
Söderköping. Vil. 85 m. SW. of Stockholm 14
Södertälje. t. 16 m. SW. of Stockholm
Soleure, Solothurn. t. 18 m. N. of Berne 10
Solihull. T. 6 m. SE. of Birmingham 5
Sölvesberg. Vil. Sweden facing Denmark
Sombourne. Vil. 7 m. W. of Winchester 5
Somersham. Vil. 8 m. ENE. of Huntingdon 6
Somerton. Vil. 17 m. E. of Taunton 5
Sonvillier. t. 10 m. N. of Neuchâtel 10
Sorau. T. 95 m. SE. of Berlin 14
Sorn. t. 13 m. E. of Ayr 2
Sotherton. Vil. 26 m. NE. of Ipswich 6
Sottens. Vil. 10 m. NNE. of Lausanne 10
Southam. Vil. 9 m. E. of Warwick 5
Southampton 5
Southampton, U.S.A. Vil. Bucks County, Pennsylvania
South Kilworth. Vil. 9 m. NE. of Rugby 5
South Mimms. t. 12 m. N. of London 6
Southminster. Vil. 16 m. S. of Colchester 6
South Molton. Vil. 25 m. NW. of Exeter 4
South Moulsham. Part of Chelmsford
South Shields. T. on mouth of Tyne 3
Southwark. Part of S. London
Southwell. Vil. 16 m. NE. of Nottingham 3
Southwold. Coast Vil. 29 m. NE. of Ipswich 6
Spalding. T. 35 m. SSE. of Lincoln 6
Speke. t. adj. Garston near Liverpool
Speyer. T. 12 m. S. of Mannheim 9
Spijk. Vil. extreme NE. of Holland
Spilsby. Vil. 26 m. E. of Lincoln 3
Spoleto. T. 100 m. SE. of Florence 13
Springfield, U.S.A. T. S. Massachusetts
Sprottau. t. 70 m. WNW. of Breslau 14
Stadhampton. Vil. 7 m. SE. of Oxford 5
Stadt-am-Hof. t. 65 m. SE. of Nürnberg 13
Stafford 5
Staindrop. Vil. 17 m. SSW. of Durham 3
Staines. t. 19 m. SW. of London 6
Stalbridge. Vil. 17 m. N. of Dorchester 5
Stalham. Vil. 14 m. NE. of Norwich 6
Stalybridge. T. Cheshire, 17 m. E. of Manchester 3
Stamford. t. Lincs, 11 m. WNW. of Peterborough 6
Stanford. Vil. Kent, Norfolk or Northants
Stanmore. Vil. 13 m. NW. of London 6
Stavanger. T. SW. coast of Norway
Staverton. Vil. 11 m. W. of Northampton or
5 m. NE. Gloucester 5
or 10 m. W. of Torquay 4
Steinamanger. T. Hungary, 75 m. S. of Vienna 13
Steiermark. District SW. Austria
Steppach. Vil. 25 m. NNW. of Nürnberg 11B
Stettin. T. 75 m. NNE. of Berlin 14
Stewartstown. Vil. 30 m. W. of Belfast 7
Steyer. T. 90 m. W. of Vienna 13
Steyning. Vil. 9 m. WNW. of Brighton 6
Stickland. Vil. 15 m. NE. of Dorchester 5
Stilton. Vil. 12 m. NNW. of Huntingdon 6
Stirling 1
Stjärnsund. Vil. in Kopparsberg Land, Sweden
Stockport. T. 6 m. SE. of Manchester 3
Stockton, Stockton-on-Tees. T. 17 m. SE. of Durham 3

Map No.

Stoke. Prob. *Stoke-on-Trent*. T. 16 m. N. of Stafford 3
Stoke Newington. Part of N. London
Stokesley. Vil. 35 m. N. of York 3
Stone. t. 7 m. N. of Stafford 5
Stonehaven. Coast T. 13 m. S. of Aberdeen 1
Stony Stratford. Vil. 13 m. S. of Northampton 6
Stora Malm. Vil. 60 m. WSW. of Stockholm
Stourbridge. T. Worcs, 11 m. W. of Birmingham 5
Stourton Caundle. Vil. 16 m. N. of Dorchester 5
Stouting. Vil. 11 m. S. of Canterbury 6
Stow-on-the-Wold. Vil. Glos, 22 m. NW. of Oxford 5
Stowmarket. t. 11 m. NW. of Ipswich 6
Strabane. t. 13 m. S. of Londonderry 7
Stralsund. T. on Baltic N. of Berlin 14
Stran. Prob. *Strand*. t. near Stavanger, Norway
Strängnäs. t. 20 m. W. of Stockholm
Stranraer. t. SW. coast of Scotland 2
Strasbourg. T. on Rhine 9
Stratford (Essex). Sub. E. London 6
Stratford-on-Avon. T. 7 m. SW. of Warwick 5
Strathavon. t. 15 m. SE. of Glasgow 1
Stratton. t. N. Cornwall 4
Straubing. T. 65 m. NE. of Munich 13
Stretford. T. adj. Manchester 3 inset
Strichen. Vil. NE. Aberdeenshire 1
Strömstad. t. 90 m. N. of Göteborg 12
Stroud. t. 12 m. S. of Gloucester 5
Strüth. Vil. in Alsace
Stuttahof. Prob. *Stutthof*. Vil. 20 m. E. of Dantzig 14
Stuttgart 9
Subingen. Vil. 25 m. S. of Basle 10
Sudbury. t. 18 m. W. of Ipswich 6
Sulzfeld-am-Main. Vil. 10 m. SE. of Würzburg 11B
Sulzthal. Vil. 25 m. NNE. of Würzburg 11B
Sunderland. T. on coast of Durham 3
Sundsvall. T. Sweden on Gulf of Bothnia
Sutton Coldfield. T. 7 m. N. of Birmingham 5
Sutton-in-Ashfield. T. 13 m. NNW. of Nottingham 3
Sutton (Lancs). T. adj. St. Helens
Sutton Maddock. Vil. 16 m. ESE. of Shrewsbury 5
Swaffham. Vil. 25 m. W. of Norwich 6
Swansea. T. Glamorgan on Bristol Channel 4
Swindon. T. NE. Wilts 5

Tadcaster. t. 9 m. SW. of York 3
Tamworth. t. Staffs, 13 m. NE. of Birmingham 5
Tanderagee. Vil. 27 m. SW. of Belfast 7
Tanfield. t. 28 m. N. of Leeds 3
Taninge. t. France, 25 m. E. of Geneva 10
Tarporley. t. 10 m. ESE. of Chester 2
Tarves. Vil. 16 m. N. of Aberdeen 1
Tavannes. Vil. 20 m. NE. of Neuchâtel 10
Tavistock. t. 12 m. N. of Plymouth 4
Teignmouth. T. 12 m. S. of Exeter 4
Temple Cloud. Vil. 10 m. S. of Bristol 5
Temple Patrick. t. 10 m. NW. of Belfast 7
Tenbury. Vil. 17 m. NW. of Worcester 5
Tenterden. t. 14 m. SSE. of Maidstone 6
Teschen. T. Czechoslovakia, 35 m. ESE. of Troppau 13
Tetbury. Vil. 17 m. S. of Gloucester 5
Tewkesbury. t. 10 m. N. of Gloucester 5
Thakeham. Vil. 14 m. WNW. of Brighton 6
Thame. t. 12 m. E. of Oxford 5
Thannhausen. Vil. 20 m. W. of Augsburg 9
Thaxted. Vil. 16 m. NNW. of Chelmsford 6
The Hague 12
Thetford. t. 26 m. SW. of Norwich 6
Thiers. T. 60 m. W. of Lyons 9
Thirsk. t. 22 m. NNW. of York 3
Tholen. t. 28 m. S. of Rotterdam 12

Map No.

Thomaston. v. Plymouth Hollow
Thornbury. t. 12 m. N. of Bristol 5
Thorne. T. 13 m. S. of York 3
Thorverton. Vil. 6 m. N. of Exeter 4
Thrapston. Vil. 21 m. NE. of Northampton 6
Three Mile Cross. Vil. 3 m. S. of Reading
Thumenberg. Vil. near Nürnberg
Ticehurst. Vil. 28 m. NE. of Brighton 6
Tideswell. t. 14 m. SW. of Sheffield 3
Timperley. t. Cheshire, 7 m. SW. of Manchester 3 inset
Tipperary. t. 43 m. N. of Cork 7
Tiverton. t. 13 m. N. of Exeter 4
Todmorden. T. Yorks, 17 m. NE. of Manchester 3
Toledo. T. 13 m. S. of Madrid
Tölz. t. 26 m. S. of Munich 9
Tonbridge. T. 12 m. WSW. of Maidstone 6
Tong. Vil. 19 m. E. of Shrewsbury 5
Topsham. t. 5 m. SE. of Exeter 4
Torgau. T. 70 m. S. of Berlin 14
Torneå. Vil. Finland, N. end of Gulf of Bothnia
Torquay. T. E. Devon coast 4
Torrington. t. 30 m. NW. of Exeter 4
Totnes. t. 22 m. SSW. of Exeter 4
Toulouse. T. SW. France 8
Tourcoing. t. 7 m. NNE. of Lille 8
Tournai. T. Belgium, 15 m. E. of Lille 8
Tours. T. 130 m. WSW. of Paris 8
Towcester. Vil. 8 m. SW. of Northampton 5
Town Malling. Vil. 4 m. W. of Maidstone 6
Toxteth Park. Part of Liverpool
Trafford. Vil. near Chester 2
Tralee. t. in Kerry, Eire 7
Trälleborg. t. S. extremity of Sweden 14
Tramelan. t. 18 m. NNE. of Neuchâtel 10
Travers. Vil. 13 m. WSW. of Neuchâtel 10
Trawsfynydd. Vil. W. Merionethshire 4
Trebinshwn. Vil. Brecon
Tredrea. Vil. near St. Ives, Cornwall
Trenton, U.S.A. T. W. New Jersey
Trèves. T. Germany near Luxembourg 9
Trévillers. Vil. 40 m. E. of Besançon 10
Trieste. T. N. end of Adriatic 13
Tring. t. Herts, 31 m. NW. of London 6
Trollhätten. t. 45 m. N. of Göteborg, Sweden 12
Trondhjem. T. N. Norway
Troppau. T. 150 m. E. of Prague 13
Trowbridge. T. Wilts, 18 m. ESE. of Bristol 5
Troyes. T. 90 m. ESE. of Paris 9
Truro. T. SW. Cornwall 4 inset
Tuam. t. in Galway, Eire 7
Tübingen. T. 20 m. S. of Stuttgart 9
Tullamore. t. 50 m. W. of Dublin 7
Tullialan. Vil. Fifeshire
Tunbridge Wells. T. 10 m. SW. of Maidstone 6
Turdoff. Vil. Dumfriesshire
Turin 9
Turriff. t. 30 m. NNW. of Aberdeen 1
Tutbury. Vil. 18 m. ENE. of Stafford 5
Tuxford. Vil. 22 m. NNE. of Nottingham 3
Twickenham. T. 11 m. W. of London 6
Tyrnau. T. Hungary near Pressburg 13

Uckfield. t. 14 m. NE. of Brighton 6
Uddevalla. Vil. 50 m. N. of Göteborg, Sweden 12
Ulm. T. 45 m. SE. of Stuttgart 9
Ulricehamn. Vil. 60 m. E. of Göteborg, Sweden 14
Ulverstone. t. 15 m. NW. of Lancaster 2
Umeå. t. N. Sweden on Gulf of Bothnia
Unterglottertal. Vil. in Black Forest, Germany
Upminster. t. Essex, 16 m. E. of London 6
Upper Broughton. Vil. 10 m. SSE. of Nottingham 5
Upper Holland. Vil. in Lancs 2 inset
Uppingham. Vil. 18 m. E. of Leicester 6
Uppsala. T. 40 m. NNW. of Stockholm
Upton. Many small villages of this name

Map No.

Urach. t. 22 m. SSE. of Stuttgart 9
Urbino. T. 70 m. E. of Florence 13
Utica, U.S.A. T. 80 m. WNW. of Albany
Utrecht. T. 20 m. SE. of Amsterdam 12
Uttoxeter. t. 13 m. NE. of Stafford 5
Uxbridge. T. 17 m. W. of London 6

Vadstena. t. E. side of Lake Wetter, Sweden 14
Valangin. Vil. near Neuchâtel 10
Val de Travers. Valley running WSW. from Neuchâtel
Valence. Vil. 40 m. SE. of Paris
Valence-sur-Rhône. T. 58 m. S. of Lyons 9
Valenciennes. T. 30 m. SE. of Lille 9
Vallée de Joux. Valley NW. of Lake of Geneva
Vallorbe. Vil. 38 m. N. of Geneva 10
Varberg. t. 43 m. S. of Göteborg, Sweden 12
Varennes. t. 14 m. W. of Verdun 9
Vasa. t. Finland on Gulf of Bothnia
Västerås. t. 65 m. WNW. of Stockholm
Västergötland. District of Sweden S. of Lake Wener
Västervik. Coast t. 120 m. S. of Stockholm 14
Vaxholm. Island 12 m. NE. of Stockholm
Växjö. t. S. Sweden 14
Venice 13
Vercelli. t. 40 m. ENE. of Turin 9
Verdun. T. 135 m. E. of Paris 9
Verneuil. t. 37 m. ESE. of Paris
Verona. T. 90 m. E. of Milan 9
Verrières. Vil. 23 m. WSW. of Neuchâtel 10
Versailles. t. 15 m. SW. of Paris 8
Versoix. Vil. 5 m. N. of Geneva 10
Verviers. Vil. 11 m. E. of Liége 9
Vevey. t. NE. end of Lake of Geneva 9 and 10
Vic-en-Lorraine. Vil. near Metz
Vice-le-Comte. Vil. near Lyons
Vienna 13
Vienne. t. 17 m. S. of Lyons 9
Viksta. Vil. in Uppsala Land, Sweden
Villeneuve. Vil. E. end of Lake of Geneva 10
Villeret. Vil. 15 m. NNE. of Neuchâtel
Villiers. Vil. 8 m. N. of Neuchâtel 10
Villingen. t. in Black Forest, Germany 11A
Vincennes. Sub. E. Paris
Visby. t. on Isle of Gothland, Sweden 14
Vorchdorf. t. 110 m. W. of Vienna
Vrigstad. Vil. S. Sweden
Vuiteboeuf. Vil. 22 m. SW. of Neuchâtel 10

Wainfleet. Vil. 33 m. E. of Lincoln 3
Wakefield. T. 9 m. S. of Leeds 3
Wald. T. 22 m. E. of Düsseldorf 12
Waldaschach, Aschach. t. Upper Austria 13
Waldau. t. 75 m. W. of Breslau 14
Waldkirch. t. in Black Forest, Germany 11A
Waldshut. t. Germany on Swiss frontier 11A
Walford. Vil. 13 m. SSE. of Hereford 5
Wallingford. Vil. Berks, 11 m. SE. of Oxford 5
Walsall. T. Staffs, 8 m. NNW. of Birmingham 5
Walsham. v. North Walsham
Walsingham. Vil. 25 m. NE. of Norwich 6
Waltham, U.S.A. T. 8 m. W. of Boston
Waltham Abbey. t. Herts, 13 m. N. of London 6
Walthamstow. Part of E. London 6
Walton. Vil. 20 m. WSW. of Norwich 6
Walton-on-Thames. T. Surrey, 17 m. SW. of London 6
Walton-on-Trent. Vil. 14 m. SSW. of Derby 5
Wandsworth. Part of SW. London
Wangford. Vil. 25 m. NE. of Ipswich 6
Wantage. t. Berks, 13 m. SSW. of Oxford 5
Warburg. t. 43 m. SSW. of Hanover 12
Ware. T. near Hertford 6
Wareham. Vil. 15 m. E. of Dorchester
Warfield. Vil. Berks, 25 m. W. of London 6
Warminster. t. 18 m. NW. of Salisbury 5
Warrington. T. 15 m. E. of Liverpool 2
Warsaw 14
Warwick 5
Wasserburg. t. 30 m. E. of Munich 13

Map No.

Waterbury, U.S.A. T. in Connecticut

Waterford. County T. Eire 7

Watford. T. Herts, 16 m. NW. of London 6

Watlington. Vil. 15 m. SE. of Oxford 5

Wattisfield. Vil. 20 m. NNW. of Ipswich 6

Watton. Vil. 20 m. W. of Norwich 6

Wavertree. T. adj. Liverpool

Weare, U.S.A. t. 60 m. NW. of Boston

Weaverham. t. 13 m. ENE. of Chester 2

Weidhofen-a.-d.-Thayer. t. 60 m. WNW. of Vienna 13

Weimar. T. 75 m. SE. of Brunswick 12

Weissenburg. Vil. 30 m. S. of Nürnberg 11B

Wel. Prob. *Wels.* t. Upper Austria 13

Wellingborough. T. 10 m. ENE. of Northampton 6

Wellington (Salop). t. 10 m. E. of Shrewsbury 5

Wellington (Somerset). t. 7 m. SW. of Taunton 5

Wells (Norfolk). t. on N. coast of Norfolk 6

Wells (Somerset). t. 17 m. S. of Bristol 5

Welshpool. t. Montgomeryshire, 17 m. WSW. of Shrewsbury 5

Wem. Vil. 12 m. N. of Shrewsbury 5

Wenlock. Vil. 12 m. SE. of Shrewsbury 5

Weobley. Vil. 10 m. NW. of Hereford 5

Wesel. T. 30 m. NW. of Düsseldorf 12

West Ballum. Vil. S. coast of Jutland, Denmark

West Bromwich. T. 3 m. NW. of Birmingham 5

Westbury. t. 24 m. NW. of Salisbury 5

West Cowes. t. Isle of Wight 5

West Derby. Part of Liverpool 2 inset

Westerham. t. Kent, 25 m. S. of London 6

Westheim. Vil. 4 m. W. of Augsburg 9 and 11B

Westport. t. in Mayo, Eire 7

West Tarring. Vil. 8 m. E. of Brighton 6

Westzaan. t. N. Holland

Wetherby. Vil. 11 m. NE. of Leeds 3

Wetzlar. T. 30 m. NNW. of Frankfurt-am-Main 9

Wexford. Coast t. SE. Eire 7

Weymouth. T. on Dorset coast 5

Whalley. Vil. 23 m. N. of Manchester 2

Whetstone. Vil. near Leicester or Barnet 6

Whiston. Vil. adj. Prescot

Whitby. T. NE. Yorks coast 3

Whitchurch (Hants). Vil. 12 m. N. of Winchester 5

Whitchurch (Salop). t. 18 m. N. of Shrewsbury 5

Whitehaven. T. Cumberland coast 2

Wickham Market. Vil. 11 m. NE. of Ipswich 6

Wicklow. County T. Eire 7

Widcombe. t. 5 m. S. of Bristol 5

Widnes. T. 12 m. SE. of Liverpool 2

Wiesentheid. Vil. 15 m. E. of Würzburg 11B

Wigan. T. 17 m. NE. of Liverpool 2

Wigton. t. 10 m. WSW. of Carlisle 2

Wigtown. Vil. SW. coast of Scotland 2

Willenhall Field. T. 10 m. NW. of Birmingham 5

Williamsburg, U.S.A. t. near Baltimore

Williamstown, U.S.A. t. Massachusetts

Williton. Vil. 13 m. NW. of Taunton 5

Wilmington, U.S.A. T. N. Delaware

Wilten. t. in Tyrol

Wimbourne. t. 20 m. SSW. of Salisbury 5

Wincanton. Vil. 28 m. S. of Bristol 5

Winchester 5

Winchester, U.S.A. t. 8 m. NW. of Boston

Winden. One of several small villages. Prob. near Carlsruhe

Windsheim. t. 26 m. W. of Nürnberg 11B

Map No.

Windsor. T. Berks, 20 m. W. of London 6

Winsted, U.S.A. t. NE. Connecticut

Winster. Vil. 19 m. NNW. of Derby 3

Winterthur. T. 12 m. NE. of Zürich 9

Winwick. t. 14 m. E. of Liverpool 2 inset

Wirksworth. t. 12 m. NNW. of Derby 3

Wisbech. T. 31 m. N. of Cambridge 6

Wishaw. T. 15 m. ESE. of Glasgow 1

Wismar. T. Germany on Baltic 12

Wissembourg. t. 30 m. N. of Strasbourg 9

Wissett. Vil. 20 m. SSE. of Norwich 6

Wiston. Vil. 11 m. WNW. of Brighton 6

Witham. t. 9 m. NE. of Chelmsford 6

Witney. t. 10 m. WNW. of Oxford 5

Wiveliscombe. Vil. 8 m. W. of Taunton 5

Wjatka. T. 500 m. ENE. of Moscow

Woburn. Vil. 12 m. SSW. of Bedford 6

Wokingham. t. Berks, 32 m. W. of London 6

Wolcottville, U.S.A. Vil. in Indiana

Wolfenbüttel. T. 7 m. S. of Brunswick 12

Wolsingham. Vil. 12 m. W. of Durham 3

Woodborrow. Prob. *Woodborough.* Vil. Notts or 18 m. N. of Salisbury 5

Woodbridge. t. 8 m. ENE. of Ipswich 6

Woodford. T. Essex, 9 m. NE. of London

Woodhead. Vil. 18 m. E. of Manchester 3

Woodstock. Vil. 8 m. NW. of Oxford 5

Wooler. Vil. N. Northumberland 3

Woolton. t. 5 m. SE. of Liverpool 2 inset

Woolwich. Sub. E. London

Wootton Bassett. Vil. 11 m. NW. of Marlborough 5

Worcester 5

Workington. T. Cumberland coast 2

Worksop. T. 15 m. ESE. of Sheffield 3

Wormerveer. t. 12 m. NW. of Amsterdam 12

Worms. T. 35 m. SSW. of Frankfurt-am-Main 9

Worsted. Vil. 12 m. NNE. of Norwich 6

Wotton-under-Edge. Vil. 20 m. SSW. of Gloucester 5

Wrentham. Vil. 17 m. SSW. of Norwich

Wrexham. T. Denbigh, 12 m. SSW. of Chester 2

Württemberg. State SW. Germany

Würzburg. T. 56 m. NW. of Nürnberg 9 and 11B

Wye. Vil. 17 m. W. of Dover 6

Wymondham. t. 10 m. SW. of Norwich 6

Yalding. Vil. near Maidstone 6

Yarm. Vil. Yorks, 21 m. SSW. of Durham 3

Yarmouth. T. on coast 19 m. E. of Norwich 6

Yeovil. T. 20 m. E. of Taunton 5

Yoel. Vil. in Surrey

York 3

Youghal. t. 27 m. E. of Cork 7

Yoxford. Vil. 20 m. NE. of Ipswich 6

Ystad. t. extreme S. coast of Sweden 14

Ystrad. t. 10 m. N. of Cardiff 5

Yvecrique. Vil. 15 m. NW. of Rouen

Yverdon. t. S. end of Lake of Neuchâtel 10

Zeitz. T. 110 m. SE. of Brunswick 12

Zelechow. t. 50 m. SE. of Warsaw

Zerbst. T. 100 m. ESE. of Hanover 12

Zittau. T. 50 m. E. of Dresden 14

Zisserstorff. Vil. 50 m. SW. of Brünn

Zug. T. 14 m. S. of Zürich 9

Zürich. T. N. Switzerland 9

Zutphen. T. 56 m. E. of Amsterdam 12

Zwickau. T. 42 m. S. of Leipzig 13

Zwol, Zwolle. T. 52 m. ENE. of Amsterdam 12

Moray Firth
Elgin
Portsoy
Fraserburgh
Banff
Strichen
ELGIN
Keith
Turriff
Peterhead
Inverness
NAIRN
Dufftown
Fyvie
BANFF
Tarves
Old Meldrum
L. Ness
Inverurie
ABERDEEN
INVERNESS
Aberdeen
57°
Stonehaven
KINCARDINE
L. Ericht
Laurencekirk
FORFAR
Johnshaven
Brechin
Montrose
L. Rannoch
PERTH
Kirriemuir
Forfar
L. Tay
Coupar Angus
Arbroath
Dundee
Firth of Tay
Perth
Errol
L. Earn
Crieff
St. Andrews
Cupar Fife
Auchterarder
L. Katrine
Auchtermuchty
Kettle
FIFE
Kinross
Kilconquhar
Anstruther
L. Lomond
Doune
Dunblane
Leslie
Leven
Pittenween
Dollar
Firth of Forth
Kippen
Alloa
Dysart
Kirkcaldy
L. Long
Stirling
Dunfermline
Burntisland
STIRLING
Inverkeithing
Grahamston
56°
Gourock
Kilsyth
Falkirk
Polmont
Bo'ness
Leith
Dunbar
Greenock
Dumbarton
Linlithgow
Prestonpans
Kirkintilloch
Edinburgh
Haddington
Kilmacolm
Bathgate
Musselburgh
Port Glasgow
Paisley
Glasgow
Mid Calder
Dalkeith
Kilbarchan
Polton
BERWICK
Lochwinnoch
Hamilton
Kilburnie
Wishaw
Cambusnethan
Dunse
Berwick on Tweed
Beith
RENFREW
AYR
Dalry
Carnwath
Lauder
Strathaven
Irvine
Kilmaurs
LANARK
Lanark
Peebles
Earlston
Coldstream
Kilmarnock
4°
Biggar
3°
2°
0
10
20
30
MILES
I

SCOTLAND

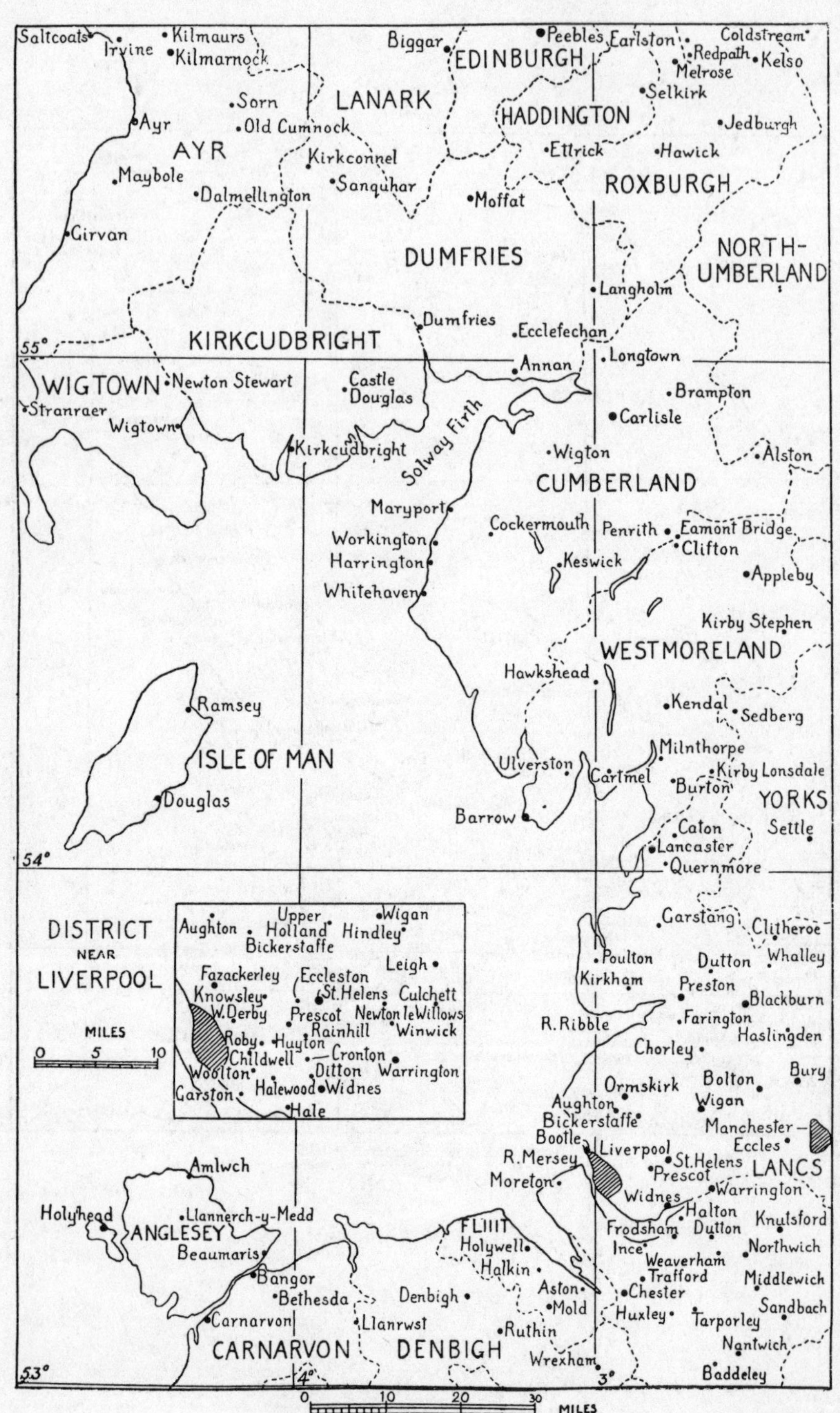

2

NORTH-WEST ENGLAND

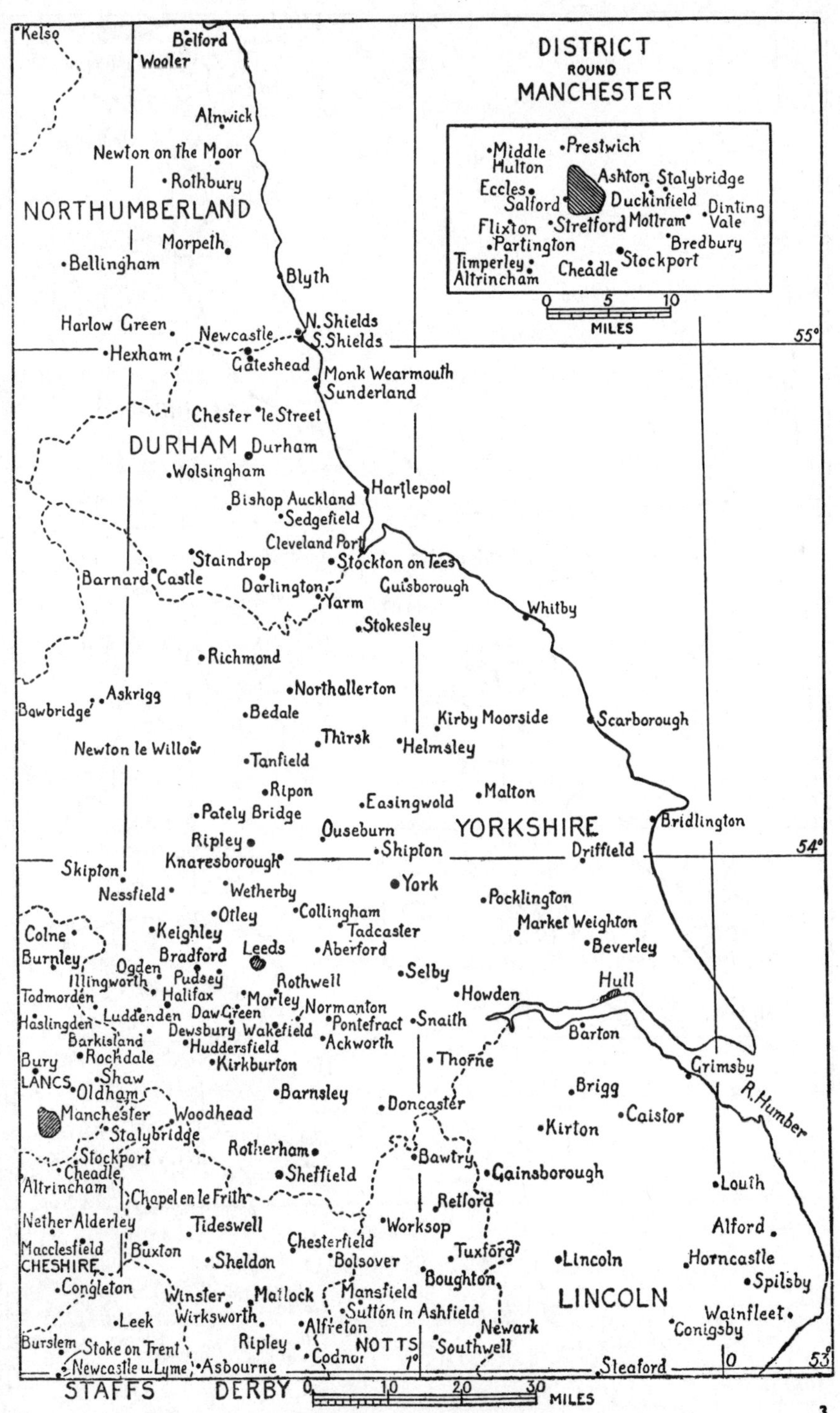

3

NORTH-EAST ENGLAND

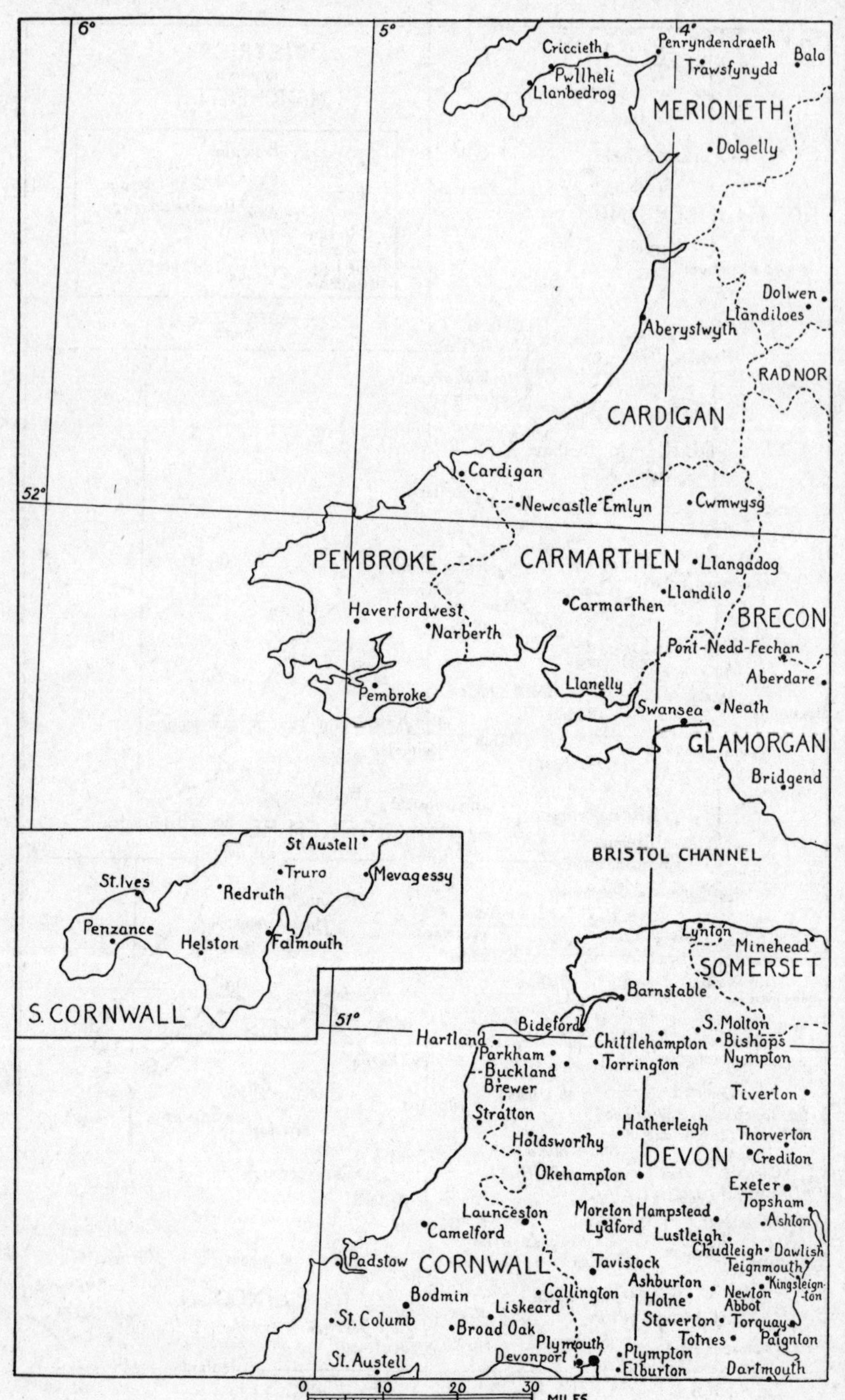

4

SOUTH-WEST ENGLAND

SOUTHERN ENGLAND

SOUTH-EAST ENGLAND

6

7

NORTHERN IRELAND AND EIRE

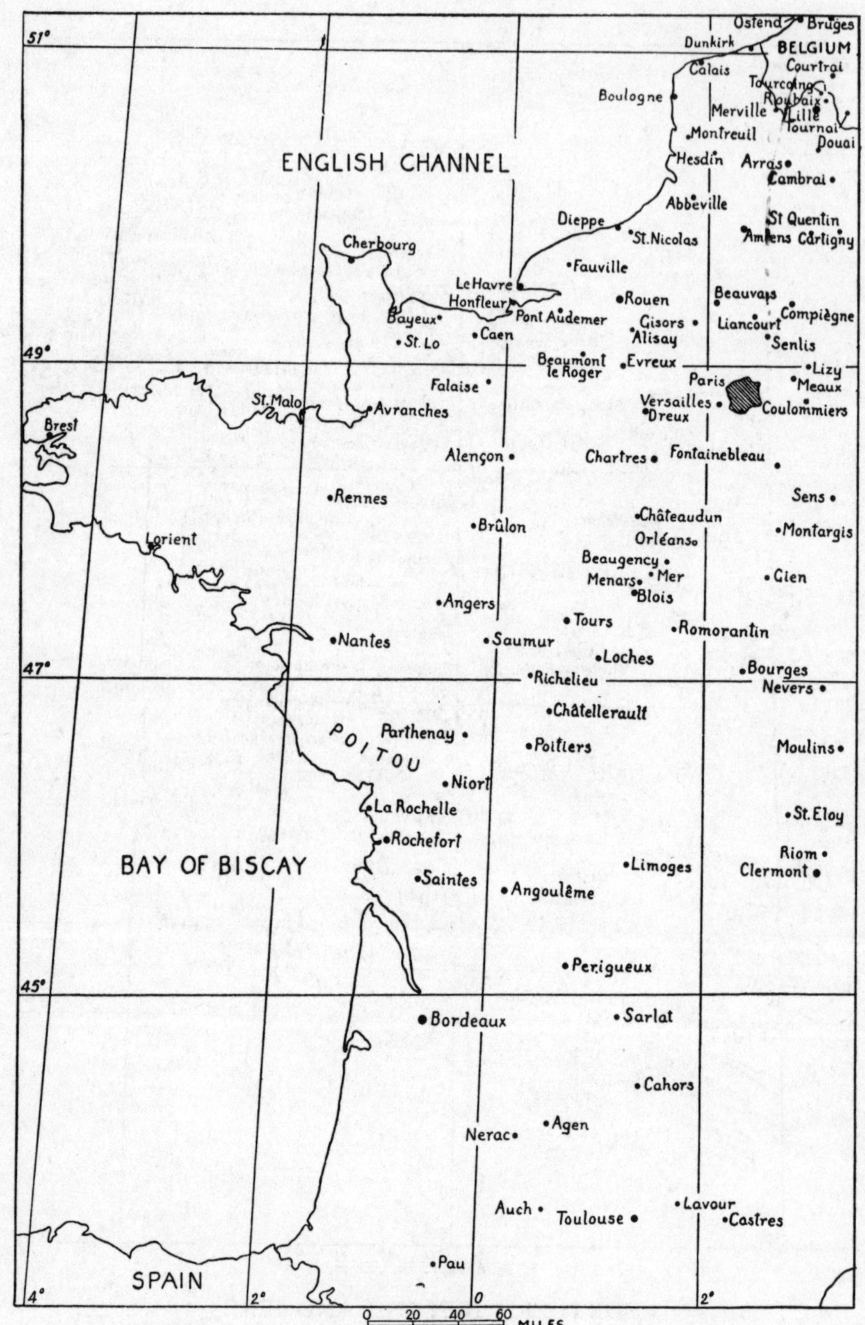

WESTERN FRANCE

E. FRANCE. S. BELGIUM. SWITZERLAND. N. ITALY SW. GERMANY

9

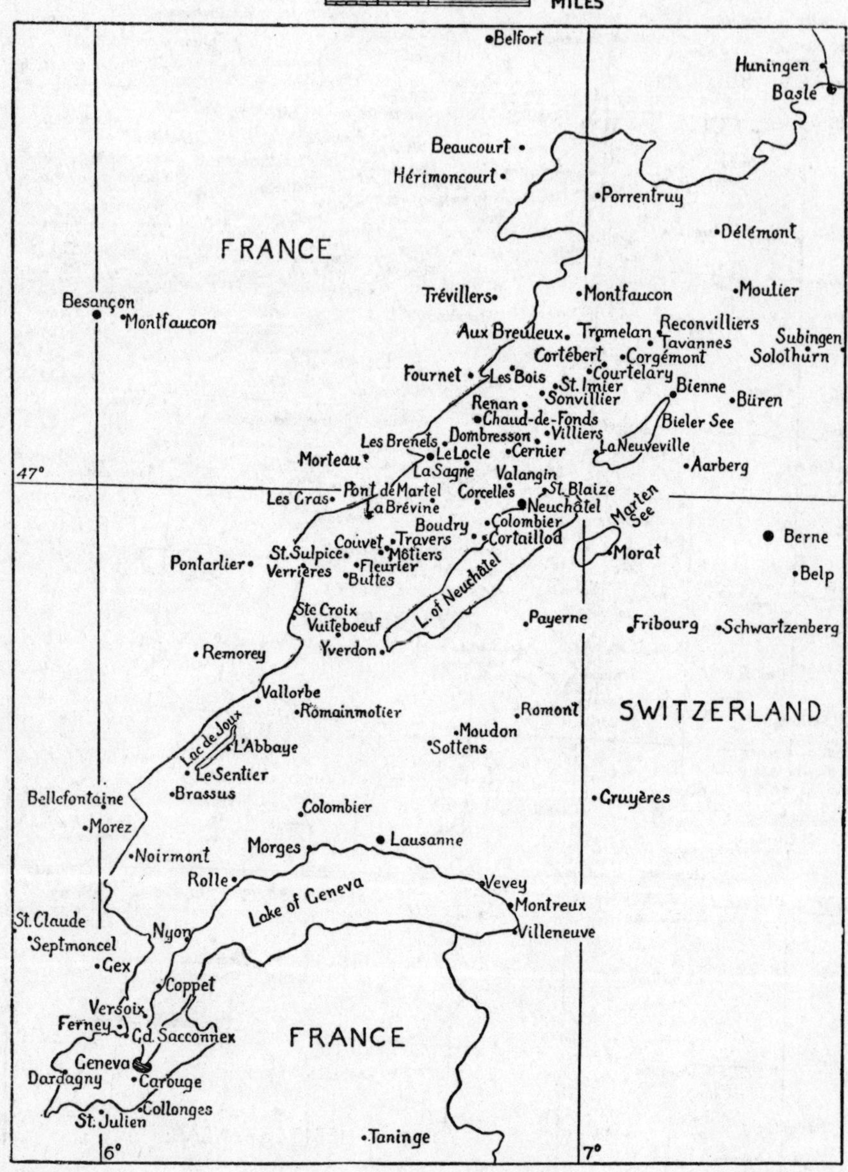

WEST SWITZERLAND 10

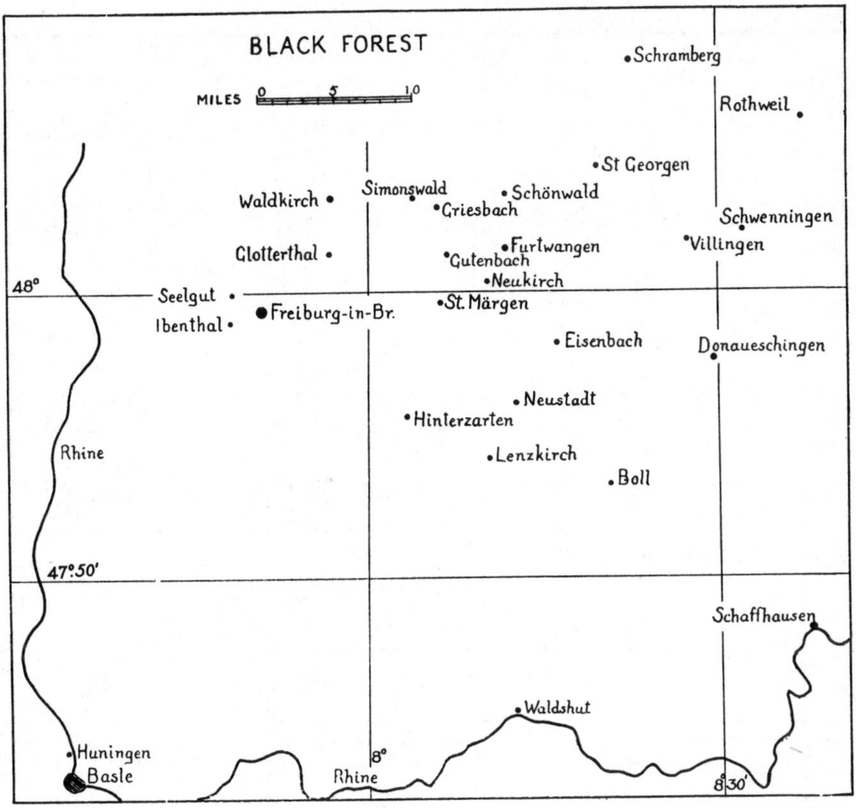

BLACK FOREST
MILES 0 5 10
Schramberg
Rothweil
St Georgen
Simonswald
Schönwald
Waldkirch
Griesbach
Schwenningen
Villingen
Glotterthal
Furtwangen
Gutenbach
Neukirch
48°
Seelgut
Freiburg-in-Br.
St. Märgen
Ibenthal
Eisenbach
Donaueschingen
Neustadt
Hinterzarten
Rhine
Lenzkirch
Boll
47°.50'
Schaffhausen
Waldshut
Huningen
Basle
8°
Rhine
8°30'

11A

NÜRNBERG AND WURZBURG DISTRICT
MILES 0 10 20 30
Neustadt-an-d.-Saale
Munnerstadt
Königshofen
Coburg
Kronach
Kissingen
Hanau
Frankfurt-a-M.
Schweinfurt
Hassfurt
Arnstein
Westheim
50°
Karlstadt
Heugrumbach
Sulzthal
Geroldshofen
Bamberg
Darmstadt
Marktheidenfeld
Dettelbach
Würzburg
Wiesentheid
Steppach
Miltenberg
Sulzfeld
Kitzingen
Amorbach
Giebelstadt
Ochsenfurt
Markbreit
Erlangen
Neustadt
Lauf
Schellenbach
Mergentheim
Windsheim
Furth
Nürnberg
Heidelberg
Rothenburg
Ansbach
Leutershausen
Heilbronn
Crailsheim
Feuchtwangen
Ellingen
9°
10°
Dinkelsbühl
49°
Weissenburg

11B

CENTRAL GERMANY

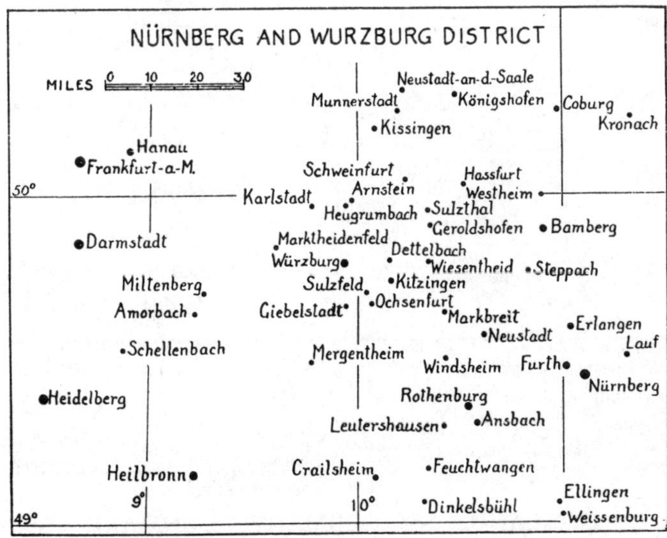

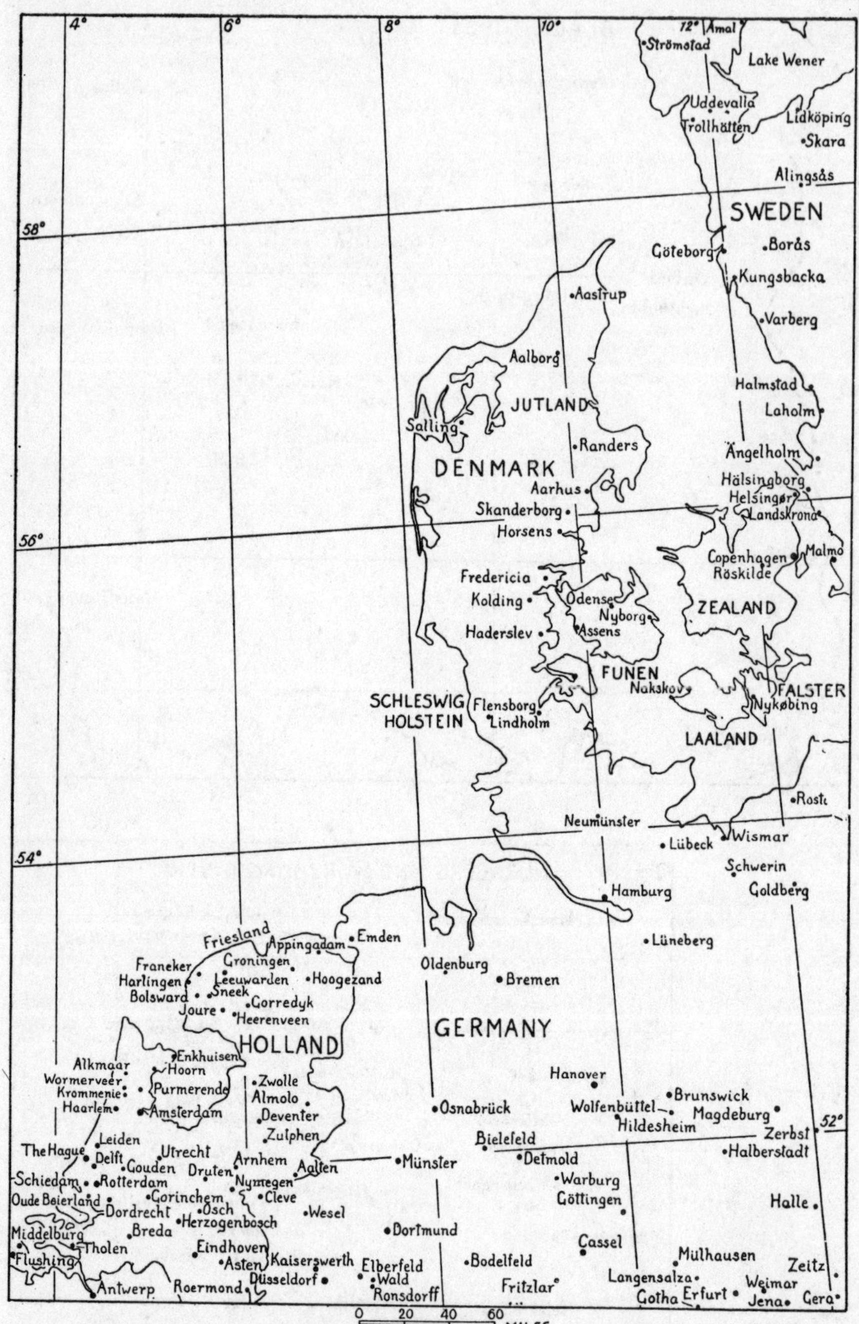

HOLLAND. NW. GERMANY. DENMARK. SW. SWEDEN

13

CZECHOSLOVAKIA. AUSTRIA. NE. ITALY

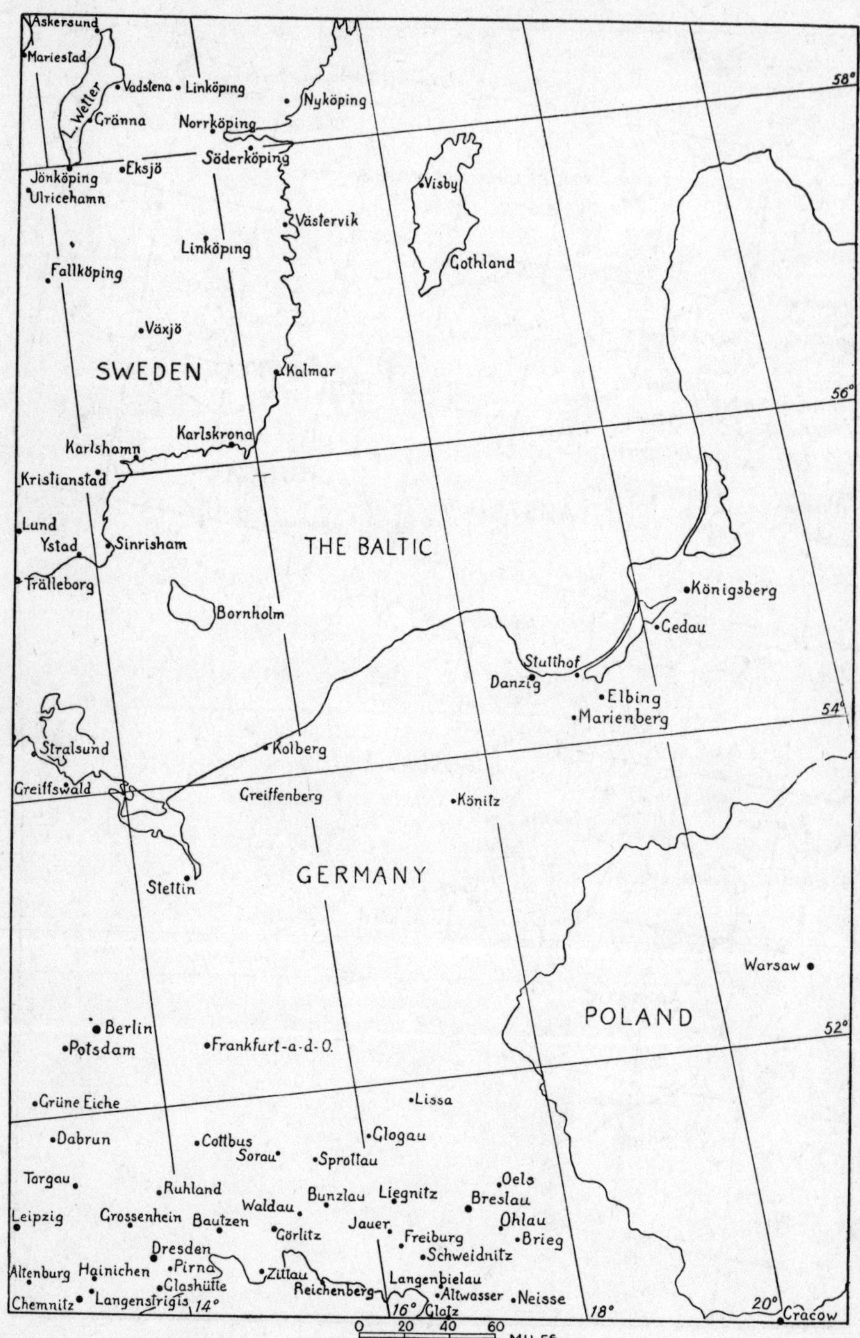

NE. GERMANY. SE. SWEDEN

14